The Children's
Encyclopedia

VOLUME ONE

Chief Contributors to
The Children's Encyclopedia

Literary	Art
T. THORNE BAKER	FREDERICK ANGER
HAROLD BEGBIE	HILDA M. COLEY
ERNEST A. BRYANT	A. FORESTIER
JOHN DERRY	F. R. HINKINS
ARTHUR D. INNES	J. R. MONSELL
MARGARET LILLIE	GEORGE F. MORRELL
CHARLES RAY	WAL PAGET
C. W. SALEEBY	S. B. PEARSE
J. A. SPENDER	T. H. ROBINSON
J. ARTHUR THOMSON	W. B. ROBINSON
R. F. TOWLER	CHARLES M. SHELDON
H. N. TYERMAN	E. F. SKINNER
SYDNEY WARNER	S. E. TRANTER
H. C. WHAITE	S. J. TURNER
PERCY M. YOUNG	

Printed in Great Britain by
The Amalgamated Press, Ltd., London

HER MAJESTY QUEEN ELIZABETH II

From the portrait by Pietro Annigoni, painted for the Fishmongers' Company
(Copyright reserved by The Times)

THE CHILDREN'S ENCYCLOPEDIA

FOUNDED
by
ARTHUR MEE

VOLUME ONE

THE EDUCATIONAL BOOK COMPANY LIMITED
LONDON

CONTENTS OF THIS VOLUME

GROUP 1   EARTH AND ITS NEIGHBOURS
The Big Ball We Live On 9
How the Earth was Made 137
Three Ways the Earth Moves 265
Inside the Wonderful Ball 393
How Fire and Water Made the World 517
How Sun and Wind Made the Hills 641

GROUP 2   MEN AND WOMEN
The First Flying Men 19
The Kings of Music 141
The Famous Men of Venice 271
Creators of Fantasy 399
Cromwell and His Men 521
The French Revolutionists 647

GROUP 3   STORIES
Sections begin on pages 27, 151, 283, 407, 529, 655

GROUP 4   ANIMAL LIFE
Nature's Thousands of Children 37
The Animals Most Like Men 159
Bats and Their Friends 291
Big Cats and Little Cats 417
The Wild Dogs 537
The Friendly Dogs 663

GROUP 5   HISTORY
Man Sets Out on a Journey 45
Man Builds Himself a House 167
Man Feels His Way to Power 297
The Wondering Egyptian 425
Man Begins to Think of God 543
A New Birth for Mankind 671

GROUP 6   FAMILIAR THINGS
Iron and Steel .. 49   Airways 429
Cotton 171   Rope 179   Bridges 547
China 301   The Piano 675

GROUP 7   WONDER
Sections begin on pages 59, 183, 307, 439, 559, 679

GROUP 8   ART
The Rich Treasure That is Ours 65
The Cave Men and their Pictures 191
The Artists of the Old Empires 315
A Great Light Shines 443
The Wonder Men of Florence 565
Leonardo and Michael Angelo 687

GROUP 9   OURSELVES
Life that Fills the Earth 77
The First Living Things 199
Why Life Left the Sea 325
Life Makes the Body 451
The Tiniest Living Things 575
Our Unseen Friends and Foes 697

GROUP 10   PLANT LIFE
How Life Goes Round and Round 81
A Plant's Struggle for Life 203
Birth, Life, and Death of a Flower 329
How Plants Work for their Living 457
How Plants Move and Feel 579
Plants and their Ancestors 701

GROUP 11   COUNTRIES
This Great World of Ours 87
Our Homeland 209
Seeing Our Homeland From the Sea 337
Our Great and Little Hills 461
England in the Long Ago 587
The Conqueror Comes 707

GROUP 12   PICTURE ATLAS
Sections begin on pages 91, 217, 345, 469, 597, 721

GROUP 13   POETRY & NURSERY RHYMES
Sections begin on pages 97, 223, 351, 475, 603, 729

GROUP 14   POWER
The Very Heart of Matter 105
What is Electricity ? 233
The Ocean of Power We Live In 359
The Electric Current 481
The Story of the Dynamo 609
The Storage Battery 735

GROUP 15   LITERATURE
The Realms of Gold 109
Poetry More Precious than Gold 239
Our First Storytellers 363
The Greatest English Book 485
The Book as Sweet as Music 613
The Poet Who Followed Chaucer 739

GROUP 16   IDEAS
Movement 113   Truth 493
Justice 243   Direction 617
Courage 371   Distance 743

GROUP 17   THE BIBLE
The Way Our Bible Came 117
The Bible Story of Creation 247
The Story of Cain and Abel 375
The First Days of Evil 497
Abraham, the Friend of God 621
Isaac and His Sons 747

GROUP 18   THINGS TO MAKE & DO
Sections begin on pages 121, 249, 377, 501, 625, 749

GROUP 19
READING   NUMBERS (continued)
Learning to Read .. 129   Adding Together .. 635
Picture Books .. 258   The Sums Get
Like A Flash .. 387   Harder 757
Making a Newspaper 509
Story Books and   MUSIC
Word Books .. 633   The Sounds We Hear 134
Some New Words   758   The Names of Sounds 262
                                  More About the
WRITING   Names of Sounds 390
Learning to Write   130   Clefs and Staves .. 513
Keeping a Diary .. 259   Melodies for Voices 636
Without Mother's   Musical Dialects .. 760
Help 386
Making a Cinema .. 511   ART
Films & Advertising 634   Your First Picture .. 132
Copying the Nursery   Patterns & Pictures 260
Rhymes 759   Patterns & Potatoes 388
NUMBERS   Colours and Mixing
Learning to Count 131   Paints 512
The Names of   Modelling in Clay .. 638
Figures 257   Ways of Modelling .. 762
Games for Counting 385
Remembering   FRENCH
Figures 510   Picture Lessons, 136, 264,
                                  392, 515, 640, 764

ARTHUR MEE

From the painting by his friend Frank O. Salisbury, C.V.O.

TO BOYS & GIRLS EVERYWHERE

You will find some day, my young friends, that, though words pretend to say what you mean, they do not say what you really mean at all, and I do not know of any words that can tell you all I want to say to you and all that this book means to me. Yet it is your book, and the story of it belongs to you.

Somewhere, in a corner of the world that a mother knows, was once a little lonely girl. When Master Jack Frost woke up from his sleep and drove the children in, our little lady would ride on her rocking-horse to Fairyland, or ring the bell on the door of her shop and pretend to sell things to somebody who was not there, or put her dolls to bed long before it was time, or tell her bear the strangest stories that ever were heard. When the sun was high in the sky she would talk to the fairies in the trees, or beg Robin Redbreast to come down and be friends.

Our little maid had friends in every flower and tree that grows, in every wind that blows ; and as the days began and ended, as weeks went by, and months rolled on, and years began to come, her little mind grew great with wonder, and she would find that behind the world and its play, behind all that she could see and hear and feel and know, was Something that she could not see and hear and feel and know, Something she could not understand.

And so there came into her mind the great wonder of the Earth. What does the world mean ? And why am I here ? Where are all the people who have been and gone ? Where does the rose come from ? Who holds the stars up there ? What is it that seems to talk to me when the world is dark and still ? So the questions would come, until the mother of our little maid was more puzzled than the little maid herself. And as the questions came, when the mother had thought and thought, and answered this and answered that until she could answer no more, she cried out for a book : " Oh for a book that will answer all the questions ! " And this is the book she called for.

That is how our book began. Let us think we are sitting by the fire, little and big children everywhere (for children are we all), with storytellers and wise men to talk to us. Such a big book must have a big name, but the name is the biggest word in the book, and you will learn to say it easily and will know when you grow up that it is the only name that will really do.

It is a Big Book for Little People, and it has come into the world to make your life happy and wise and good. That is what we are meant to be. That is what we will help each other to be.

Your affectionate Friend, **Arthur Mee**

TO ALL WHO LOVE CHILDREN
ALL OVER THE WORLD

THE Children's Encyclopedia is the first book that has ever tried to cover the chief realms of knowledge so that a child may understand.

NOTHING could be more false to its purpose than to imagine that it seeks to cram the mind of a child with things that children need not know. It conceives the bringing up of a child as the supreme task in which we can engage, but it has no sympathy with those who would set a child down at a desk before it can run. It believes that a child is largely its own teacher, and that in a right environment it will teach itself more than all the schools can teach it.

IT cannot be urged against this book, therefore, that it has come to steal away the joy of childhood and put a bitter grinding in its place. It has come to bring more joy to childhood, believing that true joy of life comes from sympathy and understanding.

ONE half of the population of the world is made up of boys and girls learning at school and little children playing at home.

Is it beyond the resources of our language to convey to this vast multitude of men and women of tomorrow such an understanding of the world they live in as shall make their lives happier and save the waste of precious years?

THE creators of the Children's Encyclopedia believe that it is not, and they have built up the simplest system of knowledge they can devise.

LEFT to wander in this field, the child will find whatever it wants. For the youngest of all the parent will find a lullaby. The child in the nursery will find nursery rhymes and the best stories that have ever been told. The child who can be left out of doors to play will find here the beginning of an interest in natural things.

FOR the boy and girl at school these pages teem with precious things ; for fathers and mothers and teachers alike, they may well become invaluable. It is a book for grown-ups and children. It is an encyclopedia of everything that comes into childhood, and by childhood it means all that period of life when the sensitive mind, the most marvellous instrument within the boundless universe, is being formed.

THE Children's Encyclopedia is what it claims to be. It is a children's book that children can understand. It is written in the words the children know. The writers of this book have been simple by being natural ; they have made a children's book without childishness, a book that children may read because it is simple, and that men may read because it is plain.

IF saving of time is lengthening of life this book should be a priceless gift of years to the generation that is growing. There can be no doubt which of two children a teacher would prefer to take—one familiar with this book or one who is not. Nor can there be doubt that this book in the hands of boys and girls will add immensely to their understanding, lessening the difficulties of their school life.

HERE is a gift to childhood ; a thing of measureless value to parents and teachers ; a treasury for children to which they may come whenever they will, for whatever they will ; an inspiration to childhood which will make these precious years a time of wise and happy building-up. It is a story of which children will never grow weary. It is the best of all stories, told in the simplest of all words, to the greatest of all ends.

Arthur Mee

PLAN & PURPOSE OF THIS BOOK

THIS book is arranged so that a child can understand it. Its purpose is to give boys and girls a conception of the world they live in and of their place in it.

It is not an Alphabet of Facts. Admirable as that is for a busy man, it is useless torture for a child. Nothing can be more forbidding to a young mind than a collection of subjects arranged in the order in which the accident of the alphabet brings them. The alphabet is for those who know ; the Children's Encyclopedia is for those who do not know.

This book presents a simple scheme of universal knowledge which opens up a vision of the world as one great whole. It seeks to stir the mind and to awake a sense of wonder. Its purpose is to fascinate and educate.

It seeks to tell the story of everything a child can understand in the plainest way in which it can be told. It believes that a child soon becomes interested in everything about it, and it tries to explain, in a logical sequence of things, whatever the child's mind may begin to think about.

In its millions of words and its thousands of pictures it brings the mind of a child up from the beginning of the world into the midst of the thrilling age we live in. It comes up from the days when a man lived in a cave to the days when he sits by his fire, touches a switch, and hears a voice on any continent. It comes up from the days when a man could send a message to another only as fast as a messenger could ride to these days when he can send a voice round the Earth in a tick of the clock.

So vast a range of interest has this book, and it seeks to deal with it in simple ways. There are thousands of things shown in colour. There are birds and insects, plants and trees, seaweeds and shells, reptiles and fishes, all in colour; there are berries, grasses and ferns, minerals and tapestries and trains ; there is the colour of old Empires, the colour of Nature, the colour from the world's great galleries. It may be claimed that in its great array of pictures and in its colour this book has not been surpassed in our time.

And the range of its thousands of pictures is as wide as it can be. It has a unique Picture Geology and hundreds of splendid views of our island home, a coloured atlas of the world, a remarkable collection of picture maps, and photographs of the peoples of the world, their homes, their industries, and their commerce.

The book has been arranged in nineteen main groups, seventeen groups of knowledge and two of practical teaching. Every group is numbered and runs through the book till it is completed ; all we have to do is to

3

turn to the group we want and read the chapters from the beginning to the end. They move forward simultaneously, so that in fact this is a book of about a thousand chapters summing up human knowledge.

Here are the Nineteen Groups of the book and their contents.

THE 19 GROUPS OF THIS BOOK & WHAT THEY ARE ABOUT

1. Earth and Its Neighbours. The story of the Universe and all its wondrous worlds. Astronomy. Geology. Geography. Chemistry. Physics.

2. Men and Women. The life-stories of immortal men and women and their achievements.

3. Stories. The great stories of the world that will be told for ever. Golden Deeds. Fairy Tales. Legends. Fables. Chivalry. Stories of all Peoples. Old Tales of Greece and Rome.

4. Animal Life. Nature's wonderful family of living things in Earth and air and sea. Mammals. Birds. Reptiles. Fishes. Insects.

5. History. The march of Man from the Age of Barbarism to the United Nations.

6. Familiar Things. The things we see about us. Our Great Industries. How things are made. Where they come from.

7. Wonder. Plain answers to the questions of the children of the world on all subjects.

8. Art. The beautiful things in the treasure-houses of the world. Pictures. Statues. Carvings. Buildings. Colour.

9. Ourselves. The wonderful house we live in and our place in the world. Body, Mind, and Soul. Citizenship. Economics. Government. Law. The United Nations Organisation.

10. Plant Life. The marvellous story of the plants that cover the Earth. Botany and its wonders. Flowers. Trees. How things grow.

11. Countries. The peoples of all nations and their homelands.

12. Picture Atlas. Maps of all nations. Illustrated maps of historic and natural events.

13. Poetry. One thousand poems of all times and all countries, with verses and rhymes.

14. Power. Where power comes from ; what it does ; how it works. Electricity. Wireless. Motor-cars. Aeroplanes. Railways. Ships. Steam. Coal. Gas. Oil. Water. Machines.

15. Literature. The imperishable thoughts of men enshrined in the books of the world.

16. Ideas. Great words that stir the hearts and minds of all mankind.

17. The Bible. The story of the world's most beautiful book, and the Life of Jesus.

18. Things to Make and Do. Crafts. Games. Needlework. Cookery. Tricks. Puzzles and Problems. Scientific Experiments.

19. School Lessons. Simple learning made easy for very little people. Reading. Writing. Arithmetic. Art. Music. French.

WE need mention only a few writers of this book to suggest the type of mind that has been enlisted in what we believe to be the greatest cause in the world, the educating of our children. Among them are Sir Arthur Thomson, the famous professor of Natural History for so long at Aberdeen ; J. A. Spender, the famous editor who had an unsurpassed knowledge of the world's affairs ; T. Thorne-Baker, with his remarkable record as a scientific investigator and inventor ; Harold Begbie, one of the most entertaining writers of his generation ; Dr. C. W. Saleeby, the popular author and lecturer ; Dr. Ronald Campbell Macfie, scientist ; Ernest Bryant, the writer on Natural History ; Charles Ray; and others whose expert knowledge has kept the information in these pages in step with the times.

Through all the things that are written here breathes a spirit which no dark days can conquer. This book is written from beginning to end in the faith that all is well. It believes in God and man and in our race. It believes in loving our country as the noblest country that has ever been, and in loving mankind no less. It believes that character is the greatest thing in the world, and that by teaching our children to do right, to love truth, and to cherish fine things, we can save mankind from all its troubles and build up the Kingdom of Heaven.

EVERY CHILD'S GOOD THINGS

I, NATURE, give to you, to be yours for ever and ever, the right to the free enjoyment of this world. I give to you the years that are before you, and the world that is about you.

I GIVE to you the Sun by day and the Moon and stars by night, with the power to wake as the Earth rolls into the light of the Sun, and power to sleep when the night comes.

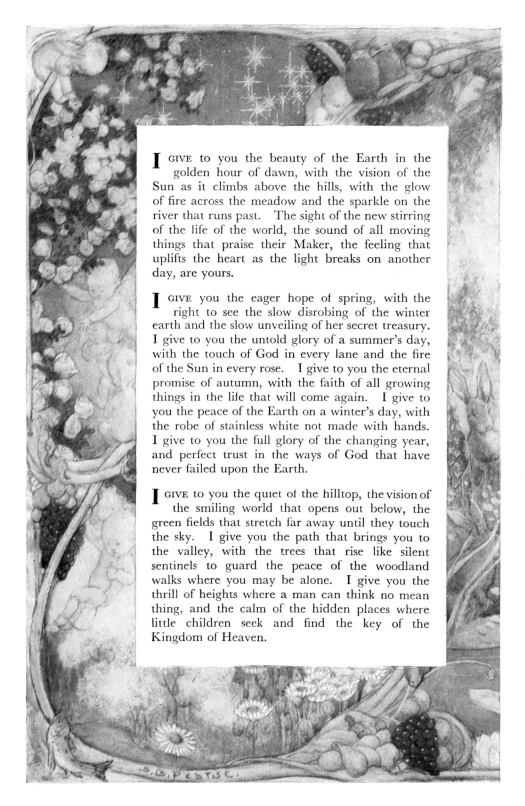

I GIVE to you the beauty of the Earth in the golden hour of dawn, with the vision of the Sun as it climbs above the hills, with the glow of fire across the meadow and the sparkle on the river that runs past. The sight of the new stirring of the life of the world, the sound of all moving things that praise their Maker, the feeling that uplifts the heart as the light breaks on another day, are yours.

I GIVE you the eager hope of spring, with the right to see the slow disrobing of the winter earth and the slow unveiling of her secret treasury. I give to you the untold glory of a summer's day, with the touch of God in every lane and the fire of the Sun in every rose. I give to you the eternal promise of autumn, with the faith of all growing things in the life that will come again. I give to you the peace of the Earth on a winter's day, with the robe of stainless white not made with hands. I give to you the full glory of the changing year, and perfect trust in the ways of God that have never failed upon the Earth.

I GIVE to you the quiet of the hilltop, the vision of the smiling world that opens out below, the green fields that stretch far away until they touch the sky. I give you the path that brings you to the valley, with the trees that rise like silent sentinels to guard the peace of the woodland walks where you may be alone. I give you the thrill of heights where a man can think no mean thing, and the calm of the hidden places where little children seek and find the key of the Kingdom of Heaven.

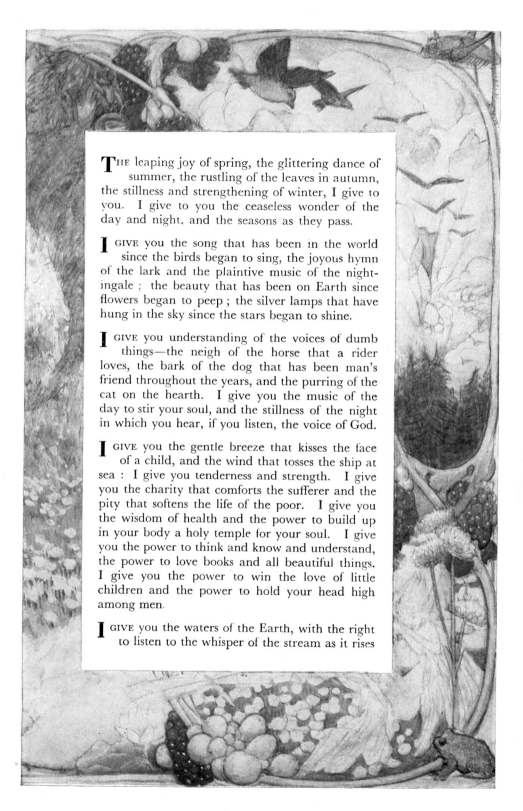

THE leaping joy of spring, the glittering dance of summer, the rustling of the leaves in autumn, the stillness and strengthening of winter, I give to you. I give to you the ceaseless wonder of the day and night, and the seasons as they pass.

I GIVE you the song that has been in the world since the birds began to sing, the joyous hymn of the lark and the plaintive music of the nightingale ; the beauty that has been on Earth since flowers began to peep ; the silver lamps that have hung in the sky since the stars began to shine.

I GIVE you understanding of the voices of dumb things—the neigh of the horse that a rider loves, the bark of the dog that has been man's friend throughout the years, and the purring of the cat on the hearth. I give you the music of the day to stir your soul, and the stillness of the night in which you hear, if you listen, the voice of God.

I GIVE you the gentle breeze that kisses the face of a child, and the wind that tosses the ship at sea : I give you tenderness and strength. I give you the charity that comforts the sufferer and the pity that softens the life of the poor. I give you the wisdom of health and the power to build up in your body a holy temple for your soul. I give you the power to think and know and understand, the power to love books and all beautiful things. I give you the power to win the love of little children and the power to hold your head high among men.

I GIVE you the waters of the Earth, with the right to listen to the whisper of the stream as it rises in the hills, to the chatter of the river as it gathers and widens, and to the shout of the cataract as it splashes through the rocks. I give you the beauty of the moving sea when it kisses the Sun, and the vision of the liquid peaks that rise and fall. I give you the slowly creeping waves that have never been still since the seas were made, and the rocks they have ground into golden sands.

I GIVE you the oceans in calm and storm, with the waters that dance in the air, the showers and the winds, the snow that clothes the world anew in a night, the rain that taps on the window, and the rainbow that springs out of the Sun.

I GIVE you, free for ever, with the right to take whom you will, the full enjoyment of the Natural Gallery of everlasting pictures, and the right to see the unveiling of all sunsets, the covering of the heath with red and gold, the floating past of the clouds that ride like mountain peaks across the sky. I give you access to all the bushes laden with berries, to the daffodils and the violet beds, to the place where ferns and mosses hide, and to the tulips when they hang their heads at night.

I GIVE to you the power to remember and the power to forget, and I give you the strength to forgive. I give you the love of the quiet places where the burden of the petty things will fall away. I give you the right to wander by the brook that babbles o'er the pebbles, to rise early in the morning and see the dew on every

I give you the time of waiting
and the time of fulfilment

buttercup, to lose yourself among the heather and in the field of the cloth of gold.

I GIVE you the Past, with its heritage of good and ill. I give you the Present, with the opportunity that knows no bound. I give you the Future, with the years that never end and know no sorrow.

I GIVE to you the long, long thoughts of youth and the memories of the years; the hope of the dawning life, the dream of the days to be, and the looking-back. I give you the yearning and the craving that make life sweet. I give you the time of waiting and the time of fulfilment. I give you the spirit that good fortune does not mar nor ill fortune break.

I GIVE you the calm that looks out upon the world and will not be discomforted. I give you the heart that does not quail ; the courage that does not flinch ; the faith that will not fail in the Valley of the Shadow. I give you the power to believe in the everlasting spirit of the world.

I GIVE you the love of true things, the love of pure things, and the companionship of sweet liberty. I give you the scorn of all ignoble things, the hate of all things evil, and the strength to march breast-forward against them until they are destroyed.

I GIVE you the promise that they shall be destroyed, that the face of the Earth shall be fair, that the mind of man shall be free, that all that come from God shall yet return to Him, that little children yet shall see the Dawn that no man knows.

The Story of the Boundless Universe and All Its Wondrous Worlds

What This Story Tells Us

HOW still the Earth seems on a moonlight night ! Yet the Earth has never been still for a moment of time. We do not know how long it has been spinning, but for millions and millions of years it has been flying like a ball through space. It began as a cloud of fiery gas ; it cooled and shrank ; and at last it became hard and round like an orange. And, as we now know, the Earth is like a speck in a boundless universe, one of the smallest of a thousand million worlds, all moving on and on in perfect order through space that seems to have no end. What are they like ? Are they alive ? Are little children playing there ? Perhaps not ; we do not know. But they have their place in God's great scheme of things, and here we will read all we can know of them until the day when our eyes shall see and our minds shall understand the marvellous purposes of God.

THE BIG BALL WE LIVE ON

THE big ball we live on, with its mountains, and rivers, and seas, and deserts, and forests, and plants, and animals, is only a speck in the vast infinity of space.

It is one of several balls, some bigger and some smaller and all turning round the Sun, which is much bigger than any of them. If the Sun was hollow, over a million balls, each the size of the Earth, could be dropped into it. Yet the Sun is only a star, and the reason it looks so different from a star is that we are nestled up close to it and so can clearly see its broad face or disc.

And there are many suns in space millions of times as large as ours. Besides suns and, probably, planets, too, there are tremendous clouds of glowing substance known as nebulae, so huge that the Earth in the middle of one of them would be like a pea in the Pacific Ocean. In space itself the Earth is quite lost. Think of the width, and breadth, and height of space !

The Sun seems a long way off, but its light takes only eight minutes to flash across to us, whereas astronomers who have been measuring the distances of stars have calculated that some of them are so far

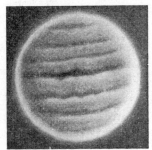

EARTH COOLING DOWN

off that light, which travels 186,282 miles in a second, takes hundreds of years to reach us. An express train would take hundreds of millions of years to cover the distance. Even farther off than that there are stars, for every time a bigger telescope is made new stars come into view. The big Hale telescope on Mount Palomar has revealed thousands of stars out beyond the stars that were previously known.

So little, then, is our big ball, when we look at it amid the suns and nebulae in the immensity of space. But we must not, therefore, think less of our Earth.

We who rush round the sun in such a wonderful chariot, with the stars millions of miles away shining into our eyes, must recognise that the Earth's place amid the suns is a place of wonder and a place of honour. Men can now fly in a jet at a thousand miles an hour ; but what an adventure it is to go flying a thousand miles a minute round the Sun, companioned by Jupiter and Venus and Mars—to go flashing with the Sun along pathless space towards some unknown goal. Life can never be a stupid and dull and sordid thing if we educate

ASTRONOMY · GEOLOGY · GEOGRAPHY · CHEMISTRY · PHYSICS · LIFE

Here our scientific artist, Mr. G. F. Morrell, gives us a Clock of the World's Life.

By their study of the radio-active elements in the Earth's crust and the time they take to lose their radio-activity and change into stable elements, scientists calculate that the Earth's crust may have been formed as long ago as 3,000,000,000 years. It is estimated, moreover, that life has existed on our planet for at least 500,000,000 years.

We can the more readily understand the period occupied by the chief forms of living creatures in their development, until at last Man appeared, by showing them as though on a clock face on which the hour hand has taken 500,000,000 years to make one revolution. On the outer edge of this clock of the world's life are shown in their proper order the names of the successive geological periods. The sections do not, of course, show the relative lengths of these periods.

In the first period came little worms in the sea, the first shellfish and the jolly little trilobites.

Between 2 and 3 sea-scorpions like big lobsters developed ; and between 3 and 4 the first fishes with backbones. It was the first appearance of the Backbone.

From 4 to 6 the armoured fishes grew strong and fought the giant lobsters. It was the first great victory for the Backbone which was to conquer all things.

From 6 to 8 giant trees flourished, and

THE EVOLUTION OF LIFE ON THE EARTH DURING 500,000,000

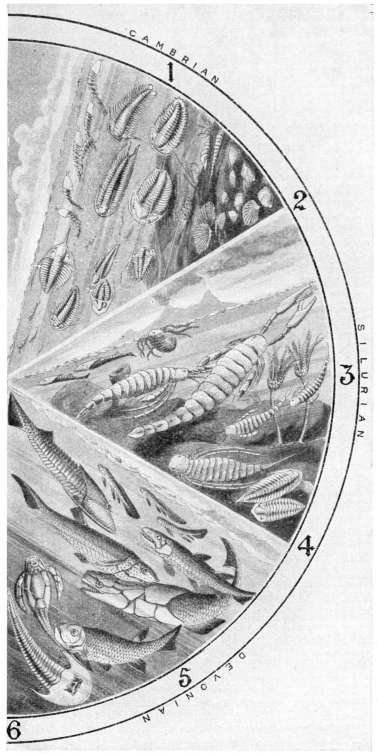

our coalfields were really fields of vegetation. So luxurious was their growth that they seem to have attracted life ashore. It was the age of the Amphibians; feet and legs appeared.

From 8 to 9 was the time of the sea lizards.

From 9 to 10 the reptiles developed; Brontosaur and Stegosaur roamed the forest; flying dragons appeared, followed by birds.

From 10 to 11 was the Cretaceous Period, when the chalk beds were laid down in the sea. The reptiles grew grotesque and terrifying, and the first birds developed, with big claws and teeth, like their reptile ancestors. Then, also, mammals developed, little creatures like opossums, and it is strange to think that they were one day to dethrone the mighty Dinosaurs.

From 11 to 12 is the Tertiary Period, at the end of which we live. During this time mammals have grown mightily, and the Dinosaurs have disappeared. Early in this period came the Dinotherium and the four-tusked Mastodon; and the six-horned Tinoceras fought the Sabre-toothed Tiger. Perhaps half-way through this period came the little lemur-like creatures which developed into monkeys and later into apes; and afterwards, late in the last half-hour of the clock, Man himself appeared.

It may have been a million years ago; we do not know. His written history—written in stone and on the rocks, or on papyrus leaves—is 10,000 years old, like a scratch of a pin in the last hour of the clock.

YEARS—FROM THE CAMBRIAN PERIOD TO THE ARRIVAL OF MAN

our imagination to realise through what a wonderful universe we are rushing.

Think, too, of the marvellous making of our little world. It is interesting to watch a sculptor making a figure out of marble, or to watch a painter putting trees and hills and faces on canvas ; but on our journey through space we see a much more wonderful artistry at work.

THE CLOUD THAT IS BEGINNING TO BE A SUN LIKE OURS

It was once thought that what we call empty space was not empty but full of an invisible substance called the Ether. It was thought that an Ether must exist to support sound, light, and other waves. It is true that sound waves can only be transmitted through some medium of matter, and this is why the Moon, which has no atmosphere, is a world of deathly silence. But we know now that light waves and certain other radiations can travel freely through space without any such medium as an Ether.

Imagine we are looking far into the heavens and suddenly we see a glowing cloud, millions of miles in diameter, which has blossomed out in space.

When astronomers examine such a cloud with telescopes and spectroscopes they discover that it is composed chiefly of the two gases, hydrogen and helium. This does not seem very wonderful, perhaps, but chemists believe that all the elements in the world are built up of atoms of these two light gases. In the cloud, hydrogen and helium are being prepared to make all the other elements that go to make suns and planets.

At this stage the cloud is very thin, thinner even than the air we breathe; but as the gases form, and as new elements are constructed, the cloud contracts, or shrinks, and grows denser and hotter. The chemical processes going on, and the shrinking of the cloud, both produce great heat, and so the cloud becomes a blazing sun like ours.

THE WONDERFUL THOUGHT THAT SO MUCH CAME FROM SO LITTLE

But at a certain point the heat leaks away faster than it is formed, and the sun cools, and as it cools down heavier elements are formed—the gases become partly fluid and partly solid.

We can see in space some suns which have reached this stage, and the spectroscope shows that they contain numerous elements, including iron and other metals. In the cloudy stage astronomers call the sun a giant sun, and in the more condensed stage they call it a dwarf sun ; and finally the dwarf sun cools down entirely and becomes a dead, dark sun.

That is a very brief sketch of how suns are made. But sometimes, while suns are contracting, their surface breaks up and the fragments become planets revolving round them. Something of that sort happened to our Sun ; and the fragments grew into the planets, and one of the planets is our Earth.

It is surely wonderful to think that the Earth was made out of a great cloud, and that at one time all its rocks and seas and animals and plants were nothing but hydrogen and helium gas ! It is surely wonderful to think that a Great Power could bring so much out of so little! And one of the most wonderful things in the making of the Earth was the final steps that made Life possible.

OUT OF THE FLAME AND FIRE CAME THE VERY THINGS LIFE WANTED

At first this big ball of ours was simply a globe of flaming gases and molten metals. As it cooled it formed a solid metallic crust, and as the metal cooled and solidified and condensed, it squeezed out slag as cooling iron in an iron foundry does. This slag formed the early crust of the Earth. And the amazing thing was that the crust contained iron and lime and sulphur and sodium and potassium—*just those elements which were necessary to life.*

More amazing still, when the cooling crust cracked, and when giant volcanoes spouted all over the world, out of the bowels of the Earth came steam which condensed into water and carbon dioxide gas, and so the Earth got rivers and seas and an atmosphere. After millions and millions of years of flame and fire, of seething and boiling and bubbling, there came out of this fragment of the Sun *exactly the right things to make life.* The water, lifted and tossed by the air, broke down the crust into soil and mud—into the clay of life.

All that is amazing and wonderful, but all would have been in vain if the Sun had not been shining across space nearly a hundred million miles away. When the Sun broke up into bits, and the bits went flying as fiery planets round it, it might have seemed an unfortunate accident ;

FROM SUCH A CLOUD OF FIRE CAME EARTH

THE NEBULA OF ANDROMEDA AS SEEN THROUGH THE BIG TELESCOPE AT THE YERKES OBSERVATORY
IN CHICAGO

1. The Earth is not flat, but round like an orange. We know this by the way a ship comes into sight at sea.

2. At first we see only smoke. Then we see the top of the mast, as if the ship were climbing up a hill.

3. Then the bows appear, and we see the vessel rising higher and higher.

HOW WE KNOW THE EARTH IS ROUND

but if the Sun had not flung forth the planets there would probably be no living things in the Solar System today. As it is often best for children to leave their parents and live their own separate lives, so it was best for the Earth to be parted from the Sun and go its own way. But the Earth still revolved round the Sun, and the rays of sunlight still reached the Earth, and it was these rays of sunlight that made living things, even as today they make food for us all.

How living things were manufactured from the materials ready in the Earth's crust and in its atmosphere nobody knows, but it probably came about in this way. On the Earth was the wonderful fluid water, with many substances dissolved in it, and the wonderful gas carbon dioxide which we can see bubbling in a soda-water syphon any day. On the gas dissolved in the water the Sun shone down, and it has been proved that when the Sun shines on such a solution some of the rays form the poison called *formaldehyde*, and other rays manufacture starch out of the poison ; and starch is perhaps the most important substance in the world in relation to life. It contains some of the energy of the sunlight which made it, and this energy comes forth when oxygen is joined to it. When we burn starch, for instance, we get the Sun's energy out of it in the form of light and heat. We know, too, that all the energy of living depends on starch food. The Sun makes starch out of water and carbon dioxide in green plants ; animals eat the starch, and all life depends on the energy of the Sun contained in that compound ; all the tissues of living bodies are built out of it by the processes of digestion.

Now many people believe that Life itself originated in some such way—first the poison that in itself is destructive to life ; then starch ; then from this starch the energetic substance of life called protoplasm. That may or may not be so ; but it is certain that today all living things depend on the energy of the Sun, and that without sunlight life could not be.

In many ways this arrangement of a Sun to put energy into the gas and water of the Earth would seem to be the contrivance of a foreseeing Mind, and it is really a much more complicated arrangement than it looks ; for the Sun's rays would not only make starch but would

4. If the Earth were flat we should see the whole ship at once, not the mast first and the rest bit by bit.

5. But we do not see it that way. We see the ship rising as if it were sailing up the other side of a ball.

6. At last the ship is over the circle, sailing clear on the top of the ball.

THE SHIP COMING UP THE HILL

THE SUN AND HIS FAR-AWAY WORLDS

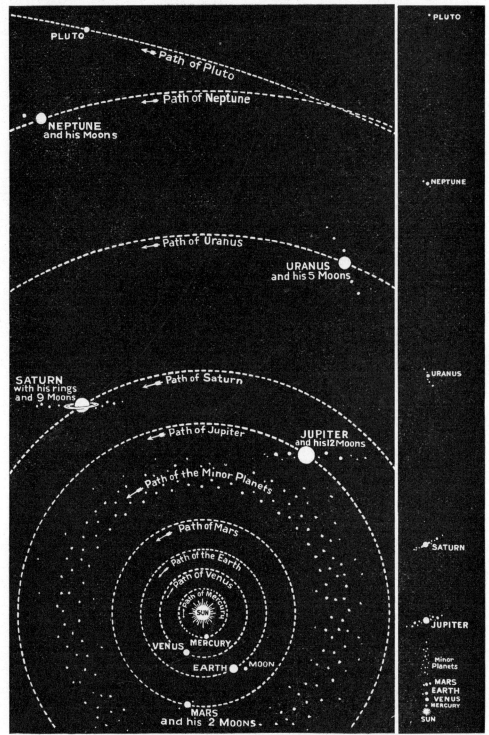

The Sun is in the centre of our part of the Universe. Around it travel for ever a family of worlds which we call planets. The Earth goes round the Sun once in a year, but Pluto takes 248 years to go round. This picture is a diagram of the Solar System; relative sizes and distances are not in proportion.

slay all living things were it not that the atmosphere holds back most of the rays. Exactly the right rays are let through to make starch without destroying life.

In some such way Life began and the conditions on the planet were such that it multiplied and developed till now Earth, air, and sea swarm with myriads of living creatures.

Not only in starch do we enjoy the energy of the Sun that was stored up in the starch of green plants for hundreds of thousands of years. Who could have imagined that all the decaying vegetation in ancient swamps and jungles would one day drive the machinery of unborn men ?

This decaying vegetation becomes coal and is used as fuel and to generate steam to turn the turbines which revolve electric generators. Coal and everything else is made up of atoms which have enormous stores of energy within them, and this energy we are beginning to use. So tremendous is the energy stored in the atom that, used wisely, it could perform all the work necessary for our lives. It can be transformed into electricity to light and heat our homes, drive our machinery, and propel our ships.

EVERYTHING ON EARTH MADE AND PREPARED FOR MAN

Everything in this wonderful planet of ours seems to have been made for us, and, in wise, far-seeing ways, prepared for us. Think of glass, and what it means to us ! Think what the microscope and telescope have revealed to us ! Think what eye-glasses mean to so many ! Yet silicon, the element essential for glass, was collected for us in sea-water by countless myriads of tiny sea organisms which made of it little glass shells, often of delicate beauty.

Wonderful changes have taken place in our world since it first became the home of living creatures. Its crust has been broken, and cracked and crumpled ; its ocean beds have been puckered up into mountain ranges ; continents have sunk beneath the seas. Most of the chalk of England was formed in the bottom of the sea ; and the granite of Scotland is the remnants of mighty volcanoes. Even the Himalayas rose from the ocean ; the Dolomites were once coral reefs ; and many parts of the Earth's surface have been alternately land and ocean floor. Earth has had its tropical periods, too, when great forests and jungles grew in the Polar regions,

and it has had its Ice Ages, when almost all Europe was under glaciers. It has had its Age of Insects, its Age of Reptiles, its Age of Mammals, its Age of Man.

Yet evermore the Earth has gone spinning round the Sun, and evermore Life has blossomed more richly. At first its most wonderful blossom achievement, Man, hardly knew where he was, and it was many ages till he discovered that the Earth was a round ball spinning on its axis and revolving round the Sun. At first he naturally thought the Earth was flat, and that the Sun went round it ; but bold men who sailed about the world proved it to be round, and other clever men discovered the revolution of the planets.

THE SPINNING OF THE EARTH AND WHAT IT GIVES US

The spinning of the Earth on its axis is a very strange thing ; but the Sun also spins, and all the other planets spin, and it is probable that it has meanings we do not understand. But some of its uses to us we do understand ; it gives us alternatives of day and night which help us to divide our lives between activity and rest. It produces the tides, and it is the cause of some of the great regular winds which regulate and modify the climate of the Earth.

The Earth does not spin quite upright, but is inclined a little on its axis, and this slanting of the Earth as it revolves round the Sun is the cause of the seasons in the North and South Hemispheres. At one point in the Earth's revolution the North Pole is leaning towards the Sun and the South Pole away from it ; and at another point in its revolution the South Pole is leaning towards the Sun and the North Pole away from it ; so we have summer and winter alternately in each of the two halves of the globe. During its revolution round the Sun the Earth turns on its axis almost exactly 365 times, and so the year has almost exactly 365 days.

THE BIT OF THE EARTH THAT BROKE OFF LONG AGO

When we are talking of the wonders of the world we must not forget the Moon which revolves round it once every 27 days. Some astronomers think that the Moon is a bit of the Earth, having been torn off by the tug of the Sun from the molten Earth ages ago. Whether this was so or not, the Moon was once much nearer to the Earth than it now is and was spinning rapidly on its axis. It must have raised great tides on

THE PROCESSION OF THE WORLDS

This is what we should see if we could stand out in the Universe and watch the great procession of the worlds that make up the Solar System. In the centre is the Sun, 93 million miles from Earth. Nearest to it is Mercury, then Venus, then our Moon below the Earth. In the picture the Earth looks the biggest world of all, but that is only because it is the nearest to us; the giant planet Jupiter, for instance, has actually a diameter about ten times that of the Earth.

the Earth, which raised much greater tides on the Moon and slowed down its rotation so much that it now always turns the same side toward us. Like the Earth, it had great volcanoes spouting fire, and it must have been a splendid spectacle as it rushed round the Earth dragging great molten tides after it. But it could not hold the gases and the water vapours within it as the Earth did; it was too small to have sufficient gravitational force, and so, even though it had probably the same elements

Venus and Mars, with the silver Moon shining on its oceans? There are bigger suns and planets than ours, but is there any with such a wonderful heritage of life?

And the Earth is the home of mankind, full of beautiful and wonderful things. We are all rushing on, no man knows where, through the ocean of infinite space. We are spinning round at thousands of miles an hour, we are revolving round the Sun at eighteen miles a second, but so smooth is the motion that we feel neither the whirl

THE LITTLE WORLD NEAREST TO THE EARTH—THE MOON THROUGH A BIG TELESCOPE

as the Earth in its crust, it never managed to produce plants or animals.

In time this fragment of the Earth got farther and farther from the Earth, and in time it cooled down, and now it is like an enormous piece of dry slag covered with huge extinct volcanoes, and it keeps always the same side to the Earth.

Could there be a more marvellous world than this planet of ours, spinning on its axis and racing round the Sun between

nor the rush. On and on we go, and when the Earth has revolved some seventy times round the Sun, you, I, and each one of us, must go perhaps on a still longer and more wonderful journey. But while we are in the world let us try to explore its wonders and understand it, seeing in all things the wisdom and love of God who made us out of a cloud of gas.

(Next chapter in this group, page 137)

The Story of Immortal Folk Whose Work Will Never Die

What This Story Tells Us

NONE of us can ever pay the debt we owe to those who lived before us—to the men who made life easier and happier and healthier for us all. Have you ever thought, when looking through the window, that once there was not a pane of glass in the world ? Then a man dug things out of the earth, mixed them, and made Glass. Who was he ? We do not know. Nor do we know the man who found fire, or the man who found iron. Here, however, we shall read of some of those immortal men and women whose work is known and will never be forgot—those who wrote books and painted pictures, who found power and made ships and railways and aeroplanes, who gave us light, who conquered plague and found out the laws of health, who gave us liberty and law and knowledge. Let us never forget the debt to them that we can never pay.

THE FIRST FLYING MEN

MEN have always been jealous of the birds. As far as legend carries us back we trace man's yearning to fly.

Think what it would have meant to men to fly in the days when they had neither trains nor ships nor roads ; when the seas were still unplumbed and mountain barriers raised their heads forbidding man to cross them ; when a trip from London to York by coach was so alarming that before starting men made their wills and took leave of their families as solemnly as if they were going forth to war.

King David sighed for the wings of a dove. The Greeks represented one of their legendary heroes with wings of wax, which melted when he approached too near the sun.

Roger Bacon, whose genius towered like a beacon-light over a dark sea of ignorance, had a flash of inspiration when he suggested that the upward way of man must be in a vessel made lighter than air by the use, in a thin metal cylinder, of either heated air or something which seems to have been a sort of gas. But he might as well have whispered his ideas to the Moon, so far ahead of his age was he. Then there were those who, through ages of experiment, cracked their skulls or maimed

THE LANGLEY FLYING MEDAL

themselves by trying to match the way of a bird in the air, with the aid of flip-flap paddles or sail-like wings worked by the arms and legs.

Nothing came of all the old experiments of our ancestors, except to set an example to posterity of courage and fearless endeavour. They could raise glorious cathedrals, but they could not think out the mechanism of flying. When the first flight was made, it took place at what seemed to be the predestined hour.

Henry Cavendish discovered hydrogen in 1766 ; the first balloon was sent up in public in 1783—but not with hydrogen, which had to wait a little longer to be harnessed. It was a puff of smoke that suggested the balloon. Two brothers, Joseph Michael and Jacques Etienne Montgolfier, sons of a paper-maker near Lyons, watching the smoke rising from a fire, speculated as to whether, being lighter than air, smoke would lift a weight. They tested the question by inflating a paper bag with smoke, and the bag floated up to the ceiling. The brothers thought some special property in the smoke was responsible for the lifting power, but they could not do much because they were unable to get enough smoke into their

EXPLORERS · INVENTORS · WRITERS · ARTISTS · SCIENTISTS

paper bags, until a neighbour's wife came in and suggested that they should tie a dish full of fire and smoke to the bag itself.

The brothers did so, and the bag went up and remained longer than ever in the air. Within seven years of its discovery hydrogen was suggested by Dr. Black, the father of English chemistry, as a method of causing light bladders to float in the air, and in the very year in which the Montgolfiers began their smoke experiments a man named Cavallo had sent up soap-bubbles filled with hydrogen. But the Montgolfiers went on using smoke. They made larger paper bags and raised them with little braziers attached.

HOW THE FIRST MEN WERE LIFTED INTO THE AIR BY FIRE

The chief terror of the flying man is fire, but the first man-carrying balloons were raised by fire ! Experiments having been made with paper-lined linen balloons of varying dimensions filled with smoke, Pilâtre de Rozier went up in a Montgolfier balloon in November, 1783, accompanied by the Marquis d'Arlandes. A wicker basket was fixed to the balloon, and a little furnace to supply smoke and heat was attached to the basket. They rose from Paris armed with bundles of wood to feed their fire, and with wet sponges to apply to any flames which might break out in the fabric of the balloon.

There have been few more adventurous voyages than that. The balloon lobbed up and down in the air, threatening to drop into the Seine. The only remedy was to fire up, and that endangered the balloon, which actually was alight in several places. But the journey across Paris was accomplished safely.

THE FRENCHMEN WHO WENT UP IN A THUNDERSTORM

This fantastic bit of gallantry was no sooner achieved than the first balloon to be filled with hydrogen carried up two other Frenchmen a height of 14,000 feet, weathering a thunderstorm and travelling thirty miles. Ascent followed ascent after this, and the public imagination was so fired that plans were soon in progress for building balloons to reach the moon ! Hydrogen now took the place of the furnace in the balloon. The light gas, of which 14 cubic feet lift one pound, was the only possible agent for continuous experiments ; without it ballooning would soon have come to an end. It came to

the use of man before the balloon, yet its possibilities as a lifting force was illustrated by a puff of smoke in a paper-maker's house. Ballooning came from smoke ; the aeroplane propeller came from the boomerang.

For over a century balloons shared the sky with the birds, with the decided difference that, while birds fly wherever they will, balloons were always the sport of any wind that blew. They could not be steered. When near the ground their course might be retarded, and in some respects directed, by a long rope with an anchor attached ; but such a rope might drag a man up into the air, whisk a cow off its legs, pull a chimney off a roof, or bring down part of a church steeple.

A TERRIBLE ADVENTURE OF TWO MEN UP IN THE CLOUDS

Balloonists did magnificent work in tapping the secrets of the upper air. They revealed the fact that air lies in layers, and that over our heads in what seems an even atmosphere there may be winds one above another ; that while a balloon is sailing serenely in a blue sky from east to west with a low wind, it may meet a terrific thunderstorm coming up on a higher wind from west to east. A great body of knowledge these men accumulated for our flying-engine men ; and they risked their lives and often gave them.

Many magnificent feats of endurance stand to their honour also. The achievement of a scientist named Glaisher and a daring and skilful balloonist named Coxwell has never been forgotten. Before we had ever heard of cylinders of oxygen for the use of airmen at great heights these two splendid fellows, one day in 1862, rose seven miles. They wanted to descend, but the rope connected with the valve was fouled, and Coxwell had to climb into the rigging to clear it. The temperature was below zero, and as Coxwell touched metal his hands were frost-bitten, and his task proved long and difficult. Glaisher found paralysis stealing over him. Power went from his limbs ; his sight failed ; he could barely breathe ; yet his mind remained intensely active till the last. Then he fell unconscious in the car of the balloon.

Coxwell had at last secured the rope he had gone up to disentangle, but when he descended he found that his hands were useless. There was the balloon mounting

STRUGGLING UPWARD THROUGH THE DAWN

Otto Lilienthal

Langley in his hour of success

Santos Dumont

Orville Wright

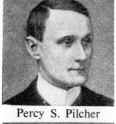

Wilbur Wright

Orville Wright's first flight, in 1903

From a photograph in the Science Museum, London.

Louis Bleriot

Percy S. Pilcher

Marquis D'Arlandes

Langley in his hour of defeat

Pilâtre de Rozier

James Glaisher

Henry Coxwell

MEN WHO WORKED THROUGH THE GENERATIONS TO WIN THE POWER OF FLIGHT

21

up into the sky and two men near death rising with her, like the phantom crew of the Flying Dutchman. But the immense will-power of Coxwell saved the situation. He gripped the rope between his teeth and tugged and tugged and tugged at it with his last gleam of energy. The valve opened; the balloon began to descend; they dropped rapidly into a warmer layer of air. Glaisher recovered, and they were saved. All honour to the men of the balloons! They worked and worried on for generations.

THE ENGLISHMAN WHO MISSED THE FAME OF BEING THE FIRST MAN TO FLY

The next step lay with the men of the motor-engine. Between balloons and aeroplanes came the men who risked their lives by constructing planes and throwing themselves off walls and buildings and cliff-faces, and gliding to earth like the so-called flying animals. A man would begin by launching himself off a bank three feet high and plane across his lawn, and would end by skimming down from a house-top.

It is thrilling to look back and realise how strangely an Englishman missed the fame of being the first man to fly. He was Percy Pilcher, who in the nineties of the last century was experimenting with gliders in a valley in Kent. He had nearly finished making a little four-horsepower engine to fit to his best glider in 1899 when he went to Lord Braye's park at Standford in Northamptonshire to give a demonstration of gliding. He took with him his second-best glider, the Hawk, and, although the weather was bad, he would not disappoint the crowd. When he was about 30 feet up, a rudder wire broke, the Hawk crashed, and he was killed. An Ionic column marks the spot.

THE AMERICAN SCIENTIST WHO INSPIRED THE WRIGHT BROTHERS

Had he lived he might well have beaten the famous American brothers, Wilbur and Orville Wright. For Pilcher, with the Frenchman, Octave Chanute, and the German, Otto Lilienthal, gave much inspiration to those brothers who were destined to solve the problem.

Before the Wrights' triumph, however, a fellow-countryman of theirs came near success. He was the American scientist, Samuel Pierpont Langley, the first of all inventors to make a heavier-than-air machine fly independently—but his was only a model. His dream of making a machine that would carry a man was never

realised. But he, too, inspired the Wright brothers, chiefly because he was a scientist who, in spite of the world's ridicule of the idea, believed that men could fly. Langley's plan was in opposition to the mighty authority of Sir Isaac Newton. Many trials showed him that an engine will carry a larger weight at 20 miles an hour than at 10 miles an hour, and a still larger weight at 40 m.p.h. than at 20.

In plain language, the faster you move from place to place in the air the better will be your support from the body of atmosphere beneath the machine.

Numberless were the tests and experiments tried by Professor Langley before at last, on May 6, 1896, he went out with his friend Dr. Graham Bell, the telephone inventor, and launched a model from the top of a house-boat moored on the River Potomac. The first power-driven aeroplane weighed only 25 pounds. It had a wing-span of 13 feet, it was driven by a little steam-engine, and it *flew!* It rose from the house-boat, glided smoothly into the air, sailed above the trees until the steam failed and the propeller ceased to work. Then it planed down into the river, was recovered, dried, and set flying again.

THE MOST DRAMATIC MOMENT IN THE HISTORY OF HUMAN FLIGHT

It was the most dramatic moment in the history of flight, and the inventor was so excited that he could not gaze upon the scene, but withdrew into the woods.

News of this great success was received with mingled rapture and disbelief. To Langley it seemed that his task was ended. He had solved a scientific problem, and it was for the commercial world now to develop the idea if it cared to do so; he wanted no financial gain. There the matter rested for some years, until Langley was persuaded to try a man-carrying aeroplane. He made one in 1903, which, with its engine, weighed 125 pounds. He could think of no better way of launching it than of starting from the roof of the same house-boat as before, and so it was all arranged. But the machine dived straight into the river. It was recovered, and more attempts made to launch it, but each time it fell into the water. Fickle public opinion turned against the hapless inventor, and poured ridicule upon him.

Langley uttered no complaint, but he

WILBUR WRIGHT AND HIS BROTHER ORVILLE THINK OUT A PROBLEM IN THEIR WORKSHOP

went home and said to a friend: " My life's work is a failure."

Only nine days later the Wright brothers made their first flight ! One would think that this would have turned the tables on those who had derided Langley as a crank. But not a bit of it. Strange as it seems to us, it was some years before the world as a whole believed that the Wrights *had* flown.

THE FIRST AEROPLANE AS A CURIOSITY IN THE SMITHSONIAN INSTITUTE

Langley knew it was true, for he was on the best of terms with the Wrights. He died a disappointed man in 1906, leaving his own machine lying as a curiosity in the Smithsonian Institution at Washington, where he had been a professor.

So that it was an American who gave us the first aeroplane; and it was an American who made the first flight. Wilbur Wright, born in Indiana, in 1867, and his brother Orville, born at Dayton in Ohio in 1871, are the actual accomplishers of human flight. Their father was a modest minister; their sister Katherine was a schoolteacher; the two lads were among Nature's nobility. They were eager scholars at school; they set up in business as printers, and added bicycle-making and bicycle-mending to their calling. It was in 1896, the year in which Langley's model flew, that they took up the study of aircraft. They read all they could read on the subject, made many experiments in their little bicycle shop, and found many theories wrong, inaccurate, even dangerous.

THE ABIDING GLORY OF ORVILLE AND WILBUR WRIGHT

They tried all sorts of gliding mechanism, and Orville once did a glide against an up-current of wind of just over one minute. But they were working towards an engine-driven aeroplane, and with their practical minds they saw that the engine most suited for the work was one of the internal combustion type, driven by petrol, and avoiding the worry and danger of carrying furnace, coal, and water up into the clouds. They went out into the wilds of North Carolina, lived in a hut at Kitty Hawk, and there carried out trials with the tiny motor-engine they had built. They were often hard pressed for money, but their father helped from his shallow purse, and Katherine, their sister, gave every penny she could save from her school earnings. At last they harnessed their plane to the puffing internal combustion engine. On December 17, 1903, one of them flew for 59 seconds !

That was a red-letter day in the history of human progress. Two young men whose friends and neighbours thought them crazy, who tinkered with an invention at the back of their little bicycle shop, were the first human beings to rise from the ground in a heavier-than-air, power-driven machine. They had made it themselves, and had had to teach themselves to fly ! The glory of Wilbur and Orville Wright will shine down the centuries.

Older people can remember when Wilbur Wright came over to Europe and startled them all by flying in France. It is strange now to remember the time when he was tapping away in a shed in the middle of a field in France, preparing the machine which was to astonish all who saw it. All day long the peasants gathered about the mysterious wooden shed, and as the days went by and nothing happened the peasants began to jeer.

THE GREAT DAY WHEN WILBUR WRIGHT WAS UP AMONG THE BIRDS

And then one day the great doors of the wooden house swung open, and out came Wilbur Wright, in grey suit and cap, and out came a great ungainly thing which is very familiar now, but was something to laugh at then—a huge thing of wood and canvas, full of wires, and bars and levers, running along on wheels; and the people laughed more than ever. This was the thing they had waited weeks to see, and as, at last, the machine was run into the middle of the field, the peasants jeered more than ever.

But Wilbur Wright cared nothing at all. He sat down in his seat and got ready.

One ! he shouted.

The crowd jeered.

Two ! he shouted.

The crowd jeered louder.

Three ! he shouted, and the crowd jeered no more, for Wilbur Wright was flying among the birds.

He came down from the skies, never, never to be jeered at again, for these people, belonging to the most emotional race in the world, hailed this hero and kissed him. They had seen the first man fly.

Not many weeks after that the Founder of this Children's Encyclopedia left his desk and went out to see Wilbur Wright fly at the foot of the Pyrenees, and this is what he wrote home that night:

"Out of this wooden shed—so rough a place for the beginning of the flight of man—came Wilbur Wright.

"There was a sound of whirring wheels; a man was oiling the propellers; Wilbur Wright was moving.

THE KEEN LITTLE MAN IN HIS BIG LEATHER JACKET

"He dragged a clumsy stool across a floor of dust, stepped in among the wires, filled a huge jug with petrol, and climbed up with it on to the stool. He could hardly reach with his great jug—he has not had time to make a pair of steps. But two jugfuls of petrol go into the pipes, and down he comes.

"He goes into his room, and comes out in his black leather jacket. He is going to fly. He goes out of the shed into the field, where is a simple little rail with a pulley arrangement, which he himself puts in order. For a quarter of an hour he moves about, while all the people who are not going to fly wish he would go up; and then the lumbering thing comes out on wheels. Slipping off its wheels, it rests on the rail. The men start the engine by turning the propellers. A dozen people take hold of a rope and pull up the weights that are to give the aeroplane momentum to start. Wilbur Wright sits down on one of the two little slabs of wood with arms like a child's swing. Then—swish!—swish!—he goes along the rail into the middle of a field, and at the end of the rail the man-bird rises in the air.

THE THRILLING SIGHT OF THE MAN-BIRD OVER THE PYRENEES

"Away he flies, on and on, and to see him is the most thrilling thing. The great lumbering thing becomes a thing of grace and beauty. It curves this way and that; it rises high and falls low; it goes straight and spins round; it dips and bends like the wings of a bird; it flies to the hills until it looks in the distance like a motor-car dashing along the snow-covered ridges of the Pyrenees. It flies at the rate of forty miles an hour over the tree-tops until it has gone from sight, and then, after ten minutes, the man-bird comes back, racing a bird that flies beside him, and comes straight over our heads.

"Now we see the man-bird clearly, see him sitting on his seat, his face set stern and straight, knowing nothing of the little crowd below, his eyes fixed ahead, his hand grasping the levers that control the engine and keep him a hundred feet above us.

"The flying machine is alive! No longer is it a great ungainly thing. It moves like the wings of a bird, under the most perfect government of this simple, wonderful man, flying above us and about us for half an hour, and coming down at our feet like—what shall I say to be true?—like a feather on the breeze. Like that exactly. The end of it was amazing beyond belief. This great thing, that had grown beautiful before our eyes, came down from the skies and rested gently on the ground without a tremor or a jolt, with less of that than if it had been a stick thrown up in the street and allowed to fall. It was a thrilling and splendid and historic thing."

WILBUR WRIGHT AND THE INSPIRER OF THE CHILDREN'S ENCYCLOPEDIA

That was the introduction of the aeroplane into Europe; and Wilbur Wright on one of these historic flights carried up with him a portrait of the child who inspired the Children's Encyclopedia.

One of Wilbur's many visitors at that period was an Englishman, the Honourable C. S. Rolls who, with Sir F. H. Royce, had already given the world the famous motor car. Charles Rolls in 1910 was the first man to fly across the Channel in both directions in a single flight, the great French pioneer, Louis Blériot, having flown one way in the previous year.

Those were the years when the new art of human flight spread rapidly. C. Grahame-White, in 1909, was the first Englishman to be granted an aviator's certificate. Sir A. Verdon-Roe (described on another page) was the British pioneer in aircraft construction; Henri Farman, the Frenchman, was in 1909 the first airman to fly a circuit of 100 miles.

There was the Brazilian, Santos-Dumont, the airship man who turned to making planes; our own Lord Brabazon, who in 1909 made the first officially observed flight in Britain; Sir Geoffrey de Havilland who, in 1910 built his own plane, and whose son was killed in 1946 while attacking the world speed record in a jet-propelled plane.

There were many others, but the leaders of them all were the two bicycle-shop boys, Wilbur and Orville Wright.

ROUND ABOUT THE FIRE DANCED A FUNNY LITTLE MAN UPON ONE LEG, SINGING, "RUM-PEL-STILT-SKIN IS MY NAME." See story on page 30

The Great Stories of the World That Will Be Told for Ever

What These Pages Tell Us

THERE is a kingdom that belongs to us all. Its gates are never closed. Yet no man has seen half the wonderful things this kingdom holds—its enchanted islands, its silvery streams, its magic caves, its mysterious rooms; its giants and fairies and dragons and gnomes; its marvellous ways down in the sea, under the earth, up in the clouds; its wondrous colour, its heavenly music, its secrets of happiness that all who will can find. This kingdom is yours and mine; it is the Kingdom of the Storybook. Here we will walk its streets together and hear the stories children have been told since human life began. We shall read the stories they told in Babylon and Greece and Rome; the fables and legends and chivalry and golden deeds and fairy tales that have come down to us in books. We shall see the imagination of the world working through all ages, among all peoples.

KING MIDAS

HERE is a story which in olden times the reeds would tell the winds that rush across the surface of the Earth.

One day, when Gordius, the ploughman of Phrygia, came up to the city in a cart, drawn by white bulls, a crowd thronged to him shouting : " The king is dead ! You are to reign over us, for the Oracle has said, *Put on the throne the first man entering the town in a cart drawn by white bulls.*"

The grateful Gordius betook himself to the temple, where he fastened the cart to the altar with such clever knots that no ends could be seen, and the Oracle declared that whoso should untie this knot should conquer Asia. It was not till long after that Alexander, conquering the world, cut the Gordian knot with his sword. But Midas, the son of Gordius, did not care about conquering Asia; he loved a quiet life and never thought of wars. Yet his quiet country life was soon to be shaken.

One day some shepherds of Phrygia carried to the palace a man they had found wandering in the country, and Midas recognised him as Silenus, the friend of Dionysus. Delighted to befriend him, he entertained him for ten days and

nights with an unceasing round of jollity, but on the eleventh day, thinking that Dionysus must sadly miss his friend, King Midas took him back.

Thereupon Dionysus, in his joyfulness at seeing his counsellor once more, offered Midas whatever he wished.

Truly a wonderful chance had come for him had Midas been wise, but the poor king, too greatly excited to think wisely, begged that everything he touched might change into gold ! Dionysus, though lamenting the astonishing choice of his friend, consented, and so it was ordained. King Midas went on his way rejoicing.

At first everything went well with him, and the king could scarcely believe his eyes. If he picked up a twig it became gold in his hands; if he touched a stone it was transformed; his very throne was turned to gold as he sat down on it. But, alas, how was King Midas going to live ?

Too late the awful truth began to dawn on him. All the food he carried to his lips, every drink with which he sought to quench his thirst, were solid gold for him ! Even worse was yet to come, for when he kissed his child she changed into a golden statue before his wondering eyes.

IMAGINATION · CHIVALRY · LEGENDS · GOLDEN DEEDS · FAIRY TALES

Burdened with this terrible affliction, the King of Phrygia strove to get rid of his fearful power ; but all his striving was in vain. At length, in his despair, he implored the god to deliver him from the consequences of his foolish prayer, and Dionysus heard him and yielded. " Go to the River Pactolus," said the god to Midas, " and plunge into the stream."

Midas went, and scarcely had he touched the waters when his power passed to the river, so that the sands have carried gold-dust ever since. From that time, hating wealth and splendour, Midas dwelt in the woods and became a friend of Pan, god of the fields. Often would he take Pan to his palace, and in the king's garden Pan would cut fresh reeds for his famous flute, on which he played tunes so sweet that lambs would follow him, enchanted.

The new happiness that had come to him greatly rejoiced the king, who became a worshipper of Pan ; but, alas, things were to take a tragic turn for Midas.

Apollo making fun of Pan one day, the god of the fields answered with a challenge, saying, " My flute is well worth your lyre " ; and Midas offered his hall for a concert.

On the appointed day a great crowd hastened to the palace. Apollo had invited his nine sisters, the Muses, who came down from the lofty mountains and arrived with Apollo, who rode on the silver wings of his famous horse Pegasus, whose flight was like the lightning flash.

Pan began. He copied the melodious call of the blackbird, the jolly chirping of the sparrow, the thrilling note of the nightingale. Midas loved the song of birds, and, applauding long, he hardly listened to Apollo's play. However, the victory was awarded to the god of the lyre, and all but Midas accepted the judgment.

The anger of Apollo with Midas knew no bounds, and, annoyed that the king's ears should be so depraved, he resolved that they should no longer retain their human form. As Midas mounted his horse on his way back to the palace, Apollo murmured some words of which only the first and last could be heard ; but none paid any attention, and Midas rode away. It was not till he was once more at the palace, with his barber, that he caught sight of his shadow and found that he had ass's ears ! Apollo had avenged himself.

The king vowed his barber to solemn secrecy on pain of losing his own ears ; and a new head-dress for Midas hid his affliction from the people.

Only the barber knew, and well he kept the secret until at last the burden of it was more than he could bear. And so one day the barber ran to a field, dug a hole, lay flat on the ground, and whispered into the hole: " Midas, King Midas, has ass's ears ! "

Then, having covered up the hole, the barber went home with a lighter heart, but little guessing what would follow.

In the following year, as he happened to pass by the field, he noticed, waving in the wind, a tuft of reeds, and hardly could our barber believe his ears, for at every touch of the wind the reeds were saying : " Midas, King Midas, has ass's ears ! "

The poor barber fell stricken to the earth, dead. Soon after a child passed by that way and heard the same words on the wind ; and the child repeated them, so that soon the secret of King Midas was known all over the world.

THE THREE LITTLE PIGS

Once upon a time three little pigs went out into the world to seek their fortunes. The first little pig had not gone far before he met a man carrying straw.

" If you please," said the little pig, " will you give me some of that straw to make me a house ? "

" With pleasure," replied the man.

Away went the little pig with the straw and built his house.

Now, an artful old wolf who lived close by determined to have the little pig for supper. So when it became dusk he went up to the little straw house and called out : " Little pig, little pig, may I come in ? "

But the little pig knew his voice, and said : " No, no ; by the hair on my chinny, chin, chin ! "

" Ho, ho ! " cried the wolf. " Then I'll puff and I'll blow till I blow your house in." And he puffed and he blew, and he puffed and he blew, till the house fell down. Then he sprang inside, pounced on the little pig, and gobbled him all up.

The second little pig met a man carrying some sticks.

" If you please," said the little pig, " will you give me some of those sticks to make me a house ? "

" With much pleasure," replied the man.

Away went the little pig with the sticks and built himself a cosy house.

That night the wolf came to the door.

"Little pig, little pig," cried the wolf, "may I come in?"

"No, no," replied this little pig, "by the hair on my chinny, chin, chin!"

"Ho, ho!" cried the wolf. "Then I'll puff and I'll blow till I blow your house in."

And he puffed and he blew, and he puffed and he blew, till the house fell down. Then he sprang inside, pounced on the little pig, and gobbled him all up.

But the third little pig was exceedingly wide awake the morning *he* set out on his travels. This little pig went on till he saw a man carrying bricks.

"If you please," said the little pig, "will you give me some of those bricks to make me a house?"

"With pleasure," replied the man.

house. But the little pig must have got up earlier still, for when the wolf arrived he found him out. The wolf hurried off to the orchard; but the little pig saw him coming and climbed up into a tree.

"These are indeed fine apples," he called out, as the wolf came up to it. "Just try this one." And he threw the apple as far away as he could into some long grass. Then, while the wolf was hunting for it, the little pig ran home.

The wolf did not like being beaten, so the next morning he went again to the little pig's house, and said: "There's going to be a fair on the village green this afternoon. You come with me and we'll have a fine time. I'll call for you at three o'clock."

The little pig said nothing, but at half-past two he started off for the fair. He bought a churn, and was rolling it home when he saw the wolf in the distance.

THE THREE LITTLE PIGS

Away went the little pig with the bricks and built his house.

Soon the old wolf came along that way.

"Little pig, little pig, may I come in?"

"No, no; by the hair on my chinny, chin, chin!"

"Then I'll puff and I'll blow till I blow your house in!"

But the house was made of bricks, and the old wolf he puffed and he blew, and still the house stood firm.

The wolf was furious; but, pretending he did not mind, he said, quite pleasantly:

"Do you like apples? I know an orchard down the lane where the trees are covered with fruit. I'll call for you in the morning, and show you the way."

The next morning the wolf got up very early, and walked round to the little pig's

Quick as lightning the little pig jumped into the churn to hide, and set it rolling down the hill. It came flying along at such a speed that the wolf became frightened, and ran home as fast as he could. When he felt braver he went to the little pig's house.

"I was just on my way to call for you this afternoon," he shouted out, "when I met an awful thing rolling down the hill all by itself. It gave me a horrible fright."

The little pig burst out laughing.

"It was I," said he; "I spied you coming and jumped inside to save my skin."

This so enraged the wolf that he jumped up on to the roof and began sliding down the chimney. But it was baking day, and the little pig had made a huge fire, and that was the end of the old wolf.

RUM-PEL-STILT-SKIN

IN a certain kingdom once lived a poor miller who had a very beautiful daughter. She was, moreover, exceedingly shrewd and clever ; and the miller was so proud of her that one day he told the King of the land that his daughter could spin gold out of straw. Now this King was very fond of money, and when he heard the miller's boast he ordered the girl to be brought before him. Then he led her to a chamber where there was a great quantity of straw, gave her a spinning-wheel, and said, "All this must be spun into gold before morning, as you value your life."

It was in vain that the poor maiden declared she could do no such thing : the chamber was locked and she was alone.

She sat down in the corner of the room and began to cry. The door opened, and a droll-looking little man hobbled in, and said, " Good-day to you. What are you weeping for ? "

"Alas ! " answered she, " I must spin this straw into gold, and I know not how."

" What will you give me," said the little man, " to do it for you ? "

" My necklace," replied the maiden.

He took her at her word, and set himself down to the wheel. Round about it went merrily, and before very long the gold was all spun.

When the King came and saw this he was greatly astonished and pleased ; but his heart grew still more greedy, and he shut up the poor miller's daughter again with a fresh task. Then she knew not what to do; but the little man presently opened the door, and said, " What will you give me to do your task ? "

" The ring on my finger," she replied. So her little friend took the ring, and began to work at the wheel, till by the morning all was finished again.

The King was vastly delighted to see all this glittering treasure ; but still he was not satisfied, and took the miller's daughter into a yet larger room, and said, " All this must be spun tonight ; and if you succeed you shall be my Queen."

As soon as she was alone the dwarf came in, and said, " What will you give me to spin gold this third time ? "

" I have nothing left," said she.

" Then promise me," said the little man, " your first little child when you are Queen."

" That may never be," thought the miller's daughter ; but, as she knew no other way to get her task done, she promised him what he asked, and he spun once more the whole heap into gold. The King came in next morning, and, finding all he wanted, married her.

At the birth of her first little child the Queen rejoiced very much, and forgot the little man and her promise ; but one day he came into her chamber and reminded her of it. Then she offered him all the treasures of the kingdom in exchange ; but in vain, till at last her tears softened him, and he said, " If in three days you can tell me my name you shall keep your child."

Now, the Queen lay awake all night, thinking of all the odd names that she had ever heard, and despatched messengers through the land to inquire after new ones. The next day the little man came, and she began with Timothy, Benjamin, Jeremiah, and all the names she could remember, but to each one he said, " That's not my name."

The second day she began with all the comical names she could hear of, Bandy-legs, Hunchback, Crookshanks, and so on ; but the little gentleman still said to every one, " That's not my name."

On the third day came back one of the messengers, and said, " Yesterday, as I was climbing a high hill among the trees of the forest where the fox and the hare bid each other good-night, I saw a little hut, and before the hut burnt a fire, and round about the fire danced a funny little man upon one leg, singing :

> Merrily the feast I'll make,
> Today I'll brew, tomorrow bake ;
> Merrily I'll dance and sing,
> For next day will a stranger bring ;
> Little does my lady dream
> Rum-Pel-Stilt-Skin is my name ! "

Then the Queen jumped for joy ; and as soon as her little visitor came she said :

" Is your name John ? "

" No ! "

" Is it Tom ? "

" No ! "

" Is it Rum-Pel-Stilt-Skin ? "

" Some witch told you that ! " cried the little man, and dashed his right foot in a rage so deep into the floor that he was forced to lay hold of it with both hands to pull it out. Then he made the best of his way off, while everybody laughed at him for having had all his trouble for nothing at all.

THE KING'S NIGHT OF TERROR

THERE was a great multitude in the streets of Palermo, for not only was the morrow a feast day, but the king was expected to go by, on his way to church.

Presently he came, the cold, handsome, haughty, and roystering King Robert of Sicily. Splendidly arrayed, he was surrounded on all sides by a glittering retinue well-nigh as splendid. The evening sun goldened his brown face and made specks of fire in his black beard. There was such a pride in his eye, such a majesty in the carriage of his head, such a masterfulness in his stride, that he seemed like a lord of the human race and emperor of all the world.

The acclaiming shout of the people drowned the ring of the spurred heels, the clatter of the swords, and the gay laughter of the king and his courtiers. In the square before the church the loud huzzas drowned the music of the organ.

The priests were singing the beautiful evening hymn of the Church, Magnificat.

"What do these Latin words mean?" asked the king of a young clerk.

"They mean, sire," came the answer, "He hath put down the mighty from their seat, and hath exalted the humble and meek."

The king frowned. Then, with a bitter laugh he said, "Tis very like sedition. But I tell you this—no person in heaven or on earth can rob me of my throne."

THE JESTER RUSHED UP TO THE POPE

A little later, and the slumbrous words of prayer had sent the king asleep in the shadows of the carven stalls.

He woke. There was darkness on every side. A vast silence held the church. He was there alone.

With an oath, he started from his seat. His scabbarded sword and pointed spurs set strange echoes ringing as he strode down the dark aisle. His heart was on fire with rage and indignation. They had gone —his courtiers and those dogs of priests—and left him in the church alone.

His great hand thundered on the door till the beams groaned and the iron rattled. The sexton came with the lantern.

"Who is there?" he cried.

"The king!"

Shaking his head and placing the key in the lock, the old man muttered to himself, "Some drunken beggar!" Then he opened the door, prepared to speak stern words. A man rushed by as if in madness, and vanished in the dark.

King Robert sped through the darkness to his palace. He gained the banquet hall, which was ablaze with light and cheerful with sounds of merriment. On the threshold he stopped dead, his cheeks blanched, his knees tottering.

Another king—himself in face and form and raiment, yet glorious with some mystic holiness—occupied his throne.

"Who art thou?" demanded this mysterious being, gravely regarding him.

"I! I am the king!" cried Robert,

with a sudden accession of strength and indignation. But as he spoke courtiers and guests leaped up, and, drawing swords, would angrily have killed him.

"Nay!" smiled the mysterious being. "You have made a mistake. You are not the king, but the king's jester. You shall be furnished with cap and bells; you shall have an ape for your companion ; you shall lie on stable straw."

And, with the laughter of his people in his ears, the king was borne away to stable straw and cap and bells.

Long he lived as the jester, making sport for all, and buffeted by his own soldiers and servants, companioned in his stall at night by a black ape that watched unmoved his bitter tears.

In vain he cried, "I am the king!" That made the courtiers laugh the more, and made the men-at-arms more scornful with their blows. They flung him scraps of food, and, smiting him with glove or lance, would say, "Long live the king!" and laugh to see the ape creep up beside the jester to share his broken meat.

Thus sadly and despairingly lived King Robert, thought by all to be a madman, till on a certain day the mysterious being on the throne announced a journey to the great city of Rome. Then did King Robert's heart revive. For the Pope was his brother, and at Rome, also, was the Emperor Valmond, likewise his brother. Surely, when he reached Rome with this false king, he would be recognised, and the usurper driven from his throne.

Never was greater pomp and glory seen than in that journey of state from Sicily to Rome. And as the cavalcade passed through sunny Italy, dazzling all eyes that saw it, behind it rolled, like the breaking of a wave, a tide of laughter, merry as a summer's day. For Robert, in his cap and bells, seated upon an ancient piebald steed with broken knees and hanging hair, his ape mounted behind him, and striving to appear a king, made men roar with joy.

But Robert said, "The Pope will know me. Wait till I return."

Up to the Pope, thrusting all men aside, the jester rushed, and, in a voice of thunder, cried, "Look on me! I am Robert, King of Sicily, your brother! This crowned impostor is a liar and a thief! I only am the king!"

The Pope turned from the sorry spectacle. And Emperor Valmond said, "I like not this bad jest—a madman for the jester of a king!"

Strong hands were quickly laid upon Robert, and he was flung into a cell, while the bells tolled for Holy Week.

All through that week he lay neglected and alone. But on the morn of Easter Day, when all the air was filled with clash of bells and hymns of joy, there entered into his cell a presence and a calm which curbed him to his knees.

There, on the floor of his mean cell, dressed in the motley of a clown, King Robert bowed down, placed his hands in prayer, felt the glory of God surrounding his soul, and asked forgiveness of his sins. And all that day he pondered on the meek and lowly Jesus, and meditated on His sorrow and His pain, and thought about Him risen from the earth and placed in glory by God's side.

So when the visit ended, with great humility and lowered gaze, the king returned, and no man laughed to see him pass, and none did smite him with a scornful heel when, with the ape, he meekly sought his stable straw.

But the mysterious being sent for him, and when they were alone he gently asked, "Art thou the king?"

"Thou knowest," answered Robert. "All I know, my sins are scarlet. All I seek, a cloister. I would pray my life away, with thoughts set heavenward."

And as he spoke the music from the chapel came, and the sound of voices :

"He hath put down the mighty from their seat, and hath exalted the humble and meek."

The mysterious being on the throne became transfigured with a shining light, and like heavenly music was his voice, "I am an angel, and thou the king."

Then Robert slowly, with fear and trembling, raised his gaze, and, lo! the throne was empty, and he stood in that proud chamber all alone, but not in rags, and not in motley, but in the panoply of royal power, splendid and glorious, with all his robes and jewels, and the great crown upon his head.

An hour afterwards the courtiers came to attend the king's commands and take his pleasure. Not on the throne they found him, but meekly kneeling on the floor, in prayer.

DICK WHITTINGTON AND HIS CAT

DICK WHITTINGTON LISTENS TO THE MESSAGE OF BOW BELLS—By James Sant, R.A.

Dick Whittington was a poor country lad, who, having lost his father and his mother, came to London to make his fortune. His only friend in the world was a cat which he had picked up and fed when it was starving ; and a very good friend it was to him.

Dick used to think that the streets of London were paved with gold, but he found that they were covered with hard stones, and on these stones he had to sleep with his cat for many nights. At last he got a place as a scullery-boy in the house of a rich merchant. Unhappily, the cook was a wicked woman, and she beat him every day and made him sleep in a garret overrun with rats and mice. These, however, were soon killed by Dick's cat, for the cat was an excellent mouser.

The rich merchant in whose kitchen Dick worked was a foreign trader. He used to fill his ships with all kinds of goods, and send them to far countries, where the goods could be sold at a great profit ; and, being a kind man, he allowed all his servants to put in his ships anything that they wished to sell. One day, when he was about to send a ship to trade with the Blackamoors, his pretty daughter Alice came into the scullery and said to Dick :

" Now, what are you going to put in for sale this time ? "

" I've only my cat," said Dick.

" Well, put in your cat," said Alice.

And to please her he parted with the only friend he had in the world.

But Dick soon began to miss his cat. The rats and the mice crept back to his garret and kept him awake at night, and the cook beat him more than ever. So hard did Dick's life become that one morning he tied all his things up into a bundle and set out to walk back to his home.

He got as far as the village of Holloway, and sat down on a stone to rest, and Bow Bells began to chime, and the sound travelled across the fields.

" Turn a-gain, Whitt-ing-ton,
Thrice Lord Mayor of London."

That was what the ding-ding-dong of Bow Bells seemed to say to him. Poor Dick tried to laugh, and began to cry.

But he turned, and went a little way along the road to Finchley.

" Turn a-gain, Whitt-ing-ton,
Thrice Lord Mayor of London."

said Bow Bells, and he turned and went a little way along the road to Enfield.

" Turn a-gain, Whitt-ington,
Thrice Lord Mayor of London,"

said Bow Bells.

" After all," said Dick, " it's only the cook who treats me harshly. How kindly Alice spoke to me ! I will turn again, as the bells say, and see what happens."

Something happened as soon as Dick regained his master's house. The ship in which he had put his cat returned with the news that his cat had been sold at a very great price.

On arriving at the land of the Blacka-moors, the captain of the ship went to the king of the country, and was invited to dine at the palace. There he saw an amazing sight. As soon as the dishes were placed on the tables, a vast crowd of rats and mice came and devoured all the food.

" Oh dear ! " cried the King of the Blackamoors. " I shall not get anything to eat again today."

" Good gracious ! " said the captain. " You ought to keep a cat in your palace to kill all these rats and mice."

" A cat ? " said the king. " What's that ? Is it a new kind of lion ? I have bought hundreds of lions and tigers but none of them would kill a mouse for me."

The captain sent a sailor to the ship to get Dick Whittington's cat. When the King of the Blackamoors saw how quickly it killed rat after rat, and mouse after mouse, he clapped his hands and shouted with joy, and said that he would buy it even if it cost him half his kingdom.

" Will you take six sacks of gold for this wonderful little animal ? " he asked.

The captain agreed, and the ship came to London laden with the sacks of gold.

The wicked cook told the merchant that Dick was only a poor scullery-boy, without a friend in the world, and that there was no need to give him the gold. But the merchant was an honest man. He gave Dick all the money, and had him brought up as if he were his own son, and years after Dick married Alice. He was made Lord Mayor of London three times, as Bow Bells had said. Such is the legend that grew up about Dick Whittington, who really was Lord Mayor of London.

LOVE LAUGHS AT LOCKSMITHS

LOVE laughs at locksmiths. This was the device which the handsome young Marquis of Hautmont engraved on his shield when he came to Paris. Being as bold as he was handsome, he began to make love to Princess Marguerite, the king's daughter, and the king was annoyed at his boldness.

" They are loud words which you have taken for your device," said he, " but are they true ? I will lock the princess up in a tower. If you can enter it within a month, you can marry her. If you fail, you must lose your life."

The marquis pretended to be dis-comfited. But he secretly ordered some woodcarvers to make a great hollow wooden nightingale. When the bird was finished and painted, the marquis got inside and played beautiful airs on a flute, while his servant drew it about the streets. Everybody began to talk about the mechanical nightingale ; the king came to see it, and Princess Marguerite asked for it to be brought to her. The king, think-ing that the music was produced by machinery, had the bird carried into the tower, and the marquis then jumped out and kissed the princess's hand, saying :

" Love laughs at locksmiths, you see, sire." And the king was forced to acknow-ledge that this was true ; and as he saw that the marquis and the princess were in love with one another, he allowed them to marry, and presented them with a really royal dowry.

THE WILLOW-PATTERN PLATE

A BEAUTIFUL Chinese girl named Koong-Shee fell in love with her father's secretary, Chang, who was poor. But the father of Koong-Shee wanted her to marry a rich man, and because she would not give up Chang her father sent her away to a little house at the end of the garden. Outside Koong-Shee's window was a willow tree, and just beyond a fruit tree, and Koong-Shee sat all day watching the

Koong-Shee read the letter, and sent back her answer. She said she would go if her lover were brave enough to come and fetch her. Chang went boldly up to the little house and took her away. They had to cross the bridge to get out of the garden, and as they were half-way across Koong-Shee's father saw them, and hurried after them. Koong-Shee went first with her distaff, Chang followed carrying her

fruit tree bloom. She was very lonely and unhappy, until one day Chang asked her to fly with him.

Chang dared not post the letter lest it should fall into the hands of Koong-Shee's father, but he found a coconut-shell, fixed a sail to it, and, putting his letter inside the shell, dropped it into the lake, and watched it sail across.

jewel-box, and behind them ran the father with a whip. But the father did not catch them, and they escaped to a little house on the other side of the lake. The rich man who had wanted to marry Koong-Shee was so angry that he set fire to the pretty little house, but Koong-Shee and Chang were transformed into a pair of doves and thus lived happily ever after.

JELLYFISH IN SEARCH OF A MONKEY

This is a tale they tell in Japan of the origin of the Jellyfish we find stranded on the beach.

LONG, long ago, instead of soft tentacles, he had a bunch of legs as graceful as a greyhound's, and as for his figure, the proudest pig in Ireland could not vie with him for firmly arched, well covered ribs.

Naturally, he was the admiration of all the other fish, for, besides being nimble and stately, he was the only deep-sea thing that could walk on land as well as swim in the water. Unfortunately, he was like only too many human beings, who simply rely on their good looks to make them popular, and do not trouble to develop their brains. This handsome creature was exceedingly stupid.

One day Jellyfish was strolling about the shore of a coral island, when a flying fish shot out of the waves, and told him that he was summoned to the palace of the Dragon King.

As he approached the audience chamber he could hear by the clanking of golden scales that the Dragon King was pacing about in the greatest agitation, but his brow cleared as he caught sight of Jellyfish.

" I thought you would never come ! " he cried. " And the Queen gets worse every hour ! Listen. The doctors say that she can be cured by swallowing the liver of a live monkey. You are the only fish who can go ashore. You must swim, as you have never swum in your life, to the nearest bit of land, and persuade a monkey to return with you. If you succeed I will make you Grand Warden of the Indian Ocean, with a right to a coronet of pearl shell and cowrie."

Jellyfish hardly stopped to bow ; in a very little while he was wading out of the breakers on to a lovely island of palm trees and scarlet hibiscus. The first animal he saw was a small grey monkey with a friendly countenance. Jellyfish hailed him gladly :

" Ho, you Master Monkey there ! I am sent by the Dragon King of all the seas ; you are to come to his palace."

The monkey's shrivelled face beamed with pleasure. Never had he dreamed of receiving a royal invitation, and he was only too ready to accept this.

For a little while Jellyfish, with the monkey on his back, swam in silence, for he was short of breath, but soon he asked :

" By the way, I hope you have got your liver with you ? "

The monkey was not handsome, like Jellyfish, but he kept his wits well polished.

" Why do you ask ? " he inquired.

" Well," said Jellyfish, " the Queen is ill, and she can only be cured by the liver of a live monkey."

At this the monkey exclaimed :

" Dear me ! What a thousand pities ! I left mine hanging out to air at the top of a coconut palm. We had better go back for the thing at once."

" We must, indeed," said Jellyfish.

No sooner was the monkey up his coconut palm than he called down :

" Go away, stupid ! I won't part with my liver for any queen, in the sea or out."

To clinch the argument he threw nuts at Jellyfish till he ran into the sea.

All his knees knocked together as he told the tale of his failure, and the Dragon King smoked with rage. When he had stammered out his last word the monarch roared to his servants :

" Beat him ! Beat him within an inch of his life ! Break every bone in his body ! Beat him to a jelly ! "

As you can see for yourself, that is exactly what they did.

HOW A SULTAN FOUND AN HONEST MAN

A SULTAN wanted to find an honest man to collect the taxes of his realm, and a wise counsellor advised him to invite all the applicants to his palace.

" I will show you the honest officer when you ask them to dance," said he.

The applicants arrived, and were told to advance to the Sultan, one at a time, through a dark and empty corridor. As soon as they were all assembled before the throne, the Sultan said : " Gentlemen, I should very much like to see you dance."

But all the applicants refused, with many blushes, except one man, who danced cheerfully and well.

" That is the honest man," said the sage, pointing to the dancer.

In the dark corridor the wise man had placed sacks of money, and all the dishonest men had filled their pockets as they passed through to the Sultan. If they had danced, their pockets would have sounded like money-boxes being shaken, and so they had refused.

Nature's Wonderful Living Family in Earth and Air and Sea

What This Story Tells Us

WHAT a marvellous family is Mother Nature's, with her host of strange and terrible and beautiful children ! Some of them have passed away for ever—gigantic creatures of the long ago, tramping the lonely world before Man came. No more will Iguanodon be seen, or Brontosaurus, or old Diplodocus, or the dragons that flew like birds, or the Dodo that lost his power to fly. Gone are they all. Nature has a vaster kingdom now, and smaller subjects. Since life first came ashore her great families have spread over the earth. The story of their lives would fill the most romantic book that could be written, and here we will read a few chapters of it. Sometimes the truth will seem too strange to believe, but nothing is more astonishing than truth. The lives of animals, like the lives of men, are far more wonderful than anything the novelist writes about.

NATURE'S THOUSANDS OF CHILDREN

A MARVELLOUS family is Mother Nature's, with thousands of children almost beyond belief. Think of a few of them.

Consider a group comprising a protozoan, an oak tree, a crocodile, a whale, an elephant, and a man. The protozoan is the very simplest form of life, all the mysteries and magic processes of existence wrapped up in a single cell. The crocodile, king of the reptiles ; the oak tree, monarch of our forests ; the whale, greatest of all existing animals ; the elephant, greatest of all the beasts that tread the ground ; and man himself—each was once a single cell. The protozoan remains one-celled today, the rest develop, multiply cells, cell upon cell, in uncountable profusion. In that rough-and-ready grouping we have the story of the rise of the living families of the world—plant, animal, human.

We cannot any longer make the old sharp division between plants and animals. A sea-lily is like a freakish plant whose stem is chiefly mineral ; yet it is an animal. A pitcher plant seems animal in its capture of insects ; but it is a plant. The no more intelligent sea anemone, so like a lovely marine blossom, is an animal. An oak tree goes to sleep for the winter as hedgehogs,

tortoises, and big bears do. In torrid lands trees and plants go to sleep till rain returns. So does a lungfish in his exhausted pool ; so do the worm and the snail during drought in parched English gardens. Trees shed bark and leaves ; shell-fish shed their covering and cast off their limbs ; reptiles cast their skins ; caterpillars jump out of one skin and grow another. We take cuttings from plants and establish new ones ; a starfish rent asunder may become five starfishes, and a worm cut in halves may become two worms.

The resemblance is repeated in the process of reproduction. As trees and flowers produce enormous quantities of fruit and seed, so in animal life we find enormous numbers of eggs. An oyster lays eggs exceeding the population of the British Isles, a ling has a progeny outnumbering the white population of our Dominions. Ingenuity excelling human invention is shown by Nature in providing for the dispersal of seeds, as if trees and flowers loved the thought of offspring.

The same astonishing principle exists in the animal world. The eel undertakes an appalling voyage from ditch and pond, far into the deepest recess of a distant

PREHISTORIC LIFE · MAMMALS · BIRDS · REPTILES · FISHES · INSECTS

28 B 1

ocean, to bring forth eggs from which will arise little eels that the mother will never see. Birds build wonderful mound nests for eggs which they will not hatch ; wasps construct nurseries and store rich larders for baby wasps which will come to life when their parents are dead. Fishes strew the sea with ova and never see their children.

Purpose and result are the same with trees and with animals. That parents shall leave one or two children to succeed them and to maintain the species—that is the lot assigned them, and all the fruitfulness, all the splendours, beauties, and harmonies of existence are means to that end.

LIFE IS MADE UP OF BEAUTY AND SPLENDOUR AND TERROR

That unseen mighty Hand which painted the flowers painted also the butterflies, gave them lustrous scales to make them equally lovely, gave them, also, their own apparatus for the creation of rich perfume to render them attractive to their fellows. All the colours of the rainbow are in the flowers, but they are repeated in the insects and again in the birds. Reptiles have many rich, strange hues ; there is luxuriant colouring for many of the mammals ; and, as if Nature has an eye for farce as well as for harmony, we find most extravagant colours on the bodies of apes.

Life is made up of beauty, splendour, wonder, skill, cunning, and also of terrors we can dimly understand. To balance the song of the nightingale we have the terrible deeds of the flesh-eating animals.

Every day and night myriads of herb-eating creatures must die to make meals for the carnivores. Every day, while the bee is performing her beneficent wonders in the hive, multitudes of insects are sentenced to lingering death by ichneumon flies, which make nurseries of them for their eggs, from which will hatch ichneumon grubs to devour the living bodies of the insects in which the eggs are laid ; and wasps carry living spiders to their nests, paralysed but not killed, to await, alive, the birth and appetite of the grubs yet to be born from the wasp's eggs.

HAS NATURE REACHED HER HEIGHT OR IS SHE IN THE CRADLE ?

These are facts to be considered as much as the vivid luxuriance of the flowers and the harmony of the song of birds. On the face of it the scheme seems desperately cruel ; but Nature is wiser than the wisest of us. Her ways may be terrible only in

appearance, not in reality. She may have her drugs which dispel the fears and soothe to sleep the senses of her victims. It is comforting to assume that. But it should make us determined not to add one pang of suffering to the inevitable total, and to prevent pain and anguish wherever we have dominion in the animal world.

For Nature will not alter. She never does. She is as ruthless as she is benevolent. She cherishes success, she tramples down failure—not suddenly, not in a century, not in an age, but slowly and surely. The things living today are her successes, though some of them—the great apes, the sloths, the giant reptiles—are failing fast, while others are improving. We do not know whether existing creation has reached its pinnacle, or whether it is only in the cradle. If man is too successful as an agent of destruction the answer may be that the bulk of wild creation is neither in the cradle nor at the summit, but on the brink of the grave. But until man rose to pre-eminence Nature pursued an even course of development, progress, trial, failure, renunciation, triumph.

THE WONDERFUL THINGS NATURE BUILT WITH HER BOX OF BRICKS

She has filled the Earth, the air, the waters, with abounding forms of life. All arose from creatures as simple as the one-celled animals of our waters. From those lowly creatures, during unthinkable periods of time, came all life. No changes effected in the crucible of the scientist match the marvels wrought in Nature's processes. She had all time and all substance for her work. The one group of elements sufficed for all the diverse outlines and characteristics known in the Book of Life. Our oak, crocodile, whale, elephant, man—all are made up of precisely the same elements, differently grouped and arranged. A boy with a box of bricks builds first a cottage and then a castle. Nature, with her box of bricks, built man and mouse and mammoth, reptile and bird and insect, at different times and from different starting-points.

In the waters of a twilight world were the first of created life forms, mere specks of living jelly. From these substances Nature evolved a succession of creatures new and strange. She changed a creature a little and changed its children more, and the changes became constant, as the changes which man effects in flowers,

THE AMAZING PROCESSION THROUGH TIME

Here our artist imagines a man with the power to look down Time and see the gigantic creatures that inhabited the world before man. If we study this picture by the Clock of Life on page 10 these creatures, going down the page, would begin to appear about 9 and go on appearing till about half-past 11.

PROWLING BEASTS OF JUNGLE AND SWAMP

THE LION, MOST TERRIBLE MEMBER OF THE BIG CAT FAMILY AND LORD OF THE ANIMAL WORLD

THE TERROR OF THE SWAMPS—THE RHINOCEROS WITH A COAT LIKE LEATHER

DESCENDANTS OF ANCIENT MONSTERS

THE FRIENDLY AND USEFUL ELEPHANT COMES DOWN TO US FROM THE MAMMOTH

THE QUEER ANT-BEAR COMES DOWN TO US FROM THE GIANT SLOTH

birds, and animals by scientific breeding are constant. Jelly-fish arose, and to protect them from creatures which would have devoured them Nature gave them stings. Worms were formed, in infinite variety, and from them came insects and the sea-urchins, brittle-stars, and so on.

Then along another line came the Crustaceans, first of all Nature's little men in armour ; then the things with shells such as we recognise in the molluscs and gasteropods ; and, as shell-design became a fixed feature of life, the way was open for the cuttlefish to take his place in the increasing army.

We are sketching very rapidly only one imaginary line of ascent, so that a thousand details are omitted. Let us hasten to the first attempt at a backbone.

Nature seems to have toyed with this idea in several forms. Two of her experiments are with us today. The lancelets and the tunicates of modern times never are, but always seem likely to be, blessed with backbones. Each young one seems about to grow one, but the promise is never realised, and the adult is grouped like its ancestors, with the backboneless. There they are today to suggest what all creation might have been like had not Nature succeeded at last in finding a line of life fit to bear spine and ribs.

THE BACKBONE COMES AND ALL THINGS ARE POSSIBLE

Lancelet and tunicate, deprived of the backbone, never got any further forward, and thousands of other failures of which we have no record must have passed out of knowledge. But at last fishes came, strong, pliant, bold ; the Vertebrates had come, and all things were possible !

Fishes multiplied in number and species, and, the idea of armour having taken root on the bodies of crustaceans and molluscs, the fish must have their armour too. And arm they did, in mail of bony plates, invulnerable to any teeth then in existence. Nearly all fish took to armour for ages, and the sturgeon and half a dozen other floating fortresses survive to remind us of what they were. Things were developing apace in the waters as each successful feature established itself, and fishes gradually grouped themselves in an ascending scale of power and merit. But the greatest adventure had yet to come. Life had to cease swimming and march! It had to come ashore.

To do so gills, which breathe oxygen in water, had to yield place to lungs, which breathe air. What a change this was we may infer from what would happen if men tried to convert themselves now from air-breathers into water-breathers, and to forsake the land for the sea. Life had to make the hazard in those old days, and vertebrates came trembling ashore, to be left high and dry when the tide ebbed, to be recovered when the tide flowed again, and finally, after millions of years, to come right inland and possess the Earth.

ONE OF THE MOST DRAMATIC EPOCHS IN THE STORY OF NATURE

That was one of the most dramatic epochs in the story of animate nature. It was the beginning of a pageant whose source was the waters and whose summit was mankind—a sea-squirt at one end of the line and Shakespeare at the other.

Once life had landed it made fast, and the developments which had begun in the deep were multiplied on Earth. The great forms were amphibian—frogs, toads, and salamanders, things which were born in the water and came ashore to live.

The early amphibians grew gigantic, some of them as big as oxen, but the reptiles, creatures born on land, were the next to advance. They also attained colossal size, but, though they possessed the Earth and ruled in horror, the future did not lie with them, for there was not a brain worthy of the name among them.

Forth from one of the reptile groups came the ancestors of the birds—not at a bound, of course. The reptiles themselves took to the air in numbers, huge, loathsome-looking things with leathery wings, the real dragons, though they did not breathe fire, as the legends say.

THE MOST TERRIBLE AGE OUR EARTH HAS SEEN

The age of reptiles was the most appalling, we must suppose, that ever Old Earth has witnessed. The sea was turbulent with the movements of the colossal swimming fish-lizard called ichthyosaurus. The marshy land trembled and squelched beneath the tread of giant dinosaurs, which, squatting on their haunches, pulled down the tops of trees to feed. Carnivorous monsters devoured herb-eating dinosaurs ; the nightmare creature called stegosaurus roamed about with its immense bulk and length, armed with great bosses of bone along the back.

MOTHER NATURE AND HER LITTLE ONES

MERRY AND CHARMING ARE THE WAYS OF SOME OF NATURE'S SMALL WILD CHILDREN, AND HERE AN ARTIST HAS PICTURED MOTHER NATURE WITH A GROUP OF THEM ABOUT HER

The incredible brontosaurus, the terrific iguanodons, creatures of the lizard order, were there, and in the air were the pterodactyls, flying reptiles with teeth as terrible as a crocodile's. These were the masters of that amazing world.

The birds began pretty much where the pterodactyls left off, for the archaeopteryx, first of birds, was lizard-like in body, in tail, teeth, and jaws. Its tail was long and jointed, but feathers grew from each joint. Here, in feathers, a new structure had come into being, and we must believe that blood—cold in reptiles and fishes—had at last become raised in temperature. Birds had come—to blossom into bulk, beauty, and a thousand forms, hues, songs, and habits. The giant moa tells us by his remains what they did with their genius for mere size ; the extinct dodo, the ostriches, and the penguins reveal to us how fatally some misused their sovereign gift of flight.

AT LAST THE HOUR SOUNDS FOR THE GREAT DAWN

At last the hour sounded for the dawn of mammal life, of life for creatures that have hair or fur, warm blood, and, the highest characteristic of all, the habit of nurturing their young on milk. They came from a reptile origin. Man bears the seal upon his body of far-away ancestors who were reptiles, The first mammals were little timid animals, and how they kept their helpless young alive in such a world of perils passes understanding. But they did it by the exercise of a new quality.

Something which made the Earth worth while appeared. It was love, mercy, the spirit of self-sacrifice ; the sublime power which makes us ready to lay down our lives for others. That was the condition which changed the face of Nature when mammals came into being. It did not happen forthwith, but the mere fact that mammals survived the early days of danger on that reptile-ridden Earth tells us that love for offspring was triumphant. The doom of brute frightfulness arrived when animal love conquered peril.

NATURE HAS STOPPED HER GIANTS AND METHUSELAHS

The same varying development which we see among fishes and reptiles took place among mammals. Armour and size were the order for the reptiles, size and weapons for the mammals ; that was the plan for most. Herb-eaters grew gigantic. The flesh-eaters grew huge, too ; bears bigger than any now existing, tigers immense and strong with tusks like sabres, lions of appalling size and power.

There is nothing tending to increase of bulk to which Nature has not given rein. Every order existing today has had its giant in the past. Nature, though she explored possibilities with every order, though she sent the whale and walrus back from the land and let them grow monstrous in the sea, has ceased her strivings for giants and Methuselahs. No more does she produce enormous trees which last thousands of years, or dinosaurs that live two centuries. She creates more trees, but gives them shorter lives. She summons into existence more animals, but gives them a briefer span.

All the giant reptiles are gone, all the giant mammals, save the whale, elephant, rhinoceros, and hippopotamus ; all the myriads of armoured fish have vanished save seven groups. Birds have lost their reptile teeth and gained a thousand graces. Mammals have increased their speed and cunning and lost inches and weight ; man himself has lost his hairy body-covering, his gloomy brow and mighty canine teeth. Much has gone of the animal world which the reptiles knew. Its secrets have now to be sought in the rocks formed from the age-old mud into which past forms sank to die.

MAN THE LORD OF ALL, WITH HIS WONDROUS POWERS

The best and highest yet remain to proclaim the wondrous story. The past is full of nightmare terror and phantasy, interpreted by creatures turned to fossils underneath our feet. Now comes Nature's highest yet—Man, the lord of all, the only creature to whom a soul is given, in whom the brain has become the master organ of the body. Though he rises from the same ancestral stock which produced apes and monkeys and lemurs, he is the supreme achievement of Nature; and, having made him master of her kingdom, its animals, its resources, and many of its secrets, it would seem as if Nature means him to act the role of Viceroy of the Earth, and himself to mould the forces which, until his coming, were wielded by Nature herself.

And what will Man do with his powers? His conduct in the discharge of his trust will determine whether the animal world generally is in its cradle, or is approaching a destiny which is to be a tomb.

The March of Man from the Age of Barbarism to the United Nations

What This Story Tells Us

WE do not know how long it is since some trembling human creature hid himself from some wild beast that threatened to engulf him, but we know this trembling man is now master of the Earth. How he rose from the mists of time, by what struggles he survived, how he overcame his enemies, how he set up kings and threw them down again, how he found fire and what he did with it, how he magnified the senses Nature gave him and won new powers from Nature's secret stores, how he made the world a better place to live in and filled it with beauty and power and music and books—this is a tale indeed ! Here we shall look at the great epochs of man's march from the days he came into the world, through the long years of his struggling and yearning, up to these days when, if only he will open his eyes to see, he stands at the gate of the Promised Land.

MAN SETS OUT ON A JOURNEY

EVERY story in the world has grown out of the story we are going to read. Every picture in the world has grown out of the picture we are going to unfold. And every discovery that has been made by the inventors and the men of science since life began has come from the discovery unveiled in this journey we now set out to take together.

JULIUS CAESAR

For we are setting out to follow the rise, the growth, and the adventures of the very greatest thing on this planet, the thing which stood up in the midst of barbarism and chose a road which led to civilisation, which found itself shut in on every side by Ignorance and broke a way through to Knowledge, which was so feeble that any beast of the field might have stamped it out of existence, yet which discovered in itself the secret of all power and dominion.

We are going to consider the wonderful journey of Man through Time.

Many thousands of years after the flames which wrapped the whole Earth had blown away, many thousands of years after the steaming vapour which clouded it all round had lifted into the sky, and many thousands of years after Life in myriad forms had appeared on its surface, there came into existence a creature different from every other creature under the shining Sun.

Millions of years had gone to the making of this astonishing creature.

A period of time, so tremendous that we may call it almost an eternity, had passed over this beautiful and mysterious Earth before there came into the world of life a creature radically different from all the other inhabitants of Earth, yet so like some of them that from an outside view it might have been confounded with them.

The difference was invisible. The thing which separated it from all other living forms was inward and spiritual. This creature had a Mind, and this mind was the most wonderful thing existing in the world.

Man stood in the dense primeval forest, and looked about him with eyes which seemed no different from the eyes of apes and tigers, elephants and birds, snakes and bears ; but behind those eyes of his was a mind which reflected on what he saw. All the rest of creation *looked*; he alone *observed*. Something within him could not rest content with the instincts he had inherited, like the rest of creation, from

MIGHTY EPOCHS OF THE WORLD & MAN'S WONDERFUL ADVENTURES

millions of years of experience. He felt within himself a power which urged him into strange ways ; a restlessness, a disquiet, a curiosity, a faint and struggling faith in himself which crossed his instincts at every step. He had no name for this movement in himself, just as he had no name for bear or tiger ; all he knew, dimly and confusedly, was that something pushed him from within into new paths.

This is what happened. The energy which had been working in matter for millions of years, which had brought into existence during those tremendous periods an infinity of living shapes, was now working in the brain of man. The great process of Evolution had taken a new turn. The body had been fashioned ; it was now the turn of the mind. Henceforth evolution was to be the story of man's soul.

Now we can see how it was that this creature of the forest felt within himself a movement away from his animal instincts. The power of Life was concentrating all its yearning for improvement on his brain. He was to be the Adam of a new race. No longer was the elephant to excel in strength, the tiger in swiftness, the serpent in subtlety, the ape in knowledge.

MAN LOOKS AT HIS WONDERFUL HAND, AND BEGINS TO THINK

No longer was the Earth to remain a vast wilderness. No longer was time to lack a chronicler. Life, pressing forward in its passion for improvement, needed a gardener, a discoverer, a historian. In man it had found its opportunity.

The first difference in man, distinguishing him from all the other creatures, was observation. Think about that word, for it is the foundation of every single thing that has happened since the dawn of human history. Man found himself looking at things with a particular attention.

Perhaps the first thing he looked at attentively was his own hand, turning it over and over, closing and unclosing its fingers, examining the bend of the knuckles, observing the tension and relaxation of the muscles. Never had the lion reflected on its paws, or the parrot on its wings, or the whale on its tail. Never had any creature wondered if it might not do something else with its limbs—something different from instinctive action. But man, observing his hand, reflected on it, and wondered.

We must remember that as yet there was no language. There was no name for

any creature, no term for any thing. Man did not say to himself, " I have a hand, and my hand is composed of four fingers and a thumb." He did not look about him and say, " This is a tree, that is a flower, and yonder goes a panther." He had no words of any kind in his mind, no speech on his lips. Like other animals he uttered sounds expressing satisfaction or fear, like other animals he could convey to his fellows in an instant the feeling of alarm or the sense of caution ; but neither the things about him nor the sensations within him had any name.

MAN WONDERS IF HE COULD NOT HAVE DONE SOMETHING BETTER

We must picture him at the dawn of human history, standing in a maze of wordless thoughts, torn between the two paths of Instinct and Reason. We must not think of him as a creature suddenly dumped down on Earth with no experience to help him. His experience reached right back to the first stir of life on this planet. He knew, indeed, many things. He knew quite as much as the elephant, the bear, and the snake. But he was more confused than any other creature because, whenever he did anything instinctively, a movement within him suggested that he might have done something quite different—something better.

This was a new birth on our planet—the birth of mind. Instinct said to man, *Do this !* so imperiously that he did it at once, just as a tiger and a jaguar do what instinct tells them ; but, after man had obeyed his instincts, reason bothered him with questions : Was that the best way to act ? Might he not have done something better ? The next time the same thing occurs let him think before he so blindly obeys the unthinking impulse of instinct.

THE MORNING WHEN A MAN RAN FOR HIS LIFE

A tragic position ! How much happier is the bird that wings and sings without thinking how or why, that builds its nest exactly as its ancestors built theirs ten million years ago. But, with the tragedy, what a marvellous romance ! Man may be torn between instinct and reason, he may be confused and perplexed, but at least he has something to console him for this civil war within his brain ; he has a feeling that he can outwit his enemies.

Imagine him setting out one morning in the fall of the year to pick blackberries for his family. He is bending over a bush when he hears a soft padding noise behind him. He turns his head. A few paces away is a huge bear. Instinct bids him fling away his berries and run for his life. He charges up a hill. Breathless and terrified he reaches the top. He looks down, and there is the bear climbing after him. Instinct says *Run!* He obeys, but catches his foot in a huge stone and falls. Reason, as quick as instinct, says to him : " Don't you remember how you took a little stone in your hand yesterday and threw it at a tree ? " He springs round, seizes the big stone in his two hands, lifts it above his head, and hurls it at the bear.

A MAN PICKS UP A STONE AND THROWS IT

A wonderful thing has happened. The stone struck the bear on the side of its head, and the bear lost its foothold and went tumbling down the hillside. Now it lies at the bottom of the valley, dead !

Man rushes back to his home in the forest, and brings his fellow-men to the hillside. He shows them the bear. He points to the stone. He acts the scene for them. He lifts the stone, raises it above his head, and flings it from him. The others imitate him.

Something has come of observing the human hand, of not taking that hand for granted, of wondering about it, reflecting about it, experimenting with it. Man has discovered that he need not run away. His hand has become his plaything. He takes up a stone and flings it at a snake, twenty yards away. A bird flies over his head, and he flings a stone into the air. He stumbles over the bough of a tree broken by a winter's gale ; he drags it along, pulls it after him, breaks an arm of it off, swings the branch over his head, flings it ahead, picks it up again, and takes it home with him.

THE MAN GOES INTO THE FOREST IN SEARCH OF FOOD

One day his family is hungry. He goes out into the forest with his cudgel and looks for prey. A rabbit starts up under his feet. A blow of the stick and the rabbit is dead. He remembers a place in the forest where rabbits came out after sunset and just before dawn. He goes with his cudgel, hides, and waits. No longer need his family fear for food.

The cudgel does something else for him ; it enables this feeble and defenceless creature to leave the woods and adventure himself more boldly in the open. He is now a hunter. He can creep up behind a sleeping animal and kill it with his club. He can throw a stone so accurately that no bird within forty yards is safe from him. He wanders farther and farther afield, and comes presently to a broad river. He sits down to observe this mighty flow of water. In a pool he sees fish, and studies them. These, too, are not to be taken for granted—these large legless things which move in water like a flash of light ; not merely as the buffalo or the hippopotamus looks at fish does man look at them.

In the midst of his observation a bough of a tree comes swirling down the river. He watches it with curious eyes. That, too, can move in water, like the fish. But this tree does not move under the water ; it moves on the water. He watches it intently. Suddenly it is caught by the branch of an overhanging tree and prevented from moving. A bird flies up the river, sees the log, and perches on it. Slowly there comes into the mind of man an idea which is destined in far-off centuries to revolutionise human life. If he stood on that tree where would it take him ? If he rode upon it, kicking his legs, could he make it bear him across the river ?

MAN FINDS AN ACORN THAT WILL GROW INTO A TREE

On his way home he thinks of riding logs of wood over great rivers, and tells himself strange stories of adventures on the other side of those flowing waters. Presently he passes a cave in the hillside. He peers into it. Nothing in there. He enters. It is warm. Nothing could attack him from inside. Only the entrance would need to be guarded. Why should he live for ever in the forest ?

One day he is sitting at the mouth of this cave when he notices little sprouts of green in the earth. He picks up the soil with his fingers and discovers at the end of each sprout a seed which he himself has flung away after eating berries and fruit. He notices that some of the sprouts are strong and others weak. They are strong where the ground is open, weak where they have fallen among thorns.

He begins to observe the earth with attention. The acorn which drops from the trees is not only food for swine ; *it grows into a little tree.* The grain he loves to chew as he walks falls into the earth and *comes up again as a plant.* He collects handfuls of their golden grains and carries them back to his cave. He breaks down the brambles, sharpens a stick to loosen the roots, pulls them up from the ground, and plants his seed.

On another day he comes upon a pile of bones at the foot of a hill. A number of wolf-like creatures start away from them as he approaches, growling as they go. How did they come there, all those bones ? As he stands watching, a buffalo comes turning over and over through the air from the top of the hill. It crashes among the bones, and lies still. At the same moment, a wolf-like creature appears breathless at the top of the hill looking down. The man climbs up the hill. He watches. One day he sees a buffalo chased by these wolves

How is he to get those things ? Is there in all nature such a thing as a steam-plough, a railway engine, a steamship ? No, but in his own mind there is the idea of a spade, a wheel, and a boat.

He has invented a crude language. He can tell others what is in his mind. They are all agreed to call a tree a tree, a bear a bear, water water, wind wind, and wheat wheat. They have names for themselves. One is father, another is mother, this child is son, and that daughter. When a fire rages through the forest they call it fire. They can speak to each other of fire. They notice that two flints struck sharply together produce the same thing on a tiny scale—fire. They have observed that fire eats up dried things quicker than damp things. They make a heap of twigs and

MAN CLIMBS UP THE HILL

across the open, headed for the precipice. He says to himself, " I need not go hunting for animals. I need not fight with them." He becomes a trapper.

His wife flings meat to some of the creatures about his cave. The smallest of them become friendly. In winter time they come even to the mouth of the cave. Presently they take meat from her hand. The man thinks to himself, " Why should not these things hunt for me ? " The hillside becomes his trap, and the wolf becomes his dog.

His needs multiply with his victories over Nature. He wants something more than a stick for breaking the earth to receive his seed. He wants something more than his two hands for dragging home his loads. He wants something more than a log for crossing the rivers.

dead leaves ; they strike flints against it, and presently it burns.

A vegetable root which has got into this fire smells good. They taste it and like it. They fling flesh into the fire, and taste that. It is good. Animals are afraid of fire. Very well, he will light fires at night and that will keep tigers away from him.

All this movement away from instinct is the work of observation. Man is unafraid of the universe. So far he is only a hunter seeking power over his prey. He has never lifted his eyes from the earth. He is like the rest of the animal kingdom except in this—that with him instinct is not enough. Superstition is yet to come. Death is not yet either a tragedy or a mystery.

The Great Journey of Man is begun.

(Next chapter in this group, page 167)

The Story of the Things We See About Us Every Day

What This Story Tells Us

ALL around us is the mystery of familiar things. How does the blade of your penknife come through the roaring furnaces into your pocket ? How does your fountain pen come from the heart of a forest, from the top of a mountain, from the depth of a mine, from the fiery crater of a volcano, to your desk ? How does a piece of cotton, growing like a flower in Egypt, come on to a reel on a sewing-machine ? How does a newspaper come out every day ? Through what marvellous processes do the familiar things about us pass before they reach us ? Here we shall look round at many familiar things—at pens and pencils and coins, at railway engines, ships, and aeroplanes, at silk and cotton and wool, at sugar and salt and tea, at gas-meters and cameras ; we shall see, too, how tunnels are made under cities and rivers ; and many other fascinating things.

IRON FOUNDATIONS OF ENGLAND

CAN we picture what Great Britain would be like if the use of iron were not known? Everything made by man would be different. There would be no great ships to carry us across the sea, for without iron and steel we could not build anything better than the rough canoes which the primitive men used before history began. There would be no fine houses—we should all have to dwell in primitive huts—for without iron we could not build houses requiring the use of metal tools.

We could not have printed books or papers; we could not have proper clothes; for there would be no machinery with which to make them. There would be no such things as aeroplanes or trains or motor-cars.

How did men manage without iron? They used stone tools—sharp pieces of flint which they chipped off larger stones. Bones served for knives and forks, and for needles with which to stitch together their garments of roughly-tanned skins. It would have been no use looking round for a knife to sharpen a pencil, for there would be no knife, and there would be no pencil. Man has known how to forge metal

tools out of ore dug up from the Earth for about 5000 years. At first, it is thought, he used copper and tin. Then someone discovered that if iron ore were heated in a fierce fire it turned into a hot, pasty lump of metal which could be beaten into any required shape, a shape it would retain when cool.

This kind of iron came to be known as wrought iron. A cutting edge, however, could not be put on any tool or weapon made from this metal. But another pioneer in ancient days found that if wrought iron were heated again while surrounded by charcoal and hammered repeatedly, the result was a blade that would take a cutting edge. A hardness had thus been given to the surface of the metal—the forging of steel had, in fact, been discovered.

For centuries there was little progress. Then, about the middle of the fourteenth century, a method was developed of making iron melt into a liquid in sufficient quantities that it could be poured into a mould where it would harden into the mould's shape. This is called cast iron.

It was not until the eighteenth century that the next big discovery was made.

INDUSTRIES · HOW THINGS ARE MADE · WHERE THEY COME FROM

Between 1730 and 1740 Abraham Darby found an efficient way of using a coke fire, instead of one of charcoal, for smelting iron. This meant that the iron became available in much larger quantities, and so the development of engineering, of railways, and all our modern manufacturing activities was made possible.

The next step followed almost immediately, about 1740, when Benjamin Huntsman, a Sheffield clockmaker, invented a method of making steel in small crucibles, by melting carbonised wrought iron and suitable scrap and freeing it from impurities. From this proceeded the wonderful high-quality Sheffield steel, world-renowned for making knives.

From then on giant strides were made in the knowledge and skill of iron and steel making, and most of the progress throughout the world was due to the genius and craftsmanship of the people of our little island.

The essential difference between iron and steel is in the amount of carbon it contains. Iron has up to 4½ per cent carbon, few steels have more than 1½ per cent, and ordinary mild steel only about ¼ per cent. To make steel this carbon must be removed from the iron.

In 1855 Sir Henry Bessemer, an Englishman, patented his famous Bessemer process of making steel by forcing air through molten iron. This burned away the excess carbon very quickly. His invention caused the annual output of steel in Britain to rise in a few years from 50,000 tons to 1,600,000 tons.

Let us consider now the practical side of iron and steel making. Men now know the chemical secrets of what happens when iron ore is melted in a furnace. It is this scientific knowledge which has made possible the enormous technical advances in production during the past 100 years.

What happens in iron-making is this. As already mentioned, iron and steel are combinations of metal and carbon in varying proportions. When iron ore is smelted in a furnace, the heat drives the oxygen out of the ore and some of the

carbon from the coke in the furnaces combines with the iron.

We show a diagram of a blast furnace, where iron is smelted out of the natural ore from the earth. Into the top of the furnace, by means of an inclined skip bucket, coke, limestone, and ore are charged. The coke burns to make the heat, the limestone helps to absorb some of the impurities out of the ore. For iron ore contains such impurities as alumina, silica, sulphur, and phosphorus.

At the bottom of the blast furnace—which is from 80 to 100 feet high—are ten holes called tuyères through which a continuous blast of very hot air is forced at the rate of between 200 and 400 mph, making the furnace blaze at white heat. The steel furnace walls, inside, are lined with firebricks which can withstand even this terrific heat.

As the ore melts it sinks in the furnace, and when the taphole at the bottom is opened, the white-hot molten iron runs out and flows along specially-made channels. From these it may be taken in brick-lined containers to a nearby steelworks, or it may be ladled into what is called a pig-casting machine. This is an endless chain of moulds in which the molten iron is cooled by water and despatched to other works in solid blocks. The iron coming out of the blast furnace is called pig-iron.

Meanwhile, the impurities of the ore, in the form of molten slag, have been allowed to run out of another hole at the base of the furnace.

The next step is to turn the pig-iron into steel. This is done by removing the carbon and the impurities which still remain in it. The pig-iron is put into another furnace, either an Open Hearth furnace or a Bessemer Converter. From either of these the molten metal is drawn off into large moulds where it takes the form of ingots of steel. These ingots, when their outsides have cooled and hardened, are ready to be forged or rolled into any required size or shape.

Diagram of a blast furnace

WHAT HAPPENS IN AN IRON WORKS

Iron ore is usually found quite near the surface of the earth, and is dug from open-cast mines by means of huge mechanical excavators, such as the one shown on the left. On the right a " walking dragline " is clearing the overburden from the ironstone face and throwing the soil across the cutting to fill the place from which the ore has been removed.

Here is a modern blast furnace, which smelts the ore after it leaves the mine. Much of the residue, called slag, is crushed and tarred for road-making, and some is used in the manufacture of cement.

A FLOWING STREAM OF WHITE-HOT IRON

From the blast furnace a stream of glowing molten iron flows into a trough. The man on the left is taking a sample for laboratory analysis. The iron is tapped four to eight times daily.

The molten iron is poured into a great ladle in which it will be taken to the steel works in readiness to be charged into a steel-making furnace.

THE BLAST OF AIR THROUGH A MOLTEN MASS

Here a ladle is filling the converter in readiness for the spectacular " blow " in the Bessemer process, which burns away the excess carbon very quickly.

The fiery cascade that bursts forth when air is blown through the molten mass in the converter, the intake of oxygen raising the metal to a fierce heat.

FEEDING A FURNACE WITH SCRAP IRON

The open-hearth process, invented by Sir William Siemens in 1867, is another method of large-scale steel production which also makes it possible to add the chemicals required for certain steels.

About half the "charge" for open-hearth furnaces consists of scrap iron and steel, and this is fed into the furnaces by means of a travelling mechanical charger, as shown on this page.

STEEL FLOWS INTO THE INGOT MOULDS

Huge ladles of this type, into which the steel is tapped after some 13 or 14 hours in the furnace, may hold as much as 80 tons of metal. Here the steel is being " teemed " into ingot moulds.

WHITE-HOT STEEL READY TO BE ROLLED

The steel ingots, lifted by travelling grabs, are placed in the " soaking pit " prior to rolling. This process brings the steel to the required temperature for exact treatment.

This picture shows the beginning of the rolling process, the 8-ton ingot being deposited by a " chariot " which has brought it from the furnace at the desired temperature.

ROLLING & CUTTING A LONG BAR OF STEEL

Now the rolling-mill takes the short, thick ingot and turns it into a long bar of glowing steel. On the right is a near view of the hot, soft metal passing between rollers.

Showers of sparks fly from the guillotine, a powerful type of circular saw, as it cuts the moving bar of hot steel into the desired lengths.

THE STEEL IS COOLED AND INSPECTED

In this stacking bay the rods and bars are left to cool before delivery to the manufacturers who convert them into all kinds of finished steel products.

A final process is an examination of the steel to ensure that it is up to standard. Minor flaws are burnt out with an oxy-acetylene flame, but a serious fault means rejection of the steel.

The photographs on these pages are reproduced by courtesy of the British Iron and Steel Federation

Plain Answers to the Questions of the Children of the World

What These Pages Tell Us

FOR ever in this life we are asking questions ; for ever, throughout this world, wise men and children are saying " I wonder why ? " Where do we come from ? Where are we going ? What happens when we are asleep ? What brings a mighty forest from a few small seeds ? Has the sea been moving for ever and ever ? Who holds the stars up and lights them at night ? Who puts the thoughts in our heads and the feelings in our hearts ? How does a bird find its way from Africa back to the same little nest in Kent ? To all of us come such questions, and never will they stop while the world goes on, because out of the answer to one question another question grows. So it must always be, for the wonder of the world has no end ; the longer we live the more we wonder about life. Here are hundreds of questions asked by readers of this book.

WHY DO I LAUGH AND CRY?

You laugh and cry because you are "made that way." It depends upon the way in which your brain and body are built. After all, you laugh when you are tickled, even though you may not be pleased, and that is really easier to explain. If a bright light suddenly strikes your eye, you shut it because your brain is made so as to make you reply in that way.

That is a simple way of replying, and laughing when you are tickled is really the same, only that instead of doing only one thing, you do a number of things all at once. You move many muscles of your face instead of merely moving the muscles of your eyelids. You also move the muscles you breathe with in an unusual way, and the muscles you make sounds with. It is this particular movement of all these muscles together that we call laughter, and it is really a reply to the tickling, just as drawing away your foot is a reply when someone tickles the sole of it.

It is the same with crying as with laughing. We do not know why our brains should be so made, for, though there is much use in tears when we are not crying, there is no use in crying when we are hurt.

When people grow older they find this out, and usually do not cry when they are hurt. The highest part of the brain is the master of the lower part, and can order it to do things, and forbid it to do things. Now, it is the lower part of the brain that replies by crying when we are hurt, so that even the tiniest baby can cry. But when we grow older we tell the lower part of the brain that it must not do as it feels inclined to do, and so we stop crying.

There is no known reason why tears should come when we cry, but there is a very good and beautiful reason for the tears we are really making all the time we are awake, though we know nothing about it. You know that every few seconds you wink both your eyelids at once. If you did not your eye would soon cease to work.

Now let us see what winking does for the eye. When the eye is open, the front of it is exposed to dust and dirt, and also the front of it is apt to get dry, and if it got dry we could not see properly. Yet, how is it that, though we never wash the front of our eyes, they are always clean ? *It is because we wash them every time we*

SUN · MOON · STARS · FIRE · WIND · WATER · LIFE · MIND · SLEEP

wink. Up above each eye, rather to the outer side, is a tiny thing called the tear-gland, and all the time we are awake this is slowly making tears. Then when the front of the eye feels itself becoming rather dry, and perhaps a little dusty, it tells the brain, and down comes the eyelid with a tear inside it, so washing clean the front of the eye.

If you look at the inner corner of your lower eyelid you will see a tiny little hole. The tear runs down this and finds itself—where do you think ? When you have been crying a great deal, do you not have to blow your nose ? The reason is that tears run down into the nose. All the time we are awake this goes on, keeping our eyes moist and clean ; but when we cry we make far more tears than we need, and so they get spilt over the edge of the lower eyelid, and run down our cheeks.

But though the tears, when we are not crying, are so useful that we could not do without them, yet it is no use to shed too many tears in this beautiful world.

What Does Encyclopedia Mean ?

This is quite an easy question even though the name of this book is longer than most words in it. *En* means *in*, and is added to make the word stronger ; indeed, the word is often used without the *en*, and just written *cyclopedia*. Then the next part of the word comes from the Greek word *cyclos*, a circle, and tells us that the book is not only about one thing only, but goes all the way round knowledge. And the last part of the word is just the English form of a Greek word *paideia*, which means teaching or instruction. So this book is a circle of teaching. But the name is better even than it looks, and perhaps ours is the only kind of book that ought to have this name ; for the word that means teaching comes in Greek from another word, *pais*, which means a child, because, of course, teaching suggests child, and a child suggests teaching. So the very word tells us that it has something to do with a child.

Could We Walk Without Our Toes ?

There is no doubt that we could walk without toes, but we should not walk nearly so well, nor so gracefully, nor so safely, for the simple reason that our toes spread out over the ground to a certain extent, and so give us a greater space upon which to balance our bodies. In these civilised times, when everybody wears boots or shoes, the toes themselves are really very little used, but in the early days of the human race they were very valuable, and capable of much more movement than now. A person without toes could easily walk, but the steps would be rather uncertain and movement more restricted.

What is the Force in Lightning that Kills a Man so Quickly ?

We use the word lightning to mean two distinct things—the light seen when electricity passes strongly from a cloud to the earth ; and the electricity which causes that light. The light itself is quite harmless, but the electricity itself is very different. If this strikes the ground close beside a man it will do him no harm ; but if it actually passes to the earth through his body it may kill him. If this should happen, it happens very suddenly, as a rule, by affecting the brain and the nerves that run from it to the heart. The electricity, in passing, excites those nerves, so that they stop the heart, and the person dies.

Is There a British Lady Mentioned in the Bible ?

Yes ; there was a British lady in Rome in the days of Paul, and we are almost certain that she would go to visit Paul in his prison cell, and comfort him. To this day we may still stand in the house in Rome in which she lived.

Claudia was the name of this British lady, and she was the wife of Pudens ; and if we look at Paul's letter to Timothy we shall find that the apostle there sends her his greetings. Her house was open to Paul and the followers of Jesus in the days when to follow Him brought peril.

Her praises were sung in poetry eighteen centuries ago, and it may be that through Claudia came the first news of Christianity to Britain.

Where Does the Tadpole's Tail Go ?

At a certain stage in the life-history of a tadpole some of the cells within the tadpole's body begin to attack and devour the cells that make up the tail. The tail is gradually eaten away and absorbed until finally, by the action of these cells, there is nothing of it left. The material thus disappears, by the process which is known as absorption ; that is to say, it is used up by something else.

What Makes the Sea Salt?

The Sun sucks up the water from the sea, but it sucks up nothing else. The salt of the sea has been brought to it by the rivers. These, as they come down from the land, melt away from the land anything that water can melt, and this they carry into the sea. River water is salt, too, only so very little salt that we notice nothing. Sea water is so much salter chiefly because it contains all the salt that the rivers have been carrying down to it for ages past. One of the commonest kinds of salt in sea water is ordinary salt that we use at table, but there are a great number of other kinds too. We must remember that, though table salt is the only kind of salt we usually think of, yet " salt " is really only a general word for a large number of compounds, like each other to some extent, yet different. It is a mixture of a great number of these that helps to make the sea salt.

What are Youth Hostels?

They are buildings of different kinds in beautiful parts of the country where young people on a walking or cycling holiday can stay cheaply.

In Britain the young people must be members of the Youth Hostel Association, to which they pay a small annual subscription, and, at the hostel, they must be willing to carry out light " chores."

Youth Hostels started in Germany where, about 1900, a movement began among young people who called themselves " Wandervögel " or Wanderbirds. A schoolmaster named Richard Schirrmann opened a shelter for them in 1910.

The idea spread to Britain and in 1929 the Youth Hostel organisation was formed. Soon afterwards there were three Associations : for England and Wales, for Scotland, and for Northern Ireland.

What Makes a Nettle Sting?

The leaves of a stinging-nettle are covered with small hairs with sharp, hooked points, that will break off when they are lightly touched. But the nettle does not merely prick ; it *stings*. This is because the hairs are filled with an acid which gets under our skin, through the hole made by the point of the hair. This makes our skin uncomfortable. *Formis* is Latin for an ant, and this acid is called formic acid because it is found in the bodies of ants. There it probably prevents other animals from eating the ants, because it is not nice to taste. This is one of the thousands of ways in which animals and plants are protected from their enemies—like the poisoned tooth of the serpent and the unpleasant and often poisonous oils found in the leaves of certain plants like the tobacco plant.

How Does the Speedometer Work?

The two types of speedometer most commonly used are the Centrifugal and the Chronometric. The first is a simple arrangement based on the fact that rotating weights tend to fly outward. Details of its working are shown on page 62.

The Chronometric speedometer is rather more complicated. It may be said to consist of four sets of mechanism in one. There are two distance-recording drums and the way they work is described on page 63. The speed-recording mechanism consists of a series of wheels engaging with one another to indicate the speed ; and an escapement and camshaft control the periods during which the speed-recording apparatus is to work.

The Geared Spindle turns the Integrator Wheel for a quarter of a second and then is out of engagement for half a second. Clearly the integrator wheel will be turned farther at 60 miles an hour than at 10 miles.

A peg on the integrator pushes forward a peg on the Recorder Wheel, turning it an equal amount, and this movement is passed to the Stabiliser Wheel to which the pointer is fixed.

The integrator and recorder wheels are locked by flat Control Springs and are held until the Camshaft releases them, when coiled springs pull them back to zero.

Now the car starts off. The geared spindle engages, carrying the integrator and recorder wheels forward. This movement is transferred to the stabiliser and pointer. The camshaft then lifts the integrator control spring, and that wheel flies back to zero, ready for the next engagement of the geared spindle. The recorder wheel does not drop back yet.

If the car is moving slower, the integrator is not moved quite so far next time; the camshaft releases the control spring of the recorder, and its coiled spring pulls it back to the integrator peg where it is stopped. If the car's speed had increased, however, the shape of the

HOW A CENTRIFUGAL SPEEDOMETER WORKS

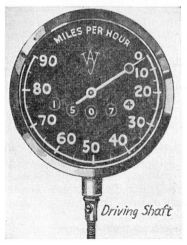

Driving Shaft

1. Here is a speedometer of the Centrifugal type registering speeds up to 90 miles an hour. It also records the distance run in miles and tenths of a mile. Usually a speedometer of this kind has a dome-shaped casing at the back, and the driving shaft enters obliquely.

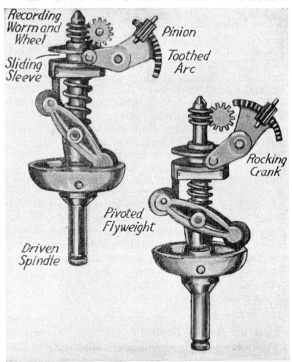

3. Here are shown the principal working parts of the speedometer at rest and in motion. The flexible cable drives the spindle, and on it is pivoted a double flyweight. Linked to this is a sliding sleeve. The weights fly outward when they turn and the sleeve is drawn down against the spring on the spindle. Thus the rocking crank is moved and the toothed arc at its other end turns a pinion on which the pointer is fixed.

2. Every modern car has a speedometer drive in its gear-box, and this picture shows how it may be arranged. The shaft which passes the engine power to the back axle may have a little spirally-toothed gear-wheel, meshing with another. To this second gear a long flexible cable is attached, and this, in a metal casing, takes the drive up to the speedometer.

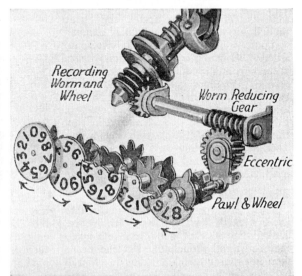

4. Here is the recording gear. A worm on the spindle turns a worm-reducing gear so that an eccentric makes one turn in a tenth of a mile. Each time the eccentric makes a downward push the pawl moves a ratchet wheel and brings the next figure up to the little window where tenths of a mile are shown. After nine figures have passed, the single-toothed wheel will next move on one tooth the ten-toothed wheel next to it, which indicates miles. When this second disc has made a complete revolution, after ten miles, it moves on the next by one tooth, and so on.

INSIDE THE CHRONOMETRIC SPEEDOMETER

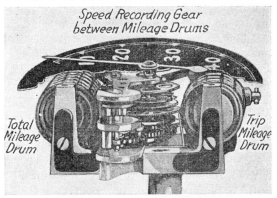

Speed Recording Gear between Mileage Drums

Total Mileage Drum

Trip Mileage Drum

1. This speedometer is of a different type altogether, known as Chronometric. It is based on a clock movement, driven from the gear-box as before. The distance-recording gives us two sets of figures, one for the trip just made and one for the increasing total.

2. Here we see inside the casing of the chronometric speedometer with the dial face half broken away to show how the parts are arranged. On the right of the trip mileage drum, which also records tenths of a mile, can be seen the connection for setting the trip back to zero, which can be done without interfering with the total mileage. The speed-recording gear is the mechanism in between the two drums.

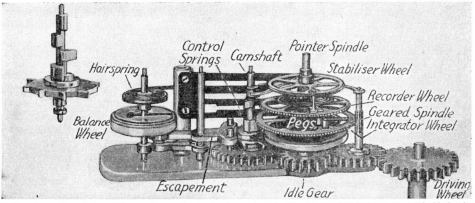

Hairspring Control Springs Camshaft Pointer Spindle Stabiliser Wheel Recorder Wheel Geared Spindle Integrator Wheel Balance Wheel Pegs Escapement Idle Gear Driving Wheel

3. Here is an enlarged view of the speed-recording mechanism and, on the left, the camshaft is shown removed. Notice the train of four gear-wheels. That on the right is driven by the flexible shaft from the gear-box. Next is that which drives the geared spindle, and following this is an idle gear. This is not connected to the spindle running through the column of wheels above it. The gear on the left is the camshaft drive, but it is not fixed to the camshaft, driving it by way of a spring clutch. This camshaft is the master of the mechanism, operating the control springs; it can only make one revolution every three-quarters of a second. The balance-wheel and escapement ensure this, as described on page 64.

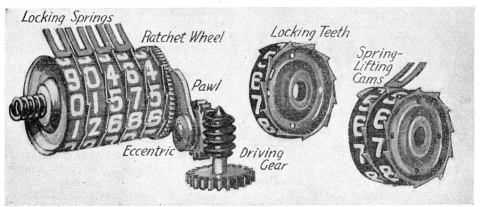

Locking Springs Ratchet Wheel Locking Teeth Spring-Lifting Cams Pawl Eccentric Driving Gear

4. The working of the distance-recording gear is shown here, on the left being the complete assembly, the five drums, each similar to that shown in the centre, being squeezed together by a spring. The eccentric and pawl step the right-hand drum round one turn in ten miles. The locking-teeth on the right edge of the next drum are held by the locking springs until one complete turn has been made by the right-hand drum. Then the spring-lifting cam on the right-hand drum levers up the spring and allows one tooth of the next drum to the left to move up. The same thing happens when the second drum has made one complete turn, and so on until 99,999 is registered, when all go back to zero again.

recorder wheels' teeth would have allowed it to be pushed onward.

A gearwheel drives the camshaft through a slipping spring clutch, and whatever the speed of this gearwheel the camshaft, controlled by the balance wheel and an escapement of clock type, cannot turn at more than 80 revolutions a minute or one in three-quarters of a second.

The top cam on the camshaft engages the geared spindle with the integrator wheel, and the two lower cams lift the flat control springs as required, releasing recorder and integrator wheels in turn.

What Wakes Me Up in the Morning ?

In order to understand this we must realise that we do not sleep in just the same way all through the night. To begin with, we sleep deeply. Now, it is good to sleep deeply. It makes us look well and beautiful.

But for some hours after this we sleep less and less deeply. We can easily find this out by noticing exactly how loud a noise is required to wake anybody up at various times in his sleep. And we find that when he has had nearly enough sleep he will be awakened by a noise which, a few hours before, he would not have noticed.

That is the sort of thing that happens when we wake. We have been sleeping less and less deeply for some time, and our brain has almost awakened of itself. Then there comes a sound or a light, or perhaps we move in bed and feel ourselves moving, and since we are already very nearly awake the sound or the light or the feeling wakes us up. Of course, we live in a way that we have made for ourselves; but if we lived out of doors, as men did long ago, and as birds do still, it would naturally be light that woke us up at last. That is what wakes the birds up now, though we are awakened by a noise.

Why Does a Tree Grow Upward ?

The first thing to say in answering this question is that the whole tree does not grow up. Part of the tree grows downward, and that is the root. Each grows to the place where it can do the work for which it was made. In the seed from which the tree grows, there are certain cells which are meant to form the part of the tree that is to live in the air and the light. Wherever the light is, they grow toward it. On the other hand, there are other cells which grow best in the dark, and which even seem to be affected by the gravitation of the Earth, so that they grow best toward the centre of the Earth.

It is possible to play tricks with the seed, as, for instance, to turn it upside down; but the rule is that the plant will do its best by curling round as it grows, to ensure that the *shoots* shall get into the air and the light, and the *roots* shall grow downward. So the tree—and this is true of nearly all plants—has two parts: one that lives in the air and one that lives in the soil. Neither part could live without the other, and the tree is so made from the first that the right part of it, that which is capable of making leaves, must grow upward into the light and air; while that part of it which will be capable of sucking up water and salts, and also of holding firm, must grown downward into the earth.

Why Is It Dark at Night ?

If you take a ball and hold it near a bright light, said the Wise Man, the half of the ball next to the light is shone upon, and the half of the ball away from the light is dark. If you mark a spot on the ball, and then turn the ball round and round like a top, that spot will be shone upon half the time and will be in the dark the other half of the time. We live on a big ball called the Earth, which is always spinning round and round, and it is shone upon all the time, day and night, by the bright light called the Sun.

The place where we live is like the spot on the ball, and, as the great Earth-ball spins, part of the time we are on the side next to the Sun and part of the time we are on the side away from the Sun. When we are on that side it is dark at night, but while it is our night it is day-time for the people who live on the other side of the ball. However dark it is where we live, the Sun is always shining some-where. The Sun does not come to the Earth, but the Earth comes into the sun-light. If you think of the ball and the light you will understand that, however dark it is, the Earth will soon carry us round into the light again. Have you ever heard one of the most beautiful lines in all poetry: " There is a budding morrow in midnight," meaning that every night a day is being born?

The Story of the Beautiful Things in the Treasure-House of the World

What This Story Tells Us

WHO shall count the treasures of the world that men have made—the lovely things that have come down to us through the ages? Nature has filled the Earth with beauty, and in the dark hours of the world it is good to remember that spring and summer have never failed to come, that the violet and the daffodil have never failed to bloom, that June will bring red roses and lift up the hearts of men. And man, too, has made a glory in the world not unworthy to compare with Nature in her glory. It is good to think of all the heritage of art that comes to every child alive, of the gems that pack our museums, the glory that enriches our great galleries, the old cathedrals that stand to witness to the faith that man has never lost in his Creator. Here we shall read of the most beautiful things that men have made—pictures and statues and buildings from all ages and all lands.

THE RICH TREASURE THAT IS OURS

THE art of the world is a glorious inheritance of which we can never be too proud, and it is our very own.

The great pictures of a nation may hang on the walls of public galleries, but every time we go and look at them it is as if we stamped them with our own names. They thus become our private collection—a treasure house of lovely things that time cannot wither nor custom make stale. And, by a beautiful magic, the more miserly we are, the more we gloat upon our treasures and count them over, the richer we become.

MICHAEL ANGELO

There is something extravagant in the world's showering of these gifts upon us, the children of a hardworking and meagre day. It is not only in our galleries and museums, in great paintings and sculptures, that we find things to gladden our eye. Art is with us everywhere. We can scarcely walk by a bookseller's shop, or a pottery store, or a jeweller's window, without being face to face with something we owe to the art of the past.

It may be a picture painted and reproduced yesterday, an enamel or china bowl fresh from the maker's hands, but its beginnings lie in the remote civilisations of the world. It may be a beautiful doorway or a pedestal of modern construction, but the first stone was laid many thousands of years before Jesus was born. The art of today is the inherited sense in large or small degree of the art of all time.

So that our treasure, our inheritance, is twofold. For centuries upon centuries the nations of the earth have been creating and storing up lovely shapes and colours that are our joy today. These are a historic possession. And every year that passes, beautiful things are made which owe their origin consciously or unconsciously to this historic possession ; and in these we are again enriched. In art, more than in any other province of the world's history, we are indeed the heirs of all the ages.

Surrounded as we are by innumerable expressions of art, we are apt sometimes to confuse an inspired picture with its imitations, and to take for great what is only cleverly shoddy. We need some standard by which to set our judgment, and we find sooner or later that the Old Masters are the best of all teachers.

PICTURES · STATUES · CARVINGS · BUILDINGS · IVORIES · CRAFTS

A picture or a statue is not necessarily good because it is old. A great deal of ancient art is mainly treasured because it is a vivid emblem of a dead civilisation, and acts as illustrations to the book of days of an extinct race. But there are certain paintings and sculptures which can be taken as great art, the work of the loftiest genius the world has known, and they owe their proud place, not merely to their antiquity, but to the judgment and verdict of history.

THE THREE CHIEF CLASSES OF THE GREAT ART OF THE WORLD

In the minds of some people there is at first an unwillingness to take the opinion of another, even of generations of men. And often, if some of us were courageous and sincere, we should confess that we preferred the pretty pictures on a birthday card to the paintings of a Titian or a Botticelli. This is, perhaps, because we have never had an opportunity of studying art seriously enough. It takes two to make a picture, one to paint it and the other to look at it. A great picture is the subject the artist painted plus the secret he painted into it. Until we understand something of that secret we cannot fully appreciate our magnificent inheritance.

The great art of the world—the art which has passed the ordeal of centuries of criticism—falls into three chief classes : painting, sculpture, and architecture. Architecture, indeed, may be called the parent of all art, because for a long time pictures were only made to decorate spaces on walls, and they were painted on the fabric of the building itself ; the framed picture is a comparatively modern adaptation of the coloured wall-panel. And statues were chiselled to adorn niches in temples and palaces, or cut in low relief, to make a long fresco pattern.

THE LOVE THAT INSPIRED THE WORLD'S GREAT PICTURES

Whatever it may be, sculpture, painting, or architecture, this work of the Old Masters owes its birth to an instinct common to its kindred. In almost every case it was inspired by one of the great emotions of the human heart—love, sorrow, reverence, or worship, and without some such feeling no great art is ever conceived.

Love has inspired more pictures than any other human emotion, but love bears a very wide interpretation. There is physical love—the love of husband, wife, or child; love of the mind—the love of abstract qualities, such as truth, courage ; spiritual love—the love of God and of the earth, which poets call the garment of God. The pictures inspired by sorrow are fewer, but move more intensely, because the tragedy of life is that death stalks our beloved, and sooner or later hurls his dart.

Love, sorrow, worship ; and in a way the greatest of these is worship and holds in itself all three. Worship painted pictures, carved statues, built temples and cathedrals, and made them greater than man because they held a sense of God-head, of eternity enclosing time.

If we think seriously of any picture the world calls great, we shall see that its subject is one of these powerful emotions ; and any work so conceived, if poorly executed, has in it the seeds of greatness because it strikes at the heart of the human race. This basic feeling, however, is, so to speak, the foundation, the scaffolding, and not the finished edifice. It is the subject the artist painted minus the secret he painted into it, which some of us spend our lives trying to discover. The secret was his own imagination and sense of beauty, and therein lay his final and unapproachable greatness.

THE FEELINGS OF THE SOUL THAT ARE PERFECTLY REAL

We ask what is beauty, what is imagination, and no one can find an answer. We know where beauty and imagination are revealed, in form and colour which satisfy the soul as food satisfies the body; but their nature is hidden deep in the mystery of life. We can think of them as senses of the spirit, as real as are the physical senses of sight, hearing, touch, taste, and smell. Just as our ears record the sound of a piece of music, and our eyes register an impression of the shape of a piece of stone, so these spirit-senses " feel " the vision of perfect sound that makes the music beautiful, the vision of perfect contour that makes the stone a lovely statue.

Beauty and imagination reach out beyond the actual to the ideal. For instance, thousands of artists have drawn portraits of old women. Rembrandt drew the portrait of an old woman, and it is one of the greatest things in the world, because, having his sense of sight, he recorded the features, by his sense of beauty and imagination he recorded something infinitely wonderful : not the face of one old woman, but the lovableness, the dignity, sorrow, and other-worldliness of old age of all time.

Hundreds of men have painted landscapes and got on to their canvases the glow of the sun and the radiance of the sea. Turner painted that same glowing sun, that same radiant sea, but his sense of beauty, his imagination, reached out to an intangible, heavenly glory, and so he put into his pictures " the light that never was, on land or sea, the consecration, and the poet's dream."

THE SPIRIT THAT BUILT THE PARTHENON AND WROTE SHAKESPEARE'S TALES

These spirit-senses of beauty and imagination are powers which the human soul has developed through thousands of years of effort to express itself. All art, poetry, and music, are forms of self-expression. Next to bodily needs, such as food, shelter, clothing, the need of self-expression is one of the most powerful of human instincts.

Every man, save the few in a generation who are born spiritually slothful, is moved by it to the doing of certain kinds of work on which he can stamp his own individuality. It is that which makes a child set up an erection of sand with patience and care, and then say, " *I* have made a house." It is that which built the Parthenon and wrote The Winter's Tale and composed the " Pathetic " Sonata. We are told by Indian mystics that it was because of God's desire to express Himself that He created the world—flung from Him a whirling atom, and on that atom, grown huge and populous, we live and are trying to express the beautiful, which, in the ultimate, is God.

THE GREAT HUNGER OF MEN TO EXPRESS THEMSELVES

Art is the very earliest form of this self-expression. Before men could read or write, while yet their clothing was the skins of animals, they could draw. They rendered the objects about them in the simple way a little one would draw its pet kitten on a slate today. They drew in their idle moments, when the chase was over and the food broiled and eaten by the cave fire. Between those early efforts and the art which today is a lofty vocation there is a great gulf fixed. Thousands of years are needed to span the gulf, and during that time, as whole civilisations rose to power and died, the craving to express himself in beautiful imagery became a spiritual hunger in man's heart.

To look back on the art of the world is, in a way, to see the story of the growing pains of this aesthetic life which is now our pride and exceeding great joy. The early art of the world was centred round the several religions of the human race, and for a long time the sense of beauty was small and stunted and responded to false ideals. Imagination went astray, and the gods men portrayed in their sculpture as high above humans were often decorated puppets.

But while his soul was thus struggling in the half-light, man's power of self-expression was becoming great. With each passing century art became more ennobled, more purified of excess, and grew to be a very real part of the life of a nation. And soon it came to pass that men were born whose sense of beauty and imagination were so powerful as to override all other instincts. They were the men we call geniuses, in whom the inward urge for self-expression in lovely imagery became a driving force that cut a wedge, so to speak, through the history of their day.

NATIONS THAT FEEL DEEPLY, AND NATIONS BLIND AND DEAF

To these gifted ones art mattered more than food or clothing ; they spent their lives working out their ideals of purity in line and colour, their spiritual conceptions. But nations, like men, are different one from another ; some races have been sensitive to beautiful impressions, and others have been blind and deaf.

The spirit of beauty and imagination filled one people as one man—the Greeks. The soul of Greece was loveliness, pagan loveliness, and there has never been another nation to whom art was so vital.

Even in Greece there were generations of immaturity. A sense of pure beauty only comes to a race in its flowering time ; when the soul of a people withers and falls asunder the art it expresses becomes depraved and false. Nature is chary of perfection. It is, perhaps, because artists have always dreamed of a realisation of perfect beauty that genius is called the sorrowful gift, always urging the soul to express the inexpressible, to attain the unattainable. It was the pent-up spirit of an artist who cried :

" Oh beauty, oh divine, white wonder,
On whom my dull eyes, blind to all
  else, peer."

But it is not only artists who yearn for the vision beautiful. Almost every man, woman, and child has inherited, in however slight degree, the instinct which is the beginning of art. And therein, as soon as we realise it, lies a wonderful happiness. It is because we have in our own souls— we who have never painted a picture or carved a statue—a latent sense of beauty and imagination that we are moved by great art, that we stand spellbound before a picture and go away haunted by its lines and colours.

WE ARE ALL DESCENDED FROM THE GENIUSES OF THE WORLD

We are all, in a way, descended from the geniuses of the world, and the longer we live, the more we cultivate our sense of beauty, the more shall we show the marks of our breeding. There is scarcely a child born into the world who carries not in himself the seeds of greatness. And the reason the greatness so rarely flowers is due to the accident of circumstance, upbringing, environment. So that we are in the position of knowing in our inmost souls what beautiful sound is, and being unable to express it in music ; of realising dimly what colour is, and of being helpless when someone offers us a palette and a canvas.

Art says for us the things we cannot say for ourselves. And, in the measure that we allow our aesthetic sense to grow, we realise that it is not only in the actual rendering of concrete shape and colour that artists are our spokesmen. Art makes articulate the dumb emotions of the soul.

Great happiness or great sorrow seals our lips and keeps us dumb, but as we look on great pictures and sculptures we find that happiness and that sorrow portrayed for ever by someone who had the power to speak it out.

ART RUNS THROUGH THE WHOLE WORLD OF THOUGHT AND FEELING

As in a greater degree, so in a lesser one, we owe to lovely things the expression of ourselves. There is not a province of thought or feeling that art does not reveal. It is as if beauty and imagination, like pagan goddesses, immeasurable in their power, had thrown over the world a finely meshed net, and caught all the outward-flying fragments of human aspirations and held them for ever in a golden web. And so we come to see that great statues and pictures are more than lovely shapes and colours : they are beautiful dreams come true, heavenly visions crystallised in stone. They are the sum of all that is best in the mind and heart and soul of the human race. They are a fragment of bygone time and yet a piece of today and tomorrow. They are the tremendous fulfilment of all the small longings of the individual soul, the ideals and hopes that flit to and fro in the chambers of the mind, the loveliness we yearn for and may not possess. The spirit senses of beauty and imagination have seized once and for all the fleeting rapture of daily life, the dawns that are full of little angels' wings, the sunsets that are full of spring flowers, the hours when earth is very near to heaven.

And we may be quite sure that a picture which does not react on our own imagination, which does not make us conscious of other qualities than colour and shape— of the artist's secret, in fact—is not great. It may be a pleasant and attractive subject, but if it ends in itself it will die. It is the secret of art for ever to tantalise us with its secret.

THE THRILL OF THE FIRST MAN WHO DREW A BEAUTIFUL THING

For all our knowledge of the presence of art as a living force in the world for some sixteen thousand years, it is still as mysterious a presence as it was in the consciousness of the first man who drew a beautiful thing and thrilled with the thought, " *I* have done that." Art has become in a way a great science, whereof the handbooks are legion, and yet a fairy tale ; a career demanding seasons of hard study and yet dependent on the elusiveness of dreams. And when painters have given their rich years to learning and toil, and have grown great, they are still what the unlearned artists of old were, magicians who make the world a garden.

The work of these inspired ones of yesterday and today lies scattered about the world like flowers which bloom for ever. We cannot think how bare our lives would be, lacking these blossoms. Colour, shape, and line, finely drawn old faces, lovely forms, green fields and tossing seas, are brought within the range of our stay-at-home eyes by means of great art. We should never count an hour wasted that is spent on looking at these treasures and making them our own, for every time our hearts are moved, however faintly, by the sense of beauty, our souls are marching on.

THE EVERLASTING GLORY OF ART

Art, the expression of the love of beauty in the soul of man is the pride and glory of the world throughout all ages. Here we give a few examples of the treasures men have left behind for all mankind to love. They show Art in many different fields—painting, sculpture, carving, and so on.

THE WONDERFUL HEAD OF DAVID AS HE LOOKS DOWN FROM THE HILL ABOVE FLORENCE WHERE MICHAEL ANGELO PLACED HIM

28 c 1

A SILVER MEDAL OF THE
SEVENTEENTH CENTURY

BRONZE HEAD FROM
HERCULANEUM

A MAJOLICA PLATE FROM
ITALY

A SIXTH-CENTURY
IVORY FROM FLORENCE

A FOURTEENTH-CENTURY
CAVALRYMAN

THE COFFIN OF AN
OLD EGYPTIAN

AN IVORY PANEL A
THOUSAND YEARS OLD

A WROUGHT-IRON WINDOW IN THE
CHURCH OF SAINT CROCE, FLORENCE

A RARE LANTERN FROM
SIENA

A GOLD MEDAL OF CROMWELL'S
MINISTER, JOHN THURLOE

A TURKISH JUG OF THE
SIXTEENTH CENTURY

A MEDAL FROM SYRACUSE
25 CENTURIES OLD

A COLUMN IN A
PALACE OF FLORENCE

A MINIATURE OF CROMWELL
By CHRISTIAN RICHTER

A PERSIAN DOOR IN
LACQUER WORK

INCENSE-HOLDER FROM THE
PITTI PALACE, FLORENCE

AN OLD GERMAN CUP IN
THE FORM OF A COCK

A DECORATED WATER-JUG
FROM GREECE

MISS LINLEY & HER BROTHER
By THOMAS GAINSBOROUGH

A DOGE OF VENICE
By GIOVANNI BELLINI

MARCUS AURELIUS

MICHAEL ANGELO'S DAVID

AN OLD LADY   By REMBRANDT

MISS BOWLES   By SIR JOSHUA REYNOLDS

MISS HAVERFIELD   By THOMAS GAINSBOROUGH

A FINE PAINTING BY FRANK HALS OF A NURSE AND CHILD

AN ETRUSCAN VESSEL
IN BRONZE

AN ANCIENT BRAZIER FROM ITALY

FOOD-CARRIERS OF OLD
EGYPT

A WOODEN BUST OF THE
SIXTEENTH CENTURY

A FOURTH-CENTURY MOSAIC
FROM RAVENNA

COPPER MODEL OF
A SHIP

A BIT OF PAVEMENT FROM FLORENCE
600 YEARS OLD

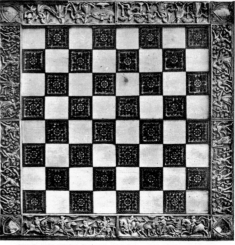

A CHESSBOARD IN IVORY 400 YEARS OLD
FROM THE BARGELLO MUSEUM, FLORENCE

VELASQUEZ'S FERDINAND
OF AUSTRIA

A CHINESE GODDESS IN
WHITE PORCELAIN

FORTUNA—A SIXTEENTH-
CENTURY STATUE

MICHAEL ANGELO'S STATUE OF
VICTORY IN FLORENCE

AUGUSTUS CAESAR IN
FULL ARMOUR

THE ANGELUS   By JEAN FRANCOIS MILLET

A STATUE OF NAPOLEON IN A PARIS MUSEUM

SALISBURY CATHEDRAL

PISA BAPTISTERY

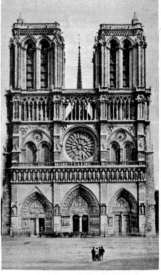

NOTRE DAME, PARIS

ST. GEORGE'S CHAPEL, WINDSOR

A TOWER BUILT BY JULIUS
CAESAR IN PROVENCE

ROMAN ARCH AT ORANGE

A BEAUTIFUL OLD GATEWAY
IN ISTANBUL

A 500-YEAR-OLD GATEWAY
AT NORWICH

THE CARVED INTERIOR OF AN
INDIAN TEMPLE

The Wonderful House We Live In, and Our Place in the World

What This Story Tells Us

HOW Life came into the world no man can tell. Certainly the first living things were plants, and from these all the life we know has come. This part of our book tells us what we know of life, and how it works, and the most marvellous things it has made—the bodies we live in. Fearfully and wonderfully are we made, and perfect and beautiful beyond words is the human frame and all that moves within it. Here we shall read how it works, of the astonishing arrangements which govern our lives, of the delicate balancing of the machinery which secures the perfect working of sight, thought, speech, hearing, breathing, moving; of the complete co-operation and sympathy existing in us all between body, mind, and soul. We shall read here, also, of the lives of those about us, of citizenship, and of our place in society and the world.

LIFE THAT FILLS THE EARTH

LIFE fills the seas, covers the dry land, and flies in the air above. Everywhere there is life and movement and birth and death and new birth; always and everywhere there is life and more life.

These are the most interesting facts of the world we live in, and we must ask many questions concerning them. For instance, what is the difference between a living thing, like a fly, or a rose, or a child, and a thing that is not living or that never has lived, like a stone, or the gravel or clay in the garden?

What are the different kinds of living things? How is it they are so different? An elephant is very different from a piece of moss, yet an elephant is much more like a piece of moss than like a piece of flint. Why is it?

We know that living creatures die, and yet Life does not die ; there is no living thing on the Earth now that was alive two thousand years ago, except, perhaps, a few great trees like the cedars of Lebanon. All the living things that were alive then, fishes and flies and birds and flowers, are dead now ; yet the Earth never was so filled with life as now.

Why is it ? It is because of the very wonderful fact that all living things have children, that these children are like their parents, and that when the parents die the children carry on their lives; and so the world goes round.

There is an old Greek story of the runners who had to carry a flaming torch, and as one runner fell, tired out, he gave the torch to another, and so, though the runners fell and could not reach the goal, the torch was not put out, but went on burning. The torch is like the flame of life, and each living creature is like the runner, handing the flame to the children who will carry it on when he is gone.

Where have all these living things come from ? We know that all things, living and dead, have come from God, who sustains them from everlasting to everlasting, but how did all these kinds of living things come into existence? What is their history? Who were their parents? It is well for us that we have been born in the days when this truth and so many others are becoming known, for the more truth we know the better it is for our lives.

Let us begin by asking ourselves how we can tell whether a thing is alive or not alive. Now, that is really silly, you may say, because anyone can tell in a moment that the fly is alive and that the

BODY, MIND, AND SOUL · CITIZENSHIP · ECONOMICS · GOVERNMENT

window-pane is not alive. We know that the fly is alive, just as we know that a boy is alive, because he is so lively. We call anything alive that moves about itself, anything that jumps, or shouts or swims, or flies. We say this, but is it true?

Really it is not true. When we come to think of it, the boy is still alive even when he is asleep. He is just as alive when asleep as he was when he was playing before he went to bed. Some wise child may say this is not a good argument at all, for even when the boy is asleep he still moves, for we can see him breathing.

A BIRD'S-EYE VIEW OF THE WORLD ABOUT US

That is true. The heart has not gone to sleep; it is still moving, and it is moving because it is alive. So that, after all, the boy is lively all the time, whether he is asleep or awake, and the real question is whether a thing which does not seem to move at all is alive like the boy. Must anything really alive be really lively like the boy? We shall see.

We can imagine how a bird flying high in the air is able to look down on the surface of the earth. A bird's-eye view is a view that the bird has of the world when it is up in the sky; it sees everything at once. Now, it is always necessary to take a bird's-eye view of anything we are trying to understand. If we take nothing but short views of one thing at a time our ideas will be as silly as a fly's idea of an elephant must be. We must see one thing at a time, and all things together—we must take both sorts of views.

When we do this we see that there are two great kinds of living things, very different from each other. The difference is not in size or quantity, but in kind or quality—the one kind of living things we call animals, and the other kind plants; and they are quite different. There are many differences, but the difference we notice first when we take our bird's-eye view is a difference of liveliness. Animals move about themselves; plants do not.

THE LIFE IN THE ANIMAL AND THE LIFE IN THE PLANT

Shall we say, then, that plants are not alive? That has often been said and thought in the past, because men thought that if a thing was to be called alive it must be lively. We know that plants are not lively, like a cat ; you can always find a rose bush where you left it in the garden,

but the cat is not always where you left it. So men thought that because plants did not walk away they were not really alive.

And then men came to see the truth of what we have already said—that, after all, there is something about a rose which makes it more like a fly than it is like a piece of stone, even though the fly can fly and the rose cannot. So men thought there were two kinds of life; one was real, true life, like the fly's life, or the tiger's, or ours, and the other was a sort of half-and-half life, not the real thing but a feeble imitation of it, just enough to make a difference; and men said that that kind of half-and-half life was the life of trees and plants. The men who said these things did not understand much about them. They knew that there was something strange about the oak and the acorn, but they could not persuade themselves that anything that was not lively was really and truly alive.

But men began to find out things at last. One man learnt something, the next man learnt a little more, the man who came after him learnt a little more still; and so the world became wiser and wiser.

THE QUIET WAY IN WHICH THE PLANT KINGDOM DOES ITS WORK

We know all that the men who lived before us knew, and we have also learned something they did not know. As men learned more about the world they were able to get a bird's-eye view, and the result of all their thinking is that we know now that plants are just as much alive as animals. In some ways plants are actually more alive than animals, even though they are not lively. The difference is that the life of the animal shows itself in liveliness, but the life of the plant shows itself in something else.

We know the animal is alive because it is lively, like the boy—like you. Your life shows itself in your liveliness. But we know the plant is alive because it helps the animal to live and to be lively, and for many other reasons.

Though the plant is very quiet and still, its life is very important, because it makes the liveliness of the animal possible. For the animal lives on the plant, and if there were no plants all animals would die.

Animals make a great noise, but plants do just as much work, only they do it quietly. We need not always be shouting and jumping and barking or blowing a

LIFE AND ITS WONDERFUL LADDER

This picture suggests the later steps in the Ladder of Life—the steps since the creation of the backbone, which the first creatures had not. The oldest backboned creatures are Fishes. Above them are Amphibians, the land and water animals. Then there is a split. On the one side the Amphibians gave rise to Reptiles, and these gave rise to Birds. On the other came the Mammals. Man came later in this last line.

trumpet to prove that we are alive. Plants do none of these things, but their life makes all other life possible.

We see now that life means more than liveliness. Many things that are not lively are really alive, but all living things do not make a noise and walk about. You may look at a thing and never see it move for a day, or a week, or a year, yet it may be alive. Life means much more than the idea of something which moves by itself.

Movement is not really life, because *everything moves.* Plants do not walk about the garden, but they move by themselves. When the acorn grows into an oak it moves upwards. When the sunflower faces the sun as it grows it moves not only upwards, but in other ways also; and if we take the leaf of a plant and look at it through magnifying glasses, in what is called a microscope, we can see for ourselves that the tiny specks of green stuff which give the leaf its colour are ever moving.

Everything is moving, whether we see it or not, so that life is more than liveliness. The tiny specks of stuff that make up a

Life moves in a plant as in a child. If we put an acorn in the ground it will grow into an oak.

In olden days a runner would carry a flaming torch, and as he fell out would hand it on to another to keep burning. So each one of us carries on life.

How can we tell whether a thing is alive or not alive? What is the difference between a living thing, like a boy or a rose, and a thing not living, like a stick?

pebble are always moving, and so are the black specks that make the ink on this page. If liveliness means life, then all things are alive, for all things are lively if we see them clearly enough.

This is important to understand if we are to think properly of the life of the plant. Perhaps movement is the most important thing in the world, and perhaps, if we could really see deep enough, we should find that life itself is really a very special kind of movement or liveliness. But if life is just a special kind of movement, it is so very special that it makes all the difference whether a thing has this movement or not.

The best way for us to understand what it is that really makes a thing alive is to study very simple kinds of life. The most simple kinds are plant life or vegetable life ; some are lively and some are not lively, but they are all alive. If there were no plants, animals could not live. Plants are older than animals; that is to say, there were plants on the Earth before there were any animals, and the first kinds of animals were the children of plants.

The Story of the Marvellous Plants that Cover the Earth

What This Story Tells Us

THE oldest living things on Earth are plants. They cover the Earth with beauty like a truly magic carpet, and they are the very foundations of our lives. We could not live without them ; but for the Plant Kingdom, spread over the whole surface of the Earth and along the surface and the bottom of the sea, the Animal Kingdom must perish. The whole world depends for its food upon plants, and the whole world depends, therefore, upon a secret that a plant has which no man knows ; for a plant knows how to take its food from air and water. It takes its supplies as it stands there rooted in the soil, nourishing itself in some mysterious way from the atmosphere direct. As we stand looking at it a plant is making its own food ; no man knows how. Here we shall read of the astonishing wonder of life in the Kingdom of Plants.

HOW LIFE GOES ROUND AND ROUND

FOR a very long time there were no living creatures at all upon the Earth.

That was millions and millions of years ago, when the Earth was too hot to be a home of life. But the crust cooled, depressions were filled with water, and there was a heavy atmosphere of gas.

Then the first living creatures made their appearance. Scientists cannot tell us whence they came. What they were like, these firstlings, we do not know— almost all beginnings are very misty— but it is probably safe to say that they were microscopically small, like the microbes which cause rotting and disease. If we can imagine an observer of the Earth in the time of the dawn of life he would not have been able to see the teeming animalcules, any more than we can see the tiny specks of bacteria.

Another thing that is almost certain is that the first living creatures were neither decided plants nor decided animals. They were, so to speak, hesitating between these two very different lines of life. They were nearer plants in this way—that they were able to feed at a low level on water and carbonic acid gas (carbon dioxide) and salts in the water ; they were able in some measure to use the energy of the sunshine to help them to build up carbon compounds from simple materials.

The genealogical tree on all living creatures must be thought of as like an ornamental V, with little twigs on each half of its fork. To the left we may put the animals, and to the right the plants, and it would be useful to make the animal line go much higher than the plant line.

Everyone feels that there is a great gulf between a beech tree and the squirrel on its branches ; but we are not quite so clear when it comes to distinguishing between a mushroom and a sponge, and some of the old naturalists thought sponges and corals were plants of the sea. Still more difficult is it to be sure whether a living creature with a single cell is a plant or an animal, especially as some simple animals have managed to get hold of the green colouring matter called chlorophyll —which is characteristic of almost all plants.

Then, at the foot of our V-shaped tree, there are creatures, sometimes called Protists, which the botanists and the zoologists both claim. They have not yet taken the decisive step.

Long, long ago, then, some simple, single-celled creatures manufactured chlorophyll, surrounded themselves with a

BOTANY & ITS WONDERS · FLOWERS · TREES · HOW THINGS GROW

cell-wall of cellulose—now sold in the shops as vegetable parchment paper—and began to build up quantities of sugar, starch, and other carbon compounds. These were the first plants, and they probably lived freely in the sea. The secret of their success was the ability to feed at a low chemical level, and to use the power of the sunlight in their chemical operations of building up. Their success meant much for future history, for *they began to form an atmosphere of free oxygen*, and they made carbon compounds sufficient to feed not only themselves but the animal world.

THE GREAT SECRET OF THE ANIMALS AND WHAT IT MEANT FOR THEM

Of course the animals had their simple beginnings too, and the parting of the ways was when certain creatures—the first animals—became addicted to the habit of not building up their own food but using what simple plants had made.

This discovery of ready-made food was the deep secret of animals, and it meant the possibility of great activity, of living adventurously! For food is just like fuel; it is a supply of chemical energy. Plants are like manufacturers of munitions, and animals explode these in the never-ending battle of life. Happily for us, plants are like misers, accumulating much more than they need; animals are spendthrifts, often living close up to their income. We can understand, then, why most animals get along comfortably without being green, and why they are nearly all free from the somewhat clogging and embarrassing material called cellulose, which forms the cell-walls of plants. Perhaps a plant may be compared to a knight of long ago, boxed in by his suit of armour. The muscles of animals could not do what they do if the wall of each muscle-cell were surrounded by stiff cellulose. It must be remembered that cellulose is chemically next door to wood.

THE SOMETHING OF THE ANIMAL THAT IS OFTEN FOUND IN THE PLANT

The two halves of the V-shaped tree of life diverge farther and farther, but it is not surprising that something of the animal may often be detected in the plant, and something of the plant in the animal. We shall have to return to the animal lurking in the plant, but let us take a few examples in the meantime.

The sundew and the Venus fly-trap and other " insect-eating plants " have turned the tables on animals; they depend in part on insects for their food, and catch them very effectively. Many leaves rise and fall, many flowers open and close, with the growing and waning light of day.

Young shoots bend and bow to the different points of the compass; the young rootlet moves in the earthworm's burrow; the tendril of the pea is extraordinarily sensitive to the touch of a twig, and its tip moves around in little paths *as if it were searching;* it is easy to see the movements of the stamens of the rock-rose, or the closing of the stigma of the musk.

All plants are sensitive in some measure, and Sir J. C. Bose, the great botanist of India, proved that a tree may answer back to a passing cloud. Many plants, if not all, have some capacity for movement, and there is a telegraph-plant in the Ganges basin—called Desmodium—whose leaves are always moving a little. When the Venus fly-trap in the Carolina swamp shuts the two halves of its rat-trap-like leaf and catches a fly there is an electrical change similar to that which occurs when we contract our muscles in shutting our hands. There is no doubt that the animal lurks in the plant.

THE SOMETHING OF THE PLANT THAT IS OFTEN FOUND IN THE ANIMAL

Many animals, like sponges, zoophytes, and corals, have relapsed into a plant-like sluggishness. Except when they are very young, they are fixed. Many of them are much given to branching, often in a very tree-like way. In the sea-squirts there is abundant cellulose in the enveloping coat—a characteristic vegetable substance in the most sluggish part of a very sluggish animal.

A number of sluggish animals resemble plants in accumulating quantities of stored material, which may be utilised in hard times or serve as a legacy for the young ones. Not a few animals have a very plant-like power of partially dying down when outside conditions are unfriendly, and some types form resting germs which last through the hard times of winter, as the seeds of many plants do.

One must not make too much of green animals, for most green animals, like the green freshwater sponge, or the green freshwater Hydra, or green sea-anemones and corals, owe their green colour to tiny partner-plants which live inside some of their cells. There seem to be just a few cases where the animal has chlorophyll belonging to itself. In many cases — in some starfishes and worms, some lizards and birds— the green colour has nothing at all to do with the green colour of plants.

So far as complexity of structure and life-history goes, the whole kingdom of many-celled plants may be compared simply to the zoophytes and corals among animals. They are all within a comparatively narrow range. But what diversity there is between toadstool and oak tree, between the lichen on the hilltop and the fields of golden wheat, between the beautifully coloured seaweeds and the flowers of the meadow ! Or, if we take a single class like ferns, what a multitude of kinds there are, each itself and no other !

One of the miracles of every summer is the building up of such a flower as this from a tiny seed

The glory of the flowers of the woodland
LIFE COVERS THE EARTH WITH BEAUTY

And we get the same impression of endless form-changes when we study a single order of flowering plants— say the Rose order. All the members have a great deal in common; they are near relations.

Yet how different at first sight seem such plants as the rose, strawberry, apple, tormentil, and salad burnet ! Who would think at first sight that the columbine, monkshood, and buttercup belong to the same order of Ranunculuses?

And, besides variety of form, there is variety of habitat. Where is there any plantless place, except in the darkness of the deepest sea? There may be " red snow," due to a very simple plant, on a floating iceberg ; there are some simple plants in hot springs; there are Alpines above the snow-line on the mountains ; there are moulds glistening on the underground passages in mines ; there is a partner-fungus spreading through and through the heather-plant, even into the flower ; and doctors sometimes speak of the " flora " of man's food-canal!

Another fact so plain that we hardly think about it is the almost universal beauty in the plant world. The exceptions are certain cultivated plants, like cauliflower and cabbage, which have lost most of the beauty of their wild ancestors. And perhaps there are some parasites which do not live independent lives, and are therefore branded with some measure of ugliness. For beauty is the hall-mark of harmonious, healthy, well-ordered living, and it may be that, though life remains half asleep in plants, the beautiful shapes and colours are their dream-smiles.

Think of the harebells swinging by the wayside, the wood-hyacinths, which the poet speaks of as the heavens upbreaking through the earth, the laburnums dropping wells of fire, the daffodils dancing by the lake-side, Wordsworth's " jocund company." No doubt there is easy beauty and difficult beauty, but the big fact is *beauty everywhere.*

BEAUTY CROWDS UPON US ALL OUR LIFE IN NATURE'S WIDE KINGDOMS

The old idea that beauty is exceptional, and to be looked for especially in such plants as orchids, has almost disappeared. Many orchids are, indeed, resplendent, and often strangely suggestive of butterflies, but one cannot say that they greatly excel some of our common flowers—the violet, the butterwort, the bog-bean, the bladderwort, the grass of Parnassus, the bog-pimpernel, and the daisy. The fact is that beauty crowds us all our life if we keep in touch with wild flowers ; and this is a fact not less important than the statement that the central secret of the green leaf is being a sunshine-trap.

We have not learned much botany unless we have come to feel the beauty of common plants. The poet Keats said that throughout his life nothing moved him more than the opening flowers, and there is something wrong with us and with our science if we do not feel the wonder of the crocus breaking through the sod. But it is worth our while, also, to discover thrills, to follow the stream up the gorge till we find the Royal Fern, glistening with spray beside a waterfall :

Plant lovelier in its own recess
Than Grecian naiad seen at earliest dawn
Tending her font, or lady of the lake
Sole sitting by the shores of old romance.

We are accustomed to think of strength in connection with animals and machines that move quickly about and do things and withstand assaults. The elephant, the railway-engine, the lighthouse, show strength. Whereas we are inclined to think of the tender plant, the bruised flax, the short-lived grass, the poppy which is broken by being plucked. As everyone knows, many of our gay garden flowers are annuals, lasting only for the summer.

THE QUIET STRENGTH OF THE FOREST TREES AND THE WORK THEY DO

But this is only one side of the picture. The grass withereth and the flower fadeth, but, after all, the grass is one of the most successful of all living things. It has covered the earth like a garment.

This power of spreading and multiplying is all very well when the plant is on man's side, as most grasses are ; but when it is an injurious plant that spreads, like bracken in this country or prickly pear in India, then we see the menace there may be in the strength of plants.

We are often impressed by the weight-lifting feats of the strong man at the show, but have we done justice to the quiet strength of the forest trees, which are continually sustaining enormous weights against gravity, every year adding to their burden and lifting it higher ? We know the explosive power of dynamite, but it is very interesting to see the roots of a tree spreading within a cleft in the rock and ending by rending it asunder. We know of the great transformations of energy which go on in chemical and engineering works, but we must do justice to the intensity of the operations that continue unceasingly through the summer day in the chemical and physical laboratory of every green leaf ; and all without a sound !

NO PLANT IN THE WORLD LIVES OR DIES TO ITSELF

What strength of a sort there is in the way that microbes multiply, killing a man in a few hours ! If one bacillus of the plague gets entrance into man through the bite of a rat-flea it may be represented by a million the next day. What strength of renewal there is in many plants ; the hawthorn is all the more vigorous because of the hedgeman's savage pruning. Then there is the strength of longevity, for the oldest living things in the world are some of the big trees of California, which may have lasted for two thousand years.

One of our poets is responsible for the magnificent exaggeration :

> Thou canst not stir a flower
> Without troubling of a star

It is but a striking way of saying that no plant lives or dies to itself. Every the basis for manufacturing the essentials of life known as starch, sugar, fats, and what are known as proteins.

Some animal eats the plant, or part of the plant, and another incarnation begins. For the nutritive material obtained from the plant—the nectar the bee changes

THE WONDERFUL CYCLE OF LIFE THAT NEVER ENDS AND NEVER FAILS

Life works in a cycle. Water, gases, and salts are absorbed by plants as food. The plants are eaten by animals, the animals die, and bacteria destroy their bodies. From these bodies arise new gases, water, and salts. These are absorbed by the plants again, and the cycle of life begins afresh.

one is the intersection of numerous threads in the web of life. Let us gather a few illustrations of the part plants play in the Natural Kingdom.

First, there is the work of plants in *the circulation of matter*. As we have seen, green plants feed on air, water, and salts ; they use the carbon of carbon dioxide as into honey, the nut the monkey cracks— becomes part and parcel of the animal's body ; it is incorporated in some measure into the animal's living matter.

As the animal lives it gives off carbon dioxide, and this carbon dioxide, when it again enters the atmosphere, may be absorbed by a green plant.

Other forms of waste from the animal pass into the soil and may help to form salts which the roots of plants may absorb. Some may pass as ammonia into the air, and this may be washed down by rain into the soil, to be again recaptured by the roots of plants. Or, when the animal dies and sinks to the ground, bacteria begin to work on the dead body, and it rots. Its complex substances are broken down into simple substances, such as carbon dioxide, water, ammonia, and some salts. Out of a dead bird on the ground the bacteria make materials which plants can utilise. Bacteria act as middlemen between the dead animal and the living plant. They make the materials of the dead body fit to enter again into the cycle of life ; and so the world goes round.

THE SMALL SPECKS OF LIFE ON WHICH THE CREATURES OF THE SEA LIVE

If we pay an early morning visit to a great fishing-port, such as Hull, Grimsby, or Aberdeen, we see what look like miles of fishes laid out for sale. We get a glimpse of the harvest of the sea, and the question arises in our minds: How is man able to take so much out of the sea, year after year, when he puts so little in ? If he did this on a farm there would soon be exhaustion of the soil, and he obviates this on land by putting in manure. But what happens in the sea ?

The answer is partly to be found in the vegetable sea-dust which is wafted outwards and downwards from the shallow water, where seaweeds and sea-grasses flourish abundantly. Minute particles, worn off by the breakers or nibbled at by animals, are washed down the slope and form the food-supply of fishes or animals, worms and molluscs on which fishes feed. It takes ten pounds of this vegetable sea-dust to make a pound of worms; it takes ten pounds of worms to make a pound of whelk; and it takes ten pounds of whelks to make a pound of rock-cod !

THE WONDERFUL CYCLE OF LIFE BY WHICH THE WORLD GOES ROUND

But the other half of the answer is to be found in what a biologist once called the floating sea-meadows of the Open Sea. Countless millions of diatoms and other minute algae form a sort of living sea-soup at or near the surface of open waters. These minute organisms depend on the air and the sea-water with its salts ; in the sunshine they go on with their work

of building up life from light, like the leaves of the forest ; they and some minute green animals form the fundamental food-supply of small crustaceans; and these, again, are devoured by fishes. The Earth is run on a plan of successive incarnations something like this :

Air, water, and salts are absorbed by green plants in sunlight.

Nutritive carbon compounds are built up out of these, and are eaten by animals.

The animals die, and their dead bodies are destroyed by bacteria.

From the decay of these bodies gases, water, and salts are formed.

These are absorbed by green plants again, and the cycle of life begins afresh.

A great transformation of energy is always going on in plants. The plant is a laboratory of complex chemical substances, and each has its own peculiar chemical routine, as every chemical factory has. But this work of building up could not keep going without help from outside, and it is the green plant's special secret to obtain this from the orange-red rays of the sunlight. The energy of the sunlight is used by the plant to help it in its manufacture of carbon-compounds, which have chemical energy just as gunpowder has.

THE MYSTERIOUS EVENT ALWAYS TAKING PLACE IN A GREEN LEAF

Thus there is a continual changing of kinetic energy into potential energy. We see the same thing when the kinetic energy of a rush of water is used by a hydraulic machine to raise a heavy weight to a height, where it has energy of position, or *potential energy*. But what takes place in the green leaf is a more intricate transformation, and it is not yet fully known.

We shall have to do with many other "between" things, or linkages. Thus, one plant may unconsciously play into the hands of another, as when the dodder gets both support and food from the nettle ; or when the mistletoe gets support and watery sap from the apple tree; or when an alga joins with a fungus to form a double plant or lichen ; or when a root-tubercle bacteria joins in with clover and enables them somehow to utilise the free nitrogen of the air. On another line are the linkages between flowers and their insect visitors, which secure fertilisation, and the linkages which secure the scattering of seeds by fruit-eating birds. But we have made a good start towards understanding the relations which bind plants to the rest of Nature.

The Story of the Peoples of All Nations and Their Homelands

What This Story Tells Us

THIS wide world, 8000 miles in diameter and 25,000 miles round, with over 57 million square miles of land and more than twice as much water, is the home of 2500 million people. Some of them are crammed up in great cities ; some are scattered here and there with vast spaces all around them. Greater London, with about seven hundred square miles, has nearly as many people as Australia, with about three million square miles. There are still forests and deserts that keep back population, but rarely do we find a spot on Earth that is not home, sweet home, to somebody. Which way is the world going ? Backwards or forwards ? In our own time the world has been thrown back by war, plunged into disaster, but we who make this book believe that still the world will go forward. Here we see the life of the peoples who share the world with us.

THIS GREAT WORLD OF OURS

ONCE upon a time, in the not very distant past of our ancestors, there was no such word as World. They used two words meaning Man and Age. When they did at last run these two into one, making it presently our own familiar word World, they meant by it *an age of man.* They never used it to suggest the whole Earth as we do now.

It is in this ancient sense that we will now speak of the world—our world, the world composed of living men, women, and children in every corner of the Earth, the rich and various humanity of this planet circling round the flaming Sun.

What is it that first strikes us as we look at our world ? Is it the difference which exists in speech, the difference which shows in raiment, the differences which mark one nation from another in complexion and size ? No ; it is something much more difficult to understand.

The first thing to strike us in looking at the inhabitants of the Earth is the extraordinary difference which separates the various peoples *in time.*

It is the same hour for the whole Earth. For the history of the entire planet, it is the twentieth century since the time of Jesus. And yet look at the vast differences which still separate the French mathematician from the Laplander, the American inventor from the American Indian, the German chemist from the Australian Aborigine, the British engineer from the peasant of Egypt.

The age of the Earth is the same for all the world, and Asia was civilised many centuries before Europe ; yet at the westernmost parts of Europe, so lately barbarian, we see more science, more art, more refinement in morals and manners than in the very heart and centre of the once regal East—the East of Babylonia, Assyria, and Greece.

At once, then, we learn to be careful how we speak of the world. It is absurd, and it is also dangerous, to speak of the world as if it were a body of people all marching together on one road towards one definite goal. It is absurd to speak of the Present as if it were the Present for all the world, or of the Past as if all the world had done with it and was pressing forward to one Future for all mankind. We must speak of the world as a long chain of humanity which at all times stretches from the very beginnings of

THE FIVE CONTINENTS & 100 NATIONS & RACES THAT INHABIT THEM

human history up to this fleeting moment which is itself passing while we read these words.

We are reminded of that old story of a traveller through Time, told in a book seven hundred years old.

In passing one day by a very ancient and extremely populous city, I asked one of the inhabitants who founded the place. He replied: " I know not ; and our ancestors knew no more than we do on this point." Five hundred years afterwards, passing by the same place, I could not perceive a trace of the city. Inquiring of one of the peasants when it was that the city was destroyed, he answered me : " What an odd question ! This country has never been other than you see it now." I returned there after another five hundred years, and I found a sea. I now asked the fisherman how long it was since their country became a sea, and he replied that I ought to know it had always been a sea. I returned again after five hundred years; the sea had disappeared, and it was now dry land. No one knew what had become of the sea, or if such a thing had ever existed. Finally, I returned once more after five hundred years, and found again a flourishing city. The people told me that the origin of their city was lost in the night of time.

So Time covers up the history of men.

EVERY NATION HAS ITS GOOD MEN AND ITS BAD MEN

But there is another way in which time enters into our view of the world. Each country is composed of people who are living at different points in this chain, people whose mental clocks are all striking a different hour.

One of the greatest of thinkers said that he did not know the way in which to draw up an indictment against a whole nation. It can never be done. Each nation has its savages, its barbarians, its illiterates, its half-civilised, and its civilised. Each nation drags the same world-chain on its journey to the future. There are saints in India and criminals in England. There are philosophers in China and ignoramuses in Germany. There are geniuses in Arabia and yahoos in America.

We see, then, that the difference of all differences in this great world is one of time ; and when we ask what we mean by time in this sense we discover that it is a question of intelligence. To be a savage is to be near the starting-post of life. To be an educated and law-abiding person is to have run some part of the race through time. To be a genius or a saint is to be nearing the goal.

There was genuine inspiration in the lines of old Andrew Marvell :

The world in all doth but two nations bear ;
The Good, the Bad ; and these mixed everywhere.

Indeed, the whole business of politics, philosophy, and religion lies now in getting the good to act together as one nation, not to crush and destroy the Bad, but to encourage them to travel a little faster. It is because the world is marching out of step, and at such different paces, that we get confusion and the constant danger of catastrophe.

THE HOME OF TWO THOUSAND MILLION HUMAN LIVES

We shall notice many other interesting differences when we come to visit all the countries of the Earth in this book. No nation will show us the same picture. Each country to which we travel in thought will tell us a tale told by no other. Every people will speak to us in a tongue quite different from the rest.

We shall be looking at the details of a tremendous canvas, at particular threads in a long tapestry, at small fragments in a vast mosaic ; and we shall have to remind ourselves from time to time of the thing as a whole—not of France, not of Italy, not of Japan, not of Mauritius—but of the world.

This mighty world consists of more than 2500 million human beings. It is divided up into a hundred nations or peoples. Here it spreads itself over an enormous space and calls itself India. Here it creeps away into a little corner of snow-capped mountains and calls itself Scandinavia or Switzerland. Here it swarms over a fierce and desolate territory and calls itself Russia. Here it captures a few little islands and calls itself Britain.

THE VAST AREAS OF THE WORLD THAT WE SHALL SEE

At one point, as in China or Japan, this world is so congested that the very roadsides must be cultivated for food ; at another point, as in Australia, every man has scores of acres to himself. We shall visit the prairies of Canada, the tropical forests of the West Indies, the sultry streets of Spain, the frozen peaks of

OUR NEIGHBOURS OF FOUR CONTINENTS

RUSSIAN COTTON-PICKER

A CHEERFUL MONGOLIAN LAD

CHIEFTAIN OF LAPLAND

YOUNG GIRL OF CEYLON

A TYPICAL ALBANIAN

MELANESIAN HEADMAN

A YOUNG ARAB

WOMAN OF BASUTOLAND

HARVESTER IN JORDAN

YOUNG GREEK BOY

A COWBOY OF NEVADA

HOPI INDIAN OF ARIZONA

STRAW HATS IN PUERTO RICO

Caucasus, the sandy wastes of Arabia, the domestic calm of Holland, the mighty waters and far-stretching deserts of Africa, the storied cities of France, the rocky fastnesses of the Balkan peoples, the dismembered empire of Austria, the slumbering islands of the South Sea, the romantic towns of Germany, the shores of Portugal, and the lovely realm of Italy.

But what will specially interest us in this grand tour, this journey round the world, is the present condition of the human mind. We shall see the average person in each country moving before our eyes in one direction or another.

THE MEMBERS OF THE BIG WORLD FAMILY WE SHALL MEET

We shall see the odd little figure of the Chinese awakening from his sleep ; the German building a new world on the ruins of an old ; the Frenchman loving art and following the path of strict logic ; the Italian turning from the monuments of a past of unrivalled glory to the factory of modern industry, a future of trade and commerce.

We shall see the industrious Norwegian harnessing his tumultuous waters to the service of man ; the Indian uncertain whether to follow his holy books or Herbert Spencer ; the Russian striving to develop his vast territories under a new system of government ; the Englishman digging his garden, building his ships, and spinning his cotton ; the Australian riding after his sheep, and the Canadian after his cattle ; the Sinhalese of Ceylon diving for pearls and picking leaves from the tea plant.

We shall see the Spaniard waiting for a sign ; the Mexican curbing his former passion ; the Hollander smoking his pipe on the side of a canal or in the midst of acres of tulips ; the American ceaselessly making new things to lift the load of labour from mankind.

WHILE A CHILD AND WHILE A FLOWER IS BORN, THE WORLD IS YOUNG

And when we have seen all these things, and thought about them, we shall not only be able to form an opinion as to whether the nations will find a way out of the financial and industrial chaos into which they were thrown by war, but we shall have at least some notion as to the spirit in which mankind should face the manifold new problems of life today.

We shall see quite clearly that one nation cannot suffer want and woe without inflicting want and woe on other nations. We shall see that while nations live like wolves and vultures there will always be suffering on the Earth ; and that until they all co-operate together, as the wheat co-operates with the soil, and the bee with the flower, and the rivers with the sea, there can be no lasting peace on this planet, and no permanent security for human life.

And, however dark seems the future, we shall learn from the troubled past that, so long as the Good strive nobly and earnestly forward, the Bad can never drag us right back to the past ;

For while a youth is lost in soaring thought,
And while a maid grows sweet and beautiful,
And while a spring-tide coming lights the South
And while a child and while a flower is born,
And while one wrong cries for redress and finds
A soul to answer, still the world is young.

So the present generation, if it has faith, if it has courage, if it has a clear conviction of the one far-off divine event to which the whole Creation moves, may be able to break down the madness of war, the wickedness of jealous rivalry, and help to carry the world over the dangers brought about by the pursuit of a blind and selfish nationalism.

And so on to the end (and the end draws nearer)
When our souls may be freer, our senses clearer
('Tis an old-world creed which is nigh forgot),
When the eyes of the sleepers may waken in
  wonder,
And hearts may be joined that were riven asunder,
And Time and Love shall be merged—in what ?

IF LOVE IS THE WAY, LOVE MUST BE THE END

The answer to that question is the great riddle of existence ; but if Love is the way, Love must be the end. At least we may be certain of this—that moral intelligence makes for Love, and that in all the nations of the world the Good are those who believe in Love as the one solution of human difficulties. No prouder boast can be uttered by the human soul than that which claims kinship with the Mind of God in the universe, and says :

On Earth there is nothing great but Man,
In Man there is nothing great but Mind.

Illustrated Maps of All Countries with Thousands of Pictures

What These Pages Show Us

HERE we shall see, in pictures and maps, what the surface of the Earth is like. Such an array of picture maps we shall have in these pages as has rarely, if ever, been brought together before. They will show us, not only the boundaries of nations, the rivers and hills and oceans, but often the insect life and plant life of a country so vital to its prosperity and the proper development of its natural resources; the animals and birds, and the remarkable migration of living things; great events in its history and where they happened, sometimes the fossils that lie under its fields. With these maps, too, come hundreds of pictures illustrating striking scenes in these lands, their picturesque landscapes, their innumerable industries, peoples, cities, and buildings, while the little pictures which have been carefully drawn on the maps must number many thousands.

THE WONDERFUL GLOBE WE LIVE ON

ON THIS SPINNING GLOBE, FASHIONED COUNTLESS MILLIONS OF YEARS AGO FROM A CLOUD OF FIRE, LIVE TODAY A HUNDRED RACES AND NATIONS

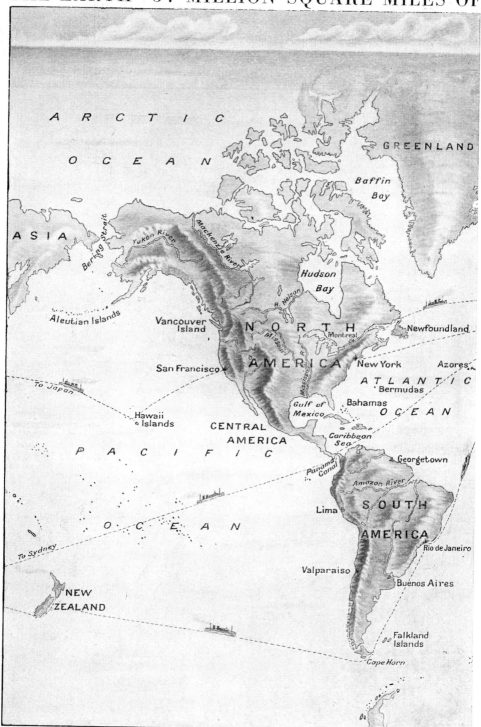

This map shows the surface of the Earth and its division into land and water. The Polar land boundaries have not been finally mapped, but the whole surface of the Earth is about 197 million square miles, of which about 57 million are land. Europe has 3,750,000 square miles, and (with the U.S.S.R.) over 600 million people. Asia, four and a half times as large, has more than 1300 million. Africa, three times the

LAND ON WHICH 2500 MILLION PEOPLE LIVE

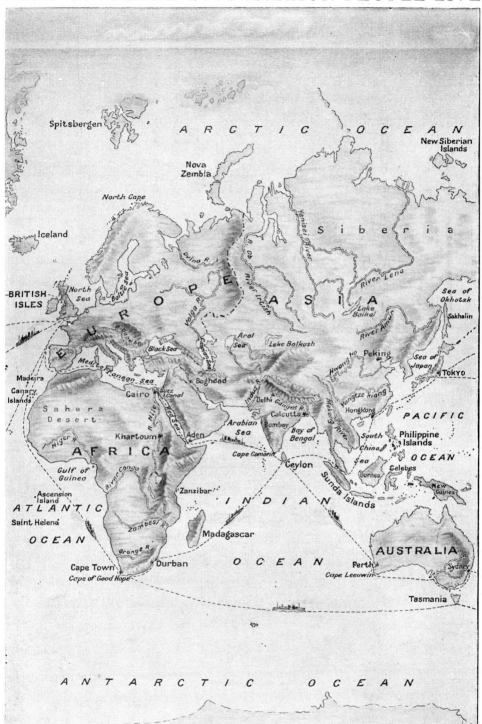

size of Europe has over 200 million people.   North and South America are four times the size of Europe, and have more than 350 million.   Australia is nearly as big as Europe, but has only about nine million people.   The oceans, covering about 140 million square miles, occupy over 80 per cent of the southern half of the world.   The Pacific covers nearly 64 million square miles, the Atlantic about half as many.

WORLD MAP OF INSECTS THAT HELP & HINDER THE PROGRESS OF MANKIND

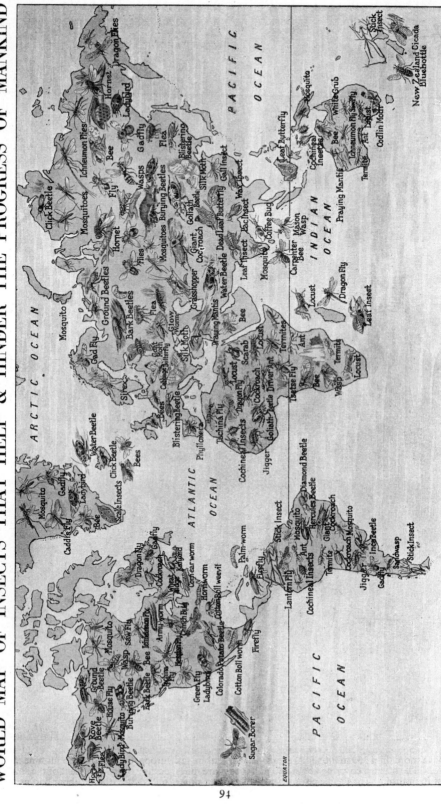

THERE ARE OVER 250,000 KINDS OF INSECTS, AND THIS MAP SHOWS THE MOST IMPORTANT OF THOSE THAT WORK FOR AND AGAINST MAN

WORLD MAP OF THE FOOD PLANTS OF MANKIND: FRUITS, NUTS, & CEREALS

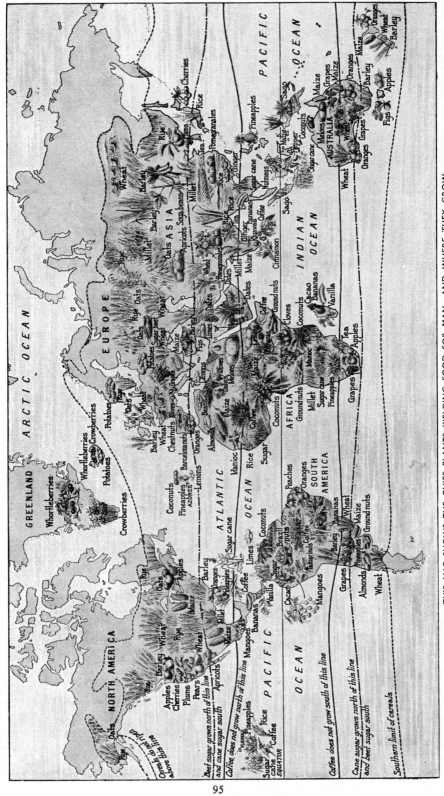

THIS MAP SHOWS THE CHIEF PLANTS YIELDING FOOD FOR MAN, AND WHERE THEY GROW

WHEN THE WORLD BECAME KNOWN

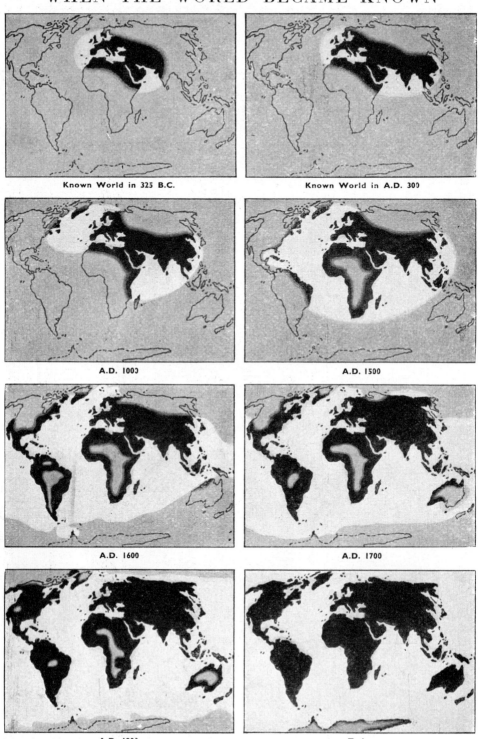

Known World in 325 B.C.

Known World in A.D. 300

A.D. 1000

A.D. 1500

A.D. 1600

A.D. 1700

A.D. 1800

Today

THE WORLD AS KNOWN IN EIGHT PERIODS IN HISTORY. KNOWN LAND IS SHOWN IN BLACK

One Thousand Poems of All Times and All Countries

What These Pages Give Us

THE poetry of the world is the noblest thing that every child inherits. It is more precious than all the gold in the mines of Africa. There are poems we would not sell for all the crowns of kings. They are the sweetest music of our tongue. They enshrine in matchless words some noble thought, some famous deed, some heart's great dream. One of our poets pictured the lark pausing to listen as the poet sang; and he goes on:

And the nightingale thought, " I have sung many songs, but never a one
     so gay,
For he sings of what the world will be when the years have died away."

It is poetry that leads us on to the vision of what the world will be, and it is the poet who, more than any other man, weaves himself from generation unto generation into the very hearts and lives and souls of men.

THE GRANDMOTHER'S TALE

Pierre Jean Béranger was a great song-writer of France. He lived through the most exciting periods of French history. He was a great admirer of Napoleon, and, though his genius was worthy of a nobler theme, we can hardly help being moved by his pathos and humanity in these lines. He was born in 1780, and died in 1857.

His fame shall never pass away!
   Beside the cottage hearth the hind
No other theme shall list to find
For many and many a distant day.
When winter nights their gloom begin
   And winter embers ruddy glow,
Round some old gossip closing in,
   They'll beg a tale of long ago—
"For all," they'll say, " he wrought us ill,
   His glorious name shall ne'er grow dim,
The people love, yes, love him still,
   So, grandmother, a tale of him,
         A tale of him!"

One day past here I saw him ride,
   A caravan of kings behind;
   The time I well can call to mind,
I hadn't then been long a bride,
I gazed out from the open door,
   Slowly his charger came this way;
A little hat, I think he wore,
   Yes, and his riding coat was grey.
I shook all over as quite near,
   Close to this very door he drew—
" Good-day," he cried, " good-day, my
     dear!"
What, grandmother, he spoke to you,
         He spoke to you?

The following year I chanced to be
   In Paris; every street was gay.
   He'd gone to Notre Dame to pray,
And passed again quite close to me!
The sun shone out in all its pride,

With triumph every bosom swelled;
" Ah, what a glorious scene ! " they cried.
   " Never has France the like beheld!"
A smile his features seemed to wear
   As on the crowds his glance he threw,
For he'd an heir, at last, an heir!—
Ah, grandmother, what times for you,
         What times for you!

Then came for France that dreadful day
   When foes swept over all the land:
   Undaunted he alone made stand,
As though to keep the world at bay!
One winter's night, as this might be,
   I heard a knocking at the door;
I opened it; great heavens! 'twas he!
   A couple in his wake—no more;
Then sinking down upon a seat—
   Ay, 'twas upon this very chair,
He gasped: " Defeat! Ah, God, defeat!"
What, grandmother, he sat down there,
         He sat down there?

He called for food; I quickly brought
   The best I happened to have by;
   Then, when his dripping clothes were
     dry,
He seemed to doze awhile, methought.
Seeing me weeping when he woke,
   " Courage," he cried, " there's still a
     chance;
I go to Paris; one bold stroke,
   And Paris shall deliver France!"
He went; the glass I'd seen him hold,
   The glass to which his lips he'd set,
I've treasured since like gold, like gold!
What, grandmother, you have it yet,
         You have it yet?

POEMS · SONGS · BALLADS · VERSES AND RHYMES WITH MUSIC

'Tis there. But all, alas! was o'er;
　He, whom the Pope himself had
　　crowned,
　The mighty hero world-renowned
Died prisoner on a far-off shore.
For long we none believed the tale,
　They said that he would reappear,
Across the seas again would sail,
　To fill the universe with fear !
But when we found that he was dead,
　When all the shameful truth we knew,
The bitter, bitter tears I shed !
　Ah, grandmother, God comfort you,
　　　　　God comfort you !

MY GARDEN

This lovely little poem, sweetest of all swallow-flights of song about a garden, was penned by Thomas Edward Brown, the Manx poet. Born in 1830, T. E. Brown died in 1897. His poems were chiefly written about the people of the Isle of Man, their quaint ways and seafaring heroism.

A GARDEN is a lovesome thing, God wot !
　　Rose plot,
Fringed pool,
Ferned grot :
The veriest school
Of peace ; and yet the fool
Contends that God is not :　　[cool ?
Not God ! in gardens ! when the eve is
Nay, but I have a sign ;
'Tis very sure God walks in mine.

THE SHUT-EYE TRAIN

The poetry of Eugene Field (1850-1895), an American, is the quaintest and prettiest that has ever been written for the entertainment of children, and The Shut-Eye Train is one of the most charming of them all.

COME, my little one, with me !
　There are wondrous sights to see
As the evening shadows fall,
In your pretty cap and gown.
Don't detain
The Shut-Eye train—
" Ting-a-ling ! " the bell it goeth,
" Toot-toot ! " the whistle bloweth,
And we hear the warning call :
" All aboard for Shut-Eye Town ! "

Over hill and over plain
Soon will speed the Shut-Eye train !
Through the blue where bloom the stars,
And the Mother Moon looks down,
We'll away
To land of Fay.
Oh, the sights that we shall see there !
Come, my little one, with me there—
'Tis a goodly train of cars—
All aboard for Shut-Eye Town !

Swifter than the wild bird's flight,
Through the realms of fleecy night
We shall speed and speed away !
Let the Night with envy frown—

What care we
How wroth she be !
To the Balow-land above us,
To the Balow-folk who love us,
Let us hasten while we may—
All aboard for Shut-Eye Town !

Shut-Eye Town is passing fair,
Golden dreams await us there ;
We shall dream those dreams, my dear,
Till the Mother Moon goes down—
See unfold
Delights untold !
And in those mysterious places
We shall see belovèd faces,
And belovèd voices hear
In the grace of Shut-Eye Town.

Heavy are our eyes, my sweet,
Weary are our little feet—
Nestle closer up to me
In your pretty cap and gown ;
Don't detain
The Shut-Eye train !
" Ting-a-ling ! " the bell it goeth,
" Toot-toot ! " the whistle bloweth,
Oh, the sights that we shall see !
All aboard for Shut-Eye Town !

LAND OF HOPE AND GLORY

Arthur Christopher Benson, the author of these lines, was the gifted son of an Archbishop of Canterbury, and one of three brothers who gained distinction. A. C. Benson was born in 1862 and died in 1925. He wrote many poems, and in these verses has deserved a nation's thanks, for we should all be grateful to a man who sings so nobly of our land. The poem was set to music by Sir Edward Elgar.

DEAR Land of Hope, thy hope is
　　crowned,
　God make thee mightier yet !
On Sov'ran brows, beloved, renowned,
　Once more thy crown is set.
Thine equal laws, by freedom gained,
　Have ruled thee well and long ;
By freedom gained, by truth maintained,
　Thine Empire shall be strong.

Thy fame is ancient as the days,
　As ocean large and wide ;
A pride that dares, and heeds not praise,
　A stern and silent pride ;
Not that false joy that dreams content
　With what our sires have won ;
The blood a hero sire hath spent
　Still nerves a hero son.

Land of Hope and Glory, mother of the
　free,
How shall we extol thee who are born of
　thee ?　　　　　　[set ;
Wider still and wider shall thy bounds be
God, who made thee mighty, make thee
　mightier yet.

ONLY A BABY

The writer of these charming lines, ending with a note so tender, was Matthias Barr, a Victorian verse-writer for and about children. He was born in Edinburgh, of German parents, and his spirit was bright and gentle.

ONLY a baby small,
    Dropped from the skies;
Only a laughing face,
    Two sunny eyes.

Only two cherry lips,
    One chubby nose;
Only two little hands,
    Ten little toes.

Only a golden head,
    Curly and soft;
Only a tongue that wags
    Loudly and oft.

Only a little brain,
    Empty of thought;
Only a little heart,
    Troubled with naught.

Only a tender flower
    Sent us to rear;
Only a life to love
    While we are here.

Only a baby small
    Never at rest;
Small, but how dear to us
    God knoweth best.

THE TWENTY-THIRD PSALM

The Psalms of David in the Bible are among the finest poetry we can read. Many of the other books in the Bible are also poetic in form, but we do not usually think of them as poems. They are not in verse. More than 250 years ago a Poet Laureate, named Nahum Tate (1652–1715) re-wrote them in rhyme, and his verses are still sung ; but he was a poor poet. Joseph Addison (1672–1719) was a far greater man, and the 23rd Psalm is here given as turned into verse by him.

THE Lord my pasture shall prepare,
    And feed me with a shepherd's care;
His presence shall my wants supply,
And guard me with a watchful eye;
My noonday walks He shall attend,
And all my midnight hours defend.

When in the sultry glebe I faint,
Or on the thirsty mountains pant,
To fertile vales and dewy meads
My weary, wandering steps He leads,
Where peaceful rivers, soft and slow,
Amid the verdant landscape flow.

Though, in a bare and rugged way,
Through devious lonely wilds I stray,
Thy bounty shall my pains beguile;
The barren wilderness shall smile.

With sudden greens and herbage crowned,
And streams shall murmur all around.

Though in the paths of death I tread
With gloomy horror overspread,
My steadfast heart shall fear no ill,
For Thou, O Lord, art with me still:
Thy friendly crook shall give me aid,
And guide me through the dreadful shade.

PIPING DOWN THE VALLEYS WILD

William Blake (1757–1827), the English poet, has always a touch of the mystical and imaginative even in his simplest verses, and this poem is no exception to the rule. What the poet means to suggest to us is the inspiration of the true singer of Nature, whose written poems should be as much in tune with Nature itself as the imaginary piper who here turns a reed into a pen to write down for ever the songs he has been piping.

PIPING down the valleys wild,
    Piping songs of pleasant glee,
On a cloud I saw a child,
    And he, laughing, said to me:

Pipe a song about a lamb.
    So I piped with merry cheer.
Piper, pipe that song again;
    So I piped ; he wept to hear.

Drop thy pipe, thy happy pipe;
    Sing thy songs of happy cheer.
So I sang the same again,
    While he wept with joy to hear.

Piper, sit thee down and write
    In a book that all may read.
So he vanished from my sight;
    And I plucked a hollow reed.

And I made a rural pen,
    And I stained the water clear,
And I wrote my happy songs
    Every child may joy to hear.

LIGHTS OUT

When General William Sherman (1820–1891), a hero of the American Civil War, died, these verses were written in commemoration of him by C. H. Adams, a fellow-countryman. The verses were appropriately read at the funeral of the author.

THE strenuous day is past,
    The march, the fight;
The bugle sounds at last
    Lights out. Good-night!

The sky is white with stars;
    The tents gleam white;
Tired captain from the wars
    Sleep through the night.

Sleep till the shadows take
    Their endless flight,
Until the morning breaks,
    Good-night! Good-night!

LITTLE VERSES FOR VERY LITTLE PEOPLE

A LITTLE KINGDOM I POSSESS

A LITTLE kingdom I possess,
    Where thoughts and feelings dwell;
And very hard I find the task
    Of governing it well;
For passion tempts and troubles me,
    A wayward will misleads,
And selfishness its shadow casts
    On all my will and deeds.

How can I learn to rule myself,
    To be the child I should,
Honest and brave, nor ever tire
    Of trying to be good?
How can I keep a sunny soul
    To shine along life's way?
How can I tune my little heart
    To sweetly sing all day?

Dear Father, help me with the love
    That casteth out my fear;
Teach me to lean on Thee, and feel
    That Thou art very near ;
That no temptation is unseen,
    No childish grief too small,
Since Thou, with patience infinite,
    Dost soothe and comfort all.
            Louisa M. Alcott

WILLIE'S LODGER

Two little boys named Willie
    Live in the house with me.
One is as good a darling
    As ever I wish to see;
His eyes are glad, his smile is sweet,
His voice is kind, his dress is neat,
    And he is the boy for me.

This Willie says : " Good-morning! "
    Happy as any bird;
A merrier laugh, a lighter step,
    No mortal ever heard.
"Thank you," he says, and "If you please?"
He will not pout, he will not tease—
    Oh, he is the boy for me!

The other Willie, sad to say,
    Is very, very bad;
I think he is as cross a child
    As ever a mother had.
"Go 'way!" he shrieks.   He squalls and
    cries:
The angry tears oft fill his eyes—
    He is not the boy for me.

He lingers round my Willie,
    And whispers evil things.
Oh, how we dread him!   For we know
    The sin and grief he brings.
Who keeps him, then?   Why, Willie's self;
He keeps this wicked Willie-elf
    Who is not the boy for me.

If I were you, my Willie,
    I'd make him stay away-
This boy who grieves your mother
    And spoils your brightest day.
For he lives in you where he doesn't be-
    long,
So oust him, Willie!   Send him along!
" Clear out ! " I'd say, " old Fume and
    Fret!
This heart of mine is not to let—
    You're not the boy for me! "
            Mary Mapes Dodge

TRY AGAIN

'TIS a lesson you should heed,
    Try again;
If at first you don't succeed,
    Try again;
Then your courage should appear,
For if you will *persevere*,
You will conquer, never fear,
    Try again.

Once or twice though you should fail,
    Try again;
If you would at last prevail,
    Try again;
If we strive, 'tis no disgrace
Though we do not win the race;
What should we do in that case?
    Try again.

If you find your task is hard,
    Try again;
Time will bring you your reward,
    Try again;
All that other folk can do,
Why, with patience, may not you?
Only keep this rule in view,
    Try again.
            William Edward Hickson

THE WORM

TURN, turn thy hasty foot aside,
    Nor crush that helpless worm!
The frame thy wayward looks deride
    Required a God to form.

The common lord of all that move,
    From whom thy being flowed,
A portion of His boundless love
    On that poor worm bestowed.

The sun, the moon, the stars, He made
    For all His creatures free;
And spread o'er earth the grassy blade
    For worms as well as thee.

Let them enjoy their little day,
    Their humble bliss receive;
Oh ! do not lightly take away
    The life thou canst not give !
            Thomas Gisborne

I SAW A SHIP A-SAILING

I saw a ship a-sail-ing, a-sail-ing on the sea, And
it was deep-ly la-den with pret-ty things for me. There were
rai-sins in the cab-in, and al-monds in the hold The
sails were made of sa-tin, And the mast was made of gold.

THE four and twenty sailors
  Who stood upon the decks
Were four and twenty white
  mice
With rings about their necks.

THE captain was a duck, a duck,
  With a jacket on his back,
And when the faery ship set
  sail
The captain he said Quack!

When I was a little boy,
    I had but little wit;
It is some time ago,
    And I've no more yet.

Nor ever, ever shall,
    Until that I die;
For the longer I live
    The more fool am I.

Pretty maid,
    Pretty maid,
Where have you been?
Gathering a posie
To give to the Queen.

    Pretty maid,
    Pretty maid,
What gave she you?
She gave me a diamond
As big as my shoe.

As I walked by myself,
    And talked to myself,
Myself said unto me:
Look to thyself,
Take care of thyself,
For nobody cares for thee.
I answered myself,
And said to myself,
In the selfsame repartee:
Look to thyself,
Or not look to thyself,
The selfsame thing will be.

Pat-a-cake, pat-a-cake, baker's man.
    So I will, master, as fast as I can;
Pat it and prick it and mark it with T,
Put it in the oven for Tommy and me.

Dance to your daddie,
    My bonnie laddie,
Dance to your daddie, my bonnie lamb!
    You shall get a fishie,
    On a little dishie,
You shall get a herring when the boat
    comes hame!

Dance to your daddie,
    My bonnie laddie,
Dance to your daddie, and
        to your mammie sing!
    You shall get a coatie,
    And a pair of breekies,
You shall get a coatie when the boat
    comes in!

Handy Pandy, Jack-a-dandy,
    Loves plum-cake and sugar-candy;
He bought some at a grocer's shop,
And out he came, hop, hop, hop, hop.

OLD MOTHER HUBBARD

Old Mother Hubbard
Went to the cupboard
To get her poor dog a bone;
But when she got there
The cupboard was bare,
And so the poor dog had none.

She went to the baker's
To buy him some bread,
But when she came back
The poor dog was dead.

She went to the joiner's
To buy him a coffin,
But when she came back
The dog he was laughing.

She took a clean dish
To get him some tripe,
But when she came back
He was smoking his pipe.

She went to the fishmonger's
To buy him some fish,
But when she came back
He was licking the dish.

She went to the ale-house
To get him some beer,
But when she came back
The dog sat in a chair.

She went to the tavern
For white wine and red,
But when she came back
The dog stood on his head.

She went to the barber's
To buy him a wig,
But when she came back
He was dancing a jig.

She went to the hatter's
To buy him a hat,
But when she came back
He was feeding the cat.

She went to the tailor's
To buy him a coat,
But when she came back
He was riding a goat.

She went to the cobbler's
To buy him some shoes,
But when she came back
He was reading the news.

She went to the fruiterer's
To buy him some fruit,
But when she came back
He was playing the flute.

She went to the sempster's
To buy him some linen,
But when she came back
The dog he was spinning.

She went to the hosier's
To buy him some hose,
But when she came back
He was dressed in his clothes.

The dame made a curtsey,
The dog made a bow;
The dame said, "Your servant,"
The dog said, "Bow-wow!"

SIMPLE SIMON MET A PIE-MAN

Simple Simon met a pie-man
Going to the fair:

Said Simple Simon to the pie-man,
" Let me taste your ware! "

Said the pie-man to Simple Simon,
" Show me first your penny! "

Said Simple Simon to the pie-man,
" Indeed, I have not any! "

The Story of Where Power Comes From, What It Does, & How It Works

What This Story Tells Us

MAN has magnified his powers a millionfold. What a wonderful world there comes to mind as we think of electricity—its waves spreading themselves about the world innocently and invisibly until they touch a thing that man has made, and, lo, there is power to drive our ships and trains and light our cities. And what a vision of the past comes as we think of oil, lying buried in the earth a million years and more to come bursting out at last to turn half the wheels of Europe. Out of the past, also, comes coal. Is it not strange to think of coal growing as a great green plant? Yet so it was. Here we shall read of all the sources of power that men have found, and of all the mechanical powers they have invented. We shall have wireless explained, the telegraph and the telephone, the motor-car and the aeroplane, ships and trains and engines of all kinds.

THE VERY HEART OF MATTER

THOUSANDS of years ago, in a certain part of the world, shepherds noticed with curiosity that bits of rocky mould clung to the crude iron hooks of their crooks. In other climes men bedecked with amber beads had noticed, with the same mere curiosity, that these beads when rubbed against their garments would sometimes attract little bits of straw or silk, which clung to the amber through some mysterious force.

These two forces were magnetism and electricity, which today have revolutionised the world, and have made the wizardry by which the voice is carried round the Earth, by which a waterfall will drive a train or light a town, and by which the common clay is turned into shining aluminium.

Electricity is the heart of matter, for recent discoveries have shown beyond all doubt that everything in the world consists of minute particles called atoms, themselves composed of tiny specks of negative electricity called electrons, which are held together by a central bond of positive electricity. Electricity is the great secret that matter has held within it for millions of years and we now know that it has weight and *is*

matter. As far as our Earth is concerned, electricity in one form or another has proved to be the sole material used by the Creator in building up its fabric.

The miracle of electricity is thus around us every day, every instant. The world, revolving round the Sun with the other planets which form the Solar system, is a tiny speck in the vastness of space ; but space itself is filled with a rare material which, because we can think of no better name, we call ether. The invisible ether is capable of being thrown into agitation just as water is if it be beaten up with a stick or disturbed by a stone thrown into it. The water of a lake may become calm and still when there is no wind to disturb it, but the ether is always in a condition of unrest.

Waves of millions upon millions of different sizes and forms are continually passing through it. The light of the sun, the heat from the kitchen fire, wireless signals and X-rays, all come from these waves, some so tiny that millions of waves go to an inch, others so long that they reach twenty miles from crest to crest. But they all travel with uniform speed through the ether, three thousand times as far in a second as an

ELECTRICITY · WIRELESS · OIL · GAS · MOTORS · ENGINES · SHIPS

express train goes in an hour ; their only real difference is the number of them which follow each other in a wave-train and pass a given point in a second of time.

Let us leave these ether waves for a while, and see what has come of the discovery of this all-pervading force in Nature.

We live essentially in an age in which we have learnt how to change the form of power. A mighty waterfall like Niagara represents natural power which for thousands of years has been running to waste; today men have turned it from a useless, churning, boiling mass of spray into a force which *produces*. The swiftly flowing water is directed through a water-wheel spinning round at an incredible rate. Fixed to the shaft of the turbine is a machine that converts mechanical power into electricity. This electricity is conveyed through the ether along copper wires, which guide it to some given spot, perhaps a hundred miles off, where it arrives ready for conversion into useful power, perhaps at a mine.

THE MOTOR THAT CHANGES ELECTRICITY INTO MECHANICAL POWER

Here the electricity is changed back into mechanical power again, by means of another invention of quite recent times— the electric motor. The current flows round the magnets of a machine, within which is what we call an armature, and this armature is forced to revolve by the electric force. The motor drives all kinds of machinery. It works the cages which take the miners down into the bowels of the earth and bring them up again. It drives their machines; it provides them with light.

Near by may be a foundry, where broken masses of ore are turned by the furnace into molten metal, and huge ingots of iron are cast—far too heavy for a man to handle. These are picked up by an electric magnet, an iron hand which, under the spell of electricity, possesses giant strength and lifts up ten tons of metal as if it were a feather. Remember that all this work, the driving of the machines, the making of the light, the lifting of the heavy mass of metal, is still the work of the waterfall a hundred miles away.

Some of this iron is turned into useful articles: bicycle-handles, perhaps. These are brightly nickel-plated, and this silvery coating of nickel is put on the steel by means of an electric current. Electricity silvered the spoons and forks with which you eat every day of your life. We can-

not get away from its power and results. The train we ride in is driven by electricity; the light we read by is made from it. Every time we press a button and ring a bell we set electricity in motion. Every time we talk with someone on the telephone, or send a telegram, we use electricity. Life as it is today could not go on for a moment without it.

HOW NATURE HAS BEEN USING ELECTRICITY FOR AGES

The development of electricity has been remarkably rapid in our time. But for thousands of years after the first signs of the existence of electricity men did no more than look upon them with wonder or curiosity. But through all these ages Nature had been using electricity, stimulating with it, for example, the growth of plants, every one of which is provided with tiny hair collectors like miniature lightning conductors, collecting the atmospheric charges that play such an important part in the chemistry of plant growth. The Chinese were the earliest to make use of magnetism, constructing crude compasses which helped them to guide their ships.

Then, a hundred years ago a greater interest was taken in these natural phenomena. Men studied magnetism. Some attempt was made to offer an explanation of the curious things that had been noticed. But no notion existed of the marvellous future of electricity, or of the intimate part it was to play in the life of the nations. Even a hundred years ago it would have seemed fantastic to think of two men a hundred yards apart talking by electricity, yet today a man in England can ring up another in Australia and talk to him on the telephone.

WHEN MEN BEGAN TO THINK ABOUT THE WONDERS THEY SAW

About a century ago, when knowledge had reached the stage at which men began to look round for a reason for anything remarkable that they observed, there came the realisation that these forces could be imitated, and produced by themselves, and even controlled. The age of scientific experimenting and thinking had arrived.

Many foolish theories were formed at first, many an explanation found for the curious things that happened which afterwards proved to be wrong ; but, as time went on, the real truth was gained largely by the endeavours of others to disprove these earlier theories. The age of real science had begun, when facts were the only things that counted, and soon philosophers in different parts of Europe, but notably in England, France, and Germany, contributed bit by bit to a knowledge of electricity and magnetism on which the world of today so largely depends.

We might turn the power of a mighty steam-engine, of a million horse-power waterfall, into electricity ; but how is it to be distributed to those who want it for light, heat, or power ? These were great problems which have been solved in a truly wonderful way.

THE POWER IN THE WIRES THAT LIE UNDER OUR FEET

At each large generating station is a switchboard from which pass the cables that carry the current to the factories, the trains, and the homes of the people. How does the electrician arrange that a train wanting a hundred horse-power for each motor shall have a hundred horse-power, and the lamp wanting only a tiny fraction of this power shall have its exact needs ?

Under our feet as we walk along the street is a maze of wires. Some of these carry power to the factory or the electric railway, others carry the feeblest of currents by which telephone or telegraph messages are being sent. Overhead, along the roads, are more wires, guides to lead the electric current through the ether to the distant towns. In the fields are the great pylons with their overhead cables carrying current at an enormous voltage from the grid stations, and throughout the surrounding space is the ether with its countless wave motions that are conveying speech and music to our homes.

An electric van may drive past, running silently on electric power which is stored up in a box that it carries.

THE FLOOD OF LIGHT A TOUCH CAN BRING FORTH

Think how we start the electric bell ringing by a touch of the finger ; how a child can turn on a switch and flood a room with light. A thousand horse-power is set in motion by the touch of a lever ; a dozen people are swiftly carried in an electric lift to the top of a high building by pressing a button. It is magic, the natural magic of electricity, so subtle that the light from a star a million million miles away can be made to set it in operation by means of a very sensitive cell.

There is a whole world of romance in the way in which electricity is created, stored, and transported to a distant spot. The submarine cable is a good example. As the cable lies along the bottom of the Atlantic Ocean, for example, there flow through it the telegraphic currents by which Britain speaks with America. And because of the currents in the cable, 35 telephone conversations can be carried on at the same time.

Today, busy as the cables are, we are sending other telegraph messages all over the globe by wireless. Ships and aeroplanes can find their bearings in foggy weather by that great invention the wireless compass, a heaven-sent safeguard to the modern navigator. The fact that selenium is sensitive to light was discovered by cable layers in the Atlantic, and this discovery led to others which have given us a new power, the electric control of machinery by *light*. The fact that we can turn light into electric power has brought about that modern marvel the talking picture, and has made it possible for a ray of light reflected from a mirror mounted on an express train to bring the train to a standstill if the signals are against it.

THE ELECTRIC WAVES THAT FILL YOUR BEDROOM EVERY NIGHT

One marvel has followed another with almost incredible rapidity ; the one that appeals to most of us more than any other is the sending of electric power through space without wires. In the year 1895 Marconi sent a wireless message a few hundred yards, shortly afterwards a mile or two, then across the Channel, then across the Atlantic ; now a telegraphic message can be sent round the world. A wireless signal will, in fact, encircle the globe in the seventh part of a second.

When we lie asleep in bed the room is full of these waves. Some of them can pass through the walls, through our bodies. A drop of water will spread in a piece of blotting-paper because it can penetrate between the tiny specks of the paper. A lump of sugar will suck up a certain amount of water without increasing in size, because the water finds its way into the tiny spaces between the molecules of which the sugar is composed. The ether finds its way everywhere, and permeates everything. It is in the spaces between the atoms that make up everything, so that there is a *continuity* of this invisible medium everywhere.

The fact that the atoms in a substance are arranged in an orderly manner in planes, and that these planes will reflect X-rays, has made it possible by X-ray photography to discover the exact structure on which substances are built up. In this way electricity has provided us with a new means of analysing materials, and has in itself produced a revolution in engineering and the study of metals.

THE WONDERFUL THING THAT PICKS UP MUSIC OUT OF SPACE

A wireless wave is often of great dimensions, and an obstacle like a house will only baulk a part of it in its progress, but everywhere in its path the ether is in motion. Put a wireless receiver into a room, and if it is sensitive enough it will pick up a human voice, a piece of music, or a song sent from a distant spot. With waves of light, heat, or wireless the ether is never at rest, and thus we go about our daily life in the home, or in the office, in the school or the street, surrounded by, immersed in, a vast sea of electric waves.

More wonderful perhaps than wireless itself is the revelation that every substance we know of is itself composed of electricity. As we shall see, there are two kinds of electricity, positive and negative, and we have discovered during this century that Matter itself, the stuff of which the world is made, is nothing more than a simply organised mass of positive and negative particles.

ECONOMIC DEVELOPMENT UNDER THE GRID SYSTEM

One of the greatest changes in our modern life has been brought about by the grid. About half a century ago a famous President of the Institute of Electrical Engineers suggested that we should convert the coal where it was brought up from the mines into electrical power. This idea was a practical one, and for many years now electricity has been generated at selected spots where coal is cheap and is transmitted to various parts of the country, to railways, factories, mines, towns, and cities by means of the overhead lines which convey current at the enormous voltage of one hundred and thirty-three thousand. With the amazing progress that has been made in electric lamps themselves, and in the devices for converting electricity into heat and power,

our industries and homes alike have been transformed. And now that electricity can be produced by atomic energy, it will play an even bigger part in our lives.

The greatest marvel of electricity is the wondrous variety of states in which it exists. First of all it is the common source from which everything is derived. Then it exists in a *static* state, as in the electric charge in a thundercloud. In an instant it turns to a blinding flash of lightning, releasing fifty million horse-power for a brief fraction of a second. It exists as an electric current, which can be controlled with the utmost exactness and made to drive a simple sewing-machine or a mammoth ship. We can make it give just sufficient heat to boil an egg or to produce the intense heat of the electric furnace, in which the chemist can melt substances that refused to melt in the hottest furnace known before.

TELEVISION AND RADAR, YOUNGEST OF ALL THE SCIENCES

The electric wave can weave its path through opaque substances such as flesh or wood, but is stopped by bone or metals. Hence photographs can be taken through the body which will reveal fractures, bullets, or shell splinters ; in this way it has saved countless lives. More intense rays will actually penetrate steel, and so will show on a photographic film the image of a flaw or crack in a metal casing or weld.

The two most wonderful things that electricity has done for us are perhaps radiolocation and television. By wireless means aeroplanes can be directed with amazing accuracy. A man on the ground can talk to another thousands of feet in the air, and so give him directions for bringing in the aircraft safely to the runway. A man on a ship can talk to the man in the air, and guide him safely down to the deck of the ship, a mere speck in the mighty ocean.

Television, which enables us to watch by electricity on a little screen in our homes events that are happening hundreds of miles away, has given us something more wonderful than the cinematograph. It is now possible for two people conversing on the telephone to see each other while they talk. The electric power to penetrate haze has made it possible to apply television to ships so that they can be safely navigated in foggy weather.

Imperishable Thoughts of Men Enshrined in the Books of the World

What This Story Tells Us

OH for a book and a shady nook! a man cried long ago, and in truth there is nothing to equal a book. Nothing has been able to stop the men who write books. Tyrants have burned their books and writers have been tortured by fire, but books have spread themselves throughout the world so that there is no land on Earth without them now. They are the only things that live for ever, for new copies are made as old ones pass away, and so through all the ages of time a book carries down the thoughts of men. A thought put into a book is stronger than a statue carved in marble, and in the story of mankind the book has been the mightiest and noblest invention conceived by the human mind. The man who writes a book can laugh at Caesar and Napoleon; they perish while he lives on. Here we shall look at the writers of the world and what they wrote about.

THE REALMS OF GOLD

WE are to go together on the rarest journey ever made by the mind of man through the wonderful treasure land of Literature, the glorious world of books, and with them to enjoy delights the greatest and the easiest that are within the reach of all of us.

To say that this is possible is no vague promise.

SHAKESPEARE

The master impulse of youth is curiosity: to see and hear and know more about the world into which it has been born, to feel and think and do more, and hour by hour take to itself a larger share of life. And this it does first, as a child, by observation, and then by activity and widening experience. But soon the child finds, or should find, that through books it can reach out, by its mind, far beyond the pleasures and knowledge it can attain through its bodily activities. And so it will be to the end of its days, however long it may live, if once it can feel the joys that await it in the great realm of bookland. We want here to make some of those joys felt by anticipation.

All that has ever been known and felt by men, everywhere, in all the years that have been, is probably treasured up somewhere in books, marvellously preserved for our use and delight. Books live and tell us of the past when most other things have faded away.

Into books men have put their very souls, as they have longed to speak their highest and dearest thoughts to those who will follow them, and perchance be influenced by them, in long distant future ages. What the world has been is embalmed in books, and the passionate hopes of men for what it may be are there passed along as an everlasting inheritance for the human race.

For, on the whole, it is the best that lives in books and retains an unending power, while what is evil or what is feeble perishes and is forgotten; and so the great permanent accumulation of books which is known as Literature is constantly growing nobler—a vital essence distilled from the mass of men's writings.

It is because books have this splendid cumulative power, age beyond age, that the great writers of them are so deeply honoured. They do not belong to their own period, but to all time. They may shape the minds of innumerable millions.

In the end no man has an earthly immortality except through books. The

ROMANCE · HISTORIES · DRAMAS · ESSAYS · WORLD CLASSICS

most stupendous men of action are only known at last by what has been written of them in books.

It is, then, no little thing that we do when we set out through the land of books and try to feel what can be found there that is noble and inspiring, delightful, cheering, comforting, and enduringly wise.

Happily, a large part of the world's riches in literature, the books that move our spirits deeply by their truth or beauty or romance, are to be reached through a knowledge of the English tongue. Our language is a gateway to this treasure-land.

THE BOUNDLESS RICHNESS OF THE KINGDOM OF BOOKS

Think of the boundless breadth and richness of the region we are to wander in. Our great English poet John Keats called it the realms of gold, and pictured the reader as a traveller. So he is, for the kingdom of books has many provinces, each tempting us to enter in.

There is, for instance, the wide region of knowledge, the books which gather up and hold in trust for us all the wisdom and skill that generations of men have won.

There is the far-reaching field of history, a vast expanse, enthralling to the observant reader, beginning with fragments from the dim past, all pieced together by careful, imaginative thought. Then come legends that have passed along the centuries from memory to memory, the tales of long ago that are one of the chief fountains of the world's poetry, and existed in outline before writing began.

With writing came more flowing narratives ; the picturing of the characters of men and women who made a deep impression on others ; the stately records of great events ; the familiar jottings of biography ; the virtues of some leaders of men and the sins of others ; the movements of the many, as they were drawn on by hope or driven by despair ; the successes and failures in forms of government ; the oratory that pleads for justice and forms men's opinions—all these things have found a record in books.

THE THOUGHTS THAT HAVE FLASHED THROUGH MEN'S MINDS IN THE AGES

But not only do books, the mind's realms of gold, tell of the knowledge men have gathered slowly and picture the varied story of all that has been : they treasure up for us also the imperishable and beautiful thoughts that have flashed into men's minds throughout the ages, and, being captured and expressed in lovely words, remain as guides, and awaken in us noble impulses to be good, and to spread happiness among mankind.

Through books, again, we may increase enormously our knowledge of life, seeing more of it in our minds than ever we are likely to see by our own observations. That is the chief use of novels. If novels picture life truly, they enlarge our range of vision and experience. If they do not picture life faithfully and wisely they mislead and deceive us, and have a bad influence.

In stories that are truthfully imagined, and choicely told, we may see family life, the tenderness of parentage, the sweetness of childhood, the pleasant claims of kinship, the faithfulness of true friendship, the romance of love, and the firm bond of duty. Or we may penetrate the secret history of the individual soul, its high endeavours, its stern endurance, its clashing passions and rivalries, its thirst for adventures and thrilling conquests, its selfless heroisms, its bold face turned to misfortune, its eager inquiries, patient virtues, its hushed reverence before what is good and beautiful. Yes, truthful fiction fills a large place in these realms of gold.

THE HOMES OF THE FAIRIES, FAYS, NYMPHS, GNOMES, DROLLS, AND GENII

It is largely in fiction that humour and laughter, those unfailing sweetnesses of life, are found. No gratitude can be too great for a combination of a humorous eye, seeing life's oddities and loving them, with a cheerful face and a tender heart. That kind of character has made itself felt in books outside of fiction, but it shows itself with much more freedom in stories.

In them are treasured for ever the gladsomeness of spirit that is seen and heard in the merry laughter and rollicking fun of the young, in the quiet smiles of the strong, and the mellowed, humorous wisdom of the aged. The world's humour is all around us in life, waiting for us to see it, but it is also condensed in the best fiction, and the observing eye is there taught what to see that will lighten the heart, and also how to see it.

It is in books, too, that we find the airy traceries of fancy which men, women, and children have been shaping since the human world began, images woven by the mind, with threads as delicate as the gossamer that bedecks the morning dew, yet so beautiful that they will endure for ever. In this region live imaginary creatures seen and felt by millions as if they were realities—the fairies, fays, nymphs, and gnomes, the drolls and genii, the giants and monsters that once peopled the world born of the perplexed guesses of simple ignorance and fear ; the legends made out of the half-forgotten materials of fading history ; the ever-increasing riches of imagination that never were life, yet may be as true to life in their effect on us as if they were actual events.

THE POETRY THAT ADORNS OUR LANGUAGE FOR EVER

And now, in our glance through the realms of gold, we are led to poetry, the choicest part of that wide territory. Poetry is present, more or less, in every nook of literature, though it also has a place of its own. It keeps step by step with advancing knowledge. It turns history into song. It inspires the lover of Nature, the patriot, and the saint. It gives their clearest voice to Life and Love and Laughter ; and Fancy is its dainty attendant. It is the finest expression in words of the soul of man. And so the most wondrous wealth of interest that awaits us as we travel through the world of books will be found in the poetry which, above all other writing, adorns our English language everlastingly.

We have tried to suggest how wide and welcoming and attractive is the great range of reading that we call our English Literature ; perhaps we may add a word as to how to approach and enjoy it.

In finding out what is delightful in books, we must never think we can know what is worth knowing only by being told about it. We must know the books themselves.

A FINGER-POST TO THE HIDDEN TREASURE OF BOOKS

Whatever may be written here will be a finger-post pointing the way to the treasures of the realms of gold, but each one of us must make the journey and seek the treasure. A guide may tell what to expect. He may quicken anticipation by promises of what can be found ; he may show specimens ; but if even every word a guide says is remembered, the reader will have failed unless the book itself is read.

Of course it is helpful to know a good deal about the interesting people who have written the books that make up our fine English literature. The more we know of the times in which they lived, and the circumstances in which they wrote, the better we shall understand their books. Also some directions about the purpose of a book are useful. We may like to know how other readers of a thoughtful kind have regarded the book, and so books about books may be welcomed rather than avoided. But from out of our own mind our opinion should come, through our reading of the book. It is only when we have seen with our own eyes, or heard with our own ears, the message sent forth in a book, in the form and with the accent the author gave it, that we can say we know the book.

One of the uses of any book, whether it be simple or great, is that it is an exercise in judgment for ourselves. We should not read to criticise with cold reproof, but to see what there is in a book that will attract, reward, and delight us. And we must remember that if we are not attracted by a book that many praise it is quite possible the fault is in ourselves. Some great books may not attract us at first, and we may leave them for a later reading, when we pass that way again.

LET US BE HONEST WITH OUR BOOKS, AND NOT PRETEND

Let us be honest and not pretend we like what we do not really care for. But let us not be hasty and condemn what we have failed to understand. Even things of beauty do not always dawn brightly on us at once ; many people have wondered, as they have grown up, how they could have missed enjoyments in books which might have been theirs years ago. The truth is that they were not ready for them.

The reading of the finest books should never become a task. It should be a natural delight. In that spirit all the best books were written, and in that spirit they should be read. Then reading becomes the chief source of pure delight, the happiest of habits, pleasing us greatly while it enriches our minds.

What we wish to do here is to help our readers to extract from books their choicest essences, as the bee extracts honey from the flowers. Books that have delighted men for hundreds and thousands of years must have rare essences of thought and feeling in them, or they would have been neglected and forgotten. We will wander with our readers in search of such books, to discover their inmost spirit, and enjoy together their unfailing charm.

FOR EVER THE WINDS BLOW, FOR EVER THE WATERS MOVE : NOT FOR ONE MOMENT SINCE CREATION HAVE THEY BEEN STILL

The Great Words that Stir the Hearts and Minds of All Mankind

What This Story Tells Us

HOW wonderful and how solemn are the words we speak! They come down to us out of the life of the past full of meaning and of mystery, often stirring great emotions in us as we think of them. One of our great poets used to say that he could never think of the words " far, far away " without a tear in his eye. So, as we grow up, the time comes when we can hardly think of great and noble words without a thrill vibrating through our being. To those who know something of the vastness of the universe the word Distance brings a thrill. To those who think of man's long fight for freedom the word Liberty brings a thrill. And so it is with many words. Here we shall talk about the really big words in our language, and consider what they mean and what thoughts they stir within us. They are like milestones in the march of life and learning.

MOVEMENT

IN waking up from sleep it is said that movement almost always precedes sensation. We move first; then we feel that we are waking up. There is a tremble of the body, then a tremble of the mind.

Movement precedes everything we know. There could have been no Earth without movement, no universe, no life. But for the movement of the ocean there would be no health on this planet. But for the movement of the seed there would be no grass. But for the movement of man's brain there would be no history.

One of the most striking phrases in the great story of Creation as told by Moses comes at the opening of that immortal epic. *In the beginning God*—— and then, after the thought of Creation enters the Divine Mind, " the Spirit of God *moved* upon the face of the waters."

We all make use of this word: it is one of the commonest words of tongue and pen. But how many of us stop to think what this word means, how long a history it has, and how greatly it helps us in trying to understand the riddle of existence?

One of our greatest men of science has laid it down that man's sole occupation on the Earth is moving things from one place to another, shifting matter about, arranging it or re-arranging it. We once told him that a surgeon of the brain had explained to us that he could make the right hand or the left hand of a patient jerk up in the air by merely touching the particular cells in the brain which connect with the arms. " I have no doubt he can," replied the scientist; " but can he, by touching those cells, make the hand do this? "—and he lifted a book from the arm of his chair and placed it on a table.

From that remark you will see at once that into all rational movement something enters which determines its nature or character. A tree moves when the wind blows, and so does a sailing ship; but the sailing ship moves to a destination because a sailor is controlling its movement. A scarecrow moves if you give it a push.

But think of the difference between the movement of the scarecrow and the movement of Handel's fingers over the keys of an organ, the movement of Van Dyck's brush over a canvas, the movement of Shakespeare's pen over a sheet of paper.

We are now taught by science that everything is in motion. Look up from this page at the door of your room. It appears to be perfectly still. Once it moved and throbbed in the forest; but it was cut

LIBERTY · JUSTICE · SPACE · DISTANCE · MOVEMENT · TRUTH · FAITH

down, sawn into a plank, ceased to be a living thing, became dead wood. So, at any rate, thought our ancestors. Now we know that every piece of wood in a house is composed of atoms, and that every atom is like a miniature firmament, a tiny solar system with particles of electricity revolving round a nucleus.

The Earth appears to be still; but we know that it is making a vast journey round the Sun, spinning at the same time like a top, and moving also with the whole universe through the voids of space. Nothing is still. You wake up and look from your window, and everything is the same as last night; a leaf may have fallen, or a window in the opposite house may have been closed, but otherwise everything is exactly where it was last night. But in truth everything you see has accomplished a journey which no aeroplane or express train could have accomplished in that time; yes, and not only trees, hills, and buildings, but the very air you breathe has also flown, like the wind—the climate of your country has swept with you through the fields of space.

LET US TRY TO UNDERSTAND THE MYSTERY OF THIS THING

What is it, this thing we call Movement? Can we shut our eyes, fold our hands, and think it out? A thing is here; then over there. A thing was red with autumn glory, now it is black as death. A thing was so small that it could lie easily in the palm of an infant's hand; now it is an oak tree with great rooks swinging in its branches. A thing was beautiful and delicious; now it is withered, hideous, ill-smelling. Look in this nest: a little white egg no bigger than a finger-nail and as still as a stone on the road—but soon a thing that flies up into the air, that sings, that builds a nest, that can feel joy, that can suffer pain.

How is it possible for us to understand the meaning of this mysterious thing?

We can begin quite simply. You want to read a book or to play a game of cricket. You take a book from the shelf or a bat from the cupboard. You have moved those things. Why have you moved them? Because you wanted to read or to play. The want comes first. Your hands obeyed your will. Then we may begin by saying that movement is the action of the will. Our hands move because we will them to move. But there are many movements, even in our own bodies, which we do not consciously will. You do not will to breathe, to digest your food, to grow taller and stronger. Obviously there are many movements into which the will does not enter. And look at the movement of the tides, of the wind, of the electrons in an atom, of the stars. What are we to say of such movements?

BACK IN TIME AS FAR AS IMAGINATION WILL TAKE US

We must go back in time as far as imagination will take us. Once there was nothing but ether—or some substance out of which everything has been made— no suns, no moons, no planets, no life, no movement. All was silence and stillness and darkness. Then came movement. The ether was swept up into flaming forms. The universe became alive. There were suns and moons and planets. Light shone in the darkness. Order came out of chaos.

Now we must make the choice of everyone: Did this first movement originate in a Will, or did it happen no one knows how? Did Will come out of that movement, or did Will ordain the movement? Did Mind come first, or Matter?

Notice that there is a difference between the movement of a scarecrow and the movement of Shakespeare's hand writing Hamlet. Out of the one movement comes nothing; out of the other an ordered work of the brain. Is the universe nothing? Is it nothing more than the movement of a scarecrow blown by the wind, or is it more wonderful, more full of order and perfection, than the play of Hamlet?

A MIGHTY WILL MOVING TO SOME STUPENDOUS PURPOSE

The great majority of thinking men have decided that behind the first movement of matter was a Will, and that we could not ourselves possess wills if there had not been a previous Will.

Those who take this view see in evolution the movement of a mighty Will working in matter to achieve some stupendous purpose of which we can only dream. They tell us that before there could be any potentiality there must have been a directing Activity—that is to say, before there could be an acorn capable of changing into an oak there must have been a Power to give it that capacity to turn into something so different. In the beginning was God, and from God came Movement.

And see the glory of this word. Out of the first movement everything we know has come to pass. For this first movement was not a case of moving matter from one position to another, but a case of giving it one single impulse capable of creative results, capable of going forward itself, and incapable of stopping. Matter was moved in a direction which not only brought suns and planets into existence, but suns to shine so long as God wills,

Evolution; now they speak of Creative Evolution. It is not the movement which amazes them, but the character of the movement. The universe is not a pebble rolling down a hill, but an arrow shot at a mark in the vast distances of Eternity.

To think about movement, to realise that every metal and plank, every stone and every leaf, every nodule of soil and

THE MOST ASTOUNDING MOVEMENT OF MATTER THE EYE CAN SEE—THE WATERS OF NIAGARA FALLING OVER A CLIFF

and planets to bring forth life capable of everlasting multiplication. Creation is not the work of successive movements, but of one movement which is continuous and creative. We may say that the electrons whirling around in every atom represent the continuing vibration of the first movement of God's Will—the whole universe still tingling with the first touch of the Creator. Once men spoke about

every drop of water, is in constant and unceasing motion is to make us wonder at the little human word *stillness*, and to prize the calm and silence of the mind in which we come into communion with the First Mover of all forms of all existences, the First Will of Creative Evolution.

There is only one stillness in the midst of a universe which is never still. It is in the soul of man.

WILLIAM TYNDALE TRANSLATING THE BIBLE

DRIVEN FROM HOME, WILLIAM TYNDALE FLED TO HAMBURG, WHERE HE BEGAN TRANSLATING THE LATIN
BIBLE INTO THE ENGLISH LANGUAGE

The Story of the Most Beautiful Book in All the World

What This Story Tells Us

THE glory of our written language is our English Bible ; of all the millions of books in the world it is the most beautiful. It is the book read in every land by scholars and peasants and little children ; it is printed in over 200 languages ; it is read by white people and black people and yellow people and brown people everywhere. It has an ancient history. It comes down to us through thousands of years, filled with the wonder of the past, with marvellous and beautiful stories, and with wisdom beyond compare. Here we shall read the wonderful stories the Bible tells, the lives of the great figures of the Old Testament, the Psalms of David and the Proverbs of Solomon ; and shall go through the beautiful life of Jesus, reading the words of wisdom that fell from His lips, and considering also the work of the Apostles.

THE WAY OUR BIBLE CAME

WHEN you look at tablets attached to monuments and buildings you find that the date is very often followed by two capital letters. These letters are either B.C. or A.D. The first means the time Before Christ; the second means *Anno Domini*, the time After Christ.

Think of time and of all human history as a picture—the picture of a vast country stretching under the sun and the moon and the stars for ever and ever ; and then, in the midst of this picture, very lonely and sad, you will see a Cross rising out of the ground, with the figure of a Man hanging upon it, dying for love of His friends and enemies. Behind that lonely Cross all the country is called B.C.—in front of it all the country is called A.D.

Jesus is the centre of history and time. From the Cross men look forward; from the Cross men look backward. Man, you see, has divided time into two great parts, two immense divisions. The first division is the time before Jesus lived among men ; the second is the time after Jesus appeared on Earth. All over the world time is now divided in this way.

Now, the Bible, the most beautiful of all the books in the world, is divided into two parts, just as time is divided. It has its period called B.C. and its period called A.D. The period called B.C. is known as the Old Testament, and the period called A.D. is known as the New Testament. The word Testament used to be called Covenant, and this word covenant is really a much better word than testament, because it is truer to the meaning. By the Old Covenant men meant a promise made by God to man before Jesus appeared on the Earth ; and by the New Covenant men meant a new promise made by God to man in the life and teaching of Jesus Christ. The New Covenant is really the keeping of the promise made by God to man in the Old Covenant.

Now we see what the Bible is. It is a book about God and man, and the hero of the book is the great central figure in the history of the human race—Jesus.

The Old Testament is a history of a certain nation called the Hebrews, or Jews, or Israelites—three names all meaning the same thing. It is their own history written by themselves. The Jews believed they were chosen by God to teach the other nations about life and the mystery of death, and that God promised that they

GREAT FIGURES OF THE OLD TESTAMENT · THE LIFE OF JESUS

should be a blessing to all the world. What God promised they wrote down, and kept the writings carefully.

They were a wonderful nation, worshipping one God when other nations worshipped sticks and stones. Then they were a poetic and kind-hearted people. They loved to live with their flocks and enjoy the simple blessings of the beautiful Earth. They made the home the great thought of their lives. What we call family life, meaning the pleasures and affections of a happy home, was the chief ideal of this brave people. What made them so happy and strong was their belief that God was watching over them. So in the midst of their sorrows they began to watch for the coming of some mighty being whom they called Messiah, thinking that this Son of God would destroy their enemies, give them back their flocks and herds, and set them up as the rulers of the whole Earth.

THE WAITING AND WATCHING FOR THE COMING OF THE MESSIAH

They watched and waited for the coming of the Messiah. The promise of the Messiah runs through the Old Testament like a little silver brook winding through a dry country towards the sea. But when the Messiah came they found that He was not a mighty warrior, but a beautiful young peasant, who sat in a weather-beaten ship with simple fishermen and taught people that to forgive their enemies was better than to fight them. And then the Jews were angry, and refused to believe that He was the Messiah. The Old Testament shows them seeking the Messiah ; the New Testament shows them rejecting the Messiah.

In very ancient times men used to write the stories of their fathers on a peculiar paper made from the pith of an Egyptian plant called papyrus. It was on this papyrus that the Jews wrote their history, and the precious writings were kept as sacred records. Even before Christ came into the world, the Greek people were anxious to learn about the Jews and their clever writing. Men took the history of the Jews told on the papyrus and wrote it down in the language which the Greek people knew.

Now, the Greek word for papyrus was *biblos*, and this word came to stand for book ; so that they spoke of the Hebrew writings as *Biblia*, or the Books. The Latin nation borrowed this word, and our first copies of the Bible were in the Latin language and were called *Biblia Sacra*, meaning the Holy Books. At last Englishmen made their own words, and, speaking of all these writings as the Book, and not the Books, called it the Holy Bible. So that *Bible* means *The Book*.

THE BOOK WRITTEN IN FAR-OFF TIMES BY MANY MEN

We must not think of the Bible as a single book written by one man. It is many books, written at far distant times, by many very different men. These different books have been collected and bound together, because they teach us so clearly about God and man.

To understand the story of the English Bible we must go back nearly six hundred years in our history. In those days the influence of the Church was not so strong as in the earliest years. England had many foreign clergy who mostly failed to understand the needs of the people, and who were not acquainted with their language ; and it was at this time that John Wycliffe arose. He was a Yorkshireman, a weak-looking man with a little body but a fervent soul. He was a scholar, and he held that all men should study the Bible for themselves, and interpret it as they thought fit.

Accordingly he sent out poor men, dressed in rough serge, through the country lanes who preached the story of Jesus in plain and homely English, and this attracted many people to his views. When he himself spoke, crowds of people flocked round to listen—peasants, nobles, and townsmen.

THE GOOD MAN WHO BELIEVED THAT TRUTH WOULD CONQUER

Wycliffe was not a Protestant, as the religious reformers came to be known a hundred years later, but he was the first man in England who, within the Catholic Church, claimed that every man should have a right and an opportunity to read the Bible for himself, and build up his beliefs on what he had read. Wycliffe's good work came to an end when he died at Lutterworth, in the firm conviction that he had discovered the true faith.

" I believe," said he, " that in the end the truth will conquer." Even thirty years after that the bones of this good man were dug up from the kindly earth and thrown into a river.

JOHN WYCLIFFE, WHO SPREAD THE BIBLE STORY

JOHN WYCLIFFE SENDS HIS PREACHERS OUT INTO THE WORLD—FROM THE PAINTING BY W. F. YEAMES

WYCLIFFE AT HIS TRIAL—FROM THE PAINTING BY FORD MADOX BROWN

About a hundred years after Wycliffe's death, William Tyndale, who had studied the writings of Wycliffe, determined to break away from the Roman Catholic Church, got together a company of scholars, went with them quietly to Hamburg, and set about translating the Latin Bible into our English tongue.

HOW TYNDALE BROUGHT HIS BIBLE TO ENGLAND AT GREAT PERIL

In his love for the Bible Tyndale faced "poverty, exile, bitter absence from friends, hunger and thirst and cold, great dangers, and other hard and sharp fightings." He set up a printing machine, knowing perfectly well that he was engaging in a most hazardous enterprise. He then decided to bring over his Bible to England, a somewhat difficult task, for he had refused to obtain the authority of the Pope to make his translation, thinking he was the better judge of how the Bible should be rendered into English. But at last Tyndale managed to smuggle his Bibles into England, and when they reached this country they were secretly sent to nobles and merchants.

The news of their arrival leaked out, and every effort was made to find the Bibles. When the Church authorities got hold of them a great fire was lighted in St Paul's Churchyard, and the books were burned. The friends of Tyndale were driven out of London, many of them going across the sea.

THE INFLUENCE OF A MAN WHOSE WORK CANNOT BE DESTROYED

Tyndale was now in great danger; he had continually to change his place of residence, and was driven from town to town. But wherever he went he continued writing the Bible in English. He lived for some time in Antwerp, but he was arrested, thrown into prison near Brussels, and first strangled and then burned. But though the body of Tyndale was destroyed, no one could destroy his work, and so great was his influence that the Reformation may be said to date from this period. The Bibles translated by Tyndale were now carried into the churches and chained with heavy steel so that no one should take them away, and the people crowded in to hear them read.

Bibles can now be bought and read freely anywhere, but things were very different then, when liberty of conscience was unknown, and when good people thought it their duty to persecute those who differed from them in religion. In those far-away times readers of the English Bible were often grievously treated, a persecution which had, as persecution always has, the very opposite effect to that which was expected.

Soon the whole country read scarcely any other book than the Bible, and talked of nothing save the wonderful book which Tyndale had introduced to the people. When Bishop Bonner set up the first six Bibles in St Paul's Cathedral, says a writer, crowds of people flocked to hear them read aloud. " One, John Porter," a book tells us, " used sometimes to be occupied in that godly exercise. This Porter was a fresh young man, and of a big stature, and great multitudes would resort thither to hear him because he could read well." Is it not good to think of this fine fellow, John Porter, giving out the sweet music of the Bible to the common people of the land?

THE SWEETEST MUSIC EVER HEARD ON ENGLISH SOIL

Think what it must have been for England to hear the Bible read for the first time! It was the strangest and sweetest music ever heard on English soil. Try to picture the crowds of London people round the six great English Bibles chained to the lecterns in St Paul's Cathedral. Try to picture the fair face of this big young man, John Porter. Try to imagine that you can hear his strong voice rolling down the mighty aisles. And then go back in your memory to the far-off days of Wycliffe, the days of Tyndale, writing in exile the first English Bible in Germany, and smuggling over those precious sheets to our island home. It is wonderful to think how greatly and how bravely men and women have struggled that we might read in our own tongue the story of Jesus.

The Bible is the Book of God,
  And unto every age it shows
The ancient path that Israel trod,
  The grave from whence our Saviour rose.

Two Covenants are found therein,
  The Old and New, and both declare
How love alone can conquer sin,
  And God alone can answer prayer.

We know not who inscribed each page,
  But this we know, where'er we look,
That men have found in every age
  The God of comfort in this Book.

(Next chapter in this group, page 247)

120

The Interests and Pleasures of Life for All Indoors and Out

What These Pages Show Us

ALL work and no play makes Jill a dull girl and Jack a dull boy. If we would be healthy and wise we must go bravely and merrily to our games. Here we shall learn how to play them, to enjoy ourselves in a hundred ways, whether in the long winter evenings by the fire or on the lovely summer days in the garden or the field. We shall learn many ways of using our time and doing things with our hands. What a boy may do with a little box of tools or a girl with a needle and her clever fingers, magical illusions, conjuring tricks, puzzles, problems, and simple scientific experiments will give us entertainment here of which we shall never grow tired.

THE BOY CARPENTER'S KIT OF TOOLS

EVERY boy should have a box of tools and know how to use them, for many useful and ornamental things may be made with a little practice. Good advice to a beginner is: Do not be too ambitious, but start with something simple, and as experience is gained a good job will be made of more difficult things.

Do not get a box of tools, but buy them separately from a reliable tool shop, taking someone older than yourself with you to help in the choice. Always buy the best tools you can afford, beginning with a few that are essential. Tools in greater variety and those for special purposes can always be added to the kit as they are required.

For a good start you will need a saw, a plane, a chisel, a screw-driver, a rule, a square, a gimlet, a hand-drill and bits, a hammer, an oilstone, an oilcan, and a pencil. A fretsaw and cutting table are also very useful; in fact, quite a lot of small articles, including wooden toys, can be made with this tool alone. You should also have some sandpaper and glue. On page 122 are pictures showing how to use some of these tools, and a careful study of these, together with the descriptions given, should enable you to handle them properly.

There are many saws, but the one you should begin with is known as a handsaw (picture 7), and its purpose is to cut the wood

to the necessary sizes. It should be about twenty inches long, and when buying it mention that it is for cross-cutting and ripping—that is, you will want to be able to cut the wood both across the grain and in the direction of the grain.

Before starting to cut, always mark the wood clearly to the size required, using the square (picture 1), the rule, and the pencil. Then lay the wood on a box or wooden chair, and hold it down with the right knee. Do not force the saw through the wood, but begin by making short cuts until the saw "grips," then move it up and down at a steady, easy rate, keeping your head above the saw so that you look down directly on to it. In this way you will be able to watch the cut along the pencil line, and keep straight. To allow for the width of the cut and for planing-off afterwards, always saw slightly outside the pencil line.

The plane is for smoothing the wood after cutting, and a useful type for a beginner is known as a jack-plane (picture 9). The main points to watch in using this tool are to keep it sharp and not to remove too much wood at once. The plane iron should be set to take off very thin shavings, which may seem slower, but it does make for better work, and is less tiring. When buying the plane, ask the shopkeeper to show you how to sharpen and set the iron. In using the

CRAFTS · GAMES · NEEDLEWORK · PUZZLES · SCIENCE EXPERIMENTS

tool, push it forward on the wood steadily, and press upon it evenly all the time.

An experienced woodworker always has a vice attached to his bench to hold the wood when planing edges, but you can manage quite well by holding the wood by the bottom edge in the left hand, and putting the front end against a table, then with the right hand you can plane the upper edge. The other edge can be done in the same way by turning

table or box, and against this place the piece which is to be planed.

The chisel (picture 5) is for cutting away the wood for joints, and for such jobs as shaping to suit hinges and locks. Here again do not try to take away too much wood at a time. If the chisel is kept sharp and thin cuts are taken, there should be no need to tap it.

A hammer (picture 4) is a tool you cannot

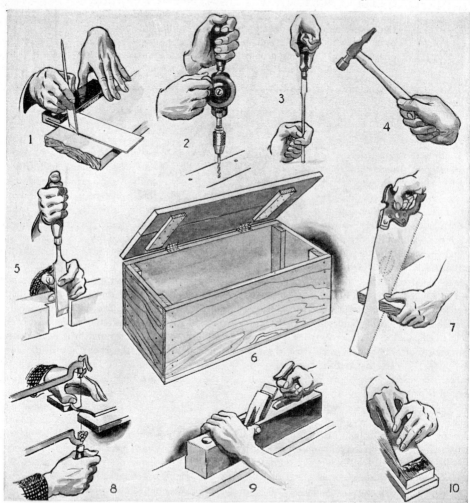

THE WAY TO USE THE NUMBERED TOOLS IS DESCRIBED IN THESE PAGES.

the wood over. When planing the ends (that is, across the grain of the wood) do not take the plane the full length of the edge, or the wood will split. Plane from each end to the middle in turn.

A carpenter's bench is provided with a stop for planing flat surfaces, but without one, the best way of holding the wood is to nail or screw a thin piece of wood (thinner than that which you are using), to an old

possibly do without, and is chiefly needed for driving in nails. Remember to hold it well down by the end of the handle.

The screw-driver (picture 3) is for putting in screws, or for removing them. It is pressed against the head of the screw with its point in the slot of the head, and turned round at the same time.

A gimlet is used principally for making holes in the wood to take screws. There are many sizes, but a small one should meet all a beginner's needs, especially if the tool kit includes a hand-drill and bits (picture 2). This, being a more elaborate tool, is one you can leave to buy later. The bits, as wood drills are called, can be obtained in various sizes to suit all requirements. The drill holds a bit, and the turning of its handle rotates this, making the hole in the wood.

Picture 8 shows very clearly how to use the fretsaw and cutting table. Hold the wood firmly on the table, keep the saw blade erect, and, with an up-and-down motion, cut round slowly and evenly. Do not attempt to force the saw through the wood, or the fine blade will be very easily broken.

Glue is used for sticking pieces of wood together. Buy any of the good brands ready for use, and work to the instructions on the container.

Sandpaper is for putting the final smoothness on the planed wood to get a better finish.

Every tool with an edge must be kept sharp, and this is where the oilstone and oil can come in. Apply a little oil to the stone and rub the cutting edge of the plane iron or the chisel to and fro on this, holding it at an angle as shown in picture 10, and *pushing* forwards but only *sliding* backwards. To finish sharpening, lay the back of the tool flat on the stone, and give one or two light rubs backwards and forwards.

Having got some tools, the first thing you will want to make is a box to hold them, like the one in picture 6.

A useful size for this would be thirty inches long, fifteen inches wide, and eight inches deep. If you have no old box about this size, you may be able to get one from a local tradesman, otherwise you will need to buy some wood. In this case it could be obtained already planed, though most keen woodworkers prefer to do this themselves.

First mark the pieces of wood the sizes they have to be cut, starting with the ends. For these you will want two pieces fourteen inches long and eight inches wide, and four pieces eight inches long and one and a half inches wide.

For the sides mark off two pieces thirty inches long and eight inches wide. If the wood is narrower than eight inches, cut two lengths for each end and two for each side, so that the two joined together will be eight inches. Every piece should then be planed all over until it is smooth.

Now take the narrow pieces, and nail or screw them to the end boards, flush with the ends—the sketch shows where they have to go. Next screw the sides to the ends, which should fit inside the sides in line with the edges. Make holes in the wood first with the gimlet or drill to take the screws, and be sure that these go into the narrow pieces.

Four pieces of wood thirty inches long and seven and a half inches wide, also two strips twelve inches long and one and a half inches wide, are now needed for the bottom and lid of the tool-box, and these also must be planed.

Screw two of these pieces on to the sides and ends to form the bottom of the box ; and, to form the lid, fasten together the other two parts with the twelve-inch strips, using either nails or screws.

To finish the box, get a pair of hinges and screw them to the lid in the position shown in the illustration. Then lay the lid on the box, and mark with the pencil where the hinges come on the top edge of the back of the box. Lift the lid off, and make small saw cuts in the back where the marks come, and with the chisel remove the wood between the saw cuts. This should be done carefully, so that when the lid is laid on the box again the hinges will fit completely into these cuts, and the lid will lie quite flat. Then, when the hinges have been screwed into position, the box is complete.

Though the box has been made in the simplest way, it would be wise before beginning to turn to page 253, and learn how to use nails and screws.

MAKE YOUR OWN GREETING CARDS

WITH the lovely coloured papers which can be bought, it is easy to make your own greeting cards, and much more interesting than buying them.

To make one, take a piece of drawing paper, twice the size you want the finished card to be, and double it in half either lengthways or widthways, whichever will suit your chosen design.

The picture parts are then cut out in various glazed or plain coloured papers and stuck down. Sometimes the paper has gum on the back, but if not, use a smooth paste and apply very sparingly, otherwise it will squeeze out around the sides and look messy.

For a beginner, flower pictures are the easiest to do, because they can be cut out by using coins of different sizes. For instance, in making the birthday card shown at the top of the next page, the bowl was marked out with a halfpenny on dark green paper, a rounded piece being afterwards cut off to shape the bowl. The flowers were made by cutting two circles the size of a halfpenny, one in dark mauve and the other in light, then a small circle was pencilled in the centre of each with a farthing, and the petals were cut in as far as this circle which served as a guide to keep them even. Then, after the bowl and the leaves, in light green, had

been stuck down, the flowers were pasted on, one slightly overlapping the other.

The leaves are just small wedges of paper, but to get different shapes, trace some from a Nature book, or from small real leaves, if necessary cutting the tracing down until it is the size you want before using it as a pattern. Usually the greatest difficulty is with lettering, and if you are not clever at this, copy some bold design from a magazine or picture book. It could be painted in or written, but it looks much more effective if cut out in the paper to match the rest of the picture.

Remember to pencil-mark only on the back of the paper, and to use a small, very sharp pair of scissors for cutting out, being careful to keep the outlines clear. The exception to this is when doing animals or birds, like the little chicks on the Easter card. Then the bird is cut out a little larger than it needs to be when finished, and the feathers are made by snipping continuously with the very sharp tips of the scissors on the very edge of the cut-out.

Coins are too big to help with these small chicks, but both the end chick and the centre one were marked out by standing upright together a fountain pen and

These cards were made from four pieces of drawing paper, each measuring four and a half inches by three and a half inches, the galleon being on blue-tinted paper which makes the sky, the others on white.

a small pencil, and outlining them, the same small pencil and another from a notebook doing the tiny chicks in the bowl. You will find all kinds of things like this in everyday use which will help in the cutting out. The chicks were all made of yellow paper with orange beaks and feet, and the bowl of brown, with brown words on yellow strips at the top of the card. The two little worms were dark red, and the tufts of grass in spring green.

The Christmas card was very quickly done with a bright blue strip down the side, vivid green leaf, red candlestick, pale yellow candle with a deeper yellow flame which has an orange wick in the centre, and the greeting in the same blue as the strip. In cutting out a motif like this large leaf, the part from which it was cut can be used in another picture as a tree or shrub design. In that way paper is not wasted, and often quite new ideas are discovered.

Almost everyone will like the galleon, though it makes a nice birthday card for a boy. It is on tinted paper, with the sea and lettering in deep blue cut-out; the cliffs, birds, wave crest, and large sails in white; the back sails in cream; the cliff top, hull, and masts in green; and the pennant, orange.

LITTLE PROBLEMS FOR ODD MOMENTS

THROUGHOUT the ages puzzles and riddles have held a fascination for old and young alike. In this part of our book are gathered many interesting and tricky problems—some old, some new—that will help to pass away spare minutes and, at the same time, will test our knowledge and quickness of wit. More problems like these appear on page 252, where the answers to the questions below will also be found.

1. Did George Walk Round the Dog?

George was playing with his dog which was sitting up on a stool, but he noticed that although he walked all round the stool, the animal always turned so as to face him the whole time.

When George had walked round the stool, had he walked round the dog?

2. How Many Apples Did Mabel Buy?

Mabel bought some pears at three for twopence, and an equal number of halfpenny apples. If she spent sevenpence altogether, how many pears and apples did she buy?

3. How Did Mary Get the Eggs?

Alice and Mary were staying on a farm and were allowed to collect the eggs. One morning Alice discovered that several eggs had been laid on a small square island in the middle of a square pond, but as she had no plank long enough to reach across, she had to leave them where they were.

Soon afterwards Mary came along and saw the eggs, and, looking round for a means to get to the island, found two planks, neither of which would quite reach from the edge of the pond to the island. But they were her only way of getting the eggs, so Mary thought for a while and then placed them so that she could step across to the island and pick up the eggs.

How did Mary arrange the planks to reach the island?

Mary's problem

4. Who Is Tom's Uncle's Sister ?

" Father, Tom says his uncle's sister is not his aunt."

" Well, I expect he is right."

If Tom's uncle's sister is not Tom's aunt, who is she ?

5. How Many Stamps Had They?

Three boys—Jack, Frank, and Harry—divided some postage-stamps between them. Jack had half of them and one more; Frank had one more than half of those left; Harry had the remaining three.

How many stamps were there?

6. How Long Was the String?

Peter had two pieces of string, one of which was just twice as long as the other. He cut six inches off each, and then found that one was just three times as long as the other. How long were they at first?

7. Whose Photograph Is It ?

One of the problems that has puzzled many people is the old one of a man looking at a portrait saying : " Brothers and sisters have I none, but this man's father is my father's son."

Whose photograph is it?

8. What Did the Cork Cost?

A bottle and a cork cost 2½d. If the bottle cost 2d. more than the cork, how much did the cork cost?

9. How Many Girls Are There?

If £3 is divided amongst fifty boys and girls, the boys getting 1s. 3d. each, and the girls 1s. each, how many girls are there?

10. The Missing Canaries

Grandfather gave a birthday party for Joan and invited nineteen of her little friends. He had prepared a great surprise for the children, each of whom, Joan included, was to be given a live canary. But when the time came to present the birds, it was found that many had flown. The old gentleman sent out for others to replace them, saying to the messenger : " Bring back as many and half as many —that is, one and a half times as many—as there are left in the cage, and two and a half more."

When the messenger came back with these, there were enough birds to go round, making twenty in all. How many canaries flew away?

11. How Fast Was the Horse Walking ?

Joe was walking along a country road steadily at the rate of four miles an hour. He saw a horse and cart going in the same direction, and when he noticed them they were exactly 220 yards ahead of him. After walking for fifteen minutes he overtook them.

At what rate was the horse walking ?

12. How Much Does a Brick Weigh ?

If a brick weighs 6 lbs. and half of its own weight, what is the weight of the brick?

13. How Much Are Pegs?

" What are pegs a dozen ? " Betty asked the shopman.

" Two more for a shilling," said the man, " would make them a penny per dozen less."

" Then," said Betty, " I will take one shillingsworth."

How many did she buy?

THROWING SHADOWS ON THE WALL

Shadow throwing is a useful party accomplishment out of which a great deal of fun can also be had at home, and all the equipment needed is the performer's own hands, a good light behind them to cast the shadow, and a white or light wall, or other flat surface, to act as a screen for the pictures.

In the illustration on this page, there are a number of shadows of animals which are quite easy to make. Imitate closely the position of the hands as shown in each picture, and practise until the shadow shows clearly and correctly. Repeat all the different forms over and over again, and after a little while the position of the hands will be remembered without having to refer to the picture.

The next step is to learn to give action to the shadows by moving the fingers or thumbs so that the animals appear to be eating, or moving their ears or legs. It also adds greatly to the effect to imitate the sounds made by the different animals and birds — barking, grunting braying, and so on.

Small children love each animal to be given a special name, and to be told a little story, either imaginary or a true Nature one, about each—the funnier this is the better they will like it, and even for grown-ups it is much more interesting if the performer can combine chatter and anecdote with his display.

The shadows here are merely a few of hundreds that can be produced by different combinations of the hands and fingers. New ideas will come with practice, and it is remarkable how the same position of the hands, or almost the same position, will give entirely different shadows by holding them at different angles to the light, and moving a finger or two this way or that.

Of course, the brighter the light the blacker will be the shadow, and the outline will be clearer or less defined according to whether the hands are nearer to the light or to the screen. For all ordinary purposes, and for an entertainment given on the spur of the moment, a light wall is quite suitable, but amateur entertainers may like a special screen upon which to give their show. This may be made quite roughly, of any size, by merely nailing or screwing four battens, or narrow strips of wood, together to form a square or an oblong, and filling in this framework with strong white material or even paper. It would, of course, be quite flat, and would pack away, when not in use, in a cupboard, or if it is likely to be carried around, it could be made to fit into a suitcase. Do be sure that the material used is suitable, before fixing it to the frame, as the audience should see the shadows *through* the screen—that is, the performer will be on one side with the light behind him, and the spectators on the other.

The screen can be much improved by painting curtains on it to give it the appearance of a stage, which naturally adds greatly to the attraction from the onlooker's point of view.

The show could finish up with this shadow-acting game which everyone will enjoy. Divide the audience into small groups, each of which must take it in turn to go behind the screen and act in dumb show—a word; a well-known book, play, or film title; represent a famous person ; or some similar idea ; while the remainder have to guess what is being shown.

Do not forget, though, that on a small screen only the head and shoulders of the actors would appear, which limits a little the choice of subject; and be careful, too, to place the light so that it does not distort the shadows, and so make it too difficult for the audience to discover what is happening. Clothes, particularly hats, for dressing up, do much to help the fun.

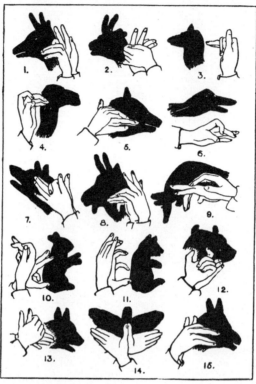

SHADOWS MADE BY THE HANDS

1. Reindeer. 2. Chamois. 3. Llama. 4. Camel. 5. Pig. 6. Goose. 7. Wolf. 8. Goat. 9. Elephant. 10. Hare. 11. Teddy Bear. 12. Ox. 13. Dog. 14. Butterfly. 15. Donkey.

CAN ONE ALWAYS BELIEVE ONE'S OWN EYES?

By fixing the eyes on the two white spaces between the lines it will appear as if the top space becomes wider at the ends, and as if the bottom space becomes wider in the middle. But both lines are perfectly straight.

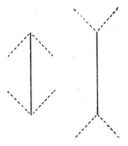

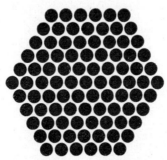

Which line is the longer? The black line on the right appears longer than the line beside it, but both lines are exactly the same length.

This shows how a circle appears to have sides and corners. These black spots, if looked at intently, seem to have six sides, like a honeycomb, but they are all quite round.

There is a blind spot in both eyes—part of the eye, that is to say, is blind. This can be proved by closing the left eye and looking at the X with the right. Hold the paper a foot away, and slowly draw it nearer. Though looking at the X, the spot can be seen, too, but at a certain point this will disappear. By drawing the paper still nearer, the spot will come into view again.

Who is the biggest? The policeman, most people would say. But the policeman is really the smallest, and the little girl is the biggest.

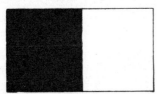

Which square is the larger? Nearly everyone would say the white, but the white is smaller than the black.

One of these sets of lines looks higher than it is wide, and the other wider than it is high, but both are square.

Turn the page round and round to the left. The plain rings will appear to revolve rapidly to the left, and the others to go slowly round in the opposite direction.

The poet was perfectly right when he said that things are not always what they seem. One cannot always believe one's own eyes. One's vision of things is never quite perfect. There is always a little error in the sight, and this page shows how the eyes can be deceived and be made to believe that things are not what they are.

HOW TO MAKE A LIVING FLAG

A LIVING flag is a very fine sight at an entertainment, whether indoors or out, and an easy one to represent is the St George's Cross, which needs thirty-five performers, eleven of whom must be dressed all in red, and the remaining twenty-four entirely in white.

If the flag is to be made up of boys and girls, eleven boys could wear red suits, made of any cheap red material or of crêpe paper, with wide trousers and a simple jumper top with long sleeves. The girls could wear ordinary white dresses and white tennis shoes.

All may, if liked, wear caps, or soldier hats, to correspond with the colour of their clothes, and these would be easily made out of white or red paper.

For the flag there must be seven rows of five performers. Each row should hold hands and stretch out to its fullest length, so that it extends nearly five yards, and all seven rows must stand close together one behind the other. Standing like this makes a flag about fifteen feet long by seven feet wide.

The fourth, or middle row out of the seven will, of course, be made up of five boys dressed all in red ; and the third, or middle, performer in each row will also be a boy dressed in red. These make the red cross of St George, while the other performers fill in the white ground.

The twenty-four girls in white should be divided into two groups of twelve, and stationed one group on each side of the stage or field. As soon as the music strikes up a patriotic air, they must file in and form four groups of six, with three pairs in each group, all facing the audience, so that when in position they form a flag with a blank cross which the boys in red will occupy.

The boys are divided into two parties, one of six and the other of five, and each party is stationed at the side of the field or stage, like the girls. When the four groups have taken up positions, the boys must march on in correct time, so that the leader of the party of six arrives at the space between the two groups farthest away from the audience just a fraction before the leader of the party of five.

Without stopping, the first of the six leads the way through the passage that has been left between the groups, the first of the five follows, and then the second of the six, and so on alternately. When they reach the front, the first doubles to the right and the second goes to the left, and so on, all except the last three, who remain and take up their places in the front of the central gangway.

Meanwhile, the first boy who marches to the right passes between the two groups on the right and down the central gangway, where he takes up his place in the back row, the first boy round from the left comes next, and so on until the cross is complete. Then, at a given signal, each row joins hands, and the flag of St George is finished.

BALANCING PENCILS ON A NEEDLE-POINT

HERE is an excellent balancing feat which any boy or girl can perform with very little practice. The task is to balance a pencil by its point horizontally on the tip of a needle, and then, on the opposite end of the pencil, to balance another pencil by its point perpendicularly.

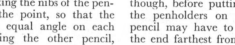

We need two penknives of almost equal weight, and two penholders also, each of which is the same weight as the other. We begin with the second pencil, sticking the nibs of the penholders into it near the point, so that the holders project at an equal angle on each side. Before preparing the other pencil, see that the balance of this one is correct by standing it on its point upon the finger-tip. If the penholders have been stuck in properly the pencil will remain upright without difficulty.

Now tackle the other pencil. Treat it in exactly the same way as its companion, but using the penknives instead of the penholders. If the knives are stuck in properly there will be no trouble in getting the pencil to balance on the needle's point, though, before putting the other pencil with the penholders on the end, the horizontal pencil may have to be tilted up a little at the end farthest from the point.

A COLOUR COMPETITION

FOR this game the umpire selects a colour, and in a given time the players have to write down as many things as they can think of which are wholly, or at least almost completely, that shade. For example take red: then pillarbox, sunset, holly berries, could be on the list. Another way is to ask the players to put down everything they can see which is a given colour. The prize goes to the one who has the most items not mentioned by anyone else when the lists are read out at the end.

Simple Learning Made Easy for Very Little People

What We Learn Here

NO book can take the place of school, but here we begin to learn many things which will help us at school and make us useful as we grow up. We shall learn what figures are and the wonderful things that can be done with them. We shall try to draw pictures of the things we see at home and in the streets. We shall learn how to read and write, so that we can read the story-books ourselves and write letters to our friends. We shall begin to understand music, and those who are learning French will find here little picture-stories that will help them with their lessons.

JOHN AND JENNIFER LEARN TO READ

JOHN and Jennifer had been to the Zoo. They had seen all kinds of animals, but best of all they liked the Panda.

Jennifer wanted to bring him home, but John said, "You can't do that; he is too big for our house, but I'll draw you a picture of a Panda when we get home, and perhaps Mother will let us pin it up on our bedroom wall."

When they got home John drew a picture of a little black and white Panda. Jennifer wanted his name written underneath his picture, so Mother took her thick pen and wrote underneath in big letters:

This is Panda

Every time John and Jennifer looked at the picture they asked Mother what she had written, and she said, "This is Panda," and they said it too.

One day John said, "I can read that"; and he did, all by himself. Jennifer said, "I know which word says 'Panda,'" and pointed to the right word.

The next day Mother said to John and Jennifer, "Why don't you both paint a picture of a Panda?" They thought it a very good idea, and John painted Panda having his tea, and Jennifer painted Panda having his dinner.

"Now write underneath these pictures, please Mother," said John.

So underneath John's picture Mother wrote these words:

This is Panda having his tea

Underneath Jennifer's picture Mother wrote:

This is Panda having his dinner

"How lovely!" said John. "Now we have three pictures to put on our wall."

Every day Mother read what she had written under the pictures to John and Jennifer, and they read it too.

"It's like a story," said John. "Let's paint some more pictures, and make the story longer." So John painted Panda playing with a balloon, and Jennifer liked it so much that she painted one too. Under John's picture Mother wrote:

Panda and his red balloon

Under Jennifer's picture Mother wrote:

Panda is having fun with his balloon

Every evening after tea, when Daddy came home, John and Jennifer read their picture stories to him.

One night, when they had gone to bed, Daddy painted a picture for their story. Mother wrote underneath:

This is Panda and his red balloon

How surprised John and Jennifer were when they saw the new picture in the morning! "Why," said John, "I can

READING · WRITING · ARITHMETIC · ART · MUSIC · FRENCH

read those words, because they are in our other story pictures," and he did.

Very soon John and Jennifer could read all the sentences under the pictures, and then they found out what the different words said. "I can find *Panda*," said Jennifer. "That's easy," said John. "I can find *balloon*." Mother said, "Who can find *red*?" John found it first.

One day John and Jennifer could find all the little words, like *is*, *and*, *his*, *tea*, *with*, and *for*.

At last the day came when they could find every word that Mother asked them.

"That's twelve words you know," said Daddy, when he heard about it.

"Yes," said John, "we can really read!"

Daddy said they had better go to the Zoo again, and take Panda a red balloon to see just what he would do with it. They bought a big, shiny, red balloon, and took it to the Zoo. Panda loved it, played with it, and had great fun.

When they got home John and Jennifer painted six more pictures to go on their bedroom wall. They put them round like a frieze.

Mother wrote the stories underneath, using the twelve words they knew, and some new words for them to learn. This is what Mother wrote underneath the six new pictures:

Panda likes his red balloon
"It is fun," said Panda
He blew it up
He pulled it down
I like my red balloon
I want it for my tea

John and Jennifer tried and tried to learn all the new words, and when they knew them they found them for Mother and Daddy.

"That is twenty-four words you know," said Mother. "Now you must try to remember them."

JOHN AND JENNIFER LEARN TO WRITE

"MOTHER," said John one day when he was looking at the Panda pictures on the bedroom wall, "I wish I could write underneath my own pictures."

"So do I," said Jennifer.

"Well," said Mother, "so you can. We will go to the shops today, and buy some large sheets of paper, some thick pencils, and some lovely coloured pencils, red and yellow, blue and green, brown and black."

They did so, and the next morning, while Mother was doing her housework, John and Jennifer drew some more Panda pictures, for he was still their favourite animal. This time, instead of painting them, they coloured them with the lovely new coloured pencils. They finished their pictures at the same time as Mother finished her housework.

"Now," said Mother, "let us see about this writing." Underneath John's picture she wrote:

This is Panda

with the thick new pencil, leaving a space underneath her writing.

Then she wrote the same under Jennifer's picture.

She made the letters slowly and clearly, and, as she wrote each word, the children told her what it said, because they were all words they had learned to read.

"Let me try," said John and Jennifer together, and try they did.

They found it much easier to draw and paint Panda than to write his name! Their writing did not look much like Mother's. John's letters wouldn't stand up straight, and Jennifer's looked as if they were trying to push each other off the page!

"Never mind," said Mother, "that's enough for this morning; it's a lovely day, and we are going for a picnic."

"Can we go to the Zoo again, Mother, and see Panda?" said John. "Yes, please," said Jennifer, "and I'll take his picture and show it to him."

They went to the Zoo, and, as they

were going in, they saw a large notice-board, on which was written:

TO THE PANDA →

" I can read some of that," said John, " but I can't read the first word." Mother told them it said " *To.*"

" I want to write that tomorrow," said John, " then we can put a notice outside our bedroom, and people will know the way to our Panda pictures."

" I'll write one too," said Jennifer, " and put it in the hall."

The next morning Mother wrote on two pieces of paper in large, clear letters:

To the Panda - this way

" Now," said Mother, " there's a new word for you to learn." So they learnt the word *way.*

John and Jennifer each wrote it underneath Mother's writing, and put up one notice in the hall and the other outside their bedroom.

When Daddy came home he said it was a good thing Mother had written it first, as he didn't think he would have been able to read many of John's and Jennifer's words.

" You wait, Daddy," said Mother, " very soon, when the children have had more practice, they will be able to write so well that you will be able to read every word of their writing."

" Wouldn't you like to learn how to write your own names? " said Mother one morning.

" O-oh yes! " said John and Jennifer together, " then we can sign our pictures."

So on one piece of paper Mother wrote:

John

and then on another piece she wrote:

Jennifer

John and Jennifer copied their names underneath. John wrote his name five times, and Jennifer wrote hers five times.

JOHN AND JENNIFER LEARN TO COUNT

WHEN John and Jennifer were at the Zoo one day it was very hot, and Mother took them to a café for a drink of lemonade.

They thought it was great fun, and liked the bottles of orange juice, lemonade, and milk. They liked the tins of biscuits, the plates of cakes, the tarts, and, best of all, the ice-cream cornets. They had one each.

On their way home John said that he thought it would be fun to have a café at home. " Yes," said Mother, " but from where will you get the things for a café? "

" Make them," said John. " I've got lots of ideas."

First of all John got two orange boxes from the greengrocer and Daddy gave them a piece of wood to put between the boxes to make a counter; then he and Jennifer painted them green.

Mother gave them some empty bottles which they filled with water. For orange-ade they added a drop of orange juice, for lemonade a spot of lemon juice, and for milk Mother spared them a little

powdered milk. They made labels to put on the bottles.

They made cakes, biscuits, tarts, and sweets out of clay and papier mâché, and painted them to look like real ones. They even made ice-cream cornets.

They had a cash box too, with some real money that Daddy gave them.

" We will be shopkeepers, Mother, and you can come and buy from our café," they said. " How can I? " said Mother. " You haven't a price-list, and I don't know the price of your goods! "

" Let's make one," said Jennifer.

So Mother made a list of all the things they were going to sell, and John and Jennifer each copied a word. Then they talked about how much things cost, and Mother wrote that down, and John and Jennifer copied it. Their price-list looked like this:

Orangeade..2d Biscuits.....1d
Lemonade..2d Tarts......4d
Milk ..... 2d Ice Creams.3d
Cakes...2d Sweets.5 for 1d

"I shall never remember the prices," sighed Jennifer. "Never mind," said Mother, "that is what your price-list is for."

"Yes," said John, "but I don't know which is figure 3 and which is figure 5!"

"I know figure 1," said Jennifer, "but I don't know 2 or 4!"

"Look!" said Mother. "I have painted a picture for you this time. I know you don't know all your figures, so I thought I would paint a picture of all the things you have in your café and put the figures with them."

Mother showed them the picture she had painted, with 1 biscuit, 2 cakes,

3 ice-cream cornets, 4 tarts, and 5 sweets. It was like this:

To help them, Mother had hung some strings of beads underneath the pictures and the figures.

"We will hang that up in front of our shop," said John, "and then if we don't know a figure we can find it."

"I'm going to paint another picture of Panda," said Jennifer, "then we can call our café the Panda Café."

ART—HOW TO MAKE YOUR FIRST PICTURE

CAN you remember when you made your first drawing, and what it was like? Was it made with chalk on a wall or a pavement, or with your finger, reaching through the side of your cot, on the nursery wall?

Most children have been to the seaside and made drawings with a stick on the firm sand of the beach. Sometimes fingers are used to draw, and shells, pebbles, and seaweed are added to make a frame for the sand picture.

You have to use your imagination when making things in this way; it is great fun, of course, and once you have done it you remember it for years. You will be surprised, too, at the number of ideas you have in your mind once you keep your eyes open for them; and not only ideas but memory pictures of things you have seen.

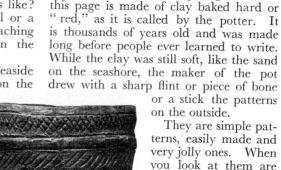

AN ANCIENT DECORATED BEAKER

Children and grown-ups have had the desire and ability to make drawings ever since the world began. Before people learned to write they made picture drawings, and in fact some of the earliest forms of writing are made of simple pictures or signs. Most children can draw very well long before they can write.

The beaker or drinking mug shown on this page is made of clay baked hard or "red," as it is called by the potter. It is thousands of years old and was made long before people ever learned to write. While the clay was still soft, like the sand on the seashore, the maker of the pot drew with a sharp flint or piece of bone or a stick the patterns on the outside.

They are simple patterns, easily made and very jolly ones. When you look at them are you reminded of plaited hair or string, or do the patterns recall wickerwork as in a basket, or do they remind you of the bones of a fish? The people who made this kind of pot also made wicker baskets, plaited hair and leather, caught fish, and certainly knew what fish bones were like.

The pattern on the pot is drawn so simply with up-down zig-zag lines that it looks well and seems to "belong" to the pot. You may have noticed similar lovely patterns on sea shells; and the wonderful ripple patterns left in the sand when the sea goes out at low tide. These ripple patterns seem to belong to the sand, just as the patterns belong to the beaker; and how finely drawn they are!

Those early people not only liked to draw patterns on their pots, but also little pictures on the handles of the bone tools they used, as well as quite large pictures of animals on the walls of the caves in which they lived. Can you see the little scratched drawing of an ibex on the piece of bone shown in the second picture? It was drawn with a sharp piece of flint. The artist must have seen it very clearly in the odd-shaped piece of bone before he drew it, for it seems so much to belong to the shape.

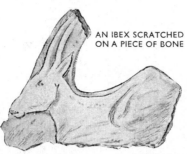

AN IBEX SCRATCHED ON A PIECE OF BONE

Such patterns and pictures were made for the sheer joy of the making. It is the most natural thing in the world for us to want to draw, and to be able to draw, and to make patterns and pictures from our ideas. We like to make them in our homes, gardens, on our clothes, on the things we use as well as in drawing books.

Just as we have drawn lovely patterns with pebbles and shells in the sand, people have made lovely patterns with sea shells, seeds, berries, and even used animals' teeth for necklaces and wristlets to wear. Some of you have probably seen in a seaside cottage an old glass bottle with a model of a ship inside it, made by an old sailor in his odd moments between voyages. It was made of scraps of wood, cork, pins, cotton, and little pieces of paper, and painted in two or three bright colours—and a lovely thing it is.

The first thing needed is an idea. Sometimes this idea comes before we know what material we are going to use to make it. At other times ideas come when we handle chalk, wood, clay, or a paintbrush, and we then say to ourselves, "I am going to make a picture," or "I am going to make a horse." Whatever it is, it should look like your idea and like the material in which you made it. When you make a man out of

snow he should look like a snowman and not an ordinary man. It is just the same with the making of the horses on a roundabout at a fair, or with a rocking horse. We think they are lovely things, and we enjoy riding on them as horses even though they are made of wood. We use our imaginations and pretend we are riding in a race, or that we are a St. George chasing a dragon.

Will you try now and see what you can imagine for a picture? First of all get a piece of chalk, or a soft B pencil, or a stick of charcoal, or a large round paintbrush and some paint, or a pen and some ink. Next get a large sheet of paper and pin it up on a wall within reach, or on a drawing board on an easel. If you are going to use the pen and ink choose a smooth sheet of paper about twice the size of this page and lay it on a table or a desk.

Now, just sit and look at your sheet of paper and imagine it has a frame round it, and that you are going to make a picture to fit it. Suppose your picture is going to be of St. George and the Dragon. In your picture you can see the great beast which looks a bit like a crocodile, with horny spines all down its back from its head to the tip of its long wriggly tail, and a bit like a bat with its great webbed wings. You can see its scaly body, and what a pattern those scales make! Big five-clawed feet, long open jaws and terrible teeth, flame and smoke coming out of its mouth, eyes that stand out like those of a frog, and long pointed ears.

The dragon is creeping clumsily out of its dark, rocky lair, and St. George is seated on a fine horse with a lovely curved neck, long mane, and long flowing tail. He is wearing a helmet and a shining

MAKING PICTURES IN THE SAND

THE BEAUTIFUL RIPPLE PATTERN LEFT IN THE SAND BY THE RECEDING TIDE

suit of armour. He holds the reins with his left hand and is just going to strike the upturned head of the dragon with the long sword held firmly in his right hand. Beside the rocky lair of the dragon you can get a glimpse of a small town on a hill far away.

When you have a clear idea of the pattern of your picture, begin to draw it on your paper and make your drawing fill your paper. It is best to draw in the big shapes first and add details later. When you feel you have drawn all your picture and it looks just as you saw it at first in your mind, finish off by writing your name on it.

If you would like to paint your St. George and the Dragon, and you have plenty of colour in your paint-box, by all means paint it.

MUSIC—THE SOUNDS WE HEAR

WE are travelling through the lovely English countryside in a train. It is a pleasant journey, for it is April and there is much to see—trees in bud, lambs at play, little rivers and little hills, old villages, and many other things.

We all enjoy looking through a railway-carriage window because we can use our eyes. Also, we use our minds. Far off we see a line of hills, and our mind says, " How like clouds the hills look ! "

In such scenes artists see subjects for their pictures, poets find inspiration for their poems. What about music and musicians ?

For music we need to use, first, our ears. We hear around us the sounds from which music is made. Wherever you are, close your eyes and listen. How many sounds can you hear ? In our train we can hear the noise of the wheels, the knitting needles of the lady sitting opposite, and the engine whistle as it enters a tunnel.

The wheels of the train go monoton-

ously on—*taa-tai taa taa-tai taa* . . ., not in any sort of melody, but in a pattern of sounds, some long and some short. A regular pattern of sounds makes a *rhythm*, and rhythm is the foundation of music. We can write down the rhythm of the train in musical notes. Here it is :

The train goes on and we notice the lady's knitting needles. Their sounds make a different pattern from that of the wheels. *Click, click, click, click* . . . We think " Why are those needles such a nuisance ? " It is because all the sounds are equal in length. How monotonous it is to have all these sounds of the same length (which we could write—   ).

Musical rhythm becomes alive as it is filled with varied sounds, some long and some short.

Our train is not very far from where Sir Edward Elgar lived. He was a great English musician who loved the sights and sounds of his native country. These find place in his music.

One day a country wagon passed by Sir Edward Elgar. The hoofs of the horses were going something like this—*clip clop clipper clop*. Elgar wrote down this pattern— ♩ ♩ ♫ ♩ And then he noticed that the driver of the wagon was whistling a tune. Elgar wrote this down too. He put the rhythm of the hooves and the tune of the whistling driver together and gave us a beautiful little picture in music called The Wagon Passes.

We hear many *rhythmic* sounds around us. Also, we hear *melodic* sounds. Here we notice not how long or short the sounds are, but how high or low. Just now the engine whistled its way through a tiny station. When a certain little boy hears an engine whistle he sings, rather high, "Boo-oo-oo." If we were to write down the whistle sound we could write it like this, in the *treble* clef:

The height of musical sounds can be shown quite accurately on a musical map, about which we shall learn later. A *clef* is a guide as to whether we are going over mountains or down the valleys.

When we see 𝄞 we expect height ; when we see 𝄢, the *bass* clef, we know that we are dealing with low sounds (this sign is often used reversed).

Stop reading for a moment. Close your eyes again. Can you hear any low sounds or any high sounds? Of course you can. High sounds might be the song of birds, a bicycle bell, or the music of the wind in the telegraph wires. Low sounds, on the other hand, may include a ship's siren, a church bell, or a noisy cow.

These sounds are the raw material of melody. Before sound becomes music it goes through several processes, just as does the wheat in the fields before it comes to our table as bread.

We notice, in any music we hear, the contrast between high and low. Nature knows quite a lot about the making of music. You have only to listen to the cuckoo. "Cuckoo" he calls; high, and then low. Sing "cuckoo." The two sounds go something like this—*Cuc-koo.*

Always the cuckoo sings the same song,

and always it looks (if we write it down) as we have written it.

Now, if a composer wishes to write down, accurately, the song of the cuckoo he does it like this :  This is a picture of the music. It is an exact picture, showing just how far the melody falls.

The cuckoo has often found his way into music. The best known piece which shows him singing is by Frederick Delius, another English composer, and it is called On Hearing the First Cuckoo in Spring.

We all enjoy finding out how things work, and music is as interesting as everything else. Look inside a piano. You will see long strings (or wires) and short strings. Look at a church organ. It has big pipes (in the Town Hall of Sydney there is one pipe 64 feet long!) and little pipes. Look at this picture of a peal of bells. They are of different sizes.

The bells are of different sizes so that they make sounds of different *pitch*. The smaller the bell the higher the sound. The larger the bell the deeper the sound. So it is with all musical instruments. The bassoon is a long pipe and makes deep sounds. Could you write down the clef in which the bassoon player would have his music? The piccolo is a tiny pipe (smaller even than the flute, to which it is a little brother) and makes high sounds. What clef would he have? Write it down.

We are near our destination. The rhythm of the wheels has changed. 1 2 3, 1 2 3, 1 2 3 . . . We can count the sounds. We write them down ♪♪♩ | ♪♪♩ | ♩♩♩ Clap that rhythm, and imagine that you are now on the railway. But here we are running into the station over the points— 1 & 2 &, 1 & 2 &, 1 & 2 & say the wheels ♫♫ | ♫♫ | ♫♫ Soon we shall be getting out of the train and listening to the sounds of a great city.

Will you, too, listen as you go about the world? Remember that you have ears as well as eyes. What you *see* helps you to look at, and to enjoy, pictures. What you *hear* gives you the beginning of music. Long sounds and short sounds are rhythmic by nature. High sounds and low sounds are melodic.

FRENCH—A LITTLE PICTURE LESSON

YOU will not be able to learn to speak French from these lessons There are some sounds in French which cannot be made clear on paper, and you will only be able to understand these by hearing them spoken. But this page will help if you are learning French at school, or if there is someone at home who can help you to understand how the words should be said. These lessons tell us the story of a visit to France and of the visitors' doings among the French people. The first line in each case is in French; the second line gives the English word for the French word above it. But the French people do not put their words together as we do, and the third line shows how we make up the words into English.

Pierre—Peter   **Jeannette—Jenny**

La bonne—The nurserymaid

Je m'appelle Pierre, et j'ai dix ans.
I myself call Peter, and I have ten years.
My name is Peter and I am ten years old.

Ma sœur Jeannette a huit ans.
My sister   Jenny   has eight years.
My sister Jenny is eight years old.

Mon petit frère a deux ans.
My little brother has two years.
My little brother is two years old.

On l'appelle Bébé.
One him calls Baby.
He is called Baby.

Bébé   va   venir et la bonne aussi.
Baby is going to come and the nurse   also.
Baby is coming and nurse also.

Nos malles—Our trunks

Notre bonne a fait toutes nos malles.
Our nurse has made all our trunks.
Our nurse has packed all our trunks.

Nos jouets sont dans la grande malle.
Our toys   are   in   the large trunk.
Our toys are in the large trunk.

L'école—The school

Jeannette et moi nous allons à l'école.
Jenny   and I   we   go   to the school.
Jenny and I go to school.

Maintenant nous sommes en vacances.
Now   we   are   in   holidays.
Now we have a holiday.

Nous allons en France.
We are going in France.
We are going to France.

Nous allons avec papa et maman.
We are going with papa and mamma.
We are going with papa and mamma.

Nos jouets—Our toys

Nous avons beaucoup de jouets.
We have   many   of toys.
We have many toys.

Bébé emporte son bateau à voiles.
Baby is taking his boat with sails.
Baby is taking his sailing boat.

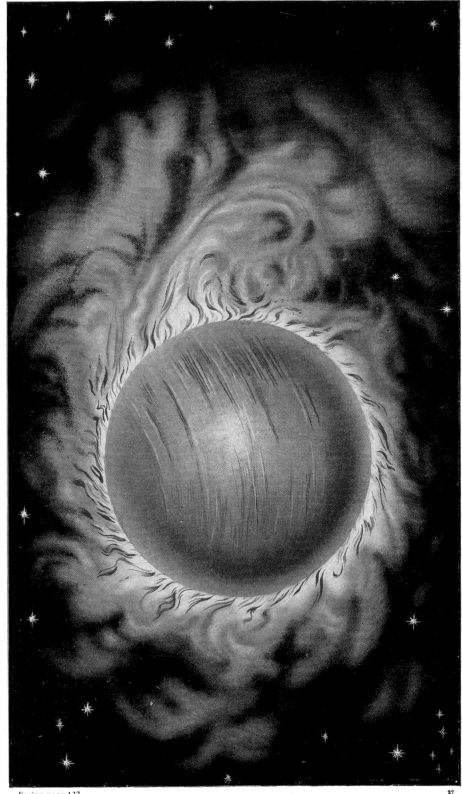

THE DAYS WHEN EARTH ROLLED THROUGH SPACE AS A RED-HOT GLOBE

Here our scientific artist, G. F. Morrell, gives us a conception of what the Earth was probably like in the days when the globe was red-hot, flaming out for thousands of miles into space, with showers of fiery rain pouring over it. Nobody knows how long that was ago: it may have been ten thousand million years

The Story of the Boundless Universe and All its Wondrous Worlds

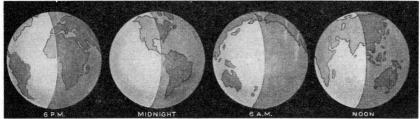

6 P.M.   MIDNIGHT   6 A.M.   NOON

The Changing Face of the Earth to the Sun every six hours

HOW THE EARTH WAS MADE

AND now we must ask ourselves more particularly the great question : Where have the Sun and the Earth come from ?

For a long time men used to think that the solar system, including the Sun and the Earth, had been from the first as they are now. No one now thinks that. We believe that they have grown, so to speak, to be what they are, but astronomers are not agreed as to how this came about. It used to be thought that in order to see what the solar system was like at first we had only to take a telescope and look up at the sky. There we see scores of thousands of wonderful bodies which are still at the stage reached by the solar system long ages ago. These bodies are called nebulae, and one of them would be called a *nebula*, which is the Latin word for a cloud. They look like little bright fleecy clouds in the sky. Some of them can be seen with the naked eye, and then they look like stars, but they are quite different from stars.

By examining the kind of light they send to us, we know that the sky contains, at the very least, 120,000 real nebulae. They are not star-clusters at all, but glowing clouds of matter. Perhaps we can get the best idea of what a nebula is like by using the name the poets often call it by—*fire-mist*.

A nebula is like a great mist of fire. Those we see in the heavens are of different shapes and sizes. Many of them are far bigger, hundreds of thousands of times bigger, than the whole space occupied by the solar system. A great many of them have a shape like the firework called St Catherine's wheel—flattened and coiled up. They are called spiral nebulae. You know what a spiral staircase is. The spiral nebulae, however, ought never to have had that name, because they are not at all like a spiral staircase; they are flat and thin, more like a St. Catherine's wheel in shape.

If we look at some of these spiral nebulae we see bright points in them here and there which suggest to us that the fire-mist has become thicker at certain places than at others. Often these bright points are so large and bright that they look like stars, and, indeed, probably they are stars. Probably all stars are made out of nebulae. Now let us come back to our solar system.

If you could look at the solar system from a great distance away you would notice many remarkable facts about it. In the first place, you would notice that all the twistings and movements are in one direction; then you would notice that the solar system is a flat thing. All the planets, so to speak, go round the Sun at much the same level.

There is another curious fact, and that is that the kind of stuff the Sun is made of is the same stuff that the various planets are made of. It almost looks—does it not ? —as if our little Earth and all the planets were once part of the Sun ?

And so men guessed that perhaps the pieces of stuff that now make the planets

ASTRONOMY · GEOLOGY · GEOGRAPHY · CHEMISTRY · PHYSICS · LIFE

had been somehow brushed off from the Sun, and that as they cooled down they had become solid and started travelling round and round him. We are sure now that that is not what happened, but various theories have been advanced as to how the solar system might have been formed.

One theory supposed that the solar system was once a small nebula which gradually contracted and left rings which, in their turn, condensed into the planets. But it has been shown that wide rings like these could not possibly condense into compact globes. Another theory is that a passing star came so close to the Sun that a great fiery arm was thrown off which broke up, and these detached pieces condensed into the planets.

Yet another theory supposes that the Sun passed through a great cloud of dust particles. Many of these dark clouds are known ; they can be seen hiding parts of the Milky Way and are quite common in space. According to this theory the Sun *gathered* the particles of this cloud into knots, so to speak, and these condensed into the planets. One thing is certain : the various planets were never very much nearer to the Sun than they are now.

Whichever is the correct theory, there is one great force that must always be at work—it is the force that has made the solar system as it exists today.

WHAT SIR ISAAC NEWTON THOUGHT AS HE LAY UNDER AN APPLE TREE

This force is called gravitation, and it acts in such a way that it causes every tiny piece of matter in the world to be attracted by all other matter in the world.

Gravitation is, perhaps, the most familiar of all facts in our daily lives. When you let a ball out of your hand it drops to the earth simply because the earth and the ball have attracted each other.

One of the greatest men who ever lived, an Englishman called Isaac Newton, was lying on his back, under the shade of an apple tree in his mother's garden. He was not just dreaming his time away, however, but thinking ; and he saw what thousands of people had seen before him, but never troubled to think about—an apple falling from the tree to the ground. The result of his thinking about this was that he discovered a law of attraction which is true throughout the whole universe, not only of the Earth and a ball, but also of the Earth and the Moon, the Earth and

the Sun, and also of all the little pieces of matter in a nebula.

From the first moment a nebula was formed, then—perhaps by a collision between two stars or more—there would begin to act upon all its parts the same force of gravitation which acts upon you if you miss your footing and tumble downstairs—a force that goes on acting all the time, never ceasing and never getting tired. So, some years after the great work of Newton, several men began to apply his ideas to the nebulae (remember that when the word is spelt like this it means more than one nebula) and to ask what must happen in the course of ages when this force of attraction acts upon a nebula.

THE HEAVENS LIKE A RICH GARDEN FILLED WITH BLOSSOMING WORLDS

One of the greatest of these followers of Newton was Herschel, who made finer telescopes than anyone had used before, and who spent all his life studying the stars and the nebulae. He was the first man who ever made a list of nebulae, and he it was who first saw that they might be arranged in classes, from those which look like little milky clouds, and nothing more, to those which are really stars with a sort of cloudy substance round them.

So it seemed to him that some " clustering power " must be at work turning these scattered and milky nebulae into brighter and smaller objects which would some day become stars or suns and solar systems, and he compared the heavens to a rich garden containing plants in all stages of their lives. This gives us the advantage, he says, that as at one and the same time we can see all the different stages in the history of plants—from their birth to their death—so also in the heavens we can see all the different stages from a nebula to a star. Then there followed a great Frenchman who saw that the "clustering power" must be gravitation, and who worked out exactly what must happen in such a case, as we know exactly the force with which gravitation acts.

THE SPACE THAT SWARMS WITH WORLDS LIKE PEBBLES

Now, in order to fill in the history of the solar system we have to reckon with two facts. We have already seen that the Sun and his family do not stand still in space, but are moving all together through it. We cannot, indeed, believe that there is rest anywhere ; everything is moving.

The Sun itself was once much bigger than it now is and there may have been a sort of small nebula around it. Perhaps that Corona is the remaining portion of what once extended much farther. The Sun is always moving through space and in doing so must, in the course of ages, approach other stars in what we call outer space.

Men used to think that outer space was quite empty as far as the nearest of the fixed stars, but we are now learning that space is very far from empty, and that really it is swarming with those little bodies like grains of sand or pebbles, or even larger bodies still, which we have already described as being found within the solar system. It is quite reasonable to suppose, then, that as the nebula went through space, gradually becoming smaller and denser by the force of gravitation causing it to shrink, it would come across millions and millions of these grains and pebbles, also rapidly moving.

THE EARTH OF LONG AGO THAT WAS LIKE THE SUN TODAY

Many interesting consequences would follow. If the nebula ran across a great swarm of meteorites, as the Earth does in November, then there might be the beginning of a planet. But, even apart from such a swarm, there would be marked results from the millions of little collisions that would be constantly happening. For one thing, the nebula would be made hotter, for when anything in moving strikes anything else, or is partly stopped by it, its motion is turned to heat, which is itself a kind of motion. We use this fact every time we strike a match. We put the match in motion and then partly arrest the motion by whatever we rub it against; so there is enough heat produced to set the match on fire.

That, then, is all that we can tell at present about the origin of the Sun and his family. Everyone is agreed that something like this is what really happened.

Now let us try to imagine what our own Earth must have been like in its beginnings. We cannot be quite certain as to the shape of the Earth at first, though some men who have made a careful study of the subject think it may have been shaped like a pear instead of like a flattened orange, as now. But, whatever its exact shape was, it was so utterly different from the Earth we know that we can scarcely imagine it. Really, the Earth of long ago must have been far more like what the Sun is now—only, of course, quite tiny compared with the Sun.

We think of the Earth as something that ends suddenly at the surface—at the level of the ground. That is, however, by no means quite correct. Even now the Earth does not end sharply all round as an orange does. We must not imagine that the Earth ends at the level of the ground or at the level of the water, and that we walk outside it.

THE SOLID EARTH THAT THINS OUT UNTIL IT IS A GAS

Not at all. Above both the ground and the water there is something which is really part of the Earth, though we cannot see it. It moves with the Earth round the Sun, and twists round with the Earth as it spins. The stuff of which it is made is constantly being exchanged in both directions with the water of the sea and the stuff of which the dry ground is made. In short, the air is part of the Earth. The air as it is at present probably extends upwards from the surface of the solid and liquid part of the Earth to a distance of about 200 miles. As we travel upwards through the air in an aeroplane we find the air becoming more and more thin, or more and more rare ; and though we cannot go very far, we are quite sure this rareness goes on increasing until there is no air to be found.

So even now, we see, the Earth does not really stop short sharply anywhere, but its stuff is spread out all round it in a layer of gas which gradually becomes rarer and rarer until it stops altogether.

THE ATOMS IN THE GREAT GLOBE OF GLOWING GAS

What we now call the Earth was at first nothing more nor less than a great globe of glowing gas. In that hot, twisting, glowing globe there were contained all the tiny little portions of matter, or atoms, which now make up the water of the sea, the soil, the rocks, the bodies even of all living things, and also, of course, the air, or mixture of gases, that still remains covering the Earth like a warm blanket.

So far are we from being really on the surface of the Earth that the whole world, sea and land together, is really covered with a great sea or ocean of air. We crawl about at the bottom of this ocean, and one of the latest things that men have learnt to do is to jump off the bottom and swim in it, as the birds have been able to do for ages without troubling their heads at all; only we call this swimming *flying*!

In the course of time we know that great changes had to happen in this glowing globe of gas. It was doubtless then giving out light and heat like a little sun, and in doing so it would gradually become cooler. If you make a poker red-hot, and then take it out of the fire, it will give out light and heat for some time; then it will give out heat only, but no light—it is still hot, but will have become dark; and it will become quite cold. It cannot give out light and heat without becoming cooler, for it does not make them out of nothing. The case was the same with the Earth, and in the course of long ages she had gradually to become cooler. At last she had to become so cool that part of the stuff of which she was made would no longer remain a gas, but become a liquid.

This is a perfectly simple thing which you must have seen for yourself a hundred times—whenever you look out of a train, for instance. As you breathe, a great deal of water comes out of your mouth and nose. This water, having come from the inside of your warm body, is itself so warm that it is in the form of a gas; but when this warm gas strikes the cold glass of the window-pane it is cooled so much that it is turned into a liquid, and will run down the pane in little drops. If you cool any gas sufficiently it must become liquid.

HOW THE EARTH COOLED OUTSIDE WHILE THE CORE WAS RED-HOT

Now that part of the Earth which would soonest become cooled would not of course be the hot inside—which perhaps consists of a gas at this very moment—but would be the part next to the surface. All the kinds of stuff that were most apt to become liquid would become so, and, being heavier, would fall towards the centre ; while the kind of stuff, like the air of today, which is not so apt to become liquid, would stay where it was.

So that we can imagine an Earth with a core of hot gas and a layer of liquid outside that, and then a layer of cool gas, or air, outside that. But soon even part of the stuff that had become liquid would become solid, or perhaps like a thick oil.

It must be remembered that all this time the Earth was twisting round and round like a top, as it has done ever since. Also it must be remembered that the great Sun is all this time pulling as hard as it can upon the Earth by means of gravitation. We can imagine, then, that the liquid stuff next to the Sun at any given moment would be apt to be pulled out towards the Sun or heaped up at the surface of the Earth. But, of course, as one point of the Earth is never opposite the Sun for long, this heaping-up of the liquid on the surface would be like a wave travelling over the surface of the Earth. Now this great travelling wave is nothing else than a tide, and every child who has been to the sea has seen its consequences. But the first tides that were raised by the Sun upon the Earth were not tides of cold water; the Earth was too hot for that, and all the water in it was in the form of a gas in the air, like the water in your warm breath before it strikes the cold window-pane.

THE WAY THE BEDS OF THE OCEANS MAY HAVE BEEN MADE

The first tides that rolled upon the Earth must have been terrible tides made of stuff like red-hot lava—the red-hot stuff that comes out of a volcano and runs down in fiery streams until at last it turns quite cold and solid.

It is much more probable that a very remarkable thing happened somewhere about this time. The men who have studied this subject believed that one day, while these tides of lava were rolling round the Earth as she spun, part of the stuff was whisked off like drops from a wet umbrella when you spin it. Perhaps at this time the surface of the Earth had become cool enough for the great gaps left by this loss to remain more or less fixed, and some people think that those gaps are now the basins of the seas.

WHAT BECAME OF THE BIT OF THE EARTH THAT BROKE OFF ?

But what became of the stuff that would then break off ? Its shape at first, of course, would be irregular, but as it went on moving and became cooler, and as its parts acted upon one another by gravitation, it would become round, and men believe that the Moon was formed from the Earth in this wonderful way. At first she was very near the Earth, and for a long time afterwards she went farther and farther away.

(Next chapter in this group, page 265)

The Story of Immortal Folk Whose Work Will Never Die

The boy Handel is discovered playing in the garret in the night

THE KINGS OF MUSIC

IT has been said that if a man were permitted to make the ballads of a nation he need not care who made its laws. In that sense the composers of the world's music have been unconscious lawgivers, moulders of national moods and aspirations. But the names and works of the earliest composers are unknown ; the story of the world's earliest music, like that of the world's earliest civilizations, is unrecorded.

That music was of great consequence to antiquity we know from the Bible ; and we also know that in Ancient Greece music was a sacred influence ranking even higher than drama and poetry. It was Aristotle who said, " To reform or to relax the manners of a people it suffices to add a string to the lyre or to take one from it."

But the music of that glorious age is lost for all time and we know nothing of the old composers ; all knowledge of them was lost in the Dark Ages.

The first men we know of who tried to exercise some sway over the kingdom of music in Europe were churchmen, for it was only behind the protection of monastery walls that knowledge of any kind could be pursued during the early Middle Ages. These men were Ambrose, Bishop of Milan in the fourth century, and Pope Gregory in the sixth. The former seems to have encouraged the congregation to join in singing the services while the latter introduced some discipline into the choral part of the service. St. Augustine brought to Britain the kind of singing called plainsong.

Three centuries later came a great musical teacher, an Italian monk named Guido of Arezzo. Under his influence the primitive way of writing down notes, by making signs on one or more lines, was standardised into the four-line staff or stave. This developed into our five-line stave.

Slowly music was growing from simple chanting in unison on a few notes, supported by the simple forms of wind or stringed instruments of those times, to what is called polyphony. This means the sounding of two or more different notes simultaneously to form a primitive harmony. You can still hear one of the earliest forms of this in the drone of the bagpipes, which keeps to one long sustained note while the chanter, with its row of finger-notes, produces the melody.

From Scotland came the thirteenth-century Hymn to St. Magnus in which two voices sing in thirds ; and to the same period belongs the famous " Sumer is icumen in," with words in the Wessex dialect and music written in six parts. Of

EXPLORERS · INVENTORS · WRITERS · ARTISTS : SCIENTISTS

course, there must have been many other hymns and songs like them, but we have no knowledge of them.

Some 150 years later, when singing masters in many cathedrals and monasteries must have been experimenting with this new and exciting game of religious song-writing, three men became famous enough to have their names handed on to succeeding generations. Two of them, Dufay and Binchois, belonged to the famous Netherlands school of musicians ; the third, and perhaps greatest of all, was the Englishman, John Dunstable.

THE GREAT MUSICAL AMBASSADOR FOR OUR COUNTRY

Little was known of his work till recent years because it was in manuscripts hidden away in various towns in Italy and France. But you hear some of his elaborate and beautiful choir music on the radio sometimes. Dunstable seems to have travelled widely, and during his time, and for two centuries after his death, in 1453, England was recognised as one of the foremost musical nations.

In those days the words were in the international language of Latin. Music itself is a tongue which every nation can speak and we can regard John Dunstable as a great musical ambassador for our country.

That great revival of learning which we call the Renaissance affected music just as it did the other arts. The greatest of the Netherlands composers, Orlandus Lassus, and Josquin Des Près, a contemporary of Martin Luther, bring us to the end of the Middle Ages and the entry upon the scene of the great Italian, Palestrina.

CHOIR MUSIC THAT BREATHES THE VERY SPIRIT OF DEVOTION

He was a fine singer and also a teacher of singing as many of his great predecessors had been and his appointment as official composer to the papal chapel was a new idea, then. It was perhaps the first public acknowledgement of a man as a composer of music rather than as a teacher of singing. Palestrina's music is, of course, primarily choir music, and it breathes the very spirit of devotion.

Contemporaries in England were John Taverner, Christopher Tye, and Thomas Tallis, all growing up in the days of Henry the Eighth and all working to improve the standard of part-song writing. They

covered the end of the Catholic era in this country, and the beginning of the Protestant.

Taverner wrote a beautiful Mass founded on a lost English folk tune, " The Western Wind." Tye later set a rhymed version of Bible stories in English, dedicating it to Edward the Sixth. Tallis, " father of English cathedral music," wrote for the newly devised Anglican service. His settings were designed to bring out the meaning of the words, pouring out upon them rich and pure harmonies whose simplicities go far deeper than the complications of many of his Continental contemporaries.

His great pupil, William Byrd, was fifteen when Elizabeth came to the throne. He wrote fine church music, both Catholic and Protestant, but he lived in a time when conditions in the country were more settled and there was time for family music.

WHEN PEOPLE MADE THEIR OWN MUSIC AT HOME

People did not go to concerts ; they made their own music at home. Every well-furnished house had a box or chest of viols—forerunners of our violin, viola, and 'cello. There was a great demand for secular music and Byrd wrote many solo songs, madrigals, fantasies for the viol, and music for the virginal, that miniature early version of the piano on which the great Queen Bess was a clever performer.

Abroad, the Spaniard Tomasso Victoria, was following in the path of Palestrina, and Claudio Monteverde, in Italy, was breaking away from it. Italians, who had been used to voice training for centuries, now wanted something else besides church music, and the new composer, priest though he was, supplied it. His first opera, written for a great wedding celebration, was produced in 1607 and was marked by a bolder and more original use of the orchestra than had been known before.

Meanwhile, the English madrigal writers of this period—John Dowland, Thomas Campion, Michael Cavendish, and many others, all contemporaries of Shakespeare —were leaving us a heritage of sounds reflecting those romantic and fateful days of our history. Thanks to the radio we have many chances nowadays to hear their music played on the very

KINGS OF MUSIC AMID THE NOISE OF WAR

When the French army was firing on Vienna in 1809, two men sat listening to the guns. In a cellar sat Beethoven, trying to shut out the sound of the guns from his ears lest they should ruin his hearing ; in another room Haydn, with his dying fingers, played the Austrian anthem to try to drown the noise. It is a wonderful picture this, of two of the world's great musicians, sitting, while life and power were ebbing from them—for Beethoven *did* become deaf, and Haydn died—helpless in the face of the great destroyer of mankind, the curse of War.

instruments, such as the lute, for which it was composed.

In 1658 there was born in a lane in Westminster the matchless Henry Purcell, greatest English composer until the nineteenth century. When he was nine he became a chorister at the Chapel Royal, and at 12 he wrote an ode for Charles the Second's birthday. He began writing incidental music for the theatre, which was then enjoying a boom, and composed a vast amount of this besides nearly two hundred songs for solo voices, many sonatas for two violins with keyboard accompaniment, much church music including some sixty anthems, besides organ and harpsichord pieces. His theatrical writings for plays and masques led him to attempt one opera, Dido and Aeneas, which is probably the earliest opera still regularly performed.

HANDEL, THE MAN WHO NEARLY SET THE BIBLE TO MUSIC

The 17th century saw the slow development of both opera and oratorio, the latter named from a type of performance originally given in Rome at a hall called The Oratory. But it was left to Johann Sebastian Bach and George Frederick Handel, both born in Germany in the year 1685, to raise the oratorio to heights which its founders could never have even guessed at.

Handel was much influenced by his three years' stay in Italy, which began when he was 21. He thoroughly mastered the style of Italian opera. Neither his music nor his personality were markedly German and when he became a naturalised Englishman he had the true cosmopolitan touch which always pleases a London public.

Handel began, then, as a composer of operas. But as the operas had no great run on the Continent he came to London to live. For long years he wrote almost nothing but operas, and he generally rented a theatre of his own. He had some successes, but he had more failures ; in fact he was twice bankrupted by his opera business.

Yet if Handel had not failed with his operas we should never have had his wonderful oratorios, with words nearly always taken from the Bible.

Somebody has said of Handel that he set the Bible to music, and he very nearly

did. He wrote more than twenty oratorios, though not more than three or four of them are performed today. But one alone of the three or four would have been quite enough to immortalise the name of Handel, for it is to Handel that we owe the Messiah. And he wrote it—this long work, which takes more than two hours to sing—in 23 days !

ORGANIST OF GENIUS WHOM HANDEL LOVED LIKE A BROTHER

When he died, in 1759, they laid him beside our own great men and women in Westminster Abbey, and there we may see a monument representing him in the act of writing " I know that my Redeemer liveth " for the Messiah. He had a fiery temper, and once threatened to throw a singer out of the window. But he was pious and charitable too, and it is pleasing to know that he gave an organ to the Foundling Hospital, together with much of the money he drew from his oratorios.

The greatest musician who was living in Handel's time was Johann Sebastian Bach. Both Handel and Bach were fine organists ; both gave great religious works to the musical world ; both were stricken blind in their later years. Beyond that, they had not much in common. Handel never married, Bach was a quiet, stay-at-home man who married twice and had a family of twenty sons and daughters. He was an organist first of all, and his organ compositions remain to this day the most perfect things of the kind ever produced. This wonderful genius died in 1750, nine years before Handel, who mourned for him as for a brother.

THE MOST ORIGINAL AND COMPREHENSIVE MUSICAL GENIUS EVER KNOWN

Now we will take another pair— Mozart and Haydn. It has been remarked as strange that Bach and Handel never met, though both were Germans, born in the same year, and living practically throughout the same period. It was not so with Mozart and Haydn ; they met often, and they were very fond of each other. It was Haydn who described Mozart as the most extraordinary, original, and comprehensive musical genius ever known.

Haydn had one advantage : his musical abilities, discovered in early childhood, were not thwarted by his father. The father insisted on a most severe training

THIRTY GREAT COMPOSERS OF THE WORLD

Elgar   Rachmaninoff

Dvorak   Gounod

Mozart

Sibelius   Schumann

Sullivan   Dr. Strauss

Handel

Beethoven

Wagner

Weber   Rossini

Palestrina   Tchaikovsky

Haydn   Schubert   Liszt   Mendelssohn   Chopin

Bizet   Purcell

Verdi   Brahms

Grieg   Berlioz

Bach

Gluck   Puccini

28 F 1

for the boy, and the young prodigy was taught his crotchets and quavers with many floggings when things went wrong. He developed a good voice, and so was sent to sing in the choir of Vienna Cathedral. But the day came when his voice broke, and he was of no more use to his choirmaster, who might have kept him resting until his voice recovered and set ; but Haydn had displeased him. One day he played a boyish prank on a fellow-singer by cutting off his pigtail, and now he was dismissed from the choir.

You would not like to hear of all the hardships he endured for long after this. He became a singing teacher's servant; he fiddled at dances and even in the streets !

HAYDN TAKES ADVANTAGE OF HIS GREAT OPPORTUNITY

But he was perfecting himself in composition all the time ; and a set of sonatas he wrote took the fancy of a wealthy countess. She introduced him to pupils who paid well. Henceforward he had no trouble in getting on. In 1760 he married, not very happily, and a year later he entered the service of the Esterhazys, one of the richest Austrian families of the time. Great families kept a permanent band of their own in those days, and Haydn was the Esterhazy bandmaster, with a good salary and a comfortable home.

This meant that he had a permanent orchestra of hand-picked players whom he could rehearse again and again. Never did a great musician have more encouraging circumstances in which to develop his art. Haydn took his opportunity with both hands.

That lasted until 1790, when the Esterhazy orchestra was disbanded. Then he came to London on a visit, and wrote for certain London concerts some of those symphonies which we still delight to hear. Altogether he wrote about 150 of these symphonies. Mozart saw him just before he left, and wept at the parting. " We shall never meet again," he said ; and it proved true. In the music of our Church hymnals we find a tune called Austria, with Haydn's name attached. It is almost as well known as our national anthem; and it was after hearing God Save the King in London that Haydn felt that he must make a national tune for his own country.

He went home and wrote God Preserve the Emperor, which is familiar to most of us as the tune for the hymn, Praise The Lord, Ye Heavens Adore Him.

He remains the great master of the sonata and the string quartette and Beethoven owed much to him. For his fine, smooth melodies he used his own country's folk songs again and again.

THE TENDER HOMAGE OF ONE GREAT MUSICIAN FOR ANOTHER

His symphonies are still played by our leading orchestras ; his piano music is in all the publishers' lists ; and his oratorio of The Creation ranks as a good third to the Messiah and Elijah. Haydn wrote The Creation in his old age, and it was in listening to a performance of it that he made his last appearance in public. The excitement was too much for him. " Not I, but a Power from above created that," he cried out at one point. They carried him away, and, as he passed, Beethoven fervently kissed his hand.

A young man once asked Mozart to tell him how to compose. The gentle Wolfgang Amadeus, for these were his Christian names, made answer that the questioner was too young to be thinking of such a serious occupation. " But you were much younger when you began," said the aspirant. " Ah, yes, that is true," replied Mozart, with a smile ; " but then, you see, I did not ask anybody how to compose." No. Mozart, born at Salzburg in 1756, was only five when he composed a minuet and trio that boys and girls of much maturer age might play with some effect today.

HOW MOZART BECAME POOR AND DANCED TO KEEP WARM

His father was a good musician, and Wolfgang had a sister, Maria Anna, who at first showed nearly as much talent as himself. Hence they all started on a musical tour, in the course of which Mozart played before the Empress Maria Theresa, and romped with the little princess who afterwards became Queen of France—the unfortunate Marie Antoinette. These great ladies used to take him on their knees, kiss him, and shower gold upon him.

It was Mozart's happiest time, for, from the day that he began life in earnest as a married man—that was in 1782—the wolf of poverty was never away from his door. He composed incessantly, but even successful composition did not pay then as it does now, and the butcher and the baker were often worrying poor Mozart for a settlement of their accounts. A friend called one winter day, and found Mozart and his wife waltzing round the room. " We are cold," they said, " and we have no wood to make a fire." Let us think of that, and then think of the glorious works that Mozart produced under such depressing conditions. He left 769 compositions in all, and he was still under 40 when he died.

In his own day he was regarded chiefly as a composer of opera, and we still think highly of his Don Giovanni, The Magic Flute, and The Marriage of Figaro. He wrote 49 symphonies, including those special favourites the so-called Jupiter symphony, and one in G minor, which has been described as his tenderest and daintiest instrumental composition. All his works are full of charming melody.

THE STORMY DAY WHEN MOZART WAS LAID IN AN UNKNOWN GRAVE

Mozart's end was very sad. He was taken ill in 1791, and during his illness he wrote a famous Requiem, a sort of funeral song, which he had sung around his death-bed, to hear its effect. Then, on his funeral day, a great storm arose, and only the undertaker and his men went to the cemetery when he was buried. He died so poor that his remains had to be put into a pauper's grave, where many other coffins lay. Nobody bothered with the grave for many years, and then it was found that nobody could point it out. So Mozart's monument in the great Vienna cemetery stands over an empty grave. It is pathetic to think of such an end of a great man.

There was another composer who went through very much the same sufferings, the same persecutions and fate as Mozart. His name was Franz Schubert. " My music is the product of my genius and my misery," Schubert said. It could hardly be otherwise. His people were poor, and he had eighteen brothers and sisters, from which we may judge that no special attention was given to his education and upbringing. But as truth will out, so will genius. Schubert entered upon music as a prince enters on his dominions. When they began to teach him they found that somehow he had learnt the rudiments for himself.

He began to compose at eleven, and consumed as much music-paper as would have made a small fortune for a stationer. He wrote all kinds of things at that time— overtures, symphonies, quartettes, operettas, Church music, piano music, and so on. But now we remember him almost solely for his songs and a few orchestral pieces. He is Germany's greatest classical song writer. He composed more than 500 songs.

SCHUBERT'S UNEARTHLY MUSIC OF THE ENCHANTED FOREST

One afternoon Schubert took up a volume of Goethe's works lying on his table. He read The Erl King. The rushing sound of the wind and the terrors of the enchanted forest were instantly changed for him into realities. Every line seemed to flow into strange, unearthly music as he read ; and, seizing a pen, Schubert dashed down the song nearly as we know it. He got a great singer to sing it, and then a Vienna music publisher, who had hitherto declined to have anything to do with his songs, asked for it.

He paid Schubert a very small sum, though in a few months the publisher made £80 out of it. That was the way with Schubert all along. Some of his finest songs were sold for the price of a meal. Grinding poverty, slights, insults, disappointments innumerable—that was Schubert's portion. He died in 1828, before he was quite 32, and they laid him to rest near Beethoven, at whose death-bed he had shed tears; and this inscription was put on his tomb: " Music buried here a rich possession and yet fairer hopes."

THE TWO MEN LISTENING TO THE BOMBARDMENT OF VIENNA

We have still to speak of Beethoven. Recall Haydn for a moment. When Haydn was dying in Vienna, in 1809, the French were bombarding the town. Haydn's servants were terrified, but Haydn took it all very calmly. He asked for the piano to be opened, and when this had been done, he played his own Austrian Hymn three times over, while the guns were thundering outside.

Now at that very moment there was another composer in Vienna, crouching in a cellar, with cotton-wool stuffed in his ears. That composer was the mighty Beethoven. His hearing had begun to go, and he was frightened that the sound of the explosions would still further endanger it. Think of a musician being *deaf!* You might as well think of a painter being blind ! Yet Beethoven, in some respects the greatest composer who ever lived, became almost totally deaf. The infliction embittered all his later years, and turned an originally lovable man into a kind of surly bear. He would throw the soup in his housekeeper's face when it did not please him, and rage and growl over most trivial annoyances. Let us be charitable to him; it must have been awful not to be able to hear his own compositions.

But Beethoven, apart from his deafness, had a very hard life. Born in 1770, at Bonn, that pretty little university town on the Rhine, where they have preserved his birthplace just as it was, he had to work his way up in a home directed by a father who was a drunkard.

THE YOUNGSTER WHO WAS TO MAKE A GREAT NAME IN THE WORLD

But the father was musical, and he set Ludwig to work at the piano, and visitors would often see the child late at night shedding tears over the keyboard. By and by he was sent to Vienna to complete his musical education.

Beethoven's works for the piano— particularly his sonatas—are the grandest things of their kind ever written. Most of the great pianists regard him as the king of composers for their instrument. And so, too, with the orchestra, for which he wrote those grand Nine Symphonies—the immortal nine as they are sometimes called. Apart from his wonderful Choral Symphony, the Ninth, he did not write very much for the voice, for he was essentially an instrumental composer; but he left one great opera, called Fidelio. He passed away in March 1827 and Vienna never before saw such a great funeral as his. The year before there had died his younger contemporary, Weber, composer of the great opera Der Freischütz.

FREDERIC CHOPIN, THE POLE, AND THE EVERLASTING MENDELSSOHN

There was another great composer for the piano, and he wrote the most beautiful things that we are ever likely to hear from that instrument. The name of this composer was Frederic Chopin, a Pole, born near Warsaw in 1809. For much of his music he was inspired by the national dances of his country, the polonaise and the mazurka. Yet neither the story of Poland nor this great national composer of hers would suggest gaiety.

The tragedy of his country combines with the sadness of his own life, dominated by illness, yet these things also encouraged intensity of feeling and this we find in the jewelled nocturnes and études. Such sharp emotions can only be expressed shortly and in these typical pieces Chopin soon says what he has to say and stops. But he leaves us to remember for long afterwards.

Another great composer who met him in 1834 was Mendelssohn, a German, born the same year as Chopin, who said of one of his pieces: " It is so perfectly beautiful that I could go on for ever playing it." One might say the same of several of Mendelssohn's own compositions. He was born to wealth and happy worldly circumstance, and never had to struggle with poverty.

So his music is bright and genial, clever and pure, manly and refined. His Songs Without Words are among the classics of the piano; and his oratorio Elijah ranks in popularity next to the Messiah. It was written specially for our Birmingham Musical Festival—for Mendelssohn had a great affection for the English people, and liked London better than Berlin or Leipzig. He had a short life, but his early death, in 1847, was hastened by grief at the loss of a favourite sister.

ROBERT SCHUMANN, THE TRAGIC GENIUS WHO COMPOSED IMMORTAL SONGS

Another short-lived genius was Robert Schumann, composer of immortal songs and of one of the best loved of piano concertos. Born at Zwickau, Saxony, in 1810, he was the son of a well-to-do publisher ; but there was a taint of insanity in the family. Schumann's sister died at 20 of an incurable melancholy; and Schumann himself spent his last years in an asylum.

We come to the great name of Richard Wagner. Musical people have been building up Wagner's fame in recent years, perhaps in return for the neglect he suffered during his life. He wrote little but those great musical dramas upon which he prided himself so much — Lohengrin, Tannhäuser, The Meistersingers, The Flying Dutchman, Tristan and Isolde, and the rest. He had an idea of his own about opera, and it was that the words are of equal importance with the music.

The older opera composers thought

THOMAS TALLIS LISTENS TO HIS CLEVER PUPIL

"Since singing is so good a thing, I wish all men would learn to sing," said good William Byrd.
Here we see him practising on his virginal, to the delight of his famous master, Thomas Tallis.

the music was everything, and the words of their operas were often silly to the verge of nonsense. Wagner changed all that. He was born at Leipzig, in 1813, and had a troubled career until the crazy King Ludwig of Bavaria, who happened not to be crazy where music was concerned, took him up and gave him money and a home.

From Wagner we may turn to that other immortal German who was born at Hamburg in the same year—Johannes Brahms. He was a great pianist and wrote much fine work for this instrument. He was also a prolific writer of songs, and reached supreme heights in his orchestral works.

As the 19th century progressed it produced musical kings at a rate never known before. Germany gave us Richard Strauss after the giant Brahms, followed by Humperdinck (with his charming Hansel and Gretel) and Mahler, great writer of symphonies.

THE GREAT FRENCH AND ITALIAN COMPOSERS OF OPERAS AND SONGS

France went steadily ahead in musical fame with Bizet and his ever-popular Carmen, a very French opera about Spain, and the delightful incidental music to the play, L'Arlésienne. Then came Saint-Saens (of the Carnival of Animals), Chabrier, Claude Debussy who caused such a stir with his six-tone scale, Gabriel Fauré of the lovely songs, and Maurice Ravel, whose Bolero must have been one of the most popular gramophone records of its time in this class of music. We can include here César Franck, a Belgian who spent most of his life in Paris; how many great violinists have delighted in his sonata in A?

First of the great Italians of the 19th century (though born in 1792) was Rossini, famous for his Barber of Seville and William Tell operas. Twenty-one years later Verdi was born. He was to give us the excitements of Rigoletto, Il Trovatore, and La Traviata, followed by Aida, written on an Egyptian story at the request of the Khedive and produced in Cairo in 1871.

Leoncavallo and Puccini were both born in the year 1858, the former achieving his first triumph in 1892 with Pagliacci. Puccini visited England in 1894 when his Manon Lescaut was produced at Covent Garden. La Bohème followed at Turin in 1896, and then Tosca at the turn of the

century, and Madame Butterfly in 1904. Slightly younger than either was the rather tragic Pietro Mascagni with one delirious success, Cavalleria Rusticana, followed by failure after failure.

COMPOSERS WHOSE MUSIC BREATHES THE SOUL OF THEIR COUNTRY

Russia reached world fame in music with Balakirev, founder of a great school of music, and his pupil Borodin whose Prince Igor comes so often over the air; also with Moussorgsky, Rimsky-Korsakov, that great master of melody Tchaikovsky, Glazounov, and the great pianist composer, Rachmaninoff.

The music of these great Russians breathes the very soul of their country, and so does that of the two Bohemians, Dvorak and Smetana, heroes of the Czechs. Scandinavia had her great national musicians, too, in Grieg, the Norwegian of Scottish descent; Sibelius, grand old man of the North; and his contemporary Palmgren who, like him, was a Finn of Swedish descent.

DAWN OF A NEW ERA IN BRITISH MUSIC

When we turn to our own land the musical horizon brightens as the century ends and passes into the twentieth. Fifty years ago the only English composer of whom many Continentals had ever heard was Sir Arthur Sullivan. Certainly he earned his fame, for never did composer more skilfully wed music to words.

When the B.B.C. began operations in the early 'twenties British music began to come into its own internationally. Millions could now experience the intensely English and deeply moving work of Elgar—the Dream of Gerontius, Enigma Variations, and the great violin concerto. There was Delius making a kind of musical lyric poetry out of the English countryside. It was Grieg, by the way, who persuaded Delius's father to let the young man study music. Gustave Holst fairly burst upon eager audiences with his invigorating " Planets," and the grandeurs of Vaughan Williams began to make their impression on a wide public.

It is because the kingdom of music has no limits that new kings can ever continue to arise, each bringing his own precious gifts. But old or new, the kings of music, in the words of Ben Jonson, are " not for an age, but for all time."

The Great Stories of the World That Will Be Told for Ever

BEAUTY AND THE BEAST

A RICH merchant had three daughters. The two elder ones were cross and ugly, but the youngest daughter was so sweet and lovely that she was called Beauty. But the day came when the merchant lost nearly all his money. He had to sell his grand house and go to live with his daughters in a little cottage. He was too poor to keep any servants, but Beauty willingly undertook all the work of the house, and even tried to find excuses for her lazy sisters when they stayed in bed till quite late in the morning and allowed their younger sister to wait on them all day long.

One day, while the merchant worked in his garden, a letter was handed to him. He opened it, and learned that if he could go to a distant town he would be able to obtain work. Overjoyed at his good fortune, the merchant embraced his daughters, and prepared to set out.

"What shall I bring you when I return?" he asked Beauty.

"I want a new dress!" cried both the elder daughters.

"I will bring you the best that I can afford," replied the merchant. "And you, Beauty, what would you have?"

Beauty knew that it pained her father to feel that he no longer had the means to buy costly presents for his children, so she said quietly: "A rose, father, just a beautiful rose, if you can find one," thinking that such a present would cost him nothing.

So the merchant set out, and, after travelling for a whole day, reached the town to which he was journeying, and received his orders. The following day he prepared to return, but he had not gone far when, to his dismay, he discovered that he had taken the wrong turning. He was in the midst of a huge forest, and knew it was very unlikely that he would meet anybody of whom he could inquire his way.

After searching in vain for the right path for many hours a terrible storm arose, and the merchant, in despair, climbed up into a tree in the hope of finding a light to guide him to some house. Sure enough, he saw a light, and, regaining the ground quickly, he leapt upon his horse and was soon before a magnificent castle.

For a moment he waited, but as nobody appeared he dismounted and strode up the steps. The house was brilliantly lighted from top to bottom, and on every side were signs of wealth and luxury.

The merchant passed through the great hall, blazing with lights, and found himself in a fine room. In the centre stood a table loaded with good things, and the merchant being very hungry, sat down and made a

IMAGINATION · CHIVALRY · LEGENDS · GOLDEN DEEDS · FAIRY TALES

good meal. When he had finished, he began to feel very sleepy. Opening a door at the end of the room, the merchant found himself in a comfortable bedroom. He got into bed, and soon fell asleep.

In the morning, to his intense astonishment, he found a new suit of clothes in the place where he had left his old ones. He thought this strange, but he put them on and went to the dining-room, where he found breakfast awaiting him.

When he had finished an excellent meal, he rose and wandered out into the garden. The flowers were magnificent, and the sight of a lovely rose tree reminded him of his youngest daughter's request. Stooping, he cut a lovely bud, and placed it in his coat. Just then he heard a noise, and, looking up, he found the ugliest man he had ever seen, for, though he had a man's body, the face was that of a beast.

The merchant shuddered.

" Ungrateful man! " roared the Beast. "Did I not feed you when you were hungry, and shelter you for the night? And yet you repay me by robbing me of my flowers. Ingratitude is a sin I cannot pardon; in an hour from this time you must die! "

" Forgive me, I pray you! " cried the merchant, falling on his knees. " I did but pick a rose for my daughter, and could I have found you sooner I would have thanked you for all your kindness."

After some pleading, the Beast consented to forgive the poor man if he would promise to send in his place the first living thing he saw on returning to his home; and the merchant, hoping that this would be his dog, who always ran to welcome his master long before anyone else had heard his footsteps, gladly promised, and departed.

To his horror, his first sight as he drew near the house was Beauty.

" Oh, what a beautiful rose! " she exclaimed, kissing him.

" Alas ! " replied the poor man sadly, " you little know how dear it has cost me." And, drawing her to him, he led her inside and told her the whole story.

" What you will do when I am gone, my poor children," he concluded, " I do not know."

" But you are not going," declared Beauty bravely, " for I shall go instead." And, in spite of everything that the merchant could say, Beauty insisted on having her own way.

And so the next day they both set out for the castle, where they found a splendid supper awaiting them. They sat down to eat, and had scarcely finished when the Beast appeared. He looked at Beauty and Beauty lifted her eyes and saw him. She shuddered and moved closer to her father. " What a dreadful man ! " she was thinking. " I do hope he will kill me quickly."

But the Beast did not want to kill one so lovely, and he told her father that if he would go home and leave her behind no harm should befall her.

So the merchant rode sadly away, and Beauty was left alone in the huge castle. The Beast scarcely went near her all day, and when night came he showed her a beautiful little room, which he told her was hers. Sure enough, on the door was written " Beauty's Room," and inside was everything she could wish for. That night Beauty dreamed that a fairy came to her and bade her be not afraid, for she was quite safe.

The next morning she rose early and wandered through the gardens, but not one single person did she see. When she felt hungry she went to the dining-room, where she met the Beast.

" Do you think me very ugly ? " asked the Beast.

" Well—yes," replied Beauty.

He spoke so gently that she felt quite sorry for him.

The Beast sighed and left her. The next day she met him again.

" Will you marry me, Beauty ? " said the Beast.

" Oh, no, no, no! " cried Beauty, for, much as she pitied him, she could not bear the thought of marrying him, and the Beast went away looking very unhappy.

Soon after this, Beauty looked into a magic glass, and saw that her father was very ill. The next time she met the Beast she begged to be allowed to visit her home.

" If you go away it will kill me," said the Beast ; " but rather than see you unhappy I would bear any pain. Go, but you must return in a week."

At parting, the Beast gave her a magic ring, which would take her home and bring her back again when she wished to return, and Beauty was very much surprised to find how sad the parting with the great, ugly creature made her.

AS BEAUTY SPOKE A WONDERFUL CHANGE CAME OVER THE BEAST

Her father was so rejoiced to see his daughter alive and well that he quickly recovered, and Beauty was so happy to be at home again that she forgot all about her promise to the Beast. The week slipped by, and then another, until one night Beauty dreamed that the Beast was dead. She burst into tears and awoke. She dressed quickly, and with the aid of her ring was soon back again in her little room in the palace.

She ran out into the gardens, and there, in a swoon, by the fountain lay the Beast. Beauty threw some water upon his face, and presently he recovered. When he saw her he smiled.

" I could not live without you," he said, "and so I tried to starve myself to death."

" Oh, you must not die ! " cried Beauty, wringing her hands. " I will marry you, dear Beast, for it is surely better to be kind than to have a handsome face."

As she spoke a wonderful change came over the Beast, and even as she looked the Beast was turned into a handsome prince, with whom she instantly fell in love.

Beauty was so astonished that she could scarcely believe her eyes. Taking her hand, the young man explained that a wicked fairy had cast over him a spell, which could not be removed till some gentle girl should promise to marry him, ugly as he was.

Beauty's father was overjoyed to hear the good news, but the disagreeable sisters were as jealous as they could be, and said such unkind things to Beauty at the wedding that the Prince turned them into statues, and placed one at each side of the palace gates, where they stand, still and cold, to this day.

THE HUNGRY FOX AND THE KITTEN

A VERY hungry fox was prowling one moonlit night about a farmhouse, and he met a little kitten.

" You're not much of a meal for a starving creature," he said. " But in these hard times something is always better than nothing."

" Oh, don't eat me ! " said the kitten. " I know where the farmer keeps his cheeses. Come with me and see."

She led him into the farmyard, where there was a deep well with two buckets.

" Now, look in here, and you will see these cheeses," she said.

The fox peered down the well, and saw the moon reflected in the water.

" This is the way down," said the kitten, jumping into the top bucket. Round and round rattled the rope-wheel, and down went the kitten into the water. Happily, she had gone down before, and she knew what to do, and, climbing out of the bucket, she clung on to the rope.

" Can't you bring up one of the cheeses ? " said the fox.

" No ; they are too heavy," said the kitten. " You must come down."

Now, the two buckets were connected, so that when one went down the other came up. As the fox was much heavier than his little companion his bucket went down and the water drowned him, while the kitten came up and escaped.

CUNNY RABBIT AND THE LION

CUNNY RABBIT was a little creature, but he was very shrewd. Even the lion was not a match for him. The lion stole a fawn from a gentle doe, and would not give it back. The doe appealed to all the great beasts for help, but they were afraid of the lion. Then she came to Cunny Rabbit, and Cunny Rabbit said : " Tell all the animals to meet in council tomorrow at my burrow."

In the meantime Cunny Rabbit dug a long underground passage from his burrow to an outlet behind a distant bush. The animals met in council and listened to the case, and they decided that the fawn was the child of the lion. None of them dared to speak the truth, because they saw that the lion was watching them with angry eyes. But Cunny Rabbit peeped out of his burrow, and boldly cried out:

" Nonsense ! The fawn belongs to the doe. The lion is a thief ! "

The lion sprang at him, but Cunny Rabbit darted down his passage and came out behind the bush, and escaped.

" I'll starve him out ! " roared the lion. He waited and waited till he grew thin and feeble, but still he would not give in, for he thought that if he went in search of food Cunny Rabbit would get away. So there he stayed till he starved to death, and the doe was able to recover her fawn.

ANDROCLES AND THE LION

ANDROCLES was a poor Roman slave who was carried away to Northern Africa many hundreds of years ago. His life was very hard and painful and his master was a very cruel man. At last he resolved that he would try to escape to the sea-coast and get back to Rome.

He knew that if he were caught he would be put to death; so he waited till the nights were dark and moonless, and he then crept out of his master's house and stole through the town, and got into the open country.

On and on he hastened through the darkness as fast as his legs would carry him. But when the day broke he found that, instead of making toward the sea-coast, he had struck into the great lonely desert. He was tired out, hungry, and thirsty, and seeing a cave in the side of some cliffs he crept into it, lay down, and very soon fell into a gentle sleep. Suddenly he was awakened by a terrible roaring, and, starting to his feet, he beheld a huge tawny lion. Androcles had been sleeping in its den. He could not escape; the great lion barred the way. Terror-stricken, he waited for the great beast to spring upon him.

But the lion did not move. It moaned and licked one of its paws, from which blood was flowing. Seeing that the animal was in great pain, Androcles forgot his terror and came forward, and the lion held up its paw, as if it were asking Androcles for help.

Androcles then perceived that a great thorn had got into the paw and cut it, and made it swell. He drew the thorn out with a quick movement, and then pressed the swelling and stopped the flow of blood.

Relieved of the pain, the grateful lion limped out of the cave, and in a few minutes it returned with a dead rabbit, which it laid beside Androcles. When the poor slave had cooked and eaten the rabbit, the lion led him to a place in the cliffs where there was a spring of fresh water gushing from the earth.

For three years the man and the lion lived in the cave. They hunted together and slept together, and the great, shaggy, affectionate creature used to lie down at night at Androcles' feet, and slowly wag his huge tail from side to side, as a cat does when it lies before the fire and feels happy and comfortable.

But at last Androcles began to weary for the society of his fellow-men. So he left the cave; but he was soon caught by some soldiers and sent as a fugitive slave to Rome. The ancient Romans were very cruel to runaway slaves, and they sentenced Androcles to be killed by wild beasts in the arena on the first public holiday.

ANDROCLES TAKING THE THORN FROM THE LION'S PAW

A vast multitude of spectators came to see the pitiful sight, and among them was the Emperor of Rome, who sat on a high seat above the arena, surrounded by his senators. Androcles was pushed into the great open space, and a lance was thrust into his hand. With this, he was told, he would have to defend himself against a powerful lion which had been kept for days without food to make it savage and fierce. So the poor man had little chance of surviving.

He trembled when the hungry lion sprang out of its cage with a terrible roar, and the lance shook in his feeble grasp as the huge beast came bounding up to him. But instead of rushing fiercely at him, and bearing him down, it wagged its tail and began to lick his hands. Androcles then saw that it was his own lion with whom he had lived in the cave, and he patted it and leaned on its head and cried.

All the spectators marvelled at the strange scene, and the emperor sent for Androcles, and asked him for an explanation of it. And he was so delighted with the wonderful story that he made Androcles a free man.

LITTLE STORIES FROM A BOOK THAT SHAKESPEARE READ

The most famous story-book of the Middle Ages was a book written in Latin called the Gesta Romanorum, which means the Exploits of the Romans. It was in this book that Chaucer, Shakespeare, and other famous poets found many of their plots; and we give here a few of these interesting stories.

THE DOGS THAT BECAME FRIENDS

THERE was a king who possessed two hounds, and these were kept chained up at some distance from one another. But directly they were let loose they flew at each other and began to fight fiercely. The king consulted one of his wise men as to what could be done to make the dogs live together as friends.

" Take them into the forest," said the wise man, " and when you see a fierce wolf, let one of the dogs loose. The wild animal will attack it. But just as it is being overcome, let loose the other dog, which will fly at the wolf, and the two dogs together will be more than a match for the wild animal."

The king did this. A wolf appeared, and one dog was let loose. When its strength had nearly failed the other was let loose, and very soon the fierce wolf was slain. The first dog was so grateful to its companion for saving its life that ever after the two animals were firm and faithful friends.

ALEXANDER AND THE PIRATE

A SEAMAN named Diomedes for a long time sailed the seas in a galley, attacking the shipping, plundering the cargoes, and sinking the vessels. At last he was captured and brought before Alexander the Great, who asked angrily how he dared to trouble the seas as he had done for so long.

" Sire," said Diomedes, " ask rather how you dare to trouble the earth. I am master of only a single galley, and do but little harm, while you are master of great fleets, and carry desolation and war. Yet I am called a robber, and you are a king and conqueror. Did fortune but change, and I become more successful while you became less successful, our positions might be reversed."

This argument so struck the king that he forgave the pirate and made him a wealthy prince, on condition that he should give up his life of robbery.

THE CONQUEROR'S TRIUMPH

A CERTAIN king, after a great victory, appointed three honours for his successful general. He decreed that the victor should be greeted with loud hurrahs, that he should enter the capital in a triumphal car drawn by four white horses, and that the captives should follow the conqueror's chariot, bound hand and foot.

The general was greatly delighted at hearing this. But when the time came for all his honours to be enjoyed he found that the emperor, to keep him humble amid success, had appointed also three annoyances to accompany the honours.

First of all, a slave rode by his side in the triumphal chariot, to remind him that even the poorest and least of mankind could attain to a position such as his; in the second place, the slave struck him a blow whenever the people cheered, so that his pride might be checked; and, in the third place, the people were allowed free licence to shout the most insulting remarks while the victor enjoyed his triumph, so that he might be reminded very plainly of his weak points.

THE GUESTS AT THE FEAST

A GREAT king made a feast, and invited everyone to it. He sent out messengers to all the cities and towns in his kingdom, asking the people to come, and promising not only food but wealth.

In one town there was a strong, robust man, who, unfortunately, was blind; and he loudly bemoaned the fact that his affliction would prevent his accepting the king's invitation. " Alas ! " he said, " is there anyone so unlucky as I ? Here is the chance of a lifetime, and because of my infirmity I am unable to take advantage of it." But presently he heard that in the same town was a lame man, who was also grieving that he would be unable to go to the feast.

The blind man and the lame man, therefore, came to an arrangement by which the blind man would carry the lame man to the feast, the lame man directing him. So the man who had sight but could not walk guided the man who could walk but could not see, and thus the two went together to the king's feast.

TRYING TO PLEASE EVERYBODY

A MAN who wanted to sell his donkey decided to take it to the nearest market town. So early one morning he set out for the town, accompanied by his son, and while the father rode upon the ass, the youth walked by his side.

Presently they passed three men going in the opposite direction.

"A nice father," said one of the men as he passed, "to ride while his poor son has to walk over the hard stones. He ought to walk himself and let his son ride."

Hearing this, the father dismounted and told his son to get upon the donkey's back. But they had not gone far when two women passed, and one remarked to the other:

"You ought to be ashamed of yourselves: two great, strapping men riding on one poor donkey!"

So father and son both dismounted, and allowed the donkey to search for thistles by the roadside, while they sat together on a bank and discussed how they could reach the town, which was not far distant, in such a way as not to displease any of the people whom they met on the road. At last a bright idea struck the son.

"Let us get a pole," said he, "and, tying the donkey's legs together, let us hang him on the pole and carry him to market. Perhaps that will please them."

"A good idea!" replied the father; so

THE FOOL WHO WOULD PLEASE EVERYBODY—BY BYAM SHAW
This picture is in the Laing Art Gallery, Newcastle-on-Tyne

other: "A fine son, that! Rides comfortably on the donkey, and makes his poor old father walk."

"It seems difficult to please people," said the father. "We had better both walk."

Just then some more people passed by and one said to another, in a loud voice:

"They seem to have little sense. Fancy walking when they have a fine strong beast like that! Why, it could easily carry both of them."

At this both the father and son mounted the donkey, and were getting along comfortably, when a man said:

they broke off the branch of a tree close by, slung the donkey across the bough and carried him to market that way.

When they reached the town the people roared with laughter, and the boys began to follow them, jeering and shouting:

"Look, here are two fools, carrying their donkey to market instead of letting their donkey carry them!"

"I'll tell you what it is, son," said the man. "By trying to please everybody we have pleased nobody. In future, we will just do what we think right, whatever other people may say."

THE SHEPHERD'S HOARD

Shah Abbas, king of Persia, having lost his way when hunting, saw a young shepherd playing the flute under a tree while his flock grazed on the mountain side.

The frank countenance of the young shepherd pleased him. He questioned him on various subjects, and the lively and accurate replies of this child of the open fields, who had grown up untaught among his flocks and herds, so delighted the monarch that he decided to take him to his Court and have him educated.

In this favourable soil the young shepherd grew up to be a man of merit, and the king gave him the name of Ali Bey and made him Grand Treasurer.

Ali Bey possessed every possible virtue. His conduct was irreproachable; absolute reliance could be placed on his fidelity and prudence in the exercise of his duties; he was generous toward strangers and benevolent towards supplicants ; and, though he was the king's favourite, he showed reserve and humility.

Yet his great worth did not make him safe from slanderous tongues, for the courtiers looked on his rise with envy.

They laid all sorts of snares in his path; they attempted to make the king suspicious of him. But Shah Abbas was no ordinary prince. His great soul knew no vile suspicion, and Ali Bey remained in peace and honour as long as his generous benefactor lived.

Unfortunately for Ali Bey, the great king died, and his successor, Shah Sefi, was a very different man. He was mistrustful, cruel, greedy; he seemed to take pleasure in the sight of blood.

Such a sovereign gave the enemies of Ali their opportunity. They heaped calumny upon calumny on the Grand Treasurer. At first the king paid little attention, but at last their chance came.

The king desired to see a precious sword which Shah Abbas had received as a present. This sword could not be found, and Shah Sefi suspected Ali Bey.

This was just what the courtiers wanted. They redoubled their insinuations, and depicted Ali Bey as the most infamous of embezzlers.

"He has built a multitude of houses to give lodging to strangers," said they. "He has spent great riches on other public buildings. He came to court without a penny, yet now he possesses un-

bounded wealth. Whence came all these valuables with which his house is filled if he does not rob the Royal Treasury? "

Ali Bey came into the king's presence at the very moment that his enemies were accusing him.

"Ali Bey," said the angry monarch, " thy infidelity is well known; I dismiss thee from my service, and I order thee to hand over thy accounts within 14 days."

"Lord," replied Ali Bey, " my life is in thy hands. I am ready, at this moment, to lay at the foot of thy throne the key of the Royal Treasury and all the marks of honour that thou hast conferred on me, if thou wilt deign to inspect the accounts in thy slave's presence."

This offer pleased the king. He accepted it and at once visited the Treasury. Everything was in perfect order, and Ali Bey convinced him that Shah Abbas had himself taken away the missing sword and had used the diamonds on it to decorate something else.

The king had nothing to say against these explanations. He therefore imagined some pretext for accompanying the Treasurer to his dwelling, so as to see for himself all the valuables of which his courtiers had spoken. But to his great surprise there too he found nothing to confirm his suspicions. He was about to leave when a courtier pointed out a heavy wooden door closed by two iron bars.

"What is there hidden behind these locks and bars? " asked the king.

Ali Bey seemed abashed but, recovering himself quickly, said : " Lord, in that little room I keep what I cherish most in all the world, my own property. Everything you have seen in this house belongs to the king, my master. What is in there is mine. It is a secret."

The suspicious monarch gave an order for the door to be opened. But all that could be seen was four naked walls, a shepherd's crook, a flute, a poor cloak, and a satchel ; such were the treasures shut up behind the locks and bars.

"O king," said Ali Bey, with the greatest modesty, " when the illustrious Abbas met me on the mountain where I was feeding my flocks these things were all my wealth. They are my only riches. Let me take them back to our peaceful valleys, where I was happier in my poverty than ever in thy opulent Court."

Nature's Wonderful Living Family in Earth and Air and Sea

THE ANIMALS MOST LIKE MEN

MAN sees a grim likeness to himself in the animals which rank next to him in the scale of life. They form the group of creatures called Primates—the apes, the baboons, the monkeys, and the lemurs.

In a sense they are our distant kindred. We are not descended from apes, nor are apes descended from men, but far, far back in time a common source of life gave rise to two new forms. One, with a soul and a mighty brain, learned to walk upright, to use the hands for work, and to become lord of creation ; the other retained its four-footed—or four-handed?— gait, kept to the trees, remained a pure animal, and came down to the present day as a wild caricature of ourselves.

Apes and monkeys have brains, but they are undeveloped, like those of the dawning mind of a human baby. But the difference from our own is in quality, not in kind. An ape appears to think as we think, though mistily ; its movements and actions are governed by the same area of the brain as human actions are. Bone for bone, muscle for muscle, with slight modifications, a man-like ape resembles ourselves. In shape, in looks, in hairiness, in life-habits, it reproduces before our eyes what science, as the result of long investigation, has built up as the picture of the earliest members of the human family.

The gorilla is the sovereign of the order, not by conquest, for gorillas do not come in contact with the others, but they come at the head of the order in bulk and power. They are peaceful giants, only roused to wrath if their homes are invaded. Then, although they flee if they can, they attack the boldest man, no matter how well armed he be, if their little ones are endangered. They are entirely confined to the dim forest lands of the western half of Equatorial Africa, and when civilisation reaches there the gorilla will vanish from the Book of Life.

For their lives cannot be lived away from trees. Enormous as is their size, six feet and upwards in height, with a weight far exceeding a man's, they are ideally suited for climbing about in the leafy roofs of their forest aisles. Each foot is a hand, and all are used in climbing ; the legs are short and sturdy, with the suggestion of a calf, the arms are so long that on the ground they serve as crutches. In the trees the giant beast goes with the ease and certainty of a huge squirrel.

It is so much like a nightmare vision of what a man might be that the gorilla is perhaps the most terrible of all things to look upon; yet when we come to know it, it is, in youth at any rate, as engaging as any creature living.

PREHISTORIC LIFE · MAMMALS · BIRDS · REPTILES · FISHES · INSECTS

No pet ever excelled the intelligence and gentle merriment of Johnny Gorilla, who lived for two years in London. Six or seven others in various stages of youth had died, all within a short time after their arrival at the Zoo, but Johnny was an exception. He was caught in the forest when about a day old, and was nursed by a native woman as if he had been human.

JOHNNY GORILLA AND HIS MERRY LIFE IN LONDON TOWN

He played with a kitten as a child does; he did all the usual monkey climbing; he romped like a child. When tickled he laughed tremendously, with a deep, hoarse chuckle : when annoyed he cried "Hock, hock." He drank six pints of milk and water a day, ate fruit of all sorts, was terribly afraid of worms or anything else that crawled, as if he had an instinctive recollection of snakes; and he would jump like a child if a leaf stirred, then tremblingly advance, pick it up with nervous, outstretched arm, and smell it.

Later, two young gorillas who became great favourites at the Zoo were Moina and Mok. Moina, the female was a mere baby weighing over seven stone when she arrived, and her companion was an infant of five stone! They lived happily together for several years until Mok died in 1938 and Moina in 1939.

Meanwhile, in the United States, Mrs Gertrude Davies Lintz was the first person in the world to bring up two gorillas from babyhood in her own house. Both were males called Massa and Buddy. Massa eventually went to the Philadelphia Zoo, and Buddy to a well-known circus to live in a specially-constructed roomy cage surrounded with glass to keep out germs. Before he left his well-loved mistress, Buddy weighed 33 stone 6 lb and stood head and shoulders above her. He was re-named Gargantua the Great and by the time he was over 39 stone he was reputed to be as strong as 20 men.

THE UGLY ORANG-UTANG WHO LIVES IN THE JUNGLES OF THE EAST INDIES

The orangs rank next in size to the gorillas, but whereas the giants are restricted to Africa, the orangs have their homes in Borneo and Sumatra. It is interesting to note that in the land of black men the skin of the gorilla is black, while the orang, whose home is where men are a reddish brown, is himself reddish brown. Terribly ugly, the orang has the great gaping mouth of its order, with a dismal bony ridge over the brow and an extraordinary bony development round the face.

Two fine orangs made history at the London Zoo. They were Jacob and Sandy. Jacob died in 1916 but his friend Sandy died of old age in 1924. These two apes were concerned in a famous breaking out. It began with Sandy, who, twisting off a piece of the stout wire of his cage, made it into a sort of chisel, then passed it through to Jacob, who was in the cage adjoining. Jacob improved on Sandy's plan, for, using the tool as a lever, he ripped open his wires and escaped into the ape-house. One night he broke through the roof of his den again, knocked out a window with a flower-pot, slipped through, descended into the ground, chose his tree, skipped up it, made a nest of broken twigs and lay down and slept like a king in a castle. The keepers got him home in the morning, and pretended to be cross with him. But they photographed the nest and wired it round as a great treasure—the first nest ever built by an ape in England, and the first positive proof that orangs do really make nests to lie on in the tree-tops.

THE CHIMPANZEE AT HOME IN THE GREAT AFRICAN FORESTS

Next in size to the orang-utang is the chimpanzee, at home in the forests of Equatorial Africa, but with a range extending farther east than the orang. Chimpanzees are heavily built, with massive arms and long, powerful hands and feet, but they are less formidable in teeth than the others, and, although grotesque and hideous, are really more like a caricature of a man than either of their relatives. A gorilla averages six feet, an orang about five, but the chimpanzee is usually smaller.

Studied at short range they seem much the same in temperament and characteristics as the orang, but, as they are hardier, they are better known, and therefore appear to eclipse the others as the authors and imitators of clever tricks. They can open doors, they learn to use cups and saucers, to eat and drink politely, to sweep out their cages, to distinguish between the sexes and show more deference to a lady than to a man. They learn to count a little, to master a bicycle and roller skates, to dress and undress. But while they are gentle and docile in their youth, they become uncertain and even dangerous to

THE ANIMALS NEXT TO MAN

ORANG UTANG

CHACMA BABOON

AN OLD GORILLA

ORANG UTANG

A BLACK APE

CHIMPANZEE

ANUBIS BABOON

YOUNG MONKEYS

A NISNAS MONKEY

WHITE-TAILED GUEREZA   COLOBUS ANGOLAN MONKEY   WHITE-COLLARED MANGABEY

The photographs on these pages are by Messrs. Gambier Bolton, D. Seth-Smith,
W. S. Berridge, T. A. Barns, W. P. Dando, C. Reid, and F. S. Bond.

22 F 1*

TWO BABY ORANG UTANGS SIT FOR THEIR PHOTOGRAPH

A BARBARY APE AND HER LITTLE ONE

A CAPPED LANGUR WITH HER YOUNG ONE

CHIMPANZEES IN PLAYFUL MOOD

THE PIG-TAILED MONKEY

JOHNNY GORILLA

MANDRILL

MACAQUE MONKEY

WANDEROO MONKEY

GALAGO

YELLOW BABOON

RHESUS MONKEY

A CHIMPANZEE TAKES A WALK

CAPUCHIN MONKEY

SLOW LORIS

A GIBBON

RING-TAILED LEMURS

human beings as they grow old. Extraordinarily long of arm and lissom of body, the gibbons come lowest in the scale of the man-like apes. Their brains are small and primitive, so naturally they are the least intelligent of the group; but they can be easily tamed, for they have brain enough readily to receive instruction and to perform wonderful feats of gymnastics. But that is a development of their natural excellence. Although they preserve a more upright, two-footed gait than the others, balancing themselves by carrying the long arms bent over the head, they are essentially creatures of the trees. They are not climbers so much as are the other three, but leapers, animals to whom a great range of forest trees is as a succession of horizontal bars to a gymnast.

THE GIBBONS THAT SWING THROUGH THE TREES BY LEAPS AND BOUNDS

They swing through a forest by leaps and bounds. Twenty feet, thirty feet, forty feet they leap. They clutch a bough with one hand, swing off and fly through the air, catch another bough forty feet away with the other hand, and then away again, hand after hand. There are nearly half a score species of gibbons, all natives of South-East Asia, and especially numerous in Malaya. To meet the lower four-handed folk—the monkeys, lemurs, and marmosets we must descend the scale. It is a great array of life, with scores of species in the Old World and the New, some of them up in the snow-laden trees of the Himalayas, most of them in the tropical forests, but one small tribe assistant guardians of the Rock of Gibraltar.

THE STORY OF THE TEN APES ON THE ROCK OF GIBRALTAR

They are called Barbary apes, but actually they are simply a species of macaque monkey. They are very interesting to us for several reasons. *They are the last monkeys at liberty in Europe.* Their ancestors thronged Britain in the old, old days before the North Sea made us an island and before the collapse of a land-bridge had cut Gibraltar off from Africa. These few on the Rock are the sole survivors in Europe of days that saw England, Europe, and North Africa all one.

These Gibraltar monkeys descend from those from which the Greeks studied anatomy. They once warned the British garrison of an attempt by the Spaniards to recapture Gibraltar. They shared the common lot in the smallpox outbreak of 1894, and were reduced in number to fifty. Alas, by 1920 they had become so numerous and so bold that they invaded houses and frightened women and children in bed; they stole; they destroyed roofs; and, worst of all, their habits fouled the garrison's supply of drinking water. So the military order was, " Let no more than ten Barbary apes survive upon Gibraltar."

Poor Barbary apes! But they abound in North Africa!

Now let us consider the monkeys in general, first distinguishing the Old World type from the New World type. The Old World species have the nostrils close together; they have food-pouches in the cheeks, and they never use the tail for anything but balancing. The American monkeys have the nostrils wide apart, have no cheek-pouches, and many of them use the tail as a grasping organ, for which purpose it serves as a fifth hand. General habits agree fairly well; a monkey is a monkey wherever you find him. Taking the average, they grow up in from five to six years, and are known to live as long as thirty years.

THE MONKEY THAT CO-OPERATES WITH MAN WHEN THE TIGER COMES

The eleven genera of the Old World monkeys have the Langurs at their head, a widely distributed group, especially famous in India, where one of the species, the Hanuman, named after an Indian god, is sacred to the Hindus, and therefore at liberty to pillage right and left. Its long age of security has made the Hanuman the tamest of free monkeys, and, alone of wild creatures, it seems to recognise Man as a friend in the forest, and to co-operate in giving him warning of the presence of the most dreaded enemy of both, the tiger.

It is known that there are many Pharaohs among the grown-up male Hanumans, and they hate and kill young males if they can. But the mother Hanuman takes her little monkey Moses off into the forest to nurse and hide him until he is big and strong and can go back and fight for life, and perhaps for leadership. If her baby is a female the mother remains safely with the troop; with a male baby she flees, and braves in solitude the terrors of tigers, snakes, leopards, and birds of prey, for her little one's sake. That is mother love in a dim-minded monkey!

We now come to the baboons, creatures with large dog-like heads and huge teeth, ranging many regions in Africa and Arabia. They are ferocious animals, yet capable of taming; and in the wilds they are masters of combination, mutual assistance, and unity in the face of a common foe. They combine to raise a rock which one cannot lift, in order to seek insects and reptiles for food beneath it. Retreating up a hillside from pursuit, they roll stones down at their foes, and at need a detachment will advance in good order to rescue an unfortunate comrade. They are hideous and savage, but have splendid qualities. The old Egyptians worshipped them as if they were gods.

QUEER LITTLE MEMBERS OF THE TEN BIG GROUPS OF AMERICAN MONKEYS

The American monkeys, all creatures of the hottest parts of the continent, abound in the forests of the Amazon and the Orinoco. They are all tree animals, and it is they who have made extra hands of their tails. Wonderful creatures many of them are, clinging, climbing by their tails, even employing them as fingers to pick leaves and other food. There are ten big groups of them. Some have faces like tiny aged men; among the squirrel monkeys we find little gems of pathos and comedy, which smile when they are pleased, shed tears when they are sad, and are all the while as mischievous as the tiny jolly baby children whom they resemble.

These are the midgets of the family; at the other extreme are the howlers, giants by comparison, 30 inches long, and with voices which can be heard for miles when a howler is really trying to howl. They have howled so long, so much, and so loudly that their throats have changed to enable them to do their vocal best.

THE BEGINNING OF THE HONOURABLE AND ANCIENT ORDER OF PRIMATES

Those delightful pets, the marmosets of South and Central America, are more like squirrels than monkeys; but they are nevertheless four-handed mammals. They have 32 teeth, as we have, whereas an American monkey has 36. They are ancient and primitive; they remain as a sort of living bridge to show how the monkeys crossed from a lower level of animal existence to the position they now occupy in the scale of creation.

Now we come deeper and deeper still, to the bed-rock of the order crowned by the inclusion of man; the lemurs! The order of Primates took its rise in the humble lemurs and their kin. More like little foxes, or squirrels, seem the lemurs today. Yet science fixes on these animals as descendants from that source which gave rise to every monkey and every man-like ape in existence. Their headquarters is Madagascar. They reached Madagascar when it was part of the African mainland. A land bridge sank, and Madagascar was an island, and to the lemurs it became what Australia has been to the kangaroo and their cousins. There, sheltered from the turmoil and striving which urged other animals along the strong current of Evolution in the outer world, they let time and transformation go by.

Infinite variety marks the forms and colours of the lemurs—some like weasels, some like mice, going to sleep during the hot months like a desert plant and waking with the rain; lemurs which are so meek and mild as to be called the gentle lemurs; and the extraordinary aye-aye. This has teeth like a rat or a rabbit and a unique skeleton-like middle finger with a hook-like claw, a wonderful modification enabling the animal to scratch out insects from their hiding-places in the bark of the trees which it explores by night.

THE GALAGO, THE LORIS, AND THE LITTLE TARSIER

On the African mainland is a well-known lemur called the galago, which has kept itself and its sluggish fight against evolutionary progress to the densest twilight forests. Seeking farther we find the lorises, whose habits suggest the beginning of sloth life; and at the end of the long procession come the tarsiers, with extraordinary little kangaroo-like hind legs, absurdly long feet and hands, and huge staring eyes. The tarsier leaps like a kangaroo, springing from bough to bough. A native of the Malay Archipelago and the Philippine Islands, it is rarely found.

This quaint little animal preserves in its body one of the forms into which life was moulded when the first experiments of Nature were begun with the newest and highest development of the greatest order then created ; when, out of the general body of mammals, the Primates were summoned into being, to yield tarsiers, lemurs, and apes, while, by a parallel ascent, man himself was painfully toiling upward to his kingdom.

The March of Man from the Age of Barbarism to the United Nations

MAN BUILDS HIMSELF A HOUSE

FOR hundreds of years after the discovery of his mind man remained in the animal stage.

Let us take a good look at him before we go on to the next step in his progress. He was a little creature, brown in colour, covered with hair, nimble rather than swift, wiry rather than strong. His forehead was low, his eyes sunken and bright, his chin heavy and underhung. There was something of the gloom of great, far-stretching forests in his face.

He wore no clothes. He knew no language. He had no conscience. His life was concerned with food. All his ingenuity was directed to outwitting his enemies. The thought of God never entered his mind. The idea of Right and Wrong had no existence for him. Like an animal, he regarded the Earth as a larder, and like an animal he spent his time in searching for food.

Because enemies were numerous in the jungle, many of them hunting in packs, man very seldom travelled alone. Thus it came about that great companies of these little brown people would leave the dark forest together and make their way with clubs and stones to the open country and to the distant hills. In the course of cen-

turies some of these hunting parties elected to live in the hills or on the banks of a river, making their dwellings in caves. Faith in their cunning, and an increasing knowledge of the Earth and its inhabitants, led the bolder of them to explore farther and farther afield, until at last the race of mankind was scattered over a considerable portion of the Earth's surface.

Then for some of these wanderers there happened a strange and alarming thing. They woke one night in their caves to find themselves shivering from head to foot. They went to the mouth of their caves and looked out. Nothing was to be seen there but a dense greyness. The Earth lay still; the Sun was yet hidden; and only a piercing coldness in the air told of something strange.

Day by day man looked at the sky. Where was the blue of the sky? Why did the Sun give no heat? How came it that the plants did not grow and the birds did not sing?

A woman picked up the skin of a dead animal and wrapped it round her babe, who was crying with cold. A new idea was born on the Earth. Clothing! An artificial skin! Henceforth to the food question must be added this new question of

MIGHTY EPOCHS OF THE WORLD & MAN'S WONDERFUL ADVENTURES

clothes. The animal man walked the Earth in the skin of an animal, looking for food and fur.

A great wind began to blow. The skies became like lead. Little specks of white blew across the world, like feathers. Some of the women said, " Let us go back to the forests." They set fire to logs of wood in their caves. It was possible to keep warm; but food? There was no fruit, no grain. The earth became like iron, and on this iron earth lay a covering of those white feathers from the sky, bright, crisp, and cold to the feet—cold and wet.

The days moved strangely in these regions. Man had discovered another climate. Winter came with a fury and a power which were sometimes terrifying. But spring returned, and summer followed spring, and for a little time before winter there was the berry-time of autumn.

MAN SETTLES DOWN TO FIGHT THROUGH THE DARK WINTER

So man established his confidence in Nature afresh, and settled down to outwit his enemies and to defeat the dark, unprofitable months of winter.

But out of his sight there was a mighty change going on in Nature—a grinding of vast masses of ice clotted together in huge and awful confusion at the Poles.

A day dawned when there would come to the ears of a few men who had long been watching strange movements of ice in the mountains, a noise of crashing thunder from the hills. The cold intensified. The air became like crystal. Some of the people picked up their children and their skins and ran in panic for the valley. " Let us get back to the forest," was their cry.

THE EXTRAORDINARY THINGS THAT HAPPENED IN THE ICE AGES

But some remained in the hills, and saw among their peaks one day a blaze of whiteness, hearing at the same moment a crash that sounded like the collapse of all the mountains. They knew no more. In the next instant they were swept away, they and their caves, their very hills and rivers, their valleys and their trees—swept away under a mighty avalanche.

Such events went on in the course of thousands of years, during which the Polar Ice cap spread farther and farther south, driving men and animals before it. Such, indeed, was the destruction of

glacial ages in the days before Man that the world itself was ploughed up into new shapes, whole continents plunged down into the depths of the sea, and new continents exposed from the depths of the Earth's interior.

The climate of the Earth was changed. Trees and plants appeared where they had never been before. Animals found themselves grazing on hills far across great oceans. Man appeared as a stranger in places where his ancestors had first learned to stand upright on their feet. And buried under the surface of the Earth were millions upon millions of creatures, among whom were multitudes of men, women, and children.

With this new birth of the world came a new birth in the mind of man. He ceased to be only a hungry animal in search of food. He became conscious of something in the world about him so much greater than himself that no cunning of his could outmatch its powers. He began to fear. The dark frightened him. A change in the weather terrified him. The sight of a dead person set him thinking.

WHO WAS BEHIND ALL THESE THINGS : THE SUN, THE MOON, AND THE WIND ?

Calamity had turned the observation of man from the Earth to the sky, and his thoughts from his stomach to the powers behind the universe. Heat and Cold! Light and Darkness! The Sun by day and the Moon by night! The Wind and the Rain! Who was it managed all these things? Who made them?

All religion has its foundation in fear, and all ritual in superstition. Glorious and sublime ideas were to come into the mind of man from religion, but its cradle was fear—a dim feeling in the human mind of powers greater than its own, controlling not only the Earth on which man hunted for food, but the sky which changed by day and night from light to darkness.

Picture to yourself this changed man on the changed Earth looking at the rising up of the Sun, watching the waves of the ocean breaking on the shore, and listening to the wind roaring through the forests. See what a gigantic change has overtaken him. He is no longer looking for bird or beast; he is no longer hungry. His mind fastens on the fact that

A BRITISH HOME BEFORE THE ENGLISH CAME

From the remains of an old British lake village discovered at Glastonbury, and from the things found there, an artist has been able to draw this picture, showing the inside of a British home 2000 years ago

things change. The mighty Sun rises, climbs the sky, and goes down over the sea, taking its heat away with it. The ocean is for ever moving—at times softly, but presently with majestic rage. The wind is gentle now, and now cruel with a suddenness which is terrifying. Why is all this? Who does it?

Speech becomes something more than grunts. Man goes to old grandfathers and asks them who made the world, and why things are always changing. The old men become conscious of a new power. They are no longer regarded as troublesome. They tell the young men stories of the past—of adventures in old huntings, and strange things seen in other lands.

The idea forms itself in the human mind that all round the human race are things which human eye cannot see. The tremendous division is made between the visible and the invisible, between appearance and reality, between humanity and the gods. Conduct becomes a master thought. How to act, so as not to offend these invisible gods? There is a line of conduct which is *right*, there is another which is *wrong*. Right becomes wisdom, and wrong dangerous. The mind of man addresses itself to this matter. He decides what is wise and what is dangerous. He makes altars, and he also makes laws.

MAN GOES ON LEARNING AND FEELING AND THINKING

Something else is born into the world, destined to merge into superstition and become one of the greatest powers in human life. Man has learned to sow his seeds in the earth, to plant his vines, to catch fish with a spear, to slay some animals with arrows, and to domesticate others. There is no longer the constant dread of hunger. He has time on his hands, those wonderful hands which can never be still. He scratches marks on bones, he shapes flints, he squeezes clay into imitations of living creatures, he carves pictures on stone. Art is born.

One day there comes to his land of plenty a host of men from the distant hills. They are tall, hard, fierce, with the look of eagles. They demand food. There is a quarrel. Blows are struck. Men fall dead. The hillmen retire with anger. They will return in thousands. War is born.

The mind of man is forced into a new channel. Safe from wild animals, he must now make himself safe from the attacks of his fellow-men. That simple mind of his, which had shared with other savage things the perils of forest life, which had learned to get food for its body with little labour, which had discovered how to placate the gods, which was beginning to study the stars, the seasons of the Earth, the movement of waters, and the habits of plants, must now turn its cleverness to a new difficulty. Politics is born.

MEN BEGIN TO WORK TOGETHER FOR THEIR COMMON GOOD

The tribe has hitherto been a body of people living together for safety, a vast hunting party united by the common danger from wild beasts, and also by its habits, its traditions, and its speech. But now something more is necessary. A thing is born in the tribe which takes away individual freedom. Discipline arrives, and Loyalty. One must do this, another must do that, for the good of the tribe. Parties must go together into the hills to spy out what those ferocious hillmen are doing behind their ramparts of stone. Boys must be taught to fight and to kill. Women must make wild music—not to frighten away wild animals, but to terrify the hillmen. New implements must be fashioned, and those who are cleverest at this work must do nothing else. The priests must find out new sacrifices to please the gods, so that the hillmen cannot conquer.

Notice in all this a strange blending of an idea which still governs the human mind —a strong sense of dependence on invisible powers coupled with a vigorous sense of personal self-reliance.

Finally, to part with the savage man, whose work will now merge into the yet unfinished work of civilised man, let us look at his last contribution to the progress of the human race. He builds a town.

TOWNS AND HOUSES TO HIDE IN, AND A WISE MAN OVER ALL

Neither the tree nor the cave can shelter him from those human vultures who swoop down upon his flocks and herds from the pinnacles of rock which pierce the blue sky. He must have ramparts in the valley, and behind those ramparts houses of mud into which his women and children can creep when the arrows fly and stones are whistling through the air. And over the life of the town there must be someone to rule. The wisest man is chosen.

(Next chapter in this group, page 297)

The Story of the Things We See About Us Every Day

Preparing the ground for the cotton seed in Egypt

THE FLOWER THAT CLOTHES US ALL

THERE is a little flower which clothes three-quarters of the human race. It is the cotton plant.

Nature fashioned it on the lines of the hollyhock. Its blooms of red, white, or yellow give place to a capsule of seed, the petals fall, the capsule breaks open, and discloses a mass of white, hairy down, and that is the cotton of commerce.

The energies of man are directed, first to enabling Nature to do her best with the plant and bloom; then to separating the down from the seed, then to getting it to the market and the mills, where the little white hairs are twisted and spun into continuous lengths, so providing the raw material from which all cotton goods are made by the weavers.

This important material in the clothing of civilised peoples had run wild for many an age before civilisation began to use it. Cotton was an article of manufacture in India when Alexander marched his army there over twenty centuries ago. It was awaiting white men in America. Columbus found it growing wild when he reached the West Indies; and the conquerors of Mexico marvelled to find the Aztecs arrayed in garments of cotton. Australia is now found to possess the same rich gift of Nature, for in the sparsely-populated Northern Territory the cotton plant blooms untended by man.

Of course there are many varieties. Cotton which thrives in India fails in America, and the best of American cotton has a struggle for mere existence in India. But, given a warm, humid climate, the cotton plant, of some species or other, flourishes under any sky.

Some of the best cotton grows in the land of the Pharaohs, along the strip of mud which the Nile throws out on each side to make a fertile Egypt. Farther south, away down through Africa, cotton is a native plant. Experience proves that the finest fibre comes from plants grown in lands where there is a long, genial summer, no matter how severe the winter. Great Britain cannot grow cotton; yet, though not a needleful rises from English soil, it is in England that the greatest quantity of manufactured cotton is produced. Every handful of cotton used for our manufactures comes from overseas, and the greater portion of all we make goes out to clothe people in climates warmer than that of the British Isles.

Nothing else that grows has influenced history as cotton has. More than almost any other thing it put England in the forefront of manufacturing races. For long

INDUSTRIES · HOW THINGS ARE MADE · WHERE THEY COME FROM

the cotton utilised was spun by hand, and trade in it was insignificant. But Hargreaves with his jenny, Arkwright with his water-frame, Crompton with his mule, Cartwright with his power loom, changed the whole character of the work and the financial position of the country.

Instead of working in cottages in the country, men, women, and children were gathered together in mills. That was the beginning of our factory system, and Lancashire was its centre.

Industries seem at a glance to spring up casually in certain areas and to avoid others without reason; but there is reason for the geography of cotton and wool and iron. The mills and factories are built on the verge of coal-fields which feed the boilers. But the special fitness of Lancashire is guaranteed by her climate. She lies westward of the Pennine hills, which convert Atlantic winds, heavy with moisture, into rain. Humidity is essential to cotton spinning, and the climate of Lancashire is ideal for this work.

Cotton is the source of our greatest wealth. English goods have rivals now in other countries, such as India, but the finest cotton goods in the world come into existence in Lancashire, which has the biggest output and the best that honest labour and skilful contrivance can furnish.

THE TERRIBLE DAYS OF THE LITTLE COTTON SLAVES OF ENGLAND

Yet there is a sordid chapter to be written in the history of cotton. Our factories, which made us among the wealthiest of nations, became the centre of tyrannous abuses of child labour. No industrial conditions have ever been more terrible than those in which little boys and girls, aged women, and ailing men toiled to found the fortunes of the pioneer manufacturers in Lancashire. They were a callous race, these builders-up of our factory system.

Our Factory Acts are a memorial to those whose hearts were touched by these cruelties, and today, though still far from ideal, a cotton mill is a model to the rest of the world. The health of the workers is now recognised as of greater importance than the profits of the owner of the mill.

But this wonderful product of a flower did not scourge England alone. It led, in the middle of last century, to the greatest war waged for two thousand years. Cotton endangered the liberties of millions of human beings in the Southern States of North America, which in spite of the ravages of the cotton boll weevil, is still the foremost cotton-yielding area in the world.

No Briton has any right to taunt the Southern States with their desire to make slavery permanent, for English ships took the slaves to America.

THE AFRICANS WHO WERE STOLEN AND SOLD FOR THE COTTON FIELDS

In the hundred years before the declaration of American Independence we carried to the United States three million stolen men and women, human beings caught like animals in Africa, and sold into bondage. About 300,000 died at sea in our horrible slave ships, and their bodies were flung into the Atlantic.

Gradually public opinion in America turned against this horrible system of slavery. For one thing, it did not pay. The broken-spirited Negroes were found hardly worth their keep in the cotton fields, for they cleaned only a few pounds of cotton a day. Emancipation was ready to be born, when an invention suddenly changed the whole situation.

Eli Whitney evolved a cotton-gin, a machine which automatically separated the cotton fibres from the seeds. At once every slave's value was increased enormously, for instead of a few pounds, he could now clean a thousand pounds a day.

The cotton-growing States determined to maintain slavery ; the non-growing States decided that they should not. The South declared its right to do business in its own way, and decided to break away from the Union; but the North refused to recognise this right.

COTTON NOW PICKED BY FREE MEN ALL THE WORLD OVER

So came about the American Civil War. The North fought for the preservation of the Union; the South fought for independence. Those were the battle-cries. But the liberty the South sought was the liberty to keep millions of Negroes in chains. It was a bitter war, lasting four years, causing terrible loss of life and property, and bringing Lancashire to starvation through want of cotton.

But Abraham Lincoln and the cause of righteousness prevailed. The enemies were reconciled, and today cotton is grown and picked by free men and women in America and all the world over.

COTTON BEGINS ITS GREAT CAREER

The U S A produces far more cotton than any other country. On the left we see cotton being picked by hand in Georgia. Very ingenious machinery, such as that on the right, is being widely used now.

Cotton is a hair covering the seeds. From the flower springs the boll, which, on ripening, bursts and displays the seeds and cotton. The destructive boll weevil threatens America's cotton supremacy.

The cotton, or lint, is separated from the seeds in the ginning machine shown here. American cotton yields on an average from 30 to 35 pounds of lint from 100 pounds of seed cotton.

The lint is packed into bales weighing about 500 pounds each, and then compressed for shipment abroad. The seeds are crushed and yield oil for making soap, margarine, and oil-cake for cattle.

CLEANING THE COTTON AT THE MILLS

At the mills spiked or fluted rollers tear the matted fibre apart and pass it forward in a flaky stream to an opener-machine which carries on the work of cleaning stray seeds, dirt, and so on from the cotton. Then the wide stream of fluffy cotton passes under rollers and goes forward to the scutcher.

The scutcher gives the cotton its final beating and, by means of air currents, its final cleaning. After that it is condensed into a broad sheet and rolled into a lap, which has been made of even thickness and weight per yard.

THE CYLINDER WITH FOUR MILLION TEETH

Good yarn is impossible unless carding is well done, on a machine like this. On a cylinder four million needle-pointed teeth tease out the lap fibres, making a fine veil. This passes through a condenser and thus is pressed into a riband.

Then the drawing-frame takes six ribands (slivers) and drafts them into one, doing this again and again until 216 slivers may be combined into one, every yard uniform in weight and thickness, with its fibres as parallel as skill can make them.

From the drawing-frame the cotton comes in cans to the flyer frame, and there begins the twisting of the cotton from a thick sliver to a fine thread. Passing between rollers the sliver is gradually drawn out thinner and thinner, being given a slight twist, and then wound on to bobbins.

MARVELLOUS WORK OF THE SPINNING MULE

The real process of spinning begins on a ring-spinning frame like that in our picture, in which the drafting, twisting, and winding of the yarn on to the tube is carried out at the same time.

The fineness of cotton is reckoned in figures. On the finest mules cotton up to 400's (equal to 336,000 yards or about 190 miles to the pound) can be spun on to spools, known as cops, without breakages. For experimental purposes a pound of cotton has been spun into 1000 miles of yarn, but cotton used for the finest goods averages about 95 miles a pound. Such is the marvellous work of the mule, which may be 120 feet long with 1300 spindles, each spinning 64 inches of thread in about 15 seconds.

THE THREAD IS MADE READY FOR WEAVING

After spinning, the threads are prepared for the weaver. Here we see the coning machine, which clears the threads of faults and winds many miles of warping, or lengthwise thread, onto each cone.

These high-speed beamers (or warpers) gather together as many as 600 threads in a running length of up to 24,000 yards, and wind them onto the beam in preparation for sizing.

STREETS OF LOOMS IN A WEAVING SHED

Each branch of the textile industry has its own type of loom, but the calico, or ordinary Lancashire, loom is that in widest use. In weaving sheds sometimes thousands of looms are at work together with deafening roar. As dryness weakens the threads, which might then break, all sheds are kept moist.

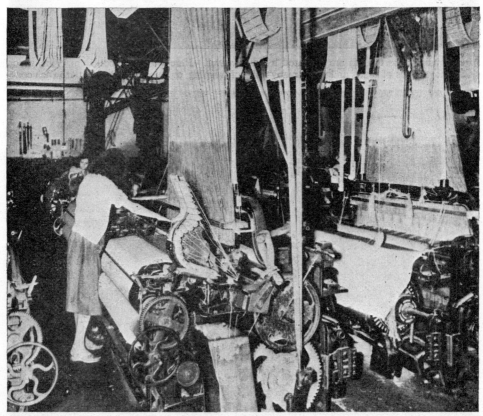

On the Jacquard loom beautiful patterns in stripes and checks can be woven, and the border and centre designs for quilts or tablecloths. The perforated card at the top of the picture is punched with holes corresponding to the pattern, and these allow the loom needles to penetrate when so required.

Many of the pictures in these pages were taken at Horrockses' Mills at Preston

PICTURE-STORY OF A PIECE OF ROPE

Rope is made of fibres from several sources—manila hemp, sisal hemp, cotton, coconut husk, and synthetic yarns; indeed, some of the strongest rope is made from nylon. In these pictures we see how rope is produced from manila hemp, the material most commonly used.

Manila hemp, made from the leaf-stalks of a plantain growing in the Philippine Islands, is the finest fibre for rope-making. It has great strength and flexibility, and when tarred, does not deteriorate in sea-water.

The tree is cut down close to the root and the leaves are cut off. The fibrous coat is then stripped from the stem and split into narrow lengths. Here we see these lengths being treated on a stripping-spindle, which leaves the coarse fibres.

The fibres are then washed and sun-cured on rails in the open, as seen here. They are afterwards graded for quality before being taken to the baling press to be packed for export. It takes two men a day to prepare 25 pounds of hemp, and to produce a ton of hemp the stems of over 3000 trees are required.

MACHINES THAT COMB THE FIBRES

After mixing different grades of fibre for the various qualities of rope, bundles of fibre of fixed lengths are fed on to a machine called a spreadboard. This combs the fibres until they are all lying in one direction in a continuous ribbon known as sliver. In this picture the women in the background are feeding the bundles of fibre on to the spreadboard, while the girl on the left waits to remove the large coil of sliver.

The sliver is passed to a series of drawing frames, each of which combs the fibre with successively finer steel pins. This process draws the sliver into an even narrower ribbon that is fine enough for spinning into rope yarn. This thin ribbon of fibre is then fed from the drawing frames into the rotating cans seen here.

SPINNING THE YARN FOR STRAND FORMING

An overhead conveyer system carries the cans of ribbon to gillspinners, where it is spun into yarn. In this general view of a yarn-spinning mill, the gillspinners are on the left and extreme right. From these the bobbins of yarn are taken to the machines seen on the right centre of the picture, which wind the yarn for strand forming.

A number of yarns, depending on the size of rope required, are next formed into strands, either on a rope-walk or on a machine like that in this picture. Here we see how the strands are formed by a strand-forming machine. The bobbins are seen on the left, with the yarn running into the strand formers and from there on to laying machines, which twist the strands into the finished rope on great spools as seen in the background.

28 G 1

STRANDS THAT TRAVEL A QUARTER OF A MILE

Here is a rope-walk, which works on the same principle as the strand-forming machine, the yarns passing through register plates to form the strands. The rope-walk travelling-machine, seen at the top of the picture, hauls out the strands for most a quarter of a mile. A second car then returns along the rope-walk twisting the strands together.

The finished product in this picture is a nine-strand rope, 20 inches in circumference, and 720 feet long. It weighs about three-and-a-half tons.

The photographs in these pages are reproduced by courtesy of The Gourock Ropework Company Limited

Plain Answers to the Questions of the Children of the World

The fire dies down in the cottage.   From the Painting by Walter Langley, R.I.

WHY DOES THE FIRE GO OUT?

A FIRE will go out if the supply of air or oxygen to it is stopped, or made so scanty that burning goes on very slowly, and so does not produce enough heat to keep the coal, or whatever is burning, at the temperature at which it is capable of combining with oxygen.

Oxygen is not always necessary for a material to burn. A piece of paper saturated with turpentine will burst into flame if it is plunged into a jar of chlorine gas. A fire will *go out* if there is not enough of the element it combines with to support combustion. Combustion is really a chemical combination which is accompanied by sufficient heat to cause flame.

When a fire goes out in the ordinary way there is often plenty of burnable stuff left in the grate. But there is not a good enough draught up the chimney, and the air of the room is not getting to the unburnt coal of the fire quickly enough. Perhaps there are many ashes in the grate, choking up the spaces between the bars, and the air cannot get to the coal. So the fire dies of suffocation; it cannot get air. If we clear away the ashes the fire goes on burning as long as there is anything combustible left. Ash itself cannot be burned any more.

A thing may be hot either because it is burning, or for some other reason. The fire is hot *because* it is burning, and gives

out heat and light. The filament in an electric lamp gives out heat and light *because* it is hot, but it is hot not because it is burning, but because it is made hot by electricity passing through it. The Sun gives out heat and light because it is hot, but the Sun is not burning. The Sun is actually so hot that oxygen cannot combine with the other elements in it.

Similarly, the centre of the Earth gives out a great quantity of heat; but it is unlike a fire in that it is not burning any more than the Sun is, or the filament in the electric lamp.

We say that the Sun and the inside of the Earth are glowing though they are not burning. The current through an electric lamp makes the filament glow though it does not burn. It would burn if there was any oxygen in the bulb, but every trace of air (a mixture of nitrogen and oxygen) is removed from the globe before it is sealed up, in what is almost a vacuum.

A fire and many other things glow when they burn because the burning makes the things so hot that they glow. Any kind of matter that is made hot enough will glow ; that is to say, will give out light and heat. The proper way of describing this condition of matter now is to say that it will radiate, or give off rays of light and heat. This is called " incandescence."

SUN · MOON · STARS · FIRE · WIND · WATER · LIFE · MIND · SLEEP

What Makes the Wind Whistle?

The howling and whistling and all the other noises made by the wind are not so easily noticed by us when we are out of doors, as when we are in a house. As the moving air forces itself through chinks of doors and windows, or perhaps even down the chimney, and so on, it sets all sorts of things that it meets vibrating or trembling, and so produces all kinds of sounds, and these are often almost musical. Often people are very much frightened by these noises, yet if they went out of doors into the wind itself they would not hear them. The wind, or current of air, does not make itself known to us in sound because what our ears can hear is not a current, but a wave in the air. You cannot hear a draught.

Is There Colour in the Sea?

Land animals and land plants are of all the colours of the rainbow, from the red plant of Arctic snow, to the peacock's gorgeous tail, from the yellow buttercup to the golden humming bird.

In the sea, too, life decks itself in rainbow colours. There we find meadows of green, and blue, and red algae; there we find blue flying fish, rosy sea-anemones, and red coral, and iridescent mackerel. In fact there is hardly a colour on land that cannot be matched in the sea.

But down into the depths of the sea the colour of life goes, as the sunlight goes. More than 3000 feet deep photographic plates bring back impressions, and so violet and ultra-violet rays must penetrate there, though most of the rays of light do not penetrate to half that depth. The Swiss naturalist, Hermann Fol, making investigations in a diving-suit near Nice, noticed that even at a depth of 30 feet red things looked black, showing that the red rays did not reach so far. It is pretty certain that below 1500 or 1700 feet no colour—unless violet—can be seen by the light of the sun; and below that depth all fishes are brown, or black, or violet-black. The last bright colour to disappear is red, and where the red ceases violet-black begins.

Even in the depth of the sea, however, there is light of a kind, for many of the deep sea fishes carry lanterns; at least, they have phosphorescent spots and organs that light up the darkness. One fish of this kind is named the midshipman, because it has a row of luminous spots on it like the gilt buttons of a midshipman.

If a man went down to the depth of the ocean and looked around he would find himself in a darkness lit only as by stars, and by the light of the stars he would see only violet and black fishes. Besides fishes there are numerous sea creatures, such as squids and bacteria which are luminous, so that the depths of the sea are never without some light.

Why Cannot Fishes Live on Land?

The answer to this is curious. Every living thing must have air or die. The fish comes out of the water, where there is very little air, into the air itself, and there it dies for lack of air. It is drowned on land for lack of air, and dies of what is called suffocation, just as you or I would be drowned in the water.

But why cannot the fish help itself to the air around it when it is put on earth? Why should it starve in the midst of plenty, like a rich man who has something the matter inside him? The reason is that in order to breathe air you must have lungs, or something like lungs, and the fish has none; while in order to get the air which is dissolved in water, which the fish does, you must have something quite different from lungs, which are called gills. The fish has no lungs, but only gills. We have no gills, but only lungs. Therefore, we die in the water and the fish dies out of it. If an animal had both gills and lungs, then it would be able to get air from the air or to get the air which is in the water, as it pleased; and it could live both on the land and in the sea.

Can a Fish See and Hear Us?

If we go to an aquarium, such as the one at the London Zoo, we shall see for ourselves that fishes can see us, and see very well and quickly, too. Every fisherman knows this. He knows, too, that fish are very particular about colour, and that they catch things by sight as well as by smell ; for a fisherman's flies are not scented, but coloured, and the fish come to them very readily if they are of the right kind. Then we all know that fishes have eyes, for we have all seen them, and they are quite highly developed eyes. But fishes are decidedly inferior to us in hearing ; though they are by no means deaf, they do not respond to music as they seem to respond to colour.

Very few of the fishes in these pages have popular names, and the long Latin names, intelligible only to a few people, are not given. The fishes are chosen as among the best examples of colour in the sea, and their gorgeous colouring is part of the idea of mimicry that runs through Nature—the idea of making creatures invisible to their enemies or attractive to their mates.

FISHES SWIMMING IN FOREIGN SEAS

DAZZLING COLOURS OF THE TENANTS OF THE WATERS

LIVING COLOURS IN THE OCEAN

What is the Loofah We Use in the Bath ?

The loofah looks like a stiff, fibrous piece of netting, and because it is tough, not brittle, it makes a capital thing to use for a good brisk rub when we are bathing. But it is not made by hands. It is the fruit of a plant, and belongs to the same family as the cucumber. The cucumber is not fibrous, or we could not eat it, and the loofah, or luffa, differs from it in this respect.

Of course the loofah is not, in its natural state, like the loofah of the bathroom. The loofah that we use is simply the fibrous skeleton of the cucumber, or gourd, that grew in Egypt. After the fruit has ripened it is dried, and the fleshy part disappears, leaving only the fibres, and these are so strong, and stand the action of water so well, that a loofah lasts quite a long time. There are about ten species of loofah, and one sort, grown in the West Indies, is used as a sponge.

Why Do We Cook Our Food ?

There are many good reasons why we should cook certain kinds of food. Perhaps the best is that cooking makes it softer and loosens it, so as to help our teeth. This is especially true in the case of meat.

Another good reason for cooking food is that the cooking kills any microbes which may be in it, and some of these might do us a great deal of harm. It is certainly much better to boil, or cook, our milk, unless we are very sure where it comes from, and a great deal of the food that we eat now, especially in some cities, would certainly hurt us, by means of the microbes in it, if it were not cooked.

A third reason why we cook food is in order to make it look nice. This is especially true of meat. We have grown to dislike the look of red meat, and we prefer it cooked, so that the red colour of the blood in it is changed.

Why Have We Lines On Our Hands ?

Some people have said that the use of these lines is to give us a better hold on things, but probably that is not their real use. If it were so we should really have to say that they were scarcely worth having. It is much more likely that the use of these lines is to help the sense of touch in our hands and fingers, where touch is so very important. By making little valleys and ridges they increase the surface of the skin, and by going in different directions they help us to feel the kind of surface that anything has which we touch. The little endings of the nerves of touch are placed to the greatest advantage by means of these lines, and that seems to be the reason why they are so very well marked on just those parts of the skin where delicacy of touch is most important. It is nonsense, of course, to say that our characters can be read from these lines. The crease in a man's trousers shows much more of his character than the creases in his hands.

Why Does Not Oil Mix With Water ?

When two lots of liquid, added together, mix perfectly, it is because the molecules that make up the one liquid are just as ready to link on with the molecules of the other liquid as with each other. The most perfect case is, of course, when the two liquids are the same, as when water is added to water, and the next most perfect case is where the liquids are very similar, so far as the linkage of their molecules is concerned, as when water and alcohol are mixed. But when oil and water are added to each other, we have two liquids which are made of very different kinds of molecules. The molecules of water are very small, and those of oil are enormous—made of great numbers of atoms, instead of only three apiece, as water is. And the large molecules of oil find it very much more natural and easy to link with each other than with the molecules of water, and the molecules of water find it very much more natural and easy to link with each other than with the molecules of oil, so that as a visible result of these invisible causes the oil and the water keep apart.

What Does Eureka Mean ?

This famous word means " I have found it," and the story goes that it was used by one of the greatest philosophers of antiquity, Archimedes, who lived in the city of Syracuse, in Sicily. The king's crown had been in the hands of the goldsmith, who was suspected of having replaced some of the gold by some other metal ; and Archimedes was set the task of finding whether this was so. He did it by putting the crown into his bath, and noticing how much the water rose ; and he is said to have run out into the streets shouting " Eureka ! Eureka ! "

And now, when we have found out something we have been searching for, we sometimes repeat his famous exclamation.

Why is a Raindrop Round?

Why does rain form drops at all? We know now that there is always something which we may call a speck of solid stuff in the inside of a raindrop, and when the drop was made it was made by the water-gas or water-vapour in the air turning liquid upon this solid speck, as steam from boiling water turns liquid on a cold plate held above it.

But you want to know why, when it is formed, a raindrop is so nearly round. The answer is the same as the answer to the question why water forms in round drops on a plate, and the question why it runs in drops down the window-pane when it rains. When water turns liquid it really consists of a kind of crowd of tiny parts, each of which is itself a part, or particle, as we say, of water, just as a human crowd is made of men and women.

Now, these little particles of water behave rather as a crowd might behave, if all the men and women making it were to catch hold of each other's hands, so that they were all joined together. If they all held on to each other as tightly as they could, and especially if all the people on the outside of the crowd held each other's hands so as to make a ring, then that crowd would be something like the crowd of particles of water that make up a drop of water. They all prefer to hold on to each other, and stick together, and that is why the drop is formed.

Why Does a Bee Sting?

The use of the bee's sting is exactly the same, in its own way, as the use of the nettle's stinging hairs. The sting is really a fine, sharp, barbed tube, through which a drop of poisonous stuff can be sent when the bee stings. It is the worker-bees that sting—those that do the work of the hive. The case of wasps is the same.

Usually bees or wasps sting only once, for the barb, which is such a nuisance to us when we are stung, prevents the sting from being quickly withdrawn. What generally happens is that a person stung instantly knocks the offending insect away, tearing the sting from its body before the wasp or bee had time to withdraw it naturally; and the insect is so injured that it dies. Thus it is true to say that a wasp or a bee

can sting as often as we let it, but in practice we stop it by dragging out its sting and so killing it.

The stings of bees and wasps were not originally weapons of warfare. Originally they were ovipositors, or instruments connected with the laying of eggs; and only in the course of time have they become poison needles. Indeed, there are some bees in which the apparatus is quite useless for stinging purposes.

Only very rarely do bees attack anyone, unless they have received provocation. As a rule, they sting only when people try to kill them or drive them away, when they get alarmed and use in self-defence the weapons Nature has given them.

What Holds the Stars in Their Place?

This is a question that thinking people have been asking for many ages, and you are quite right to ask it, but the answer is that the question is not really a correct one. The stars are not kept in position, but are all in movement, and sometimes the stars *do* fall on to one another, we now believe. The stars are so distant that although they are moving quite fast there is no noticeable change in their position in the sky for many centuries.

No one has any idea at all how this process started, nor what the results of it will be, but at any rate we are quite certain that there is no such thing as what for so long has been called a fixed star, anywhere. It is now generally believed that there is a centre about which all the stars move round rather like planets around the sun.

Where Does the Water Go at Low Tide?

The shortest answer to this would be that, at low tide, the water goes to the places where it is high tide. As the Earth spins, under the pull of the Moon and the Sun, the water is always being moved about. Of course, it is always somewhere, and if it is not in one place, it must be in another. When it is pulled to one part of the Earth and heaped up there, that makes high tide.

As we watch the tide rising, what we see is the water being heaped up in our neighbourhood, mainly under the influence of the Moon. But if it is heaped up there, it is being drawn away from somewhere else, and that somewhere else is the place where the tide is ebbing. No tide rises but some other tide falls.

The Story of the Beautiful Things in the Treasure-House of the World

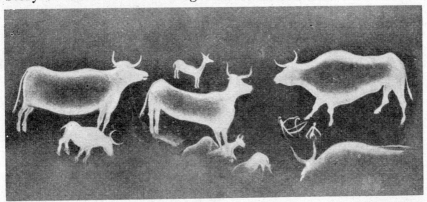

THE CAVE MEN AND THEIR PICTURES

THE story of art begins with a kind of fairy tale so wonderful we can scarcely believe it. Like all fairy tales, its first words are *once upon a time*, and the opening paragraph takes us back at a stride to the Long, long ago.

We cannot at first realise what this Long, long ago means. We think of the period of ancient Greece, but our story lies in the dawn of a much remoter day. We think then of the dynasties of early Egypt, and say there can surely be nothing older; but the tale is about some people who lived and made beautiful pictures thousands of years before the Pharaohs set up their huge, fantastic statues.

When we have allowed ourselves to be carried back to this Long, long ago, we look for the place of our fairy story, and we find it, not a historic temple, hill, or in the sunlit ruins of great Asiatic cities, but hidden underground, in the half-light of the caves of Europe.

We have been so used to thinking that the oldest of all artists lived in the far-off East, that it is very thrilling to realise they are our own millionth great-grandfathers, and that their art belongs to the Western Continent. Also, until about eighty years ago, nothing was known or guessed of these age-long treasures.

The most wonderful was found quite by accident in the year 1868 by a hunter who fell down through some brushwood into a deep hole that led to a long, underground cavern. So that this incredibly old art is new, and is more truly concerned with hidden treasure than any story that a novelist has ever written.

In order to get to the beginning of the tale we have to go farther back than even the pictures themselves.

Geologists have divided the history of the Earth's development into four great periods and, during the last of these, Europe and North America were held in the grip of an intense Arctic cold. From the heights of Europe grew great glaciers, and compared with them the Swiss glaciers of today are like snow hills down which children slide in winter time.

Before this bitter cold had seized the world, and in between the various epochs of the Glacier Age, the primitive tribes of Europe had been basking in a long summer, living an indolent, semi-tropical life, their food chiefly fruits and berries which were easily gathered. The Mediterranean Sea was so shallow that land bridges were possible, and men and animals trekked across into Europe from Africa and Asia. When Europe slowly cooled to the

PICTURES · STATUES · CARVINGS · BUILDINGS · IVORIES · CRAFTS

PICTURES FROM THE WORLD'S FIRST GALLERIES

THE WILD BOAR

AN OX

AN ELEPHANT FEEDING

MAN ATTACKING A STAG

A COMICAL FIGURE

THE MAMMOTH

A REINDEER RUNNING

QUAINT GROUP OF FIGURES OF THE STONE AGE

LIVELY PICTURES DRAWN BY CAVE MEN

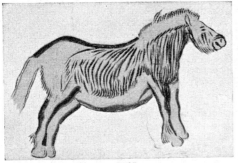

A HORSE

A BISON

AN ODD PROCESSION OF HUMAN AND ANIMAL FIGURES

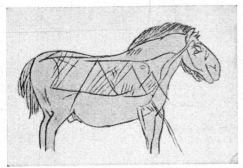

A PICTURE ON A PICTURE

A BEAR

THE WAR MEN OF THE STONE AGE

temperature of an ice-house, these earliest of all men found that life had become very hard. Their food disappeared, and they must either find new sustenance or die. They turned for the means of life to the flesh of animals, and this hard necessity made of them the greatest race of hunters the world has ever known.

THE AGE OF DARKNESS WHICH WENT BEFORE THE DAWN OF HISTORY

They had only one weapon—a flint knife or dart. A perfect specimen of this implement was found, together with an elephant's tooth, in central London at the end of the 17th century, and this historic treasure was kept and vaguely described as a British weapon. Not till over a hundred years later did scientists learn that the stone dart belonged to an incredibly remote age of the world—that it was used by primitive man in the darkness which preceded the dawn of history.

We can go to the British Museum and see this ourselves, the weapon with which our millionth great-grandfathers faced and slew mighty beasts. Because of their skill in hunting, the men who lived in Europe during the Glacier Age are often called reindeer hunters, and because the only tools they knew were flint, their period is known as the Stone Age.

The Stone Age, however, merely marks off a stage of human culture, and has nothing to do with measurements of time. The Stone Age lasted for thousands and thousands of years ; there are parts of the world where it has not long been dead, or even where it still is; for all the continents did not grow up at the same rate ; its most ancient home is in Europe.

THE STRANGE LOVE OF BEAUTY THAT CAME TO THE RACE OF HUNTERS

The reindeer hunters were driven to take shelter in caves—very often rocky holes which had been bears' dens—and to keep themselves alive dressed in the skins of the beasts they slew. Arctic animals—the reindeer, musk sheep, mammoth—roved over the frozen fields where formerly the hippopotamus, the African lion and elephant, the hyena and tiger had basked in the sun. As centuries passed by, the reindeer hunters made a kind of rude civilisation of their own. They developed their knowledge of the use of flint instruments, had factories for their manufacture; had cook-houses, and knew something of domestic management in their caves ;

their dead were buried with peculiar and mysterious rites.

And there grew up in the minds of this race of hard, cruel hunters a strange love of beauty and decoration. It was as if their souls, struggling for expression, turned to Art. We have no knowledge of their speech ; they had not developed the first coarse signs which are the beginnings of an alphabet; they knew nothing of spinning or weaving or making pottery.

Of the branches of elementary knowledge which underlie our present civilisation they were as ignorant as the Arctic fox or the prairie buffalo today. They were very much like animals themselves, rough, ugly, hairy beings with enormous jaws and small skulls. Their whole scheme of life centred round their hunting—the finding of food and skins for clothing, and their thoughts were continually on the animal world around them. We may be quite sure that they had more knowledge of Nature in their queerly-shaped little heads than ever we shall be able to acquire, and they drew animals which show us how marvellously accurate were their observations.

THE MEN WITH FLINT KNIVES WHO WERE REALLY GREATER THAN RAPHAEL

The early drawings, it is true, are crude, and in some cases almost unintelligible. Many are in part undecipherable, for the natural reason that they have lain for thousands of years deep down in the earth. In order to find them, archaeologists have to dig first through depths of the deposits of many ages, and then remove stalactites—which we know take an incredibly long time to form—before they can touch the original cave wall or ceiling where the pictures are.

Not all of the hundreds which have been discovered are worthy of mention, but there are among them some amazingly beautiful drawings. And the men who made them were far greater in their day than Raphael in his, because Raphael was the child of a civilisation that was already old, his tools and medium were ready to hand, the traditions of art established. These reindeer hunters were the heirs of nothing but brute life and naked instincts.

Most of the work of the Cave Men was a kind of rude engraving, done with the flint knife. Before they reached the stage of making frescoes on their walls, they tried their hand on all the small properties of their daily life—the bones, tusks, teeth,

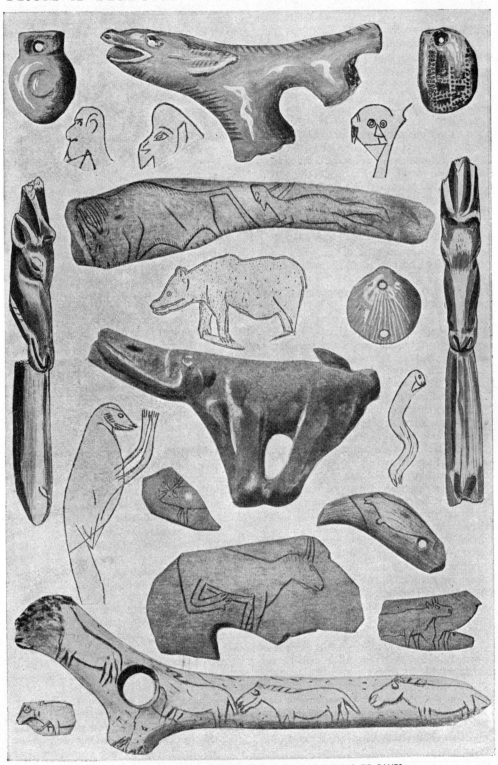

DRAWINGS OF THE CAVE MEN ON BONES AND WALLS OF CAVES

horns of the animals they slew. They made ornaments of perforated shells, horn needles, tiny plaques of schist, ear pendants of various material. For wood they apparently had a slight scorn.

As their civilisation progressed, they learned to make daggers of horn to supplement the stone dart. These were set in bone handles whose decoration was their special delight. Dagger handles and some mysterious horn or bone sticks, beautifully carved, are among the most wonderful of the remains which have been dug up out of the debris of the cave dwellings. The sticks were certainly not a means of defence—more probably do they belong to the class of sticks we call sceptres, or staffs of office; they may have marked the headship of a family; they may, on the other hand, have been wizards' wands. Archaeologists have given them the name of *bâton de commandement*.

THE OLD-TIME ARTIST SITTING AT THE MOUTH OF HIS CAVE

Upon them the primitive men concentrated their daintiest and most imaginative skill. One can see in the mind's eye these dark-skinned, uncouth men squatting at the mouth of their caves, tossing the hair out of their eyes as they scratched away at their dagger handles or batons. The designs were of various kinds, sometimes repetitive strokes, sometimes a leaf pattern, but more generally adaptations of animal life. For the most part, although the creatures drawn were of course too long, in order to conform with the shape of the handle, they are recognisable, and the lines are peculiarly free and life-like.

In addition to these two special pieces of ornament, the Cave Men made pictures on objects for which we have not been able to think of any definite use. Bits of mammoth's tusks and branched reindeer horn were their favourite materials, and it seemed to be the height of their achievement to draw all over the surface.

HOW THEY COVERED THE GALLERIES OF THEIR CAVES WITH PICTURES

Sometimes they made a procession of animals, sometimes a medley of differing forms of life. In the same way a child given a piece of paper to draw on will cover every inch, upside down and cornerwise. And again, in this delightful, childlike manner, when the artists had used all their available space, they would often begin again on the drawings they had already made. Inside the outline of a reindeer they would draw something else —a fish, or the head of another reindeer, or a horse's head ; or they would find room for something which seems like a serpent.

Interesting as are these smaller objects of the Cave Men's art, they give place in importance to the wall, floor, and ceiling decorations of their cavern and rock shelters. There the love the artists bore for animal shapes and their growing joy in self-expression found an almost endless scope. They covered the galleries of their caves with isolated drawings, long frescoes, and sometimes they attempted to represent the massing of a herd of the creatures of the wild.

The animals they were most fond of portraying were the horse, reindeer, mammoth, bison, and goat. Occasionally they outlined a kind of ox, or deer. Here and there a man is drawn, but it would seem that the cave dwellers were not much interested in themselves, perhaps because they fell short of the brute strength of the four-footed creatures.

THE FAITHFULNESS OF THE PICTURES OF THE FIRST ARTISTS

The pictures of animals which still flourish on the Earth we can judge from our own knowledge. From the skeleton of a mammoth found in perfect condition in Siberia, we can judge how faithful were their drawings of this huge creature.

For the most part, these pictures were made on the rock with the point of a flint tool. Sometimes the artists scratched an outline and chiselled the interior rock away to give an illusion of " relief."

As their sense of art grew, they supplemented the engraved line with a brushwork line. In their latest stage they had learned to paint. The substance they used, the " pigment," was a mixture of charcoal, oxide of manganese, and some oily material ; and their tubes were hollow bones. Their brushes were of a fine nature, and the result is a freedom of line that artists of today might envy. It is because the art of the Cave Men was in a way so "artless," so free from conscious construction, that it is so great.

We find this simplicity marking the work of famous men all through the ages, for a perfect picture, like a perfect poem, should give the impression of having written or painted itself. If we are conscious that one rhyme is dragged in to supplement another, one shape to explain another, the poem or the picture falls short of greatness. Such a work may be clever, but, generally speaking, cleverness is the enemy of greatness. Or, to put it another way, *cleverness steps in where pure inspiration fails.*

in others it would seem that the artists left the engraving unfinished.

In the south-west of France, in the district of the Pyrenees, and in Northern Spain, about forty of these underground picture galleries have been discovered. The conditions of life in this part of

AN ARTIST BEFORE HISTORY—SCRATCHING A PICTURE ON BONE

One kind of cleverness the reindeer men allowed themselves in their work, and that is very interesting to us because it reveals their unconscious hunger for true shape. They took every possible advantage of the uneven surface of their rocky walls. Where a bump came that in any way suggested an animal's head or a shoulder, they would avail themselves of it as if it were natural statuary, and make a line round it. In some cases this blending of relief and contour made a startlingly good, vivid piece of work;

Europe seemed to be the happiest and most productive of art.

There have not yet been discovered in England any great wall engravings like those of the Continent, but the search has only just begun, so that it is quite possible that, hidden about eighty feet below the earth's surface, there are rocky walls with beautiful frescoes drawn by the Cave Men.

In this most fascinating branch of archaeology it is impossible to say definitely to what district belong the greatest treasures. Scientists are continually exploring, and classifications are made to-day to be undone tomorrow. At present, the finest and most famous wall pictures are at Niaux near Tarascon in France, and Altamira in North Spain. There are few things more wonderful in the history of art than the horde of animals that chase each other across the rocky roof of the Altamira cave. We wonder were they done by one man or many, by a family or by a generation, and still more do we wonder what kind of art the Cave Men would have evolved had their strange civilisation developed. All we know is that, about 12,000 years before Christ was born, there came another of those mysterious slow Earth changes. The ice fields melted and Europe became a bed of rushing rivers and swollen lakes; the face of the Continent was altered. The bed of the Mediterranean was filled, the English Channel and North Sea divided Britain for ever from Europe. The mammoth and the reindeer retreated to the Arctic Circle, one to disappear from the world before the world had really begun.

The Cave Men died out, gave place to a new order who discovered metals and grain, and learned to spin and make pottery. The first of the layers of earth and debris began to grow on the cave floors. The Bronze Age, another of those stages of human culture, superseded the Stone Age. The dawn of history, for Europe at any rate, then began.

The Stone Age, of course, was not confined to Europe, but it existed in different parts of the world at different times. Among certain semi-civilised races the retreat-ing Stone Age is still within hail, so to speak. Even so late as the close of the eighteenth century, one third of the habitable globe had not advanced beyond the use of flint tools.

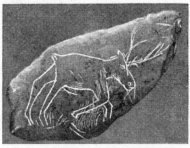
An elk scratched on a flint in Norfolk perhaps 6000 years ago

From Egypt, Palestine, and the still uncultivated peoples come traces of the Stone Age, its rude, harsh way of living, and its arts. But the use of flint has been overlapped in time in many countries by the use of other tools and the knowledge of other medium and material, so that we do not get anywhere else such an isolated splendour as the cave drawings of Europe, such an epoch so set apart from the con-flict of different kinds of development. The expressions of art among the back-ward peoples of the earth are, generally speaking, flavoured by superstition.

Only here and there do we find a faint family likeness to the pure art of prehistoric man in France and Spain. The early Red Indians chiselled drawings on the face of the rocks of the Pacific coast. The Eskimos still engrave beautiful and very small designs on walrus tusks and teeth, and so on. But the Red Indian art degenerated into the carving of the mysterious and hideous totem poles of the various tribes. Strangely enough, the real primitive art of the Red Indian is a craft—basketry. The most perfect and delicate basketry in the world—woven from strands of the pith of certain trees—comes from a quite uncivilised tribe in California. In Polynesia we find skilful en-graving done on turtle shell—queer, clever, and grotesque carvings in wood. The Maori races in New Zealand have left some amazing engravings on whalebones and wood, and their wonderful canoes show to what an extent they have developed the art of carving.

But all these peoples lack the sim-plicity of thought that underlay the work of the reindeer hunters. They revel in coarse representatives of the human body and superstitious idolatory. When we think of their work and then turn back to the art of the European Cave Men, we get a sud-den sense of purity and vigour, of a strong, clear wind after a foul atmos-phere. The art of the reindeer hunters is sep-arate and distinct, and can never be forgotten.

Some fifteen thousand years have rolled over the world since those early cave pictures were made. Thousands of generations of men have walked across the hidden roofs where animals chase each other in an eternal line of beauty. As we think of those artists long ago it is im-possible not to be moved by a sense of awe. It is like looking back on a world of dreams ; and, indeed, it seems that those dim, remote figures are the stuff that dreams are made of, their little lives rounded by a sleep.

The Wonderful House We Live In, and Our Place in the World

The ivy spreads out its leaves to catch the sunshine

THE FIRST LIVING THINGS

WHEN life first appeared on the Earth, there was nothing for it to feed on but lifeless things, like air and salt and water ; and the only kind of living creature that can live on such things is the plant.

So we may be quite sure that the first living things were plants, not animals. Now what the first plants did at first all plants do still. The trees, different in so many ways, living for hundreds of years, and sometimes so large that you could drive four horses abreast through the trunk of one of them, yet feed in just the same way as the first plants that were formed at the bottom of the sea ages ago.

Now let us study the history of plant life and see how plants have grown ever more numerous and more wonderful.

If we dig down very deeply into the Earth we find ourselves passing through the first layer to another layer of a different kind, and then to another and another, and so on. We know that these different layers, lying below the one that we live on, were once at the surface and have been covered up ; and so as we dig down, and find remains of different kinds of animals and plants, we can tell something of what the story of life has been on the Earth.

You can guess, perhaps, what kind of plants the first ones were. There were no trees or flowers, but there were plants rather like seaweed, and also simple plants of a very humble kind that were close relatives of simple plants of today, such as the mushroom and the toadstool. Those men who know most about this matter are also sure that near the very beginning of life there were to be found the kinds of plants which we now call microbes, some of which are apt to enter our bodies now and make us ill.

Then, higher up, later in history, and nearer our own days, we find evidence that plant life was becoming richer. This stage is the stage of the ferns, and in those days everything seems to have been just exactly right for the life of ferns, which flourished richly for a long, long time. They became very large, too—giant ferns, such as we cannot see nowadays. The remains of these are now changed into coal, and very useful we find them today all over the world.

But all this time there is no sign at all of what are called the higher plants ; there were no flowers, or, to use a general sort of word, there were no *flowering plants*. But in time flowering plants did appear, and they soon made room for themselves.

Many of the kinds of plants that had a good time of it before died out, either

BODY, MIND, AND SOUL · CITIZENSHIP · ECONOMICS · GOVERNMENT

altogether or very nearly. The flowering plants were cleverer than any of the older kinds ; they were fitter to live in the world that they found around them, and so they succeeded. Just as animals with back-bones are the masters of the animal king-dom, so the plants that bear flowers are the masters of the vegetable kingdom, though they have not entirely destroyed all the older kinds.

We can still, indeed, find living plants of lower kinds, which are really not very different from many of the plants found deep down in the Earth, which lived at a time when there were no flowering plants at all. But nevertheless the story of the plants is a story that leads steadily up from very small beginnings to the flower-ing plants, including all the mighty trees.

THE OXYGEN THAT EVERY LIVING THING IN THE WORLD MUST HAVE

And now let us see what we mean when we say that a plant breathes. If we can understand the breathing of a plant, we shall understand the breathing of every living thing, including you and me. When we talk about breathing, we usually think of the way in which our chests move up and down, as we draw the air into our lungs, and then let it out again.

But a plant has no chest or lungs, and many animals have neither chest nor lungs, yet they must all breathe. There are many different ways of breathing, but they are all really the same at bottom, whether it is the breathing of a plant or a fish or a man.

Wherever living things are to be found, whether under the water or out of the water, there must always be a particular kind of stuff called oxygen. This is a thing we may have never seen or heard of, and yet, whenever we see anything at all, we see through oxygen—because it is part, and the most important part, of what we call air. Oxygen is found in air, and it is also found in water. If a living thing lives in air, it takes oxygen from the air. If it lives in water, it takes oxygen from the water.

HOW THE FIRST PLANTS FOUND THEIR FOOD IN WATER

The first plants took oxygen from water because they lived in water, like many plants of today, and like crabs and fishes and many other animals. But later plants, like the flowering plants, moved out of the water on to the land, just as animals have done, and so they take their oxygen from the air, just as cats and horses and birds and men do.

Breathing is an act that has two parts, and the first of these two parts is this taking in of oxygen. Every living thing does this, and must die if it ceases to do it. But what is the second half of this act of breathing ? Directly we think about it we shall see that the oxygen which is taken in by breathing must go somewhere, something must happen to it, and the second half of the process of breathing consists simply in giving back oxygen to the air or to the water.

But if that were all, of course there would be no sense in it ; it would not be worth doing. But the point is, that while the oxygen comes in alone, " by itself," it always comes out again joined to something else ; and it is that which makes all the difference. This something else, though you could hardly believe it, is the same stuff as that which makes coal and diamonds and the writing part of lead pencils, and its name is carbon.

NO LIVING THING CAN GO ON LIVING WITHOUT BREATHING

When the carbon which the oxygen meets in the body of the animal or the plant is joined to the oxygen, it is turned into a new kind of stuff, like the stuff which comes through pipes into houses, and is burnt at the end of them—a kind of gas, the special name for which is carbon dioxide. Every living thing, from its first moment of life to its death, breathes in oxygen and breathes out this stuff which is made of carbon and oxygen, and is call carbon dioxide.

Now, plants must do this because they are living things, and no living thing can continue to live without breathing it. But this breathing is not one of the things that a plant is very good at. Indeed, a plant breathes just enough to keep itself alive. It is quite easy to prove that a plant must breathe to some extent, at any rate, because you can suffocate a plant as easily and certainly as you can suffocate an animal. If you keep away all oxygen from an animal you suffocate it, and it will die, and the same is true of a plant.

Indeed, we may be sure that every living thing will die of suffocation if it does not have enough oxygen all the time, day and night. But a plant needs far less oxygen than an animal, because it breathes much more slowly, and the curious thing, as we must now see, is that most plants are specially good at doing something which is just the opposite of breathing, something which no animal can do, and which every animal depends upon plants to do for it. The plants that do this wonderful thing that we are going to talk about are all green plants, or, at any rate, if they are not green, like grass, they are brown, like seaweed. But the little difference in colour does not matter, for the stuff that makes the seaweed brown is really the same as the stuff that makes grass green. This stuff is so important that we must think of all plants in the world as divided into two great kinds—those which have this green or brown stuff,

stuff can do nothing ; it is of no use to the plant, and is only a burden to it. Indeed, if plants are cut off from sunlight altogether, they die at once, or, at any rate, lose all the green stuff in them. It is the Sun that makes the green stuff in the plant, and the green stuff's only use is to help the plant to profit by the Sun.

Now this is just a tremendous fact, and we should make a very great mistake if we went on to talk about what the green stuff does without making quite sure that we understand what the Sun does. Without the Sun there would be no life at all upon the Earth : *No Light, no Life.*

The green stuff, then, though necessary

ONE OF THE FIRST OF ALL LIVING THINGS—THE SEAWEED, IN THE SHALLOW WATERS WHERE LIFE IS SUPPOSED TO HAVE BEGUN

and those which have not. The first kind we shall call green plants.

Very nearly all plants are green plants, but we have already mentioned one or two that are not—such, for instance, as the mushroom.

The green stuff of all other plants is really one and the same everywhere—even when it is brown, as in some seaweeds. It has the long name of chlorophyll, but we may just call it green stuff.

This green stuff is most important because of what it enables the plant to do, and that is what we must now talk about. But we must begin at the beginning—and that beginning is not the green stuff itself, but the Sun, the great and glorious Sun. By itself the green

for life, is only an instrument, something the light uses to make life. If the Sun were to go out all the green stuff in the world would not help us at all, and all the plants and animals would soon die.

Yet though we have learnt how important the Sun is, we can still look at the green stuff, since it is the means by which light can produce life.

This green stuff is to be found in other parts of plants besides the leaves. We know that the stalk of a rose is green. But most of the green stuff of plants is found in their leaves, and it is for the sake of the green stuff that leaves exist at all. The leaves of a plant are its tools for using the green stuff. Directly we think of a leaf we see that it is made in a particular way. It is a flat, thin thing. So much are leaves flat, thin things that we call other things which are flat and thin " leaves," though they are not parts of a plant at all—like leaves of the Children's Encyclopedia.

Now, there is a very good reason why leaves should be flat and thin. Leaves exist in order to expose as much green stuff as possible to the light. If a leaf were shaped like a ball, only the green stuff on the outside of it, and, indeed, only the green stuff on the side of it which was turned to the Sun, could receive the sunlight. All the rest would be darkness, and that is as good as to say that it would be quite useless.

WHAT THE SUNLIGHT DOES WITH THE GREEN STUFF

Perhaps you never asked yourself before why a leaf is shaped like a leaf ; but the question is worth asking, and the answer is that no other shape can be even thought of that would be so useful.

We have said that there is something the green stuff does by means of the sunlight, or, better still, there is something which the sunlight does by means of the green stuff. What is it ?

If we go back to what we said about the plant's breathing, we shall remember that the plant is surrounded by air. We have seen that this air contains oxygen, which is a gas, but it also contains many other gases, for the air we breathe is nothing else than a mixture of gases. Now plants, as well as animals, breathe air, but all green plants do also what no animal can do—they eat air. The gas in the air which plants eat, or feed upon, is, curiously enough, the same gas as that which the plant gives out while breathing—carbon dioxide.

THE GREATEST DIFFERENCE OF ALL BETWEEN A PLANT AND AN ANIMAL

The only way in which the plant can get food out of the carbon dioxide is to split it up into the two things of which it is made—carbon and oxygen, to keep the carbon, which is good food, and to give back the oxygen to the air. In the long run it takes from the air far more carbon than it gives to the air, and builds up this carbon into its own body.

The greatest difference between animals and plants lies in this great power that the plant has of taking carbon dioxide from the air, splitting it up into its carbon and oxygen, giving back the oxygen to the

air, and building up the carbon into its own body. As it is building the carbon up into its own body, it fixes the carbon on to other kinds of stuff in such a way as to make things which animals, including ourselves, can eat.

All animals, like all plants, require carbon, but if we were left with nothing but the carbon dioxide in air to get our carbon from, in a coal-mine, with tons of carbon all round us and tons of lead pencils and millions of pounds worth of diamonds, we should die of starvation in a day or two.

The carbon becomes of use to us only after it has been built up into food substances by the green plant, and if carbon food were not made for animals in this way the whole animal world would starve.

Let us try to see what it is that happens. Carbon dioxide, as we have seen, is made up of carbon and oxygen, and these two things are joined together so strongly that it needs very great power, used in just the right way and at just the right moment, to separate them. But what men find so difficult is quite easy to the green leaf in the sunlight.

HOW THE GREEN LEAF BEATS THE CLEVEREST MAN IN THE WORLD

The green stuff in the green leaf has no power of itself, and you understand that it is power which is wanted in order to separate things which are rightly joined together. The more tightly a nail is in a wall the harder you must pull to get it out.

Now, there is no power in the world stronger than the power of sunlight. The sunlight which pours down upon the green leaf is power. Clever men can help themselves to far more power than the green leaf can get, but they cannot apply it, and so they can scarcely do what the green leaf does. The green leaf beats the clever men because of the green stuff it contains. It is its green stuff that makes it able to apply all the sunlight it gets to the business in hand, which is to split up the carbon dioxide gas of the air into its carbon and oxygen, and to keep the carbon for the use of the plant. This is done without any noise, without any fuss, without any machinery, without great heat, without any waste at all, and without any wear and tear of anything.

And now we know the miracle that is going on in every green leaf in the world.

The Story of the Marvellous Plants that Cover the Earth

A PLANT'S STRUGGLE FOR LIFE

Up to a certain point the outer world is what we may call a friendly home for living creatures. They are not strangers in a strange land.

Thus the circulation of water by mist and cloud, wind and rain, helps them greatly. The atmosphere is a useful curtain, and it contains the Big Four elements—carbon in the form of carbon dioxide, hydrogen in the form of water-vapour, free oxygen which has been formed for the most part by green leaves, and abundance of free nitrogen which a few plants are able to capture. There are many other ways in which the Earth is hospitable to living creatures, and the question rises, Why must plants and animals struggle as they do?

The outer world is in a measure friendly to plants, but it is very changed. Not only are there regular changes to be faced —night after day, winter after summer— but there are irregular vicissitudes, such as tempests, floods, hailstorms, drought, and severe frost. The plant must answer-back to these changes or perish.

Just as we, in a small way, must change our clothing according to the season and weather, so in a deeper and subtler way the plant must. This is the *Struggle with Fate*, and Darwin, whom everyone knows as the great student of struggle, pointed

out that the plant's struggle with drought at the edge of the desert was as real as the plant's struggle for room and light in the crowded jungle. Where water is abundant at a rainy season, and scarce for a long time, we find water-storing tissue, as in cactuses, a thickening of the plant's skin, a reduction of foliage, and a greening of the stem. When the cold is apt to be excessive, we find many precautions, which have become in the course of time established, all without taking thought for the morrow, such as the curious woolly covering of edelweiss.

The second reason for struggle is to be found in the rate at which many plants multiply. The river of life is always over-flowing its banks. A single plant of hedge-mustard may produce 730,000 seeds, and it has been calculated that if each seed germinated and developed into a plant which seeded, the members of the next generation would be touching one another all over the earth. Of course, this does not happen—*because of the struggle for life*. The director of Brooklyn Botanic Garden tells us that a fern of moderate size produces every year about fifty million spores. If each of these spores (he says) ultimately produced a mature fern-plant, and if we allowed only one square foot of elbow-room for each plant, the progeny of one

BOTANY & ITS WONDERS · FLOWERS · TREES · HOW THINGS GROW

parent only, in one season, would require 50 million square feet, nearly two square miles.

If each of these plants produced 50 million offspring the next season, the descendants of only one fern plant would in two years cover the stupendous area of over 89 million square miles, half as much again as the land surface of the Earth.

We see, then, that plants have to struggle not only because the outside conditions are very changeful, but also because of the rate at which plants tend to multiply.

THE LIVING CREATURE ROLLS UPHILL AS WELL AS DOWN

But is there not a third reason for the struggle—a reason wrapped up with the central secret of life? Every vigorous living creature is *always asking for more*. It is of the nature of the living creature to assert itself, and to answer back to difficulties and limitations.

Just as the loosened stone rolls down the hillside, crashing through obstacles until it reaches the level ground or is jammed, so the living creature soon gets some way on and will not be hindered. But the living creature rolls uphill as well as downhill—that is its secret. Plants and animals alike may be compared to clocks that can wind themselves up. We must not dwell on this reason for struggle, for it is very difficult ; but the fact is that the more a plant succeeds, the more it asks for. It is a hustler and a jostler, though it looks so quiet. To put it another way, the plant does not readily submit to being hindered, whatever the difficulties in its way.

We know that a young plant can burst its way through the hard asphalted pavement at the side of a street. Without the aid of tools or explosives a plant will make its way to the light by the gentle force of growing. So we see that plants must struggle—because the outer world is changeful and callous, because they tend to have such big families, and because it is their very nature to assert themselves against difficulties.

CARING FOR SELF AND FOR OTHERS IS THE BUSINESS OF LIFE

For plants, as for animals, the business of life is twofold—caring for self and caring for others ; and the most important part of caring for self is the quest for food.

We have already seen that all ordinary green plants feed on the carbon dioxide mixed with the atmosphere, and absorbed by the leaves, on water, usually from soil, and on salts like saltpetre, which are taken in by the rootlets along with the soil-water. As there is in all ordinary cases an abundance of this simple kind of food the struggle must be *in tapping the supply and competing with other plants* which are doing the same. We shall come to this competition later ; it is useful first of all to notice some of the more or less unusual ways in which plants feed.

In boggy and marshy places the soil is poor in nitrogenous salts like saltpetre, and this makes plant life difficult. For living matter is in part a complicated mixture of nitrogenous carbon compounds called proteins—like the gluten for the sake of which we eat bread—and if the living matter is to be kept going and growing there must obviously be *nitrogenous* food. Therefore, boggy and marshy places cannot be peopled except by plants which have some special fitness for thriving in the poor and peculiar soil. Immediately we see why bogs and marshy places should show so many insect-eating plants, like sundew, butterwort, Venus fly-trap, bladderwort, and some pitcher plants, which are able to eke out the scanty nitrogenous food supplies by capturing insects and other small animals.

THE PLANT THAT FLOATS IN THE POOL WITH HUNDREDS OF LITTLE TRAPS

The bladderwort floats in the pool in the marsh; it has not even roots; it absorbs everything through its green leaves and shoots. But it has hundreds of little traps, each about the size of the head of a blanket-pin, and these serve to capture water-fleas and other small fry. The small animal pushes its head against a swinging door and enters the trap. The door closes automatically behind it, and the prisoner dies, rots, and is absorbed.

The beautiful sundew spreads its leaves on the bog moss—each somewhat like a flattish spoon with a narrow handle. The expanded part of the spoon is surrounded by tentacles which are tipped with dewlike drops of sticky secretion, and these tentacles are exquisitely sensitive to the touch of a small insect. They bend inwards like the fingers of a closing hand, the insect is securely captured, digestive juice is poured out upon the prisoner and what is useful in its body is dissolved and absorbed. The tentacles then expand again. So the sundew flourishes.

The Venus fly-trap whose leaves close like a spring trap over insects that alight on it. The plant then proceeds to digest the body of the insect.

The prickly spikes with which Nature has endowed the gorse as a defence against browsing animals. The gorse therefore grows freely on open heaths.

The pitcher plant whose acids digest the insects attracted into it by the honey glands.

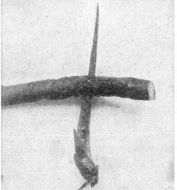

The force exerted by a plant as it grows—a blade of grass that has penetrated a piece of root.

The cup on the stem of a teasel plant that fills with rain and drowns insects that fall in.

The hairs on the stem of the begonia that serve as a rampart against climbing insects.

Clusters of mistletoe, the parasite that makes its home on the oak tree and the apple tree.

The convolvulus, struggling to the sunlight by winding itself round the stem of a neighbour.

In the same way, but less sensationally, insects are captured by the glistening, light-green leaves of the butterwort, which are so often spread in starfish-like fashion on the sides of the ditches in the bog. The margins of the sticky leaves curl inwards and shut in entangled flies, which are then digested by the secretion of numerous glands on the surface of the leaf.

Another mode of life is thievish, or *parasitic*, when one plant filches food material from another. This is a sort of back-door escape from the struggle for existence. Farmers know that the pasture land is bound to be poor when there is great abundance of the beautiful little flowers called eyebright. And why is this?

The soil does not yield enough to keep ordinary plants going ; those that get on there must have some peculiarity, such as very long roots, or very much branched roots, and very much cut-up leaves as in millfoil, or very long not-overlapping leaves like grasses. The little eyebright has discovered another way out—hardly worthy of its beauty and its pretty name. It is a root parasite. Some of its rootlets fit on to the rootlets of the grass like a saddle on a horse, and there is absorption of supplies from the grass. This weakens the grass, of course, but it is also an indication that the soil is far from generous.

THE CLIMBING DODDER AND HOW IT STEALS ITS FOOD

The thievish habit seen in the eyebright is found also in the yellow-rattle and in the lousewort. Farmers say that sheep get out of condition where the lousewort is very abundant, and they used to blame the plant for giving the sheep lice! What this means is probably that lousewort, as a root parasite, manages to thrive in very poor pasture. It is the poverty of the pasture that weakens the sheep.

The dodder is a rather beautiful climbing plant that has lost the usual green pigment called chlorophyll. It twines round the stems of nettles, hops, wheat and other vigorous plants, and sends its suckers into the zone of the stem—the bast—where the nutritive materials manufactured in the leaves pass down to places of storage. The dodder gets its water and salts from the soil, but, being unable to build up carbon compounds on its own account, it steals them from its host.

Very different is the mistletoe, which has plenty of green pigment, but no con-nection with the ground. The thrush eats the white berry with its sticky pulp, and the seed, passed through the bird's food canal undigested, is deposited on the branch of a tree, such as an apple or an oak. Sometimes, perhaps, the thrush, having failed to swallow the sticky fruit, wipes its bill on the branch, and the seed is anchored. In any case, the seed of the mistletoe germinates on the branch of a tree, and sends its rootlets into the wood-zone of the stem where the crude sap, consisting of soil-water and dissolved salts, passes up. Being green, the mistletoe plant can make plenty of carbon compounds on its own; but, having no con-nection with the earth, it must steal water and salts from its host. These are but three examples of plant parasites—eye-bright, dodder, and mistletoe—but they illustrate this seamy side.

THE BIGGEST FLOWER IN THE WORLD AND WHERE IT GROWS

Another possibility in the quest for food is to batten on the dead. Many bacteria, many moulds and rusts, besides some big funguses, live on living plants ; many bacteria and some moulds live on living animals. But others feed on what is dead and rotting, and they are called *saprophytes*. We are familiar with the fungoid plants that feed on decaying leaves and branches, utilising the ready-made organic matter which, being without green pigment, they cannot make for themselves.

Many of these saprophytes play an important part in keeping the earth clean. Among the saprophytes are some flowering plants of high degree which have lost caste and become, to a greater or less extent, dependent upon rotten vegetable matter. The biggest flower in the world (*Rafflesia*), more than a foot across, is the flower of a saprophyte that grows on the floor of the tropical forest.

HOW SOME PLANTS ENTER INTO PARTNERSHIP, AND WHY

Let us look for a moment at the very interesting way in which plants enter into partnership with other plants, and occa-sionally with animals, to the great ad-vantage to both parties; it is one of the alternatives in the quest for food. There are bacteria which form partnerships with the roots of clovers, peas, lupins, and other plants of the bean family, and enable them, in some mysterious way, to capture and utilise the free nitrogen of the air There are many fungi which wrap themselves round the roots of plants and form a most useful sponge. The heather gets on well, as we have mentioned, on very poor soil, *because it has a partner - fungus.* This is another solution of natural difficulties.

In the early summer we see men and women busy thinning the turnips with a hoe, destroying ten and leaving one. Sometimes we see women on their knees laboriously thinning or singling out the young carrots. There are too many young plants; they crowd one another and dwarf one another. If the farmer is to get full-grown vegetables, he must single them out. Similarly, in wild nature, there is natural thinning. The young plants that get a good start, either through some virtue of their constitution or some accident of environment, elbow out their neighbours. There is ceaseless sifting. As Tennyson said of Nature, " So careful of the race she seems, so careless of the single life."

But while the sifting is often effected in early life by a great " infantile mortality " of seedlings, there are

A CACTUS OF ARIZONA WHICH GROWS MORE THAN FORTY FEET HIGH

THE PRICKLY CUSHION CACTUS

THE PRICKLY FLOWERS OF THE DESERT

sheltered and luxurious places where many plants get past the juvenile stages, and where there is extraordinary crowding, and, therefore, great competition for foothold, for light, and for air. Such places are sheltered —self-sown woods, tropical jungles, thick-set hedgerows, and rich meadows. We get a key to what goes on in such places if we realise that plants are struggling, each in its own way and all in the plant's way, to find self-expression, to get on, to obtain satisfaction, or to overcome obstacles and limitations. Let us think of a few of the moves in the life or death game.

What light is shed on the variety of climbing plants when we understand that they are conquerors in a fight ! They have remained young and mobile in their stems, or leaf-stalks, or tendrils, or some other part of their body, and they have risen on the shoulders of their neighbours to thrive on fresh air and light.

It is very interesting to think of the different ways in which plants escape from deadly overcrowding and the literal shadow of death. Brambles, with their long shoots and gripping prickles, are *scramblers* ; and so is the Jack-Run-the-Hedge, which is helped by attaching roughness on its rapidly-growing shoots. The ivy is a *root-climber*, giving off numerous brown roots on the shady side of the lanky stem. Then there are *twiners*, with stems that encircle the support, as in the case of honeysuckle and dodder, and the lianas of the tropical forest. But the artists in the business are the *leaf-climbers* and the *tendril-bearers*, where the leaf-stalk, or a specialised sensitive filament, bends round a support. Think of clematis, vine, bryony, and pea ; what masterpieces they are !

We see a new significance in the spiral arrangement of leaves on the stem, for this means that they shadow one another less ; in the mosaic of leaves on the horse-chestnut branch where many leaves make the most of the available light without overlapping ; of the success of long, grassy leaves that run parallel without overlapping ; of much cut-up leaves, like millfoil, which have an enormous surface for absorption and exposure to light, like countries with a big coast-line. We must realise the intensity of the struggle. Every meadow is like a tropical jungle, every hedgerow like a tropical forest.

THE MONGOOSE THAT FIGHTS A SNAKE WITH TEETH AND WITS

When man struggles with wild beasts or poisonous serpents or injurious insects, his weapons are often *ideas*. His struggle is rational. When a mongoose fights a snake his weapons are not only teeth but *wits*. His struggle is intelligent. When a mother digger-wasp struggles with a cricket, which she will paralyse to form food for her young ones, her weapons are not only her sting, but that inborn power which we call instinct.

Now, the struggles of plants against animals are at a lower level than all these. There is no reason to believe that the plant ever really *knows* what it is doing, even when it catches a fly, and that is the most active answer-back that a plant ever gives to an animal. In most cases all that we can say is that in the course of time some plants have changed in the direction of having stings and poisons, thorns or spines, hard skins or unpalatable crystals, which have turned out to be very profitable—indeed, life-saving—in warding off the attacks of animals.

The answer-back is an unconscious constitutional change which pays ; and sometimes the change occurs without there being, so far as we can see, any need for it. We must not learn what we shall afterwards have to unlearn. The lilies of the field do not toil or spin ; and no plant thinks out devices which save its life.

THE STRUGGLES OF PLANTS GO ON UNCEASINGLY

To come to the facts of the case, let us give two or three examples of the ways in which many plants are protected from the assaults of animals. Everyone who loves a garden knows that among the worst enemies of plants are the snails and slugs, and their depredations go on all over the world. But there are some plants that snails leave alone, because of hard skins, rough prickles, stiff hairs, poisonous stings, strong odours, and other defences. Thus there are few if any snails that attack the quaint plant of the woods called Cuckoo-pint or Lords-and-Ladies ; and one good reason for this is that the leaves are crowded with minute sharp crystals which would pierce and irritate the lips of the snail.

The struggles of plants are world-wide, rarely ceasing, and many-sided. They include all the answers-back, all the thrusts and parries, that plants make against the difficulties and limitations that beset them. There are struggles with Fate—the physical world ; struggles with Fellows—other plants in the crowded area ; and struggles with Foes—hungry and injurious animals of high and low degree. There is struggle for food, for foothold, for freshness, for light, for moisture—for everything a plant needs. There are ways of evading the intensity of struggle—as for instance, by becoming a parasite, but this usually means some degree of degeneration.

THE FIGHT FOR THE PLACE OF A PLANT IN THE SUN

The great fact for plants and animals is the same—that success means struggle. Not only must plants struggle to win a place in the sun ; they have often a struggle to keep it.

But struggle among plants is usually a dreamy business ; it includes all the answers-back that it is in them to make, as they care for themselves and for their race. The central principle of all life that goes forward is : *Test all things, and hold fast that which is good.*

The Story of the Peoples of All Nations and Their Homelands

OUR HOMELAND
A SURVEY OF THE BRITISH ISLES

IT is natural for people of all nations to love the land in which they were born, just as it is natural for them to love their parents.

Here, in our own homeland, the British Isles, we have gained our early knowledge of life. Other places, more beautiful perhaps in some ways, we do not know till later, but by that time the love of our homeland is fixed. Let us, then, consider why our homeland should be admired and loved; let us glance over its several parts, recall what they have been, outline what its people have done, are doing, and are hoping to do in friendship with all other nations.

We will make our approach by the English Channel. Many people returning home, and foreigners who come to see us, land at Plymouth or Southampton or Dover. Of course many other ports (as well as our airports) receive other arrivals, but the Channel is the chief sea-way for travellers.

By it the traveller sights the part of the land where its earliest history begins. The Channel route is a historical panorama. For many centuries the national story centred on southern England. Long before Julius Caesar briefly raided the south of Britain the civilised nations round the

Mediterranean Sea knew of island lands beyond the Pillars of Hercules where much-needed metals abounded, and their most adventurous mariners braved the stormy seas outside the Gibraltar Strait to secure those treasures. A sense of great age pervades the jutting corner which South-Western England thrusts into the broad Atlantic.

Whether it is seen from the land or is approached by sea the Land's End of Cornwall seems to be possessed by a gaunt eeriness. In early times that jagged rock-bound coast was strewn with wrecks. Now warning lighthouses surmounting outlying rocks and lofty headlands flash a welcome across the seas, but the whole region, though inhabited by a most friendly race, seems old and grim. That it is so is not surprising. It is the only part of England where the ancient British still predominate.

For about four centuries, while the legions of ancient Rome garrisoned the southern part of Britain, as part of the Roman Empire, the Celtic and earlier British were protected from other invaders. Then, through six centuries after the Romans went away, nearly all that is now England and Southern Scotland was largely re-peopled by invaders from Northern Europe (Saxons, Danes,

THE FIVE CONTINENTS & 100 NATIONS & RACES THAT INHABIT THEM

and Norwegians), and, though there has been much intermixture with the earlier Britishers, the bulk of the present English and Scottish people are descendants of these pagan northern sea-rovers, and the earlier Britons have only held their own in the peninsula of Cornwall, the mountains of Wales, and the Scottish Highlands. Wherever we go we shall find signs that the people of this varied and delightful land have been gradually mixed from several human sources through thousands of years, beginning long before the arrival of those who are commonly known to us as Ancient Britons.

THE DIM, UNREADABLE STORY OF OUR HOMELAND'S VANISHED LIFE

We shall miss much of the romance of our Motherland if we do not feel that behind her known history there is a dim, unreadable story of vanished life. All the way up the English Channel from Cornwall to Kent, high on the Moors and Downs which rise behind the rocky coast, are many remains of earthen fortresses or camps of refuge whose first builders are not clearly known. Some of these defensive works were occupied by the Roman legions in the course of the first four centuries after Christ and later served in turn as battlegrounds for Saxons and Northmen through 600 more years of recurrent strife. Some of them had marked the lines of defence of tribes who had held the land long before the Romans came, tribes that had been only partly superseded by the Celtic Ancient Britons.

IMPRESSIONS OF THE TRAVELLER COMING FROM THE SOUTH COAST

Whether anyone lands in Southern England at Falmouth in Cornwall, or at Plymouth in Western Devon, at Weymouth in Dorset, Southampton in Hampshire, or Dover in Kent, and proceeds to London by air, or rail, or road, two or three clear impressions will be received from the changeful landscape. One is that of neatness and finish in the farming of the land. It is the tidiest of countries.

The fields are small and edged by hedges in the lower lands, or by stone walls in hillier parts. The villages, mostly in wooded recesses, are homely and cosy, and the little gardens are adorned with flowers. Another broad effect is that of a tree-clad countryside. Trees are sprinkled wherever there are hedgerows. A further impression is that, while all farmed lands are trim, there are considerable portions of open, hilly grazing grounds with an almost primeval wildness.

One sees patches of this character in Cornwall, particularly the central knot of Bodmin Moor, with its rocky crowns of Brown Willy and Rough Tor. We pass at once from the cultivated to the wild.

It is the same with Dartmoor, the central mass of Devonshire, with its granite tors and lonely, peaty, hilly expanses, the source of many little rivers, and a common grazing ground for sheep, cattle, and ponies. Somerset has the broad, lofty, heathery, combe-trenched Exmoor, and the sudden gorge-gashed Mendip plateau ; Dorset has breezy embattled heights, and on lower levels darkly ancient heathlands. Wiltshire and Berkshire have their grazing Downs, Hampshire its Forest venerable with age, and Sussex, Surrey, and Kent vie with each other in their alternations of noble Downs and gracious woodlands.

WHY THE SOUTH IS SO LARGELY A HOLIDAY-MAKER'S REGION

This southern expanse of England, benevolent in climate, has become in a large degree a holiday-maker's region. The whole coast from the North Foreland to the Land's End, in town and village, offers a welcome to people in search of relaxation or of quiet retirement. Its people, in the main, are of the Saxon variety, softer in speech and manner and more restful than the breeds of the more rugged North. The milder climate of the southern counties and their long Channel coast make them favourite holiday resorts and also favourite places of retirement when a man's business or professional life is over. The chief centres of southern population are still all connected with the sea, either as seaports or as naval stations, or as health resorts.

In all this southern district there is no concentration on distinctive manufactures similar to the industrial Midlands and the North. It is a continuous range of pleasant scenery, with quick diversity from open sheep-rearing Downs to fertile valleys where dairying and orchards seem to be the commonest interests, though in parts there is a good deal of corn grown on the Downs, even on Salisbury Plain, which once was chiefly a sheep run.

In very early times the central parts of these counties, between hills near the coast and the bare Downs farther inland, were densely wooded, and the forests served as a protection against invaders.

The easy ways of travel then lay high on the hills, the Wiltshire hills having a central position. The middle of Somerset was swampy. Eastern Hampshire, Sussex, and western Kent had an almost continous forest, and in Sussex particularly at a later period the woods were burned in smelting the iron that was then fairly abundant in the county. But the metal wealth of the South, such as Sussex iron and the Mendip lead in Somerset worked by the Romans, is now almost exhausted, except in Cornwall. Coal, however, is worked in Somerset and in Kent.

There is valuable quarrying for stone of various kinds such as granite, slate, and building stone—Bath, Portland and Purbeck—and for china clay, in Cornwall, Devon, Somerset, Dorset, and Wiltshire, but the main resources of all these southern counties are drawn from the land and sea, and from entertaining visitors who live in less genial parts of the homelands.

WHEN THE ANGLO-SAXONS GRADUALLY HUSTLED THE BRITONS WESTWARD

The distinctions of the British southlands are that they have on the whole a softer beauty than any other large areas of England. Historically they form the base of the British pyramid. They were the most civilised parts of Britain when the Roman Empire introduced its civilisation, and when the Empire collapsed in Britain our invading Anglo-Saxon forefathers, coming in pirate swarms, gradually hustled the Celtic Britons westward as the Celts had before hustled the earlier Iberian invaders into the mountains.

It was on the southern Downs and in these wooded valleys that the first English settled as cultivators of the soil, became Christianised, and in their turn helped to check the later invasions of the pagan Northmen who were endeavouring to uproot Christianity, finally absorbing them into the Christian system. The fabled Celtic King Arthur and the much more substantial King Alfred each played his part in this region. Winchester as capital of Wessex, when Wessex was a kingdom, shared with London the claim to be the capital of England.

The influence of the South in the religious life of our country is reflected in the fine list of its ancient cathedrals : Canterbury, Rochester, Winchester, Salisbury, Chichester, Wells, and Exeter, to which have been added Truro, Portsmouth, and Guildford in modern times. It is a noble array, but is very far from exhausting the national record.

London, the most important city in the British Commonwealth in many ways (historical, financial, political, commercial, and industrial, to mention only a few), began its career in a rather obscure way. It was not at once made a capital city.

THE CHIEF CENTRES OF CELTIC POWER BEFORE THE ROMANS CAME

The chief power of the Celtic rulers in Britain before the Romans arrived to conquer it was massed a little way north and east of the Thames and London, at St Albans in Hertfordshire and at Colchester in Essex. The Romans went straight for those strongholds, took them, fortified them in their own way, and garrisoned them. Then they found that the easiest way of bringing up their supplies and supports was to sail up the chief waterway, the Thames, as far as the pool below the present site of London Bridge. There they developed a thriving seaport and made it a walled town where the old City of London now stands, and from it they began their wonderful system of roads.

It is still a thriving port, but much else besides. Sixty million tons of shipping arrive in it yearly. It is also the historic centre and the biggest city of the great British Commonwealth, whose aim is to help all nations toward prosperity through peace, co-operation, and friendship.

LONDON, ITS TEEMING MILLIONS, AND ITS VAST TRADE AND VARIED INDUSTRIES

Increasingly it is a centre for an immense variety of miscellaneous manufactures as well as a place of storage and sale for materials from all the world. Its population is more than eight millions, and that does not include a vast and ever-increasing number whose work is in London but whose residences are outside its official borders. There are other great British centres of specially organised industries, as we shall see, but none is so impressive as London, and all the rest of our industrial centres maintain close affiliation with it in business.

London is the main centre of Britain's clothing, furniture, and printing industries. Its excellent transport and electric power services have attracted much private enterprise from elsewhere and its 600 square miles of built-up area, with a population greater than that of Sweden, forms in itself a great market.

The wonderful changes made in transport during the present century, particularly by road, have amazingly affected London. The country year by year knows more of London, but in a far greater degree London knows more about the country.

The way in which Londoners and all city dwellers have organised themselves into innumerable clubs for cycling and rambling, bird-watching or visiting places of historic interest, is of mutual profit to themselves and the country village and town which must cater for them.

THE LONG-FAMED HIGHWAY OF THE GREAT NORTH ROAD

We have reached London by way of the southern counties bordering the English Channel, and we will leave it northward to glance first at the counties east of the Great North Road, and then those on that long-famed highway. Essex, Suffolk, and Norfolk, the coastal counties between the Thames and the Wash, formed the East Anglia of our forefathers from whom the name England is inherited.

East Anglia, the kingdom of the Anglians, was not a very stable kingdom, for it readily accepted the sovereignty of either Mercia or of Wessex, as those neighbour kingdoms rose above it in power and prestige. One of the most dramatic periods in its history came about 400 years before the Angles arrived. The chief power of the Celtic British centred on Essex when first the Romans came.

THE REBELLION OF BOADICEA AND HER DEFEAT BY THE ROMANS

After they thought themselves firmly established there, and, contrary to the Roman custom, began to act tyrannically, Boadicea, Queen of the Iceni tribe in Norfolk, rose in fierce rebellion, recaptured Colchester, St. Albans, and London from the Romans, burned them, and massacred many thousands of Romans and their British friends. The chief Roman general, Suetonius, was far away in Anglesey, uprooting the evil power of the priestly Druids. Returning, he utterly defeated Boadicea and restored the Roman

power. But that did not satisfy the Roman sense of justice. Suetonius had won a great victory, but he was ordered to return to Rome and was reprimanded for allowing the misgovernment that had caused the rebellion. In the meantime Boadicea had poisoned herself.

The east side of London long ago overflowed into Essex. One of the most striking of these developments is the town of Dagenham, serving the big Ford motor works whose blazing furnaces beside the Thames make it seem as though a piece of the industrial North had come south to the very outskirts of the capital. There are large residential extensions in the neighbourhood of Epping Forest. Essex was formerly almost covered with woodlands, of which Epping Forest, though much reduced, is the principal survivor, and an inestimable boon to the East End of London.

Neither Essex nor Suffolk nor Norfolk can be generally said to vie with the southern counties in regard to natural beauty, but they are very valuable from an agricultural point of view.

THE CORNLANDS OF ESSEX WHICH HAVE HELPED TO FEED LONDON

Essex has fertile cornlands and has played a big part in feeding London through a long past. Its towns, Colchester and Chelmsford, away from the London area, have a fine history. The county shares with Suffolk the sweet scenery of the River Stour that found an interpreter in Constable, the most English of painters, who was a Suffolk man. Ipswich, the county town of East Suffolk, and Bury St. Edmunds, the county town of West Suffolk, have much historical interest.

Cardinal Wolsey was born in Ipswich, George Borrow lived at Oulton Broad, and the county has literary claims through its poets, Edward Fitzgerald, who was a native of Woodbridge, and George Crabbe, who was born at Aldeburgh.

Norfolk is a county with strong claims peculiar to itself. It has a great variety of soils, and people who only know one part of it are astonished to hear of the difference in other parts. Viewed as a whole it is a fine agricultural county, with patches of very attractive scenery, including unexpected heathery expanses. The Broads, which are natural widenings of some of its rivers that invite small sailing craft, fascinate many lovers of quiet holidays. Norwich, the capital, and far the most important city in all the Eastern counties, has been a busy manufacturing centre since the fourteenth century, when it became the pioneer of the new woollen English trade. It has changed its business but has never ceased to be manufacturing as well as agricultural. Its cattle market is the largest in the land.

HOW THE FEN COUNTRY HAS BEEN TRANSFORMED SINCE MONASTIC TIMES

The English coastline between the Thames and the Humber leads the way in the marketing of fish. Cornwall and Devon have their fishing fleets, and each maritime county participates in some degree, but Grimsby, Yarmouth, and Lowestoft dominate the trade, with help in the busiest season from Scotland.

Norfolk brings us, at King's Lynn, to the Fen country. It includes all the district of Holland and strips of Norfolk, Lincolnshire, Cambridgeshire, and Huntingdonshire. Nowhere has England changed so much. The Fenland is almost entirely flat, and very little above sea-level. For many centuries it was a swampy plain subject to tidal inundations from four or five considerable rivers, and from floods.

Its villages were built on slight rises : islands in the midst of quagmires. Fishing and fowling were natural occupations, for wild birds abounded. There was much rough vegetation and the floods gradually deposited good soil. Then pious men began as hermits to influence the rude dwellers in these watery wilds, and presently assembling in brotherhoods founded abbeys, began drainage, made roads, and developed fertility in the gloomy fens. After the dissolution of the monasteries, big schemes of drainage were carried out, and now the fens are reclaimed and healthy and grow splendid crops of all kinds. The monks who began this marvellous change long ago are kept in memory by the dignity of many churches they founded in the Lincolnshire fens.

EAST ANGLIA AND ITS PART IN PUBLIC AFFAIRS IN CROMWELL'S TIME

Lincolnshire outside of its fen district has pleasing scenery and skilful agriculture. Its central city, Lincoln, stands out in history as a dominating place toward the North, like Chester, York, and Durham.

Eastern England, over which we have been glancing, played its most con-spicuous part in public affairs during the period of the Civil War, when it was almost solidly united in support of Parliament. That was largely owing to the relation of Oliver Cromwell to Huntingdon, his birthplace, his association with Cambridge, and the fact that London, staunchly parliamentarian, traditionally had a powerful influence in Essex, though it did not prevent Colchester from holding out on the other side. London, the East of England, the manufacturing towns, the seaports, and Oliver Cromwell made up the successful opposition to Charles Stuart's methods of government.

The counties round London have much territory now included in what is called Greater London. Its area of 693 square miles has eight million people.

A CHANGE WHICH ALTERED THE FACE OF MANY PARTS OF ENGLAND

It is not till Northants, Leicestershire, Notts, and Derbyshire are reached that we see how the conditions of work arose in the past which enabled manufactures to be massed in the form of factory production, a change which altered the face of many parts of England. Well into the nineteenth century woollen garments were made on a machine worked by a man in a cottage. We can see these machines in some of our museums, and very quaint they sometimes look.

It was coal that first brought the factory into being, and the inventions that work machinery by steam or gas or electricity. It was coal and iron, often found together, that blackened the face of many an English countryside, but also gave the country a long lead in the chief industries of the world. Every one of our large towns that has prosperous manufactures, except Norwich, is either near a coal or an iron deposit, or is on the coast where coal may reach it cheaply. But petrol may be equally used as engine-driving power anywhere, and coal has a dangerous rival until it can be turned into a more handy power. Meantime England and Scotland and Wales have their coal and iron works and their manufactures massed in the same neighbourhoods.

Of course agriculture is everywhere, more or less, but there is a considerable difference where minerals are found and worked. There agriculture takes a second place as employing less labour. In the

Midlands there is a mixture between prevailing mineral and manufacturing industry on the one hand and quiet agriculture on the other hand. Northants has steel works, and the manufacture of boots and shoes widely spread, without having any coalfield, but it has coal-bearing neighbours and a good deal of ironstone. Warwickshire, Leicestershire, Derbyshire, and Nottinghamshire all have coalfields : Warwickshire and Leicester-shire each in its north-west, Derbyshire in its east, and Notts in its west. Vigorous manufactures flourish in their principal cities and towns in consequence, with room being left in other parts for delight-ful unspoiled scenery and distinctive agri-culture. Warwickshire has in Birmingham and the towns adjoining it (chiefly in Staffordshire) a remarkable accumulation of metal manufactures, numbering thou-sands of different articles large and small.

THE FOREST OF ARDEN AND THE GREEN MEADOWS OF STRATFORD

Leicester and Nottingham are manu-facturing cities, and Derby is a great railway centre. But not far away from Birmingham are Shakespeare's Forest of Arden and the green meadows of Strat-ford-on-Avon, while Leicestershire has, adjoining its coalfield, the granite plateau of Charnwood Forest, the most ancient hills of England, and elsewhere the great hunting grasslands of Melton Mowbray and Market Harborough.

Nottinghamshire's collieries reach the great aristocratic domains of what are known as the Dukeries and Sherwood Forest, the fabled haunt of Robin Hood, and the county has good farming in the lower vale of the Trent.

Derbyshire is halved between a fine coalfield in the valleys of the Rother and the Erewash, and the scenery of the River Derwent and its tributaries, as beautiful as anything to be found any-where. Thus, in the northern midlands, mining with manufactures is accom-panied by agriculture as a secondary.

The great county of Yorkshire is distinguished in agriculture and more dis-tinguished in manufactures. In very early times it was divided into three Ridings, or Thirdings, for convenience in government. The East Riding, except for the fine seaport of Hull, its one centre of popula-tion, is entirely occupied with agriculture and seaside relaxation at Bridlington,

Filey, and smaller places. Its soil is fertile and its gentle hills, called Wolds, are cultivated to their summits. The North Riding is all the county north of the city of York, and a line eastward to Filey mostly along the Derwent, and a line westward to Westmorland along the southern water-shed of the River Ure. The rest of York-shire is in the West Riding except York itself. That proud old city is a county to itself and not in any of the Ridings.

THE BUSY TOWNS, FARMLANDS, AND COAL-FIELDS OF YORKSHIRE

The great agricultural tract of York-shire is down the Vale of York in the middle of the county, on either side of the rivers Swale and Ouse as far as the Humber and spreading into all the three Ridings. Near the Humber the lower Vale is fenlike. The city of York, in the middle of the Vale, has long been a notable agricultural centre.

The West Riding and the North Riding are filled on their western side by hill spurs from the Pennine Chain which pour seven rivers eventually into the Humber, and the lower courses of several of these rivers pass, in the West Riding, through the great south-west Yorkshire coalfield. Here has been gathered in nearly the whole of the English woollen manufacture in its many forms, and also other manufactures, by Leeds, Bradford, Huddersfield, Halifax, and many other towns.

When England began to make its own cloth instead of selling its wool abroad to be made up there, the trade started in the eastern counties and passed on gradually to the west, near the Cotswold district, where indeed some forms of cloth are still made ; but west Yorkshire has become the chief centre of the manufac-ture, and England is the greatest purchaser of the world's wool. Here we see the massing of men together in large numbers for a single purpose which is the most distinctive feature of modern life.

SHEFFIELD'S WORLDWIDE FAME AS A CENTRE OF THE STEEL INDUSTRY

Another Yorkshire instance of the same tendency is the steel trade in all its branches.

More than 500 years ago Sheffield, in south Yorkshire, was known widely in England for its steel tools, and its fame for the most valuable forms of steel is now worldwide. Similarly the iron industry is specialised in various districts such as Staffordshire, the north-east (Cleveland) corner of Yorkshire, South Wales, and the north-west corner of Lincolnshire. There is concentration in the most suitable places, formation of huge firms, and the absorption of smaller firms in smaller towns. Agriculture is everywhere, and much of the machinery of agriculture has been made by famous country firms in comparatively small towns, such as Ipswich, Bedford, Grantham, and Gainsborough, but in the years between the two World Wars large mass production at bigger centres tended to swallow up local industries. This, with the resulting risk of periods of mass unemployment, has been partly offset by the establishment of new light industries in many parts of the country.

CHARMING WOODLAND SCENERY AND LOFTY MOORLAND SOLITUDES

Manufacturing towns are rarely attractive anywhere, but those in the West Riding have alleviations not far away. Nearly all the middle courses of the Yorkshire rivers have charming patches of woodland scenery, and their upper courses come from lofty moorland solitudes. Nidderdale, Wharfedale, and upper Airedale are fine rambling grounds, as also are Wensleydale and Swaledale in the North Riding, and the dales inland from Whitby drained by the Derwent and its tributaries.

Durham is so famous for its coalfield and heavy industry that its rich agriculture is often overlooked. It is also notable for livestock, and the famous shorthorn cattle were first developed here. Once we go westward from the coal-tips this county has some fine scenery especially along the splendid valley of the Tees.

Northumberland is solidly industrial, with its great shipyards, from Newcastle to the sea, and is also a mining county. But northwards are the grand Cheviot Hills and westward runs Hadrian's Wall, the most impressive relic of the Roman occupation left in our island. For miles it runs from the Tyne to the Solway, often broken but still to be marvelled at, running like a ribbon over the fells. It was the " farthest north " of a vanished empire.

The cathedrals of historic note along our northward route from London to the Scottish border are Norwich, Ely, Peter-

borough, Lincoln, York, and Durham, and, returning southward by a western route, are Carlisle, Chester, Lichfield, Worcester, Hereford, Gloucester, Oxford, and Bristol, all worthy of study.

Cumberland and Westmorland have the supreme distinction of containing, with the Furness part of Lancashire, the most impressive expanse of English scenery, the Lake District. They are both agricultural except that Cumberland has a small coalfield on its coast, also they have a little lead mining. No one can be said to know England who does not know the Lake District and its many forms of beauty and grandeur. Its two largest lakes are in the Furness district of Lancashire, which, outside the lakeland area, has rich deposits of iron that account for the industrial town of Barrow-in-Furness.

Lancashire, the sixth English county in size, has more than five million people, or nearly three-quarters of a million more than Yorkshire, which is about three-and-a-half times as big. That is, Lancashire is a mass of towns in about half of its extent, the other half being well farmed. Nowhere else are manufactures and agriculture so contrasted in a single county. The cotton fabrics on the making of which the county chiefly depends, are made from material that is all imported.

ONE OF THE MOST VARIED IN SCENERY OF THE ENGLISH COUNTIES

Cheshire, largely manufacturing, has as its capital city Chester, a romantic place that for centuries was a fortress safeguarding England from Welsh invasions. Staffordshire, north and south, is given up to manufactures and mining. Shropshire, one of the most varied in scenery of the English counties, has an historic capital, Shrewsbury, finely placed on a loop of the River Severn. It has in Ludlow Castle the seat of the Lord of the Marches who kept watch upon Wales. The remainder of the Western counties, Hereford, Worcester, Gloucester, and Oxford, with the Malvern and Cotswold Hills, are all agricultural, with special charms in their mild airs and subtly English feeling. And so we see England given up in part to agriculture, but crowded where minerals call men together and manufactures are produced to offer to the world. Agriculture is still an important English business, but manufactures support the greater mass of the people and by trade with the world have brought her into touch with all nations.

The problems of our own country are just the same in all parts of the island, in England, in Scotland, and in Wales. Wales is a very beautiful country in almost every part of it, with a people rightly proud of the way in which they have preserved their individuality and language. It is extremely mountainous, but the valleys have good grazing. The farming is chiefly pastoral.

THE COALFIELDS EXTENDING ACROSS NEARLY THE WHOLE OF SOUTH WALES

The mineral resources are a small coal-field in the north, and one of large extent, fine quality, and exceptional thickness across nearly the whole south of the country.

Copper, tin, lead, and ironstone are worked, the latter extensively, and there are valuable slate quarries. The populous part is of course the mining area—Monmouthshire and Glamorgan, with Cardiff, Swansea, and Newport as the principal towns. More than a million-and-a-half of the two-and-a-half million Welsh people live in the coal-mining districts. The coal of South Wales is particularly suitable for steamships. The use of oil by shipping has not deeply affected the coal industry, and manufacturers, not only in this country but all the world over, are clamouring for the magnificent grades of coal which are mined in the Principality.

The 1931 census revealed that, for the first time in a hundred years, the population of Scotland had decreased. But the 1951 census showed that there had been an increase once more. It is a land to be loved. Its beauty, its industry, the splendid progress it made when it got into its stride, and the wonderful part taken by the Scottish race everywhere overseas have commanded the world's attention and admiration.

HOW SCOTLAND HAS HELPED HERSELF TO THE WORLD'S CHIEF BUSINESSES

Three hundred years ago there was not a poorer nation than Scotland. Much of it had not the means then to be anything but poor. However, since coal and metals began to dominate industry, Scotland, having a fair share of both, went ahead comparatively, and Glasgow is our second city in population. The country has all

the manufactures its natural resources make possible—iron and steel, railway equipment, woollens, cottons, silk, linen, jute, materials for seafaring, tobacco, spirituous beverages, well spread over the country, and granite and fish from the east coast, papermaking, and printing.

So Scotland may be said to have helped herself freely to all the world's chief businesses, and though a good deal of her land is not available for high-class agriculture she uses what she has that is good so well that, in farming most kinds of crops, in gardening, and in forestry, she gives others instruction.

Scotland's slight loss of population in the years before the two World Wars was, of course, mainly due to lack of employment. The Scots with their characteristic determination and energy sought better prospects elsewhere. But in the strenuous years in which Britain was fighting for the world's freedom Scotland's output of shipping and manufactures was as flourishing as it had ever been.

OUR COUNTRY THE MOST UNSELFISH ADVISER AND FRIEND OF THE WORLD

What is the prospect for our country generally now that she has emerged victorious from her long years of stress ? We ought to ask that, for the true test of every nation is the spread of reasonable happiness to all peoples.

Even in the dark days of industrial depression between the two World Wars we met the shock of changing customs in trade and kept a larger proportion of our own trade than any other country. Even our unemployed were fewer in proportion and better cared for than in other lands. The spirit of our men and women had not been broken, and this was clearly proved immediately the hardest trials of all time faced them.

No task then proved too difficult to attempt, no hours of labour too long. Making a proportionately greater contribution to the fighting forces than any other Allied Nation, except Russia, in the factories and in the fields the men, women, and children of this island toiled without respite.

By her devotion to the cause of Freedom Britain enhanced her high reputation in the eyes of all mankind, and now the battles are over she is in high heart to act once again as an unselfish world partner in the more fruitful paths of peace.

Illustrated Maps of All Countries with Thousands of Pictures

ATLAS HOLDING UP THE WORLD

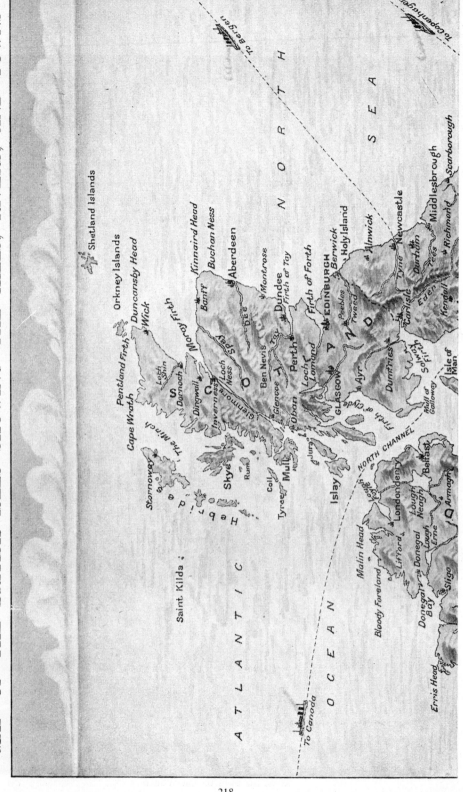

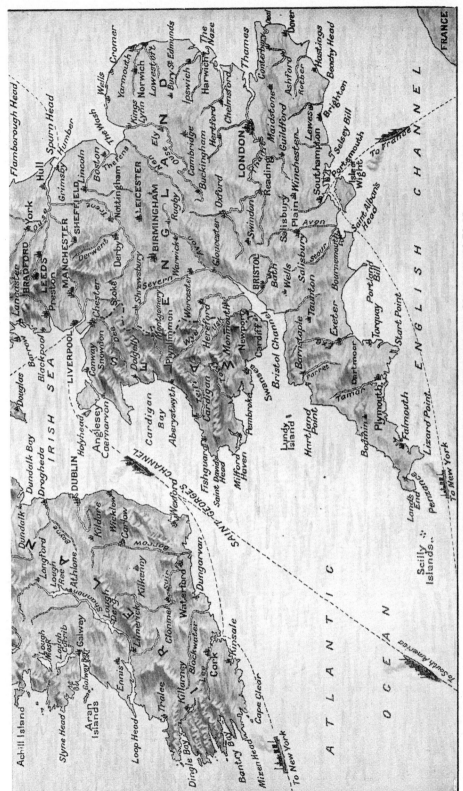

LAND OF OUR BIRTH, WE PLEDGE TO THEE OUR LOVE AND TOIL IN YEARS TO BE

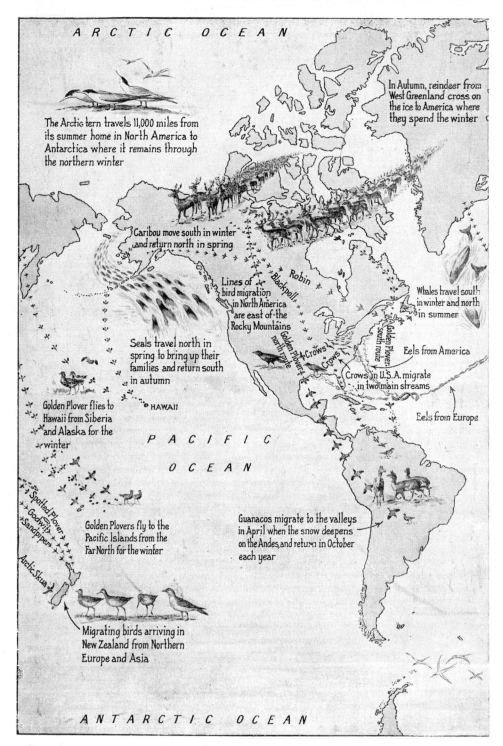

A NATURAL HISTORY MAP SHOWING THE ANNUAL MIGRATIONS OF ANIMALS

CREATURES THAT TAKE PLACE EVERY YEAR

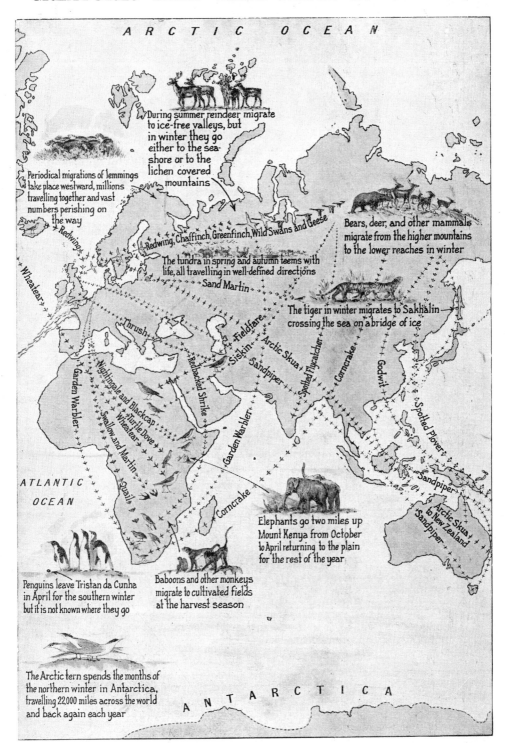

During summer reindeer migrate to ice-free valleys, but in winter they go either to the sea-shore or to the lichen covered mountains

Periodical migrations of lemmings take place westward, millions travelling together and vast numbers perishing on the way

Redwing, Chaffinch, Greenfinch, Wild Swans and Geese

Bears, deer, and other mammals migrate from the higher mountains to the lower reaches in winter

The tundra in spring and autumn teems with life, all travelling in well-defined directions

Sand Martin

The tiger in winter migrates to Sakhalin crossing the sea on a bridge of ice

Wheatear

Redwing

Thrush

Fieldfare

Siskin

Arctic Skua

Sandpiper

Spotted Flycatcher

Corncrake

Godwit

Garden Warbler

Nightingale and Blackcap

Redbacked Shrike

Turtle Dove

Wheatear

Swallow and Martin

Quail

Garden Warbler

Corncrake

Spotted Plover

Sandpiper

Arctic Skua to New Zealand

Sandpiper

ATLANTIC OCEAN

Elephants go two miles up Mount Kenya from October to April returning to the plain for the rest of the year

Penguins leave Tristan da Cunha in April for the southern winter but it is not known where they go

Baboons and other monkeys migrate to cultivated fields at the harvest season

The Arctic tern spends the months of the northern winter in Antarctica, travelling 22,000 miles across the world and back again each year

ANTARCTICA

AND BIRDS, WITH THEIR ROUTES FROM PLACE TO PLACE. See Index for Migration

ANIMALS OF THE LONG AGO & WHERE THEIR REMAINS ARE FOUND TODAY

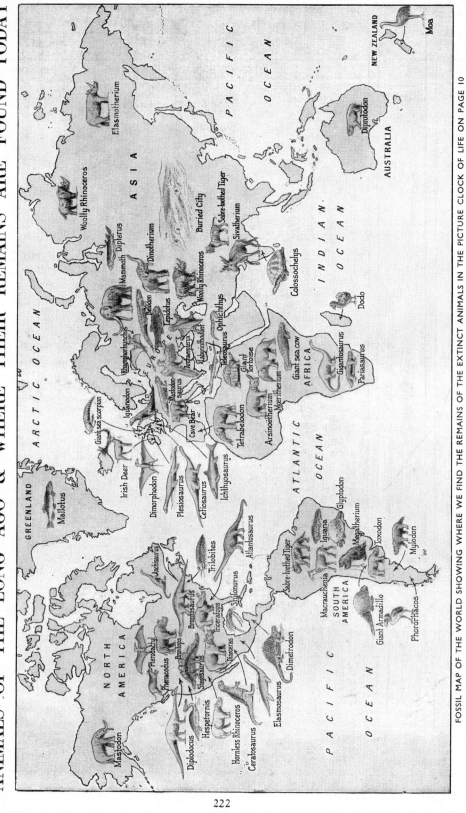

FOSSIL MAP OF THE WORLD SHOWING WHERE WE FIND THE REMAINS OF THE EXTINCT ANIMALS IN THE PICTURE CLOCK OF LIFE ON PAGE 10

One Thousand Poems of All Times and All Countries

THE BOY AND THE ANGEL

Robert Browning seeks to illustrate in this poem one of the greatest truths of life. The poor boy Theocrite, sincerely praising God each day, foolishly comes to think that God would be better pleased to be praised in the " great way " of the Pope of Rome, and so his ambition is to become the Pope. The poet imagines the angel Gabriel coming down to Earth to take the place of the poor workman Theocrite, while Theocrite has climbed into the papal chair. Thus in the end the angel shames the boy. The lesson is that we are all free to praise God in any way we choose.

MORNING, evening, noon, and night,
" Praise God ! " sang Theocrite.

Then to his poor trade he turned,
By which the daily meal was earned.

Hard he laboured, long and well;
O'er his work the boy's curls fell.

But ever, at each period,
He stopped and sang: " Praise God! "

Then back again his curls he threw,
And cheerful turned to work anew.

Said Blaise, the listening monk: "Well done;
I doubt not thou art heard, my son.

" As well as if thy voice today
Were praising God the Pope's great way.

" This Easter Day the Pope at Rome
Praises God from Peter's dome."

Said Theocrite: " Would God that I
Might praise Him that great way, and die."

Night passed, days shone,
And Theocrite was gone.

With God a day endures alway,
A thousand years are but a day.

God said in heaven: " Nor day nor night
Now brings the voice of My delight."

Then Gabriel, like a rainbow's birth,
Spread his wings and sank to earth;

Entered, in flesh, the empty cell,
Lived there, and played the craftsman well.

And morning, evening, noon, and night,
Praised God in place of Theocrite.

And from a boy to youth he grew;
The man put off the stripling's hue.

The man matured and fell away
Into the season of decay;

And ever o'er the trade he bent,
And ever lived on earth content.

(He did God's will; to him all one
If on the earth or in the sun.)

God said: " A praise is in mine ear;
There is no doubt in it, no fear:

" So sing old worlds, and so
New worlds that from my footstool go.

" Clearer loves sound other ways:
I miss my little human praise."

Then forth sprang Gabriel's wings, off fell
The flesh disguise, remained the cell.

'Twas Easter Day; he flew to Rome,
And paused above Saint Peter's dome.

In the tiring-room close by
The great outer gallery,

With his holy vestments dight,
Stood the new Pope, Theocrite:

And all his past career
Came back upon him clear,

Since when, a boy, he plied his trade,
Till on his life the sickness weighed,

POEMS · SONGS · BALLADS · VERSES AND RHYMES WITH MUSIC

And in his cell, when death drew near,
An angle in a dream brought cheer:

And rising from the sickness drear
He grew a priest, and now stood here.

To the East with praise he turned,
And on his sight the angel burned.

" I bore thee from thy craftsman's cell
And set thee here; I did not well.

" Vainly I left my angel-sphere,
Vain was thy dream of many a year.

"Thy voice's praise seemed weak; it dropt;
Creation's chorus stopped!

" Go back and praise again
The early way, while I remain.

" With that weak voice of our disdain,
Take up Creation's pausing strain.

" Back to the cell and poor employ:
Become the craftsman and the boy! "

Theocrite grew old at home;
A new Pope dwelt in Peter's dome.

One vanished as the other died:
They sought God side by side.

TO A WATERFOWL

William Cullen Bryant, who was born at Cummington, in
the State of Massachusetts, November 3, 1794, and died in
New York, June 12, 1878, was one of the greatest poets
America has produced. In his poetry we find a deep understanding of Nature and a steady, serene faith in the Providence which guides the wondrous life of earth. The
manner of his poetry is, however, rather that of a scholar.

WHITHER, midst falling dew,
While glow the heavens with the
last steps of day,
Far, through their rosy depths, dost thou
pursue
Thy solitary way?

Vainly the fowler's eye
Might mark thy distant flight to do thee
wrong,
As, darkly painted on the crimson sky,
Thy figure floats along.

Seek'st thou the splashy brink
Of weedy lake, or marge of river wide,
Or where the rocking billows rise and sink
On the chafed ocean-side?

There is a Power whose care
Teaches thy way along that pathless
coast—
The desert and illimitable air—
Lone wandering, but not lost.

All day thy wings have fanned,
At that far height, the cold, thin atmos-
phere.
Yet stoop not, weary, to the welcome land,
Though the dark night is near.

And soon that toil shall end;
Soon shalt thou find a summer home
and rest,
And scream among thy fellows; reeds
shall bend
Soon o'er thy sheltered nest.

Thou'rt gone, the abyss of heaven
Hath swallowed up thy form; yet on
my heart
Deeply hath sunk the lesson thou hast
given,
And shall not soon depart.

He who, from zone to zone,
Guides through the boundless sky thy
certain flight,
In the long way that I must tread alone
Will lead my steps aright.

LORD, IT BELONGS NOT TO MY CARE

Richard Baxter (1615-1691), the writer of this hymn, was a
famous broad-minded minister, who wrote many books,
beautiful in spirit and style, and won universal respect in
days when persecution was common. His health was always
precarious, and that fact gives these verses their tone, and
some of their beauty.

LORD, it belongs not to my care
Whether I die or live;
To love and serve Thee is my share,
And this Thy grace must give.

If life be long I will be glad
That I may long obey;
If short—yet why should I be sad
To soar to endless day?

Christ leads me through no darker rooms
Than He went through before;
He that into God's kingdom comes
Must enter by His door.

Come, Lord, when grace hath made me
meet
Thy blessed face to see;
For if Thy work on earth be sweet,
What will Thy glory be?

Then I shall end my sad complaints
And weary, sinful days;
And join with the triumphant saints
To sing Jehovah's praise.

My knowledge of that life is small,
The eye of faith is dim ;
But 'tis enough that Christ knows all,
And I shall be with Him.

AT SEA

There is a fine sense of the swift movement of a great ship across the salt sea in this poem by Allan Cunningham, a Scottish author who lived from 1784 to 1842, spending half of his life in London, where he wrote a great deal about art.

A WET sheet and a flowing sea,
  A wind that follows fast,
And fills the white and rustling sail
  And bends the gallant mast ;
And bends the gallant mast, my boys,
  While, like the eagle free,
Away the good ship flies, and leaves
  Old England on the lee.

O, for a soft and gentle wind !
  I heard a fair one cry;
But give to me the snorting breeze
  And white waves heaving high ;
And white waves heaving high, my boys,
  The good ship tight and free—
The world of waters is our home,
  And merry men are we.

There's tempest in yon hornéd moon,
  And lightning in yon cloud;
But hark the music, mariners !
  The wind is piping loud ;
The wind is piping loud, my boys,
  The lightning flashes free—
While the hollow oak our palace is,
  Our heritage the sea.

A CHRISTMAS HYMN

This spirited hymn by Alfred Domett (1811–1887) gives a new turn to an old theme. Though the story of Christmas is a story that changed for ever the whole course of human life and thrilled the world with a new hope, so that there is a sense in which it will never grow old, it has been sung by countless poets, and he may be regarded as something of a genius who can bring a new thought to it.

IT was the calm and silent night !
  Seven hundred years and fifty-three
Had Rome been growing up to might,
  And now was queen of land and sea.
No sound was heard of clashing wars—
  Peace brooded o'er the hushed domain:
Apollo, Pallas, Jove, and Mars
  Held undisturbed their ancient reign
    In the solemn midnight,
      Centuries ago.

'Twas the calm and silent night !
  The senator of haughty Rome,
Impatient, urged his chariot's flight,
  From lordly revel rolling home;
Triumphal arches, gleaming, swell
  His breast with thoughts of boundless
    sway;
What recked the Roman what befell
  A paltry province far away
    In the solemn midnight,
      Centuries ago ?

Within that province far away
  Went plodding home a weary boor;
A streak of light before him lay,
  Fallen through a half-shut stable-door
Across his path.   He passed—for naught
  Told what was going on within;
How keen the stars, his only thought—
  The air how calm, and cold, and thin,
    In the solemn midnight,
      Centuries ago !

O strange indifference ! low and high
  Drowsed over common joys and cares;
The earth was still—but knew not why
  The world was listening, unawares.
How calm a moment may precede
  One that shall thrill the world for ever !
To that still moment none would heed
  Man's doom was linked no more to
    sever;
    In the solemn midnight,
      Centuries ago !

It is the calm and solemn night !
  A thousand bells ring out, and throw
Their joyous peals abroad, and smite
  The darkness—charmed and holy now !
The night that erst no shame had worn,
  To it a happy name is given;
For in that stable lay, new-born,
  The peaceful Prince of earth and heaven
    In the solemn midnight,
      Centuries ago !

THE MOUNTAIN AND THE SQUIRREL

Emerson was a famous 19th-century American writer. Seldom humorous in his poems, this is one of the exceptions. Though the verse is humorous, its lesson is quite serious, for it reminds us that we have each our particular work to do and our special abilities for doing it. The all-wise Creator has not made us all alike, and we must do our best with the gifts He has given us.

THE mountain and the squirrel
  Had a quarrel,
And the former called the latter " Little
  prig ";
Bun replied,
" You are doubtless very big;
But all sorts of things and weather
Must be taken in together
To make up a year
And a sphere.
And I think it no disgrace
To occupy my place.
If I am not so large as you,
You are not so small as I,
And not half so spry;
I'll not deny you make
A very pretty squirrel track.
Talents differ; all is well and wisely put;
If I cannot carry forests on my back
Neither can you crack a nut."

225

EXCELSIOR

Written by the famous American poet Henry Wadsworth Longfellow, this poem may seem strange at first reading. We must know that the word excelsior comes from a Latin word which means higher ; then the poem is quite clear. The youth wished to excel and he heeded no warnings, no inducements to remain in comfort and safety, but went striving upward, and at last suffered death in the snow-storm. But to the end he stood bravely by his motto.

THE shades of night were falling fast
  As through an Alpine village passed
A youth who bore, 'mid snow and ice,
A banner with the strange device :
    Excelsior !

His brow was sad; his eye beneath
Flashed like a falchion from its sheath,
And like a silver clarion rung
The accents of that unknown tongue :
    Excelsior !

In happy homes he saw the light
Of household fires gleam warm and bright;
Above the spectral glaciers shone,
And from his lips escaped a groan :
    Excelsior !

" Try not the pass," the old man said;
" Dark lowers the tempest overhead;
The roaring torrent is deep and wide ! "
And loud the clarion voice replied :
    Excelsior !

" Oh stay," the maiden said, " and rest
Thy weary head upon this breast ! "
A tear stood in his bright blue eye,
But still he answered with a sigh :
    Excelsior !

" Beware the pine tree's withered branch !
Beware the awful avalanche ! "
This was the peasant's last good-night !
A voice replied, far up the height :
    Excelsior !

At break of day, as heavenward
The pious monks of Saint Bernard
Uttered the oft-repeated prayer,
A voice cried through the startled air :
    Excelsior !

A traveller by the faithful hound
Half-buried in the snow was found,
Still grasping in his hand of ice
That banner with the strange device :
    Excelsior !

There, in the twilight cold and grey,
Lifeless, but beautiful, he lay,
And from the sky, serene and far,
A voice fell, like a falling star :
    Excelsior !

THERE'S A GOOD TIME COMING

Charles Mackay (1814-1889), who wrote these spirited words of cheer. was a fine Christian Englishman. and his songs have the ring of downright sincerity. The good time he sang of has not yet come, but it is nearer, and more and more people feel that it would indeed be a good time.

THERE'S a good time coming, boys,
  A good time coming :
There's a good time coming, boys—
  Wait a little longer.
We may not live to see the day,
But Earth shall glisten in the ray
  Of the good time coming.
Cannon-balls may aid the truth,
  But thought's a weapon stronger;
We'll win our battle by its aid —
  Wait a little longer.

CHORUS

Oh, there's a good time coming, boys,
  There's a good time coming :
There's a good time coming, boys,
  Wait a little longer.

There's a good time coming, boys,
  A good time coming;
The pen shall supersede the sword,
And right, not might, shall be the lord
  In the good time coming.
Worth, not birth, shall rule mankind
  And be acknowledged stronger.
The proper impulse has been given—
  Wait a little longer.

A FAREWELL

Charles Kingsley (1819-1875) was the author of some of our finest adventure stories. He also wrote verse, and this is one of the best-known of his smaller poems. It was written for a girl as farewell advice. Kingsley loved children and delighted to write for them. The poem reminds us that it is better to be good and to do good than to be clever and win fame. " A Farewell " is printed here by permission of Messrs. Macmillan, the publishers.

MY fairest child, I have no song to give
  you;
  No lark could pipe to skies so dull and
    grey,
Yet, ere we part, one lesson I can leave you
  For every day.

I'll teach you how to sing a clearer carol
  Than lark that hails the dawn on
    breezy down,
To earn yourself a purer poet's laurel
  Than Shakespeare's crown.

Be good, sweet maid, and let who can be
  clever;
  Do noble things, not dream them, all
    day long,
And so make Life, Death, and that vast
  Forever
  One grand, sweet song.

MEMORY

The American poet Thomas Bailey Aldrich (1836–1907) here expresses a curious fact which most people have experienced. Some unimportant events in our lives will be remembered by us far better than we can ever remember dates which are supposed to be of the greatest importance. Perhaps Memory is wiser than we are in thus calling to our mind the things of which we had taken least account.

My mind lets go a thousand things,
  Like dates of wars and deaths of
    kings,
And yet recalls the very hour—
'Twas noon by yonder village tower,
And on the last blue moon in May—
The wind came briskly up this way,
Crisping the brook beside the road;
Then, pausing here, set down its load
Of pine-scents, and shook listlessly
Two petals from that wild-rose tree.

THE VOICE OF THE GRASS

We are not apt to look upon the grass as a thing of life and movement, and yet, of course, it shares the silent, steady life of all the plants. In these verses, by an American poet named Sarah Boyle (1812–1869), the grass is personified as a living thing, with striking and truthful effect. It is thus that the poet can make us see familiar things in a new light

Here I come creeping, creeping every-
    where;
  By the dusty roadside,
  On the sunny hillside,
  Close by the noisy brook,
  In every shady nook,
I come creeping, creeping everywhere.

Here I come creeping, smiling everywhere;
  All round the open door,
  Where sit the aged poor;
  Here where the children play,
  In the bright and merry May.
I come creeping, creeping everywhere.

Here I come creeping, creeping every-
    where;
  In the noisy city street
  My pleasant face you'll meet,
  Cheering the sick at heart,
  Toiling his busy part—
Silently creeping, creeping everywhere.

Here I come creeping, creeping every-
    where;
  You cannot see me coming,
  Nor hear my low sweet humming;
  For in the starry night,
  And the glad morning light
I come quietly, creeping everywhere.

Here I come creeping, creeping every-
    where;
  More welcome than the flowers
  In summer's pleasant hours ;
  The gentle cow is glad,
  And the merry bird not sad,
To see me creeping, creeping everywhere.

Here I come creeping, creeping every-
    where;
  My humble song of praise,
  Most joyfully I raise
  To Him at whose command
  I beautify the land,
Creeping, silently creeping everywhere

WHAT I LIVE FOR

George Linnaeus Banks, who was born in 1821 and died in 1881, was well known in his day as a poet and a writer, though the novels of his wife were more read than his own writings. He was a man of lofty ideals, and endeavoured by voice and pen to forward the education of his fellow-men, for he was an orator as well as a writer. Of his short poems the following is perhaps the best known, and it sums up the life-work of the true Christian. The last four lines form a favourite quotation with writers and speakers pleading for workers to come forward in any good cause.

I live for those who love me,
  Whose hearts are kind and true;
For the heaven that smiles above me,
  And awaits my spirit, too;
For all human ties that bind me,
For the task by God assigned me,
For the bright hopes left behind me,
  And the good that I can do.

I live to learn their story,
  Who've suffered for my sake;
To emulate their glory,
  And follow in their wake;
Bards, patriots, martyrs, sages,
The noble of all ages,
Whose deeds crown history's pages,
  And time's great volume make.

I live to hold communion
  With all that is divine;
To feel there is a union
  'Twixt Nature's heart and mine;
To profit by affliction,
Reap truths from fields of fiction,
Grow wiser from conviction,
  And fulfil each grand design.

I live to hail that season,
  By gifted minds foretold,
When men shall live by reason,
  And not alone by gold;
When man to man united,
And every wrong thing righted,
The whole world shall be lighted
  As Eden was of old.

I live for those who love me,
  For those who know me true;
For the heaven that smiles above me,
  And awaits my spirit too;
For the cause that lacks assistance,
For the wrong that needs resistance,
For the future in the distance,
  And the good that I can do.

THE SOLDIER

The pathos of this beautiful poem is redoubled when we know that the writer, Rupert Brooke, a young officer, lies buried, as he felt he might be, in " some corner of a foreign field," for early in the First World War he died for the England he loved. What could he have left behind more beautiful than this idea of his spirit for ever echoing in the world what is best in England ? It is from his Poems, published by Sidgwick and Jackson.

IF I should die, think only this of me:
  That there's some corner of a foreign
    field
That is for ever England.   There shall be
  In that rich earth a richer dust con-
    cealed;
A dust which England bore, shaped, made
    aware,
  Gave, once, her flowers to love, her ways
    to roam;
A body of England's breathing English air,
  Washed by the rivers, blest by suns of
    home.
And think this heart, all evil shed away,
  A pulse in the eternal mind, no less
Gives somewhere back the thoughts by
    England given;
Her sights and sounds; dreams happy as
    her day;
  And laughter, learnt of friends; and
    gentleness,
In hearts at peace, under an English
    heaven.

SALLY IN OUR ALLEY

Few songs are better known or more popular than this, supposed to be sung by the apprentice who loves his pretty Sally so dearly, although she *does* live in a humble alley. He will be true to her, too, in spite of the disagreeable neighbours, who " make game " of him and his sweetheart. Of course, Sunday is " the day that comes between a Saturday and Monday." Henry Carey (1690-1743), the author of this song, was also a musician of some note in his day. It has been said that he wrote our National Anthem, but the evidence in his favour is not very strong.

OF all the girls that are so smart,
  There's none like pretty Sally;
She is the darling of my heart,
  And lives in our alley;
There is no lady in the land
  That's half so sweet as Sally;
She is the darling of my heart,
  And lives in our alley.

Of all the days within the week
  I dearly love but one day,
And that's the day that comes between
  A Saturday and Monday;
Oh ! then I'm dressed in all my best,
  To walk abroad with Sally;
She is the darling of my heart,
  And lives in our alley.

When Christmas comes about again,
  Oh! then I shall have money;
I'll save it up, and box and all
  I'll give unto my honey;

I would it were ten thousand pound,
  I'd give it all to Sally;
She is the darling of my heart,
  And she lives in our alley.

My master and the neighbours all
  Make game of me and Sally,
And, but for her, I'd better be
  A slave and row a galley;
But when my seven long years are out,
  O, then I'll marry Sally;
O, then we'll wed, and then we'll bed,
  But not in our alley.

JOHN ANDERSON

This famous song is a love song—with a difference. In it Robert Burns pictures a happy couple not at the beginning of their married life, but toward its close ; and it says much for the enduring affection each has cherished for the other that the old lady is able to sing so tenderly of her " jo," or sweetheart.   The Scots words in the song are easy to understand, but " brent," it may be said, means smooth or unwrinkled ; " pow," head, and " canty," happy.

JOHN ANDERSON, my jo John,
  When we were first acquent
Your locks were like the raven,
  Your bonnie brow was brent;
But now your brow is bald, John,
  Your locks are like the snow;
But blessings on your frosty pow,
  John Anderson, my jo.

John Anderson, my jo John,
  We clamb the hill thegither,
And mony a canty day, John,
  We've had wi' ane anither;
Now we maun totter down, John,
  But hand in hand we'll go,
And sleep thegither at the foot,
  John Anderson, my jo.

THE SHEPHERD BOY SINGS IN THE VALLEY OF HUMILIATION

John Bunyan, whose Pilgrim's Progress is the greatest allegory in the world wrote very little verse. But the snatches of poetry he introduced here and there into his story were quaintly expressed.   The song which he placed in the mouth of the Shepherd Boy in the Valley of Humiliation, however, is entitled to warm praise, even on the literary side.   The lad had already found out the secret of happiness and peace. A contented mind is a continual feast.

HE that is down needs fear no fall,
  He that is low no pride;
He that is humble ever shall
  Have God to be his guide.

I am content with what I have,
  Little be it or much;
And, Lord, contentment still I crave,
  Because Thou savest such.

Fulness to such a burden is
  That go on pilgrimage;
Here little, and hereafter bliss,
  Is best from age to age.

GOOSEY GOOSEY GANDER

Goosey, Goosey, Gan - der, Whither shall I wander?

Up - stairs and down - stairs and in my lady's chamber.

There I met an old man who wouldn't say his prayers; I

took him by the left leg and threw him down the stairs

28 H 1*

HIGGLEDY, Piggledy,
My black hen,
She lays eggs
For gentlemen ;
Sometimes nine,
And sometimes ten,
Higgledy, Piggledy,
My black hen.

HERE we go up, up, up,
And here we go down, down,
downy ;
And here we go backwards and forwards,
And here we go round, round,
roundy.

PEASE-PUDDING hot,
Pease-pudding cold,
Pease-pudding in the pot,
Nine days old.
Some like it hot,
Some like it cold,
Some like it in the pot,
Nine days old.

JACK SPRAT had a pig, who was not
very little nor yet very big ;
He was not very lean, he was not
very fat ;
He'll do well for a grunt, says little
Jack Sprat.

GO to bed first,
A golden purse;
Go to bed second,
A golden pheasant;
Go to bed third,
A golden bird.

HERE we go round a ginger ring,
A ginger ring, a ginger ring ;
Here we go round a ginger ring,
Around about merry my Tansy.

A bowlful of nuts we sat down to
crack,
Sat down to crack, sat down to crack ;
A bowlful of nuts we sat down to
crack,
Around about merry my Tansy.

What will you give us to tell his name,
To tell his name, to tell his name;
What will you give us to tell his name,
Around about merry my Tansy ?

The last time is the catching time,
The catching time, the catching time ;
The last time is the catching time,
Around about merry my Tansy.

PLEASE to remember
The fifth of November,
Gunpowder, treason, and plot ;
I know no reason
Why gunpowder and treason
Should ever be forgot.

WHEN little Sammy Soapsuds
    Went out to take a ride,
In looking over London Bridge
    He fell into the tide.

His parents never having taught
    Their loving Sam to swim,
The tide soon got the mastery,
    And made an end of him.

DANCE, little baby, dance up high,
    Never mind, baby, mother is by ;
Crow and caper, caper and crow,
There, little baby, there you go ;
Up to the ceiling, down to the ground,
Backwards and forwards, round and
    round ;
Dance, little baby, and mother will sing,
With the merry coral, ding, ding, ding !

ONE misty, moisty morning,
    When cloudy was the weather,
There I met an old man,
    Clothed all in leather ;
Clothed all in leather,
    With cap under his chin—
How do you do, and how do you do,
    And how do you do again ?

HERE'S Sulky Sue ;
    What shall we do ?
Turn her face to the wall
    Till she comes to.

COME, let's to bed,
    Says Sleepy-head,
Tarry a while, says Slow,
    Put on the pan, says Greedy Nan,
Let's sup before we go.

RUB-A-DUB-DUB,
    Three men in a tub ;
The butcher, the baker,
The candlestick-maker ;
And they all jumped out of a rotten potato.

Sybil Burnside

DAME TROT and her cat
    Sat down for to chat ;
The Dame sat on this side,
    And Puss sat on that.

Puss, says the Dame,
    Can you catch a rat
Or a mouse in the dark ?
    Purr ! says the cat.

LITTLE Tom Tucker
    Sings for his supper ;
What shall he eat ?
    White bread and butter.
How shall he cut it
    Without a knife ?
How can he marry
    Without a wife ?

ROBERT BARNES, fellow fine,
    Can you shoe this horse of
        mine ?
Yes, good sir, that I can,
As well as any other man.
Here's a nail and there's a prod,
And now, good sir, your horse is shod.

THERE was an old woman
    Lived under a hill,
And if she's not gone
    She lives there still.

HERE am I, little Jumping Joan ;
    When nobody's with me
        I'm always alone.

THERE was an owl lived in an oak:
    Whiskey, whaskey, weedle!
And all the words he ever spoke
    Were fiddle, faddle, feedle!

A gunner chanced to come that road;
    Whiskey, whaskey, weedle!
Says he, I'll shoot you, silly bird!
    So fiddle, faddle, feedle!

The Story of Where Power Comes From, What It Does, & How It Works

Syrian women with their distaffs

WHAT IS ELECTRICITY ?

THE first kind of electricity that was known was the kind produced by friction. In ancient Syria the women often used for their spinning distaffs made of amber, and the spindles as they ran merrily round would often touch against the garment of the spinner and become electrified. Then, when placed on the ground, they would attract dry leaves or dust, which would cling to them with a mysterious force.

All unconsciously these spinning-women were driving an electrical machine, making the electricity which thousands of years later was to light the homes of the people. Take a glass rod or a fountain-pen, rub it briskly with a silk handkerchief, and hold it over some tiny piece of tissue-paper. The bits of paper will suddenly become lively ; they will move about and jump up to meet the rod, clinging to it by what is known as electric attraction.

Some three hundred years or so before the birth of Jesus, one of the early philosophers of Greece, Theophrastus, found out that some unknown force must be at work when amber was excited by friction, and, as far as we know, his thoughts were the first to be directed on any sort of scientific lines to this curious phenomenon. Experiments began, and Theophrastus found

that amber was not alone in this power but that it was possessed also by a mineral called tourmaline. Pliny, seventy years after Christ, again drew attention to these things, and followed up the early studies of Theophrastus.

Many other evidences of the existence of the same sort of curious force were noticed later ; probably they were not really new, but men had begun to link up these various happenings, and to seek some explanation of them. Aristotle tells us how the " torpedo fish " would benumb both men and fishes. This curious creature has an organ with which it produces electricity, and it can benumb another fish with a powerful shock by merely touching it. The electric eel has similar powers; in fact, several varieties of these remarkable fishes are now known.

An interesting fact can now be recorded: the first endeavours of man to put electricity to any real use. These electric fishes were actually used to give shocks to people suffering from gout, as a cure, probably with very doubtful results. Yet such crude attempts to use the yet unknown forces of electricity were the beginnings of the vast electro-medical science of today.

Electricity owes its name to amber, the earliest substance known to show the

ELECTRICITY · WIRELESS · OIL · GAS · MOTORS · ENGINES · SHIPS

property of attraction; and the Greek word elektron, which means amber, has clung to the force that rules the world, although it was not given the name Electricity until so christened by Dr. Gilbert, the famous physician of Queen Elizabeth.

Very little more was heard of electricity throughout the whole of the Middle Ages. A few facts were handed down to history, but were of little importance. Eustathius told of a philosopher who, while dressing and undressing, would at times emit crackling sparks, flames blazing from him without burning his clothes, but it was nothing more than the electricity we get from stroking a cat on a frosty day. The old philosophers saw lightning without thinking of electricity ; they looked upon it as a little flame falling from heaven.

Homer, in his famous Odyssey, described the sulphurous smell that follows lightning, due to the electrified oxygen's conversion into ozone—a process that we copy today for purifying the air of tube railways and large buildings. But everyone groped in the dark through the centuries for the real power that was to revolutionise the world, until the real beginning of electricity was made by Dr. Gilbert of Colchester, toward the end of the sixteenth century.

THE FIRST MAN WHO FOUND THAT ELECTRICITY CAN BE STORED

This distinguished physician first of all repeated the experiments that history had recorded with amber, and then set himself to see what other substances would become electrified when rubbed. Suspending a fine needle by a piece of silk, he held the rubbed object near it, and observed whether it attracted the needle. In this simple way he discovered that a whole number of substances could be electrified by friction, and he drew up a list of what he called " electrics," or substances with which electricity can be produced.

Robert Boyle, who lived from 1627 to 1691, now set himself to discover the origin of electricity. We may look upon him as being the first man to discover that electricity can be stored. For he found that a piece of amber, when it had been rubbed, did not immediately lose its powers, but that the charge of electricity remained upon its surface for some time. The importance of this simple observation has become immense today, for no force is of use to man unless it can be stored and used in the form required.

These little experiments had shown that the new force could exert power—the power of lifting. A contemporary of Robert Boyle next showed that the mysterious force could produce light. This was Otto von Guericke, who cast a ball of sulphur in a glass bowl, broke the glass, and, extracting the sulphur ball, mounted it on a spindle. When it was rapidly revolved, and the hand held against it, the rubbing (or friction) caused it to glow in the dark. The first electric lamp had been made.

A SIMPLE EXPERIMENT TO PROVE THAT LIKE REPELS LIKE

Another discovery was made by von Guericke about the same time—one of the greatest importance, for it led to the further discovery that two kinds of electricity must exist—the two kinds which later became known as positive and negative electricity. He discovered that if a substance is attracted by an electrified body, and touches it, it is at once repelled.

This attraction, so swiftly followed by an exactly opposite effect, is due to the fact that any electrified body tries to share its electricity with a non-electrified one. Having done so, each of the bodies now possesses a charge of the same kind of electricity, and they no longer agree, because like repels like. Any boy or girl can prove this at home by a simple experiment. If two balls of dry pith, the size of a large pea, are suspended by pieces of silk thread so that they hang quite near together, and if they are then touched with an electrified rod—a stick of ebonite, for instance, rubbed with a piece of silk—they will instantly fly apart. The rod has shared its electricity with the balls, which become then charged with a similar kind of electricity, and similarly charged bodies will repel each other.

THE THREE WISE MEN WHO HELPED FORWARD OUR KNOWLEDGE

Three illustrious countrymen of our own next come into prominence: Newton, who made pieces of paper leap about in the air by an electrified glass ; Hawksbee, who made many new discoveries about the attraction of electrified bodies ; and Stephen Gray, who made the important discovery in 1729 that certain substances would conduct or carry electricity, while others would not. Without conductors and non-conductors we could do none of the things we do with electricity today. Look at the telegraph wires at the side of the railway track as you go along in the

THE ELECTRIC LAMP & THE LEYDEN JAR BEGIN

A WHIRLING BALL OF SULPHUR GLOWS WITH FRICTION, AND THE FIRST ELECTRIC LAMP IS BORN

A LEYDEN PROFESSOR RECEIVES A SHOCK FROM A JAR OF WATER, AND THE LEYDEN JAR IS BORN

train, and on each pole you will see little white porcelain insulators ; porcelain is a non-conductor, and as it carries the copper telegraph wires it prevents the electric current from escaping.

These early philosophers carried the making of electricity to a really practical stage. We have already seen how von Guericke electrified a sulphur ball by revolving it with the hand rubbing against it to provide the friction. Newton and Hawksbee built primitive electric machines, the forerunners of quite powerful ones used later to produce X-rays and so on.

THE ELECTRIC CURRENTS THAT WERE LOST ALL TOO QUICKLY

This turning round of a glass cylinder or disc and rubbing it by something to cause friction, was really the primitive electric machine. But the currents were so quickly lost that men now tried to devise some way of storing them. Various attempts in this direction led to the discovery of the Leyden jar, which for years played so important a part in wireless telegraphy. A professor of Leyden named Musschenbroek one day electrified some water in a glass bottle, and his assistant, who was holding the bottle, tried to disengage the wire that had been used to conduct the current to it from the machine. In touching it he received a strong electric shock, which showed that electricity had been stored up in the bottle, which had instantly communicated it to his body on being touched. The first Leyden jar had been charged and discharged.

It can be seen now to what a wonderful stage men's knowledge of electricity had been brought. This mysterious force had been made by *work*, or friction; power had been turned into electricity.

THE MAN WHO WORE TWO PAIRS OF STOCKINGS, AND WHAT HE FOUND

This force could now be conveyed from one spot to another by means of conductors. Some substances would not conduct electricity, and by making use of such substances the new force could be kept apart; while by storing it in a Leyden jar, standing on some non-conducting substance, the power could be accumulated and then discharged when it was required.

To Symmer must be given the credit of having first discovered that there are two distinct kinds of electricity—positive and negative. Putting two stockings on the same leg, one black and presumably woollen, the other white and of silk, he found that when he drew them off, drawing the white one off from the black one, the friction charged each one with electricity, but of a different kind ; each stocking stood up as if blown out, owing to its charge.

If brought together the two stockings *collapsed*, because the two different kinds of electricity neutralised each other. But when he repeated the experiment with two stockings of the same material, the two pairs would repel each other when electrified and held together. We now know that whenever electricity of one kind is made by any method, an exact amount of electricity of the opposite kind is always produced, and that, while similarly charged bodies repel each other, *oppositely charged bodies attract one another.*

If we rub a glass rod with a piece of silk it will become charged with positive electricity, while a piece of sealing-wax rubbed with flannel will be charged with negative electricity. Both the glass rod and the stick of sealing-wax will pick up bits of paper or pith, yet the kind of electricity is quite different in each case.

THE GOLD LEAVES IN THE BOTTLE AND WHAT THEY TELL US

The presence of either kind may be shown by a little instrument called the electroscope. Two pieces of gold leaf are attached to a brass rod or wire which may be fitted through a cork in the neck of a wide-mouthed bottle. The gold leaves are suspended inside the bottle from the bottom of the wire, and a metal disc is attached to the top of the wire outside the bottle. If we touch the disc with an electrified object, the charge will at once be shared by the disc, and will be distributed to the gold leaves. Each leaf being thus electrified with the same kind of electricity, the two will repel each other, and will stand apart and form an inverted ∨, thus ∧. In this way the most extraordinarily minute charges of electricity can be measured. If, when the leaves are standing apart, we touch the disc with the finger, the leaves will at once fall together again ; the electric charge will run through our body to the earth and be lost.

Many kinds of electric machines have been devised for producing large amounts of static electricity, which can be stored up and discharged in order to perform various experiments. Stroking a cat on a winter's

SIR ISAAC NEWTON HAS A LITTLE GAME

It delighted Sir Isaac Newton, who used to play with soap bubbles to learn about Light, to play with an electrified stick and little bits of paper, to learn about Electricity

day near the fire is perhaps the most primitive of natural " machines." The friction of the hand will electrify the hair of the cat, which will stand up, and a crackling noise will be heard as tiny sparks pass between the cat's fur and the hand. We can see the sparks if the room is dark.

The elaborate machines, in which the charge is accumulated in Leyden jars, are made by revolving cylinders or circular plates against substances which produce the necessary friction. A Wimshurst machine, which can be made of sufficient power to produce electric sparks several feet long, has two (or several) pairs of varnished glass-plates revolving in opposite directions, on the outsides of which are cemented a number of sectors made of tinfoil. Brushes of tinsel, fixed on arms, excite the tinfoil sectors as the plates revolve. Metal combs placed at each side of the wheels collect the electricity.

The earth itself may be looked upon as a huge store-house of static electricity, and indeed, as a giant generator of current. The globe itself, and the layer of atmosphere round it, may be looked upon as the two plates of an enormous spherical condenser, the earth itself being the negatively charged plate, the atmosphere the positively charged one.

THE ELECTRICAL ILLUMINATION OF THE SKY 200 MILES ABOVE THE EARTH

When a liquid evaporates, electricity is formed, the evaporated vapour carrying up with it a positive charge. One authority tells us how the evaporation that is continually going on all over the world bears a constant stream of positive electricity to the upper atmosphere, and how discharges occur between layers of air and cloud, giving rise under certain conditions to what we know as the aurora borealis.

These electrical effects are always greatest at the Poles, and it is in the polar regions that the aurora is most brilliant. the luminous discharges taking place sometimes at heights of more than two hundred miles above the Earth. Such remarkable development occurs in the vegetation in these regions, such remarkable yields from the crops, that Lemström and others were led, towards the close of the last century, to look into the matter, and it was found that the needle-formed leaves of the northern pine, the beards on the ears of cereals, and so on, were very much more pronounced than on those of warmer climates. Plants, in fact, continually collect the static electricity from the atmosphere with their myriads of hairs, spikes, and sharp points—to which a static charge will always fly—and by transmitting the electricity to the earth they help to produce their own nitrogenous food.

These discoveries led later to experiments in which positive electricity, generated by a machine, was distributed by means of wires, supported by poles, to the crops growing below, and in this way wheat and barley have been made to yield more than half as much again as normally.

THE LIGHTNING FLASH AND ITS FIFTY MILLION HORSE-POWER

In wonderful contrast to the feeble currents of electricity caused by friction, are the intensely powerful discharges that occur during a thunderstorm. The angry clouds of the storm were the first electric dynamo, and they remain today vastly more powerful than any electric machine made by man. Fifty million horse-power is released from the huge storage ground of the clouds, and discharged in the hundred-thousandth part of a second in the form of the blinding flash of lightning.

A Swedish scientist named Norinder has discovered that two things happen in the sky during a thunderstorm. There is what he calls a " first variation " in the conditions, which is connected with the movements of the clouds and with silent discharges of electricity—the movement of electric charges *without* a spark ; this condition lasts for about ten seconds. Then there come a series of very rapid changes in the electric field, which result in the pent-up electricity bursting the bonds which hold it—the resistance of the air between the clouds and the earth—so that it is discharged to the earth.

HOW THE LIGHTNING CONDUCTOR GUARDS A HOUSE FROM DANGER

The charge in a Leyden jar will fly to a finger held near it. In this we see what the lightning conductor does. It is a pointed metal rod placed on the highest part of a building, and to it leaks the electricity stored up in the thunder clouds. The result is that in the immediate surroundings enough electricity to break through to earth is never able to accumulate, and the safety of the building is thus secured. The conductor is connected to a metal plate buried in the earth, to which it conveys the electricity it collects.

Imperishable Thoughts of Men Enshrined in the Books of the World

POETRY MORE PRECIOUS THAN GOLD

IT is a splendid thing to say something the world will never forget. That splendid thing has been done often by great men and women who have written fine thoughts in words so beautiful that the books in which they are found will never die.

Most of these thoughts that cannot be forgotten are in poems, for poetry is far more easy to remember than the ordinary reading called prose. There are thousands of poems that everybody ought to read because they preserve the world's choicest thought in the choicest words, and those who do not read these poems can never know how fine a thing reading is.

True poetry is more precious than gold. Not only does it make us good and happy and hopeful, but it is so pleasant that the words sound like music.

When we write a story, or tell about a place, or a thing, or an event, in words like those we use in speaking to each other, but choosing them carefully to express our meaning, and also to have a fine and pleasing sound, we use Prose. But when grander events and more beautiful scenes are described, or nobler thoughts stir our spirits deeply, demanding words more thrilling or sweeter and more musical in sound, we use Poetry. Poetry is expression made perfect, the best thought in the best words.

At first poetry was great joy or great sorrow put into song. Long ages ago, when our far-off forefathers could not even read or write, they had poets who went with them into battle to compose fine-sounding verses to celebrate the victory, or laments for defeat. These verses were sung while they played a harp, so poetry then was feeling expressed in musical words suitable for singing.

We think of poetry now as it is read in books, but at first, before books came, it was only known by being heard, either sung or recited; and making it in simple forms was quite common. The earliest English poet we hear of, Caedmon, tells us how ashamed he was when, as he sat with a circle of companions and the harp was passed to him, he could not make and sing his verse in turn. It was in this way that the short stories in verse, which we call ballads, were first composed, not by one poet but by many, and then passed on by memory.

Poetry is grouped into three kinds— Epic, Dramatic, and Lyric. Epic poetry is an extended description in grand and noble words of some great event, or of the career of a hero, or of a period in the history of a nation. Dramatic poetry is written in the form of people speaking to each other, and is acted on the stage. Lyric

ROMANCE · HISTORIES · DRAMAS · ESSAYS · WORLD CLASSICS

poetry was originally intended to be sung to the playing of the lyre, an ancient form of the harp. All beautiful songs come into lyric poetry.

Sometimes poetry is written in rhymed lines, the words at the ends of the lines having similar sounds, as in

> The world is so full of a number of things,
> I'm sure we should all be as happy as kings.

The lines in which the rhyming words occur need not be next to each other. They may be alternate, as in

> Arabia's desert ranger
> To Him shall bow the knee,
> The Ethiopian stranger
> His glory come to see.

Or the rhymes may be otherwise separated, as in the lines

> Ring out, wild bells, to the wild sky,
> The flying cloud, the frosty light;
> The year is dying in the night
> Ring out, wild bells, and let him die.

Some lines, too, may have rhymes and others be unrhymed, as in

> Blue were her eyes as the fairy flax,
> And her cheeks like the dawn of day,
> And her bosom white as the hawthorn buds
> That ope in the month of May.

THE POETRY THAT TELLS OF GREAT EVENTS AND HIGH IMAGININGS

Here day and May rhyme, but flax and buds do not. The advantage of rhyme is that it pleases the ear, and helps us to remember the words, the sound speeding us on to the next similar sound. But rhyming does not make poetry. It is the beauty of the thought and the balance and melody of the words that make true poetry.

And, indeed, much of the finest poetry has no rhymes, but is balanced in lines with such dignity and sweetness that it is grander than rhymed verse. This form of poetry, called blank verse, is used to tell us of great events, tragedies, high imaginings, and noble deeds. Shakespeare and Milton wrote most of their works in this way. Here is an example from Shakespeare, describing Brutus:

> His life was gentle; and the elements
> So mixed in him that Nature might stand up
> And say to all the world, This was a man!

How fine these lines sound! They have the solemn music of a grand organ, and need no rhyme ; but each line balances with the other in syllables and accent.

Lyrical poetry is divided into verses' Strictly speaking, a single line of poetry is a verse; but usually any two lines, if they come together and rhyme together, are called a couplet, and three or more lines may combine into a verse. Another name for a verse is a stanza. Four rhymed lines are called a quatrain.

THE LONG, LONG HISTORY OF OUR SWEET ENGLISH TONGUE

The Sonnet is a form of poetry that has been used with beautiful effect by nearly all the greater poets. It develops and illustrates one main thought in fourteen lines. An Elegy is a mournful poem about the dead. An Ode is a song of praise, and was originally written to be sung or set to music. Psalms and Hymns are the poetry of worship.

English poetry has a very long history. It began when the English language was so different from the language we speak now that few of us would understand it. But for five hundred years our language has had nearly its present form, and though in modern times it has been written in more varied forms than before, its poetry has not been written more sweetly or nobly than it was written three hundred years ago. An anthology of the best poetry is given in another part of this book where we have the work of all those poets whose songs come echoing to us down the corridors of Time.

POETRY THE MUSIC OF THOUGHT AND FANCY AND NOBLE FEELING

It is our great hope that we may lead our readers into a love of poetry, which should be as natural for us to love as it is to love music; for poetry is the music of thought and fancy and noble feeling. The liking for it should be as quick as the liking for sweet sounds and scents, the colour of sunsets, or the thrill of splendid deeds.

Better than all other means it expresses these delights. It can record them for us and bring them back to us as fresh as ever, and with the added magic of haunting words with a beauty of their own. Life has no greater enrichment than the love of poetry. It never loses its charm. That, in ever-varying beauty, is the offering we make in these pages to all who read them.

In reading poetry we should always understand that it is of many different kinds, appealing to widely different minds, and sometimes suiting one mood of our own mind and sometimes another. Great mistakes have been made, even by critics who have had a love of poetry, in refusing the name of poetry to verses that do not happen to suit their own taste at the moment. We should beware how we try to fix the bounds of poetry too narrowly.

Clever people will sometimes try to rule out simple songs for children, and will say they are not poetry. And those who enjoy simple verse will not trouble to understand what others can enjoy in blank verse and the majestic measures of the greater poets. Both are often looking at poetry too narrowly, for it covers a very wide field, varies greatly from age to age in its form and spirit, and, when it rings true, moves the hearts of nearly all mankind by some of its strains.

It is like the wind in its changeful moods, now whispering softly to the leaves, now fanning laziness with a lulling breeze, now blustering along masterfully, now piping shrilly round the cosy home, and again smiting the ill-clad deeply with cruel blows, or raging in wild commotion with its companion the trackless sea. None of these moods, gentle, commonplace, or terrible, can claim for itself the full and exclusive name of the wind. It is all of them.

And so it is with poetry. The simplest song of childhood may lisp it, sweet and low. The daily life of the home is electric with it. It wings the messages of religion on their way to the human heart. If there are people who show a contempt for the poetry of childhood, or for the verses that express the sentiments of family life, or deny the right of hymns to a generous share in true literature, they are, by such narrow views, proving that they have yet something to learn about true poetry.

It is true that poetry was first of all at home amid scenes where men's hearts were stirred by strong passions. War has always, in its dreadful agony, aroused men to poetic fervour; as have bold adventures, staunch heroism, and noble sacrifice.

The tumult of men's passions and the mysteries of their fate have inspired poems, powerful and profound. So, too, have all the wonderful charms of Nature, changing day by day, and present everywhere; but these fine materials for poetic treatment must not blind us to the simpler forms of poetry that satisfy plain people.

One of the objects of the poems that will follow through this book is to broaden the appreciation of British poetry, and avoid slavery to any fashion. For the history of verse is a history of the rise, the reign, and the decay of a series of fashions in writing, thinking and feeling. Elizabethan song, the well-drilled writing of Pope's day, and the overflowing sentiment of the first half of the nineteenth century were fashions that left the world weary of their sameness. Each of these movements was popular, and then left the reader tired and seeking a change. First praised to the skies, each became rejected and neglected. Knowing that this injustice is always happening, the wise reader will enjoy what is permanently good, whether it be simple or great, and will be unmoved by all exaggerations, praise, or blame.

The coinages of song are of varying value, but each, if it is to be preserved, must have some measure of the pure gold of poetry. It may have the small value of trifling fancy, or the higher stamp of glowing and noble feeling, or the inspiration of lofty thought, and each will appeal to some minds; but happiest are they who can give a due welcome to all.

A FIGURE DRAWN BY RAPHAEL TO REPRESENT POETRY

THE FINE PICTURE OF JUSTICE BY THE FRENCH ARTIST PASCAL DAGNAN-BOUVERET

The Great Words that Stir the Hearts and Minds of All Mankind

JUSTICE

IN ancient times the king would come down from his palace to the gates of the royal city, or the gates of its chief temple, and there administer justice to his subjects. Many of the gates of great churches were sculptured with lions to suggest the strength and dignity of the law. Thus came the phrase *At the gates,* or *At the lions;* and so to this day men speak of *The gate of justice.*

But before ever temple was built, or king reigned, the idea of justice lived like a lion in the minds of savage men. They were brutal, fierce, ignorant, and cruel; they had " their living to get," and to get it they had to fight cunningly and unscrupulously against all the forces of Nature. Nevertheless, they were conscious in their minds of certain laws, of a right way and a wrong way of doing things, and of a Power, higher than anything they could see with their eyes, which was somnolent when they did right, but seemed to them like a roaring lion whenever they did wrong.

These men regarded justice with great fear. They were superstitious. If they did right, they would prosper; if they did wrong, they would be smitten hip and thigh. They did right chiefly because they feared the consequences of wrong. But when they had partly outgrown this

fear, when they discovered from long experience that wrong might sometimes be done without visible suffering on their part, still they kept in their minds the idea that there is a vast difference between right and wrong, and nursed the faith that above all the laws of man is an abiding and unchanging justice.

Plato taught the sublime doctrine that, though a man might have to suffer evil for the sake of justice, he would suffer a yet greater evil, even if he prospered, by doing injustice.

This faith has now become the very centre of man's social life. It is the very soul of civilisation. "Justice, sir," said Daniel Webster, " is the great interest of man on Earth."

What do we mean by Justice? We do not mean the law. Law is a thing that changes; it has as many coats as a dandy, and as many reflections as the glass of Fashion. In Cromwell's day, and later, a man might be hanged for stealing a shilling. There is a bridge in Dorsetshire, crossed in these days by motor-cars and motor-lorries, which bears the warning that anyone who damages the structure will be transported for life. Once there was a thing called Jedburgh Justice, which meant " hang first and try afterwards." Little more than a century ago children

LIBERTY · JUSTICE · SPACE · DISTANCE · MOVEMENT · TRUTH · FAITH

were suffocated to death in London's smoky chimneys, and fell fainting and dying on the floors of cotton-mills.

The law allowed these things. No chimney-sweep could be prosecuted for sending a little, shrinking girl up a crooked chimney; no cotton-spinner could be tried for murder when a delicate workhouse child dropped dead at the foot of a loom. Today such frightful things are impossible. Why? Because the law has been altered. But why has the law been altered? The answer lights up for us the whole dark night of man's heroic past. The plain answer is simply this—*Because Justice demanded that the laws should be altered.*

HOW HAS THE GREAT IDEA OF JUSTICE COME ABOUT?

Now, we know very well that no statue of Justice opened its lips and told men that these laws should be altered, and that no handwriting to this effect appeared on the walls of Parliament, and that no voice spoke from the sky bidding men to change their wicked laws. How, then, did Justice make known its demand?

The idea of justice is the creation of man's mind. It does not exist in Nature. There is no justice between wolf and lamb, fox and fowl, hawk and sparrow. Great men like Pericles, and many smaller men, have even denied that justice can exist between strong nations and weak nations. " The strong do what they can, and the weak suffer what they must," we are told. Yet the idea lives. It is here in the world. It has never been burned out of man's mind by fire or cut out of his soul by the sword. It has triumphed over all tyrants; it has outlived all despotisms. It is pronounced and still is the great interest of man. How has this come to pass?

THE SOUL OF MAN ACHIEVES SOMETHING NOT FOUND IN NATURE

It is because Justice, arising in man's mind, has ever been making its demands known by the voice of conscience. We often hear the words " It may be law, but it is not just." Men do away with a bad law and make a better law, and Justice whispers, not "Well done," but "Better still."

It can never be satisfied with any of our enactments. It is the mind of man himself, raising itself up to see the next turn in the road, the next height to be scaled. It is a sign to us that we are travellers to a noble goal and heirs of a glorious destiny.

For this idea of justice is man himself, the soul of man acting on a brute body and achieving something not to be found in all the realms of Nature.

Justice is not represented even by the splendid figure of the judge. The judge in his scarlet and ermine represents the majesty of the law. He is there to see that the cunning of contending advocates does not mislead the minds of the jury, and to see that the prisoner, guilty or not guilty, is given a fair trial according to law. But men feel and know that there is a justice higher than the justice of the law, even the most just law.

"Look with thine ears," says our clear-sighted Shakespeare; "see how yond justice rails upon yond simple thief. Hark, in thine ear; change places; and, handy-dandy, which is the justice, which is the thief?"

The preacher John Bradford, seeing a condemned man pass to the gallows, exclaimed, " There, but for the grace of God, goes John Bradford! " The symbol of Justice is a pair of scales. What son of man can hold them even?

ONE OF THE VERY NOBLEST THINGS IN HUMAN HISTORY

Earth's justice can never be perfect. Above any form of justice conceivable by the mind of man hangs the eternal and absolute justice of that great God " from whom no secrets are hid." Early in the history of the human race came that marvellous cry, " Enter not into judgment with Thy servant, O Lord; for in Thy sight shall no man living be justified." This thought it was which led the most inspired of all our poets always to associate mercy with justice.

But, imperfect as man's justice is, it still stands for one of the very noblest achievements of human history. It might almost be said, indeed, that the strongest movement in the tide of moral progress has come from man's longing after justice. Of justice he has dreamed in the midst of oppression, and for justice he has fought even in the chains of slavery. No voice rings so persistently and powerfully through all the despotisms and tyrannies of times past as the voice of the bondman claiming justice as a right. No hands were lifted more heroically in the history of mankind than those manacled hands of the oppressed slave striking for the liberty of justice.

Kings have destroyed prophet after prophet who uttered this divine word, and king after king has been destroyed by the people who listened to those prophets. The grandest of all struggles in the chronicles of humanity are those in which the conscience of simple men contended for justice against the cruel sword of resentful and implacable authority. Despot after despot exclaimed, "I am the Law, I am Justice, I am Authority"; but each time the people answered, "Nay, for you, too, are a man; above you, O King, is the Justice we will abide by, the Law we will honour, the Authority we will reverence, even the God of our conscience." Has not man prayed for two thousand years, "Thy will be done on Earth, as it is in Heaven"?

In these great struggles the thought which impelled the people was noble and splendid, but their idea of justice was crude. They claimed the right to tax themselves, to manage their own lives, to make their own laws, to live in freedom of mind and body. All these things we now take for granted. We cannot imagine ourselves in a state of slavery—told what we must do, ordered to think only as the Sovereign ordains, our privacy and our property for ever at the royal mercy.

THE FARTHEST JOURNEY OF ALL THAT JUSTICE HAS TAKEN

Has justice, then, reached the end of its journey? By no means. Indeed, the farthest-reaching of all its journeys is only now begun.

The law tells us that we may enjoy the fruits of our labour. If a burglar enters our house he is guilty of breaking the law, for he is taking from us what we have the right to keep for our own enjoyment. But how speaks the voice of conscience when a starving man looks in at our window or a famished child stands at our door? Is it just that we should eat and drink as if there was no starving man near by? Nay; is it *possible* for us to do so without a feeling of guilt?

And yet why should there rest upon our conscience this feeling of guilt? We are breaking no law at our feast. The food is ours. We have worked for it, paid for it, and it is necessary to our health; whereas the starving man may be a rogue, and the hungry child may be the daughter of a wicked mother who will be all the wickeder if we relieve her of the moral duty to feed her child. All the same, that feeling of guilt remains. No logic can still the voice of conscience. We hear no whine from those hungry and homeless creatures outside in the wind and rain, but conscience says to us, "Justice, justice!"

WHAT IS IT THAT MAKES LIFE SO GREAT AN ADVENTURE?

Thus does virtue grow with a man; thus does the human race never attain any of its ideals. All we can do is to reach stages in those ideals, never their ends, which are lost in eternity. This it is which makes human life so splendid and so unendingly a great adventure. For to conquer a wrong and to possess ourselves of a right is not to find a throne and sceptre awaiting us, but a long road and a pilgrim's staff.

A right is not an easy chair and a footstool, but a hard duty. It is just that man should be free, but it is not just that he should use freedom to prey upon others or to gratify his own selfish interests. It is right that men and women should have votes to decide who shall make their laws for them, but it is not right that they should use that power carelessly or only to promote their own welfare. Justice says, "All power is responsibility. You are strong to make others strong, free to make others free, wise to make others wise." The law says we have a right to possess learning and riches. Justice says we have a duty to share those privileges with others. Every virtue is a door to service, and every great attainment of man is the first page in a book which never ends.

WE CAN BE UNJUST IN OUR THOUGHTS AS IN OUR ACTS

True justice is yet to come. We shall have moved a little on that shining path when we recognise that we can be unjust in our thoughts as well as in our acts, and that to be just to our friends, just to those who are kind to us and whose prosperity is akin to ours, is not enough.

Perfect justice will bring not only peace to a warring world, but brotherly help between nations. It will purge the heart of man of all hatreds, calumnies, jealousies, and scorns, and ignoble egoisms. It will draw men together. It will make this Earth like Paradise, and even then a man will know in his heart that pure justice is still ahead of him in the heart of God.

THE EXPULSION FROM EDEN, FROM THE PICTURE BY A. T. NOWELL IN THE WALKER ART GALLERY, LIVERPOOL

The Story of the Most Beautiful Book in All the World

The Creation of the Sun and the Moon—Raphael's picture in the Vatican, Rome

THE BIBLE STORY OF CREATION

THE Bible, in the beautiful Story of Creation told in the Long Ago, tells us that in the beginning there was a great darkness, and that there was nothing which had any shape or form. Try to think of this black darkness and this dreadful emptiness ; everywhere, darkness and nothingness. There were no stars, no lovely Sun, no wind blowing through trees, no waves breaking into foam at the foot of the cliffs. There was no Earth, no heaven, no light, no heat and cold— only darkness, silence, and emptiness everywhere.

But God was there, and the Bible tells us that the Spirit of God moved upon the face of the waters which filled the whole of the shapeless universe, like the ether, the mysterious stuff that is in all space. Out of this strange element God created the heavens and the Earth.

The first words breathed by God, the Bible tells us, were those wonderful words :
Let there be light.
The first thing God wished to do was to send away the great blackness. So God spoke, and in speaking He did two things. He broke the awful silence that reigned throughout the world, and created Light.

Then the Bible tells us that God called the light Day, and the darkness which visits the Earth when the Earth turns her face away from the Sun, He called Night. This was the beginning of the acts of creation. Then the Bible tells that God divided the waters which filled the great universe, setting heaven in the midst of it. Then the water which was under heaven He gathered into one place and called them the Seas of the Earth, and the dry land appeared out of the midst of the seas, and God called the dry land Earth.

Then came the grass springing out of the dry land, and many strange and lovely herbs, and trees throwing their shadows on the grass. God made the herb and the fruit tree, each with its own seed, so that they could sow themselves and gradually cover the Earth with beauty and joy.

Then God filled the sky with stars, and gave the Sun power to rule the day and the Moon power to rule the night.

And now, this story of creation tells us, came a greater wonder still. Out of the deep waters upon the Earth God called forth Life. He spoke, and from the water issued living things that could move and utter sound, and swim and fly—tiny and unseen things, millions of them; huge and mighty things, thousands of them; so that the whole Earth, the water, the land, and the air became filled with life.

GREAT FIGURES OF THE OLD TESTAMENT · THE LIFE OF JESUS

Finally God said: " Let us make man in our image, after our likeness; and let him have dominion over the fish of the sea, and over the fowl of the air, and over the cattle, and over all the Earth, and over every creeping thing that creepeth upon the Earth."

Then came forth Man and Woman, whom God created in His own likeness, and into whom he breathed the breath of life. And God set this man, whom we call Adam, and this woman, whom we call Eve, in dominion over all the Earth, to rule it, to conquer it, and to enjoy it.

THE BEAUTIFUL PICTURE OF THE MAKING OF THE EARTH

How beautiful is this picture of God making the wonderful Earth for Adam and Eve and their children to enjoy in happiness and peace! The animals came to them when they were called; the birds sang over their heads as they walked; and the fishes came to the side of the lake to watch them as they stood in the sunlight. Do we not feel that we should like to live in such a happy world for ever and ever?

But this happy Paradise did not last. The Bible story fills our eyes with tears that man should have been so foolish and so ungrateful to God.

God had given man everything on the Earth except one thing. There was one thing which man was not to do. If man did this one thing he would lose all his happiness and all his peace. *And man did do this very thing.*

The Bible tells us that this one thing man was not to do was to eat of the fruit growing on a certain tree in the Garden of Eden. There were a thousand other fruits of which man might eat, but this one was forbidden. If man loved God he would not eat of this tree; if he did not love God he would disobey. So, you see, this was God's test of man's love.

THE STORY OF ADAM AND EVE IN THE GARDEN OF EDEN

Well, we read how Satan, the Evil One, took the form of a serpent and glided into the Garden of Eden, sought out Eve while she was away from her husband's side, and suggested to her that she should eat of the fruit. And, although Eve did not at once obey the Evil One, she argued with him, instead of driving him from her. So the temptation to eat the fruit stayed in her mind ; she allowed herself to think about it ; and at last the temptation was too great for her. She ate the fruit, took it to Adam, her husband, and persuaded him also to do this forbidden thing.

Then, the Bible tells us, Adam and Eve heard the voice of the Lord God " walking in the garden in the cool of the day," and they were afraid and hid themselves in the trees. And God said because they had done evil they must suffer. But the punishment God sent them was not a cruel punishment. He made them go out into the world to toil for their existence.

Now, though work is hard, it is far better than idleness ; and in setting man to till the Earth God has provided him with the opportunity of making himself better and kinder and purer. So that when we see pictures of Adam and Eve going out with tears and shame from their beautiful garden of Innocence, we must remember that over them the face of God is smiling with love and pity, knowing that His children shall one day return to their Garden and to Him.

THE SEVEN DAYS

The first day God created light:
He made the day and made the night.

The second day of His intent
He made the heavenly firmament.

The third day came both land and sea,
And grass, and herbs, and bush, and tree.

The fourth day Sun and Moon had birth,
And stars that twinkle over Earth.

The fifth day, from the waves of strife,
God called great creatures into life.

And in the sixth day of His plan
In his own image God made man.

Then when His work the Lord had blest
The Seventh Day He gave to rest.

This account of the origin of all things is an inspired vision that was placed first in their sacred book by the Hebrews, before they began to tell the story of their race and its descent from Abraham. It was natural to ask who lived before Abraham, and so, when the Hebrew records and traditions were gathered into one book, not by Moses but about 800 years after his death, this fine vision of the Creation was prefixed to the book. The various backward races of mankind have their legendary accounts of how the Earth came to be, but nothing has been imagined by the mind of man to compare with this Bible story in beauty, dignity, and truth.

(Next chapter in this group, page 375)

The Interests and Pleasures of Life for All Indoors and Out

AN EASY-TO-MAKE FIDDLE

ANYONE with a good ear for music who can sing or whistle an air correctly after having heard it once or twice, would soon be able to play a one-stringed fiddle or violin. There is no need to study music, or even to learn to read the notes. Experience teaches where to put the finger on the string of the violin to get any note and in a very short time simple tunes can be played.

These instruments may be bought, but it is very easy and much more interesting to make one. The work is already half done if a wooden box, about 8 or 9 inches long, 5 inches wide, and 2½ inches deep, with a well-fitting lid, can be obtained.

A cigar-box for fifty cigars is usually near this size, and would do splendidly. Begin by taking off all the paper that is stuck round the edges of the box. In this case the easiest way to do this is to scrub it off with a hard nail-brush that has been dipped into hot water. But do not make the wood wetter than can be helped or it will warp. The lid will now come right off, because it was only the paper that formed the hinge. On the box lid draw with a pencil the two little figures, something like an S in shape, shown in the picture. These shapes can be cut out with a fret-saw in a few minutes, but try to do it neatly for the appearance of the finished violin depends upon its being done well.

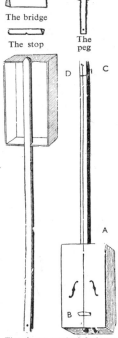

The bridge

The stop

The peg

The picture on the left shows the fiddle without box-lid and that on the right the complete violin. (A) Box ; (B) bridge ; (C) peg ; (D) stop.

Now get a piece of hard wood about thirty inches long. Walnut or mahogany will do. It should be about three-quarters of an inch wide and half an inch thick. Plane away the sharp edges on one side and leave the others square. Then, looking at the end of the wood, it is seen to be shaped like a D—round on one-side and flat on the other. With a sharp penknife cut two notches in the ends of the box for this piece of wood to fit into. When these notches have been made almost big enough with the knife, wrap a piece of sandpaper round the wood that is to fit into them and rub it steadily backward and forward in the notches until they are quite smooth. In this way the wood is fitted into them in workmanlike fashion.

Now glue the wood into the notches, leaving about one inch projecting at one end. Then put a little glue all round the edges of the box and on the wood between the two sides, and fix the lid into its place. A few tiny brass screws put in round the edge of the lid will make it all quite firm.

About one inch from the end of the long piece of wood, make a hole about one-third of an inch in diameter, and fit into it a small wooden peg shaped like the one shown in the picture.

CRAFTS · GAMES · NEEDLEWORK · PUZZLES · SCIENCE EXPERIMENTS

The violin is now practically complete. Only two tiny pieces of some hard wood are needed. One will form what is called the bridge, and the other will be merely a thin strip which is glued close to the peg and called the stop. They can be cut out of a boxwood ruler, and the picture shows how they are to be fixed.

Now go to a music shop and ask for one A string for a violin. These strings are generally made double the length required for ordinary violins, so they will be just right for this one. Mention that a double-length one, uncut, is wanted, and then the shop assistant will understand.

At the same time take the opportunity of buying a violin bow. Often music shops have second-hand ones, and these are sometimes very much better than those that have never been used before.

Before attempting to fix the string, cut the little piece of wood that projects from the bottom of the violin to a point. Then make the box perfectly smooth with sandpaper and give it a coat of varnish.

When the varnish is quite hard, take the string and make a loop at one end large enough to slip over the projecting point. Then stretch the string to the other end, make a small hole through the peg, and thread the string through it. Now put the bridge into its proper place, as shown in the picture, and make the string tight by turning the peg. When tight, draw the bow across it gently, and if it gives out a clear note the fiddle is properly made.

The instrument is not held like an ordinary violin. The box part is placed between the knees, the string is fingered with the left hand, and the bow is, of course, held in the fingers of the right hand.

The player will soon learn how to slide the finger up and down the string to get the right notes, and, as confidence and experience are gained, there will be hours of fun in trying out new tunes.

QUAINT PICTURES BUILT UP FROM SQUARES

THIS quaint group of pictures is drawn by using squares as a basis, building up square upon square, and adding what lines are needed to complete the illustrations. It shows four subjects, a man, a cat, a horse, and a dog. Look at the man. First four squares are made, one on top of the other; then two lines at each side of the top square give the outline of the arms; a tiny square, a horizontal line, and a rectangle represent the head and the hat; four lines give the features of the face; a series of simple straight lines in the topmost large square make the coat and the tie. The arms are easily completed. Then an inverted V separates the two legs, the feet are made by two triangles, and the stick and moustache are added; finally, the man is complete. To make the cat with three squares as a basis is even simpler, and the method to be followed for it, and also for the horse and the dog, is clearly shown.

HOW TO FEEL THE PRESSURE OF THE AIR

THERE is a very simple scientific experiment by which the pressure of the atmosphere may be felt.

Take a board measuring about two feet long by four or five inches wide, and, say, a quarter of an inch thick. Place this upon a table, with about six inches projecting beyond the table, and cover it with an opened newspaper, smoothing this down all over so that it may lie as flat as possible.

Now, clenching the hand, bring it down with a sharp hard blow upon the projecting wood. One who has never tried the experiment before naturally expects that the board will be knocked off the table. But no matter how hard the blow the projecting end may be broken off, but the board itself cannot be moved. And yet, with slow and gentle pressure upon the end with only one finger, it can easily be pushed to the floor.

The explanation of the apparent mystery is to be found in the scientific fact of the pressure of the atmosphere. The air presses upon everything on the surface of the earth with a force equal to fifteen pounds on every square inch. But this pressure is unnoticed in ordinary circumstances, because it works equally in all directions.

THE BOARD THAT WILL NOT MOVE

When, however, the pressure of the air is removed from one side of a body, it is felt with great force on the other side. It is this removal of the air-pressure from one side that happens when the projecting end of the board is struck.

The blow is given sharply, and the air has no time to rush in between the table and the newspaper. The result is that the pressure of fifteen pounds to the square inch is exerted in a downward direction only, upon the surface of the paper, and when the end of the board is struck, this pressure is felt just as though the other end of the board was held down by heavy weights. The blow must be short and sharp, the fist being removed instantly, for if the hand rests upon the board for more than a moment, it will go down, because that is practically the same thing as deliberately pressing upon the board. If the hand continues to press on the board, the air has time to rush in under the paper, and the pressure of the atmosphere then being the same both below and above, there is nothing to counteract the blow as is the case when striking sharply and quickly; then the air-pressure is exerted on the top of the board only. This experiment could be performed as a trick at a party.

A MUSICAL INSTRUMENT MADE FROM OLD BOTTLES

A CLEVER musical instrument can be made from a number of old bottles. Any kind will do as long as they are all the same size. Having collected the bottles, take an ordinary broomstick and rest this on the backs of two chairs, tying it firmly. Then tie the bottles to this stick, so that they hang loosely and not too close together.

Now comes the work of tuning up, and this is done by pouring water into the bottles, a different quantity into each, putting more water for a low note and less for a high. To get the note of each, tap it with a stick—the edge of a boxwood rule is a very good thing for this purpose. With patience and perseverance and a little ordinary care and skill, the bottles will at last be all tuned and ready for use. This curious instrument can now be played

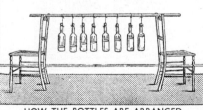

HOW THE BOTTLES ARE ARRANGED

by striking the bottles with the edge of the rule, gently at first, partly for fear of breaking the bottles, and partly to learn the different notes and get the " feel " of the instrument.

After some practice, it will be found that simple tunes can be played on the bottle-bells, and then two sticks can be used and quicker tunes tried. Be careful to hang the bottles far enough apart so that they do not knock against each other when struck ; and perhaps it would be wise for the first attempt to take place out of doors, just in case of accidents.

If any difficulty is found in tuning a bottle to the right note at the first attempt, start again, and put in the water in very small quantities, tapping the bottle each time a little more is added. In this way the required tone is reached gradually.

LITTLE PROBLEMS FOR ODD MOMENTS

THESE problems are continued from page 125, and their answers, together with more questions, will be found on page 382.

14. The Clock Strikes Twelve

George and his sister stood under the church tower and heard the clock strike six. George looked at his watch while it did so, and said to his sister: "It took thirty seconds to strike six."

His sister, hoping to catch him out, said: "Then how long would it take to strike twelve?"

George replied: "Sixty seconds!" But he was wrong.

What is the correct answer?

15. How Did He Measure the Vinegar?

Mrs. Thomson ordered four quarts of vinegar from a roundsman who had eight quarts in his barrel, but no measure by which he could measure it. Mrs. Thomson had two jugs, one able to hold five quarts and the other three quarts. The man said that he could not measure four quarts with these, but Mrs. Thomson's little boy, Charlie, showed him how to manage, using only the two jugs.

How did he do it?

16. How Many Eggs?

If a hen and a half lays an egg and a half in a day and a half, how many eggs will one hen lay in six days?

17. Twelve Bananas in a Dish

There are 12 boys, and on the table is a fruit bowl containing 12 bananas. Each boy took one banana and there remained one in the bowl.

How was this?

18. The Farmer and the Tramp

A tramp lying down for a nap at the side of a haystack, heard the farmer approaching. He ran round and round the stack, chased by the farmer. They started from opposite corners, the tramp taking forty seconds to run completely round, and the farmer thirty seconds.

How often must the farmer run round before catching the tramp?

19. How Old is Tommy?

In another three years Tommy will be exactly three times as old as he was three years ago.

How old is he now, assuming that today is his birthday?

THE ANSWERS TO THE PROBLEMS ON PAGE 125

1. No; George never saw the dog's back, which he clearly would do if he had walked round the animal.

2. Mabel bought six pears, which cost 4d., and six apples at ½d. each, making 3d. for the apples and 7d. for the whole.

3. Mary put the planks as shown in the picture, and thus reached the island.

4. Tom's uncle's sister was Tom's mother.

5. Find first of all how many stamps were left when Jack had taken his share. Seeing that Frank had one more than half, Harry must have had one less than half. It was known that Harry had three, therefore four must have been half the quantity that Harry and Frank divided. Four is the half of eight, so that Frank had five, which is one more than half of eight. Jack's share was one more than half of the total quantity, and therefore the quantity divided by Frank and Harry must have been one fewer than half of the total. Frank and Harry's share came to eight, as seen; and the half of the total quantity, being one more than eight, was nine. Jack had ten, which is one more than half of the total quantity, and there were thus eighteen stamps altogether.

How Mary got the eggs

6. To begin with, one piece of string was 12 in. long and the other piece 24 in. After cutting 6 in. off each, the shorter piece was 6 in. long and the longer piece 18 in. long.

7. If a man says that he has no brothers and sisters, his father would have only one son—himself. Thus, if what he says is put in simple language, it is: "That man's father is myself." This means that the picture at which he looked was that of his own son.

8. As the bottle cost 2d. more than the cork, if we take away that 2d. it leaves the other ½d. to be divided equally between bottle and cork. The cork, then, cost ¼d.

9. Suppose the children were first given 1s. each. This will use £2 10s. There is then 10s. left, which is to be used in giving another 3d. each to the boys. Now, there are 40 three-pences in 10s. so that there must be 40 boys. Therefore there are 10 girls.

10. The messenger brought 2½ canaries, and 1½ times as many as there were left in the cage. Counting those in the cage, then, there were 2½ times as many as were left, and 2½ canaries. But there were 20 altogether. Taking away the 2½ canaries, we see that 17½ canaries is 2½ times as many as were left in the cage. Or, what is the same thing, 35 canaries is 5 times as many as were left in the cage. There were 7 left in the cage, and so there were 13 which flew away.

11. In fifteen minutes Joe had gone 1 mile and the horse 220 yards less than 1 mile. In one hour the horse would walk 880 yards less than 4 miles—that is, 3½ miles in one hour.

12. The brick weighed 12 lb. The weight of each of two halves is the same, so that if a brick weighed half its own weight and 6 lb., the 6 lb. must represent the other half.

13. Betty got 16 for a shilling, being ninepence per dozen. Had there been 18 for a shilling the price would have been eightpence per dozen.

HOW TO USE NAILS AND SCREWS

Everyone thinks he can drive a nail or put in a screw ; and while such tasks may be quite easy, there are a number of hints about nails and screws that every boy, and every girl, too, should know.

To drive nails into hard wood touch the end of the nails with some grease, and they will be found to go in much more easily and to drive more accurately than if this simple precaution is not taken.

Deal boards, such as are used for rough shelves, often split when nails are driven into them. To prevent this, hold the nail upside down with its head on the ground and give the point a tap with the hammer to blunt it slightly.

Ordinary nails used for fences and in other exposed positions very quickly rust, and lose their strength and value. For this purpose buy galvanised nails.

Use a claw hammer to draw out nails. Lay the head of the hammer on the wood with the handle upright and with the nail-head in the claw. Then by pulling the handle backwards the nail will be levered out. Work carefully to avoid splitting the wood.

To draw a rusty nail from wood is sometimes rather difficult, but it may be rendered easier by giving the nail a sharp tap with the hammer first. This will loosen the rust that holds the nail so tightly to the wood.

In driving in nails always hold the hammer by the end of the handle, and get a good swing on it. This adds to the force of the blow. Short, sharp taps are of very little use. They drive the nail only a short way and usually send it in a wrong direction. Good, firm blows right on the head of the nail should be given.

When buying screws see that the heads are sound and the groove for the screw-driver well cut. The body and the thread should have no flaws, and the point should be sharp and turned like the point of a gimlet.

Screws used in outdoor work should be galvanised iron or brass. These will not rust.

A rusty screw is often very difficult to remove, but it may be loosened by holding a punch or big nail to the head of the screw and giving one or two sharp taps with the hammer. If this has no effect hold a heated iron upon the head till the screw is hot, and it will turn easily.

In driving screws, first drill a hole about the same length as the screw with a gimlet or drill about half the diameter of the screw. The screw-driver, when used, should be held in a straight line with the screw, so that it may exert its full force.

Another carpentry article describing different methods of joining wood, is given on page 379.

A TRICKY GYMNASTIC EXERCISE

No elaborate apparatus is needed in order to practise some useful gymnastic feats at home, and here is one which is worth learning, not only because it is a good physical exercise, but also because it is a splendid trick to show to friends, and to get them to try.

Take in the hands a fairly stout stick, about 18 inches long, as shown in the picture. This may be the straight branch of a tree, a round ruler, or any similar piece of wood that is available. Standing in the

position given, with arms rigid and extended, keep both feet together, and then try to jump over the stick through the loop formed by it and the two arms. It is not easy to do at first, and so it is wise to practise on the grass or on a mat indoors, where a fall will not hurt.

This same stick can be used to improve the carriage and correct round shoulders. Put it behind the back and walk with the elbows hooked round each end.

HOW FAST DO YOU WALK ?

There is a very simple way of telling at what speed one walks. Take a piece of thin string, say, 80 to 100 yards long. To one end tie a weight—a piece of lead or other metal, or even a stone. At a point 44 feet from the weight put a knot or a loop. Then put a second knot 44 feet from the first, and so on along the entire length of the string put a series of knots 44 feet from each other.

Take in one hand a watch with a second hand. Now drop the weight upon the ground and walk along at an ordinary pace, letting the weight remain where it fell, and allowing the knots or loops to slip through one hand.

The number of knots that pass through the hand in half a minute are the same as the number of miles walked in an hour.

It is always well to know the reason for what you do. It is not enough to know that the number of times you walk 44 feet in half a minute is the same as the number of miles you walk in an hour. You ought to know *why* it is so. The reason is that 44 feet is the 120th part of a mile, because a mile contains 5280 feet, and a half-minute is the 120th part of an hour. Therefore you are able to walk 120th of a mile just as many times in 120th of an hour as you can walk miles in an hour.

SPEAKING IN CODE LANGUAGE

HERE are three secret codes which, with a little practice, will enable friends to talk together, so that no one else can know what is being said.

In two of them the words are all spelt, but the letters are so disguised that when spoken quickly they give a foreign sound which might give the impression to anyone overhearing it that some strange tongue was being spoken.

The first is very easy : every letter of the alphabet has the syllable *ker* (pronounced just as it is spelt) added to it, and each letter is said in its usual way first—for example, a-ker, b-ker, c-ker, the only exception being w, which for speed and clearness is called *worker*. To indicate the end of every word, the last letter has *tug* added, and this short sentence will show just how this talk code works.

S A L L Y
Sker - aker - lker - lker - ykertug

I S   G O I N G
iker-skertug   gker-oker-iker-nker-gkertug

A W A Y
aker-worker-aker-ykertug

With the second code, it takes rather longer to learn to carry on a conversation, because there is more variation in the letters and the words run on, with only a short pause at the end of each sentence. The idea is to make of every letter a palindrome—that is a word which reads backwards and forwards alike—with *u* in the centre, but in many cases this is too awkward to pronounce, and some letters have to be left just as they are.

The *u* in every case has a short sound as in rub, and j, w, and y are exceptions to the general rule for easy speech. Here is the complete alphabet:

a	fuf	kuk	pup	u
bub	gug	lul	q	vuv
cuc (*suck*)	h	mum	rur	wuv
dud	i	nun	sus	x
e	jug	o	tut	yuv
				zuz

Sally is going away in this language would be : Sus-a-lul-lul-yuv i-sus gug-o-i-nun-gug a-wuv-a-yuv.

More difficult to grasp at first is the third code, but when it is mastered and can be spoken quickly, it sounds much more like a real foreign language than either of the others, and it is almost impossible for anyone who does not know its secret to work out what is being said.

In this, the first letter of every word is taken from the front and put at the end followed by the letter a, pronounced *ah*, so the sentence already used as an example, would in this case be written like this, and said as shown underneath :

Allysa	sia	oingga	wayaa
Ally-sah	see-ah	oh-ing-gah	way-aye-ah

With these suggestions as a guide, it will be easy for anyone to work out a private language of their own. These could also, of course, be used as written codes, especially the last one, though they are not so clever as the Secret Ciphers which will be found on page 383.

TAKE CARE OF YOUR BICYCLE

A cycle which is well looked after, regularly cleaned, and carefully ridden, will look much better and last longer than one which is carelessly treated. So take a pride in your machine, and thereby get greater comfort and pleasure out of your rides.

SPEND a little time altering the saddle to the height and slope which suits you best. It may need to be tilted slightly backwards for real pedalling ease. Handlebars, too, can be very uncomfortable on long spins if the wrists are twisted in holding them, and it may be necessary to adjust these as well. Then tyres should always be kept well pumped up. The reward will be longer life for them, and much easier riding for you. In summer time remember that hot sunshine spoils rubber, and when leaving your machine in the open for any length of time, be sure to park it in the shade.

Watch for wear and tear on vital parts. It is particularly important that brakes should be kept in perfect working order, and brake blocks should be renewed as soon as they show signs of deteriorating. Now and then examine all nuts to see that they are tight, especially before a tour or long ride. Before trips of that kind, make sure that the puncture outfit is complete, and put in a spare battery and bulb.

When the bicycle is brought home wet and muddy, wipe the spokes and enamelled parts with a cloth. Paraffin will clean the chain, which should afterwards be thoroughly oiled—soaking it in the oil is the best way. Stainless metal parts should only need washing in warm soapy water, rinsing and drying well, though if they have been neglected they may require a patent cleaner. The same applies to white mudguards. Tyres must be wiped clean with a wet house-flannel. The best way to clean the bearings is to run paraffin through them until the dirt has been washed out, and then apply lubricating oil. Oil on any rubber parts, such as tyres or brake blocks, should be wiped off at once as grease perishes rubber.

FUN WITH PAPER AND PENCIL

ON rainy days or long winter evenings, these games played with pencil and paper will provide much amusement.

INITIALS

THE umpire tells the players that they will be asked to write down the name of a tree, an animal, a flower, a bird, a fish, a town, and a country, each beginning with the letter A. This list may be extended by including such names as those of statesmen, cricketers, authors, the umpire fixing the time limit accordingly. Then each player in turn reads out his list, scoring a point for every name that has not been duplicated by someone else. In the second round the letter B is the initial, and so on.

UP TO LONDON

THIS game is for two players. The paper is ruled up as shown in the diagram, and a counter placed at each starting point. The players then take separate sides, and the first to begin flicks his counter up the paper.

LONDON	
START	START

If it stops between two lines, he draws there a tiny circle to represent a man's head. If, when his turn comes again, he succeeds in flicking the counter into the same space, he may add a body to the head ; the third time means legs; the fourth time, arms; and the fifth time, a stick is drawn in his hands so as to reach across the central line and stop the opponent from drawing any men in the space it enters. Should the opponent have already begun to draw one, it must be rubbed out. The first player to get a man in *all* his spaces wins the game, and the quickest way to do this is to reach " London " every time, for, once there, means a head in every space; twice there, means a body in every space; three times, legs; and four times, arms. If the counter flies off the paper, or rests on a line, the player scores nothing.

CAPPING VERSES

THE first player writes down a line of poetry, and, turning the paper down to hide it, hands it to his left-hand neighbour, telling him only the last word in the line. The second player must add another line to rhyme with this word, then cover it over and pass the paper on. The third player starts a new rhyme for the fourth to " cap," and so on. The poem is then read aloud.

NOUGHTS AND CROSSES

THIS game is played by two players. The paper is ruled with a double cross so as to form nine spaces. One player agrees to be "noughts,"and the other " crosses."

If " noughts " begins the game, he does so by drawing a little circle in any space he chooses. The " crosses " does the same with his own mark, and the first to get three of his marks in a line wins the game. This line may be from side to side, or up and down, or from corner to corner. Each player should place his mark so as to take up part of the line his rival is trying to make. The pictures show how the game might begin.

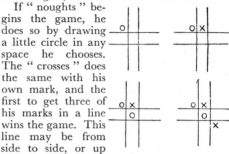

A COMPETITION MEDLEY

ASK each player to draw what he considers the right size of a halfpenny, a penny, and a sixpence. It will not matter if the circles are a little irregular, the correct diameter counts.

Open a book at random, holding it so that no one can read the actual number on the page, and ask everyone to write down how many pages there are in the remaining unopened portion of the book.

Give a time limit during which the players must make a list of persons or things that usually go in pairs, like St George and the dragon, bread and butter, first and last.

OUTLINES

AT a given word each player scribbles on his or her paper a thick zigzag line any shape. The pieces of paper are then exchanged, and everyone must try to turn the line into part of a picture. Another way is

to make five dots instead of a line—that is, one for the eye, two for the feet, and two for the hands. However awkwardly these dots may be placed, they must be worked into a drawing of some living creature.

THE RIGHT WAY TO CLEAN THINGS

THERE is one golden rule about cleaning anything, whether it is a stained coat, a slimy sponge, or soiled paint-work—*Do it without delay.* The straightforward hints given here will help in putting this maxim into practice.

WICKER GARDEN FURNITURE

Brush thoroughly to get out as much of the dust as possible ; wash with warm soapy water, and to this add a little liquid bleach if the furniture is white. If very dirty, use a soft scrubbing brush, and when quite clean rinse with plenty of cold water. Running the garden hose over it is a good idea, then leave to dry in a breeze.

KNIVES

Campers may like to note that a dirty, greasy knife can be cleaned by pushing the blade into the earth slantwise several times, then wiping it off with paper.

BOTTLES

A glass bottle can be cleaned by pouring some household ammonia into it ; shake it well, empty it, and rinse it with warm water. If the neck be wide, tea-leaves, or small pieces of raw potato mixed with salt and water can be shaken up in the bottle. Perhaps less trouble than any of these methods is to keep handy a well-corked little bottle containing some lead shot and vinegar. This shaken around the stained insides of glass bottles and vases cleans them splendidly, and can be used over and over again.

STAINED CLOTHES

Before being brushed with a clothes-brush, dusty or muddy garments should be well shaken out of doors. It is better to let splashes of mud dry on cloth, and then remove them with a hard brush, always brushing the way of the nap. To rub the splash with a piece of the material itself before applying the brush is a good plan. A grease-spot can sometimes be taken out of cloth or silk with eau-de-Cologne; and when grease is dried on cotton or woollen material it may be removed by moistening it with warm water and soaping it. Carbon tetra-chloride is an excellent grease-remover, but *do not inhale it.*

Another method is to place a piece of blotting-paper or porous brown paper over the spot and press a hot iron on it, moving the paper every now and then until the grease is completely absorbed. Black or navy blue cloth is freshened by sponging with cold tea or ammonia diluted with water. Lay the cloth flat on a table and sponge very carefully, moistening the sponge every now and then, and hang the cloth in the air to dry. Ink-spots can be removed by rubbing with milk and salt. This must be done at once, otherwise the application is of no use. Fresh tomato juice is very helpful, too, in taking recent ink marks out of white or coloured material, and does not leave a stain when rinsed out. If the ink-spots are old, the best method is to soap them and then sponge with well-diluted salts of lemon. Remember this is poisonous, *so handle very carefully,* and do not use on coloured materials, as it is a bleach. Fruit stains will yield to salt and boiling water. Hold the material taut over a basin, cover the stain well with common salt, and pour boiling water through.

PAINT

Dirty painted woodwork should be first dusted and then washed with a cloth and warm soapy water, using a soft brush for crevices. Very hot water and a hard brush spoil the paint. Wash from the bottom upwards, and finish off from the top downwards; in this way streaks which, once made on dry paint are difficult to remove, are avoided. Then go over the surface with a chamois leather which has been wrung out in clean water, and polish till dry. If preferred, one of the many good patent paint-cleaners could be used, but the directions *must* be carefully followed, as a number are also used at strength for removing paint.

Paint can be removed from brushes by dipping these in linseed oil or turpentine, and then washing them in soap and water in the palm of the hand. The soap must be rinsed out in clean water, and the bristles shaped to a point, before being stood upright to dry. The simplest way, though, is to clean the brushes in paraffin, immediately after use, and stand them handle downwards in a jar to dry thoroughly, before putting carefully away.

DIRTY WET SHOES

If the shoes are very muddy the mud can be wiped off with a damp cloth; cakes of it may be removed with a knife, but this needs skilful doing, or the leather may be cut. Wet shoes should not be dried before a fierce fire, for great heat spoils the leather. It is better to place them on their sides in a good draught. When dry, any remaining dirt can be brushed off before the shoes are cleaned in the usual way.

A SPONGE

Sponges are liable to become disagreeable and slimy if used long without being cleaned. This can be done by washing the sponge in ammonia and hot water, and then leaving it for some hours to soak in cold water in which some coarse salt has been dissolved. Soaking in sea-water, its native element, freshens up a sponge. Another way is to soak the sponge for a while in lukewarm water to which a little vinegar—about a teaspoonful to a pint—has been added. Afterwards rinse thoroughly, and dry in a draught.

Simple Learning Made Easy for Very Little People

NUMBERS—THE NAMES OF FIGURES

JOHN and Jennifer played lovely games with their café, and learned the prices of their goods, and how many pennies to take for anything they sold.

One morning when they went to open the café they found a box on the counter. In the box were some cards, each with a figure on it, and Mother said they could match the figures and hang the cards on the little dresser hooks she had screwed into the picture which hung in front of their café.

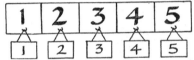

John and Jennifer went on making things for their shop, and one day Mother said, " I want to buy more than 5 sweets today, please. I want to buy 8."

" Oh," said John, " I don't know how many 8 is. Does 8 come next to 5 ? "

Then Mother showed them a new number board that she had made. It had a lot of figures on, a lot of dresser hooks, a lot of loose cards and figures, and a lot of bead strings.

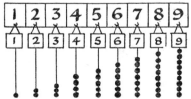

The beads were different colours: 1 red, 2 red, 3 red; 4 was 3 red + 1 yellow, 5 was 3 red + 2 yellow, 6 was 3 red + 3 yellow; 7 was 3 red + 3 yellow + 1 green, 8 was 3 red + 3 yellow + 2 green. Mother told them the names of the figures, and John very quickly learned

which was figure 8. He and Jennifer soon could match the figures and hang the right bead string underneath each one.

" Now I know my figures to nine," said John. " I'm going to make some tickets for our café, and you can help me, Jennifer." The children made some little price tickets out of cardboard, like this:

BISCUITS	SWEETS	MILK
6 for 6d	10 for 2d	3d

One morning Mother and Daddy came to the café, and each asked for a glass of milk. Mother paid 3d. and Daddy paid 3d. John counted the pennies, and found the two threepences counted up to six.

Another day Mother bought a jam tart for 4d. and a glass of lemonade for 2d. This time Jennifer counted the pennies, and she soon found that 4d. and 2d. made 6d. Mother told them that six pennies were of the same value as a silver 6d.

John and Jennifer went on making new things to sell in their café. They decided to sell fruit too, so they made oranges, apples, lemons, and bananas out of papier mâché, painted the right colours.

For Christmas, Jennifer had a tea-set.

" Now," she said, " we can sell cups of tea in our café, at 1d. a cup."

So they had to make a new price list, and Jennifer painted

Orangeade and Lemonade	2d a glass
Milk	3d a glass
Tea	1d a cup
Cakes	2d each
Biscuits	3 for 3d
Tarts	4d each
Ice cream cornets	3d each
Sweets	5 for 1d
Oranges and Lemons	2d each
Bananas	3 for 6d
Apples	1d each

the pattern round it to make it look gay.

READING · WRITING · ARITHMETIC · ART · MUSIC · FRENCH

READING—PICTURE BOOKS

ONE day Mother said to John and Jennifer, " I think it would be a good idea to make your paintings of Panda into a picture book."

The twins agreed, so Mother made a book of large sheets of brown paper. John and Jennifer took their pictures down from the bedroom wall, and stuck them into the new book.

" What shall we call our book? " said Jennifer.

" I know," said John, " let's call it The Panda Book, and it will be our very own picture book."

So Mother printed the words on the cover; John painted a Panda, and Jennifer painted balloons.

" Now," said Mother, " we must learn some more words. You know twenty-four, but that's only a beginning. I will write you a story book, and you two can paint the pictures."

" That will be fun," said John, " and then, as soon as we can write properly we can write our own books."

So Mother bought an exercise book with plain pages, and made up a story of Panda, using the twenty-four words the children already knew, and more new words. The children helped her to think of things to write. There were 12 pages in the book, and Mother wrote:

1 This is Panda.
  He lived at the Zoo
  He was black and white

2 Panda had black ears and black legs
  He had black-ringed eyes
  He was like a ball of black and white fur.

3 One day John and Jennifer
  saw Panda having his dinner.
  He had green leaves.

4 He had green leaves for his tea.
  He liked bamboo stems, but
  they were very hard to get.

5 Another day John and Jennifer
  went to the Zoo with Daddy.
  They took Panda a red balloon.

6 Panda liked his red balloon.
  He liked its lovely shiny colour.
  He blew it into the air.

7 He held the string, and pulled
  it down.
  He had great fun with it.

8 Panda liked his red balloon
  so much.
  He wanted it for his tea.

9 One day when he was hungry
  and his keeper was late with
  his dinner, he tried to eat his
  red balloon

10 At first he held it in his two
   paws, and smelled it; then he
   tried to taste it.

11 It had no smell and no taste.
   So Panda thought he would
   see what was inside. He bit it,
   and it went off bang !

12 Poor Panda ! Just then his
   keeper came with his dinner.
   John and Jennifer bought
   him a new balloon.

" We can make books of other animals, if you like," said Mother.

" Yes," said John, " and I would like to write a book all about boats."

" I wouldn't" said Jennifer. " I'd like to write one about my dolls."

" Well, so you shall," said Mother. " You draw the pictures, and we'll talk about them, and you shall tell me what to write."

258

WRITING—KEEPING A DIARY

WHEN John and Jennifer wanted Daddy to take them out, he would say, " Wait a minute, I must look in my diary and see if I am free."

" What is a diary? " said John and Jennifer together, one day.

" Well," said Daddy, " a diary is a book in which I write down all the things I am going to do, and all the people I have to see, and in which I keep a day-to-day record of what I have done. So, really, it is like a little story-book all about myself."

That night when John and Jennifer were in bed they talked about Daddy's diary, and decided that they, too, would like to keep a diary. So, in the morning, they told Daddy about it. He thought it a very good idea, and that evening he brought them each a nice note book, full of clean pages. One book had a blue cover, for Jennifer, and one had a red cover, for John. On the first page of their diaries they wrote their own names. They tried so hard that they wrote them beautifully.

" My diary is going to have pictures in it, as well as writing," said John.

" So is mine," said Jennifer, " because I like drawing."

Mother said it would be a good idea if they coloured their pictures with their crayons.

The first day they both drew a picture of Daddy, coming home from work, carrying their diaries ! When the picture was finished, Mother wrote on the opposite page:

This is Daddy bringing home my diary.

And John and Jennifer each copied it underneath.

This is Daddy
This is Daddy
bringing home
bringing home
my diary
my diary

The next day being a Saturday, Daddy did not have to go to work ; so he took John and Jennifer for a drive in his car. They took a picnic lunch with them and went into the country. They climbed trees and rocks and collected shiny pebbles from a little tumbling stream. Jennifer picked a bunch of wild flowers for Mother, who had stayed at home because she had some work to do.

When they got home, they at once got out their diaries. When they had finished they looked like this:

John's Diary:

This is me
This is me
fishing
fishing

Jennifer's Diary:

I saw flowers
I saw flowers
and a cow
and a cow

Every day John and Jennifer drew a picture in their diary, and told Mother what they wanted her to write. Then they copied her writing underneath.

Sometimes they wrote about what they had been doing, and sometimes they just drew a picture, and asked Mother to write about it, such as:

This is a boat

This is me dancing

I went to see the Queen.

Here is my cousin Jane.

Daddy said that when their diaries were full he would buy them some new ones. John and Jennifer said they would try to write in their new diaries without Mother writing all the words first.

ART—PATTERNS AND PICTURES

HAVE you ever thought how exciting are some of the patterned papers in which your birthday or Christmas presents were wrapped? And not only parcel wrapping papers, but those used in the making of Christmas crackers or wrapped round sweets and chocolate boxes. Perhaps you may have wondered how you could use them.

Some children collect the little cut-out printed pictures of places, people, flowers, or animals, which are stuck on crackers, until they have enough to use with other picture and pattern scraps to cover a screen. Lovely screens have been made by covering the panels with patterns made of hundreds of different kinds of old postage stamps.

Whole sheets of coloured and patterned papers of many different kinds can be bought from a fancy goods or fancy paper shop. You will be surprised if you go to such a shop to discover how many kinds of paper there are. If you ask for samples you will be shown dolls' house papers, flint papers, marbled papers, tissues, foils, velvet papers, batik papers, and paper d'oyleys.

Some are smooth, some rough, some thin, some thick, some you can almost see through, some with patterns raised on their surfaces. Try to get a large collection of them, including some paper d'oyleys, and add them to any others you have kept from your parcels and sweets wrappings, and old newspapers. You can also make some coloured and patterned papers yourself. When you have a collection of such papers you will have the material for making a picture.

A POLISH PAPER-CUT

Next time you go to the theatre keep a lookout for the man who entertains the queue by folding newspapers or coloured tissue papers, carefully tearing out little pieces here and there from the folds and then, when he has finished, unfolding the paper and showing a wonderful torn paper pattern like a Christmas decoration.

In Poland people use scissors to cut out all sorts of lovely patterns like the one shown on this page.

In making these patterns the great thing is to tear or cut away as little as possible to give the best effect, and to make sure the pattern does not fall to pieces through taking too much paper away. It is a good plan afterwards to try placing the torn or cut patterns on a piece of paper of a different colour and to notice the change in effect this makes.

Now try folding a piece of paper about the size of this page—a piece of newspaper will do. Fold it into four and then with your finger and thumb try very carefully to tear out little shapes from the folded edges and also from the outside edges. Some of the shapes can be tiny, others big, some with curved edges, some straight.

When you have done this, open out your paper again and see what has happened and what you think about the pattern you have made. You will understand now how it works, and will want to try making another pattern. Next time you might like to try cutting away the shapes with a pair of scissors and to get finer and smaller cuts in your pattern. Birthday cake bands and all sorts of lovely Valentine cards can be made from this cutting paper method, and you will probably think of other uses for it too.

But these coloured and patterned papers can also be used for making pictures. For this you need a fairly large sheet of dark paper as a background on which to work. Ordinary dark brown paper or one of the dark coloured papers sold for drawing on with chalks or water colour would be suitable. Ordinary dark brown paper, paper d'oyleys, black flint paper, and bits of grey, red, and gold paper were used by the Indian who made the picture of the elephant.

For your first picture a piece about four times the size of this page should be tried. Have all your coloured papers ready to hand, as well as a pair of scissors, paste, and pastebrush.

Handle the papers and have a good look at them, and notice the way one colour looks next to another. You will be excited to discover the way one little piece of bright colour stands out against a large piece of dark. Some torn pieces make patterns like those of the bits of coloured glass in a kaleidoscope. Notice, too, the difference in the surfaces of the papers, some rough and some smooth.

Now for an idea for your picture—a coloured and patterned paper picture

PAPER PICTURE BY AN INDIAN

which will look as though it were made of large and small pieces of coloured and patterned papers.

Imagine you are looking through a window into a dark room. The window has lace curtains pulled back on either side like the curtains of a theatre. In the centre of the window ledge is a big bunch of flowers in a vase. The pattern of the lace curtains looks light against the dark room, like a piece of beautiful lace, or like a d'oyley on a table. The flowers in the vase are of different shapes, sizes, and colours— some are round like the Sun, with lots of petals growing from it; some are delicate bell shapes, others are like little trumpets with six-pointed star frills; some have soft edges like torn paper, others have sharp edges like cut paper ; some have thick stalks with big leaves, while others have thin stalks.

The petals of some of the flowers have fallen off on to the window ledge.

Now choose the papers you are going to tear or cut to look like flowers, and those for your curtains and for the window ledge.

Make the shapes of the big things first and arrange them on your sheet of dark paper. It is a good plan to have a coloured paper frame round your picture, so leave a little space for this as part of the picture. When you have got the big shapes as you want them, take your pastebrush and paste and stick them down. Then add the little pieces of paper on top.

Perhaps you will feel like using some of the flower colours in the pattern of the frame of your picture. This will help to make the picture and frame look as though they belonged to each other.

TORN-PAPER PICTURE BY AN AFRICAN

MUSIC—THE NAMES OF SOUNDS

As soon as we find something new in life we give it a name. Elsewhere in this book you will learn of countries which were discovered by brave explorers. These were countries about which no one (except the natives) knew anything until they were discovered, and about which no one could talk until they were named.

The music which you hear from your radio set, from your aunt's piano or your uncle's violin, or from the organ in your church, would not be there for you to enjoy unless, many years ago, explorers had set out in the realm of music. These explorers were the great composers, the great teachers, and the great performers. Each one in that great company discovered something about music which no one else had found out.

In one way or another we are all explorers as we go about the world of music. We, like the birds, can sing naturally. Little children make up their own tunes long before they have learned anything about music. A little boy is singing himself to sleep—high notes, low notes, and middle notes—and it is possible to draw a picture of the tune. It will then look like this :

Long, long ago, shapes of melodies were drawn in this way so that music could be remembered. Many tunes were composed. Many shapes were drawn. When the shapes of tune after tune were studied some important points became clear.

The most important was that sounds which you or I can sing are few in number, and they can be arranged as if on a staircase. Sing a low note, now the next one higher, higher again . . . like this :

When you arrive at No. 7, you go up one more step and find yourself on a sound which agrees so well with No. 1 that for the sake of convenience we can regard it as No. 1 in a new position. If you find

someone to play  on the piano

you will see exactly what this means.

We shall understand this when we hear

and say " cuckoo "; also when we hear

and say " ding, dong, ding, dong." We here give names to collections of sounds. Sing " cuckoo." You sing two notes, one high and one rather lower. But if you are asked to sing the same sounds in the opposite direction, first the lower and then the higher, a request for " Koo-cuc " only sounds funny and does not help very much. If you are asked to sing " dong, dong, dong ; ding, ding, ding," you know that three low notes and three high notes are wanted. But you do not know how low and how high.

There was once a choirmaster taking a practice with his boys. He was an Italian, and lived in a little town in the mountains. The town was Arezzo and the choirmaster, a monk, was named Guido—or, as we should say in English, Guy. Guy had long wondered how he should teach the hymns and psalms of the church accurately. When the boys sang the wrong notes we may be sure that the other monks were cross. " Look here," they would say, " why can't your boys do better than this ? They always seem to be practising." As they were not very musical they did not know that music teaching was difficult, particularly when the notes had no names.

One summer's day Guy was practising a hymn. The first line of the hymn started on sound 1, the second line started on 2, the third on 3, and so on. " I have it at last! " said Guy. He repeated the first note of each phrase and added to it the proper Latin syllable (for they were singing in Latin)—*Ut, re, mi, fa, sol, la,* and *si.* " Now boys," said Guy, " sing that after me and don't forget in future that those are the names of the notes of the scale."

That was seven centuries ago. Sol-fa was born, and ever since the time of Guido d'Arezzo it has been a key to the meaning of music. Two of the names have changed, and now we learn :

262

The main sounds out of which music is made live in one street in seven houses.

Now let us think of a real street. Mr. Jones and Mr. Smith live next door to one another. But when they go to work on the morning bus Mr. Jones often sits with Mr. Robinson, who lives three doors away, while Mr. Smith accompanies Mr. Brown.

In the same way *doh* lives next door to *re*, but in a melody may be seen rubbing shoulders with *me*. Let us look at a tune which we all know:

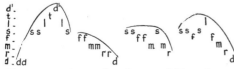

There you have the shape of Baa, baa, Black Sheep. Notice also that we have four sentences; for music, like words, is built in sentences. And we can measure

two pegs and then plucking it in the the middle. The elastic says " *twang !* " and you will see it shiver from side to side.

If you shorten the elastic you will hear a higher sound. The " shivering " will be quicker than the first time. So we learn that the quicker the vibrations the higher the sound. A circular saw sings a higher note as it gains speed. An empty glass gives a deeper note than one of the same size which has some water in it. The water leaves less room for the sound vibrations.

It is important to know this much about sound because we can then understand that a violinist lengthens and shortens his strings by taking off or putting on the fingers of his left hand; and that a wind instrument player alters the length of his pipe by stopping or unstopping holes. A tin whistle will

PLAYING TUNES ON BOTTLES FILLED TO DIFFERENT LEVELS WITH COLOURED WATER

exactly how far up and how far down we have to go.

What are the sol-fa names to the melody of God Save the Queen ? Write them down and then look at the foot of the page to see if you have them correct.

Train yourself to listen to melodies so that you can say to yourself on hearing Annie Laurie, " That starts with three low *dohs* and then jumps up to high *doh*." Or, if our tune is the Old Hundredth, say "*d-d,t,l,s-drm*" (we can use just one letter of each of the sol-fa names and save space). Learn, too, to make up tunes of your own with these names.

What makes sound? The answer is, Vibrations in the air. This you can find out by stretching a piece of elastic between

show you how any wind instrument works. In all these instruments different notes can be made because there is some mechanism to produce vibrations of different length.

One instrument is in tune with another when each produces the same number of vibrations in each second. A pianist, when he is to accompany a violinist, plays one note. It has 440 vibrations a second. The violinist plays a note which has 440 vibrations a second. Each plays exactly the same sound, and we say that they are in tune with each other. For the sake of convenience we call the 440-vibrations-a-second note A.

The sol-fa names of God save the Queen :
ddrtdr : mmfmrd : rdtd : ssssfm : ffffmr : mfmrdmfs : lfmrd.

FRENCH—A LITTLE PICTURE LESSON

HERE we read of the arrival at the railway station. We must remember that the first line under the picture is the French, the second gives the English word for the French word above it, and the third line shows how we make up the words into our own language.

Le taxi—The taxi

Le taxi arrive à la porte.
The taxi arrives at the door.
The taxi arrives at the door.

Le chauffeur—The driver

Le chauffeur met les bagages sur le taxi.
The driver puts the luggage on the taxi.
The driver is putting the luggage on the taxi.

Dans le taxi—In the taxi

Nous sommes six dans le taxi.
We are six in the taxi.
There are six of us in the taxi.

1	2	3
Un	deux	trois
One	*two*	*three*
4	5	6
quatre	cinq	six
four	*five*	*six*

Nous aimons aller en taxi.
We like to go in taxi.
We like riding in a taxi.

En route—On the way

Le taxi va très bien.
The taxi goes very well.
The taxi goes very well.

La gare—The station

Nous arriverons bientôt à la gare.
We shall arrive soon at the station.
We shall soon arrive at the station.
Nous sommes maintenant à la gare.
We are now at the station.
We are now at the station.

L'horloge—The clock

Il y a une grande horloge à la gare.
There is a big clock at the station.
There is a big clock in the station.
Il est dix heures et demie du matin.
It is ten hours and a half of the morning.
It is half-past ten in the morning.

The Story of the Boundless Universe and All Its Wondrous Worlds

Our Face to the Sun in Winter   Our Face to the Sun in Summer

THREE WAYS THE EARTH MOVES

THE first thing we are inclined to say when we are told the Earth moves is that we do not feel it moving, but the answer to that is easy.

When you are in a train in a station, you sometimes cannot tell whether the train is moving or not, except, perhaps, by looking at another train standing at the other platform, and sometimes you think your train is moving, until you see that the platform is quite still. It was the moving of the other train that made you think *your* train was moving.

So it proves nothing to say that we do not feel the Earth moving with us. If you are travelling in a train, or on a boat, or in a balloon, or on this great Earth, you have only two ways of judging whether you are moving or not. One is by feeling the movement under you, and the other by noticing that things outside seem to be moving past you.

Now, certainly we cannot feel the Earth move under us, but this is simply because the movement is so smooth. The best proof of the smoothness of the Earth's motion is that no one has ever felt it moving. Sometimes a little bit of the outside of it moves by itself, and then people feel it. That is called an earthquake, and is quite different. No one has ever felt the movement of the Earth as a whole.

What would happen if the Earth suddenly stopped moving? If suddenly it *did* stop moving, as a bus pulls up sharp, or as you pull your arm up sharp when you throw a ball, what would happen to us? When a bus stops suddenly all the passengers are jerked forward. The Earth is going so fast that if it were suddenly to stop moving all the loose things on it, and many of the fixed things on it, would be hurled across space. Indeed, the shock would render the Earth red-hot and probably tear it to pieces. But nothing except collision with a sun or a planet could stop the motion of the Earth, and there seems to be no likelihood of such a collision occurring. The Earth is likely to rush on smoothly for thousands and thousands of years and meantime men will not feel its motion.

If you cannot *feel* that the thing you are travelling on is moving, there is only one way of finding out that it is moving, and that is by looking at things outside it and seeing what they seem to do. Clever men have been doing this for ages, and there seemed to be no doubt at all about what they saw. As we have already seen, when we look up at the

ASTRONOMY · GEOLOGY · GEOGRAPHY · CHEMISTRY · PHYSICS · LIFE

sky we find the Sun, for instance, seeming to travel once round the Earth every day.

But, as a boy in a train can sometimes make a mistake and think that the other train is moving when it is really *his* train that moves, so all the men who thought they saw the Sun moving across the sky were wrong. It was not the Sun that was moving, but the Earth. We still talk of the Sun rising and setting, and no doubt men will go on doing so for ages, but the Sun does not rise and set. It is simply the Earth that is spinning round like a top. If you have got a globe, a little round model of the world, you can easily learn from it something about the first kind of movement of the Earth.

THE TURNING OF THE EARTH THROUGH THE SUNLIGHT INTO SHADOW

There are at least three different movements of the Earth, and we must look at them all. The one we shall begin with explains why the Sun seems to rise every morning in the east and to set every evening in the west. Take your little globe—if you have not a globe an india-rubber ball or an orange will do—and hold it in your hand opposite a lighted torch in a room where everything else is dark. The side of the ball next to the torch will be lit up, and the side away from the torch will be dark. Put a spot of ink on the ball and call it your house, and hold the ball so that the spot is opposite the torch. Now turn the ball slowly round, and the spot will travel round until at last it loses the light of the torch. Then, as you go on turning, the spot will become lit up again.

The torch stands for the Sun, and when the spot is just opposite the torch, that is *midday*. Then, as the ball goes on turning, the spot loses the torchlight : that is to say, the Sun sets, and it is night. Then the spot turns to the side where the ball is lit up, and if you were on that spot you would say the Sun had risen once more.

WHAT WOULD HAPPEN IF THE EARTH WERE TO STOP MOVING

Imagine the ball to be the Earth and the spot your house, and you will begin to understand how day and night occur. It is night because your side of the Earth passes out of the sunlight; it is day because it comes into the sunlight again.

Think what it would be like if it were always day, or if it were always night. If the Earth were not for ever spinning round and round like a top, and if it were quite still, one half of it would always be in daylight, while the other would have an endless night. So long as you hold your ball or globe or orange still, one half of it must be facing the torch, and the other half is turned away from it.

What do you think would happen to us all if the Earth were to stop moving round and round, and if it slowed down quietly like a top so as not to jerk us all off ? Suppose it stopped with our part facing the Sun, we should say: "The Sun is standing still in the heavens." The lamplighters would do their work at the ordinary time. People would say: "It is a very bright evening," and then they would say: "Whatever has happened?" There would be no night at all; it would go on being day. Do you think that all the people from the other side of the world, where it was night all the time, would jump into their ships and come over to our side so as to see the Sun again? Probably they would, but before long we should all be very glad to get on to the dark side of the Earth—for a time, at any rate. The best thing for us is that the Earth should go on spinning as it spins now, and that we should have the day to be awake in and the night for sleep.

THE BEES THAT WERE DECEIVED AND DIED FROM OVERWORK

There is a story of some bees that had worked hard all day and gone to rest when someone lit a brilliant electric light and brought a sham day back to them. The bees started work again until the light was put out, and then, soon after, the sun rose, and they started again. At the end of that day they were all worn out, and died from overwork. But the natural and proper thing for bees—and for men, too, who live on a great spinning top —is to be awake when the part of the top they are on is facing the Sun, and to sleep when it is turned the other way.

But the spinning of the Earth, which gives us night and day, is by no means the Earth's only movement. You will have noticed, when spinning a top, that sometimes it stands in one place and spins there, but sometimes it moves along the table. When this happens the top is moving in *two ways at once*.

It is spinning on itself, so to speak, and also being moved as a whole from one place to another. The Earth is like the

ROUND AND ROUND THE SEASONS COME

SPRING

SUMMER

AUTUMN

WINTER

top. All the time the Earth is spinning on itself it is also moving as a whole, as the top does when it moves along the table. We do not feel this, but it is the most important movement of the Earth, even though its results are not so startling as the day and night which the spinning movement gives us.

There is no need now to ask " What holds the Earth up ? " We know that the Earth is not supported by anything, but flies through space without stopping from one year's end to another.

A year, you know, is a real thing—not like a week. We may think a week is a real thing because Sunday always comes back every seven days, and so do the other days. But we might just as well miss out Wednesday, Thursday, Friday, and Saturday, and make the week three days. Long ago, men agreed to call seven days a week and we do so still, but a week is an *artificial* thing; a day is a *natural* thing, and so is a year. We say a week is an artificial thing because nothing in Nature makes it; but a day is a natural thing because a great fact in Nature makes it, that fact being the spinning of the Earth. A year is also a natural thing, because it is made by this second kind of movement of the Earth, which is like the movement of the top *along* the table.

Let us think of a spinning ball now, instead of a spinning top. We know very well that a ball can spin as it goes along, because we can set it spinning on a table, and as it spins it will also run in one direction or another. What direction does the Earth move in, then ? We have already seen that day and night, which never fail us, are due to its spinning. Now, on the whole, one night is just about as dark as another, and one day as bright as another.

This means that the Earth does not get much nearer to the Sun or go much farther from it. It stays at about the same distance, yet it always goes moving onwards, onwards, onwards. That means that it

HOW THE EARTH IS
TILTED TODAY

HOW THE EARTH WILL BE
TILTED IN 12,000 YEARS

must go round the Sun. If you tied a string from your ball to your candlestick you could make the ball fly round the candle, only it would not be so easy to make the ball spin as it flew.

If you could make the ball spin, and if you could make it spin on itself about 365 times while it was going right round the candle once, that would be what the Earth is doing. The Earth is always flying round the Sun, and if you made a mark at some point, and then waited until the Earth came back to that point after going round the Sun once, the time the Earth took in its journey would be a year, and during that journey round the Sun the Earth would have spun round on itself 365 times. Really, it is about 365 and a quarter times, and it is so that we may not forget that quarter that every four years we have what we call leap year, making the year 366 days long by giving February 29 days instead of 28.

In its course round the Sun, however, the Earth does not move in a perfect circle, but in a circle very slightly oval, so that it is sometimes a little nearer the Sun and sometimes a little farther away. Nor does it always move at exactly the same speed, but quickens as it nears the Sun. This is necessary, for if the Earth moved no more quickly when near the Sun than when farther away, it would be drawn into the Sun; and if it moved as quickly when farther away as when near, it would fly away from the Sun altogether.

We have mentioned two of the three great motions of the Earth—its spinning on its own axis and its revolution round the Sun—and we now come to its third motion, which is a kind of wobble.

If you have a globe, you must have noticed that it is not set squarely in its frame. The North Pole is not at the very top and the South Pole at the bottom, but the globe is tilted. This tilting of the Earth as it goes round the Sun is very important indeed, for it is responsible for the seasons. It means that the northern half of the Earth will get the Sun's rays pouring very directly down upon it during one part of the year, which we call summer, but not so directly during the other part of the year, the winter.

That is why summer is hot and winter cold. You might perhaps think that when the Earth was nearer the Sun this would make summer; but, as a matter of fact, the

axis. The Earth is always tilted at about the same angle, but the axis does not always point toward the same direction in space. One wobble takes about 25,000 years. Then the orbit of the Earth is sometimes more oval than at others ; and when the orbit is very oval then one season will be much longer than another. For instance, if the northern half is turned

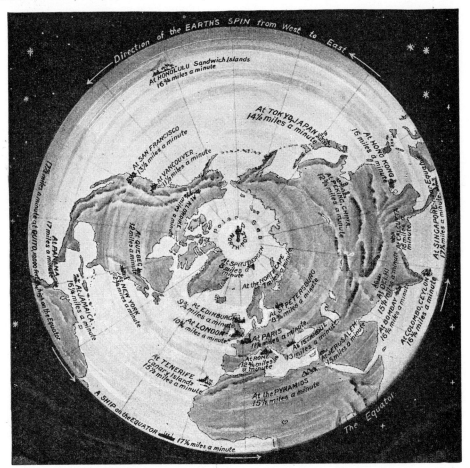

THE WORLD FOR EVER MOVING ROUND AND ROUND—A PICTURE-MAP SHOWING THE RATE AT WHICH THE VARIOUS PARTS OF IT TRAVEL ROUND ITS AXIS

Earth is nearer the Sun during our winter. Our winter, also, is summer for the Australians, who live on the opposite side of the world, and when we have summer they have winter. So the distance of the Earth from the Sun has nothing to do with the seasons, and they are due, as we have said, entirely to the fact that the Earth is tilted.

Now, the wobbling we have mentioned has to do with this tilting of the Earth's

from the Sun when the Earth is at the far part of the very oval orbit, then the winter will be long and cold, and the heat of the summer, which will of course be short, cannot melt it.

This explains why in times past all the northern part of the Earth was always covered with ice.

(Next chapter in this group, page 393)

TWO FAMOUS SONS OF VENICE

YOUNG TINTORETTO PAINTS HIS MOTHER'S PORTRAIT

ANDREA VERROCCHIO FASHIONS THE HEAD OF HIS FAMOUS HORSE FOR THE COLLEONI STATUE

The Story of Immortal Folk Whose Work Will Never Die

Carpaccio   Donatello   Tintoretto   Giovanni Bellini

Andrea Palladio   Giorgione   Verrocchio   Paul Veronese

THE FAMOUS MEN OF VENICE

VENICE is old, but age does not disfigure her. Our admiration and love for her increase. She is very beautiful in her old age, and very pathetic. All her glories belong to the past. Venice is slowly decaying.

She stands like some beautiful vision on the sands of the seashore, and men, as they see her image reflected in the gleaming waters of the lagoon, wonder if it be not some fairy fancy that they picture. Such cities as Venice seem to belong more to dreams and poetic visions than to this world of ours.

Hundreds of years ago, when barbarians overthrew the might of Rome, a small number of Roman descendants were driven before the conquering Goths and Lombards down to the coast of the Adriatic Sea. They hid in swamps and in little islands near the coast, and became fishermen and sailors.

Each island was controlled by its own tribune, appointed by the people. After two centuries, however, the people appointed one man a duke (or doge, as they called him) to rule over them all. No longer did they fear attack from the mainland. They constructed bridges to join the islands together, and canals were made along the channels where the water had previously flowed unchecked. They built a powerful fleet, and this fleet they sent, in 827, to Alexandria, where it is said to have recovered, and carried back to Venice, the body of St Mark.

Venice became a crowded, wealthy, and important city. She sent out her soldiers and her ships with the Crusaders. She built up a great trade. She bought from the East and sold to the West ; she bought from the West and sold to the East ; and her own manufactures became famous.

While her citizens were prosperous they had ample means for making their city beautiful. Her richest residents could not build great castles, for there would not have been room for them in Venice ; so they built gorgeous palaces of marble. The Republic could not build huge forts, so they devoted their money to erect splendid halls, council chambers, and palaces.

They had very little space on which to build, so they made a small city unequalled in beauty.

Her widespread trade brought her into relationship with all the civilised world, and she gleaned knowledge from far and wide. The fall of the Greek Empire sent the learned Greeks to Venice for refuge. They taught the Venetians all that they knew, gave them the treasures of the old writers, and so implanted a love of learning in

EXPLORERS · INVENTORS · WRITERS · ARTISTS · SCIENTISTS

them that it is to the Venetians we owe some of our finest literature.

Great works which would have perished for ever were translated by them, and preserved for all the world. The Arabs, then among the masters of learning in the world, taught them how to make gunpowder and how to make glass, and taught them also the first principles of decorative art. East and West, wherever they went, the Venetians were always learning.

Their early building combined many styles, the elaborate fancy of the East with the sterner simplicity of Northern Europe; but all was so beautifully blended that there was nothing in the world quite like it.

It is not easy to point to many notable architectural features of Venice and say that they are the work of such and such a man. Their building took too long, and engaged too many men in successive generations for that. Thus it was with the famous Palace of the Doges, and the Cathedral and Campanile of St Mark. The cathedral and palace still stand, and the campanile stood until 1902, when, through gradual decay and neglect, the lovely tower crashed suddenly one morning to the ground. A terrible disaster to art, it was, but happily it came about with little damage to life or property. The Venetians have since rebuilt the tower on the old foundations.

THE MAN WHO BUILT THE SPLENDID LIBRARY OF VENICE

Among the famous architects of Venice come the names of Giovanni Giocondo and Michele Sanmichele, both of the sixteenth century; but a greater architect than either arose in the person of Jacopo Sansovino, who was born at Florence in 1477, and lived in Venice from 1527 up to his death in 1570. Several churches stand to his credit in Venice, but the work which immortalised him was the building of the famous Library of San Marco, and the Mint which adjoins it. He built them at the same time, joining wall against wall, to form the most striking contrast. The library, now called the Royal Palace, is one of the sights of the city—a building of two storeys, each supported by a series of arches of the greatest beauty.

Next followed a man to whom English architecture owes much. This was Andrea Palladio, who was born at Vicenza in 1518, and died there when sixty-two. He gave practically all his life to beautifying Venice. He built splendid churches and other edifices, but not palaces. He loved space for his work, and to rear buildings distinguished by dignity and simplicity.

Much excellent sculptural work was done by the Lombardo family—the Lombardi, as they are called.

THE SOLDIER WHO GAVE HIS FORTUNE TO BE REMEMBERED FOR ALL TIME

In their workshops many other sculptors received their training, among them being Alessandro Leopardi, whose name is familiar to every visitor to Venice. Born in the latter half of the fifteenth century, he died about 1545, but his fame remains fresh. Two things make him always notable—the majestic flagstaffs which rise in front of St Mark's, and the work which he did in connection with the statue of Colleoni.

Colleoni's deeds of war are of no account today; he is of no more importance to the world than if he had never lived, but he is of interest as having called forth a supreme work of art. He gained great wealth from the wars, and at his death he left all his money and horses and arms to the State, on the condition that they should raise a statue to his memory.

The Venetians faithfully carried out their part of the bargain. Although Venetian sculpture was making progress, they could not trust one of their own citizens to do this work. They sent to Florence for Andrea del Verrocchio, who was famous as painter, sculptor, and goldsmith, and memorable to us as a teacher of Leonardo da Vinci. He was born in 1435, and was 44 when sent for to make the Colleoni statue. He—Verrocchio—had only nine years to live, and we might fancy that he realised that this was to be the last and greatest work of his life.

THE SCULPTOR WHO COULD AFFORD TO LAUGH AT VENICE

Verrocchio went to Venice to make the statue there, and the story is told that he had just modelled his horse when he heard that the Government of Venice meant to ask a scholar of Donatello to set the rider on the horse's back. Verrocchio was indignant. He broke his horse's head to bits and went home to Florence, and there followed him a decree forbidding him ever to set foot in Venice again under penalty of death. But artists can always laugh at governments; they have a power that politicians know not of. Verrocchio

VENICE IN ALL HER GLORY

VENICE RISING FROM THE WATERS

THE DUCAL PALACE THAT HAS STOOD FOR CENTURIES

28 I I*

THE SQUARE OF SAN MARCO WITH THE GRACEFUL CAMPANILE

SAN MARCO, THE MARVELLOUS DOMED CATHEDRAL OF VENICE

THE LOVELY COLUMNS OF A VENETIAN PALACE

A RARE PIECE OF THE TWELFTH CENTURY ABOVE THE DOORS OF SAN MARCO

A SQUARE IN VENICE

THE COLLEONI MONUMENT

A STAIRWAY IN THE MINELLI
PALACE

THE OLD COLUMN OF
ST. MARK

DOORWAY OF THE DUCAL
PALACE

ONE OF THE BEAUTIFUL DOOR-
WAYS OF SAN MARCO

A LOVELY FIGURE IN A
VENICE CHURCH

THE BRIDGE OF SIGHS BETWEEN
PALACE AND PRISON

smiled at the decree of the proud Republic, and wrote back that he would never run that risk, as if his head were once cut off the Government of Venice could never put it on again, while he could at any time replace his horse's head. The Government of Venice felt that this was true. They cancelled their decree, begged Verrocchio to return, doubled his fee, and promised to leave him alone.

THE MOST SOLDIERLY FIGURE ON THE EARTH, BUT A NOBODY

He came back to Venice, and began his work again ; but he had only begun to restore his broken model when the penalty of death was carried out indeed. Not the Republic of Venice, but a Power that neither men nor governments can contradict carried the artist to his grave ; a short illness, and his life was done.

He left behind him an appeal that one of his pupils should be employed to complete the work, but Venice chose Alessandro Leopardi, who had fallen into evil ways and some years before had been driven from the city as a forger and criminal. In their need they recalled him, and told him to make the casting. He atoned for his sin by the way in which he executed the task. He produced a splendid work from Verrocchio's model.

The statue is still without comparison. Horse and man seem alive. John Ruskin thought it one of the noblest monuments ever set up on the face of the earth. Colleoni rides with defiant features, proud in his strength as a man, fierce and disdainful in his skill as a general. The horse moves heavily, but with great strength, as upon some dreadful battlefield. Leopardi was not satisfied with the fame which the pedestal gave him, but wrote his name upon the girth of the horse, as though the whole design were his. But nothing can rob Verrocchio of the honour of modelling one of the greatest masterpieces in the world.

THE FAMOUS FAMILY THAT STARTED PAINTING IN VENICE

Yet, after all, the great splendour and wonder of Venice belong to her paintings. There never was another place where such a notorious kingdom of art grew up. Venice is as supreme in painting as for the beauty of her situation and buildings. For a long time she had painters of no special merit, and then the Bellini family arose. With them came new light. The glory of Venetian art dawned with them. They began to paint finely in distemper before ever the art of oil-painting had been heard of in Venice.

The improvement began with Jacopo Bellini, who was born probably about 1400, and died about 1464. Jacopo never became a great artist himself. His work was an improvement upon anything ever done before in Venice, but his chief credit is that he was the father of two notable sons, who carried out his own splendid ideas.

They worked together with him, and all the young artists of Venice who desired to become great in their art flocked to their studio to become pupils. Giorgione and Titian were of the number. Gentile Bellini painted scenes from the life of Venice ; Giovanni Bellini painted religious subjects as Venice had never before seen them painted. Gentile painted portraits, and gained such fame that he was sent for by the Sultan of Turkey to paint his portrait.

THE BELLINIS WELCOME THE NEW MANNER OF OIL PAINTING

Gentile went and painted a famous picture of the cruel man who then ruled over Turkey. This wretch one day wished to show that Bellini had not correctly painted the head of John the Baptist after death, so he drew his sword and cut off the head of a slave standing near. So horrified was the artist that he never rested until he was back in Venice.

But a great change had now come over the art of Venice. An artist named Antonello, of Messina, appeared in the city, bringing with him a new art. He had learned from Hubert and Jan van Eyck, the great Flemish artists, their secret of painting with colours mixed with oils. Let us look for a moment at a scene painted for the stage of a theatre; it is done in distemper, the medium in which the artists of Venice had been working. Then let us remember one of our glorious oil-paintings at the National Gallery, which is the style of work that Antonello introduced. It set all Venice wondering.

The story runs that Giovanni Bellini went in disguise to Antonello to have his portrait painted, solely that he might learn for himself the great secret. Whatever the truth of this story, we know that the grand secret was soon mastered in Venice, and that the Bellinis were the first to help to make it famous by their work.

PICTURES BY THE FAMOUS PAINTERS

THE MARRIAGE AT CANA—BY PAUL VERONESE, IN THE LOUVRE

ADMIRAL VENIERO—BY TINTORETTO

INDUSTRY—BY PAUL VERONESE

SAINT STEPHEN IN DISPUTE WITH THE DOCTORS—BY CARPACCIO

VIRGIN AND CHILD, BY GIOVANNI BELLINI

PORTRAIT OF A GENERAL, BY GIORGIONE

PORTRAIT OF A WOMAN, BY TINTORETTO

GIRL WITH A LUTE, BY CARPACCIO

Venice was now glorified by many brilliant works of the brothers.

But the Venetian authorities feared that death would come too soon and carry off Giovanni Bellini before his work for them was done. Though they paid poorly for the work, they loved his art, and were determined to get as much out of him as possible. They therefore decreed that he should work every day in one of the great State apartments he was decorating, and should have assistants.

THE MIGHTY GENIUS WHO LEARNED PAINTING AS A WORKMAN

These young men had only four or five ducats a month as payment, and the great Titian was one of the workmen. The document stating the terms of his engagement refers to him with as little ceremony as if he were a poor man called in to white-wash a ceiling. He became one of the greatest painters of all time, and his story is told elsewhere. The mighty genius of Titian could never have developed in the way that it did had not Jacopo Bellini and his two illustrious sons given a new turn to the world of art.

Gentile Bellini died in 1507, nine years before his brother Giovanni. Both of them had the happiness to meet Albert Dürer, Germany's greatest painter. Born at Nuremberg in 1471, Dürer had a hard struggle for education. His father was a poor goldsmith with a family of eighteen children, and Albert had for a time to support his aged mother and a brother as well as his own family. He worked like a slave to master the elements of painting. His father, bitterly disappointed that the lad had wasted his time by years of study of the goldsmith's art, at last allowed him to adopt painting for his profession.

THE GREAT BELLINI SITS AT A YOUNG MAN'S FEET

There was little money for Albert in Nuremberg, but elsewhere others made money by copying his designs and selling the copies as his work. These pirated copies reached even Venice, and it was to prevent this dishonest trading in his productions that Albert, in 1505, went to Venice. His paintings astonished the Venetians.

The younger men were jealous. Not so the Bellinis. Giovanni went to Dürer as humbly as if he had been an apprentice, and asked to see the German painter's work. He could hardly believe that he had painted some of the things said to have been done. Giovanni asked to see the brushes with which the work had been carried out. Even then he could not understand, so Dürer picked up one of the brushes, and, while the old artist looked on, painted a lock of hair so much like nature and so beautiful that it might have been taken from a human head and laid upon the canvas.

Giovanni was delighted; he praised and honoured the young German, and gave him an order for his portrait. Dürer died at his home in 1528. A great painter and skilled engraver, he was also the father of etching, as well as one of the men whose art helped Venice on toward the glorious goal to which she was tending.

CARPACCIO, GIORGIONE, AND THE GREAT LITTLE SON OF A DYER

One of the first of the new school of artists to be influenced by the Bellinis was Vittore Carpaccio. He was born in Istria, about 1450, and lived 72 years. We have seen how the idea of painting scenes from life began to take the place of pictures which had been painted again and again in the same flat style. Carpaccio carried on the work in the noblest way. Some of the painters of his age took subjects from heathen books for their pictures. Carpaccio painted beautiful stories upon his canvases. His pictures told the story of the lives of saints and heroes ; they were made to appeal to the mind and the soul, not, like some others, merely to the eye.

Another great man arose in these days. In 1477 Giorgione was born. As Giotto perfected the changes introduced by Cimabue, his master, into Florentine art, so Giorgione ennobled the art schemes of his masters, the Bellini family. Giorgione not only enriched the city by his wonderful frescoes and other paintings, but had a most powerful influence on the artists of his own day. He died when only 33.

This was a wonderful age for Venice. Every rich man was willing to employ artists. They may not have paid well, but there was no very serious competition ; and we find Giorgione, Titian, and others, painting articles of furniture, and other artists rivalling goldsmiths in the splendour with which they decorated buildings.

Much talent was wasted in this way. Some of the artists would do anything for money ; Titian was, perhaps, the most grasping of them all. His mean nature

TITIAN, THE IMMORTAL COLOUR MAN

THE EMPEROR CHARLES THE FIFTH HONOURS HIMSELF BY PICKING UP TITIAN'S PAINT BRUSH

TITIAN, THE MASTER COLOURIST OF THE WORLD, TOUCHING A CANVAS "WITH A WARMTH DIVINE"

was never more apparent than in his treatment of another great man, Tintoretto, to whom we now come. His real name was Jacopo Robusti, and he was born at Venice in 1518, and died in 1594. His father was a dyer—a tintoro—and so they called Jacopo, his son, Tintoretto, or Tintorettino, meaning " the little dyer." The clever boy was a born artist.

He used to dabble in his father's dyes, and to splash the colours all over the walls and furniture until his parents must have found him a nuisance. Seeing which way the lad's genius was inclined, the father took him to Titian. Jacopo's apprenticeship lasted but a few days.

Titian went into the studio one morning and saw, lying on the floor, papers covered with drawings. He picked them up, and asked who had done them. Little Tintoretto shyly confessed that he had. Titian saw that they were the work of a genius; he saw that this boy might soon become a rival to himself. He left the studio at once, and that day had the poor boy turned out. It was a shameful thing, but brave young Tintoretto was not to be beaten. His life became a miracle of activity. He set before himself two models—Michael Angelo for design; Titian, his cruel master, for colour.

THE IMMORTAL PAINTER WHO LEARNED FROM WORKING MEN

He made models of wax on which to hang draperies for the figures he meant to paint. He copied tombstones and bits of broken statuary. He studied the methods of every artist in every studio into which he dared to peep. He went down into the square where the poor painters worked who painted common furniture and cabinets for sale, and studied how they got some of their effects. He followed the work of architects. He used to beg builders to let him decorate houses which they were erecting. Once he painted designs all round the clock which the builders were erecting in a tower. Another builder was putting up a new house, and Tintoretto insisted on painting the walls with lovely frescoes, simply for the cost of the materials he used. He would do paintings for chapels and churches and other buildings for practically nothing.

He did anything and everything to perfect his art and make his name known. He worked with marvellous speed, and, of course, the effect was not always good. But in time he made a very great name,

and became one of the very greatest painters of all time. One story must suffice to show his passion for work and the marvellous ways in which he carried it out.

HOW TINTORETTO ASTONISHED THE VENETIANS ONE DAY

The ceiling of the San Rocco School was to be decorated with a painting, and the artists of Venice were asked to send in sketches for the work. There were not many days for the preparation. The other artists made their rough plans. Not so Tintoretto. He had the space measured, and, with that zeal and speed which nobody could match, he painted his whole picture, and had it secretly fixed up on the ceiling and covered over.

When the day of trial came the others showed their sketches, while Tintoretto stood by. At last he drew away the linen covering the ceiling, and the company saw his splendid picture already fixed.

The last of the greatest Venetian painters was Paul Veronese. He was born in 1528 at Verona, whence his title, his real name being Caliari, or Cagliari. He lived in Venice from 1555 till his death in 1588. His pictures were characterised by the brilliance of colouring proper to works of the great Venetian school, but he had caught the spirit of painters in Rome, and gave to his work more dignity, grace of pose, and ease of movement than had been possible before his day.

Paul Veronese was a painter more for the palace than the church. His scenes were scenes of splendour, of great space and riches and luxury, so that it has been said that one of his paintings would convert a garret into a palace of vast size and delight. He was a great worker, but different in type from Tintoretto, taking careful pains with all that he painted.

PAUL VERONESE AND HIS FAMOUS PICTURE OF A MARRIAGE FEAST

In the Louvre at Paris hangs his picture called The Marriage Feast at Cana, showing 160 portraits of people who lived in Venice in his day.

With the death of Paul Veronese the sun of Venetian art set. But the afterglow has lighted the world for more than three hundred years, firing the enthusiasm of all the artists who have lived since.

While the glory of Venice as a sea power is departed for ever, her glory in art will never die. So long as her pictures last they will remain the treasures of the world.

The Great Stories of the World That Will Be Told for Ever

ALI BABA AND THE FORTY THIEVES

ALI BABA was a poor man who lived with his wife in a town in Persia, and one day he went into the forest to cut some firewood. He saw a band of forty thieves, and so he climbed into a tree and hid himself. The tree grew beside a great rock, and the forty thieves came to this rock, and cried : " Open, Sesame ! "

A door opened leading into a cave, and the forty thieves went in and placed there the gold and silver they had stolen. Then they came out, and cried : " Shut, Sesame ! "

Then the cave closed up, and they rode away. Ali Baba then came down from the tree, and cried: " Open, Sesame ! "

Again the cave opened, and he entered and found himself in a sort of treasure-house, stored with sacks of gold and silver; and, seeing that it had all been stolen, Ali Baba seized as many sacks as he could carry, and took them home.

"Now," he said to his wife, "I will soon grow as rich as my brother Cassim."

And this thought pleased him very much, for his brother was a proud and haughty man, who had married a very wealthy woman.

" We must measure how much gold we've got," said Ali Baba's wife joyfully.

So she went to Cassim's house and asked for the loan of a measure. Cassim's wife wondered what sort of grain her poor sister-in-law had got. So she put some wax under the measure, and when the measure was returned to her she found, to her immense surprise, a piece of gold sticking to it. She at once told Cassim, and Cassim went to Ali Baba and asked him where he had got his gold from. Ali Baba frankly told his brother about the treasure-house in the rock, and told him how to open and shut the cave.

" I'll have all that gold carried away before Ali Baba gets a share of it," said Cassim to himself.

He at once took ten mules to the cave with the idea of loading them with all the sacks. He cried, "Open, Sesame!" and got into the cave, and danced with delight when he saw how much treasure there was. But at last he became so excited that when he wanted to take away the sacks he forgot the words that opened the cave.

"Open, barley!" he cried. "Open, wheat!"

While he was trying to think of the right words the forty thieves returned and found him in the cave, and killed him.

The next day Ali Baba went to get some more gold, and he discovered in the cave the body of his brother, and carried it away and had it decently buried. Then, in accordance with the Persian custom,

IMAGINATION · CHIVALRY · LEGENDS · GOLDEN DEEDS · FAIRY TALES

he took his widowed sister-in-law to live with him; and with her came a clever female slave, whose name was Morgiana.

When the forty thieves found that the body of Cassim had been removed from the cave they were full of fear.

" So there's another man who knows our secret!" said the captain. " But I know how to find him!"

He disguised himself and went to the town, and inquired if a man who had been slain by the sword had recently been buried; and he at last learned that just such a man had been buried by Ali Baba.

"Now," said the captain of the thieves to his men, "I must arrange to get all of you quietly into the house of this Ali Baba; and you must come out at night and kill everybody there, and escape without being seen."

So he brought some of the huge leather jars in which the Persians used at that time to keep their oil, and he got a thief to get into each one of them, and covered them up, leaving a little space for air. He then put them all on some mules, and took with him one jar really filled with oil in case he should be called upon to show what he carried, and travelled at night from the forest into the town, and stopped before Ali Baba's house.

" I have brought my oil from a good distance," he said to Ali Baba, "and it is now too late to go to an inn. Will you kindly put me up for the night?"

Being a kind-hearted man, Ali Baba welcomed the captain of the forty thieves, and told the servants to look after the mules, and bring in the jars. Morgiana was sent to cook a supper for the strange guest. Finding that she had no oil to fry the meat in, she went to take a little out of one of the jars. When she approached the thief thought she was the captain, and whispered cautiously:

"Is it time?"

"Not yet," said Morgiana.

She went from jar to jar and found there was a thief in each, and at last she came to the jar which was filled with oil. She heated the oil in a great kettle, and then crept up to the jars and poured in the hot liquid, scalding all the thieves to death.

" Now we shall see what will happen," said Morgiana.

In the dead of night the captain tried to arouse the thieves ; but after peeping into the jars he saw that his men were all dead, and he rushed quickly out of the house. In the morning Morgiana told Ali Baba the whole story, and Ali Baba, much astonished, buried the dead thieves secretly the next night.

"But remember," said Morgiana, "there is one thief still at large; and you must be on your guard, for he will never rest until he has killed every one of us who know his secret."

Morgiana was right. For the captain of the forty thieves soon returned in a new disguise, and set up as a shopkeeper, and tried to make friends with Ali Baba and get an opportunity of killing him. One day Ali Baba invited the captain to come to supper.

Now, there is a very strange law of honour which all Persians and other Mohammedans strictly observe. Even the very worst men among them will not kill anybody with whom he has eaten salt. So the captain of the thieves said to Ali Baba: "I should be pleased to sup with you, my friend, but I must confess I have a very curious taste. I cannot bear the least bit of salt in any dish."

" Oh, that's easily arranged!" said Ali Baba. And he told Morgiana not to put any salt in the meat for supper; and that made Morgiana suspicious.

"So your new friend is a man who will not eat salt with you ! " she said. " I must have a look at him."

She did so and, in spite of the new disguise, she saw that he was the captain of the thieves. Moreover, she saw a dagger hidden in his dress. So she said to Ali Baba: "Tell your strange friend that one of your slave girls will come and dance before him after supper."

When the supper was over she entered the room attired in a beautiful dress, and began to dance the dagger dance. She whirled round and round in graceful movements, holding a dagger in her hand, and then rushed at Ali Baba and pretended to stab him. Then she lightly danced up to the captain of the forty thieves, but, instead of pretending to stab him, she drove the dagger into his heart.

"I recognised the villain!" she said.

Then she showed the dagger hidden in his dress. Ali Baba then married Morgiana to his eldest son, and gave her as a dowry a large share of the treasure in the cave in the forest.

THE CARGO OF WHEAT

Seven hundred years ago Stavoren was the greatest and most beautiful city in Holland. An immense dyke protected it from the sea ; and the townspeople were very rich because they had many ships sailing to different parts of the world and bringing back riches from the strange countries they visited.

The people of Stavoren were very proud and hard. The wealthiest and the hardest and the proudest of them all was a lady. One day she sent for the captain of her greatest ship, and said to him:

" Set sail at once, my man, and bring me back a large cargo of the most precious thing in the world."

" I do not understand," said the captain. " Do you want fine silks, or golden jewels, or diamonds ? "

" I have given you my orders," replied the lady. " I am the richest person in Stavoren, and I am resolved to astonish all my neighbours. Find out what is the most precious thing in the world, and bring me a large cargo of it."

The captain ran to the port and set sail at once. On reaching the open sea he called his men around him, and told them what his mistress had ordered him to do.

" Now, what, in your opinion," he said, " is the most precious thing in the world ? "

" Gold," said his first mate.

" No," said the second mate. " Fine silks are worth more."

" In my opinion," said the third mate, " diamonds are the most precious things in the world."

The captain asked each of his men in turn, and each gave him some different advice. But a little cabin-boy said:

" I really know what is the most precious thing in the world, because I have known what it is to be without food. It is wheat."

The captain saw the truth of this. Setting full sail, he steered into the Baltic Sea and landed at the town of Danzig. There he bought a cargo of magnificent wheat, stowed it in the ship, and put out on the return voyage.

In his absence his proud mistress called on all the rich townspeople of Stavoren, and said to them:

" I have sent my captain to bring me a cargo of the most precious thing to be found in the world."

Naturally, everybody in Stavoren be-came very curious, and they waited in great impatience for the return of the ship. In a few days the captain came back.

" How quick you have been! " said the lady. " What have you brought me ? "

" A large cargo of the finest wheat in the world," said the captain.

" Wheat ? You wretch! Wheat ? " cried the furious woman. " I asked for the most precious thing in the world and you bring me some vulgar, ordinary, common wheat ! I shall be the laughing-stock of Stavoren! Throw the whole cargo into the sea! "

And, in spite of the pleadings and the cries of the crowd of poor, hungry beggars, this was done.

On her way home the lady met the captain. His face was set and stern.

" You bad woman! " he said. " The day will soon come when you will know what it is to feel hungry. Then you will think of the good wheat you cast away."

The woman laughed scornfully, knowing she was the richest person in Stavoren. But when she reached her house a great storm began to rage, and some days afterwards she received news that all her ships had been destroyed.

In the tempest a great bank of sand was thrown up by the waves before the port of Stavoren. The ship in which the captain had sailed was wrecked and buried in the sandbank, and all the commerce of Stavoren was ended.

For some months the proud lady managed to live in luxury by selling her jewels, but when the springtime came all her money was gone. She went to her rich friends and begged for food, but they laughed at her, and turned her from her doors.

One morning in April, as she was passing by the old seaport and looking at the sandbank, she saw that it was covered with green verdure. The wheat she had thrown into the sea had been cast up by the storm, and had sprouted in the mud.

" It is a miracle! " she said.

Knowing now what hunger was, she waited patiently until autumn came and all the wheat was ripe, and then she led the poor people of the town to the sandbank, and told them they could gather the corn. When it was all harvested they went into the inland country, and took the repentant woman with them.

THE KNIGHTS AND THE SHIELD

In the days of old a gallant horseman was riding along a lonely road. Presently he came to a wide, open space, where he was attracted by a magnificent statue, which stood facing the south. He had travelled the world over, but never had he seen anything more imposing.

On the summit of a lofty pedestal stood a figure representing Victory. Her sword was sheathed, her shield lay at her feet, and her brows were entwined with a wreath of laurel.

" Ah," he exclaimed, " what a costly monument ! I declare the shield is of solid gold ! "

He was so much taken up with wonder that he did not hear the approach of another traveller from the opposite direction. He, too, stopped to admire the statue. Great was his astonishment when he heard a voice exclaim, " The shield is of solid gold," for from where he stood it was clearly silver.

" What a strange mistake to make ! " he thought. " I must see this man who does not know gold from silver. Pardon me, my friend," he said, " but your eyes are playing you some trick; the shield is not gold, but silver."

" How mean you, sir ? " returned the first knight. " Do you dare to tell me that I don't know gold when I see it ? "

" I do not wish to tell you anything," exclaimed the second knight; " but I know silver when I see it, and I declare that this shield is silver and not gold."

" It is gold, I say."

" Nonsense! " replied the other knight.

" You insult me, sir," said the first knight angrily, " and I would have you know that I listen not to such talk from any man."

" I never thought to cross swords with one who knew not gold from silver; but if you will make a quarrel of it I am not the man to refuse you," was the reply.

So the two men drew their swords and prepared to fight. Hardly had their blades crossed, however, than they heard a voice calling:

" Oh, my good masters, be not hasty; take care what you are about ! "

The knights paused. They saw a girlish figure clad in white running toward them. She placed herself between them, and asked as she looked at their flushed faces:

" What is it you are about to do, good sirs ? For what cause is it you are about to fight ? "

" The cause for which we are about to fight is just," said one. " Yon knight accuses me of having said what is not the truth."

" And he says no less of me," exclaimed the other. " Come, stand out of our way, little maid. And you, sir, prepare."

" Stop ! " said the maiden, in a voice so commanding that the knights obeyed in spite of themselves.

" Say no more, maiden," said the first knight, " for men of honour do not look at such matters with women's eyes. Come," he added to his enemy, " are you ready ? "

Once more the swords clanged together; once more the voice of the girl sounded bidding the combat cease.

" Stop, I tell you! " she cried. And the men could not but lower their weapons. " Now, sir," she went on, " you who have come up the north road, step in front of the statue and tell me what you see."

The knight looked, and answered in a humble voice:

" I see, my lady, a golden shield."

" And now, sir knight from the south, do you step behind the statue and tell me truly what you see."

The knight looked carefully, and answered humbly:

" I see a silver shield."

" Even so," answered the maiden; " the shield is silver on one side and gold on the other. Thus both of you are right, and both of you are wrong. Now tell me what you will do."

" Our quarrel is at an end," said the one, " for we were both right."

" Yes," answered the maiden, " that is so. And now," she added, " let me see you shake hands and be friends."

The two knights laughed heartily as they did so. And the little maiden suddenly changed into a tall and stately woman. She was so fair and so queenly that the two knights fell at her feet.

" Go," she said, " and be my knights faithful and true—my name is Peace."

Even as she spoke her name she vanished.

And the two knights followed down the path, talking like old friends.

There are two sides to every question.

THE BOY FIDDLER OF SICILY

PERO was a merry, simple lad, and he lived in a village in the beautiful island of Sicily. His parents died when he was young, and when he was fourteen he set out to make his fortune. On the road he met a beggarman, who said: "My son, I am starving. Give me something to buy some bread."

"You can take my wages," said Pero, "and I will go back and serve three years more."

"You are really as kind as you are simple," said the beggarman, and as he spoke he changed into a bright Spirit. "I give you three wishes."

"Stop, Pero!" he cried at last, "and I'll give you a thousand crowns."

Pero received the money, but as soon as his back was turned the farmer ran to the magistrate and denounced him as a robber. There was little mercy for robbers in Sicily in those days. Pero was quickly arrested, tried, and condemned. But just as the hangman was putting the rope round his neck he asked the magistrate to let him play one tune.

"Don't give him the violin!" cried the farmer.

But Pero had the gift of speech, and nobody could refuse him anything. The

HE PLAYED TILL THEY WERE WEARY HE PLAYED TILL THEY WERE WORN OUT

"Well," said Pero, "give me, please, a violin that will make everybody dance, and a gun that will never miss, and the gift of speech, that nobody can refuse me anything."

The Spirit granted Pero these wishes, and Pero turned back to the farm. Seeing a pheasant fly by, he fired at it to test his magic gun. The bird fell, but before he could pick it up the farmer seized it.

"Well," said Pero, "you can have it if you like to dance for it."

He played on his violin, and the farmer capered like a madman.

magistrate gave the violin to him, and Pero played on it, and the magistrate and the farmer and the hangman and the spectators danced to his playing. He played till they were weary; he played till they were worn out; and still he played. And the magistrate at last promised that if he would stop he should go free. Pero then came down from the scaffold, and took his gun and his violin and his thousand crowns, and returned to his native village, and, having the gift of speech, he won the prettiest girl in Sicily as his wife, and settled down.

PUNCH AND JUDY

IT was all the fault of Toby. You know Toby, of course—Toby, the wicked little dog belonging to Mr. Scaramouch, the showman. Punch one morning was in a very merry humour. He had got up early, and put on his scarlet and yellow dress and his peaked hat with tassels at the corners, and he was dancing and singing to himself upstairs as he waited for his wife Judy and the baby, to take them out for a walk. Toby, however, ran up into the room where Punch was dancing, and Punch tried to stroke him, saying:

"Hallo, Toby! How do you do, Mr. Toby? Hope you are well, Mr. Toby?"

But the wicked little dog jumped up and bit poor Punch's long nose. This made Punch very cross, and he seized Toby and threw him out of the window just as Scaramouch, the showman, was passing by. Scaramouch rushed into the house, with a long stick in his hand, and said to Punch:

"Hallo! Hallo! Hallo! What have you been doing to my dog? Do you want to learn how to play the fiddle?"

"Yes," said Punch, getting over his bad temper in an instant. "I should like to know how to play the fiddle."

"Well, isn't that sweet music?" said Scaramouch. And he gave poor Punch a hard, ringing blow on the back. But, just as he was going to strike again, Punch wrested the stick from his hand, knocked his head clean off his shoulders, and then threw him out of the window.

Punch then became a very dreadful person to live with. When Judy brought him the baby to mind he at first rocked it softly on his knee, but as soon as it began to cry he threw it out of the window.

"I'll teach you to throw the baby out of the window!" cried Judy, hitting him with the big stick.

"Oh! Oh!" squealed Punch. "I don't like such teaching. But perhaps you do."

And he seized the stick and thumped Judy unmercifully, and threw her also out of the window.

"Now all the house is quiet at last," said Punch. "I'll go for a ride."

But Hector was a very savage horse, and it threw Punch on the ground; and a doctor ran up to give help.

"Have you had a fall, or are you taking a nap on the grass?" said the doctor.

"I'm dead! dead!" shouted Punch. "Or, if I'm not dead, I'm speechless."

"You are shamming," said the doctor. "This is the sort of physic you want. The more you take the better you'll feel."

And he began to belabour Punch with the big stick. But, by a desperate effort, Punch got up, and wrestled with the doctor, and got the stick from him, saying:

"What's good for the patient ought to be good for the doctor. It is now your turn to take physic."

And Punch killed the doctor with one tremendous blow, and set off home, saying to himself: "Doctors always die when they take their own physic."

On the road home a footman and a blind man got in his way, and Punch felled them to the earth with his big stick. But when he opened the door of his house there was a policeman waiting for him.

"I didn't send for you," said Punch.

"No, I'm sent for you," said the burly policeman.

"But I don't want a policeman," cried Punch angrily.

"But a policeman wants you," was the reply. "You've been murdering people in a frightful way."

"Yes," said Punch. "This is how I do it."

And he knocked the policeman down with the big stick. An officer then entered, and after the officer came Jack Ketch, the hangman.

"I'm come to take you up," said the police officer.

"And I'm come to take you down," said Punch, knocking the officer over, with a great shout of laughter.

"But I'm Jack Ketch," said the hangman, in an awful, hollow voice.

"Well, ketch that, then!" cried Punch. And down Jack Ketch tumbled.

At last, however, Punch was taken to prison to be hanged, and the hangman got the fatal noose ready.

"How shall I put my head into that thing?" said Punch.

"Like this," said the hangman, thrusting his neck into the noose.

Punch at once pulled hard at the rope, and so hanged the hangman, and in the excitement Punch got out of prison; and you can still see the old rascal wandering about at the present day with Scaramouch, the showman, and Toby.

PROVERB STORIES

Every nation has its proverbs—short, pithy sayings in which are contained much wisdom. The stories on this page illustrate some of these proverbs.

THE FARMER AND HIS SACKS

Repay Kindness with Kindness

A FARMER was taking his grist to the mill in sacks thrown across the back of his horse. On the way the horse stumbled, and one of the sacks fell to the ground. It was too heavy for him to lift, and he was at a loss to know what to do. As he stood wondering he saw a horseman coming toward him.

When, however, the rider came nearer the farmer saw that he was none other than the nobleman who lived in the great house at the top of the hill. It was impossible to think of asking help from one of his rank.

The nobleman, however, was something more than a man with a title—he was a gentleman, and he dismounted.

" I see you have had something of a mishap, friend," he said. " It is fortunate I came along just now, for help is not always handy on these roads."

So saying, he took one end of the sack, the farmer took the other, and the load was once more placed on the horse's back.

" My lord," said the farmer, lifting his cap, " how can I thank you ? "

" Easily enough, my good fellow," said the nobleman. " Whenever you see any-one in a difficulty, help him all you can, and that will be thanking me."

THE BAG OF PEAS

There's no Luck in Laziness

" Do you believe in luck ? " said a king to one of his officers.

" Yes," answered the officer, " I do."

" Ah! " laughed the king. " I am afraid you could not prove to me that there is any such thing in the world."

" That may be, your Majesty," answered the officer ; " but, if it please you, we might try to find out. I have thought even now of a plan."

He whispered in the king's ear, and his Majesty replied:

" Very good, very good indeed; let us try it without loss of time."

So that night the officer hung a bag from the ceiling of one of the rooms in the palace. What it contained none but the king and the officer knew. Then two men were put into the room. When the

door was shut one of the men who believed in luck laid himself down in a corner and prepared for sleep; the other looked about him, and at once saw the bag hanging from the ceiling.

He reached up and put in his hand, and found some peas. " One might have a worse supper," he thought, as he took out a handful and ate them.

Presently he came on some diamonds, but in the dark he thought they were mere stones, and of no value. So he threw them toward his companion, saying:

" You may take the stones for your idleness."

In the morning the king and his officer came to the room, and told each man he might keep what he had found. The one man got the peas which he had eaten; the other got the diamonds.

" Now, your Majesty," said the officer, " Truly," answered the king, " you seem to have the best of the argument. There may be such a thing as luck; but it is as rare as peas mixed with diamonds, and so let none hope to live by luck."

THE TWO KINGS

The Second Word Makes the Quarrel

THERE was once a king who sent a message to the king of a neighbouring country, saying:

" Send me a blue pig with a black tail, or else——"

To this the other king replied:

" I have not got one; and if I had——"

When the first king got this answer he flew into a great rage, and declared war against the other. For many weary months fighting went on, but at last the two kings arranged a meeting.

" What did you mean," said the first, " by saying: Send me a blue pig with a black tail, or else——? "

" Why," answered the other, " I meant a blue pig with a black tail, or else some other colour. And now let me ask you what you meant by your message: I have not got one, and if I had——? "

" My meaning was simple enough; for, of course, if I had had such a pig I should have sent it."

" Dear me, how foolish we have been ! Let us make peace and be friends."

So peace was made, and the story was written in the annals of both countries to serve as a warning to those who should come after to be slow to take offence.

MEMBERS OF THE GREAT BAT FAMILY

THE GREAT BAT—OR NOCTULE BAT

THE AFRICAN FALSE VAMPIRE

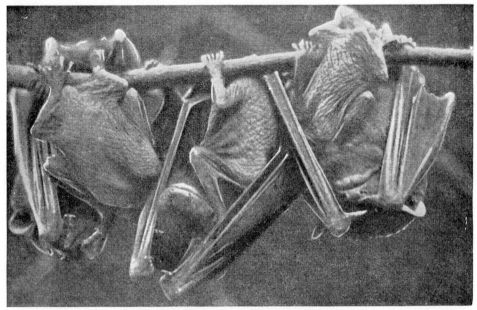

NOCTULE BATS AS THEY SLEEP

LONG-EARED BAT

NATTERER'S BAT

GREATER HORSESHOE BAT

MALAY FOX BAT

THE HAIRY-ARMED BAT

THE ABYSSINIAN EPAULETTED BAT

The photographs on these pages are by Messrs. Douglas English, J. J. Ward, and C. W. R. Knight

Nature's Wonderful Living Family in Earth and Air and Sea

BATS AND THEIR FRIENDS

Where the bee sucks, there suck I :
In a cowslip's bell I lie;
There I couch when owls do cry.
On the bat's back I do fly
After summer merrily :
Merrily, merrily, shall I live now,
Under the blossom that hangs on the bough.

Shakespeare's song, sweet and melodious on the lips of his happy Ariel in The Tempest, is like an allegory, a burst of anthem from kindly life's own pulsing heart. Insect, flower, bird, and mammal are all there, with the poor bat as the dainty sprite's own courser.

Four great orders of created wonder march to the music of that verse, and it is wonderful to think of the ages Nature must have taken to fashion the picture Shakespeare gives us in a flash. Repeatedly Nature has given a long, slow turn to her kaleidoscope, and many an age elapsed before the outline of bee and cowslip, bat and owl, was perfected.

The bats did not come singly. They issued from reptile forms, they and their kindred, among the first successful mammals.

The mammal is warm-blooded, and, of course, hairy. A wide multitude of such mammals appeared, little timorous, insect-eating creatures. They succeeded, but not all by following the same line.

Many were driven by fear for their lives to hide in the Earth, but the bats did a thing like magic. They must have followed their prey about the rocks and have had many a tumble; they pursued them into the trees and flopped from branch to branch, and to the ground, spreading out arms and legs to break the shock of their fall. Undoubtedly, there were countless bats that never got beyond the parachute stage.

What that was like we see in many animals which glide through the air but do not fly. The so-called flying lemur, the cobego, is the best example of the type. It arose from the same stock as the bats and the other insect-eaters, but instead of wings it has flexible folds of skin, one on each side, from the throat to the hind quarters, and this natural parachute, expanding at the will of the animal, carries it through the air, in a downward direction, 200 feet and more. But that is no more flight than the air-trips of the flying fish.

Something better was needed. The birds were urged into feathers and flight; the reptiles flaunted their scaly leather-like wings up in the clouds, and still Nature demanded better and better. Then came this line of insect-eaters which gave rise to the bats, animals which created real wings from flesh and blood and bone, without scales, without feathers. An entirely novel and marvellous creation branched off from the same ancestral stock to become the ancestors of all the bats, whether they eat insects or fruit, or draw blood. Consider this natural

PREHISTORIC LIFE · MAMMALS · BIRDS · REPTILES · FISHES · INSECTS

wonder, this little winged mammal, which has sacrificed free arms and legs, invested them in a living webbing, and flies superbly.

If you could take away the webbing you would see a little animal with two arms and hands and two hind legs. But though it has the same number of fingers as we have, they are strangely formed. The thumb is very short, and, instead of a nail, has a claw or hook which is used when the bat is not flying, to enable it to walk or to hang itself to anything upon which it means to rest when it folds its wings to go to sleep.

THE LITTLE BIRD WITH THE VERY LONG WINGS

The bones of the palms of the hand are not short and like ours, but very long, and joined to them are the finger-bones, which again are very long. This great length of bone is to support the web of the wings. The web stretches from the shoulders down the two bones of the arm over the bones of the hand, and down the tips of the four fingers. Then, from the under side of the arms, it reaches down to the legs, as far as what would be our ankles, and between the legs to join on to the tail.

Thus the spread of the wings is very big for the size of the bat. The biggest bat in England has a body three inches long and a tail one and a half inches long—only four and a half inches all told, yet its wings, when spread out, measure fourteen inches from tip to tip.

There is no other animal in England that we know less of than the bat. The reason is that it only comes out at night. Its eyes are so formed that it must sleep when the sun is shining, but at night it can see splendidly. It lives entirely on insects, and by eating these does good work for man. We cannot see the insects it catches, but the insects are in the air all the same; and if the bats did not catch them they would be a great nuisance to us.

THE BAT'S AMAZING SENSE OF FEELING WITHOUT TOUCH

There is something about the bat which none of us can understand. Added to its good sight, it has the most wonderful power of feeling its way through the air. There is a great network of nerves and veins all over its wings, and there are clusters of nerves about its nose which act as a sort of telegraph to control the wings as the little animal flies about in the dusk. A man who gave his life to the study of

animals once tested bats in a strange way. He got some bats whose sense of sight and smell and hearing had gone from them. He turned them loose in a room in which were many corners and obstacles against which they were likely to dash themselves. They flew without fear about the room, and never came in contact with anything that might hurt them. Then the man strung many threads across the room, but the bats flew between them as easily as if nothing were there. When the man placed his hand in the way of their flying, though they could neither hear, see, nor smell, they avoided it.

Bats are like birds in this—that their blood is very hot, but there is a strange difference. The bird dies if it cannot keep warm. The bat, however, goes to sleep in winter. Its sleep is so like death that you would think the bat in its winter sleep dead. It almost ceases to breathe, and its body, so warm in summer, is in winter almost quite cold.

THE GIANT BATS OF THE EAST THAT LIVE ON FRUIT

All the English bats, of which there are about a dozen varieties, eat insects, but there are foreign bats which do great mischief. The fruit-eating bats do not live in this country, but in Japan, Australia, most of the Pacific Islands, the Malay Islands, India, Ceylon, and Madagascar. The biggest of these measures about five feet across the wings. It is called the flying fox because it has red-brown fur and a head like a fox. As they eat a great deal, they cause much damage to the crops, and in some places the natives have to tie up the growing fruit in baskets, to keep the bats from eating it at night.

The most repulsive bat is one of the vampire bats, called the desmodus. This attacks cattle and horses and poultry, and even human beings, as they lie asleep. With its sharp teeth it makes a tiny hole in the flesh, and draws large quantities of blood from its victim. In some parts of the world it has been found impossible to keep poultry, owing to the dreadful habits of these bats. It used to be supposed that the bite of a bat was fatal to life, but that is not so. It is true, however, that should they find a sleeping man's feet uncovered, they can make a wound without waking him, and draw blood enough for a vampire bat's meal.

QUEER LITTLE INSECT-EATERS

THE COMMON SHREW

THE PYGMY SHREW

THE MOLE

THE LONG-NOSED JUMPING SHREW

THE WATER SHREW

THE QUAINT-LOOKING SOLENODON OF CUBA

THE TENREC THAT ROAMS BY NIGHT

THE HEDGEHOG HAS A DRINK

There is nothing more startling than the operation of the vampire. It performs its surgery at dead of night in a darkened room, and, while drawing its meal, supports itself in the air by the beating of its wings. We marvel at the kestrel as she hangs with rapidly moving wings in the air, at the humming-bird poised at the gateway of a flower; but this winged mammal, stealthily sucking blood while poised like a living helicopter, displays a proficiency not excelled by any creature.

THE TERRIBLE ANIMAL THAT WILL HAVE TO PERISH

The bloodsucking bat will have to go. It cannot alter. Unlike the rest of the bats and insect eaters, it has no grinding teeth, and it is so accustomed by ages of habit to a diet of blood that its throat and stomach have grown too small for anything but fluid. Yes, the vampires which have this hateful way of gaining a living will have to be exterminated, and so will the flying foxes, which live near plantations and ruin the fruit of men's labours. So destructive are they in the fruit-growing areas of Australia that shooting parties are organised to drive them from their regular nesting places.

But with the exception of certain fruit bats and the vampires all the bats are helpful allies of man. The British group is a splendid array—the greater and lesser horseshoe bats, the long-eared, the barbastelle, the pipistrelle, the noctule, the hairy-armed, the serotine, the rough-legged, Natterer's, the whiskered, and one or two believed not to be residents but visitors, like chance migrant birds.

THE MODEST, HARMLESS, AND QUEER LITTLE BATS OF BRITAIN

They haunt belfries, barns, old sheds, trees, clefts, and crannies, anywhere and everywhere, and issue at night to hunt and munch as they fly. England has some fantastic forms, which have appendages to their noses like leaves and blossoms sprouting on an animal instead of a plant; but ours are modest and unassuming contrasted with foreign bats. Ceylon has in the Kerivoula picta, bats which are so brilliantly coloured as to look like butterflies. There is an American species which catches and eats small fish. Some bats are white, and a Malayan bat is naked but for a fringe of hairs round the neck.

Bats are devoted mothers, and carry their young with them, clinging to their fur, but the naked bat, having no fur for baby bats to cling to, has evolved a living cradle; a deep fleshy pouch on the underside of the body in which the thriving infant is carried. With that in mind, and the further strange fact that some bats have added sucker discs, like the implements of the octopus, to their thumbs and feet, so enabling them to climb the smoothest surfaces, we must bid adieu to the wing-handed folk, one of the most fantastic of all Nature's experiments.

What that same wizard Nature can do from the same materials we shall now see as we turn to the great assembly of animals called the Insectivora. They have that name because the peculiar character of their pointed teeth enables them to penetrate the horny cases in which many of their victims are sheathed.

THE WINGLESS LONG-NOSED COUSINS OF THE BATS

They are all long-snouted, they all have furry coats, and the majority of them are creatures of the night and the underworld. But note the exceptions. The hedgehog has converted part of his hairy covering into spines, and can roll himself up like a woodlouse. Some, like the tupaias, have taken to the trees, and many forms have adapted themselves brilliantly to life chiefly spent in the water. The variety in habit and structure is immense, and, though the mole is extremely primitive, with all the evidence of its lowly origin manifest, still it is full of wonders. We see our mole, not yet blind, behaving with as fatal an indifference to its eyes as the penguins to its wings. Indeed, its cousin, the golden mole, is now absolutely sightless.

We see a supreme wonder of natural economy in the largest of animal necks—the giraffe's, which consists of only seven vertebrae, like a man's or an elephant's; yet it requires nearly seven times as many vertebrae to make up the tail of one of the little tenrecs.

Such things are not to be explained. What we have to remember is that tremendous tests have been applied to this order. From the ancestors of the insectivores came not only the bats, but the great cats. Down in the rocks is the connecting link between the leopard and the shrew, between the tenrec and the tiger.

The insect-eaters that survive remain truest to the ancestral type; yokels in a rustic school which has given the world some of its grandest and most powerful forms. There was a place for modest stupidity, and with smooth inferior brains these animals have filled it, in many climes, leaving ambition and betterment to those of their cousins in whom the latent fire of animal genius burned.

And glad we are that it is so. The insectivores owe almost nothing to man, but unchecked myriads of tiny foes. They would starve us by eating all herbage off the face of the Earth. The Insectivora are our dull uncomprehending guardians against that appalling contingency.

We have noted the progressive weakness of the common mole's sight, so must see what he gains by his sacrifice. Probably it is increasing engineering skill. Next to the worm he has done more than anything

FLYING FOXES AT REST IN A TREE

man owes half his fortune and more to the insectivores.

It is always so close a fight between man and insect, always so grave a hazard that the insect may win, that, were some fell stroke of destiny suddenly to withdraw the aid of the Insectivora, our crops and harvests, the things we grow for food, medicine, and clothes, would fall before to plough the world's soil. He is a superb tunneller, a master engineer who constructs beautiful galleries leading to a marvellous hall or fortress. And he prepares an almost equally elaborate nursery for the little ones.

Perhaps there has been exaggeration of the directing skill with which these hidden wonders are wrought, but critics go to the opposite extreme in suggesting that many of the galleries are purposeless. They forget that the mole, which is a voracious feeder, is constantly burrowing for worms and larvae, and sinking wells for water—hence tunnels and descents are condemned by them as useless.

Damage may be done here and there to lawns and flower-borders by moles, but the balance in the little sable gentleman's favour is enormous. To estimate his night's labour we have to imagine a man excavating, between sunset and sunrise, a tunnel 37 miles long !

Far and near the mole and its allied forms roam. The desman is of the family tree, long-muzzled, flat-tailed, a superb swimmer, whose webbed feet dig tunnels 20 feet deep in the banks of Asian streams where leeches and water insects afford it ample diet. There is a web-footed mole in North America which lives far inland. The waters which called for the special faculty for swmiming have left the mole, or the mole has left them, but the webs on the feet proclaim the past.

THE USEFUL SHREW, AND HOW HE HAS DAMAGED HIS CHARACTER

Next in order comes our old friend the hedgehog, born blind, with prickles soft and white as cotton, and squeaking when its mother is long absent, like a baby pig. Hedgehogs are dull, stupid things, content with their magnificent armour and the security of night-hunts and hidden beds for day and winter.

We once had near relatives of the hedgehogs in Europe, but now we must go to Asia for them and find them in rat-like creatures called the gymnuras. Although rat-like in externals, the gymnura, stripped of his jacket, is marvellously like a hedgehog in his bones, but he cannot convert himself into a ball as his spiny cousin does.

The shrew is often called a destructive mouse, whereas he is a priceless aid to us as an insect-eater. If he escapes that penalty of misunderstanding, he is the victim of an age-long superstition which attributes to him poison, paralysis, and pestilence to man and beast. His only offence is against the nose, for he has a strong disagreeable odour. In that he is not exceptional, for this defence is common to many shrews, of which the world has no fewer than 120 species.

"There's richness for you," as Mr. Squeers said of the watered milk to the poor scholars of Dotheboys Hall. It is, numerically, a rich assemblage. The tupaias or tree-shrews are kings of the greenwood tree, wonderfully like squirrels, in spite of their long flexible snouts. This feature, however, finds its most extravagant development in the shrews whose trunk-like nose gives them the name of elephant shrews. Yet they are as agile as crickets, leaping, by means of their abnormally long hind legs, as if they had once tried to be little kangaroos.

THE FINE WORK DONE BY THE LOWLY ORDER OF INSECT-EATERS

As bats have a fish-eater, so have the shrews, in a wonderful creature called the otter-shrew, a name which carries its own story of the apparent lines of progress followed by this species. Yet perhaps the web-footed shrew is even more notable for a novel method of mastering fate. Not only is it web-footed; it has produced extraordinary little sucker-pads on its feet for an unparalleled purpose—so that in seeking its food at the bottom of the water it may cling to stones and other smooth faces and not be carried up against its will by buoyancy, unfed.

We should like that type in our English ponds, but we do not envy our Indian friends their musk-shrew whose odour makes uneatable anything it touches; and we do not covet the king of the order, the Madagascar tenrec, tailless, 16 inches long, with spines hidden in his hair, and a ferocious bite. Tenrecs might become too numerous: the female of one species has as many as 21 infant tenrecs at a birth. Fortunately, these animals are generally insectivorous, and the solenodon, a dismal rat-like creature with alarming claws, is devoted to similar good work.

THE BEAUTY IN A RACE OF PLAIN AND SOBER LITTLE FOLK

There, all too briefly sketched in, we have something of this great but lowly order of insect-eaters. It gives us the tiniest mammal in the pygmy shrew; it gives us hair, fur, prickles; it gives us the lustre of the golden mole's fur. Is it not a mystery that such beauty should have been wasted on an animal which has let itself become blind ? The moles are generally plain, sober, even repulsive little folk, but this gaudy one might stand for the emblem of their order. In their lives and occupation they are to mankind like the hue of that lustrous coat, pure gold.

The March of Man from the Age of Barbarism to the United Nations

Man at the Cross-Roads—To the Town and Civilisation or back to the Wilds ?

MAN FEELS HIS WAY TO POWER

LET us halt for a moment and remind ourselves of the nature of the hero whose adventures we are following, chapter by chapter, in his journey through Time.

Never was such a hero. We are not reading of a magic horse, or a grisly giant, or a comical dwarf, or an Arctic explorer, or a millionaire. We are reading about something which has never been seen, which cannot be handled, which cannot be defined or described even by the greatest man in the world. But is there anything in the world more real to us?

It is something which has produced giants and dwarfs, dragons and fairies, mythical kings and fabulous monsters. It is something which has also fashioned the world of actuality in which we live—the world of great temples and marvel-working hospitals, of ships that fly in the air and ships that swim under the sea; the world of comfortable houses with hot-water pipes, electric light, and windows through which we can look at sunshine and storm ; the world of the daily newspaper filled with tales from every quarter of the Earth ; and the world of the wireless telephone, anaesthetics, antiseptics, the telescope, and atomic energy.

Everything we know in ourselves, everything that has made history and changed the course of human life, is the work of this wonderful thing, this invisible and intangible and indefinable thing, the Mind.

But cannot we form some rough and ready notion of what it is like before we follow it from savagery to the first adventures of Civilisation? What is Mind?

At least we can say this : *It is Life trusting to itself.*

We know that each bird builds its nest exactly as its parents built theirs before it was born. We know, too, that a caterpillar makes itself a wonderful dwelling called a cocoon, although it has never seen such a thing before. There we are looking at Life trusting to instincts, leaving itself entirely in the hands of impulses which come from it knows not where. But in *mind* Life is self-conscious and self-reliant.

It *experiences* things consciously, reflects upon them, stores them into a wonderful department of the brain called Memory, and makes use of them for fresh adventures. It receives from the outside world all sorts of impressions, and weaves them into a garment which we may call *habit*, but a garment which is always being patched and improved by fresh experience and enlarged reflection. The animal is driven ; *the mind drives*. The animal accepts; the mind questions.

The mind, then, is Life seeking adventure. Now, Life exists everywhere. But so

MIGHTY EPOCHS OF THE WORLD & MAN'S WONDERFUL ADVENTURES

far as we can see it is only in the brain of man that Life has fashioned an instrument which enables it to push on into the fields of new experience and across the oceans of fresh discovery.

But wait a moment. There are a few human beings less intelligent than animals, whose lives are far lower in the scale of being than the lives of many birds and insects. Life, then, can only push on *when the brain of a man is willing ;* when it responds, that is to say, to Life's longing for new experience and greater power.

LIFE CAN ONLY TRAVEL AS FAST AS MAN'S BRAIN ALLOWS IT

It is like this. In many countries of the world Life is still travelling on foot; in many other countries on horseback or camelback; and in even the most civilised countries it is travelling in all sorts of ways—on foot, horseback or camelback, donkey-cart and carriage, bus and train, motor car and helicopter, aeroplane or submarine. That is to say, Life can only travel as fast as the brain of individual man will allow it to travel, and the brains of men are as different as the means of locomotion in a modern nation.

Now we can turn again to our Adventurer, where we last left him, with a feeling that at least we know something about him. He has climbed up from the stationary plant to the moving reptile, from the reptile to the mammal, and from the mammal to the human mind. He has pushed the body of man through all these changes, and now is putting forth all his mysterious energies to enlarge the organ of understanding in that body—the body of savage man.

Savagery, wonderful as it is, far transcending the power of birds and beasts, is nevertheless not enough. Onward, onward ! No rest till the Earth has been turned topsy-turvy to discover its ultimate mystery. Who is it that can do this ? It is Life in partnership with the willing brain of man, and that partnership is mind—the Human Mind.

MAN BEGINS TO FEAR THE LIGHTNING AND THE THUNDER

Picture to yourself the savage in the first town ever built, probably under the shadow of the Kurdistan mountains, somewhere between those two great rivers called Tigris and Euphrates. He has lost much. He is no longer perfectly free. He is no longer as fearless and as careless as the animals. He fears lightning and thunder, he prostrates himself at an eclipse, he sacrifices some of his animals to gods who are at once cruel and indifferent. And he fears man. Other creatures like himself— who have learned to stand upright and to use their front legs as arms—descend upon him in ordered packs, brandishing terrible weapons of death, beating drums of terror, shouting battle-cries which make the knees tremble with fear.

But something he has gained. He need no longer hunt for his food. He has heads of cattle, flocks of sheep, and fields of corn. Nor need he seek his food in its raw state. His women grind the corn between stones and roast his meat over a fire. And he has amusements. He has learned to draw pictures. He has invented a speech which enables him to tell stories. He can make sounds of music. He has discovered that clay can be not only worked into many shapes, but also put into his fires and baked almost as hard as stone. Yes, he has many amusements.

All the same, he is bothered by laws. Something inside him says, *This is right— That is wrong.* The head of his tribe sends him here and there. He must make things for other people, do things for other people, expose his body to the risks of death for other people.

MAN STANDS BETWEEN THE HILL AND FOREST AND THE TOWN

And the gods! Surely it was happier when men lived like the animals. What animal makes an altar of stone, and beats itself till the blood comes, and sacrifices other animals on the fire of the altar ?

This town, too, smelling and crowded and noisy, and threatened by war, can it compare with the happy cave on the hillside, where the freshness of dawn woke one like the song of a bird, and twilight fell with a peace that descended as a blessing ?

These questions represent a crisis in the fortunes of human history. On the one hand was the noisome town, pointing like a finger-post to Civilisation, and on the other, the hills and the forest calling man back to Instinct and Stagnation.

To some men the town was the clear road of the future, but to others the call of the wild was the irresistible call of happiness. Thus it came about that the great family of mankind split up into two branches, the one following Reason, the other following Instinct ; and to this day

THE PEOPLE OF PERHAPS TEN THOUSAND YEARS AGO

these two branches still flourish in every quarter of the globe.

Life's one hope of advance lay in the brain of those savage men who saw in the town not only a means of safety from wild beasts and man-enemies, but a means of endless amusement. They saw the advantage of co-operation. Their brains told them that in partnership with others they might do many wonderful things. This man loved carving, this man could only be happy making pots, this man thought of nothing in the world but making shields, this man spent his days in learning from the patriarchs of his tribe stories of the past; and the women—

were they not happier grinding corn together, going in great companies down to the river for water?

Then came another step towards civilisation. Men sat watching for their enemies from the hills, and a spy came to them with a report that their enemies were quarrelling among themselves. Into the brain of one of those watchers came a new idea. Instead of waiting to defend their town, why should they not swarm out together, climb the mountains, fall upon their enemies, and destroy them?

There was no one in those days to speak of Peace. It has taken the human mind more than ten thousand years to realise that war is the maker of war. To the savage his enemy was a wild beast, and the way to deal with a wild beast was to kill it.

Do not let us sigh over this sad past of the human mind. Just as all the glory of religion has ascended from the darkness of fear and the mire of superstition, so also have the loveliness of Peace and the beauty of moral character—self-sacrifice, courage, chivalry, and mercy—risen from the savagery of the battlefield. The human mind had to rise from the pit of its animal ancestry, just as all life had to climb out from the ooze of ocean shores. The glory of Florence Nightingale was her ascent from savagery ; the sin of the Nazis was their descent into the past of that savagery.

THE LITTLE TRIBE IS TO BECOME A GREAT NATION

When the townsman fell upon his enemies in the hills, and slew the warriors and dragged off the women and children into slavery, he was taking a tremendous stride, however bloodstained and terrible, towards civilisation, for he was giving a breathing space to Peace, and Peace is the first necessity of true science and art. By that incursion into the hills, that first war of aggression, savage man enlarged the borders of his town and the borders of human life. He pushed out his frontiers and made them safe, and within his territory he pressed on to the farthest frontiers of the mind. The tribe was to become a nation, and the country an empire.

All this happened at least ten thousand years ago, probably much farther back. Strange to say, we have better records in writing of a civilisation older than Egypt than we have of Egypt itself. For by the time Man had journeyed to Egypt he had learned to write on papyrus, and papyrus crumbles and decays; but before the human mind had discovered papyrus it had written its record on stone.

WHAT THE SCHOLARS OF EUROPE FOUND IN RUBBISH HEAPS

But there was an older way still of leaving a record of the first steps in civilisation—a record stamped upon the surface of the Earth. Far away in Chaldea are the remains of a system of irrigation, proving that the first makers of civilisation had a knowledge of Nature and science, and that they supported in those plains a vast population. It is as if the savage, emerging into civilisation

for the first time, took a pen in his hand and wrote upon the earth, " I am a man." To look upon those remains is to be deeply moved by the thought of man's sublime courage and his indestructible faith in his power of self-reliance.

Also in Chaldea there are many humps of earth which remained there undisturbed till a hundred years ago. Then came scholars from Europe who dug down through those waste-heaps and came upon cities built of brick, and wandered through streets, entered the palaces of unknown kings and found libraries, with inscriptions on walls and other signs of civilisation.

The toil of scholarship has worn away the mystery of a writing unknown for a hundred centuries. Older than any Semitic language, some of the cuneiform inscriptions—as we call the wedge-like characters of the early empires—bear witness to the human mind in ages beyond all other record. At least that mind had conceived the idea of leaving a record. At least it could draw pictures, convey a meaning by signs, place its signature to the work of its hands. And there, too, it left a record of a considerable city built of brick; and a city is the first work of art on the border-line of savagery and civilisation.

THE DISCOVERY OF SPEECH AND SONG AND HAPPY LAUGHTER

A marvellous journey already! Let us think of it as the Odyssey of the human soul travelling from a grunt to a song, from a frown to a smile.

In some remote parts of the world there are still savage men whose eyes are filled with the same perplexity which we see in the eyes of monkeys, whose brows are scored with the deep wrinkles of a perpetual frown, and whose lips have never learned to smile as the child of civilised parents smiles almost from the hour of its birth. Speech, song, and laughter were first heard in that wonderful dawn of civilisation when the human mind knew that it had found a path to more knowledge and more power, and felt itself already capable of Egypt, Athens, Rome, and civilisation.

Always on our journey we shall find the shadow of savagery dogging the advance of Mind, but henceforth we shall see that unconquerable Mind pressing forward with irresistible power.

(Next chapter in this group, page 425)

The Story of the Things We See About Us Every Day

This series of ancient pictures shows an Egyptian potter working at his trade

THE CHINA ON THE TABLE

POTTERY making is one of the oldest crafts in the world. Its story goes back thousands of years, long before recorded history. Indeed, much of our knowledge of prehistoric man is derived from the pottery he left behind.

In the china cups and saucers we use at breakfast there are the powdered remains of ancient mountains and the roasted bones of oxen. Much of the clay used in the manufacture of pottery has been formed by the gradual wearing-down of rocks by the weather until they became powder. It was in this way that the famous china and ball clays of Cornwall, Devon, and Dorset were formed.

Before these clays are used for making high-quality pottery, they are washed and prepared. Different types of clay, each chosen for its special properties, are mixed with other ingredients.

For the manufacture of earthenware in this country, the " ball clay " or " blue clay " of Devon and Dorset is mixed with china clay and china stone from Cornwall and finely ground flint stones from the seashore. Each of these ingredients has its special qualities. Ball clay is easy to mould ; flint imparts strength and whiteness ; china stone serves to fuse or unite

the other ingredients during the firing process ; and china clay not only increases whiteness but also helps to maintain shape during firing. Such is the composition of earthenware, which is an opaque (or non-shiny) material.

In bone china, the shining porcelain for which England is famed, the principal ingredients are china clay, china stone, and bone ash. Bone ash, which is obtained by calcining (roasting) and grinding selected ox bones, is chiefly responsible for giving bone china its great strength combined with a delicate translucent appearance. It has been aptly said that " bone forms the skeleton of English china."

After the different materials have been ground to the required degree of fineness they are blended into a creamy fluid known as " slip."

The liquid " slip " is forced by powerful pumps through fine-mesh screens and then flows over electro-magnets which extract every particle of iron, which would discolour the finished ware.

The next stage is the removal of the water from the " slip." This is done by forcing the liquid into filter-presses. The surplus water is removed under pressure, leaving flat sheets of plastic material

INDUSTRIES · HOW THINGS ARE MADE · WHERE THEY COME FROM

which are then placed into a machine resembling a gigantic mincing-machine. From this, the clay emerges in just the right consistency and texture for the potter.

Now comes the shaping. The throwing-wheel is a device which in principle is not unlike the one used by the potters of ancient Babylon. Hand-throwing is the shaping of a mass of clay on a revolving horizontal disc ; by skilful manipulation the potter is able to create an infinite variety of beautiful shapes.

This method is still in use today for the making of individual pieces of ware, originals of vases, and jugs, and new patterns for cups, but it is being superseded more and more by semi-mechanical throwing machines (known as " jollies " and " jiggers ") which reproduce the effect of the thrower's hands, but more swiftly, and more cheaply. Such machines are used in making most of our cups and saucers and plates.

THE THREE FIRINGS THAT GIVE THE POTTERY ITS BRILLIANT FINISH

Another modern method of shaping is that of casting, in which liquid clay is poured into plaster moulds. Plaster being porous, it absorbs some of the moisture from the liquid leaving a skin of firm clay adhering to the inside surface of the mould. As soon as this skin is thick enough the excess liquid clay is poured away, the mould opened, and the article removed.

After shaping and drying, pottery is subjected to the first (" biscuit ") firing. In the case of earthenware, the decoration is usually applied before the ware is glazed and the colours are fixed by a second (" hardening-on ") firing. Finally, the ware is glazed and then fired for the third and final time in a " glost " kiln.

Bone china, however, is more often than not decorated by the " on-glaze " method ; that is to say, the decoration is applied on top of the glaze. Enamels, themselves containing minute particles of glaze, are applied to the plain already glazed ware and are fixed by an " enamel" firing.

Decorating with ceramic pigments may be done entirely by freehand brush-work, by the use of transfers from engraved copper plates or lithographic stones, or by a combination of transfers and freehand painting. To get special effects there are several other methods of decorating, such as the application of coloured clay " slips."

Our English potters were remarkable men. The first with whom we need concern ourselves is John Astbury, who was born about 1688, and died in 1743. He was the first to manufacture cream-coloured pottery. He did more than that. One day he saw an ostler trying to cure a horse by blowing into its eyes the powder from a red-hot flint-stone. Astbury thought that flint-stones burnt to powder might be more usefully employed, and, after experimenting with the powder, he found that it was a valuable substance for making pottery.

THE BROTHERS WHO DISCOVERED THE SECRET OF GLAZING POTTERY

At about the same period there were two brothers from Amsterdam, named Elers, at work near Burslem, the English home of the pottery trade. These were the men who discovered how to glaze common pottery by scattering salt in the oven. But they had another secret—the making of a pretty red ware which they called Japanese. By pretending to be an idiot, Astbury got into their works and learned their secret.

Josiah Wedgwood was born at Burslem in 1730, and died in 1795.

After very hard struggles he built up a great business. He did so solely by merit. He discovered new materials for his pottery. He found out new processes.

While he continued making good crockery for the table, he developed the artistic side of the industry until his porcelain ware was famous throughout the world.

After Wedgwood's death the artistic side of the pottery industry showed signs of decline, but a revival took place, though on somewhat different lines, in the Lambeth works of Sir Henry Doulton.

FROM THE MAKING OF DRAINPIPES TO FAMOUS TABLE WARE

Sir Henry's father was in a very small way of business, making blacking bottles and other common things. But Henry was given a good education and later discovered the art of making drain-pipes of glazed earthenware. Until that time our drains had been simply channels of bricks, which let poisonous matter leak through in all directions. The Doulton pipes created a revolution in sanitation.

From that kind of work Doulton went on to the making of the world-renowned Doulton ware.

WHERE THE CHINA COMES FROM

From pits in Devon and Cornwall is obtained the finest china clay. Here is a pit near Land's End.

The granite rock from which china clay is derived is crushed and washed, and the clay allowed to settle in pits. It is then mixed with finely ground flints and ball clay.

Iron particles in the mixture which would make brown specks in the finished ware are drawn out by magnets. Water is now pressed out, and the clay is dried in a shed.

So that the clay may be thoroughly mixed it is put through a pug-mill, kneaded, rolled out, and cut off in pieces suitable for the potter to handle. Here clay is being fed into the pug-mill, and is seen on the left emerging as a block.

HOW THE CLAY IS SHAPED AND GLAZED

The master mould from which the tea cups will be made is carefully examined by the head mould-maker.

On a revolving horizontal wheel the "thrower" fashions the clay in the mould.

After it has left the thrower the tea cup is turned on a lathe. The rough edges are trimmed and the base is shaped.

The handles, which are made separately, are then added. Precision is needed to ensure that they set accurately.

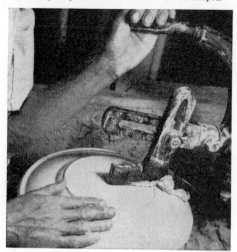

Plates are shaped on a machine, known as a jigger, which is an adaptation of the traditional potter's wheel. After it is shaped the ware goes for firing.

After being fired the ware is dipped in a mixture known as glaze. It is again fired to give it a hard-wearing and attractive gloss finish.

THE ARTISTS WHO DECORATE POTTERY

When pottery is to be decorated, a skilled craftsman engraves the outline of the design on a copper plate. The pattern is then transferred by taking an impression on thin paper and printing it on the ware. After this the colour details are filled in by hand. Earthenware is usually decorated before glazing and bone china after glazing.

Here we see a dinner plate being decorated by the " on-glaze " method. After this the ware receives its final firing. This is one of several different methods of decoration employed in the making of fine English ware.

THE POTTERY IS READY FOR THE OVEN

When the ware is ready for the final firing it is placed on special heat-resisting trucks which carry it into the kiln. The long tunnel oven is divided into various zones in which the temperature gradually rises and then falls again. The trucks pass through each zone in turn and the time taken for the final firing is about 24 hours.

Here we see the trucks of ware entering an electric kiln for the last firing. Gas and electric kilns are taking the place of the old coal-burning bottle-neck kilns which for centuries have been a familiar feature in the Potteries. Apart from their greater efficiency, they do not pollute the atmosphere with dust and smoke.

Many of the pictures in these pages were taken at the Royal Doulton potteries

Plain Answers to the Questions of the Children of the World

WHY DOES A BALL BOUNCE?

THERE are two kinds of balls which bounce—those which are solid, like a hard indiarubber ball or a golf ball, and those which are hollow, like a tennis ball.

No matter whether a ball is solid or hollow, its bounce is due to the fact that it is what we call elastic. This simply means that when the ball is pressed out of its shape it tends to return to the shape it had at first.

We must not, however, think that only indiarubber is elastic. On the contrary, steel is much more elastic than india-rubber, and, as can easily be proved, steel balls bounce splendidly.

Into almost every question we can ask there comes, sooner or later, the greatest and deepest law of all science, which is that nothing is lost or created, and that everything has to be paid for.

When the ball starts bouncing it has a certain amount of motion in it, which is force, or power, or energy. When it stops, that has gone. Either we must show that the energy has gone somewhere and has not been destroyed, or, according to the great law of the persistence of power, the ball should bounce for ever. If it did not bounce for ever the law would be false. It is, however, quite easy to show that the ball does lose the power with which it started. To begin with, it is moving, both up and down, through the air, and forcing millions of particles of air aside. All the motion it gives to them it loses.

If a ball were bounced in a space as far as possible emptied of air, it would bounce far longer than it does in the atmosphere, just as a top will spin longer in the same circumstances. Suppose that, instead of bouncing the ball on something hard, we bounce it on a pillow or on loose sand. It will not bounce long in such a case. Its power has gone in moving the pillow or sand as well as the air. The ball itself, too, is not quite elastic, nor is the ground. If the ball and the ground were quite elastic, and there were no air to move, and the ball never turned and rubbed the ground in falling, it would bounce for ever.

In the case of a hollow rubber ball, it is not by any means the indiarubber only that explains why the ball is so elastic. The ball is filled with a mixture of several gases, which we call air. We can see how much this ball bounces if we compare an ordinary soft indiarubber ball with another one which has a small hole in it.

The air is expelled from the hole when the ball is bounced, and we find that it bounces very little, because the elasticity of the ball is so poor. But the other ball bounces exceedingly well, because, when it is bounced, the air in it is not squeezed out through any hole, and thus gives the ball its elastic rebound.

SUN · MOON · STARS · FIRE · WIND · WATER · LIFE · MIND · SLEEP

How were the Pyramids built? We are almost sure that they were built as shown in this picture. When the first stones had been fixed in their place a bank was made up to the top, sloping down to the level of the ground. Up this slope the next great stones were dragged, and as the pyramid rose the sloping way rose too, until it became a wonderful road for thousands of slaves to walk upon, dragging the stone blocks behind them. By the time the pyramid was finished this roadway must have been hundreds of yards long, and it had, of course, to be removed before the great monument could be seen as we see it today.

What is Pain, and Why Does It Hurt ?

Not the wisest man can answer this question, but we know some things about it. We know, for instance, that certain nerves run to the skin, and that when they are excited the result is a painful sensation in the affected part. We know that when these nerves are damaged and cannot work the skin cannot feel pain. Also, we know that when any other nerves are excited too intensely, the result is painful. Loud music may be very pleasant, but there is a point beyond which it quite suddenly becomes painful. Similarly, a bright light may be beautiful and pleasant, but beyond a certain point it suddenly becomes painful.

No one, however, has any idea what happens in the nerve or in the nerve-cells when this change comes, though it has been suggested that when a nerve is very highly excited it changes in shape. This, however, does not tell us in the least why pain should go with it. No one could explain what pain was to a person who had never felt it, except by causing him pain. Similarly, you cannot describe sight to a person born blind. Words cannot describe these things, except to people who know them by experience.

What are our Eyebrows for ?

There are two good reasons why we have eyebrows. One is a reason of use, and the other of beauty. In the first place, if we had none, the drops of sweat that form on our foreheads when we get warm would run into our eyes ; and this would be bad, not only because it would blur our seeing, but also because sweat is really poisonous and a thing to get rid of, which is one of the best reasons for washing.

Now, our eyebrows catch the drops of sweat, and turn them aside. That is quite a good enough reason in itself, but there is another. The eyes are the most beautiful and interesting part of our faces, not only from their form, but also because they and the eyelids move so quickly, and so give the idea of life. That is why a face looks so different when the eyes are shut.

Now, the eyebrows are not only beautiful in themselves, but have the special purpose of calling attention to the eyes, just as we draw attention to a specially important word in a letter by underlining it. That is why some people make their eyebrows and eyelashes darker than they really are ; but if you keep fit and healthy your eyes will not need any treatment to make them more attractive.

How Do We Know the Height of a Mountain ?

There are various methods of measuring the height of a mountain, but the most accurate is by means of a type of theodolite, an instrument used by surveyors.

With a theodolite the surveyor measures the angle between the ground and the top of the mountain. Calculations based on his measurements give the height of the mountain. This explanation is, of course, a very simplified account of a very complicated operation.

Another method, less exact, is possible if you can get to the top of the mountain. This is by measuring the pressure of the air at the top of the mountain by means of a barometer.

Now, a barometer simply measures the weight of the air above it. The higher you go the less air there is above you, and so, as you ascend, the mercury in the barometer moves in a tube as less weight presses upon it from above. If you take the pressure of the air at the top of the mountain a simple calculation will give a rough idea of the height.

It is on this principle that the pilot's altimeter works, although instead of using mercury in a tube his instrument records changes of pressure on a collapsible metal capsule exhausted of air.

Why Does a Pin Get Hot if Rubbed Against a Stone ?

All rubbing, or friction, produces heat. If you had a really delicate thermometer you could easily prove that paper and indiarubber and the air around them all get hotter when you rub out something you have written. The motion that starts the rubbing is changed into the special kind of invisible motion called heat. In the case of a pin rubbed against a stone, we notice the heat-effect of friction particularly well. This is, in the first place, because the pin has a sharp point, which hinders easy movement on the uneven surface of the stone; and, second, because the pin is made of metal, and all metals are very good conductors of heat. So the heat runs up the pin very easily and quickly, and that is why we feel it so distinctly and quickly.

HOW DOES A GRAMOPHONE WORK?

EVERY year many millions of gramophone records are sold throughout the world. They represent a vast industry.

These flat black discs bring music into homes to be played at will. With their aid we can hear the songs of our choice sung by world-famous singers, or the great classical symphonies played by world-famous orchestras ; and we can hear them whenever we wish—they are at our command. Such is the wonder which the gramophone has made possible.

It is a far cry from the faint metallic scratchings of the first phonographs to the

of all the magnetic tape recording is played over on the tape machine and the electrical signals (corresponding to the original sound waves) are fed to the disc recording head. This head is fitted with a cutting stylus or needle, and when the electrical signals pass through the recording head they cause the stylus to vibrate from side to side in sympathy. As the lacquer disc revolves with the recording head travelling slowly across it, a fine spiral groove of constant depth, but containing the side to side variations of the stylus, is cut into the lacquer. So now

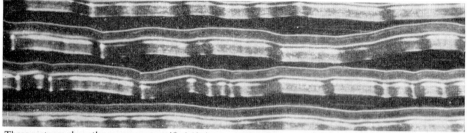

These pictures show the grooves, magnified 40 times, on the surfaces of different gramophone records. That above is of a 78 revolutions per minute record, in which there are 90 grooves to the inch. The picture below is of a long-playing record, which has from 200 to 320 grooves to the inch.

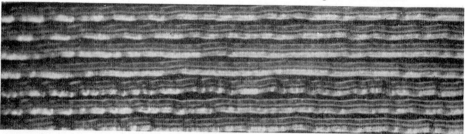

exact, clear reproduction of the modern gramophone or the combined radio and gramophone which we call the radiogram. But before we begin to see how our gramophone works we must understand how a record is made.

Usually the performers are gathered in a sound-proofed recording studio where outside noises cannot interfere or intrude into the record. As the artists begin their performance the sound waves produced by them are picked up by microphones which transform them into minute electrical impulses corresponding to the original sound waves. These electrical signals are amplified and recorded by a special machine on magnetic tape ; wax discs are no longer used.

The recording is then transferred from the magnetic tape to lacquer discs. First

at this stage the original sound waves, converted first into electrical signals, have found their way on to the disc in the form of the spiral, wavy groove.

By special chemical processes, metal discs, or " stampers " as they are called, are produced from the lacquer disc, and from these thousands of gramophone records are made for sale in the shops.

When we put a gramophone record on to our record player or radiogram, it is able to reproduce the sounds of the original performance in this way. As can be seen from the top drawing on the next page, the record player consists of three basic parts : the turntable and pick-up, the amplifier, and the loudspeaker.

The pick-up has a needle (or stylus), and when the record is placed on the revolving turntable and the pick-up

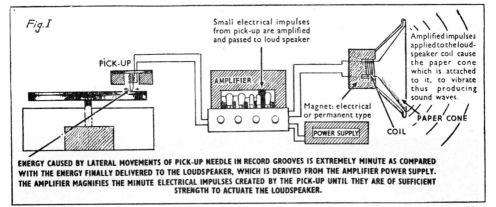

Fig.I

Small electrical impulses from pick-up are amplified and passed to loud speaker

PICK-UP

AMPLIFIER

Amplified impulses applied to the loud-speaker coil cause the paper cone which is attached to it, to vibrate thus producing sound waves.

Magnet: electrical or permanent type

POWER SUPPLY

PAPER CONE

COIL

ENERGY CAUSED BY LATERAL MOVEMENTS OF PICK-UP NEEDLE IN RECORD GROOVES IS EXTREMELY MINUTE AS COMPARED WITH THE ENERGY FINALLY DELIVERED TO THE LOUDSPEAKER, WHICH IS DERIVED FROM THE AMPLIFIER POWER SUPPLY. THE AMPLIFIER MAGNIFIES THE MINUTE ELECTRICAL IMPULSES CREATED BY THE PICK-UP UNTIL THEY ARE OF SUFFICIENT STRENGTH TO ACTUATE THE LOUDSPEAKER.

needle placed on the record, the wavy grooves cause the pick-up needle to move from side to side. These movements generate electrical signals in the pick-up which correspond to those that the microphones produced from the sound waves in the studio. The amplifier in the record player performs the task of strengthening these electrical impulses so that they can operate the loudspeaker. The loudspeaker is really the counterpart of the microphones in the studio. The microphones turn sound waves into electrical signals while the loudspeaker transforms the electrical signals back into sound waves.

The diagram below illustrates a modern high fidelity record reproducer designed specially to make the re-created sound

waves as near to the original as is scientifically possible. The basic principles of operation are the same as the machine in Fig. 1, but many special refinements are incorporated. One of these is an automatic mechanism which plays several records automatically to save having to change them by hand. Notice, too, that there are three loudspeakers instead of one. Each of these loudspeakers is designed to handle a particular range of notes : two of them for the low and middle register, and a special one for the very high notes. The filter is simply an electronic device which sorts out the electrical impulses from the amplifier and sends them to the proper speaker according to the range of notes it is designed to reproduce.

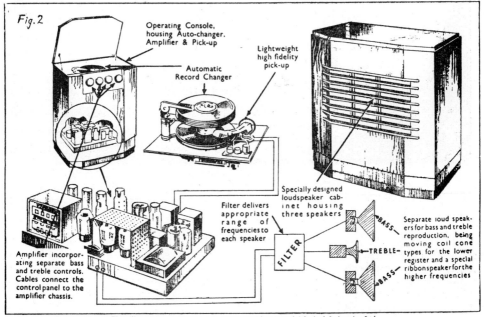

Fig.2

Operating Console, housing Auto-changer. Amplifier & Pick-up

Automatic Record Changer

Lightweight high fidelity pick-up

Specially designed loudspeaker cab-inet housing three speakers

Filter delivers appropriate range of frequencies to each speaker

FILTER

BASS

TREBLE

BASS

Separate loud speakers for bass and treble reproduction, being moving coil cone types for the lower register and a special ribbon speaker for the higher frequencies

Amplifier incorporating separate bass and treble controls. Cables connect the control panel to the amplifier chassis.

The illustrations on these pages are by the Electric and Musical Industries Ltd.

How Does a Soap Bubble Hold Together?

The tiny particles of water which make a soap bubble are held together by the force we call " surface tension."

Surface tension is a force that acts in the particles at the surfaces of fluids, and acts in such a way that each attracts each see it, too, in the rounded form which little drops of fluid take, for this form is made by the pull, or surface tension, of the particles. On the surface of every liquid there is such an elastic skin. A bubble is all surface; it is simply such an elastic surface skin stretched, by air pressure. As the air pressure presses equally in all direc-

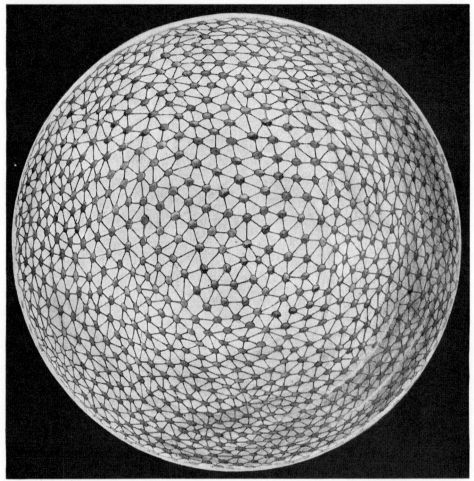

THE WONDERFUL WAY IN WHICH A SOAP BUBBLE IS MADE TO HOLD TOGETHER

This picture shows us how a soap bubble holds together. Of course no microscope could show us a bubble like this, but the picture gives us an idea of how a bubble is made. The molecules of water should really be infinitely smaller and greater in number than here, and the lines between the molecules are merely drawn to suggest the way in which the pull, or surface tension of water, draws the molecules together. There are not really any lines. See explanation on this page.

and pulls on each, and will stretch rather than separate from its neighbours. In this way the united particles come to make, as it were, a very thin elastic skin.

We see surface tension acting when we fill a tumbler of water above the brim, for the particles form a rounded skin which prevents the water from overflowing. We tions, and the particles pull equally on each other, the skin is blown up into a round balloon just as any other elastic skin might be. But the bubble must burst in time, for the particles which hang together, and compose its skin are subject, like other particles, to the action of gravitation. They are not only stretched by the air inside the bubble, but are pulled downward by the force of gravity, and that force is greater than the other force called surface tension. So some drops run down the bubble and the bubble becomes thinned and weakened in parts, and in the end so thin and weak that it cannot resist the pressure of the air inside it and accordingly bursts.

What Makes a Soap Bubble Rise and Fall ?

If a soap bubble lasts long enough, and does not burst too soon, it will begin to come down again after a little.

The simplest explanation of this would be to remember the case of a balloon filled with hot air. It goes up, for a time, and then it comes down again. It goes up because the hot air inside it is lighter than the air round it, and, being lighter, must rise, just as hydrogen would have to rise.

When it cools, the weight of the covering of the balloon brings it down again. Now, a soap bubble is really a little hot-air balloon, for the air that fills it is warm air from our lungs, and the air is so much lighter than the air outside that it goes up with force enough to carry the weight of the water that makes the skin of the soap bubble.

But this cannot last long, for the skin of a soap bubble is very thin, and so the heat from our breath that is inside the soap-bubble soon escapes, and the bubble becomes as cool as the air around it. Then there is nothing to hold up the water of the bubble, and it begins to come down. The early experiments for ballooning were actually made with soap bubbles.

Why Do We Hear Better on Water than on Land ?

Sound is composed of waves of different lengths transmitted through the air, and these waves can be interrupted and broken up by coming in contact with any obstacle, as the waves of water are broken up when they strike a rock.

On the land, sound waves cannot travel far without striking against houses, or trees, or mountains, or other obstacles to their progress, and these prevent the sound travelling to a great distance. On the sea, however, or on a great lake where the surface is perfectly level, it is possible to hear for a very long distance, simply because there is no hindrance to the path taken by the sound.

Why Does a Match Go Out When We Blow It ?

When a match or fire burns, it makes a certain amount of heat. Now, it needs heat in order that it shall burn at all, and that is why we have to put a match to a fire. Once it has started burning it will keep itself hot enough to go on burning as long as there is stuff to burn and air to burn it with.

Now, we can blow a match out because we blow away the heat in the hot gases which are just going to burn, and the whole thing becomes so cold that it will burn no longer, any more than the match would before it was struck. Any fire, the heat of which is in the gases it makes, can be blown out in the same way if we have a big enough wind to do it. You must have seen the wind blow out a fire at a picnic. But the wind cannot blow out a coal fire, because much of the heat which keeps the fire going is in the glowing coal itself, and the wind cannot blow that away. We can make a match burn more quickly by blowing on it gently enough, so as not to blow its heat away altogether, but so as to keep up a brisker supply of air than if we were not blowing at all.

What Does a Worm Know ?

A worm knows a great deal. It knows when to come out of the rain. When the ground becomes too sodden with moisture it seeks the upper air. It knows how to get a living and it knows how to protect itself, as we may see by the way it slides into the soil again when exposed by the gardener's fork.

The worm has no brain in which to store memories. Yet it has a memory, stored probably in its nervous system ; and experiments have shown it.

Some worms were tested in a passage shaped like a T. They crawled along the upright till they came to the cross-bar of the T. About half of them turned one way and half another. Then, by putting in a mild electric current, the left-hand passage of the top of the T was made disagreeable to the worms. At first they were puzzled, but after about 200 shocks they learned to prefer the right-hand way. Then the current was put into the other leg of the T, and this time the worms learned the error of their way in 65 times. Evidently they were cultivating a memory.

Why Do We Ever Stop Growing ?

What we call growth is the power the cells of the body have of taking nourishment into themselves and so becoming larger, and of dividing and giving rise to other cells like themselves. This power, however, is limited, and every kind of cell can only grow within the limits of its own law—the law of growth. No matter how much food or exercise is taken, the law of growth prevents any number of cells becoming more numerous or larger than a given limit.

When the body is young the growth is very active, but as the body grows older the limit of growth is gradually reached, and growth stops.

Why Do Owls Come out by Night ?

Quite a number of animals, and some other birds besides owls, are *nocturnal* in their habits—that is to say, they are adapted for living their lives generally during the hours of night.

If we want to understand why an animal comes out at night, or why it comes out in the daytime, we must, as a rule, ask ourselves : What is it that makes an animal active at one time of the day rather than at another ? The answer to this question is generally to be found in the search for food. So it is in the case of the owls. Owls feed chiefly upon mice and other small creatures that are active during the hours of the night, and so the owl, with its peculiar noiseless flight, due to the fact that its plumage is so soft, comes out at night in search of food. It is because of this habit that the pupils of the owl's eyes are adapted for seeing at night, being made to open very widely to catch every ray of light that there may be.

Why Does a Wet Plate Get Dry if We Leave It Alone ?

This is due simply to what we call the evaporation of water, and the great fact about this is that it occurs at all temperatures. It is true that on a hot day, or when put before a fire, a plate may get dry much more quickly than otherwise, but water everywhere evaporates at all temperatures, though the rate varies according to the amount of water already present in the atmosphere.

Sometimes, whatever the temperature, we may find that the wet plate does not get dry when we leave it, and even that dry things get damp. Matches will not strike, we find, and writing-paper is quite moist. In such cases the air has been holding more water than it needed, and has deposited it on everything exposed to it. That is what happens when the dew falls, and then a wet plate laid on the grass would become wetter.

Where Does the Fog Go When it Clears Up Suddenly ?

The answer to this question is not fully understood, but we know quite well what happens in certain cases. For instance, a wind, warm or cold, may come in and drive the fog before it, exactly as the air of a room where several people have been smoking may be cleared by making a draught. Or sometimes a fog clears suddenly because the air gets warmer, as may happen in various ways. A fog is only possible when the air is below a certain temperature, and if the sun, coming through clouds, or an inrush of warm air, should raise the temperature above this point, the fog will disappear.

But electricity is also concerned in this question. We know that it is possible to disperse a fog artificially with great speed by means of electricity ; this was most clearly proved by the great English scientist, Sir Oliver Lodge. Now, electrical changes constantly occur in the atmosphere ; and it is very likely that sometimes, when a fog suddenly disappears, as if by magic, it is because of some electrical change in the air, of much the same kind as that produced by Sir Oliver Lodge's machine for dispersing fogs.

What is a Cenotaph ?

Cenotaph is an English word made up of two Greek words meaning an empty tomb, and that is exactly what a cenotaph is. It is a monument erected in honour of some dead person or persons buried elsewhere.

Cenotaphs are almost as old as architecture itself and have been erected by people of all nations ; but until the end of the First World War the word was little used in Britain. Soon after the war, however, a great national cenotaph was erected in Whitehall, in the heart of London, to commemorate all who had died for their country.

When we speak of *the* Cenotaph we always mean the monument in Whitehall.

The Story of the Beautiful Things in the Treasure-House of the World

A Famous Greek Picture Probably Nineteen Centuries Old—The Aldobrandini Marriage.

THE ARTISTS OF THE OLD EMPIRES

THERE are few things more remarkable in the history of the world than the complete eclipse of the art of the Reindeer Hunters when the Stone Age came to an end. The impulse which forced men to make those beautiful and simple pictures went out suddenly, like a candle flame.

The Stone Age, as we have seen, was a period of rough, rude existence, when wild animals supplied man's every need. The Bronze Age which followed lasted many thousands of years, and it would appear, looking at this stage of human development, that life was almost as simple then as in the Stone Age.

But in glancing back over the bounds and fields of Time as over a landscape, we see the Bronze Age in its true perspective. This slow-seeming period held nothing short of a revolution, for early during its span men discovered the use and growth of corn, barley, millet, flax, and they learned to tame animals. The world has rolled on over a hundred centuries since then, but until the dawn of steam power there had been no development so vital to human life as these apparently simple discoveries of the far-off Bronze Age. At a slightly later date men also discovered metal— first gold, then copper; some happy accident led to the mixing of copper and tin, and so the name of the mixture was given to the period. A little later again, the art of making pottery was discovered.

Many relics of daily life in Europe at this time have come to light, and they show a certain skill in decoration, although it is of a primitive kind. Yet the workmen of those days knew a good deal of the technique of engraving on metal, and we can judge their skill by the decorated swords, bracelets, daggers, plaques, and so on, which have been found. The potters also made rough patterns on their bowls and dishes. And the interesting thought which arises about these is that, crude though they may be, they mark the beginning of what we might call domestic decoration. Nearly all our cups and saucers and jugs and basins today bear some design, and this habit of making useful things attractive is thus about ten thousand years old.

In addition to these small objects, the men of the Bronze Age left mysterious and huge decorated granite blocks, which they set up, generally in avenues of approach to their stone-built tombs, or dolmens as they are called.

The most famous of these are on the island of Gavr'inis, off the coast of Brittany. Other examples have been found in various parts of France, in Denmark, Sweden. Spain, and Portugal. There is

PICTURES · STATUES · CARVINGS · BUILDINGS · IVORIES · CRAFTS one fine specimen at Newgrange, near Dublin. All bear the peculiar stamp of the Bronze Age ideal of decoration; patterns made of repeated triangles, circles, and crosses, and—in the dolmens—minute lines that follow each other much like those on sea-charts of a coast-line.

We have been unable to find out why there was nothing alive, so to speak, among these patterns of geometric lines. Save for one or two clumsy attempts at engraved figures there is no representation of human or animal life. It would seem that superstition had laid a ban on the representation of living beings.

In the meantime, it is to Egypt that we must turn for art in that distant period. While the men of the Bronze Age in our continent were making their small, skilful patterns, a great and national art was rising in the country of the Nile.

Egyptian art was immensely removed from the quality of the art of any other early nation because it was inspired by a definite system of religious thought. It is the first such art in the history of the world; it is the next big thing, in time, to the art of the Reindeer Hunters, that, as we remember, was warm and natural and beautiful, and was the work of men who had thought very little; while Egyptian art was cold and unnatural and beautiful, the work of men who had thought a very great deal.

THE TWO THOUSAND STRANGE GODS OF OLD EGYPT

The Egyptians had worked out for themselves a curious religion, a system embracing over two thousand gods and goddesses divided into certain families or groups. If it had not been for their animal worship—there were many animal deities, and numerous birds, reptiles, and insects were sacred—the religion of the Egyptians would have been lofty and rather wonderful. Some of the chief gods have interesting titles. There is Osiris, the man-god who rose from the dead, and was deified and became King of the other world and judge of the Dead; there was Set, the principle of evil, the enemy of Osiris. There was Nu, the God of the watery mass whereof the world was made.

There are the goddesses of wisdom, of literature, of Earth, sky, rain; almost every physical and mental force has its divinity in the old mental outlook of the Egyptians. Portraits of them are shown in the sacred books and paintings, and, generally speaking, from the shoulders down they are very much alike, but distinguished one from another by the most wonderful head-decorations.

These divinities imposed upon their subjects a certain way of thinking and behaviour which had for a foundation two strong beliefs—that this world is of little moment save for the passing happiness it may afford, and that the wicked are punished and the good rewarded in the world to come. It was on the idea of the future life, of which they were so wonderfully sure, that the Egyptians based most of their literature and art, and we cannot appreciate either their paintings, sculpture, or architecture without first understanding this fact.

THE OLD EGYPTIANS' RESTING ROOMS FOR THE LONG, LONG SILENCE

A Greek historian once said that the Egyptians looked on their houses as mere places of passage, and on their tombs as their permanent dwellings. They made tombs fit to outlast time itself, and in them buried their dead, wonderfully embalmed so that the bodies would be preserved for thousands of years; and they placed in these houses of a long silence very beautiful things. It seems strange to us that a nation should concentrate its art on its sepulchres, and perhaps we shall understand it better when we realise that to these far-off people death was only a suspension of life; sooner or later the spirit would reinhabit the body.

This idea was so real to them that they furnished the house of the dead with as great a solicitude as if the dearly-loved person had been alive ; tables, chairs, stools, beautifully decorated bowls for oils and spices, painted and inlaid boxes containing mirrors, hairpins, scents, were among the furniture of the tomb. In a child's tomb they placed its toys, in that of a warrior his spears, in that of a hunter his bows and arrows, in that of a state dignitary his staff of office.

THE LOVELY BOOK LEFT WITH THE DEAD FOR THEM TO READ

In all tombs of any importance they put a most wonderful set of writings called the Book of the Dead, which was supposed to have been written in the first case by Thoth, the scribe of the gods. It contained religious teaching, stories of the life of the gods, and so on. Each copy was separately

A PORTRAIT FROM ONE OF THE OLDEST PICTURE GALLERIES IN THE
WORLD ; KING SIPHTAH OF EGYPT, FROM THE MILES OF PAINTED WALLS
AND CEILINGS LEADING TO THE TOMBS IN THE VALLEY OF THE KINGS

This fine piece of Egyptian colour was rescued in the excavations
carried on at Biban-el-Muluk by the generosity of Mr. Theodore Davis

A PAGE FROM THE BOOK OF THE DEAD LEFT IN THE TOMBS OF EGYPT FOR THE DEAD TO READ

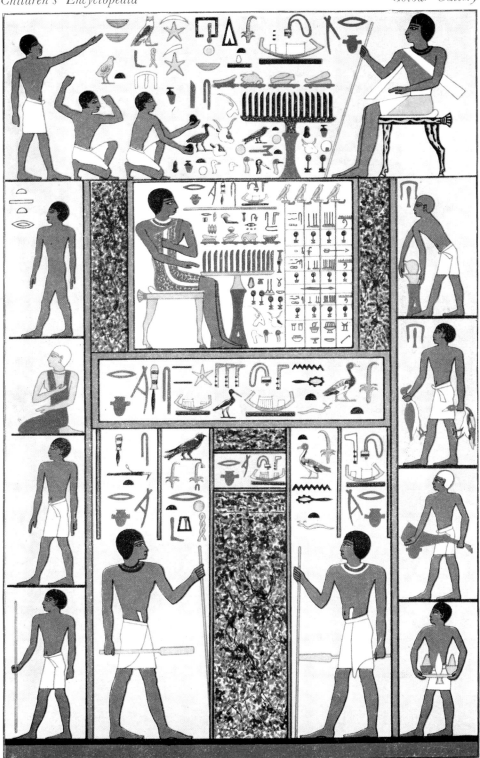

THE PAINTED WALLS OF A TOMB AT GIZEH ON THE NILE

A KING'S PALACE IN ASSYRIA IN THE TIME OF NINEVEH

written and painted by scribes and artists in bright colours and hieroglyphics—picture-words ; and these men put into a work which would only be seen by the spiritual eye of the dead all the skill generally put in pictures meant to win world-wide fame.

We can see the kind of illustrations that were painted in the Book of the Dead from the magnificent specimens shown in the Egyptian Galleries of the British Museum. Our collection of these papyri is the finest in the world, and it brings back to us a race and a religion and an art that will have a definite place in history as long as history endures.

THE ROYAL TOMBS THAT MADE KINGS SEEM MORE KINGLY

The tombs on which so much time and art were spent were of various kinds, the mastabas of the earlier dynasties—heavy, rectangular constructions, the pyramids of the later centuries, and the rock-hewn tombs of the mountainous parts of the country. Of these the most famous are the tombs of the kings at Biban-el-Muluk, near Luxor, on the banks of the Nile, and it would seem on entering them that death had made royalty thrice royal.

They all contained several chambers and passages, and a shaft leading to a remote chamber where the sealed sarcophagus was laid. There was generally placed in or near the tomb a statue of the dead, to which offerings were made. These tombs were built and endowed by the wealthy " for ever." In some there was generally a chamber where " the sad and solemn priests " made daily offerings for the dead. A temple built near the later tombs took the place of this room. The walls of the chambers, and in some cases the ceilings, were covered with wonderful decoration showing men and animals, gods and goddesses. Figures were often outlined or engraved, or sculptured in relief.

WHERE THE DEAD WAIT IN QUIET HOPE OF THE LIFE TO COME

In later days the decoration of the tombs developed more on the lines of painted frescoes, and some of the chambers can only be described as gorgeous. Rows of figures were underset and surmounted by brilliant lines of patterns.

The Egyptians had a curious idea in the frescoes of their tombs and temples and vignettes in their " books," and throughout the entire history of the nation it was never quite cast aside. The paint is all flat ; no light and shade or modelling is attempted, and the laws of perspective had no place whatever in their backgrounds. Their figures were always wilfully " out of drawing," as we say. They showed faces in profile set on shoulders and bodies in full view. This distortion is all the more marked because the eye shown in the profile is always the eye as it would appear in a full view of the face.

Another of their peculiar conventions is shown in the position of the feet. The Egyptians as a race had small hands and long feet, and the feet were always shown flat to the ground. Any attempt at a light poise, a resting on the toes, or one foot flying, would have seemed to them a contradiction of their standards of art. After a little thought we see that it could not be otherwise. The whole spirit of Egyptian art is the clamping down of a human being on the Rock of Eternity.

THE WHITE RACES POURING FROM ASIA INTO EUROPE

The idea that they could not possibly die crept into the work even when the artist had no thought of portraying something of a religious kind. The keynote of their art, so to speak, is a quietness, a waiting, an immobility. In portraits and statues their kings and queens are often shown seated, knees together, feet together, no twist in neck or shoulders, eyes looking calmly out, the face in complete repose. If the figure is standing it is pulled out to an abnormal length, and has the same quality of serenity. Egyptian art, alone in the world, is intensely still.

Meantime, across the blue sea, there was another kind of art rooting itself in the soil of history, and its first seed was sown in one of the big changes of the world, like that of the coming and going of the Stone Age civilisation. About 2000 B.C. from out of Central Asia, across the tract that lies in between the Caspian Sea and the Ural Mountains, there came a race of white-skinned, fair-haired people called Aryans. They came in a succession of waves, so to speak, and one of the waves, in the fulness of time, brought the Celts to our shores. The Aryans settled all over Europe and founded a civilisation which reached its highest point in Greece.

A new life sprang up about the Eastern Mediterranean ; there was one small part of it—the islands and coast of the Aegean

Sea, where wonderful things were made. The chief of these islands, colonised from Greece, and the centre of their life, was Crete, and her art reached a very high standard indeed. But in course of time another civilisation rose on the islands, and the work of the early artists was buried beneath sand hills and new towns.

We should know very little about it all were it not for the work of a great British archaeologist, Sir Arthur Evans. About 1900 Sir Arthur began excavating in Crete, and he astounded the world by his discoveries during the next few years. He revealed the island's proud and important place in art.

THE WONDERFUL PALACE THAT WAS LOST TO HISTORY

Near Candia, on the site of the ancient town of Knossos, he laid bare the wonderful palace where the fabled King Minos lived, to which the Greek legend gave the name of Labyrinth. Italian archaeologists have since unearthed another palace at Phaestus, another ancient Cretan town.

The palaces are built on a very intricate plan, and show a tangle of rooms and corridors where strangers might very easily lose their way.

These royal houses were adorned with a wealth of beautiful things, chiefly plaster reliefs, painted frescoes, and pottery. The wall paintings show a wonderful freedom and vividness in their treatment. All sorts of subjects are painted on these frescoes, and when we realise how new was the culture of the islanders we can but look in amazement on the work.

The artists were of a fresh, pliant nature, and went from one subject to another in a cheerful, unbiased way. They painted landscapes, towns, ladies on terraces, scenes of royal life, pictures of the chase. A great treasure among our discoveries at Crete is a heavy stone vase sculptured to show reapers in a kind of triumphal procession bearing heavy sheaves on their shoulders.

THE HAPPY PEOPLE WHO LEFT CHEERFUL PICTURES OF THEIR LIVES

The Cretan artists—they are sometimes called Minoan, from the ancient king's name—were skilled makers of pottery, and they painted vases in floral designs in orange, red, and white on a polished black ground. The Cretan vases, and those of Cyprus, were forerunners of the famous Greek vases.

The artists of the islands also made dainty carved and cast tablets in marble and bronze. We can imagine them a happy, sun-kissed people, pleasantly occupied in painting whatever came to hand.

Troy is another legendary town which was buried and has been brought to life again near Hissarlik on the Dardanelles, Lovely little ivory tablets and figures have been found in the ruins, beads and jewels which the ladies wore, ornaments that decorated the houses sacked by the Greeks in the Trojan wars.

People who are interested in beautiful things ought to be very glad they are alive now, for no one knows how many more treasures will be dug out of the past before another few years have gone by. In the meantime, in continental Greece, on the site of ancient Mycenae and Tiryns, archaeologists have found more works of art that belong to the early days of that famous nation—some wonderful wall paintings and vases. A fragment of painting on plaster from Tiryns shows in itself how wild and free was their work. It is a picture of a hunter either vaulting over a galloping bull, or, lightly poised on knee and toe, riding the heavy beast. There is something in the look of the bull that reminds one for the first time since the Stone Age of the art of the Reindeer Hunters. We can only wait for time to show if there is any link between this new and old of the far past.

THE GREEKS WHO MADE BEAUTIFUL EVERYTHING THEY TOUCHED

Crete, Mycenae, and Cyprus have given their name to a group of the famous Greek vases which made a kind of art of their own on the eastern shores of the Mediterranean. Looking back on the minor art of vase making, one is newly amazed at the wealth of Greek genius. All the world knows the grandeur of their statuary and it would seem that the gift of sculpture alone was sufficient to make Greece famous for all time. But it is clear that the Greeks could not touch anything without making it beautiful.

Like the Egyptians, they buried a great many articles with their dead, and these, found in the tombs in an almost perfect condition, are an astounding revelation of the high standard that obtained among jewellers and potters. The burial places in Greece, Asia Minor, Southern Russia, and Etruria have yielded

PICTURES THOUSANDS OF YEARS OLD

A ROMAN PORTRAIT
THOUSANDS OF YEARS OLD

A GREEK VASE IN THE
BRITISH MUSEUM

A MUMMY PICTURE FROM
OLD EGYPT

A FRAGMENT FROM THE WALL OF THE THRONE ROOM AT KNOSSOS IN CRETE

WALL PICTURES FROM POMPEII BURIED IN THE EARTH FOR 18 CENTURIES

a veritable harvest of these beauties; gold and silver vases so costly that had they not been buried with the dead, they must have been bartered for gain long ago; vessels of glass, beautiful jewellery, and hundreds of terra-cotta vases and tiny figurines. Of the small figures there is a very fine show in the wall cases of the Terra-cotta Room in the British Museum.

DAINTY FIGURES THAT HAVE DANCED ON VASES THROUGH 3000 YEARS

They must have been " turned out by the dozen " by Greek artists, yet no two are exactly alike, and each one is fresh and vibrating with life and a sense of great art. They show on our shelves a multitude of dainty figures which seem to go dancing, walking, loving, and talking through life. The best of them were found at Tanagra, in Boeotia, and they bear the stamp of the Great Age of Greece.

When we think of the minor arts of this nation, however, we instinctively turn to the vases. Here, again, in the British Museum is a carefully arranged collection, and we can see the wonderful pottery advance from the early Cretan and Mycenaean ware to the last of the vases made in Greece when her " beauty eye " was a little dimmed.

The shape of the vases altered as time went on. The finest are the most simple, and have the severest handles. There are, roughly, about a dozen types, and we can see them—labelled " Set of vase shapes," in the room of Greek and Roman life. This set acts as a key to the great array of pottery in the vase rooms.

The uses of the vessels were as varied as their shapes. Some are drinking-cups, some jugs, some are bowls for mixing, others are jars to hold oil.

THE CHANGING COLOURS THAT COUNT THE TIME FOR US

The ornament, like the shape, varies with the passing centuries and mirrors the rise and fall of Greek art. The free, flowing decorations of Crete and Mycenae, which belong to about 1500 B.C., gave way in the course of five hundred years or so to a kind of very stiff, geometric pattern with conventional figures in keeping with the designs. A very famous set of vases belongs to this period, jars on which are painted naval battles and funeral processions. They are called Dipylon vases, from the Dipylon (double-gate) cemetery at Athens where they were found. These were fol-

lowed, about 700 B.C., by a class of vase called Corinthian, where the ornament is of another style, more florid and less severe. In them reddish-brown figures with white and black relief are painted on a light yellow ground.

After the Corinthian vases came another style of painting—black figures on a red ground. Then, about 200 years later, the ornament became red on a black ground. There are some very fine designs on the Athenian vases of this time, and a few of them are signed by the artist. The names of the chief of these vase painters are Euphronios, Brygos, and Douris. About 200 years still later came the end, where the pure terra-cotta vases were concerned. A period of imitation followed, as is always the case when an inspired art dies out.

Unfortunately very few specimens of Greek wall painting have been preserved for us, and that is one of the reasons why we treasure the vases which show the wonderful technique of brush drawing.

THE DYING LIGHT OF GREECE KEPT BURNING IN POMPEII

We can only guess how great the pictorial art must have been from a famous painting called " The Aldobrandini Marriage," which hangs in the Vatican Museum in Rome. There were innumerable frescoes painted by the Greek artists and their scholars, but all except those of a late period have perished. Some few were found in Egypt, and eleven of them are in our National Gallery. The rest we mainly owe to the excavation of the buried towns of Herculaneum and Pompeii, which were buried beneath a volcano eruption in A.D. 79 and discovered about the middle of the eighteenth century.

These two towns were by no means the home of what we should call Greek art of the high order, but they were freely and lavishly stored with art treasures executed under Greek influence. The paintings are chiefly compositions dealing with Greek mythology. There is an ancient Judgment of Paris, which has inspired many later pictures; another is " Achilles recognised by Ulysses." A great many of these frescoes were done by the Roman scholars of the Greek masters.

Some of these paintings make us realise what the great work of the Greeks in their prime must have been. But the great fire of their genius had burned down, and here we see it going faintly by in thin flames.

The Wonderful House We Live In, and Our Place in the World

WHY LIFE LEFT THE SEA

WE know for certain that there was a time in the story of the Earth when there was no life whatever, because the Earth was far too hot for any living thing. Now, in our story of life, which leads up to the story of our own lives, we have plainly to make a beginning at that very time when life first appeared on the Earth, which, up till then, had shown no life at all.

The story of the origin of life and of the nature of the first living things is a most interesting romance, but at present we are trying to tell in the shortest way the different stages of life upon the Earth, and we need remember only that the first living things must have been plants, because, being the first living things, they had nothing but the simplest kinds of food to live on, and it is only plants that can live on the simplest kinds of food.

As the ages went on the first living things gave birth to many more, and of these some differed in many ways from their parents, so that the seas would hold not only many living creatures, but many different kinds of living creatures; and among these certainly appeared the first forms of animal life.

Now at one time or other something very remarkable must have happened. Living creatures, born and bred in the sea and needing liquid water for their life, must actually have dared to leave the water—a very brave and big thing to do.

Life *swam ashore*. Now, we put it in that way because perhaps it will help us to remember; but this great event did not happen exactly like swimming ashore.

It may have been the moon that came to the help of life, and that really led to making life possible upon the land, for the moon makes the tides, and it may have been the tides that made it possible for life to swim ashore.

The tides do what nothing else could do; they make possible the change from the sea to the land, because they prevent the change from being too sudden.

We know hosts of living creatures today that teach us this lesson. Their proper place is in the water, especially the shallow water near the shore. Very often they live on the rocks, and as the tides come and go they often learn to do without the water for a time until it returns. Can you not imagine how they might learn, so to speak, after a long time, to do without the water altogether, and so live on the land? Of course, we do not mean that they or any other living things can do without water, for all life is in water, and

BODY, MIND, AND SOUL · CITIZENSHIP · ECONOMICS · GOVERNMENT

²⁸ L 1

though we should be drowned in the sea our bodies themselves are more than three-fourths water. But we must understand that these creatures could learn to live without being covered by water.

This step from the water to the land was really the greatest step that life ever took after its first beginning, and the reason is a very good one.

What is the real reason why life has made so little progress in the sea and so much on land? Well, before we answer the question let us remind ourselves that life *has* made very little progress in the sea. The highest kinds of living things that are natural to the sea are the fishes, and even the cleverest fishes and the biggest are very stupid and humble things. They are quite cold, like the water round them; they have scarcely any sense at all, and they will never come to anything more so long as they stay in the sea.

It is true that there are certain wonderful creatures, like the whales and the seals, whose blood is warm, who live in the sea. But, though they look like fishes, they are not really fishes but far higher, and far younger in their history. Though these live in the sea *they breathe air*, and even the cleverest whale must sometimes come to the surface to get a new supply of air. Now, that is the whole point.

HOW THE BREATH OF LIFE IS CARRIED TO THE BOTTOM OF THE SEA

As we know, every living thing must breathe or die—that is to say, it must get supplies, and always fresh supplies, of the gas called oxygen. Now, the rate at which it gets and uses up oxygen decides the rate at which it lives. The rate at which it can get oxygen depends, of course, on the amount of oxygen that is there to be got—that is plain enough.

Though life began and continued for many ages in the water, it could never make any more progress in the water than is allowed by the very small amount of oxygen that water contains; just as, if you only have a very little money, and cannot make or get any more, there must plainly be a limit to the amount of spending you can do. Life in the water went on for ages and ages learning how to make the most of the oxygen that is in it; and, when it had learnt how to make the most of that, it could make no more.

The whole of the small amount of oxygen in sea water is got from the air.

Thus, there is a fair supply of oxygen near the surface of the water, which is next the air, and much less down below. It is believed that the oxygen which supports life at the bottom of the oceans is carried there in streams of cold water, which were once near the surface in the cold regions of the Earth, and which, as they are carried to the warmer regions, sink down and down, carrying the necessary oxygen to the life in the depths.

HOW THE FIRST LIVING THINGS MAY HAVE COME ASHORE SLOWLY

Now, if we think about it, we shall see that the waters near the shores of the seas, which are very shallow, and which the tides are constantly spreading out into thin layers, must really be the best-off in the way of oxygen; and that is why there is so much life of so many kinds in the waters and on the rocks of the shore. We may be sure that it would be the creatures which were accustomed to a good supply of oxygen that at last would learn to " make the plunge "—only it was a plunge not into the water but out of it into the great ocean of air.

Now, while the amount of oxygen in water is so small, the oxygen in the air is actually one-fifth part of the whole air, so that the difference between water and air in this respect is like the difference between bitter poverty and boundless wealth.

So life was abundantly rewarded for the great step from the water to the land. No doubt times were hard at first, because the arrangements which do very well for breathing oxygen in water are of no use at all for breathing oxygen in air. That is very strange, yet we all know it very well, for we know that when a fish is taken out of water it dies, and though it is surrounded by far more oxygen than it has ever known before, it actually dies for want of oxygen—that is to say, it is suffocated. It has no lungs, you see, but only what are called gills, which are arrangements for filtering oxygen out of water which contains it.

THE GREAT STEP WAS TAKEN, AND LIFE BEGAN ITS WONDERFUL MARCH

So that when life first came ashore it had to learn how to invent lungs which would enable it to use the oxygen of the air. Without them life would die in the midst of plenty, just as the fish does, dying for want of oxygen in the midst of a boundless amount of it.

This great difficulty was got over, however, in one way and another, and we have already seen how the tides came to the help of life by giving it opportunities to learn how to breathe air when the tide was out, and coming to its rescue with water when the tide was in. And so, after a long time and many failures, the great step was taken ; for, while much life remained in the water, and remains there to this day, all the great, high, and wonderful stages in the story of life came after this.

Now, when living things came to land and got abundance of oxygen what ad-

little bit warmer, though you cannot notice it. The rule is simply that the amount of heat, or warmth, in any place spreads itself about over everything, until no one thing is hotter or colder than any other. This is the case with a cold-blooded animal, such as a fish. It is just as hot as its surroundings. If it is in very cold water, it is very cold ; and if it swims into warm water, it becomes warm, too.

But now let us contrast with the fishes the case of warm-blooded animals. The fish in your hand is cold, but your hand is warm ; your whole body is warm, and

A cat-fish which drowns if kept in the water

A fish from the Congo River which drowns if deprived of air

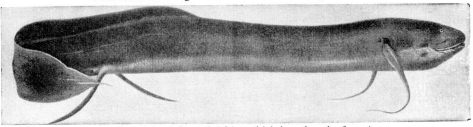

The lung-fish of Central Africa which breathes the free air
LIFE ON THE BORDER LINE BETWEEN SHORE AND WATER

vantage exactly did they gain ? In the sea there is so little oxygen to be had that the fish cannot use any of it for the purpose of keeping itself warm. And so the fish, like other cold-blooded animals, behaves, so far as its warmth is concerned, like a piece of stone. If you have a number of different things in a room, and leave them there for some time, each of them will soon be just as hot as the others ; if, now, you bring a tumbler of hot water into the room, it will get cold, and the other things in the room will get a

that is why other things feel cold to your hand. The truth is that air-breathing animals can help themselves to as much oxygen as they please, and after they have taken all they need for necessaries, they can help themselves to more for luxuries. They simply light a fire within themselves and so keep themselves warm. The warm-blooded animal is hotter than its surroundings, because it is making quantities of heat inside itself with the help of the large supplies of oxygen it can get from the air. This does not mean that the animal just makes itself as hot as it pleases—one day very hot, and another day not so hot. The great fact about the warm-blooded animals is that they are just as hot one day as the next, and as the day before, and that all warm-blooded animals are about equally hot. We might expect, perhaps, that a little bird would have a certain degree of hotness or temperature, and an elephant something quite different, and a man something different again ; but when we compare the hotness of all the warm-blooded animals we find that it is about the same for every one of them.

THE FIRE WITHIN ALL LIVING THINGS IS KEPT STEADILY BURNING

The birds are generally slightly hotter than other animals, but the difference is very small indeed. It is fair to say that all warm-blooded animals live at about the same point of hotness, and this means, we may be quite sure, that *there is a particular hotness, or temperature, at which life goes on best.* When this hotness is reached and kept, all the changes that go on in living matter do so with the greatest ease and success. So long as life lived in the water, which holds only a very little oxygen, it could never hope to reach this point of hotness at which it lives best. One or two fishes have been found which are always, it seems, a little hotter than the water around them.

It was not until the great step was taken to the land, until living things learnt to breathe air and to make the most of all the oxygen in the air, that living creatures could keep themselves warm enough all the time to do the very best that is possible for them. So that the abundance of oxygen gave land life a great advantage. It is interesting to remember that, though the plant-world has covered the land as well as the bottom of the sea, it has not taken any advantage of the large supplies of oxygen in the air. It only breathes very slowly, and though some plants, like some fishes, are sometimes found to be rather hotter than their surroundings, they are never very much hotter, and never so hot as the warm-blooded animals.

LIFE'S STEP INTO THE AIR IS NOT OF GREAT IMPORTANCE

You might think, perhaps, that yet another great step was taken when life left the land for the air, as in the case of the birds ; but this is not a step of any great importance. Animals that do not fly live just as much in the air as the birds do. It is true that birds spend much of their time actually in the air, and can swim about in the great ocean of air, while we crawl about at the bottom ; but, of course, the bird really lives on land just as much as we do. It does not sleep in the air, and does not make its nest in the air. The real beauty of the bird's life is that, though its home is on the land, it can soar about in the air when it pleases.

So really there is only one great step, so far as mere place is concerned, in the story of life, and that is the step from the water to the land. The bird is really a land animal, and though it can soar it never really roams from its home on the Earth.

We have spent some time in seeing why it is that the step from the water to the land was so important, and now that we have reached land we shall not have very much more to say about the life in the waters. Yet we must never forget what we said at the beginning—that life, though it has left the water for the land, can never exist anywhere, in any creature, without water.

MILLIONS OF LIVING THINGS ON LAND NO BETTER THAN THE FISHES

This is true not only of animals or plants that live in water, but also of those that live in air ; and it is as true of the lark soaring in the sky as it is of a flat fish lying at the bottom of the sea. When the lark goes up in the sky he takes with him all the liquid water in his body, and it is really in that liquid water that his life is lived. Take it away, and the lark must die ; it is true of every living thing.

A clever Frenchman once made a study of the water contained in the bodies of animals, and he has shown that this water has in it a quantity of different kinds of what are called salts, the most important being the ordinary salt of the dinner-table. These salts are the same as are found in sea-water, and occur in just about the same proportions.

It is a most wonderful thing to have found this out, for it teaches us that, whatever life may do on land, it yet requires water very much like sea-water ; and even when most of the sea is dried up, and the Earth becomes smooth with land, like our wonderful neighbour Mars, we do not doubt that life will still be needing water every hour if she is to carry on.

The Story of the Marvellous Plants that Cover the Earth

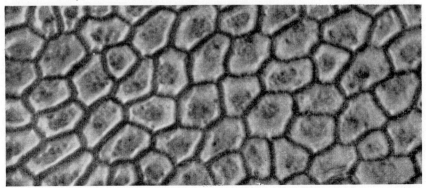

The Cells of a Leaf—The most wonderful laboratories in the World

BIRTH, LIFE, AND DEATH OF A FLOWER

LIFE is like a rhythm. There is a time of saving, and a time of spending. A period of accumulating energy—the power of doing work—is followed by a period of expenditure. There is winding-up and there is corresponding running-down in the living clock.

Probably this was established at the dawn of life, when simple creatures throve on the energy of the sunlight during the day and lived during the night on their gains. In ordinary green plants there is sunlight capture during the day and manufacture of sugars and proteins; in the darkness this stops, but there may be other internal activities such as cell-division, fermentation, and transport of material from one part of the resting plant to another.

The so-called sleep-position of many leaves, such as the clover, is very different from their position during the day, when they are busy transforming the Sun's rays into food. The life of the plant is naturally a see-saw between work and rest, but it is also in tune with the alternation of day and night.

But there is a larger rhythm in the plant's life, and that is related to the march of the seasons. In warm countries there is the sprouting, leafing, growing period of spring; the maximum industry

and the flowering of summer; the fruiting and seed-scattering of autumn; and the entrenchment and rest of winter. Two ways of looking at this must be combined.

First, it is in the nature of every life to have a youthful growing time—the ascending part of the life-curve; then there is a period of maturity and great activity; then a time concerned with reproduction, or the continuance of the race; and finally there is the downward part of the curve during which activity wanes and ageing leads to death.

There are four great chapters in the life of man—youth, maturity, love, and ageing; and there are four great chapters in the life of a plant—leafing, flowering, fruiting, and withering away. These chapters depend on the nature of the organism; they are determined from within.

But the second point of view is that in warm countries there are the regular changes of the seasons; and to these the life of the creature must be adjusted. There are many annual animals such as an ordinary queen humble-bee. A young queen lies in a sleep-like rest throughout the winter; she awakens in early spring and, after visiting early spring flowers and collecting pollen and nectar, she becomes the mother of a large family. She ceases to go out of doors at all, and her working

BOTANY & ITS WONDERS · FLOWERS · TREES · HOW THINGS GROW

daughters do everything but lay eggs. She usually dies in the autumn. But among her daughters there are young queens, some of them fertilised by drones, sleepy through the winter and beginning the story afresh next spring.

The point is that the chapters in the life-history are adjusted to the variation of the seasons, and so is it with the plant— with its spring foliage, its summer flowers, its autumn fruits and seeds, and its winter rest, or death. In the case of an annual, the whole life-curve rises and falls with the four seasons ; when the plant lives for many years the external ups and downs have to be faced many times, and they leave their mark on each of the great chapters of life, maturity, maximum vigour, and ageing. The annual plant has its single spring in its youth ; the perennial plant has many springs, and enjoys a period of youth and renewal every year.

Spring is the season of young things, and we see this in the crowds of seedlings that rise from the ground. The seeds were formed in the sunshine of the previous summer; they were scattered and sown in various ways in the autumn; they have lain dormant in the ground through the winter. But the waiting has not been a mere marking time ; there have been preparations within the seed itself.

Towards the end of winter, if we unearth some of the seeds in the ground, we find that their protective envelopes have been weakened by rotting. Bacteria help in birth. As the spring showers moisten the ground and the water soaks into the seeds

the living matter re-awakens, and this is helped by the rise of temperature. The stores of starch and proteins in the seed are fermented and made more available for the young plant, which develops rapidly and bursts out. The young stem grows towards the light, and, rising above the surface, moves round and round, bending and bowing to the different points of the compass. The young roots grow downwards and they also move in the cavities in the soil. The first leaves are expanded in the light and air, and when they are thickly sown there is often keen competition among neighbour seedlings.

Another feature is the opening of the leaf-buds. They, too, were formed in the plenty of the previous summer. They are young shoots with closely packed young leaves — well wrapped up in tough bud-scales, often varnished which keep out the cold and the damp during the winter. The spiral arrangement of the young leaves inside these protective coats allows many leaves to be economically packed away in a small space. The spiral arrangement in the bud corresponds to the spiral arrangement of the full-grown leaves on the branch or stem, and there it has the advantage of lessening the risks of the over-shadowing of one leaf by another. The full-grown shoot, of course, is due to the lengthening-out of the minute axis in the core of the bud. The two main factors that start growth within the bud are the rise of temperature in the spring, and the ascent of sap from the stem. Living matter contains 70 or

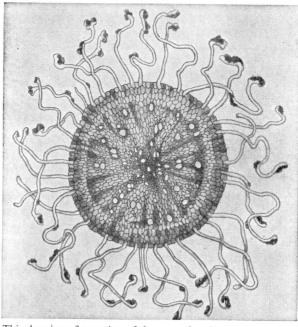

This drawing of a section of the root of a plant shows the fine root-hairs through which the plant obtains nourishment from the soil. Particles of earth are seen clinging to the root-tips.

THE LEAF OF THE SYCAMORE OPENS

April 30

May 1

May 2

May 3

May 4

May 5

May 6

May 15

May 22

THE DEVELOPMENT OF THE WINTER BUD OF THE SYCAMORE INTO FULL LEAF

more per cent of water, and the increase in the amount of living matter implies plenty of watery sap.

If we look in spring at a cut surface on a birch-tree, where a branch has been lopped off, we see that it is very wet. This is an overflow of the sap which is ascending from the roots. It is possible, by inserting a tube into the young wood of a tree like the maple, to show that the sap rises with considerable pressure, and this pressure has often been measured. This ascending sap, which comes up from the roots through tiny tubes in the young wood, consists of soil-water and dissolved salts. It is necessary for the re-awakening and growth of the buds, and for the manufacture of carbon compounds in the sunlit leaves.

THE WONDERFUL AND DIFFICULT PROBLEM OF THE CLIMBING SAP

We cannot give a short answer to the question: What causes the ascent of sap? But the two most important factors are root-pressure and the breathing-out of water-vapour from the leaves. The soil-water passes by diffusion through the surface of the rootlets into the concentrated sugary fluid of the living cells. As a cell receives fresh supplies it must pass on its surplus water to another cell, so enabling itself to absorb water from the soil.

So the water passes with considerable pressure up the stem from cell to cell ; perhaps it brings to mind the way firemen used to pass buckets of water from hand to hand. But then there is a supplementary process, working from the leaves backward and downward, for the using-up of water in the leaves, and the loss of water-vapour into the air, must make one cell more dense than another, so that it is able to draw on its neighbour. But it is a difficult problem—the ascent of sap.

THE POLLEN-GRAIN THAT STARTS A NEW FLOWER ON ITS WAY

As we have seen, summer is the time of the plant's greatest activity, when foliage is at its best, when there is the richest supply of sunshine, and when the process of splitting up carbon dioxide and building up carbon compounds is at its height. There is an enormous chemical industry going on, though all is so quiet ! But no one can fail to associate summer with flowers. Although there are many flowers in spring, they are few compared with the pageant of summer, and they are usually, though not always, of paler colours. White and yellow flowers are common in spring; reds, blues, and purples are more characteristic of summer.

Just as the leaf is the organ through which food is taken, so the flower consists of the organs of reproduction. It was a great discovery, part of the credit of which rests with the poet Goethe, that a flower is made up of four whorls of transformed leaves. In the centre, at the top of the floral axis, or flower-shoot, are the carpels which produce the possible seeds (or ovules), each containing an egg-cell which will develop into an embryo plant if it is fertilised by the pollen of another flower. The next tier consists of stamens, whose heads (or anthers) produce the fertilising golden-dust (or pollen), which is carried by insects or by the wind from blossom to blossom. Each pollen-grain includes a male element (or nucleus), which unites in an orderly way with the nucleus of the egg-cell when a tiny outgrowth from the pollen-grain penetrates into the ovule.

On the tier below the stamens are the petals, forming the corolla. They are in most cases brightly coloured, and they help to attract useful flower-visiting insects in various ways—by their brilliance, by their fragrance, or by producing nectar, or by several of these methods at once.

THE SUMMER-TIME WHEN LIFE IS QUICKENED EVERYWHERE

The petals often shelter the essential parts from the rain; they may ward off useless intruders; and they make certain that welcome visitors, such as bees, get well dusted with pollen.

Lowest of all are the sepals, forming the calyx, usually green and substantial, protecting the rest of the flower during the bud stage and steadying the upper tiers against the wind. In many cases the calyx, or part of it, is carried on into the fruit, as in the strawberry. In some cases the sepals are brightly coloured and make the petals attractive, and it may be noted that nectar may be produced by various parts of the flower beside the petals.

But the big thing is this—the flower consists of four tiers (or whorls) of transformed and often glorified leaves—sepals, petals, stamens, and carpels. As John Ruskin said, " When leaves marry, they put on wedding-robes, and have feasts of honey— and we call them flowers." The flower is the crown of the plant's life, and when we know a little more of botany we shall see that Erasmus Darwin was not wholly fanciful in writing a long poem on *the loves of the plants*.

Summer is the time when the Earth gets its largest dividend of solar energy. Much

tions than they can possibly need. They thrive and grow, they multiply and spread, and all the more adventurous life of animals rests in the end on the large capital that plants place so liberally at their disposal.

The Seeds of an Apple

The Seeds of a Lemon

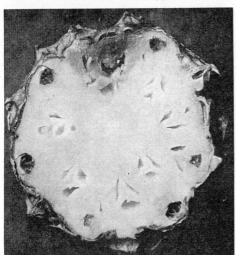

Pine-apple Seeds sheltered by the Wall

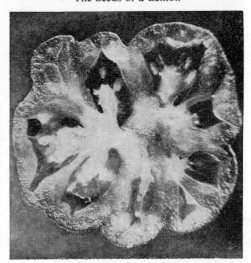

The Seed Chambers in a Tomato

THE BEDS THAT MOTHER NATURE MAKES TO PACK HER FRUIT CHILDREN IN

of that warms the land and the sea and the air, and so quickens life. But much of the energy is in the form of light, and, though that is health-giving in many ways, quickening the pulse of life, and in some cases *energising* animals, its chief importance is that it is a source of energy to green plants, which trap it so successfully that they accumulate more stores and muni-

All higher plants, especially the ordinary flowering plants, are very complicated organisms. There is great intricacy in their make-up, as, for instance, in the architecture of a green leaf. Each cell is like a laboratory, and when there is much work being done, transforming matter and energy from one form to another, there is bound to be wear and tear in the furnishings

THE LIFE-STORY OF A BUTTERCUP

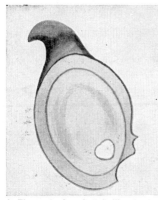  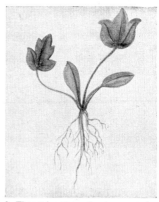

1. The seed of a plant is like the egg of an animal, the product of male and female parents, and here we see the seed of a buttercup inside the female organ of the flower, with the young plant (the embryo) in its earliest stage.

2. The seed (which we call an ovule) absorbs water, and chemical changes take place inside which cause it to sprout, or germinate, throwing out a tiny white thread which is really the root, and always grows downward.

3. The seed-coat now bursts open and a stem begins to grow upward, which we can see is a continuation of the root. Presently tiny leaves that were folded up tightly inside the seed begin to open out and expand.

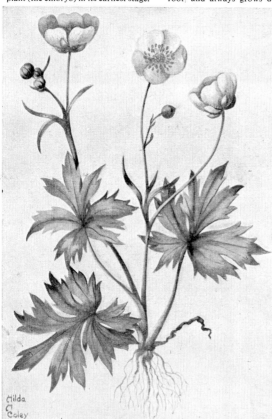

4. The flower is not only beautiful to look upon, but a wonderful and complicated piece of work, as we can see if we cut a buttercup down the centre so as to uncover the inside.

5. The plant now grows rapidly until at last we have a perfect buttercup with stem, leaves, flowers, and roots, a wonderful work of art containing within itself all the power of carrying on the race. We should appreciate the beautiful flower more if it were rare and costly instead of growing in every field and being within reach of all.

6. Still more wonderful is a horizontal section of the flower, showing the orderly arrangement of the parts. Outside there are the five green leaves (sepals), then the five yellow petals, then the male organs, and then the female organs.

These pictures show the wonderful life-story of a flower, the flower chosen by our artist being the common meadow buttercup. We see it from the seed to the flower and from the flower to the seed again. It is the wonderful story of mother and child, repeated for ever by nearly all living creatures, whether

7. If we take one of the yellow petals, we shall find at its base a tiny pocket (or gland) which contains a honey-like fluid called nectar, and is called a nectary. This nectar attracts insects.

8. These are the stamens (or male organs) of a buttercup, a back and front view being shown. The stamen is divided into pockets called anthers, which contain the pollen to fertilise the flower.

9. Here is another view of a stamen showing the anther open and shedding its pollen, which is in the form of a fine powder consisting of tiny grains, which vary in shape in different plants.

 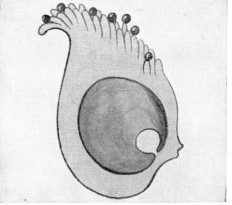

10. The female organ (or pistil) of the buttercup is made up of a number of modified leaves called carpels, clustered round the top of the flower stalk, and this picture shows such a cluster of carpels, with one detached and magnified.

11. The top of the carpel, called the stigma, receives the grains of pollen that come from the stamen, and here we see the pollen resting on the stigma, while inside the seed-vessel (or ovary) a seed is waiting to be fertilised.

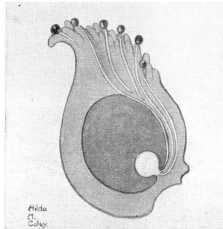 

12. A sticky substance on the stigma holds the grains of pollen prisoner, and these at once begin to form little tubes which make their way down into the ovary and penetrate into the seed, so promoting fertilisation. The seed is in this way made capable of producing another plant, and so the race of buttercups is carried on from year to year.

13. Here is a cluster of carpels after being fertilised, one of them detached showing the seed developing. This brings us to the stage of our first picture, and now we have to imagine the whole process going on again. A buttercup will fertilise itself, but the child-plant is stronger if the stigma receives pollen from the stamen of another plant.

they be animal or plant. Everywhere the principle is the same in all cases, but the buttercup has been taken for the purpose of these illustrations because it is the most familiar of all our common flowers.
In the buttercup, as in many other flowers, both parents appear on the one plant.

of the laboratory—that is to say, in the microscopic framework of the living cells. In other words, *ageing is inevitable*. As Shakespeare said :

And so, from hour to hour, we ripe and ripe,
And then, from hour to hour, we rot and rot,
And thereby hangs a tale.

To a long-lived plant, every spring and summer bring opportunities of becoming more or less young again, and this is taken advantage of. Ageing is staved off, but in the end it wins. In many other cases there is a sacrifice of hard-worked parts, and the plant automatically sheds what has become a source of weakness, as we see in the falling of the dead and exhausted leaves of trees. But there are limits to this saving of the life by losing. In the end age must win, and what we see so characteristically in autumn is the waning of life, either for the year or for ever, as far as the individual plant is concerned.

The fall of the leaves is characteristically autumnal. They have worked hard; the furnishings of the laboratory show wear and tear; the leaves are ageing. Moreover, with lowered temperature and frozen ground they could not continue the use they make of water. The supply cannot be kept up, and even if water were available, it would be liable to freeze in the leaf and burst the cells. Thus, the leaves *have to fall*, and it is well for the plant that this should be so.

THE WITHERING AND FALLING OF THE LEAVES IN AUTUMN

A very interesting point to remember is that before the leaves are shed there is a migration of most of the useful material into the stem of the plant. The remnants of the green colouring matter (chlorophyll) account for the yellowness of the leaf when it is ready to fall.

And along with the withering and the fall of the leaves we must take the dying down of the stems of many herbaceous plants, so that nothing is left exposed to the cold of winter. If a sudden frost comes the parts above ground may be killed in a night, while there is still much life in them, and that means great loss to the plant. When cold sets in gradually there is a retreat of almost all that is valuable into the root. Thus what withers and is swept away as rubbish is often as empty as a fallen leaf.

But there is another very distinctive note in the life of the plants in autumn. Just as we associate sprouting and leafing with spring, and flowering and intense growth with summer, so we must recognise autumn as the season of fruiting and seed scattering. The fruit is what remains of the flower after the ovules have become genuine seeds. Stamens and petals fall away ; the sepals often wither ; the supplies which may still be coming up the floral axis are drafted into the fruit, which often becomes very substantial, or into the seeds, which receive a useful legacy of proteins and fats.

HOW THE PLANT SAVES ITS LIFE IN HARD TIMES

As the flower withers the nectaries close, and the sugary material which overflowed in these glands may be drafted into the fruit. Besides juicy fruits there are multitudes of dry pods and capsules, which liberate the seeds by breaking up; though transformed in connection with the production of young trees, they are really leaves, and it is natural that they should wither.

In the warm countries of the northern hemisphere, most plants pass into a state of rest. The leaves have fallen; the buds are well wrapped up; it may be that there are no parts left above ground; there are stores in underground parts; the seeds are sleeping in the crannies. This is partly the natural reaction after a period of great activity, and partly an adjustment to hard external conditions. The plant needs a rest, as the fall of the leaf shows; it saves its life in hard times by lying low.

Evergreens, like the holly and the pine, have leaves specially suited, by their tough skins, to stand the cold and to go on slowly capturing winter sunshine; but we have only to walk under these trees to see that their leaves also have a very limited lease of life. They fall off piecemeal, as it were, not all at once as in ordinary trees.

THE PAUSE IN THE PLANT'S LIFE BEFORE A FRESH START

Then there are woolly plants, like edelweiss, which are so well wrapped up that they do not need to die down as so many herbaceous plants must. Besides evergreens and woolly plants, there are many exceptional cases, but these do not affect the truth of the general idea that winter is a time when the fires of life burn low, if they do not go out altogether. It is a time of retreat, retrenchment, and rest. It may be a full-stop in the life-history, but it is often a semicolon, a pause, a preparation for a fresh start, a crouch before a spring.

The Story of the Peoples of All Nations and their Homelands

The Needles and their lighthouse

SEEING OUR HOMELAND FROM THE SEA

LOVELY it is to look at our Homeland from the sea. Let us imagine ourselves sailing Westward Ho! from busy Southampton. Passing Calshot Castle on our right to enter the Solent, with the Isle of Wight on our left, we turn south and west, passing Beaulieu River creek, gateway to the New Forest. The shore is fairly high with a vista of hills and woods behind.

Reaching Christchurch with its Priory we look down the coast to Bournemouth, Poole Harbour, and Swanage, a pleasing prospect of low, sandy cliffs crowned with pines and rich in gorse. From the tideway of Poole Harbour, through a gap, we may see Corfe Castle against the background of the Purbeck Hills. Beyond Swanage Bay, from Durlston Point to St Albans Head, the coast is bold and steep, receding in a wide bay scarred with quarries. Here runs a jumble of dark water, the Race. To the south-west is Portland, to the north the wooded pinnacle of the Nothe rises above Weymouth Bay. The pale cliffs of the Dorset coast are like a chain of gables, with slopes of downland behind, and here and there a mustard field among the green, and here and there toy villages. Coppices come down to the water's edge.

Passing Lulworth Cove and Durdle Door we reach Weymouth Bay, Portland Isle,

and Portland Bill and its lighthouse with another Race at its foot. This Race has helped to pile up the famous Chesil Beach, one of the great natural breakwaters of the world. Beyond is Bridport, then Lyme Regis, from which four ships sailed to aid Edward the Third and two to join in the attack on the Spanish Armada. The coast is hilly ; behind it rises Golden Cap, and farther west is the chalk cliff of Beer Head.

From here to Sidmouth, sheltered by its high Peak Hill, there is a succession of red cliffs with narrow valleys in between. Salcombe Regis Chine is one, and after Budleigh Salterton, behind the shingle bank, is pretty Ladram Cove with its pinnacle rocks and Otterton Point. As Straight Point is weathered the beautiful valley of the Exe lies before one. From Exmouth to Teignmouth the coast is fairly steep, with the red rocks of Dawlish halfway between. Thence we pass Oddicombe Beach to Hopes Nose, round which, in Torbay, lies on one side Torquay, and on the other Brixham with its trawlers. To Torbay Napoleon was brought in the Bellerophon and to Brixham came William of Orange on a Protestant wind.

From Brixham and Berry Head the coast is dangerous as, after sighting the Start Lighthouse, we pass Mewstone Peak to Dartmouth Harbour and the

THE FIVE CONTINENTS & 100 NATIONS & RACES THAT INHABIT THEM

mouth of the entrancing River Dart, with lofty Kingswear facing the romantic old town to which the river gives its name. There is no lack of rocks hereabouts and the headlands are in keeping, but after passing Prawle Point, the sandy bar of Salcombe, magnificent Bolt Head, and the entrance to Bigbury Bay and Wembury Bay, all is plain sailing to the mouth of the Yealm and Plymouth Sound.

PLYMOUTH AND THE HARBOURS ON THE WAY TO THE LIZARD

Plymouth, with green Mount Batten, lies half-revealed and half-concealed. Its old red town and famous Hoe must be singled out before they can be seen. From Plymouth Sound to Fowey is a short sail. The Eddystone Lighthouse rises 152 feet above high water, a grey circular tower with red gallery and lantern. The stump of the old Smeaton Tower stands a little to the north. The coast is rugged to Port Wrinkle, and between here and Looe are the Sherberterry Rocks. More steep coast and then come Polruan, Fowey Harbour, and St Austell Bay.

There are busy little harbours all the way to Dodman Point, a cliff as high as St Paul's and, like St Paul's, with a cross at the top. Then come Porthloe, with many rocky outliers, and Zone Point (more familiarly known as Zoze Point), opposite Pendennis Castle, and we are at Falmouth, to which the Romans may have come for corn, the Greeks for hides, and the Phoenicians for tin. A little south are the dreaded Manacles and rocky coast, with Coverack Cove, Cadgwith Cove, and Housel Bay breaking it, on the sail to The Lizard.

PICTURESQUE ST. MICHAEL'S MOUNT AND GREY-FRONTED PENZANCE

The twin lights of The Lizard, with the Stag Rocks at its base, shine across Mounts Bay. Round the Point are Kynance Cove with its two pretty islets, lofty Rill Head, Mullion Island and its cove, Loo Pool, and Porthleven. Then we reach Marazion and the causeway that at low water joins it to St Michael's Mount, whose central tower rises 250 feet above the sea, and grey-fronted Penzance, whose stony streets climb up the hill past Newlyn on the west. From Mousehole Harbour to Land's End the coast is an epitome of Cornwall. Breaking its rocky contours are Lamorna Cove, with the guardian Carn Dhu and the stream running past the mill to the sea; and Treen Castle, with the Logan Stone, and Porthcurnow, where the Atlantic cable comes in.

Land's End is not the end. Some miles away are the Scilly Isles, islands of flowers on which anything will grow; while beyond them is the Bishop Rock and its lighthouse. At the entrance to Whitesand Bay is the Longships Lighthouse, and Cape Cornwall rises about 200 feet as against 260 feet at Land's End. Off the Cape are the rocky Brisons. Just beyond the Cape is Botallack Mine, some of whose galleries run below the sea. Beyond rises the tower of St Just. Turning in east we come to Pendeen Point and the dark mass of Gurnards Head, with Mulfra Quoit and its cromlech crown behind, and pretty Zennor below.

WHERE LOFTY TINTAGEL BREATHES THE VERY SPIRIT OF ROMANCE

Beyond Carn Naun and Battery Point is St Ives, looking toward Gwithian and Godreva Head across the bay. Passing St Agnes Head, Perran and Holywell Bays, and Kelsey Head we reach Newquay, Watergate Bay, and then Trevose Head, with Padstow Bay between it and Pentire Head. Padstow with its Doom Bar and inlet are not impressive, but lofty Tintagel breathes the very spirit of romance. Opposite is High Cliff, the termination of Resporvel Down, rising 850 feet. Tintagel is lower, but noble and steep, its castle beautifully placed, and the church tower behind. Two miles farther is the inlet of Boscastle, with a legend of bells sounding beneath the waves. The cliffs rise 700 feet and more till we come to Cambeak Head and Widemouth Bay, Bude, Chapel Rock, and Efford Beacon. Round dark Hartland Point, with its lighthouse, and then Clovelly Cove and Bideford Bay and the Bristol Channel are before us, with Lundy Island about midway between Hartland Point and St Anne's Head in Pembrokeshire.

East of Clovelly the rocky coast gives way to sandhills as it sweeps round to the mouths of the Torridge and the Taw, with Bideford at the head of one and Barnstaple at the head of the other. Just by Appledore is Northam Burrows, and behind it are the links of Westward Ho! The coast runs north to Baggy Point, then round and to the east of Morte Point we come to Ilfracombe. Beyond Combe Martin Bay the Great and Little Hangman hills rise nearly 1000 feet, the romantic cleft of Heddons Mouth points the way to Exmoor, the steep shores become wooded, and Borthaven, Lynmouth, and Lynton attract by their beauty, a delightful panorama continuing all the way to Porlock.

AN ISLAND WHENCE WIRELESS MESSAGES WERE SENT BEFORE MARCONI'S DAY

Behind Porlock is Dunkery Beacon ; then come Minehead and Blue Anchor, and Burnham, and half-way across the narrowing channel are the islands of Flatholm and Steepholm. It was from Flatholm that some of the early wireless messages were sent to the mainland before Marconi came on the scene. Weston-super-Mare is reached beyond Brean Down, and beyond the mouth of the Yeo is Clevedon, whence a tall hill edges the coast to Portishead. Then it sinks again and Dumball Islet marks with its beacons the mouth of the River Avon, with Clifton and Bristol six miles inland. Some way beyond New Passage the Ship Canal reaches the Severn at Sharpness Dock. Now we cross to the north side of the Severn and sight Chepstow standing impressively above the River Wye.

THE VARIED SCENE BETWEEN CARDIFF ROADS AND THE CHESTER FLATS

Between Cardiff Roads and the Chester Flats Wales has more than 500 miles of coast, with towering cliffs, majestic headlands, submerged and jagged surface reefs, sandbanks and sand dunes, old castles and churches, estuaries, and mountainous backgrounds, with many signs of the ebb and flow of erosion and reclamation. Soon after leaving the Rhymney Estuary we reach that of the Taff and the great docks of Cardiff and Penarth, with Barry just round Lavernock Point. Between Barry and Porthcawl promontory are the Tressilian Caves and St Donat's with its ancient church and restored castle (the poor man at the rich man's gate). Then two lighthouses give warning of the grim Tusker Reef.

Next come the wide sandy sweep of hill-encircled Swansea Bay, with Port Talbot's limestone ridge on our right and, across the bay, Oystermouth and the Mumbles islets off the south-eastern point

of the rugged grandeur of the Gower Peninsula, with Langland, Caswell, Oxwich, and Port Eynon bays. At the south-west corner of the peninsula is Worms Head with its dragon crag, and round it delightful Rhossili Bay. Then we reach the salt marshes of the shallow Burry Inlet, the eastern arm of Carmarthen Bay, the mouths of Taf and Towy, and, on the farther shore, pleasant Tenby, Caldy Island with its priory, and St Margaret Island with its light.

Between Oldcastle and Stackpole headlands can be sighted ruined Manorbier Castle, and beyond St Gowans Head and Linney Head the coast bends northward to the splendid harbour of Milford Haven, with Pembroke Dock well inland. Rounding the promontories of St Ann and Great Castle and passing the islands of Skokholm, Grassholm, and Skomer, we come to the wide opening of St Bride's Bay, north-west of which, off Ramsey Sound, are Ramsey Island and the Bishop and Clerks islets with their light.

CADER IDRIS COMES INTO VIEW WITH DOLGELLY IN ITS SHADOW

Beyond the bold St David's Head, with its lighthouse, the much indented coast runs north-east to Strumble Head, also with a lighthouse, and round Pen Caer we reach Fishguard Bay, the G.W.R. port for Rosslare and Cork, with lofty Dinas Head dividing it from Newport Bay. Another notable headland is that of Cemmaes, which protects Port Cardigan. Beyond are New Quay on its rocky hill, Aberayron, Aberystwyth, and the mouth of the Dovey. Soon Cader Idris comes into view, with Dolgelly in its shadow, and the fine estuary of the Mawddach, with Old Barmouth overlooking the new town below it.

Soon after passing Mochras Island and its submerged reef (St Patrick's Causeway), historic Harlech and its castle are seen, and we come to the treacherous sands and legendary inlets of Traeth Bach and Traeth Mawr. Criccieth and its castle crag overlook Tremadoc Bay, which washes the eastern shore of the lonely and rockbound Lleyn Peninsula. Facing Harlech, on the farther side of Tremadoc Bay, is Pwllheli. To the south of Pwllheli are the St Tudwall Islands with a lighthouse, Gimlet Rock, and a deep indentation between Wylfa Head and Penkilan Head, round which is the long sandy reach of Porth Nigel, more familiar to sailormen as Hell's Mouth. Westward we come to the rushing waters of Bardsey Sound and Bardsey Island and lighthouse and the Yellow Rock of Lleyn.

Rounding Braich-y-pwll we enter the broad waters of Caernarvon Bay and, some distance up the coast, which shelves to the east, Porth Dinlleyn, the finest natural harbour of North Wales, and the prehistoric hill-fort of Dinas Dinlle. Beyond it The Rivals rise above 1800 feet, with Gwydir and its lighthouse still farther on.

THE HAZARDOUS MENAI STRAIT AND CAERNARVON'S NOBLE RUIN

There is little more of interest till we come to the entrance to the hazardous waters of the Menai Strait running between Anglesey and the mainland to Bangor and Penrhyn on the east and Beaumaris on the west, with Caernarvon and the superb ruins of its castle at the mouth of the Seiont. Anglesey, the ancient Mona, and at one time a stronghold of the Druids, has few picturesque features beyond Beaumaris Castle, Redwharf Bay, Puffin Island, and Penmon Priory on the north coast. On the west is Holy Island with the port of Holyhead. where the boats leave for Dublin. Holyhead Mountain rises 719 feet. Off Holy Island is the South Stack Lighthouse and off Carmel Head to the north-west are the Skerries and their light.

Returning to the mainland, across Beaumaris Bay, we come to Conway and its walled castle, above Conway River. To the north the huge promontory of the Great Ormes Head (680 feet) shields popular Llandudno, with lovely Ormes Bay between it and the imposing Little Ormes Head (463 feet) and its interesting caves. Eastward are Rhos-on-Sea, Colwyn Bay, Rhyl, and Prestatyn, and round Point of Air, whose light is a lofty companion to that of the Great Ormes Head, we come to the sandy shores of the Dee washing the northern shores of Flintshire for some distance beyond Flint and the ruins of its old castle.

The long neck of land which divides the Dee, from the Mersey extends north-west to Hilbre Point, north of Point of Air, and New Brighton, nearly opposite Bootle on the Lancashire side of the Mersey.

Birkenhead and Liverpool face one another a little way up the river. Between Hilbre Point and Formby Point, for about eight miles out to sea are sandbanks, including the Blundells; and north of these are one lighthouse and three lightships to warn the mariner of the perils in his way.

WHERE LANCASTER OVERLOOKS THE FINE ESTUARY OF THE RIVER LUNE

The coast is dull and uninteresting past pretty Southport, as far as the Ribble Estuary, sands and sandhills alternating to the south shore of Blackpool, though between St Anne's and Blackpool the sands draw in more to the shore. From the sea Blackpool looks an imposing place. Red clay cliffs rise behind it, and between it and Rossall Point ; but beyond the ports of Fleetwood and Heysham the sands resume their sway. Morecambe is one of the gates of the Lake District, with Lancaster near by, overlooking the fine estuary of the Lune.

Off the western extremity of Morecambe Bay is the long and straggling Walney Island, north of which are the Duddon Sands. Beyond these Black Combe is seen rising 2000 feet above the shore. North of the Selkar Rocks and their beacon is the Ravenglass Inlet, and beyond this St Bees Head, a perpendicular cliff of red sandstone and the nearest point of England to the Isle of Man, 27 miles away. Next is Whitehaven, and then comes Harrington, where cliffs rise behind the low foreshore, and there are rocks and ledges out to sea.

BOLD MAUGHOLD HEAD AND THE WOODED STEEPS OF THE ISLE OF MAN

There is little change to Workington and the mouth of the Derwent, a low coast leading to Maryport, whence to Allonby Bay sandbanks extend and encroach till the Solway Firth narrows above Wampool Mouth and, beyond Bowness and Port Carlisle, we come to Rockcliff Marsh between the Eden and the Esk and so reach the Scottish border, where the little Sark enters the Esk estuary just below Gretna Green.

Before dealing with Scotland's coastline we may look for a moment at the Isle of Man. From Ayre Point, its northern extremity, behind which North Barrule and Snaefell are seen, the east coast to Ramsey is edged with sand and shingle leading to low, gravelly cliffs, which rise to bold Maughold Head. Behind this are wooded steeps climbing up to North Barrule. Here is clearly seen the island's mountainous backbone rising south-west above its central valley to South Barrule. Southward of Maughold Head steep hills are close to the edge of low cliffs with copses in the valleys.

THE HEADLAND WHICH RECALLS THE FATE OF THE SPANISH ARMADA

At Laxey Bay Snaefell dominates beautiful scenery and the coast is bold and rugged and indented to steep Douglas Head and St Ann's Head. Round Langness Point and its lighthouse is the complete horseshoe of Castletown Bay. The most southerly point is precipitous Spanish Head. Here is the little Calf of Man. Beyond, to the north, is the promontory of Bradda Head above Port Erin, with, beyond, Peel and its castle and a coast that never loses its charm.

Returning now to the shallow and sandlocked Solway, in which the tide rises 20 to 26 feet and is extraordinarily variable in the speed and direction of its ebb and flow, we come to the beginning of Scotland's no less extraordinarily variable coastline, its innumerable sea lochs, straits, and islands, stacks and lofty heights of gneiss, sandstone, limestone, granite, and so on. Above Blackshaw Flats, between the Esk and the Nith, is Caerlaverock's fine ruin.

The shore then becomes rocky to Kirkcudbright and Wigtown bays and round Burrow Head, the southernmost point of the Machers Peninsula, the scene of St Ninian's brief mission. At the entrance to Luce Bay are the Scare Rocks and the gaunt headland (or Mull) of the double peninsula (or Rhinns) of Galloway, on the north-west of which are Locknaw Castle and Corsewall Point, rounding which we come to Loch Ryan, with Stranraer, the port for Larne and Belfast.

THE IMPOSING CLIFFS OF THE BLEAK CARRICK COAST TO GIRVAN

Imposing cliffs mark the Carrick coast from Ballantrae to Girvan, seaward from which Ailsa Craig with its lighthouse rises 1114 feet above the water. Then come Turnberry, the reputed birthplace of Robert Bruce; Dunure Point and castle; Ayr and its memories of Burns ; Troon, with harbour, docks, and fine sand; Irvine Bay, Saltcoats, and Ardrossan; Fairlie,

with another castle ruin ; Largs, Skelmorlie and its castle, and Gourock. East of Bute, famous for its kyles (straits) as the Firth of Clyde narrows, are the islands of Great Cumbrae and Little Cumbrae. South of Bute Sound is mountainous Arran and west of Kilbrennan Sound the long peninsula of Kintyre. Lying off the Mull of Kintyre is Sanda Island and off its west coast Gigha Island, to the east of which West Loch Tarbert almost divides Kintyre Peninsula from the equally mountainous Knapdale. Across Jura Sound on the west are the islands of Islay and Jura, southernmost of the Inner Hebrides.

Off Jura lie Oronsay and Colonsay, and, west of the Firth of Lorne, cut off from Morven by the Sound of Mull, is the massive island of Mull with rugged coasts and smaller islands off its western shores, among them Iona with its relics of St Columba and Staffa with Fingal's Cave. Between Mull and the Argyll coast is little Kerrera Island sheltering the popular resort of Oban, to the north of which is Lismore Island, in Loch Linnhe, with Fort William at its head and, north-eastward, Telford's Caledonian Canal with its famous Neptune's staircase.

STARTING-POINT FOR THE MISTY ISLE OF SKYE

Passing through the Sound of Mull we have Loch Sunart and Ardnamurchan on our right and, on our left, the islands of Coll and Tiree, with remains of Danish forts on the first-named. Rounding Ardnamurchan Point, off Arisaig Sound, we see the islands of Muck, Eigg, Rum, and Canna. North of Arisaig is Mallaig, a starting-point for the misty Isle of Skye. Beyond the Minches, to the west, lie the Outer Hebrides, including the Barras, the Uists, Harris, famous for its tweeds, and Lewis.

Through the Inner Sound to the north of Skye we pass Applecross, Loch Torridon, Gair Loch, Melvaig, Loch Ewe, Greenstone Point, and the islands beyond Gruinard Bay and Loch Broom. Then come the Cape of Rhu Coigach, west of Enard Bay, the Point of Stoer, at the southern point of Eddrachillis Bay, Scourie, and Kinloch Bervie. Finally we reach Cape Wrath and its light rising 523 feet, having realised on our journey how true it is that Scotland is best seen from the sea. Along the deeply indented north coast of Sutherland

and Caithness we pass to Thurso with its episcopal palace ruins and its bay ; Dunnet Head, Scarfskerry, and Gills, off which is Stroma Island, John o' Groat's and Duncansby's bristling stacks.

Between Dunnet Head and Duncansby Head are the swiftly rushing waters of the Pentland Firth, with the Pentland Skerries to the east and to the north those stepping-stones to Norway the Orkneys (with historic Scapa Flow) and Shetlands.

Southward from Duncansby is Sinclairs Bay, a deep indentation between Castle Keiss and Noss Head, with Girniga Castle and Castle Sinclair north and south of it. South of Wick the shore slopes inward, its general contour and lack of islands contrasting strangely with Scotland's western coast, to Occumster, Latheron, Dunbeath and its castle, the Ord of Caithness, Helmsdale, Port Gower, Brora, Dunrobin Castle, Golspie, and Little Ferry to Dornoch and its firth. Here a spur of land juts out to Tarbat Ness. Then we enter Moray Firth, coming first to the narrow opening to Cromarty Firth between Dunskeath and Cromarty.

A LOW AND CURVING COASTLINE STRETCHING EASTWARD

Cromarty Firth runs along the north shore of Black Island from Nigg Bay to Invergordon, Dingwall, and Strathpeffer. South of Black Isle are Beauly Firth, Inverness, and Inverness Firth, at the mouth of which are Fortrose and Fort George. To the east is Nairn. Then, past the Bar, a low and curving coastline stretches eastward to Kinnaird's Head and Fraserburgh by Findhorn, Burghead, Lossiemouth, Spey Bay, Buckie, Portknockie, Cullen, Portsoy, Whitehills, Macduff, Pennan, and Rosehearty. There is a slight outward slope to the whaling port of Peterhead and Buchan Ness, after which comes a gradual inward slope past Port Errol and Cruden Bay to the great fishing port of Aberdeen between the mouths of the Dee and the Don and Girdle Ness.

South of Stonehaven cliffs is Dunottar Castle. Then comes Bervie, Montrose, Arbroath, Carnoustie, and Broughty Ferry, at the mouth of the sandy Firth of Tay, some twelve miles seaward of which is the Inchcape Rock. The shore now extends south-eastward to St Andrews and Fife Ness, rounding which we enter the Firth of Forth, with Inchkeith and its lighthouse

about midway between Kirkcaldy and Leith, with Edinburgh in the near distance. From Musselburgh, near Leith, the shore rises past Prestonpans to North Berwick, east of which is Tantallon Castle, and seaward of which is the Bass Rock with its sea birds, and the Isle of May to the north of it. A much indented coast, rising from 300 to 400 feet, leads past Dunbar and Eyemouth to the English border at Berwick-on-Tweed.

ISLANDS PRESERVING THE MEMORY OF ST CUTHBERT AND GRACE DARLING

Berwick stands on a hill to the north of the Tweed, with a lighthouse on its massive stone pier. Southward the coast is rocky, with a sandy strand. The barren Kyloe Hills rise above the Fenham flats. At Beal Point the sand widens and at low tide Holy Island, the ancient Lindisfarne, is connected with the mainland. The rocky hill of the Heugh is marked by a ruined lookout; what is left of the priory and the church is near to it, and on St Cuthbert's Islet is the ruined chapel. Farther south is Bamburgh Castle on a rocky height, the square tower of the church serving sailormen as a landmark. Out to sea are the Farne Islands, Longstone with a lighthouse memorable for its association with Grace Darling.

Next come North Sunderland Harbour and Snook (or North Sunderland) Point, Beadnell Bay, and Embleton Bay.

DUNSTANBURGH CASTLE ON ITS RIDGE OF BLACK COLUMNAR BASALT

The noble ruin of Dunstanburgh Castle is seen on the crest of a ridge of black columnar basalt amid the monotony of the sandhills. On the north side of the River Aln stands Alnmouth with its belfry chapel.

Warkworth Harbour is formed by the lower reach of the Coquet. Warkworth Castle has towers and a tall eight-sided keep. Coquet Island serves chiefly as a foundation for its lighthouse. The shore is low and sandy all along Druridge Bay to Snab Point. Cresswell Point, low and rocky, breaks the sandy shore. Then come Cambois Bay, the boulder stones of Horsebridge, the stone and timber piers of Blyth Harbour, and one sees Tynemouth Castle. A little way from Curry Point is St Mary's Island with its lighthouse. Past the cliff at Seaton Sluice, with Cullercoats at its edge, the land becomes a steep, grassy bank with a sandy foreshore.

The entrance to the coaly Tyne is marked by the sandstone cliff of Tyne-mouth Head, made more imposing by the remains of priory and castle. From Tyne-mouth and South Shields the River Tyne runs through the heart of a great coal district, taking Newcastle on its way. More sandhills follow when the river is left behind, varied by an occasional crop of limestone, as at Trow Point, or of rock, as at Marsden. Sunderland Harbour is marked by Roker Cliff and its old battery. The ensuing grassy bank of the coast beyond the River Wear is intersected at Henden, Ryhope, and Seaham by deep ravines.

THE TALL MONUMENT TO CAPTAIN COOK THAT RISES FROM EASBY MOOR

Southward of Seaham Harbour, with its piers and decks, low limestone cliffs are interrupted by stretches of sand, with the castellated tower of Kinley Hill prominent. Then we reach Tees Bay and Hartlepool on the low rocky extremity of the Heugh, where the noble church of St Hilda and the spire of St Mary's stand up finely. From Seaton Carew to the Tees Estuary are more sand-hills, which continue to Redcar. The moors are behind.

Between Redcar and Marske the tall monument to Captain Cook on Easby Moor can be seen, and at Saltburn the land climbs to Whitby, with its memories of Caedmon and St Hilda, whence cliffs from 100 to 600 feet high extend for eleven miles, broken only at Staithes, near Sandsend and Mulgrave Castle. Redcliffe is one of the boldest features of the Yorkshire coast, its deep red sandstone face rising 672 feet. Staithes Old Nab is low and black, and from it alum cliffs reach to Runswick Bay.

SCARBOROUGH, WHICH RISES PROUDLY WITHIN ENCIRCLING HILLS

From Whitby to Robin Hood's Bay high dark cliffs continue to Hayburn Wyke, but fall gradually toward Scarborough, which rises proudly within encircling hills, with the ruined keep of its castle and the war memorial on Oliver's Mount. There is another line of red cliffs along the coast of Filey, where they give way to sand and grassy slopes till the chalk cliffs of Speeton are reached, and from here to Flamborough Head they are nearly perpendicular.

From Bridlington low cliffs of clay extend along Bridlington Bay to Kilnsea,

beyond which is a narrow neck of land to Spurn Head and the mouth of the Humber, where the Bull light-vessel lies off Cleethorpes and Great Grimsby. Both shores of the Humber are skirted by wide flats. Outside and south of Grimsby is the Dogger Bank, and sandhills front the shore to the mouth of the Wash, the way marked by Saltfleet, Theddlethorpe, Mablethorpe, Sutton-on-Sea, Chapel St Leonards, and Ingoldmells Point.

Into the Wash, in which are the Boston and Lynn Deeps and Wisbech Channel, flow the Welland, Witham, Nene, Ouse, and other rivers, and its entrance is ten miles across between Skegness and Burnham flats. Passing Hunstanton with its light-house and cliff on the Norfolk coast we come to Gore Point and its sandy hummocks, which stretch eastward to Scald Head, broken only by Thornham and Brancaster Harbours. Then we come to Wells and Blakeney, whose church is the most conspicuous object on the coast, and Cromer. On Blakeney marshes is a bird sanctuary. Sandy shore continues to Weybourne, whence to Cromer are quickly eroding cliffs, of boulder clay, gravel, and sand, with Cromer Church perilously near the edge.

WHERE YARMOUTH STANDS BETWEEN THE YARE AND THE SEA

Beyond Cromer, the cliffs rising and falling to Winterton, we pass Overstrand, Trimingham, Bacton's square church, and Happisburgh's embattled church tower ; and beyond Winterton Ness are sand hills and sandy cliffs to Caister Point. Then come the notorious shoals of the Yarmouth Roads and Yarmouth standing on a strip of land between the Yare and the sea, making a brave show with its old church of St Nicholas, its naval hospital, its Nelson monument, and its fishing fleet.

From Yarmouth to Lowestoft Ness, the most easterly point of England, there are cliffs for three miles, succeeded by sandy beach. Low cliffs then extend to Southwold and Thorpeness, when shingle succeeds them, continuing past Aldeburgh, near where much erosion has caused the disappearance of once familiar landmarks. Soon after we reach Felixstowe, and Landguard Point at the entrance to Harwich Harbour, where the Orwell and the Stour meet and British Railways have a port for Continental traffic.

From the Naze, past Walton-on-the-Naze, Clacton, the low, marshy, embanked coastline of the Thames Estuary runs south-west to Shoeburyness past the mouths of the Colne, the Blackwater, and the Crouch. Between Foulness Point and Shoeburyness are the Foulness and Maplin Sands. Eastward of the Isle of Grain, at the confluence of Thames and Medway, we come to the Isle of Sheppey, separated from the Kent coast by the narrow winding Swale, with Sheerness and its dockyard at its north-west corner, Queenborough where the Swale joins the Medway, and Minster. Then follow Shell Ness, Whitstable, the home of the "native," Swalecliffe, Herne Bay, Reculver (the Roman Regulbium) and its two towers, Birchington, Westgate-on-Sea, and Margate. From Margate to Long Naze are low chalk cliffs with a stony foreshore.

SHORES ON WHICH ST AUGUSTINE LANDED AND WHERE CAESAR CAME

Round the point are the North Foreland with one of our oldest lighthouses, Broadstairs, Ramsgate, Pegwell Bay, and Ebbsfleet where St Augustine landed, and the low shore with hills behind it where Caesar came. Near by are the Sandwich flats and Richborough. From the Downs, off which are the Goodwin Sands, we see Deal and Walmer Castle, where the Duke of Wellington died, and as Kingsdown is passed the land rises to delightful St Margaret's Bay.

Round the South Foreland and its lighthouse is Dover Bay with two high cliffs and a valley between, and the ancient castle, great harbour, and Shakespeare Cliff. Soon afterwards we pass the harbour of Folkestone with its splendid Leas, whence to Sandgate and Hythe the coast gradually diminishes in height, with a few protuberances here and there. Romney Marsh behind its shingle bank is saved from the sea only by Dymchurch wall, but Dungeness Point is said to be pushing out seaward at the rate of 14 feet a year. Beyond the shallow indentation of Rye Bay lies Winchelsea, which is now high and dry.

Towards Hastings the coast rises again and sweeps in a long ridge from Battle to Fairlight cliffs, to diminish again as Pevensey Bay opens and we see among the marshes the ruins of the Roman fort of Anderida. Eastbourne comes in sight nestling in the shadow of Beachy Head, off which is Belle Toute lighthouse and beyond which a fine succession of cliffs, with Cuckmere Haven between, rise to Seaford ; then the Ouse, emerging at Newhaven, breaks their line to Brighton.

EMSWORTH AND BOSHAM ON THE LARGE LAGOON OF CHICHESTER HAVEN

A low foreshore follows to Portsmouth, broken by low gravel cliffs between Hill Head and Brown Down opposite Wootton Creek in the Isle of Wight. On the way are Shoreham, Lancing, Worthing, Littlehampton, with Arundel Castle in the distance, and Bognor Regis. From Selsey Bill, reminding us of the Selsea now under the sea, to Chichester Harbour the coast is very low, with Emsworth and Bosham, to the east of Hayling Island, on the large lagoon of Chichester Haven.

Beyond Langston Harbour and Hayling Island, with a high shingle beach, Southsea opens before us as we approach Portsmouth and historic Spithead. On the eastern side of Portsmouth Harbour are the White Hot Walls and redoubts, on the west Gosport and Haslar Hospital, and, in the distance, Porchester Castle.

To the south the Isle of Wight spreads westward from Bembridge, with Seaview, Ryde, climbing up its hill, Cowes on its little River Medina, Newtown, and Yarmouth. Rounding Sconce Point and Cliff End and passing through Colwell, Totland, and Alum Bays we come to the Needles and their lighthouse jutting out below the frowning Downs above. On its southern front the isle is continued to St Catherine's Point past Freshwater Bay and the cliffs crowned by Tennyson's Cross. To the north of St Catherine's are Ventnor, Shanklin, Bonchurch, and Culver Cliff, and we are at Bembridge again.

A WATERWAY NEVER WITHOUT INTEREST AND ATTRACTIVENESS

From Portsmouth the coast toward Southampton Water rises little above the sea. Stokes Bay and Lee-on-the-Solent are backed by woods. The shore is broken by creeks and there are mudbanks at Hamble Point, where the Hamble flows in past Bursledon. Netley Hospital seems set in green. Behind it is Netley Abbey. At low water the shoals stretch out. But the waterway, with its varied shipping and yachting, is never without interest and attractiveness.

THE COASTS OF OUR HOMELAND

HOLY ISLAND OFF NORTHUMBERLAND WITH ITS SIXTEENTH-CENTURY CASTLE

THE SEASHORE NEAR THE DELIGHTFUL DEVONSHIRE VILLAGE OF BEER

SHAKESPEARE'S CLIFF AT DOVER

QUIET BEAUTY AT BORTH-Y-GEST, CAERNARVONSHIRE

THE LITTLE HARBOUR AT PENZANCE, CORNWALL

THE LITTLE FISHING TOWN OF STAITHES IN YORKSHIRE

DURDLE DORE, A NATURAL ARCHWAY IN THE CLIFFS NEAR LULWORTH COVE IN DORSET

347

THE FISHING FLEET AT LOWESTOFT

THE FRONT AT FELIXSTOWE

THE HARBOUR AT SCARBOROUGH IN YORKSHIRE

IONA CATHEDRAL ON ONE OF
THE INNER HEBRIDES

ST ANDREWS CASTLE ON THE
COAST OF FIFESHIRE

THE ROYAL DOCK AT GRIMSBY

THE POPULAR RESORT OF BROADSTAIRS, KENT

THE PASSENGER TERMINAL AT SOUTHAMPTON DOCKS

FINGAL'S CAVE IN THE ISLAND OF STAFFA

THE KYLES OF BUTE, ARGYLLSHIRE

EDDYSTONE LIGHT

CAPE CORNWALL AT LAND'S END

BLACKPOOL TOWER

SUTTON HARBOUR AT PLYMOUTH, FROM WHENCE THE PILGRIM FATHERS SET SAIL

TINTAGEL HEAD, CORNWALL

LIZARD POINT, CORNWALL

One Thousand Poems of All Times and All Countries

THE FORSAKEN MERMAN

Matthew Arnold, if not in the very first rank of English poets, is still to be regarded as one of the greater of our modern writers. He was a lover of all that is manly, pure, and of good repute. The eldest son of Dr. Arnold of Rugby, one of England's most famous schoolmasters, he was born on December, 24, 1822, and died on April 15, 1888. Most of his active life was spent as an inspector of schools, but for ten years he was also Professor of Poetry at Oxford. The poem we give here is one of his most delicate and fanciful pieces. Its charm is never lost.

Come, dear children, let us away;
　Down and away below.
Now my brothers call from the bay;
　Now the great winds shoreward blow;
　Now the salt tides seaward flow;
Now the wild horses play,
Champ and chafe and toss in the spray.
Children dear, let us away.
This way, this way!

Call her once before you go,
　Call her once yet
In a voice that she will know:
　" Margaret! Margaret! "
Children's voices should be dear
(Call once more) to a mother's ear;
Children's voices, wild with pain.
Surely she will come again.
Call her once and come away,
This way, this way!
" Mother dear, we cannot stay."
The wild horses foam and fret.
Margaret! Margaret!

Come, dear children, come away down.
　Call no more.
One last look at the white-walled town
And the little grey church on the windy
　shore.
　Then come down.
She will not come though you call all day.
Come away, come away.

Children dear, was it yesterday
We heard the sweet bells over the bay?
In the caverns where we lay,

Through the surf and through the swell,
The far-off sound of a silver bell?
Sand-strewn caverns, cool and deep,
Where the winds are all asleep;
Where the spent lights quiver and gleam;
Where the salt weed sways in the stream;
Where the sea-beasts, ranged all round,
Feed on the ooze of their pasture ground;
Where the sea-snakes coil and twine,
Dry their mail, and bask in the brine;
Where great whales come sailing by,
Sail and sail, with unshut eye,
Round the world for ever and aye?
When did music come this way?
Children dear, was it yesterday?

Children dear, was it yesterday
(Call yet once) that she went away?
Once she sat with you and me
On a red-gold throne in the heart of the
　sea,
And the youngest sat on her knee.
She combed its bright hair, and she tended
　it well,
When down swung the sound of the far-off
　bell.
She sighed, she looked up through the
　clear green sea.
She said: " I must go, for my kinsfolk pray
In the little grey church on the shore today.
'Twill be Easter-time in the world—ah
　me!
And I lose my poor soul, Merman, here
　with thee."

POEMS · SONGS · BALLADS · VERSES AND RHYMES WITH MUSIC

I said: " Go up, dear heart, through the
    waves.
Say thy prayer, and come back to the kind
    sea-caves."
She smiled, she went up through the surf
    in the bay,
Children dear, was it yesterday?

Children dear, were we long alone?
" The sea grows stormy, the little ones
    moan.
Long prayers," I said, "in the world they
    say.
Come," I said, and we rose through the
    surf in the bay.
We went up the beach, by the sandy down
Where the sea-stocks bloom, to the white-
    walled town,
Through the narrow, paved streets, where
    all was still,
To the little grey church on the windy hill.
From the church came a murmur of folk at
    their prayers,
But we stood without in the cold-blowing
    airs.
We climbed the graves, on the stones
    worn with rains,
And we gazed up the aisle through the
    small leaded panes.
She sat by the pillar; we saw her clear;
" Margaret, hist! Come quick, we are here
Dear heart," I said, " we are long alone.
The sea grows stormy, the little ones moan."
But, ah! she gave me never a look,
For her eyes were sealed to the holy book.
Loud prays the priest; shut stands the
    door.
Come away, children, call no more.
Come away, come away, call no more.

Down, down, down;
    Down to the depths of the sea.
She sits at her wheel in the humming town,
    Singing most joyfully.
Hark what she sings: " O joy, O joy,
For the humming street, and the child
    with its toy,
For the priest, and the bell, and the holy
    well,
    For the wheel where I spun,
    And the blessed light of the sun."
And so she sings her fill,
    Singing most joyfully,
Till the shuttle falls from her hand
And the whizzing wheel stands still.

She steals to the window and looks at the
    sand;
And over the sand at the sea;

And her eyes are set in a stare,
And anon there breaks a sigh,
And anon there drops a tear
From sorrow-clouded eye
And a heart sorrow-laden,
    A long, long sigh,
For the cold, strange eyes of a little
    Mermaiden,
And the gleam of her golden hair.

Come away, away, children,
    Come children, come down;
The hoarse wind blows colder;
    Lights shine in the town.
She will start from her slumber
    When gusts shake the door;
She will hear the winds howling,
    Will hear the waves roar.
We shall see, while above us
    The waves roar and whirl,
A ceiling of amber,
    A pavement of pearl.
Singing: " Here came a mortal,
    But faithless was she;
And alone dwell for ever
    The kings of the sea."

But, children, at midnight,
    When soft the winds blow;
When clear falls the moonlight,
    When spring-tides are low;
When sweet airs come seaward
    From heaths starred with broom,
And high rocks throw mildly
    On the blanched sands a gloom;
Up the still, glistening beaches,
    Up the creeks we will hie:
Over banks of bright seaweed
    The ebb-tide leaves dry.
We will gaze from the sand-hills
    At the white, sleeping town,
At the church on the hillside—
    And then come back down.
Singing: " There dwells a loved one,
    But cruel is she;
She left lonely for ever
    The kings of the sea."

THE END OF LIFE

These four fine lines are those most quoted from the long
poem " Festus," by Philip James Bailey (1816-1902), a
Nottingham poet, once much admired but now seldom read.

WE live in deeds, not years; in thoughts,
    not breaths;
In feelings, not in figures on a dial.
We should count time by heart-throbs.
    He most lives
Who thinks most, feels the noblest, acts
    the best.

GIRLS AND BOYS COME OUT TO PLAY

{Girls and boys come out to play, The
{Leave your sup-per and leave your sleep:

moon doth shine as bright as day.}
Come to your play-fel-lows in the street.}

{Come with a whoop and come with a call,
{Up the lad-der and down the wall, a

Come with a good will or not at all.}
half-pen-ny loaf will serve you all.}

THIS IS THE HOUSE THAT JACK BUILT

THIS is the House that Jack built.

THIS is the Malt that lay in the House that Jack built.

THIS is the Rat that ate the Malt
That lay in the House that Jack built.

THIS is the Cat that killed the Rat
That ate the Malt
That lay in the House that Jack built.

THIS is the Dog that worried the Cat
That killed the Rat that ate the Malt
That lay in the House that Jack built.

THIS is the Cow with the crumpled horn
That tossed the Dog that worried the Cat
That killed the Rat that ate the Malt
That lay in the House that Jack built.

THIS is the Maiden all forlorn
That milked the Cow with the crumpled horn
That tossed the Dog that worried the Cat
That killed the Rat that ate the Malt
That lay in the house that Jack built.

354

THIS IS THE MAN ALL TATTERED AND TORN

THIS is the Man all tattered and torn
    That kissed the Maiden all forlorn
That milked the Cow with the crumpled horn
That tossed the Dog that worried the Cat
That killed the Rat that ate the Malt
That lay in the House that Jack built.

THIS is the Priest all shaven and shorn
    That married the man all tattered and torn
That kissed the Maiden all forlorn
That milked the Cow with the crumpled horn
That tossed the Dog that worried the Cat
That killed the Rat that ate the Malt
That lay in the House that Jack built.

THIS is the Cock that crowed in the morn
    That wakened the Priest all shaven and shorn
That married the Man all tattered and torn
That kissed the Maiden all forlorn
That milked the Cow with the crumpled horn
That tossed the Dog that worried the Cat
That killed the Rat that ate the Malt
That lay in the House that Jack built.

THIS is the Farmer that sowed the corn
    That fed the Cock that crowed in the morn
That wakened the Priest all shaven and shorn
That married the Man all tattered and torn
That kissed the Maiden all forlorn
That milked the Cow with the crumpled horn
That tossed the Dog that worried the Cat
That killed the Rat that ate the Malt
That lay in the House that Jack built.

I LOVE little pussy
    Her coat is so warm,
And if I don't hurt her,
    She'll do me no harm.
So I'll not pull her tail,
    Or drive her away.
But pussy and I
    Very gently will play.
She will sit by my side,
    And I'll give her her food,
And she'll like me because
    I am gentle and good.

SEE a pin and pick it up,
    All the day you'll have good luck;
See a pin and let it lay,
Bad luck you'll have all the day.

MY house is red—a little house,
    A happy child am I;
I laugh and play the livelong day,
    I hardly ever cry.
I have a tree, a green, green tree,
    To shade me from the sun;
And under it I often sit,
    When all my work is done.
My little basket I will take,
    And trip into the town.
When next I'm there I'll buy
        some cake,
And spend my bright half-crown.

MY dear, do you know,
    How a long time ago
Two poor little children,
    Whose names I don't know,
Were stolen away on a fine
        summer's day,
And left in a wood, as I've
        heard people say?
And when it was night,
So sad was their plight,
    The sun it went down,
And the moon gave no light.
They sobbed and they sighed,
        and they bitterly cried,
And the poor little things, they
        lay down and died.
    And when they were dead,
    The robins so red
        Brought strawberry-leaves,
    And over them spread.
    And all the day long
    They sang them this song :
" Poor babes in the wood!
    Poor babes in the wood!
And don't you remember the
        babes in the wood? "

I NEVER saw a Purple Cow,
    I never hope to see one;
But I can tell you, anyhow,
    I'd rather see than be one.

POETRY

MARY MORISON

This most lovely song was written by Robert Burns while he was still at home, working on his father's farm and unknown to the world. There is a doubt who was meant by Mary Morison. The last two lines of the second and third verses are beautiful examples of saying much in the simplest of words. *Trysted* means *appointed;* *bide the stoure* means *endure the dust;* and *braw* means *handsome.*

O MARY, at thy window be,
    It is the wished, the trysted hour,
Those smiles and glances let me see
    That makes the miser's treasure poor.
How blithely wad I bide the stoure,
    A weary slave frae sun to sun,
Could I the rich reward secure,
    The lovely Mary Morison.

Yestreen, when to the trembling string
    The dance gaed through the lighted ha',
To thee my fancy took its swing;
    I sat but neither heard nor saw;
Though this was fair, and that was braw,
    And yon the toast of a' the town,
I sighed, and said amang them a',
    " Ye are na Mary Morison."

O Mary, canst thou wreck his peace
    Wha for thy sake wad gladly die?
Or canst thou break that heart of his
    Whase only faut is loving thee?
If love for love thou wilt na gie,
    At least be pity to me shown:
A thought ungentle canna be
    The thought o' Mary Morison.

CONSIDER IT AGAIN

Arthur Hugh Clough, who wrote this poem, was a favourite scholar of Dr. Arnold, the famous headmaster of Rugby School. Clough had an undecided mind. He loved to think of every side of any question, and seldom came to any fixed conclusion. In the last verse he seems to regret that other people do not turn things over and over in their minds in the same way. But he did it too much. Yet he was a real poet, and made a considerable reputation.

OLD things need not be therefore true,
    O brother men, nor yet the new;
Ah, still awhile the thought retain,
And yet consider it again!

The souls of now two thousand years
Have laid up here their toils and fears,
And all the earnings of their pain;
Ah, yet consider it again!

We! What do we see? Each a space
Of some few yards before his face;
Does that the whole wide plan explain?
Ah, yet consider it again!

Alas, the great world goes its way,
And takes the truth from each new day;
They do not quit, nor can retain,
Far less consider it again.

THE STARS

Barry Cornwall (1787–1874) was one of our lesser poets. His real name was Bryan Waller Procter. You will notice that in these verses, instead of expressing wonder as to what the stars may be, he is content to think of them as among the glories of God's world, that fill our souls with reverent joy.

THEY glide upon their endless way,
    For ever calm, for ever bright,
No blind hurry, no delay,
    Mark the Daughters of the Night;
They follow in the track of Day,
    In divine delight.

And oh! how still beneath the stars
    The once wild, noisy Earth doth lie;
As though she now forsook her jars,
    And caught the quiet of the sky.
Pride sleeps; and Love (with all his scars)
    In smiling dreams doth lie.

Shine on, sweet orbed souls, for aye,
    For ever calm, for ever bright:
We ask not whither lies your way,
    Nor whence ye came, nor what your light.
Be still—a dream throughout the day,
    A blessing through the night!

AN EVENING HYMN

One of the most beautiful of hymns for the evening hour is the following, written by the Rev. James Drummond Burns, a Scottish minister, who was born in 1823 and died at Mentone in 1864. Samuel, of course, was one of the great prophets of Israel, and in this hymn his qualities of mind and heart are chosen as worthy of our emulation.

HUSHED was the evening hymn,
    The temple courts were dark;
The lamp was burning dim
    Before the sacred ark,
When suddenly a voice divine
Rang through the silence of the shrine.

Oh, give me Samuel's ear—
    The open ear, O Lord!
Alive and quick to hear
    Each whisper of Thy word;
Like him to answer at Thy call,
And to obey Thee first of all.

Oh, give me Samuel's heart!
    A lowly heart, that waits
When in Thy house Thou art;
    Or watches at Thy gates
By day and night—a heart that still
Moves at the breathing of Thy will.

Oh, give me Samuel's mind!
    A sweet, unmurmuring faith,
Obedient and resigned
    To Thee in life and death:
That I may read, with child-like eyes
Truths that are hidden from the wise.

357

A LAUGHING SONG

Many of William Blake's Nature songs, such as that given here, might be described as songs of the joy of the earth. The idea of Nature being glad is, of course, as ancient as thought; and we find such phrases in the Bible as " Let the hills be joyful " and " The trees of the field shall clap their hands."

WHEN the green woods laugh with the
    voice of joy,
And the dimpling stream runs laughing
    by;
When the air does laugh with our merry
    wit,
And the green hill laughs with the noise of
    it;

When the meadows laugh with lively
    green,
And the grasshopper laughs in the merry
    scene;
When Mary, and Susan, and Emily,
With their sweet, round mouths sing,
    " Ha, ha, he! "

When the painted birds laugh in the shade,
Where our table with cherries and nuts is
    spread:
Come live, and be merry, and join with me
To sing the sweet chorus of " Ha, ha, he! "

MY BOAT IS ON THE SHORE

Lord Byron, a great poet, was a wayward, unwise man, and managed his life so badly that he had to leave his native land in great disfavour. In this poem to his faithful friend Tom Moore he pretended he did not care, but he was really very bitter in spirit. Byron's trust in his friend was well deserved. If he could have thought about more people in the same way he would have lived and died a far happier man.

MY boat is on the shore
    And my bark is on the sea;
But before I go, Tom Moore,
    Here's a double health to thee!

Here's a sigh to those who love me,
    And a smile to those who hate;
And, whatever sky's above me,
    Here's a heart for every fate.

Though the ocean roar around me,
    Yet it still shall bear me on:
Though a desert should surround me,
    It hath springs that may be won.

Were't the last drop in the well,
    As I gasped upon the brink,
Ere my fainting spirit fell
    'Tis to thee that I would drink.

With that water as this wine,
    The libation I would pour
Should be: " Peace with thine and mine,
    And a health to thee, Tom Moore! "

THE PATRIOT

The first line of this poem by Robert Browning is one of the most quoted in modern poetry. The poem was written to illustrate the fickleness of popular applause. History abounds in examples of men who have been hailed as heroes by the mob and a little later been hounded to death by the same mob. The wise man is he who has the strength to look with contempt upon the favour of the crowd, knowing that they who acclaim him as a patriot would, if it served their purpose, denounce him as a traitor.

IT was roses, roses, all the way,
    With myrtle mixed in my path like
      mad;
The house-roofs seemed to heave and sway,
    The church-spires flamed, such flags
      they had,
A year ago on this very day.

The air broke into a mist with bells,
    The old walls rocked with the crowd
      and cries.
Had I said, " Good folk mere noise repels;
    But give me your sun from yonder
      skies! "
They had answered, " And afterward,
    what else? "

Alack, it was I who leaped at the sun
    To give it my loving friends to keep!
Naught man could do have I left undone:
    And you see my harvest, what I reap
This very day, now a year is run.

There's nobody on the house-tops now—
    Just a palsied few at the windows set;
For the best of the sight is, all allow,
    At the Shambles' Gate; or, better yet,
By the very scaffold's foot, I trow.

I go in the rain, and, more than needs,
    A rope cuts both my wrists behind;
And I think, by the feel, my forehead
    bleeds,
    For they fling, whoever has a mind,
Stones at me for my year's misdeeds.

Thus I entered, and thus I go!
    In triumphs people have dropped down
    dead.
" Paid by the world, what dost thou owe
    Me? " God might question; now, in-
    stead,
'Tis God shall repay; I am safer so.

THE SELKIRK GRACE

Robert Burns made rhymes to suit all occasions. This one is generally used at dinners held in his memory.

SOME hae meat, and canna eat,
    And some wad eat that want it;
But we hae meat and we can eat,
    And sae the Lord be thankit.

The Story of Where Power Comes From, What It Does, & How It Works

An electric magnet used for unloading scrap-metal. *Reproduced by courtesy of Electrical Review*

THE OCEAN OF POWER WE LIVE IN

EVERY ship in the world owes its safety and its guidance to the compass.

Every boy and girl knows that a compass needle points to the North. Whichever way you turn, the little compass held in the palm of your hand will show you where to look for the North.

It does so for two reasons. The compass needle is a magnet, and the Earth is a huge magnet ; and magnets affect each other by means of some invisible power which can pass through a stone wall, a glass window, a plate of wax, or any of the simple materials that would entirely shut out electricity.

It is very important to try to imagine magnetism as a force spread out in space, and existing throughout space, no matter what it may be otherwise filled with.

The mysterious force of magnetism was discovered over 2000 years ago by the shepherds of Asia Minor. As we have already seen, on the slopes of the mountains there is found an abundance of hard, black mineral, and the shepherds noticed that bits of this rocky substance would cling to the iron-shod ends of their crooks.

This mineral was an ore of iron, and was found in the district of Magnesia, from which the power of magnetism took its name. The ore became known as the magnes-stone ; then, when it was found that a piece of the stone, if hung on a thread, would always point in one direction, it came to be called the leading-stone, or the lodestone.

There were wonderful legends about the mysterious lodestone in the Middle Ages. Magnetic mountains were supposed to exist which would draw the iron nails out of ships if they approached too closely. Even after the first primitive compasses were made with bits of the lodestone itself sailors would fear that evil mountains of magnetic power would lead the compass astray and bring them to destruction.

The compass first appeared in Europe sometime during the twelfth century. A tiny bar of iron was touched with a piece of lodestone, whereupon it acquired the powers of a magnet, and it was then mounted on a little piece of wood or cork which floated in a dish of water; later on it was rudely pivoted, but in neither case was there anything to show the points of the compass; it was merely known that the "needle" pointed North and South.

Now, if a magnet, when free to run, will always point to the two poles of the Earth, we can easily understand that there must be some special power possessed by the poles, and it is not surprising to learn that

ELECTRICITY · WIRELESS · OIL · GAS · MOTORS · ENGINES · SHIPS

the Earth is itself a huge magnet, floating, as it were, in an ocean of magnetic force which we can discover, measure, and make use of at any point on the globe.

To understand how this can be we must first learn how the magnet force of a substance shows itself. William Gilbert, physician to Elizabeth the First, did much good work in the early days of frictional electricity, and made many remarkable discoveries about the magnet. He found that the power of a magnet has nothing to do with its *shape*; but it will always display a maximum of power at two opposite spots—the magnetic poles. If you stroke a steel knitting needle a few times from end to end with a magnet, and thus make *it* a magnet, and then roll it in some fine iron filings, you will find on lifting it up that a tuft of filings clings to each end, but that none cling to it anywhere else. All the power seems to pour out of the poles, but the poles are always connected by a field of magnetic power that falls outside the magnet itself, in the form of invisible lines running from one pole to the other.

WHY STEEL HOLDS MAGNETISM AND IRON LOSES IT

One of the most remarkable things about magnetism is that so very few substances can be made into a magnet. In spite of all the scientific research that has gone on, we are left today with nothing more than the iron of the ancient lodestone.

A few other things are mildly magnetic —the metals nickel and cobalt, liquid oxygen, and so on; but iron is so powerful in this respect that it stands out among metals as absolutely unique. An electric current can turn a lifeless lump of iron into a living giant with more than human strength. A spell can be cast upon a piece of iron which endows it with this gigantic power for just the period an engineer desires; with a movement of his hand he can destroy its power and leave it a lifeless piece of metal. Soft iron behaves quite differently from hardened steel; soft iron is magnetic only as long as it is under the influence of another magnet; steel, once made a magnet, remains so.

We know that iron, like any other substance, is composed of molecules. These molecules, the "bricks" of which iron, and every other substance, is built, are thrown together by Nature with no sort of arrangement, no order. But once the

magic influence of magnetism is used on a piece of iron the molecules arrange themselves in line and lie in an orderly manner, all pointing in the same direction. It is this orderliness which is the secret of the magnet. Soft iron is like an undisciplined regiment of soldiers; once the influence of the master magnet is removed the molecules fall out of place, there is no more order in them, and the magnetic power is lost.

Steel is stiff and enduring; the molecules, once arranged, never go back to disorder, and so the magic power bestowed on steel remains. We thus have what are known as *permanent magnets*, of which the horse-shoe pattern is known to every boy and girl.

HOW THINGS ALIKE PUSH AWAY AND THINGS UNLIKE COME TOGETHER

What a wonderful thing it would be if we could see this invisible power at work! Yet we can actually watch it through the agency of tiny pieces of iron. If we put a magnet under a sheet of paper, and sprinkle some iron filings on the paper, the filings will be drawn to the lines of force or magnetic power of the magnet, and will take up quite definite paths.

We can not only see that lines of force between a north and south pole seem to show the two poles trying to clutch each other in their eagerness to come together, but we can see the obvious repulsion which one north pole feels for another north pole, or a south pole for a south. The lines of force clearly show what the "like" poles think of each other. Magnetism, in fact, follows the same rules as electricity—like poles repel one another; unlike poles attract one another.

THE EARTH AS A VAST MAGNET WITH LINES OF FORCE ACROSS IT

Although the Earth is a sphere, it is also a vast ball-shaped magnet with two ends, each of which is a magnetic pole of opposite properties. We might compare it with an orange, with its stringy core running through the middle. The core itself represents the true magnet, terminating in a top and bottom which are the North and South Poles, and from these poles a field of magnetic force stretches over the skin of the orange. In the Earth this means that lines of force stretch from the Northern Arctic regions to the South Pole, so that the whole surface of the world is clothed with a magnetic field which can be measured at any spot, and will always have such an effect on a compass needle that its north pole will point to the top of the core, and its south pole to the bottom.

There is something a little wrong with the Earth in this respect, because the magnetic poles are not quite the same as the actual North and South Poles. A compass needle does not point to the true North, but to the magnetic north, so that a ship which followed a course directed by a magnetic needle would not sail quite in the right direction. The mariner must take into consideration this difference, which he calls the *variation* ; more often it is called the *declination*.

A wonderful feature of this declination is that it varies from day to day, even from hour to hour. The magnetic poles of

the position of the magnetic poles was found to take about 470 years.

Another important feature of a compass needle was discovered in 1576 by Robert Norman, an English instrument-maker. He used to make compass needles and balance them 'in a horizontal position before magnetising them. In this way he discovered that as soon as the needle was made magnetic it no longer remained horizontal, but its north pole always pointed downwards towards the earth. This was afterwards known as the *dip*, and Norman found that in London the angle of dip was about 71 degrees. It is quite easy to see this for ourselves. If a steel knitting needle be suspended by a piece of fine thread tied exactly at the middle so that it hangs parallel with the table, and

An electric magnet lifting a heavy ball used for crushing scrap metal by falling on it.

An electric magnet doing the work of dozens of men.

These photographs are of electric magnets made by E. G. Appleby and Company.

the Earth are always changing, ever so slightly, in position. It is as if this immense world-force were fidgeting about in its great prison. In addition to this daily change in position of the magnetic north and south poles there are bigger, but much more gradual, changes, one taking place in a regular way every year and known as the *annular change*, another taking several centuries. In 1580 the magnetic north was more than 11 degrees too much to the east of the true North, as indicated by a compass needle in London; in 1800 it was 24 degrees too much in the West; by 1940 it had come back to within 13 degrees of the true North. This gradual cycle of changes in

if the needle is then magnetised by stroking it a few times with a good horse-shoe magnet, the needle's north pole will point towards the table. In doing this, care must be taken that when suspended the needle points due North and South, which it will quickly do if allowed to swing freely of its own accord. The line pointing due magnetic north and south at any part of the world's surface is called the *magnetic meridian*.

No satisfactory explanation of this marvellous natural power has yet been discovered. The strength of the Earth's magnetic field at any spot is certainly slight, but its value is infinite merely because it has made possible the navigation of the seas, without which there would have been no intercourse between the nations. What could be done were all the magnetic power of the Earth concentrated at one spot? We can obtain a little idea of this when we see what remarkable lifting power even a piece of lodestone has.

Sir Isaac Newton is said to have worn in a ring a tiny lodestone which weighed three grains, and this scrap of magnetic rock could lift nearly 250 times its weight, or 746 grains. A large and powerful lodestone sent by a Chinese emperor as a present to a king of Portugal could lift a weight of 300 pounds. But what must have been the delight of early philosophers when they discovered, by stroking a piece of steel with a bit of lodestone, not only that the magic power was passed on to the steel, but that the lodestone itself lost nothing of its power by so doing! A thousand magnets can be made with a permanent horse-shoe magnet, which becomes actually stronger as the result. Does there not seem to be here a clue to the secret of perpetual motion!

THE MANTLE OF MAGNETIC POWER WHICH CLOTHES THE EARTH

In the beginning of the seventeenth century Galileo discovered this method of making magnets of steel by means of the lodestone, and thus the *natural* magnet gradually gave place to the *artificial* one. Soon afterwards William Gilbert discovered that magnets could indeed be made by means of the Earth's magnetic field, and bundles of thin magnets in this way were bound together, the north poles all at one end and the south poles at the other, and from these stronger magnets were made, and from them stronger magnets still.

We shall see later that by passing an electric current round a piece of iron it can be so strongly magnetised that it can be made to lift far heavier weights than any artificial magnet ; the electric magnet has today entirely replaced the artificial steel magnet, except for a few simple purposes and for the mariner's compass.

The mantle of magnetic power with which the Earth is clothed is often upset by changes in the magnetic state of the Sun—itself a gigantic magnet of doubtless much vaster power. Magnetic storms take place from time to time, when the delicate instruments of observatories are much disturbed. Magnetic storms are usually more frequent at times when we see the aurora borealis, or northern lights. The effect of these storms is seen by means of delicate recording instruments, which trace hour by hour the changes in the *angle of declination*. Imagine a delicately-poised magnetic needle on some part of which is fixed a tiny mirror. A spot of light is reflected by this mirror on a moving photographic film which travels at a steady rate by means of a small clock-work motor.

WHAT HAPPENS TO A NEEDLE IN A MAGNETIC STORM

As long as the needle remains steady the spot of light will remain still, and when the film is developed a perfectly straight line will appear in the photograph. During a magnetic storm the declination of the needle will vary, and the needle will move from side to side of the magnetic meridian. Instead, then, of getting a straight line in the photograph, we shall get a zigzag line, due to the spot of light from the mirror dancing about. In this way every tiny change in the declination of the needle is registered with amazing accuracy, and thus we can obtain records of the effects wrought by all magnetic storms.

Great disturbances of the Earth's magnetism are usually accompanied by disturbances on the surface of the Sun on the same day, and as a rule we are warned of a really big magnetic storm by smaller disturbances which occur three or four days beforehand. These storms are always prevalent and of unusual severity when large sun-spots are observed, and in years of great activity on the Sun's surface the magnetic variations are most marked.

The marvellous displays of light which we see in the northern regions, especially in summer time, are closely connected with sun-spots and their magnetic storms.

MYSTERIES OF MAGNETISM WHICH REMAIN UNSOLVED

In spite of all the knowledge we have today, of all that modern science has revealed, we are still supremely ignorant of the real causes of natural magnetism and of the things that are wrought by it, and it is only in this century, the greatest century of science, that we have discovered that even electrons in the atom, whirling round in spiral paths with incredible speed, create their own magnetic fields in their tiny worlds.

Imperishable Thoughts of Men Enshrined in the Books of the World

Chaucer as we find him in an old book, pointing to the poem of his friend Occleve

OUR FIRST STORYTELLERS

THE first Englishman who wrote in our language poetry that is felt to be great, used it to tell tales; and the first writer of an English book in prose that remains a great classic work was also a famous tale-teller.

The poet was Geoffrey Chaucer, who died in the year 1400; and the prose-writer was Sir Thomas Malory, who died about 70 years later. These two stand out as founders of English literature, because they wrote in language we can still understand with very little trouble, books that will always be read for pleasure.

The two books of old yet living stories, one in verse and one in prose, were among the first to be printed in England by William Caxton, the earliest English printer. Geoffrey Chaucer's Canterbury Tales had been spread about the land in manuscript for 90 years when Caxton printed them in 1477; and Sir Thomas Malory's Morte d'Arthur, of which no manuscript copy exists, was printed in 1485, about 15 years after it was written. Here we start the story of English books by giving glimpses of these two first collections of romances, and by telling something of the men who wrote them.

Geoffrey Chaucer will always be read because his poetry is full of beauty; because very largely he shaped our fine English language into its present form; and because he pictured the English people as they were six centuries ago, and has shown us that they were then the same kind of people we are now, with the same kind of thoughts, and caring for the things we still admire.

When Chaucer was a young man of about 22, that was in 1362, the language spoken by the common people of England was adopted, both in Parliament and in the Law Courts, as the official language of the country. Before that, for nearly 300 years, French had been the language of the governing classes.

But it had never been accepted by the mass of Englishmen. The people's older language, however, which we now call Anglo-Saxon, and only understand when we have studied it, had changed greatly, and had absorbed many words from the French; and, as time went on, the kings and governing people felt themselves to be English and not French, and learned the rapidly altering common tongue.

So the time came for a new English, based on Anglo-Saxon and including many words from the French, to be made the standard tongue.

Here was a fine opportunity for a great writer to use this enriched language, and pass it on through books which all would admire. Chaucer, who was thoroughly English in birth, character, and spirit, was the man who did this. He made the English people proud of their national language as it was used in his books to express every necessary shade of meaning.

OLD CHAUCER'S PICTURES OF THE MEN AND WOMEN OF HIS TIME

He was just the man to do it, for he was in touch with all kinds of people, rich and poor, lofty and lowly. His father was what we should call a London business man. Geoffrey himself was well educated, brought up as a page in a prince's household, with service as a young soldier following, in France, where he was captured and then ransomed. Later, he was sent abroad on the king's business to several countries, and afterwards became what we now call a civil servant, and a knight of the shire for Kent, and a Member of Parliament. So he was a man of wide experience, acquainted with all sorts and conditions of people.

At first, his writings were chiefly translations from the French, or imitations of French models in poetry. Afterwards, he was attracted and influenced by Italian poetry; and it was not till he was 40, and had settled down in England, that he wrote the distinctively English poems which have made him for ever famous.

Though Chaucer's writings chiefly take the form of tales, it is not his stories that are most interesting to us today, but the pictures he gives of the men and women of his time. And this side of his genius—his observation, humane spirit, and descriptive power—is best seen in the Prologue to the Canterbury Tales.

THE PILGRIMS THROUGH KENT, AND THE TALES THEY TOLD

The shrine of Thomas à Becket at Canterbury was a great place of pilgrimage at that period, and Chaucer, as knight of the shire for Kent, must have been familiar with all the features of the pilgrims' progress, which he finally used as a framework for a number of tales he had been writing for many years.

He imagines twenty-nine people, including himself, gathered at the Tabard Inn, in Southwark, to travel together to the Canterbury shrine, the landlord of the inn acting as guide, and as manager of the procession. To amuse the pilgrims on the journey the landlord proposes that each member of the company shall tell two tales on the way to Canterbury, and two more during the return journey, and that the teller of the best tale shall be entertained at supper by the rest of the pilgrims when they reach the inn again.

Twenty of these tales are told, and four more are left unfinished, or are interrupted. The collection of tales remains a fragment; we do not know who won the supper. Nor does it matter. For it is the array of old-time travellers, and the character sketch of each, that fascinates us—the courtly knight, the lively squire, the honest yeoman, the dainty prioress, the friar, an adept at begging, the Oxford clerk in his threadbare cape, and lean as his horse, the poor parish parson, the lawyer pretending to be busier than he is, the doctor more than half a quack, the pardoner seeking a sale for forgiveness of sin, the country gentleman, or franklin, the tax-collector, the miller, cook, dyer, sailor, merchant, wife of Bath. These, with London burgesses, the landlord, and the poet himself, fill up the human picture and bring a dead world to life.

THE POETRY THAT IS ALWAYS SMOOTH AND REGULAR

The opening lines of the Prologue show us Chaucer's love of country scenes—a delight he shares with his country's poets, before his time and ever since; his style in verse; his use of syllables which we do not pronounce; and his accenting of words from the French on their last syllable, where we accent their first syllable.

Chaucer's verse is always smooth and regular. If, in reading it, we make it limp and hobble, we are not reading it aright.

Thus Aprille (April) has three syllables; showres (showers) two; croppes (crops) two; younge, halfe, smalle, fowles (fowls or birds) all have two syllables; while liquor, virtue, Nature, and corages (meaning hearts) are all stressed on the second syllables, not the first. If this is remembered, the lines will run and will rhyme quite smoothly.

When that Aprillé with his showrés soot (*sweet*)
The drought of March hath piercéd to the root,
And bathéd every vein in such liquor
Of which virtue engendered is the flower,
When Zephirus eke with his sweté breeth (*breath*)
Inspiréd hath in every holt and heath
The tender croppés, and the youngé sun
Hath in the Ram his halfé course y-run,
And smallé fowlés maken melodye,
That sleepen all the night with open eye—
So pricketh them Natúre in their coráges—(hearts)
Then longen folk to go on pilgrimages.

Paraphrased into present-day prose, the poet says that when the sweet showers of April have moistened the roots that have been dried by the March winds, and have caused the sap to rise and give birth to the flowers, and the mild spring wind, early in April, has given life to the tender growths of every wood and common, and the birds make music late and early, scarcely sleeping by night, then Nature also touches the hearts of men, and makes them long to go journeying afield.

With the poetry of spring, then, Chaucer begins his poem before he brings his pilgrim company together, in these smoothly running lines.

> Befell it in that season on a day,
> In Southwark by the Tabard as I lay,
> Ready to wenden on my pilgrimage
> To Canterbury, with full devout coráge (*heart*)
> At night were come unto that hostelrye
> Well nine-and-twenty in a companye,
> Of sundry folk, by áventure y-fall (*chance*)
> In fellowship, and pilgrims were they all,
> That toward Canterbury wolden ride.

As a sample of the old-time pilgrims travelling with the poet, and telling their tales on horseback to relieve the tedium of the road, note this:

THE PERFECT, GENTLE KNIGHT

> A Knight there was and that a worthy man,
> That from the timé that he first began
> To riden out, he lovéd chivalry,
> Truth, and honoúr, freedom and courtesy.
> Full worthy was he in his lordés werre, (*war*)
> And thereto had he ridden, no man ferre. (*farther*)
> At mortal combats he had been fifteen,
> And foughten for our faith at Tramysene
> In listés thriés, and aye slain his foe. (*thrice*)
> This ilké worthy Knight had been also (*same*)
> Sometime with the lord of Palatye
> Against another heathen in Turkye,
> And evermore he had a sovereign prize.
> And though that he was worthy he was wise,
> And of his port as meek as is a maid.
> He never yet no villainy ne'er said
> In all his life, unto no manner of wight. (*person*)
> He was a very perfect, gentle Knight.

The Knight's son, The Young Squire, is described with equal delicacy and charm.

THE YOUNG SQUIRE

Crulle means curled ; delyvere, nimble ; chyvachie, active service ; space, opportunity.

> With him there was his son, a young Squiér,
> A lovyere and a lusty bachelor, (*lover*)
> With lockes crulle as they were laid in press.
> Of twenty years of age he was, I guess.
> Of his stature he was of even length, (*average size*)
> And wonderly delyvere and great of strength.
> And he had been sometime in chyvachie
> In Flanders, in Artois, and Picardy,
> And borne him well, as of so little space,
> In hope to standen in his lady's grace.
> Embroidered was he, as it were a mead (*meadow*)

All full of freshé flowrés white and rede. (*red*)
> Singing he was or fluting all the day,
> He was as fresh as is the month of May.
> Short was his gown, with sleevés long and wide,
> Well could he sit on horse and fairé ride.
> He couldé songés make and well indite,
> Joust and eke dance, and well pourtray and write.
> Courteous he was, lowly, and serviceáble,
> And carved before his father at the table.

This picture of the character, dress, and accomplishments of a young gentleman of the period has as companion portrait a pen drawing of a lady, a Prioress, whose dainty manners are a guide to etiquette in the fourteenth century.

THE PRIORESS

Fetisly means fluently ; ferthing, morsel.

> There was also a nun, a Prioress,
> That of her smiling was full simple and coy,
> Her greatest oath was but by Seinté Loy,
> And she was clepéd madame Eglentine. (*called*)
> Full well she sung the servicé divine,
> Entunéd in her nose full seemély. (*seemly*)
> And French she spake full fair and fetisly,
> After the school of Stratford-atté-Bow,
> But French of Paris was to her unknowe.
> At meaté well y-taught was she withal,
> She let no morsel from her lippés fall,
> Nor wet her fingers in her saucé deep.
> Well could she carry a morsel, and well keep
> That no drop ever fell upon her breast.
> In courtesy was set full much her leste. (*pleasure*)
> Her over-lippé wipéd she so clean
> That in her cup there was no ferthing seen,
> Of greasé when she drunken had her draught;
> Full seemély after her meat she raught. (*reached*)

The most complete and tender of the sketches is that of the parish parson, the fore-runner of several similar pictures in later English literature.

THE GOOD PARSON

> A good man was there of religioún,
> And was a pooré parson of a town;
> But rich he was of holy thought and work:
> He was also a learnéd man, a clerk
> That Christé's gospel truély would preach
> His parish'ners devoutly would he teach.
> Benign he was and wonder diligent,
> And in adversity full patiént.
> Wide was his parish, and houses far asunder,
> But he nor lefté not, for rain or thunder,
> In sickness nor in mischief to visite
> The farthest in his parish, much and lite, (*little*)
> Upon his feet, and in his hand a staff.
> And though he holy was and virtuous
> He was to sinful man not despitous, (*merciless*)
> Nor of his speeché dangerous nor digne, (*proud*)
> But in his teaching discreet and benign,
> To drawen folk to heaven by fairness,
> By good ensample was his business.
> A better priest I trow that nowhere none is;
> He waited for no pomp and reverence,
> Nor makéd him a spicéd conscience,
> But Christés lore and his Apostle twelve
> He taught; but first he followed it himself.

As a character sketch of a common type that of the landlord of the inn is perhaps the most vivid. Big, bright-eyed, outspoken, jolly, he acts as the master of the ceremonies. When he asks Chaucer to tell a tale this is how he calls the attention of the company to the poet.

And then at erst he lookéd upon me,
And sadé thus: "What man are thou?" quod he;
"Thou lookest as thou wouldest find an hare,
And ever upon the ground I see thee stare.
Approaché near, and look up merrily.
Now, ware you, sirs, and let this man have place:
He in the waist is
  shape as well as
  I;
This were no poppet
  in arm t'embrace
For any w o m a n,
  small and fair of
  face.
He seemeth elvish
  in his counten-
  ance
For unto no wight
  doth he dalliance."
(*Gossips with no one*)

Chaucer hav-
ing begun a story
in s i n g-s o n g
rhyme, the land-
lord p r e s e n t l y
stops him ab-
ruptly with the
words:

Thou doest naught
  else but depend-
  est time (*waste*)
Sir, at a word, thou
  shalt no longer
  rhyme.

W h e r e u p o n
Chaucer breaks
o f f a n d t e l l s
another tale, this
time in prose.

We have another picture of Chaucer sketched by himself in the prologue to his Legend of Good Women.

And as for me, though I ken but lite, (*but little*)
On bookés for to read I me delight,
And to them give-I faith and full credénce,
And in mine heart gave them in reverence
So heartily that there is gamé none
That from my bookés maketh me to gone,
But it be seldom on a holiday,
Save certainly when that the month of May
Is comen, and that I hear the fowlés sing, (*birds*)
And that the flowrés ginnen for to spring—
Farewell my book and my devotión.

CHAUCER AS THE ARTIST IN THE FAMOUS ELLESMERE MANUSCRIPT DREW HIM

This, then, was the great English poet who, knowing the world, and delighting in the study of his fellow-men, and writing with grace and ease, in a spirit of tolerance and kindness, but of sly humour, helped Wycliffe and Malory to give our language its lasting form.

Of Wycliffe something must be said when the literary influence of the English Bible is considered later. Malory has but a dim existence as a man. All his life for us is found in his book describing the romance of King Arthur and his noble Knights of the Round Table

It m a y be inferred w i t h confidence t h a t Malory w a s a W a r w i c k s h i r e knight w h o, i n the Wars of the Roses, supported t h e Lancastrian side, and when the Yorkists were triumphant, was not forgiven but s u f f e r e d i m-prisonment, and illness while he was in confine-ment. F o r h e turns aside in the story of Sir Tristram to say that sickness is "t h e g r e a t e s t pain a prisoner m a y h a v e." And, again, in the closing sen-tence of his book, he says:

"I pray you all, gentlemen and gentlewomen, that readeth this book of Arthur and his Knights, pray for me while I am alive that God send me good deliverance, and when I am dead I pray you all pray for my soul."

Apparently while he was in prison he collected French books in which various legends that centred on the life of the half-fabulous British King Arthur were preserved, and occupied his solitude by translating them into English. These legends had passed from Wales into France and

CHAUCER AT THE KING'S COURT

had been developed there by French poets, and Malory brought them back by his translations in a more poetic form, though he wrote in prose, than ever they had worn before.

Whether Malory died in prison is not known. It is clear he had no opportunity of revising his book and removing contradictions and blemishes. Caxton received the manuscript, from an unmentioned source, it seems, after Malory's death, and himself prepared it roughly for publication.

In this way one of the most haunting books in any literature reached the public, and has proved itself a mine of rich, though vague, romance for generations of poets. Milton thought of taking it as the theme of his masterpiece before he decided

THE JOLLY PROCESSION OF PILGRIMS WHO RODE WITH CHAUCER ON THE

on Paradise Lost. Tennyson has transposed Malory back into verse in his Idylls of the King ; but, notwithstanding his skill and all the poetic art of four centuries since Malory, he improved little on the wonderful prose of this pioneer in the writing of simple yet beautiful English.

Many parts of the Arthurian Legend preserved by Malory are shadowy, remote, and unreal if we examine them coldly for facts; but as examples of exquisite English these early simple narratives, almost the first in the slow approach toward modern English, remain unsurpassed, and are equalled only in the lovely language of the English Bible. They should all be read; but as a typical example of his perfect style, here is the last look one gets of King Arthur, the central figure in the many stories that make up his Legend.

Then Sir Bedevere took the king upon his back and so went with him to the water side. And when they were at the water side, even fast by the bank hoved a little barge, with many fair ladies in it, and all they had black hoods, and all they wept and shrieked when they saw King Arthur. "Now put me into the barge," said the King. And so he did softly ; and there received him three queens with great mourning ; and so they set them down, and in one of their laps King Arthur laid his head. And then that queen said : "Ah! dear brother, why have ye tarried so long from me? Alas, this wound on your head hath caught over-much cold." And so they rowed from the land and Sir Bedevere beheld all those ladies go from him.

Then Sir Bedevere cried, "Oh, my lord Arthur,

WAY TO CANTERBURY, TELLING THE TALES THE POET WROTE DOWN

what shall become of me, now ye go from me and leave me here alone among mine enemies ? " "Comfort thyself," said the king, "for in me is no trust for to trust in; for I will into the Vale of Avilion to heal me of my grievous wound; and if thou hear never more of me, pray for my soul."

And as soon as Sir Bedevere had lost sight of the barge he wept and wailed, and so took the forest; and so he went all that night, and in the morning he was ware, betwixt two hills, of a chapel and an hermitage.

And read, too, the lament of Sir Hector over his brother, Sir Launcelot.

"Ah! Sir Launcelot," said he, "thou wert head of all Christian knights. And now that there thou liest I dare say thou wert never matched of none earthly knight's hands ; and

thou wert the courtliest knight that ever bare shield ; and thou wert the truest friend to thy lover that ever bestrode horse ; and thou wert the kindest man that ever struck with sword; and thou wert the goodliest person that ever came among the press of knights; and thou wert the meekest man and the gentlest that ever ate in hall among ladies; and thou wert the sternest knight to thy mortal foe that ever put spear in the rest."

In that tribute to Sir Launcelot may be discovered the qualities which Malory and true knights like him looked for in the best type of men; and in the noble writings of Malory, over four and a half centuries ago, one may hear a cadence that harmonises with the idea then generally held of what a fine man should be

"GENTLEMEN, I SALUTE YOU," SAID MAJOR REED TO THE AMERICAN SOLDIERS WHO OFFERED THEMSELVES, AND THEIR LIVES IF NEED BE, TO SAVE THE WORLD FROM YELLOW FEVER

The Great Words that Stir the Hearts and Minds of All Mankind

COURAGE

THERE are many meanings to almost every word we use about human beings, but perhaps there are only two or three of these words which have more meanings than this great and noble word Courage.

Why is that? You have only to find out the origin of the word to discover the reason. It comes to us from a Latin word *cor*, which means *the heart*. What a thing is the heart of man, how full of power and servitude, of goodness and badness, of love and hate, of the godlike and the beast-like; why, it is a whole world in itself—every emotion is there, every feeling, every thought, every vision, every strength; look into the heart of a man, and you see the history of the human race.

See how difficult it is to use the word justly. Many men have been accused of cowardice in war who were full of superb courage in civilian life. Many a man who fought against terrible temptations in civil life, and who kept his heart pure and his soul unblemished, who was a good man and a noble brother, who lived a life of self-sacrifice and loving-kindness—many a man of this order has found it impossible to master his nerves in battle and has had to face a charge of cowardice.

But it is nonsense to call such a man as this a coward. The word comes too easily to our lips. In the sight of God he was no coward. His fault was simply this, that in an unnatural situation he was unable to control his nerves.

We see at once that this word is well worth thinking about. It is something much bigger than a bottle-fly, and something much finer than the sound of a trumpet. In our first story-books it is a brave and glorious word, warming our hearts, stirring our imaginations, making us long to grow up valiant and unconquerable. We say to ourselves, " I too could face a dragon." And we fall asleep at night dreaming that we have drawn a sword against a giant, and that behind the giant are seven roaring lions, each of them more terrible than the other, all of which must be killed by us before we can rescue the enchanted princess from the castle. A grand thing is courage!

But, later on, we get a little tired of this courage, and when we are old enough to think about the words we use, ceasing to speak like parrots, we find that this word courage is like a house of many rooms, each room different from the rest, and all of them leading us on and on till we come to a roof which shows us nothing but the stars.

Let us enter the first of these rooms. There is the daily courage of the miner who descends into the darkness of the

LIBERTY · JUSTICE · SPACE · DISTANCE · MOVEMENT · TRUTH · FAITH

earth and burrows his way for many miles through tunnels, the roofs of which are propped up by logs of wood. There is the courage of the diver who descends to the bottom of the sea, and whose safety depends on a frail mechanism which provides him with air from above. There is the courage of the fireman who faces a tempest of flame to rescue a child's life. There is the courage of the airman flying a new machine, and the courage of the crew of a submarine going down to the depths of the sea. And there is the simple, unheroic-looking courage of the policeman who stands in the midst of the racing traffic of crowded roadways directing the vehicles this way and that.

THE COURAGE OF INQUIRY THAT MAY KILL THE INQUIRER

Pass into another room and you find a man injecting into his veins a fluid which never before has entered the human body. He believes he has discovered a cure for some deadly disease. But he does not know that his cure will work. There is only one way to that knowledge. He must risk his life to prove it.

Enter another room: three men are huddled up in furs, starving to death near the Pole. One of them is writing to a friend in England, the creator of Peter Pan, and his pen sets down these words: " We are pegging out . . . feet frozen, no fuel, and a long way from food; but it would do your heart good to be in our tent, to hear our songs."

Enter another room: a man is here doing some hard and laborious work, which he hates, which he knows can never give him pleasure or satisfaction—dull, dreamy, meaningless, mechanical work.

THE GREAT COURAGE THAT SMILES TO HIDE THE AGONY WITHIN

And his whole outlook is hopeless. At such work he can never rise to be anything else. To the end of his days he will have to go on doing this dull and dreary thing— never something else, never something that he wants to do. Why does he stick to this dull work, cheerfully, happily, making the best of a bad job? Because it brings him wages, and with those wages he can keep his children in decency and happiness, bringing them up to love life, and keep their hearts unspotted from the world.

Enter another room: a child is lying in bed, very pale and very thin. The mother is there at the bedside reading to the child

a funny story. Every now and then she comes to a picture and shows it to the child, and asks: " Look, darling, isn't this a funny picture? " and no one could tell from her voice or the look in her eyes that her heart is breaking. The doctor has told her the worst. But she goes on amusing the child, keeping a brave face, though her agony of soul and brain is greater than any language can express.

Enter another room: it is filled with people who are very happy and playful together. They are wonderfully kind to one another, and yet there is a good deal of chaffing among them, particularly of those who happen to complain. The great thing in this room is to be lively in a subdued way, to tease your companions in a friendly manner, and to be extremely interested in books, or politics, or flowers, or clothes, or even food. Yet most of the people in this happy room never go beyond the four walls in which they dwell in the house with the tragic name—the Home for Incurables.

Now we come to a room which calls for shrewd observation. Do not let us speak until we have looked about and made quite certain that we know what it is we have to do with. A man is here with a rifle. He stands by the window, peering out wild-eyed at the people in the street. He has opposed himself to the will of his nation. He says they are wrong. He will die rather than submit to them.

THE PEOPLE WHO THINK THEY ARE COURAGEOUS IN STICKING TO AN IDEA

What courage! you say. Are you quite sure? Look at the man more closely. Does he strike you as one likely to be right? Is there not something feverish in his eyes, something terribly like arrogance on his lips? Does he not seem to you more like a fanatic than a hero?

That is one of the dangers of this great word—it can give a sort of glory to obstinacy, can throw a sort of halo round pigheadedness. A man may show courage in a bad cause. A man may be marvellously brave in stupidity.

Suppose we found a man who was drinking himself to death, who was impoverishing his family, and bringing dreadful dishonour on a noble name. And suppose we brought doctors to him who proved to him that he was drinking himself into madness and death, and he laughed at them and exclaimed: " I don't

THE RIDE TO THE VICTORY OVER DEATH

THE BRAVEST GIRL WHO EVER LIVED—JOAN OF DOMREMY, THE STAINLESS MAID OF FRANCE

This fine painting by Roland Wheelwright is from a photograph by the Autotype Company

To Face Page 373

care; I am not afraid of madness or of death!" Should we say he was brave?

So, in like manner, you may find in the world people who think they are courageous because they stick to an idea in politics or religion which appeals to them, and which they persist in saying is a right idea and a true idea, although the whole world is against them. These people do not care how much misery they cause to other people. They see poverty widening around them. They see murder on every hand. They see cruelty and brutality on every side of their cause. But they still persist in saying that they are right.

THE POOR SORT OF COURAGE THAT IS BOLD IN DOING WRONG

We realise at once how courage can be debased. It is like music, or literature, or religion: it can be used for wrong things. There is literature that ennobles and literature that degrades. A book by one author makes you feel you will always try to do your best; another makes you feel it does not matter whether you are good or bad.

This is one of the most arresting thoughts that can enter your mind—the power of man to use a sublime thing for a bad purpose. You know that the coinage of a country must be genuine if life is to flourish there, and you know that there are men who make bad coins in order to enrich themselves, never mind how many people they make poor in consequence. So it is with the whole world. It is essential to our safety that we should cherish good thoughts, and keep the moral law, and think more of other people than of ourselves. But there are some people who say : "What do I care for the rest of the world ? I will do whatever I like "; and they persist in doing what they like, even when it is bad, and dangerous, and fatal to the world's happiness.

UNSELFISHNESS THE GREAT TEST OF THE TRUEST COURAGE

True courage lies in the suppression of self. That is the essence of it. Wherever self enters it is a questionable courage. Wherever selflessness is the heart of it, there you may be certain the courage is fine. Wonderful is this test of all truth. We may deceive ourselves here and there, but everybody knows when he is truly unselfish.

There is another form of courage which is worth looking at. We call it Spartan courage. The Spartan mothers told their sons when they went into battle that they were to come back either with their shields or on their shields, that is to say, as victors, or as dead. The mother of John Wesley was a veritable Spartan; she used to whip her children till they could bear pain without weeping.

A few years ago people used to say that Spartan courage was a fine thing. We are not so certain about it now. We are inclined to think that a hardening of the nerves is not good ; that to blunt the senses is to spoil the fineness of the spirit. We say that endurance is a noble thing, but that it is only at its highest when the nerves are sharp and sensitive.

Some people do not feel pain. Some people do not hear a discord in music. Almost any child can be trained to bear pain without a whimper, but many a child brutalised into such a state of insensibility never knows the highest and rarest pleasures of human existence. Courage of this order does not move our admiration. We say that the brave soldier is he who wants to run away and does not. When a man tells us that he does not know what fear is, we do not feel that he is a brave man; we know he is a man with no imagination.

THE MOST BEAUTIFUL COURAGE THE WORLD HAS EVER KNOWN

Compare such courage with the purest and most beautiful courage the world has ever known. There once lived on this Earth a Being who had no thought in His heart except love. He loved children, He loved flowers, He loved birds. So wonderful was His love that he could look through the sin to the heart of the sinner and love that poor troubled heart. He was gentle, tender, compassionate. Everything we can think of as beautiful and gracious was in His soul. Yet, for the sake of His idea, the idea of love, He laid down His life. In silence and meekness He laid it down. He fell into the hands of a brutal soldiery. He suffered every ignominy that flesh can bear. He was reviled, scourged, beaten, spat upon, and finally put to a cruel and lingering death—this gentle and tender creature who shrank from all pain and all cruelty. And He prayed for those who mocked him as He died, prayed for those who spurned His idea that love alone can save mankind from desolation.

This is the courage which unveils for us the stars of God.

THREE MEN OF THE EARLY DAYS

CAIN WHO KILLED HIS BROTHER   TUBAL CAIN WHO WORKED IN BRASS   NOAH WHO BUILT THE ARK

THE BUILDING OF THE ARK

The Story of the Most Beautiful Book in All the World

The First Rainbow—By J. James Tissot

THE STORY OF CAIN AND ABEL

Two sons were born to Adam and Eve. The first was named Cain; the second Abel. Cain worked as a gardener; Abel was a shepherd.

The two brothers heard from their father and mother about God, and they felt how good it was to worship the great Creator of the Earth.

But there was a difference between the characters of these two brothers. Cain, as he dug the soil and tended his plants, thought of God as a great and terrible King. Abel, as he wandered through the valley with his flocks, thought of God as a kind Father. Cain was half afraid of God; Abel loved his Maker.

These two men worshipped God by sacrifice. That is to say, they gave up something which was theirs, and offered it to God. In our day people still make sacrifices to God, but they do it in other ways; they give up money or possessions or pleasures; they help the sick and the needy. Cain gave up some of his fruits and Abel gave up some of his flocks.

But Cain's sacrifice was made grudgingly. It was a sulky gift. He gave because he was afraid not to give. Abel, with purer heart, gave his very best to God, and gave cheerfully, because he loved God and trusted in His goodness.

And when Cain saw that Abel's sacrifice was better than his, instead of making his own like to it, he hated Abel.

He would think bitterly of Abel as he dug in his garden or walked home through the fields at sunset. He would hate him for being better than himself.

And so long did he dwell on this angry thought that at last he could think of nothing else. Directly he thought of his herbs, his thoughts flew to Abel; directly he thought of God, his thoughts flew to Abel. Eating and working, resting and sleeping, his thoughts fastened themselves like a swarm of angry wasps on the beautiful character of his brother Abel.

One day they met in the fields, and talked together. Soon the talk became an argument. In the midst of the argument rage suddenly seized upon Cain. He felt his brother to be a better man than he. The thought was more than his wicked temper could bear. With a wild and desperate fury he sprang upon his brother, struck him, and killed him.

In an instant the Voice of God sounded in his soul:

" Where is Abel, thy brother? "

" I know not," he cried back. " Am I my brother's keeper? "

But the Voice in his soul continued:

" What hast thou done? "

GREAT FIGURES OF THE OLD TESTAMENT · THE LIFE OF JESUS

And Cain knew that he had done murder. The Voice spoke again, and spoke of another voice which Cain himself could hear. *The voice of thy brother's blood crieth unto Me from the ground.*

Cain knew then the horror of his crime. He had done something which could not be undone. A moment before Abel had been a living man; now he lay dead and still. Cain could never restore him.

With a bitter cry of agony he called upon God: " My punishment is greater than I can bear."

He went forth a fugitive. Henceforth there could be no rest for him; no hours of peace and contentment ; no days of happiness and joy. On his soul was the mark of murder. In his mind was the voice of his brother's blood. In his heart was despair.

Though Cain had such a sad story, his family recovered its position among men in the sixth generation, when Tubal Cain became the inventor of metal working and of stringed musical instruments.

The first crime told in the Bible is the crime of murder, and that crime was caused by the same spirit which makes people today wish to be richer, grander, cleverer, and prouder than their neighbours. God's law is that we shall be unselfish, and love one another.

THE BIBLE STORY OF NOAH'S ARK

IT is sad to read in the Bible that men and women became so wicked that God was sorry He had made the Earth.

The Bible story tells that God looked at the way men and women were living, and determined to punish them by sending a great flood; but that, for the sake of one upright man, God saved the Earth from destruction. This man was Noah.

He called Noah, we are told, and bade him build a great Ark out of gopher wood, with rooms in it for his wife and his sons, and his sons' wives ; with one great window and with a mighty door in the side. The Ark was to be covered with pitch inside and outside, and to be built so well that it should have room for two of every living thing.

Noah, having made the Ark, called two of every living thing upon the Earth — animals, birds, and insects ; and, laying in a great quantity of food, he himself, and his wife and his children, with all these other living things, entered the Ark. The Bible tells that, when they

THE DOVE THAT RETURNED NOT AGAIN
From the painting by G. F. Watts. R.A.

were all entered in, the springs of the Earth and the fountains of the sea burst their bounds, the windows of the heavens were opened, and the water covered the highest mountains. And in the flood the wicked perished.

But God remembered Noah. The rain ceased, the waters passed away, and the sunlight entered into the Ark.

Then Noah let a raven fly from the window of the Ark, and it did not come back to him. Noah then sent out a dove, but the dove flew terrified above the waters, and returned to the window of the Ark. After seven days more Noah sent out the dove again, and this time it returned bearing in its beak a leaf of olive. Noah then knew that the Earth was dry, and when he again sent the dove forth it did not return.

Then Noah came out from the Ark with his family. God was pleased with Noah, and set a bow of light in the sky after the rain. That is the Bible story of the first rainbow.

(*Next chapter in this group,*
page 497)

The Interests and Pleasures of Life for All Indoors and Out

LEARNING TO BE A GOOD COOK

Cookery, like every other Art and Science, is based on certain principles which sometimes appear dull to people longing to make showy dishes, iced cakes and pastries. But rules do not seem so dreary if directly you have learnt one by heart you copy it into the beginning of your own Cookery Scrapbook, or on to a sheet of paper to put in your own indexed Folder for Special Recipes.

A washable canvas cover for your scrapbook can be embroidered sampler fashion, or just with your name on it in cross-stitch. A folder can be made from varnished cardboard or stiffened oilcloth, decorated with a magazine print of a modern kitchen. Make either book or folder large enough to hold your recipes for years to come and hand it on as a family heirloom.

Fashions in foodstuffs and cookery vary, but however much recipes may alter, there is one rule that remains unchangeable, the rule for Cleanliness and Method. Wash your hands and nails. Put a protective overall or cloth over your clothes. Read your recipe carefully, and if an oven is needed, light and set it to the degree given in the recipe.

Collect all the utensils you want to use. Collect all the ingredients you need. Put them tidily on your work table, not on the edge where they are so apt to uptip and make a mess on the floor, particularly if you have forgotten to protect this with newspapers. Read the recipe a second time to check ingredients and utensils.

Do not stand with your back to a stove in hot weather. It will cook you as well as your food; and always work in a direct light,

not in your own shadow. Measure all ingredients carefully. Study the chemistry of cookery; why custards turn watery and nasty in over-hot ovens; why cold ovens make pastry as hard as dog biscuit.

Avoid flurry, and fluster, and muddle. Wash and put away used utensils as the work proceeds, and replace ingredients on their shelves.

Cook by the clock. Write on the margin of every new recipe you test the exact time it takes to prepare, cook, and dish up in your kitchen, for it is the cook, not the recipe, who makes or mars the dinner.

Serve meals punctually. Put plates, dish-covers, sauceboats, and serving spoons to heat in plenty of time before dishing-up a hot meal. For serving salads, jellies, or other cold food be sure plates are icy cold.

Unavoidable spill-overs and splutters in or outside an oven should be wiped off with a damp cloth before the stove cools. Do not handle hot pots or dishes with a damp cloth; it may cause them to crack. If you have not a non-inflammable asbestos oven mit, make your kitchen a present of a heavy woollen one.

At the end of every meal transfer all eatable left-overs to clean plates, away from sunshine, dust, and flies. If no pigs or poultry need the plate scrapings, burn them or put them in folded newspaper, then they will not soil the dustbin. Wash-up in hot, not lukewarm, water. Use plenty of soap or washing powder, and rinse well. Work methodically, with all dirty things stacked on one side, and all clean things draining on the other. First wash the glass, then silver-ware, then china. Lastly, scrub any messy pots you may have left to soak in cold water.

CRAFTS · GAMES · NEEDLEWORK · PUZZLES · SCIENCE EXPERIMENTS

Think ahead, remembering that damp cloths are useless for drying-up. After scrubbing the draining board, sweeping and wiping over the floor, wash all the cloths you have used, putting them to dry, if possible in the open air, and finish up by cleaning the sink thoroughly.

Make a fire extinguisher and first-aid box part of your kitchen furnishing. Homes have been burned down by a fire started through a wooden tray put on an electric hotplate that did not look hot, so do not use your electric stove as a sideboard. Remember clothes have been set alight by an oil stove flaring in a sudden draught. Think of the scalds caused by an uptipping pot some careless cook has put, handle outwards, on the stove to catch against a passer-by.

Besides these accidents, which it is within a cook's power to prevent, cooks in certain Eastern countries are credited with the power to create happiness in the people who eat the food they have prepared. Whether this be the case or not, *Cook Happiness* is a good motto for any cook, for it makes a pleasure of the work and helps to get the best result from any recipe.

One of the most important principles of all good cookery is accuracy, particularly when weighing and measuring. If no accurate measure is available you can make one for yourself out of a standard size two-pound glass jam jar, measuring 11¾ inches round and 5¾ inches high.

On a sheet of thin paper very accurately trace and then cut out the measuring strip drawn on this page. Using waterproof glue, fix this upright on to the jar, so that the bottom of the *inside* of the jar and the bottom edge of the strip are level. Then varnish over the paper to prevent its coming off if damped. Another way to make a measure is to paste the paper inside the jar and very accurately paint the measures on outside with any bright-coloured enamel you fancy. The paper inside can then be soaked off after the enamel has dried.

When tea, dessert, or table-spoons are used as measures, they should be of standard

size, as shown in the drawing on this page. Test the spoon by placing it over its equivalent pattern, and if it is correct it should fit exactly.

Then here is a list of weights and measures for some dry ingredients in everyday use, which will enable you when no scales are at hand, to convert a recipe in which any of them are given, from ounces to spoonfuls. In each case the figure given shows the number of level tablespoons which equals an ounce.

Cocoa, 2; Custard Powder, 2; Dried Beans, 1; Dried Milk, 2½; Flour, 2; Lentils, 1; Oatmeal, 2; Syrup or Treacle, 2; Sugar, 1½.

Measuring fat is simple when it is done up in halves or quarters of a pound: divide the half into eight equal pieces, or the quarter into four portions of the same size to get an ounce. But if using dripping from a bowl, it is worth remembering that a level dessert-spoonful is about an ounce.

To level a spoonful (and unless otherwise stated a spoonful should be measured level) fill the spoon level with the edge and then smooth off with a knife.

To measure a half, or a quarter spoonful, fill the spoon, level it off and then cut the ingredients across in half, and for quarters in half again lengthways.

When measuring sticky ingredients, like treacle and honey, if you dip the spoon into the liquid there will be as much sticking to the bottom as is in the spoon, so pour it into the spoon.

In America one table-spoonful contains three tea-spoonfuls instead of four as in Britain, and a liquid half pint contains eight ounces as against the British ten ounces; whilst the continental half a kilogramme, or 500 grammes, roughly equals one pound two ounces, and the measure for liquids, a litre, is a fraction over one and three quarter pints.

The next article, on page 507, explains some special cookery terms.

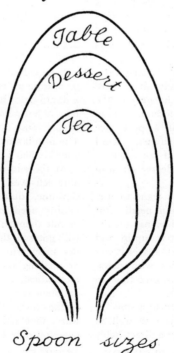

1pt

¾ pt

½ pt.

¼ pt. or 1 gill

Liquid measure

Table

Dessert

Tea

Spoon sizes

JOINTS THE BOY CARPENTER SHOULD KNOW

THE joint you will use most to begin with is the simplest one of all, and is known as the *butt* joint. It is for corners, and so it is very important that the ends of the two pieces of wood should be sawn off square or the joint will not fit properly. It can be glued together before nailing, and to give it extra strength the nails should be driven in on opposite slants as in the picture.

When you come to building up frame-works of any kind, you will find the *halved* joint a much stronger one to use, either for corners or for fitting cross-pieces, the two different types being shown in the illustrations. This joint is made by cutting away half the wood with the saw, marking it first very clearly so that there is no danger of sawing too far, and going very carefully until you have gained experience.

When the joint comes in the length of a piece of wood, then it is necessary to make two saw cuts across the wood, and chip away the wood between them with the chisel. Do not work from one side only, but make the chisel cuts from both sides equally. This joint is used in making the dog kennel, described on page 756, and will be found valuable for household jobs of many different kinds.

An even stronger joint is made by the *dovetail*, which is the fastening of two pieces of wood together by letting one part into another in the form of a dove's tail. This is used for the corners of drawers and good boxes, and in frameworks, too, but is not an easy joint for a beginner. The two halves of the dovetail should be equal in size for the strongest joint. Here again the main cuts are made with the saw, and the wood cut away with the chisel.

For fitting shelves into the sides of a bookcase or a cupboard, the *housed* joint is the one to learn. The housing, as the groove which is made to take the shelf is called, is cut with the saw, and then the wood is cleaned out with the chisel.

All these joints should be fixed with glue, and, except the dovetail, nailed or screwed.

When you are able, add to your tool set a tenon saw, which is shorter and squatter and has much finer teeth than the hand-saw, and is the best one to use for making the joint cuts, or for cutting across the grain of the wood.

It is very important that all joints should fit perfectly, and too much care cannot be taken. Make sure that the saw cuts are on the inside of the marking, for it is better to cut away too little than too much. More can always be pared off if the joint is too tight, but a loose joint can never be made to fit properly, and the work will not be firm.

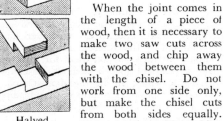

Butt

Halved

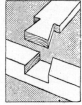

Dovetail

Dovetail

Housed

A RAILWAY TRAIN BUILT UP FROM SQUARES

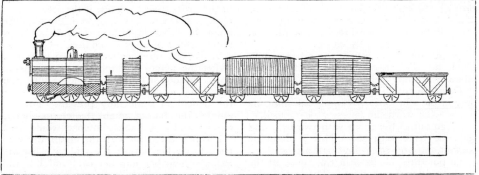

Here is a train which can be built up from squares. The little sketches below show how to start building with the squares as the foundation. Some quaint animal pictures made like this are on page 250.

FORFEITS AND HOW TO PAY THEM

A FORFEIT is some curious and amusing task that has to be performed by a player who failed to do what was required in some game, and part of the fun at a party is to get the victims to choose their own penalties either by drawing from a hat, or by shutting their eyes and stabbing with a pin on a forfeit list. This should be as long as possible, so that all the players could pick out something different.

FORFEITS THAT ARE DIFFICULT

Some forfeits sound quite easy, but prove difficult to do. One of these is to lie at full length on the floor with arms folded and then to rise, keeping the arms tightly folded all the time. Another is to pay a compliment to five friends in the room, and not to use any word in which occurs the letter A in speaking to the first, or the letter E to the second, or I to the third, or O to the fourth, or U to the fifth. A third difficult forfeit is to go round the room and give to everyone present a piece of good advice, and yet another is to wrap up a parcel and tie it with string, using only one hand.

Eating forfeits are difficult and are always funny to watch. There is the old one of trying to take a bite out of an apple, hung up with string, while the hands are tied behind the back. Another is to eat a piece of ice cream or jelly, using two straws chopstick fashion.

FORFEITS THAT ARE TRICKS

But most forfeits are the opposite of those given already; they are tasks that sound impossible but are really easy. Here is a list of interesting ones that cause much amusement if carried out, but puzzle the victim if he does not know how to do them.

To bite an inch from the poker. For this, of course, hold the poker so that the end is about an inch from the mouth, and imitate the act of biting.

To put yourself through the keyhole. Write the word " yourself " on a slip of paper, fold it up into a narrow strip, and pass it through the keyhole. There are other forfeits of a similar kind, for instance, to sit upon the fire. The words " the fire " are written on paper, which is promptly sat on.

To put one hand where the other cannot touch it. This is easy : just hold the left elbow with the right hand.

To ask a question that can be answered only in the affirmative. Simply ask someone to say what word the letters y—e—s spell.

To go out of the room with two legs, and to come back with six. This is done by walking out and returning with a chair.

To put three chairs in a row, take off the shoes, and jump over them. The victim puts the chairs in a row, then, taking off his shoes, jumps over *them*—the shoes—not the chairs.

To place some small object, like a book, upon the floor in such a way that none present can jump over it. This is done by putting the book close up against the wall of the room.

FORFEITS THAT CAUSE GREAT FUN

There are some forfeits which are good fun because the task set is impossible without the player getting into difficulties, or being able to escape from saying something foolish about himself. Here are four of this kind:

1. That was I. The player has to go all round, asking each person present what he has seen lately, and to every answer he must reply " That was I." Of course, the objects that are mentioned are such as a donkey, a baby, a dunce.

2. To act as a statue. In this forfeit the victim has to remain perfectly passive while one player after another puts him into some ridiculous position, and at each change he has to remain still till permission is given to move.

3. To act as a dummy. This is something like being a statue. The player has to keep perfectly silent, and to do whatever he is commanded by the different members of the company in turn. Good ideas for this are : make a political speech without, of course, uttering a word; sit in the dentist's chair and have a tooth out; imitate animals feeding, such as lap like a cat, drink like a bird, and chew like a cow.

4. To laugh in one corner of the room, to weep in another, to sing in another, and to dance in another.

FORFEITS THAT NEED SKILL

Another class of forfeits needs real skill and tact and quick thought, as these two do:

1. To make a sentence according to the letters given. Each member of the company in turn mentions a letter of the alphabet to the payer of the forfeit, and he then has to speak a sentence in which the words begin with the letters that were given to him, and in the order given. Thus, if the letters were n, d, y, t, t, i, v, f, a, i, o, y, o, the sentence might be " No doubt you think this is very funny, and I'm of your opinion."

2. To use three articles named. In this forfeit the names of three articles are given, and, without a moment's hesitation, the player has to say how he would use these for the benefit of some lady present. For example, the names might be chain, hand, cloak ; and a suitable sentence would be : " I would fasten up with the chain any who tried to do her harm ; I would give her my hand to help her into her car; and I would gladly lay my cloak in the road, so that she should not soil her shoes."

A GAME OF LIKES AND DISLIKES

IT was a rainy afternoon, and Phyllis was alone, feeling bored with everything, when in burst Donald, who lived next door. He was always full of fun, and never at a loss for something new to do.

"Hallo, Phyllis!" he called out, "you do look fed up. I know a good game we can play together."

"What is it called?" asked Phyllis.

"Likes and Dislikes," said Donald. "I'll soon show you what to do, it's so simple. Got some spare paper, and a good sharp pencil? That's right, a few pages out of that old exercise book will do splendidly. Now, this is what you do. Starting with the letter A, I'll put down something I like, and you put something down that you dislike. Now, here goes: I like Apples." Phyllis thought a moment, and then put down her dislike, Arrowroot.

"Good shot!" cried Donald. "Now for the letter B. Banana for me." Beetroot, Phyllis quickly wrote down.

"C for Chocolate, of course," exclaimed Donald. "Cabbage," called out Phyllis.

For D Donald chose Dates, and Phyllis surprisingly chose Damsons.

E for Egg-sandwiches, Donald preferred. "Epsom Salts," declared Phyllis with a shudder.

For F Donald wrote Figs, and Phyllis's dislike was Fried Onions.

Under G Donald wrote Grapes, and his companion Gorgonzola Cheese.

Honey was Donald's choice for H, while Phyllis had no hesitation in writing down Haddock.

And so the absorbing game went on until they came up against the last letters, X Y Z, but while they were puzzling their heads about the answer, Phyllis's mummie called to them to come at once for tea.

PICTURES MADE WITH 12 LINES AND A DOT

These clever pictures are all made up of twelve straight lines and one dot, neither more nor less. It is far more difficult to draw anything if you are confined to a few lines than if you can put in as many strokes as you like. Now see if you can make some drawings with twelve lines and a dot as good as these. Sketch them in pencil first before attempting to rule them in ink.

LITTLE PROBLEMS FOR ODD MOMENTS

THESE problems are continued from page 252, and their answers, together with more questions, will be found on page 502.

20. When did Alfred Reach School?

Alfred had a fairly long walk to school every morning. When he got as far as the church he had walked one-quarter of the way, and it was usually half-past eight on the church clock when he passed it. When at the railway station he had walked one-third of the way, and it was twenty-five minutes to nine on the station clock when he passed. At what time did he usually reach school?

21. When was the Watch Right?

At noon on Monday Herbert asked his father what o'clock it was. His father told him that it was noon, and said that his watch was two minutes fast. On Wednesday morning Herbert again asked the time, and his father replied that the exact time was eight o'clock, but added that his watch was one minute slow. Herbert then told his father at what time his watch had been exactly right. How did he work it out?

22. What Cars were Sent?

An order had been received at the garage for accommodation for a party of 59 children. The manager had big saloons to seat nine and some four-seaters, and he sent some of each, so that every one had a seat and there was no place vacant. How did he do it?

23. The Hare and the Hound.

A hare was sixty of her own leaps in front of a greyhound, and took three leaps while the hound took two; but the hound went as far in three leaps as the hare did in seven. In how many leaps did the greyhound catch the hare?

24. How were the Sweets Divided?

" Pastries are 4d. each, caramels two a penny, and chocolate drops four a penny," said the assistant. " I have just twenty pence," said the customer, " please make me up a bag of twenty." How many of each did she get?

25. How did the Sheep Stand?

" I saw an odd sight the other day," said Brown. " Two sheep were standing in a field, one looking due north and the other due south. How do you think that each could see the other without turning round? " What is the answer?

26. How Many Seats in the Hall?

" Is there a good audience? " asked the lecturer. " Only one-third of the seats are filled," he was told; " but I think we should have filled the hall if the tickets had been 6d., including tax, instead of 1s., and in that case we should have taken five pounds more." How many seats were there?

27. How Many Boys Were at School?

A schoolmaster divided £10 among the boys in his school Ten were away ill and he kept their share back. Had he not done so the others would each have received a shilling more. How many remained at school?

28. How Long Did He Wait?

" You have missed the train by a minute," said the station-master, " but there is a train every few minutes." " If there were three more trains an hour," said the traveller, " and I had just lost a train by a minute, I should have a minute less to wait for the next." How long had he to wait?

29. How Fast Was the Current?

Duncan rowed three-quarters of a mile up-stream in half an hour. If there had been no current he would have taken only a quarter of an hour. What was the speed of the current?

30. How was the Ferry Crossed?

Fred and Albert, with their father and the village postman, stood at the ferry, waiting to cross. Fred and Albert each weighed 8 stone, and their father and the postman each weighed 16 stone. But the boat could carry only 16 stone at once. How did they all cross the ferry?

THE ANSWERS TO THE PROBLEMS ON PAGE 252

14. The clock would take sixty-six seconds to strike twelve. Between the first stroke and the sixth stroke there were five intervals of time, each interval being six seconds. Between the first and the twelfth stroke there were eleven intervals of time, each interval of six seconds, so that the clock would take sixty-six seconds to strike twelve.

15. Charlie filled a three-quart jug from the roundsman's barrel, and then poured it into the five-quart jug. He filled the three-quart jug again from the barrel, and from it filled up the five-quart jug, leaving one quart in the three-quart jug. Now he emptied the five-quart jug back into the barrel, and poured the one quart in the three-quart jug into the five-quart jug. Then, by filling up the three-quart jug from the barrel again, and adding it to the one quart in the five-quart jug, he had the four quarts required.

16. Four eggs. One hen would lay one egg in a day and a half—that is, two eggs in three days, or four eggs in six days.

17. The last boy took the bowl as well as the banana that it contained.

18. As the tramp ran round the stack in forty seconds, and the farmer in thirty seconds, the farmer can run round four times in the same time that the tramp takes to run round three times. This means that in four rounds run by the farmer, he would gain one round upon the tramp ; but, as the tramp had a start of only half a round, the farmer would overtake him after running two rounds, which is the answer.

19. In another 3 years Tommy will be 6 years older than he was 3 years ago. If his age is then 3 times what it was 3 years ago, 6 years must be twice his age 3 years ago, so that he was 3 years old 3 years ago, and he is 6 years old now.

HOW TO KEEP A SECRET IN WRITING

To keep a secret it is a wise and safe rule never to put it on paper, though it is easy for friends to write to one another, in code or cipher, in such a way that no one else can find out what the letter means.

For a cipher is a method of writing, in any language, so that even those who know the language cannot understand the message unless they have the key which makes it clear. There are many simple ciphers which can quickly be learned.

This sentence might puzzle some if they saw it in a book: "Ihopeyoucanreadthis," but it is really only six words joined together.

That is the simplest kind of cipher, and not really one at all. Here are some others, three letters written in different ciphers. The first looks like a Chinese puzzle, but the key will show how easy it is.

The alphabet is divided up so that it is possible to indicate the position of any one letter by a dot, as is seen here:

writing a letter in this way remember to *put a full stop after each word* and *three stops at the end of each sentence*. Always take care that these stops come *outside* the space. Commas and stops may be used as usual.

This code looks more mystifying if the lines are varied slightly in thickness and length, and it makes no difference to the key as long as the dots are carefully placed in the correct positions between them.

Now, with this key, the cipher letter can easily be read. It says:

Dear Elsie,

I hope you can read this. Have you ever had a letter like it before? It is the first I have written in this way, but it does not seem very hard. When are you coming to see us? Father has bought me a beautiful pony, and I want you to ride him. With love from Eva.

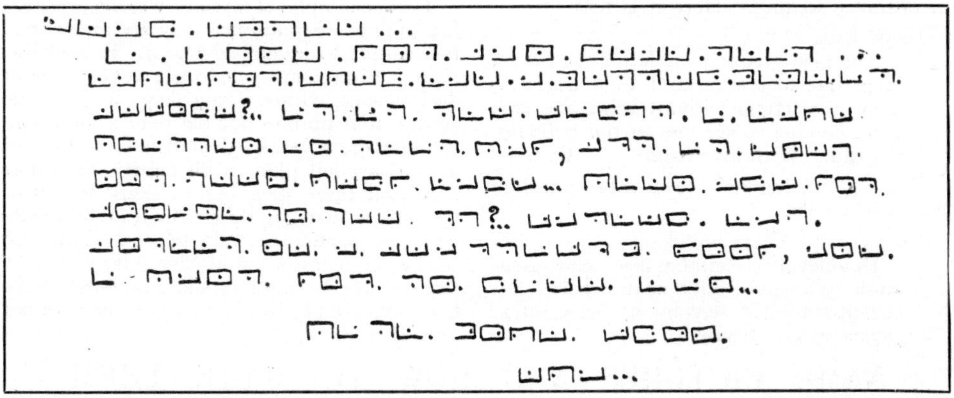

possible to indicate the position of any one letter by a dot, as is seen here:

a b c	d e f	g h i
j k l	m n o	p q r
s t u	v w x	y z

It will be noticed that there are three letters of the alphabet in each space, except the last. To write the key, begin with the first letter in the first space, then write the alphabet *across* the row of spaces. Next the position of each letter in each space must be noticed ; for instance, *a* is the *first* letter in the space marked by the lines. Thus instead of writing *a*, write, being careful to place the dot in the *first position* in the space. In the same way *b* is written, where the dot is in the *second position*. The letter *d* is the first dot in the second space, thus ; *e* is, and so on for the remainder of the letter. Instead of using dots the figures 1, 2, 3, may mark positions, so that *a* would be 1, *b* 2, *c* 3, and so on; but the dot system is better and more puzzling. When

Here is another cipher—a letter in figures:
13.2.1.43—2.51.1—
45.23.2—21.3.43.44.45—41.1.43.45—
4.21—54.4.5.43—33.2.45.45.2.43—
45.4.4.32—34.2—1—33.4.35.22—
45.3.34.2—45.4—43.2.1.13, 11.5.45—
3—44.4.4.35—11.2.22.1.35—45.4—
32.35.4.52—45.23.2—33.2.45.45.2.43.44—
52.3.45.23.4.5.45—5.44.3.35.22—
45.23.2—32.2.54.·· 3—1.34—
12.4.34.3.35.22—45.4—44.2.2—54.4.5—
3.35—45.23.2—23.4.33.3.13.1.54.44—
3.21—3—12.1.35.··
52.3.45.23—33.4.51.2—21.43.4.34—
2.33.44.3.2.

To get the key of this cipher write out the alphabet in this way, numbering the five vowels in order:

a b c d e f g h i j k l m n o p q r s t u v w x y z
1   2   3   4   5

Thus, a is 1; e is 2; i is 3; o is 4; u is 5.

To find any other letter, first get the number of the vowel before it, then count the number of letters after the vowel until the required letter is reached. Thus, *b* comes after the *first* vowel, and is the first letter after it; so instead of *b* write 11—the first figure for the number of the vowel, the second for the number of the letter past the vowel. In the same way, *c* is 12—that is, the second letter past the first vowel; *f* is 21—that is, the first letter after the second vowel. Great care must be taken, of course, to put the number of the vowel in its proper place.

Now write the whole alphabet in figures according to the cipher:

a-1	e-2	i-3	m-34	q-42	u-5	x-53
b-11	f-21	j-31	n-35	r-43	v-51	y-54
c-12	g-22	k-32	o-4	s-44	w-52	z-55
d-13	h-23	l-33	p-41	t-45		

In writing this cipher, *put a full stop after each letter,* and *a short line at the end of each word.* Finish a sentence with three full stops ; use commas and other stops as usual. Now it will be easy to read the figure-letter in ordinary writing. Here it is :

DEAR EVA,

The first part of your letter took me a long time to read, but I soon began to know the letters without using the key. I am coming to see you in the holidays, if I can. With love from   ELSIE.

The third cipher may seem more puzzling still at first sight.

DEEEEAYARE EEELLESSEYEEE,

Doubleyouee aitchaydee essyousea-aitch effyouen ohveceeare teaaitchee elleeteateaeeare wyohyou esseeentea. Jayayseakay teaaitch eyeenkayess wyohyouare seaeyepeaaitcheeare eyeess veeeearewy geeohohdee. Eye ayem jayyouesstea geeoheyeengee ohyoutea ohen emwy peaohenwy, essoh geeohohdee-bewyee.

Doubleyoueyeteaaitch ellohveeee

effareohem EEVEEAY

If this letter is read aloud, the mystery will become clear. The secret of it is that every letter is *spelt*. Some letters of the alphabet can be spelt in more than one way, but it does not matter which is chosen if the same spelling is kept throughout the letter.

In ordinary writing the letter reads :

DEAR ELSIE,

We had such fun over the letter you sent. Jack thinks your cipher is very good. I am just going out on my pony, so good-bye. With love from

EVA.

These examples of mystery-writing are great fun to practise, and once they are understood it is simple to invent new ones. Remember, though, that some people are very clever at deciphering without any key, and to be certain that no one but the person for whom the message is intended shall be able to read it, it is a good plan in all ciphers to scatter here and there meaningless signs, letters or figures—in fact, anything which fits in neatly with the particular code in use. This will completely confuse inquisitive folk, while the receiver of the note should previously have been told simply to ignore whatever does not appear in the key.

NAME PICTURES AND HOW TO MAKE THEM

To make a name-picture or smudge-graph, first fold a piece of paper, then open it out flat, and with pen and ink, using a fairly thick nib, scribble a few words quickly on the mark made by the fold. At once, before the ink gets dry, fold the paper over on the same line as before, and rub it down with the thumb-nail. When it is opened again, a quaint design will be seen. It is interesting to keep a special book, like one used for auto-graphs, in which friends can make their smudge-graph signatures; and for a party competition get everyone to do a smudge-graph of a zigzag line, instead of words, and then turn it into a funny picture, a small prize going to the one who makes the best effort.

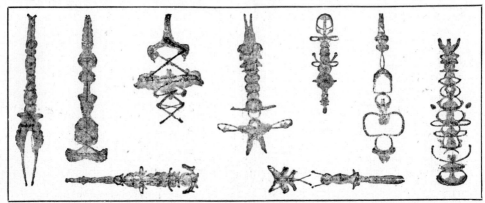

Pictures made by folding over smudges, zig-zag lines, and crosses.

Simple Learning Made Easy for Very Little People

NUMBERS—GAMES FOR COUNTING

Like most children, John and Jennifer loved playing with toys, and now they had had their fifth birthday they liked playing games with balls and skittles. Mother and Daddy said that if they would spare some of their toys, they would make some new games which would help them with their numbers.

John gave Daddy nine skittles, and he enamelled them, and painted a number on each. Then John found a ball, and the game was to stand up the skittles in a row, roll the ball, and see which number they could knock down.

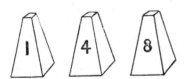

John was very proud of his new game, and Jennifer wanted one of her own, but it must be the same as John's! Alas, there were no more skittles!

Daddy said he would make some. He asked Mother for an empty cocoa tin and all the other empty tins she could find. Mother very soon found nine, and Daddy enamelled them and found another ball, so Jennifer had a game of her own.

Mother gave them some patty-pans, like the ones she used when she made little cakes. Daddy enamelled these and painted a number on each one. John and Jennifer collected shells, and beans, and acorns, and put as many in each patty-pan as the number Daddy had painted on the bottom.

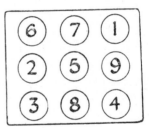

One day Mother bought three little boxes. In two of them were lots of beads of two colours and a long, thin bootlace. In the third box were a lot of little tickets with the numbers on.

John and Jennifer each chose a ticket and threaded it on their laces, then they threaded as many beads of each colour as the number on the ticket.

Another day, when John went upstairs to fetch Mother a handkerchief from her drawer, he found a whole collection of bus and tram tickets. He wanted to know what they were for, and Mother said she was going to use them to make a new number game.

She got a piece of cardboard and stuck some of the tickets on it.

READING · WRITING · ARITHMETIC · ART · MUSIC · FRENCH

Then she put all the loose tickets into a box, and John and Jennifer matched them with the tickets on the board.

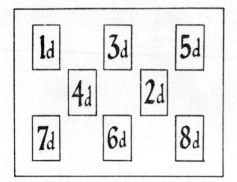

Daddy had been very busy at his work-bench, and John, who loved wood and nails and hammers, wanted to help him;

but Daddy said it was a secret, and he would show them when it was finished.

At last the day came, and Daddy showed John and Jennifer what he had made. It was a set of wooden figures, and with a brace-and-bit Daddy had made some little holes in the figures. These holes did not go right through, and he bought a box of tiny coloured balls to put in them.

The tiny balls just fitted into the holes. Daddy said he expected he could have bought the figures, but he thought it was much more fun to make them

WRITING—WITHOUT MOTHER'S HELP

DADDY liked reading very much. He had what he called his " library." The first time he came home with a new book to add to his library, John and Jennifer did not know what a library was. Daddy explained that it was a collection of books.

That gave John and Jennifer an idea for his birthday. They would write a book for Daddy! It was to be a secret and it was to be all their own work. They made up their minds that they were going to make even the book themselves.

" We will get some white paper, all the same size, and do a page each," said John.

So he and Jennifer set to work.

" We must have clean hands every time we write or paint," said Jennifer, " because Daddy wouldn't like a dirty book in his library."

John and Jennifer wondered what they would do if they wanted to write a new word, one that they had not had before. Mother said she would help them. She took a large sheet of paper, and said she would write on it any word they could not spell, and could not find for themselves in their picture books or diaries.

The children talked a lot about what they would write in Daddy's book. They talked it over with Mother too, and at last decided to write a book about themselves, so that when they grew up Daddy could read about them when they were little.

They folded each piece of paper in half

so that they had a page for writing and a page for a picture, like this:

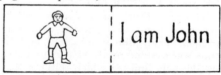

Here are twelve pages that John wrote:

I am John

I am a little boy

I am five years old

I have brown eyes and brown hair

I can run fast

I like to draw and paint

I am learning to read and write

We have a café

We made things to sell in our café

My sister's name is Jennifer

I am taller than Jennifer

We are twins

Here is what Jennifer wrote in her part of the book:

I am a little girl

My name is Jennifer

I am five years old

I have blue eyes and curly hair

I can jump high

I like flowers

I can read about Panda

Daddy bought me a diary

I like to go to the Zoo

My brother's name is John

He is my twin

I like John and Mummie and Daddy

When John and Jennifer had finished their book Mother showed them how to put it together. Jennifer sewed the pages together, and John made the cover. For the cover Mother found two pieces of cardboard just the same size as the book, and John joined them together with two pieces of adhesive tape, one inside and one outside.

When the strips of tape had stuck properly he painted the inside of the cover blue, and the outside green, because they were Daddy's favourite colours. Then Jennifer sewed the pages inside the cover, taking her stitches right through the tape. On the outside John wrote what the book was called, and when it was finished it looked like this:

The book of John and Jennifer

READING—LIKE A FLASH

JOHN and Jennifer were so delighted with the book Mother had made for them that they wanted her to make another, but she said it would be better to be quite sure of the words in the Panda book before they learned any new words.

One morning Mother told them she had a surprise for them after breakfast. When they had eaten their breakfast and helped Mother to clear up, she fetched a packet of cards that she had printed. On each card was a sentence out of their Panda book, like this:

This is Panda

On the back of the cards Mother had written the sentence in smaller letters.

Mother said, " You have read all these sentences in your reading books, and now we will see how many you really know. We call these Flash Cards, because I am going to hold them up for you to see, and

put them down very quickly, like a flash, and you must see who can recognise the sentence first."

Mother held the card so that the twins could see the side on which was printed the sentence in large letters, and the side with the small letters was facing her.

Mother had made a card for each sentence in their Panda book. John said it seemed much harder to read the sentences from the cards than from their reading books. Jennifer kept " guessing "—she looked at the first word and guessed the rest! So Mother said they had better take it in turns at reading a sentence from the Flash Cards, and she would keep the score to see how many each got right.

It was a lovely game the first morning they tried it that way. John got six sentences quite right, and Jennifer got five sentences right. The next morning John got 15 and Jennifer 16. Quite soon the children could read all the sentences with only a little help from Mother.

Mother then made more cards, smaller

this time, and on each card she printed just one word, in large letters on the front, and small letters on the back like this:

lived	lived

They used these in the same way as they had used the sentence Flash Cards, and Mother had made a card for every word in the book. The children found this the hardest thing they had yet done; but it

is fun to do hard things, and each tried to beat the other.

When Mother was busy John and Jennifer used to match the word cards with the sentence cards, like this:

Panda had black-ringed eyes
Panda	had	black-ringed	eyes

The children got very quick at this, and it helped them to learn the words, too.

ART—PATTERNS AND POTATOES

HAVE you ever noticed how much we are surrounded by patterns? The patterns made by the woven threads of the clothes you wear, the covering of chairs or the seats in railway carriages, in wallpapers, curtains, carpets, tablecloths, dresses, handkerchiefs and scarves, the covers and lining of books, the punched holes in a nutmeg grater, the cane seat of a chair, motor-car tyres and the prints they make in the mud of the road, wicker baskets, and many other things.

These patterns are made by repeating some simple pattern, called the unit, and in so doing making an all-over pattern. Repeating, running, or flowing are words which could be used to describe these all-over patterns. Usually the simpler the pattern of the unit the better is the pattern which it makes when repeated.

There is no end to the kinds of patterns in the branches of trees, of leaves, in the skins of animals, the feathers of birds, the clouds in the sky, the waves in the seas, as well as on the surface of sea shells.

Nature has countless ways of making exciting and wonderful patterns. In a tree there is the big bole and the branches tapering as they reach out to their tips where they become lacelike twigs. There are many different kinds of bark on the boles of trees. The London plane has a bark like a crazy pavement with odd-shaped pieces of green, black, and brown; the sweet chestnut has a pattern on it like the carved patterns on a column in a Norman cathedral ; while the holly has a fine and dainty little spot pattern.

The leopard's spots are larger and closer together on his back than on his sides and underneath. The variety of pattern looks right and we feel it belongs

to the creature. The stripes of the zebra and the tiger are thicker on the back, too—in fact these animals are nearly white underneath.

Have you noticed the shape of a sycamore leaf? Folded down the middle it will look something like the folded paper patterns we made with the edges carefully cut into delicate shapes. It often has dark patterns on it made by some insect.

Quite a different thing happens with the oak leaf. You will remember that the two halves are quite uneven in shape, but often you will find underneath it little round discs made by insects. Seashells, too, are mostly very regular shapes, but the patterns on them are often just blobs, or spots, or dashes, or zigzag lines, and yet they all seem to belong to the shells on which you find them.

There are many ways in which flowing patterns can be made, and much depends on the ideas we have, and what we use when we carry out an idea. The Greeks made simple patterns with their paint brushes on vases by doing dots and dashes in rows.

There is a way to print patterns from little stamps or blocks made with a piece of potato or carrot or swede or turnip. Obtain some sheets of thin paper, such as the kind sometimes used to wrap round bread, or old newspaper, or (if you can get it) a kind of paper called whitey-brown. Next take a piece of felt or flannel and cut it to fit in an old tin lid about three inches across.

A fairly large piece of felt or flannel, the size of the paper, should be laid on the table with the paper on top of it. Now mix up some paint to put on the felt in the tin lid. Mix a strong colour—a dark red or brown; or you could try soaking the felt with ordinary writing ink. All you need now is a potato and a pen-knife to scratch or cut a pattern in it.

Cut the potato in two with a dinner knife, and make sure the cut surface is flat and even. If you rub the cut surface on a brick or a piece of glass-paper you will be sure to have it smooth and level. Next cut off pieces from the sides so as to make an oblong of the oval surface. Now all is ready to begin. In this oblong try to imagine some simple unit which, if you repeat it, will make a flowing

Just hold the potato block in your hand and imagine some very simple pattern on it—a pattern which will join up well when printed. Try closing your eyes and imagine how it will look as you repeat the prints of your block. When you know what your pattern is going to be like, open your eyes and get your penknife and cut or scrape away the lines or dots which will make it.

The printing should be done evenly—dipping the potato block in the paint on the felt in the tin lid for each print you make. There are many ways of making patterns and you will enjoy discovering

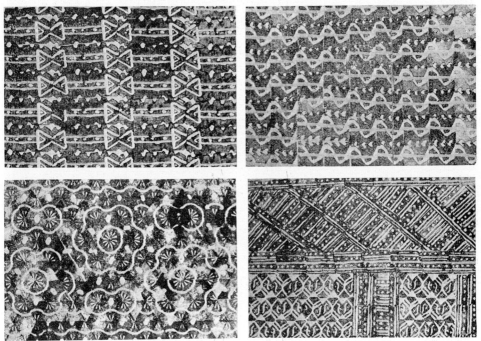

PATTERNS MADE WITH POTATO-CUTS, SHOWN HERE MUCH REDUCED IN SIZE

pattern. The repeating is done by dipping your potato block into the colour in the tin lid and making prints of the unit on your sheet of paper. It is a good plan to start printing at the top of your paper in even rows from left to right, and just let each print from the block touch the next one to it.

As for ideas, you can imagine a unit made up of straight lines or curved lines which will flow into a zigzag or a fish scale pattern. You can also cut little pieces away from the sides of the oblong which will make lovely leaf shapes when you join them up in the printing.

some of them. The shape of the block can be cut to a square or triangle, and each print or impression made like bricks being laid in a wall, or like the squares on a draughtsboard, or like the cells in a honeycomb. Of course, your pattern should join up nicely, apart from the edges of the prints.

When you have printed a fair-sized piece of paper, and can see what the pattern looks like, try to make a different one. Cut off the used surface of your potato and start again as before.

Sometimes it is a good idea to add little touches of another colour. This can be done with paint on the finger-tips, or with paint on a brush, or by cutting another small potato block and printing it in between the first block prints.

You can also make quite large patterns by using more than one potato block. One block can be used to print a great wavy stalk, something like the one that Jack climbed up, and with another block you could print leaves or flowers growing out of it.

When you have printed the sheet of patterns, stand back and look at it and see what you feel about it. Does the unit lose itself in the whole pattern? Would you like to use your pattern for a scarf or a dress or a curtain, or do you think it would do for the cover of a book? The patterns you make from potato-cut blocks may be suitable for any one of these.

When we looked at the skin of the leopard we felt that the spots somehow " belonged "; that they looked right in size and place; and when we look at the patterns on a dress or on a curtain we ought to feel that it " belongs " too. Some things need big units ; others look better with small ones.

There is one other thing to look out for, and it is in the pattern itself. As well as being a good flowing pattern, it should look calm, and not fussy or restless.

With some pieces of linoleum and a set of lino-cutting tools you can go much further with your pattern-making. You can make the size of your unit block much bigger, and it will last longer, and you can print long lengths of cloth with it.

At school you could make a pattern for the curtains of the hall, and at home you could make patterns for cushions or small window curtains.

The shop which sells the lino-cutting tools will most likely sell special inks for printing on cloth. These are called fabric inks. You can also use ordinary oil colour paint for printing on cloth. Lots of gay clothes can be made in this way for plays. As with the potato-cut, you can use more than one colour in the printing, and you can do this by cutting another lino block or painting in the colour. For the printing you need to have a large pottery tile or a slab of smooth stone or thick glass on which to put the fabric ink and spread evenly with a rubber-covered roller with a handle—the kind of roller used by photographers will do.

When you have spread the ink evenly and got the roller evenly covered, you then roll it up and down and across your lino-block to make sure it gets a good even coat of ink. Then you turn the block upside down in place on the cloth and press hard on the back so as to leave a good even print. You will have to be careful to place the block in the right place each time you make a print. You can either press hard with your fingers or, if you have one, roll the back with another clean roller.

Both the potato-cut and the lino-cut blocks and the use of inks and paints are simple ways of doing what the big firms do who print all the rolls of coloured cloth which you see in the shops.

MUSIC—MORE ABOUT THE NAMES OF SOUNDS

Sometimes, no doubt, you will be able to go to concerts. Half the fun of listening to music comes from watching players make the sounds—the right sounds, we hope!—come from their instruments.

Let us peep inside a concert hall just before a rehearsal is due to start. The conductor (perhaps in his shirt sleeves, because conducting is warm work) says, " May we have an A, please?" The organist, the pianist, or the oboe player sounds a note— the one with 440 vibrations a second. The rest of the orchestra play what they hope is the same sound. " Clarinet a little sharp " (a little too high), says the con-

ductor. The clarinet player pulls the joints of his instrument a little farther apart. This makes his pipe a little longer and the sound a little lower. " All right, Mr. Clarinet," says the conductor, " but now the violins are out of tune." The violins tighten or loosen the pegs which control their strings, and sooner or later everyone is happy and in tune.

Then you will notice that the A which everyone plays sounds quite agreeable. You can tell when instruments (or voices) are out of tune. When you are playing or singing it is very important to listen all the time so that you do not go out of tune.

But why do we have to call a note A? Could not we simply say *doh*? If you were to ask a passer-by the way to St. Paul's Cathedral he might say, "Go straight up Ludgate Hill, and you will see the cathedral in front of you." But he could only say that if you were both in London. If you were, say, in Manchester, he would need to say a good deal more. "Take a train to London," he would start, "and get off at Euston station . . ."

If you were singing Unto Us a Boy is Born, the conductor would sing a note and tell you that that note was to be *doh*, and you should all get along happily together. But if you wanted to sing the same tune when you were a long way away from the conductor he must say, "Find C on the piano, or the violin, and that is, for this song, *doh*."

It is common for people to have two names. Perhaps you have two names, and sometimes you will be called by one and sometimes the other. So it is with music.

Look at the keyboard of a piano.

G A B C D E F G a b c d e

Each key plays one sound, and one sound only. Each is called by a letter of the alphabet. When we have run through seven names we start at the beginning again. The black keys—which are as brothers and sisters to the white keys, and have the same alphabetic names—we shall come to again.

Find A. Find it on the piano itself, if you have one; if not, point to it on the picture. That is the orchestra's tuning note. The violinist first of all puts his A string in tune. Then he tunes the other strings. How many strings has a violin? Do not read on until you have thought. Now, here is the answer. The violin has four strings, so has the viola, and the 'cello.

The four violin strings are tuned to **G**, **D**, **a**, and **e**. Those notes are specially marked on the picture so that you can play them. If you can borrow a violin (you must be very careful with it) you can pluck the strings and find out which sounds G, which sounds D, and so on. Now, if a string player wants to play any note other than those which come from the *open* strings he has to shorten the strings with the fingers of his left hand.

On the piano the notes are ready made. Look inside. There are long strings for the deep notes, and little strings for the high notes. The harp, a very old instrument, is made similarly.

When we touch a key on the piano the mechanism causes a hammer to jump up and hit the string, which makes the sound we want. If we hit the key hard we get a loud sound, but if we are gentle we get a quiet sound. The instrument can play both *soft* and *loud*. The Italians would say *piano* and *forte*. This is how our piano (which we should really call a pianoforte) gets its name.

We were talking about Unto Us a Boy is Born. You could play this tune on the piano if the names of the keys to be played are written as at the foot of this page.

But what a lot of space it takes to write it down this way! How can we use less paper? and how can we make the reading of music less difficult? That is what we must find out next.

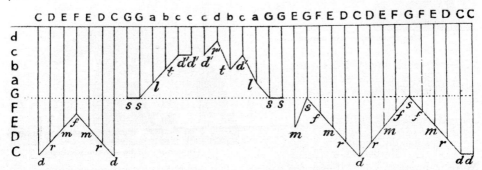

This diagram shows us which keys we must play, the length of the piano string for each sound, and the ups and downs of the melody. It shows, too, how all these things are related to one another.

FRENCH—A LITTLE PICTURE LESSON

HERE we read of the little party on the platform. We must remember that the first line under the picture is in French, the second gives the English word for the French word above it, and the third shows how we make up the words into our own language.

Une machine automatique—An automatic machine

Nous voyons une machine automatique.
We   see   a   machine   automatic.
We see an automatic machine.

J'ai mis dix sous dans le trou.
I have put ten sous in the hole.
I have put a penny in the slot.

Papa et maman viennent nous chercher.
Papa and Mamma come us to find.
Papa and Mamma are coming to find us.

Une locomotive—An engine

Ils nous font voir les trains.
They us make to see the trains.
They show us the trains.

J'aime les locomotives.
I like the engines.
I like the engines.

Notre train est en vue. Il entre en gare.
Our train is in sight. It enters in station.
Our train is in sight. It is coming in the station.

La fumée—The smoke

La fumée nous entre dans les yeux.
The smoke us enters in the eyes.
The smoke is getting in our eyes.

L'employé—The porter

L'employé met nos malles dans le train.
The porter puts our trunks in the train.
The porter is putting our trunks in the train.

Un compartiment—A compartment

Papa choisit un compartiment.
Papa chooses a compartment.
Papa is choosing a compartment.

HOW THE FIRES BURST FROM THE EARTH

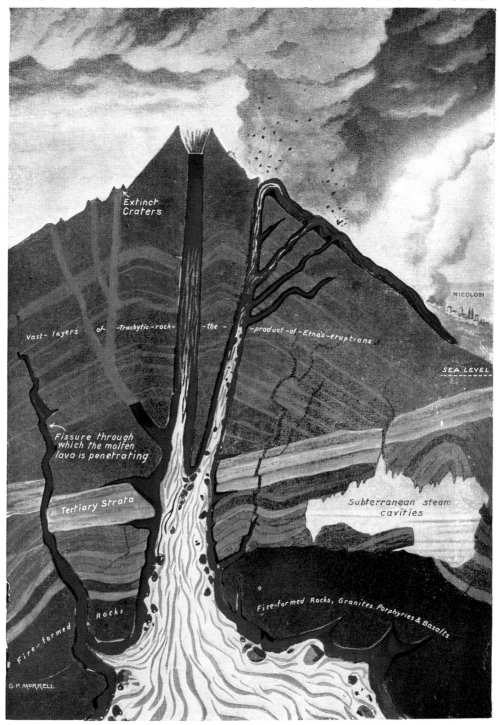

Extinct Craters

Vast layers of Trachytic rock the product of Etna's eruptions

NICOLOSI

SEA LEVEL

Fissure through which the molten lava is penetrating

Tertiary Strata

Subterranean steam cavities

Fire-formed Rocks

Fire-formed Rocks, Granites, Porphyries & Basalts

G. F. MORRELL

THE CENTRAL FIRES OF THE EARTH SEEK AND FIND THE WEAKEST PARTS OF THE ROCKS AND BURST
THROUGH THE CRUST AS VOLCANOES

25

The Story of the Boundless Universe and All Its Wondrous Worlds

The boy's iron ball and the girl's balloon have the same *volume* but different *mass*

INSIDE THE WONDERFUL BALL

LET us think of the Earth as a colossal ball, a cricket-ball of a size unthinkable.

A cricket-ball has a certain weight, it has a cover, and inside this there is a core made of certain materials put together in a particular way. A cricket-ball is elastic, so that when you throw it against a wall it comes back again instead of spreading out and sticking to the wall, as a lump of mud would. Now, in the same way, we must look at the qualities of the great Earth-ball, tiny little pieces of which we put together to make cricket-balls, cathedrals, and other things.

In the first place, let us consider the size of this big ball. It measures round its circumference, roughly speaking, 25,000 miles. It is difficult to imagine such a great distance as 25,000 miles ; yet, compared with some other things, the Earth is really small. There is a very good way of comparing the size of the Earth with that of the Sun. If we can imagine the Earth being placed at the centre of the Sun, the surface of the Sun would reach far beyond the distance that the Moon is from the Earth—that is to say, the Sun occupies far more space than the whole of the space swept by the Earth and the Moon moving steadily round her.

We will not bother with the figures which say how many square miles there are on the surface of the Earth, or how many millions of millions of tons it weighs, because we cannot realise what these figures mean, and so, they are of no use to us at present. There is, however, one enormously interesting thing about the Earth which can be expressed in a way which we understand, and which is interesting because it means so much ; and that is the question of the density of the Earth. Let us see what density is ; how the density of the Earth can be found out ; and what the Earth's density is, and what it means.

A lawn-tennis-ball is bigger than a golf-ball but it is not so heavy. There is more stuff in the golf-ball than in the tennis-ball. A big piece of coal is heavier than a small piece of coal ; there is more stuff in the bigger piece. But if you took two pieces of the same size and kind they would be the same weight—that is to say, they would have the same amount of stuff in them. Now, there is a special word for the size of a thing—for the amount of space it occupies. This special name is volume, and it not difficult to understand, for it only means size, or bigness.

Now, as the tennis-ball and the golf-ball show, the volume of a thing tells us nothing about its weight, or, rather, about the amount of stuff in it—unless we can

ASTRONOMY · GEOLOGY · GEOGRAPHY · CHEMISTRY · PHYSICS · LIFE

compare it with a different volume of the same material, as in the case of pieces of coal of different size. So we want a special word to express the amount of stuff there is in any particular kind of thing as compared with a similar volume, or size, or bigness, of something else. You know what a cube is—a thing like the bricks you used to use for making pictures. If you can imagine a cube of water, such as you might have by pouring water into a cubical vessel, that would have a certain amount of stuff in it according to the size of the cube. If you poured the water out and filled the cube with mercury instead, you would have the same volume, or size, or bigness, of mercury, but it would be much heavier.

The mercury gets more stuff into the same space than the water does. Now, the proper way of saying this is that the mercury is *denser*, or has a greater *mass*, than the water. Perhaps you will say that you do not see any reason why we should not say the mercury is heavier than the water, but the objection is that, though it is quite true for here and now, yet the heaviness, or weight, of a thing depends upon the Earth's pull for it and its pull for the Earth ; whereas the amount of stuff in it would remain the same even if the Earth were moved a million miles away, and so could hardly pull at all.

WHY THE SAME THING DOES NOT ALWAYS WEIGH THE SAME

Therefore, instead of describing the amount of stuff in a thing by the word *weight*, we use the word *mass*, or *denseness;* and the mass of a thing would remain the same even if it were moved to the Moon, where it would weigh far less, as the Moon is smaller and therefore pulls less hard.

Now, in order to compare the density, or *mass*, of different things, we take a certain volume of water under definite conditions, and call its density *one ;* then, if we find that something else is twice as massive, or dense, as water, we say that its density is *two*—and so on. If the thing we were comparing with water were at the same distance from the centre of the Earth, then, if it were twice as dense as the water, the same volume, or bigness, of it would be twice as heavy, or would weigh twice as much.

Let us take one more illustration of why it is that the same thing does not always weigh the same. If we take two metal cubes of exactly the same size and

material, and place them side by side on a flat table, then, besides being of the same density, or mass, they are also of the same weight. But if, instead of having the two cubes side by side, you put one on top of the other, though they are still of the same density, though there is still the same amount of stuff in the one as in the other, it can be shown that the one which is above weighs less than the other, because it is *a little bit farther from the Earth*, and therefore the Earth and it do not pull each other quite so hard ! Let us agree, therefore, that there is some sense in distinguishing between mass and weight.

HOW DO WE FIND OUT THE MYSTERIES OF THE EARTH ?

How are we to find out what is the density of the Earth ? How are we to find out whether this great ball is less massive or dense than water, or more massive or dense ? This is a problem which men of science have thought out in various ways. Just now, perhaps, it is enough to say that if we can measure the extent to which the Earth makes a pendulum swing, and the rate at which the pendulum swings, we can measure the force with which the Earth acts upon it, and, therefore, as we already know the size, or volume, or bigness, of the Earth, we can say how dense it is—that is to say how tightly the stuff in it is packed.

Now, the extremely remarkable conclusion to which we come is that the Earth is somewhere between four and six times as dense as water, and the stuff in the inside of it must be squeezed together more tightly than we can imagine. None of the things we know and can examine at the surface of the Earth, no rocks or coal, or anything of that sort, are as dense as this average density of the Earth, and, therefore, away down beneath us, the stuff of which the Earth is made must be so tightly packed that the densest things we know, such as lead, can be almost nothing compared with it.

THE THIN CRUST OF THE EARTH UPON WHICH WE LIVE

This is not only very interesting in itself, but it is also important because of what it tells us as to the tremendous forces which are, so to speak, chained up underneath the Earth's crust.

Sometimes, as we know, these show themselves by means of earthquakes. It is also interesting to know that the crust of the Earth, compared with the whole size of the Earth, is really extremely thin. It feels firm enough under our feet, and there is no fear of its cracking and letting us through, but if the Earth could be cut right through the middle like an orange we should be very much astonished, if we could take a sort of bird's-eye view of the whole cut surface, to see how thin is the crust on which we walk, and from which all living things have been produced.

Of course, when we learn that the inside of the Earth has this extraordinary density, we are apt to think of it as solid—far more solid than lead. But another great fact about it is that it is intensely hot, so hot that no heat we know on the surface of the Earth can compare with it. It is indeed probable that the inside of the Earth is so hot that the stuff of which it is made is not really solid at all. On the other hand, we may be wrong in thinking of it as liquid or as a gas, for it is more than likely that matter inside the Earth, owing to heat and pressure, has a state which is like nothing that we know.

IF WE COULD THROW THE EARTH AT A WALL IT WOULD BOUNCE !

We said something a little while ago about a cricket-ball being elastic, so that when it is thrown against a wall it comes back again, instead of spreading out and sticking there like a lump of wet mud. When we say that a thing is elastic, we simply mean that when it is put out of its shape it comes back to its old shape as soon as it can. When the cricket-ball hits the wall, it is flattened at one part for a twinkling of time, and then it springs back to its original shape, and that makes it bound back from the wall.

Now, if you could throw the great ball called the Earth against a wall, it would spring back more perfectly than a cricket-ball, more perfectly than a ball of steel.

There is a cheap kind of cricket-ball which is called a composition cricket-ball, often called compo, for short. This means that it is a composition of a number of things put together. Well, the Earth is also a compo, made up of a large number of different materials put together in a particular way, and this question of the composition of the Earth is immensely interesting. But before we go into that let us look at one of the latest things we have learnt about the composition of the Earth, because it tells us far more than ever we knew before about the Earth's history, about what is happening to it now, and about the wonderful way in which it is kept warm.

The special kind of stuff with which it deals is very rare, but it is one of the substances which make up the Earth. There is so little of it, that if the stuff were not so wonderful in itself, it would not be worth mentioning. Its name is radium. Before we consider why it is so important, we will ask ourselves in what ways the Earth might be kept warm.

YEAR IN, YEAR OUT, THE EARTH IS LOSING ITS HEAT

In the first place, the Earth might be kept warm by the heat of the Sun—of which we catch only a very tiny amount, of course, but still enough to produce all the life on the Earth, our own included. However, during the night the Earth throws back into space the heat which is got from the Sun during the day, and as we know what night and day mean, we know that all the time one half of the Earth is getting heat from the Sun the other half is losing it.

Secondly, we know that the Earth is kept warm by the heat in its inside. The heat from the inside simply soaks outwards and keeps the crust warm, and then it passes away from the crust into the air, and is finally lost.

Year in, year out, then, the Earth is slowly giving forth heat, and, clearly, this could not go on for ever. The Moon, of course, was hot when it began, but it has got cool much faster than the Earth, because it is so very much smaller. A small thing always loses its heat faster than a big thing, because a small thing has a bigger amount of surface to lose its heat by in proportion to the amount of stuff in it. That is one reason why a baby has to be kept so very warmly clad.

WHILE THE EARTH GIVES FORTH HEAT IT MAKES NEW HEAT FOR ITSELF

But, in spite of all we have said, the Earth is not losing heat. Early this century the astonishing discovery was made of another way, previously dreamt of by nobody, in which the Earth is kept warm, and has for ages past been kept warm—and will be kept warm for no one can say how many ages to come.

It is true that the Earth is giving forth its heat, but we have discovered that, while it is giving forth heat, it is actually making new heat for itself.

Of course, you see the importance of this. If you have six pennies in your pocket, and spend one every day, when a week is out you will have nothing left. But if, while still spending, you can also make a new penny every day—well, you can go on for a long time at that rate ! Now, that is what the Earth is doing. It is spending its heat, but it is also making new heat. Nay, more; there is every reason to believe that the Earth is making at least as much heat as it loses. Now, the wonderful stuff which makes the new heat for the Earth is radium.

THE MOST WONDERFUL OF ALL THE ELEMENTS WE KNOW

It used to be thought that there were four elements—earth, air, fire, and water —and boys and girls still play a game based on that idea. But now we know that none of these is really an element. There are real elements, however, such as lead and gold and silver and quicksilver, and oxygen. Well, radium is just another of these elements. It is one of the rarest of all elements; but it is far more wonderful than all the other elements put together.

Now, one of the wonderful things about radium is that it is all the time making heat out of itself. Lead and silver and oxygen cannot do this. If they are warm it is because something has made them warm from outside, just as the poker— which is made of the element iron—becomes warm if you put it in the fire. But radium left by itself, without any warmth from outside, makes heat for itself, and, wherever you find it, it is always a little hotter than its surroundings —like nothing else in the whole world, except, of course, fire itself, and the heat produced by a fire is really heat from the Sun, which was stored up in the coal and was given out again.

THE STRANGE POWER IN RADIUM THAT WILL HEAT THE EARTH FOR AGES

The extraordinary thing about radium is that it does not require to be burnt in order to make heat, and that the heat which it makes is not the Sun's heat of the past given out again, but is absolutely made brand new, so to speak, on the spot.

Our discovery, then, does not mean that the Earth has a source of heat which can never be used up, but that it has means of making heat which will probably not be exhausted for ages longer than we can think about.

But we have left out something ; we have not satisfied ourselves that there is enough radium to do all these things. For some years all the radium in the world that chemists had been able to extract from mineral ores could be contained in an egg-cup. It was obtained chiefly from a uranium oxide called pitchblende, found at Joachimsthal in Czechoslovakia, in Hungary, in Colorado, and in the Belgian Congo; a little radium also exists in the pitchblende of Cornwall in our own country. But when its tremendous importance was realised, in that endless power and energy could be obtained by splitting up the atoms themselves through its agency, a frantic search for uranium ores was started, and during and soon after the Second World War many new sources were discovered.

THE NEW POWER WHICH WILL TAKE THE PLACE OF COAL AND OIL

Uranium, however, contains only rather more than three parts of radium in ten million, so we can see what a lot of uranium ores must be found before we can get really big supplies of the wonderful element. A little of it, nevertheless, goes such a long way in the creation of new power that there is little doubt that " atomic disintegration," which really means " power from radium," will one day take the place of coal and oil.

As radium occurs, in the crust of the Earth, in such tiny amounts, you might wonder if it could ever make up, day by day, for the amount of heat which the Earth is always losing into space. But the extraordinary fact is that this very small amount of radium added to the heat received from the Sun is sufficient to keep the Earth as warm as it is, as warm as it has been for ages past, and as warm as it will be for ages to come.

Now let us think over something very wonderful. Here we are on this Earth of ours, and we cannot leave it ; but you might at least think that, though we cannot leave it alive, and perhaps do not want to leave it, at any rate we can thoroughly examine every part of it. Now, this is not so. Even today there are still parts of the Earth that have not been explored, and only in comparatively recent years have we reached the North and South Poles. The ocean of air that floats above us is part of the Earth, of course, and it probably extends at least something like two hundred miles high. It seems likely that one day man will fully explore this mysterious region.

It is unlikely, however, that a human being will ever penetrate right down to the interior of the Earth. His whole body would have turned into gas long what it would look like. What have we done in the way of cutting into this thin crust that supports us ? Practically nothing. We measure coalmines by thousands of feet, but as we go down it gets very hot, and it is a very serious matter to get air enough down to these levels. When all is said and done, the deepest coalmine has only got as far as the coal level,

INSIDE THE EARTH—THE SOLID CRUST AND THE RAGING FURNACE BENEATH

before he got there. But take this thin crust, which has produced such wonders. Compared with the whole thickness of the Earth, it is a mere nothing—40 miles out of 8000 ; its crust is 200 times thinner than the Earth itself.

A little while ago we were talking about cutting the Earth in half and seeing and that, compared with the whole crust of the Earth, is almost nothing at all.

Yet every day the mind is teaching us more about the Earth. Every day the eyes of our mind are getting to see farther and farther, and wider and wider.

(Next chapter in this group, page 517)

LEWIS CARROLL TELLS HIS LITTLE FRIENDS THE STORY OF ALICE

The Story of Immortal Folk Whose Work Will Never Die

Charles Kingsley   Sir J. M. Barrie   Jacob Grimm   Wilhelm Grimm   Hans Andersen   George MacDonald

Hawthorne   Lewis Carroll   Madame d'Aulnoy   Charles Perrault   J. C. Harris   Carl Ewald

CREATORS OF FANTASY
Their Tales of the Land of Make-Believe

IN Venice, that marvellous city which is itself a fairy story, there lived in the early years of the sixteenth century Giovanni Francesco Straparola.

We know very little about this Straparola, except that he was a writer of stories. In those days Venice was the wonder of the world, and all sorts of clever men were drawn to the town because of its riches, and the splendid company to be found there.

Straparola was a clever Italian who had gone there doubtless because it was a famous place for printing books; and there for many years, in some unknown house by the side of an old canal, this man with the strange-sounding name wrote his stories and got them printed in the lovely city of the sea. He first wrote Puss in Boots, except that his Puss wore no boots.

Towards the end of the seventeenth century, and in the early years of the eighteenth, the pleasant land of France was noted for its writers of fairy tales. It was then that Blue Beard, Little Red Riding Hood, The Sleeping Beauty, Mother Goose, Beauty and the Beast, and many another of our old favourites first took the form in which we know them.

The two great writers of fairy stories at that time were a Parisian named Charles Perrault, and the French countess, Madame d'Aulnoy. We see how grateful we should be for many of our happiest hours to that forgotten Straparola, when we are told that both Perrault and the countess got most of their ideas from his writings.

He must have been a kindly old gentleman, this Monsieur Perrault—who was busy with the affairs of State, being the official in charge of the Royal buildings, and a member of the great French Academy—to have found time and delight in telling his own children these charming stories, and writing them down for the children of the world. He was nearly seventy when his principal book of fairy stories appeared, and he made believe the stories were told by his son, Pierre, which was perhaps a device for commending them to other young folk; for Perrault, though a learned scholar, was not ashamed to set the fashion of writing fairy stories. The proper title of his book was Stories or Tales of Past Times, but it had another and better title, Tales of Mother Goose.

One of the many grand ladies who lived in France at the same time as Perrault was Madame d'Aulnoy. The White Cat, The Yellow Dwarf, The Fair One with the Golden Locks, Cinderella, and many another nursery favourite were shaped by her pen from the earlier tales of Straparola. There were many other ladies who, about the time of Madame d'Aulnoy and somewhat later, practised this delightful art of weaving fairy tales, but, as they all borrowed from the little-known writer who plied his pen by the sparkling waters of Venice a hundred years before them, our thanks for the pleasure of these old tales are perhaps more due to him.

THE GRAVE AND LEARNED SCHOLARS WHO TOLD THE JOLLY TALES

What delight is associated with the otherwise forbidding name of Grimm! Tom Thumb, The Queen Bee, Hansel and Gretel, The Frog Prince, Rum-pel-stilt-skin, and many other stories that boys and girls for more than a hundred years have been reading with endless entertainment, were all written down by two brothers named Grimm, who lived in Germany during the first half of last century. Jacob Grimm was the elder of the two brothers, being born at the town of Hanau on January 4, 1785, while his brother Wilhelm was born on February 24, 1786.

These two brothers were probably not in the least like the sort of people one would expect to be fond of telling fairy tales. As a matter of fact, they were sober, industrious scholars whose whole lives were devoted to literary studies and teaching, both of them becoming professors at the University of Berlin. Grave and learned gentlemen they were, whose greatest concern was to produce books of a kind that only students read, yet they quite unconsciously made themselves famous for ever by collecting the old German fairy stories into a book, which has been translated into all the principal languages of the world, and has made the name of the brothers Grimm as well known in England and America as it was in their native land.

HANS CHRISTIAN ANDERSEN, THE LONG AND LANKY COBBLER'S SON

They went out together, these two industrious scholars, among the country-people of Germany, and induced them to tell such stories as they knew of the fairies. What a charming occupation, and how delightful were the results !

The other name that stands beside the Grimms in fame is that of Hans Christian Andersen, the great Danish storyteller, who is really a much abler writer than the Grimms. Hans Andersen was certainly one who knew the fairies, as most of his wonderful stories—such as Little Klaus and Big Klaus, The Little Mermaid, The Tinder-Box, The Wild Swans, The Ugly Duckling, and The Snow Queen—were told to him not by the peasant-folk, but by the fairies of his own brain.

A wonderful and strange man was Hans Christian Andersen. The son of a poor cobbler, he was born in the year 1805 in the ancient city of Odense, in Denmark. The poor cobbler was a learned man in his way, and used to read books at night with his son Hans, who was growing up a long, lanky lad. But neither his father nor mother was sufficiently strict about his attending school, so that as a boy his education was irregular.

He was perhaps more sensitive than most children, being of a nervous, highly-strung nature, and his mother found it necessary to arrange at the first school he attended that he should never be birched. One day, when the mistress gave him a slight tap with the rod, he immediately took up his books and slate and marched off home. His mother then sent him to another school, where was a tiny girl who once told Hans that her ambition was to be a dairymaid at a large country house.

WHAT HAPPENED WHEN HANS ANDERSEN TOLD HIS FIRST FAIRY TALE

" You shall be a dairymaid at my castle when I am a gentleman," said the boy in jest, and he drew upon his slate a rough picture of what his castle was like. The little fairies of the brain were already at work prompting him to tell strange stories about himself. So he went on to assure the little scholar that he was really of noble birth, but that the fairies had changed him in his cradle.

It would be a long story if we were to follow the incidents of Hans Andersen's life, though everything concerning this strange genius would be well worth telling.

His father died when the lad was eleven, and even at that age he had made very poor use of his schooling, dreaming and idling his time away.

It was not very long before he had a stepfather, and soon he had to think of making his way in the world by going to Copenhagen, the capital of his country.

It was all because of having appeared on the stage of the theatre at Odense in a very tiny part in Cinderella, and having

holding with admiring confidence the hand of Old Mother Goose, Henry the Eighth (our real and royal Bluebeard) in his jolliest mood, and Rip Van Winkle who went to sleep for twenty years; the Cow that Jumped over the Moon, Joan of Arc, the Three Bears, showing that, after all, their sizes were not so very different; the Cock that Crowed in the Morn, Old Mother Hubbard and her hungry Dog, Dapple Grey, George Washington grown up, and many more of the immortal friends that live with us for ever in the magic world of childhood. What a merry company they are, all in their colours!

to recall the names of the many strange characters, such as The Mad Hatter, Tweedledum and Tweedledee, The White Rabbit, and all that varied throng with which every boy and girl loses no time in making acquaintance.

But what sort of a man was he from whose brain of teeming fancies these strange and delightful creatures came? Should we picture him as a jolly, middle-aged gentleman, leading a life free from care, and happiest with his children round his knees, telling stories?

A BRILLIANT PROFESSOR WITH A LIVELY IMAGINATION

Such a picture would be curiously incorrect, for Lewis Carroll was in certain ways as strange a character as some of his own fairy folk. In the first place, he was, of all things in the world, a mathematician, and lectured at Oxford University on that science which is the terror of most young scholars. Perhaps it was because he spent so much time over difficult problems in mathematics that he liked to clear and refresh his brain with humorous thoughts and happy fancies, which he turned into the shape of fantastic stories for the amusement of the children of his friends.

Perhaps he was just a little moody, being sometimes rather a dull companion to grown-ups, and although he was 66 at the time of his death, on January 14, 1898, he had never been married.

One of the queer things about children's books is that they often interest and delight grown-ups as much as the little people for whom they are intended. Alice had a great admirer in Queen Victoria, and it is said that she was so charmed with the story that she asked to see a copy of the author's next book.

Carroll must have received the Royal request with some amusement. As it happened, he was already at work on a new book, and in due course it was sent to the Palace—an advanced treatise on Pure Mathematics!

HOW LEWIS CARROLL TOLD ALICE A STORY ON THE RIVER BANK

He was young when he wrote his immortal story of Alice's Adventures in Wonderland, first published in 1865. There really was a little girl named Alice, one of the many little girls who were delighted when Lewis Carroll came to visit their parents, as they had never any difficulty in getting him to tell a story. The real Alice was a daughter of Dean Liddell, and she herself has told us how the story was begun.

We cannot do better than let the words of the real Alice be heard again. " Most of Mr. Dodgson's stories," she says, " were told to us on river expeditions to Nuneham or Godstow, near Oxford. My eldest sister, now Mrs. Skene, was Prima, I was Secunda, and Tertia was my sister Edith. I believe the beginning of Alice was told one summer afternoon when the sun was so burning that we had landed in the meadows down the river, deserting the boat to take refuge in the only bit of shade to be found, which was under a new-made hayrick. Here from all three came the old petition of ' Tell us a story,' and so began the ever-delightful tale."

Another of Lewis Carroll's young friends was a lad named Greville, the son of George MacDonald, who was a great preacher, a popular novelist, and a poet. George MacDonald, too, was one who knew the fairies, and he wrote for us many books of fairy tales—At the Back of North Wind, The Princess and the Goblin, and many more. George Macdonald was born in Scotland in 1824 and died in 1905.

THE BEST OF ALL THE FAIRY PLAYS, PETER PAN

There are, of course, many other fairy-story tellers. Joel Chandler Harris, the American writer, who was born in 1848, and died on July 4, 1908, told those wonderful Negro tales of Uncle Remus, in which Brer Fox and Brer Rabbit and the Tar Baby have such wonderful parts to play; and Carl Ewald, a Danish schoolmaster, born in 1856 and died in 1908, who wrote Mr. Two-Legs, and seventy other fairy tales. When we have mentioned them, we have noticed most of those who knew the fairies.

Though, after all, we may be asked, " What about Peter Pan? "

Certainly Sir J. M. Barrie, the writer of that most charming of all the fairy plays, knew the little folk as well as anyone ; and no man seems to have had in him a finer touch of fairy life than he had. But we read of him elsewhere, as a writer of greater books than Peter Pan.

Nearer to our own day is the ever popular Toad of Toad Hall, which is a play by A. A. Milne based on Kenneth Grahame's book, The Wind in the Willows. This book has a romantic but sad history. One of its chief characters, the genial, boastful adventurer, Toad,

HANS ANDERSEN SITS DREAMING AMONG THE FRIENDS HE MADE FAMOUS IN HIS FAIRY TALES

began life at the beginning of this century. His creator, Kenneth Grahame, was then Secretary of the Bank of England. He was a busy man, but could always find time in the evenings to go to the nursery of his little son Alastair, and tell him some more about the doings of Toad. Later, Kenneth Grahame made the stories into a book, The Wind in the Willows. But the little boy for whom Toad had been invented was killed by a train when he was only 20 and an undergraduate at Oxford.

THE TINY BOY WHO ASKED SO MANY QUESTIONS

Even as a child he had been a remarkable personality. When he was hardly more than a baby he asked, " Why is there trouble in the world? " and one day when with his governess he passed a shop which had a picture of Jesus in the window, he said, " That is my friend. He came to see me when I was ill." This young foster-father of Toad was a very human little boy. A certain treat depended on his being good all day. Had he been ? " Yes," he said slowly, and added, " but there was a good deal of vulgar eating and arms on the table."

Kenneth Grahame died in 1932.

A. A. Milne, who died in 1956 at the age of 74, gave us that bedtime favourite, Winnie the Pooh. His poems, When We Were Very Young, were as popular with grown-ups as with children when they were first published, though nowadays they are for most of us a pleasant memory of the days when we were very young. He wrote the poems and the Winnie the Pooh books to amuse his son, Christopher Robin, and the little boy's toys live on in the stories as Winnie the Pooh, Piglet, Kanga and Roo, and Eeyore. But among the favourite books on Christopher Robin's bookshelf was a set of this work, The Children's Encyclopedia.

BEATRIX POTTER, AND HER FOUR FAMOUS RABBITS

Another creator of charming fantasy, who created pictures as well as stories, was Beatrix Potter, who died in 1943 at the age of 77. She gave the world the famous Peter Rabbit and those other well-loved folk, Squirrel Nutkin, Jemima Puddleduck the over-trustful goose, the expansive but puddly-footed Mr. Jeremy Fisher, neat, industrious Mrs. Tiggy-Winkle, Hunca Munca, The Tailor of Gloucester, and others who have called forth dimples of laughter and round eyes of wonder in many a small countenance.

The celebrated Peter Rabbit began life in September 1893, in a letter written by young Miss Potter to a friend's little son who was ill in bed. " Dear Noel," she wrote, " I shall tell you a story about four little rabbits whose names are Flopsy, Mopsy, Cottontail, and Peter. They lived with their mother in a sand-bank under the roots of a big fir tree." The letter was illustrated with those skilfully drawn sketches of Peter and his family which were destined to become known all over the world.

Although she gladdened the childhood of many thousands, Beatrix Potter herself had not a very happy childhood. Her parents were rich people who lived in London and, perhaps without realising it, they neglected little Beatrix. She spent most of her days alone in her nursery with no other children to play with. She never went to school and was educated by governesses.

THE LONELY CHILD WHO CREATED HER OWN PLAYMATES

The most exciting periods of her life were when she went with her parents for summer holidays in Scotland. There she made acquaintance with the little furry people of the woods and the hedgerows, and the farmyard characters who were to make her famous in her books. The lonely child was building up a world of her own in her imagination—but it was a world she was to share with millions of others.

When she was grown up she longed for a country life, but a strong sense of duty kept her living with her parents, mostly in London, until she was well advanced in middle age. However, with the profits from her books she bought a farm in the Lake District, which she visited as often as possible.

She was nearly 50 before she found happiness. She married a lawyer, Mr. William Heelis, a Westmorland man, and at last settled down to live the life of a farmer, which pleased her far more than being a famous writer.

Thus this lovable woman, who has enriched the lives of millions of children, spent the evening of her days among the fells and lakes she had often sighed for when cooped up in a stuffy old-fashioned London house.

The Great Stories of the World That Will Be Told for Ever

LITTLE GOODY TWOSHOES

ALL the world must allow that Twoshoes was not her real name. No : her father's name was Meanwell, and he was for many years a well-to-do farmer in the parish where Margery was born ; but bad times came ; he and his wife died, leaving Margery and her little brother to the mercies of the wide, wide world.

Little Margery and Tommy were both very ragged, and Tommy had two shoes, but Margery had but one. They had nothing, poor things, but their love for each other. Their relatives took no notice of them; but Mr. Smith, a good-hearted clergyman who lived in the parish where little Margery and Tommy were born, sent for the children. A friend of his ordered little Margery a new pair of shoes, gave Mr. Smith some money to buy her clothes, and said he would take Tommy to make him a sailor, while Mr. Smith promised to look after Margery.

Next morning the shoemaker came in with Margery's new shoes. She ran out to Mrs. Smith as soon as they were put on, and cried out:

" Two shoes, Mamma; see, two shoes! "

And so she behaved to all the people she met, and thus got herself the name of Goody Twoshoes, though her playmates called her Old Goody Twoshoes.

Little Margery was very happy in the home of Mr. and Mrs. Smith. She saw how good and how wise Mr. Smith was, and concluded that this was owing to his great learning, therefore she wanted, above all things, to learn to read. For this purpose she used to meet the little boys and girls as they came from school, borrow their books, and sit down and read till they returned. By this means she soon learned more than her playmates, and devised a scheme for teaching those who were more ignorant than herself.

She knew that only twenty-six letters were required to spell all the words we ever need; but as some of these letters are large and some small, she, with her knife, cut out of several pieces of wood, ten sets of each of the small ones and six sets of each of the large ones.

Every morning she used to go round with the wooden letters in a basket to teach the children

Mrs. Smith once went with her on her rounds. The first house they came to was Farmer Wilson's. Here Margery stopped, and ran up to the door, giving a tap.

" Who's there? "

" Only little Goody Twoshoes," answers Margery, " come to teach Billy."

" Oh, little Goody," says Mrs Wilson, with pleasure in her face. " I am glad to

IMAGINATION · CHIVALRY · LEGENDS · GOLDEN DEEDS · FAIRY TALES

see you! Billy is quite ready for you, for he has learned all his lessons."

Then out came the little boy, Billy.

" How do, Doody Twoshoes? " says he, not being able to speak very plainly.

Yet this little boy had learned all his letters; for she threw down the alphabet all mixed together, and he picked them up, called them by their right names, and put them in order.

The next place they came to was Gaffer Cook's cottage. Here some poor children met to learn. They all came round little Margery at once; and, having pulled out her letters, she asked the boy next her what he had for dinner.

He answered, " Bread." Indeed, they were so poor that they lived on little else.

" Well, then," says she, " put the first letter down here."

He then put up the letter *B*, to which he next added *r*, and the next *e*, the next *a*, the next *d*, and it stood thus: *Bread*.

" And what had you, Polly Comb, for your dinner? "

" Apple-pie," answered the little girl; and so the lesson went on.

The next place they came to was Farmer Thompson's, where there were a great many little ones waiting for her.

" Little Mrs. Goody Twoshoes," says one of them, " what have you been doing all this time? "

" I have been teaching," says she, " longer than I intended, and am afraid I am come too soon for you now."

" No, but indeed you are not," replied the other, " for I know my lessons, and so does Sally Dawson, and so do we all."

" Why, then," says she, " you are all very good, and God will love you; so let us begin our lesson."

They all huddled round her, and, though at the other place they were concerned with words and syllables, here were children of much greater ability, who dealt in sentences, which they set up and read aloud.

Mrs. Williams, who kept what we should call today an old-fashioned Dame's School, was at this time very old and infirm, and it was decided that Margery should take up her work. Henceforth she was known as Mrs. Margery.

One day Mrs. Margery brought home a fine raven which she had rescued from the cruel hands of some village boys.

Now, this bird, whom she called Ralph, she taught to speak, to spell, and to read. He sat at her elbow, and when any of the children were wrong she used to call out, " Put them right, Ralph."

She had also a pigeon, which she had taught to spell and read, though not to talk. He was a very pretty fellow, and she called him Tom.

Soon after this a present was made to Mrs. Margery of a little dog, Jumper, and a pretty dog he was. Jumper was the porter of the college, for he would let nobody go out or come in without the leave of his mistress.

One Thursday morning Jumper all of a sudden laid hold of his mistress's apron, and endeavoured to pull her out of the school. She was at first surprised; but she followed him to see what it was he wanted her for.

No sooner had he led her into the garden than he ran back and pulled out one of the children in the same manner; upon which she ordered them all to leave the school immediately, and they had not been out five minutes before the top of the house fell in.

The downfall of the school was a great misfortune to Mrs. Margery, for she not only lost all her books, but was without a place to teach in. But soon after a friend had it rebuilt for her.

Mrs. Margery was much esteemed by her neighbours. One gentleman, Sir Charles Jones, had conceived such a high opinion of her that he offered her a considerable sum to take care of his family; but she refused. This gentleman sent for her afterwards when he had a dangerous illness, and she nursed him so well that he made her promise to marry him.

The wedding day arrived, and they went to church. But just as the clergyman had opened his book a gentleman ran into the church and cried : " Stop! Stop! "

This gentleman turned out to be Mrs. Margery's brother, who had just come from beyond the sea, where he had made a large fortune, and, hearing of his sister's intended wedding, he had ridden in great haste to see that a proper settlement was made on her.

Mrs. Margery, after her marriage, still went on with her good works. She was a mother to the poor, a doctor to the sick, and a friend to all in distress, and she was loved by everybody.

THE OLD MAN OF THE PIT

ONE misty summer's morning two Indian braves came slowly over the mountains carrying a wounded comrade on a litter.

By and by they laid it on the ground, and sat down to rest a little way off, talking in sullen whispers. This accident had spoiled their hunting expedition ; it was weary work bearing the youth all this long way back to camp. Presently they took up the burden again, and, marching with it to the edge of a narrow cleft in the rocks, they suddenly flung the litter down it.

At first the wounded youth was stunned by the fall, but when he came to his senses he ardently wished that his neck had been broken. How much more dreadful it would be to starve to death in this pit!

All at once he heard footsteps close at hand. Looking up, the youth perceived that an old man was coming slowly toward him in the fast-gathering twilight.

"My son," said the ancient stranger, "I have been examining your injuries. They are great. I can cure them, but I make this condition —when you are well you must go hunting for me, as I am too feeble to go." The youth was only too thankful to accept these terms, and could not thank his deliverer enough.

THE HERMIT BECAME A PORCUPINE

The old man was skilful in the use of medicine; before long the youth recovered. All day he spent in hunting, and would have been quite content if he had not thought of his mother, who would be mourning him as dead.

One day he killed a bear, and was bending over his prey when he heard a rushing sound in the air. Looking up he beheld three beautiful beings whose feet did not touch the ground. Their limbs shone like gold through the thin, rainbow-coloured garments which fluttered about them, and their faces were as bright as stars.

The brave fell on his knees.

"O, Indian," they said, "we are the Thunderers. It is our task to watch over the Earth, to foster the good, and to drive out evil spirits. We have come to you to seek your alliance."

"How can I serve such mighty ones?" asked the youth. "I will do whatever you command."

One of the Thunderers replied: "Then we will take you back to your mother's lodge. Know that the old hermit whose huntsman you are is really an evil spirit in disguise. For fear of us he hides in that cavern where we cannot reach him. Your task is to draw him out into the open."

The youth leapt to his feet and hurried back to the cave.

"I have killed a fine bear," he said, "but it is much too heavy for one man to drag. You must help me to bring it in."

The old man frowned and sighed. He was silent. Then he asked :

"Are there any clouds about?"

The youth said there were none, and the hermit followed him unwillingly. When they reached the dead bear the old man lifted it on his back, and set off for home with great strides.

But a little black cloud suddenly appeared in the midst of the blue sky. In a moment or two it had grown to a gigantic size. There was a flicker of lightning, a roar like the falling of mountains, and a thunderbolt was suddenly hurled in the direction of the old man.

He dropped the burden and fled. A second thunderbolt was flung, and the ancient hermit became a porcupine as big as a calf, which ran along shooting out a shower of quills like arrows. As he was gaining the cave a third thunderbolt fell, and this time the aim was perfect. The monster rolled into the cavern dead.

Then the clouds parted, and the Thunderers appeared before the trembling Indian. Two of them took him between them, with his arms about their necks, and bore him swiftly over the hill and forest to his mother's feet.

THE IDOL AND THE WHALE

AMONG the trees of Kamakura there sits an enormous bronze Buddha.

He is fifty feet high, and ninety-seven feet round about; his face is eight feet long and the girth of his thumbs is three feet. There he sits, smiling gently to himself as though he remembered the fine times of the Middle Ages, when Kamakura was a capital city and he lived in a temple, instead of having no roof but the sky over his mighty head.

All this is a matter of fact. But we are not prepared to say quite as much for the story of his encounter with the whale.

The whale was a monster among his kind, and he took as much pride in his bulk as soldiers take in their medals, or as some queer folk seem to take in their ailments. Others might be more beautiful, more clever, more useful to the community, but no one was as big, and somehow he felt that this gave him a kind of kingship over his fellow-citizens of the water. He patronised them all; yet, as he was good-natured, they put up with his airs and graces.

One day some fishermen gossiped about the bronze Buddha while they were at sea. They spoke of the scores of pilgrims who flocked to Kamakura because of the image, which they said, was *the biggest thing in the world.* They were overheard, and of course some little busybody of a sprat must needs fly off to tell the whale.

At first the monster roared with laughter, and made several tidal waves. Nothing could be as big as he was. But by-and-by he began to grow jealous. He would have liked pilgrims to make journeys to see *him.* He took a dislike to the Buddha; he brooded, he sulked; at last he began to fear that the image might really be bigger than he was, and at that he flew into a passion like a naughty baby, dashing about the sea and blowing water spouts through his nose till all the other ocean people were dizzy.

When he was forced to pause for breath an elderly shark approached him cautiously, and asked what was the matter. The whale poured out his cares.

"Don't meet trouble half-way," said the shark, " you may still be the biggest thing there is. Wait here quietly, and I will find out if these rumours are true."

The shark swam to the coast, and there he saw a rat cleaning his whiskers as he sat on a junk in the sunlight. He was an obliging little beast, and agreed to go inland and measure the idol.

When he returned to the shark he was quaking all over. Never in his life, he said, had he seen anything so immense as the bronze Buddha. He had plucked up courage to crawl round the base of it, and it was five thousand paces.

The whale could hardly believe the shark's message. Rest and happiness were no longer possible to him. He decided that he must see the Buddha for himself, and settle his mortifying doubts once for all. Tradition says that he borrowed a pair of magic boots so as to be able to travel over land, though how he wore them it is difficult to imagine. Thus equipped, he set out for Kamakura without delay.

He arrived at night, which was fortunate, or the population would have died of terror. There was no mistaking the great temple. He knocked on the door.

A voice that rang like a mighty bell bade him enter.

" Pray come out to me," replied the whale.

There was the sound of heavy footsteps, the doors opened, and a vast figure appeared towering under the stars.

At first the two immense beings were so amazed at the sight of each other that they could not speak. But the whale presently began to tell his story.

The sound of voices woke a priest who had fallen asleep over his vigil in the temple. He saw the idol's pedestal empty; he rushed out, and, beholding the colossal pair, fell upon his face with a scream. But the Buddha picked him up, and bade him take their measurements with his rosary.

The whale's heart almost cracked with suspense, and the priest thought that his master's beautiful face did not look quite so calm as usual in the moonlight.

At last the priest said, " The whale is taller by two inches."

There is no need to add that the whale lived happily ever after. Really, in spite of his conceit, we must be glad he did not lose, for the consequences might have been so dreadful. As for the Buddha's feelings, if we may judge by his expression today, his defeat did not rankle very long.

HOW MR. CAT BECAME KING

ONE morning Mr. Cat found himself without a home. He had been living for years with an old man in a fine house on the edge of the forest. But the old man died at last of old age, and the house was bought by a woman who did not like cats. She had a dog, and this dog would never let Mr. Cat enter the house.

So Mr. Cat set out to explore the forest, and he found a little empty hut in a valley which he thought would suit him. Here he lived for some time, and no one disturbed him; and, though he did not get much food, he managed to keep well and active. One afternoon he was strolling down to the stream for a drink when he met one of the daughters of Brer Fox. She had never seen a cat before, and she looked at Mr. Cat with great interest.

"Who are you, and what is your name?" said Sis Fox. "And what are you doing in this forest?"

Mr. Cat looked very important.

"I have come from town," he said very grandly, "to govern this forest and to keep all the animals in order. I am a cat, and, as of course you know, the cat is the king of beasts."

"Oh," said Sis Fox, "I wish you would come and have dinner with me!"

Mr. Cat had not found anything to eat that day, and he accepted the invitation. And during the dinner Sis Fox said: "My lord, are you married or single?"

"I am a bachelor," said Mr. Cat, stroking his whiskers in a knowing way.

"And I also am single," said Sis Fox. "Would you like to marry me?"

Mr. Cat, he agreed to this, and the wedding took place with a great deal of ceremony. But at the request of Mr. Cat none of the big animals was invited.

The morning after the marriage Mr. Cat said to his wife: "Sis, I am already growing thin with hunger. Go and get me a good dinner."

Away went Sis Fox, and while she was hunting she met Mr. Wolf.

"My dear little sister," said Mr. Wolf, "I have not seen you for days! What ever have you been doing with yourself?"

"I have been getting married," said Sis Fox. "I am now the wife of the governor of the whole of this forest."

"What! You married?" said Mr. Wolf, starting back in surprise. "I must go and call on your husband."

"Very well," said Sis Fox. "But I must warn you that he is an absolutely terrible creature. Before he sees you you must try to win his favour by some gift. Bring him a nice young fat lamb. Leave it at the door, and run away and hide yourself, or he will surely devour you."

Mr. Wolf was rather frightened, and he scuttled off to fetch a lamb for Mr. Cat. Sis Fox went on her way, and in turning a corner she met gruff old Mr. Bear.

"Good-day, my pretty friend," said Mr. Bear. "Where do your come from?"

"From my husband's house," she replied. "I have just married the governor of the forest."

"Really!" exclaimed Mr. Bear. "I must go and call on him."

"Certainly," said Sis Fox. "But my husband has a distressing habit of devouring every animal he does not like. Go and find a bullock, and bring it to him as a gift. Mr. Wolf is bringing a lamb."

The bear shuffled off and got a bullock, and on his way he met Mr. Wolf carrying a lamb.

"Hallo, Mr. Bear!" said Mr. Wolf. "Where are you going?"

"To the governor of the forest, who has married Brer Fox's daughter," said Mr. Bear. "I am taking this bullock to him."

"And I this lamb," said Mr. Wolf. "I understand he is absolutely terrible."

The two animals came together to the hut in which Mr. Cat lived.

"Go and knock at the door," said Mr. Wolf to Mr. Bear.

"I am afraid," said Mr. Bear. "You go."

"I daren't," said Mr. Wolf. "But here is Brer Hare. He will go for us."

Brer Hare had come for a drink at the stream in the valley, and the two big animals asked him to knock at the door of the hut for them. He did so. Mr. Wolf, he hid himself under a bush; and Mr. Bear, he climbed up a tree.

The door of the hut opened, and Mr. Cat and his wife came out.

"He is a very small creature," said Mr. Wolf to Mr. Bear.

"Yes," said Mr. Bear, rapidly climbing down the tree, "he is remarkably small."

He looked at Mr. Cat with scorn, but Mr. Cat leapt on the bullock, and looked it over, and said in an angry voice to his wife: "This is very little! Who has dared to make me so paltry a gift?"

Mr. Bear drew back in surprise, and scrambled again up the tree and said to Mr. Wolf:

"He is so small, and yet has such an appetite. Why, a bullock is a good meal for four grown-up bears! This husband of Sis Fox is really a terrible creature."

Mr. Wolf, hidden under the bush, began to tremble. Mr. Cat heard a slight noise among the leaves. Thinking that a mouse was stirring there, he sprang forward, and his claws scratched the muzzle of poor Mr. Wolf. Mr. Wolf yelped, thinking he was going to be devoured; and, backing out of the bush, he fled away as fast as his legs would carry him.

But Mr. Cat had seen him, and, fearing that Mr. Wolf would attack him, he scrambled up the lowest branch of the tree.

"Oh," said Mr. Bear, "the terrible creature has seen me! He has seen me, and he is climbing up here, and he is going to devour me!"

Down he came from the tree, and away he went after Mr. Wolf. And all the time the wife of Mr. Cat kept on screaming: "My husband will devour you! My husband will devour you!"

Mr. Bear and Mr. Wolf were well-nigh terrified out of their lives, and they went about the forest relating their awful adventure to all the other animals, and all the other animals grew horribly afraid of their new governor. But Mr. Cat and his wife were very happy, for they had an abundance of food to eat. Presents were heaped up every morning at the door of their little hut.

THE WITCH'S RING

A MILLER of Mayfield had three sons, who all fell in love with the same girl. Her name was Marjorie, and she was the daughter of a farmer at Rotherfield, and the prettiest maiden in Sussex. But a rich old miser who lived in the village began to court her, and the farmer favoured his suit and kept the miller's sons away.

At last Richard, the eldest son, determined to propose to Marjorie before the miser won her. On his way to the farm he met Mad Molly. She was an old, feeble woman, suspected of being a witch.

"Good-day, my son," said Mad Molly. "Where are you going this morning?"

Richard hurried on without replying. On reaching the farm he blurted out a proposal of marriage, but Marjorie only laughed at him.

Rowland, the second son, then tried his luck. He also met Mad Molly and hurried on without answering her, and he, also, returned in a downcast mood. Then Robin, the youngest boy, went to the farm. But he set out without hope. He was a strong, clever, and gentle lad, but he had a very long nose, and this, as he knew, made him look ridiculous. When Mad Molly asked him where he was going, he said: "On a hopeless errand, Granny. I am about to call on Marjorie and ask her to be my wife."

"And your wife she shall be," said Mad Molly. "Look at this ring, my son. Put it on your finger and say 'Bless it'!"

Robin did so, and his nose grew half an inch shorter, and he became a very handsome youth.

"Now," said Mad Molly, "if Marjorie refuses you, give her the ring to wear. Then every time you say 'Drat it!' her pretty nose will grow half an inch longer, and she will become ugly, and be very glad to marry you. Then you have only to say 'Bless it!' and her nose will grow shorter and she will recover her beauty."

Robin ran to the farmhouse, and, as Marjorie was out, he sat on a chair and closed his eyes. Just then the miser entered, and saw the ring on his finger.

"An engagement ring!" he said. "I'll keep that."

He pulled it off Robin's finger and put it on his own. But Robin was awake, and he began to whisper "Drat it! Drat it!" and as he said these words the miser's nose grew longer and longer.

"Something is stinging me!" cried the miser, running off to a doctor.

Happily, Robin did not want his ring any more. Marjorie was surprised to see how handsome he looked. She had always liked him for his gentleness, and she now fell quite in love with him, and agreed to marry him as soon as he got a farm.

"Return my ring and I'll cure you for one thousand pounds," said Robin to the miser when he came back.

The miser at last did so, and Robin and Marjorie then married and bought a farm, and lived there very happily together.

THE PEDLAR OF SWAFFHAM

In the days of Henry the Seventh, in a little town called Swaffham, there lived a pedlar, John Chapman by name.

He lived in a cottage on the Peddar Road, with a small garden, in which there was an almond tree he loved.

He delighted in all beautiful things, and he loved the old church in Swaffham, often wishing he were a rich man so that he might add to its beauty.

John was not rich; indeed he had a struggle to make both ends meet. One night, going to bed anxious and dis-

replied: "I have come to London because of a dream I have had."

The shopkeeper, a bluff, matter-of-fact man, laughed heartily.

"How foolish you are!" he said. "Why, I had a dream the other night in which a man named John Chapman, from some place called Swaffham, came to me, and in my dream I told him that if he dug a hole under a tree in his garden he would find a pot of gold there. A fine fool I should look if I went about telling folk to dig for pots of gold because of a dream!"

"I HAVE COME TO LONDON BECAUSE OF A DREAM I HAVE HAD"

heartened, he had a dream in which a man said to him:

"If you walk to London you will meet someone on London Bridge who will give you good news."

The next morning, he set out for London with his pack on his back and his dog at his heels.

When he at last reached London Bridge he waited about for three hours, but no one came up to greet him with good news. He was about to turn disconsolately away when a shopkeeper said to him:

"What is your business here?"

In a burst of confidence the pedlar

The pedlar did not disclose the fact that his name was Chapman and that he came from Swaffham, but set off for home as fast as he could.

When he arrived the first thing he did was to dig a hole beneath his almond tree, and there, sure enough, he found a great pot of gold.

He was now a rich man, and one of the first things that he did was to have a beautiful north aisle—which is to be seen to this day—built in Swaffham Church, and in it a seat for his own use, with a carving on it of the Pedlar of Swaffham with his pack upon his back.

SNOW-DAUGHTER

BJORN always told his wife Dagmar that it was a good thing they had neither sons nor daughters, seeing that they lived in the Naerodal, in Norway, in a pine-built house which was perched among the heights where for half the year they never saw the Sun.

No, their home would be a gloomy one for children ; all the same, the couple secretly longed for them.

One winter, when the snow was deep, Bjorn came down the steep mountain path rolling a big snowball before him, which gathered size as it went.

"Make a snow baby," said Dagmar.

The fancy pleased her husband. He patted and moulded the snowball with what seemed to them both to be almost magical ease.

Presently little limbs made their appearance, chubby arms were outstretched. Dagmar stooped and kissed them.

There was a sound like ice cracking. Out of the crust of snow, like a chicken breaking through its eggshell, came the Snow Baby, pure as a pearl, with hair as pale as silver and eyes of the scilla's blue.

"You woke me to be your wish-child," said she, clasping Dagmar round the knees. "Call me Snow-daughter."

How happy then was the mountain home in the Naerodal all through the long winter, though Dagmar dared not kiss her treasure too warmly and they had to put the child's bed on the roof and heap snow on her for blankets ! No longer could their house be called lonely, as from far and near the children came to visit Snow-daughter.

At last the days of the year drew round to summer. A party of young people came to Bjorn's door.

"Mother Dagmar, we have come to take the Snow Maid down to the valley to see the Sun and the flowers."

"Children, I am afraid the Sun will hurt her."

"Let me go !" cried the Snow-daughter eagerly.

Down the zigzag mountain road they went and reached the river. In the woods and meadows around were flowers. The children cried out with delight to see them ; but Snow-daughter came running to Dagmar, moaning, "Oh, Mother, the Sun is stealing me away !"

And even as she spoke she pined and dwindled.

"Come down to cool yourself in the river," cried Dagmar.

But Snow-daughter had changed to a white vapour which the wind blew away.

Frantic with grief, Dagmar followed the drifting wreath of mist through the pine-woods and up the bleak mountain side. When she came to the ancient snows, which thaw not, she found Snow-daughter, grown to a maiden's shape again, seated in a lofty cleft in the glacier, spreading her hands to the blue ice, as others do to a fire.

"Come back, my darling," Dagmar called across the gulf.

"If I did, next morning you would only find my tears, not me," she replied. "But another winter I shall come and peep through your window at the real baby, the daughter of flesh and blood, whom Heaven is going to send you."

THE WANDERING SHEPHERDESS

IN the days of King George the Third all the beaux of Exeter vainly waited for a sign of love from Maria Selwyn, the gentle, beautiful heiress of Squire Selwyn. But Maria had already given her heart to a handsome shepherd, and she used to steal out at dawn and meet him in the silent meadows.

But one unhappy morning the old Squire also rose early, and he saw the two lovers sitting together under a thorn. The sight drove him mad with anger, and he had the shepherd lad attacked, and the next morning Maria found her sweetheart nigh to death.

"All I have in the world, dearest, are my sheep. I leave them to you. They shall follow you," he said, as he died.

The girl was crazed with grief. Her father shut her up and hunted the sheep away ; but she got out of the house, and began to wander aimlessly about England, and the sheep followed her.

She at last crossed the Scottish border with her strange flock, and she perished on the wild moors near Kingswell. Her sheep then would neither eat nor budge. They pined away, and some kindly Scottish peasants buried them around their mistress.

THE KNIGHT'S TEN THOUSAND JEWELS

A JAPANESE knight was once walking near the shore when he was amazed to see a hideous monster creeping inland.

He drew his sword, but the creature turned its eyes on him meekly, and made no show of resistance.

"What are you?" cried the knight.

"My name is Samébito," replied the creature. "I have been exiled because the Dragon King of the Sea is angry with me. On land I shall soon perish, even if you do not kill me."

The knight was moved to pity. He took the monster home, and let it live in a lake fringed with lilies and graceful trees. Every day the knight fed it with freshly-caught fish.

All went well till the man fell in love with a beautiful damsel who vowed she would not marry him unless he gave her ten thousand jewels. Even if he sold his land and his armour, his house and his furniture, the unfortunate knight would not be able to make her such a present.

He went to bed, turned his face to the wall, and lay there without tasting food or water, for he no longer cared to live.

Samébito could not understand what had become of his master. At length he crept out of the water and drew his long scaly body into the house. The knight turned his head and murmured faintly:

"Alas, Samébito, we must part for ever, for I am dying."

At these words the monster burst into tears. And lo, every tear was a ruby!

The knight leapt out of bed, and began to pick up the jewels with exclamations of wonder and delight.

"You have saved me, Samébito!" he cried. Then his face fell, for he saw that there were not ten thousand jewels yet.

"Please weep again," he asked.

Samébito was indignant.

"I cannot weep at will," the monster exclaimed. "My tears welled up from the anguish of my heart. Now you are well I sorrow no longer."

However, when the knight explained his difficulty, the ruffled monster became pensive. After remaining for a moment deep in thought he said:

"Take me to the sea, and perhaps as I gaze at my old home I shall grow mournful and weep."

So they brought a large wagon, and drove the monster to the sea. He had not contemplated the blue ocean for long before the precious tears began to ooze from his sad eyes. There was soon quite a mound of jewels, and the knight could hardly contain his exultation.

Suddenly a voice cried from the sea:

"Samébito! You are pardoned. You may return."

The two friends took a tender farewell, and parted, one for his bride, the other for his native sea.

HOW THE THIEF WAS FOUND OUT

MOSTAFA, a wise and rich merchant of Damascus, had an only son, Said, whom he wished to train up in prudence; but Said trusted too much in a young Armenian, who managed to cheat him several times without in any way raising his suspicions.

One day Mostafa and Said were compelled to go on business to Bagdad.

"Now, whom can I trust my money with during our absence?" said the merchant.

"With my friend the Armenian, of course," said his son. "He is the most honest man in Damascus."

"Very well, Said," replied the merchant. "For once I will rely upon your judgment."

He gave his son a large, heavy strong-box to entrust to the keeping of the Armenian, and when Said returned he took him to Bagdad. Two months afterwards they returned to Damascus, having made a considerable amount of money.

"Now, my son," said Mostafa, "go to your friend and get my strong-box."

Said went to the Armenian, and quickly returned in great anger.

"You have insulted my friend," he exclaimed. "It was not money you entrusted to his safe keeping, he says, but a mass of broken stones!"

"Pray, how did your very honourable friend find that there were only stones in my strong-box?" said Mostafa. "He must have broken the three locks, and this, I think, will now prove to you that it was well I entrusted him with nothing of any value."

Said hung his head, and thenceforward he allowed himself to be guided by his father's wisdom and experience.

EIGHT COUSINS OF PUSSY-BY-THE-FIRE

THE TIGER CAT

THE AARD-WOLF

THE OCELOT

THE MEERKAT AT ATTENTION

WATERHOUSE'S GENET

THE MANX CAT

THE MONGOOSE

THE GENET

Nature's Wonderful Living Family in Earth and Air and Sea

BIG CATS AND LITTLE CATS

IT is a disturbing and terrible thought that one of the most magnificent orders in the scale of Nature lives by unceasing slaughter. For fierce and insolent beauty, for grace, strength, speed, and audacity, there is no living thing to excel the animals that feed on flesh.

Long process of refining of wits, of sharpening of natural weapons, has brought these Carnivora—so they are called—to the highest pitch of efficiency in the capture and killing of other animals.

Day and night the Carnivora are playing their appointed part in keeping down numbers. They themselves are without visible foes, yet have a mysterious check on over-multiplication. All the flesh-eaters are more numerous at a birth than the herb-eaters. But an unseen agency takes off cubs from every nursery, or the flesh-eaters would be too numerous, and would destroy all herb-eaters.

Check and counter-check are constantly at work to maintain the balance, and as for the terrors of it all—they hardly exist! The deer and antelope tribes, the stock source of the flesh-eaters' meals, are possibly the happiest things in dumb creation. They are born with a sense of caution in the presence of lions, leopards, and tigers, as emphatic as their instinct to find food and water and mates.

The conditions of jungle and plain and forest are not more frightful to animals than the traffic dangers of Hyde Park Corner to a Londoner, born to elude such perils. We must imagine that a cheery gazelle is not more worried by the possibility of an encounter with a lion than we are by the possibilities of motor-buses, wasp-stings, and bites from the mad dogs we may never meet.

The Strand or Trafalgar Square would be more horrifying to a lion or an antelope than the jungle or the forest to us. Life is anxious, full of responsibilities to all that inherit. Humanity has to cross Ludgate Circus in the high tide of traffic, and to confront the viper in the wilds; yet it is happy, unquailing. The eland approaches its Ludgate Circus when a lion is near; a gazelle must avoid its wasp-sting when a hyena lurches at it. The balance is on the side of escape and happiness for the great majority, human and animal.

Freed from any challenge from animals, the cats are the necessary tyrants of the world, by right of might. Like the other carnivores, they have claws, not nails, and teeth which tear and chop or shear like scissors, but do not masticate. Lion, tiger, leopard, lynx, the domestic pet on the hearth—they are all cats, with the lion at the head of the family as the king of beasts, at home in Africa and Persia, but now almost extinct in India.

The majestic appearance of the male lion is crowned by a great mane, sometimes black, but always darker than the tawny skin. Added to that it has the most

PREHISTORIC LIFE · MAMMALS · BIRDS · REPTILES · FISHES · INSECTS

stupendous voice in nature ; its ground-shaking roars sometimes unnerve animals so that they are incapable of flight.

This is its armament: teeth which can crush at one bite the bones of a buffalo's, an eland's, or a zebra's neck ; claws like grapnels of yellow horn, which can hold a horse from its gallop and strip the flesh from its flanks; a gape which admits a man's head into its mouth; strength which enables it to leap a fence when hauling a dead bullock in its mouth; speed which makes it, for a short distance, a kind of flesh-and-bone thunderbolt.

Although it is called the king of beasts it is really less formidable than the tiger, which has greater strength of jaws and claws. Yet the lion is sufficiently terrible. As a rule, it does not attack man; now and then it eats only human flesh; sometimes it takes man or beast by turns.

THE LIONS THAT CREPT OUT OF THE JUNGLE NIGHT BY NIGHT

One which entered the camp of a white traveller had already slain six native women, but on leaping into the enclosure it struck not at men, but at a donkey, five yards from the fire. The donkey fell dead, and two others, tethered near, broke their ropes and fled. The lion bounded after them and killed first one, then the other, and lay down to eat the third.

The two most notorious lions in all African history began their public career by raiding the sheep and goats collected for the workers who were building the Uganda Railway. Then they invaded the camp of men at Tsavo, and for nine months caused a reign of terror there. Night after night they crept from the jungle into the little city of tents ; night after night each carried off a man. As darkness fell, the beasts would be heard roaring in the forest. Silence would follow, then a cry of anguish would ring out, " Beware, brothers ; Satan is here," and all knew that another poor native had gone to make a ravening lion's supper.

The resources of the British Empire were behind the building of that railway, but the slaughter by these two lions became so terrible that at last panic paralysed the undertaking, and all work ceased for about a month. Finally the two brutes were shot, and the line again marched forward.

Tigers often create havoc in the domes-tic life of India. One animal may kill over a hundred people in a year as the people go at night to draw water from a well. In due course this tiger will be shot, but another is almost certain to appear on the old beat, and the remnants of a village population, terrorised beyond endurance, will flee.

THE TIGERS AND LEOPARDS, AND THE TERRIBLE WORK THEY DO

Giants of the tiger tribe live in Manchuria, monsters, huge of bone and muscle, long of fur, at home in the snow and rigours of a bitter climate; but the Indian tiger is full lion size—ten feet long and up to 550 pounds in weight. With its ability to live in swamps, in reeds, grasses, in caves and clefts of rocks, in old buildings and deserted cities, it has a wider range than the lion, and is the foremost death-dealer among Indian animals. What the casualty list is in Africa no man knows, but in India tigers kill scores of people every year, to say nothing of all the thousands of domestic cattle.

Next to the tigers come the leopards, the second animal scourge of India. Although about 5000 leopards are killed every year, they are still responsible for much loss of human life, and greatly feared. Indeed, leopards are more to be feared than lions and tigers, for leopards climb superbly, either to catch a fugitive or to lurk in hiding ready to pounce down on one. In Africa the leopard is viewed with special abhorrence for this reason. All these great cats are extremely difficult to kill. If dying animals do not feel the pain inflicted by the big cats, the big cats seem to experience none themselves.

THE LION THAT KILLED A FAMOUS STATESMAN'S BROTHER

The lion which killed the brother of Viscount Grey was first shot through the right shoulder, then through the lower jaw, then through the body, and finally through the heart. Between the second and third shots it charged home at Mr. Grey, and bit him frightfully. After the third shot it turned on him again, and with its damaged lower jaw " worried him as a dog worries a rat," as the unhappy man's friend said. The last of the four shots, all fired at close range, was fatal; but so were Mr. Grey's wounds.

Now in the presence of these horrors, it is consoling to find that Mr. Grey was able to assure those about him that he felt no pain. He did not suffer at all ; shock and loss of blood, not agony, caused his death. Sir Edward Bradford had his left arm munched away up to the elbow by a tiger, and sat at dinner one night with Rustem Pasha, who had lost his right hand and left arm to a bear. Both men were able to say that they had no suffering during the mutilation. They agreed that probably their intense desire to defend themselves prevented them from feeling the pain.

THE LION WHICH SHAKES A MAN AS A CAT SHAKES A MOUSE

Dr. Livingstone, who was terribly bitten by a lion in Africa, had a different and deeply significant theory. The shock, said he, produced a stupor, similar to that which seems to be felt by a mouse after the first shake by a cat. It caused a sort of dreaminess, in which there was complete consciousness of what was happening, but no sense of pain, no feeling of terror. It annihilated fear, and allowed no sense of horror in looking round at the beast. This peculiar state, Livingstone urges, is " probably produced in all animals killed by the Carnivora, and, if so, is a merciful provision by our benevolent Creator for lessening the pain of death."

There is comfort in that thought as we consider the daily lives of this splendid but pitiless order of flesh-eaters, animals which would perish within a week if other animals were not available as food.

Lion, tiger, leopard, we have named, but a special type of leopard must be added—the ounce, or snow leopard, which haunts the towering Himalayas. In summer it ranges up to 18,000 feet, lithe and formidable at a height where a man is so exhausted that he thinks twice before undergoing the exertion of turning over in bed. There this redoubtable great cat lives, never coming lower than 6000 feet.

THE PUMA THAT WILL ONLY ATTACK A MAN TO SAVE ITSELF

So far we have kept to the Old World, but now we must cross to the New, where we find no lions or tigers but interesting parallels. The American jaguar is a big leopard, with huge, powerful limbs, decorated with rosettes instead of spots like its Old World cousin ; an accomplished swimmer and climber, a deadly foe to cattle and horses, and as ready to kill an unarmed man as to look at him. The jaguar slays an ox, and drags it lightly into hiding.

America's lion is the puma, which, if men were not there to dispute its path to progress, ought to have a future, and for this reason that the more varied an animal's diet, the greater that animal's success in life. The puma eats anything, from a pig to a porcupine, from a horse to a snail, from a sheep to a bullock. It is a terrible scourge to ranches, and in olden days exterminated the half-wild horses which roamed free in Patagonia.

The one thing in its favour is that in no circumstances will it attack man unless it has to fight him to save its own life. The tradition is persistent that it will do battle with the jaguar in defence of the man whom the jaguar seeks to assail.

THE FASTEST SHORT-DISTANCE RUNNER IN THE WHOLE ANIMAL KINGDOM

Prosperity has attended the campaign waged by teeth and claws, and abundant species have arisen to carry on in lesser ways the tradition of the giants. There is one beast, called the clouded leopard, which is as much a tree-dweller as a sloth. The lynx and the caracal are also cats. Then we launch into a world of lesser cats; the golden cat of the Indo-Malay area, which has a grey Chinese cousin; the fishing cat which truly catches fish, but little children and hosts of animals as well; the leopard cat, the serval, the tiger cat, the eyra, a weasel-like type; the Egyptian or Kaffir cat, from which our own puss is believed to descend; all these and more, including the fine old wild cat of Britain, stupid and untamable up in its last retreat, the Highland deer forests, come into the cat family. Each one is Destiny to some order of grass-feeders.

There are others, and we must note the cheetah, more cat than dog, yet not quite cat either, a leopard-like beast with claws resembling a dog's, and therefore not capable of freely working in and out of their sheaths. This animal is remarkable as the one which is caught young and trained to hunt like a dog, its quarry being the swift deer of India. A cheetah runs down the fleetest of grass-feeders, and is regarded as the fastest of all runners for any distance up to about 400 yards.

The cheetah and the domestic cat are the only animals from the feline group that we have brought home with us from the wilds, but our puss shows what man's selective care can do. Arising from a common stock we have dozens of breeds of pet cats.

It is a wonderful choice—white, black, blue, cream, tabby, sandy, silver, brown, and all the combinations desirable from a blend of those colours. There are long-haired cats, there are short-haired cats, there is even a horrid hairless Mexican cat. Chinchillas, tortoiseshell, Persians, Russians, Manx, without a vestige of a tail beyond a tuft of hair; Abyssinian, Indian, Siamese; white cats that are deaf, white cats that are tailless—what would you have? Every sort and size, every colour and disposition, is available, a triumph for scientific breeding.

Farewell, then to lion and family, and now to their near kindred. These are found in the civets, a tribe which, beginning with the cat-like fossa, has thrown up a great number of species, all in the Old World. Without dealing with anatomical niceties, we may note that they are all long-bodied and short-legged.

THE PLUCKY LITTLE MONGOOSE THAT WILL FIGHT A SNAKE

The group includes the remarkable true civets, which develop a well known perfume. Africa, India, Malay, Java, Malabar, all give their name to civets; there are civets that rob the Java coffee trees of their ripe berries, civets that frequent the palm trees of Africa and Asia, and civets in the East which are otter-shaped and supremely adapted to life in the water—though sleeping, of course, on land.

In the same family we come next to the mongooses or ichneumons, as varied a group as the civets, distinguished into genera and species by colour, teeth, toes, thick tails, thin tails, short tails, white tails, red tails. Those which chiefly interest us, however, are the true mongooses.

These little animals have long been the natural guardians of Indian and Egyptian homes. They are great snake fighters. Long ago there was an unspoken bargain between man and mongoose, that man should furnish the home and mongoose should fight and eat all the snakes that appeared in the family circle. The mongoose has redeemed his bond. He is the arch-enemy of the deadly cobra and he fights with such agility as rarely to be bitten ; and with what satisfaction he converts a cobra into a meal! Master

mongoose is not so pretty a pet as the jolly South African meerkat, but he is a fearless little ally when snakes come.

From the cats to the civets, from the civets to the hyenas, with that strange animal, the aard-wolf, to act as connecting link. Built like a long-legged fox, and resembling a starveling striped hyena in appearance, this creature, living in burrows, seldom seen by day, and eating carrion and termites, seems an isolated freak ; but it shows us how civets developed along one line and hyenas along another, from a far-away common ancestry.

A HIDEOUS CREATURE THAT WAS ONCE COMMON IN ENGLAND

The hyenas themselves are creatures with a past. They were once common in England, and cracked bones that the sabre-toothed tiger had stripped of flesh. Now, restricted to three species, and to the warmer parts of the Old World, they act as scavengers for more powerful animals, though they will attack a donkey or bullock if it be tied and helpless.

The striped, the brown, and the spotted hyena, make up the family today, the most repulsive of all mammals; powerful, ungainly, ferocious, but cowardly beasts. They will not face a waking man, but they will bite his face off if he is sleeping, or too ill to defend himself. In Syria and Palestine the striped hyena haunts rock-cut tombs ; in India it is at home in rocky crevasses. Everywhere it despoils the couch of the dead.

Its chief wonder is the might of its jaws. This feature is most pronounced in the ignoble king of the tribe, the spotted hyena of Africa. Here is a pair of jaws which can crack the thigh-bone of an ox as easily as we could crack a walnut. This is the fiercest of the three species, and will raid camps and kill small cattle and ponies. The brown species, which is the least common, is restricted to South Africa.

THE UGLY MEMBERS OF NATURE'S ORDER OF SCAVENGERS

They are members of Nature's order of scavengers. They come after the gigantic feasts of the warrior animals. A lion has a kill and eats seventy pounds of flesh at a meal. The jackal and the vulture follow. But the hyena performs the last rite. He rids the scene of its pitiful evidences of tragedy. He is the receptacle of the bones. So even this noisome animal has its niche in the scheme of the living world.

MEMBERS OF THE GREAT CAT FAMILY

PUSSY ON THE HEARTH

THE FIERCE TIGER OF INDIA

THE MAJESTIC LION OF AFRICA

THE FINE HEAD OF THE SNOW LEOPARD

THE HANDSOME JAGUAR

FIERCE-LOOKING WILD CATS OF SCOTLAND

THE STRIPED HYENA

THE LEOPARD

THE CLOUDED TIGER

A LIONESS LOOKS OUT

THE BEAUTIFUL SNOW LEOPARD

THE JAGUAR

THE LYNX

THE PUMA OF AMERICA

THE KING OF BEASTS

THE WEST AFRICAN SERVAL

THE TIGER AT HIS EASE

THE LEOPARD CAT

THE BINTURONG CIVET

THE CARACAL

THE AFRICAN CIVET

THE CHEETAH

The March of Man from the Age of Barbarism to the United Nations

A Funeral Procession at a Great Feast in Ancient Egypt

THE WONDERING EGYPTIAN

WHILE the people who lived near the Tigris and Euphrates were fighting like wild animals, there was another set of people living in Egypt who were more peacefully disposed. In these people Mind pressed forward to the true adventure of life, making wonderful advances from barbarism.

These Egyptians were the first human beings to enjoy the blessing of peace. Their little country was guarded from enemies by sea and desert. For centuries no other race seems to have troubled them. They had probably escaped into Egypt to get away from war. And so, because they had peace, the mind of man, working in those Egyptian bodies, was able to give its attention to the mystery of existence, and that means progress.

Every year between July and September the river flowing through Egypt lifted itself up, washed over the banks, and spread far afield in a shining flood. When those waters had disappeared the barren earth was covered with a soft ooze of mud, and under the rays of the sun there soon appeared through this rich river mud a mantle of green herbage.

The mind of the peaceful and observant Egyptian told him that if he sowed grains of corn in that river mud, and drove his sheep over it so that the seed was trodden into the soil, he would reap a wonderful harvest. Not only, then, was he free from enemies, but free from many of the more arduous labours of agriculture. The Nile did for him what other people had to do for themselves.

Thus we find in these Egyptians those first stirrings towards a wider and more gentle life, which we call civilisation. They cultivated fruits and made ropes of papyrus; they built irrigation works and raised gigantic buildings greater than any seen on Earth before them; they became artists and authors.

Finally, they established religion. How did the Nile rise every year and overflow its banks? Who was it that performed this annual miracle? A man could not do it. A man might lift a bucket of water, but what man could lift a great river and spread it over miles of land? Clearly it was the work of a very big man, the biggest of big men, a god.

They looked up and saw the stars. Nothing is more memorable in the history of our race than the early lifting up of man's eyes to the shining firmament. No animal, we may be sure, bothers its head about the planets. No bird, we may be certain, has studied an eclipse. No

MIGHTY EPOCHS OF THE WORLD & MAN'S WONDERFUL ADVENTURES

creature save man has ever felt that the heavens are sublime in beauty and majestic in power. Quite early in the history of civilisation, which means the history of the human mind, we find men studying the stars, watching their movements, associating them with events on the Earth. It is as if men felt instinctively a kinship with the universe. Their curiosity was aroused. The Nile overflowed its banks. The stars moved through the heavens. How? Why? Curiosity is one of the greatest powers in science and civilisation.

THE EGYPTIAN BEGINS TO THINK THAT MIND MUST BE BEHIND MATTER

The mind decided that behind the vast forces of Nature there were powers like its own, but much greater. It said there was a good power, and named it Osiris; and an evil power, and named it Set. Osiris had a wife named Isis and a son named Horus. It was possible to secure the favour of Osiris by offering little gifts to Isis.

We observe much error in all the first guesses of the mind at the mystery of Nature, but there is always a grain of truth. Before astronomy there was astrology; before chemistry there was alchemy. Bad shots, perhaps, but shots in the right direction. So it was in religion. What we call heathenism contains at least an element of truth. Superstition is a bad shot, but it is a shot in the direction travelled by the noblest of religions and the very greatest of the sons of men. Like the child learning to walk, the mind staggers in its first steps toward truth. It, too, must learn to walk before it can run.

Thus did the mind in man very early connect itself with the Mind which is behind the universe. Very early, too, it began to feel itself responsible to this great Mind. That great Mind wished it to act in a particular way, not in another way; moreover, after death the human mind would live again, and the great Mind would call it to account for all the deeds done in the body.

THE EGYPTIAN PRIEST AS MORALIST, SCIENTIST, AND OWNER OF LAND

In this wonderful conviction the people of Egypt took a tremendous stride toward civilisation. For if man felt himself to be an animal, and was certain that he would not live again after death, he would submit to no laws which stood in the way of his own animal pleasures. But religion gave him an inward law, a law of right and wrong, and set that law in his conscience, and left him alone with the tremendous thought of God.

The greatest person in Egypt was the priest. To him were unveiled the mystery of the stars and the knowledge of life and death. No one else was a student. The rest were drilled in the army to protect their land from invasion, or were farmers, or were artisans. The priest contemplated the stars, studied Nature, cross-examined travellers, and wrote books on papyrus leaves. It was from him that the rest of the nation learned how to answer the questions which arose in their minds. He was the brain-worker.

Enormous power was given to these Egyptian priests, and they used it well. They owned most of the land. They made all the laws. They helped to subdue the animal side of man's nature. Magnificent temples arose in Egypt, so that the thought of the gods was ever before man's mind; and magnificent tombs were raised for the dead, so that the thought of immortal life was impressed on the people's mind. But, unfortunately, religion became to the Egyptian another word for fear, and he lived with very little joy, thinking only of pacifying the gods, the terrible thought of death haunting him.

THE DEBT THAT CIVILISATION OWES TO EGYPT AND ITS PRIESTS

In spite of this sad feature of Egyptian civilisation, we look back to it as the first creative movement of the human mind in those fields of energy and achievement which have given us such extraordinary power over Nature.

You may still see in Egypt the relics of this amazing civilisation. Columns of a sublime grandeur still lift themselves clear of the dust of many centuries, and the tremendous Pyramids still witness to these present times of the astonishing mechanical power of these people. No shaped or fitted stones have so strange a tale to tell as these creations of the Egyptian mason. Far back in the past there was an uprush of the human spirit to express itself with great glory and a magnificence that would never die. At a time when our ancestors were the lowest of savages, and these British Isles were a jungle, men in Egypt flashed back the sunlight from temples which were like the courts of heaven and caught the moonlight on stones set up in the desert as monuments of man's faith in immortality. Glorious was this achievement of those ancient Egyptians, and it expressed their answer to a movement in the human soul which carried humanity away from the savage and some distance at least toward the divine. Four thousand years before the birth of Jesus, twice as long a space of time as has elapsed since that supreme event, the Egyptian bowed himself in the dust of the

and could scarcely have built their amazing Pyramids without a knowledge of mathematics. Their cities were large and noble. Their temples had no equal in the world. They trained dogs for hunting, domesticated the cat to catch birds, and rode on the backs of horses.

If the priests had not written their records on perishable papyrus leaves they would have bequeathed to us a library of immeasurable value. In spite of their superstition, they were keen seekers after

THE DEATH OF CLEOPATRA, THE LAST QUEEN OF EGYPT BEFORE THE ROMANS CAME
This picture by the Hon. John Collier is in the Oldham Art Gallery : the picture on page 425 belongs to the Fine Art Society

desert before his Great Pyramid and shuddered at the thought of God.

In later years a far greater people was to carry this movement of the mind away from fear and superstition, but the Egyptians were the first of all the races of mankind to conceive grandly of human life and to advance along the road of observation and discovery.

These people cultivated barley as well as wheat, and grew crops of radishes, lentils, and peas. They made use of wool as clothing. They understood arithmetic

truth, and this spirit showed itself in their arts and crafts, as well as in their science.

The fame of their country became known all over the world, and many nations travelled there with goods to seek and exchange for the Egyptian's merchandise. His caravans travelled far across the deserts. His ships were to be seen on every sea. It was some 4000 years before the birth of Jesus that the Great Pyramid was built and the Nile was canalised. Ancient indeed are the glories of Egypt. Think of their temples and their astounding tombs, of which we have read in our group on Art.

The influence of their civilisation extended far, and must have been felt even in the most advanced cities of war-harassed Mesopotamia. We know that the people of Babylonia were very much in earnest about education, and that women there knew how to read and write as well as men. Two thousand years before the birth of Jesus, Hammurabi, a king of Babylon, issued a Code of Laws which show us clearly how far the mind of man had advanced from barbarism as many years before the birth of Jesus as the world has seen since. Here are a few of those laws, as translated in a book by the Rev. Claude H. W. Johns :

If a builder has built a house for a man, and has not jointed his work and the wall has fallen, that builder at his own cost shall make good that wall.

If a man has stolen a watering machine from the meadow, he shall give five shekels of silver to the owner of the watering machine.

If a doctor has treated a gentleman for a severe wound with a bronze lancet and has cured the man, or has opened an abscess of the eye for a gentleman with the bronze lancet and has cured the eye of the gentleman, he shall take ten shekels of silver.

THE WEAKNESS OF A CIVILISATION FOUNDED ON SLAVERY AND WAR

There are punishments for men who neglect to keep the bank of a canal strengthened, showing the communal nature of society, and one or two terrible punishments showing that the mind had not yet reached the idea of mercy:

If a woman has not been economical, a goer about, has wasted her house, that woman one shall throw into the waters.

If a man has caused the loss of a gentleman's eye, his eye one shall cause to be lost.

If a man has made the tooth of a man that is his equal to fall out, one shall make his tooth fall out.

All these ancient civilisations, we must remember, were built up on the labour of slaves. From war man had learned this bad idea. It came to him as perfectly natural, for what could be wiser than to enslave those who might try one day to take his land from him ? War will justify every wickedness. It is the great denial of man's spiritual nature. If there had never been any war in the world we should now be thousands of years in advance of our present ideas ; and yet, as we have seen, war did teach men certain virtues and did hasten them toward the first foot-hills of civilisation.

But slavery is one of the most dreadful records in the history of mankind, and a record which always ends in retribution. Among the slaves in Egypt were the Hebrews, destined to make a marvellous contribution to human history, yet so marked by slavery even to this day that they creep in among other nations, and do not always, as they mostly do in England, associate themselves with the fortunes of their adopted countries.

THE FATE THAT MUST ALWAYS FOLLOW CRUELTY AND FEAR

Egypt was destined to fall because she depended on slavery. Her own people had become soft and effeminate. Everything hard and healthful was done for them by slaves. The greater their prosperity the greater the temptation they offered to other nations. There they lay, in a rich land covered with fertile fields and studded over with noble cities, a people who almost called to the invader.

Thus far had the human mind travelled onward when Egypt fell into alien hands. Man had learned something about Nature, had risen to great heights in architecture, had learned to sail ships across the sea, had become a craftsman, an artist, an astronomer, a writer, a physician, and a priest ; but he was still cruel with the cruelty of an animal; he had learned to extend his natural fear of wild beasts, not only to his fellow-men, but to the invisible Power of the universe.

THE SLOW ESCAPE FROM A CREED OF FEAR TO A CREED OF LOVE

We leave him for the present in the grasp of this terrible fear which we call superstition, observing that one body of the human race, escaped from Egypt, had conceived the idea of a God greater than all other gods in the world, and had made the worship of this righteous God the supreme concern of existence. But even among the Hebrews seeking their freedom in Palestine superstition was an immense power, in spite of the inspiration of their poets, who sang with joy and exultation of the mercy and loving-kindness of this God of gods. Not easily was the human mind to recover from the stunning effect of its first realisation that there existed an unseen Power.

(Next chapter in this group, page 543)

FAMILIAR THINGS
The Story of the Things We See About Us Every Day

Airliners on the tarmac outside the passenger reception buildings of London Airport

HIGHWAYS IN THE SKY

BREAKFAST in London, a mid-morning cup of coffee in New York, lunch in San Francisco, dinner in Honolulu. Half-a-century ago such a feat would have been beyond man's wildest dream ; today, by means of the jet airliner, it is an accomplished fact.

Carrying their passengers swiftly over the clouds, airliners are making the Earth smaller and drawing people of different races closer together, and thus forming bonds of friendship and understanding never before possible.

More than forty million people fly every year, for business and pleasure, on domestic and international airlines throughout the world. On the wings of a huge fleet of 4000 civil airliners, they daily soar in comfort and safety over the great oceans, deserts, forests, and mountains.

Prior to the air age a sea voyage to Australia took great-grandfather 35 days. By air in 1947 the same journey took 4½ days. Now, in a jet airliner, the travel time can be reduced to a mere 40 hours.

We are all familiar with the sound and outlines of airliners as they pass overhead on their way to distant lands ; but to learn more about these wonderful machines and how they operate, let us start on an imaginary journey in one. A particularly interesting flight—one that would take us over colourful and varied scenery—is to South Africa in a B.O.A.C. Britannia.

To begin our journey we go to Airways Terminal in Buckingham Palace Road, London, provided with passport, ticket, and our full quota of 66 pounds of luggage. A streamlined coach bearing the familiar B.O.A.C. " Speedbird " badge completes the first stage of our journey—down the Bath Road to London Airport.

Two remaining formalities are completed on arrival : our passports are checked by the Immigration Officers, our luggage is examined by Customs officials. This procedure over, we are guided to the departure lounge to await our call to board the Britannia.

Within a few minutes a receptionist announces that our aircraft is waiting and leads us across the concrete apron to the huge airliner, with its highly finished surfaces glinting in the sunlight.

We reach the Britannia, climb the short staircase leading up to the fuselage entrance door, and are welcomed by a neatly-dressed stewardess who takes us to our seats. These, incidentally, are luxurious, foam-filled slumberseats ; by pushing

INDUSTRIES · HOW THINGS ARE MADE · WHERE THEY COME FROM

a button we can take our ease in a low, reclining position.

The interior of the Britannia is finished in dark blue and grey. It is divided into three main compartments : a control cabin for a flight crew of five, a pantry, and a main cabin seating up to 90 passengers. The flight crew consists of a Captain, First Officer, Third Pilot, Communicator, and Engineering Officer ; two stewards and our stewardess form the cabin crew.

Before an airliner takes off it is carefully inspected to make certain that all the controls and engines are working perfectly, that tanks are filled with oil and fuel, and that there is suffi-cient food for the journey. It is most important that an adequate fuel sup-ply is carried to get the aircraft to its destination. If the pilot flies into bad weather the trip may take con-siderably longer than scheduled.

The fuel is sup-plied by stream-lined bowsers, petrol-carrying lorries, which quickly fill the tanks of piston-engined machines with petrol ; or (in the case of our turboprop Britannia) with kerosene.

Airways Terminal, one of the flying traveller's starting points in London

Through the windows at our side we can see passengers boarding and disembarking from other airliners, and, in the distance a car is being driven up the ramp and through the nose doors of a Silver City Freighter.

Air freight is responsible for more than a quarter of the total scheduled airline traffic today. For perishable goods, such as fruit, air transport is invaluable ; and animals of many kinds show a marked preference for this mode of travel.

In the freight sheds at London Airport we may see a wide variety of cargoes—ranging from racehorses on their way to America, to leather and cotton goods, cameras and surgical instruments being exported to the Middle East. Extra heavy cargo may be on its way overseas, too ;

perhaps a giant 2½-ton propeller shaft for a disabled ship at Singapore, or a big ice-cream machine for Australia.

Soon comes the moment for departure. A faint whine tells us that the four Proteus turboprops have been started. The Captain in his cabin calls by radio to the air traffic controller for permission to taxi to the end of the runway and take off. No machine may take off—or land—without permission from the control tower, nerve-centre of the whole airport.

Permission is given right away, and our plane runs swiftly round the taxiways. There is a brief halt while the Captain lines up the air-craft with the two-mile stretch of concrete, then he opens up the en-gines to full pow-er. Slowly the straining brakes are released and we shoot down the runway.

Aircraft, hang-ars, airport build-ings, and the con-trol tower flash by as we gather speed ; within seconds we are airborne.

Sitting back in our comfortable seats we leave the earth far below and climb steadily upward through the woolly cumulus clouds, heading for Rome —our first port of call. Flying at between 22,000 and 26,000 feet, and cruising at 360 to 380 m.p.h., our Britannia will cover the 950 miles from London to Rome in about 2 hours 30 minutes.

We are now on the first leg of an air voyage of more than 6000 miles. But how do we manage to breathe at the great height at which we are flying, where the air is very thin and there is little oxygen ? The answer is that our cabin is "pres-surised."

At 25,000 feet, we breathe without dis-comfort because the air in the cabin is equal in density to that inhaled at 5000 feet. A supply of specially heated fresh air is pumped into the cabins at the required density by the main engine compressors, and is changed every three minutes. From the turboprop engines, too, comes hot air to de-ice the wings.

Our airliner is equipped with a library and a refreshment bar. Delicious meals—cooked before flight, frozen, and then heated in an electric oven in the aircraft—are served by the stewardess in climates like our own ; in tropical climates there are always salads, fruits, and iced drinks on the menu.

We took off from London Airport at 2 p.m. and by about the same time to-morrow we shall touch down at Johannesburg having stopped at Rome, Khartoum, and Nairobi.

This is, of course, only one route we might have followed in our imagination. It is known as the "Springbok" route and is run in conjunction with South African Airways. Had we wished we could have chosen one of the other major air routes.

The busiest international air route is that across the Atlantic —over which 17,000 flights are made every year. Another route is down to the Gold Coast of Africa, passing through Lisbon.

Alternatively we could have flown to India and the Far East. The "Kangaroo" route would have taken us to Zurich and Beirut and from there to Karachi, Calcutta, Singapore, Darwin, and Sydney. From Calcutta we could have taken the "Dragon" route to the Orient—through Bangkok to Hong Kong.

From these big international airports domestic airlines run a network of services linking with the major towns and cities. In relatively undeveloped countries like Australia, even the smaller communities have their own airstrip. All this means that we can now fly across the world in any direction, experiencing all types of climates, visiting the homes of widely differing races and colour ; and the whole travelling time would take less than three days.

Growing apace with this increased speed is increased safety ; from the moment an aircraft is first thought of, to the time that it enters regular service, every possible measure is adopted to ensure reliability and airworthiness. And regular inspections ensure that reliability is maintained.

Modern navigational aids also play their part in making flying simple and safe. Radar and radio aids, for example, enable pilots to land safely at night and in fog.

Precision Approach Radar (P.A.R.) enables the pilot to be "talked-down" to the airfield even though he cannot see it.

The Flight Log, a radio aid, is an automatic navigator that not only shows the pilot his exact position on the map but records his previous course.

A signpost on Nairobi Airport points to the skyways of the world

Over Britain and America airliners fly within a system of air lanes. In these flying highways the aircraft are controlled so that there is no chance of a collision. We can see therefore that everything possible is done to make our flights and landings as simple and safe as possible.

The present-day airliner represents standards of safety, comfort, and speed never before attained. With the further development of gas-turbine engines and the ever-increasing passenger accommodation, it is possible that one day the airliner and flying-boat will supplant the steamship.

PICTURE-STORY OF AIRWAYS

The crew of a B.O.A.C. airliner receiving final briefing instructions before setting out from London Airport for New York. More than 17,000 planes annually cross the Atlantic on this most important of all air services.

The crew of a B.O.A.C. Stratocruiser check their instruments prior to take-off. On the left are the Navigator and Radio Officer ; at the controls, the Captain and First Officer ; and on the right, the Engineering Officer.

COMPLETE COMFORT HIGH IN THE AIR

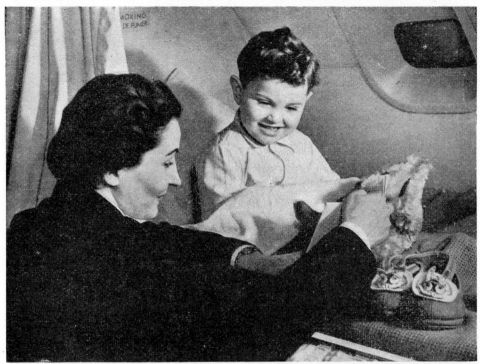

A young passenger snuggles down in his berth while a B.O.A.C. stewardess reads him a bedtime story.   Hundreds of children, visiting parents abroad, are looked after by B.O.A.C. every year.

A library of books and magazines is always carried aboard a large airliner, lighter literature being provided for the younger air travellers.   Here a stewardess is offering journals to the passengers.

28 01

CARGO PLANE AND PASSENGER PLANE

A special cargo transport version of the Super Constellation, which has a capacity for a 38,000-lb. load, and flies at 330 m.p.h. Freight is loaded through large doors in the nose and rear fuselage with the assistance of mobile lifts.

Fastest of modern piston-engined airliners is the Douglas DC-6B. Fitted with four Pratt & Whitney radials, it has a cruising speed of 311 m.p.h. at 20,600 feet. The transoceanic model seats 54 passengers, and the short-range version carries 92. Span is 117 feet, and length 105 feet 7 inches.

PORTS OF CALL ON THE WORLD'S AIRWAYS

One of the biggest of the inter-Continental airports is Ciampino Airport at Rome. Here we see airliners from many parts of the world lined up on the tarmac for unloading or refuelling.

Something of the difficult conditions under which airliners often have to operate is seen in this picture of a Constellation on a snow-covered airfield at Goose Bay, Labrador.

Passengers embark on a B.E.A. Elizabethan airliner at Le Bourget Airport, Paris.

AT WORK ON PLANES BY DAY AND NIGHT

This picture of a Stratocruiser being serviced clearly shows the double-deck fuselage. Its " figure 8 " section simplified the problem of pressurising the cabins for high altitude flight. The upper deck seats 60, and the lower has a 12-seat refreshment lounge and holds for freight. It has a cruising speed of 340 m.p.h. at 25,000 feet.

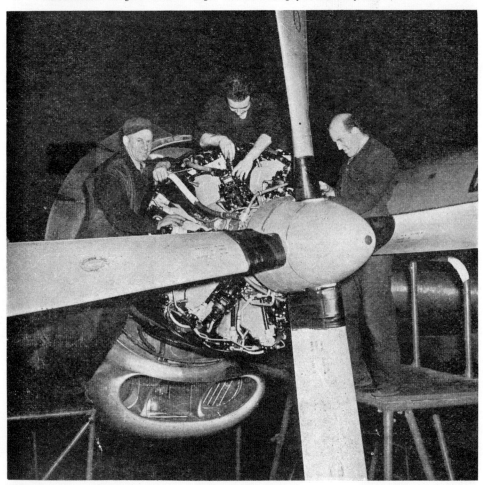

Maintaining and overhauling by night one of the four 28-cylinder radial engines on a Stratocruiser. A Pratt & Whitney Wasp Major, it develops 3500 h.p. at take-off and drives a four-bladed feathering airscrew.

IN THE CONTROL TOWER OF AN AIRPORT

Here is the aircraft approach room, which keeps in touch by wireless telegraphy and radio telephony with every aircraft approaching within 20 miles of the airport.

This switch panel in the control tower at London Airport controls the system of lights and beacons which help pilots to pick out the runways at night or when visibility is poor.

The great airport is in constant wireless communication with other air and meteorological stations and with machines in flight. Here are wireless operators at work.

With this radar approach instrument, aircraft 20 miles away can be seen and given exact bearings. Radar has also become an essential feature of all large aircraft.

In the operations room this officer is recording on his graph the position of an airliner which is somewhere between England and Australia.

Wireless messages give the whereabouts of machines flying between this airport and other lands. As each message comes in the new positions are plotted on charts.

BRITISH PLANES ON THE WORLD'S AIRWAYS

One of the newest of British planes to go into service on the world's airways is the turboprop airliner Bristol Britannia. Carrying up to 100 passengers, it flies at 360 m.p.h. at 25,000 feet.

First turboprop airliner in the world to go into scheduled service is the Vickers Viscount. Flown by many major airlines, it cruises at 340 m.p.h. and carries up to 53 passengers in vibrationless comfort "above the weather." Conversation within the cabin can be carried on in normal tones, and at its operating height of 20,000 feet the pressurisation system maintains conditions comparable to 5000 feet.

Plain Answers to the Questions of the Children of the World

WHY CANNOT WE SEE IN THE DARK?

"THE dark" is the absence of light. Now, what is the name for the absence of sound? What do we call the state of things when we hear no sound? The answer is silence. Let us remember after this always to think of darkness and silence as if they were a pair of things. By darkness we mean the absence of light, just as silence is the absence of sound.

But there is more to say. There may be a wave motion in the ether, but it is hardly proper to call that light until someone sees it. Similarly there may be a wave movement in the air, but it is hardly proper to call that sound unless someone actually hears it.

Seeing and hearing, then, depend, first of all, on there being something outside of us—a particular kind of wave ; and, secondly, on our being able to feel that something. In order to see, it must be there.

That is why we cannot see in the dark, because there is no light, and it is only light that we see. But, also, the seeing eye is necessary. A table in a dark room is there, though we cannot see it. There is no light, and so we see nothing. When we do see the table, as we say, we really see the light coming from it, and the form of the light tells us that the table is there. A blind man cannot see, even in the light.

Our great poet Milton, in his poem on Samson, makes Samson say, when he had lost his sight :

"Oh, dark, dark, dark amid the blaze of noon!"

That famous line will help us to understand what darkness may depend on—either the absence of light, or the absence of the power to see light.

It is often supposed that cats and tigers can "see in the dark," but we must know that nobody at all can see if it is perfectly dark—that is to say, if there is no light at all coming from anywhere. When we speak of being in the dark we usually mean that there is so little light that we see hardly anything.

That is because our eyes are so made that they cannot alter themselves to suit the conditions of very dim light; but some animals can make the pupil of the eye so wide as to get the benefit of whatever rays of light are about. This is the case with cats, and if we watch the cat's eyes when it is in the dark, we see that the pupils appear much enlarged. This allows all the light possible to enter the eyes, and the cat, and other night-prowling animals that have eyes like the cat, are able to see very much better in dim light than we can. But even among human beings some people, especially seamen, can see farther in the dark than others.

SUN · MOON · STARS · FIRE · WIND · WATER · LIFE · MIND · SLEEP

Can a Poisonous Snake Bite Without Poisoning?

Some can and some cannot. The way that poisonous snakes use their fangs to inject poison is one of the most wonderful things in Nature, and in the case of some of them—for instance, the common adder or viper, which lives all over Great Britain —this poison fang and its venom are only used as a means of self-defence, or for getting food.

But the adder as a rule does not use its poison fang when it bites the animal on which it feeds, and so it has a very curious arrangement, by means of which these fangs are laid flat back in the roof of the mouth out of the way of the ordinary teeth which are used for feeding. Thus the adder can use one or other sets of teeth just as it likes when it wishes to kill its foe, and it can tuck its fangs securely out of the way and use its ordinary teeth when it wishes to swallow food. In some of the other poisonous snakes the fangs are fixed, and cannot be used in this way.

What is a Mirage?

A mirage is an optical illusion due to certain atmospheric conditions. It occurs especially in certain conditions of the air when the air is very hot.

Sometimes in deserts there are spots called oases, where there is water, and, as there is water, there are also green trees and shade. We are told that sometimes travellers think they are coming to an oasis only a few miles away, where they can get water and shade; and then, as they travel on, it disappears. A great explorer once " discovered " and named a mountain which did not exist, but which he had seen as a mirage.

But a true mirage is not an appearance in the sky due to nothing at all, and it is not pure imagination on the part of those who see it. When the traveller sees an oasis in the desert, and it fades and deceives him, what he has seen is the image of a real oasis, much farther on, below the horizon. The light from the real oasis has been reflected from a layer of air, as we see in the picture on page 441, and the traveller sees it as if there were a huge mirror placed in the sky to give a view of the oasis to the traveller's eyes.

The reason of this is that there are layers of air of different temperatures, and therefore of different density, and whenever light passes from one thing into another of different density, part of it does not go on, but is deflected back. Appearances due to a similar cause are often seen at sea. A ship near the horizon may seem to have another ship, exactly like itself, perched upside down upon it.

Why Do Empty Vessels Sound More Than Full Ones?

In the study of sound we soon discover the existence of things which help to magnify a sound. The virtue of these things is that they resound, and so they are called *resonators*. The body of a violin is a resonator, and so are our chests and the spaces of the mouth and nose when we sing. If we play a violin from which the body has been taken away, the sound is weak and thin, and ugly, and the difference between a violin worth £2000 and one that is not worth £5 is to be found in the body, or resonator.

The whole point about a resonator is that the air inside it can be thrown by it into sound-waves. If there is no air inside it, of course, its use is gone. An empty vessel is a resonator. If it is filled with liquid, it can no longer act; it makes far less sound, and the weight of the liquid quickly stops what sound it does make, acting like the dampers in a piano. If we were to fill the body of a violin with water, we should get the same result as if we held the body of a violin tightly in our hand when playing it.

Do Animals Know When They Are Being Treated Kindly?

Not even the wisest man can tell you how much animals know and how much they do not know, and it is still more difficult to say how much they can appreciate; but what we do know is that all the animals that man makes use of, or lives much with, can feel pain very readily, and are capable of great suffering. Whether they know they are feeling it is a different matter, much too deep a question for us here.

But the most important point about this subject is this—that whether animals appreciate kindness intelligently or not, it makes a very great difference to the human being who treats his animals well. No one who is cruel or unkind to animals will be kind to his fellow-creatures, and therefore we should always try to treat animals as kindly as one of ourselves.

SEEING WHAT IS NOT THERE

In this picture we see a mirage in the desert. The trees seem reflected in water, but there is really no water, and the inverted image of the trees is due simply to the refraction, or bending, of the rays of light.

This picture shows a mirage at sea, where the conditions are the opposite of those in the desert, the colder and denser air being lowest. The light rays from the ship strike upon layers of different density in the upper air and are refracted downwards. When the densities vary much, several images will be seen, some of them inverted.

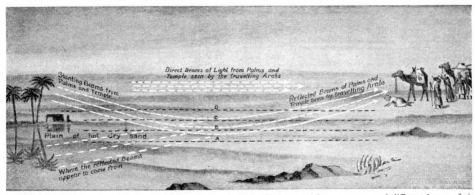

This diagram explains the mirage. The layer of air, A, next to the hot sand is very warm, and different layers of air above, B, C, and D, have different temperatures, and therefore different densities. Now, beams of light passing through gases of different densities are refracted, or bent, in varying degrees, and, as shown here, the trees, as well as being seen by direct beams, are seen by the reflected beams as if reflected by water.

What Makes the Earth Quake?

The first reason that probably accounts for all earthquakes is simply that the Earth is shrinking as it gradually loses the heat which it encloses. We know that the Earth has a very thin crust, which is comparatively cool, and a very hot inside. The crust rests upon the inside of the Earth, and as the inside shrinks it is bound to leave parts of the crust unsupported, so that they are apt to sink or crack. This will happen especially where the crust of the Earth is thinner and more liable to crack than in other places. It is very common in Japan, for instance, and very rare in England.

But when an earthquake happens at any part of the Earth it starts a wave of disturbance that travels right over the Earth, and can be detected anywhere if we look out for it. Then, if we notice the time when the wave reached a place, and find out what the time was when it started, we can learn how quickly the earth-wave travels. But sometimes no one knows where the wave started, and then very often we can guess that it started under the sea ; for earthquakes may start in the Earth's crust where it forms the beds of great oceans as well as anywhere else.

When I Walk in a Moving Train Do I Move Faster than the Train?

We ought to know which way you are walking. The answer to the question is yes, if you are walking in the direction that the train is going. But if you are walking from the front of the train to the back, then you are moving more slowly than the train. There can be no doubt about it, for you can prove it by experiment, that is, by trying.

If two of you got into the back of the train when it started, and one of you walked right through the train, if he could, to the front, then when the train stopped, he would get out on the platform much farther forward than the other. He would have travelled farther in the same time than his friend, and farther than the part of the train his friend was in, and thus farther than any part of the train. He has added his own movement compared with that of the train to the movement of the train compared with that of the Earth.

The Earth is moving too, and if the train is moving on the Earth in the same direction as the Earth is moving through space, then the train is moving through space faster than the Earth. And if you are walking from the back of the train to the front, you are travelling through space faster than the train, and still faster than the Earth. And if a fly is walking across your cheek from your ear to your nose it is travelling through space faster than you, or the train, or the Earth!

Does the Brain Need Food?

The brain is made of nerves and nerve-cells. These taken together we call nervous tissue, and we know that nervous tissue is more richly supplied with blood than any other tissue in the body, not even excepting the muscle tissue of the heart itself. The blood carries the food materials without which nerve tissue cannot act, and nerve tissue has practically no reserve at all of food supply in it. If the supply of blood is stopped for a moment, nervous tissue gives out sooner than any other tissue in the body.

A simple and wonderful little experiment will show you this for yourself. The screen or curtain at the back of your eye, which receives the rays of light from everything you see, is made of nervous tissue. It is packed with blood-vessels. If you shut one eye and look out of the other, and then press your finger firmly on the open eye (pressing on it through the lid), in three or four seconds everything will grow quite dark. The eye is open and there is plenty of light, but it is quite blind. Move your finger away and in a second or two you will see again. The reason is that when you pressed on your eye-ball you prevented the blood running through the screen or curtain at the back of the eye, and after about two seconds, during which it was using up what it had taken from the blood, it could do no more, and your eye became blind.

Is Every Seventh Wave a Bigger One?

No. Another superstition we may add to this is one which says that every third or every ninth wave, when the tide comes in, is bigger than the others. It is untrue and without any basis of fact. Most of these assertions about three and seven are nonsense, and are derived from long ago, when those numbers were thought to have some special value in Nature.

The Story of the Beautiful Things in the Treasure House of the World

A decorative mosaic from an old castle in Sicily

A GREAT LIGHT SHINES

THE dying out of classic art left the world cold and bare, and something like ten centuries were to pass before a new glory rose on the ashes of the old. Meanwhile, in an obscure corner of Asia Minor, the greatest event of the world's history had taken place—the birth of Jesus at Bethlehem. Let us think of the influence of Bethlehem on the fortunes of those days. It was the shining of a great light for Art.

For many generations Christianity had no real home, but was the guest of several countries and states. It was impossible for a people so scattered to have in themselves the dominant power which produced the art of Egypt, Assyria, or Greece ; it was equally impossible to be neighbours to such greatness without copying it.

In early Christian art, therefore, it is natural that certain influences should be traced—Greek, Syrian, and to some extent Persian. Alexandria was then the centre of Greek painting, and although the Grecian genius was worn out, and its ideals rather battered, it still had command of technique, and was able to give valuable lessons to a new art. Greek painters taught the Christians how to fill spaces, and group figures and ornament. The secret of great composition—the avoidance of over-crowding—was still a part of the Greek tradition, but the early Christian artists, like the Romans, failed to learn this lesson. To its dying day, the spirit of Greek art was beauty for beauty's sake. A very different purpose underlay Syrian art.

The Syrians were less interested in their painting than in the subjects they portrayed. It was their instinct to represent the gentle Jesus as an arrogant figure, tinged with the egotism of the Egyptian and Assyrian art of which the Syrians themselves were heirs. The Founder of their religion was always in a central position, and drawn on a larger scale than any other figure. We can always trace this Eastern influence, so contrary to Greek ideals, when we see pictures by the early Christians painted in what is called *inverted perspective*.

This peculiar treatment showed the foreground figures, which should have been larger than the rest, actually smaller, so that the Christ in the middle of the composition might stand out more convincingly. The Syrians, in a word, did not paint pictures as pictures; they merely illustrated an idea in colour and shape; their art was the expression of their religious thought.

The Persians, on the other hand, who also had an effect on this new art, were without any sense of perspective whatever. In its place they adopted a curious convention. Their compositions of groups

PICTURES · STATUES · CARVINGS · BUILDINGS · IVORIES · CRAFTS

of people show figures always painted in flat tints, with no attempt at modelling, no rendering of a background. And, in order to show that some persons were nearer the front of the picture than others, they painted figures in zones or layers, one set above another; the highest group in the picture was supposed to be in the farthest background. The Persian strain in early Christian art is shown mainly in this strange un-lifelikeness and in the introduction of a certain kind of ornament—a conventional scroll of vine leaves and branches wherein birds and beasts are most incongruously set.

PICTURES IN THE MEETING-HALLS OF THE FIRST CHRISTIANS

Generally speaking, Christian art of the first few centuries was divided into two branches, that of the Western world, centring in Rome and Ravenna, and that of the Eastern world, centring in Constantinople (now Istanbul). This school is known as Byzantine, and takes its name from Byzantium, the ancient name for Constantinople, which the Christian Emperor Constantine, in the fourth century, made the new capital of the Roman Empire.

Traces of the work of early Christian artists, gold and enamel objects, and pottery, have been discovered in most of the Mediterranean cities. The chief monument to their art is found in the wall paintings of the catacombs during the first four centuries. These were burial places, and, in the years of their persecution, the secret meeting-halls of the followers of Jesus. Catacombs were known to exist in Naples, Syracuse, Alexandria, Cyrene, and the Holy Land. The most famous are at Rome, where about fifty have been discovered from time to time.

THE UNDERGROUND GALLERIES WITH THE SECRET ENTRANCES

The Christians, like the Romans, built their catacombs outside the city wall, on the great high-roads that led from Rome to the outer parts of the Empire. Some of them lie in the famous Appian Way; one of these, the catacomb of St. Domitilla, is supposed to be the most ancient.

The catacombs were long, narrow, subterranean galleries, with recesses and small chambers breaking their gloomy lines. They formed a network of underground galleries, and when, during the bitterest spell of their persecution, the

emperor Diocletian ordered the catacombs to be closed, the Christians burrowed fresh entrances and made new and mysterious passages whose winding mazes were known only to themselves.

As time went on, the existing catacombs proved in some cases insufficient for needs of burial. The workmen then sank shafts until they found a lower stratum suitable for excavations; when those galleries became surcharged with their ghostly burdens they found another stratum.

In the walls of the catacombs horizontal, rectangular spaces were cut for the reception of the dead, and afterwards closed by marble slabs. At a later period it was the habit to place beautifully chiselled stone coffins in these niches. When the " peace of the Church " came with the reign of Constantine, the practice of burying the dead in catacombs ceased. Cemeteries and chapels were made, and the underground galleries and chambers became meeting places for the cult of martyr worship which arose. In later centuries the catacombs ceased to have this hold on the Christians and they became merely a dim tradition.

HOW THE CATACOMBS WERE LOST FOR AGES AND FOUND AGAIN

Medieval pilgrims who walked across Europe to the Eternal City used to visit a catacomb in the Appian Way, near the little church of St. Sebastian, but for the most part the ancient burial-places were forgotten. Late in the sixteenth century the accidental falling of a vault laid bare some wall-paintings, and these excited the interest of archaeologists. Most of the catacombs have since been excavated, and thus a period of remote Christian history of unparalleled interest comes to light.

In spite of the dim light and most unpleasant and foul air, the chambers and recesses of the catacombs were decorated. Some of the wealthiest families of Rome were Christian, and spared no pains or expense in making beautiful the halls of their dead. The Christian religion had taught them that death is the least misadventure which can befall a man, and thus there was nothing morbid in their interest and devotion to this mural art. Just as in Syrian paintings it seemed that the artists were speaking aloud, saying a tremendous creed about a Great and Jealous I AM, so in the timid, shy art of the catacombs it seemed that the artists

444

PICTURES ON THE WALLS OF LONG AGO

A SPLENDID RAVENNA MOSAIC OF THE SIXTH CENTURY

SAINT MICHAEL IN
AN OLD MOSAIC

FIGURES FROM THE WONDERFUL MOSAIC
WALLS OF SAINT MARK'S, VENICE

FROM A MOSAIC OF
THE SIXTH CENTURY

A PORTRAIT OF JESUS SAID TO
BE BY SAINT LUKE

PICTURES ON THE WALLS
OF A CATACOMB IN ROME

A PORTRAIT OF JESUS IN THE
CATACOMB OF ST. CALIXTUS

were praying aloud and holding communion with their dead in Paradise.

There is nothing of outstanding merit in the paintings of the catacombs, but looked at now across a span of about twenty centuries one can see in those dark, underground places the first blossoming of the eternal spring-tide and hope and Christianity, the spirit of the One who said, " Behold, I make all things new."

This " joyful sorrow " for those who had found a happier home was never far from the thoughts of the Christian artists; and so they painted dainty friezes of peacocks, typifying eternity; trees which meant the garden of Paradise; the turtle dove—the picture of the soul at peace; the lyre—signifying the divine word. It was the early Christians who inscribed on their tombs that most beautiful phrase—*Sit tibi terra levis*—" May the earth rest lightly on thee "—a whole poem in one line.

The Roman catacomb decoration of the first century was chiefly of this delicate, lyrical kind—symbols, floral designs, vine tendrils. At first only the walls were painted. In the second century the treatment of the figure in design appears, the walls were set apart for subject paintings, and the daintier symbolic work was reserved for the ceilings of the chambers.

THE FIRST PICTURES IN THE WORLD OF MARY AND JESUS

Some of these ceiling decorations are a delightful mixture of paganism and Christianity. On the roof of the catacomb of Lucina a delicate geometric pattern appears, with tiny figures subjugated to the lines of ornament. Looked at casually, it might seem to be a repeat on a ceiling paper in our grandmothers' houses; closely examined, it reveals a figure of the Good Shepherd in the centre, persons representing the four seasons at corners of the design, and little heads and praying figures set round about which appear very Greek in their treatment. Another ceiling decoration—the famous catacomb of St. Calixtus—shows Orpheus with his lute in the centre, surrounded by small Scriptural groups, such as the raising of Lazarus, Moses drawing water from the rock, Daniel in the lions' den. This same catacomb of St. Calixtus has excellent examples of the wall-work of the early artists.

In the catacombs we find the first of the innumerable representations of the Madonna and Child which Christian art has given to the world. These pictures are very simple, and, as in the case of the paintings of Christ himself, are not in any sense portraits. Mary is shown as an ordinary Roman woman with her baby. In the early paintings Jesus has the appearance of a Greek youth. The traditional bearded face in the pictures of Christ dates from a later time.

CHRISTIANITY SET FREE BRINGS ABOUT A CHANGE IN ART

The art of the catacombs was a mere apprenticeship, leading up to the important work which followed when Christianity became a great power. In the fourth century, Constantine issued an edict giving full liberty to the followers of Jesus, and permission to build churches. The Christians had been waiting for this; their faith had assured them of ultimate freedom; their suppressed activities blazed into life. As we look back on these early centuries it almost seems that we can watch the actual progress of Christian art as of a living thing.

Within a few years of her release from suppression, Christianity had evolved a church entirely unlike any other religious building in existence, and lavished a wealth of beauty on its decoration. In two hundred years or so art in Italy developed on these lines. During that time the centre of progress had moved from Rome to Constantinople, and the splendour of Byzantine art arose, to find its culmination in the church of St. Sophia.

While thus the art of church decoration became a great force, the quality of Christian art, the motives which had inspired it, had changed. The spiritual feeling of the catacomb pictures, born in a period of persecution and humility, gave place to the proud glorification of Jesus, Mary, and the Saints. The artists were no longer praying aloud, they were singing the songs of the Church triumphant.

THE GREAT THING THE FIRST CHRISTIAN ARTISTS DID

Paintings in fresco and coloured friezes were not rich enough as a medium for this glorious sentiment; the artists began to make pictures in mosaic—in small squares of gold and coloured glass embedded in cement. Only in the less important churches did wall-painting continue.

The Romans had learned the art of mosaic work from the Greeks, and had used it beautifully in their pavements. The

A MOSAIC FIGURE OF THE VIRGIN IN SAINT MARK'S, VENICE

MARY AND JESUS—A MOSAIC IN THE CHURCH OF SAINT GREGORY, MESSINA

A SEVEN-CENTURY-OLD MOSAIC IN SAINT MARK'S, VENICE

Christians took up mosaic work at this point—that is to say, their first mosaic pictures were executed in colours on a white ground. Very soon, however, they obtained a style of their own, and a mastery of technique; in two or three centuries they evolved a distinctive and wonderful scheme of decoration.

THE SHINING COLOUR OF THE BYZANTINE ARTISTS REACHES ITALY

The early churches were peculiarly adapted for this wealth of colour display. They were huge buildings, erected, with certain adaptations, on the plan of the Roman basilica—a large hall for public gatherings. Their lines were long and straight, their weight more horizontal than perpendicular; the exteriors were severely plain, and the interiors unhampered by any breaks in the walls. Rome and Ravenna were the home of the most famous basilican churches. Several were built by Constantine himself.

We can faintly surmise how beautiful their interiors must originally have been, what a glory of shining colour must have mapped the walls, from the mosaics which still exist. On some of them time has laid a ravaging hand; many have been destroyed by fire; those that remain mark a period in the development of Christian art. When the tide of progress had set toward the Byzantine shore, a backwash touched the ground of Italy, and for two or three hundred years an art flourished that was half Italian and half Byzantine. We can trace the curious development from the basilican structures of this time in many Italian towns, such as Milan and Brescia, but chiefly in Ravenna, which during the sixth century became really a Byzantine city.

THE LIGHT FROM THE EAST THAT SPREAD ITSELF IN THE WEST

It would seem that the mosaics in the basilicas showed almost at once that tendency toward the Eastern influence in Christian art which was to become so marked in the Byzantine churches. Just for a short time there was the artless mixture of paganism and Christianity noticeable in the catacomb paintings. There is, for instance, a beautiful narrow frieze in the architecture of the nave in St. Maria Maggiore, Rome. The mosaic is blue and red on a gold ground and it shows a long spiral design based on the acanthus. Little doves flutter through the classic ornament; every now and then the design breaks and there is a white lamb standing alone—the symbol of Christ. A great many of these mosaics proclaim that Western Christian art was born in a land saturated with classic influence.

Very soon, however, the work was given up more to religious subjects, and the art native of Italy showed itself only in the border-friezes and curious garlands which the mosaic-makers crowded in abundance about their figures.

The growing Eastern influence in Christian art showed itself in several ways. The Syrian idea of a magnificent deity crept into the work, and we see Christ enthroned on a shining seat beneath a cross sparkling with jewels, Christ between Peter and Paul, Christ between the old law and the new, Christ surrounded by hosts of shining ones. But, generally speaking, the chief characteristic of the mosaics of the Christian churches, Italian and Byzantine, was a kind of narrative art—stories told in colour. The walls are unending illustrations of the history of the Church and the life of its Founder.

THE JEWEL-LIKE MOSAICS AND THE CHURCH'S CROWN OF GLORY

So real was this instinct to preach, to declare a creed from the structure itself, that the art of the churches developed a scheme of ornamentation. The dome was usually set aside for paintings of a visionary nature, and the body of the church for more earthly subjects. From this grew the idea of portraying Christ in the crown of the dome with heavenly legions of angels and archangels ranked around. In the apse the Virgin was generally shown, and subjects connected with the sacraments of the Church. The upper walls of the nave were set apart for figures from Old Testament history and scenes from the life of Jesus.

The mosaics were not ordinary pictures. Artists took advantage of the fact that they were dealing in a very artificial medium to fill in spaces with wedges of colour and brilliance. They were not content to place isolated panels or circular decorations in the sacred halls; they literally filled them with mosaic following the lines of the arches, and running up to the roof. The work reached its height in the jewel-like mosaics of the later Byzantine churches which sprang up; its crown of glory was St. Sophia in Constantinople.

This very brilliance was presently the death of Byzantine art. The life it should have portrayed became pomp and glitter, Oriental pageantry and display. Convention overrode beauty, and mural decoration of the Church, which had begun in the mysticism of the catacomb paintings and grown to the imagery of the basilicas, became under later Byzantine sway a mere mass of gorgeous but petrified ornament.

Gothic which was to transform Medieval Europe. A great many beautiful Romanesque churches were built in France; the oldest and most famous lie south of the River Loire. In England the Romanesque tradition, taking root with the Norman Conquest, gave rise to another kind of architecture adapted to the island genius. These new buildings were known as Norman, to distinguish them from the earlier Saxon edifices.

HOW THE FIRST CHURCHES WERE DECORATED FOURTEEN CENTURIES AGO—A MOSAIC IN THE CHURCH OF SAN VITALE, RAVENNA

In the meantime, although early Christian art was centred in Italy and Byzantium, the religion had spread over Europe, founding a new civilisation. North of the Alps, after the reign of Charlemagne, this spiritual force found its expression in a new class of architecture. The timber-roofed structure of the south gave way to vaulted buildings called Romanesque. The churches of this period stand midway between the severe basilicas and heavy Byzantine and the upward-reaching, airy

The Gothic style followed hard on the heels of the Romanesque. By the twelfth century it was established in England and France; by the thirteenth in Germany. With it came an instinct for internal decoration on the lines of sculptured figures and reliefs. The reason for this change was that the Romanesque churches had proved unsuitable for wall-paintings or mosaics, owing to their bad system of lighting, and the lines of Gothic buildings did not lend themselves to long friezes.

Of the Romanesque wall-paintings only a few fragments remain. A fine example is in the church of St. Savin, in Poitou, France; another in St. George's Church, Oberzell, on the Reichenau Island on Lake Constance. There is a beautiful painted altar-panel belonging to the Münster Museum.

By a pleasant exchange, as the art of wall-painting died out, that of window-staining arose, and enriched the churches with a shadow of the Byzantine brilliance. A school of coloured glass painters grew and reached its highest power in the thirteenth century.

Side by side with this smaller branch of religious art was growing another—the illumination of manuscripts.

From about the first century of our era, books were made of sheets of vellum—a fine parchment, originally made from calf-skin—beautifully and marvellously inscribed. There was no limit to the loving and laborious care spent on these manuscripts. Some were written in black ink, with red ink for use in headings and titles.

THE LOVELY OLD BOOKS ILLUMINED WITH PURE GOLD

Some were written in gold and silver. The British Museum possesses a copy of the Gospels written entirely in gold.

Vellum was very costly, and in many cases sheets were cleaned of their original matter and used again. Manuscripts written on second-hand vellum are called palimpsests, and are of the greatest value to archaeologists, as the ghost of the original characters lie under the new, and by restoring the first writing, texts of great value have been recovered underneath.

When paper was introduced for literary purposes in the thirteenth century, the character of the writing and illumination changed with the rougher surface of the new medium. The invention of the printing press was naturally the beginning of the decline of both writing and illumination, except for specific purposes. A very beautiful and spiritual art has thus been almost lost to the world.

The real meaning of illuminated manuscripts is a book "lighted up" with gold and clear, radiant colours. The earliest Gospels and Prayer Books are in this form. Lovely colours run riot in their pages; the earliest reflect the spirit of classic art, but for the most part their ideal of ornament was Byzantine, the style of illumination which reached its highest point in the ninth century and for two hundred years was a strong influence. Its decadence, in the thirteenth century, is marked by the same stilted artificiality that stamped the later church mosaics.

THE FAITHFUL MEN WHO SPENT THEIR LIVES IN MAKING BOOKS

The decorations of these illuminated manuscripts took the form of full-page pictures, vignettes and miniatures, marginal designs, and very lovely initials. The initials of the finest vellum books are truly a great joy. They flung out their dainty designs to any part of the page; some of them hold a picture within the compass of the letter.

The monasteries were largely the source of illuminated manuscripts, and as monasteries spread over Europe the art of vellum painting was taken up in England, Ireland France, Germany, and Flanders. Num, berless copies of the Gospels, Books o- Hours, missals, hymnals, and the lives of the Saints were produced. They were made for members of the wealthy class and for the inmates of the abbeys and monasteries themselves. There is a wonderful collection of illuminated manuscripts in the Grenville Library of the British Museum. There we can see displayed the strangely lovely design in which little birds and animals and vine tendrils get so delightfully mixed up, and strands of ornament are flung about the text as if they had been living things and the wind had entangled them.

THE MARVELLOUS BOOK OF KELLS MADE BY IRISH MONKS 1000 YEARS AGO

One of the most beautiful things in the world is an illuminated manuscript by the monks of the Irish monasteries. It is a copy of the Gospels known as the Book of Kells, written and illuminated about the eighth century, and now treasured in the library of Trinity College, Dublin. The Irish monks, unlike Byzantine scribes, did not use gold; their ornament is both dainty and rich at the same time. When we see a page of the text of the Book of Kells containing an initial or a marginal design we feel that, with all our art and improvements and reproduction of pictures everywhere, with all our wealth of illustrated books, we have nothing to surpass these shining glories achieved by the monks of the Long Ago.

The Wonderful House We Live In, and Our Place in the World

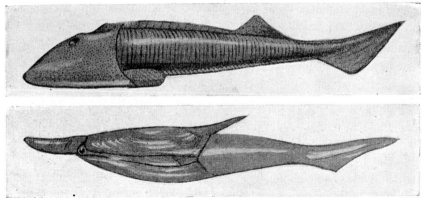

Two of the earliest backboned animals that lived, perhaps 25 million years ago

LIFE MAKES THE BODY

WE read here of the way in which life became clothed—that is, of the making of the body. The first animals were never able to do much in the world, for two reasons. They lived in the sea and could not get enough oxygen, and they had no backbone, and no animal without a backbone has ever been of much importance in the world.

If we could summon before us all the animals that exist, and look at them carefully, we should be able, in spite of all their differences, to divide them up into two great classes, so that all the animals in one class would be far more like each other than they would be like any animal in the other class. In the one class we should place all the animals that have a backbone, and in the other all the animals that have not.

It is true that we should find a few animals about which we could not be sure, or which we should have to place between the two classes, for there are a few kinds of animals still living which have only half a backbone, or something that looks like a rough model of a backbone. These animals are immensely interesting, because they teach us how the backbone began.

Let us begin first with what are much the least important class of animals—those which have no backbone. We deal with them first because they actually came first. For ages there were animals of many kinds living in the sea, and others living on land, which had no backbones; and if you had searched the whole Earth and all the seas you would not have found a backbone anywhere—or a brain.

These animals which have no backbones are very difficult to arrange in any kind of order. Some are more wonderfully made than others, and have not existed so long. But they differ from each other so widely that it is really impossible to arrange them in a simple order. In any case, however, these backboneless animals, such as insects, oysters, and worms, are very humble and unimportant.

None of them has a brain. This does not mean that they cannot feel, nor that some of them, such as the bees, are not wonderful in many ways ; but, after all, until the brain came into existence no great progress could be made. So we need here say no more about the backboneless animals.

Nor need we here say anything about the curious kinds of animals which show us the first hints of a backbone. We may begin with those animals in which the first complete backbone—though a very simple one—is to be found. They are the fishes.

BODY, MIND, AND SOUL · CITIZENSHIP · ECONOMICS · GOVERNMENT

If we study all the kinds of backboned animals, we find they can all be arranged in a simple way. More than this, it is possible to show which class came first, which last, and so on.

Here, then, are the five great classes of the backboned animals—fishes, amphibia, reptiles, birds, mammals. Some of these words are strange, but they are really not difficult, and we shall easily explain them. For instance, if you have not heard of amphibia before, at any rate you do know a frog when you see it, and if you have never heard of mammals, it is easy to remember that mammals are animals which feed their young by means of milk, as, for instance, a cow, which feeds her calf. A human mother feeds her baby in the same way.

THE HISTORY OF THE ANIMALS THAT HAVE BACKBONES

There are very great differences between a fish, a cow, a sparrow, and a frog ; yet they all agree entirely in the main lines on which their bodies are made, because they all have a backbone. And we shall see soon that they agree in many other things besides. It is true that the fish is cold-blooded, and breathes water (or rather, the air dissolved in water), while a cow or a sparrow is warm-blooded, and breathes air, but, so far as the great history of the body is concerned, all these backboned animals are far more like one another than like any animal that has no backbone.

Now we want to trace upwards, if we can, the history of these various kinds of backboned animals. The first, we are certain, were the fishes. The backbones of the fishes are the principal part of what we call their skeleton; and this skeleton, inside their body, is covered with soft parts like muscle and skin. This fact, the possession of a skeleton inside the body, built up around the backbone, is true of all backboned animals.

But on no account must we confuse the fishes with animals like the whale, which is a newcomer compared with the fish; and we must here give up, once and for all, the utterly wrong notion that all the animals found in the sea are fishes. Some of these animals have existed ages and ages longer in the sea than any fish. They have no backbones, no hints of a brain, and are as inferior to the fish as the fish is to a cow. We have no more right to call crabs fishes because they live in the

water than we have to call a worm a bird because it breathes in the air.

Backboned animals very often have limbs—fore legs and hind legs, or arms and legs, or wings and legs—and the making of these limbs is one of the most important facts in the history of the body.

THE MAKING OF THE BODY—THE FISH THAT GROWS INTO A LAND ANIMAL

The nearest approach to anything like limbs in fishes is in their fins. We believe that certain fishes which had a long fin stretched right along each side of the body, from head to tail, played a great part in the making of the bodies of higher and later animals, for from these long side fins there were gradually formed, as the ages went on, two pairs of limbs, one pair in front and one behind, which are found after this time in all backboned animals.

Now, we remember the great step taken by life when first it swam ashore. We know, even now, certain fishes which can get along for some time in the air, and they give us a little hint of what happened, especially as some of these fishes are very clever at hopping along in the mud. If now we turn to the next class of backboned animals, which have that difficult name amphibia, we shall be able to guess what happened.

Amphibia is really a Greek word, and means " both-life." It is a word made up to say that animals of this kind, such as the frog, lead both kinds of lives— in water and on land; each amphibian begins by leading the one kind of life and goes on by leading the other, and this gives us a hint—the history of life in the great chain of backboned animals.

THE ANCESTORS OF THE FROGS LAID THE PLAN FOR BACKBONED ANIMALS

When the frog is very young, it is called a tadpole. This lives in water and breathes water. If it never went any farther, we should properly call it a fish. So long as it is a tadpole it is a fish; but, of course, if it were no more than a fish it would live in water all its days. The tadpole does not do this, but after a time it begins to make great changes in itself; there begin to be hints of limbs and, what is even more important, of lungs; and at last the little tadpole grows into a frog—which is not a fish—which has arms and legs, or fore limbs and hind limbs, and breathes air by means of lungs. But this is not the only development; for the frog has hands,

THE BACKBONE—NATURE'S STAMP OF MERIT

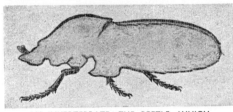

AN INVERTEBRATE—THE BEETLE, WHICH
HAS NO BACKBONE

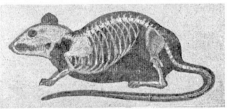

A VERTEBRATE—THE MOUSE, WHICH HAS
A BACKBONE

THE ANCIENT MONSTER DIPLODOCUS, ONE OF THE GREATEST VERTEBRATES EVER KNOWN

RECONSTRUCTED SKELETON OF DIPLODOCUS AT SOUTH KENSINGTON, WITH BACKBONE 80 FEET LONG

A FAMILIAR INVERTEBRATE—THE COMMON LOBSTER

The backbone is Nature's stamp of merit. The backboned creatures we call Vertebrates; those without backbones are Invertebrates. The backbone may be long, as in old Diplodocus, or short, as in a mouse; but it always means a highly-developed nervous system. The animals without backbones, like the lobster, may have splendid armour, but they always belong to a much inferior type of Life.

as we have, each having four fingers and a thumb, while it has five toes on each of its feet. Ages and ages ago, the first frogs laid down the plan of the kind of limbs which all backboned animals since then have had ; though some of them, like the bird, do not keep this kind of five-fingered limb all their lives.

Now, when the frog is grown from the tadpole into a backboned animal with four limbs, breathing air by means of lungs, it is really very like certain of the next class of backboned animals, which are called reptiles. It is not like a snake, but it is like a small lizard—especially if the lizard has no tail. Indeed, the simplest way of looking at this is to think of the amphibia as fishes when they are young and reptiles when they are grown up. The young frog or tadpole is practically a fish, because it is made as a fish is made, and does what a fish does. The grown-up frog is practically a reptile, because it is made as reptiles are made, and does what they do.

WHEN THE REPTILES WERE THE MASTERS OF THE EARTH

Now we leave the amphibia and may pass on to the next class of backboned animals that appeared upon the Earth, which were the reptiles; and of these we need not say much, except that many of the reptiles gradually lost their limbs and became extremely long and round and crawling, until at last they took the shape of snakes and serpents. Snakes and serpents in their very earliest stages show that they are the children of creatures that had limbs, and we are certain of this. A snake has no limbs that we can see; it moves about in a different way.

Now we are getting much higher, and coming to times nearer to our own. There was a stage in the story of life when the reptiles were masters. There was then nothing to beat them. They grew to great sizes, and if you go to museums you may see the remains of their bodies, sometimes sixty feet long. Some of them, especially the smaller ones, grew great stretches of skin between their outspread fingers, a sort of web such as we find in the feet of many swimming birds, and so they were able to fly more or less. Some of them were perhaps very fierce and powerful, and they had terrible teeth. It must have been a very strange Earth in the age of reptiles.

Then, somehow, a wonderful thing happened. This was guessed at long ago, but it was proved only last century by the discovery of the remains of certain curious animals which do not now live on the earth at all.

HOW THE BIRDS FIRST CAME INTO THE WORLD

If you think of a snake, and then of a lark, you would never guess that the birds have sprung from reptiles ; but if, instead, we take a reptile, such as a small lizard, which has not lost its limbs, and then look at the remains of certain creatures which once existed, we discover that birds have sprung from reptiles.

Of course, there are a great number of very marked differences between reptiles and birds, both in their appearance and in their ways of life. No bird now living has teeth, for instance ; birds have feathers, and so on. Yet we discover the remains of birds which once had teeth, and we know that birds have sprung from the reptiles.

Lovers of birds are almost inclined sometimes to place them on a level with the mammals themselves, and it is true that in some ways the birds are equal to the mammals, and in some ways even superior to them. But really no one, not even the best lover of birds, questions that the highest group of animals, and indeed of living things of any kind, are the mammals. Where did they come from ?

It seems most likely that the mammals did not spring, like the birds, from the reptiles, and it is quite certain that birds did not spring from mammals, or mammals from birds. We must go right back, not so far as the fishes, but at any rate as far as the amphibia, to find where the mammals have sprung from.

THE GREAT UPWARD CLIMB OF THE ANIMAL WORLD

The picture on page 79 shows us how from the fishes there sprang the amphibia; how from some of the amphibia there sprang the reptiles and birds ; and how from other amphibia sprang the mammals. A few of the earliest mammals must have led a hard life on the Earth.

They cannot have had anything like the strength of the reptiles, yet they survived and flourished—partly by keeping out of the reptiles' way, and by going to corners where the reptiles did not want to live, but more especially because of the great care they gave to their young—a care far better and finer than anything to be found in the rest of the world of life. And so they went on from strength to strength, until now man, the highest of the animals, is the master of the Earth.

Now, throughout all these long ages, while so many changes have been happening, and so many different kinds of animals have come into being, nothing has ever happened to cause the disappearance of the backbone.

THE CHIEF FACTOR IN THE MAKING OF OUR BODIES

On the contrary, it has steadily become more and more perfect. You know what the backbone of a herring is like; it is a very useful thing, without which no herring or other fish could grow; but it is very simple, and only fit for a creature which leads a very simple life and from its birth to its death makes practically only one kind of movement.

As we pass upward we find—in the frog, for instance—that the backbone is becoming at the same time stronger and less simple, and as we pass up higher still we find this process going on until, in a mammal, the backbone is so complicated that we might spend a lifetime in studying it.

In ourselves, as in the fish, it is the chief factor in the making of our bodies. It is something like the keel of a ship, upon which everything else is built; but it is, at its simplest and smallest and weakest, a million times more wonderful than the keel of the biggest ship ever made.

THE BUILDING UP OF THE BACK-BONE OF THE BODY

We know that the backbone is not really one bone, but is made up of a number of little bones laid in a line. Indeed, these bones are built or placed on one another, just as we may place a number of stones on one another in building. For this reason the backbone (or spine, as it is often called) is as often called the spinal column. The little bones of which it is made have the not really very difficult name of vertebrae, a single one being called a vertebra; and the scientific name for animals that have a backbone is Vertebrates, while those which have none are called Invertebrates.

All backboned animals above the fishes either have two pairs of limbs all their lives; or have them at the very beginning

and lose them afterwards, like the snakes; or have them when they are grown up, but not at first, like the frog. No backboned animal ever has more than two pairs of limbs.

The serpent loses its limbs, the whale turns its fore limbs into flippers, and in order to find its hind limbs, or legs, which have fallen out of use altogether, you have to dig deep in its blubber, or fat. But there you will find them all the same —toes and all. The birds have learnt to turn their fore legs into wings. When the chick is very young, it has five fingers on each hand, like its forefathers, but later finds that these are more than it needs to build a wing upon, and when it is grown up we find that the wing is really only built upon three and a half fingers. The other one and a half have disappeared, as they were not wanted.

The use of limbs is for movement; but if we trace limbs upwards from the days of the frog, or at any rate from the days of the earliest mammals, we find that the fore limbs begin to be used for other purposes. For instance, we know for what terrible purposes a tiger uses its claws.

HOW IMPORTANT IS THE FREEDOM OF MAN'S ARMS

If we go to a higher mammal than the tiger—as, for instance, to the monkey— we find that he does much more with his fore limbs. The cleverest lion or tiger, though it will steady its food with its claws while gnawing at it, cannot pick up its food in the way that we can and take it to its mouth. The monkey does this; it has learnt the art of grasping.

In man, the spinal column has been made into a real column because he stands upright; only babies now use their fore limbs for walking. Once the crawling stage is passed, our arms are freed for ever from purposes of walking, and are used instead as the great servants of the brain, without which man could have done nothing in the world, and, indeed, would have been starved and hunted out of the world by animals long ago.

It is almost impossible to say how important is the freedom of man's arms, or fore limbs, from the mere purpose for which he now uses his feet, and for which the hands of all other backboned animals have been used for so many ages. But the hands of man, as we said, are the servants of the brain and the nerves.

THE EXTRAORDINARY WORK OF A TREE

THE AMAZING ROOT THAT FEEDS AND ANCHORS A TREE

THE HUNDREDS OF LITTLE ROOTS FORMED BY
THE IVY FOR CLIMBING AND CLINGING

HOW A ROOT WILL TURN SHARPLY ROUND IN
SEARCH OF FOOD

A MOTOR-CAR INSIDE THE TRUNK OF A TREE

The Story of the Marvellous Plants that Cover the Earth

Always the young shoot goes up and the root goes down

HOW PLANTS WORK FOR THEIR LIVING

BECAUSE plants spend but little energy in the form of movement, we are apt to underrate their working powers.

Only some of the simplest plants, swimming about in the water, show any sign of locomotion, but the majority are very busy. As among animals, the business is mainly twofold—caring for self and caring for others. It is the first of these that we have to do with here, and it means capturing raw materials, manufacturing these into carbon compounds—sugar and starch, fat and oil, and, above all, *proteins* (like the gluten of wheat) ; and using this self-made food for upkeep, for growth, and for storage.

A great part of the work of green plants is devoted to increasing the amount of living matter; to growing, in fact; and we cannot look at an oak tree 100 feet high without feeling that to build this up from an acorn the plant must have done an immense amount of work. Some of the Big Trees of California (the Sequoias) are about 300 feet high, and this is near the limit, for there is a limit beyond which a tree cannot grow without tumbling down, and we sometimes see healthy trees laid prostrate because, when a strong wind came, their foundations would not stand the strain. Some of the great sea-weeds, such as oar-weed, grow to a very great length without having any hard tissues for support, but in these cases the heavy plant is floating in the water.

The most ancient plants lived probably in shallow water near shore, and when we look at the great beds of seaweeds exposed at low tide, we get some idea of the primeval vegetation—after ages and ages of the simple free-swimmers. The first use of the root was to anchor the plant so that it could not be swept away into deep and dark water, and that is the use of the so-called roots of seaweeds today.

But land vegetation, when it began, meant among other things the need for a new water-absorbing organ, and this is the main use of the root. A seaweed absorbs the water by the general surface of its fronds, and similarly the beautiful bladderwort of bog pools, having no roots, must absorb water by its leaves. This is not possible in ordinary land plants, and thus the chief use of the root is to absorb water and salts from the soil. Of course, when the stem of the plant rises high, as in trees, the roots serve as foundations, or anchors; and another use of roots is to form a storehouse for reserve food supplies. This is plainly seen in the case of edible roots like carrots.

BOTANY · ITS WONDERS · FLOWERS · TREES · HOW THINGS GROW

The tip of a root is clear and delicate. It remains ever-young and growing; it is always feeling its way farther into the soil. Its growing-point is protected by a root-cap which saves the delicate, rapidly-dividing cells from being punctured by sharp particles in the soil. A little way behind the growing part we see the origin of numerous root-hairs which are of fundamental importance to the plant. They are the water-absorbers.

There are often many hundreds of root-hairs to a square inch, and they grow like delicate fingers into the gaps among the soil-particles. They are outgrowths of the very living skin-cells of the root, and their use is to absorb the soil-water which occurs in delicate films round the minute particles. The wall of the finger-like processes that probe and bend in the gaps is very delicate, so that water passes readily through it into the denser cell-contents. Moreover, towards the tip of the root-hair the cell-wall is soft and gummy, so that a soil-particle sticks to it.

HOW THE ROOT-HAIRS WORK THEIR WAY INTO THE DARK SOIL

All that the plant gets out of the soil passes in by the delicate root-hairs, and no individual root-hair lasts very long. They shrivel away as the part of the root from which they arise gets older ; and new ones are formed nearer the tip. It is important to understand that the growing of the root deeper into the ground is always just at the tip, below the youngest hair-roots ; otherwise the growing would tear the root-hairs from their grip of the soil-particles, and of this there is no trace.

In the core of the young root there is a column of pipes or vessels (wood and bast), surrounded by a slightly corky sheath. There is another corky sheath just below the outermost cells that form the root-hairs. Between these two slightly corky sheaths there is the rind (or cortex) of the root, a sort of intermediate reservoir for the absorbed water. But as the root gets older the rind often becomes unimportant, or disappears altogether. What is most important is this—that the water captured by the root-hairs passes into the wood-elements of the root's core, and then into similar elements in the stem, until it finally reaches the leaves.

Before we leave the root it is of interest to notice two or three other points. Often

as the root grows older it shortens as a whole, and this gives a plant a stronger hold in the ground. With the growth of the plant as a whole there is an increase in the total size of the root-work, and this is in great part due to the giving off new rootlets. It is very striking to find a boulder that has been cracked and has then allowed roots of plants to grow into it, with the result that it is eventually split in two. Then we may see the whole root-work of a heather plant, much larger than the bush above ground. Rootlets begin in the core of the root and their emergence is very striking, for a kind of digestion takes place in front of them as they penetrate the rind. They may be said to *eat* their way.

THE STRANGE WAYS IN WHICH THE ROOTS CLING AND HOLD UP WATER

Finally, there are roots that do strange things. Thus, the little brownish air-roots of the ivy are used for climbing purposes, binding the stem tightly to tree or wall. In some of the perched plants of tropical forests, that live quite off the ground, the roots absorb water-vapour from the moist air. In the orchid which yields vanilla some of the roots serve as tendrils, and others dangle. They are able to absorb dew and rain, for they are surrounded by a sheath of large empty cells opening by pores to the outside, very much like the water-storing cells of the bog-moss.

In the bog-moss more than half the cells are dead and empty, but are kept from collapsing by delicate spiral and circular bands. Twenty times the plant's own weight of water may be stored in these cells, and this is used by the living elements which the others enclose.

THE BRICKS AND RAFTERS AND VENTILATORS OF THE LEAF

Thus, when there is prolonged drought the bog-moss is still able to flourish, and it is also in part to be thanked for holding-up the rain that falls on the hills, so that the springs are slow in becoming dry. The use of bog-moss for soaking up moisture from wounds is well-known. It is interesting to find the same sort of device in situations so different as the bog-moss and the vanilla roots.

Beyond any doubt, the green leaf is the most marvellous laboratory in the world. For there, in perfect silence, is brought about the raising of simplicity into complexity, the making of the organic out of the inorganic. It is also the most important laboratory in the world, for all animal and human life practically depends on the nutritive material the green leaf builds up.

A leaf is a sheet of living tissue, sometimes as thin as tissue-paper, as in a young beech leaf; sometimes as thick as leather, as in a cabbage. Some leaves are so small that we can hardly see them with the naked eye, while some palm leaves are six feet long.

No self-supporting higher plant can get on without leaves unless an expanse of green is attained in some other way—notably by having a large area of green stem. Thus in cactuses the leaves are turned into spines, and the whole stem is green. What look like floating leaves in the case of the little duckweed on the surface of the pool —the smallest but one of all British flowering plants—seem to be tiny flattened shoots.

To understand the work of leaves we must know a little about the microscopic architecture.

THE BUSY FACTORY IN THE ROOT OF A TREE

Here, in a highly magnified picture-diagram, we see the wonderful structure of a root, and the scene of a root's astonishing activities. The delicate growing point is protected by a hard cap. Immediately within the outer wall are the layers of cells which bring down food from the leaves, and next to them are the quill-like tubes which bring up food from the soil. In the heart of the root are the cells which store the starch from which the root nourishes itself and grows. At the top we see a few of the countless root-hairs which absorb salts and water from the soil.

Think of a leaf hardly thicker than this paper, and even there is room for no small degree of structure. The upper surface is covered by a layer of skin-cells, and the outer walls of this are often thickened to protect the delicate, more intensely living units below. The skin-cells often bear non-conducting hairs, giving the leaf a woolly surface; or they may be, as it were, varnished with protective wax.

To the lower side of the leaf there is another skin (an epidermis), but set here and there on this surface there are pores called *stomata*, which allow of an exchange of gases between the leaf and the air. If the leaf is floating on the surface of a pond, as in the case of a water lily, there would be no use in having the openings on the lower surface which touches the water ; and we are not surprised to find them on the dry upper surface.

Now, between the two skins there is the middle green tissue of the leaf. Towards the upper surface the cells are arranged like bricks or posts, and often in two layers. They are called palisade cells. Towards the under surface there are more green cells, less closely fitted together, and the gaps between them communicate with the openings (or stomata). This is called the spongy tissue. The green colour of the palisade layers and the spongy layers is due to numerous green discs (chlorophyll corpuscles) lying in the living matter of the cells.

Finally, the leaf is supported by a framework or network of veins, which form the skeleton of the leaf. If we are not familiar with the appearance, we should collect some skeleton leaves, and, after washing them, hold them against the light to see the beautiful lace-work. The wood-elements of bundles that support the soft tissue of the leaf are also of use as conducting pipes by which the water and salts from the roots may be distributed to the green cells of the leaf, and by which the nutritive organic materials manufactured in the green tissue of the leaf may be carried downward, as " elaborated " sap, to the stem and the roots. It is useful to take a few leaves of the plantain from the side of the road, and break the stalk to see the four or five firm strands which are thus exposed. These are the conducting pipes up and down from root to leaf, and from leaf to stem or root.

THE GREAT CHEMICAL LABORATORY IN THE CELLS OF THE LEAF

The all-important fact is that the green cells in the middle tissue of the leaf, with thousands of chlorophyll discs turning their edges to the light, are able, with the help of the energy of the sunlight, to split up the carbon dioxide of the atmosphere, liberating the oxygen and fixing the carbon in the form of carbon compounds. This building up by the power of light is what is called *photo-synthesis*.

The conditions for this photo-synthesis, which is the most characteristic work of green plants, are thus summed up by Professor F. O. Bower in his masterly book on The Botany of the Living Plant.

1. Chlorophyll must be present in the cells which carry on the building-up process.
2. Carbon dioxide must be accessible to them.
3. Light must reach them, and in sufficient intensity.
4. Temperature must be within certain limits.
5. Mineral salts must be available.

" These necessary conditions being met (says Professor Bower), the constructive process consists in the absorption of carbon dioxide, fixation of the carbon, release of free oxygen, and the appearance in the active cells of material formed from the carbon which has been fixed."

STARCH AND SUGAR MADE BY SUNLIGHT AND THE GREEN LEAF

The first visible product of the leaf's industry is starch, but this is preceded by the formation of formaldehyde and sugar. If a green leaf is covered with a plate of tinfoil or cardboard with the letters S-T-A-R-C-H cut out on it, and if the plant is kept in the dark for two days so that any starch already formed may pass down into the stem ; and if the leaf is then exposed to sunlight for a morning, we can easily prove that the building-up process has been working only in the illumined parts.

For if the leaf be pulled off, boiled for a minute in water, then decolourised with alcohol and stained with iodine solution, the word Starch will be seen in purple letters on the exposed parts of the leaf, while the shaded parts will be yellow. The fact is that the starch is formed in the *illumined* chlorophyll discs.

If a shoot of Canadian water weed is fixed in a glass tube, with the cut end upward and exposed to light, bubbles of gas are seen escaping from the cut surface. It is easy to capture these and prove that they consist of oxygen. They are the result of the splitting-up of the carbon dioxide captured from the water, and by counting the bubbles and using glass of different colours it is not difficult to show that the red, orange, and yellow rays are much more important than those of the blue or violet.

THE TINY MOUTHS OF THE LEAF AND HOW THEY BREATHE

Every living creature must take in oxygen and give off carbon dioxide, for living cannot go on without slow combustion (or oxidation). If we have in a room at night a lighted candle, a sleeping cat, and a green plant, all three are taking in oxygen, burning away carbon compounds, and giving off carbon dioxide.

It is at night that we must study the breathing or respiration of plants, for during the day the breathing process is quite disguised or masked by the feeding process. The little openings (stomata) on the under-side of the leaf are breathing pores, and it is also by these important apertures that water-vapour is given off to the atmosphere. The stomata open and close regularly, so that, though too much water is not given off, there is enough to maintain the up-current from the roots.

To sum up. Water with salts in solution is absorbed by the roots. It passes by the stem to the leaves, where it meets carbon dioxide which the leaves have absorbed. Starch and other materials are formed. They steal away by the bast of the bundles to the place where they can be used and stored. This is the daily work of a plant.

The Story of the Peoples of All Nations and Their Homelands

Mountains of the Lake District overlooking Grasmere

OUR GREAT AND LITTLE HILLS

ENGLAND's little hills, with their graceful outlines and peaceful sheltering woods, are familiar presences to most of us, but there is nothing in them to abash our human conceit. Not so the mountains. Let us look at them first. Whether we see them bare in the sunlight, or wreathed in mists, or swept by stormy winds, they are profound and impressive in their solemn grandeur. Fully to realise this, however, we must match ourselves against their steepness and sternness and feel the influences of their upper solitudes.

If we trace the Cheviot range along the Northumberland border to the south-west, and then southward to the Pennine Chain by the boundaries of Cumberland, Durham, Westmorland and Yorkshire to its end in Derbyshire, we shall find more than 40 fells and moors and pikes and dodds of 2000 feet and more in height. If we add the Lake District peaks, the number of mountains of 2000 feet and more in England is increased to over 200.

The Cheviot range culminates northward in the Cheviot, or the Great (Scottish Muckle) Cheviot (2676 ft). Several of the summits hereabouts are over 2000 feet, by far the finest being the conical-peaked and rock-crowned Hedge-hope, which, like the Big Cheviot itself, is in Northumberland. The massive height that gives its name to the whole range is quite a simple mountain, though with a steep slope. Its rocks are granite, but it is almost entirely a grassy sheep-walk.

From the top of the Muckle Cheviot there is a view over Northumberland that includes many miles of the coastline, from Berwick to Warkworth; but the top is so flat that half a mile of boggy ground must be crossed before Scotland comes into view. There are 30 mountains in the Lake District higher than the Great Cheviot.

The Cheviots continue south-westward from their topmost height at an average elevation of about 2000 feet for half a dozen miles to Windygate Hill (2034 ft), and then sink to an average of 1600 feet as far as Peel Hill, where they almost reach the 2000 feet level again. Then they turn southward at lower levels down the boundary of Northumberland and Cumberland and become the Pennine Chain. Throughout they are a fine, grassy sheep-rearing range, cleft on either side by narrow glens, each with its infant stream flanked by hills that become more and more rounded as they sink away into Northumberland.

THE FIVE CONTINENTS & 100 NATIONS & RACES THAT INHABIT THEM

The most chain-like part of the Pennine range is where, to westward of the range, the River Eden clearly makes a valley between the Pennines and the mountains of the Lake District. The chain may be said to begin where the Newcastle to Carlisle railway breaks through. North-ward of this gap the range is a continuation from the Cheviots, and it falls short of the mountain standard. Southward of the River Irthing there is a succession of mountains between the headwaters of the South Tyne, Wear, and Tees on the east and the Eden on the west, their western slopes descending sharply into the Eden Valley while the range spreads more broadly into Northumberland, Durham, and Eastern Westmorland.

This well-marked range continues for more than 30 miles, its central and highest mountain being Cross Fell (2930 ft), in the extreme east of Cumberland. The Shap Fells reach out eastward from the Lake District and link with the Pennines beyond the Eden at Appleby and beyond the Lune at Tebay. Along this Cross Fell ridge are more than a dozen fells all rising above 2000 feet, some looking out across the Eden Valley and some sending their waters down to the Tyne, Wear, and Tees. The next highest summits to Cross Fell in this part of the range, are Milburn Forest (2780 ft), Mickle Fell (2596 ft) in Lune Forest, Hilton Fell (2446 ft), and Burnhope Seat (2452 ft).

INDUSTRIAL ENGLAND AND THE NORTHERN FELLS OF THE PENNINE RANGE

South of Kirkby Stephen, and around the sources and upper courses of the rivers Eden, Lune, Swale, and Ure, the chain expands eastward and westward, and becomes a series of short ranges, mainly north to south in their trend. Here there are more than a dozen fells rising from 2000 to 2300 feet such as The Calf (2220 ft), north of Sedbergh, and Baugh Fell (2216 ft) to the east; Wild Boar Fell (2323 ft) and Swarth (2235 ft) between the headwaters of the Lune and the Eden; High Seat (2328 ft), Nine Standards Fell (2008 ft), Rogan's Seat (2204 ft), and Water Crag (2176 ft) around the early course of the Swale; and Great Shunnor Fell (2346 ft) and Stags Fell (2213 ft), draining chiefly to the Ure.

These northern fells of the Pennine system are partly grazing grounds of rough grass and partly heathery moorland with broad, and often boggy summits, with sides deeply cut here and there by narrow water courses, inhabited very thinly in their lower valleys, with rarely visited solitudes above. Their roads or tracks are several miles apart and rarely cross the summits. Some of them lead to lead-mines that began their workings centuries ago. The uplands act as gathering grounds for the chief rivers of the North, and as they spread more broadly at lower levels, with wider valleys and lower heights, and reach the coal-bearing regions, they become on either side the great manufacturing areas of Northumberland and Durham, Western Yorkshire and Eastern Lancashire, North Derbyshire and Eastern Staffordshire. Industrial England is largely based upon the fringes of the Pennines where coal has been found.

A BREAK WHICH LEADS US INTO THE FLAT PLAIN OF YORK

West to east, Wensleydale makes a break in the hills right into the flat agricultural plain of York. The Pennines continue south of the gap, the rivers Lune and Ribble making their way down the western watershed of the chain to the Irish Sea, and the tributaries of the Yorkshire Ouse—the Nidd, the Wharfe, the Aire, the Calder, and the Don—reaching the North Sea after making various confluences. South of Wensleydale the 2000-feet Pennine heights are more scattered. On the western flank, between the Lune and the Ribble are Whernside (2414 ft), Gragreth (2250 ft), and Ingleborough (2373 ft) ; between Ribblehead and Wensleydale, Dodd Fell (2189 ft) and Weather Fell (2015 ft) ; between the Upper Ribble and the Upper Wharfe, Penyghent (2273 ft) and Fountains Fell (2191 ft); between Wharfedale and Nidderdale, Buckden Pike and Great Whernside (2310 ft). In Derbyshire are Kinderscout (2088 ft) and Bleaklow (2061 ft).

SCENERY THAT CHARMS BY ITS VARIETY SOUTH FROM WENSLEYDALE

The northern hills of the Pennine Chain are mostly composed of carboniferous limestone, which here and there is topped by millstone grit. Where the millstone edges are found the scenery becomes more impressive. The limestone has rounded contours, whereas the gritstone is strong and bold. The scenery that charms by its variety is mostly found southward from Wensleydale. Ribblesdale is the first valley where individual hills stand out and command attention, the massive bulk of Ingleborough being contrasted across the valley with the fine peak of Penyghent. Perhaps the greatest change from beauty to sternness is in Upper Teesdale.

A feature of the limestone regions is the extensive honeycombing with caverns in the Ingleborough region and on the limestone side of the River Derwent and its tributaries in Derbyshire. The change from grimness to softer beauty is most suddenly seen between precipitous Kinderscout and bare Bleaklow and the quick succession of sylvan beauty in the valley of the Derwent. Kinderscout lords it over the Pennine hills of the south as Cross Fell does over the northern Pennines.

WHERE WE MUST GO TO FIND THE SPIRIT OF THE MOUNTAINS

It is, however, to the Lake District that we must go to catch the real mountain spirit, for the Earth has no mountains on an equal area excelling them in variety of beauty. It all lies within an area of thirty miles by twenty-five ; but so broken up into groups is this wonderful region that it cannot be even glanced at by passing straight through it. There is no highway from east to west, and only one from south to north, and that one, though it passes scenes of great beauty, with fine historical memories, is not representative.

None of the beauties can be adequately seen from the road. This grand highway, south to north, from Bowness or Windermere by Ambleside and Grasmere to Keswick, is at the bottom of a natural trench in which four lakes lie—Windermere, Rydal Water, Grasmere, and Thirlmere. It is beautifully wooded and shoulders of mountains rise from the road, but the mountains themselves can only be seen in peeps.

THE MOST IMPOSSIBLE ROAD IN ENGLAND FOR THOSE WHO WALK

To get anything like a general view of the mountains on this side of the group they must be viewed at a distance, from a Windermere steamer between Lakeside and Waterhead ; or by turning aside from the road at Windermere to Orrest Head, or before reaching Ambleside to Jenkin Crag on the lowest slope of Wansfell Pike. From the lake the positions of the Kentmere range in the east, the Fairfield semi-circle in the north,

the Coniston mountains (The Old Man and Wetherlam) in the west, and the Langdales can be fixed for further study.

The central road, as it approaches Keswick, does disclose the two terminal mountains, Skiddaw and Saddleback, on the north, and gives a distant view of the north-western group, in which Grisedale Pike is most conspicuous ; but the chief west-central mass, incomparably the finest of all, clustered around England's loftiest mountain, Scafell Pike, is not seen at all.

The plain truth is that the hundreds of thousands who rush across this fascinating district in motor-coaches and motor-cars, making its one thoroughfare the most impossible road in England for those who walk, think they have seen it but have not seen it, though they have had a glorious ride. Let us state, then, how the mountains can be seen.

They are grouped in seven blocks. Looked at from east to west the first is the High Street and Kentmere block, from which radiate the Fusedale, Mardale, Long Sleddale, Kentdale, and Troutbeck valleys, with Hawes Water nestling in their midst and five other waters resting on their shoulders. The only usable road into the heart of these mountains comes from the east and runs to a dead end in Mardale.

THE GLORIOUS THREE-MILE WALK TO THE HIGH STREET PLATEAU

This block of hills, eight miles long and rising 2000 feet or more, is separated from the Helvellyn-Fairfield block by the Kirkstone Pass, between Ambleside and Patterdale, which receives its waters chiefly from the Helvellyn, or western side. The Travellers Rest Inn, near the head of the Kirkstone Pass, is at the foot of Caudale Moor, one of the outlying heights of the High Street range. This Kirkstone Pass road, which connects Windermere with Ullswater, shears off the High Street block and leaves these hills comparatively unvisited ; but no one knows the Lake District who does not know them.

The best way to reach High Street from Ambleside is to begin the walk behind the Kirkstone Traveller's Rest, cross Caudale Moor to the extreme head of the Troutbeck Valley, and climb Thornthwaite Crag, where the Kentmere hills (Froswick, Ill Bell, and Yoke) join the High Street plateau. It is about a three-mile walk and leads to a splendid view.

From Thornthwaite Crag, on which is a large cairn, reached by a steep climb alongside a wall, the view opens out over Windermere to the sea beyond, and includes the Coniston Fells, the lofty heights round Scafell Pike, and the rugged eastern side of the Fairfield range and Helvellyn. Within a mile, north-eastward, are the steep descent into the upper vale of the River Kent from which rise the precipices of Froswick and Ill Bell, the summit of the Nan Bield Pass (2100 ft) with its entrancing view into Mardale, and, more northward, the summit of the High Street range (2718 ft), all reached by crossing to the edges of a mile-wide almost flat plateau.

Along the grassy and peaty summit of High Street once ran a Roman road, now but faintly marked.

Here, then, is a range, flat on the summit, declining gradually to the north, sending forth lateral ridges enclosing lofty rocky dales from which rise bold crags, and embosoming half a dozen lakes, large and small. Glorious prospects, from Morecambe Bay to the Pennines, are visible in a two-hours walk around the edge of the High Street plateau.

THE THIRTY SUMMITS AND FELLS OF THE HELVELLYN-FAIRFIELD RANGE

Between the car-crowded motor-road from Ambleside to Keswick and the road which winds up the steep zigzagging Kirkstone Pass from Ambleside on the way to Patterdale and Ullswater rises the Helvellyn-Fairfield range. It has at least 30 summits and fells. There are half a dozen pony tracks going up Helvellyn or crossing it to the main road, the chief being the Grisedale Pass, from Patterdale to Grasmere, reaching its highest point (1929 ft) at the junction between Helvellyn and Fairfield. The length of the Helvellyn mass above 2000 feet is seven miles as the crow flies, and the length of the continuing Fairfield mass is six miles, beginning with St Sunday's Crag and ending with Red Screes overlooking the top of the Kirkstone Pass.

The western side of Helvellyn is dull and unromantic, and its ascent presents no difficulties, though the gradient is stiff occasionally. But Helvellyn decidedly commands respect if approached from the east, whether the ascent be by the Grisedale Pass, from Grasmere, or from Patter-

dale, or Glenridding. The most dramatic approach is up Ullswater on a steamer. Though lumpish St Sunday's Crag and pointed Catchidecam are the most prominent heights seen at first from the lake ; the gradual revealing of Helvellyn and the Low Man as Glenridding is ascended is finely staged. The true Helvellyn looks down its precipices into the hollow where the Red Tarn lies. Scott was not exaggerating when, in his poem on the dog that watched three months in this hollow by the undiscovered body of its master, he wrote of climbing " the dark brow of the mighty Helvellyn."

THE VISION THAT GREETS US FROM THE LOFTY SUMMIT OF HELVELLYN

Wordsworth, in his poem on the same tragedy, describes the scene truly.

It was a cove, a huge recess,
That keeps till June December's snow ;
A lofty precipice in front,
A silent tarn below.
There sometimes doth a leaping fish
Send through the tarn a lonely cheer ;
The crags repeat the raven's croak,
In symphony austere.
Thither the rainbow comes, the cloud,
And mists that spread the flying shroud,
And sunbeams ; and the sounding blast
That, if it could, would hurry past ;
But that enormous barrier holds it fast.

From the top of Helvellyn (3118 ft) nearly all the principal monarchs of the district can be seen, with six lakes, and parts of the sea from Morecambe Bay to Solway Firth ; while eastward the Cross Fell range and Ingleborough in the Pennines are clearly visible. The view from Fairfield is equally fine. Fairfield and Helvellyn meet at Grisedale Tarn near the top of Grisedale Pass, with which only the passes of the Scafell mountain group will compare.

The descent from Helvellyn over Dollywaggon Pike to the Grisedale Tarn is 1350 feet, and the immediate ascent from the tarn to the top of Fairfield is 1095 feet. The summits are about three miles apart. From Fairfield eight lakes are visible.

AN UP AND DOWN WALK ALONG THE CREST OF THE FAIRFIELD RANGE

The mountain drops eastward into Deepdale by magnificent cliffs, which continue the ruggedness of Helvellyn on the same side. By going to Cofa Pike, along the narrow ridge that joins Fairfield to its northern continuation, St Sunday's Crag, a view can be obtained of the sheer ruggedness of both Helvellyn and Fairfield.

An up and down walk along the whole crest of the Fairfield range, by Hart Crag and Dove Crag to Red Screes overhanging the head of the Kirkstone Pass, is the middle part of the best circular walk from Ambleside, by Nab Scar, Heron Pike, Rydal Fell, and Great Rigg to Fairfield, but it is only for stalwarts; whereas almost anybody can reach the summits of Helvellyn and Fairfield by taking enough time. Five pony paths up Helvellyn and one up Fairfield serve those who cannot walk. The High Street summits, and still more the Scafell summits, are comparatively remote from residential or holiday centres, but Helvellyn is neighbourly.

The third separate group east of the central highway between Windermere and Keswick is the most northerly pair of all—Skiddaw and Saddleback—beyond the Penrith-to-Keswick railway. Side by side they form a mountain boundary, with Keswick town nearly at their feet.

SKIDDAW AFFORDS A FINE FRAME TO ONE OF NATURE'S CHOICE PICTURES

Skiddaw (3054 ft), the fourth in height of the Cumbrian system, is an imposing mass, best seen from Derwentwater. By far the easiest to climb and close to a considerable town, it forms a fine frame to one of Nature's choice pictures, but closer acquaintance is disappointing. In going up Skiddaw one has his back to the scenery, the forward views are ordinary, while from the top the northward outlook is commonplace. On the other hand, the descent improves at every stage, and the panorama becomes particularly fine over Derwentwater, Borrowdale, and the Newlands, from halfway down the path. It must also be said of Skiddaw that its fine buttresses seen from the Bassenthwaite road below enhance its dignity, and looked at from the Scottish side its grand uplift from the plain is welcome to English eyes.

Though the bases of Skiddaw and Saddleback run down to each other, with a single valley between, no sensible person crosses the wet waste from one to the other. The ascent of Saddleback is a separate undertaking, usually made from Scales on the Penrith road.

Saddleback (2847 ft), when climbed, is far more impressive than Skiddaw. A mile and a half of it is over 2500 ft high. The mid part, which has given it its popular name, is a lofty grassy slope, but at either end it sinks down wild precipices to deep gorges, and the whole mass has a stern grandeur fitting its high-sounding ancient name of Blencathara. In the ascent of Scales Fell, Scales Tarn may be reached, deep-set at the foot of a towering cliff in a lonely recess. There are parts of the ridge of Blencathara that need careful walking. The descent toward Keswick is usually made by the farm of Derwentfolds.

WORDSWORTH'S POEM ON THE SHEPHERD LORD OF BLENCATHARA

It was on the grim slopes of Blencathara that Sir Lancelot Threlkeld (Threlkeld is now the station near the mountain) concealed as a babe and for 24 years Sir Henry Clifford from the vengeance of the House of York until Henry the Seventh became king. Then the hidden shepherd lord regained his estates.

The poet Wordsworth tells the story in his poem Lord Clifford. The child, the last of his race, lived unsuspected as the shepherd of Blencathara. When his estates were restored he was expected to " head the flock of war," but No.

Love had he found in huts where poor men lie ;
His daily teachers had been woods and rills,
The silence that is in the starry sky,
The sleep that is among the lonely hills.
In him the savage virtue of the Race,
Revenge, and all ferocious thoughts were dead;
Nor did he change, but kept in lofty place
The wisdom which adversity had bred.
Glad were the vales, and every cottage hearth ;
The Shepherd-lord was honoured more and more;
And, ages after he was laid in earth,
" The good Lord Clifford " was the name he bore.

A lovely instance this of the genius of Wordsworth in blending the spirit that is in Nature with the spirit of Man.

THE MUCH PHOTOGRAPHED FELLS AND TARNS OF THE LANGDALE PIKES

A fourth group sinking northward into lower fells rises between the central road from Grasmere to Keswick on the east, Borrowdale, Langstrath, and the Stake Pass on the west, and Langdale on the south. The conspicuous southern edge of this region is formed by the Langdale Pikes, perhaps the most photographed mountains in Lakeland. The higher pike, Harrison Stickle (2401 ft), appears from the eastward like a lion couchant, and its mate, Pike of Stickle (2323 ft), seems to be lying alongside with only a head projecting. They gain effect by their steep descent. Really they are the rocky edge of a plateau, ten miles long by three or four miles wide, on which are eight or nine summits about as high as themselves. The fells are swampy, and their few tracks difficult to follow.

In misty weather the stranger finds this upland region as easy to get lost in as any place in England. But Langdale Pikes are conspicuous, and so climbing people like to steer their way through the bogs behind them to High Raise (2500 ft) and Sergeant Man (2414 ft), and even to Ullscarf (2370 ft). To the north is High Seat (1996 ft), which has a remarkable range of vision paid for by wet feet.

PEAKS WHICH SEND THEIR WATERS DOWN TO NEWLANDS VALE

To the west of Derwentwater and Borrowdale, and the north of the Honister Pass and Buttermere and Crummock Water, is a fifth group of a dozen peaks that have Newlands Vale as the centre to which their eastern waters flow, while their western waters reach Buttermere, Crummock Water, or the River Cocker. They are divided into three ranges, which may be seen from above during two walks from Keswick. One walk is over Cat Bells, Maiden Moor, Eel Crags, Dale Head (2473 ft), Hindscarth (2385 ft), and Robinson (2417 ft), bold mountains the last four, at the head of Newlands Beck, and the other over the Causey Pike Scar Crags, Eel Crag, the massive, moss-covered Grasmoor (2791 ft), across Coledale Pass to Hobcarton Crags and Grisedale Pike (2593 ft). The views, near and far, on both journeys are fine.

CAIRN-CROWNED CONISTON OLD MAN AND BULKY WETHERLAM

The sixth detached group is Coniston Fells in Lancashire, separated from the rest by the Wrynose Pass and the upper part of the River Duddon. To those who only see it from afar it is represented by the cairn-crowned Coniston Old Man and the bulky Wetherlam, but the whole mass, when known from above, is nobly moulded, with deep and craggy recesses in its sides concealing half a dozen loftily placed tarns. From Walna Scar, in the south, to the Wrynose Pass is a central ridge five miles long, throwing off lateral extensions east and west, Wetherlam being to the north-east. The Old Man (2663 ft) is the highest summit, but there are seven others over 2500 ft. The southern end of the mass is scarred by copper mining, and the Tilberthwaite side by quarrying. The Coniston Old Man has a finer seaward view than any other height in the district.

In the dominant centre of these Lakeland giants Scafell Pike reaches 3210 ft in the middle of a block that for three miles do not fall below 2500 ft: Scafell 3162, Broad Crag 3050, Ill Crag 3040, Long Pike 2940, and Great End 2984.

Esk Hause, the highest pass in England, crosses by Great End and is the meeting-place for nearly all tracks converging toward the crowning summit. From the Hause the main ridge, losing height, goes northward to Glaramara, and south-east and north-west lateral ranges rise.

The south-east range, almost challenging in height the main ridge, goes by Esk Pike (2903 ft), Bow Fell (2960 ft), Crinkle Crags (2816 ft), and lower heights to the valley of the Duddon. The western range, beyond the Sty Head Pass, rises into the noble pyramid of Great Gable (2949 ft) and continues on the southern side of Ennerdale in Kirk Fell, the Pillar (2927 ft), and The Steeple (2746 ft), and on the northern side as Brandreth (2344 ft), and as High Crag (2443 ft), High Stile (2643 ft), and Red Pike (2479 ft).

THE GREAT CULMINATION OF ENGLAND'S GLORIOUS MOUNTAIN SCENERY

We have mentioned a dozen and a half of mountains diverging from the Scafell block, but there are fifty of 2000 ft or more. Happily, this rugged apex of Old England is preserved for free access. It is a scene worthy of England, its grim strength a foil to her gracious beauties. Wordsworth said of it:

On the summit of the Pike, which we gained after much toil, though without difficulty, there was not a breath of air. The stillness seemed to be not of this world. We paused and kept silence to listen, and no sound could be heard. The Scafell cataracts were voiceless to us, and there was not an insect to hum in the air. Round the top not a blade of grass is to be seen. Cushions or tufts of moss, parched and brown, appear between the huge blocks and stones that lie in heaps on all sides, like skeletons or bones of the Earth not needed at the Creation, and there left to be covered with never-dying lichens. Flowers and even gems scarcely surpass in colouring some of those masses of stone which no human eye beholds, except the shepherd or traveller led thither by curiosity—and how seldom must this happen.

It is not so now, for thousands come yearly, many again and again, and as love of every form of beauty spreads it may yet be an ambition of all of English birth to see this culmination of their country's mountain scenery. The view includes all the Lakeland mountain groups we have named, but most of the lakes are hidden in their vales. Part of Derwentwater is seen over the Sty Head Pass, part of Windermere between Bow Fell and Crinkle Crags, and part of Wastwater beyond Scafell. The calm that Wordsworth felt is a rarity.

VIEWS THAT MAY BE DESCRIED FROM THE BROW OF SCAFELL PIKE

The most distant views from Scafell Pike cannot, of course, be descried at any single visit, even when the day is clear, but the Scottish mountains and the Isle of Man are often seen, the Mourne Mountains in Ireland sometimes, and also the mountains of North Wales. Ailsa Crag has been reported. Eastward, Ingleborough is a common sight. The chief features, however, are the immediate surroundings of the dominant summit, the Mickledore Chasm between the Pike and Scafell, the fine cliffs of Scafell and Great End, the craggy dip into Eskdale, the fine array of neighbour peaks—Great Gable, Bow Fell, the Pillar—the more distant mountain passes, Helvellyn, Blencathara, and Skiddaw, the deep dales around, and the passes that climb from them to Esk Hause.

With all who travel it should be a duty to see something of this most fascinating region in all England from some mountain brows, and preferably from Scafell Pike.

SOME OF THE BEST BELOVED HEIGHTS TO BE SEEN IN ALL THE WORLD

Let us now turn to England's little hills, the best beloved heights in all the world. Apart from the Fen area of the Wash on the east coast our land is ribbed with more than a score of small hill groups. The South Downs run west from Beachy Head in Sussex to Winchester in Hampshire, reaching their great height of 889 feet at Butser Hill Their grassy slopes can be seen to advantage from the Devil's Dyke near Brighton, from Ditchling Beacon six miles from that watering-place, from Blackdown near Haslemere, where Tennyson loved to walk and where he died, from Cissbury Ring near Worthing, and from Chanctonbury Ring some three miles farther inland. The Forest Ridges of the Sussex Weald, between the North and South Downs, reach to near 700 feet and are finely wooded.

The North Downs, on the whole more attractive than the South, run north-west from the South Foreland on the Kent coast to Maidstone, and there is a northerly branch to Canterbury. From Wrotham and Westerham the direction is westerly to Dorking and Guildford, the Hog's Back, and Farnham, beyond which Hampshire is entered, with Sidown Hill and Pilot Hill rising over 800 feet. From Harbledown the old Pilgrims caught their first sight of Canterbury, and from Ide Hill near Westerham we can see over the valleys of the Darent and the Medway. Other excellent viewpoints are Box Hill (590 ft), Leith Hill (965 ft), the Hog's Back, and Hindhead.

The North Downs are supposed to stop at Inkpen Beacon (1011 ft) in Berkshire, but they only change their name to the Wiltshire and Marlborough Downs on the other side of the Kennet Valley.

FOOT-ROADS WHICH HAVE BEEN TRODDEN FOR THOUSANDS OF YEARS

From Avebury on Marlborough Downs, foot-roads have been trodden for thousands of years to the North and South Downs, and the Lambourn Downs and White Horse Hills of Berkshire which, running east to Streatley, make the Chiltern Hills of Buckinghamshire; and these, running north-east through Hertfordshire, join with the hills of Cambridgeshire near Newmarket and those of Suffolk at Bury St Edmunds, entering Norfolk by Thetford.

Similarly, in the south-west, the Mendips, the Quantocks, the Blackdowns, Exmoor, Dartmoor, Bodmin Moor, and the central Cornish hills are linked up by little intermediate heights. The Dorset heights begin in Wiltshire, between Shaftesbury and Salisbury, and run through Dorset to Lyme Regis. On several of them are ancient camps. Pilsden Pen rises 909 feet and Bulbarrow 902 feet. To the south is the Purbeck range, culminating in Creach Barrow, with Corfe Castle in a gorge.

The Mendips of Somerset are a limestone plateau with several points slightly over 1000 feet, among them Black Down (1067 ft). On their south side they drop suddenly 800 feet. The way down to the plain, where lies historic Glastonbury beside its tor, is through the impressive grandeur of the Cheddar Gorge, with jagged precipices 400 feet high, stalactite caves, and remains of prehistoric life. The Quantocks, more interesting for their literary associations and more picturesque in their quiet beauty, are about 12 miles long and three miles broad. The Brendons, separated from the Quantocks by a valley about two miles wide, are only cut off from Exmoor by the Dulverton-Dunster road. They culminate in Lype Hill (1391 ft).

On the borderland of Exmoor wild land and sea views, colour and romance, arrest the traveller as the moor comes down the coast from Lynton to Porlock. But its heart is primitive and untamed. About 120 square miles of it are above 1000 feet high. Its highest peak, Dunkery Beacon, reaches 1707 feet. On the Devon border is the Doone Valley. Dartmoor, which covers about 200 square miles between Brent and Okehampton, is, like Exmoor, wild and waterlogged in parts, Yes Tor and High Willhays rising 2000 feet. Below the 1000-feet line, however, trees appear, the little valleys smile, and rippling waters sing and babble.

Cornwall is undulating, but where the rocky summits of Brown Willy (1380 ft) and Rough Tor (1296 ft) top Bodmin Moor the born hill-lover will be well satisfied.

THE COTSWOLDS, WHERE VILLAGES AND LOVELY LITTLE CHURCHES HIDE

Coming to the valley of the Bristol Avon we reach the Cotswolds, a medley of sheep pastures where lonely villages and lovely little churches hide. One of the most important hill systems of Southern England, the Cotswolds, are the source of all the rivers that reach the Thames above Oxford. They run north-east from Bath, through Gloucestershire and Oxfordshire to the borders of Northamptonshire, and touch both Worcestershire, where is Bredon Hill (960 ft), and Warwickshire, where is historic Edgehill. On the east their long slopes are seamed with valleys and on the west they overlook the plain of the Severn, the mountains of South Wales, and the Malvern Hills. Cleeve Cloud, east of Cheltenham; Birdlip, south of that city; and Broadway Hill, in the far north, are famous viewpoints.

The Chilterns are an attractive range of chalk hills running from Goring-on-Thames for nearly sixty miles in a north-easterly direction. They continue the line of the White Horse Hills of Berkshire, cross South Oxfordshire, are most conspicuous in Buckinghamshire, spread over South Bedfordshire and Hertfordshire, and pass on into Cambridgeshire, Essex, Suffolk, and the East Anglian heights. They are gentle, grassy, and on their lower slopes well wooded. Their greatest height is about 900 feet, their general level between 500 and 600.

WHERE THE MALVERN HILLS RISE BOLDLY FROM THE SEVERN PLAIN

The Malvern Hills, in Worcestershire and Herefordshire, rise boldly from the Severn Plain. From Worcestershire Beacon (1395 ft) may be seen a long stretch of the Cotswolds, the Clee Hills of Shropshire, and the Black Mountains of South Wales. The Clee Hills rise near the hill town of Ludlow, Titterton Clee (1749 ft) and Brown Clee 50 feet higher. In a line with the wooded Edge of Wenlock is the Wrekin (1335 ft). At Church Stretton, Long Mynd rises 1674 feet.

In North Leicestershire is Charnwood Forest, a plateau with 6000 acres above 600 feet, rising here and there into granite outcrops. Bardon Hill reaches 912 feet. From the summits of the forest ridge Leicester, Nottingham, Derby, and Coventry, may be easily seen if the weather is at all favourable. In Lincolnshire, from Rutland northward, the land is undulating up to more than 300 feet for a width of four or five miles, and beyond Grantham a range known as The Cliff continues to Lincoln. Farther north the ridge, less plainly marked, continues to the Humber, but gathers again at Burton Stather (200 ft). Between Spilsby and the Humber are the Lincolnshire Wolds. Midway, south of Caistor, the ridge reaches 525 feet.

THE LITTLE KNOWN SOLITUDES OF THE GREAT MOORS

On the east of Yorkshire are the Wolds, with some points of between 500 and 600 feet. At Malton the Howardian Hills link the Wolds with the Hambleton Hills. The Yorkshire Moors, between the Tees and the Derwent, include the Cleveland ironstone district which, at Boultby Cliff (666 ft), near Staithes, has the loftiest headland on the English coast. A final ridge fronts the Yorkshire Plain east of Northallerton and Thirsk, its highest point, Black Hambleton, rising 1289 feet. The hills stretch from the Hambleton escarpment to Scarborough and Whitby. Comparatively few people know the inner recesses of the Yorkshire Moors, but those who do, love them for ever.

HILLS AND MOUNTAINS OF ENGLAND

THE NORTH DOWNS NEAR REIGATE

CLEY HILL SHELTERS THE WILTSHIRE HAMLET OF UPPER WHITBOURNE

THE WHITE HORSE AT WESTBURY IN WILTSHIRE

THE MALVERN HILLS SEEN FROM THE WORCESTERSHIRE BEACON

CARDING MILL VALLEY IN THE LONG MYND, A SHROPSHIRE HILL RANGE

THE HAMBLETON HILLS IN YORKSHIRE

HAY TOR ON DARTMOOR

IVINGHOE BEACON IN THE CHILTERN HILLS

THE SOUTH DOWNS NEAR BRAMBER IN SUSSEX

THE CLEVELAND HILLS IN YORKSHIRE   GLASTONBURY TOR IN SOMERSET

SKIDDAW AS SEEN ACROSS BASSENTHWAITE LAKE IN CUMBERLAND

LANGDALE PIKES IN THE
LAKE DISTRICT

STRIDING EDGE, HELVELLYN, ON THE
WESTMORLAND AND CUMBERLAND BORDER

SCAFELL PIKE IN CUMBERLAND, ENGLAND'S HIGHEST MOUNTAIN

PEN-Y-GHENT IN THE PENNINES
NEAR SETTLE

GREAT GABLE, ONE OF LAKELAND'S
FINEST VIEWPOINTS

IF I want to be happy
    And quick on my toes,
I must bite my food slowly
    And breathe through my nose.

I must press back my shoulders,
    And hold up my head,
And *not* close my window
    When going to bed.

I must soap my bath-flannel,
    And scrub all I know;
I must then take a towel
    And rub till I glow.

I must never be idle,
    And loll in my chair;
Or shout like a demon,
    And act like a bear.

I must lay and not fidget,
    Read books and not flop!
Begin all with a purpose,
    And know when to stop.

I must love what is noble,
    And do what is kind;
I must strengthen my body
    And tidy my mind.

Yes, if I would be healthy,
    And free from all cares,
I must do all I've told you,
    And *mean* all my prayers.

               Harold Begbie

One Thousand Poems of All Times and All Countries

THE CRY OF THE CHILDREN

Callous as the heart of England was when Lord Shaftesbury was seeking to save the children from their slavery, this poem by Mrs. Browning, not quite complete here, stirred the nation to the depths, and led to a great awakening.

Do ye hear the children weeping, O my
    brothers,
  Ere the sorrow comes with years?
They are leaning their young heads against
    their mothers,
  And *that* cannot stop their tears.
The young lambs are bleating in the
    meadows,
  The young birds are chirping in the nest;
The young fawns are playing with the
    shadows,
  The young flowers are blowing toward
    the west,
But the young, young children, O my
    brothers,
  They are weeping bitterly!
They are weeping in the playtime of
    the others,
  In the country of the free.

Do ye question the young children in
    their sorrow
  Why their tears are falling so?
The old man may weep for his tomorrow
  Which is lost in Long Ago;
The old tree is leafless in the forest,
  The old year is ending in the frost,
The old wound, if stricken, is the sorest,
  The old hope is hardest to be lost.
But the young, young children, O my
    brothers!
  Do you ask them why they stand
Weeping sore before the bosoms of their
    mothers
  In our happy Fatherland?

For oh, say the children, we are weary,
  And we cannot run or leap;
If we cared for any meadows it were merely
  To drop down in them and sleep.
Our knees tremble sorely in the stooping,
  We fall upon our faces trying to go;
And, underneath our heavy eyelids
    drooping,
  The reddest flower would look as pale
    as snow
For, all day, we drag our burden tiring,
  Through the coal-dark underground—
Or, all day, we drive the wheels of iron
  In the factories, round and round.

And all day the wheels are droning,
    turning;
  Their wind comes in our faces,
Till our hearts turn—our heads, with
    pulses burning,
  And the walls turn in their places.
Turns the sky in the high window blank
    and reeling,
  Turns the long light that droppeth down
    the wall;
Turn the black flies that crawl along the
    ceiling—
  All are turning, all the day, and we with
    all.
And all day the iron wheels are droning,
  And sometimes we could pray:
O ye wheels (breaking out in a mad
    moaning),
  Stop—be silent for today!

Ay, be silent! Let them hear each other
    breathing
  For a moment, mouth to mouth!

POEMS · SONGS · BALLADS · VERSES AND RHYMES WITH MUSIC

Let them touch each other's hands in a
   fresh wreathing
   Of their tender, human youth!
Let them feel that this cold, metallic
   motion
   Is not all the life God fashions or reveals;
Let them prove their living souls against
   the notion
   That they live in you, or under you,
   O wheels!
Still, all day the iron wheels go onward,
   Grinding life down from its mark;
And the children's souls, which God is
   calling sunward,
   Spin on blindly in the dark.

Now tell the young children, O my
   brothers,
   To look up to Him and pray;
So the blessed One, who blesseth all the
   others,
   Will bless them another day.
They answer, "Who is God that He should
   hear us,
   While the rushing of the iron wheels is
   stirred?
When we sob aloud the human creatures
   near us
   Pass by, hearing not, or answer not a
   word.
And we hear not (for the wheels in their
   resounding)
   Strangers speaking at the door;
Is it likely God, with angels singing round
   Him,
   Hears our weeping any more? "

And well may the children weep before
   you!
   They are weary ere they run;
They have never seen the sunshine, nor
   the glory
   Which is brighter than the sun.
They know the grief of man, without its
   wisdom;
   They sink in man's despair, without its
   calm—
Are slaves, without the liberty in Christdom,
   Are martyrs, by the pang without the
   palm;
Are worn, as if with age, yet unretrievingly
   The harvest of its memories cannot
   reap—
Are orphans of the earthly love and
   heavenly.
   Let them weep! Let them weep!
They look up with their pale and sunken
   faces,
   And their look is dread to see;

For they mind you of their angels in high
   places,
   With eyes turned on Deity.
"How long," they say, "how long, O cruel
   nation,
   Will you stand to move the world on a
   child's heart,
Stifle down with a mailed heel its palpita-
   tion,
   And tread onward to your throne amid
   the mart?
Our blood splashes upward, O gold-heaper,
   And your purple shows its path!
But the child's sob in the silence curses
   deeper
   Than the strong man in his wrath!"

LIFE

Mrs. Barbauld (1743-1825), a well-known writer in her day, was the author of these thoughtful lines, in which there is the quiet beauty of a contented and hopeful spirit.

LIFE! I know not what thou art,
   But know that thou and I must part;
And when, or how, or where we met
I own to me's a secret yet.

Life! We've been long together,
Through pleasant and through cloudy
   weather.
'Tis hard to part when friends are dear,
Perhaps 'twill cost a sigh, a tear;
Then steal away, give little warning;
Choose thine own time;
Say not good-night, but in some brighter
   clime
Bid me good-morning.

LITTLE LAMB

This is one of the curiously beautiful little poems written by William Blake. He loved this world, but the idea of a spiritual world made a haunting appeal to him.

LITTLE lamb, who made thee?
   Dost thou know who made thee?
Gave thee life, and bade thee feed
By the stream and o'er the mead;
Gave thee clothing of delight,
Softest clothing, woolly, bright;
Gave thee such a tender voice,
Making all the vales rejoice?
   Little lamb, who made thee?
   Dost thou know who made thee?

Little lamb, I'll tell thee;
Little lamb, I'll tell thee:
He is called by thy name,
For he calls himself a lamb.
He is meek and He is mild,
He became a little child.
I a child, and thou a lamb,
We are called by His name.
   Little lamb, God bless thee!
   Little lamb, God bless thee!

ANNIE LAURIE

When William Douglas wrote this song he reached at once the pinnacle of fame and of merit as a song-writer. It has every quality of the perfect love-song—simplicity, poetic imagery, and a delicate passion of tenderness unsurpassed. The light of romance is shed for ever on Maxwelton braes by this burst of pure feeling.

MAXWELTON braes are bonnie
　　Where early fà's the dew,
And it's there that Annie Laurie
Gie'd me her promise true—
Gie'd me her promise true,
Which ne'er forgot will be;
And for bonnie Annie Laurie
I'd lay me doune and dee.

Her brow is like the snawdrift,
Her throat is like the swan,
Her face it is the fairest
That e'er the sun shone on—
That e'er the sun shone on;
And dark blue is her ee;
And for bonnie Annie Laurie
I'd lay me doune and dee.

Like dew on the gowan lying
Is the fa' o' her fairy feet;
Like the winds in summer sighing,
Her voice is low and sweet—
Her voice is low and sweet;
And she's a' the world to me;
And for bonnie Annie Laurie
I'd lay me doune and dee.

SAY NOT THE STRUGGLE NAUGHT AVAILETH

Arthur Hugh Clough was a noteworthy poet who never made his full genius felt. Born at Liverpool on New Year's Day, 1819, he died at Florence on November 13, 1861. His poetry is not only beautiful in form but is weighted with thought, and these four short verses make up a little gem of poetic form and enlarging thought. They are a warning to us not to take a narrow view of life.

SAY not the struggle naught availeth,
　　The labour and the wounds are vain,
The enemy faints not, nor faileth,
　　And as things have been they remain.

If hopes were dupes, fears may be liars;
　　It may be, in yon smoke concealed,
Your comrades chase e'en now the fliers,
　　And, but for you, possess the field.

For while the tired waves, vainly breaking,
　　Seem here no painful inch to gain,
Far back, through creeks and inlets making,
　　Comes silent, flooding in, the main.

And not by eastern windows only,
　　When daylight comes, comes in the light;
In front the sun climbs slow, how slowly,
　　But westward, look, the land is bright!

THE SONG OF THE BOW

This vigorous song, with the ring of open-air England all through it, was written by a famous author, Sir Arthur Conan Doyle. It is from his "Songs of Action," but was first printed in his tale of early English life "The White Company," one of the best historical stories. It is supposed to be sung by a bowman at a New Forest meeting.

WHAT of the bow?
　　The bow was made in England,
Of true wood, of yew wood,
　　The wood of English bows;
　　　So men who are free
　　　Love the old yew tree,
And the land where the yew tree grows.

What of the cord?
　　The cord was made in England:
A rough cord, a tough cord,
　　A cord that bowmen love;
　　　And so we will sing
　　　Of the hempen string,
And the land where the cord was wove.

What of the shaft?
　　The shaft was cut in England:
A long shaft, a strong shaft,
　　Barbed and trim and true;
　　　So we'll drink altogether
　　　To the grey goose-feather,
And the land where the grey goose flew.

What of the mark?
　　Ah! seek it not in England:
A bold mark, our old mark,
　　Is waiting over-sea.
　　　When the strings harp in chorus,
　　　And the lion flag is o'er us,
It is there that our mark will be.

What of the man?
　　The men were bred in England:
The bowmen, the yeomen,
　　The lads of dale and fell.
　　　Here's to you—and to you!
　　　To the hearts that are true,
And the land where the true hearts dwell.

LIGHT

This lovely example of a simile, with an exquisite meaning cast into simple verse by perfect art, is from the pen of Francis William Bourdillon (1852–1921).

THE night has a thousand eyes,
　　And the day but one;
Yet the light of the bright world dies
　　With the dying sun.

The mind has a thousand eyes,
　　And the heart but one;
Yet the light of a whole life dies
　　When love is done.

LITTLE VERSES FOR VERY LITTLE PEOPLE

The happy verses on this page and the next are by Laurence Alma-Tadema (died 1940), daughter of Sir Lawrence Alma-Tadema (1836–1912), Anglo-Dutch painter, whose pictures of the glory of Greece and Rome are so widely known. Many of these verses have been set to music.

MARCH MEADOWS

A LARK

Lark-bird, lark-bird, soaring high,
　Are you never weary?
When you reach the empty sky
　Are the clouds not dreary?
Don't you sometimes long to be
A silent goldfish in the sea?

Goldfish, goldfish, diving deep,
　Are you never sad, say?
When you feel the cold waves creep
　Are you really glad, say?
Don't you sometimes long to sing
And be a lark-bird on the wing?

LAMBS

O little lambs! the month is cold,
　The sky is very grey;
You shiver in the misty grass
And bleat in all the winds that pass;
　Wait! when I'm big, some day—
I'll build a roof to every fold.

But now that I am small I'll pray
　At mother's knee for you;
Perhaps the angels with their wings
Will come and warm you, little things;
　I'm sure that, if God knew,
He'd let the lambs be born in May.

A TWILIGHT SONG

Baby moon, 'tis time for bed,
　Owlet leaves his nest now;
Hide your little horned head
　In the twilight west now;
When you're old and round and bright
You shall stay and shine all night.

Baby girl is going, too,
　In her bed to creep now;
She is little, just like you,
　Time it is to sleep now;
When she's old and tired and wise
She'll be glad to close her eyes.

THE NESTING HOUR

Robin-friend has gone to bed,
　Little wing to hide his head;
Mother's bird must slumber too,
Just as baby robins do.
When the stars begin to rise
Birds and babies close their eyes.

THE LITTLE SISTER

BATH-TIME

Baby's got no legs at all;
　They're soft and pinky, crumpled things.
If he stood up he'd only fall;
　But then, you see, he's used to wings.

BED-TIME

　Baby, baby, bye,
　Close your little eye!
When the dark begins to creep
Tiny-wees must go to sleep.

　Lammy, lammy, lie,
　I am seven, I;
Little boys must sleep and wait
If they want their bed-time late.

　Fidgy, fidgy, fie,
　There's no need to cry!
Soon you'll never dress in white,
But sit up working half the night.

PLAYGROUNDS

In summer I am glad
　We children are so small,
For we can see a thousand things
　That men can't see at all.

They don't know much about the moss
　And all the stones they pass;
They never lie and play among
　The forests in the grass.

They walk about a long way off;
　And, when we're at the sea,
Let father stoop as best he can
　He can't find things like me.

But when the snow is on the ground,
　And all the puddles freeze,
I wish that I were very tall,
　High up above the trees.

THE NEW PELISSE

Baby's got a new pelisse,
　Very soft and very neat,
Like a lammy in her fleece
　She's all white from head to feet.

Thirty lambs each gave a curl,
　Mother sewed them, stitch by stitch—
All to clothe a baby girl:
　Don't you think she's very rich?

IF NO ONE EVER MARRIES ME

IF no one ever marries me—
   And I don't see why they should;
For nurse says I'm not pretty,
   And I'm seldom very good—
If no one ever marries me
   I shan't mind very much;
I shall buy a squirrel in a cage,
   And a little rabbit hutch.

I shall have a cottage near a wood,
   And a pony all my own,
And a little lamb quite clean and tame
   That I can take to town.
And when I'm getting really old,
   At twenty-eight or nine,
I shall buy a little orphan girl
   And bring her up as mine.

KING BABY ON HIS THRONE

KING BABY on his throne
   Sits reigning O, sits reigning O!
King Baby on his throne
Sits reigning all alone.

His throne is mother's knee.
   So tender O, so tender O!
His throne is mother's knee,
Where none may sit but he.

His crown it is of gold,
   So curly O, so curly O!
His crown it is of gold,
In shining tendrils rolled.

His kingdom is my heart,
   So loyal O, so loyal O!
His kingdom is my heart,
His own in every part.

Divine are all his laws,
   So simple O, so simple O!
Divine are all his laws,
With love for end and cause.

King Baby on his throne
   Sits reigning O, sits reigning O!
King Baby on his throne
Sits reigning all alone.

Laurence
Alma-Tadema

479

HOW YOUR ELECTRIC TORCH WORKS

A SIMPLE FORM OF CELL

LECLANCHÉ CELL

DRY CELL

Here we see three types of electric cells. The first is a simple form of electric cell, in which energy is produced by chemical action. A zinc plate and a carbon plate, connected by a wire, are standing in a jar of sulphuric acid. The acid eats into the zinc and liberates hydrogen, which drifts across the liquid to the carbon plate, as the upper arrow suggests. The ions of hydrogen travel from zinc to carbon, and start an electric current flowing in this direction, which causes swarms of electrons to crowd upon the connecting wire; these electrons continue to travel over the surface of the wire from the carbon to the zinc plate, and so set up a continual circulation of electricity just as long as the carbon and zinc are joined together. The hydrogen set free adheres to the carbon, and sets up an opposing force which soon puts the cell out of action, but in the Leclanché cell, where sal ammoniac takes the place of sulphuric acid, this trouble is overcome by a chemical mixture which removes the hydrogen. In the dry cell the zinc case takes the place of the zinc plate and the carbon is surrounded by manganese dioxide packed in a damp paste of sal ammoniac.

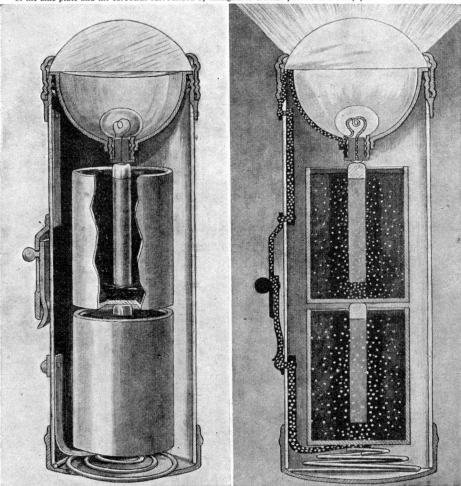

In a pocket torch a number of cells are connected to form a battery. These pictures show how it works. The wire connecting the two ends of the battery is represented by the filament in the lamp and by two metal strips, one attached to the zinc of the bottom cell, and the other to the metal cup into which the lamp is screwed. Until the gap between these two strips is bridged, however, there can be no circuit. In the left picture the switch is off, but as soon as it is brought down to the lower metal bolt, as seen in the right picture, the circuit is completed. Then the electrons flow from one cell to the next, along the metal strip, up to the bulb, and so on to the cells again. As the electrons flow along the delicate filament in the lamp, they cause the filament to become white hot and we have a bright light.

The Story of Where Power Comes From, What It Does, & How It Works

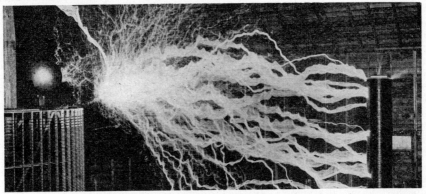

Electricity made visible—A powerful electrical discharge at a wireless station

THE ELECTRIC CURRENT

Towards the end of the eighteenth century new discoveries were made in electricity which brought about a wonderful change, and introduced an era that has entirely revolutionised the world.

Very little had been done with the static electricity produced by friction. But a *new* electricity was now discovered, the effects of which far transcended anything that could possibly be done with the electricity already known.

Two great names, those of Volta and Galvani, will be associated for all time with this discovery. We speak today of this new power as voltaic or galvanic electricity.

It may be imagined as a current flowing through a wire, and endowing the wire with a wonderful power that can be turned to account in a thousand ways.

In the year 1790, Luigi Galvani, an eminent doctor of Bologna, had skinned some frogs to make broth for his wife who was ill, and the leg of one of these frogs, being accidentally touched by a knife which had lain near an electric machine and had become charged with electricity, was seen to kick violently. Other frogs suspended from an iron railing by copper hooks were similarly made to give jerks each time they touched the railing. The mystery was explained by the discovery of current electricity, a form of electricity set up by the action of two dissimilar metals.

In 1800 Volta made the first electric battery by using two different metals, separated by some porous substance such as cloth moistened with water. By using a number of discs of tin, and silver or copper alternately, separated by moistened material, Volta produced what was afterwards termed Volta's Pile. The first description of his discovery was given in a letter written by Volta to the president of the Royal Society in London.

The secret of the battery had been discovered and was used as a means of producing quantities of electricity hitherto undreamed of.

A number of glasses containing acidulated water was used, with a zinc and copper strip dipping into each glass, the zinc of one pair connected to the copper of the next, and so on. In this way, Volta produced a " crown of cups," from which a current of what was then quite large power was obtained. Volta proved that the electricity he got from this chemical method was of exactly the same character as that which had previously been got from friction. Although he was a professor in the University of Pavia, Volta recognised that there were others who could advance the new science better than he could, and for the last twenty-five years of his

ELECTRICITY · WIRELESS · OIL · GAS · MOTORS · ENGINES · SHIPS

life he made no further attempts at electrical discoveries.

There is probably hardly a home today without its own battery, for this chemical generator of electricity is used for ringing electric bells, for lighting pocket lamps, and for many other purposes where only moderate power is required. There were afterwards discovered more powerful kinds of electric cells than the simple pieces of copper and zinc standing in acidulated water, though for many years something very similar was used for working the post office telegraphs.

THE REMARKABLE FORCE THAT FLOWS LIKE WATER FROM METAL TO METAL

Volta had found that when any two different metals are made to touch each other, one of them immediately assumes a different electric state from the other. If two different metals be put in a vessel filled with acid, one metal will always become electrified to a higher degree than the other. The word *potential* has been given to this state, and the secret of the battery is that if the two metals are connected by a wire, that is, by a conductor, an electric current will always flow from the metal at the higher potential to that at the lower potential.

One of the most powerful cells was invented by the famous chemist Bunsen. It consists of a cylinder of zinc standing in a jar filled with sulphuric acid. Inside the cylinder is placed a porous pot of unglazed earthenware through which gases can pass, containing a rod of carbon and filled with nitric acid. Three or four such cells joined up so as to form a *battery* would produce enough electricity to drive a sewing-machine motor, or light a six or eight candle-power lamp.

The electric battery, it will be seen, introduced the era of electric *power*, though little real use was ever made of it owing to the advent of the much more practical generator known as the dynamo.

THE FORCE THAT CAN BREAK UP COMPOUNDS INTO ELEMENTS

The real importance of the discovery of voltaic, or galvanic, electricity was that it gave a new force to man, with which he made a quick succession of other discoveries that laid the foundation of our vast knowledge of today. Even in the same year that Volta made his electric pile, two Englishmen, named Carlisle and Nicholson, discovered that the new current which it produced possessed the remarkable power of breaking down the bonds of Nature, and releasing hydrogen and oxygen from water.

A few years later Sir Humphry Davy found that the voltaic current would split up many other substances into their elements. The electric current could do what up till then fire alone had done, and far more. Science had entered a new era.

Then, in 1820, came perhaps the greatest of all electrical discoveries in so far as it paved the way for the dynamo, the motor, the telephone, the telegraph, and all the wonders of the electric world of today. Hans Christian Oersted, a Danish scientist world-famed for his lucid writings, found that if a current from a voltaic battery was made to flow through a wire, some new and mysterious force was created around the wire which caused a compass needle to turn around.

It had long been thought that some connection must exist between the forces of magnetism and electricity. It was left to Oersted in Copenhagen to show that the two powers were actually related, and in what way.

NOTHING IN NATURE CAN BE HAD FOR NOTHING

If you wind a spiral cord of copper wire round a pencil, and connect the two ends of the coil to the two " poles " of a battery, the passage of the electric current through the coil makes it a magnet. The coil possesses magnetic power, and one end of it will act like the North pole of a magnet, the other end like a South pole. As long as current flows through the coil, it remains an electric magnet. Place a rod of iron through the coil, and the iron becomes powerfully magnetised.

A magnet of this kind no bigger than a horse-shoe, excited by the current from a couple of Bunsen cells, becomes strong enough to lift an iron scuttle filled with coal. The chemical waste going on in the battery is turned into *force*.

It is the experience all through Nature that nothing can be gained without cost, and in the electric battery the same holds good—a battery will not go on for ever producing current. A destructive action is, indeed, going on. The battery is a little world in itself, in which all kinds of interesting things are happening. A good example is found in the Daniell's cell, for years used in telegraphy because of its constancy. Here we find a copper plate or cylinder standing in a solution of a blue salt called sulphate of copper, and inside the porous pot is a zinc rod standing in a solution of sulphate of zinc or weak sulphuric acid. As soon as the copper and zinc plates are joined by a wire, or connected up with an electric instrument through which a current flows, everything within the battery gets busy.

In order to understand what happens we must try to imagine what the mysterious *ion* is. Chemistry tells us that all substances are made up of molecules, each molecule being the simplest arrangement of the atoms that can exist in a free state. A molecule of salt consists of one atom of sodium and one atom of chlorine. But, if an electric current were passed through water in which salt has been dissolved, these molecules would be gradually split up into ions of sodium and chlorine, each ion of sodium bearing a charge of positive electricity ; each ion of chlorine bearing a charge of negative electricity. The sodium ions would gradually travel through the water towards the negative pole, an equal number of chlorine ions would travel towards the positive pole, and this process would go on steadily until all the salt had been used up.

We have already seen how it was discovered that electricity broke up water into hydrogen and oxygen in a similar way.

This marching along of the ions takes place in every battery. To return to the Daniell's cell, the zinc rod gradually becomes used up through ions of zinc being set free, and these travel towards the side of the porous pot. In the outer vessel, the sulphate of copper is being turned into ions of copper and what we may call ions of sulphate.

OERSTED TRIES AN EXPERIMENT

The copper ions travel to the copper plate, and instantly they meet it they become transformed from invisible atoms to solid copper metal, and they actually build up and increase the weight of the copper plate. The ions of sulphate travel in the opposite direction, and make their way to the porous pot. Here they meet the zinc ions, at once join forces with them, and produce more zinc sulphate.

This busy little world of travelling ions is present in every battery. Every time you press the switch of a pocket-lamp the little battery that supplies the lighting current begins producing ions of ammonium and chlorine, which in turn set up new chemical processes that gradually exhaust its power. This is why a battery will only give so many flashes and has then to be renewed.

One of the best batteries for boys to experiment with is known as the *bichromate* pattern. In its usual form a zinc plate and two carbon plates, one on either side, are immersed in a solution of bichromate of potash acidulated with sulphuric acid. A powerful current is generated sufficiently strong to drive a toy motor or to operate a small two-volt electric lamp.

Perhaps the most useful and most widely employed battery is the Leclanché. This is used for working electric bells and pocket flash-lamps, and is the type employed for wireless high-tension batteries.

The negative element of this battery is a zinc rod, or often a zinc box, forming the container of the cell; the positive element is a carbon rod enclosed in a porous pot—or a little canvas or linen bag—filled with black oxide of manganese. A liquid is used containing a salt sold by every ironmonger, and known as sal ammoniac—in chemical language, chloride of ammonium. In what is called a dry battery, the sal ammoniac is made in a paste with sawdust, so that there is no liquid to spill, but it is not really dry, as without the presence of a liquid there would be no fluid in which the ions could travel.

While the cell is in use, hydrogen gas is often set free at the negative element, in the form of tiny bubbles which cling to the metal and form a protective coating that keeps the fluid away from it. When this happens the chemical action can no longer go on, and the cell is said to be polarised. Given a short rest, the bubbles of gas disappear, and the metal is once more in contact with the fluid of the cell, which will work again. Batteries thus require frequent rests, and cannot be worked continuously for too long a period.

Let us now come back for a moment to the early part of the last century, when the powers of an electric battery were first being revealed. The next illustrious name after Oersted is that of Ampère, a famous physicist of France, who made very great advances in electrical knowledge, and whose name will be used for all time as the unit of current flowing through a wire.

THE TWO GREAT FACTS OF ELECTRICAL RESISTANCE AND ELECTRICAL HEAT

It became possible to measure the strength of an electric current by the magnetic power which it could produce, and instruments were invented by which these currents could be measured; and, just as a piece of iron placed near a magnet is itself made into a magnet, so it was found that on passing a voltaic current through a coil of wire a current could be set up in another coil of wire placed near to it.

Two great facts had also been discovered: one, that certain metals offered greater resistance to the flow of a current through them than others; another, that the passage of an electric current through a wire made it hot. Ohm discovered that the amount of current which can flow through a conductor depends strictly on the *resistance* of the conductor, and ever afterwards this property of resistance was measured in units called ohms, after his name.

The fact that materials with a great resistance cause an electric current to generate heat has proved of the greatest importance, and today we are able to heat a house, a cooking-stove, or a furnace by passing electricity through materials which offer great resistance. The day will come

when coal and gas are no longer used for direct heating ; coal will be used to make steam, the steam-engine will drive a machine which generates electricity, and the electric current will be turned into heat by making it flow through metallic wires which offer great resistance, and, in consequence, generate great heat. This is already done, of course, on quite a large scale; but it will be the general rule at a time not far distant, for science has triumphed over the present wasteful methods of turning fuel into power.

THE MYSTERIOUS FORCE CONTROLLED, STARTED, AND STOPPED

The effect of an electric current upon a magnet had led the way to the first means of measuring the strength of this new power that was to rule the world, and men of every nation set to work to make electricity an exact science. But for very many years its real nature was not to be understood, and electricity was looked upon as a mysterious fluid which flowed in, or perhaps, around the wires that conducted it.

The interest of the whole world had, at any rate, been roused, for here was a power which, produced by the action of dissimilar metals excited by a chemical liquid, could make light and heat, create magnetic power, and decompose matter and other substances into the elements of which they were made. The new power could be controlled, started, and stopped; it could be led to any spot by means of conductors, and be made to do work there. Greatest of all, it was shown not only how electricity could produce magnetic power, but how magnetic power could in its turn produce electricity, and from these early observations was evolved the dynamo, the machine which today enables us to generate all the electricity we want from the mechanical power of the steam-engine, the oil-engine, and the waterfall.

THE POWER THAT CAN BE SENT THOUSANDS OF MILES

Without its magnetic effects, the voltaic battery would have been very limited in its uses, though it might have been developed on wonderful lines. But this remarkable connection between the two forces, separately revealed to man thousands of years ago, has brought about the harnessing of power, and the means of turning power into a force that can be led to some distant spot, there to be used again.

Imperishable Thoughts of Men Enshrined in the Books of the World

When Bibles were scarce they were chained up, as in this picture of a library at Hereford Cathedral.

THE GREATEST ENGLISH BOOK

No book, considered as literature, has had so great an influence on the English people as the Bible.

No other book has done so much toward moulding the English language. Though in origin it is not an English book at all, it is the greatest book in the English tongue, the one best known and best deserving to be known as a literary work.

Of course, because of the subjects it brings before its readers, it is a supremely great book in any language, but we are not here referring to its religious teaching. It is the influence of its style on British speech and writing that concerns us for the moment.

For more than 500 years the Bible has been popular in England beyond all other books, more read, more listened to, more known than any other writing. For more than 300 years it has set the standard and been the great example of English prose, with effects on our speech that cannot be overestimated in value.

From the earliest days of Christian England there seems to have been a desire to read the Bible. Bede's eagerness in translating the gospel of Saint John on his death-bed and Alfred's unfinished translation of the Psalms are illustrations, but of course these beginnings have no bearing on the Bible as English literature, for the language used was not English as we know it, but Anglo-Saxon, unreadable by us except as a strange tongue.

The first translation that counts was Wycliffe's, who was a contemporary of Chaucer, and whose version, not from the original tongues, but from the Latin, though rough and ready, and never printed till quite recent times, had a lasting influence during the next 150 years, till William Tyndale produced his beautiful version direct from the original languages, Hebrew and Greek.

Eighty years after Tyndale had paid with his life for his noble ambition that " every boy that driveth the plough should know the scriptures," the noble Authorised Version was produced from the various versions that had gone before, but chiefly from Tyndale's, and " England became the people of a book and that book the Bible."

What is it in this wonderful book that has given it such a great and lasting influence on our literature, an influence far more powerful than any it has had on other languages?

An important fact is that Hebrew, the language of the Old Testament, is very simple, with clear imagery readily understood and conveying its meaning in plain

ROMANCE · HISTORIES · DRAMAS · ESSAYS · WORLD CLASSICS

words that represent common objects, even when the thought is most poetical and beautiful. " The Lord is my Shepherd, I shall not want." What could be simpler, or more tender and consoling? " A thousand years in Thy sight are but as yesterday when it is past, and as a watch in the night." What could be grander and more impressive ?

HOW OUR ENGLISH VERSION PRESERVES THE OLD BEAUTY OF THE BIBLE

And these definite images and thoughts by comparison were changed into as simple English words at the very time when the English language was being formed, and they fitted in with it so perfectly that in modern days most of the translations of the Bible into 500 languages and dialects have been made, not from Hebrew and Greek, but from the English version which preserves, with a wonderful fidelity, the combined simplicity and grandeur of the language originally used.

That England's earliest printed language widely circulated among her people should have been so plain and clear and pure as it is in the Bible has been a continuing blessing that will never be lost. Really, it is not what might have been expected. And it is not what was happening in many other directions in the formation of our noble English prose.

It must be remembered that learning was largely restricted to the clergy in those early days ; that they often lived a secluded life ; that Latin was their chief study; and the natural tendency in writing was to parade any knowledge which most of the people did not have. And so writing in prose was likely to be learned, cumbrous, and over the heads of unlearned persons. That is what happened then, and does happen to this day.

THE BOOK OF NATURAL MUSIC AND ITS MIGHTY INFLUENCE

Any special set of men with exclusive knowledge are inclined to create a formal language for themselves that does not readily give up its meaning to plain people. It is so with philosophy, religion, the law, medicine, education, and most of all with science. Apart from the special, technical words involved, there has always been a convention that these dignified subjects cannot be discussed in plain speech, and so a special jargon is invented for each learned clique; and in no instance does

the jargon become literature. The dialects of special learning have to be shed before any piece of prose can be read with pleasure for its own sake. How fortunate it was then that, from the first, there was a book in the language of the people, plain, strong, full, with a natural music in it, and that book one with an extraordinary variety of expression, rich in interest, and exhaustless in meaning. Theology swiftly hid its meaning in a clumsy jargon from which it has never escaped, but the Bible is clear, simple, and beautiful.

And this purity in language and style, drawn from common English speech, has been influencing sincere writers ever since.

The most popular books have always been written in words akin to those of the Bible, and so literature is refreshed from the wells of common speech. It has been said with truth that though the Bible language was that in common use, it is impossible to be vulgar with it, for it is everyday language refined by choiceness and dignity.

THE RAREST STORIES IN THE BOOKS OF THE WORLD

Nor is there lack of breadth and variety in the contents of the Bible. The most vigorous of minds will not be narrowed, but will be expanded by its use. Properly studied, the Bible provides a generous education from a literary point of view. It covers a wide range of history, touching all the great nations of antiquity, and there is no form of human expression that it does not illustrate.

No book in existence illustrates so well the writing of history, for it is a library of books combined into one. The separate parts now brought together as a volume were written and edited by hundreds of authors working through at least a thousand years, and using historical records and orally conveyed memories that reach back several thousand years.

It contains examples of every form of writing and speech. There are bare lists of family names showing how ancestry was treasured in the East. There are the legends of national origin, like those of every other race, besides the Jewish, that has emerged from a wandering life into a settled civilisation.

Then, early and late, there are the choicest examples of narrative—the telling of a story, simple, graphic and beautiful—

THE NOBLE BEDE WITH HIS SCHOOLBOYS

BEDE, TRANSLATOR OF THE BIBLE 1200 YEARS AGO, TEACHING HIS BOYS IN THE SCHOOL AT JARROW

that the literatures of the world afford. Whether one is following the exquisitely told story of Joseph in Egypt forgiving his brethren, or the wanderings and talks of our Lord, or the stormy life of Paul, the telling of the story is equally perfect in its simplicity, and its feeling of reality.

Of formal writing of history there are abundant illustrations, which, when they are closely examined, disclose how in ancient Palestine as in modern Europe the telling of the tale of the past depends quite as much on the point of view of the historian as on what actually happened. Then as now, one must know to which side the historian belonged.

Of controversy in politics and religion here is a fairly continuous, but rather confused, record in the works of the prophets, who were the journalists of their day—the first men in Israel to use deliberately the power of the pen in public affairs, as well as warning oratory. But how earnest those ancient politicians and preachers were, how terrible in their warnings, how eloquent in their outbursts of golden hope !

Of oratory there is no lack through the story of two thousand years, down to its most formal example in the pleadings for justice by Paul, the eloquent and fearless.

Poetry is scattered lavishly through the long range of books from Genesis to Revelations, beginning with the majestic vision of the creation of all things and ending with the vision of eternal day.

Not only is there the poetry of sublime imagination, but also that of song, adapted to a wide variety of circumstances—odes of victory, tender laments, outbursts of pious adoration, and magnificent Nature poems saturated with the feeling of God in all that is lovely or grand or beneficent.

Then, too, there is sublime drama, as in the book of Job, and allegory in the Book of Jonah rebuking the hard exclusiveness of the fanatical Jews, who would allow no other people to have access to God.

And lastly, oldest of all the writings in the New Testament, there are letters in many styles—some familiar notes about everyday things, some good advice, some closely-reasoned argument, some lofty expositions of the mysteries of death. What a vast field of literature is here, vast in time, in subject, in method of writing, in complexity of authorship, but one in feeling to a very large extent.

And all this, though the product of many minds, of other races, and reaching us by translation by many minds, is in effect an English book, the greatest and most distinctive English book, accepted and belonging in its entirety to the British race more than to the Jewish race from whom it came. And so it is that in thinking of English literature, and how prose writing came to be what it is, we are obliged to give not only an early place, but a commanding place to the Authorised Version of the Bible in English. Shaped by study and piety, it is the book which beyond all others forms the kernel of our speech and literature, our greatest national classic, the delight alike of the scholar and of the unlearned. It finds expression for us in our most solemn moments and invites us to the noblest heights of thought.

In the world's treasure-house of literature the share of space for the English tongue is generous ; but in all that wide compartment the rarest gem is the translation of the Hebrew Bible and the Christian New Testament given to us by 47 studious men.

A TWELFTH-CENTURY PICTURE OF BEDE WRITING

THE LOVELY BOOKS OF LONG AGO

The glorious books, which the old monks designed and copied by hand have never been surpassed in beauty by the countless products of the printing press. Here we give a few pages from old illustrated manuscripts that have come down to us through the centuries, and are now in the British Museum.

A GLORIOUS PAGE FROM A BOOK MADE BY A MONK ABOUT 600 YEARS AGO

A RIDER ON A WHITE HORSE GOES FORTH CONQUERING AND TO CONQUER

FROM A BOOK MADE BY THREE ENGLISH ARTISTS 600 YEARS AGO

A PAGE FROM A HOLY BOOK BELONGING TO A LADY OF THE HOUSE OF SALUCES, IN FRANCE, IN THE
MIDDLE OF THE FIFTEENTH CENTURY

These pictures are from Bibles illustrated by English artists between the years 1250 and 1400

From a Book 600 years old　　From a Book made about the year 1300　　　　　Six centuries old

15th century Picture of Abraham

From a Book of Psalms made 600　　From a Book of Psalms of about　　Initials from an English-made
years ago for an abbey of nuns　　　　the year 1270　　　　　　　　Bible 650 years ago

The Great Words that Stir the Hearts and Minds of All Mankind

The most terrible test Truth could endure was to face the Spanish Inquisition

TRUTH

It fortifies my soul to know
That, though I perish, Truth is so :
That, howsoe'er I stray and range,
Whate'er I do, Thou dost not change.
I steadier step when I recall
That if I slip Thou dost not fall.

ALL down the ages men have forsaken their homes to seek treasure islands and to find things no one has found before. Adventure is in our blood.

We can never rest content for a long time with the familiar and the customary. Perhaps you have heard your mother say: " I am tired of this wall-paper, and these curtains ; we will have something new in the spring." She is moved by the same spirit which sent the brave Magellan, the two Cabots, Sir Francis Drake, Sir Walter Raleigh, and Captain Scott to perilous seas forlorn.

But one of the wisest men who ever lived saw in this passion for the new, the inexperienced, the unknown, something far deeper and far grander than a mere thirst for physical adventures. He saw in it that movement of man's spirit which has carried him from savagery, darkness, and ignorance to civilisation, light, and the power which is born of knowledge. In other words, this wise Frenchman, Montaigne, saw in adventure the hidden force of progress and evolution, the energy which makes the wheels go round, the

power without which the universe would be stagnant and dead. We are born, he said, to inquire after truth.

That is a great saying. We should keep it constantly before our minds. We should make it so completely a part of our inmost life that we always think of ourselves as the adventurers of truth—every day a new search, every night a new record.

But Montaigne teaches us another lesson. We are indeed born to inquire after truth, but " it belongs to a greater Power to possess it." He died 24 years before our Shakespeare died. He did not say that truth was hidden in a well. He said it was in the heights of the Divine. Truth is God, and in seeking truth we are seeking our Creator.

Now, think what a wonderful thing human life is, what an exciting and delightful thing ! *We are born to seek what we can never find !*

It is the greatest game of hide and seek that was ever invented. God has hidden his truth, and we shall never find it on this Earth; but He has made the search for it so exciting and splendid that, although we know we can never discover it, the greatest of the sons of men have found their highest happiness in this search. To this every age bears witness. Do you remember those striking words of

LIBERTY · JUSTICE · SPACE · DISTANCE · MOVEMENT · TRUTH · FAITH

a great German writer of the eighteenth century ? Lessing said :

> If God held in his right hand all truth, and in His left the everlasting desire for truth, although with the condition that I should remain in error for ever—and if He said to me, Choose, I should humbly bow before His left hand, and say, "Father, give; pure truth is for Thee alone."

He said that the worth of a man does not lie in what he knows, but in the earnest efforts he has made to know it—" for it is not through the possession of truth, but through the search for truth, that he develops those powers in which alone consists his ever-growing perfection."

There is this to be remembered, that in seeking after pure truth, although we can never find it here on Earth, we do collect certain and definite grains of truth. All our power over nature comes from this living collection of infinitesimal fragments of truth. For example, men once believed the world was flat and immovable, and because of this wrong notion they could not understand the movements of the stars. But as soon as they discovered that the Earth is a sphere, that it rotates on its axis, and that it swings round the Sun, they were able to begin those august adventures among the stars which have given us the marvellous science of astronomy.

THE TRUTH THAT MAY BE HID FROM US FOR THOUSANDS OF YEARS

That is perhaps the most wonderful thing about the search for Truth. Though we never grasp her " flying robe and fluttering hem," yet ever, as we pursue, we are led from height to height and from star to star, obtaining wider views of both the physical and moral universe.

We do not know the truth of Evil. That is a problem which may be hid from us for thousands of years, perhaps never solved on Earth. But at least we know that Good is finer than Evil. We know as certainly as we know anything that a merciful man is higher in the scale of being than a cruel man. Such things we call truths, and we guide our lives by them.

But many great thinkers find their happiness in attending to this tremendous problem of evil. They do not think they will ever understand it, but because it is such a terrific puzzle they love to try to understand a part of it, or at any rate something about it. One man says that there is no such thing as evil—that it is merely the absence of good, as darkness is the absence of light. So they argue together, and in their argument they find little bits of truth which help us to think rightly and to make juster laws.

SIR ISAAC NEWTON'S APPLE AND EINSTEIN'S CURVE

The great Greek Eucleides, whom we call Euclid, laid down several laws in mathematics which were regarded as self-evident truths. For two thousand years they have been unquestioned, and on the basis of those truths many wonderful engineering feats have been performed. But now we begin to see that some of these accepted " truths " must be modified, in view of the changes that have taken place in our conceptions of physical things. Einstein himself has said that by the truth of a geometrical proposition we understand its truth for a construction with ruler and compasses, but that Euclid's geometry cannot hold good under certain conditions. However, on another occasion Einstein tells us that our Universe differs only slightly from the one for which Euclid propounded his geometry.

Sir Isaac Newton saw an apple fall to the ground. Why did it not fall up ? He came to the conclusion that the Earth *pulled* the apple towards it, and this pulling of the Earth he called gravitation. This truth was accepted by everybody until Einstein showed that even the gravitational pull was not in a strictly straight line, but that it is a *curve in space* which brings all things into order. Newton and Einstein are both right, except that even a truth must be modified to conform to newer discoveries which make all things *relative*.

WE ARE BORN TO SEEK WHAT WE CAN NEVER FIND

You will see from these examples that truth itself must always remain relative— that is to say, it may have to be referred to circumstances. We have been told that a ray of light travels in straight lines; Einstein has told us that rays of light are propagated along a curve due to gravitational fields. Relative to these the lines are straight. Actually they are not. Many chemical theories hold good for years and by their application great progress may be made ; yet later it is found that the theories themselves, no longer " truths," must be modified. Thus we continue to seek the truth ; *we are born to seek what we can never find!*

TRUTH, IT IS SAID, IS AT THE BOTTOM OF A WELL—AN IDEA ILLUSTRATED
IN THIS PICTURE BY ARTHUR DIXON

You see a man running down the road, and you say, " How fast he is moving !" That is quite true. But a horse gallops by, and the man seems to be walking; then a motor-car dashes up, and he appears to be crawling; and then a low-flying aeroplane flashes past him, and the man actually appears to be standing still.

A MOST USEFUL FOUNDATION
FOR ALL OUR THINKING

This fact of the relativity of truth is a most useful foundation for all your thinking. Suppose somebody brought you a very bad and ugly picture, and said to you: " This is a most beautiful picture, and you must admire it "; what would you say? It would be foolish merely to assert that in your opinion it was a bad picture. The man might be stronger than you, and he might say, " I will fight you to prove I am right." That is how all the wars of the world have been made; as if force could prove what is true! No; your true answer would be to hang the ugly picture beside a picture which all the intelligent people of the world declare to be beautiful, and to make its champion compare his idea of beauty with this other idea of beauty.

We call this way of arriving at truth, *judging by standards*. It is the best way we know for protecting ourselves against the dangers of wrong thinking.

One of the chief values of education lies in this, that it forms in our minds certain definite standards for judging new things. If a boy came to you with a blunt knife and recommended it as a pencil-sharpener, you could prove to him he was wrong by showing him what a sharp knife can do. In the same way, if you have read the poetry of Shakespeare and Keats, you will not rave about a modern ballad as if it was the highest kind of poetry, however fresh and interesting it may be.

CIVILISATION WOULD FALL TO PIECES
IF EVERYONE DID AS HE LIKED

Without these standards in the mind we cannot properly and safely judge of truth; they are the measures by which we test the claims of fresh ideas. That is why education steadies the mind, and enables it to form just opinions.

So we have our moral standards. People sometimes break away from the normal behaviour of civilised nations and try to attract attention to themselves by being noisy, or irreverent, or challenging.

Others say, " How original!! " and follow their example. If you argue with them, they will laugh at you, and perhaps they will call you a prig or a kill-joy. You can never argue them out of their badness. They are not judging by your standards. You judge them by the useful, beautiful and unselfish lives of people like St. Francis, John Howard, Elizabeth Fry, Florence Nightingale, the good Lord Shaftesbury, and Dr. Barnardo. By such standards their lives are seen at once to be contemptible. But these people say, " We have no standards, except our own will and pleasure! " and they become anarchists of the moral life.

Human existence could not continue in a civilised condition if every individual in a community acted in this way. You will see how important truth is if you imagine life in England without these standards. Suppose bankers and solicitors denied the claims of honesty; suppose doctors came to their patients in a drunken condition; suppose the drivers of express trains took no notice of signals; and suppose policemen lived like burglars and assassins. Civilisation would fall to pieces if everybody did as he liked, and if there was no general acknowledgment among men that certain things are right and certain things are wrong.

THE SAFETY OF OUR LIVES DEPENDS
ON LOYALTY TO TRUTH

The safety of civilisation depends on loyalty to the moral law, and the moral law is the result of man's adventure in the fields of truth. We are born to inquire after truth—not only physical truth, not only the truth of our bodies, of the Earth, of the winds, of the tides, of the stars, but the truth of our own souls. What is best for a man? What is the conduct which helps us most, and what is the conduct which hinders or destroys us?

We can never know the absolute truth, but we can know and do know that love of knowledge, love of goodness, and love of truth, these three great affections of the human spirit, lead us away from error, and guide our feet into the way of happiness.

There may be fools and fools, wise men and wise men—everything is relative; but between folly and wisdom, between false and true, between knowledge and ignorance, there is a great gulf, and we are standing, each one of us, either on the one side or the other of that tremendous chasm.

The Story of the Most Beautiful Book in the World

Job and His Friends

THE FIRST DAYS OF EVIL

THE Ark rested in a place where it was easy for the sons of Noah to spread themselves over the Earth. God wanted men to cultivate the Earth, and so He brought the Ark to anchor where they could most easily cross into all lands. But the sons of Noah settled down in one place and built a great city, and in the midst of the city they erected a vast tower.

Then, says the Bible, when God saw that they were determined to disobey Him, He caused the people to speak in different languages, so that no one could understand the other.

So the Lord scattered them abroad from thence upon the face of all the Earth ; and they left off to build the city. Therefore is the name of it called Babel, because the Lord did there confound the language of all the Earth ; and from thence did the Lord scatter them abroad.

But even after God had made a mock of this foolish Tower of Babel, men continued to stumble and fall, and behave like infants learning to walk. Instead of praying to God, they made images of many gods and prayed to them. They prayed to the Sun because it warmed them. They prayed to fire because they were afraid of it.

God wished them to understand that everything they saw with their eyes— the Sun, fire, animals, and the whole world—was the work of His hands. He wanted them to understand that the Sun warmed them and made the Earth beautiful because He had ordained it. More than everything else, He wanted man not to be a coward, but a strong, intelligent creature, trusting in the power of the great Creator, and setting himself to get dominion over the Earth.

At this time there lived in the world a mighty man named Nimrod, who obeyed God in going forth to conquer the world. He was a great hunter, and men feared him and obeyed him. He gathered people about him, and went across the world to found cities. He is the first monarch that ever existed, for men made him their king.

But Nimrod's empire was poisoned by idolatry; for, although he built mighty cities, the people who dwelt in them were weak and cowardly. They made images and prayed to them. They were superstitious and worshipped animals.

God could not be pleased with such people. He had ordained that men should have dominion. He had purposed that men should count the stars, weigh the suns, and harness the waters to their service, and control the mighty forces of Nature. How could He hope for such things from a people who trembled at a shadow, grovelled in the dust before images, and worshipped animals?

GREAT FIGURES OF THE OLD TESTAMENT · THE LIFE OF JESUS

But all men at that time were not sunken in folly and wickedness. There was one, at least, we are told, who had the soul of a hero. This was that great and splendid spirit called Job. Job's story is told late in the Old Testament, but it is possible that he lived in the evil time between the Flood and the call of Abraham.

Job was a rich man. He was a great lord, the master of servants, the owner of much land, the farmer of many flocks destroyed his flocks; robbers made away with his camels, his oxen, and his asses; and upon Job himself there fell the terrible and awful doom of leprosy. His wife hastened from him; his friends withdrew themselves; the poor, stricken man was left alone, deserted and cursed, smitten with sores from the sole of his foot even unto his crown, and childless. In this appalling ruin Job uttered words which we say to this day when we bury our dead:

JOB IN DEEPEST SORROW—FROM THE PAINTING BY A. ACLAND HOOD IN MAIDSTONE MUSEUM

and herds. He was also a happy man, living cheerfully with his family, enjoying life with a good appetite, and praising God who had blessed him with so much happiness and comfort.

There were, no doubt, many who said: " It is easy for this great lord to believe in God, but how would it be with him if he became poor and miserable like us? Where would his faith be then? It is easy enough to be good when you are rich."

But God tried Job. A storm arose from the desert, and, sweeping down a house in which Job's children were assembled, crushed them to death. Another storm

" The Lord gave, and the Lord hath taken away; blessed be the Name of the Lord."

But Job was not perfect, and when three of his old friends journeyed to see him from far countries, and comforted him by saying he must have sinned to bring this calamity upon his head (such to this day we call Job's comforters), he suddenly rebelled against his doom, and cursed the day that he was born.

But as he talked, often in a strain of fine poetry, he regained his composure and faith.

Here is his picture of what man, even in Job's day, could do in mining—his description of work underground.

JOB AND HIS FAMILY IN THE DAYS OF THEIR PROSPERITY

JOB RECEIVES BAD TIDINGS—THE BEGINNING OF HIS TERRIBLE SUFFERING

Surely there is a vein for the silver and a place for the gold where they fine it ?

Iron is taken out of the Earth, and brass is molten out of the stone.

He setteth an end to darkness and searcheth out all perfection.

The flood breaketh out from the inhabitant, even the waters forgotten of the foot ; they are dried up, they are gone away from men.

As for the Earth, out of it cometh bread, and under it is turned up as it were fire.

There is a path which no fowl knoweth, and which the vulture's eye hath not seen ;

The lion's whelps have not trodden it, nor the fierce lion passed by it.

He putteth forth his hand upon the rock, he overturneth the mountains by the roots :

He cutteth out rivers among the rocks ; and his eye seeth every precious thing.

He bindeth the floods from overflowing, and the thing that is hid he bringeth to light.

THE FEAR OF THE LORD IS THE BEGINNING OF WISDOM

All this man can do, says Job, in the deep darkness of the Earth, but there is much he cannot do, so Job continues:

But where shall wisdom be found ?
And where is the place of understanding ?
Man knoweth not the price thereof.
The depth saith, It is not in me ;
And the sea saith it is not with me.
It cannot be gotten for gold,
It cannot be valued with the gold of Ophir.
Whence then cometh wisdom? and where is the place of understanding ?
Behold, the fear of the Lord, that is wisdom ;
And to depart from evil is understanding.

So in the midst of the argument which followed between Job and his comforters, the poor, smitten man regained some of his faith, and uttered many noble words concerning the providence of God.

But finally God showed Job the whole truth of the matter. He showed that no man can judge God; first, because no man existed when God created the heavens and the Earth, and therefore no man knows His purposes; and, secondly, because no man has passed through the gates of Death, and therefore no man knows what God has prepared for us in the endless ages of eternity. A man can only judge a tiny part of a great whole.

These are some of the mighty words, unequalled in all the books of the world, which came to Job from God:

Who is this that darkeneth counsel by words without knowledge ?
Where wast thou when I laid the foundations of the Earth; when the morning stars sang together, and all the sons of God shouted for joy ?
Have the gates of death been opened unto thee ? Or hast thou seen the doors of the shadows of death ?
Canst thou bind the sweet influence of Pleiades, or loose the bands of Orion ?

Knowest thou the ordinances of heaven ? Canst thou set the dominion thereof in the Earth ?
Hast thou given the horse strength ? Hast thou clothed his neck with thunder ?
Doth the hawk fly by thy wisdom ? Doth the eagle mount up at thy command ?
Shall he that contendeth with the Almighty instruct Him ? He that reproveth God let him answer it !

Then Job answered and said:

Behold, I am vile : what shall I answer Thee ? I will lay mine hand upon my mouth.

THE PATIENT AND OBEDIENT JOB IS BLESSED AT LAST

So when God had tried Job, and had made him humble and obedient, He blessed him again, and Job lived in honour and health, praising God all the days of his life.

Not only is the story of Job one of the greatest in the world, but it is the story of one of the first faithful men in the history of the race. Very probably Job lived in the dark and evil days after the Flood. He lived at a time when men were cowardly, superstitious, disobedient, and foolish. He lived at a time when mankind was likely to perish through sin and ignorance, and he is a great hero. But he was not the man chosen by God to raise the human race from the slough of sin, and help it forward once more on its path of clean and healthy progress.

There was another and a greater man, a man whose title is sublime, for he is called "The Friend of God," and his story we shall read at another time.

But we should pause here a moment to consider those early days of our history. God wanted men to advance and develop their reason. They disobeyed, and lived wicked lives of pleasure. They prayed to sticks and stones; they were afraid of dead bodies; they made gods of animals. There are people still in the world, after all these thousands of years, doing exactly the same thing.

THE MAN WHO TRUSTED THE INVISIBLE CREATOR OF THE VISIBLE WORLD

Then God chose a man who trusted in Him—a man who worshipped, loved, and trusted the invisible Creator of the visible world, and God said:

I will make of thee a great nation, and make thy name great, and in thee shall all the families of the Earth be blessed.

It is from this man, The Friend of God, that we ourselves are descended.

(Next chapter in this group, page 621)

The Interests and Pleasures of Life for All, Indoors and Out

THE YOUNG MAGICIAN

No one is in greater demand at parties than the amateur conjurer, and any boy with plenty of patience and nimble fingers, who is interested in magic, can easily become one. There are, though, some important points to be borne in mind in order to make a real success of this.

To begin with, do not attempt too much. Choose one or two simple tricks such as those given in this series, and some catches which anybody can do, and if necessary supplement these by one or more ready-made tricks which can be bought at most toy shops.

Practise all tricks—the bought ones as well, for even these require a certain amount of ability to present attractively—over and over again until they become quite automatic. A simple trick perfectly done is much more effective than a complicated one fumbled, and the amateur needs to be so sure of himself that he is not put out by interruptions ; for sooner or later he will come up against the clever fellow who will proceed to tell the audience how the trick is done. The young magician must be prepared to turn the tables on the heckler neatly and quickly, and often it is quite enough just to suggest that if he lets the show finish he can then come up and demonstrate his knowledge.

Because of such people, it is as well to practise in front of a mirror to see exactly how a trick looks to the audience, though some boys find this confusing at first, and like to master the trick before trying it this way.

Patter, the idle and usually amusing chatter that is such a necessary part of the professional's showmanship, is equally important for the amateur. Some are naturally good at this, others have to put in a lot of hard work to acquire it; but it does come with practice, and is so worth while because it keeps everyone in happy humour and distracts attention at the vital moment of the trick.

Borrow the apparatus whenever possible, and get members of the audience to help, too. It gives them a personal interest, and they do know that the props are genuine and have not been previously prepared in some way.

Never repeat a trick unless it can be presented in a slightly different way. The spectators know what to expect and will be watching for its weak spot. This applies particularly when working in a room, where the onlookers would be close in front.

But, in the event of getting caught in a really small space, it is as well to have a few tricks which can be done with a crowd all round—like this one:

The conjurer puts a penny in the centre of a handkerchief, then borrows a ring from a lady's finger, or uses a small curtain ring, pulls the four corners of the handkerchief through the ring (until this is quite close up to the coin), and gives them to four members of the audience to hold, announcing that he will now remove both coin and ring.

Then, covering his own hands with another handkerchief, he gently works one edge of the held handkerchief through the ring. Directly this happens the coin will slip out, followed by the ring, leaving the handkerchief still in the surprised spectators' hands.

No magician's kit would be complete without a wizard's wand, so instructions for making one are given on page 631.

CRAFTS · GAMES · NEEDLEWORK · PUZZLES · SCIENCE EXPERIMENTS

LITTLE PROBLEMS FOR ODD MOMENTS

THESE problems are continued from page 382, and their answers, together with more questions, will be found on page 626.

31. How Long was the Train?

As Tom was waiting at the station, a train took 9 seconds to pass him, and to go through the station, which is 88 yards long, it took 21 seconds.

How long was the train ?

32. What Were the Distances ?

A farmer drove to Chester at 8 miles an hour, and returned home by a road 2 miles longer at 10 miles an hour. He found that the return journey took 12 minutes less than the outward.

How long was each road ?

33. What Did the Large Sack Contain?

" There are 40 bushels of corn in those 2 sacks," said the corn chandler, " and the smaller has 5 bushels less than half the quantity in the larger."

How many were in the big sack?

34. How Many Trains ?

A train leaves New York for San Francisco every morning at 9 o'clock, and another leaves San Francisco for New York every morning also at 9 o'clock. Each train takes exactly six days to make the journey across the continent. If a man travels in one of these trains, how many trains will he pass coming in the opposite direction ?

35. Was it Quicker to Cycle ?

James and John were cycling from Liverpool to a village 20 miles distant, and when they had gone only 4 miles John's machine broke down. They wished to reach their destination at the same time. They could both walk or they could use the cycle alternately. They can walk 4 miles an hour and cycle 8 miles an hour, and they chose the quicker way.

Which was it?

36. How Long Were the Candles?

There were two candles, one of them an inch longer than the other. The longer was lit at 4.30 and the shorter at 6. At 8.30 they were both the same length. The first burnt out at 10.30 and the second at 10 o'clock.

How long were they before they were lit?

37. When Will Harry Have a Pony ?

Harry, aged 12, has been promised a pony when he is one-third the age of his father, who is now 56 years old.

When will Harry get the pony?

38. How Much Water was Spilt ?

A boat leaving a wreck had water to last 13 days, allowing each man one quart each day. After 5 days some water was spilt, and one man died on the same day. The water then lasted just the expected time.

How much water was spilt?

THE ANSWERS TO THE PROBLEMS ON PAGE 382

20. By 8.30 Alfred has walked one-fourth of the way, and in another 5 minutes he has walked one-third of the way. The difference between one-third and one-fourth is one-twelfth, so that he walks one-twelfth of the distance in 5 minutes. At 8.30 he still has three-fourths, or nine-twelfths, of the distance to go, and this will take him 9 times 5 minutes, or three-fourths of an hour. He therefore arrives at school at 9.15.

21. From noon on Monday to 8 o'clock on Wednesday morning is 44 hours. His father's watch, therefore, lost 3 minutes in 44 hours. But it was right when it had lost only 2 minutes, which it would do in two-thirds of 44 hours—that is, in 29 hours 20 minutes. This number of hours from noon on Monday would make it 5.20 on Tuesday afternoon.

22. Try 1 saloon first. This will seat 9, and leave 50. There is not an exact number of 4's in 50, so that four-seaters would not do. Next try 2 saloons. These will seat 18, and leave 41, which, again, cannot be fitted in. Next, 3 saloons will seat 27, and leave 32. Now 8 four-seaters will seat exactly 32, so that the manager must have sent 3 saloons and 8 four-seaters.

23. The hare makes 3 leaps while the hound makes 2, so that she makes 9 while the hound makes 6. But the hound goes as far in these 6 leaps as the hare does in 14, so that the hare loses a distance equal to 5 of her own leaps in every 6 leaps the hound takes. She will therefore lose 60 leaps while the hound takes 72—that is, the hound catches her when he has made 72 leaps.

24. The customer received 3 pastries (worth 1s.), 15 caramels (worth 7½d.), and 2 chocolate drops (worth ½d.), making 20 in all for 20 pence.

25. This is what is usually known as a " catch " ; and the answer is that, as they stood, they faced each other, one looking north and the other south.

26. One-third of the seats were filled at 1s. each. At 6d. each two-thirds would have yielded the same amount. Therefore, had the hall been filled, the remaining third would have yielded £5, so that there were 200 in that third, or 600 seats altogether.

27. Forty boys remained at school, and when the master divided up the ten pounds among the scholars he added the ten who were away sick to the forty who were there, making fifty portions into which the ten pounds had to be divided. This gave each boy the sum of four shillings. If the ten absent boys had not received their share then, of course, the forty would have had five shillings each.

28. Divide 60 minutes by the number of trains an hour, to get the number of minutes between each train. If there were 3 more trains per hour there would be 1 minute less between each train. Therefore two numbers whose difference is 3, and which, when divided into 60, give results which differ by 1, have to be found. The numbers which divide 60 are 2, 3, 4, 5, 6, 10, 12, 15, 20, 30. First, those which differ by 3 are 2, 5 ; 3, 6 ; and 12, 15. Of these, the pair which give results differing by 1 when divided into 60 is 12, 15, Hence there were 12 trains an hour, which is a train every 5 minutes. The passenger waited 4 minutes.

29. With no current Duncan would go three-quarters of a mile in one quarter of an hour—that is, 3 miles an hour ; but he actually went only at the rate of 1½ miles per hour, and the difference between 3 miles and 1½ miles was the speed of the current, which was, therefore, 1½ miles an hour.

30. Fred and Albert crossed the ferry first, and Fred brought back the boat. Then the father crossed alone, and Albert returned with the boat. The boys again crossed together ; and Fred brought back the boat in which the postman crossed alone. Albert then rowed across to the start and brought back his brother.

ELECTRICITY AT HOME

On another page is told the story of electricity and its marvellous powers. It is one of the most powerful and the most mysterious forces in the world. Yet the knowledge of it is comparatively new. It is easy to push a button or press a knob up or down and so light up a room with electric light, but this has been possible only since the beginning of the century.

Though the experiments which made the powers of electricity known go back much farther, and it is more than two centuries since Benjamin Franklin began to find out something about this mysterious power. Some of the methods he used were very simple, and any boy can try them for himself.

Take a piece of ordinary brown paper, and warm it before the fire. When it is hot, lay it on the table and brush it briskly with a warm, dry clothes brush. Then pick it up quickly and hold it to the wall. You will find that the paper has become electrified, and that it will cling to the wall. It clings because it is *electrified* and is attracting the wall to it. If you warm the paper and brush it as before, and then hold it over some little bits of lighter paper, small pieces will fly up and cling to the electrified paper.

It is even possible to get sparks from electrified paper. Take a large sheet of stout drawing-paper, warm it till it is thoroughly dry, lay it on a dry wooden table, and rub it very briskly with a piece of flannel. Then put a piece of metal—a bunch of keys would do very well—in the middle and lift the paper off the table by two corners. Then, if some-one else puts his knuckle or finger to the metal, a bright spark will pass between his finger and the metal, which, however, he will not feel. If the weather and the paper are thoroughly dry, there may be a spark an inch long.

But paper is not the best thing with which to try these experiments. For one reason, it will not retain electricity very long, and for another it is not the easiest substance to electrify.

A piece of glass rod or tube is a better *exciter*, as anything electrified by rubbing is called. A solid rod is the better, and a piece can be bought from a chemist. To excite or electrify this, rub it briskly with a piece of dry silk. Or an alternative is to take a stick of ordinary sealing-wax, and rub this with flannel. Another kind of exciter, and a very

good one, is a piece of vulcanite rubbed with flannel. Vulcanite is hard rubber, and fountain-pens are often made of it.

Take the glass rod, sealing-wax, or fountain-pen, and excite it by rubbing with the silk or flannel. Then hold it near some tiny scraps of paper or bits of bran, and it will pick them up, as seen in picture 1.

Be careful that everything is quite dry, and the articles could be warmed before the fire to make sure of this. All experiments with this kind of electricity will fail most disappointingly unless everything is warm and dry, including the weather. Sometimes it will be found that the rod will pick up the paper, and afterwards will not attract the same piece. This is because the little bit of paper has received a charge of electricity from the rod, and when two electrified bodies come together they repel one another, if both are electrified with the same sort of electricity.

If the bodies are charged with opposite kinds of electricity they will attract one another. These two sorts of electricity are called *positive* and *negative* electricity. Glass rubbed with silk gives positive electricity, and sealing-wax or vulcanite rubbed with flannel gives negative electricity.

Take a piece of thin paper—the white edge of a newspaper would do—and cut a strip, say, about four inches long and about an inch wide. Double it over and bring the two ends together. Now draw a man as shown in picture 2, and cut it out, taking care not to cut the hat, so that the figure when folded along the dotted line will stand up. If you excite the glass rod, and hold it near one side, the figure will roll over toward it, and if you then hold the excited vulcanite or sealing-wax at the other side he will roll back that way, and so you can attract him all round the table.

Another experiment is to make a tiny ball of pith out of the centre of an elderberry stick. This pith is very light when it is dry, and can easily be made into a small ball about as big as a pea.

Fix the ball to a silk thread, and the silk to an electric fitting, or something where it can hang down. Now excite the rod by rubbing and hold it near. The pith-ball will fly toward the rod, but after touching it will fly away again, and will keep off as long as the electricity remains in the rod. But if you have used the glass rod

1. Exciter picking up paper.

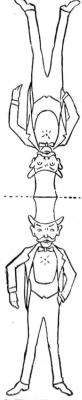

2. The rolling man.

and then bring the vulcanite or sealing-wax near, the ball will fly to it. This shows the difference between the two kinds of electricity.

In place of the pith-ball you can use a little piece of feather, but pith is the better. Instead of hanging the pith-ball from some bracket, you can easily make a stand as shown in picture 5. This is made of a bottle with a piece of copper wire stuck through the cork. Bend the wire over as shown, and make a loop in it to which to tie the silk thread.

With the pith-ball you can prove that when you rub the glass with silk, or the vulcanite or the sealing-wax with flannel, the silk or the flannel also becomes electrified. If you roll the silk or flannel into a ball, and after rubbing the rod with it hold it near the pith-ball, the effect will be the same as if you held the rod near the ball.

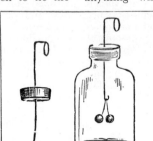

3. Cork and bent wire.   4. The electroscope.

The pith-ball electroscope is a contrivance which will be very useful in many electrical experiments, and it is easily made. With the electroscope you can always test the presence of electricity, and make a good estimate of its strength. Take a glass pickle bottle with a big neck, and clean and dry it thoroughly. Then put a piece of copper wire through the cork, through which a hole has been made with a skewer or a nail.

The wire should be a little thicker than ordinary electric-bell wire. If buying it, ask for No. 14, but any piece of fairly stiff copper wire will do. When you have put it through the cork, bend one end—the one to go *inside* the bottle—into a small hook-shape. The other end first has

5. An easily-made stand.

to be bent round like a ring, and then the ring must be bent down at a right angle. The result will be a piece like picture 3.

Now make two small pith-balls and hang them each on a piece of cotton, both pieces being of the same length. Tie the two ends to the hook in the wire and put them into the bottle and fix in the cork.

The pith-balls should then be about two inches or three inches from the bottom of the bottle, as shown in picture 4.

Of course, do not forget to see that the bottle and everything else is quite dry. Then if you excite the rod and touch the top of the wire with it, the two pith-balls will become excited ; and, as both will be charged with the same sort of electricity, they will stand out apart from each other, and if you bring anything which is electrified against the copper wire the pith-balls will move.

You can make electricity on a larger scale than this. Borrow a lacquered wooden tray and cut out a piece of thick, heavy brown paper, the same size as the inside of the tray, so that it lies flat on the bottom of the tray.

Gum two slips of paper at each end of the sheet to serve as handles. Have the tray supported on two dry glass tumblers — to prevent the electricity leaking away—and warm the sheet of paper at the fire until it is thoroughly dry and hot. Rubbing will help to dry it. Then put it quickly on the table and brush it hard with a warm and dry, stiff clothes brush. Put it on your tea tray which is resting on the tumblers, touch the tray with your finger, and lift away the sheet of paper by the handles you have fixed to it. Then put your knuckles close to the tray and you will get a spark, which you can get half a dozen times if you repeat the process of touching the tray, lifting away the brown paper, and putting your knuckle to the tray.

These experiments are the simplest you can undertake, and it was by such experiments that great inventors came to understand the mysterious powers of the force that makes possible all the marvellous electrical inventions and discoveries which are in use today ; including the telephone and the telegraph, wireless and radar.

MUSICAL CHAIRS WITH A DIFFERENCE

So much easier than ordinary musical chairs, especially if space is limited, is this game in which half the players provide seats for the other half by kneeling on the floor in a wide circle, each facing outwards with one knee up.

While music plays, the others run round the outside of the circle, and sit down on the knees when it stops. The one who has no

seat is out, for there should always be one knee less than the number of runners—there is no need for the " chairs " to get up, it can be managed by simply dropping a knee to the floor. When all are out except one, the teams reverse positions, the two winners finally competing against each other, unless there are enough grown-ups to provide knees for everybody in the first place !

HOW TO DRAW HUNDREDS OF FACES

With the diagram on this page hundreds of different pictures can be made by anyone. First take a piece of good tracing paper and trace the sketch upon it carefully and accurately. Then ink over the lines, and when the ink is quite dry paste this traced design on to a piece of cardboard. To do this, cover the card with a smooth paste and lay the tracing paper upon it, easing out all wrinkles with a clean cloth. When this is

of eyes comes into position within the outline of the face that has just been drawn, and trace them. Finally turn the paper round to another position and trace a nose and mouth. There is now a complete face with eyes, nose, mouth, hair, and hat.

By turning the paper round and drawing different eyes in the different face outlines, and putting sometimes one hat or mouth and sometimes another, an endless variety of

dry, take another piece of tracing paper and pin it down upon the card, pressing the pin through the centre of the diagram where a star is marked. Now trace any one of the hats upon the transparent paper. Then turn the paper round until the hat that has been drawn comes over one of the other hats in the diagram, and trace the shape of the face that appears underneath. Again turn the tracing paper round until one of the pairs

pictures can be made. But in order to do a good portrait gallery the tracing paper must be pinned down firmly upon the card, and must not be allowed to shift about, or the different parts of the faces will not join up properly. Use a soft blacklead pencil and do not press too heavily.

Some amusing women's faces can be drawn by omitting the moustaches, and by adding trimming to the hats, and some curls

VERSES MADE WITH FIGURES AND LETTERS

SOME writers of verses show a great deal of ingenuity in using for their rhymes words that can be expressed by figures or single letters, which, when pronounced, give the sound almost exactly of the words represented.

It makes a good game on a winter evening to gather a group round the table with pencils and paper, and see who, in a given time, can make up the best rhymes in this way. The examples given here will show how the letters and figures are worked into the lines. The first little poem is a good specimen of the use of single letters as a substitute for actual words.

The Chinaman praiseth his T's,
  The mandarin praiseth his Q ;
The gardener praiseth his turnips and P's,
  But I praise U.

The mariner loveth the C's,
  The bagatelle-player his Q ;
The husbandman loveth his cattle and B's,
  But I love U.

The foolish have need of the Y's,
  The actor needeth his Q ;
The pilot hath need of two excellent I's,
  But I need U.

The hunter seeketh the J's,
  The shepherd seeketh his U ;
The college boys seek their final B.A.,
  But I C Q.

Here is one of the nonsense rhymes called Limericks in which figures are very cleverly worked in to represent syllables.

There was an archbishop named T8,
Who dined with a friend at 8.8 ;
  But, sad to relate,
  I'm unable to state
What T8's t8-à-t8 8 at 8.8.

Another Limerick in which the figure 8 is introduced in a very similar way is this.

They dined all alone at 8.8,
On oysters they dined and 8 8 ;
  And he asked his dear K8
  To tell him his f8
When they 8 t8-à-t8 at 8.8.

This is another verse in which letters are used to take the place of a word.

A budding author, something new
Submitting, signed himself X Q ;
The editor the paper read,
And begged he might be X Q Z.

One little verse was headed U C I D K, and, after puzzling over this title for some time, the editor to whom it had been sent managed to discover what it meant.

The title was, of course, " You see I decay."
And this is how the verse ran.

Surely, good sir, you follow me ?
It is as plain as A B C ;
Repeat it in a treble clef,
For I am rather D E F.

In this example double letters are used all through for the rhyming words. This is more difficult to arrange. The double Y, of course, stands for "Wise," and so on.

There is a farmer who is Y Y
  Enough to take his E E,
And study Nature with his I I,
  And think of what he C C.

He hears the chatter of the J J,
  As they each other T T,
And sees that when a tree D K K
  It makes a home for B B.

A yoke of oxen he will U U,
  With many whoas and G G,
And their mistakes he will X Q Q
  When ploughing for his P P.

He little buys, but much he sells,
  And therefore little O O ;
And when he hoes his soil by spells,
  He also soils his hose.

Perhaps one of the best poems in which letters are used for words is A Maid of R K D.

A dainty maid of R K D
  Is F E in her bower;
Smart as U C A honey-B ;
  And sweet as N E flower.

Does she S A herself 2 please,
  X Q Q the little miss,
She sings an L E G 2 T T,
  Or blows an M T kiss.

B mine, I say, U bonny J,
  B4 U R mine L (my knell) ;
When U R gay, my hopes D K,
  In T-sing U X L.

Without ado she takes the Q.
  Her I I B9 and B D ;
O, sir, I do not N V U,
  I C U R so need E.

O F E U I C R true,
  Y need I C Q less ?
I'll never D V 8 from U,
  But end my cares with S.

Most of this is good, except the last line, which needs to be explained. By "ending cares with S," the maid ends with "caress."

THE A B C OF COOKERY

Here is a list of some of the special words and terms used in the course of preparing everyday meals, arranged in alphabetical order for easy reference.

Aspic. A jelly made from meat and bones boiled down sufficiently to become firm when cold; also vegetable, fish, fruit, or tomato juice set with gelatine.

Au Gratin. Food covered with bread-crumbs and cheese or butter, and baked or put under the grill till golden brown.

Balanced Meals. Meals containing a correct measure of all the body-building, warmth, energy-making and protective *Vitamin Foods, Mineral Salts and Water* that our bodies need to make them strong and keep them healthy. Later you will read more about these foods and about how to combine them in the way best suited to a body's digestive machinery, but it may help you to understand how they work if you imagine that you yourself are a motor car and that all the food you put inside your body is the fuel that makes your engine go.

The difference between your fuel food and the petrol fuel for a motor car is that your food, besides having to keep your engine going non-stop night and day, also has to make your body grow as it goes.

Every engine must burn up the fuel fed into it in order to make it run well. The word scientists use for measuring the heat-energy or fuel value of food is Calories, and one Calorie denotes the amount of heat necessary to raise the temperature of one kilogramme of water one degree Centigrade.

Bain-marie. A bain-marie consists of several saucepans in a bath of water. Its name comes from a witch called Marie who invented it. A double-boiler saucepan works on the same principle of preventing the food in the inner pan from burning or cooking too fast.

Baking. To cook by dry heat, usually in an oven, though dishes thus cooked are still apt to be spoken of as roasted which really means cooked by direct rays from an open fire.

The correct temperature when baking is always important and, in an oven without thermostatic control or a thermometer, the paper test can be used : *For a Hot Oven.* A sheet of white paper placed where the

The way to knead dough. Press with the knuckles, or lower part of the palm, pushing forward and working lightly.

baking-tin will stand that turns DARK brown in five minutes shows that the oven temperature is hot, that is between 375° and 400° F. *For a Medium Oven,* about 350° F., the paper takes about five minutes to turn golden brown. *For a Slow Oven,* the paper takes nine minutes to turn golden brown.

Basting. To keep the surface of meat or fish moist by spooning hot fat or liquid over it during cooking.

Blanch. To dip food in boiling water for a few moments, and then to plunge it into cold. When blanching offal, or meat sundries, it may be necessary to bring the food which needs blanching to the boil in cold water.

Boiling. Water boils at 212° F., when bubbles rise constantly to the surface and break; milk boils at 230° F.; lard at 210° F.; clarified fat at 250° F.; and oil at 400° F., when the surface of the oil is quite still with a faint blueish vapour rising from it.

Bouquet Garni or Broth Posy. A small bunch of mixed herbs, (thyme, mint, parsley, a marigold flower, and a bay leaf) used as a flavouring for sauces, stock, or stews, and removed before serving. If fresh herbs are unobtainable, dried herbs with peppercorns and a blade of mace tied in muslin, can be used.

Braising. A combination of stewing and pot roasting in a lidded braising pan.

Caramel, or Caramelise. To heat sugar till it turns brown by adding water to turn it into a syrup or a browning for gravy.

Cereals. The word used to describe all grains such as wheat, rice, oatmeal, and semolina.

Cream. To work butter, or any other kind of shortening, with the hand or a wooden spoon until it looks and feels like thick whipped cream.

Dissolve. To melt a solid food into a liquid.

Dough. A thick mixture of flour, liquid, or other ingredients.

Dripping. Fat from cooked meat, or from chopped fat rendered down or melted.

Dry Ingredients. Flour, sugar, salt, baking powder, and similar products.

Fold in. To add a beaten ingredient, such

as whipped cream or egg-white to another ingredient without loss of the air gained by beating. To do this, heap the lighter ingredient on to the heavier, then blend it with a down-up-and-over motion of the knife or spoon.

Forcemeat. A savoury stuffing.

Fry. To cook in *deep* fat.

Glaze. This word has two meanings—(1) A meat, fish, or vegetable coating of aspic. (2) Some preparation like sugar and water brushed on top of pies or buns to improve the look when cooked.

Grill. To cook food by exposing it to direct red heat : or when an oven is not in use, to brown the top of a dish placed beneath the grill for a few moments. Grill racks need greasing before uncooked food is placed upon them, and when turning food on a grill care must be taken not to pierce the surface with a fork, so letting nourishing juices escape.

Knead. To work dough, as shown in the picture on the previous page, with a pressing action of the knuckles, or lower part of the palm of the hand, pushing the dough forward then lightly folding the outside over itself towards the centre. Kneading must be done in a warm room away from draughts.

Marinade. A mixture of four tablespoonfuls of salad oil to one of vinegar seasoned with chopped onion, peppercorns, one teaspoonful salt, and a teaspoonful each of chopped mint, thyme, and parsley. Tough

meat rubbed with, and then left to absorb this mixture, usually becomes tender.

Parboil. To boil half the usual time, the cooking then being finished by some other means.

Purée. Cooked food of any kind rubbed through a sieve.

Roux or Liason. Butter melted at the bottom of a saucepan over gentle heat, and thickened with double its weight in flour.

Sauté. To cook in a small amount of fat.

Shortening. Any fat suitable for baking.

Simmer. To cook in liquid just below boiling point.

Soufflé. A dish with a base of whipped egg and sauce—light as air.

Stock. Liquid left from the cooking of meat, fish, or vegetables.

Stew. To cook in a closed vessel in liquid at simmering point.

Tepid. A temperature between 80° and 98° F., or one part really boiling liquid mixed with two parts cold.

Vitamins. The word vita means Life, and vitamins are the unseen life-givers found in certain foods, and easily destroyed by careless cookery. You will read more about those vitamins, A B C D and E, which you need to keep you fit and happy, later in this series, but in the meantime learn how to make breakfast one of the nicest meals of the day by turning to page 628.

PARTY GAMES WITH BALLOONS

These games are always very popular, often because they are noisy, and so they are good to play between paper and pencil competitions.

BURSTING THE BALLOON

WHEN balloons are plentiful (substitute paper bags if they are not), a favourite game is to see who can blow up and burst the most. Limit the time allowed for this according to the quantity of balloons available.

PASSING THE PLATE

Divide the players into two teams standing opposite one another, and give each a balloon on a flat plate. This has to be passed from hand to hand up the line and down behind the players' backs, the winning team being the one to return their balloon to the starting point first. Let small children pass it up and down in front, as they find the behind-hand work too difficult.

If the balloon falls to the ground, or is handled by a player, the defaulting team has to start from the beginning again. Another way is to give a penalty mark for every fault, in which case the winning team would be the one with the least number of blots on its record.

RELAY RACE

This is similar to the plate game, but the two teams stand in a line at one end of the room, the leader of each holding the plate with the balloon on it. At a signal they have to carry their slithery burdens as quickly as possible to the other end of the room and back again where the next member of each team takes over.

If the balloon falls to the ground, it can be picked up again, but only with the plate— the player must not touch it.

THE FAN RACE

This also is a relay race, run in exactly the same way as the last one, except that, instead of the balloon being carried, it has to be fanned along the room and back. On no account must it be batted. If fans are not obtainable, make them from paper.

AIR FOOTBALL

Sitting on the floor opposite one another for this, and using right hands only, the teams have to hit a balloon from one to the other, the aim of each being to knock it to the ground behind their opponents' line, when a goal is scored. If any player rises off the floor, a free hit is given to the other side.

Simple Learning Made Easy for Very Little People

READING—MAKING A NEWSPAPER

JOHN and Jennifer loved their Panda books, and they loved, too, having stories read to them; but every day when Daddy read his newspapers and read out the things he thought might interest them, they longed for the day when they would be old enough to read the newspapers for themselves.

Daddy said it would be a long time before that day came, so the twins decided they would have to do something about it. Mother heard them talking, and suggested that they should write their own newspaper. They could write it in the same way as they wrote their diaries, but not only about the things which they did, but also of things which happened in the family, in the town, even in the world, which interested them.

" We will have a monthly newspaper," said John, " and we will collect pictures and write about them, and advertisements to stick into our paper, as well as writing stories and news; then it will be like a real newspaper."

Jennifer agreed, but said that she was going to paint pictures for the paper too! Mother said that would be splendid, as anything of real interest could be put into a newspaper.

" What shall we call our paper? " said Jennifer. The twins and Mother thought of all kinds of names, and Daddy too was asked to suggest a good name for it.

At last they decided to call their newspaper The Treasure Box. Jennifer painted a cover for it, and John printed the name. Daddy brought home some large sheets of paper, 20 inches by 30 inches, which they folded in half. Then Mother sewed these inside the cover Jennifer had painted,

and they had a strong book in which to paste their items of news, their pictures, and so on. The outside was like this:

Some of the news the children wrote themselves, writing the words they knew, or could find in their other books, or asking Mother to write the words they did not know, and then they copied them. Sometimes Daddy or Mother wrote a piece of news for them to put into the Treasure Box. One day Daddy wrote :

WANTED—two children and a Mummie to come to tea with me in town, because it is my birthday. Daddy

He addressed it to "The Editors of The

READING · WRITING · ARITHMETIC · ART · MUSIC · FRENCH

Treasure Box." Here is one of the pages out of the children's Treasure Box:

The Treasure Box is a Paper written by John and Jennifer.	Mother went shopping to buy some meat and potatoes for dinner.	We made some new sweets for our café.
I have a doll; her name is Susan.	We went for a ride on a big red trolley bus.	We had eggs for our breakfast.
		Our grown-up cousin is going to be married.

One day John made up a piece of poetry, and Jennifer painted a picture for it, and they stuck them on a new page of their newspaper and called it the Poetry Page. This was the piece of poetry:

I saw an aeroplane
Having a fly
Up in the sky,
High high high.

The twins had a Nature page in their newspaper, and wrote things like this:

The daffodils are coming out.

We planted some seeds.

Our cat had four kittens.

When people came to the house they were given the newspaper to read.

NUMBERS—REMEMBERING FIGURES

ONE morning Mother said they would have a little talk about *nought*. She told John and Jennifer that 0 stood for nothing, no things, none.

" If you sold all the sweets in your shop," she said, " there would be none left, and you would write on your *Sold Out* notice, *Sweets—none left*. But when you learn how to do sums, you do not write none or nothing, you write 0.

" There is a glad nothing and a sad nothing. If we had no milk and no bread and no babies in the world, that would be very sad, but when we look at our socks and see no holes, then we are glad!

" Now this next figure with a straight back—he is easy to remember and to write. One tall father, one nose, one neck, one mouth, one teapot, one milk jug, one sugar basin. Here he is : 1.

" The next number is two," said Mother. " Think of all the things of which you have two." John and Jennifer thought of 2 eyes, 2 ears, 2 hands, 2 feet, 2 arms, and 2 legs.

" When two things are alike, or nearly alike, we call them pairs," said Mother.

" I know," said John—" a pair of socks, a pair of gloves, a pair of shoes, and a pair of horses."

" A pair of twins," said Jennifer, " that's us ! "

Mother said they were quite right, but could they think of some pairs of things that are joined together? They thought of a pair of scissors, a pair of eyeglasses, a pair of shorts, and a pair of trousers.

John and Jennifer played games with their toys, putting them in pairs; they put their farm animals in twos, their soldiers in twos, and their bricks in twos.

" Now," said Mother. " What about 3 ?"

" Oh," said Jennifer. " We know a song about 3." And she sang Three Blind Mice.

" I know one, too," said John; and he sang Baa, baa, Black Sheep.

" I like threading my beads in threes," said Jennifer. " It's a nice number, and easy to remember."

" I expect baby bear knew all about 3," said John, " because there were 3 bears, 3 bowls of porridge, 3 spoons, 3 chairs, 3 beds."

The next day Mother asked the children to look round and see how many fours they could find.

They could see lots of fours: 4 legs on a table, 4 legs on each chair, 4 legs on the cat, 4 legs on the dog, 4 corners in the room, 4 corners on each picture.

Then they played a game : 2 twins—how many eyes? 2 twins—how many hands? 2 twins—how many legs?

"We will have a talk about figure 5," said Mother. "We've all got lots of fives."

"Five fingers on each hand," said John.

"And five toes on each foot," said Jennifer.

"Yes," said Mother ; "and do you remember when you were babies I used to sing to you, 'This little pig went to market,' when I played with your little pink toes?"

"We are five years old," said John.

The twins decided that figure 5 was the nicest number of them all.

WRITING—MAKING A CINEMA

JOHN and Jennifer, like other girls and boys, liked going to the films, but Mother and Daddy did not like them to go too often, partly because it made them so excited that they couldn't sleep, and partly because there were not many really good films for children.

As we know, John and Jennifer loved stories, and now that they were beginning to write quite well they loved writing stories, and painting pictures, particularly Jennifer.

One day Daddy had a really brilliant idea. He told the twins that if they painted their own pictures and wrote their own stories, he would make a cinema of their very own. They could work it themselves, and show the films to all their friends when they came to tea.

John and Jennifer thought this was the very best idea that Daddy had ever had, and at once got to work. For a long time they couldn't decide on a story. At first they wanted another Panda story, but Mother suggested that they thought of a new one. John did not want to wait while they made up a story, and neither did Jennifer, so Mother said, "Why don't you have a story that you know and like? You could choose your favourite story."

So after much discussion, John and Jennifer decided on The Three Bears. Mother said that twelve pictures and writing would be enough for their first film. She also said that they must try very, very hard with their writing, for if people could not read it the film would be wasted.

These are the twelve sentences they decided to write, and for which they would paint pictures:

Goldilocks went for a walk in the woods.
She found the Three Bears' house.
They had three bowls of porridge.
They had three chairs and three beds.
Goldilocks ate Father Bear's porridge.
She broke Mother Bear's chair.
She slept on Baby Bear's bed.
The three bears came home.
"Who has been eating my porridge?" said Father Bear.
"Who has been sitting on my chair?" said Mother Bear.
"Who is this, fast asleep on my bed?" said Baby Bear.
Goldilocks ran home to her mother.

They painted a picture for each sentence and wrote the words underneath—having copied them from Mother's writing on another piece of paper. Here is one of their pictures:

Goldilocks went for a walk in the woods

When they had finished each one Mother stuck the pictures, in order, on to a piece of butter muslin, leaving a space in between each picture. Then she nailed each end of the butter muslin on to a piece of broom handle, cut about four inches longer than the width of the butter muslin. In one end of each broom handle she put a large screw, and in the other end a large dresser hook. She then rolled the pictures round one piece of the broom handle, like this:

Daddy, as soon as he knew the depth of their roll of film, made up the frame for the cinema. While Daddy was doing this they made a travel picture for their cinema. They wrote of a bus ride through London, but did not make it as long as The Three Bears, because they knew that travel and news films are never so long as the big picture. They called it A RIDE THROUGH LONDON.

We saw the Houses of Parliament, and heard Big Ben strike 2 p.m.

We saw the guard in Whitehall.

We saw Nelson on his column, and the fountains.

A man was feeding the pigeons.

There were boats on the River Thames.

John and Jennifer had great fun and made a lot of different films of stories they knew, stories they made up, news films, and advertisements for their café.

They learned many new words, and tried so hard with their writing that it grew better every day.

ART—COLOURS AND MIXING PAINTS

WE tend to think of certain colours when we think of some things or ideas. Winter is thought of as cold dark greys or browns or black and white. Spring with millions of little spots of coloured buds opening out of the cold grey of winter. Anger, too, may look like deep flaming reds; miserliness like cold dark greeny-greys and yellows. Happiness makes some people see pictures of lovely blues or golden yellows.

In Nature there is endless variety in colour, from the bright yellows, blues, and scarlets of cockatoos to the modest browns and greys of a sparrow. Gardens filled with coloured flowers usually have a great deal of green in the background, and you

have noticed how many different kinds of greens there are even in the leaves of one tree. English people are specially fond of their gardens as well as their country-side, and artists have enjoyed making pictures of both.

Artists use paints to give us an idea of what they feel about colour in their pictures, and you will find that the pictures of one artist are very different from those of another because each tends to choose the colours he likes best, and uses them in his paintings.

Have you tried mixing yellow, red, and blue together to see how many colours you can make from those three? If not, do try. If you have done some mixing of colours, set yourself a special task of mixing several different kinds of greens or browns or greys and see what a variety of each you can make. You could do either of these trials with water colours or powder colours or oil colours.

The way you use your paint brush, too, plays a big part in your use of colours. A large round hog-hair brush with ample supplies of powder paint is the ideal, and some kind of palette on which to mix colours is essential. In a well-made brush the hairs are all arranged to come to a point, and the spring of the hairs makes it possible to paint many kinds of brush marks, from brush-tip touches to bold, flowing lines. Try to feel something of the harmony of music or dancing in the way you use your brush. There is no one way to paint, and as long as you apply the colour with real feeling for paint, you are doing well.

When you go to the art galleries look at the way different masters have used their paints, and you will be surprised at the number of ways there are. An artist uses his brush strokes of colour to complete the pattern of his picture—to express his ideas in terms of paint.

It is simpler and better to use few colours rather than many. White, black, yellow ochre, Indian red, Prussian blue, ultramarine, and raw umber will be the most useful, though you may find you need chrome yellow, vermilion, crimson, cobalt blue, and viridian green.

One way to mix them is to buy the powder of a colour and mix it in a small bowl with sufficient liquid gum and water to make the powder stick together when painted on to paper. Another way is to buy tins of powder colour ready mixed with gum powder, and all you have to do is to add water.

Jonah and the Whale, painted by a girl of 13. The whale is black, with pink mouth and vermilion eye, the boat is yellow, while the sea and sky are bluey-grey.

MUSIC—CLEFS AND STAVES

WHAT useful things lines are! They guide tramcars and trains. They help us to obey the rules in cricket, in football, and in hockey. Lines are not only useful, they are often beautiful. One of the most beautiful lines is the horizon—the line which divides, in the distance, sea or land from sky; and as we look at the horizon we think of contrast, the contrast between high and low.

Music, as we have found out, shows the same sort of contrast. Always we are saying, " That is a high note," or " That is a low note."

Draw a line on a piece of paper, like this: _____
As we look at this line we think: " Above the line is high ; below the line is low."

Play C on the piano. Play it again; and again ; and again ; you hear CCCC —a straight line of sound. To make it quite clear, you could put the four Cs

on a line: ̶C̶C̶C̶C̶-. Take C as *doh* and sing what you have written. If you saw 100 Cs on a straight line it would mean that you were to sing C 100 times—but it would make a very dull tune !

Long ago church music had melodies which were very simple. There would be one principal note with perhaps two or three others for contrast. In its early days the Church thought that the words of the service were all-important. Melody was expected to help the words, but not to get in the way.

Sometimes when we go to church we hear $\overline{\text{C CC}}$ | $\overline{\text{CCC C}}$
         B|B   B
This is a simple melody, but it can sound quite fine when sung by many people. The most important note in the melody is C and we can call C *doh*. If C is *doh* then B is ——— ? Can you fill in the gap ? The answer is, of course, *te₁*.

513

We have C (*doh*) on the line and B (*te₁*) below. What note can we put above? D (or *re*). Round and on our one line, then, we can build a melody of three notes.

There is an old French nursery song which only has three notes. This is a lovely tune, so simple and yet so interesting. Pianists will notice here that A is on the line. For the rest of you *doh* is below the line. Notice that we can have any note on the line so long as we know which it is. Here it is for you to play and sing:

If you listen to a choir you will find that women (or children) sing high notes, while the men sing much lower notes. A comfortable note for you to sing is G, the note on which we usually start God Save the Queen. This note crops up often in our songs. Let us have a G line 𝄞——

Now let us write our G as it was writtten hundreds of years ago 𝄞. Now it has come into our everyday music surrounded by a number of other lines.

Men have a comfortable note of their own—nine notes lower than yours (work this out on the piano). The note is F. And so we have F, favoured in music for men's voices, and in "left hand," or low, music in general.

F was first written 𝄢. Then came 𝄢. And now we have 𝄢: or even 𝄢:

Music on one line does not take us very far with many of the tunes which we know. If we learn, however, to use a single line, we find out how it works, and we can also learn to write melodies of our own. Perhaps you will try some tune-making. When you have made a tune around one line, play or sing it to see how it sounds.

On our railway journey the other day we noticed sometimes a track branching off the main line and going to some small village or town. On the main line we had, for the most part of the way, two tracks. But near important towns there were four tracks, and at a big junction so many lines that we could not count them.

Music runs on lines too. A tune which is very compact, like Fais Dodo, needs only one line. But what about our carol —Unto us a boy is born?

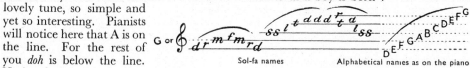

Sol-fa names   Alphabetical names as on the piano

We may start with one line, but before we have gone very far we need five lines. To save the trouble of having different numbers of lines in any piece we now have five line sets.

This is a sensible number of lines, for if you listen to the notes which can be put on the lines, and in the neighbouring spaces, you will find that they are just those that you can sing.

People with high voices or instruments have their music written on a stave which is marked by a treble clef:

𝄞 . . . . the G line

Low voices or instruments use another clef, the bass clef:

𝄢 . . . . the F line

If you were to look over the viola player's shoulder in the orchestra you would find yet another clef—the alto or C clef:

𝄡 . . . . the C line

What a lot of new words we are meeting! Later we will talk about treble, alto, bass, and a word of the same family which we have not yet mentioned, tenor.

Clef is a French word. It means key. A clef in music is a key which helps us to solve a problem.

We look at the clef and the clef tells us that on these lines (and in the spaces) we can put notes which can be sung by people with high voices or played by high sounding instruments. Also the second line from the bottom will always carry the sound which on the piano we call G. From this we can work out precisely what each line and each space stands for. A different clef would give us a different solution.

FRENCH—A RIDE IN THE TRAIN

HERE we read how our little party spent their time in the train. We must be sure to remember that the first line under the picture is the French; the second gives the English word for the French word above it: the third line shows how we make up the words in our own language.

Nous montons dans le compartiment.
We mount in the compartment.
We get in the compartment.

On crie: " En voiture ! "
Someone calls: " In carriage ! "
Someone calls: " Take your seats ! "

Un monsieur court—A gentleman runs

Un monsieur court de toutes ses forces.
A gentleman runs with all his might.
A gentleman is running with all his might.

Il manque de tomber. Que c'est drôle !
He misses to fall. How it is funny !
He nearly falls. How funny it is !

La portière—The door

Maman nous installe, chacun dans un coin.
Mamma us settles, each in a corner.
Mamma settles us, each in a corner.

On ferme les portières.
Someone shuts the doors.
The doors are shut.

Le train part. Nous sommes en route !
The train starts. We are on way !
The train starts. We are on our way !

Maman et Papa—Mamma and Papa

Maman et Papa lisent les journaux.
Mamma and Papa read the papers.
Mamma and Papa are reading their papers.

La poupée—The doll

Nous jouons à la poupée.
We play at the doll.
We play with the doll.

Je suis le papa. Jeannette est la maman.
I am the Papa. Jenny is the Mamma.
I am Papa. Jenny is Mamma.

Bébé et la poupée sont nos enfants.
Baby and the doll are our children.
Baby and the doll are our children.

Nous les aimons beaucoup.
We them love very much.
We love them very much.

Bébé pleure—Baby cries

Bébé pleure et fait le méchant.
Baby cries and makes the naughty child.
Baby cries and is tiresome.

A FRENCH PICTURE LESSON: NAMES OF FAMILIAR THINGS IN A DINING-ROOM

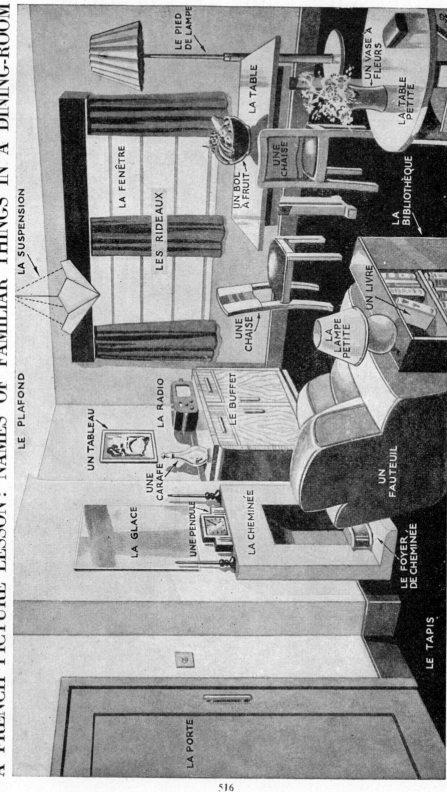

This picture of a dining-room will help us to learn the French for the familiar things around us. The objects named are the ceiling, electric-light pendant, mirror, picture, window, decanter, radio set, curtains, door, clock, lamp-stand, fireplace, sideboard, chair, bowl of fruit, table, hearth, armchair, table lamp, book, bookcase, small table, flower-vase, floor.

The Story of the Boundless Universe and All its Wondrous Worlds

Molten lava from the Earth's interior pours forth from the crater of Kilauea, a volcano in Hawaii

HOW FIRE & WATER MADE THE WORLD

The hills are shadows, and they flow
  From form to form and nothing stands ;
  They melt like mist, the solid lands,
Like clouds they shape themselves and go.

WE have seen that the Earth blossomed, as it were, from the Sun, and grew into a huge hot ball denser than steel, with a wonderful substance called radium in its crust to keep it warm.

Many people think that when it first hardened it was probably pear-shaped, and even today, if we were to remove the seas, the Earth would roughly resemble a pear, or peg-top ; at least it would have a bigger rounded end at the North Pole and a smaller more pointed end at the South Pole. But the early pear-shaped Earth had still much smelting and forging to go through.

When ore is melted in a furnace the stony materials rise to the top, forming slag such as we see heaped round iron foundries, and the metals collect in the lower part of the furnace. In the mighty fiery furnace of the blazing Earth the same sort of separation occurred, so that it grew to have a core of iron and other heavy metals surrounded by a crust of slag. Nobody has ever dug right through the slag, now in the form of mudrock, to the metal core, but it is believed to be about forty-five to seventy-five miles thick. The slag consisted chiefly of two beautiful rocks—granite and basalt; and it is these two rocks which have made the Earth the home of life.

Now if the Earth had been composed wholly of metal it would have made a giant cannon-ball; but it could never have become a world of living things. The granite and the basalt slag contained iron, magnesium, silicon, phosphorus, lime, sodium, and potassium; indeed, all the elements necessary for life—even water and the gases carbon dioxide and nitrogen. That is surely a marvellous thing—that the stuff of the whirling fiery furnace of the Earth should have contained *exactly the things necessary for life !*

But granite and basalt are hard rocks ; and Life at that stage might have complained: " I asked for bread, and you give me a stone." In that stage the crust was not even a crust of bread. Yet the elements of life were there ; the rocks had been made, and now they had only to be ground down into soil. So the great mills of God began to grind; and

  Though the mills of God grind slowly,
    Yet they grind exceeding small.

They ground the granite and the basalt into mud and dust.

ASTRONOMY · GEOLOGY · GEOGRAPHY · CHEMISTRY · PHYSICS · LIFE

As the hot slag cooled down it contracted and puckered up into mountain ranges, or was torn asunder, leaving great cracks through which poured rivers and seas of steam and lava ; and everywhere volcanoes flung hot ashes and gases to the sky, and filled the heavens with dust and clouds. Probably the gas from the torn and twisted crust grew to be the atmosphere, and almost certainly the steam from earthquake cracks and volcanoes grew to be the water of the world. The steam condensed on the top of high mountains and became rivers and seas ; and the air and the water began their great work of wearing down the granite and basalt mountains.

Millions of years they worked away, while the volcanoes steamed and the earthquakes thundered, and the tortured crust was twisted and torn ; and during these years of mountain-making and rock-grinding the whole geography of the crust was ever changing, so that great mountain ranges rose out of the sea, and the floors of seas became dry land.

MOUNT EVEREST RISES FROM THE WHALES AND VISITS THE EAGLES

At one time the Himalaya mountains were at the bottom of the sea, and were slowly lifted out of it—" once with the whales, now with the eagle skies "—and at one time there was almost certainly a great continent in the middle of the Atlantic Ocean. Some of the rocks and mountains of the world are composed almost entirely of sea-shells, great and small. " The white cliffs of Dover " are built up of such shells which collected on an ocean floor, and some of the limestone rock in the state of New York contains as many as 40,000 tiny shells in each cubic inch. And all this lime had been worn off granite and basalt mountains by rain, washed into the sea, and collected by the little living creatures there! The Dolomites in the Tirol are actually made of coral, that is to say of lime and magnesium collected from the sea by coral-making creatures, and originally basalt slag and granite slag worn down by rain and rivers. Well did Tennyson write:

> There rolls the deep where grew the tree.
> O Earth, what changes hast thou seen !
> There where the long street roars hath been
> The stillness of the central sea.

Yes, not so very long ago, as we count time in geology, Regent Street, Oxford Street, and Hyde Park were deep under salt water; and only in a few little areas in the British Isles are there any bits of rock that have not at one time been mud in the bottom of the sea.

It is extremely difficult to know how land and sea were arranged ages ago, but it is quite certain that there have been tremendous changes. At one time, as we said, the Himalayas and the Dolomites were at the bottom of the sea, and that is the history also of the Alps, and of practically all the mountains except volcanoes.

THE VOLCANOES THAT BURST THROUGH THE NEW CHALK FLOOR OF BRITAIN

Not only is there reason to believe that at one time there was a continent in the middle of the Atlantic, but it seems likely that once we could have walked overland all the way from where New York is to where Australia is, and could have gone by boat all the way from where Stockholm is to where Peking is. Anyhow, it is certain that only after tremendous changes, heavings, sinkings, crumplings, crackings, did the Earth reach its present form.

Even after the seas were formed we find evidences of tremendous eruptions. At one time, when Ireland and Britain had been raised from the sea as one great island of chalk, a tremendous volcano—or, it may be, several volcanoes, burst through its white floor and covered many thousand miles of the white chalk with molten lava a thousand feet deep. The remains of this lava outflow are still to be seen in the massive basalt columns of the Giant's Causeway, and at some time there must have been a basalt causeway all the way between Ireland and Scotland. But a still greater lava outflow took place in Iceland, coming forth like a deluge from a colossal crack, covering fifty thousand square miles, ten thousand feet deep, and uniting Iceland with the Faroe Islands, the Hebrides, Ireland, and Scotland in one huge island.

THE MILLS OF GOD GRIND ON, AND THE RIVERS WASH AWAY THE EARTH

In later years, when the Earth's crust was harder and more stable, such tremendous eruptions did not occur; and the changes on its surface were less violent; but changes continued; fire, water, frost, wind, glacier, and animal life all worked unceasingly, shaping and re-shaping the surface of the world.

As we now know it, Earth seems a finished planet. It has mountains and

FIRES OF THE EARTH BREAKING THROUGH

EUROPE'S GREAT VOLCANO—VESUVIUS, WHICH DESTROYED POMPEII AND IS STILL ACTIVE

VESUVIUS SEEN IN ACTION FROM AN AEROPLANE

seas, and rivers and forests. Its granite and basalt have been ground down into soil for roses and trees and wheat, and it is teeming with plant and animal life. The furnace has wrought it into perhaps the most wonderful orb in the universe. But still the mills of God grind on. Still the rain and the rivers are ceaselessly washing the land into the sea. Still we can hear

The sound of streams that fast or slow
Draw down Aeonian hills and sow
The dust of continents to be.

Still the waves are nibbling and gnawing at the coasts of islands and capes. Still the wind is wearing sandstone hills into sandy deserts. Still chalk cliffs and coral peaks and continents may be slowly rising from the depth of some ocean: even still some volcano yet unborn may overtop Chimborazo and Aconcagua.

Once more England may be submerged: once more men may walk dry-foot across the Atlantic. We live only a short time, and the mills of God grind on so slowly that in a human lifetime little change is to be seen on the face of the Earth; but even in one lifetime we can watch the mountains "flow from form to form"; and the gradual sinking or rising of parts of the Earth's

unforeseen happens, it has still a changeful life before it for millions of years to come.

To what great goal all these changes are working we cannot tell; we cannot see far enough. But as we spin through space we can study the changes and take interest in them, knowing that they are directed by the same far-seeing Wisdom that melted the world in a furnace, and brought forth the magic slag which grew into the wonderful world of plants and animals.

It may seem to us that the Earth could not be much better than it is: we and the plants have just the right gases—oxygen and carbon dioxide—which we need for life. With less oxygen and more carbon dioxide we could not flourish so well, and might die. The plants, too, have just the right food in air and water to make food for themselves and for us. We even find coal ready for our use prepared by the sunbeams and forests millions of years ago; and we find iron and salt and other useful elements all assembled in accessible places. Beauty, too, we find everywhere—flowers and trees and blue skies, and rivers and seas and mountains.

Altogether it seems a very perfect and wonderful world, with all things fitting

THE MOUNTAIN RANGES FORMED BY THE CRUMPLING UP OF THE EARTH AS IT COOLED

The ranges shown in these pictures were all formed by the wrinkling and folding of the Earth's crust ; and they are formed mainly of mud accumulated at the bottom of the sea, though in many cases—as in the case of the Andes—volcanoes broke through the folds and increased the height of the general range.

surface, the slow nibbling of the coasts by the breaking waves. Within the last hundred years volcanoes such as Krakatoa and Bandai San have been blown to pieces, and great earthquakes have occurred which have made new cracks in the Earth's slaggy crust. Our Earth is not yet dead; it has still a hot heart; and so long as there are water and wind, and a Sun to move them, it will go on changing. Some day, millions of years ahead, when the Sun is extinct, our planet may spin as a cold dead ball covered with frozen air; but unless something

like the wheels of a watch, and we may find it difficult to believe that further change will bring forth yet more wondrous things. But all the changes through all the past, spread over millions of years have led upward and onward. The beautiful blazing Earth cooled down till its outside was slag and mud and dust; but it died to live again, and we who can look back through the ages, and see the blossoming of life, can still believe that the future holds beauty.

(Next chapter in this group, page 641)

The Story of Immortal Folk Whose Work Will Never Die

John Pym

Thomas, Lord Fairfax

Prince Rupert

Admiral Blake

John Hampden

Sir John Eliot

General Ireton

John Bradshaw

CROMWELL AND HIS MEN

THERE was a great painter called Van Dyck, who made many portraits of King Charles. If you have ever seen one of them, it is easy for you to understand why, with all his faults and his follies, he was loved with a passionate devotion, and how he still casts a spell over the minds of men.

There is a dignity, a majesty, in the grave, delicate face, a charm in the haunting, melancholy eyes, a kingly air in the pose, which makes you feel that this was a man for whose sake many would die gladly. And yet we can see that it is not the face of a man wise in counsel or strong in action.

Now, if you look on the face of Cromwell, it is as though it had been hewn roughly out of solid granite, grim and massive and hard; there is power in every line, but of grace or graciousness no whit. This man is a born fighter and a born leader. The other is born for defeat.

From his youth, Charles had evil counsellors. His father, King James the First, was a rickety-legged bigot; who was well described as "the wisest fool in Christendom." Never was a monarch so undignified as he; perhaps that is one reason why Charles bore himself always with such dignity. James gave the prince

for a companion a young gentleman who was handsome, brave, proud, and worthless. Him he made a lord, and he became famous as the Duke of Buckingham.

Buckingham utterly won the heart of Charles, and taught him to think that princes and their favourites are altogether above the law. Moreover, it was due to Buckingham that Charles married the pretty French princess Henrietta Maria, who proved a counsellor fully as bad as Buckingham himself, after the duke had been slain by a crazy assassin. So that the two people whom Charles loved best in the world were the worst advisers he could have found, yet it was their advice he always followed.

But of all the ill counsel he got from these two, or from his father, the worst was their teaching that the word of a king may be lightly given and lightly broken. This, more than aught else, brought Charles to his final ruin. For, though the people were wroth with him before he signed the promises in the Petition of Right, they were far more angry afterward, because they felt he had played them false. Again, when he gave up Strafford to his doom, all knew that he had broken his word; and when Parliament

EXPLORERS · INVENTORS · WRITERS · ARTISTS · SCIENTISTS

resolved to fight, it was because they would not trust him. When, at last, Cromwell and his party resolved that the king must die, it was because they had lost all hope that he would keep his promises if he were allowed to live.

Yet Charles really believed he was in the right, except when he surrendered Strafford, for he held that the king is appointed by God, and should rule his people, not as the people think good for themselves, but as the king thinks good for them ; and that, whether he rules ill or well, none can call him to account save the King of kings. Besides this, he saw that Parliament was now demanding rights which it had never claimed before, and he thought that if he gave way there might remain to the king no power at all.

After the king had most openly broken the law by entering the House of Commons, seeking there to arrest the five men who were the chiefs of the party that opposed him, he went away from London, and there was little hope that war could be avoided. Some months later Charles unfurled his standard at Nottingham, and this was the beginning of the great Civil War.

OLIVER CROMWELL, THE MAN WHO WAS TO CONQUER THE KING

Let us see, now, what manner of life had been lived by the man who was to conquer the king. Oliver Cromwell had farmed his lands in Huntingdonshire, seeking to make no stir in the world. Once, indeed, he had come forward in his own part of the country as champion of the people's rights in the matter of certain lands of which they were being robbed, but for the rest he was known chiefly as a very religious man, who for his religion's sake had been willing to leave his own home and seek a new one in America. But he and his company were stayed by the king's orders when they were about to cross the sea.

In Parliament, at first Cromwell was a rough, uncouth figure, unskilled and confused of speech, yet a man of mark by reason of his deadly earnestness.

When the war broke out and the tide of battle ran against Parliament, it was Cromwell who saw how the tide must be turned. He saw that what made the King's soldiers so irresistible was the proud sense of honour which made them fear nothing but disgrace, and that these men must win unless they were fought by soldiers who feared death as little as they.

Cromwell went down to the eastern counties, and gathered troops of men picked out for their zeal in religion, but also for their strength and valour and horsemanship. These men he trained in utter obedience, so that when they came to the shock of battle these Ironsides swept all before them, yet were ready to rally to their chief's command and hold back from needless pursuit and plunder.

THE BATTLE OF NASEBY AFTER WHICH CHARLES GAVE HIMSELF UP

So, at Marston Moor and Naseby, under Cromwell and Lord Fairfax the Ironsides smote the gallants whom none had been able to resist. But after the rout of Naseby the king's cause was lost, and Charles gave himself up to the Scots, who were in arms to aid the English Parliament; and after some time the Scots handed him over to Parliament.

But now Cromwell and the soldiers grew ill content with Parliament, because it was willing to make terms with the king without having secured the liberty of religion, which was the thing they most cared about. Therefore, they sent a troop of soldiers to bring the king from Holmby House and keep him under charge of the Army itself. And then, because the Army and Parliament were in disagreement, the king tried privately to treat with each of them, and to make them the more obstinate in their disagreements with each other, hoping he might yet win the day.

But when he tried to escape from the country, and was stopped in the Isle of Wight and held prisoner at Carisbrooke Castle, the Royalists rose in insurrection, and Cromwell saw that the king had been only making pretences. He felt that when the insurrection was put down there could be no peace in the land until the will of the Army was made to prevail.

THE STRANGE SPECTACLE THAT ENGLAND SHOWED THE WORLD

Then England showed the world a strange spectacle. They, who had risen in arms against the king in the name of the law, now set up a tribunal to judge the king which was itself without rights from any law. So that now it was the king who stood for the law, and his judges who stood for arbitrary power, or the power that is not restrained by law. And the Army, having this power, cut off the head of the king in the name of the people of England, though all knew that the chief part of the people of England shrank in horror from the deed.

Thus, in the last days of his life, the false king who had wrought so much ill to the land became a martyr, and throughout those days he acted with a most royal dignity and showed great tenderness and courage. He would make no defence before judges who had no right to try him. In his prison he remained calm and collected, mindful of his friends and his children, but with his thoughts bent on eternity. And when the last hour came, and he stepped through the window of Whitehall to the scaffold, and looked on the crowds that had gathered to see how a king can die :

> He nothing common did or mean
> Upon that memorable scene,
> But bowed his comely head
> Down as upon a bed.

When the executioner struck off his head and raised it, with the words, " This is the head of a traitor," the crowd answered with groans and tears.

THE MANNER OF MAN THAT OLIVER CROMWELL WAS

Let us turn now to the man who, more than any other, had brought about this just and necessary, but terrible deed. Cromwell had striven his hardest to make terms with Charles and to restrain the Army, which would willingly have made away with him long before; but at last he had judged that there was no way left but the way he took. When his mind was made up he never faltered. On the king's death warrant there is no signature written more firmly than Oliver Cromwell's.

For no man could be more utterly merciless than he if it seemed to him that the need arose for firmness, as he showed when he slew and spared not at the pitiless taking of Drogheda and Wexford in Ireland. Yet he had no love for bloodshed; his mercilessness was doubtless caused by his religious fanaticism. He made himself King of England in all but the name, just as he slew King Charles—because he could see no other way of restoring order in the land.

He established order and made the country prosperous. The foreign nations which at first treated England as an outcast State when she had put her king to death, became eager for Cromwell's friendship and feared his hostility. At his bidding the French stopped persecuting Protestants. Since the days of Elizabeth the foreign nations had cared nothing for England's will or wishes, till Cromwell trained his army, and Blake proved himself a match for Van Tromp on the seas. And Cromwell did this when the country had just been rent with a great civil war, and when one-half of it was thirsting to overthrow his government.

OLIVER'S STORMY LIFE ENDS IN A STORM ON HIS GREAT DAY OF TRIUMPH

Perhaps it is not easy to love a man so rugged and ungainly; it was easy to hate him. His enemies hated him so much that during the last years of his life he always wore mail under his dress, lest he should be slain by an assassin.

With all his massive, uncouth force, Oliver was tender of heart. It is pleasant to think how, when the grim soldier had become the greatest man in the land, he brought his old mother up to live in his house; and because the poor old lady lived ever in fear that his foes would kill him, he made a rule to show himself to her every evening, so that she might go to sleep knowing he was safe.

Cromwell had taken up the task of fighting the king, of killing the king, and of ruling the country because he saw things that must be done, and no other was fit or able to do them.

" God knows," he said, speaking sober truth, " I would have been glad to have lived under my woodside, and to have kept a flock of sheep, rather than to have undertaken this government."

He was willing enough to lay the task down. " My work is done," he said as he lay on his death-bed; " yet God will be with His people."

He lived a stormy life; it was fitting that a great storm was raging when the hand of Death laid hold upon him. On the anniversary of two of his great victories, Dunbar and Worcester, the spirit of the great Protector passed away.

HOW THEY SNATCHED CROMWELL'S BODY FROM THE ABBEY

No Englishman has been more abused than Oliver Cromwell. The Royalist historian of the period, the Earl of Clarendon, summed him up as " a brave, bad man," and that estimate was passed on into several school histories, and warped the judgment of generations.

The bitterness of the supporters of the Stuarts was such that after Charles the Second had succeeded to the throne of his

CHARLES STUART, THE FAITHLESS KING

It is easy, in looking at this picture by Van Dyck, to see why with all his faults men loved King Charles with a passionate devotion. There is a dignity in the delicate face, a charm in the haunting, melancholy eye, a kingly ease in the pose, which makes us feel that this was a man for whose sake men would die. Yet he was a faithless king.

father, Cromwell's body was torn out of its grave in Westminster Abbey, hanged on a gallows at Tyburn, and then beheaded, the head being placed on a pole on the top of Westminster Hall, and the body buried at the gallows. This vengeful course was timed to take place exactly twelve years after the beheading of Charles the First.

But the judgment of later times is shown in the fact that a tablet to his memory has been placed in the Abbey by the authorities of that venerable pile; his statue stands between the Abbey and the Houses of Parliament, one of the finest statues, in one of the finest positions, in London; and the sober mind of history declares him to be not only one of the greatest but one of the most honest of Englishmen. It is remembered in his favour that at the height of his power he remained true to his principles and refused the English crown; that he was tolerant toward all forms of religion in an intolerant age; and that his piety was attested by the purest minds of his generation who knew him best.

It was the life of Cromwell written by Thomas Carlyle, with evidence clear as noonday from Cromwell's own letters, that brought justice to his memory, and almost silenced the voices of hatred and ignorance. Faults he had, of course, but the final verdict of history is that he was a great, good man.

Now let us look at some of the leaders who gathered about Cromwell in those great and stirring days.

At first there were three men who stood up in Parliament against the king—Sir John Eliot, John Pym, and Thomas Wentworth. Of these three the first died, as men say, a martyr to his cause.

The Parliament, headed by these three, made the king sign a declaration, which was called the Petition of Right, that it was not lawful for him to make the people pay taxes without consent of Parliament, or to put people in prison unless they were brought to trial and it was proved that they had broken the law. But he had hardly signed it when he began to demand certain taxes and put people in prison if they refused to pay. But when Parliament came together, Eliot made a great speech which stirred everyone to be more resolute in resisting the king's unlawful demands. This made Charles so angry that he had Eliot thrown into prison and kept in close confinement so that he became very ill; and, as Charles would not make the imprisonment any the less severe, Sir John died. Men loved his memory, for he had been a very noble gentleman, caring nothing for his own ease, but ready to endure all things if so he might help to keep England a free nation.

Very different was Wentworth, who had been Eliot's friend; for just after Charles had signed the declaration, Wentworth went over to the king's side, so that the other side, of which he had been a chief, gave him the name of the Apostate, which means a man who has deserted a great and worthy cause.

From that time there was no man who wrought so shrewdly or so sternly to make the king all-powerful; either because, having seen that there was no hope of agreement, he thought the rule of the king would be better than the rule of Parliament, or because he loved the king and hoped thus to save him.

At any rate, this Wentworth, with the grim face and

OLIVER CROMWELL, THE MAN OF IRON

This picture by Ford Madox Brown shows Oliver Cromwell on his farm, and we see in his face, calm and hard as if hewn out of granite, the power that is missing from the face of Charles, as we see in Charles's face the grace that is missing from the face of Cromwell. Few Englishmen have influenced the course of our history more than Cromwell.

the fathomless, unsmiling eyes, was sent first to rule the North of England and then Ireland. With an iron hand he ruled, careless of law, but careless, too, whether the foes he crushed were strong or weak; and all had to obey his will while for eleven years he ruled without the help of any parliament.

But a time came when Charles needed more money than he dared demand without Parliament's consent; and when the Parliament met, seeing how strong and clever a servant Charles had in Wentworth, who was now Lord Strafford, and that if Strafford lived he might make the king too strong for Parliament, they charged him with treason and passed an Act declaring that he was dangerous to the State and must be beheaded. Fearing the wrath of the people, and that if Strafford were not slain they would clamour for the life of the queen whom they hated no less, Charles yielded his consent, even though he had promised Strafford that not a hair of his head should be harmed. Can we wonder at Strafford's bitter exclamation when he heard of the betrayal: " Put not your trust in princes! " This man who had served both parties was slain, and the king gave up to death his most faithful servant. And now there was none left who could save him from his own impending doom.

JOHN PYM, WHO ROSE AGAINST THE MAN WHO HAD BEEN HIS FRIEND

The third great opponent of King Charles was John Pym, a country gentleman who was also a lawyer. When Parliament met again it was John Pym who first ventured to attack the king, and who did everything in his power to bring about the destruction of Wentworth, who had once been his friend. It was Pym who most roused the people in the country, and whose words carried most weight in Parliament. He was the boldest as well as the shrewdest of all Parliament men. Beside him stood one who was not indeed so skilled an orator, but who was not less honoured for nobility of character, John Hampden, the champion of the people.

These two had some ado both to give heart to those who feared the evils of a civil war more than they hated tyranny, and to restrain those who were too hasty to take thought how best liberty might be secured.

But so great was Pym's influence that he came to be called King Pym, by his opponents in mockery, but in admiration by his friends. And those two, more than any others, the king himself sought to overthrow, so that one day he came suddenly down to the House of Parliament, where the Commons were sitting, having with him a band of soldiers, and willing there to arrest them with three others even in Parliament itself. But they, having warning, had gone down the Thames by boat into the city of London, where they were too well loved for the king to dare attempt their capture. So Charles retired in wrath, and after that it was but a few months before there was open war between the king and Parliament.

BRAVE JOHN HAMPDEN IS STRUCK DOWN BY A BULLET IN BATTLE

When the war began John Pym remained in London to direct the counsels of Parliament, and this he did with great wisdom until he died, about a year and a half after the war began. But John Hampden went at the head of a troop of horse which he had raised at his own cost, to be one of the leaders of the army of the Parliament in battle.

It was Hampden who, when the king ruling without Parliament put an unlawful tax upon the people, refused to pay it, and was punished by the judges who were afraid to give judgment against the king.

He was a man who tried always to do what he counted right, at whatever cost, so that even his foes honoured him; and once it was said that it was only his coolness and wisdom which had restrained the king's party and the parliament party within the House of Commons from falling upon each other in the House itself. Therefore all men were grieved, even the king's men, when John Hampden was struck down by a bullet in the fight of Chalgrove Field; for they knew that when he died the chance was less than it had been that the sides might yet find some way of agreement.

PRINCE RUPERT—CAVALRY LEADER, SEA ROVER, AND MAN OF SCIENCE

The most active leader on the king's side when war broke out was Prince Rupert of the Rhine, a son of Charles's sister. His courage was much greater than his discretion, for his impetuosity lost more than his bravery won.

When the war was lost to the king on land Rupert tried to keep an opening for new attempts by maintaining himself

ADMIRAL ROBERT BLAKE IS SUMMONED BEFORE CROMWELL TO RECEIVE HIS
COMMISSION AS GENERAL OF THE SEA IN THE COMMONWEALTH PERIOD

at sea as the leader of a Royalist fleet.
The Scilly Isles and the Channel Islands
were his bases for a time, but he was
finally driven out of the seas around England by the bravery and skill of Admiral
Blake, who left him no rallying place,
but declared that any country which gave
Rupert's ships a place of refuge was forthwith by that act an enemy of England.

But Rupert was more than a dashing

cavalry leader on land and a daring rover
on the seas ; he was a keen student of
science, and the discovery of the process
of printing pictures known as mezzotint
stands to his lasting credit.

Also on the king's side was that fine
character Lucius Carey, Lord Falkland.
When the Parliament met which was
called the Long Parliament he stood on
the same side as Pym and Hampden,

hoping the king and the Parliament might both learn wisdom and come to agreement, but when he saw them growing more bitterly at enmity, till the Parliament seemed to be grasping at the whole power, he went over to the king's side, fearing the tyranny of Parliament more than the tyranny of the king. For this reason, in sadness of soul, Falkland chose loyalty before liberty; and when he was slain in battle men said that he had died willingly.

CROMWELL'S CLOSEST FRIEND IN THE ARMY THAT WON THE WAR

Henry Ireton was Cromwell's most intimate friend in the army that won the war. He was a Nottinghamshire gentleman, who had been educated at Oxford and trained for the Bar, and quite early he saw that Cromwell was a military genius. Cromwell, on his part, knew the value of Ireton's superior education, knowledge of the law, and force of character, so he made him his cavalry leader and took him as his intimate adviser; and presently Ireton married Bridget Cromwell and was his leader's son-in-law.

At first Ireton's views of the king were quite moderate. He believed in giving Charles every chance of winning back the people's favour. When, however, he found that Charles could not be trusted, he became sternly bent on punishing him for what he thought was treason to the nation, and he signed the warrant for his execution. When the war passed over to Ireland, Ireton acted there as Cromwell's second-in-command, and there he died on active service. His body was brought to England and buried with honour in Westminster Abbey, but after the Restoration of the revengeful Stuart family to the throne the grave was opened and the body of Ireton was hanged aloft at Tyburn (near the place where the Marble Arch now stands) and then buried at the foot of the gallows.

THE BLIND PEOPLE WHO TOOK THEIR REVENGE ON THE DEAD

John Bradshaw, a Cheshire lawyer who had removed to London, was chosen to preside over the Council that tried the king in Westminster Hall. Bradshaw was not present at the meeting which elected him President of the Council, and at first he wished to be excused from taking the office, but as he was urged to consent, he gave way, and he conducted the trial with great sternness. As a convinced Republican, Bradshaw was an outspoken opponent of Cromwell when he feared the Protector might allow himself to accept the kingship. He died before the Restoration, and was buried in the great Abbey, but his body also was brutally dug up, carted away to Tyburn and exposed there.

An indignity only a little less abominable was practised on the body of the heroic Admiral Robert Blake, General of the Sea in the Commonwealth period. It was disinterred from the Abbey by order of Charles the Second and, along with the bodies of Cromwell's mother and daughter, was buried in St. Margaret's churchyard.

Yet Blake had not taken any part in the trial and execution of the king. His offence, in the eyes of the people who were wreaking their revenge on the dead, was that he had been the man who chased Prince Rupert off the seas when the prince tried to continue the Civil War there. That Blake had defended England against attacks from abroad was not counted as patriotism, though again and again the country had offered him enthusiastic thanks for gallant exploits.

THE MOST FAMOUS SEAMAN OF HIS TIME IN THE WORLD

Blake was a Somersetshire man who, after an education at Oxford, became a sea-trading merchant, and then a Member of Parliament. When the war began, he helped to defend Bristol for the Parliament and was the last to surrender. Later he made successful defences of Lyme and Taunton, and then was transferred to a command at sea. Against the Dutch, in many desperate battles, the Spaniards, the Portuguese, and against Algerian and Tunisian pirates, he won great victories that made the open sea a safe highway for British ships. Worn out by incessant toil, he died as he came homeward, the most famous seaman in the world.

Any fair review of Cromwell and the men who gathered about him must admit that, after great patience, they took up arms reluctantly, though the cause they defended was just, for it was resistance to forms of oppression which the laws and traditions of the nation did not allow to kings. They developed in England a sturdy public spirit, and individually they were men of a rare strength of character, who in a time of turmoil and chaos raised the nation to a high level in the opinion of all mankind.

The Great Stories of the World That Will Be Told For Ever

WILLIAM TELL

We do not know whether he lived or not; but he lives in the story books of all the world.

ONE fair day there walked across the market square of Altdorf, in Switzerland, as fine a looking man as one could wish to see. Tall and straight, broad and shapely, with ruddy, bearded face and proudly-held head, this man of the mountains strode with clean, swinging stride across the square, a look of bright happiness in his eyes, and a cheerful word of greeting for his friends.

Many turned to say, " There goes William Tell, the crossbowman of Bürglen."

This man, who was said to be the finest crossbowman in Switzerland and the best handler of a boat on the storm-swept lake of Uri, lived quietly in a mountain cottage with a wife who shared his every thought, and children for whom it was his pleasure and delight to work.

He hunted deer in the mountains, and went a-fishing on the lake. His children never lacked good food and decent clothing. His home was trim and neat. There was no family in that district more firmly established in peace and content.

Tell had sold the pack of deerskins which he had brought with him to Altdorf. He was on his way now to buy winter clothing of warm wool for his children. He had money enough and to spare, and he was in a mood of great happiness. In an hour or

more he would be singing a song on the road to his mountain home.

Suddenly he felt his arm seized, and found himself in the grip of an Austrian soldier. In another instant he was surrounded. The soldier who had seized his arm pointed to a pole with the ducal cap on the top of it.

" It is death not to bow to that cap, and you know it! " said the soldier.

A silence fell upon the whole square. People left their trading and crowded round the group. A thing greater than trade was at stake now—a man's freedom, a nation's liberty.

William Tell had flushed a deeper red. He brought his eyes from the cap on the pole to the soldier's face.

" I have done nothing unlawful," he said slowly.

" You have insulted the majesty of the Duke! " said the soldier.

William Tell kept a steady eye.

" Why," said he, " should a man show more reverence to an empty cap than to any empty cloak or a pair of hose? "

At this there came from behind the soldiers the figure of the governor of the district, the tyrant Gessler.

It was this Gessler who, set over the once free Swiss by their conqueror and oppressor, the Duke of Austria, had trodden liberty under foot, had murdered

IMAGINATION · CHIVALRY · LEGENDS · GOLDEN DEEDS · FAIRY TALES

and imprisoned all who stood against him, and, as a last barbarity, had declared that everyone who did not do homage to the badge of Austrian rule set up on the pole in their market-place should die.

William Tell faced the governor. He feared no man. No man could break his proud spirit. On his mountain he had brooded upon the shame of the slavery which enchained his country, and had already spoken with his friends of resistance. Never, never, would he do homage to the hated badge of the tyrant's mastery.

"So you would make a jest of the sign of majesty?" asked the governor, approaching him, while the soldiers saluted. At that moment there came from the crowd a child's cry of "Father! Father!"

The crowd turned about, opened out, and presently William Tell's little son, who had come without leave to the fair, was rushing to his father.

The governor caught the boy's arm.

"Is this the brave traitor's son?" he asked scornfully.

"Hurt him not," said Tell. "He is my first-born."

"Oh, I won't hurt him!" answered the terrible Gessler. "If any harm should come to him it will not be by me, but by you." A horrible smile lighted his eyes. "Here," said he to a soldier, "take the boy and tie him to the trunk of that linden tree over there, and place an apple on his head."

"What is this for?" demanded Tell.

"I am told that you are called the crossbowman of Bürglen," replied the governor, "and I should like you to give me an exhibition of your skill. Your life is forfeit. But I am in a merciful mood; I will give you a chance of redeeming it. Come, listen to me. If at this distance you can shoot an arrow so as to split the apple on the head of your first-born I will let you go free. If not—if you miss the apple or kill your child—I will execute you, here and now."

"Have you no mercy!" cried Tell, trembling with indignation. "And do you think I will attempt to save my own life at the risk of my son's?"

"I am doing you a favour," replied Gessler. "Think. By a lucky shot you may save your life and go home!"

Tell held out a hand which trembled.

"How can a man who loves his son aim with a steady hand an inch above his temples? Ah, look at the child! My lord, look at him! He is no kin of yours; you know nothing of the pretty ways by which he has climbed into a father's heart, the innocence of his eyes, the beauty of his face! Am I to risk that life?"

Gessler laughed brutally.

"Well, you either shoot or die."

"Then I will die."

"And first your child shall have his neck wrung before your eyes."

A blinding passion of indignation overswept the noble soul of the mountaineer.

"Give me the bow!" he said. "One thing in mercy I ask. Let the child's face be turned away from me."

A way was cleared between father and son. The boy, with his face to the tree, bound by ropes to its trunk, felt the apple weigh like lead upon his head.

A dreadful silence fell upon the market square. William Tell chose two arrows. One he thrust in his girdle; one he fitted to his bow-string. Then for a moment he stood, a little bowed of shoulder, with his eyes downcast; he was praying. You might have heard a leaf fall, so still were the people gathered round.

Then Tell raised his head; his eyes were steady, his hands had become still, his face was like iron. He brought the cross-bow to his shoulder and laid his eye to the feather of the shaft. Twang!

The arrow shot forward, and, as it were at the same moment, buried itself deep in the tree. The apple fell in equal parts on either side of the boy's head.

A roar of cheering went up to Heaven, and Gessler turned to Tell.

"A good shot, traitor!" he said cruelly. "But tell me, for what reason did you take two arrows?"

Tell laid his hand upon the arrow in his girdle.

"If the first arrow had hurt my child," he said, "this one by now would be through your heart!"

"Oh! So I run in danger of my life?" said the governor. "But I will keep the pledge I gave you. You shall not die. I will give you your life. But the rest of that life you will spend in the dungeons of my castle, and your bowstring will not then be a danger to me."

At this, Tell was seized again, and rushed by the soldiers through the scowling mob to the quay where the governor's ship was moored.

"HURT HIM NOT," SAID WILLIAM TELL; "HE IS MY FIRST-BORN"

But as the ship crossed the lake of Uri a storm arose, and it seemed as if everyone would be drowned. The Austrians could not manage the vessel, and began to abandon all hope of saving her.

In their panic they remembered that Tell was reputed to be the best handler of ships in that part of the world, and they spoke to the governor.

"Loose him, and let him take the helm," said Gessler.

Tell got the vessel to right herself, and set her head for the opposite coast. But he was now thinking, not of Gessler and the

Austrian soldiers, but of freedom—his own freedom, and the freedom of Switzerland.

He brought the ship close to a rock that jutted out from the coast, and then sprang suddenly upon that rock, and left the Austrians to save themselves.

Swift of foot, he scaled the rocks, climbed the cliff, and made his way across the mountains to a place on the road which Gessler, if he saved himself, would have to pass. Here he lay concealed among the bushes with an arrow fitted to his bow-string, his heart set on delivering Switzerland from the tyrant.

Presently as he waited there came to him the sound of the tramping of feet.

"And if I live to return to Altdorf," Gessler was saying, " I swear I will destroy the whole brood of this traitor Tell, mother and children, all in the same hour."

" You shall never return ! " said Tell to himself. And, as the soldiers went marching on, he let fly the arrow, and Gessler dropped dead in the dust.

William Tell inspired the rising of the Swiss people which led to the overthrow of the Austrians and made Switzerland a free country.

They would have made him king, but he shook his head, and went back to his home among the mountains, which was more to him than many palaces.

THE FRIEND OF THE WITHERED TREE

NEAR the city of Benares there was once a great forest which trembled one noon to the steps of a god. Indra of the Thousand Eyes came walking through the earthly groves. Even in Heaven he had hardly seen fresher leaves or more beautiful cascades of blossom.

Then, in the midst of this luxuriant life, he came on a great tree which was withered and blotched and rotten.

Indra approached the dying tree, and was amazed to see a parrot sitting on its boughs looking lean and sickly.

"What are you doing there, foolish bird ? " he cried. " Are there not fair and fruitful trees enough? Why do you sit in the shadows of decay? "

The parrot bowed till its beak touched its claws, and replied:

" Glorious king! Once this tree was peerless in its beauty and strength. I was born under its leaves; I learned to fly from one of its branches; here, since my earliest days, I have found shelter and

friendship. But the other day a hunter's poisoned arrow glanced aside into its bark, and its sap has turned to fire, and it is dying. O king, how could I leave the tree in its misfortunes? "

Indra was moved.

" Lowly bird! " he cried, " I would that men also were as true and compassionate to their friends ! I will reward your devotion by granting you any boon you may ask."

The parrot did not hesitate.

" Restore the tree, great king," it said, " and I will sing your praises for ever."

Indra laid his hand on the bark. Instantly the fungus and mildew dropped away, the rotten leaves fell to the ground, fresh sap darted through its boughs, impetuous as a spring river, and buds of green and crimson burst out on every twig.

Wise is he who chooses a friend like the tree's; blessed is he who has a heart, compassionate and grateful like the heart of the parrot.

THE ANGEL OF THE DIMPLES

AN angel, about to leave the world, saw a child sleeping in some long grass.

" What a lovely child! " exclaimed the angel. " Surely it must have been stolen from Heaven."

And to make quite sure that the little one really belonged to the earth, and that its body was made of perishable stuff, the angel, with two fingers of his divine hand, fingers rosy with the beauty and tint of Heaven, touched the baby cheeks.

He touched them quite close to the mouth on each side of the lips, at the place

where ends the circle of the smiles. Then, reassured, the angel said: " The child is really human after all," and, leaving the child alone, the angel flew away.

But where they had rested his fingers had left their prints.

That is why, the story goes, on each of a baby's cheeks, when it smiles, two little dimples appear—two pretty little dimples of the angels!

That is why we so often amuse ourselves by making them laugh, just to see the dimples from the angels of Heaven.

IN THE STRANGE HOUSE

ONE day a scholar fell into talk with an Irish peasant who was resting for a while from his work.

They spoke of what they both loved, the old stories of their country, and although the scholar thought he knew all that books could tell him on the subject, he soon found that the peasant knew more. Songs and stories that can live for hundreds of years without the help of being written down must be good ones indeed; here is the pretty tale of Dermot that the professor heard for the first time from the peasant.

First let it be told that Dermot was a famous character in Irish legend, something like our Lancelot, belonging to an order of Chivalry that corresponds to our Round Table. He was as remarkable for his comeliness as his valour. It is recorded that he had bright-blue eyes, ruddy-brown cheeks, and hair that shone under his helmet. On his forehead was a little mark, and the peasant's story relates how Dermot came by it.

Once, when Dermot and three other knights were hunting, they went astray into a dark and desolate country. They wandered

SHE PUT HER FINGER ON HIS FOREHEAD

there for some time, until at nightfall they came to a hut. They knocked on the door. A voice bade them enter. Dermot lifted the latch, and they saw an old man, a lovely maiden, a ram, and a cat, all assembled together before a blazing hearth.

When Dermot asked for shelter the old man bade the strangers welcome, but there was an air of something strange about him and about everything in the hut.

A meal was prepared for the guests in silence. As they were about to partake of it the ram leapt up on to the table. One of the knights seized him by the fleece to fling him down, yet, though he wrestled with all his force, he could not move the creature. One after another his companions struggled with the ram, and one after another these mighty champions were discomfited.

Then the old man told the cat to fetch it down. She overcame the ram in a moment, threw it to the ground, and drove it to a corner, where it lay down meekly to be tethered.

The old man said to the mortified knights: "You need not hang your heads, spear-men. The ram is the World, and the cat is Death, who overcomes all things."

At these words the knights were more amazed than ever, and they slept little, partly for the wonder of what they had heard, and partly for love of the maiden whose beauty made a soft light about her in the darkness.

In the morning when they made ready to go one of the knights took courage and asked her to be his wife.

"No," she said, "I belonged to you once, and I never can again."

He stood astonished, for he was certain that he had never seen her before. The same reply she made to all, but to Dermot she said: "Ah, Dermot! I belonged to you once, and I never can again, for I am Youth who never returns. But I will make you a gift so that all others shall love you in my stead."

She put her finger tip on his forehead, and it left a little shining mark. From that hour everyone who saw Dermot loved him.

Then the knights rode away very pensive; and never again could they discover the desolate place, or the maiden who was called Youth.

THE THIRTEENTH MAN

THE story of Heligoland is going to surprise you very much.

For us this word means a naval base: it means ruthless war; it will always bring to the minds of this generation a picture of a grim fortified island in the grey North Sea, bristling with huge guns, a haven for deadly submarines, a fortress rock that was at last dismantled by the Allies after the Second World War.

Yet this sinister place is called Holy-land, and its legend is a tale of peace.

Tradition says that a long time ago the Frisians determined to draw up a code of laws. They entrusted this solemn task to their twelve noblest men. First, the elders collected the rules that various tribes and powerful families had made for them-selves; from these they meant to frame one code which should serve for all the Frisian people. A quiet place was neces-sary for their discussions, so the twelve set sail for a certain isolated spot.

But Aegir, the savage sea-god, seems to have had no kindness for law-makers. He sent a storm which blew them far out of their course. The boat was tossed help-lessly about, and it looked as if the twelve men would perish, and with them half the wisdom of the Frisians.

Then they thought of the gentle god Forseti. In Asgard, that home of the violent and battle-loving Northern Deities, he was the law-giver and peace-maker. As the patron of justice and reason the elders called upon him in their peril.

All at once they became aware of a thirteenth man on board. Silently he took the rudder, and steered the boat into the teeth of the storm. The twelve men felt as if their lips were sealed and their limbs enchanted.

Presently land appeared. The boat ran aground. The new-comer stepped out, and flung his axe; where it struck the ground there gushed up a stream of water. He drank of it, and sat down. The twelve men followed his example in awed silence.

Then, in a low, ringing voice he began to expound a code of laws. It was so clear that a child could understand it, so just that the most subtle mind could not find fault with it. As the twelve listened entranced they felt that divine justice itself was speaking.

Suddenly the voice ceased, and there were only twelve men sitting together on the shore.

" Forseti has been here! " they cried.

The code which was so miraculously dictated to them became the law of the Frisian people. The place where it hap-pened was called Holyland in honour of Forseti's visit. All the great councils of justice were held there, and each man who took part in them first drank silently of the cold spring in token of allegiance to pure justice. If any quarrelled or shed blood on the island he was held accursed.

Such was the tradition of the place. Even the most avaricious Viking did not dare to raid its sacred shores ; all the Northern nations looked upon it as the place of peace; none dreamed that it could ever belong to Tyr, the sword-god!

THE PROUD KING OF KAMERA

THE Negro king of Kamera, in Africa, was a proud, stern man, and his men feared him, and instantly carried out his slightest wishes. But one day, when he was boasting that all men were his servants, a wise old Negro called Boukabar reproached him, saying: "All men are servants of one another."

" So I am your servant, am I ? " said the king in great anger. " Then prove it. Force me to work for you before sunset, and I will give you a hundred cows. Fail, and I will kill you."

" Very well," said Boukabar.

Being a very old man he had to use a stick in walking, and just as he took it up to go out a beggar came to the door.

" Permit me," said Boukabar, " to give this poor man something to eat."

Taking some food in both hands, he tottered past the king, and his stick slipped from under his arm and got entangled in his dress, and nearly tripped him up. And he cried to the king: " Please pick up the stick, or I shall fall."

The king picked it up without thinking, and Boukabar then laughed merrily and exclaimed: " You see, all good men are servants of one another. I am waiting on the beggar, and you are waiting on me. But I do not want the cows. Give them to this poor man."

The king did so, and took Boukabar as his chief counsellor.

THE STORY THAT HAD NO END

THERE was a certain king who was very fond of hearing stories.

To this amusement he gave up all his time; for ever he listened to tales, yet he was never satisfied. All the exertions of his courtiers were in vain. The more he heard, the more he wanted to hear. At last he made a proclamation that if any man would tell him a story that lasted for ever he would make him his heir, and give him the princess, his daughter, in marriage; but if anyone should pretend that he could tell such a story, and should fail—that is, if the story did come to an end—he was to have his head chopped off.

For such a rich prize as a beautiful princess and a kingdom many candidates appeared; and dreadfully long were the stories that some of them told. Some lasted a week, some a month, some six months: poor fellows, they all spun them out as long as they possibly could, we may be sure; but all in vain; sooner or later they all came to an end, and, one after another, the unlucky storytellers had their heads chopped off.

At last a man came who said that he had a story which would last for ever, if his Majesty would be pleased to give him a trial and listen.

He was warned of his danger; they told him how many others had tried and lost their heads; but he said he was not afraid, and so he was brought before the king. He was a man of a very composed and deliberate manner of speaking; and, after making all requisite stipulations for time for his eating, drinking, and sleeping, he thus began his story:

"O King, there was once a king who was a great tyrant; and, desiring to increase his riches, he seized upon all the corn and grain in his kingdom, and put it into an immense granary, which he built on purpose, as high as a mountain.

"This he did for several years, till the granary was quite full to the top. He then stopped up doors and windows, and closed it up fast on all sides.

"But the bricklayers had, by accident, left a very small hole near the top of the granary. And there came a flight of locusts and tried to get at the corn; but the hole was so small that only one locust could pass through it at a time.

"So one locust went in and carried off one grain of corn; and then another locust went in and carried off another grain of corn; and then another locust went in and carried off another grain of corn; and then another locust went in and carried off another grain of corn; and then another locust went in and carried off another grain of corn——"

He had gone on thus from morning to night, except while he was engaged at his meals, for about a month. Then the king, though a very patient king, began to be rather tired of the locusts, and interrupted his story with:

"Well, well, we have had enough of the locusts; we will suppose that they have all the corn they wanted; tell us what happened afterwards."

The storyteller answered, very deliberately: "If it please your Majesty, it is impossible to tell you what happened afterwards before I have told you what happened first."

The king listened with admirable patience six months more, when he again interrupted him with: "O friend, I am weary of your locusts! How soon do you think they will have done?"

To which the storyteller made answer: "O King, who can tell? At the time to which my story has come the locusts have cleared away a small space, it may be a cubit each way, round the inside of the hole, and the air is still dark with locusts on all sides; but let the king have patience, and no doubt we shall come to the end of them in time."

Thus encouraged, the king listened on for another full year, the storyteller still going on as before.

At last the poor king could bear it no longer, and cried out:

"O man, that is enough! Take my daughter, take my kingdom, take anything, take everything, only let us hear no more of those abominable locusts."

And so the storyteller was married to the king's daughter, and was declared heir to the throne; and nobody ever expressed a wish to hear the rest of his story, for he said it was impossible to come to the other part of it till he had done with the locusts.

The folly of the foolish king was thus at last stopped by the ingenious device of a very wise man.

THE WILD WORLD COUSINS OF THE DOG

LONG-EARED FOX

MANED WOLF

CAPE HUNTING DOG

THE BUSH DOG OF GUIANA

FENNEC FOX

DESERT FOX

BLACK-BACKED JACKAL

SILVER GREY FOX

SIBERIAN WILD DOG

COYOTE OR PRAIRIE WOLF

SIBERIAN WOLF

Nature's Wonderful Living Family in Earth and Air and Sea

An Arctic fox out in a blizzard

THE WILD DOGS

WHEREVER men venture into the wilds, a creeping murmur is heard. It is the voice of the dog tribe, stirring in the night-time.

Wolf, jackal, fox, and wild dog, they are spread like a living coverlet over the greater part of the Earth. Where we go, there they are, before us or in pursuit. Where we can barely maintain life, they find food; where we starve and die, they can flourish. Let us look at their haunts.

Sledging through the Russian night, Miss Marsden, an English missionary, says to her driver: " The cold and darkness make me afraid. Let us shelter in one of those cottages whose lights I see."

" Madame," answers the Russian, " they are not cottage windows that you see; *they are the eyes of wolves.*"

When 25 men lay dead in that expedition which enabled Bering to discover the strait which bears his name, it took a dozen men hours to bury a comrade; not because of snow and icy sand, but because hundreds of little white and blue foxes fought wildly for the body.

The man who takes his life in his hands to seek for hidden gold in Alaska finds there a grim, grey giant stalking him from afar.

" Who goes there ? " he cries.

" Wolf! " is the answer which does not come to his question.

A sound disturbs the quiet of the prairie darkness, and the Red Indian, with his ear to the ground, explains its meaning in a word, " Coyotes."

In the raging heat of India a tiger, lord of so much and so many, is seen fighting a running retreat with a changing cloud of animals worrying at his flanks. In the morning, where the fight has ended, a strip or two of striped hide and a dismal wreck of carcase are found, and hunters know that the wild dogs were the victors.

From a noble tomb in a silent city of India, where splendour and magnificence once proclaimed the power and majesty of the rajah now within the tomb, steals a lurking figure to cry to the rising moon. It is a jackal, reigning where mysterious tragedy has vanquished human grandeur. The jungle has come back to the city, and the jackal, whose kind were there before the city, has ventured in and made his home in the abode of death.

So, wherever the eye may turn, this great tribe is either in possession as original owners, or surging back where civilisation has failed, or disputing right of way with us as we breast the current of wild life which is their home.

Brains and courage have made this widespread tribe what it is. The dogs have not a pawful of talons between them.

PREHISTORIC LIFE · MAMMALS · BIRDS · REPTILES · FISHES · INSECTS

They are blunt-nailed, so they cannot climb trees after the fashion of leopard and jaguar, nor pull prey down with their claws like a lion. But they have grand teeth, they have sturdy limbs, they have speed and endurance, which carry them fast and far from the setting of the sun until the dawn. They have the wit to combine, to hunt in concert, and they are in intelligence far above the cats, their natural enemies.

THE UNCONQUERABLE WOLF, KING OF ALL THE GALLOPING TRIBES

They are one of the most courageous, fierce, and venturesome of all the animal groups, and it is thrilling to remember that from this assembly our rude forefathers took his first partner in life—the first of man's aids to hunting, his first guide in the dismal wilds, the first sentinel to guard the little cave he called his home.

King of all the galloping host is the unconquerable wolf, an animal whose history in relation to the human family is the most impressive in all life's annals. It is nothing to him that he has given hostages to man. It is nothing to him that some of his line have been wooed to service with human beings.

He remains a splendid and terrible savage, worth his place assured in the scheme of nature by reason of his audacity, his cunning, his ability to front adversity and counter changing conditions with modified tactics. Civilisation has advanced with all its armament against him. He has given ground on a broad front, but he has doubled back, broken through on our flanks, and is still a terror in lands civilised for over two thousand years.

THE TERRIBLE ANIMAL PERSISTING THROUGH AGES OF PERSECUTION

In spite of the organised measures of a population numbering scores of millions, the wolf is still with us, and remains the most formidable and deadly animal in Europe after thousands of years of persecution. His hold on life is marvellous. He no longer shares Great Britain with us, but he was here two centuries ago. The enclosure of land made it possible to slay all the wolves in our little islands, but Europe is big, and the wolf is there.

Don Quixote travelled to glorious and comic adventures in Spain, and made rare havoc with his tilting at windmills, but he might have had really good hunting had he set his lance against wolves. For the land of that delightful hero still has wolves. Smiling France still has these terrors, too, lurking in her dim, mysterious woods. Italy, with oranges and lemons ripening in her golden valleys, looks with foreboding to the innocent-looking Apennines, for wolves hide there in summer. But when snow and famine touch the hills, they launch themselves on the plains to devour sheep and cattle, and in their raging hunger they assail human beings.

In any year when conditions menace wild life, the same story may be traced. Take the winter of 1921-1922, for example. At a time when French wolves were spreading terror in the department of Meurthe-et-Moselle, wolves tracing back to wolves that Caesar hunted swarmed down into the plains of Northern Italy and attacked human beings as their ancestors attacked before Italy was a civilised land. At the same time the Rumanian wolves were out in the Ploesti district, killing in one night five peasants and injuring 30 more. As for Russia and Asia generally, a whole literature of tragedy might be written on the sad tale of life sacrificed to make wolf feasts.

GIANT WOLVES AND PYGMIES, COYOTES AND JACKALS

Our European wolves are small compared with the great timber wolf of America, and puny compared with the giant wolf of Alaska. This Alaska wolf is a superb animal, nearly six feet from the muzzle to the tip of the tail, and almost 32 inches high, and with a head which suggests a great bear.

Dimensions such as those enable us to imagine the outline of some of the terrific beasts which once flourished in the dog family, and attained the size of polar bears! They are gone to the kingdom of fossils, and today it is not the largest wolf that is most feared. It is the European species which carries off the palm for ferocity. Men who have met both would rather grapple the giant of Alaska than the smaller animal in Spain or Scandinavia.

Probably the reason is simple—that European wolves have been so long in contact with massed humanity that the necessity of living under fiercely competitive conditions has permitted only the most savage and audacious to survive. The fight between man and wolf in Alaska, and in the wide ranges of the timber wolf, has yet to grow intense.

All over Europe, except in Britain and North and Central Germany ; over wide spaces of Russia; throughout the greater part of Asia as far east as Japan and ranging throughout North America, the wolf still clings with fierce teeth to life.

Yet, wide as is the distribution of the group, it has its curious gaps. Wolves are not found in Africa—though dogs are there. They are not found in South America proper. Yet down in the Falkland Islands, in conditions so inclement that the wind blows the grain out of the growing ears of corn—there we have wolves, an amazing

separated by 250 miles of deep sea from Patagonia, the nearest land, there are no other wolves south of Mexico, yet here these make their home. The man who solves this mystery will add a first-class romance to the wonders of animal distribution. There is no other case in the world where so small and broken a landmass, far from a mainland, has ever supported so large a native animal. It is to be feared that the Antarctic wolf will not long enjoy his supremacy, for his tribe is almost exterminated.

The coyotes, from which these mysteries

A PACK OF SNARLING WOLVES ON THE HUNT FOR FOOD

fact. Ordinary wolves move in packs, and that mainly at night. The so-called Antarctic wolves of the Falklands stalk about by daylight, singly, or at most in family groups. They do not, like the majority of the dog tribes, hide in rocks or indeed anywhere above ground, but burrow like foxes.

They have distinctive features, unique fur and peculiar size, neither that of wolf nor coyote, though apparently they sprang from coyote strain. But how came they in the Falklands ? These British islands are

apparently sprang, belong entirely to North America, half a world away, though the stress of existence has driven later generations south as far as Costa Rica in Central America. In common with its island relative, the coyote will burrow; but it packs, it has the true wolf cry on the hunt, and it is not dangerous to man, except when desperately pressed by famine.

But we must turn to the jackal, which the East calls " The Belly That Runs on Four Feet." Asia and Africa are the home of this industrious scavenger, but South-

Eastern Europe still has its jackal packs. There are several species, and all can be tamed, but they are unreliable when grown up. Nearly all wild animals are.

They slink through life as parasites, occupying in freedom much the position that homeless mongrels have in some cities.

They kill birds, young animals, and so on, and they eat anything from a lizard to a banana or a coffee-berry. But they take service with the swaggering tyrants of the wilds. When lion or tiger has made its kill and filled itself, up come the jackals to fight with the gorging vultures for the broken remains. And the curious thing is that where men go out to hunt, these timid and confiding creatures follow, just as they follow the great cats—to snap up anything left by the lord of the gun. They will clear a carcase in a night.

But we must not forget the service they render to towns and villages where sanitation is an unknown science. Holes are left in walls and stockades to enable the jackals to creep through at night. Anything which a jaw can master is food to the scavenger. A saddle or a pair of boots, left out by accident, goes the same way as a skeleton.

Horrible fevers and pestilence arise in such centres of human life, and Europeans die like stricken birds. But what would happen were it not for the loathsome feastings of the nightly jackal brigades?

THE TERRIBLE WORK OF A WOLF WITH 78 CAMELS

Well, these two groups, the wolves and the jackals, have given the world " the friend of man," for they are the ancestors of the dog. What a life of terror our ancestors must have lived when breaking in the enemy of the flock to become the guardian of the fold. Again and again, one fancies, there must have been scenes such as were witnessed in 1906 in a little British camp out in Seistan, on the borders of Afghanistan and Persia. Our party was marking out a boundary amid hundreds of miles of wild, inhospitable country thronged with wild beasts. Jackals and wolves abound there, and as sometimes happens to domestic dogs at home, the jackals were seized with the madness we call hydrophobia. That was bad enough, but the mad jackals attacked the wolves, and those in turn became mad. The natives, fearing that their dogs might be infected, killed them all, and so left themselves defenceless against the raging packs around their homes.

One fearful night, when the wave of animal frenzy was at its height, a pack of wolves attacked the camp, all raving. By some miracle of courage the men in camp beat off the howling terrors, but a worse night and a worse adventure followed. With a wind blowing at 120 miles an hour, a lone, ravening wolf, with madness heightened by the horror of the night, set out on a mission of hate. Before he could be detected he had bounded with blood-curdling howls into the little settlement. He bit like fifty wolves. He sank his envenomed teeth in the flesh of a horse; he leapt into the camel lines. Like an embodied fury he ran from animal to animal, biting each as he came to it so that before he could be killed he made his foaming teeth meet through the legs of 78 camels.

THE BRAVE TAMERS OF THE WOLF WHO GAVE US THE DOG

Imagine a camp with a horse and about fifty camels mad with hydrophobia! Imagine the fearful potency of the poison borne on the teeth of the one evil-working animal. Well, that staggering little picture from a dark night in Seistan must have had many forerunners during the ages when man lived always in the wilds, exposed to similar dangers. Do we not feel the prouder of our sad-browed forbears for triumphing over such horrors and bringing in from them a dog to help us through the toils and trials of life beneath the stars?

There is one animal which is wolf in name only, and that is the maned wolf, which is a long-legged, foxy-eared wild dog, whose lengthy coat, exaggerated on the back of the neck, suggests a mane which exists less in fact than in the description. Solitary, timid, and inoffensive, this curious animal has Brazil, Paraguay and Northern Argentina for its home; and where its borders end those of several small species of fox-like dogs begin.

DOGS THAT EAT FRUIT AND DOGS THAT CATCH CRABS

Azara's dog is the title which describes this group. They are commonly called foxes, but they are more allied to wolves and jackals, and range from Paraguay and the Chilean Andes down to Patagonia and Tierra del Fuego, a stretch of territory never reached by foxes. These dogs have a diet which embraces fruit, and that peculiarity is shared by several local races

FOXES, JACKALS, & WOLVES OF THE WORLD

NORTH AFRICAN JACKAL

TIBETAN MASTIFF

AMERICAN TIMBER WOLF

ARCTIC FOX

HIMALAYAN FOX

ASIATIC JACKAL

SCARCE WILD DOG OF TIBET

PALAEARCTIC WOLF

AUSTRALIAN DINGO

WOOLLY WOLF

INDIAN WOLF

CRAB-EATING DOG

COMMON FOX

of South American animals whose crab-catching habits give them the name of crab-eating dogs. These are creatures of the jungle and forest, where another fox-like type, the colpeo, is also to be found. Another fisher of the waters is the raccoon dog, an Old World species wonderfully resembling the raccoon in build, and found in Japan, China, and Amurland. Fish is only part of its diet, and those members of the group which have not this commodity available, sleep away the winter fasting, a unique distinction among dogs.

The true wild dogs are confined to Asia and Africa. The Asian species are big, bold animals which pack and hunt anything that runs on four legs. The African representative of the breed, the African hunting dog, is similar in habit, and runs down the swiftest antelope—an amazing feat, but the species seems to stand among untamed dogs where the greyhound stands among the domestic breeds.

HOW TRICKY REYNARD JUSTIFIES HIS REPUTATION FOR CUNNING

Amid the snows, on the plains, in the forest and jungle, dogs are everywhere, and when we come to Brazil and Guiana, we have specialised dogs, too. These are called bush dogs, extraordinary little creatures resembling badgers, foxes, and martens. They are shy and retiring, but very fierce. Though we know little about them, they are an old variety, as we know from fossil remains in Brazilian caves.

Wide as is the range of these animals, the range of the foxes is even more extensive. The fox is at home throughout Europe and Asia, from Ireland to Japan. It is in America, and in Africa north of the Sudan, and the Sahara desert. As might be expected, a great variety of species has developed in widely-differing conditions.

The common fox of Britain is the most astute of all wild animals left to us, and we might feel inclined to attribute its skill and cunning to its long competition with its surrounding foes. But high intelligence marks all the species. How well our British example lives up to its reputation for cleverness we all know. Its tricks to baffle hounds are almost incredible. Crossing a stream repeatedly to destroy its scent, running through flocks of sheep to hide the same fatal clue, leaping from heap to heap of farm produce rather than continue on level ground where its scent would lie, climbing seemingly impossible

places, hiding where one would think a rabbit could not conceal itself—in these and a thousand ways agile Reynard justifies his title to exceeding intelligence.

Poultry, game, young lambs and fawns, insects and frogs, are among his food, and his daring in getting his meals is at times astonishing.

THE STOUT-HEARTED LITTLE WELSHMAN AND HIS FORTY MILES RUN

We have more than one variety of fox in Great Britain. There is the common red beauty which we all hate and admire by turn; there is the stout-hearted little Welshman which can cover 30 or 40 miles of mountaineering at a stretch and then escape; and there is the long-legged, fleet-footed masterpiece of Cumberland and Westmorland of whose grandsire John Peel sang his song.

Fruit, carrion, fish, reptiles, birds, and animals which are young and small or enfeebled when adult, yield food to foxes of various sizes, colours, and other distinctive peculiarities throughout Europe, India, Siberia, China, and Arabia. Black fox, silver fox, grey fox, the Arctic fox which is blue in summer and white in winter, the little kit fox which runs like the wind, the desert fox of south-western Asia whose entire living depends on the flesh of the gerbils; the corsac fox which is under ground by day and comes out to banquet at night on little rodents of the Central Asian deserts; the neat and nimble little Indian fox, fat from a diet of land-crabs, grasshoppers and beetles; the sand foxes and fennecs of Africa which burrow almost as quickly as a dog could dive into water—these are among the species into which the fox family has branched out. Their origin from a common ancestry is obvious. Their variety of size, colour, homes, and habits is another object-lesson in Nature's way of making animals fit their surroundings.

THE WILD DOGS THAT STILL SNAP AT THE HEELS OF CIVILISATION

No race of animals has done more to arouse enmity among men than these members of the family which has given man his greatest animal friend, the dog; for where civilisation marches up to their frontier they live at our expense. There is a constant challenge out to them from men. But they were here before us, they are with us still, and they will continue where they are until towns cover their lairs. There is life in the Dog Tribe yet.

The March of Man from the Age of Barbarism to the United Nations

Israel in Slavery—By Sir Edward Poynter, from an Autotype photograph

MAN BEGINS TO THINK OF GOD

THE most bewildering fact in the history of the human mind is the spring it suddenly makes in times of great crises toward a grandeur and even a sublimity which seem so out of reach for normal people as to be almost non-human.

We talk about the Evolution of Man, and that useful but dangerous phrase tends to make our thoughts false to the everlasting records of history. We think of a savage slowly emerging from the complete darkness of ignorance to the light of the present times, his orderly and unbroken evolution checked only by war and disease.

This is a wholly wrong idea. There is no smooth line of progress from savagery to civilisation. It is not even a spiral of ascent and descent. It is a thing indescribable by a phrase of any kind. Far back in the mists of antiquity there were men greater than any man of the present time, and even in the history of our still youthful Europe we look back to periods of grandeur in architecture, poetry, painting, and music which we are convinced will never be excelled.

Therefore, let us think of the development of the human mind as a wonderful part in the spiritual mystery of existence, guarding ourselves from thinking of it as anything mechanical, or anything which can be wholly controlled by the schoolmaster and the statesman.

The incident of the Hebrew slaves who escaped from Egypt and made their way into Syria will help us to think more correctly of the history of man's mind.

These people had a feeling for nature unknown among other nations. They loved beauty ; they felt the glory of the Earth in their blood like a passion. Moreover, they had ideas about human life which were altogether superior to those of other people. Slaves they had been, and slaves of a nation so sunk in superstition that it placed food and raiment in the graves of its dead, that they might not be hungry or naked in the next world. Yet these slaves, sweltering in the Egyptian sunshine, and cowering under the lash of their cruel taskmasters, cherished in their minds an idea of the world nobly grander than that of the Egyptians who despised them.

How are we to account for this ? Whence came to the Hebrew slave his idea of one supreme God, ruling the whole universe, *and making for righteousness* ? We can only answer that he was inspired. As Shakespeare was inspired above all other poets, and Michael Angelo above all other sculptors, and Handel and Beethoven above all other musicians, so

MIGHTY EPOCHS OF THE WORLD & MAN'S WONDERFUL ADVENTURES

the Hebrews were inspired above all other nations in the truth of the universe.

By some power of which we have no knowledge, they broke the heavy chain which bound the soul of man in the prison-house of superstition. They took a leap in history which has never been equalled since. At a single stroke they flung off the craven fears of the Egyptian and all the dark forebodings of man's past, and stood up in the hills of Syria, singing songs of liberation and joy, as though conscious of the presence of God.

THE HEBREWS GIVE UP GRAVEN IMAGES AND WORSHIP THE TRUE GOD

Think for a moment of such utterances as these: "The morning stars sang together, and all the sons of God shouted for joy"; or, "Man doth not live by bread alone"; or, "The heavens declare the glory of God; and the firmament showeth His handywork"—marvellous phrases these.

The Egyptians had worshipped animals; other nations around them had worshipped gods made half in the image of men and half of animals; almost all these gods were horrible, repulsive, and contemptible. But the God of the escaped Hebrew slaves was the Power in the universe which was working for righteousness, and so sublime was He, so glorious beyond all human imagining, that they would suffer no one to make an image of Him.

This absence of any graven image in the ritual of the Hebrews made an enormous difference to the history of the human mind. It drove the Hebrews to an *inward-ness* which we now know to be the rock and strength of all true religion. Their religious thoughts were always turned inward upon themselves. "The righteous God trieth the hearts and reins." God was no idol made with hands, but a Spirit who read the secrets of the heart, and the demands of God were the demands of morality—no murder, no stealing, no lying, no envy, no mutiny in the heart, the home, and the nation.

THE HIGHEST WORSHIP IS TO LOVE RIGHTEOUSNESS AND WALK NOBLY

Thus could they best worship Him—by loving righteousness and walking up-rightly. He had chosen them; they were to enlighten the world; through them the Earth was to be blessed and all the nations brought into the way of peace. Note in particular that the Hebrews laid stress on the reality of this divine Power by speaking of Him as the *living* God. They felt His presence in the loveliness of the Earth and His voice in the whisper of their own conscience.

Remember that all this was a sudden uprush of the human mind into spiritual consciousness. It had not been prepared by other nations. It was not a mere development. It was not something the Hebrews had picked up here and there and so pieced together. In no literature of past times is there anything in the least comparable with the ancient scriptures of these extraordinary people—these Semitic tribes spreading themselves over Palestine, fighting their enemies like barbarians, practising cruelties which shock and appal us, plunging into a racial vanity which disgusts us; but all the way through their astonishing history holding up to the gaze of mankind the idea of a living God whose concern was the moral law.

MOSES THE FIRST HEALTH MINISTER AND THE FOUNDER OF SANITATION

Remarkable, too, is the fact that in the beginning of this wonderful religion the idea of immortality had no place. The Israelite was told to act rightly for the sake of rightness, not in the hope of entering Heaven or escaping Hell. It is true he was taught that righteousness brings a blessing here upon Earth, but the best of these Hebrews held that righteousness was its own reward, and one of them exclaimed, in words which are now known throughout the whole world: "The Lord gave, and the Lord hath taken away; blessed be the name of the Lord!" and "Though He slay me, yet will I trust in Him."

This spirit, so marvellous in a primitive people recently escaped from slavery, did not confine itself only to the contemplation of the divine Majesty. The Hebrews became the first nation seriously to perceive the immense importance of health. In them we find the fountain head of the whole science of sanitation. Moses, it has been said, was the really first great health statesman.

Again we must stop and strive to put out of our heads the thought that we are reading a history of the Israelites. Again we must remind ourselves that we are studying the history of the human soul. We have seen that soul waiting for its prey with stone and cudgel; we have seen it leaving the forest for the cave, the cave for the town; and we have seen it watching the stars, observing the seasons, investigating the mysteries of the Earth, inventing language and writing, becoming husbandman, astronomer, artist, author and physician; and finally we have seen it cowering before death, trembling at the sound of thunder, and offering up pitiful sacrifices to the fearsome gods who seemed to be bent on its destruction.

THE SOUL OF MAN FLINGS OFF THE CHAINS OF SUPERSTITION

All of a sudden, and in a place where it might least be expected, this soul of man rescues itself from superstition, flings off the chains of slavery, feels itself to be in the hands of a righteous God, and bursts into songs of gladness which have never been excelled in any religion of the world.

At the same moment, too, the soul of man becomes enthusiastic about personal cleanliness, and breaks away, not only from the spiritual defilements of slavery and superstition, but from the physical defilement of uncleanness. Moral law becomes supreme over human life, the home becomes a centre of instruction and deep love, disease is fought with the intelligence which recognises in cleanliness a great ally.

It is a jump into the future. It is as if Life had felt itself imperilled by the worship of superstition, checked by the hard and fast rules of the priests, and had found in these strange Hebrew slaves an opening for one of those tremendous springs forward which, in times of stagnation, save humanity from slipping back into the barbarism of the past. Along Egyptian lines there was no hope of progress, and a grave danger of falling back; but in Israel there was this opportunity for a plunge ahead, a dash toward the future, which would save mankind from the fearful risk of moral downfall and a return to primitive savagery.

THE AMAZING MOVEMENT OF MIND IN THE DAYS OF MOSES

However we may try to interpret it, certainly there was a movement of mind in the days of Moses which will for ever fill the student of history with amazement. If you would see how a student of history feels about this astonishing spiritual uprush, glance at the headlines of a daily newspaper, particularly a Sunday newspaper, and then read the 38th chapter of Job, the 103rd Psalm, and the 53rd chapter of Isaiah. It will seem to you that the newspaper must have been printed in a barbaric age, and that the other words are the final utterance of the highest spirits of the human race.

Glorious and incomprehensible as was this tremendous movement of the mind, tragedy was to overtake it. The mass of the Israelites kept the sanitary law, and remained true to the idea of one supreme God; but the passion of this first impulse went from them, they became formal, and they set their thoughts more on earthly well-being and comfort than on direct spiritual experience.

Some seven hundred years before the birth of Jesus the kingdom of Israel fell before the sword of Assyria, and the ten tribes were again carried off into slavery. Two hundred and fifty years later the kingdom of Judah fell to Babylon, and it seemed that never again was Palestine to be free from an alien despotism.

THE IDEA THAT WAS TO LEAVEN THE LIFE OF ALL MANKIND

But Life is concerned with the mind of man, not with empires and kings, and in Israel it had made a contribution to the history of mind which is immortal. Henceforth the idea of one supreme God was to leaven the life of the human race, the thought of righteousness was to inspire all the greatest of mankind, and to give a new beauty and a rich content to family life, while the notion of cleanliness was to work like magic in the sphere of science, and to make huge cities like London a possibility of the future.

Let us make it an immovable part of all our thinking that a little body of slaves from Egypt, suddenly inspired by the beauty and majesty of the Earth, held fast the idea of a Power in the universe which made for righteousness, found in the worship and adoration of this invisible Power a strength and gladness hitherto unknown among men, and burned into the consciousness of the human race a sense of moral law which continues to operate to this day.

Such a sense of the Divine, present constantly in our inmost thoughts, will give to our lives a dignity they must otherwise lack, sustain us with loftier hopes, shape our conduct when inherited faults assail us and, if it be widely felt, will have a social influence causing us to live more happily with our neighbours.

(Next chapter in this group, page 671)

THE BRIDGE WORKSHOP DOWN IN THE RIVER

A bridge must support the weight of the materials in it, as well as the loads it has to carry, and it must withstand snow, wind, and storms. What we call the cantilever in bridges is simply an overhanging bracket which would tend to overturn ; but if two cantilevers are built out simultaneously from opposite sides they will counterbalance one another. Each of the sitting men here represents a double cantilever. The outer sticks are tied to weights and cannot collapse inwards, and the inner sticks fixed to the chairs support a board the weight on which is equally distributed, and so easily carried.

In making foundations for a bridge men work inside what is called a caisson, a large chamber sunk to the bed of the river. This picture shows a caisson 70 feet wide, built of stout wrought-iron plates, in position at the Forth Bridge. At the bottom of the caisson is a working chamber seven feet high, lighted by electricity and filled with compressed air.

As the men dig away the river bed the caisson, which has a sharp steel edge at the bottom, sinks into it, and more plates may have to be added at the top to keep the water out.

The Story of the Things We See About Us Every Day

The wonderful Forth Bridge in Scotland

FOOTPATHS IN THE AIR

No one can say who built the first bridge. Nature herself would no doubt be man's first teacher. Man would find a path across a chasm by clinging to a twisted vine; or he would see a ready-made bridge consisting of a fallen tree-trunk lying across a stream. Those were the first bridges, and they were the sort which were made for hundreds of years.

One day a genius arose who dumped high heaps of stone on a line across a stream, and on the top of these placed slabs of slate or stone or fallen trees. Then, a long, long while afterwards, came bigger, real bridges. The Romans were the first to learn how to make these. They built splendid bridges on arches, some of which exist today.

Men had a long time to wait before they got good bridges in England. The twelfth century had almost ended when the first great London Bridge was built. There were wooden houses and shops on it, but these often caught fire and damaged the bridge, and they were all pulled down before the bridge was destroyed.

A great reform was made in bridge-building by John Rennie. It had been customary to make the arches very high, so that the roadway sloped very sharply up on one side, and very sharply down on the other. But John Rennie made his arches, not like the half of a circle, but in the shape of an ellipse, that is, a flattened half-circle, something like the half of an egg, cut lengthwise.

There still exists a famous single-arch bridge of the old type, the famous bridge at Pontypridd, in Glamorganshire. The first bridge there had three arches, but the river washed them away. Then the builder, William Edwards, put up another in its place, but it had only one arch, and the bridge soon fell in.

Edwards discovered the cause of its fall. There had been too much weight on the supports, and not enough in the centre. By being too light on top, the crown of the bridge was forced up and made to fall. Then he built a third bridge in which the haunches were lighter and the top heavier. That bridge still stands, after nearly 200 years, and it is now preserved as an ancient monument.

When the eighteenth century was drawing to a close men began to build bridges of cast iron. But engineers soon found that, though cast iron can bear great pressure, it will not bear much pull. It cannot be easily crushed by a weight, but it can soon be snapped by weights which pull at the two ends. So they then used wrought iron, which cannot easily be pulled apart. That served until steel came into use in the nineteenth century.

The first great bridge built of wrought iron was the Britannia Bridge, which crosses the Menai Straits in North Wales.

INDUSTRIES · HOW THINGS ARE MADE · WHERE THEY COME FROM

The builder was Robert Stephenson, son of the famous George Stephenson, who made the Rocket. He made a huge square tube of iron—iron at the top, iron at the sides, iron at the bottom, and through this tube of iron the trains pass. To increase the strength of the bridge he made the iron at the top and bottom tube-shaped, instead of solid, because it would better stand the pull of the weight.

THE IRON TUBES IN WHICH THE TRAIN CROSSES THE WATER

These tubes are built on huge columns of masonry, one being founded on an island half-way across the water, and the others on the land at the sides. As ships were constantly passing, it was impossible to put up great scaffolds on which to build up the ironwork. So Stephenson had the two tubes, nearly 500 yards long, built in four sections on shore. When all was ready the big tubes were floated on many boats, and ferried out to the towers.

As the tide went down the boats gradually sank, and the tubes, weighing 5000 tons each, came to rest in grooves prepared for them in the masonry. Then the boats were drawn away and the enormous masses of iron were hoisted up to the proper height, 100 feet above the water, by great engines.

The finest of all bridges is the great steel cantilever bridge. A cantilever is copied from the oldest of simple bridges. If two trees lean over the water from different sides of a stream we have only to run a plank from the end of one trunk to the end of the other, to make a simple cantilever bridge. That is one way of applying it. The other is to consider the cantilever a bracket. Secured firmly at one end, a bracket will bear a shelf with a heavy weight of books, and the steel cantilevers forming a bridge are merely huge brackets. The best example is the great Forth Bridge.

THE GREAT BRIDGE-BUILDER WHO DIED BROKEN-HEARTED

There had been many schemes for bridging the River Forth, and at last the work was begun by Sir Thomas Bouch, who had built the famous Tay Bridge. But suddenly, one dreadful night in the winter of 1879, part of the Tay Bridge was blown down, carrying with it into the river a trainload of people. Everybody in the train was drowned, and the country was horrified. Sir Thomas Bouch died broken-hearted, and the Forth Bridge was

designed by Sir John Fowler and Sir Benjamin Baker.

They had to cross two swift channels of water each 1700 feet wide, divided by an island. It was impossible to sink piers in these channels, so the central pier was founded on the island, and two others built nearer the shores.

The cantilevers, of which there are three pairs, carry the bridge across the two wide stretches of water. Each pair is 1360 feet long, and the three, stretching out toward each other, leave a space of 350 feet to be covered between the ends of the first and second, and a similar space between the ends of the second and third. Here ordinary steel girders are used. In order that ships may pass under it, the bridge is made 150 feet above high tide, and the top parts of the structure are 360 feet above the water.

The cantilever-bridge plan has since been used for many other bridges. One on this plan crosses Niagara at a great height above the water. The cantilever is used in suspension bridges also. Huge columns are erected on land, and from them chains or wire ropes are stretched across the gulf, carrying a roadway.

HOW KITES AND ROCKETS ARE USED FOR BUILDING BRIDGES

The best suspension bridge in England is at Clifton. This is 702 feet across, and 31 feet wide. It is more than 200 feet above the River Avon, and it is said that the first string attached to the rope which pulled across the cable was sent over by means of a kite.

A still stranger way was adopted for starting a great bridge across the River Zambesi, in South Africa. The bridge is the highest in Africa—420 feet above the water, and runs from cliff to cliff; so they had to fire a rocket fastened to the end of a cord. The rocket took the cord across, the cord was used for hauling across a wire, and the wire was used to pull over a small cable. On this a truck was sent across carrying the main cable of the bridge, which is over 200 yards long, and one of the greatest engineering wonders in South Africa.

The great bridge which crosses Sydney Harbour in Australia is one of the engineering marvels of our time. It has a massive steel arch with a span of 1650 feet to support the track across the harbour, and the bridge cost nine million pounds to build.

BRIDGES AND HOW THEY ARE BUILT

Here we see how the Forth men worked inside the caisson shown on page 546. Mud was diluted with water and blown out of the caisson by compressed air ; clay was hauled out, and when a firm foundation was reached, nearly 90 feet below water level, the caisson was filled with concrete, and on this solid base the massive stones of a pier were laid.

BEGINNING OF THE GREAT FORTH BRIDGE

The Forth Bridge, designed by John Fowler and Benjamin Baker, marked an epoch in the history of bridge building. Over 1½ miles in length, it took seven years to build and cost nearly £3,000,000. Three main piers, each consisting of four circular masonry supports built upon a caisson, carried pillars of hollow steel 360 feet high and 12 feet in diameter bolted down to each support with 48 steel bolts 2½ inches in diameter and 24 feet long.

From these pillars the bridge was gradually built out, over 50,000 tons of steel and 140,000 cubic yards of concrete and masonry being used. The two great openings have each a span of over 1700 feet, or nearly one-third of a mile, and offer a clear headway for ships 150 feet above high water for a width of 500 feet. The Forth Bridge was opened in 1890.

SAN FRANCISCO'S TWO MIGHTY BRIDGES

Spanning the entrance to San Francisco Harbour is the Golden Gate suspension bridge, with towers 746 feet high. The span is 4200 feet, and at the centre the roadway is 200 feet above the water.

The Bay Bridge, a series of bridges, joins the city of San Francisco to the suburb of Oakland across the bay, with a "rest" on Yerba Buena Island. It has two suspension spans each 2310 feet long, three of 1160 feet, and a cantilever span 1400 feet long. An interesting feature of this bridge is its decks. The lower deck has two railway tracks and three lanes for heavy goods vehicles, and the upper has six lanes for light traffic.

LOFTY BRIDGES OVER VALLEY AND RAVINE

A bridge of somewhat novel appearance is the Faux-Namiti Bridge on the Yunnan railway in China. It is 220 feet long, spans a wedge-shaped fissure 350 feet above the water, and is approached on each side through a tunnel. In building it a bascule was lowered from each cliff-face by cables and winches, as seen in the first picture, and French engineers then made the connection at the centre. With these bascules as supports the railroad was laid across.

The Swiss valleys afford numerous opportunities for the bridge-builder's skill. This picture shows the construction of a viaduct (seen below) across the Sitter Valley, near St Gall, Switzerland, with a column of scaffolding 300 feet high.

This is the bridge seen above in the making. It carries the Bodensee-Toggenburg railway, and such are its graceful proportions that it does not spoil the beauty of the mountain valley seen through its arches.

THE GREAT BRIDGE ACROSS SYDNEY HARBOUR

Here is the Sydney Harbour Bridge in Australia. Its great steel arch has a span of 1650 feet and is 160 feet wide. Its track, 170 feet above high-water, has accommodation for four lines of electric railway, a roadway with space for six lines of traffic, and two footpaths each 10 feet wide. The bridge was built by a British firm and cost £9,000,000.

This picture shows how the arch grew simultaneously from both sides of the harbour, with great cranes mounted on the structure itself to place the massive steelwork in position. Each crane weighed 605 tons and could lift 122 tons.

Here the arch is seen nearly completed. The Sydney Harbour Bridge is the greatest single-arch bridge in the world, the arch itself containing 37,000 tons of steel, though New York's Bayonne Bridge is slightly longer. It was opened in 1932.

THREE OF AMERICA'S WONDERFUL BRIDGES

Like the Sydney Harbour Bridge the Bayonne Bridge which spans the Kill van Kull, an important New York waterway, depends for its main support on an enormous steel arch. It is the longest steel arch in the world, having a span of 1675 feet.

Here is another of New York's great bridges, the George Washington. It is a suspension bridge which crosses the Hudson River with a span of 3500 feet between the towers.

The Delaware River Bridge, which connects the cities of Philadelphia and Camden, has a splendid roadway for six lines of traffic. It bridges a channel 1750 feet wide.

FOUR FINE BRIDGES IN FOUR CONTINENTS

The Hardinge Bridge which crosses the Ganges about 120 miles from Calcutta carries a double line of railway and has a footway five feet wide. It has fifteen river spans of 345 feet each and three smaller land spans.

This fine bridge at Makurdi in Northern Nigeria carries a roadway and a single-line railway across the Benue River. It is 2584 feet long, has 22 spans, and it was opened for traffic in 1932, replacing a former train ferry.

The Victoria Bridge crossing the St. Lawrence at Montreal was cleverly built round an old tubular bridge which was gradually removed. It is 6592 feet long and has 25 spans. It carries double railway tracks and roadways.

The magnificent Tyne Bridge at Newcastle, opened in 1928. Built progressively from both sides, the great arch rises at the centre to 193 feet above the river. The roadway is 84 feet high.

THE TRANSPORTER AND THE LIFT BRIDGE

On transporter bridges foot-passengers and vehicles are carried across in an enclosed car suspended by steel wire ropes from a trolley running on rails on the under-side of the bridge and worked electrically. A car may carry about six vehicles and 300 passengers at each trip. The picture shows a transporter at Middlesbrough.

Sometimes when a bridge is needed to cross a busy waterway a lift bridge is built. The roadway of this wonderful example at Middlesbrough is shown in its raised position where it allows a clearance of 120 feet above water-level for shipping to pass on the Tees. It has a span of 270 feet and is said to be the biggest vertical lift bridge in the world.

BUILDING AFRICA'S HIGHEST BRIDGE

Spanning the Zambesi Gorge, 400 yards below the Victoria Falls in Rhodesia, in the heart of magnificent country is the highest bridge in all Africa. It is 420 feet above the water and 650 feet long, the centre arch having a span of 500 feet. It was designed by G. A. Hobson, a partner of Sir Douglas Fox, and completed in 1905.

A rope was sent across the gorge by rocket and a cable was hauled across. Then work was begun and here one side is beginning to reach out over the depths.

Bridge building is perilous work. The men work at great heights with little foothold, and here we see a fabric device to save them from falling into the torrent below.

Building is carried on from both sides until the minute calculations of the engineers bring the ends together with beautiful exactness. Looking upward, we see that the chasm has been successfully spanned.

Here is the single span girder bridge finished, a thing of graceful beauty and an important link in the great railway, the dream of Cecil Rhodes, that some day will run from the Cape to Cairo.

The photographs on this page are by courtesy of the High Commissioner for the Union of South Africa.

A BRIDGE THAT BROKE DOWN TWICE

Quebec Bridge, carrying the Canadian Government Railways across the St Lawrence, was completed in 1917 after much trouble. In 1907 half the bridge collapsed under its own weight ; in 1916 the great central span, when being hoisted into position, fell into the river. 66,480 tons of steel and 8,000,000 rivets were used in the bridge, which cost £4,000,000.

The span from pier to pier is 1800 feet, exceeding the Forth Bridge spans by about 100 feet, and the railway tracks are 150 feet above water. This picture shows the upper chord eyebars being hoisted into position.

The large post over the main pier, seen on the left, is 310 feet high and weighs over 1200 tons. The centre span, 640 feet long and weighing 5000 tons, was erected on pontoons and towed to the bridge by tugs ; it took four days to raise it into position. On the right, workmen are connecting the first panel of the cantilever arms.

Plain Answers to the Questions of the Children of the World

DOES LIGHT DIE AWAY?

THE light of a star will disappear if the star grows cold and " goes out." Any star we see tonight may already have gone out, for the light we see it by left it long ago. Though light may be so steady and seem so permanent, yet we must think of it as we do of an electric current. Light really is a sort of electric current. It has to be made and kept up from moment to moment. To make light a star must *spend power*, and if the new power is not forthcoming the light will cease, just as an electric current will cease if the battery runs down. So that light dies away if you do not continue to make it.

It is true, of course, that light often appears to our eyes to die away, but that is merely because our eyes are not strong enough to follow it beyond a certain distance, especially if the light is not very bright.

We can see lightning for very many miles; probably only the roundness of the Earth prevents us from seeing it still farther than we do, for, of course, the time comes when the light, as it flashes through the air, will be cut off from the eyes of people far away, because they are, so to say, " round the corner " of the Earth. In questions like this we must remember that light can travel any distance, and will, indeed, travel infinite distances so long as nothing stops it. Therefore, if the light remains bright enough

for our eyes to be affected by it, we can see to the distance of the thing which is giving out the light. Thus, when we see a star, we see to a distance of billions of miles.

We know that the farther off a bright thing is, the less bright it seems. We know that the Moon, or a planet like Venus, is brighter than the stars to our eyes, though not a ten-thousandth part so bright in reality, because it is near. Yet light will travel on for ever unless it is stopped. So far as we can judge, light as it travels suffers no loss at all; none of it is absorbed or lost.

Yet we know that somehow light gets fainter as it travels. The reason is that the light spreads in all directions as it travels, and so gets less intense at any particular place—as, for instance, where it strikes the curtain, or retina, of our eyes. The law governing this phenomenon is known exactly. If the distance is doubled, the light is one-fourth as bright; if trebled, one-ninth as bright; if quadrupled, one-sixteenth as bright. To get the intensity, we must take the square of the distance—that is, multiply it by itself—and then the intensity is so much less. We say that it varies *inversely* as the square of the distance. In other words, when a light is moved two yards away from us it seems four times less bright to us; if it is moved ten yards it seems a hundred times less bright to us.

SUN · MOON · STARS · FIRE · WIND · WATER · LIFE · MIND · SLEEP

How Much Water is There in the Sea?

Most of us know that much more than half the whole surface of the Earth is covered with water, and if the Earth had been of a slightly different size from the size it is, the whole of its surface would be one great ocean. A recent estimate of the extent of the ocean's surface may be trusted as a very precise one. It is that *five-sevenths* of the Earth's surface is covered with water. If, now, we could learn the average depth of the sea all over the world, it would only need a big multiplication sum to answer this question.

We find great variations in the depth of the oceans—places where the highest mountain might be buried, and great shallow areas, too; but the result of an enormous number of soundings taken in every part of the sea, except at and round the Poles, is that the average depth of the oceans of the world is rather less than two and a half miles. This is probably a great deal deeper than you would have thought, and it means a rather long sum if you want to learn the number of *cubic miles*. As a matter of fact the scientists who went on the Challenger expedition of 1872-1876, estimated the amount of water in the sea at 323,722,000 cubic miles.

Why Does Blotting-Paper Absorb Ink?

It is mainly a question of the surface of the paper. A very hard, very smoothly glazed paper will scarcely absorb any ink. If we write on such a paper, the ink takes a long time to dry; and what makes the writing is simply a layer of the solid matter left by the ink that lies on the outside of the paper.

All other papers absorb ink to some extent. Ordinary paper, such as these words are printed on, absorbs a good deal. The drying of the ink means that the water of it has evaporated into the air, while the solids that were dissolved in it remain in or on the paper. But a paper of loose texture, with a rough, unfinished surface like blotting-paper, absorbs ink just as a sponge sucks up water; and the water of the ink, instead of mainly remaining on the outside of the paper until it dries, runs into the substance of the paper, according to the amount of ink we use. That is why the letters are blurred when we write on blotting-paper.

Can We Think Without Words?

There are some kinds of what is really thinking, where the things which are put together or related are not words, but something else. Some men, for instance, in doing what is called algebra, can think without using words at all. They can find out, for instance, what this means : $A + B \times A - B$. Somebody actually wrote to ask the Editor to have the Children's Encyclopedia written in figures as well as in words! Or, instead of thinking in words or figures, men can think in lines and angles and curves, and find out all sorts of wonderful things in this way.

Euclid could think in this way about as well as anyone who ever lived. Other men can think in sounds. One of the greatest musicians who ever lived, Beethoven, wrote some of the most marvellous music in the world, which will be listened to as long as men have ears, long after he had become stone-deaf. He put the ideas of the sounds together in his head. He could think in notes as easily as you and I can think in words.

Is Iron Heavier When It Rusts?

We have to find out what happens when iron rusts, and then we shall have the answer to this question. What happens is that the outside of the iron which is exposed to the air is burnt, or oxidised. A certain amount of the oxygen of the air is added to the iron, therefore. This oxygen, like everything else, has weight, and its weight must be added to the weight of the iron itself when the iron is rusty. Therefore, the answer to the question must be yes. The iron increases in weight by the weight of the oxygen which it has added to itself. But the rust, or *oxide of iron*, is friable, a Latin word which means crumble-able.

The rust will crumble away under the influence of water or wind or anything else rubbing against the iron, and so the iron thing will lose not only the oxygen that it has taken unto itself, but also the part of the iron which has combined with the oxygen. So an iron thing, when it rusts, loses weight, and that is very serious, of course, for it means that the thing loses its strength. And if an iron or steel bridge were allowed to crumble in this fashion, it would soon break. That is one reason why we must keep such a bridge thoroughly painted.

Is the Country Healthier Than the Town?

The country is healthier than the town for two reasons. They are that the country gives us purer air to breathe, and more sunshine, as the country air is clearer and does not stop so much of it as town air does. On the other hand, the towns are usually much better off than the country in the matter of drains and of water. Further, if people are wise and reasonable, it is better for their health of mind to see people, and to be not too much forced in upon themselves. In this way, the town is better than the country; and it is a fact that there is more insanity in the country then in towns. It is foolish to abuse cities blindly, as many people do. There never has been a civilisation without cities. Athens, and Rome, and Jerusalem, to which we today owe almost everything, were cities.

The time will come when people will see this, and will try to make their cities as healthy as the country in air and sunshine. They will not allow smoke to make the air impure, and so they will get better air into their lungs and more sunshine; they will build all houses with gardens; they will stop the unnecessary noises of cities; and so will make places where men can meet, and hear each other speak, and discuss things, while still keeping the advantages of the country.

Is there a Colour our Eyes Cannot See?

It is our brains that translate into colour something outside them which we call waves of light. If there were no brains, those rays of light would still exist, but, plainly, it would not be proper to say that there were colours.

Now, what happens in the case of light is that, if we compare all the possible kinds of light to the notes on a piano, there is just about one octave in that large compass that our eyes can see. The note above and below that octave are there though we cannot see them.

If our eyes could see them, they would certainly be of different colours from the light that we can see. The notes below the red end of the octave that we can see would appear as some other colour which, of course, we cannot imagine ; and the notes above the violet end of the octave we can see would appear as another colour.

It has been clearly proved that some insects, such as ants, can see these rays of light beyond the violet to which our eyes are blind. But what colour it looks like to them, of course, no human being can ever tell. It is very interesting to know, however, that there are animals which can see notes of light which we cannot see, just as there are animals which can hear notes of sound too shrill for us to hear.

What Does " Safety First " Mean?

Safety First is a motto that has been very much used in recent years, and is a tribute to the growing appreciation of the value of human life. It originated as an industrial term, and was used in connection with factory life as a short and convenient way of enjoining on both employers and workpeople the importance of taking every precaution against accident.

A Safety First Council was formed, and gradually the scope of the movement was extended to cover other spheres, as, for example, the crossing of roads, the entering and leaving of public vehicles, and so on. The Royal Society for the Prevention of Accidents is the present title of this organisation, which has State recognition.

The term rapidly became so familiar that its use was still further extended, as when a distinguished admiral, speaking of the importance of the British Navy being adequate in size and equipment, summed up the need in the words of the motto " Safety First."

What Does a Bird Sing About?

Whenever a child or a bird or anyone else sings naturally, it sings about its feelings. If you have no feelings you ought not to sing. Sometimes we sing just to show that we are cleverer than other people, and when we do that we do not feel what we are singing, and everyone is glad when we stop. But the birds only sing when they must—when their feelings find their way out somehow. Then they try to tell the world how happy they are. The feelings that birds sing about are always happy feelings. When a bird is ill, or miserable, or unhappy, it never sings. It only sings when it is well.

Generally, birds sing to express their feelings of love, and to tell other birds that they have acquired a hunting territory of their own and will not permit trespassing.

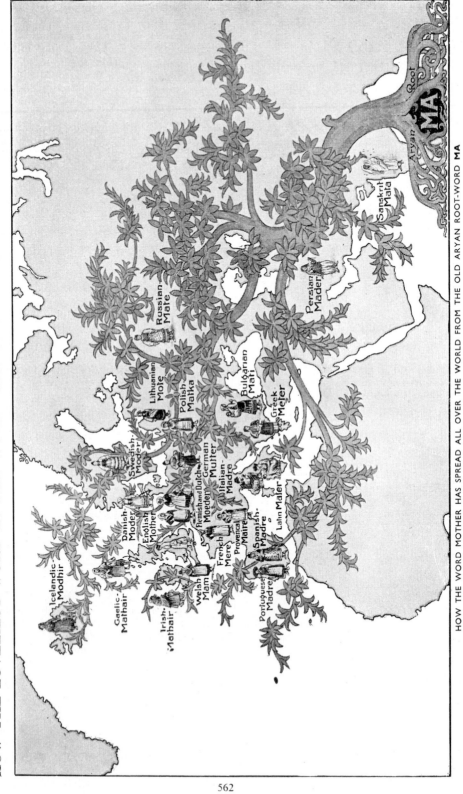

Aryan Root MA

Sanskrit Mata

Persian Mader

Russian Mate

Lithuanian Mole

Polish Matka

Bulgarian Mati

Greek Meter

Swedish Moder

German Mutter

Flemish and Dutch Moeder

Italian Madre

Latin Mater

Danish Moder

English Mother

French Mere

Provencal Maire

Spanish Madre

Icelandic Modhir

Gaelic Mathair

Irish Mathair

Welsh Mam

Portuguese Madre

HOW THE WORD MOTHER HAS SPREAD ALL OVER THE WORLD FROM THE OLD ARYAN ROOT-WORD **MA**

What Makes the White Marks on Our Nails?

Our nails are made of a very special kind of horny material. It is in some ways like the material that makes the outer skin; it is also still more like part of the material that makes the hair; but it is different from either of these, and comes closer to horn than any other part of our body does. It is made by special cells of the deeper part of the skin at the base of the nail, and the health of our nails, therefore, depends entirely upon the perfect health of these wonderful cells.

In cases where a person's skin is not healthy it is very commonly found that the nails suffer, dropping out or becoming cracked or brittle; and if for any reason the blood is out of order, and so supplies what is not quite suitable, or may even be poisonous, to the cells at the base of the nail, their work will be interfered with, and though they may go on producing nail stuff, it will not be quite what it ought to be.

In this way we can often see white marks across the nails, sometimes on all the fingers of both hands, corresponding to the date when we were out of health, and when the proper nail substance could not be made. The toe-nails may also show indications of these white marks.

Are There Families in Words?

Words and languages are grouped in families in exactly the same way as the peoples who speak the languages. Philologists, the men who study words and compare the words in different languages that stand for the same things, find words closely resembling one another, and come to the conclusion that they must be related, especially when other groups of words in the same languages show similar resemblances.

A good example is the word for Mother, which is very similar in many of the languages of the great and important group known as Indo-European, including Sanskrit, the ancient religion of India, Latin and Greek, and the modern languages of Europe.

Though these mother-words are very much alike, it is clear that one did not come from another. Our word mother, for instance, is not derived from the Latin mater, although it closely resembles it. The resemblances of the various words for mother are too great to be accidental, and so men of science conclude that they are sisters and cousins, all derived from one mother language, the so-called Indo-European tongue.

Exactly where that was spoken we do not know. Some have thought the home of the Aryan people, who spoke it, and from whom the nations referred to are descended, was in Asia, but no one can say definitely.

Philologists, however, by comparing the many mother-words, trace these all back to a common root, the old Aryan root Ma, which must have existed at some time, or all these words for mother in the many Indo-European languages could never have grown up so like one another.

Why are the Words "Ancient Lights" Put Outside Windows?

When we see these words placed on the outside of a building we know that the owner of the property is warning other people not to build in such a way as to keep out the light from the windows or openings over which he puts his notice.

The Law is that if for 20 years without interruption we have enjoyed the light which comes through a window or opening in our house without anyone's consent in writing, we have acquired the right to the continued enjoyment of the light, and we can object if anyone does anything which interferes with the light to a substantial extent. For example, we can prevent anyone erecting a building close up against us, so that no more light comes through our windows. The notice is to warn all who may be concerned that we claim this right which is known as "Ancient Lights."

In order to guard against having to pay for such a privilege, builders will sometimes, before the necessary twenty years have passed, deliberately darken other people's windows.

A selfish person, for instance, once put up a huge black hoarding as high as the top of some cottages, entirely blocking up the view from the front of those houses, in order that they might not have twenty years of light, thus hoping to prevent the landlord from claiming compensation for ancient lights when the time came for new houses to be put up on land adjoining. He did not think of the misery he was causing the poor cottagers.

Why Does the Chameleon Change its Colour?

The object of the change of colour of the skin of the chameleon is to enable it to become like its surroundings at the time, and so aid it in concealing itself.

This capacity the chameleon shares with many other lizards, and they are able to change because they possess within the skin a great number of small cells closely packed together, filled with small granules. This causes a white colour by reflecting light. Other cells are full of oil drops and appear yellow; others contain brown or reddish pigment, and the changes in colour are brought about by contraction of different parts of the skin, and the movement of the different pigments.

Thus, when all the pigment is forced toward the surface the animal looks quite dark. When the pigment is not so near the surface the colour is changed to green, and where there is no pigment the skin appears yellow. The mechanism which causes these changes appears to be under the control of the will of the chameleon, but, in addition, the external surroundings, such as heat or cold, also cause some changes in the colour.

What Makes a Dimple?

In order to understand a dimple, we should know the structure of the skin and what lies underneath it. In most parts of the body the skin, with its outer horny layer, and the inner living layer, which carries nerves and blood-vessels and makes the horny layer afresh from day to day, lies very loosely upon the layer of tissue beneath it. This is a loose layer, containing a certain number of fibres running in all directions, with fat-cells laying between them in healthy people—except under the skin of the eyelids, where fat is never found. A few of these fibres are attached to the under surface of the skin, so that, though we can move the skin about very freely over what lies beneath it, there is a limit to this movement.

But where there are dimples, as on the face, and often round such joints as the knee and the elbow, the number of fibres attached to the under surface of the skin is much increased, and they are rather short, so that the skin is depressed, or dimpled, at these points. We see what is really the same thing produced accidentally in the case of many scars, which are often a little depressed below the general level of the skin because they are tacked down in the same way. But the skin over a scar has been lost, and is replaced by a new thing called scar-tissue, whilst the skin over a dimple is true skin.

Is it Darkest just Before Dawn?

There is probably very little ground for this belief. At any rate, we may be quite certain that in all cases like this, where we compare darkness and lightness, or loudness and softness, it does not do to trust to the evidence of our senses, because they do not judge fairly.

There are various ways by which we can measure the brightness of light. In order to prove that it was darkest just before dawn it would be necessary to use some kind of light measurer—not our eyes —and compare the amount of light recorded just before dawn with what it recorded previously. Our eyes and senses in general do not judge things on their own merits, but always by comparison with other things.

The proper way to say this is that all our sensations are relative. A room may be light relatively to a room that is less light. If we go to the room from darkness we call it bright; if we go to the room from blazing sunlight we call it dark. And so we judge the darkness before dawn by the dawn. When daylight begins to come, we think how dark it was before.

Why is Salt Damp When it is Going to Rain?

When we say that the salt is damp, we mean that it has taken a lot of water into itself, and of course it has absorbed the water from the air. Common salt, like a host of other things, will help itself to the water which exists as vapour in the air, though many other salts will do so far more readily than common salt does.

Plainly, the reason why salt becomes damp before it rains is that before it rains there is an unusual amount of water-vapour in the air. Indeed, the rain is due to the fact that the water-vapour in the air has become too great in amount for the air to hold it any longer, and so down it tumbles in the form of rain. When raindrops form, we know that the water-vapour of the air condenses in little drops around particles of dust, and so on, in the air. Similarly the water-vapour in the air condenses upon the particles of salt.

The Story of the Beautiful Things in the Treasure-House of the World

St. Francis and St. John with the Madonna, by Pietro Lorenzetti—On the church walls of Assisi

THE WONDER MEN OF FLORENCE

THERE is a little town in Tuscany called Siena, a tranquil if a dirty place, sitting in the sun. Lovers of beautiful things have a warm feeling for Siena; here in the thirteenth century were shown the first tender manifestations of that spiritual force called the Renaissance, the awakening of art after its long sleep.

The Renaissance in art was due to the workings of the Gothic movement north of the Alps. A very great beauty sense lay behind this movement, as mysterious as beauty always is. It was something intensely airy and alive, with wild-flying wings; and very different from the heavy brooding of the Romanesque movement.

This lightness, this airiness, captured men's hearts and found its expression not only in buildings which flung up their lines like wheeling birds, but in statuary and coloured shapes. From Southern France the joy in lovely forms and natural beauty spread like a heavenly contagion. It touched the heart of Duccio di Buoninsegna, the Sienese, who became the first great Italian painter ; and it presently touched the hearts of his fellow townsmen to such an extent that when he had finished his great altar picture they turned out in a body and carried it triumphantly to the cathedral. Bells rang from the

steeples; the town had a holiday in honour of the beautiful thing.

This event, not the only one of its kind in the history of Italian art, throws a light on the peculiar workings of the Renaissance. For several hundred years ordinary citizens cared intensely about art. We can realise into what a far country we have travelled, how great is the gulf separating our cold selves from those ardent medieval people, when we try to imagine any community today making a triumphal procession for no other reason than that someone had painted a picture.

Duccio lived from about 1255 to 1340. Although he was a child of the Gothic period, his painting was a strange mixture of the new sense of beauty and the lifeless Byzantine grandeur which hung about Christian art in Italy like a gorgeous, stifling pall. Duccio tried to begin to understand and express what a living line meant. Byzantine lines were all dead. The Sienese artist must have known that a living figure has a certain vibration; he almost found it; he was obviously groping for it all his life, and in doing so he founded a style in which a delicate pale emotion, a struggling for vitality, are evident. Duccio's followers founded a school within a school ; the Sienese within the Tuscan.

PICTURES · STATUES · CARVINGS · BUILDINGS · IVORIES · CRAFTS

We are coming to a period in the story of art when men's names and dates crowd thick on the pages, and, as there is nothing quite so meaningless as a long string of words in an unfamiliar tongue, we will look at the painters in groups. If we can learn the characteristics of the various schools, we shall have gained enough knowledge to walk into the National Gallery or turn over a book on art, and say, without looking at the name of a picture, " that must be Sienese "; " that is Florentine, and that Venetian."

THE STRANGE COUNTRY IN THE ROOMS OF THE NATIONAL GALLERY

The great men of the periods we shall unconsciously learn in learning the schools; then we shall be in the happy position of knowing the language of a strange country.

For, there is no doubt about it, the National Gallery, or any other gallery owning a collection of *primitives*, is, on the first dozen visits or so, a strange country to most of us. To thousands of people it is never anything else. They go there as a duty; it is one of the shows of London. They have been told by enthusiastic people that the National Gallery contains certain beautiful pictures, but they themselves find them simply ugly; they walk away, and in future avoid the gallery. Thus one of the richest treasures of our national inheritance becomes meaningless and void.

This is partly because our eyes are untrained and partly because beauty is a relative term. All artists strive for the expression of the beautiful, and some succeed better than others. Each man's work is important in itself as an expression of his individual sense of beauty, and also important in the part it plays in the world-movement of all the arts *toward the expression of absolute beauty*.

WHAT WE MUST REMEMBER IN STUDYING PICTURES

The paintings of the Sienese have more of a historic than an individual sense of beauty. The painters were ignorant of technique, perspective, often of ordinary drawing. They worked in water-colour on linen stretched on wood, the fabric having been first dressed with glue. They used a great deal of gold, laying it on the canvas in leaf, and afterwards burnishing it, according to the dying-out Byzantine tradition. Their art was elementary, and they were truly called Primitives. But it marks the first step away from the real Byzantine, and that, in the history of art, was a step toward the realisation of ultimate beauty.

In trying to understand pictures which, according to the judgment of history, are great, we have to take into account more than drawing and colour and subject. A point of great importance in the study of the early Italians is the period of the various artists. For this reason we should always look at a Renaissance picture from the standpoint of the painter himself, and forget that we are the curious on-lookers of a far later day.

For instance, painters of early Italian religious pictures were used to seeing, every time they went to church, wall-paintings or mosaics of Biblical subjects. These decorations had been made by order of the Church, certain subjects to fill certain panels, the type of person in the picture settled once and for all, it seemed, by the council of Nicaea.

THE NEW JOY PREACHED BY SAINT FRANCIS WHO LOVED THE BIRDS

There was no room for individual treatment. Imagine, therefore, when these rules were relaxed, the intense joy the early artists had in painting a saint *not* to pattern. Imagine how they would look on the work as a labour of love, and not as an order to make a picture, thinking more of their own ideas than the quality of the work. We should try to remember this when we see the quaint, wry-necked saints of the Sienese school, or Duccio's very badly drawn Madonna with a worse drawn toy Child in her lap.

Another point we should remember is that artists are always influenced by what they are thinking about. The Sienese school grew up just after Dante had written his wonderful allegory, and the visions of the poet had been set free to creep into other men's thoughts. That dear saint, Francis of Assisi, had been going to and fro, preaching and teaching.

The spiritual life of the thirteenth-century Northern Italy is largely bound up in that good man. He was in literature and religion what the Gothic spirit was in architecture and statuary—something alive and tender, unbound by tradition. To ourselves, now, the book called The Little Flowers of Saint Francis is very precious. What must it have been to have lived in the very place where the

PICTURES BY FOUR ARTISTS OF FLORENCE

BOTTICELLI'S MADONNA AND CHILD

LORENZO DI CREDI'S MADONNA AND CHILD

THE VISITATION—BY DOMENICO GHIRLANDAIO

MADONNA ADORING THE CHILD—BY FILIPPO LIPPI

memory was warm of the saint who spoke of his little sisters the Birds, his big brother the Sun?

The new joy preached by St. Francis was the secret of the greatness and the weakness of the Sienese artists. Their best work is warm with an individual feeling, a struggle to make a personal, living thing out of lines and colours and tones. They did not think and plan sufficiently, allowing a beautiful emotion to take the place of mental effort. Their greatest artists were Duccio, Simone Martini, known as Memmi, Ambrogio and Pietro Lorenzetti, and Bartolo. After the fourteenth century the art of Siena died out for sheer want of strength and vigour.

Side by side with the Sienese school grew another, the Florentine. A number of pictures showing something of the Sienese spirit have been attributed to C i m a b u e, the early Florentine, and many charming stories cluster around this captivating figure. But art historians b e l i e v e that many pictures said to be Cimabue's work were painted by someone else—probably by Duccio or his followers —as the Florentine was a worker in mosaics and followed the Byzantine tradition.

THE MADONNA AND CHILD PAINTED SIX HUNDRED YEARS AGO BY DUCCIO

Florentine art was a very great movement—an intellectual force producing a number of the most wonderful artists of the world, among them two giants— Leonardo da Vinci and Michael Angelo.

The first of the stalwarts was Giotto. He may quite possibly have been influenced by Duccio in the neighbouring town, but he showed in his work the clear precision which was to mark the Florentine school and separate it from the gentle and poetic Sienese.

There are many legends about Giotto, one being that he was discovered as a shepherd boy in the mountains, drawing sheep on the rocks; another that he was apprenticed to a wool merchant and spent his time watching artists at work. Be his origin what it may, Giotto himself is beyond argument a forceful genius with a mind open to all that was beautiful in thought, and with an instinct for what writers call strong situations.

He had a keen dramatic sense, and could seize upon the most vivid actions and attitudes in the people he was painting. Intensely as he cared about his work, he never allowed sympathy to overweigh judgment. For instance, while portraying the grief and horror of some persons at the sudden death of a friend, in one of his great pictures, The Knight of Celano, he still kept his attention clear for the innumerable details of character, dress, and personal appointments which, if treated in the right proportion, make for s t r e n g t h in a picture. Giotto took the second step along the road to the realisation of the Italian ideal of beauty—he turned completely away from the chilling Byzantine traditions which still lingered in the Sienese. When we look at his work we see many faults of drawing, but we see that he battled with the problem of making a projection of colour and shape on a flat surface look as much a solid human being as if it had been sculptured in the round. Giotto's colouring was always clear and pale—another step away from the heavy Byzantine richness.

To understand the work of this pioneer among artists it is necessary to look, not only at his picture, but at his frescoes in Padua and Assisi, and especially in Florence, remembering that a fresco is painted on the wall itself in water-colour, before the plaster is dry. A great many Italian artists painted in fresco, and, as in the case of Giotto, this class of their work forms a most important study.

Some people are very much disappointed when they go to Italy and see the frescoes of Giotto for the first time; they are faded, and at first sight appear a little unconvincing.

THE DAWN OF ITALY'S GOLDEN AGE

THE VIRGIN WITH THE INFANT CHRIST. BY GHIRLANDAIO IN THE UFFIZI GALLERY, FLORENCE

AN ALLEGORICAL PICTURE OF SPRING. FROM THE PAINTING BY BOTTICELLI IN THE
ANCIENT AND MODERN GALLERY, FLORENCE

THE FLIGHT INTO EGYPT. FROM A PAINTING IN THE ARENA CHAPEL AT PADUA, BY GIOTTO

THE NATIVITY. FROM THE PAINTING IN THE SAN MARCO MUSEUM, FLORENCE, BY FRA ANGELICO

THE VIRGIN WITH THE INFANT JESUS. FROM THE PAINTING BY BOTTICELLI
IN THE UFFIZI GALLERY, FLORENCE

ST. AUGUSTINE READING PHILOSOPHY AT THE SCHOOL OF ROME. FROM THE PAINTING
BY BENOZZO GOZZOLI AT SAN GIMIGNANO

ONE OF THE THREE WISE MEN
BY GOZZOLI

THE ANGEL OF THE
ANNUNCIATION. BY MEMMI

PORTRAIT OF A LADY
BY PIERO DELLA FRANCESCA

SAINT FRANCIS
BY BARTOLI TADDEO

THE BETRAYAL BY JUDAS. FROM THE PAINTING BY
CIMABUE IN THE CHURCH OF ST. FRANCIS AT ASSISI

THE VIRGIN. BY
LORENZO DI CREDI

THE DEATH OF SAINT FRANCIS, BY GIOTTO, IN THE CHURCH OF ST. CROCE, FLORENCE

But such people have not learned the lesson we have been learning—of looking at an artist's work from the point of view of the painter and the period. Keeping that in our minds, we can never make a wrong judgment, and we should not at the outset expect the brilliance of a modern oil painting in plaster pictures which have been exposed to light and heat for close on a thousand years, and were painted by a man who, though a great genius, could not draw properly.

THE IMMORTAL GIOTTO WHO "TOOK HILLS AT A STRIDE"

Most of Giotto's frescoes are subjects from the life of St. Francis, cycles of beautiful stories. They adorn churches in Florence, Assisi, Padua, and Rome. One of Giotto's paintings is in the Louvre.

Giotto died in 1337, but he really lived on over a hundred years, seeing that it took many generations before painters reached the point where his progress was stayed. Giotto had taken hills at a stride. His followers plodded on, content merely to try to " catch up." They imitated and copied his style and work and developed little or nothing on their own account. They were a numerous company, and are known in art history as the Giotteschi.

The chief among them and the next best to the master was Andrea Orcagna. Another, Taddeo Gaddi, Giotto's favourite pupil and his godson, rather caricatured his master's style, exaggerating the long noses and faces and almond eyes which Giotto had introduced in place of the staring, round-faced Byzantine personations. But he was humble, and knew his limitations. Sometimes he signed his work, "Taddeo, a disciple of Giotto, the good master."

FRA ANGELICO, THE GENTLE PAINTER WHO WEPT OVER HIS WORK

After Orcagna and Gaddi, perhaps the best of the Giotteschi was Giovanni da Milano; then came Cennino Cennini, Andrea da Firenze, Antonio Veneziano, Spinella Aretino, Lorenzo Monaco. One of these men, Cennini, is chiefly remembered for a book on painting that he wrote, describing, among other things, Giotto's technique, and incidentally throwing a light on Tuscan habits and customs of the thirteenth century.

The greatest artist produced by the Giotto school was the famous monk Fra Angelico of Fiesole, who lived from 1387 to 1455. He was a gentle and saintly painter, who felt intensely the inwardness of all the subjects he portrayed and would frequently weep over his work. Fra Angelico's work lacks the strength of Giotto's, but it has a devoutness almost unrivalled. He accomplished an amazing amount of work and comparatively little of it has survived. One of the treasures of the National Gallery is the predella for his altar picture *Christ in Glory*, which was painted for the church of St. Domenico in Fiesole, the hilltop village above Florence. This panel picture is a wonderful and lovely thing, one of the rare flowers of the Renaissance.

Perhaps Fra Angelico used a little too much gold, because he thought that nothing short of gold was rich enough for portraits of Christ and the saints. In this way his work reminds us of the Sienese. But his careful composition and construction of figures is far indeed from the vagueness of the Primitives.

Fra Angelico's most favourite subject was the Annunciation; another theme he often painted was the Last Judgment. He was perhaps most happy in his pictures of Paradise. Earthly loves and hates existed not for him; all his affections soared outward to the heavenly land.

THE EXQUISITE PAINTER OF MAGICAL AND BEAUTIFUL EVENTS

Fra Angelico's pupil Benozzo Gozzoli was an idealist of another kind, loving to picture earthly as well as heavenly things. He has been called the most exquisite storyteller of the Ranaissance, a painter of frescoes in which magical and beautiful events are shown. There was a slight tendency in master and pupil to make art visionary and apart from real life. Fra Angelico being first a saint and then a painter and Gozzoli more an illustrator than either. Two of Gozzoli's pictures are in the National Gallery, and from them we can learn something of his style. While Benozzo was but a child, however, a man was working who in his short life—he died in 1428 at the age of 27—brought a very different influence to bear on Florentine art. This was Masaccio.

Masaccio's work was like a powerful, salt-nipped wind blowing through a languorous garden. He was very vigorous and realistic, explaining by his work that art should explain life, that life is not an affair of dreams, and that Nature is the mistress of all masters. In Italian art, Masaccio was the next strong force after Giotto;

and like him, he influenced a century of followers.

Masaccio's greatest work was the decoration in fresco in the Brancacci Chapel of the Carmine monks in Florence. The subjects are various—the Fall of Man, the Expulsion from Paradise, and then onwards, skipping the rest of the Bible to the Acts of the Apostles. This work makes an epoch in art. It is one of the stages by which progress can be counted. One of the pictures best showing Masaccio's strength is the expulsion from Paradise. It is fortunate that Masaccio, unlike Giotto, is represented in our National Gallery.

BOTTICELLI, WHO WOULD SACRIFICE JUDGMENT FOR HIS LOVE OF LINE

Artists of varying qualities were influenced by Masaccio. There was Filippo Lippi, whose work showed a curious mixture of Fra Angelico's saintliness and Masaccio's realism. One of Lippi's pupils was Botticelli, who has perhaps been loved a little more than he deserves.

Botticelli was uneven in his work, allowing himself to be swayed by his passion for a lovely line; and in order to achieve this he sometimes sacrificed both judgment and reason. At his best, as in the Allegory of Spring in the Florence Academy, he is a very fine product of the Tuscan school, but his best does not often happen. Like all the Italians, he painted many Madonnas and kindred subjects, and numerous artists after him worked in his manner. Some of his pictures of Mary and the little Jesus are in the National Gallery, and show all his virtues and failings in one group. Botticelli was a little like an organist who uses the Vox Humana stop too frequently.

THE GREAT VARIETY OF THE PICTURES OF PIERO DI COSIMO

Piero di Cosimo, whose work is not at first sight as attractive as Botticelli's, was really a much stronger artist. His Death of Procris in the National Gallery is said by some people to be the finest picture there; but that is a matter of opinion. Another very fine picture of his, also in our collection, is a portrait of a Florentine general. The paintings of Cosimo are an excellent study to lead up to the work of the great Leonardo da Vinci, who was his contemporary. He painted all kinds of subjects, classical and Biblical; he also painted exquisite portraits, of which La Bella Simonetta—a beautiful Genoese girl whom Botticelli also painted—is the most famous. There was a mingled delicacy and strength and distinction in Cosimo's work that marked it out, even in a century of great artists.

Two more Florentines call for mention —Domenico Ghirlandaio and Lorenzo di Credi. Ghirlandaio, much the stronger artist of the two, was living at the same time as Botticelli, and shared with him many of the commissions upon which artists depended then, as now. Ghirlandaio had a strong instinct for large compositions, and he painted in vivid and clear colour. He had an extraordinary capacity for work, and was said to declare that he would like to paint all the walls of Florence in fresco. Naturally he fell short of this achievement, but in the forty years of his life he accomplished a great deal. He was content to paint subjects as subjects, people as people; he had no spiritual insight, and thus his work is marked by none of the idealism that distinguishes other men of his century. As decoration it is very fine, however.

LORENZO DI CREDI WITH THE GHOST OF THE GREAT LEONARDO WITHIN HIM

Lorenzo di Credi was the fellow student of the great Leonardo da Vinci. Two of his pictures of the Madonna are in the National Gallery, and there we can see, when we have learned to judge this illustrious company of Florentines, that Lorenzo was a good second best. Like most of the men of his time, he ardently admired Leonardo and studied his style. Perhaps it may be said that a ghost of the other's greatness hides in di Credi's work.

Another artist who lived in this amazing fifteenth century was Piero della Francesca, the Umbrian. His work was strangely cold and aloof; he preferred strength to beauty. Luca Signorelli was his pupil, and he had a strong feeling for composition for its own sake, regardless of individual figures. Examples of Francesca's and Signorelli's pictures are in the National Gallery.

After a little patience in sorting out these names and getting used to the idea of Italian art, we shall see how the work of the Florentine painters grew. It was a truly miraculous development, the mystical, unskilled Sienese and the adventurous, intellectual Florentines following one after another, until Leonardo came, and Michael Angelo.

The Wonderful House We Live In, and Our Place in the World

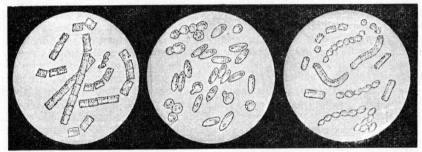

Microbes of all shapes and sizes occur in Nature, and all have their particular chemical qualities. In these three circles are seen, enlarged about a thousand times, some of the many microbes found in milk, butter, cream, and vinegar. Some turn milk and wine sour ; and some give flavour to cheeses.

THE TINIEST LIVING THINGS

WE have to talk now about the simplest kinds of living creatures that we know, and about the things they do, not only because they are very interesting in themselves, but also because their life affects the story of the Earth, which they are constantly helping to change in many ways.

These living things are extremely small; they have many names, and are often called *germs*—the germs of disease. But the great Frenchman Pasteur who found out that some of these things often make us ill called them *microbes*, a word which really means small life.

As they so often make us ill, most people think all microbes are evil. But only a very few microbes make us ill; by far the greater number of the microbes are not merely harmless to us, but we could not live without them.

The first thing to learn about microbes is that they are very small—so small that unless we have some way to help our eyes we can never see them; and, indeed, some people believe that there are many microbes so small that, however much we help our eyes, we cannot see them.

Men, therefore, could not know that microbes existed until the invention of the wonderful instrument called the microscope—an arrangement of pieces of glass in a tube, which magnifies small things so that we can see them. Yet even the microscope would not be sufficient alone to show us how many kinds of microbes there are, and to teach us that they are almost everywhere. They abound in ordinary air, they are on everything you can touch, in the house or out-of-doors, and they have even been found in the snow in the Arctic regions. They are to be found in all water. So, practically, they are everywhere—tiny living creatures, living their own lives, and employed in doing things all the time.

It is a very easy thing to grow microbes. You may take a few by dipping the point of a needle in something containing them, and then put them into milk—one of the best things for growing microbes in—or you may stroke the needle across the cut surface of a potato; and in many other ways you can watch microbes growing. You cannot see the separate microbes with the naked eye, but you can see a colony of them, and, as different kinds have different ways of spreading, anyone who knows them can pick up the tubes in which they are growing and say what kind of microbe a tube contains.

Microbes are too small for us to see their structure, but they seem to be all made very much alike. Every microbe simply consists of one little piece of living matter, called a *cell*. That is its

BODY, MIND, AND SOUL · CITIZENSHIP · ECONOMICS · GOVERNMENT

whole body, and does all the work of a living creature for it. Some microbes are round, and some are like little short rods; some are very thick, and some, like those which cause influenza and tuberculosis, are very slender; but all microbes, whether harmless or dangerous, and wherever they live, consist of a single cell, as it is called.

YOU COULD PUT A HUNDRED MILLION MICROBES ON A SHILLING

It is very important to realise that a complete living creature which moves and grows can do these things, even though it has no mouth, or lungs, or muscles. We have to learn that many of the things we do by means of many different parts of our body, made specially for the purpose, can be done by living creatures that simply consist of a single living cell, which, so far as we can see, is the same throughout, and in which no different parts at all can be observed.

When they are growing in one place perhaps they are round or very short, but when they are growing in other surroundings they may become long or thin. This is very likely a question of the kind of food they get, and it reminds us that the people who grow up in the slums are usually very short, while people who have good food and grow up in fresh air are generally many inches taller.

Considering the great things they do, the smallness of microbes is wonderful. A fair average size would be a twenty-thousandth part of an inch across. If you took some of the little rod-like microbes and could place them end to end, nearly ten millions would be required to reach a yard, while a hundred millions would be necessary to cover a shilling in a single layer, and 640,000 billions to make a solid cubic inch. (You know, of course, that an English billion is a million millions.)

SEEING A THING TEN THOUSAND TIMES AS LONG AS IT REALLY IS

This gives us some idea how tiny these tiniest of living things are, and we should not forget that there may be many others which are tinier still, so that we cannot even see them with microscopes, which are able to make a thing look ten thousand times as long as it really is. When a microbe has reached its full size—though that is not much to boast of—it does not stop feeding and growing, but splits into two. Now, there must be some reason why a living cell, which is quite strong

and young and has plenty of food, never goes on growing and growing without limit, but always after a certain point either stops growing altogether and gets no bigger, or else splits into two cells.

The rate at which microbes grow and multiply can scarcely be believed. Starting with only one microbe, and giving it sufficient food, in only twelve hours we should have something like eighteen millions, and six hours later we should have nearly eighty thousand millions. All this would simply be the result of taking in food, growing and dividing, and repeating the process at a tremendous rate. They cannot grow unless they get enough food of the right kind, and this is far from always being the case.

Microbes grow at rates something like this when we cultivate them on purpose, and give them the kind of food they like best; and also unfortunately, they multiply like this sometimes when they attack us and make us ill, especially in the case of people whose bodies are just suited for microbes to grow in.

MICROBES THAT ARE REALLY PLANTS BUT LIVE LIKE ANIMALS

But we must understand that not many kinds of microbes can grow in our bodies at all, and that most of them are killed at once when they enter our bodies. It is also well to remember that there are certain kinds of microbes which our bodies will kill at once, if we take care of our health and live sensibly, but which may kill us if we have been doing foolish things, and so have lessened our powers of resistance.

The various shapes of microbes, we have said, matter very little, but what does matter a great deal is the two different kinds of ways in which microbes feed, and this we must very carefully understand. Microbes belong, on the whole, to the vegetable world rather than the animal world, but though they are really tiny plants none of them contains any of the green matter which enables plants to live on air as well as to breathe air. Therefore, so far as their feeding is concerned, microbes are in the same position as animals. They are all compelled, like animals, to live upon food furnished them by the bodies of other living creatures.

This is the great mark of microbes— that they live upon the bodies, either alive or dead, of other living things. These may be animal or vegetable. The great distinction between microbes is that some of them live merely on the dead remains of living things, while others will attack and feed upon other creatures, animal or vegetable, when they are still alive. Here we will speak of those much more numerous microbes which live on dead matter, though always matter that has once been alive. These play a great part, for we could not possibly live without them.

Consider how many countless millions of living creatures, human, animal, and vegetable, are on the Earth, and in the air, and in the sea, at this moment. For untold ages this has been so. Yet as we know, these creatures die, and those who came before them have been dying in countless numbers every day for ages past. Now, if we consider for a moment, we shall see that if there were no means by

next spring. Microbes, then, do for the dead bodies of all living things what they do for the dead leaves. They keep the world young and fresh and green. It has very often been said that they are scavengers, meaning that they are like the men who empty the dustbins and keep the streets clear of all refuse. Microbes do this, it is true; but that is only the beginning of their work, and not nearly the most wonderful part of it. Far more wonderful is the way in which, living their own lives, they take things which would be disagreeable, or, at least, would be useless and cumber the Earth and turn them into sources, of new life.

One of the most important lessons we have to learn is that there is really nothing useless in the world. Microbes are the humblest kinds of living creatures, but

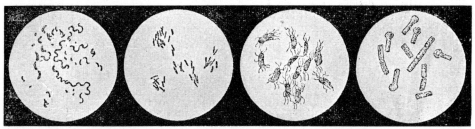

Our microbe enemies enlarged 1000 times. The first are the microbes that cause cholera the second cause tuberculosis, the third cause typhoid fever, and the last cause lockjaw.

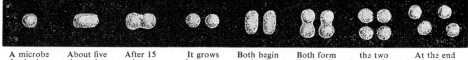

| A microbe beginning | About five minutes later | After 15 minutes | It grows into two | Both begin to develop | Both form "waists" | the two become four | At the end of an hour |

THE WONDERFUL WAY IN WHICH MICROBES ARE BORN WHILE WE LOOK AT THEM

which the bodies of all these creatures were disposed of, the Earth must long ago have been heaped up with them.

The truth is that life simply could not go on if there were not something at work which, all the time, is taking the bodies of plants and animals as they die, and doing something to them, so that they simply disappear and are got out of the way. But, more than this, there is something at work which takes these bodies—in themselves dangerous and disagreeable—and turns them into simple materials which are used as food by the new creatures living at any time.

We see in the story of Plant Life how microbes take the dead leaves in the autumn and turn them into stuff which can be used for making new leaves in the

they are not contemptible. Without the work they do in the course of their humble and unnoticed lives, no higher form of life upon the Earth, vegetable or animal or human, would be possible.

We can get some idea of the unceasing way in which these microbes are everywhere doing their work if we examine ordinary earth and find how many microbes it contains. One grain of ordinary earth will contain anything from one thousand to three hundred thousand microbes, their number being greatest in earth in which many plants are growing. If we think of the thousands of microbes in a single grain of earth, and think how tiny that quantity is, we begin to realise that it is not possible to say how many microbes there are in the world.

A BRITISH PLANT THAT EATS AN INSECT

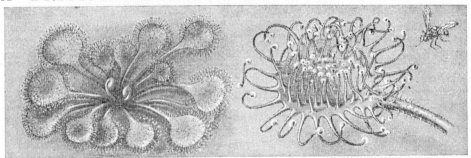

1. The round-leaved sundew, common on British bogs and heaths, is one of the most interesting of our native plants, for it catches insects and eats them.

2. Its leaves, the size of a threepenny-bit, are covered with about 200 hair-like tentacles, clubbed at the end and covered with a sticky substance that glistens in the sun.

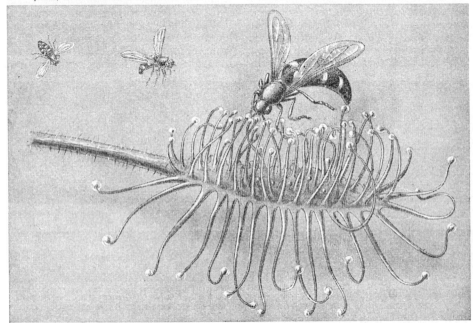

3. The tentacles remain spread out till an unwary fly in search of nectar happens to touch one or more with its antennae. At once it is held and the more it struggles to free itself the more hopelessly it becomes involved in the grip of the flower. Slowly the tentacles close in on the fly.

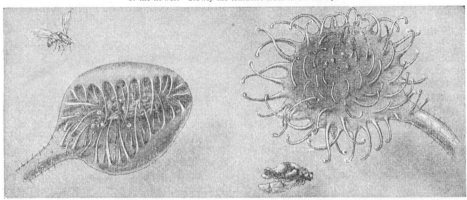

4. When the insect is completely enveloped it is suffocated in about a quarter of an hour, and acids from the leaf help the plant to digest it.

5. At last, when the insect has been thoroughly digested, the tentacles open and the remains are dropped or blown out by the wind. A sundew with 233 flies has been seen.

The Story of the Marvellous Plants that Cover the Earth

The Sensitive Plant whose leaves close up at the slightest touch, as shown in the right-hand picture

HOW PLANTS MOVE AND FEEL

SOME of the simplest plants, which are single cells, so small as to be seen only under the microscope, swim about by means of living lashes, just as many of the simplest animals do. On the other hand, there are many animals, such as sponges and corals, which have no sort of locomotion except in their earliest days.

Yet, when we have allowed for the travelling activity of some single-cell plants and the standstill habit of many animals, the big fact stands out that plants are usually fixed, while animals are usually free. Plants expend little energy in locomotion ; animals spend much.

It is important · to avoid extreme or fanciful statements in this connection, for while plants retain a power of movement in many of their parts, they have nothing corresponding to the muscles of animals; and while plants often show an exquisite sensitiveness to changes in light and warmth, to gravity and moisture, and even to touch, they have nothing at all like a nervous system.

It is altogether a mistake to use words like sagacity or intelligence in speaking of plants ; what we are sure of is that they show a sort of feeling, even an *irritability*, and a shrinking away, as it were. They answer-back to outside influences, and a

tree may respond even to the shadow of a passing cloud. They also move part of their body in an effective way. If we go on to say that plants must have something corresponding to man's mind, we may be right ; but we have passed beyond a point at which science can prove what we say.

The stem of the giant bamboo may grow a foot in a day, and a naturalist reports that he saw with the naked eye the growing of a bamboo in Java. Growth means increase in size ; the amount of the living matter is added to, and there is a *redistribution of material*. The growing units or cells are very *tense*, for there is a pressure on the cell-wall exerted from within by the watery living matter and the cell-sap. The living matter just inside the cell-wall controls the give-and-take between the cell-sap and the cell-wall, and thus controls the tenseness.

Everyone knows the limpness of a shoot that has been cut off from its water-supply ; it is worse than a punctured tyre. It is losing water into the air and gaining none back ; its cells lose their tenseness and the shoot withers. If we put the cut end into water before the withering has gone too far, the shoot will become stiff once more.

The relation of the tense cell-substance and the resisting cell-wall may well be

BOTANY & ITS WONDERS · FLOWERS · TREES · HOW THINGS GROW

compared to the relation between the bladder of a football and the leather skin. When the bladder is blown up, the outer skin is firm and rigid ; when the air is withdrawn from the bladder, the outer skin is soft and limp. But in the case of the football the pressure is gaseous, while in the case of the plant-cell the pressure is fluid. It is worth while to dwell a little on the tense state of growing and active plant-cells, for the movements of growing parts, and of full-grown parts, depend on changes in tenseness.

Charles Darwin detected the bending and bowing of seedlings. On the apex of a growing shoot he fixed a fine glass bristle with a bead at the tip, and from time to time he registered the position of the bead on a horizontal glass plate above the plant. He found that the tip of the shoot does not grow straight up ; it bends and bows to the different points of the compass.

The movement is very slow, but it goes on whenever growth is going on ; and it is due to the fact that the growth does not take place equally all round. What comes to the same thing is that there are changes in the tenseness of the growing cells in different parts of the shoot; and these seem to depend on the constitution of the plant, not on outside changes. They are movements from within.

THE TWINING AND COILING MOVEMENTS OF THE SENSITIVE TENDRIL

Of great use are the movements of tendrils, for they attach the plant firmly but elastically to its support, and help to pull it up. The tip of the slender green lasso of the bryony in the hedgerow moves slowly round in a circle, and this increases its chance of touching some support. If the under surface be rubbed a little, the tendril grows faster on the opposite side. The distinguished botanist Dr. Macgregor Skene has described what follows ·

As the tip curves, new points come into contact with the support, and the stimulus is thus constantly renewed, so that the tendril goes on twining round the support until the whole of the free tip has been used up.

The coiled part hardens and becomes woody, clasping the support firmly. The long, straight portion, between the support and the base of the tendril, twists into a tight corkscrew, reversed once or twice—for a thread fixed at both ends cannot be forced into a spiral, without at least one reversal in the direction of the hoist—and then becomes woody.

The corkscrew is of great mechanical importance. Did the free part of the tendril remain straight, any gust of wind, or shock from a passing animal, would throw a great, perhaps a breaking, strain on it. The tight spiral acts as a spring. If pulled, it opens out a little, to contract again when the pull ceases, bringing the plant back to its original position, and avoiding a rupture.

Here we have many striking things : a searching movement of the tip; an exquisite sensitiveness to contact ; a twining round the support; and a spiral coiling of the free part of the tendril.

HOW THE TIP OF THE GROWING ROOT IS SENSITIVE TO GRAVITY

When a seed sprouts, the young shoot naturally grows upward and the young root grows downward. If the seedling starts rightly, and is then turned upside down, it will soon have its root growing down once more, and its stem growing up. Of course, it may come about that the root's tendency to seek moisture may be strong enough to counteract the tendency to grow toward the centre of the Earth.

Very careful experiments have shown that the root's sensitiveness to gravity is situated at its very tip, and that this affects the area of most rapid growth a little higher up. It is the living matter of these quickly growing cells that answers-back by altering the direction of growth. In the tip-cells of the root there are starch grains which normally settle on the lower side of the cell. If the root-tip is forcibly pointed upwards, the starch grains will change their position, and some botanists think that this pulls the trigger of the answer-back. If so, the starch grains might be compared in this respect to the tiny particles of sand or lime found in the ear cavities of many little creatures. When the animal is suddenly moved, these particles in the ear have also to move; their movements affect nerve-endings in the ear; and the animal *answers-back*. In any case, what is certain is that the tip of the root is sensitive to gravity, and that the root adjusts the direction of its growth if it is interfered with.

THE THIRSTY ROOTLETS OF TREES THAT INVADE A DRAIN-PIPE

From a beautiful well a clay drain-pipe led away the water for use elsewhere ; but every year or two there was a blocking of the pipe and a flooding at the well. There was nothing for it but to dig up the pipe, and then it was seen that string-like rootlets of adjacent trees had got in at the joints, or through tiny holes. Inside the

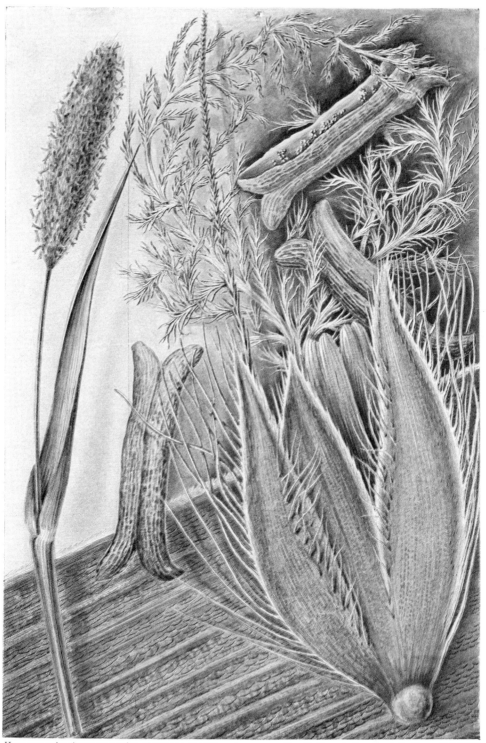

Here our artist shows us a spike of meadow fox-tail grass as we see it with the naked eye, and the flower as it looks through a magnifying lens. A glume, or husk, is shown on the point of opening, and we see the feathery stigmas (or female parts), and the anthers (the parts of the male organ called the stamen which bear the pollen).

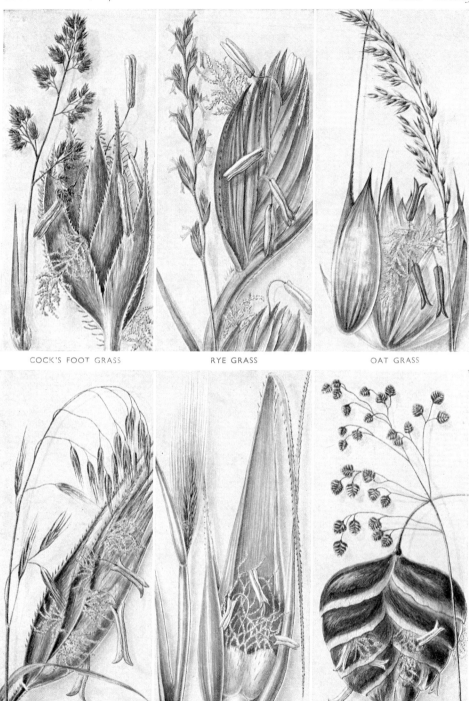

COCK'S FOOT GRASS   RYE GRASS   OAT GRASS

UPRIGHT BROME GRASS   WALL BARLEY   QUAKING GRASS

The grass family exceeds all other plant families in the number of its individual plants, and in its wide distribution over the Earth. Grasses range from the Equator to Spitsbergen in the North and to the extreme tip of South America in the South. Nine out of every ten plants in the world are grasses. Here we see the marvellous colour and beauty of various grasses of the field as seen when we penetrate their inner recesses in the microscope.

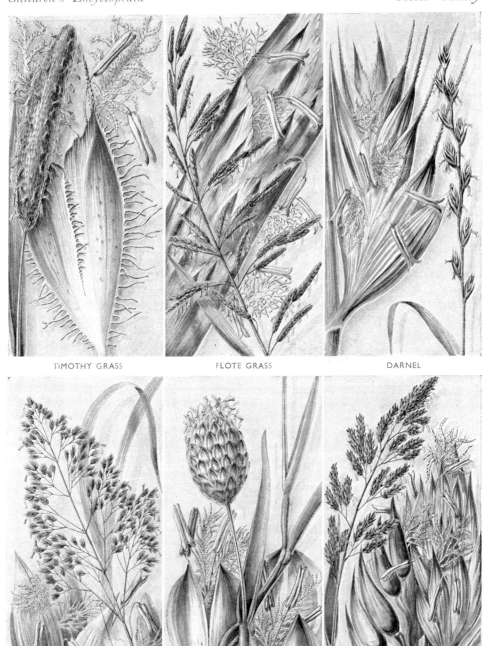

TIMOTHY GRASS   FLOTE GRASS   DARNEL

TUFTED AIRA   CANARY GRASS   REED GRASS

Grasses are mostly fertilised by the wind, and, in order that their pollen may be easily shaken off to be carried from plant to plant, the anthers which bear it are suspended on the most delicate filaments. The slightest breeze sets them in motion, and a field of grass, or a prairie, is like the sea ; it is never still. The grass responds to the faintest puff of wind, yet the fiercest hurricanes cannot destroy it, for it bends but does not break.

THE COMMON REED AND PART OF ITS MANY-FLOWERED HEAD GREATLY MAGNIFIED

A SPIKE OF COUCH WHEAT-GRASS ON THE RIGHT AND THE FLOWERS MAGNIFIED ON THE LEFT

As all these pictures show, the flowers of the grasses are alike in two things. Their pollen-bearing anthers are suspended on very fine supports, which can be moved by the slightest wind, and their stigmas have a feather-like form, so that they may easily catch the pollen as it falls upon them.

pipe the invaders branched out into a remarkable mass almost like tangled hair, and the result was a block of the pipe.

Now the interesting point was that the roots grew from a considerable distance to the water-pipe, following the increasing dampness in the soil, and that they found their way into the water almost as if they were boring animals. There is no real reason for supposing that the roots were consciously aware of the water at a distance, or that they " made up their mind " to reach it; all we are sure of is that roots are sensitive to moisture and grow toward it, altering the direction of their growth according to the conditions in the soil around them.

Plants grown in a window turn towards the light, and they would become lopsided if the flower pot were not turned round. It seems a very sensible thing to do, to spread themselves so that they get the most of the light which comes in. But what the plant does is done automatically; it is due to inequalities of growth. The stem grows less rapidly on the more illumined side, for light has a delaying influence on growth. This is just the opposite of the influence of heat, which hastens growth, as we see in hothouses. Now, if the growing part of a shoot in a window grows less rapidly on the side next to the light the result must be a bending towards the window.

LITTLE LENSES LIKE EYES IN THE SURFACE-CELLS OF SHOOTS

It is interesting to watch a growing shoot of ivy—to notice that it bends away from the light. Moreover, before it attaches itself, it gives off brownish aerial rootlets, and these are all toward the shaded side. This is obviously all the better for gripping a wall or a tree. The same is well seen in the fixing discs of the Virginia creeper, so that it is not necessary that a shoot structure must grow toward the light; it is, indeed, occasionally the other way. It has been suggested that the surface-cells of the growing shoot sometimes act like little lenses, concentrating the light on the more living growing cells within. If so, they would be rather like the very simple eyes of some backboneless animals.

So that plants answer-back to gravity, to moisture, and to light; and their answers are seen in movements of their growing parts. There are other influences to which plants are sensitive, such as electricity, chemicals, and even air. If plants have not what we call senses, they have at all events an exquisite sensitiveness.

Another point of importance is that a change in the growth of a part of a plant may become stereotyped when the part becomes older, and therefore stiff. Thus some peculiarity stamped on the growing portion may last throughout life. It remains as a record of something the plant has experienced; it is a dint from without, not an outcrop from within; and it does not seem likely that it can be handed on as such to the next generation. But if the same peculiar influences play on the children plants, then they will show the same answers-back as their parents.

THE MOVEMENT AND FOLDINGS OF THE " SENSITIVE PLANT "

So far we have dealt with sensitiveness and movements in growing plants, or, we may say, in parts which are still young. Let us now consider full-grown parts.

Thus the beautiful three-bladed leaves of the clover and the wood-sorrel are spread out during the day, but folded downward at nightfall. This may protect them from over-cooling at night; but it is not very clear. Similarly, many flowers, like daisies, close up at dusk; and others, like the yellow sorrel, when the day is dull. Most attention has been given to the sensitive plant, which has its beautiful feathery leaves expanded horizontally during the day, but folded up like a closed umbrella in the evening. The opposite leaflets of each division of the compound leaf fold their upper surfaces together; the divisions of the compound leaf seem to huddle together instead of being like an expanded fan; and the leaf-stalk sinks from a more or less erect position and hangs downward at a sharp angle. The same remarkable movements may be brought about in a minute by shaking the plant, and we know that they are due to changes in the tenseness of cells at the hinge of the leaf-stalk, or at the base of each division of the leaf.

MESSAGES THAT TRAVEL BY DELICATE TUBES FILLED WITH SAP

If we pinch a leaflet at the tip of one of the divisions of the leaf we can follow the message. One pair of leaflets after another may be seen folding together, and finally the leaf as a whole droops down. There is evidently the handing-on of an influence from one part of the leaf to another part at a considerable distance, and it may be from one leaf to another. It is probable that the message travels by long delicate tubes filled with sap surrounded by a delicate sheaf of living matter.

WHAT HAPPENS WHEN THE BEE VISITS THE CORNFLOWER

Professor Bower compares what happens to a wave of pressure in a rubber-tube filled with water. " If one observer pinches one end of the tube (he says), the stimulus is felt by an observer at the other end." If we are asked why a gentle touch to the tense cushion at the base of the leaf-stalk should make the leaf sink down, we may answer that there is a rapid change in the tenseness of certain cells in that position; but why the touch should produce the change in tenseness we do not know. We can only say that the living matter is irritable.

In the cornflower there is a neat movement of the stalks of the five stamens which surround the pistil. They are united by their anthers and curved outwards between these and their base of attachment. When a bee visits the cornflower and touches the sensitive hairs of the stamens, the curved stalks straighten and contract, drawing the anther tube downwards. The effect is to brush out the pollen on to the bee's body, and the insect is thus in a position to dust another flower which has its stigma expanded. In this case there is sensitiveness to touch, and a real usefulness in the change.

THE CAPACITY FOR MOVING AND FEELING THAT A PLANT HAS

On sunny slopes where the soil is loose we often see the rock rose, a low-growing plant with beautiful yellow flowers. If we touch the numerous stamens when the flower is basking in the sun, they exhibit a very marked movement which, perhaps, helps to dust the insect-visitor's legs. The flowers of the barberry have also irritable stamens, and there are other cases. It looks as if the capacity for feeling and moving was always lurking in the plant, ready to be used should occasion arise.

In the flower of the musk the sensitiveness is in the stigma, the tip of the pistil, which has two lobes and gapes like a mouth. If you touch this stigma with a piece of grass the two lobes close together, and this is what happens when pollen-grains are dusted by an appropriate insect-visitor. The closing of the lobes ensures that the pollen is not lost.

The opening of flowers such as daisy and goatsbeard when there is sunshine, and their closing when it is dark or cloudy, may be of use in protecting the stamens and pistil from rain and cold; and, of course, there will not be many insect-visitors about in darkness or bad weather.

In the case of the crocus and the tulip, and of some other flowers, it is the heat and not the light of the Sun that pulls the trigger of the movement. In some cases the opening and closing movements have been registered in the constitution of the plants. Thus the marigold opens in the morning and closes in the evening, even when it is kept in darkness. *An internal rhythm has been established as part of its nature.*

THE FINGERS OF THE SUNDEW THAT CLOSE ROUND THE INSECT LIKE A FIST

It has been already admitted that we are not very clear as to the usefulness of all the known movements of plants. One of the best illustrations of this is the Indian telegraph plant, which grows in the basin of the Ganges. Its leaf has a main leaflet which is stationary, and two small ones which describe circles with jerky movements. There are also almost constant movements in the leaflets of wood sorrel.

The beautiful reddish leaves of the sundew, which often grows among bog-moss on the moor, bear numerous radiating tentacles, both sensitive and mobile. Each tentacle bears at its tip a dew-like drop of insect lime which entangles the legs of small insects. The tentacle is stimulated by touch, but this requires to be confirmed by the chemical influence of the victim. When one tentacle is touched a message travels down it and influences other tentacles, which slowly curve inward. What looked like an outspread hand with many sensitive fingers becomes like a closed fist. Digestive juice is secreted round about the victim, which is then absorbed. After a while the tentacles expand again.

Still more striking is the Venus fly-trap of Carolina. If the fly-trap has been induced to shut on something it does not want, it opens again quickly, and when it has been cheated two or three times in rapid succession the plant ceases for a time to respond. Perhaps this is the nearest to Mind that a plant ever gets.

The Story of the Peoples of All Nations and Their Homelands

The proud British chief Caractacus faces the Romans

ENGLAND IN THE LONG AGO

THERE are some stories of which we never tire, and among them are those that we like to hear when we sit round the hearth, and the dancing firelight plays on the faces of those who are our home-makers. As the stories flow on, we step for a while into the quiet land of yesterday.

And what about the times before yesterday ? What happened in them ? What about the people of the far-off Past ? We know, in a way, that life has been going on in these British Isles for many years; most likely some great names belonging to them stand out for us. We realise, too, as we look about us or study pictures, that buildings such as Westminster Abbey, the great cathedrals, the Tower, and many now ruined castles and churches scattered all over the country were the work of the men of by-gone days. We can piece together the story of those days by looking carefully at the work and relics that have come down to us from them, and by reading in books and letters the descriptions of the times in which their writers lived.

By these means we can follow a written history of this country of ours back for nearly two thousand years.

Perhaps you may think the twenty centuries which hold our country's written history a long enough time to look across,

filled as they are with stirring deeds and great changes. But if you wish to peer farther back, and ask who were the very first men who lived in the country that is now ours, we must go back through ages of unknown length to seek them.

The very oldest things found in this country are some roughly chipped stone tools, which dropped from the hands of the men who made and used them when this island home of ours was not an island, but was part of the continent now called Europe. Wild animals, as well as wild men, could therefore roam about as they pleased, with neither English Channel nor Irish Sea, as they are now called, to stop them.

The poor, rough tools, found in the gravel beds or drift of old rivers, are ranged in numbers round the upper shelves in the Prehistoric Room in the British Museum; it is called prehistoric because the times to which they belong were before written history began. The owners of these tools looked out on a Thames whose opposite banks were as far apart as Hampstead and South London are to-day.

What became of the Drift Men, or the Cave Men who followed, we do not know. The Cave Men's tools are better made and in greater variety; there are harpoons to catch fish, arrow-heads to shoot birds, and

THE FIVE CONTINENTS & 100 NATIONS & RACES THAT INHABIT THEM

bone needles to sew skins together, besides the sharp pear-shaped weapons for defence or for hunting.

The most interesting things the Cave Men left behind are their drawings and carvings of the animals they saw before them; the great long-haired mammoth as he crashed along, the reindeer fighting, the oxen feeding, are all sketched from nature. Many specimens of these drawings are found in the caves of France and Spain; we read of them in our study of Art.

The Earth rolled steadily on through space year after year, century after century, and at last, as the ground sank in some places and rose in others, the sea rushed in over the lower levels and formed what is now called the North Sea, the English Channel, and the Irish Sea, and Father Thames shrank to a mere shadow of his former great size. Men came again to this country from over the sea; many different tribes followed each other, the newcomers pushing the others northward and westward, even across to Ireland and to Scotland.

NECKLACES THAT WERE WORN IN ENGLAND LONG AGO

As we look back to the far-off times of these settlers we find them very dark. They have left us no names, no writing. Perhaps the great stones set up at Stonehenge were used by them as a temple; perhaps they were set up about seventeen centuries before Jesus, that is, more than thirty-seven centuries—3700 years—ago !

The long and rounded grave-mounds, called barrows, still to be seen in many parts of the country are also believed to belong to the peoples of these times. In them are found skeletons and burnt bones, together with the rougher cups and vessels you can see in the museum below the Drift Men's and Cave Men's tools. Sometimes a little child had a whole barrow to itself; sometimes many people are buried together. The ornaments, brooches, and necklaces found in them will interest us; also the tools of bronze found often in spots where they are supposed to have been made. In these early metal factories lumps of copper and tin, of which the bronze is made, often lie side by side with old tools to be re-melted and made into new ones. Then there are iron tools which gradually came into use as time went on.

We get a few scattered beams of light on these times from the visits of some travellers who came chiefly to look after the tin found in Cornwall and elsewhere. When they reached home they wrote books about what they had seen. These were copied into other books, and in this way we hear of the barns in which corn was stored, the rich, sweet drink that the natives offered them, and so on.

THE BOOKS OF TRAVEL THAT JULIUS CAESAR WROTE

A few centuries later, in the first century B.C., a great light suddenly lit up the country in which we have been groping. By its help we can now see plainly the people who lived in it. The nations who lived on the shores of the Mediterranean Sea were very different from the Britons and other tribes living in the islands set in the wild Atlantic. They traded with each other; some were very learned; some produced the most beautiful temples and sculpture, as well as the bravest men, the world has ever seen. One of these Mediterranean nations had succeeded in conquering all the others, so that it was master of the whole of the then known world. This was the Roman nation and a great Roman soldier who stands out in this first century B.C. was the light-bearer.

As we study the calm, determined face of Julius Caesar we find out what made him so powerful. He could make himself do what he believed to be best as well as he could control others. He was always at work, conquering and settling his conquests, looking after his soldiers, and yet he found time to write books about his travels which our schoolboys read now when they begin Latin. He gives many particulars about the Britons and their relations, the Gauls.

WHEN BRITONS AND ROMANS LIVED SIDE BY SIDE

He did not conquer Britain; he visited it with his army two summers running, and described it to the civilised Roman world, who kept it in mind till a hundred years later. Then they were able to send enough soldiers to meet the warriors with faces stained blue to terrify them, to disperse the chariots with scythes on their axles, to take the hill-camps fortified with stakes and logs of wood, and in time to subdue all the country of the plains.

Little by little many of the Britons were swept farther and farther west to the high moors of Cornwall, to the mountains of Wales and Cumberland. It is to these

THE ROMANS BUILD A HOUSE IN KENT

A ROMAN GENERAL DIRECTING THE BUILDING OF A GOVERNOR'S HOUSE BY THE DARENT, WHERE THE
FOUNDATIONS STILL LIE BENEATH THE GRASS

parts we turn, especially to Wales, to find the people whose forefathers were mainly Ancient Britons, and to find echoes of the language spoken by them. It was here, too, that the old religion of the Britons, with the white-robed Druids, lasted longest.

Scattered all over the country, but chiefly in Wales, we find place-names that come from British words meaning a wood, a rock, a plain, an island, a waterfall, and many others more or less connected with the soil. Numbers of the Britons settled down, as time went on, among their Roman masters, from whom they learnt many things. Some helped the soldiers to drain the marshes and cut down trees, and to make the fine roads which crossed the country, and are still a pleasure to use, so well and straightly are they laid.

BOADICEA, QUEEN OF ENGLAND, AND THE BRAVE CHIEF CARACTACUS

Two great British names stand out in this first century A.D. Perhaps you know the statue of Boadicea, queen of one of the British tribes, which stands on the Embankment, by Westminster Bridge? With all her might she resisted the Romans, who had treated her very cruelly. Caractacus was another great British chief. He not only lost everything, in spite of his brave resistance, but was also taken prisoner to Rome with his wife and children. He did not behave at all as a frightened captive, but proudly, as a free-born king, said to the Roman emperor: " You fight to gain the whole world, and to make everybody your slaves. I fought to keep my own land, and for freedom."

For nearly four hundred years Britain was part of the Roman Empire. Great generals like Agricola came to push the conquests even farther; he built a line of forts between the Forth and the Clyde to keep out the wild mountaineers of the north—built it along the very valley that is today crowded with coal and iron mines, factories and ports, fine farms, and thousands of workers.

Emperors came and went ; we see their faces in the Roman Portrait Gallery in the British Museum, and one may read the stories of where they stayed, and how they built walls to keep out invaders.

The remains of the wall between the Solway and the Tyne are still to be seen; a railway runs in that direction now, and the name is still before us when we speak of Wallsend coal, found at the end of the Roman *vallum*. Other Roman names on our maps still show where the *castra*, or camps, were raised to house the soldiers at Chester, Lancaster, Leicester. A colony was settled in Lincoln, and many places are called Street from their position on or near the great *strata*, or roads. Stratford is an example of this.

WHAT THE ROMANS LEFT BEHIND NEAR THE EDITOR'S HILLTOP

The thousands of soldiers who came during these centuries from every part of the empire—the British lads were sent just as far away—left many remains on the soil of the country in which they worked so hard. Many of these remains are now in the great museums of the country, especially in the cities founded by the Romans—in London, York, Colchester, Winchester, and Bath. There are the altars they set up to their gods; their weapons and armour; the tablets to show long and faithful service, which gave them their discharge from the army; the memorial stones put up in their honour.

Many treasures of money and jewellery, perhaps buried in a hurry when danger arose, and never reclaimed, have been found among the foundations of cities, along the line of the walls, and on the sites of the beautiful country villas. The Editor of the Children's Encyclopedia found coins of Constantine in his garden, where Roman soldiers probably dropped them; and he dug up Roman tiles and bricks and mosaic flooring in a field near his hilltop home in Kent. The Roman houses were built in the sunniest and healthiest places, generally with a fine view, in gardens with fountains and statues.

LIFE IN THE CITY THAT LIES BENEATH OUR FEET

We can well picture the life in these villas, as we look at the fine pavements, the shoes of the ladies and children, the lamps, writing materials, mirrors, and other treasures found buried among their ruins. Some of the pottery and glass were made in Britain, for the Britons were quick to learn, but the finest came in through London.

London rose to be an important city in Roman times. Twenty feet below the pavements of the City of today are the remains of its greatness. Strong walls were built for its protection. Perhaps you have noticed how many stations have the word gate in their names—Aldgate, Moorgate, Ludgate, and so on, and from these gates in the walls started the great roads which passed over the country to connect the City with Roman stations at Lincoln, York, Chester, Bath, Chichester, and many others. Traders, therefore, found it a convenient spot to bring the goods they had for sale, especially as there was then and for many years after, a short cut for their ships from the Channel by the streams that surrounded the Isle of Thanet.

PIRATES FROM OVER THE SEAS WHO CAME TO ENGLAND IN BOATLOADS

The time came—probably in the third century—when the Romans as well as Britons began to give up worshipping the gods of their fathers, and listened to the preaching of Christian missionaries; so that there arose British churches and bishops. The country improved in many ways—more corn was grown, trade increased, and it seemed as if Roman law and order, and the liking for fine and comfortable lives, had all come to stay.

But this was not to be. In Britain itself troubles thickened as the Picts and Scots became more and more daring, and pirates from over the sea landed on the east and south coasts. Year by year, as the spring came round, fresh boatloads landed on the most desirable spots they could find, and took by force whatever they needed. In other parts of the great empire troubles thickened too, as fierce tribes poured over its distant borders and made their way towards the beautiful and wonderful capital itself. The only thing to be done, as the Roman empire grew weaker and weaker, was to give up the most distant provinces and recall the soldiers who held them to defend those nearer home.

THE ROMANS LOSE THEIR POWER AND ABANDON BRITAIN

So the Romans had to leave the walls they had built, the cities and camps, with the theatres and baths, and the castles—such as those at Richborough and Reculver which guarded the way to London. There must have been many a sad good-bye, for often Romans had British wives and relations, and the departure of those who had helped to make the country so prosperous must have sown despair in the hearts of those left behind to cope with the difficulties and dangers as best they might. They had so long been taken care of that they had forgotten how to make plans for themselves and fight all together.

Listen to a letter they sent to Rome, asking for soldiers to come back and help them: it is so sad that it is called "the groans of the Britons."

The barbarians drive us to the sea; the sea drives us back to the barbarians. We are either slain or drowned.

Many sad relics of this time are found in the caves, where families took refuge when their homes were destroyed. Thus it was that the light shed over Britain by the presence of the civilised Romans went out as the last boats carried away the last soldiers across the Channel.

The wild Picts and Scots burst over the now undefended wall, and burnt what they could not carry away back to the hills; the sea-rovers who had been coming year after year to settle and stay, came ever thicker and faster. They burnt the villas and towns, destroyed the camps, starved London to death because trade was stopped, and provisions could no longer come in by the land and water-gates from the roads and the river.

OUR FIERCE, FAIR-HAIRED, AND BLUE-EYED FOREFATHERS

Once more Britons had to flee to the mountains in the west, and most of those who were left behind became the servants of the heathen newcomers.

We want to find out all we can about these newcomers, for it is they who are the fierce forefathers of our race. Great changes have taken place, as many generations have been born, have lived and died, during the fifteen centuries between their time and ours.

But still, as a nation, we keep up a family likeness, and in many ways take after our great-grandfathers. Many of us are as fair-haired and blue-eyed as these sea rovers were; we love the sea and adventure, though in a quieter way, as much as they did. Half the words in our language —all the everyday words—come from the speech in which they shouted directions to each other as they shipped their oars and grounded their boats on these shores.

Besides all this, and much more, most of our laws, our ways of governing, our customs, have grown through the centuries from those they brought with them, together with the passionate love of freedom which we inherit, from their old homes across the North Sea.

There were long, cold winters on those flat and sandy shores round about the south-east corner of the North Sea whence the newcomers into England came in their long boats.

The meadows by the marshes, the dark woods behind them, could not afford enough food for the people who lived in the homesteads around; for, as time went on, more and more tribes of the same family of nations pushed nearer to the sea, till all were overcrowded. So it came to pass each spring, "when the birds began to twitter in the sunshine and the brooks and rivers ran gaily singing to the sea," that some of the youngest and strongest of the people set out to find new and more roomy homes, where they could hunt and fish, and where they could grow corn in order to feed their families.

NAMES STILL ON OUR LIPS AND WRITTEN ON OUR MAPS

Truly a desperate sight it must have been for the poor guardians of the shore in Kent or elsewhere when the long, narrow boats, with imposing figureheads, came swiftly toward them. In most cases resistance was useless. The tall, strong men, with flowing hair and bronzed faces, glittering swords and shields, leaped ashore one after the other, and before long were masters of some desirable piece of land, if possible near the mouth of a river or in a sheltered bay.

Then and there it was that chiefs such as Alfred or Clapa, or families like the Billings or the Harlings, set up their *ham*, or home, their *ton*, or town, as at Clapham and Alfreton, Billingham and Harlington. By names such as these and many others—such as *wick*, meaning a village ; *staple*, a store—we trace their settlements along the shore, up the courses of the rivers, and across the fertile plains. These names are still on our lips and are written on our maps.

WHERE THE JUTES, SAXONS, AND ANGLES SETTLED ON OUR SHORES

Our maps also still show us, to some extent, where the different tribes of newcomers settled. Although they belonged to the same great family they bore different names. The Jutes settled in the Isle of Wight and in Kent, which still keeps its name from an old British tribe. Branches of the Saxons, the South, East, and Middle Saxons, made their homes in Sussex,

Essex, Middlesex. There was also Wessex of the West Saxons. In course of time the Angles took up their abode in East Anglia, the country of the North and South folk—Norfolk and Suffolk ; and in Lincolnshire. It was the Angles who in the end gave their name to the whole country, which became Angleland, or England.

The settlement fighting went on for a long time, but gradually the families began to feel at home in their *hams* and their allotments, for which they really cast " lots."

In the commons of today, which are so glorious with golden furze and old whitethorn trees, we can tread, as they did, the piece of land left open and *common* to those settled near it. They had common rights, as here and there people have now, to gather wood and bracken, and let their animals roam about.

The first-comers in this greatest of all invasions that made England England were Jutes, under Hengist and Horsa, who settled by invitation in the Island of Thanet to drive away the dreaded Picts, now pressing into the country from the North. But soon the fearless sea-rovers from the country we call Jutland, or the peninsular part of Denmark, seeing that the land they had been engaged to defend was a goodly land, that it was a land rich of soil and warmed by the sun, determined to conquer it for themselves, and with that began the settlement here of the English race.

EGBERT, THE FIRST OF THE MANY RULERS OF ENGLAND

The hosts of Horsa suddenly left their camp on Thanet—then a real island—struck westward into the valley of the Medway. And at Aylesford, at the ford where the river could be crossed—about midway between what are now Maidstone and Chatham—took place the first battle ever fought by Englishmen on English soil. This was in 455.

Though Horsa himself was slain by the Britons who defended the ford, the invaders won the victory, and a step that never would be retraced was taken by the Jutes in their choice of a new home. The true founding of England took place in mid-Kent at the battle of the ford over the Medway.

For some years the country was divided up into several kingdoms, such as Kent,

ALFRED AT WAR AND ALFRED AT REST

ALFRED APPEALING TO THE PEOPLE TO DRIVE THE DANES OUT OF ENGLAND

THE ANGRY HOUSEWIFE SCOLDING THE UNKNOWN KING FOR LETTING HER CAKES BURN

In the midst of the misery of the English people caused by the fighting Danes there arose one of the noblest of our kings, Alfred. But he had a troubled life, and once hid in a cottage. The housewife let him mend his bow by the fire if he would promise to see that her cakes did not burn; but Alfred was too deep in thought to notice the cakes, and was scolded severely by the housewife when she came back to find them like cinders.

Wessex, Mercia, Northumbria. Often they were bitter enemies ; but at last, at the beginning of the ninth century, they all acknowledged one overlord, Egbert. He has been called the first King of England. There have been more than 60 rulers since his time.

The shires, or divisions into which the country is cut up, so that each part can govern its own affairs, were formed by degrees in those old times. It is interesting to remember here that the word shire comes from a word like shears, meaning cut off. Sometimes the shire was one of the old kingdoms, or a part of one ; sometimes it was named after a town of importance, such as Derby-shire.

Our family treasures, as we can see in the Anglo-Saxon Room at the British Museum, are dug up from all parts of these shires. In Lincolnshire a railway cutting goes right through a large cemetery. On the breezy downs of the Isle of Wight many warriors were laid to rest, with their weapons and ornaments beside them. Numbers come from Kent.

THE MISSIONARIES WHO CAME TO PREACH TO THE WILD NORTH

How beautiful those swords and knives must have looked when they were new. It was the mother who gave the weapons to the lad when the time came for him to follow his father to battle or the chase, bidding him keep them and to treasure them till the time came when death should take them from him.

The names of the children of those days, such as Edith, Edgar, Edwin, and Edward, have come down to us.

Sculptured stone crosses remind us that missionaries came over from Ireland to preach to the wild North; others came from Rome to the South to persuade men to give up the gods of their forefathers and become Christians. There was a long, fierce struggle before they succeeded. Woden, King of the Gods; Thor, the god of thunder; Freya, the goddess of love and fruitfulness still come to mind as we speak of Wednes-day, Thurs-day, Fri-day.

A fine cross marks the spot, near Minster, in the Isle of Thanet, where Augustine the Roman missionary landed in 597 and was welcomed by Ethelbert, king of Kent. Headed by a painted cross and waving banners, Augustine and his clergy set out for Canterbury from here, chanting hymns and prayers as they went along.

The pillow-stones which were found under the heads of nuns make one think of the numbers of women, as well as men, who were often thankful to retire in those rough times to the quiet of a religious house, to read and write, to think and pray.

EDWIN, THE GREAT KING WHO FOUNDED EDINBURGH, OR EDWIN'S TOWN

Edwin was one of the greatest of the first Christian kings. It was he who founded Edinburgh—Edwin's burgh, or town. He needed a strong fort to protect the fertile lands to the south of the Forth —our Lothians of today—and to hold the roads from the North. The castle rock gave the needed protection to the town which grew up round its base.

About this time arose Caedmon, the first English poet, from a religious house or monastery on the cliffs above Whitby in Yorkshire, to which he had retired when his great gift of song was discovered.

On the same coast, a little farther north, where now is heard the great noise of iron shipbuilding, there lived and died the great scholar and writer Bede, often called the Venerable Bede. He spent his whole life learning and teaching, and translating and writing books for the pupils who gathered round him. His chief work, perhaps, is the history of the Church of the country, which has gained him the title of the first English historian.

THE BOOK OF THE OLD SCHOLAR BEDE AND THE STORY IT TELLS

There is still a copy of Bede's book to be seen, written in Latin, in one of the most precious cases in the British Museum. Bede's book is open at the page which tells the old story of how Augustine came to be sent to preach to the English. The handsome, fair, blue-eyed boys, being sold for slaves in the market at Rome, attracted the pity of a young monk, afterwards Pope Gregory. He made a joke on their name when it was told him. " Not Angles, but Angels," he said, " they are so beautiful." As soon as he had the power he sent Augustine and a band of missionaries to carry Christianity into the boys' country.

Many another story does Bede tell. He sent all over the country to gather all the information he could, and as one reads the account of his gentle ways and his hard work to the very end of his life, one feels a great love for the saintly man.

But once more dark and bitter times fell upon the land, and learning and peace were again destroyed. Hardly had Egbert of Wessex made himself overlord of the country from the Forth to the Channel when more sea-rovers poured eagerly into it.

HOW THE FURIOUS DANES CAME DOWN UPON ENGLAND

They were even more fierce and wild than the English tribes had been three centuries before. They, too, came in fine boats, often blazing with colour, sometimes black as night, with high, carved figureheads and the dreaded Raven banner at the mast. They came across the North Sea, like the Jutes, and Saxons, and Angles. Their homes were in the lowlands of Denmark, in Sweden, and along the jagged coast of Norway. All were of the same stock—Danes ; North, or Norse, men ; Vikings, or men of the creeks. "From the fury of the Northmen, good Lord, deliver us! " was the prayer of the Christians they attacked.

All the Northmen particularly hated and despised the religion which had taken the place of the old one to which they fiercely clung. So over the stricken land flames went up from the monasteries and churches, and those who had sought refuge in them were slain. Think of it! Caedmon's haven of rest at Whitby was not spared, nor Bede's at Jarrow, nor the beautiful abbey on the little island of Lindisfarne, where Columba and Aidan, missionaries from the West, had lived. London was burned, and the whole country harried and plundered.

THE STORY OF THE TROUBLED LIFE OF ALFRED THE GREAT

In the midst of all this, toward the end of the ninth century, there uprose one of the noblest of the English kings, Alfred the Great, the Truth-teller, the Wise. His titles and the very stories about his good nature, bravery, and industry which have been handed down to our times show how beloved he was by his subjects—a thousand years ago.

When he first became king the Danes were quiet for a while, and he made good use of this peaceful time to build ships to prevent the sea-rovers landing. This was the beginning of our Navy. He also did his best to get the country into order, and soldiers trained to fight.

For a time after the return of the Danes things went against Alfred, and he had to hide. He hid one day in a swineherd's cottage where the swineherd's wife was making cakes. Not knowing the king, she let him sit by the hearth mending his bow and arrow if he would promise to see that the cakes did not burn while she was out. By the blazing red fire on the hearth sat the young king, deep in anxious thought—so deep in thought that he did not notice the strong smell of the cakes as they burned to cinders. It was rather provoking for the housewife, and, not knowing to whom she was speaking, she scolded the king severely for letting her cakes burn.

Another story from this time is of his venturing alone, disguised as a singer, into the Danish camp night after night, to find out their plans. Soon after this he won a great victory, and the treaty or arrangement which followed gave peace for many years. In his wisdom he saw that the country would be ruined unless fighting could be stopped ; and arranged to share the country with the Danes.

HOW ALFRED RULED WITH THE HELP OF THE ASSEMBLY OF WISE MEN

The part which the Danes had was called the Danelaw, because there the people were under Danish, not Saxon, laws. Part of the boundary was the Roman road which ran through London to Chester, called Watling Street.

It was not long before Alfred made his half kingdom stronger than the whole had been before his time. He improved his army and built up forts. Then he turned his mind to making good laws with the advice of the Witan, an assembly of wise men who helped him to rule the country as the Privy Council later helped our sovereigns to rule. Next he did all he could to teach his people. Since the Danes had destroyed the monasteries there was great ignorance everywhere, for the monasteries had been really schools in which people learned to read and write English and Latin.

So Alfred called together learned men from other countries—they all understood Latin—and they wrote and translated and taught as hard as they could. Alfred himself worked with them. He won a beautiful book as a prize for learning to read quickly, and he continued to study all his life. Some think it was he who started the first history of England in English, called the Anglo-Saxon Chronicle. There is a copy of it in the British Museum. King Alfred had all the information collected that could be found about older times than his, and then added the story of his own reign.

ENGLAND AFTER ALFRED'S DEATH, AND THE SPREAD OF CHRISTIANITY

After his death more was added to this, giving the history of the years as they passed for nearly three centuries. Alfred's work was carried on by his son and a very brave daughter and three grandsons, and for a time it seemed as if the Danes were going to settle down as part of the English nation without further trouble. We can see where they settled by the place-names on our map. Where the English said *tun* or *ton* for town, the Danes said *by*, and so we get Whitby, Derby, and Appleby. Many other parts of names are Danish, too, such as *toft* meaning an enclosure, as in Lowestoft; *scar*, a cliff, as in Scarborough. The long Danish swords in the British Museum remind us of the way in which they swung them round in battle; and the combs recall the flowing hair for which they were so famous.

THE PATIENT WORK OF THE MONKS AND THE MISSIONARIES

In a corner of the Anglo-Saxon Room at the British Museum are some relics which take us across the Irish Channel, to the land of those missionaries we saw preaching in the North of England. As we have seen, when Christianity was preached to the Britons in the time of the Romans, the new faith spread to Ireland, and flourished there exceedingly when the heathen Angles and Saxons had stamped it out in Britain. Churches and monasteries were built everywhere, and many people crowded into the only refuges there were in those rough times.

The country was divided into separate kingdoms, as it was in England before Egbert. Fierce fighting went on among them for many a long day. What a contrast there is between this state of things and the peace of the monasteries in which were gathered learned men from all parts ! The fame of the beautifully painted manuscripts from these monasteries spread abroad, and other arts that filled up the long days were working in metal and ivory and stone.

The missionaries who poured over the narrow straits near the Giant's Causeway, as the wild tribes of the Scots had done before them, found as beautiful a country as the one they had left in the Western Highlands, but it was wild, waste land they had to pass over in Northumbria.

Roman Britain stretched as far north as Agricola's forts between the firths of the Forth and Clyde, and later the kingdom of Northumbria, under Edwin, the founder of Edinburgh, also reached as far. The tribes that for long had fought together north of this were united at last under a king called Kenneth, in the first part of the tenth century.

Scotland, too, suffered much from the Northmen, who, pouring out of their creeks, called fiords, sailed right round the coast, taking the Shetlands, the Orkneys, and Hebrides, the rocky head of Scotland north of Glenmore, on their way down to the Isle of Man. Many traces of their rule remain to this day.

EDGAR THE PEACEFUL KING, ETHELRED THE UNREADY, AND CANUTE THE DANE

The name of Edgar stands out in the same century as Kenneth's. He was called the Peaceful King, which shows that he lived on good terms with his neighbours, even if the story is not true about eight kings rowing him on the River Dee.

In the time of his son, Ethelred, called the Unready because he would take no man's counsel (or *rede*), fresh bands of Danes appeared in England. Ethelred, at his wits' end, paid them money to go away, but they soon came back for more. Matters became worse and worse, so Ethelred fled away over the Channel to Normandy to his wife's relations. Then Canute, the Danish king who also ruled Norway, added England to his empire.

Canute was a good king in the end, and the country settled down for a time in peace. It was he who gave up to the Scottish king the land between the Forth and the Cheviots. For many centuries these hills remained the border between the two countries, with a wide road on the east by Berwick-on-Tweed, and a narrow one on the west by the marshy ground near Carlisle. Along these roads the east and west railway routes from England to the North pass today.

Illustrated Maps of All Countries with Many Thousand Pictures

KIT'S COTY HOUSE, THE ANCIENT BRITISH MONUMENT LOOKING DOWN ON AYLESFORD, THE FIRST
BATTLEFIELD OF THE ENGLISH PEOPLE ON ENGLISH SOIL

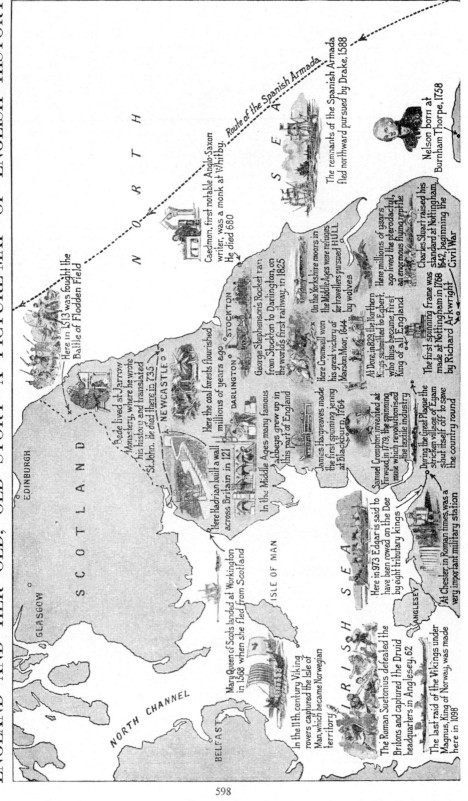

Here in 1513 was fought the Battle of Flodden Field

Caedmon, first notable Anglo-Saxon writer, was a monk at Whitby. He died 680

Route of the Spanish Armada

NORTH SEA

The remnants of the Spanish Armada fled northward pursued by Drake, 1588

Nelson born at Burnham Thorpe, 1758

SCOTLAND

EDINBURGH

GLASGOW

Bede lived at Jarrow Monastery, where he wrote his history and translated St. John. He died there in 735

NEWCASTLE

Here the coal forests flourished millions of years ago

George Stephenson's Rocket ran from Stockton to Darlington, on the world's first railway, in 1825

STOCKTON

DARLINGTON

On the Yorkshire moors in the Middle Ages were refuges for travellers pursued HULL by wolves

Here millions of years ago lived the pterodactyl, an enormous flying reptile

Here Hadrian built a wall across Britain in 121

In the Middle Ages many famous abbeys grew up in this part of England

James Hargreaves made the first spinning jenny at Blackburn, 1764

Here Cromwell won his great victory of Marston Moor, 1644

At Dore, in 829, the Northern Kings submitted to Egbert, who thus became first King of all England

Charles Stuart raised his standard at Nottingham in 1642, beginning the Civil War

The first spinning frame was made at Nottingham in 1768 by Richard Arkwright

Samuel Crompton invented at Firwood in 1779, the spinning mule which revolutionised the textile industry

During the Great Plague the stricken village of Eyam shut itself off to save the country round

ISLE OF MAN

Here in 973 Edgar is said to have been rowed on the Dee by eight tributary kings

At Chester, in Roman times, was a very important military station

IRISH SEA

ANGLESEY

Mary Queen of Scots landed at Workington in 1568 when she fled from Scotland

In the 11th century Viking rovers captured the Isle of Man, which became Norwegian territory

The Roman Suetonius defeated the Britons and captured the Druid headquarters in Anglesey, 62

The last raid of the Vikings under Magnus, King of Norway, was made here in 1098

NORTH CHANNEL

BELFAST

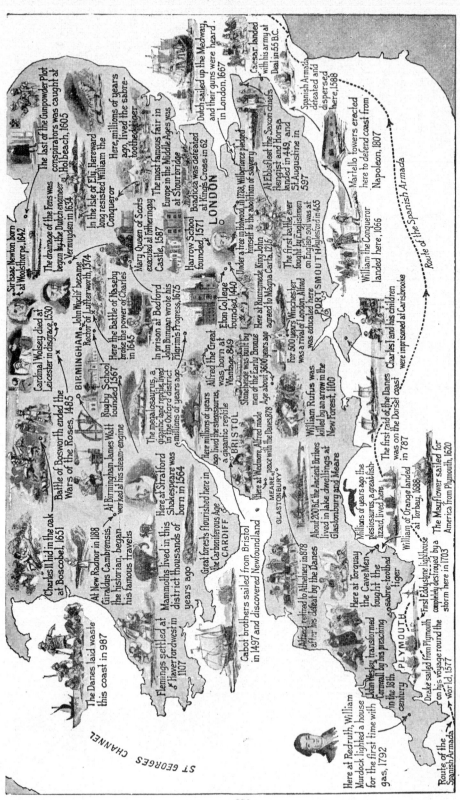

The last of the Gunpowder Plot conspirators was caught at Holbeach, 1605

Sir Isaac Newton born at Woolsthorpe, 1642

Cardinal Wolsey died at Leicester in disgrace, 1530

The drainage of the Fens was begun by the Dutch engineer Vermuyden in 1634

In the Isle of Ely, Hereward long resisted William the Conqueror

BIRMINGHAM. John Wyclif became Rector of Lutterworth, 1374

Battle of Bosworth ended the Wars of the Roses, 1485

Here, millions of years ago, lived the sabre-toothed tiger

Dutch sailed up the Medway, and their guns were heard in London, 1667

Caesar landed with his army at Deal in 55 B.C.

The most famous fair in Europe in the Middle Ages was at Stourbridge

Mary, Queen of Scots executed at Fotheringay Castle, 1587

Boadicea was defeated at King's Cross in 62

LONDON

Harrow School founded, 1571

Spanish Armada defeated and dispersed here, 1588

At Ebbsfleet the Saxon chiefs Hengist and Horsa landed in 449, and St. Augustine in 597

Martello towers erected here to defend coast from Napoleon, 1807

Rugby School founded 1567

Here the Battle of Naseby broke the power of Charles in 1645

In prison at Bedford John Bunyan wrote his Pilgrim's Progress, 1675

Eton College founded 1440

Under a tree at Olney in 1788, Wilberforce pledged himself to the abolition of slavery

Here at Runnymede, King John agreed to Magna Carta, 1215

The first battle ever fought by Englishmen on English soil was at Aylesford in 455

William the Conqueror landed here, 1066

At Birmingham James Watt worked at his steam-engine

The megalosaurus, a gigantic land reptile, lived in the Oxford district millions of years ago

Alfred the Great was born at Wantage, 849

Here millions of years ago lived the stegosaurus, a gigantic reptile

Stonehenge was built by men of the Early Bronze Age about 3600 years ago

For 500 years Winchester was a rival of London. Alfred was educated here

PORTSMOUTH

William Rufus was killed by an arrow in the New Forest, 1100

Charles I and his children were imprisoned at Carisbrooke

Here at Stratford Shakespeare was born in 1564

BRISTOL

At New Radnor in 1188 Giraldus Cambrensis, the historian, began his famous travels

Great forests flourished here in the Carboniferous Age

CARDIFF

Here at Wedmore, Alfred made peace with the Danes 878

MEARE "LAKE VILLAGE"

GLASTONBURY

The first raid of the Danes was on the Dorset coast in 787

The Mayflower sailed for America from Plymouth, 1620

Flemings settled at Haverfordwest in 1107

Mammoths lived in this district thousands of years ago

Cabot brothers sailed from Bristol in 1497 and discovered Newfoundland

About 200 B.C. the Ancient Britons lived in lake dwellings at Glastonbury and Meare

Millions of years ago the plesiosaurus, a greatfish lizard, lived here

William of Orange landed at Torbay, 1688

The Danes laid waste this coast in 987

Alfred retired to Athelney in 878 after his defeat by the Danes

Here at Torquay the Cave Men fought the sabre-toothed tiger

First Eddystone lighthouse completely destroyed by a storm here in 1703

Charles II hid in the oak at Boscobel, 1651

PLYMOUTH

Here at Redruth, William Murdock lighted a house for the first time with gas, 1792

John Wesley transformed Cornwall by his preaching in the 18th century

Drake sailed from Plymouth on his voyage round the world, 1577

ST GEORGES CHANNEL

Route of the Spanish Armada

Route of the Spanish Armada

IN THIS MAP OUR ARTIST HAS PICTURED, IN THE PLACES WHERE THEY HAPPENED, SOME OF THE MOST IMPORTANT EVENTS IN ENGLISH HISTORY

SCOTLAND AND HER OLD, OLD STORY—A PICTURE-MAP OF SCOTTISH HISTORY

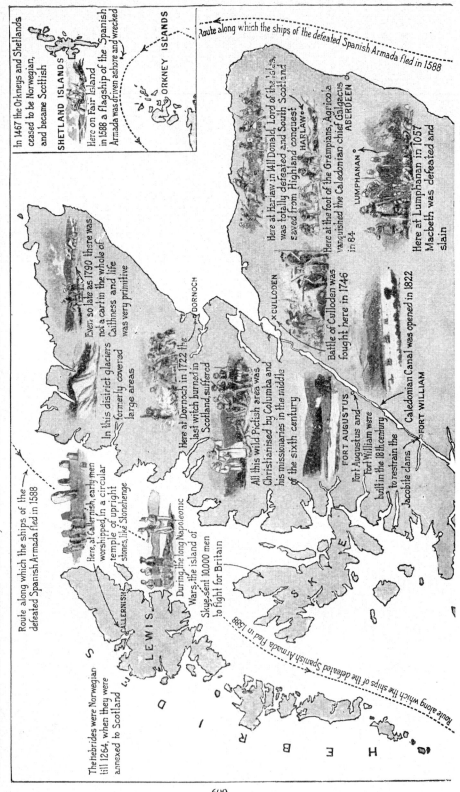

Route along which the ships of the defeated Spanish Armada fled in 1588

In 1467 the Orkneys and Shetlands ceased to be Norwegian, and became Scottish

SHETLAND ISLANDS

Here on Fair Island in 1588 a flagship of the Spanish Armada was driven ashore and wrecked

ORKNEY ISLANDS

Route along which the ships of the defeated Spanish Armada fled in 1588

Here at Harlaw in 1411 Donald, Lord of the Isles, was totally defeated and South Scotland saved from Highland conquest

HARLAW

Here at the foot of the Grampians, Agricola vanquished the Caledonian chief Galgacus in 84

ABERDEEN

LUMPHANAN

Here at Lumphanan in 1057 Macbeth was defeated and slain

×CULLODEN

Battle of Culloden was fought here in 1746

Caledonian Canal was opened in 1822

FORT AUGUSTUS
Fort Augustus and Fort William were built in the 18th century to restrain the Jacobite clans

FORT WILLIAM

All this wild Pictish area was Christianised by Columba and his missionaries in the middle of the sixth century

×DORNOCH

Here at Dornoch in 1722 the last witch burned in Scotland suffered

In this district glaciers formerly covered large areas

Even so late as 1790 there was not a cart in the whole of Caithness and life was very primitive

Route along which the ships of the defeated Spanish Armada fled 1588

The hebrides were Norwegian till 1264, when they were annexed to Scotland

S

LEWIS

CALLERNISH

Here, at Callernish, early men worshipped in a circular temple of upright stones, like Stonehenge

During the long Napoleonic Wars, the island of Skye sent 10,000 men to fight for Britain

S K Y E

Route along which the ships of the defeated Spanish Armada fled in 1588

O U T

H E B R I D E S

600

Here in Tobermory Bay in 1588 a treasure galleon of the Spanish Armada was blown up and sunk by an ancestor of Smollett, the novelist. Other ships were also wrecked and driven ashore on Mull

Here on the Island of Iona in 563 Columba, an Irish Chief's son, founded a monastery, missionaries from which were sent out to different parts of Scotland

Massacre of Glencoe took place here in 1692

The Wall of Antonine built here by Lollius Urbicus 140 to 142 A.D.

Here at Dunkeld in 815 the Culdees founded a Christian Church

Here at Scone in 1057 Malcolm III, the last of the Celtic Kings of Scotland, was crowned

Battle of Bannockburn fought here in 1314.

Here at Lochleven Castle in 1567 Mary Stuart abdicated

GLASGOW ○ Mary Queen of Scots was born at Linlithgow in 1542

By his great victory here at Largs in 1263 Alexander III defeated the King of Norway and saved the Western Isles for Scotland

Here at Balsarroch Loch in 1788 William Symington successfully tried his first steamboat

Here at Alloway in 1759 Robert Burns was born

Here at Wigtown in 1685 two women were tied to stakes and drowned by the incoming tide for their religious and political opinions

Here at Dunnichen in 685 the Picts defeated and slew Egfrid, the Saxon king, and the Highlands were saved from Saxon domination

From Leith in 1698 sailed the ill-fated Darien Expedition

Here at Haddington John Knox was born, in 1505

Here at Edinburgh in 617 Edwin, King of Northumbria, built a fort and called it Edwin's Burg

Here, in 1136, Melrose Abbey was founded by David I

For centuries fierce border raids took place here, herds and flocks being driven off

This border-line between Scotland and England was settled practically as it is now in the early years of the 13th century

DUNNICHEN ○
○DUNKELD
DUNDEE ○
SCONE ○
LEITH
○ EDINBURGH
WIGTOWN ○
MULL
IONA
NORTH CHANNEL
IRELAND
ENGLAND

601

IN THIS MAP OUR ARTIST HAS PICTURED, IN THE PLACES WHERE THEY HAPPENED, SOME OF THE MOST IMPORTANT EVENTS IN SCOTTISH HISTORY

Orkney and Shetland are shown only one-third scale of the main map

PICTURE-MAP OF IRELAND'S HISTORY

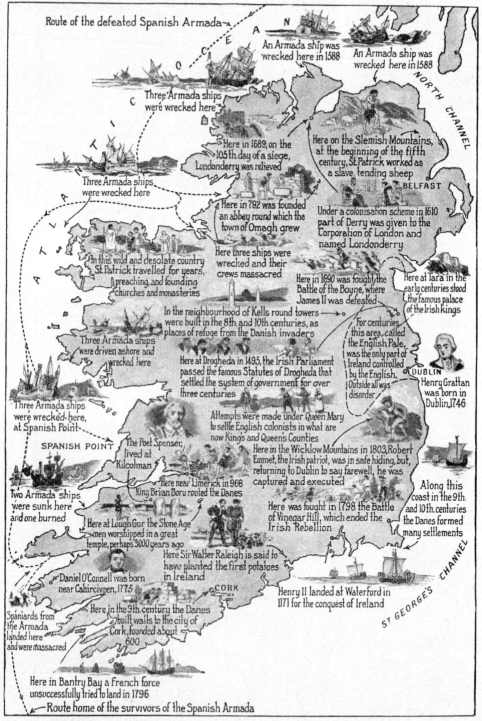

Route of the defeated Spanish Armada

An Armada ship was wrecked here in 1588

An Armada ship was wrecked here in 1588

Three Armada ships were wrecked here

Here in 1689, on the 105th day of a siege, Londonderry was relieved

Here on the Slemish Mountains, at the beginning of the fifth century, St. Patrick worked as a slave, tending sheep

BELFAST

Three Armada ships were wrecked here

Here in 792 was founded an abbey round which the town of Omagh grew

Under a colonisation scheme in 1610 part of Derry was given to the Corporation of London and named Londonderry

In this wild and desolate country St. Patrick travelled for years, preaching, and founding churches and monasteries

Here three ships were wrecked and their crews massacred

Here in 1690 was fought the Battle of the Boyne, where James II was defeated

Here at Tara in the early centuries stood the famous palace of the Irish kings

In the neighbourhood of Kells round towers were built in the 8th. and 10th. centuries, as places of refuge from the Danish invaders

Three Armada ships were driven ashore and wrecked here

Here at Drogheda in 1495, the Irish Parliament passed the famous Statutes of Drogheda that settled the system of government for over three centuries

For centuries this area, called the English Pale, was the only part of Ireland controlled by the English. Outside all was disorder

DUBLIN

Henry Grattan was born in Dublin, 1746

Three Armada ships were wrecked here, at Spanish Point

SPANISH POINT

The Poet Spenser lived at Kilcolman

Attempts were made under Queen Mary to settle English colonists in what are now King's and Queen's Counties

Here in the Wicklow Mountains in 1803, Robert Emmet, the Irish patriot, was in safe hiding, but, returning to Dublin to say farewell, he was captured and executed

Two Armada ships were sunk here and one burned

Here near Limerick in 968 King Brian Boru routed the Danes

Here was fought in 1798 the Battle of Vinegar Hill, which ended the Irish Rebellion

Along this coast in the 9th. and 10th. centuries the Danes formed many settlements

Here at Lough Gur the Stone Age men worshipped in a great temple, perhaps 3000 years ago

Here Sir Walter Raleigh is said to have planted the first potatoes in Ireland

Daniel O'Connell was born near Cahirciveen, 1775

CORK

Henry II landed at Waterford in 1171 for the conquest of Ireland

Spaniards from the Armada landed here and were massacred

Here in the 9th. century the Danes built walls to the city of Cork, founded about 600

ST GEORGE'S CHANNEL

Here in Bantry Bay a French force unsuccessfully tried to land in 1796

Route home of the survivors of the Spanish Armada

In this picture-map the chief events in Irish history are shown in the places where they occurred. The birthplaces of famous men, the scenes of social changes, famous battles and sieges, are all shown. One of the most interesting features of the map is the route taken by the defeated Spanish Armada on the way home. By comparing this map with the history maps of England and Scotland the Armada's path round the British Isles may be traced.

One Thousand Poems of All Times and All Countries

PLANTING THE APPLE TREE

William Cullen Bryant, the American poet, was the author of these verses, which, in all likelihood, were suggested to him by his having himself planted an apple tree. The planting of any tree is a favourite subject of the poets, leading the mind in the most natural way to contemplate the continuous growth of the tree possibly for centuries after the hand that planted it lies still. Tree-planters are at work all over the world, however, who never give a thought to the poetic side of their occupation, yet their labours are as suggestive of romance as any we can engage in.

COME, let us plant the apple tree,
    Cleave the tough greensward with the
      spade.
Wide let its hollow bed be made;
There gently lay the roots, and there
Sift the dark mould with kindly care,
And press it o'er them tenderly.
As, round the sleeping infant's feet,
We softly fold the cradle-sheet;
So plant we the apple tree.

WHAT plant we in this apple tree?
    Buds, which the breath of summer
      days
Shall lengthen into leafy sprays;
Boughs, where the thrush with crimson
    breast
Shall haunt and sing, and hide her nest;
We plant, upon the sunny lea,
A shadow for the noontide hour,
A shelter from the summer shower,
When we plant the apple tree.

WHAT plant we in this apple tree?
    Sweets for a hundred flowery springs
To load the May wind's restless wings
When from the orchard-row he pours
Its fragrance through our open doors;
A world of blossoms for the bee,
Flowers for the sick girl's silent room,
For the glad infant sprigs of bloom,
We plant with the apple tree.

WHAT plant we in this apple tree?
    Fruits that shall swell in sunny June,
And redden in the August noon,
And drop when gentle airs come by

That fan the blue September sky,
While children come, with cries of glee,
And seek them where the fragrant grass
Betrays their bed to those who pass,
At the foot of the apple tree.

THE fruitage of this apple tree
    Winds, and our flag of stripe and star,
Shall bear to coasts that lie afar,
Where men shall wonder at the view,
And ask in what fair climes they grew;
And sojourners beyond the sea
Shall think of childhood's careless day,
And long, long hours of summer play
In the shade of the apple tree.

EACH year shall give this apple tree
    A broader flush of roseate bloom,
A deeper maze of verdurous gloom,
And loosen, when the frost clouds lower,
The crisp brown leaves in thicker shower.
The years shall come and pass, but we
Shall hear no longer, where we lie,
The summer's songs, the autumn's sigh,
In the boughs of the apple tree.

WHO planted this old apple tree?
    The children of that distant day
Thus to some aged man shall say;
And, gazing on its mossy stem,
The grey-haired man shall answer them;
" A poet of the land was he,
Born in the rude but good old times:
'Tis said he made some quaint old rhymes
On planting the apple tree."

POEMS · SONGS · BALLADS · VERSES AND RHYMES WITH MUSIC

TO MY FRIENDS BECOME MINISTERS

Béranger, the celebrated French poet (1780–1857), was, like Robert Burns, a lover of the common people, and, although he greatly admired Napoleon and sang his praises, he preferred the friendship of humble people and their simple ways of life, as we find from this poem, addressed to certain friends of his who had become important officials.

No, no, my friends, my wants are few;
  Elsewhere with your good things
    make free;
Courts may be well enough for you,
  But spread no royal snare for me.
All that I ask is Love's caress,
  Blithe comrades, and a crust of bread;
Bending my lowly cot to bless,
  " Be nothing," the Almighty said.

Splendour would but embarrass me,
  Who idly sing from day to day;
Were Fortune's crumbs my share to be,
  " I've never earned them," I should say.
On honest Labour's humble board
  More fitly far they would be spread;
At least my wallet's amply stored!
  "Be nothing," the Almighty said.

One day, upwafted in a dream,
  From Heaven I gazed down on the world;
There, all in one vast living stream,
  Were monarchs, nations, armies swirled.
I heard a shout, 'twas Victory's strain;
  One name from realm to realm was sped—
Ye great, and thus your glories wane!
  " Be nothing," the Almighty said.

Nevertheless, all praise to you
  Intrepid pilots of the realm,
Who, bidding each his ease adieu,
  Haste to the storm-struck vessel's helm;
" Good luck," I holloa from the shore,
  " Right nobly may you speed ahead! "
Then in the sun I bask once more—
  " Be nothing," the Almighty said.

Your graves will be superb, no doubt,
  Mine but a nameless mound of grass;
Crape-covered crowds will see you out,
  I in a pauper's hearse shall pass.
Yet to us all doom is but doom,
  Your glow is quenched, my glimmer fled;
The only difference is the tomb!
  " Be nothing," the Almighty said.

Then let me be myself once more,
  To pomp I make my last salute;
Behind your grandly gilded door
  I've left my hobnails and my flute!
Though Freedom, to us both so sweet,
  Your painted halls need never dread;
I'll pipe her praises in the street—
  " Be nothing," the Almighty said.

THE FLAG GOES BY

The writer of this poem, Henry Holcomb Bennett (died 1913), was an American of the Western States. Men of each free nation can apply these words to their own flag : but more than all should British people be thrilled by the thought of the long-won and wide-won honour of the British ensign—the first flag of the free that ever floated on the wind.

Hats off !
  Along the street there comes
A blare of bugles, a ruffle of drums,
A flash of colour beneath the sky:
  Hats off !
The flag is passing by!

Blue and crimson and white it shines
Over the steel-tipped, ordered lines.
  Hats off !
The colours before us fly;
But more than the flag is passing by.

Sea-fights and land-fights, grim and great,
Fought to make and to save the State:
Weary marches and sinking ships;
Cheers of victory on dying lips;

Days of plenty and years of peace;
March of a strong land's swift increase;
Equal justice, right, and law,
Stately honour and reverend awe.

Sign of a nation, great and strong
To ward her people from foreign wrong;
Pride and glory and honour—all
Live in the colours to stand or fall.

  Hats off !
Along the street there comes
A blare of bugles, a ruffle of drums;
And loyal hearts are beating high:
  Hats off !
The flag is passing by!

ENVOY

An envoy, from the French word envoi, means the verses at the end of a poem in which some general idea of the poem is summed up and emphasised. The envoy is thus the message which the poem has carried to the reader. Here it is a way of saying that the life to which this is the envoy had been of itself a poem. The writer is Charlotte Becker.

Say not, because he did no wondrous deed,
  Amassed no worldly gain,
Wrote no great book, revealed no hidden
    truth,
  Perchance he lived in vain.

For there was grief within a thousand
    hearts
  The hour he ceased to live;
He held the love of women and of men:
  Life has no more to give!

POLLY, PUT THE KETTLE ON

Pol - ly, put the ket - tle on, Pol - ly, put the ket - tle on, Pol - ly, put the

ket - tle on, We'll all have tea. Sukey, take it off a - gain,

Suk - ey, take it off a - gain, Suk - ey, take it off a - gain, They've all gone a - way.

WHO KILLED COCK ROBIN?

Who killed Cock Robin?
  I, said the Sparrow,
  With my bow and **arrow**,
I killed Cock Robin.

Who saw him die?
  I, said the Magpie,
  With my little **eye**,
I saw him die.

Who caught his blood?
  I, said the Fish,
  With my little dish,
I caught his blood.

Who made his shroud?
  I, said the Eagle,
  With my thread and needle,
I made his shroud.

Who'll dig his grave?
  The Owl, with aid
  Of mattock and spade,
Will dig Robin's grave.

Who'll be the parson?
  I, said the Rook,
  With my little book,
I'll be the parson.

Who'll be the clerk?
  I, said the Lark,
  If not in the dark.
I'll be the clerk

I, SAID THE SPARROW

Who'll carry him to the grave?
  I, said the Kite,
  If not in the night,
I'll carry him to the grave.

Who'll be chief mourner?
  I, said the Swan,
  I'm sorry he's gone,
I'll be chief mourner.

Who'll bear his pall?
  We, said the Wren,
  Both the cock and the hen,
We'll bear the pall.

Who'll toll the bell?
  I, said the Bull,
  Because I can pull,
And I'll toll the bell.

Who'll lead the way?
  I, said the Martin,
  When ready for starting,
And I'll lead the way.

All the birds in the air
  Began sighing and sobbing
When they heard the bell toll
  For poor Cock Robin.

To all it concerns
  This notice apprises
The Sparrow's for trial
  At next bird assizes.

J.A.S

IF the old woman who lived in a shoe
   Had lived in a cottage instead,
Her children could have played at
   hide-and-seek,
   And needn't have been sent to bed.

If little Bo-Peep hadn't lost her sheep,
   She wouldn't have had to find them.
If Little Boy Blue had not any sheep,
   He wouldn't have had to mind them.

If the goose that laid the golden eggs
   Had not been killed that day,
She'd still be laying golden eggs
   As hard as she could lay.

In fact, if we could manage things,
   How different they would be!
But as we can't, we'll let them stay
   Just as they are, you see.

ONE, I love; two, I love;
   Three, I love, I say;
Four, I love with all my heart;
   Five, I cast away;
Six, he loves; seven, she loves;
Eight, both love;
Nine, he comes; ten, he tarries;
Eleven, he courts; and twelve, he
   marries.

The Story of Where Power Comes From, What It Does, & How It Works

One of the first Dynamos   A later Dynamo   A modern Westinghouse Dynamo

THE STORY OF THE DYNAMO

IF you followed the little silk-covered twin wires from which an electric lamp is suspended, and could trace their path from the house into the underground tubes which run along below the street, you would finally end up at the electric generating station; and these wires, together with a formidable bundle of other wires, would end in two huge cables joined to the switchboard of the *generator*. It is almost like following the pipe from a gas-lamp to the huge dome-shaped reservoirs familiar to us as the " gas-works." One central generating plant of sufficient size to supply the needs of a whole town distributes its power in the form of gas or electric current to the thousands of users, each of whom wants his own little quantity.

A great romance lies round the manufacture of the huge quantities of electricity needed to light the homes, run the trams, and supply the power for a town of tens of thousands of people. It is only possible as the result of combining the knowledge and discoveries of all the great men of science who followed the famous physician of Queen Elizabeth, Doctor Gilbert. As far apart as the poles of the Earth are the glowing sulphur ball of von Guericke—the first electric light—and the brilliant half-watt and mercury vapour lamps which today illumine our shops in a busy street. Little by little, one discovery, one invention, has followed another, until we can today have as much electric light as we want, or use as much electric power as is needed for the motors which run the electric trains and the machines of the factories.

The secret of the dynamo—the electric machine which produces this current—is very simple. If a coil of wire is joined to the poles of an electric battery, the coil acts as a magnet, the current producing a magnetic field. But if such a coil be itself moved about in the field of a magnet, an electric current is set up *within the coil*.

The dynamo is nothing more than a number of wire coils driven round between the poles of a powerful magnet, and as they cut the lines of force thrown out by it, an electric current is set up which is collected in a way very similar to that of storing up the current from a frictional machine.

In the early dynamos the coils in which the electric currents were set up were revolved in the field of a steel horse-shoe magnet, but in order to obtain greater power an electric magnet excited by a battery was used. Later, a great advance was made by actually taking some of the electricity created by the dynamo to excite its own magnet.

ELECTRICITY · WIRELESS · OIL · GAS · MOTORS · ENGINES · SHIPS

It must be understood that there are definite rules which magnets and coils obey when the coils are revolved in a magnetic field. According to the direction in which the coil turns, and its relation to the north and south poles of the magnet, the current will flow in a certain direction. When a coil has turned through half a circle it has become reversed, so to speak, and for the next half of the turn the current produced in it will flow the opposite way. Thus, in the simplest form of dynamo, the current is changed twice in direction during every revolution; such a current is said to be *alternating*. The *armature*—the arrangement of coils used in a modern dynamo—can be so built up that the " brushes " which collect the current will produce either alternating or direct current.

To the electrical engineer direct current is essential for charging accumulators or storage batteries, for electro-plating, and for big arc lamps. Alternating current is equally necessary for long-distance transmissions; it can be sent at a very high voltage with little loss over immense distances, and easily reduced to lower voltages at the point where it is used. It has become practically universal in England today for all ordinary purposes.

THE TERRIFIC PRESSURE OF ELECTRICITY AS IT COMES FROM THE DYNAMO

This brings us to the subject of the pressure of an electric current. Suppose we wanted to supply water from a tank through a pipe to some spot a long way off. We know that the tank would have to be higher up than the spot to which the water was being sent. The higher the tank was raised the greater would be the pressure of water, the better the driving force to send it through the pipe.

We can liken the dynamo to the water tank and the pressure of the current to the pressure of the water. Whereas water pressure is measured by saying there is so much *head* of water, electricity is measured by saying that its pressure is so many volts. In the early days of electric lighting a hundred volts was quite a usual pressure, but it was soon felt that a higher pressure was better, and today it is usually 220, 240, 440, or more.

When the problem arose of sending electricity over really great distances, when electric power was generated by using the driving force of waterfalls and sending it to spots perhaps a hundred miles away, much higher pressures had to be used, and currents at more than a hundred thousand volts pressure are in use today.

Now, why does an electric current at 1000 volts pressure travel a hundred miles with less loss than one at 100 volts?

The great pioneer Ohm discovered a law which is perhaps the most useful of all electrical laws. It is that when a current flows through any completed course, which we shall in future call a circuit, the amount of current is *equal to the voltage divided by the resistance*.

WATERFALLS AND RIVERS THAT DRIVE LARGE ELECTRIC GENERATORS

Three great philosophers gave their names to the units in which these electrical quantities are given: Ampère, Volta, and Ohm. Current is measured in *ampères*, pressure in *volts*, and resistance in *ohms*. If a current of one volt pressure flows through a circuit the resistance of which is only one ohm, the current strength will be one ampère.

We can see, then, that if a current is sent through a wire of great length, having therefore great resistance, it will be greatly diminished in strength. But it is diminished less and less as the voltage is made bigger, so that for very long distances a really enormous voltage is used.

Tens of millions of horse-power are generated today by harnessing the natural power of waterfalls and swiftly-running rivers to drive water turbines. Modern water-wheels are as far ahead of the old water-wheels of the mills as the huge turbines of an Atlantic liner are ahead of the old-fashioned paddle-wheels in steamboats. These power turbines, driven by natural forces which have for centuries past flowed to waste, are made to drive large electric generators. But waterfalls and water-power are very rarely situated near a big manufacturing town or a big city which requires current for its lighting and its tramways.

HOW POWER IS CARRIED ALONG WIRES FIFTY OR A HUNDRED MILES LONG

The electricity has thus to be *transmitted* from the scene of a waterfall or big generating station to towns and cities miles away—sent through wires perhaps 50 or 100 miles long. It is in such cases as these that high voltages are used, and the conducting wires are suspended high up in the air from steel towers called pylons ; if the wires were suspended too low there would be a leakage of electricity to the earth. The grid current being alter-ternating, the wires have to be suspended a considerable distance apart, and being " three-phase," we see generally one or two sets of three wires for each circuit. In order to reduce the voltage to one that can be used for power or lighting, static transformers are used, which provide a suitable pressure. Many factories, for

immense speed. It is so beautifully bal-anced that its motion is smooth. The most striking feature of a generating station is its apparent simplicity, its lack of com-plication ; yet the winding and arrange-ment of the field magnet, the extraordinary complexity of the armature, are things to wonder at even today.

The switchboard of a generating station is like the office of a big factory. It collects the current from the dynamos and directs it into the conductors, and so to the sub-stations whence it is put to practical use.

In this picture we see a steam engine which drives an electric dynamo. The current generated by the dynamo flows to a switch controlling a motor, which in turn drives the printing press.

example, take in current at 11,000 volts and with their own further transformers cut this down again to 440 volts, the cus-tomary pressure for works' motors. The lower voltages from the grid sub-stations are led through conductors underground.

The first impression of a large power station is generally one of wonder that this huge force, driving the tramways of a city and supplying its myriad lights, is being produced by a machine so calm and still. There is a peculiar majesty about a modern generator. At first sight it appears to be still—the only sensation of life that it gives is the buzzing, whizzing, or peculiar singing noise of its giant armature. This armature, bearing the coils of wire that cut across the lines of force of the powerful electric magnets, seem at first sight to be still, but actually it is running round at

On the switchboard we find :

1. Resistances (or rheostats), for regulating the voltage ; as only a very definite voltage or pressure must be supplied.

2. Switches, with which the different dynamos are connected to what are termed the bus-bars.

3. Cut-outs for protecting the dynamos them-selves and the wires that convey the current.

4. Instruments for measuring the amount of current produced, the power supplied, and the pressure of the current.

Very often the current is not supplied directly to the mains which carry the electricity to the consumer, but is poured, as it were, into a large storage battery, which in its turn supplies live current.

The dynamo does not, by any means, stand by itself in an electricity supply station. It is one thing to produce this great amount of current, another thing to distribute and control it. Special measures have to be taken, too, to protect lighting circuits and motors provided with current from the effects of lightning.

If the two ends of a large battery or dynamo are made to touch each other, and then drawn a little way apart, an intensely powerful flame called an *arc* will flash between them, and may do considerable damage. The switch which makes or breaks the current from a dynamo has to complete the circuit, or make a break in the continuity of it; the current must have a metal path to flow through, or else be stopped by a gap of air, which does not conduct electricity. But the very making of this gap may " strike an arc," and the current would still flow across the flame, the hot gases of the burning metals acting as a conductor. Massive switches which break the continuity of both wires leading from the dynamo, and which break away the conducting parts with a quick jerk, are used. The parts which " make " and " break " are made to work in a metal chamber filled with oil so as to quench the spark and prevent it doing harm. The switchgear of the big power stations feeding the overhead lines of the grid are far more complicated.

THE SAFETY FUSE-BOX AND WHAT IT DOES

In case any positive wire should accidentally touch a negative wire, and so cause a short-circuit, fuses are used on a large scale. A home lighted with electricity is sure to have a fuse-box somewhere, containing a number of fuse-wires which protect the electric circuits from danger.

If a big current flows through a thin wire it will heat it to such an extent that the wire will melt. This is exactly how a fuse is made. Every here and there in lighting or motor circuits—in fact wherever electricity is used—the electrician puts a fuse-wire contained in a little porcelain box. This wire is often made of tin —which melts at very low temperature— sometimes of other metals. If, through any accident, too much current flows through the circuit, the fuse-wire will melt, and an air-gap will be instantly made in the circuit, so that the current can no longer flow.

Much more elaborate fuses or " cut-outs " are used in circuits where really high power is being used, but the principle is always the same; as soon as an excessive current flows, something gives, and an air-gap is made in the circuit.

The wires leading from the generating station, known as the electric mains, are heavy copper cables carefully insulated and laid in wood, earthenware, or iron troughs under the ground. These tunnels are usually placed about fifteen inches below the footway, or twice that depth below roadways.

ONE OF THE MOST WONDERFUL INSTRUMENTS IN THE WORLD

Thus, beneath our feet, as we tread the streets, are the sinews of the power that feeds the city or the village; the electric wires convey the mysterious force that can be instantly turned into light, or heat, or mechanical power. In each office, factory, or house, the current must first pass through a meter, or measuring instrument, which keeps a record of all the current used. Coal gas is measured in therms (according to its heat), electricity in units. A unit means the use of a thousand watts for one hour. A watt means the flow of a current of one ampère at a pressure of one volt. A modern 20-candle-power lamp consumes a current of a tenth of an ampère at 200 volts pressure; 200 multiplied by one-tenth gives us 20 watts; 20 multiplied by 50 gives us a thousand. Thus fifty such lamps lighted for an hour would consume a unit of electricity.

The electricity meter is one of the most delicate, intricate, and wonderful instruments in existence today. Several different kinds of meter are in use, some depending on chemical action caused by the current, others on a motor made to turn and count by the current passing through it, and others, again, in which a clock drives a counting machine.

THE GREAT BUSINESS OF CONTROLLING AND DISTRIBUTING ELECTRICITY

The lighting of a lamp, or the switching on of an electric motor, is thus by no means as simple a thing as it appears. Every unit of electricity has to be accounted for. The demand for current from hour to hour, from minute to minute, has to be watched by the engineer at the generating station. The electricity poured out by huge dynamos has to be controlled, directed, and distributed among some thousands of users.

Imperishable Thoughts of Men Enshrined in the Books of the World

Augustine tells the Bible Story to King Ethelbert and his Queen

THE BOOK AS SWEET AS MUSIC

WE have said that the Bible is the most precious book in the English language, not only because of its religious teaching, showing how God has been revealed to mankind in truer ways as the ages have passed, but because, as a collection of books—written by many people living in many centuries, and now welded into one book—it has been translated into English so beautifully that its teaching has been set to the music of sweet words.

Here we want to show that this is so by looking at a few scenes, or teachings, and recalling the words in which they are described in our English Bible. We say there is no other book in which language is used so simply and sweetly, and with effects so profoundly true.

Take one of the earliest scenes—the finding of a wife for Isaac, Abraham's son, at least thirty-five centuries ago. When the account in the Book of Genesis was actually written no one knows, but it almost certainly was in existence 2750 years ago, and of all the books of the world not one tells a story more clearly or with greater charm.

Abraham was a very old man, and he wanted to see his quiet and studious son Isaac married to a wife of his own clan;

but he had travelled a long way from the region where they pastured their flocks. So he sent a trusted servant to find a suitable wife, believing that God would guide him aright in his search. It is a pastoral desert scene that follows ; we have slightly shortened the story here.

And it came to pass that Rebekah, the daughter of Bethuel, came out with her pitcher upon her shoulder. And the damsel was very fair to look upon, and she went down to the well and filled her pitcher and came up. And the servant ran to meet her, and said, " Let me, I pray thee, drink a little water of thy pitcher."

And she said, "Drink, my lord"; and she hasted and let down her pitcher on her hand and gave him drink. And when she had given him drink, she said, "I will draw water for thy camels also, till they have done drinking." And she hasted and emptied her pitcher into the trough, and ran again, and drew water for all his camels.

And the man, wondering at her, held his peace, to wit whether the Lord had made his journey prosperous or not. And it came to pass, as the camels had done drinking, that the man took a golden earring, and two bracelets for her hands, and said, " Whose daughter art thou ? Is there room in thy father's house for us to lodge in ?"

And she said, " I am the daughter of Bethuel. We have both provender and straw enough, and room to lodge in."

And the damsel ran and told them of her mother's house these things. And Rebekah

ROMANCE · HISTORIES · DRAMAS · ESSAYS · WORLD CLASSICS

had a brother named Laban, and Laban ran out unto the well, and said, " Come in, thou blessed of the Lord; wherefore standest thou without ? For I have prepared the house, and room for the camels."

Abraham's servant, thus offered entertainment, revealed his errand of finding a wife for his master's son, and finished, "And now, if ye will deal kindly and truly with my master, tell me; and if not, tell me; that I may turn to the right hand or to the left." And Bethuel answered and said, " Behold, Rebekah is before thee, take her and go, and let her be thy master's son's wife, as the Lord hath spoken."

ISAAC TOOK REBEKAH, AND SHE BECAME HIS WIFE, AND HE LOVED HER

Next morning, however, the girl's mother and brother counselled delay by saying :

"Let the damsel abide with us a few days, at the least ten; after that she shall go." And he said unto them, " Hinder me not, seeing the Lord hath prospered my way."

And they said, " We will call the damsel, and inquire at her mouth." And they called Rebekah and said unto her, " Wilt thou go with this man ?" And she said, "I will go."

Here is the sequel, happy in itself, and as delightfully told :

And Isaac went out to meditate in the field at the eventide, and he lifted up his eyes and behold the camels were coming. And Rebekah lifted up her eyes, and when she saw Isaac she lighted off the camel. For she had said unto the servant, " What man is this that walketh in the field to meet us ?" And the servant had said, "It is my master." Therefore she took a veil and covered herself. And the servant told Isaac all things that he had done. And Isaac brought her to his mother Sarah's tent, and took Rebekah, and she became his wife, and he loved her; and Isaac was comforted.

Many narratives equally graphic and charming are found throughout the Old Testament. One of the most striking of the literary outbursts is David's poetical lament for the fallen heroes Saul and Jonathan, the most authentic of the songs attributed to the shepherd-king. It pictures the luxury of those early times ; also it expresses in agonised words the fate of those who take to the sword and perish by it.

LOVELY AND PLEASANT IN THEIR LIVES AND IN THEIR DEATHS NOT DIVIDED

The beauty of Israel is slain upon thy high places;
How are the mighty fallen!
Tell it not in Gath;
Publish it not in the streets of Askelon;
Lest the daughters of the Philistines rejoice,
Lest the daughters of the uncircumcised triumph.
Ye mountains of Gilboa, let there be no dew,
Neither let there be rain upon you, nor fields of offerings;
For there the shield of the mighty is vilely cast away,
The shield of Saul, as though he had not been anointed with oil.
Saul and Jonathan were lovely and pleasant in their lives,
And in their death they were not divided.
They were swifter than eagles,
They were stronger than lions.
Ye daughters of Israel, weep over Saul,
Who clothed you in scarlet, with other delights,
Who put ornaments of gold upon your apparel.
How are the mighty fallen in the midst of the battle !
O Jonathan, thou wast slain in thine high places.
I am distressed for thee, my brother Jonathan;
Very pleasant hast thou been unto me;
Thy love to me was wonderful,
Passing the love of women.
How are the mighty fallen,
And the weapons of war perished!

NO GOD LIKE HIM IN HEAVEN ABOVE OR ON EARTH BENEATH

The weakness of the Hebrew religion was its narrowness and bigotry. Too often it saw no room in God's favour for any except the Hebrew race. But that was not so in the prayer that is placed in the mouth of Solomon at the opening of his gorgeous temple.

And Solomon stood before the altar of the Lord in the presence of all the congregation of Israel and spread forth his hands towards heaven; and he said, "Lord God of Israel, there is no God like thee in heaven above, or on Earth beneath, who keepest covenant and mercy with thy servants that walk before thee with all their heart.

"But will God indeed dwell on the Earth ? Behold the heaven and heaven of heavens cannot contain thee ; how much less this house that I have builded ? Yet have thou respect unto the prayer of thy servant, that thine eyes may be open to this house night and day; and hearken thou to the supplication of thy servant and of thy people Israel, when they shall pray towards this place; and hear thou in heaven thy dwelling place, and when thou hearest, forgive."

The most splendid minds that ancient Israel produced were those of the prophets who were in fullest activity from about the year 750 B.C. to 300 B.C. They sought to make religion lead to personal goodness instead of empty ceremony, and their eloquence resounds through the oldest parts of the Bible—judging age by the time when the books were written, and not by the time about which they were written. Isaiah, the son of Amoz, was the prophet who most impressed his countrymen, by appeals like this :

Hear, O heavens, and give ear O Earth: for the Lord hath spoken. "I have nourished and brought up children and they have rebelled against me. The ox knoweth his owner, and the ass his master's crib; but Israel doth not know, my people doth not consider."

THE OUTLOOK OF THE HEBREWS WIDENED BY THEIR CAPTIVITY

To what purpose is the multitude of your sacrifices to me? saith the Lord: I am full of the burnt offerings of rams, and the fat of fed beasts; and I delight not in the blood of bullocks, or of lambs, or of he-goats. When ye come to appear before me, who hath required this at your hands to tread my courts ? Bring no more vain oblations; incense is an abomination unto me; the new moons and sabbaths, the calling of assemblies I cannot away with; it is iniquity, even the solemn meeting. Wash you, make you clean; put away the evil of your doings from before mine eyes ; cease to do evil; learn to do well; seek judgment, relieve the oppressed, judge the fatherless, plead for the widow.

The carrying away of the Hebrews into Babylon had a great effect on them. They learned much there. Their outlook widened. Their view of God as majestic in power yet kind, the ruler of all the sons of men, was expressed in glorious strains; and as the time for the return to Palestine grew near, the feelings of the poet-prophets were expressed in rapturous outbursts. The splendid fortieth chapter placed under the name of Isaiah was an encouraging prelude to the journey back across the desert from Babylon to Jerusalem. It is to meet these circumstances that the prophet exclaims :

Comfort ye, comfort ye my people, saith your God. Speak ye comfortably to Jerusalem, and cry unto her that her warfare is accomplished, that her iniquity is pardoned; for she hath received of the Lord's hand double for all her sins.

SAY UNTO THE CITIES OF JUDAH, BEHOLD YOUR GOD

The voice of him that crieth in the wilderness Prepare ye the way of the Lord, make straigh in the desert a highway for our God. Every valley shall be exalted, and every mountain and hill shall be made low; and the crooked shall be made straight and the rough places plain; and the glory of the Lord shall be revealed, and all flesh shall see it together, for the mouth of the Lord hath spoken it.

O Zion, that bringest good tidings, get thee up into the high mountain ; O Jerusalem, that bringest good tidings, lift up thy voice with strength; lift it up, be not afraid; say unto the cities of Judah, Behold your God !

He shall feed His flock like a shepherd; He shall gather the lambs with His arm, and carry them in His bosom, and shall gently lead those that are with young.

At this time, too, began those sublime views of God as the omnipotent Creator which ever afterwards continued through the best Hebrew literature, and showed traces of the study of astronomy and a vision of a universe wider than the Earth. This had been gained on the Mesopotamian plain during the exile.

Who hath measured the waters in the hollow of his hand, and meted out heaven with the span, and comprehended the dust of the Earth in a measure, and weighed the mountains in scales and the hills in a balance? Behold, the nations are as a drop of a bucket, and are counted as the small dust of the balance; behold, he taketh up the isles as a very little thing. To whom then will ye liken me, or shall I be equal, saith the Holy One. Lift up your eyes on high, and behold who hath created these things, that bringeth out their host by number; he calleth them all by names by the greatness of his might, for that he is strong in power; not one faileth.

THE IDEA OF GOD AS CREATOR OF THE UNIVERSE

The same note is heard again and again in the later Psalms:

The heavens declare the glory of God;
And the firmament showeth his handywork.
Day unto day uttereth speech,
And night unto night showeth knowledge.
There is no speech nor language
Where their voice is not heard.

It vibrates through that later drama, the wonderful Book of Job :

Where wast thou when I laid the foundations of the Earth?
Declare, if thou hast understanding.
Whereupon are the foundation stones thereof fastened?
Or who laid the corner stone thereof;
When the morning stars sang together
And all the sons of God shouted for joy?
Canst thou bind the sweet influences of the Pleiades,
Or loose the bands of Orion?
Canst thou bring forth Mazzaroth in his season?
Or canst thou guide Arcturus with his sons?

The beauty in style that makes the Bible first among all books is in no way lessened when the change is made from the Hebrew

Old Testament to the Christian New Testament. Almost any narrative will serve as an illustration, but take one where description is interwoven with profound teaching :

He left Judaea and departed again into Galilee; and he must needs go through Samaria. So he cometh to a city of Samaria called Sychar, and Jacob's well was there. Jesus, therefore, being wearied with his journey, sat thus by the well. It was about the sixth hour. There cometh a woman of Samaria to draw water. Jesus saith unto her, Give me to drink. For his disciples were gone away into the city to buy food.

THEY THAT WORSHIP HIM MUST WORSHIP HIM IN SPIRIT AND IN TRUTH

The Samaritan woman therefore saith unto him, How is it that thou, being a Jew, askest drink of me, which am a woman of Samaria? (For the Jews have no dealings with the Samaritans.)

Jesus answered and said unto her, If thou knewest the gift of God, and who it is that saith to thee, Give me to drink, thou wouldst have asked of him, and he would have given thee living water.

The woman saith unto him, Sir, thou hast nothing to draw with, and the well is deep ; from whence then hast thou that living water ? Art thou greater than our father Jacob, who gave us the well, and drank thereof himself, his children and his cattle?

Jesus answered and said unto her, Whosoever drinketh of this water shall thirst again. But whosoever drinketh of the water that I shall give him shall never thirst; but the water that I shall give him shall be a well of water springing up into everlasting life.

The woman said unto him, Sir, I perceive that thou art a prophet. Our fathers worshipped in this mountain; and ye say that Jerusalem is the place where men ought to worship.

Jesus saith unto her, Woman, believe me, the hour cometh when ye shall neither on this mountain nor yet at Jerusalem worship the Father. But the hour cometh, and now is, when the true worshippers shall worship the Father in spirit and in truth, for the Father seeketh such to worship him. God is a Spirit; and they that worship him must worship him in spirit and in truth.

THE BEAUTIFUL STORIES IN THE NEW TESTAMENT FULL OF DEEP THOUGHT

Simple, graphic, deep, here is the true union between natural narrative and profound thought. Among the many examples of exquisite New Testament narrative that may be read, in all the Gospels, stands high the description of Peter's denial of the Lord, especially in Luke's account, where the Lord is described as turning and looking at Peter, whereupon he went out and wept bitterly.

Or, again, for plain, yet unsurpassed telling of a story, take the account of Paul's shipwreck on the island of Malta in the last chapter but one of the Acts of the Apostles. For argument in a style of transcendent dignity there is the discussion of immortality by Paul in I Corinthians 15, used in the burial service.

But, in truth, from the noble poetic vision of the Creation in Genesis—not in date of writing one of the earliest parts of the Bible—to the Revelation, with its poetic picture of a future beyond death, the beauty of the writing of the Bible is at times divine, and it is felt the more if we know something of the circumstances surrounding the writers who, in a rapture of vision, poured forth their eloquence.

A last instance may fitly be taken from the closing book of the Bible. Apocalyptic writings—visions of the future, as seen in dreams, chiefly comforting—were very common during the centuries immediately before and after Christ.

THE RICH SIMPLICITY AND IMAGINATION OF THE EASTERN MIND

Such writings took that form often because it was safest, perhaps the only safe way. Thus the revelation attributed to St. John is a concealed denunciation of Nero, a commemoration of innumerable martyrs, and an appeal to Christians who expected and often hoped for martyrdom. and who finally believed that the end of the world was close at hand. These writings were the uplifting call of faith to myriads to whom Christianity meant suffering and death. Of them it was asked :

These which are arrayed in white robes, what are they, and whence came they ? These are they which came out of great tribulation, and have washed their robes and made them white in the blood of the Lamb. Therefore are they before the throne of God and serve him day and night in his temple; and he that sitteth on the throne shall spread his tabernacle over them. They shall hunger no more, neither thirst any more, neither shall the Sun strike upon them nor any heat; for the Lamb which is in the midst of the throne shall be their shepherd, and shall guide them unto living fountains of water; and God shall wipe away all tears from their eyes.

Only through the Bible do we come into close and intimate touch with the refined imagination of the Eastern mind, and its expression in a rich simplicity that has gloriously haunted the strong but rugged speech of our British race.

The Great Words That Stir the Hearts and Minds of All Mankind

Even the birds know the way they go—they have a sense of Direction

DIRECTION

ONE of our greatest men of science said to us in conversation one day that two of the words which helped him most in his thinking were the words Direction and Personality. Let us now think a little about Direction.

Suppose you stood by the side of a motor-car and set it going. You would see it start off along the road just as if someone was steering it. But soon it would swing to the left, then swerve to the right, and finally crash violently against an obstacle on the wayside.

But if you saw in the distance another car approaching you, which kept to its path and steered intelligently past obstacles, you would say to yourself: " There is a man at the wheel, directing it."

You will often see a baulk of timber floating in the sea. It goes hither and thither. It has no power in itself. No one is steering it. The waves wash over it, the tide bears it onward, and the currents carry it whither it knows not. How differently does a steamship move through that waste of waters! It may be steered by a man on the bridge, or even by a man in an aeroplane overhead; but so long as it is steered by a mind it will follow a certain direction. It will not be at the mercy of winds or waves. It will triumph over the set of the tide. It will avoid rocks and shoals. It will arrive.

Now, when we come to consider the works of Nature we see in everything signs of a direction. It is quite plain to us that the sea does not move like the log of wood floating on its waves, or that the seasons of the year do not move like a motor-car without a driver. They may not be always the same. The sea may be rough at one moment, and smooth at the next. Summer may one year be cold and wet, winter in that year may be warm and muggy; but all the same there is a certain direction in the seasons. They are not permanently in disorder. Nature never appears to us in the least like a motor-car without a driver or a baulk of timber floating in the waves.

Moreover, we go back in our minds to a past which no man can measure, and we see this planet roaring round the Sun in sheets of flame. We look at it with the mind's eye, and watch it cool down, and see the atmosphere enfolding it, the water shining on its surface, the green herb appearing on the marge of those waters, and Life appearing out of the deep.

We say to ourselves: " There is a movement in Nature. Things are changing. The planet is no longer like an oven; it

LIBERTY · JUSTICE · SPACE · DISTANCE · MOVEMENT · TRUTH · FAITH

is more like a garden. Someone must be steering this movement, for it is not only movement; it is movement with direction." This seems sensible. But someone comes along who loves to argue, and he says to us, " It is true things are changing; it is true things could not change without movement; but why should you say *someone must be steering this movement?* Is it not the movement itself which does everything?"

NATURE NOT A TOPSY-TURVY CHAOS BUT AN ORDERLY MOVEMENT

This sounds as if it might be true. We cannot see anyone steering the movement. Suppose, after all, there is a movement which steers itself, a very odd movement, to be sure, but a bare possibility. Then someone else comes along and says:

I have been studying the movement of Nature, and I have come to the conclusion that it is following a very remarkable direction.

It is not moving aimlessly. It is seeking something. It is like a man who has lost his way and is trying all sorts of paths to reach his goal. Or it is like a woman who has lost a coin in her house and is searching through all the rooms to find it.

What Nature is seeking I cannot say for certain, but she is seeking *something*, and it looks to me as if she were struggling to reach beauty and power. She was not content with grass : she must have the violet and the rose. She was not satisfied with the jellyfish, she must have the elephant.

At any rate, I am quite convinced that Nature is not a topsy-turvy chaos, but an orderly movement following an intelligent direction.

We now begin to see light. If we would discover our mystery we must study the character of the movement in Nature. Then we shall be able to say something about the direction it is following. There is movement. But what is its character?

NATURE ON THE SIDE OF CO-OPERATION AND OPPOSED TO SELFISHNESS

Watch this movement of Nature and you will at once notice a very strange thing about it. It produces with infinite care a number of living forms *only to fling them away*. Dig down into the earth and you will find the fossil remains of marvellous creatures nowhere now to be found among the living. They have been cast away. You will notice that a number of other living creatures are dying out, as if Nature no longer bothers about them. Our museums and zoos collect these things and preserve them because they are dying out, which means that Nature has now no use for them.

Let us look at the things which Nature does appear to want, the things she really does care about. There are plenty of bees and plenty of flowers, plenty of sheep and plenty of green fields, plenty of men and plenty of corn.

What strikes us about these things? They are useful to one another. The bee helps the flowers, and the flower helps the bee. The sheep helps the grass, and the grass helps the sheep. Men help wheat, and wheat helps men.

It is quite different with tigers and wolves and eagles. They think only of themselves. They kill and destroy. They help nothing. It looks, then, as if this movement in Nature is *on the side of Co-operation and opposed to Selfishness*. Nature wanted swiftness and produced the tiger; but the tiger used its swiftness only for selfish purposes, and Nature abandoned it.

Well, then, it looks as if the natural movement is moral. It is not following a bad direction, but a good one. It does not want creatures to help themselves, but to help one another.

Look closer at this movement. Is it on the side of intelligence or stupidity? Is it trying to produce foolish things or wise things? Is it struggling to make Matter act reasonably or unreasonably?

THE MIND DIRECTING LIFE TOWARD TRUTH, BEAUTY, GOODNESS

We have only to think of the marvellous instinct in animals, insects, and plants to answer that question. Instinct ! What a wonderful word! How comes it that these creatures possess so extraordinary a power? How could the movement in Nature produce this instinct if it was not itself intelligent?

Let us take a look at Man. What is it that first strikes us about our fellow-creatures? We say, This man is good, and that man is bad. We mean by such a division that some men are following a wise direction and some are following a foolish direction. All the difficulties of life are made by the men who are following a foolish direction: all the hopes of making the world happy and prosperous are raised by men who are following a wise direction.

People who love to argue say: " Why should you say good and bad: good is only your idea of what suits you, and bad is your idea of what does not suit you." They wish us to think that goodness is simply an idea of Man, and that badness is not really so important as good people would make out. This is what we call shallow thinking. We can prove how shallow is such thinking. In our own time large bodies of people have agreed that murder is not a crime, and that stealing is a thing which may be practised with impunity by those who are armed. What is the result? Civilisation in their unhappy countries is brought to a standstill. Immorality means barbarism, anarchy, and stagnation.

No State can exist which is not founded on morality. You may have a low condition of morality or a high condition, but you must have morality of some kind or other before you can organise a State. There must be certain things which a man may do, and certain things he may not do. It is impossible to think of a civilisation composed of bad people. Goodness is essential to order and progress.

Ask yourself, What is goodness? You will find that it is a striving after perfection. This movement in the soul of man is not only intelligent, it is moral: it seeks to attain Excellence.

THE MOVEMENT IN NATURE AWAY FROM BADNESS AND TOWARD GOODNESS

Thus we find throughout Nature a movement away from badness, and toward goodness. This movement is so wonderful in producing beauty and virtue that we cannot believe it would produce badness. Is it possible to think that the same movement which produced the cowslip and the gazelle, the shining star and the soul of Florence Nightingale, also produced the many hideous and abominable things we find in Nature? Is it so tremendously powerful and so infinitely stupid?

No; it is easier to think that this movement produces nothing of itself, that it was set in motion by a Mind, and that the badness in the world is the result of opposition to this movement. The movement can do nothing without the co-operation of that which it seeks to move. The Mind of the Universe wants truth, beauty, goodness: it sets a movement in motion directed to these ends; the movement encounters the opposition of Matter and is twisted out of its path—it cannot go on by itself; but elsewhere it presses forward, and where it meets with co-operation it produces the loveliness of Nature and the grandeur of the soul of man.

Wheat was given the direction which led to producing more wheat; the rose was given the direction which led to beauty and scent; and man was given the direction which led to reason and love. It is the opposition of matter, not the movement, which produces disease in the wheat, canker in the rose, and sin in man. It is not the nature of wheat to be barren, of the rose to die in bud, of man to be bad. These things only prove that the direction has not been followed.

THE GOAL THAT IS SOMETIMES FAR OFF AND DIFFICULT TO SEE

In many cases, it is true, it is difficult to find the final goal of direction; it may, indeed, be centuries away, and the path to it may be dark and hazardous, but we may at least be sure that there is a divine directing influence everywhere at work, that morality and intelligence are the forces behind the evolution not only of our little world but of the whole universe, and that there is indeed, "one far-off divine event to which the whole Creation moves" —an event which we may faintly imagine in our ideas of truth, goodness, and beauty.

Now we see why the word Direction is so helpful to right thinking. It enables us to say that the universe in which we find ourselves is moral and intelligent. We are not entirely in the dark. We are not lost in a maze of confusion and perplexity. Behind movement is a Mover; behind things is a Mind. We may not know the final answer to all our questions, but because we know that there is a movement in Nature from anarchy to order, from ugliness to beauty, from selfishness to co-operation, from ignorance to knowledge, from weakness to power, from instinct to reason, we may at least be certain of this, that Life is a grand thing and a glorious thing; we may at least confess that we can help the Mind of the Universe, or hinder it, according to the direction of own own lives.

THE WISE TRAVELLER WHO WILL ONE DAY ARRIVE

The wise traveller is he who makes sure of his goal before he sets out on his journey. He may make more mistakes than the man who is on the wrong road, but at least his face is set in the right direction, and one day he will arrive at the place where he would be. Direction is the soul of living. It is what men call Destiny.

THE BITTERNESS OF HAGAR IN THE DESERT

HAGAR AND HER SON ISHMAEL IN THE WILDERNESS—From a photograph by Braun and Company

The Story of the Most Beautiful Book in the World

ABRAHAM, THE FRIEND OF GOD

IN the early days of history a procession of men and camels was seen crossing the vast Syrian desert from the direction of Mesopotamia. Among the men was a tall and noble chieftain named Abraham, whose eyes often gazed across the terrible desert as though in quest of some end to his journey. By his side went a younger man, his nephew, named Lot.

It was a sad journey they were making, and only the iron will of Abraham kept the others to their duty. For this caravan was moving away from their homes, from their friends, from people who spoke their own language, and whose customs were the same as their own ; and they were journeying to discover a new country, where everything would be strange to them, and where they might encounter enemies and treachery, and meet with slavery or death.

We can understand how Abraham's wife Sarah listened on her camel's back to the murmurs of her women, and sometimes shared their terrors. When at each day's end the tents were set up and the camels knelt down to rest on the sand, when darkness fell across the great round circle of the desert, and under the shining stars men and women sat silently round the fires thinking of the comfortable homes they had left behind, Abraham's

young nephew Lot would, we can imagine, look towards his uncle, and feel rebellious in his heart.

But no one dared to withstand this splendid king of men, Abraham. He had seen a vision. God had spoken to him in a dream, and he was following his dream. How the men and women must have looked across the dark of the encampment toward this old, stern man, with the firelight on his rugged face and sweeping beard of snow—this old man who believed the God of heaven had spoken to him— this old man who was following his dream across the desert!

These were the words Abraham declared God had addressed to him:

Get thee out of thy country, and from thy kindred, and from thy father's house, unto a land that I will shew thee. And I will make of thee a great nation, and I will bless thee, and make thy name great, and thou shalt be a blessing. And I will bless them that bless thee, and curse him that curseth thee ; and in thee shall all families of the Earth be blessed.

It was this command, this magnificent promise, which kept Abraham upon his way. The end of the long journey came at last, and Abraham found himself in Palestine, a lovely and a fertile country, beautiful to the eye and comfortable to the heart. Glad and grateful were the hearts of his company as they gazed

GREAT FIGURES OF THE OLD TESTAMENT · THE LIFE OF JESUS

upon this gracious country. Here he settled, he and all his people, and they grew very rich, and fortune smiled upon them. But so rich and powerful did they become that jealousy crept in between the shepherds and herdmen of Abraham and the shepherds and herdmen of Lot, his nephew.

HOW ABRAHAM PARTED FROM LOT HIS NEPHEW AND BEFRIENDED HIM

Then Abraham said to his nephew:

Let there be no strife, I pray thee, between me and thee, and between my herdmen and thy herdmen, for we are brethren. Is not the whole land before thee ? Separate thyself, I pray thee, from me. If thou wilt take the left hand, then I will go to the right ; or if thou depart to the right hand, then I will go to the left.

These gracious words were spoken on a high tableland; and Lot, turning from his uncle, looked down to the beautiful valley south of the Jordan, stretching far away in richness and loveliness, and promising great happiness and wealth. This was his choice, and Abraham parted from his nephew with love and kindness.

Afterwards, when he heard that his nephew had been involved in a great war and had been carried away a prisoner, Abraham did not forget him, but armed his servants and went in pursuit of the captors. Abraham prevailed against them, and the kings who rejoiced in his victory would have given him gifts; but Abraham refused, saying that he would take nothing, "from a thread even to a shoe-latchet." He sought nothing but to do his duty and wait upon the will of God.

So he returned to his pastoral life, and again God visited him in visions, with the assurance that his children should inherit the Earth.

ABRAHAM'S WIFE AND HAGAR THE LITTLE EGYPTIAN MAID

In the midst of this peaceful and pleasant existence, Sarah, the wife of Abraham, had many sad and tragic thoughts. She was, as we shall see, a strange mixture of strength and weakness, kindness and unkindness. We know that she was beautiful, for a king of Egypt had greatly desired her for his wife, and we know that Abraham was devotedly in love with her. She must have thought many times of God's promise that Abraham's children should inherit the earth ; and as the days went by, and no son came, she began at last to fear that she was unworthy of Abraham.

In those days men married more than one wife, and Sarah went one day to Abraham and persuaded him to take for a second wife a little Egyptian maid in her service, named Hagar.

She said to Abraham, "Marry my slave-girl, and perhaps she will give us a son for our home." So Abraham did what his wife said.

When poor Hagar found herself so honoured she was at first a little proud, and her pride made Sarah angry. Sarah drove her out with angry words, and the poor slave-girl who had been so proud found herself an outcast in the wilderness. While she was weeping there, God sent a messenger to tell her to return to Sarah. "Return to thy mistress, and submit thyself under her hands," said a Voice in the wilderness. And the frightened slave-girl exclaimed, in words that ever since have been spoken in all languages, in all countries, "Thou God seest me." She went back obediently and submitted herself to the harshness of Sarah.

THE THREE MYSTERIOUS STRANGERS WHO APPEARED TO ABRAHAM

One day, as Abraham sat in the doorway of his tent, when the sun was at its highest, and the land lay dazed in an Eastern noon, there suddenly appeared before him three strangers. Abraham rose, struck by their wondrous appearance, and received them with the highest honour. While he was entertaining these visitors, one of them foretold that Sarah should have a son.

We can imagine the joy of the old father and the old mother. The preparations made by the rejoicing parents for the feast when the child Isaac was born passed everything they had ever done in splendour and magnificence. Sarah was just as excited as Abraham, and gave herself up to the glory of the feast.

And Ishmael, Hagar's son, the lad who hitherto had been everything to Abraham, looked on at all this and laughed mockingly, so that Sarah, in a sudden outburst of rage, called to Abraham, "Cast out this bondwoman and her son; for the son of this bondwoman shall not be heir with my son."

Abraham grieved because of his son Ishmael; but a Voice comforted him, saying, "Let it not be grievous in thy sight because of the lad, and because of thy bondwoman ; in all that Sarah hath

THREE FIGURES IN ABRAHAM'S STORY

REBEKAH AT THE WELL—FROM THE FINE
PAINTING BY FREDERICK GOODALL, R.A.

HAGAR, THE EGYPTIAN SLAVE GIRL, AND
MOTHER OF ISHMAEL

ABRAHAM SENDS OUT HAGAR AND HER LITTLE LAD—FROM A SEVENTEENTH-CENTURY PAINTING IN THE
BRERA GALLERY, MILAN

said unto thee, hearken unto her voice; for in Isaac shall thy seed be called. And also of the son of the bondwoman will I make a nation, because he is thy seed."

Abraham listened to this Voice in his soul, and he trusted it. He brought himself to the agony of parting with his son, the gay and spirited young Ishmael.

There is something touching in the brief story of this parting. Abraham rose up " early in the morning," evidently before his angry wife was stirring, and, providing poor Hagar and his son with food and water, took a loving farewell of them, telling them, we may be sure, of God's promise, and watching them through tears in his eyes as they departed.

Alas! for poor Hagar. She set out very sorrowfully, making no protest, but quietly submitting to her hard fate. And when her food and water came to an end, and they could go no farther, she laid her son down and went a good way off from him, saying, " Let me not see the death of the child." And she wept.

THE SORROW OF POOR HAGAR AND THE TERRIBLE TRIAL OF ABRAHAM

And God heard the voice of the lad; and the angel of God called to Hagar out of heaven, and said unto her, What aileth thee, Hagar? Fear not, for God hath heard the voice of the lad where he is.

Arise, lift up the lad, and hold him in thine hand; for I will make him a great nation.

And God opened her eyes, and she saw a well of water; and she went and filled the bottle with water, and gave the lad drink.

And God was with the lad; and he grew, and dwelt in the wilderness, and became an archer.

And he dwelt in the wilderness of Paran; and his mother took him a wife out of the land of Egypt.

But another and a greater sacrifice lay before Abraham. A vision came to him, and the Voice to which he had always listened obediently seemed to tell him to take his son Isaac and offer him as a burnt offering on the mountains.

What a frightful command! How Abraham must have shrunk from it! We can imagine how he tried to persuade himself that it was not God who had spoken to him, that it was only a dream, a thing he should put out of his mind and forget. Many a man, even a pious man, who is confronted with a painful duty, manages to persuade himself that God could not mean him to make such a great sacrifice.

He shuts his ears, as it were, to the Voice of God, and listens to the pleadings of his own wishes and desires rather than to the commands of duty. But Abraham was honest with himself; the command was terrible, but his glory was that he trusted in God, and he felt the voice to be from God.

ABRAHAM TELLS ISAAC THAT GOD HIMSELF WILL PROVIDE A SACRIFICE

So he rose up early in the morning and saddled an ass, and split wood for the fire, and took with him Isaac and two young men, and started out upon his journey of death. At the end of three days in the mountains he said unto his young men, " Abide ye here with the ass, and I and the lad will go yonder and worship, and come again to you." Then Isaac said suddenly, " My father! Behold the fire and the wood; but where is the lamb for a burnt offering? " And Abraham, in great trouble, answered, " My son, God will provide Himself a lamb for a burnt offering."

Then Abraham made an altar, laid the wood upon it, and took Isaac into his arms, and laid him for a lamb upon the altar. But just as he was about to slay this beautiful victim, a Voice sounded to him from heaven. He looked up from the angry mountains to the rolling clouds of dawn, and the Voice said, " Lay not thine hand upon the lad, neither do thou anything unto him; for now I know that thou fearest God, seeing thou hast not withheld thy son, thine only son, from Me."

This was the last trial of Abraham's splendid and almost terrible faith. He did not know, as we know now, that God is a loving Father. He thought of God simply as great and powerful.

ABRAHAM KNEW THAT GOD WOULD FULFIL HIS PROMISES

The rest of Abraham's life was calm and beautiful. He lived to see his son Isaac married to one of his kindred, the beautiful Rebekah; and when he died he was laid by the side of his wife in the cave of Machpelah.

He did not know how the nations of the Earth were to be blessed through Isaac; but it is quite certain that he contented himself with the knowledge that God would fulfil His promises.

(Next chapter in this group, page 747)

The Interests and Pleasures of Life for All Indoors and Out

FEEDING THE BIRDS

EVERYONE who is fond of birds should try to help them during the cold weather, when fields and hedges are bare and they are not able to find much food.

Household scraps scattered on a bird table in the garden, whether it is a town or country one, soon attract a crowd of little feathered creatures, and there is a great deal of real pleasure in studying their quaint antics at close quarters.

The table is quite easy to make from an old wooden box. Saw up enough of the wood for a board about two feet long by a foot and a half wide. If this cannot be cut in one piece, join several bits together by screwing two battens across them, so that the bird table looks very like the lid of the tool box shown on another page (see Index).

Turning the board up the other way, fix on to it four French nails, and using these as miniature posts, tie several lengths of black cotton round and round like a little wire fence.

This is to keep the greedy sparrows away, so that the more interesting birds may have a chance to get some food.

Now make a hole at each corner of the table and run strings through, by which to hang it up. The best place to choose for this is a verandah outside a window; or perhaps it would be possible to fix a staple in a wall, put a light pole in the staple, and hang the table from the end of this rod. In this way it could be quite near the window, and the birds could be watched having their meals, and their habits and appearance studied.

As to the food, almost anything will be welcome. Fat, suet, cheese, table scraps, breadcrumbs, coconut and other nuts, apples, and potatoes are all eagerly eaten by the visitors. A baked potato, warm but not hot enough to frighten them, seems to be a particular treat to some of the birds.

Chaffinches, great tits, cole tits, blue tits, marsh tits, starlings, song thrushes, robins, and blackbirds are all very familiar and frequent visitors to the bird table. Others, though more cautious, can be attracted, such as rooks, jackdaws, hooded crows, magpies, hawfinches, greenfinches, bramblings, bullfinches, nuthatches, missel thrushes, pied wagtails, grey wagtails, ringdoves, greater spotted woodpeckers, moorhens, partridges, pheasants, and herring gulls.

Of course, all these are not to be seen on the bird table in every part of the country, but there is nowhere, not even in the centre of a big city, where several kinds of birds cannot be attracted. In the heart of London, robins, tits, wood-pigeons, thrushes, will come regularly to the table. And all the year round the birds will come, too.

A delightful sight is to see a number of tits hanging, back downward, on nuts put out for their benefit, eagerly pecking at the fruit. Brazil nuts, almonds, or walnuts are best for this purpose, and, after being cracked and having best part of the shells removed, they should be tied in rows up the strings by which the table is suspended. When there are no nuts about, the tits will thoroughly enjoy chop bones strung up in the same way.

To give the sparrows a meal without depriving the other birds, stand the bird table with the cotton fence upon another table, and put food on both. Or make a larger table and fix the cotton fence several inches inside the edge of the wood. The sparrows then will feed all round the cotton fence, but will not venture inside where the other birds are eating.

CRAFTS · GAMES · NEEDLEWORK · PUZZLES · SCIENCE · EXPERIMENTS

LITTLE PROBLEMS FOR ODD MOMENTS

*T*HESE *problems are continued from page 502, and their answers will be found, together with more questions, on page 750.*

39. Which Farm was the Bigger?

A Canadian farmer boasted that he had a farm of 4 square miles. "Ah," said a neighbour, " it is not as big as mine—that is 3 miles square."

Was the second farm really the bigger?

40. Which Road did Charlie Take?

Charlie started from his home intending to cycle to a village 10 miles away. He came to cross-roads, and found that the sign-post had been pulled up and lay in the middle of the road. Yet he made the signpost tell him which was the proper way to go.

How did he do it?

HOW DID CHARLIE KNOW THE WAY?

41. Which is the Heavier?

" Which is the heavier," asked Herbert, " an ounce of gold or an ounce of feathers? "

" An ounce of gold, of course," replied his sister Jean.

Was she right?

42. How Many Men to Finish the Railway?

A contractor took an order to build 50 miles of railway within one year, and he engaged 225 men upon the work. After 7 months only 21 miles were finished.

How many extra men would he then need to engage to complete the whole line by the time agreed upon?

43. How Far did William Go?

John met his friend William starting out from his house at 5 o'clock. "How far are you going? " said John. "Perhaps you can guess," replied William. " If I walk at the rate of four miles an hour I shall be there five minutes late, but if I walk at five miles an hour I shall arrive at my destination ten minutes too soon."

How far was William going?

44. How Many Rugs were There?

" This is awkward," said the carpet manufacturer to his accountant; " there is an entry for a sale, and many of the figures have been obliterated. It reads: rugs at £10 0s. 2½d. each=£1... 0s. 2½d." " Then we can work it out," said the accountant, and he did. Can you?

45. What was the Cargo?

A ship's cargo was unloaded by 25 barges, each barge taking three loads. But if each barge had been large enough to hold 160 tons more there would have been only one load each.

How heavy was the ship's cargo?

46. How Many Ducks?

" How many ducks did you drive home? " asked Farmer Bell. " There were two ducks in front of a duck, two ducks behind a duck, and a duck in the middle."

What was the smallest number of ducks Farmer Bell could have had?

THE ANSWERS TO THE PROBLEMS ON PAGE 502

31. The train passed Tom—that is, travelled its own length—in 9 seconds, and it travelled its own length and 88 yards in 21 seconds. Therefore it went 88 yards in 12 seconds, and, seeing that it travelled its own length in 9 seconds, its length is three-quarters of 88 yards—that is, 66 yards.

32. Ten miles an hour is 1 mile in 6 minutes, so that if the farmer had gone home by the road he took on the outward journey he would have saved 24 minutes instead of 12 minutes. Eight miles an hour is a mile in 7½ minutes, and at 10 miles an hour he therefore saves 1½ minutes in each mile. As the saving in time would have been 24 minutes (which is 16 times 1½ minutes) by the shorter route, it must have been 16 miles. Thus the outward journey was 16 miles long, and the homeward journey was 18 miles.

33. The large sack contained 30 bushels.

34. The man would meet 11 trains coming in the opposite direction, not including the one that would be arriving as he started and the one that would be starting as he arrived. There is 24 hours' difference between the starting times of the trains ; but as the trains from opposite sides are going toward each other at the same speed, each train will pass another train every 12 hours. Thus, the man's train will in

6 days pass 12 trains, including the train that will be leaving as he arrives at his destination.

35. It would take 4 hours to walk the 16 miles still to go, but cycling was the quicker way. If James rode 8 miles in 1 hour, and then, leaving the machine, walked right on, he would complete the journey in 3 hours. If John walked for 2 hours he would come to the machine and could ride it the remaining 8 miles in 1 hour, thus arriving at the same time as James.

36. The first candle burns for 6 hours and the second for 4 hours. In 2 hours (8.30 to 10.30) the first burns as much as the second burns in 1½ hours (8.30 to 10). Hence, in 6 hours the first burns as much as the second in 4½ hours, so that the second would require one half-hour to burn 1 inch, and it would have been 8 inches long originally, while the first must have been 9 inches long.

37. When his father is three times as old as Harry, the difference between their ages must be twice Harry's age ; but the difference between their ages is always 44. Therefore Harry will be 22 when his father is three times as old. Harry, then, will get the pony in ten years.

38. The amount spilt would have served the man who died for 8 days, and this, at 1 quart each day, would have been 8 quarts.

PUZZLING CARDS—WHICH IS THE LARGER?

AN old proverb says that things are not always what they seem, and this is something everybody finds out for himself sooner or later. Especially in regard to the size of things the eyes are liable to deceive, and they are particularly untrustworthy when asked for details. Ask any friend to point to a spot on the wall of the room or upon the door that would indicate the height that a silk hat would be if it were placed upon the floor. It is almost certain that he will touch a spot very much higher than the right one. Probably he will indicate a point about twice as high as the hat will actually reach.

Here is an interesting proof of the tricks that sight plays. Trace on card and then cut out with scissors the two drawings given here, and then get a good deal of amusement by showing them to friends, and asking which is the larger. Forty-nine people out of fifty will at once point out the card on the left, declaring that it is considerably the larger of the two. Then ask the friend by how much it is larger than the smaller one, and he will probably say that it is about one-fourth, or one-fifth larger than the other. As a matter of fact the pieces are the same size. There are two things that assist each other in deceiving the eyes: one is the shape and position of the pieces and the other thing is the markings.

Here is another illusion. Put a dotted line down the centre of a piece of white paper. On one side and a little away from this, draw a flying bird; on the other side the same distance away, draw a cage, making the pictures bold. Then cover the dotted line with a small white card held on edge; look steadily at this edge, and in a little while the bird will appear to move across into the cage.

SITTING DOWN WITHOUT SEATS

IF twenty or thirty boys were asked to sit down and there were no seats available, they would probably think that they would have to sit upon the ground. But it is quite possible for them to sit down without seats, and yet not to rest upon the ground, as the picture clearly shows.

The boys sit in a circle, and each sits upon the knees of the boy behind him, the last boy's knees forming a seat for the first boy, who in his turn allows the second boy to sit on his knees, and so on. This method of resting for a number of men or boys is not a mere trick or game, for it has been used by French soldiers in Africa over and over again. Where the district is wet or swampy, and it would be unhealthy for the soldiers to sit upon the ground, they are ordered by their officers to rest in this way.

It is not quite so simple as it looks in a picture, but with a little practice any number of childern can sit down. Of course, it is not necessary to have a large number to adopt this clever plan, and half a dozen can sit upon one another's knees, but not so comfortably as a large number, as, the circle being smaller, the boys are not so directly in front of one another. This is a good way for children to rest at a large party.

THE BEGINNING OF A COOK'S DAY

The best cook is not necessarily the one who crowds the greatest number of dishes on the table, and thinks there is no need to bother about a trifle like good tea-making. It is so often care in the seemingly unimportant things which makes all the difference between a good meal and a bad one, and so that everyone will start the day well, breakfast should belong to the first kind, beginning beforehand with the perfect cup of early-morning tea.

There is no single recipe for making this, because each preparation of tea-leaves has its own peculiarity and should be chosen for the kind of water with which it is to be brewed; but generally speaking a homely brown earthenware pot makes better tea than a metal one.

Every teapot should be thoroughly heated with some of the water from the kettle just before it boils. Then this water must be completely emptied out before the tea-leaves are put in, and the *pot taken to the kettle* for the absolutely-boiling water to be poured on. Allow two or more level teaspoonfuls of tea for each half pint of water.

Heating more water in the kettle than is needed wastes both time and money, and all water for tea-making should be fresh from the tap or spring, not that which has previously boiled.

Tea quickly takes up the taste of anything smelly like onions or cheese, so keep it in a tightly-lidded caddy.

Coffee also needs to be stored in an airtight tin; in fact if there is not a coffee grinder in your house, the coffee will taste better if it is brought home in a tin from whichever store in your neighbourhood grinds the newly-roasted berries fresh for each customer. Every whiff of that lovely coffee smell that comes from coffee packed in paper is part of the best of it getting lost in the air instead of going into the coffee pot.

Provided you do not use less than two level tablespoonfuls of coffee for every half pint of freshly-boiling water and half a saltspoonful of salt, your coffee-making utensils can be as simple as you please, as long as you keep them scrupulously clean, well washed and dried, and leave them to air each time after use.

How to level a spoonful of coffee; all dry ingredients can be measured in the same way.

Perhaps all that you have in which to make coffee is a clean enamel pan or jug. Aluminium should not be used. When the water comes to the boil stir in the coffee and salt, and give it time to froth up in the pan without boiling over. Take it off the fire to settle, then let it froth up again. Repeat this three times with a stir between each. Then stand the pan in a warm place for fifteen or twenty minutes before straining into a well-heated coffee pot through coffee filter paper, or a piece of clean muslin, inside a fine wire strainer.

It you possess a patent coffee machine, follow the directions given with it, but as already stated do not use less than two tablespoonfuls of coffee for every half pint.

Coffee cups, like teacups, should always be warmed before use in cold weather, and to avoid having what in the old days used to be called The Dairymaid's Apron, but which is now often referred to as that horrid skin on your heated coffee milk, make it hot over boiling water in a double saucepan, whisking it constantly.

To make good toast, use a loaf two days old, as new bread turns moist and tough. For soft toast or buttered toast, slice the bread a quarter to half an inch thick and toast fast near fierce heat, just before it is to be eaten.

To make crisp scrunch, sometimes called Toast Melba after the famous singer who loved it, cut the bread leaf thin, and dry in a very slow oven until golden.

A slow oven, though, of course, not as slow as for scrunch, is needed for baking bacon, which tastes nicer done this way than fried.

Eggs to go with it are delicious broken on to a hot plate rubbed with bacon fat, and placed over a pan of boiling water till the eggs have set sufficiently (usually after eight or ten minutes) to be lifted on to the bacon.

For boiled eggs, the water should be gently boiling in the pan, and should completely cover the eggs when you slowly lower them in with a large metal spoon. To boil lightly, leave them for three to three and a half minutes; medium take four to five minutes, and hard ten minutes.

Hot scones are specially nice for a change for breakfast, so get up early one morning and make some with the recipe on page 752.

SIMPLE EXPERIMENTS WITH AIR AND WATER

A GREAT deal of science can be learned from the most familiar objects in the home, and an interesting half-hour may be spent in doing simple experiments that will teach much that everyone should know.

First of all, here is an experiment that will show how the air, which is invisible and does not seem to have any weight, is actually pressing down upon everybody and everything on the earth's surface. Take a wide-necked bottle, such, for example, as a glass water-bottle, and also prepare a hard-boiled egg, carefully removing all the shell.

Now put into the bottle a piece of lighted paper, and, after a second or two, place the egg in the neck of the bottle as though it were the stopper. The egg will, of course, remain there as if it were in an egg-cup. At least, that is what some people would expect. But watch the hard-boiled egg, and after a time,

driven out owing to the fact that the heat from the lighted paper has expanded the air, and the glass will not hold it all. A few moments after, the water is seen to rise in the tumbler. The cause of this is that when the paper is burnt out the air cools again, and as it does not now fill the glass the pressure of the air on the surface of the water drives it up into the tumbler.

Still another experiment will prove that the air exercises a pressure, not only downward but upward as well. Take a wine-glass, and fill it carefully to the brim with water. Then take a thin sheet of paper and place it on top so that it touches both the surface of the water and the rim of the glass. Now, holding the paper carefully in position, turn the glass of water upside down, and the water will remain in the glass apparently suspended. Of course, it is not really suspended, but the

EASY EXPERIMENTS THAT CAN BE TRIED IN EVERY HOME

it will be noticed that it is gradually going down the neck of the bottle as though it were being sucked in. Then, suddenly, it will enter the bottle with a loud noise.

What is the explanation of this? It is very simple. The burning paper heated and expanded the air in the bottle, and some of it was driven out through the opening at the neck. Then the egg was placed in the neck and the opening stopped up. Presently the air in the bottle cooled, and, as it lost its heat, it contracted, or filled less space, so that there was a partial vacuum in the bottle, and the air outside pressing upon the egg drove it into the bottle. The report was caused by the outside air rushing in as soon as the egg dropped.

There is another simple experiment which shows clearly the pressure of the atmosphere. Take a basin of water, and on the surface of the water let a cork float. Now place on the cork a piece of lighted paper, and over these invert an empty glass, pressing it down gently into the water. Bubbles will be seen to come from under the glass. This is the air being

air is pressing it up into the glass. The air must not be allowed to get into the glass while it is being turned upside-down, or the water will come out; so in case of an accident make the experiment over a basin.

If another experiment is needed to prove the downward pressure of the air, use the basin of water again, and take a small ear-syringe such as is found in almost every house. Fill it with water, and invert it with the point in the water in the basin. Now press down the rod and empty the syringe. But directly the rod is pulled up again the water rushes up and fills the syringe. The reason for this is that the pressure of the air all over the surface of the water in the basin drives the water up into the syringe.

An interesting experiment, this time with a pair of ordinary domestic bellows, proves that the pressure of the atmosphere is exerted, not only above and below, but sideways and in all directions. Having blown all the air out completely, stop up the nozzle and the vent-hole with corks, and then, if the bellows are in proper order and air-tight, no

629

one will be able to open them, no matter in what position they are held. The air outside pressing equally on all sides holds the bellows firmly together.

All bodies, solids, liquids, and gases alike, when heated, expand—that is, they fill more space—and two simple experiments will show this clearly in the case of liquids and gases.

Take a small bottle, fill it with some coloured liquid, such as water in which a little Condy's Fluid has been dropped, and cork it up. But first see that the cork is pierced, and a piece of glass tube, open at both ends, inserted. Now, if the bottle is plunged into a vessel of warm water as in picture 6, the coloured liquid will be seen to rise in the tube to A. This is because the warm water in which the bottle was plunged has heated the liquid in the bottle, and caused it to expand and overflow into the tube.

To show that gases expand, use a glass tube closed at one end. Take the tube, which is, of course, full of the gas known as air, and put it into a tumbler of water, as shown in picture 7. The water rises to point B. Now hold a lighted taper to the upper part of the glass tube, and after a second or two the water descends in the tube from B to C. This is because the heat expanded the air in the tube, and as this wanted more room, it drove some of the water out.

Another experiment with a wine-glass and a jar of water will show that gases, such as the atmosphere, possesses the property of compressibility—that is, they can be pressed into smaller space. Take the wine-glass and invert it on the surface of the water. The glass is full of air, which occupies the whole of the space A in picture 8. Now press the glass down to the bottom of the jar, and notice, as in picture 9, that some water has risen in the glass, and the air that formerly occupied the whole glass now fills only the space B. As the glass is gradually lifted out of the jar the air expands and fills the glass as easily as it was compressed.

There is a simple experiment to show that liquids, like gases, exert a pressure equal in all directions. Take an ordinary lamp-glass and place below the widest opening a piece of cardboard. Hold this against it and plunge the whole into a jar of water. Now remove the hand that held the cardboard, and it will be found to remain in position, the upward pressure of the water holding it against the glass. Now pour water gently into the lamp-glass from above; the card continues in position until the water in the glass reaches the level of the water in the jar. The pressure of water top and bottom being then equal the card will be displaced, and sink to the bottom of the jar by its own weight.

A BOX THAT DRAWS VOICE PICTURES

IT is possible to draw beautiful designs with the voice, the designs varying in form according to the strength or pitch of the note that is spoken or sung, with a simple instrument that any boy can make.

Get a small tin saucepan with a round handle. Open the end of the handle, if it is not already open, and make a hole in the saucepan where the handle joins it, so that the handle is really a tube into the saucepan. Now take a piece of thin indiarubber and tie this tightly over the top of the saucepan, in the same way that covers are tied on to jampots, taking care that the indiarubber is well stretched. A piece of a bladder or toy balloon does excellently for this purpose. A paper funnel with the edge stuck down, should be inserted in the end of the handle, and the eidophone, a name which means " to copy sound," is complete so far as its construction is concerned. The picture shows how it should look.

Now prepare the surface of the rubber covering so that a voice may be able to draw designs upon it. There are various ways of doing this. A very thin layer of coloured glycerine may be put over the drum, or the

finest sand spread evenly on the surface. Then, if a note is sung steadily and continuously down the funnel, the sand or glycerine will gradually take a regular form until some beautiful and delicate geometrical design is produced. With practice, of course, it can be learned how to sing the notes continuously at suitable pitches, so that as the notes change the designs change. Some will come like flowers, some like ferns, and some like trees. To get even more delicately detailed designs than the fine sand produces, try lycopodium powder, a fine yellow powder that is the seed of the plants called lycopodiums. This is to be obtained at a chemist's shop, where glycerine can also be bought. The chemist will colour the glycerine according to order.

In place of the paper funnel, a tin funnel might be used by knocking the narrow tube off, and having the wide funnel part soldered into the handle. This makes a stronger and more permanent instrument, the results from which are very striking and astonishing. A good way of passing a winter evening would be to see whose voice makes the best picture.

THE CANDLE THAT CAN BE EATEN

THIS trick needs an accomplice (someone in the audience) who, under some pretext that a light is required, is sent to fetch a candle. A candlestick containing a short stump of candle about an inch high, is duly brought in and lit.

"Why, whatever is the use of this scrap of candle?" the performer grumbles. "I could quite easily eat a dozen like it!"

"Well, eat it then," suggests the partner, and without any fuss the light is blown out by the performer, who puts the candle in his mouth and munches it up as if thoroughly enjoying it.

The explanation is very simple. The so-called candle is prepared beforehand by cutting a portion of apple exactly to the shape and size of an ordinary piece of candle, and by sticking into it, in place of a wick, a wedge of brazil nut or almond. This will light quite easily and keep burning for a while.

The apple should not be prepared too long before it is wanted or it will turn brown, as peeled apples always do, though if it is put in brine—salt and water—until needed, then rinsed and dried, it will keep white long enough for the purpose of the trick.

When this trick is being done on a platform it can be made even more impressive if the piece of apple is moulded with white sugar icing to fit on top of a longer bit of real candle. This should be very neatly done, so that the join does not show, and a trickle of white icing be allowed to fall down the side from the nut wick as if the candle had been used before. The nut wick, too, must be darkened at the tip to look like an ordinary wick which had previously been lit.

THE WIZARD'S WAND

THE young magician's wand is a very important part of his outfit, for it serves several useful purposes. When introducing his act, it prevents him from looking and feeling awkward by giving him something to occupy his hands; it can be used to distract the attention of the audience when some vital move is being made by the other hand; while holding the wand a small object can also be concealed; and there is, of course, its traditional use—the mysterious tap with the wand which claims to cause some magical change, and which goes a long way to convince the spectators that the trick really happened.

So one of the first things a conjurer should learn is how to handle a wand. Though this could be bought, it is quite easy to make at home. From a nicely rounded rod of hard wood, about half an inch thick, cut a piece twelve inches or so long, and cover it neatly with black glazed paper. Over the last two inches of each end paste the same sort of paper, but white or cream in colour, and there is an excellent wand.

One very effective plan is for the conjurer to produce it from his purse, where he professes to keep it together with his hard-earned pocket-money. Coming forward and making a few introductory remarks, he looks about as if seeking for something. " I am sorry, ladies and gentlemen, but I have mislaid my wand; till I find it I cannot do anything. Ah! I remember now, I put it in my purse." Of course, the last statement is not strictly true; but a conjurer has a sort of special licence to romance in this way. As a matter of fact, the wand is not yet in the purse, but is hidden in the left sleeve, its outer end resting against the lower joints of the bent second and third fingers. If the first and fourth fingers be left partially extended the other two will appear natural.

There must be two purses, bag-shaped, and alike in appearance. One of these is unprepared, but the bottom seam of the other is ripped open for about an inch and a half, making a secret passage into the inside. The inner pocket remains intact, and in this put a few coins. The other purse is left empty. The two are placed, one against the other, in the left trouser pocket. Remember which is outermost.

To work the trick place the left hand in the pocket, and take out the prepared purse. Transferring it to the right hand, open it and pour out the coins upon the table. Returning it, still open, to the left hand, and placing the fingers of the right hand inside, take hold, through the opening, of the end of the wand, which then draw out through the mouth of the purse.

If it is done neatly, standing with the left side toward the spectators, no one can detect that the wand comes from the sleeve.

When the wand is clear, close the purse, put it back into the pocket, and remove the hand. Then saying, " I mustn't forget my money, though," thrust the hand into the pocket again, and bringing out the *unprepared* purse, place the coins in it.

Do not offer it for inspection, but if any inquisitive person asks to examine it, it would be quite safe to let him do so, though no one must be allowed to look at the magic matchbox in the trick described on page 753.

TONGUE-TWISTERS

Everyone knows the curious sentence with many saws in it : Of all the saws that ever I saw I never saw a saw to saw like this saw was to saw. That is quite easy to say, but there are many sentences with the same word or syllable or sound that are hard to pronounce, especially to repeat several times in quick succession, and they have been aptly called tongue-twisters. Truly rural ; short soldiers ; school coal scuttle ; soft shot-silk sash ; mixed biscuits ; and critical cricket critic all seem quite simple expressions, and yet there are very few people who can say any one of them quickly several times running without mixing the sounds of the letters.

These are the shortest type of tongue-twister. Longer ones are sentences like : Crisp crusts crackle; She saw six sick sheep; Blane's back brake block broke; while some of the most familiar are in verse, like this well-known example:

Peter Piper picked a peck of pepper.
Did Peter Piper pick a peck of pepper?
If Peter Piper picked a peck of pepper,
Where's the peck of pepper Peter Piper picked?

Here is another tongue-twister in the form of a verse:

Oliver Oglethorpe ogled an owl and oyster;
Did Oliver Oglethorpe ogle an owl and oyster?
If Oliver Oglethorpe ogled an owl and oyster,
Where are the owl and oyster Oliver Oglethorpe ogled?

Perhaps even more difficult to repeat than either of these is a verse in which the sound of q occurs in almost every word.

Quixote Quicksight quizzed a queerish quidbox;
Did Quixote Quicksight quiz a queerish quidbox?
If Quixote Quicksight quizzed a queerish quidbox,
Where's the queerish quidbox Quixote Quicksight quizzed?

The sound of c, too, mixed up with the sound of cr, is difficult to repeat over and over again in a sentence. Here is a sentence combining these sounds:

Captain Crackskull cracked a catchpoll's cockscomb ;
Did Captain Crackskull crack a catchpoll's cockscomb ?
If Captain Crackskull cracked a catchpoll's cockscomb,
Where's the catchpoll's cockscomb Captain Crackskull cracked ?

Here is a prose tongue-twister which should be repeated very rapidly:

How much wood would a woodchuck chuck if a woodchuck could chuck wood ? If a woodchuck could chuck wood, the wood that a woodchuck would chuck is the wood that a woodchuck could chuck, if the woodchuck that could chuck wood would chuck, or a woodchuck could chuck wood.

Two or three other tongue-twisters, all of them rhymes, may be given here:

Betty Botta bought some butter,
"But," she said, "this butter's bitter,
But a bit of better butter
Will but make my butter better."
So she bought a bit of butter,
Better than the bitter butter,
And it made her butter better.
So 'twas better Betty Botta
Bought a bit of better butter.

A very good tongue-twister is the verse about the sea-shells :

She sells sea-shells on the sea-shore;
The shells she sells are sea-shells I'm sure.
So if she sells sea-shells on the sea-shore,
Then I'm sure she sells sea-shore shells.

Here is a series of sentences that Dr. Moberly, headmaster of Westminster School, and afterwards Bishop of Salisbury, used to make his boys read, placing the emphasis on the right words. They are all perfectly correct, but take a good deal of examination before the sense can be understood in each case:

I saw that C saw,
C saw that I saw,
I saw that that that C saw was so.
C saw that, that that that I saw was so.
I saw that, that that that that C saw was so.
C saw that that, that that that that I saw was so.
I saw that that, that that that that C saw was so.

Repeat this twister six times in quick succession without mixing up the words:

Six sieves of sifted thistles,
Six sieves of unsifted thistles,
And six thistle sifters.

It is very amusing to try to repeat this:

Mrs. Biggar had a baby. Which was the bigger ? The baby was a little Biggar ! Which was the bigger, Mrs. Biggar or the baby ? Mr. Biggar was father Biggar ! Mr. Biggar died; was the baby then bigger than Mrs. Biggar ? No, for the baby was fatherless!

There are many variations and elaborations of "the saw that sawed wood." This one is very difficult to repeat quickly:

Esau Wood sawed wood. Esau Wood would saw wood! Oh the wood Wood would saw! One day Esau Wood saw a saw saw wood as no other wood-saw Wood saw would saw wood. In fact, of all the wood-saws Wood ever saw saw wood Wood never saw a wood-saw that would saw wood as the wood-saw Wood saw saw wood would saw wood.

Simple Learning Made Easy for Very Little People

READING—STORY BOOKS & WORD BOOKS

"WHAT a lot of lovely things we have done since we learned to read!" said John one morning.

"Yes," said Jennifer. "Pictures and picture books, newspapers and news books, and diaries. I want something harder still."

"Well, I think we are getting too big for picture books," said John. "I'd like to make a real book with stories and perhaps one or two pictures; then we can read them."

"Real books have lots and lots of words in them, and I'm sure I couldn't spell them all," said Jennifer.

Mother said they could certainly make their own reading books; and as for all the new words they would want—words which they could not read or spell—they could soon learn those by making word books. She gave them two little exercise books, and on the top of each page John and Jennifer printed a letter.

Aa on the first page, Bb on the second page, and so on right through the book until they got to Zz. As they printed the letters Mother told them the names of the letters, and it did not take them long to learn the alphabet.

Mother had first of all printed all the letters, large and small, on a sheet of paper.

"Now," she said, "when you are making up your stories for your reading books, you can come and ask me any word you don't know, and I will write it on the right page, and you can copy it. Then if you want the word again you can look

it up, until you know how to spell it without looking for it."

John called his book My Railway Train, and Jennifer called hers All About My Dolls. Their first books were not very long, but John said they could make quite a number of short story books and have a lot to read.

This is a page from John's word book:

S s	Tt
steam	train
signal	too
so	time
shrill	tree
seat	tide
stoker	their
smoke	ticket
sheep	trunk

Mother and Father were so pleased with the way that John and Jennifer were getting on with their reading that they decided to write a book for them. They kept it a secret, and wrote it after the children had gone to bed. Daddy liked drawing, so he did some pictures for both books.

One morning when John and Jennifer came down to breakfast they found a story book by the side of their porridge plates. How excited they were! John's book was called The Train That Went For

READING · WRITING · ARITHMETIC · ART · MUSIC · FRENCH

a Holiday, and was all about a train waiting in a smoky railway station, and of how the engine hooted with impatience to hurry up the passengers. It told how at last the guard waved his green flag, blew his whistle, and they were off!

It described the places they passed and the things they saw on the journey, until at last they got to the seaside. Mother wrote John's book. Daddy wrote Jennifer's book, and called it Susan Ann. It was about a little girl who had her eighth birthday. She had eight little girls to tea, eight birthday cards, eight birthday presents, eight candles on her birthday cake, and even her name had eight letters, which her mother wrote in pink icing on the cake.

Quite simple little books they were, but just right for John and Jennifer. Mother read them aloud, and they read them with her help, and copied the words they did not know carefully into their word books.

WRITING—FILMS AND ADVERTISING

Daddy said that John and Jennifer could help him to make the framework for their cinema. First of all he got some boarding, two pieces 36 inches, by 2 inches by 1 inch, and two pieces 8 inches by 2 inches by 1 inch. These he joined together with angle brackets, and made a frame which stood up like this :

could roll the film off, and when it was finished roll it back again.

When they were showing the film they rolled until each picture in turn was between the rollers, and waited while they read out what they had written underneath, before turning on to the next picture.

She found the three bears' house

He screwed two blocks of wood to each end to make it stand steady. With brace-and-bit he made two holes in the top piece of wood for the dresser-hooks to come through, and two holes exactly underneath these in the bottom piece of wood. These last two holes he only made half-way through the wood, just deep enough to take the heads of the screws in the bottom ends of the broom-sticks.

John and Jennifer took out the dresser-hooks from the top ends of the broom-sticks, slipped the screws into the sockets, and then rescrewed the dresser-hooks through the holes in the top of the broom-sticks, and the cinema was finished. By turning the broomsticks, the children

As soon as the roll was finished they rolled it back, ready to begin again.

Jennifer said she thought it would be nice to have a Nature film, and call it My Garden. John said he would like to make an advertisement strip. Mother suggested that they should think of all the things they would like to write, and tell her; then she would write the sentences down for them to copy.

Then followed a very busy time while Jennifer painted her pictures and John got on with his advertisement strip. They left space at the bottom of each picture for the wording. When they had finished their paintings Mother wrote the sentences and the twins copied them.

Jennifer's Nature film read like this when it was finished:

My Garden

I have a garden of my own.
My Daddy bought me some seeds.
I planted them.
I watered them every day.
The seeds began to grow.
There were yellow sunflowers at the back.
There were orange marigolds in the front.
Nasturtiums were in the border.
The bees came to my garden.
They wanted nectar from my flowers.
They filled the pockets on their legs with pollen.

I picked a bunch of flowers for Mother.

John's advertisement strip had pictures of all the things he liked best. He found out the prices, and wrote them down so that other people could know them too.

Bananas are 2d each today.
Toffee apples are cheap at 1d.
Eat more fruit.
Milk is good for children.
Tin soldiers are 6d each.
Jellies – 4½d a packet.
Candies – 1s a lb.
1d a glass for ginger beer.
Peaches are 4 for 1s.
Burn less coal and save money.
A motor-bus to the shops costs 3d.
Come to the fair on Saturday.

They made some curtains for their cinema, which Mother threaded on to string so that they could be pulled back when the film started.

NUMBERS—ADDING TOGETHER

"AFTER 5 comes 6, 7, 8, and 9," said Mother, " now what can you tell me about 6 ?"

" There was the story of the crooked man who found a crooked sixpence," said John.

" Yes," said Jennifer, " and about the six little mice who sat down to spin."

" Think again," said Mother. " What about your café ?"

" Why 6d., and we changed it into six pennies, and we sold two bananas for 6d."

" What about 6 o'clock ? " said Mother.

But the twins did not like 6 o'clock, because it was bedtime!

" I like 7 o'clock better," said John, " because then we can get up in the morning."

" There are seven days in the week," said Jennifer. " I can say them."

Sunday Monday Tuesday Wednesday Thursday Friday Saturday

" Yes," said John, " and there is that guessing story you told us about the man with seven wives who was going to St. Ives."

Then they talked about 8 and 9.

They liked 8 because at 8 o'clock the postman brought the letters, and figure 8 looked rather like a crusty loaf of bread that Granny made when they went to tea with her.

John and Jennifer knew a lot about 9 because they had a box of ninepins. They loved to knock them down, and count how many were left, so they soon learnt number 9.

Mother said that as they had talked

about each number by itself, it was time they learned to add numbers together. So the twins and Mother went to their café. Mother wanted 1 glass of orangeade, 1 glass of lemonade, and 1 glass of milk. John fetched them, and saw that 1 and 1 and 1 are three. Jennifer wanted 2 oranges and 1 lemon, so they found that 2 and 1 are 3.

Mother told them that when numbers are added together, the big number they make is called the " sum."

Then Mother asked them to get for her 2 biscuits and 2 tarts; and the twins said, 2 and 2 are 4. Mother said we can't be always writing words between our figures, so we use little signs instead, such as + for *add*, and = for *are*. The hard name for the second one is " equals." The twins first learned all the things which made the bigger numbers, like this:

$$1 + 0 = 1$$
$$1 + 1 = 2$$
$$2 + 0 = 2$$
$$1 + 1 + 1 = 3$$
$$2 + 1 = 3$$
$$3 + 0 = 3$$
$$1 + 1 + 1 + 1 = 4$$
$$2 + 2 = 4$$
$$3 + 1 = 4$$
$$4 + 0 = 4$$

Right up to $9 + 0 = 9$

Mother made them some number boards out of cardboard, to help them to do their sums. They were like this:

Then they did upright sums like this:

$$\begin{array}{c} 4 \\ +4 \\ \hline 8 \end{array} \qquad \begin{array}{c} 6 \\ +3 \\ \hline 9 \end{array} \qquad \begin{array}{c} 3 \\ +4 \\ \hline 7 \end{array}$$

MUSIC—MELODIES FOR VOICES

THE first type of music making was singing. We cannot help singing. When we are happy we sing cheerful songs. When we are sad we sing mournful songs. When we are in church we sing hymns and psalms.

Long before concert halls, theatres, and cinemas there were churches. Many centuries ago monks, priests, and musicians worked in the quiet churches. Between them they made books for people to read, pictures for people to look at, and music for people to hear. The music they made was mostly for voices.

Tunes were made to fit the words of the hymns and psalms. When St. Gregory sent St. Augustine to England he sent with him many of the songs of the church, so that they might be taught to the English. In those days there were no magnificent organs, and all the melodies were sung without accompaniment.

Some people had voices higher than others, of course, and music had to be arranged for everyone to sing. Some people sing better than others. Because of this we have choirs, for choirs are collections of trained singers. The monks made their churches beautiful in many ways. They did not forget music, and the best way in which music could be used to beautify the church was through the choir.

The first church music was composed as a single line of melody. The first choirs were choirs of men. These men were called *tenors* because they "held" the tune (*tenere* is a Latin word meaning to hold). But some men had higher voices and were given higher tunes to sing. They were the *altos* (*altus* means high). When composers learned to write two tunes which would fit together they were not satisfied. "We must have a third part," they said. The third part, given to the boys who were educated in the church schools, was called the *treble* (from *triplex*, meaning three-fold). And then there were the men who said that they could only sing very low notes. They were given a part of their own, and it was the *bass* part (*bassus* for low). All these Latin words came into music because Latin was the language in which psalms and hymns were sung.

If you had been able to go to a church in the reign of Henry the Eighth you would have heard, as you may hear now, choirs of trebles (*soprano* is a later word which means the same thing, although it is more often applied to lady singers), altos, tenors, and basses. You would have noticed, as you may still notice, that each part has a separate tune. All the parts, however, fitted together agreeably. They harmonised. Composers gradually learned how to make melodies and how to fit melodies together. Most of the music which we hear is made of separate tunes joined together. Just as a carpenter takes different pieces of wood and joins them together to make a chair or a table, so the musician takes different pieces of melody and fits them, one with another, to make an anthem or a sonata.

In the days of Henry the Eighth and Queen Elizabeth—both of whom were keen musicians—there were very great composers of church music. In Italy there was Palestrina, in England William Byrd, in Flanders Orlando di Lassus. One day you will hear the music of these men and you will find it as beautiful as the churches for which it was made. It is all music for voices without instruments.

There came a day when men learned to live at peace together—at any rate, within their own countries. The barons built large and forbidding castles because they did not trust their neighbours. Their spare time was spent in sharpening swords, in polishing armour, in exercising war horses. Sometimes a minstrel came to the castle on a winter's evening to charm the baron with soft songs to the accompanying harp. If the minstrel did not sing a folk song he would sing such songs as the Agincourt Song or Men of Harlech, songs of heroism and daring deeds. The baron listened.

In the days of Queen Elizabeth castles were no longer built. There were comfortable houses which were homes. The men who lived in these old brick, or timber, houses spent much time with their families. They listened to the words of one of their great contemporaries, and one of our greatest composers, William Byrd:

> Since singing is so good a thing,
> I wish all men would learn to sing.

The Elizabethans and the Jacobeans (who lived in the reign of James the First) asked composers to come and live in their homes to teach them to play the virginals, the lute, the viol, the recorder, and to sing. The songs which they sang were known as madrigals.

Madrigals were songs made to poetry—beautiful poetry, because it was a great period for poetry—and often about the countryside. Madrigals were for trebles, altos, tenors, and basses, just as the church music. But they were meant to be sung at home, not by accomplished musicians but by quite ordinary music lovers.

One madrigal is about the month of May. It was composed by cheerful Thomas Morley. Here is the melody. Ask someone to sing it to you. Then learn it yourself. As you hear it and as you sing it imagine the picture which it paints. Try to feel how the tune itself gives the sense of cheerful pleasure that we feel on a fresh morning in early summer. (Notice that this melody really needs only four lines.)

should know. It is The Silver Swan, by Orlando Gibbons. He was once a choirboy in the chapel of King's College, Cambridge. There has been a choir there since the days of Henry the Sixth. Orlando Gibbons, who knew Charles the First, was one of the most famous of

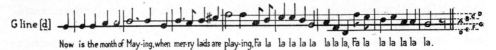

Now is the month of May-ing, when mer-ry lads are play-ing, Fa la la la la la la la la, Fa la la la la la la.

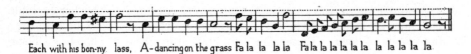

Each with his bon-ny lass, A-dancing on the grass Fa la la la la Fa la la la la la la la la la la la.

Learn to listen to music and to remember it. As you grow older you will find your memory filling with the titles of the pieces you enjoy, just as you remember the titles of the books you love.

There is one more madrigal title you

Cambridge choirboys. He grew up to become a great organist, a composer of church music and of madrigals, and of keyboard music. Keyboard music is a special branch of music, and we must save that for another time.

ART—MODELLING IN CLAY

Most boys and girls at some time or other have been given the odd bits of dough or pastry left over after Mother has made the pie, and have shaped them into a little man, or a mouse, or a little girl. In this way they have been doing some modelling.

Perhaps you have modelled a snowman or sand castle, or got some lumps of clay from the heaps thrown up by men digging, and made all sorts of models with them. It is great fun to model, to feel the shape of things and to be able to make them in clay with your fingers. You soon find out just how much you can do with the material you are modelling, and just when to stop.

An artists' colour and materials shop will be able to sell you some modelling clay, and if you happen to be near a pottery you can usually buy some there of two or three kinds in a nice soft state ready to work with.

An old tile or a slate or a piece of wood will do to make your model on; and if you use clay, and want to keep it soft in between times when you are working, get a piece of rag soaked in water and cover your model with it. If you can get a big square biscuit tin with a lid, and put

your model with the wet rag inside, the clay will keep soft and damp for a long time. To begin with, however, you will probably want to finish your modelling at one sitting, while you have a clear idea in mind of what you are going to make.

Ideas for things to model come in all sorts of ways. Perhaps you have made a doll's house with furniture as well as dolls and their clothes, and you want some toy vases or crockery for your kitchen dresser. All these can be modelled in clay, and when dry could be painted with your powder colours, making the kitchen look very gay. If you knew of someone who had a pottery kiln they might even fire them for you. The need for these things sets your imagination to work, and you will see what to model and have ideas of how to go about it.

At other times you will want to model somebody you have seen, and to make a figure several inches high. It may be the figure of an old newspaperman who sits on a box at a street corner with piles of newspapers on another box beside him, and more under his arm ready to sell to passers-by. Or you might have seen one of London's flower girls sitting with a basket of flowers on the pavement on either side of her and arranging bunches of flowers. The roast chestnut seller with his box-like oven on little wheels, and he himself leaning over to turn the nuts to prevent them from burning.

There are plenty of people who would make subjects for modelling—the coalman, milkman, postman, policeman, the chimney sweep with his brush, bundle of handle sticks, sack and shovels, and so on.

Perhaps you are fond of animals, and would like to make a model of your pet—a dog, a cat, a rabbit, or a guinea-pig, all of which would be interesting subjects to model.

If you wanted to model different kinds of animals you could start by making a model of the Zoo or Noah's Ark, and you could model all the animals you chose in clay or Plasticine.

A CLAY DOG

Once you know what you want to do you are well on the way to doing your modelling; and once you start handling clay you will soon get the feel of it, and discover the way to use it.

Clay is a material in which you can express your ideas easily, and the result of your work should look as though it had been made in clay. Modelling in clay with thin little bits sticking out in all directions (certain to be broken off as soon as they dry and become brittle) is not a good way to use it. Keep your modelling fairly solid, and any parts which are meant to stand out should be strong.

This model of a dog is a good one to illustrate this. He is nice and solid, sits well, and his nose stands out, but is very strongly and firmly modelled on to the body. He looks well from all sides. The model was made by a girl of eleven.

All the four animals shown in the lower illustration were modelled in clay, and the calf with the arched tail and the smaller horse were painted, when dry, with powder colours. They are all first efforts in modelling by young people who have left school.

The big horse is about nine inches long, and is a fine model of a farm type, with great shaggy feet. The sheep was part of a Nativity group, and lay on straw with a model of a shepherd. If two or three people combine on a piece of modelling work, a Nativity group offers lots of opportunity, as in addition to the Holy Family, it is possible to model sheep, cattle, shepherds, dog, donkey, and camels for the Three Kings.

FIRST ATTEMPTS AT MODELLING ANIMALS IN CLAY

FRENCH—IN SIGHT OF THE SEA

HERE we read of the arrival of the travellers at Dover. We must be sure to remember that the first line under the picture is the French; the second line gives the English word for the French word above it; the third line shows how we make up the words in our own language.

Nous sommes fatigués de jouer.
We   are   tired   of to play.
We are tired of playing.

Bébé dit qu'il a faim.
Baby says that he has hunger.
Baby says he is hungry.

Nous avons tous faim.
We   have   all hunger.
We are all hungry.

Maman nous donne des pommes.
Mamma us   gives some apples.
Mamma gives us some apples.

Toutes les pommes sont rouges.
All   the   apples   are   red.
All the apples are red.

Bébé laisse tomber la sienne.
Baby   lets   to fall   his.
Baby lets his fall.

Il recommence à pleurer.
He begins again to   cry.
He begins to cry again.

Papa se baisse pour la chercher.
Papa himself stoops in order   it   to find.
Papa stoops to find it.

Papa donne la pomme à bébé.
Papa gives the   apple to baby.
Papa gives the apple to baby.

Le train s'arrête.
The train itself stops.
The train stops.

Papa perd ses lunettes.
Papa loses his spectacles.
Papa loses his spectacles.

Maman les ramasse.
Mamma them picks up.
Mamma picks them up.

Nous sommes à Douvres.
We   are   at   Dover.
We are at Dover.

Nous descendons du train.
We   get down   from the train.
We get out of the train.

The Story of the Boundless Universe and All Its Wondrous Worlds

The waves of the ocean that have played their part in the shaping of the Earth

HOW SUN AND WIND MADE THE · HILLS

Most of the wonderful things that happen in the world depend on things working together, and nothing is more interesting than to discover and study the working of the great and little partnerships in Nature.

Probably the most powerful and most important partnership ever formed was the partnership between Sun and wind to make mud. Both are mighty workers, never idling and never resting: they have factories all over the world, and their production is, and has been, stupendous beyond imagining.

When the Earth was first formed its surface, as we have seen, was merely a veneer of slag some thirty or forty or fifty miles thick, and it probably would have remained simply a crumpled crust of grey and green and black slag, covered here and there with water, if the Sun and the wind had not put their heads together and started to make mud-pies.

The Sun toiled ceaselessly to lift water to tremendous heights in the sky, where it formed clouds, and the wind carried the clouds about, and made them fall in rain, mostly on the top of hills, the rain collected into streams and rivers, and the streams and rivers broke up the basalt and granite into mud, until the whole Earth was nothing but a big mud-pie.

The Moon seems to do pretty hard work when it lifts the tides—sometimes forty feet high—and some pumping machines can raise many tons of water a day; but such work is child's play compared with the work done by the Sun. The clouds seem light, but they contain enormous quantities of water, and the total weight of water raised by the Sun during the year must be millions of millions of tons, for it is enough to keep the Amazon and the Nile and the Mississippi going, not to speak of Niagara and the Victoria Falls, and a thousand other rivers. It is calculated that the rain which falls yearly upon England and Wales alone weighs nearly 70,000 million tons, and every drop of it is lifted by the Sun!

Indeed, the work the rivers do is really the work that has been done by the Sun and the wind; all the rivers themselves do is to let themselves fall into the sea.

Yet, as they fall, they wear away the hard rocks of their beds, and ages ago they wore down into mud all the granite and basalt surface of our planet.

The wind, of course, does a great deal to assist the Sun in the mud-making. It lifts the clouds higher and carries them about, and, with the help of the Moon, it hurls the waves on the coasts of the world and gradually breaks them down. Also it

ASTRONOMY · GEOLOGY · GEOGRAPHY · CHEMISTRY · PHYSICS · LIFE

28 X 1

blows about sand, and wears down rocks as with a sand blast. The carbon dioxide is also of assistance, for it is dissolved in the rain-water, and acts chemically on lime and marble, and other materials in the crust.. Frost and ice, too, are rock-grinders, rock-breakers, and mud-makers. But the Sun is the most strenuous worker in the great mud firm, and most of the mud in the world is due to his strong arm.

If we look at the rivers nowadays we get some idea of what they, with the sun-lift in them, are able to do to turn the dry land into mud.

ENOUGH SALT IN THE SEA TO COVER DRY LAND AS DEEP AS ST. PAUL'S

Consider the salt in the sea, practically all of which they collected! It is estimated that the sea contains 144 billion tons of it—enough to cover the whole dry land 400 feet deep; that is to say, to cover the Earth with salt higher than the cross on St. Paul's. That is surprising, but more surprising still are the estimates of the mud carried yearly into the sea by great rivers. The Mississippi carries more than 400 million tons of sediment yearly into the sea—enough mud to cover a square mile 68 feet deep; while the Yellow River of China brings down every year more than twice as much. Altogether the rivers of the world must make a big mountain of mud every year. Egypt is made of Nile mud, and the Netherlands chiefly of mud of the Rhine.

That is how the world has been sculptured and planned. The peak of the Matterhorn, the great limestone masses of the Dolomites, the vast canyons in Colorado, the great sierras of the Andes, were all shaped by the wet fingers of the Sun.

With a cloud the Sun made the magic clay that was to grow into roses and wheat and men. With clouds the Sun rubbed away the dry, hard, slaggy crust of the Earth and turned it into soil and food and living things.

THE GREAT MOUNTAINS THAT ARE WASHED INTO THE SEA

But this mud-making has been going on for millions of years, and even the yearly mud-pie of the Yellow River is merely a drop in the bucket compared with the mud of the past. All over the world we see not only mountains worn half away, but signs that mountains have been worn down to their very base— not only the crumpled granite ranges of

the early crust, but great volcanoes that pierced through the early mud. We find—more astonishing still—that the mud of destroyed mountains has risen again as rocky mountains from the bottom of deep seas, and has again been worn down. We find that this has happened many times in succession, until now the Earth is covered miles deep in mud and mud rock, and the only bits of its surface that are not mud or mud rock are the volcanoes and the granite and basalt lavas that have forced their way through the mud.

All the great mountains of the world, except the volcanoes, are composed of sea-mud rock, and a great part of them—as the Alps, the Himalayas, and the Apennines— are built of lime mud previously built into sea shells. Rocks made out of mud deposited in the sea are usually known as *aqueous* rocks (from the Latin word *aqua*, meaning water), because they have been formed in water; or as *stratified* rocks (from the Latin word *strata*, meaning layers), because they have been laid down in layers on the sea bottom.

THE ROCKY DEEPS IN WHICH IS WRITTEN THE HISTORY OF THE EARTH

They were all originally part of the slag of the crust—either as slag actually in the crust, or as slag-lava driven through the earliest coatings of mud. Limestone and chalk and clay and sandstone are all examples of aqueous or stratified rock. The original rocks, such as are seen in granite and basalt and other lavas, are called *igneous* rocks (from the Latin word *ignis*, meaning fire), because they were forged by fire, and are not directly made from mud. Less than a tenth of the rocks are of this nature.

The making of mud from igneous rocks, and the destruction and reconstruction of mud rocks, has been going on for millions of years, and the examples we have given to show how quickly rivers make mud show that in millions of years huge quantities of rock must have been made and remade. How deep would all the layers reach if they had not been destroyed, but had been piled on each other! Calculations, of course, are only very rough, but it has been said that from first to last they would reach at least 30 or 40 miles high, and some authorities say at least double that height. One English geologist thought that since the first backboned animals appeared in the world mud 34 miles deep has been deposited. It is quite plain that, if the floor of the sea had not time after time risen into continents and mountains there would be no land above water today. Even within three million years England will be worn away and washed into the sea if there is no rising of the land to save her.

Of mud all life was made ; on rock made of ancient sea mud and filled with ancient sea shells most men and plants now live; and without mud there would be no world as we know it. But the layers of the mud are also the illustrated history of the Earth.

When men began to study the *aqueous*

it tells the history of the Earth millions of years ago when the mud was made, and we can say that in these early days England—or New Zealand, as the case might be—was under water and the sea was full of sharks or seaweeds; or that in these days the Arctic region had a tropical climate, with ferns and mosses growing to a great height, or that in other days the ancestor of the horse appeared; or at another time there were huge reptiles. By comparing the contents of layers with their position and their position with their contents, we can put the layers of mud rock with their fossils—as the remains are called—in their correct position.

It does not follow that, because a layer

WHY WE FIND A SEA SHELL ON THE TOP OF A MOUNTAIN

These two pictures explain how the mountains arose from the bed of the sea. The top strip shows layers of sedimentary rocks beneath the sea, and the bottom picture shows the gigantic folding of the rocks through the contraction of the Earth. Since this happened Sun, rain, wind, and frost have worn away the parts indicated by the dotted line.

rocks they found in them the remains of animals and plants; and geologists soon discovered that the remains found in the deepest layers of mud were very different from the remains we find in the layers nearer the surface.

By comparing the position and contents of such layers it is found that they could be arranged in chapters and leaves like the chapters and leaves of a history book, and that we could read the history of the world in this history book for millions of years. We know by the amount of mud laid down above a certain layer that

is now on the top, therefore it is newly laid down. It may be on the top—as in the case of the very old rock in the island of Lewis—because the other layers have been worn off it. But geologists, by a process of comparison, got over that and other difficulties, and now, in the strata of the Earth, we can read the story of some of the changes in its crust and of the evolution of life—of the lifting of Mount Everest from the sea, the blossoming of the first flowers, and the coming of the first birds, and the slow ascent of man. This is a long, long story; its pages are

THE CHANGING EARTH FROM AGE TO AGE

1. The history of the Earth for millions of years is written in its rocks, and men are able, by reading the rocks, to give us a vivid panorama of the Earth's long story. We can see also how that story came to be written in the rocks. A million years ago, a little stream trickled down a mountain, carrying sand and stones to the sea. In the sea swam the ichthyosaurus.

2. The ichthyosaurus was a reptile living in the sea, and its name means fish-lizard. It had a great head with powerful jaws and teeth, and its body had four limbs like paddles which enabled it to swim. One day this great creature died, and its body fell to the bottom of the sea. Meanwhile, the stones and sand brought down by the stream continued to fall.

3. As the ages passed, the stream wore away a wider and deeper bed for itself and became a river ; and the rains falling on the mountain loosened the soil and formed hundreds of tiny streams, each running into the river. As the river became wider it brought down more earth and stones, which fell in a never-ceasing shower on the bed of the sea, and buried the reptile's body.

THE WONDER-STORY TOLD IN THE ROCKS

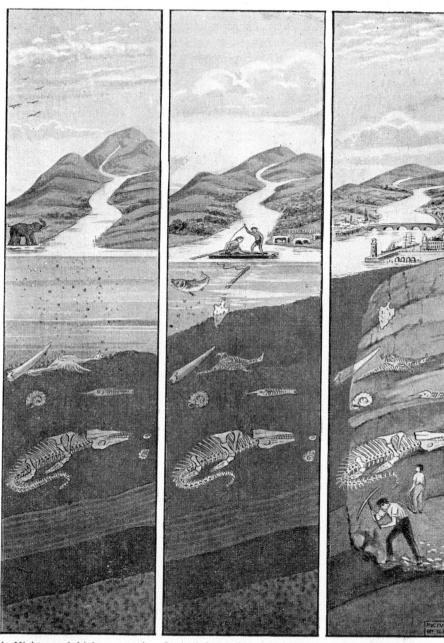

4. Higher and higher rose the ocean-bed as the mud from the mountain continued to fall, and the lower layers became hard rock. One day an elephant going to the river to drink broke off his tusk, and this was carried to the sea. Another day a bird was drowned, and fell on the ocean-bed. Dead fishes and shells also sank, and all were buried.

5. And then at last, hundreds of thousands of years after the ichthyosaurus died, men began to live on the Earth. One day a man who had made a boat out of a hollow tree-trunk took his wife and went out to fish, and the head of his harpoon broke off and fell to the bottom of the sea, and this also became buried in the mud.

6. The bottom of the sea crept higher and higher till at last it became dry land. Then one day men began to dig, and the world's wonderful story was revealed as we read it here. First the spear-head was found, then the tusk, the bird's skeleton, the shells, the fish, and at last the skeleton of the great reptile; and all were turned to stone.

at least 30 or 40 miles thick; and all we have time to do here is to skim over some of the chapters. But the torn and fragmentary pages—some early, some recent—which lie open to our gaze in Britain, are specially explained and illustrated in these pages by our scientific artist, who, like a wizard, can call up animals and plants long dead.

THE CHIEF CHAPTERS OF THE LONG STORY-BOOK OF HISTORY

Skimming, then, through the wonder story told on Nature's tables of stone, we find that there are four chief chapters of the world's history since life appeared.

1. The chapter of very ancient life which we call Palaeozoic, from the two Greek words meaning ancient and life. This was the Primary Era, with periods which we call Cambrian, Ordovician, Silurian, Devonian, and Carboniferous.

2. The chapter of ancient life which we call the Mesozoic, from the two Greek words meaning middle and life. This is the Second Era, with periods which we call Triassic, Jurassic, and Cretaceous.

3. The chapter of more recent life, which we call the Kainozoic, from the two Greek words for new and life. This is the Tertiary Era—the Third Era—and its chief periods are the Eocene, Miocene, and Pliocene.

4. The chapter of life embracing the time of human history in which we live, called the Quaternary, or Fourth Period. It includes what we call the Pleistocene Period, named after the Greek words for newest and life.

THE FORMS OF LIFE FOUND IN THE EARLIEST ROCKS

Much the longest of these chapters is the first, containing the oldest certain remains of living things. There are hints of life in still deeper layers of the Earth's crust, and probably life in its simplest forms began long before the Palaeozoic rocks were made; but the deepest pages of the stony history of life have been so crushed and heated that their story has been obliterated, and our history begins with the Palaeozoic Era. It is, of course, intensely interesting to find out what plants and animals existed then, millions of years before man.

Bits of this ancient chapter are found all over the world. In Britain it is found especially in Wales, and the first sub-chapter, the Cambrian, takes its name from the Latin name for Wales—Cambria.

But wherever the pages or fragments of pages occur, we find only rather primitive life—seaweeds and corals, crab-like creatures and sponges, and, toward the end, fishes and insects and scorpions. As there were insects and scorpions, there was, of course, vegetation, and toward the end of the chapter we find great fern trees and giant mosses. Indeed, most of the coal we use is the decayed remains of the luxuriant vegetation that flourished toward the end of this chapter. The creatures most characteristic of this period were the trilobites—little lobster-like animals in shells, with compound eyes on the tops of their heads. Toward the end of this period amphibians appeared.

THE EIGHTY-FEET LIZARD, AND THE REPTILE WITH LEATHERY WINGS

The Mesozoic Period was rich in life, but especially rich in reptiles. It was indeed, the age of reptiles, and the rocks of this chapter are full of the fossils of strange reptiles now extinct. In the sea swam huge lizards such as the Plesiosaurs and Ichthyosaurs, and on land reigned the tremendous Dinosaurus, Brontosaurus, and Diplodocus. Diplodocus was over eighty feet long from the end of his snout to the tip of his tail, and Brontosaurus was even larger.

But more interesting and extraordinary than these was the Pterodactyl—a creature half reptile and half bird with leathery wings twenty feet long, and at first with teeth in their jaws. Another reptile called the Archaeopteryx had feathered wings and a feathered tail; we call this the first bird. In this period, too, even while the Plesiosaur and the Ichthyosaur swam about in the sea the little sea-creatures called Foraminifera were making the little chalk-shells which we see today in the white cliffs of Dover. Now also appeared the first mammals—probably little rat-like creatures.

The Kainozoic Period is the Age of Mammals, and toward the end of it appeared the greatest of all mammals—the mammal Man, whose large brain and skilful hand have made him lord of the creatures that inhabit the Earth.

(Next chapter in this group, page 765)

The Story of Immortal Folk Whose Work Will Never Die

Louis XVI   Robespierre   Danton   Carnot   Mirabeau   Voltaire

Jean Paul Marat   St. Just   Charlotte Corday   Madame Roland   Lafayette   Diderot

THE FRENCH REVOLUTIONISTS

BETWEEN the years 1789 and 1792 there were very great troubles in France, and violent changes took place. The French monarchy was turned into a republic, so that there was no longer a king at the head of affairs, because it was said that every country ought to be ruled according to the will of the whole people who live in it, and not according to the wishes of one man or of the few who have wealth and power. Yet after all, it was not very long before the French found themselves again being ruled by the will of one man, who became the Emperor Napoleon, of whom we read elsewhere.

But the changes which took place before that make up the story of what is called the French Revolution ; and some of these changes in the government of the country and the life of the people have continued to the present time in France itself, and some have been adopted since that time in other countries of Europe.

We are going to learn something about the men and women who made the French Revolution, or tried to prevent it ; but we shall not be able to understand much about them unless we first of all try to imagine the state of affairs which made people so determined to have a change that they allowed all sorts of terrible things

to be done rather than stay as they were. In England there was a free government— that is, the people ruled through the Parliament, and the king and the ministers had to obey the law like everyone else. But in France the king and his ministers could do very nearly as they liked, so long as they did not interfere with the privileges of the clergy or the nobles.

But the common people suffered grievously by these privileges ; for in the country places the peasants were almost the slaves of the great landowners, who were called the seigneurs. In nearly all the land, except in Brittany and the district called La Vendée, the seigneurs cared nothing for the needs or sufferings of the peasants; and although the seigneurs and the clergy had to pay no taxes, the peasants were compelled to pay heavy taxes, as well as to labour for the seigneurs without pay —all of which was very unlike anything known in Great Britain for more than 400 years. There were many people who for a long time past had been saying that all this was very wrong, and had been pointing out that people in England were much more prosperous; and among these were Voltaire and Diderot. But these two men did not arouse so much excitement as Jean Jacques Rousseau, who came from

EXPLORERS · INVENTORS · WRITERS · ARTISTS · SCIENTISTS

Switzerland; for he had been brought up hardly, and had led a strange, wandering, discontented sort of life, failing in everything at which he tried his hand, until he took to expressing his ideas in books which at once made him famous.

The idea he had got hold of was that civilisation was all wrong, and that people would be much happier living in what he called a natural state, with very little law or government at all. He said that people who were strong and rich had persuaded the rest to serve them by pretending they would protect them, and so had got the rulership into their own hands, and used it for their own advantage.

ROUSSEAU WHO TAUGHT THAT THE WILL OF THE PEOPLE SHOULD TRIUMPH

He maintained that everybody ought to make a new agreement or social contract, according to which everything should be settled by the will of the people; and that there should be no more kings or seigneurs or people who had privileges, but everything should be arranged in the way the people thought best. This teaching of his about the rights of man and the social contract became very popular.

All the seigneurs belonged to a group of great families who kept themselves aloof from ordinary folk, and they are spoken of sometimes as the *noblesse*, and sometimes as the aristocrats. There were a few of the aristocrats who were very much in favour of some of the new ideas that Diderot or Voltaire or Rousseau were talking about. The king had not nearly enough money to carry on the government, especially as there had been great expense owing to a war with England, and he was advised that the only thing to be done was to summon an Assembly of the Three Estates—as the Noblesse, the Clergy, and the Commons were called—and to consult them as to whether better arrangements could be made for governing the country.

THE TWO MEN WHO MIGHT HAVE SAVED FRANCE FROM THE GREAT TERROR

At this time there were two men who became notable as leaders of the people, both of whom belonged to aristocratic families—the one was Mirabeau, the other was Lafayette.

It was a very unfortunate thing that these two could not be friends, for what both of them wanted was to set up in France a government in which the voice of the people should be heard as well as the voice of the king and his ministers. Both of them had learnt a good deal in England or in America; for Lafayette had gone to America when he was only 20, and had served under the great George Washington in the war which ended in the separation of the United States from England ; so he had seen what Americans and Englishmen meant by freedom, and also how wise and great a man Washington was.

Mirabeau had lived for some time in England, and had seen there how it was possible for justice and law to rule everywhere without oppression, and for both king and people to have a share in the government. But the least that either of them wanted would have made so great a change in France that the Court and most of the aristocrats and the clergy would have nothing to say to them. And perhaps the saddest thing is that if King Louis had been a wiser man, those three working together —Lafayette, Mirabeau, and the king— might have made the French Revolution a peaceful affair, which would have set up in France a government not very unlike that of our own country.

THE GOOD KING LOUIS WHO TRUSTED BAD COUNSELLORS

Louis himself was a good man who wished to do what was right and just. He was a brave man, too. But he was not clever himself, and he was not like some other kings who have had the wit to choose good advisers and trust them. Instead of that, he trusted people who gave him bad advice, and who could see nothing but harm in the changes Mirabeau and Lafayette demanded when the Three Estates were assembled in what was called the States-General and afterwards the National Assembly. It seemed to them that to take away the privileges of the noblesse and clergy would be robbery, and that the proper thing for the common people was not to govern but to obey their betters.

Mirabeau understood what was needed better than any other man in France. He was a man who lived a wild life privately, and was always greatly in debt, which set a good many people very much against him; and he was domineering, so that it was not easy to be friendly with him. But he was a wonderful orator ; so that, when the Assembly had come together bent on doing one thing, he could sometimes persuade it to agree to something altogether different. He would

MADAME ROLAND, WHO WENT TO EXECUTION SAYING: "O LIBERTY, WHAT CRIMES ARE COMMITTED IN THY NAME!" IS MOCKED IN THE PRISON GROUNDS

THE PROUD COURAGE OF CHARLOTTE CORDAY IN THE HOUR OF HER DOOM

rouse people to be enthusiastic when they were timid and hesitating; and in this way he had a great deal of power, though people were really afraid to trust him.

He was called the Tribune of the People, because he was so bold in demanding what he considered the people ought to have, and because he wanted the " privileged orders " to have their privileges taken away and to pay their proper share of the taxes.

HOW MIRABEAU TRIED TO BRING THE KING AND THE PEOPLE TOGETHER

But Mirabeau saw, too, that many who had come to the Assembly had no idea of what good government meant. The Assembly was not fit to be the real ruler; he wanted it to have power, but he knew that the only way to prevent terrible things happening was for him to become the real ruler himself. He wanted the people to trust him, and he wanted the king to trust him; but presently it came about that, while the king suspected him of being on the side of the people and against the crown, the people, and those who had most influence with them, suspected him of being really on the side of the crown against the people, when the thing he was actually striving to do was to unite crown and people for the good of both.

Several of the changes Mirabeau wanted were made, but unfortunately, before there was any real chance of bringing the king and the people into agreement, Mirabeau died; he tried to do such an immense amount of work that he wore himself out.

Lafayette was a very different kind of man. He was a popular and high-minded gentleman, who had won great praise as a soldier when he was fighting in America under Washington. After the States-General had come together, and had been turned into the National Assembly, it was found very difficult to keep order, because everyone was in a state of excitement.

LAFAYETTE, WHO TRIED TO KEEP ORDER IN PARIS AND DISPLEASED ALL PARTIES

So the better class of the citizens in Paris were enrolled as soldiers in what was called the National Guard, to keep order; and Lafayette was made their general. He was very popular among them, and some people began to think he meant to make himself the real master by the help of his soldiers, like Julius Caesar in Rome or Oliver Cromwell in England. Besides, it was not very easy for the poor people to believe that so fine a gentleman as Lafayette cared much about them; and the noblesse hated him because they thought he had deserted their order; while the queen and court disliked him because they thought he was trying to become dictator.

At last, when there was a great riot and Lafayette had to order his soldiers to attack the mob, the common folk liked him less than ever, and he found that even his soldiers were only half inclined to obey him. He always wanted to check violence; but he could not sway men as Mirabeau could. So, when more violent men got the upper hand, Lafayette no longer commanded the National Guard. Later, when France declared war against Austria and Prussia, he was sent to command the French army; but Paris became so disturbed that he wanted to take the French troops back there, and when he found that he could not do so he would not remain in command, but left the country.

HOW LAFAYETTE HELPED TO BRING BACK A KING TO FRANCE

As for what befell him afterwards, he was made prisoner by the Austrians, and after spending some years in prison he was set free again. Later, he helped in the restoration of the Bourbons, as the French dynasty was then called, and, at the end of his long life, he helped in another little revolution when the Bourbons were turned out again, and their cousin, Louis Philippe, was made king in their place.

Now let us look at the king and queen, whose story is so tragic. Louis always meant well, and would have been quite willing to grant much more power to the people and to put an end to bad laws and customs; but the people round him were always persuading him that if he allowed one thing or another to be done the king would never again have any power; and Louis thought a king had no right to give up his power. So he could never make up his mind to trust either Mirabeau or any other of the leaders of the people, or, on the other hand, to take up his stand boldly as a monarch determined that his will should be obeyed. In one way he was a brave man, for he had no fear of death, but he had not the other kind of courage which enables a man to resolve on a plan of action in which there are risks, and to carry it through in spite of all dangers and difficulties.

TWO MEN WHO LED THE REVOLUTION

THE MONSTER ROBESPIERRE FACING HIS CAPTORS. HE IS THE SITTING FIGURE

THE FIRST SINGING OF THE MARSEILLAISE, THE SONG OF THE FRENCH REVOLUTION, COMPOSED BY THE SINGER IN THIS PICTURE, ROUGET DE LISLE

Soon after the death of Mirabeau the king and queen thought the best thing they could do was to take flight out of France; they thought that then other kings would help them to recover their power, for the queen was the sister of the Emperor of Austria.

They made preparations secretly, and fled by night from Paris in a carriage, pretending to be just a gentleman and his wife. But at a place near the frontier the king was recognised when he got out of his carriage, and they were stopped and sent back to Paris, where they were kept under strict guard.

Louis accepted the new rules for governing the country which the Assembly had prepared, and so he was still king. A new liberty. The queen, too, had to set one on the head of the little Prince Royal, the heir to the throne. No real harm was done that time; but when ill news came from the war, and the Prussians made a proclamation that Paris would be punished if the king suffered any hurt, the people became furious.

The royal palace was attacked by a mob thirsting for blood; the valiant Swiss Guards, who defended it stoutly, were cut to pieces. But the king and queen had fled with the rest of the royal family and taken refuge with the Assembly. Then there came another new Assembly, which was full of Jacobins, and of others who wanted a republic, and who were called Girondins; and the new Assembly pro-

PRISON SCENES IN THE REIGN OF TERROR DURING THE FRENCH REVOLUTION

Assembly was called, but the king had no able men about him now whom he could make ministers, and the cleverest men he tried would not do as he wished, or serve him if he did not do as they wished. And at this time, because the Austrian Emperor and the King of Prussia threatened to interfere, Louis was forced to declare war against them; while the men who were called Jacobins, which was the name of a club to which they belonged, were stirring up feeling against the monarchy, and Paris was getting very excited.

One day there was a great procession, which found its way into the royal palace of the Tuileries; and the King of France was made to set on his head the red cap of claimed that France was now a republic, and the king and queen were merely citizens. And even before this the Jacobins had put to death a number of supporters of the king who had been thrown into prison, in what were called the September massacres. The next thing was to bring the king himself to trial, as Charles Stuart had been tried in England 140 years before. Louis was tried by the Assembly itself, and condemned to death.

Like Charles the First, Louis showed a royal dignity and fortitude. He was beheaded, not with an axe like Charles, but by an instrument called the *guillotine*, which had been brought into regular use in France by this time.

MARIE ANTOINETTE WALKS TO HER DEATH

MARIE ANTOINETTE, LOUIS XVI, AND THEIR CHILDREN IN THEIR PRISON CELL
From the painting by E. M. Ward, R.A., in Preston Art Gallery

The poor queen and her children remained prisoners for a long time. Marie Antoinette deserves to be pitied, for, though she had not always been wise, when misfortune came upon her she behaved with splendid courage; and it has always been counted among the wickedest deeds of the Jacobins that she, too, was sent to the guillotine by them, nearly a year after her husband.

She was not yet 40 when she was slain; but the long, terrible months of anxiety had so changed her that she seemed almost an old woman. When she became Queen of France she was still a beautiful and attractive girl who had never known what it was to have her will crossed, and had been taught to take it for granted that kings and queens have a right to go their own way, so that she always encouraged the king to resist. She died her ignoble death like a queen.

One woman was famous who was on the side of the Revolution. The party who wanted a republic in France was divided in two, the Girondins and the Jacobins; and of these the Jacobins were much the fiercer. The Girondins wanted a republic like that of ancient Rome; they did not wish to destroy for the pleasure of destroying.

THE NOBLE MADAME ROLAND, WHO DIED BECAUSE SHE TRIED TO SAVE OTHERS

Madame Roland had great influence among the Girondins, and was accounted a woman both noble and wise; but after the king had been slain the Jacobins got the upper hand altogether, and turned upon the Girondins, who wished to check bloodshed. Many of them were flung into prison, among whom was Madame Roland; and many were sent to the guillotine, though they had striven their hardest for liberty. And so it was that Madame Roland died in the same way as Marie Antoinette. " O Liberty! " she cried on her way to the guillotine, " what crimes are committed in thy name! "

No space is left for extended mention of lesser actors in the drama of this wild period—men like St. Just and Carnot—but three who are commonly named together must be pictured. One of these came very near to being a great man.

This was Danton—terrible, fearless, ruthless. It was he who caused the September massacres, because he thought that was the only way to make sure that there would not be a rising of the Royalists, just at the moment when it seemed that foreign armies might be marching on Paris. And it was he who spoke these fierce words when the kings of Europe seemed to be gathering their forces to crush the French Republic: " To the kings we will fling down the head of a king as the gage of battle "—meaning that Louis would be beheaded. After that he would have joined hands with the Girondins in checking bloodshed, but they would not join with him; so he held by the Jacobins, yet still strove to stay their bloodthirstiness. And again the more cruel among them got the upper hand, and Danton, in his turn, was sent to the guillotine.

HOW A YOUNG GIRL RID FRANCE OF A BLOODTHIRSTY TYRANT

The second of the three was Marat, who called himself the " friend of the people," foul of speech, craving for blood, ever urging death for the aristocrats. He did not die by the guillotine, for his wickedness so stirred the heart of a girl named Charlotte Corday that she thought it was her mission to free the world from such a monster. So she came to Paris, and, being admitted to speak with him, drew a dagger and slew him; for which deed she, too, died under the guillotine.

The third was, for a time, most powerful of them all. This was Maximilian Robespierre, a little, unhealthy-looking man, who would have been simply a respectable citizen if he had remained in private life. But he had one idea in his head which he was quite determined to carry out. This was that the will of what he called the Sovereign People must rule, and the way to bring that about was to destroy everything that could possibly stand in the way—kings or aristocrats, Girondins or Jacobins, men or women, young or old. He got all the power in his own hands, till at last the guillotine was killing fifty people every day.

THE END OF THE TERROR AND THE DEATH OF ROBESPIERRE

Then even his own supporters grew weary and disgusted, and turned upon him, and he, too, went to the guillotine. When his head fell, those who stood by shouted for joy. With his death, the Reign of Terror came to an end, and the ruling of the French Republic passed into the hands of a group of people called the Directory, until Napoleon arose.

The Great Stories of the World That Will Be Told for Ever

JACK THE GIANT KILLER

IN the days of King Arthur there lived a farmer's son named Jack. Not far away from Jack's home was a cave, and in the cave lived a horrible giant, who was called Cormoran.

Cormoran was three times as big as any other man; his appetite was so enormous that the only way to get enough food to eat was by stealing all the sheep and oxen that he could find. For one meal the giant could eat as much as six oxen and twelve sheep, and Jack's father said that if this went on much longer all the farmers for miles round would be ruined.

This set Jack thinking, and, being a brave lad, he determined to plan out a way to kill the giant.

So one night Jack set out for the mount on which was the giant's cave. With a spade he dug a deep pit and covered it with sticks and gravel, so that it looked like earth. Then, when all was ready, he blew a loud blast on his cow-horn and waited to see what would happen.

The giant awoke in a terrible rage, and came stamping down the mount to see who had dared to come so near his cave. Suddenly he caught sight of Jack.

" You young rascal ! " he cried. " I'll kill you and eat you for my supper ! "

He rushed after Jack, but just before he reached him his foot caught in the pit, and down he came, crash ! Up jumped Jack, and in a twinkling he drew out his axe and chopped off Cormoran's head.

Jack ran all the way home, and the farmers were so delighted at being rid of the monster that they presented the hero with a sword, and named him " Jack the Giant Killer."

Jack was so proud of his success that he determined to rid the world of another monster, named Blunderbore, who lived in a castle in the midst of a lovely forest.

Jack set out bravely, but the day was warm, and he had not gone very far when, overcome by the heat, he lay down under a tree and fell asleep. Soon Blunderbore came along, and, catching sight of Jack, he picked him up, flung him over his shoulder, and carried him to his castle.

When Jack awoke and he found himself in the Giant's castle he was in a terrible fright. Through the windows he could hear the cries and groans of the giant's other victims, and his teeth began to chatter.

" This is dreadful," he said to himself. " I must find a way out somehow."

Just at that moment Jack heard voices in the courtyard below, and, peeping through the rails of his prison window, he saw Blunderbore and another giant enter the castle. Looking round, he caught sight of a coil of rope which lay in a

IMAGINATION · CHIVALRY · LEGENDS · GOLDEN DEEDS · FAIRY TALES

corner. He made a noose at each end of the rope, and, grasping the middle firmly in his hand, he flung an end over the two giants' heads. Quick as lightning, he swung the rope round a beam by the window, and then, holding on to it with all his might, he pulled it tighter and tighter until both giants were strangled.

Jack set free all the knights and ladies whom Blunderbore had imprisoned in his castle, and set out again in search of new adventures.

The next evening he found himself at the door of a lonely castle in Wales. He knocked, and, to his amazement, the door was opened by a tremendous giant with two heads. Jack was startled ; but the giant seemed so friendly that when he offered him a bed for the night, Jack, who was beginning to feel very tired, gladly accepted his hospitality.

Now, Jack knew that this two-headed monster had four valuable treasures, which he determined to possess—a coat that made the wearer invisible, a cap that told him all he wanted to know, a sword that could cut anything, and shoes that could carry him as swiftly as the wind. Jack went to bed, and soon fell asleep. In the middle of the night he was awakened by someone singing ; and these were the words he heard :

Though you shall lodge with me this night,
　You shall not see the morning light;
My club shall dash your brains out quite.

" Ho, ho! " cried Jack, looking round for a log of wood which he had noticed by the fireplace. Jack put the log in his bed, and waited. Presently the door opened, and in came the giant and strode up to the bed. Down came the club—crash! again and again, and very thankful Jack was to have escaped the blows.

" Farewell, my young friend," the giant bellowed. " You'll make me a fine dinner by and by."

Jack had a good laugh over this, and when he was quite certain the giant had gone he crept back into bed, and was soon fast asleep.

In the morning Jack walked boldly into the room where the giant was breakfasting from a huge basin of batter pudding. The giant was so tremendously astonished at seeing Jack alive that he scarcely knew what to say to him.

Jack sat down, and began to make a good breakfast. But all the time he ate he was thinking. Suddenly a grand idea came into his mind, and when the giant was not looking he hid as much of the pudding in his jersey as he could possibly squeeze in. As soon as they had finished breakfast Jack said to the giant:

" *You* can't plunge a knife into your chest without hurting yourself. Just watch and see *me* do it."

Picking up a knife, Jack thrust it into his jersey, and out fell the pudding, piece by piece, upon the floor.

The giant did not like to be outdone by such a little creature as Jack, so he drew out his own knife, and, without more ado, plunged it straight into his chest—and fell down dead.

Then Jack caught up the cap and the shoes and the coat and the sword, and went on his way. At the next castle to which he came a grand ball was taking place. The knights and ladies, who had all heard of Jack, made him welcome, and he was just beginning to enjoy himself when in rushed a messenger to say that a hideous giant was on his way to the castle.

" Have no fear," cried Jack, hastily fastening on his invisible coat. " Leave everything to me."

He put on the shoes which carried him as quickly as the wind, and went out.

Round the castle ran a moat, and when the giant reached the drawbridge that stretched across it he sniffed the air around, and roared in an awful voice:

Fe, fi, fo, fum,
I smell the blood of an Englishman;
Be he alive, or be he dead,
I'll grind his bones to make my bread.

" You must catch me first! " cried Jack; and then, throwing off his coat, he led the giant a fine dance round the castle.

Jack ran on swiftly until he came again to the drawbridge. He ran across, but as he reached the other side he bent down, and with one stroke of his magic sword severed the bridge in two just as the giant was half-way across. Down crashed the drawbridge, and into the moat fell the giant; and that was the end of him.

Jack had many other adventures, and when he was tired of them all he went home again, and married a beautiful princess whom he loved dearly.

THE MAN WHO DID NOT FORGET

Alone in a chamber of his palace at Baghdad the great Caliph Haroun-al-Raschid reclined upon a divan, his hands motionless in his lap. So still did he sit, so set and fixed was his posture, that one might have thought him dead but for the extraordinary brightness of his eyes. The ceiling of this little chamber, chamber, the floor of which was strewn with rugs, deep and soft.

A fine piece of tapestry hung across the arch which gave an exit from this delicate chamber to the rest of the palace.

The light was dim, the air was cool and fragrant, the soft spraying sound of a fountain came from an inner courtyard. The

"THIS ALSO DO I OWE TO THEE, O JAFFAR!"

gemmed with precious stones, was carved into the likeness of a flower; the hexagonal marble walls, save only at the entrance and where a balconied window looked down through the tops of trees to the roofs of the city, were panelled with fretted ivory, so beautifully wrought that, while the Caliph could look out from them, no one could look in upon the perfumed branch of a creeper hanging across the window stirred lightly in the breeze, all the little leaves shimmering with sunlight.

Silent and motionless sat the great Caliph in this chamber, but in his soul there was a storm of passion. By his order, in a fit of jealous rage, the Vizier had been slain—the great Vizier Jaffar, adored by the city and held in highest honour throughout the Caliph's dominions, a man of goodness and purity, of kindness and justice, of truth and mercy.

Haroun had killed him. And now, troubled by the murder, bitterly repentant and filled with remorse for that wanton and abominable crime, he was afraid— afraid of the people. For the people, shocked by the murder, had uttered a universal cry of sorrow and grief, a wailing that had risen up from the huddled streets of Baghdad, even to the chambers of the Caliph's palace.

Jaffar was dead—Jaffar, the friend of the poor and helpless, the just judge, the kind governor, the good and holy man of simple honour and true courage ! He was dead, this protector of the poor, this merciful and humane judge. Who would now befriend them?

Very ill came this cry of the city to the ears of Haroun. It accused him and it threatened him. He had the right to slay whom he would; none had dared ever to question this right. But now—now——

In his wrath he had sent an order throughout the length and breadth of Arabia that any man who dared from that hour ever to utter the name of Jaffar should surely die. The man was dead; the name was to die too. Haroun commanded that his memory should be utterly blotted out.

And now he sat alone, knowing that he was defied. For messengers had come to him saying that a man in the city—named Mondeer—stood daily in the central square crying out the name of Jaffar, and telling men to mourn for him, to cherish his memory, and to tell their children of his goodness and justice and mercy, even if death were the cost.

Haroun had trembled in his soul at the tidings. But his brow had darkened, his eyes flashed, and in a voice of storm he had commanded this disobedient dog to be brought into his presence.

Suddenly he rose from the divan, tall, magnificent, and full of grace, a handsome man indeed, and strode swiftly, silently, to the archway of the chamber, thrusting the tapestry aside, and descending marble stairs to the courtyard where the fountain was playing.

Slaves rose in the shadows of this wide and darkened place, and salaamed to the ground as the Caliph crossed the floor and went on his way.

He descended more stairs and came to the audience chamber, where soldiers stood at the entrance and a crowd of his ministers was gathered before the throne. He strode through these people, who fell back at his approach, salaaming to the ground, and at last he reached the throne, where he stood with his back to the silent company for a long while, thinking within himself how he should act.

Then, turning abruptly and seating himself, he made a sign. Mondeer was brought in, slaves fastening the knots of the cords which bound him.

" Tie well, friends! " cried the prisoner. " Bind fast, and fear not to hurt me! " He raised his eyes, looked upon the Caliph, and said, " Welcome to me, very welcome, are these wounding cords that bind me powerless and fast; for I was bound faster and my lot was more sorrowful still when Jaffar found me, loosed me, set me free. And these cords bring back to my memory that gracious deed of his, they awake in my heart new love for him, new love, fresh reverence, and deeper gratitude, and therefore are they welcome. Honoured be thy glorious name, O Jaffar, for ever and evermore! "

While he spoke the soul of the great Caliph was kindled. To kill such a man were beneath the dignity of a king; to honour and befriend him might turn the tide that had gone out so far from the palace walls.

An overmastering hunger to deserve such love and gratitude from his people visited the heart of Haroun. He envied Jaffar in his grave. He coveted the loyalty of the living prisoner rejoicing in his cords.

" Friend," said he, bending his eyes upon Mondeer, " you have gratitude in your heart, and gratitude excuses all excess. I pardon and forgive you. More, since gifts so touch your heart, with my pardon and forgiveness I bestow upon you liberty and this great diamond, unequalled in the world, the proudest stone that shone in the Tartar's crown. Take it, and hold me in your heart as you deem fit."

The prisoner was unbound. He stretched forth his hands, his eyes shone more brightly than the diamond, and lifting the priceless gift heavenward, his eyes raised, he cried out in a voice of love:

" This also do I owe to thee, O Jaffar! Honoured be thy name for evermore ! "

THE MONKEYS' BRIDGE

Once upon a time lived in India a great hero named Rama. No one had ever fought such great fights as Rama, or performed such wonderful deeds ; and the people of India reverenced him like a god.

One day Rama went to a distant court where lived Sita, the most beautiful princess in India. He fell deeply in love with her, but was told by her father, the king, that the man who won his daughter Sita was to prove his strength and bravery and endurance in many ways.

Rama was determined either to win Sita or die, so he set himself to overcome the obstacles. Many of them proved quite simple, but the last of the deeds to be done was of such an impossible nature that all previous men had been unable to accomplish it. The task was to bend a mighty bow made and given by the gods to the father of Sita. Now, until this time, no man had ever been able so much as to lift the bow out of its iron case; but Rama not only lifted the bow, he bent and broke it, with a mighty crash.

So Rama won and married the beautiful Sita, and, accompanied by his brother, Lakshmana, went away from the court to his hunting lodge in the forest.

There they were very happy, for Rama was a mighty hunter and the forests were full of game. Every day either Rama or his brother went abroad to the chase, leaving the other to guard Sita from the evil beings who lived in those days in India.

From one demon in particular were they anxious to guard her, and that was Raksha, a terrible monster, part man, part beast, who had sworn to capture her. Raksha had always been Rama's greatest enemy. Time after time had he crept up to Rama to kill him, and after a terrible battle had been driven away.

One day Raksha sent a great golden deer roaming through the forest, such a deer as had never before been seen. Sita herself saw the beautiful animal, and implored Rama and Lakshmana to capture him that she might have the skin. Raksha, lurking in the forest, saw in the distance the two men stalking the deer, and his evil eyes shone with fiendish delight. He flew to the hunting lodge, and swooped on Sita as she sat singing in the sun.

No words can tell the anguish of Rama when he returned from the chase. For miles and miles in the forest he sought his lost princess, and in every nook and corner of the house. Then round and round the building he ran, calling on the name of Sita till the woods echoed again and again with the sound.

Now Rama had many friends, not only among human beings, but among the animals. Jambuvana, the king of the bears, worshipped him ; and Hanuman, the monkey god, loved him.

"Grieve not, my beloved Rama," cried Hanuman; "we will find her."

Now Hanuman, though a monkey, was the son of a god and had great power. He made a magic circle in the clearing and called a great council to help in his search. First he called the below-earth animals that live in rivers or burrow their way in and out of the earth's surface—the crocodiles, frogs, snakes, rabbits, moles, rats, and sloes; but none had seen Sita.

Then Hanuman called the over-earth animals, those who travel from place to place—the leopards, panthers, cats, jaguars, bears, elephants, rhinoceroses, tigers, boars, and wolves; but none had seen Sita.

Then Hanuman called the air people, the birds; but none had seen Sita.

Then he called his own people, the tree-top people, the monkey folk, who live neither in the air nor on the earth, who are neither animals nor humans, but something between; and none had seen Sita.

The grief of Rama became too great to bear, and he lay on the ground like one dead. All the animals waited in silent droves, and Hanuman wept till the grass was drenched with his tears.

Presently a commotion arose among the air people, for the king of the vultures was descending through the skies.

"I have found her, O Rama the Great!" he cried. "The demon Raksha is carrying her southward to his territory."

Then the chase began.

Hanuman, whose strength was boundless, took Rama and Lakshmana on his back, and bore them, swifter than a hurricane, through the tree-tops. The monkeys followed in joyous, chattering hordes; the birds flew overhead; the droves of animals followed through the forest; the vulture king soared among the clouds, with unerring eye leading the way; and all tracked Sita.

The chase went on, and day followed day, until the pursuers reached the strand

and the blue sea. There they halted, for the bird was descending.

"The demon has carried her over to Ceylon," cried he to the monkey god.

Then Rama trod the beach in furious anger, baffled; and Hanuman fell into thought. It was not possible for even him to carry Rama across to Ceylon. How could that gulf of water be bridged?

At last the idea came to him. He called his own people to a private council in the trees. And the monkeys understood. There came from them such a wild chattering of joy as was never heard in the wide land of India. It was they who were to construct the bridge, and help to fight the demon hordes in Ceylon.

Swiftly the deed was done. One grey and savage leader of a tribe picked up a huge boulder and hurled it into the sea. Then the next monkey found another rock and threw it a little farther than the first one. All the other monkeys found rocks and cast them into the Straits.

So the bridge of rocks grew until it stretched right across the water to Ceylon.

Raksha, the demon, with his unhappy prize, had gained Ceylon, and fancied himself safe. He pictured the return from the chase and the search for Sita. He knew no living animal had seen him, and he thought Rama would for a long time be unable to trace him. But even as he gloated over his successful capture there came on his ears a terrible sound—the sound of thousands of monkey folk shrieking and yelling for joy because Rama, their beloved, had crossed their bridge and was safely landed in Ceylon.

Then he called his hordes of evil beings to him, and a great and terrible battle took place between the monkey folk and the followers of the demon. But Rama and Hanuman were always at the front of the battle, fighting fiercely; and at last, Raksha was captured and slain, and the beautiful princess, happy once more, was carried back in safety to India.

A KING INDEED

Twilight was falling on the Himalayas, but still the man and the dog toiled uncomplainingly on.

The animal was a stray which had been following for some time. The man was a king and a hero. Yudhishthira had been one of the five young princes whose heroic adventures will be sung as long as the land of India stands above the sea. Now he was the last left; his gallant brothers and Drupadi, the bride whom they had won in such peril, who had shared exile and danger and final triumph—all were gone. Life held no sweetness without them; he was old, and weary of his crown; in the mountains he sought a peace that he could not find in the world.

Suddenly there appeared a bright spot in the sky. The radiance drew nearer and nearer. Yudhishthira beheld a Heavenly being in a golden chariot; it descended to his very feet. As he gazed in wonder the vision spoke:

"Just and valiant king! I am Indra, and I come to carry you to the skies, for your life has made you worthy to sit with the princes of the stars."

Yudhishthira replied with awe and sorrow, "Holy one! Even if I were fit to mingle with the kings of the sky I would not go without my brothers and Drupadi."

"They await you," replied Indra, and joy and thanksgiving filled the old man's heart. He prepared to mount the chariot but stood aside to let the dog enter first.

"No!" cried Indra. "I came to fetch a hero, not a dog. The humblest peasant holds a dog to be unclean; if it be refused the poor man's hut how shall this scavenger enter the home of the gods? Heaven itself would be polluted."

"Then," said Yudhishthira, "I cannot come with you either. All that you urge against the dog binds me to him. Because he is despised and friendless I must protect him. It is the duty of a king."

In vain Indra argued. On the one hand was celestial happiness with his kinsfolk; on the other earthly misery with the dog.

Yudhishthira only replied that in Heaven itself he could not be at rest with such a treachery on his conscience.

Nothing could move him. But as he turned away from Indra he saw a shining youth where the dog had stood. The Immortals themselves had not shrunk from putting on the likeness of the unclean animal to test his kingship.

Then the king, who would give up his crown, but never a follower, consented to enter the chariot of the stars.

THE THREE BEARS

Three bears lived in a house in a wood. There was the father bear, the mother bear, and the baby bear. The first was a great big bear, the second was a middle-sized bear, and the third was a tiny wee bear. In the kitchen was a table, and beside the table there were three chairs. The first was a great big chair, the second was a middle-sized chair, and the third was a tiny wee chair.

One day the three bears went out for a walk. Before they started Mother Bear prepared the dinner, and poured it into three basins.

While they were out a little girl named Goldilocks passed by that way, and looked

Soon the bears came back, and they went straight up to the table.

"Someone's been sitting in my chair," cried the great big bear in a great big voice.

"Someone's been sitting in my chair," cried the middle-sized bear in a middle-sized voice.

"And someone's been sitting in *my* chair," cried the tiny wee bear in a tiny wee voice.

Then they looked into their basins.

"Someone's been tasting my dinner," cried out the great big bear in a great big voice.

"Somebody's been tasting my dinner,"

GOLDILOCKS DISCOVERED BY THE THREE BEARS

in at the window. The food in the basins looked very tempting, so she walked in.

She sat down in the great big chair, but it was much too large for her. So she tried the middle-sized chair, but that was not high enough; so she sat down in the tiny wee chair, which just fitted her.

She took up the spoon and soon ate up all the little baby bear's dinner.

When she had finished she began to feel very tired, and thought she would like to lie down. So she went upstairs into the bedroom, where she found three beds. The first was a great big bed, the second was a middle-sized bed, and the third was a tiny wee bed. First she tried the big bed, but it was much too big. So she got out again and tried the middle-sized bed. But *that* was too big, so she jumped into the tiny wee bed and at once fell fast asleep.

cried the middle-sized bear in a middle-sized voice, looking very indignant.

"And somebody's been tasting *my* dinner and eaten it all up," cried the tiny wee bear in a tiny wee voice.

"Who is it?" cried all the bears together. And they all ran upstairs.

The great big bear ran in a great hurry to the great big bed.

"Somebody's been lying in my bed," he cried.

The middle-sized bear ran to the middle-sized bed.

"Somebody's been lying in my bed," she cried.

And the tiny wee bear called out in a tiny wee voice: "And somebody's been lying in *my* bed—and, oh, here she is!"

Just then Goldilocks woke up. She was so frightened that she ran out of the house, and they never saw her again.

THE COBBLER AND THE ELVES

Hans Stumpie was a cobbler who lived with his wife in the Forest of Thuringia, in Germany, where all the countryfolk wore wooden shoes.

As Hans made only leather shoes he had a hard task to get a living. Things went from bad to worse, and at last he had nothing left in the house but a bit of leather scarcely large enough to make one pair of shoes. Hans cut the leather out very carefully, and went to bed.

When he came down in the morning— oh, wonder of wonders!—there, on the board, were the shoes already made. And a customer came in and bought them at a good price, and with the money Hans got some food and also purchased a larger piece of leather. He cut this out into the stuff for two pairs of shoes, and in the morning he found the two pairs made, and he sold them in the course of the day.

Then he purchased leather enough for four pairs of shoes, and cut them out, and in the morning there were four pairs made. So it went on. No matter how many pairs he cut out overnight, they were all made for him the next day. And the end of it all was that he became a very prosperous man.

Just before Christmas Hans and his wife sat up to see who it was who made the shoes, and at midnight in jumped two wee men. They at once squatted down on the board and took up the pieces of leather, and sewed away so quickly that Hans and his wife could not follow the movements of their hands. When all the work was done the two wee men went quietly away.

The next morning Hans's wife said: "Now that the two wee men have made us rich we must do something for them. I have it! I will make them some clothes, and you must make them some shoes."

So the next night Hans and his wife put the clothes and shoes on the board for the little creatures, and watched to see what they would do. The two wee men were at first astonished to find that no leather had been cut for them to work on. Then they saw the clothes and shoes, and put them on, and danced merrily about the room, singing:

> Neat and natty boys are we;
> Cobblers' elves no more we'll be.

They hopped over the chairs, they hopped over the tables, and at last they hopped out of the window, and they never came back. But Hans always prospered in his work, and he and his wife lived in ease and happiness all the rest of their lives.

HOW GOTHAM GOT A BAD NAME

Everybody has heard of the Wise Fools of Gotham. But perhaps we do not know who these men were, or where Gotham is, or exactly what is meant by calling them "Wise Fools." This is the story.

Gotham is a village in Nottinghamshire, and one day his Majesty King John of England, marching toward the town of Nottingham, commanded that his retinue should pass through Gotham meadow.

Now, it was popularly thought that any land over which the king passed became ever after a public road; so the men of Gotham, who valued their meadow, took steps to prevent King John from crossing that way. The king, angered by their proceedings, sent his officers to conduct an inquiry in the village.

When the officers arrived they found some of the men shouting and making a tremendous din over a pond. These noisy fellows had an eel on a string, and were trying, so they said, *to drown it in the pond!* Others were found rolling cheeses down the road, giving them a push and letting them bowl along of their own accord. They were sending their cheeses, they said, to Nottingham market. Others, in a tremendous hurry, were dragging carts and wagons up a hill. They were going to shade a wood, they said, from the hot rays of the Sun. And others were building a hedge round a bush on which a cuckoo had settled to prevent the bird from flying away.

The officers went away and reported that Gotham was a village of fools utterly beneath the king's notice.

But others, who knew more of the story, said that there were some very wise fools in Gotham, and so the phrase came to signify folly which was assumed for a wise purpose.

A charming old English writer, named Thomas Fuller, says: "Gotham doth breed as *wise* people as any which causelessly laugh at the simplicity."

Nature's Wonderful Living Family in Earth and Air and Sea

Eskimo dogs, from the fine painting by Miss Maud Earl of The End of the Trail

THE FRIENDLY DOGS

IT was an important day for the human race when one of the wild men of old went into the wilderness, captured a creature with twice as many legs as his own and twice the speed that he could command, tamed and trained it, and so started an everlasting partnership between mankind and the brutes.

Man lived by tracking, trapping, and killing. In the wolf or the jackal, which was to become his dog, he found a fresh and notable addition to his powers. The friendly dog became new ears, new nose, new eyes to him, and so doubled and trebled the forces which discovered and led him to his quarry.

Moreover, we know from primitive peoples still living after the fashion of our ancestors that the dog early became a living weight-shifting power. The Eskimos with their teams of sledge-dogs, the Tibetans with their caravans of dogs crossing the mountains with packs of merchandise on their backs, mirror for us the ways and works of primeval man who moved loads of dog-drawn property when wheels were known only in very few parts of the world.

By a sort of free and easy enslavement of an animal early man began his own emancipation from the level of the beasts. He became an owner for the first time,

with duties and responsibilities to dumb creatures. The need to keep his ally healthy and vigorous for the chase and for hauling made man think, made him considerate and kind in a rough way to animals. Care for brutes helped to humanise the untutored savage who won the affection of the first of dogs.

Which was the first dog? It was none of the species that we now know as wild dogs. Differences of structure show us at once that it was none of these. And certainly it was not the fox. There remain the wolf and jackal. They are probably the source from which every dog we have comes to us.

It may be that we have dogs tracing back entirely to wolves, and dogs tracing back entirely to jackals. The Eskimo dog is practically pure wolf; so is the wolf-dog of Florida; and the line of descent of the Alsatian wolf-dog is clear. Dogs owned by Red Indians are scarcely to be distinguished from the coyotes of the prairies, but the dogs of South-Eastern Europe seem only tamed jackals.

It is just possible that the blood of wolf and jackal mingles in most of our fashionable breeds of dogs, and that only the tamed animals of savages and semi-wild peoples remain full-blooded modifications of wolf in one area, of jackal in

PREHISTORIC LIFE · MAMMALS · BIRDS · REPTILES · FISHES · INSECTS

another. There is no strain of alien life in our dogs. Wolf and jackal have yielded us all we have.

The tiny pet of the dog-show, spoiled by unnatural luxuries; the giant mastiff or St. Bernard which lorded it over patrician courtyards; the dog which guards the poultry or the flocks, which saves us from drowning in rough seas, or keeps the burglar from the house—they are all the posterity of wild hunting beasts that tore other creatures to pieces or gorged with ecstasy on the carrion fouling the ways over which their keen noses led them.

TWO HUNDRED BREEDS OF DOGS FROM ONE OR TWO ORIGINAL STOCKS

With this limited store to draw upon, man has done marvels. We know how many breeds of pigeons have been evolved from the single parent stock, the wild rock pigeon, and how many varieties of poultry have been created from the wild jungle fowl; but the man who has studied dogs by careful selection has evolved nearly 200 breeds from one or two original stocks.

Perhaps the dog most loathed of all dogs is the semi-wild Australian dingo, the dog that does for our kinsmen's sheep what the rabbit did for his pastures. It has always been regarded as a modern introduction into the island continent, the only highly developed flesh-eater in a vast land where all other animal life has remained at the stage to which it had advanced throughout the world hundreds of thousands of years ago, but a dazzling discovery has revealed the dingo as an ancient aristocrat of Australia! In 1884, fossilised remains were found, washed out by a flood from their age-old grave, seven or eight feet below the surface of the ground, at Talgai, on the Darling Downs of South Queensland.

THE PRICE ON THE HEAD OF EVERY DINGO IN AUSTRALIA

Man and these creatures lived together in Australia so long ago that we cannot even guess the time that has since elapsed. We can only put the time in geological language, and say that the period was when Britain was covered with ice. One distinguished professor at Adelaide University believed that between that far-away expedition and modern times no man reached the Australian mainland until Captain Cook visited it. We cannot but feel that man dared not have ventured into that mysterious land of extraordinary animals without his fearless dingo.

For ages he has been free in Australia, living upon small game and doing no harm. But white men arrived and brought sheep, and the sheep multiplied. They proved easy prey and good food for poor dingo.

Dingos, receiving a new impetus from this fresh source of nourishment, have increased as fast as the sheep, and have become the chief foe of the flocks in the land which their far-away ancestors sailed to seek and guard. Today there is a price on every dingo's head.

That is ever the case when tame dogs run wild. In England they kill sheep; abroad they rival the jackals as scavengers and thieves, or, in the vicinity of wolves, take up the life and liberty of those dreaded animals. Left to themselves, all the pets of our homes today would become as wild as the dingo, and as destructive.

THE MANY QUALITIES WE FIND IN ALL KINDS OF DOGS

There is no danger of this happening in civilisation where the dog stands first of all animals in our affections. The tendency is to increase the number of the breeds. This is easily done by preserving those of distinctive shapes, sizes, markings, type of coat, and so on.

The result is that we have fashions in dogs as in clothes and shapes of motor-cars. The favourites of the day are soon neglected. Today's favourites may be the Alsatians among big dogs, the Pekinese among small ones, the Bedlington and Sealyham among small sporting dogs. We also have poodles of various sizes, Boxers, setters, Corgis, many kinds of spaniels, and all sorts of little terriers. Tomorrow, perhaps, yet a new variety will arise, like a new flower or a new fruit, to become the rage.

All sorts of qualities are treasured from time to time—speed and staying power, indolence and placid home-contentment; ferocity and strength for fighting; gentleness and fidelity for the drawing-room. The one thing that men have never sought to breed in dogs is intelligence.

In spite of this the dog brain is a fine natural instrument. Which is the most intelligent dog in the world? That is known to every one of us who loves a dog: the most intelligent dog in the whole, wide world is our own!

A KENNEL-FULL OF DOGS

FRENCH POODLE

IRISH WATER SPANIEL

MASTIFF

NEWFOUNDLAND

BOXER

RETRIEVER

TOY POMERANIAN

BULLDOG

KING CHARLES SPANIEL

ST. BERNARD

BORZOI

SETTER

POINTER

BULL TERRIER

COCKER SPANIEL

WHIPPET

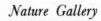

PUG-DOG

GREYHOUND

WHITE CHOW-CHOW

COLLIE

WEST HIGHLAND WHITE TERRIER

WIRE-HAIRED TERRIER

SAMOYED

GREAT DANE

AIREDALE

FIELD SPANIEL

KERRY BLUE TERRIER   BOARHOUND

SCOTCH TERRIER

SMOOTH-HAIRED FOX TERRIER   LABRADOR RETRIEVER   BASENJI

SKYE TERRIER   WELSH CORGI   DACHSHUND

ALSATIAN WOLFHOUND   YORKSHIRE TERRIER   PEKINGESE   MINIATURE PINSCHER

DEERHOUND   FOXHOUND   DANDIE DINMONT   DALMATIAN

Scientists quarrel as to whether the dog has any reasoning powers. Let them quarrel. All of us who have grown up with dogs, have been taken out as children and led about by them, who have been saved from injuries and from drowning by them, have been tricked and deceived by their cleverness, and been loved and worshipped and benefited by them—we feel that we know.

Whatever we call it, dogs have a mental quality that enables them to do things that no quite unreasoning animal could do.

Take the astonishing case of two terriers which lived in a shop near a hospital in Central London. One day while they were outside their home, a collie was run over in the road. They immediately rushed to the collie's aid and then, having guided him to the hospital entrance, barked until they were all let in for the sufferer to be treated by the doctors.

SOMETHING AKIN TO REASON AT WORK IN THE DOG'S BRAIN

How are we to account for that ? The proud owner of the dogs gave his opinion in these words : " The dogs were accustomed to see injured patients carried into the hospital. They themselves never went in, but they somehow grasped the meaning of those visits by injured people on stretchers, and, by some unfathomable process of thought, when they saw a stranger of their own kind also in distress, they led him to the help which they realised others received at the hospital."

The explanation is not scientific; it may be full of flaws, but science has none more plausible to offer. The incident is commemorated in an oil painting hanging in the hospital board-room; and doubtless the Governors would not scorn the theory built up by the owner of the two delightful terriers that are the heroes of the picture.

When we see a dog who wants the chair in which its master sits run to the door as if to go out, and then, when its master gets up to open the door, rush back and seize the empty chair with delighted barks, we feel that something akin to reason must be at work in that little brain.

When we see the marvels that are performed by dogs in shepherding sheep—turning so many to the left, and so many to the right, driving them gently round obstacles, penning them, letting them out, identifying one familiar sheep and bring-

ing it out from a flock of strangers—we know that training has made the wonder possible. But what are we to say of the animal mind capable of such an education ?

Intelligence and ability to receive instruction have made dogs the friends of man. If only they had been bred for intelligence!

SIX GROUPS OF DOGS FROM WHICH ALL THE REST HAVE SPRUNG

Let us glance at some of the results of the practices that have for ages been followed; and that have fixed six groups of dogs as those from which all the rest have sprung. These are : Wolf-like dogs, greyhounds, spaniels, hounds, mastiffs, terriers.

Some of the relationships are a little surprising. The Eskimo dogs, which draw the sleighs, like the lusty little heroes which take the mail to snowy Alaska, are obviously more or less polite wolves; but it is startling to know that the big Pomeranians, wolf-hunters in old-time Germany, come next, with the tiny poms of the drawing-room as their smaller brethren. And in the same group come the delightful Schipperkes, owning as close kindred the handsome, but rather sharp-tempered, chow-chow of China.

What a range of life that covers: a handful of fish or offal, a piece of stolen harness, or the body of a dead comrade is the meal of the wolf-like Eskimo dog, which took Amundsen to the South Pole and Peary to the North Pole. At the other end of the line are the spoilt poms for whom no food is too dainty. The hard-working, handsome collies and sheep dogs are in the same collection—all sons of wolves, as far as we know.

THE RUSSIAN BORZOI THAT WILL TACKLE A STOUT WOLF

The greyhounds, fleetest of dogs and among the least intelligent, are unique not only for their speed, but for hunting by sight. Ordinarily, dogs track by scent. Not so these specialised speed machines. They are the result of intensive breeding: they and their Italian whippet cousins.

Related to them is the Scottish deerhound, stouter and coarser of hair; the ancient Slughi of Persia, the long-haired Afghan greyhound; and distinct breeds from Greece, Albania, and elsewhere. Next comes that beauty, the Russian borzoi, over 30 inches at the shoulder and a match for a stout wolf. It was dogs from the breeds in the present group which figured in the life of the Pharaohs and were carved upon Egyptian monuments.

Merely noting the existence of unpleasant hairless freaks from China, Central and South America, and sometimes seen in England, we pass to the spaniels, of which the famous ones are the Clumber, the Sussex, the Norfolk, and the little Cocker spaniels. The King Charles and Blenheim spaniels are small varieties of the Cocker breed.

The normal spaniels all have some taste for the sports of man, and will find game and pick it up when it has been shot. But the little Pekingese, which are Eastern spaniels, do not share the common avidity of the breed. How should they, after generations of scented sanctuary and foolish pampering?

Setters, which find game, and then stand rigid over it, are specialised spaniels. The retriever, fine in the water as well as on land, is also a spaniel, and so is the noble Newfoundland. The Newfoundland is without comparison, as a breed, as the saviour of lives in the water, but one has known an untrained curly retriever just as brilliant, clever, and courageous as a water-dog as any Newfoundland.

THE HOUNDS THAT USED TO TRACK DOWN MEN

Next come the hounds, with the bloodhounds at their head. They have lost their place, we are thankful to say, as trackers of men. Once they did track, and tore when they found their man. That quality has been bred away, and the modern bloodhound fawns with delight upon the person whom it is set to find.

The feats of the bloodhound result from fineness of nose; but it is doubtful if its scent much excels that of its kindred, the foxhounds, which hunt the fox entirely by a scent that soon evaporates. Harriers and beagles, which are used to hunt hares, have the same faculty; and otter hounds have keen noses, as well as woolly coats to keep out water when pursuing their quarry.

Dachshunds, big and little, are badger-hunting dogs at home in their native Germany, and are keen of scent. Our pointers also are famous for their noses, but instead of following the trail left by the feet of the quarry, as the foxhound does, they detect victims by body scent, which rises higher in the air. The old "plum pudding" Dalmatians, now nearly extinct, are hounds, and so are the uncommon griffons.

Mastiffs include not only mastiffs proper but the Great Dane or German boarhound —biggest of all the dog tribe except the Alaskan wolf. They were used as fighting dogs by the Romans and other ancient peoples.

Allied to this breed are the bulldogs and bull terriers, once bred to fight bulls and other animals. Fortunately, this so-called " sport " was abolished in early Victorian times, but the dogs remain popular in many parts of the world. Despite its ferocious appearance, the bull-dog (emblem of British tenacity) can be a gentle companion for children.

THE WEALTH OF TERRIERS THAT WE HAVE TO CHOOSE FROM

Two of the finest dogs, the huge wolf-fighting Tibetan dog, which guards the native villages, and the noble St. Bernard, long the hero of rescues of lost wanderers in the snowy Alps, all but complete the mastiff group. The plump and gasping pug, a dwindling race, is also a mastiff.

The terriers remain, very near to our hearts, some of them, whether they guard us from rats and mice, or share our walks and hunts, become partners of the study and dining-room, or stay at home when we are out, faithfully to guard the house against unwelcome visitors.

No one need lack a favourite with such a wealth to choose from : fox terriers smooth and rough, Irish, Scotch, Skye terriers with drop ears and smooth coat, Skye terriers with prick ears and rough coat, the Yorkshire terrier with hair three or four inches long on the body, the merry Cairns, the big Labradors, the very clever poodle, the sturdy Airedale, the Maltese, the Mexican lapdog, and so on—a breed for everyone.

One of the newest comes from the Sudan, the Basenji barkless dog, which is believed to have been common in ancient Egypt.

THE GOLD OF AFFECTION THAT DOGS BRING TO US

There is something to admire and grow fond of in each. Every dog has its faults and commits its follies, but when did ever one betray its master or mistress ? When did the affections of one ever grow cold? We have done much for and with dogs, but they brought in with them from the wilds a nature whose savagery was redeemed by a vein of pure gold. And that native gold of loyalty and friendliness is what makes them so dear to us.

The March of Man from the Age of Barbarism to the United Nations

Sculptured figures from the marbles of the Golden Age of Greece

A NEW BIRTH FOR MANKIND

WHILE the wonderful Egyptians were building their temples to Osiris, and while the Hebrews were lifting up their voices in hymns of exquisite loveliness to the one true God of Righteousness, a race of people, to whom history had paid little attention hitherto, was taking a step into the future destined to change the whole face of human existence.

These people, the Ionians, were Greeks: and Greece at that time was a country of scattered villages and little primitive townships, both inhabited by people whose main interest in life was concerned with agriculture. They were constantly at war and most of their traditions were concerned with war, yet on the whole they were a peaceful peasant people, and their wars were marked with a touch of chivalry.

Few people stop to think about two extraordinary features in the great war poems of Homer. He never once abuses the enemy; and he utters the prayer that war may cease. Further, he is quick to seize upon any domestic event which appeals in the midst of war's savage brutalities to the feelings of love and pity. Who can ever forget the incident of Hector taking off his crested helmet to embrace his little son who had turned away frightened by his appearance?

These things should find a permanent lodging in our minds, for they tell us more about Greek character than many volumes of history. They tell us that here was a poor people living seven and six hundred years before the birth of Jesus, who had noble ideas about so horrible a thing as war—though a thing which might well have appeared to them as natural—and who were quick to respond when any appeal was made to those feelings of tenderness and affection which sometimes seem to us the creation of our civilisation.

Less craven and superstitious than the Egyptians, these Greeks were distinguished from all the nations of the Earth by a certain lightness and gaiety of temperament which enabled them to look at life with greater freedom and a keener curiosity than could be found among other peoples.

Very curious is it to reflect that the flash of Greek humour was a light in the darkness of man's earliest struggle with the universe, and a light so lasting that it still illuminates for many scholars a world which sometimes seems plunged in gloom.

How wonderful it is to look back into the heavy darkness of savage times and to see how many centuries rolled over this Earth before there came a *mental* smile to the face of man, and to observe how

MIGHTY EPOCHS OF THE WORLD & MAN'S WONDERFUL ADVENTURES

that first smile of intelligence was like a flash of daylight.

These Greeks loved their fields, and they made songs and dances to celebrate the seasons of the year. Many of their kings were peasants whose sons were shepherds, and the greatest in the land was not too great for making music with the pipes and joining in the dance of harvest-time. Their little towns were overgrown villages and there they would sing, dance, and make merry ; and out of those pastoral festivals grew the great drama of Greece and the stately architecture which expressed their joy in beauty and their love of making things.

At the same time these Greeks worshipped many gods who were unworthy of respect, and they feared others whose malignity entitled them to be ranked as fiends. For them, as for the savages in other lands, the heavens were filled with beings who had to be pleased or hoodwinked if the vines were to prosper and the goats were to give milk.

THE SHINING SOUL OF THE GREAT THALES OF MILETUS

We must think of them as a people standing midway between the darkness of barbarism and the first glittering dawn of civilisation—the most marvellous people yet seen on the Earth, but still trammelled by the superstitious past of mankind.

Some six hundred years before the birth of Jesus there lived in Anatolia, the Land of the Rising Sun, a man called Thales. He lived in Miletus, which was the chief city of Ionia, and the age in which he lived was an age filled with excitement by discoveries made in the East. All the wonders of Babylon and all the marvels of Egypt had become the property of Ionian gossip. Strange tales poured into Miletus of the gods worshipped by these Eastern nations, of the mysterious knowledge possessed by their priests, of the splendour of their cities, the glories of their monarchs, and the amazing achievements of their builders.

Thales is one of the greatest men in the history of the human mind because he did not allow his natural excitement in these wonders to overwhelm his intelligence. He listened; but he reflected. He looked; but he did not gape. He admired; but he also criticised.

No priest in Egypt or Babylon could deceive that shining Ionian soul. Thales studied their works, examined their instruments for searching the heavens, and agreed that these priests were wonderful men whose knowledge was surprising indeed; but he said to himself, "They prove too much by their knowledge."

Then he set out upon a career which has been followed ever since by thousands of the greatest of the sons of Earth, the career of science.

THE NOBLE PHRASE THAT " ALL THINGS ARE FULL OF GODS "

He put all the religions of paganism on one side with the noble phrase, "All things are full of gods," and set himself to study Nature with no preconceived idea from any teaching known among mankind.

It was a superb act. It was the first definite break with superstition. It was the first movement of the human mind toward a fearless pursuit of truth. This citizen of Miletus opened a door of the human race through which we have been able not only to find freedom from the shameful or disfiguring fears of superstition, but to discover in ourselves a power over the forces of Nature of which no king in Babylon, no priest of Isis, can ever have dreamed in his wildest nightmare.

Thales looked at the Oriental's work in mathematics and astronomy, and saw them as human efforts to arrive at truth. He did not say, " These things are revelations from the gods: these things are mysteries before which we must bow our heads in the dust." He said, "These things belong to knowledge." And what do you think he did? *He predicted the eclipse of 585 B.C.*

THE MAN WHO THOUGHT ALL THINGS WERE MADE OF WATER

Thales looked at the world about him, at the fields, at the rivers, at the stars, at the hills, and at the sea; he saw the majesty of Nature's power; he felt the glory and the beauty of the living world; but he did not say, "Let us hold our breath lest the hills fall upon us, or offer sacrifices to the gods lest the sea rise and overwhelm us." He said, "These things belong to knowledge."

Then he said something which has become immortal. He said, "All things are made of water." We laugh at him now for that saying, and many good jokes have been made about it; but at the time of its utterance it was as revolutionary a saying as the words of Jesus some six hundred

THE LADY WITH THE BOWL

years later. "The sabbath was made for man, not man for the sabbath." It meant a definite breach with the past, and an entirely new attitude to the future. It meant that man had brushed aside as absurdity all the legendary stories of the creation of the world, and had set himself to discover by his reason how things had come to be what they are. Also it meant —and herein lies its essential grandeur, which no ridicule can ever destroy—that in all the marvellous and beautiful variety of Nature there was unity of composition.

THE UNITY OF NATURE AS THALES TAUGHT IT

Think what it must have meant to those primitive sons of the Earth, those men so nearly savage and so deeply pagan, to be told that rock and herb, metal and river, beast and sand, were all made of one and the same thing.

Think, too, that this great utterance in Anatolia was made six hundred years before the time of Jesus.

It was a mistaken utterance, but never did any truthful utterance work a greater revolution in the history of man's mind. For this dogma of Thales changed the whole current of human thought, and turned the attention of men away from the priest and his sacrifices, away from terror and stupefaction, away from apathy and a soul-destroying indifference, and awakened in them the idea that Nature was a riddle to be read, and a document to be studied without fear. All things were in reality only one thing ! Find that one thing, and the whole mystery of the universe is solved! Is it not in this very faith that modern science, twenty-five centuries after the time of Thales, is pressing on to the discovery of truth? Thales said *Water;* today we say *Ether.*

THE SUDDEN APPEARANCE OF MEN AHEAD OF THEIR DAY

Probably we are right; certainly Thales was wrong; but should we now be near to truth if it had not been for the idea of Thales that there is one single thing fundamental to all the manifold wonders of the universe?

How did such a man arise? We cannot answer. From the earliest beginnings of history we find that suddenly and inexplicably there appears on the Earth from time to time some unique figure who seems to leap far forward from his own generation and to know what the mass of

mankind will not really know till centuries after his death. And we notice that the appearance of these mysterious beings is always accompanied or followed by some great movement of the human mind—a movement from things that have been towards things which are to come.

We find something of the same sort when we study the evolution of the bodies of animals. We find at certain times sudden great inexplicable leaps forward on quite new lines of development, and these new lines, once started, are permanently continued, directing the development of all succeeding generations.

Thus it was with Thales. There sprang up in Ionia a body of men who regarded the universe as an object of study, and life as a search after truth. A new dignity came into human life. For the sake of truth men were content to forgo all the riches of trade and all the power of politics. And truth was to be sought, not for the sake of terrifying the ignorant and preying on the credulity of the superstitious, but solely for its own sake. It was to be sought in poverty, and by a devotion and self-sacrifice not excelled by the priests of religion. It was to be sought because it was the highest thing the soul of man could ever seek.

THE GREAT DEBT OF CIVILISATION TO THE ANCIENT GREEKS

By the work of these few men the mind of mankind was so utterly changed that it does not seem a mere figure of speech to say it was born again. An age of glory came to Greece which has no parallel in the ancient world, and without which it is impossible for us to imagine the subsequent history of the human race. Our English poet Shelley has expressed in a few simple and immortal words the debt of civilisation to those ancient Greeks, and at the same time has given us a true notion of the only glory that endures. The glory of Greece, he says, is

Based on the crystalline sea
Of thought and its eternity.

It was by a thought that Greece changed the history of the human race, and because of Greece we now know that the true history of humanity is the history of thought. We shall see in the next chapters how much we owe to the great thinkers of Greece.

(Next chapter in this group, page 795)

The Story of the Things We See About Us Every Day

HOW WE GOT THE PIANO

WHEN Nebuchadnezzar set up his golden idol on the plain of Dura, the ancestor of the piano was among the instruments at whose sound Shadrach, Meshach, and Abed-nego were ordered to bow.

At what time ye hear the sound of the cornet, flute, harp, sackbut, psaltery, dulcimer, and all kinds of musick, ye shall fall down and worship the golden image.

Two lines of descent may be traced from that formidable orchestra. The psaltery was the parent of the piano-like spinet and its more ambitious successor, the harpsichord. The dulcimer comes down to us in two main streams. In one it is the toy dulcimer of the children's nursery. In the other it is the grand piano!

A musician gifted with prophecy could have predicted both harpsichord and piano from the instruments whose idolatrous overture rang out before the burning fiery furnace.

Psaltery and dulcimer seem generally to have been companion instruments in English orchestras of Bible days. The two instruments were not unlike, but melody was produced from them by two distinct methods.

The player of the psaltery drew his fingers across the strings of his instrument, or twanged them with ivory or horn, like the mandoline player. The dulcimer player struck his strings with a little hammer.

There we have the distinction between the spinet and harpsichord on the one hand and the piano on the other. The harpsichord group has wire strings, like the piano. When a key was pressed it caused a lever to rise, having at its summit either a piece of hardened leather, or a quill, or even a piece of brass. The quill was pushed past the string, tugging or jerking it in its passage, so causing it to vibrate and produce its note. The lever, on descending, allowed the quill to pass the wire without a second note. In shape, in the use of wires, of a keyboard, and in other little details, the spinet and harpsichord established a convenient outline for the piano.

The first piano as we know it seems to have been made in Italy late in the 16th century; its Italian name, Piano e Forte, means Soft and Loud. Its ancestry runs back through Greece and Egypt, Babylon and Assyria, and its ultimate creation was assured when first a man hammered melody out of two sounding materials.

Gradually the piano has become more and more popular, and the best kinds are truly noble musical instruments. As an accompaniment to singing it is second to none. and as a solo instrument it has long had pride of place. Much of the loveliest music in the world has been specially composed for the piano.

INDUSTRIES · HOW THINGS ARE MADE · WHERE THEY COME FROM

PICTURE-STORY OF A PIANO

It has taken hundreds of years and scores of inventors to give us the piano. The work is difficult, but is so skilfully done that it seems simple. The wood, which has been carefully chosen and seasoned so that it shall not crack or warp, must first be cut into the required sizes, and here we see end-pieces being shaped with a band-saw. With this ingenious machine parts can be turned out both quickly and accurately ; and much time and trouble are saved.

The wood for the outer case of the piano is passed through rollers in which glue is applied evenly. The veneer, a thin sheet of hard wood, is then placed on the glue-covered board, as in the left-hand picture, and placed in a press. When it is dry the wood is French polished, as shown on the right.

BUILDING-UP THE PIANO'S SOUNDBOARD

Parts of the soundboard which have been glued together are placed in this press, in which the bent wooden stays apply an even pressure while the glue is drying.

The parts now being firmly joined, a skilled craftsman with a chisel carves the notches in the bridge which carries the strings, or wires, over the soundboard.

Here is a scene in the shop where the soundboards are assembled and very accurately marked out for the fitting of the iron frames, one of which the man in the foreground is placing in position before screwing it down firmly. If the frame to which the strings are attached were fitted flat to the back of the wood, we should get a very deadened sound, so the soundboard is needed, on which the frame can rest clear of the rest of the wood.

PUTTING THE STRINGS IN THE PIANO

By this time an iron frame has been made ready. This frame looks something like a harp, and the strings, or wires, are attached to metal pegs which can be turned with a key to give the required tension. Iron is used because it cannot be pulled out of shape to let the instrument get out of tune. Here the frame is being strung.

When the frame is in the case a worker begins to insert the intricate part which is known as the action—the keys, the levers to which they are attached, and the hammers that strike the wires and produce the notes.

Finally an expert tuner tests every note, tightening or slackening the wires until he is satisfied that they are perfectly in tune. When the front has been put on the piano is ready to bring music into our homes.

Plain Answers to the Questions of the Children of the World

WHERE DOES AN APPLE COME FROM?

WE know that when we sow seeds properly they grow, and from a very small seed we may get a very big tree. It may be an apple tree, and it may produce hundreds of apples, year after year. Where do they all come from?

Or, to take another instance, we plant the seeds from one pound of tomato fruits and get a hundred pounds of tomatoes. Where does all the difference come from? It almost looks as if the hundred pounds of tomatoes were new weight in the world; but the world gets scarcely any heavier, so that cannot be the truth. We are also quite certain that the stuff in the apples or the tomatoes is not made out of nothing, but comes from somewhere.

The apples, then, and the tomatoes have been made by the wonderful power of the living tree or plant out of the stuff which surrounds them. In the case of the tomatoes, we are quite sure that if we could have weighed the stuff taken as food to produce the new crop of a hundred pounds of tomatoes it would have weighed practically a hundred pounds. The Earth as a whole is not any heavier; merely, some of the things that make up the weight of the air, such as oxygen, and the carbon from the carbon dioxide on which the plant feeds, and some of the things which make up the weight of the ground, such as water and many salts, have been built into its body.

It is as if you had a house that could build itself, and make its own bricks into the bargain. And so it is in the case of the apples or the tomatoes—or you. Part of the Earth has been built into apples and tomatoes, and the builder in this case is the living plant. After a time— and this is true of every living creature— it dies, and the stuff which is taken from the Earth and the air for making its body is restored to them, and other living creatures use it in the same way; and so there is a circle or cycle—the cycle of life—through which much of the stuff of the Earth and the air goes on passing from age to age.

It might be thought, then, that, as the air gives so much to the apple, the air would be lighter in summer, when the apple grows, than in winter, but we should not like to say that the air is lighter in summer than in winter on this account. In the first place, the weight of the air is so enormous that all the oxygen taken from it for the purposes of life would only be like a drop compared to the ocean; and, in the second place, there are many other things happening which might work in the other direction.

For instance, under the influence of the Sun, many of the products of past life lying on the surface of the soil are broken up, and the oxygen they contain is given back to the air.

SUN · MOON · STARS · FIRE · WIND · WATER · LIFE · MIND · SLEEP

What is a Thunderbolt ?

Long ago it was supposed that something, a "bolt," was actually thrown from the sky during a thunderstorm, and men thought God threw these thunderbolts to destroy those with whom He was angry. The Romans taught that the thunderbolt was the bolt of Jupiter, who was their chief god. But we know now that there is no such thing as a thunderbolt, and the damage it was supposed to do is really due to the violent passage of an electric current, lightning, from the air to the Earth, which damages anything it passes through.

What is Beauty ?

We call anything beautiful which gives us pleasure, and that depends as much upon ourselves as upon what is outside us. Perhaps the majority of people find the sea, for instance, most beautiful when it is blue, and especially love the blue Mediterranean, where the skies are clear and intensely blue, and so the sea is blue, too. If someone has lived in Italy as a child, and has to live beside our grey sea when he is grown up, he will think that the grey sea is ugly, and that nothing can be so beautiful as the blue sea. But suppose a Scotsman who loves Scotland had to go and live in Italy. He might find the blue sea after a while very uninteresting, and only when he went home and saw the grey sea again would he find the sea beautiful.

We are made in different ways, and grey may be just as beautiful as blue if you find the right persons to look at it, just as the cry of a baby may be found more sweet in someone's ears than the finest note of the finest singer that ever lived. Nothing is beautiful or ugly in itself, but " thinking makes it so."

What is Greenwich Time ?

It is plain that as the Earth spins round the Sun must appear to rise in the east sooner, the farther east we are, and later, the farther west we are. So the apparent time, judged by the Sun's rising and setting, is different in different places, according as they are east or west of each other; indeed, midday on one side of the Earth is midnight on the other side. It is not a question of north or south, because the Earth does not spin in the north-south line, but in the east-west line.

So it is necessary to have some agreed place from which to take our time, and the place on which the nations have

agreed is Greenwich. They have their own time for their own purposes; but for general purposes, as, for instance, events occurring in the sky, they refer to Greenwich time—that is to say, the time reckoned by what the Sun seems to do at Greenwich. The lines on maps up and down the earth's surface from north to south are called lines of longitude. They are narrower in the north and south than at the Equator, of course, and meet at the Poles—like the lines usually made by the knife when we cut a melon in the usual way. Places on the same line of longitude as Greenwich have Greenwich time exactly, and no other place can have it.

Why Do We Swing Our Arms When We Walk ?

It is rather difficult to say exactly why we swing our arms when walking, but there is no doubt that it is much easier to walk in comfort if the arms are allowed to swing naturally than if they are held stiffly by the sides of the body. Probably, therefore, the swing of the arms assists us in unconsciously keeping accurate balance as we move along, first on one foot and then on the other. Perhaps, too, it may be partly a relic of the time when primitive animals used their arms as well as their legs in walking, as a chimpanzee will do.

In any case, the fact that it is so much more comfortable to walk swinging the arms seems to suggest that Nature may have intended the swinging to help us in accurate movement.

What Makes Us Hungry ?

We have had many questions about animals which we have answered by saying that animals know things by *instinct*, and now we come to one or two questions about human beings which *we* know very much in the same way. No one needs to tell us when we are hungry. We know quite well without being told. It is one of the few instincts that human beings have.

It is a fortunate thing that the cells of which our bodies are made have this power to make their wants known to us. As soon as there is too little food in the body, it means that the blood has not enough nourishment in it. There is a sinking feeling in the pit of the stomach, and it is this feeling which we call hunger. This is one of the few things that a human being knows without having to learn it.

What is a Water-spout ?

Just as the waves of the sea are due to movements of the air, so the very astonishing disturbance of the sea called a water-spout is also due to an unusual disturbance of the air. Sometimes parts of the air get started in a twisting motion, rushing through the air and at the same time turning round and round very quickly, somewhat as the earth rushes through space and turns round all the time.

When this happens the sea may be very violently disturbed; and sometimes in the middle of this twisting portion of air there is very little air indeed—it is almost like a hollow twisting column of air. Then the water just beneath may be suddenly sucked up so as to fill the almost empty space inside this twisting column of air, and that makes a water-spout.

Where Does All The Dust Go To ?

Dust is made of very different things, and its fate varies accordingly. Some dust is mainly made of particles of carbon, and these are gradually washed into the soil by the rain. We do not know whether they are useful there. Some of them get into our lungs and stay there. Then much dust is made of substances derived from living creatures, such as horses.

These street deposits of animals are a very important part of town dust. They find their way into the sewers, and so to the seas; or often to the soil, where, like all organic matter, they are extremely useful for the growth of vegetable life. This dust often gets into our eyes and throats, and probably helps to cause the colds that are so common in towns. Town dust will be really healthier when horses, dogs, and cats are kept under better control. Also, a considerable part of the organic matter in dust is consumed and oxidised by the oxygen of the air, partly under the influence of the sun, and partly by the action of the microbes.

How Does Rubber Rub Out Ink ?

When indiarubber rubs out ink or pencil, or pumice-stone rubs out ink-stains on our skin, what happens is really the same in every case. It is the rubbing, or the friction, that actually rubs away the outer layers of the paper or the skin, and so removes anything that they may contain. Soft indiarubber rubs away only the surface-layer of paper, but that is enough for pencil-marks, which only deposit a thin layer of carbon on the surface of the paper. A harder rubber will rub off a thicker layer of paper, and so will remove ink-marks, which penetrate much more deeply. Pumice-stone is hardest of all, and removes ink-stains, which are deeply absorbed by our outer skin.

Is the Stuff in Earth and Air and Sea Always Changing Places ?

The answer to this is certainly Yes. There is a ceaseless circulation going on between the surface of the land and the water, and the bottom layers of the ocean of air which covers them both. Wherever water is, for instance, it is often being sucked up in the form of a gas into the air, of which it then forms part ; while, on the other hand, water vapour from the air often passes from it to the Earth—as, for instance, in the form of dew. Then the gases of the air, especially oxygen and carbon dioxide, are ceaselessly passing between it and the bodies of all the living creatures on the Earth ; and from moment to moment, various gases are either leaving the air to be dissolved in the ocean, or are leaving the ocean to join the air.

Why Do We Lose the Sense of Smell When We Have a Cold ?

The sense of smell depends upon scented things coming in the air to the lining of our noses, especially certain parts of the lining of the nose. When we have a cold, this lining, or mucous membrane, of the nose gets swollen, and produces a much greater amount of mucus than usual.

The chief reason why we cannot smell so well when we have a cold is probably that this mucus, constantly pouring out of the lining of the nose and running over it, prevents the scent of things getting to the sensitive part of the nose, and washes away any solid scented particles that there may be in the air. Also, it may very likely be that the poisons produced by the microbes that cause a cold, poison the living cells of the mucous membrane, and also poison the tiny ends of the nerves of smell that run to it, so that if scented things do reach the sensitive part of the mucous membrane, they cannot be felt.

This applies alike to scents coming in from outside and also to the scents of food, which pass up through the mouth into the nose, and which, when we have not a cold, help to give our food half its flavour.

How Do Fish Live in a Frozen Pond ?

Ordinary ice, we know, is lighter than water, and therefore it floats. So what we call a frozen pond is a pond of which the surface is frozen. Skaters are perfectly aware of this. They want to know how thick the ice is, for they know that there is liquid water underneath it. So when we speak about fish living in a frozen pond, we mean fish living in liquid water that has a layer of frozen water above it.

The really serious part of this for the fish is not, as we might think, the coldness of the water they are in, but the question how that water is to be supplied with enough air for the fish to live by. When a pond is not frozen, oxygen from the air above it is passing into the surface of the water as fast as it is being used up by the fish and other living creatures in the water.

When a pond is frozen, this process is very nearly stopped. There may be gaps in the ice here and there—air-holes, such as air-breathing creatures will make in the frozen North—but perhaps there may be none of these. A little oxygen may get through at the edge of the ice, but the best hope for the fish is that there is a supply of new water coming into the pond below the ice from somewhere else, and bringing enough oxygen dissolved in it to keep the fish alive. If the supply of oxygen is kept up in one of these ways, then, when there is no more of it left, the fish will surely die, as must every living creature that is prevented from breathing, whether it be man, mammal, bird, reptile, fish, or moss.

What is an Escalator ?

An escalator is a flight of stairs, always moving, so that it carries us to the top while we stand still. The escalator—which simply means moving staircase—originated in America, but there are many now at the Underground railway stations in London and in big stores in many towns.

The escalator developed from the endless band used for conveying goods in factories, and many years ago such a band, placed at an incline, used to carry visitors from the lower parade at Southend to the top of the cliff. It was an early form of escalator without steps.

The escalator differs from the moving inclined plane in having stairs which travel up or down, the steps being horizontal all the time. Passengers going up can increase their rate of progress by walking up the stairs while they are moving, thus adding their own motion to that of the escalator.

When the steps reach the top they form a horizontal plane and carry the passenger to the stationary landing, where he is left while the steps travel on and, turning round a roller, go upside down underneath the staircase to the bottom again.

The average escalator travels about forty feet a minute, which is not too fast to allow passengers to step on or off with perfect ease and safety. An endless hand-rail of leather on each side moves with the stairs and enables inexperienced people to steady themselves. The great advantage of the escalator over the lift is that it is always moving and can be used at any time by any number of passengers.

Why is a Needle No Heavier When Magnetised ?

This question puzzles us because we have not clearly distinguished in our own minds what weight really means and what it does not mean.

All weight is a direct consequence of gravitation, and of nothing else. Were there no gravitation, there would be no such thing as weight. The power of gravitation entirely depends upon the amount of stuff that is concerned, or the mass of matter that is acted upon. In other words, the weight of a thing depends entirely upon its mass—the amount of matter in it. Everything goes to prove that nothing affects gravitation except this question of the amount of matter present.

If we take a needle and heat it or cool it, magnetise it or unmagnetise it, or do anything else to it, so long as we do not take away any of the matter from it or add any new matter to it, its weight remains the same. When we magnetise it, we endow it with a new power which is very strong and wonderful, and which, for instance, can be brought to bear in such a way that it will overpower the force of gravitation, and will thus enable the needle to lift ten times its own weight. But the weight of the needle itself absolutely depends upon its mass, and upon nothing else. Our bodies weigh just the same whether we hold a weight in our hands or not; the amount of stuff in our bodies is the same in either case. Of course, our bodies and the weight together weigh more than our bodies would alone, but that is a different thing.

HOW THE MOVING STAIRCASE WORKS

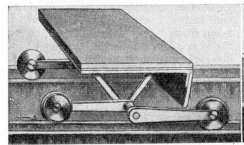 

The moving staircase, or escalator, is made up of a number of separate steps, each consisting of a tread to stand on and a riser or perpendicular piece below the tread. This picture shows one of the steps in its horizontal position before it begins to move up an incline.

Here is one side of the same step moving up an incline. We must imagine a similar pair of wheels at the other side of the step. Two wheels, one on each side, follow a lower track and two an upper track, and the next picture shows the reason for this arrangement.

This picture shows how it is that the steps of an escalator, moving up an incline, keeps always horizontal. The whole staircase is kept moving by means of an endless chain, shown in the next picture. When the steps reach the top they are carried over a big wheel, or roller, and return upside down to the bottom.

Here the escalator is seen with the treads or steps taken away. We see the pairs of wheels at each side of the staircase that carry the tread, and the great endless chain in the middle that keeps the whole staircase moving. An escalator like that at some of the Underground stations in London can carry up from the platform 11,000 passengers an hour.

Why are there More Stars Some Nights than Others?

There are not more stars some nights than others, but we see more. What really happens is that the state of the atmosphere differs very much at different times, quite apart from the presence of actual clouds. Even when there are no clouds anywhere, and all over the sky the brighter stars can be seen, the state of the air may be such —whether owing to the presence of a lot of dust high up in it, or to other causes— that the less bright stars cannot be seen. The temperature and the pressure of the air have their own effects in this respect. Much of the recent advance in astronomy has been due to the fact that great new observatories, containing the finest telescopes in the world, have been specially built on the tops of mountains, or, at any rate, as high up as possible in parts of the world specially chosen for the clearness of the air; and the higher the telescope, of course, the less the amount of air that the light from the stairs has to pass through before it reaches the eye of the astronomer or the lens of the camera.

What is Papyrus?

The papyrus is a kind of sedge from eight to ten feet high, found chiefly in Africa. It has been almost as important for the growth of man's mind as wheat for the growth of his body. From its pith was made the first paper, and for hundreds of years papyrus paper was the chief medium for the record of the thoughts of men. The paper was made of strips of the pith cemented together into sheets, which could be rolled up into scrolls, but later the sheets were bound into pages in book form. Some of the sheets were seven feet long. In Egypt many valuable and interesting scrolls have been found, including previously unknown fragments of Euripides, and a famous but lost work of Aristotle on the constitution of Athens.

Do Things Weigh Heavier or Lighter when Hot or Cold?

This question about gravitation is really extremely interesting, because it so happens that this is one of the very questions on which a great many remarkable experiments have been made this century.

There is no doubt about the answer to it, but we must understand what that answer really is. It is that the power of gravitation is not in the slightest degree affected by temperature; in other words, one and the same thing—if nothing is taken from it or added to it—weighs just the same, however much it is heated, or however much it is cooled.

But we must not be confused. When a thing is heated it swells, as a rule, and as there is no more of it than there, but it is occupying more space, it is made lighter *in proportion to the space it occupies.* Thus, hot water will float on the top of cold water; hot air will rise in cold air, and so on. This, however, is not a question of absolute weight, but of the relation between that weight, *which is not changed*, and the volume of the thing.

Does a Light-Wave go through Glass?

Light is *not* a wave of air, but a wave in the ether, which is everywhere—in the air and in the glass, too. When the light passes through glass, it is a wave in ether all the time, though during part of its journey the kind of matter called air is there, and in another part glass.

This is not to say that matter has no effect on these ether-waves, for we know that it has. All we can say is that some kinds of matter offer no great obstacle to their passage, as, for instance, glass; while other kinds of matter, such as wood or stone, interfere very much with their passage. Sound *is* a wave of air, and where sound passes through glass, the air-wave on the outside throws the glass into a wave of the same kind, and the wave in the glass starts a new wave in the air on the other side, and so the sound goes on.

How Can We Tell How Many Days There are in Another World's Year?

If we know how long a planet takes to go once round the Sun, we know the length of its year. Then, if we can watch the planet, and see how long it takes to spin round once on itself, we know the length of its day. Divide the length of the year by the length of the day, and we have the number of days in the year. But though that is quite easy in some cases, in others it is impossible, and so we cannot yet tell the number of days in a year of all planets.

The trouble is that, though we know how long the planet takes to go round the Sun, in some cases—as in the case of Pluto— we cannot make out any of its features, and therefore cannot tell at what rate it spins, and we do not know the length of its day, though we do know the length of its year.

HOW MEN WROTE IN THE DAYS BEFORE PAPER

The Egyptians painted the walls of their temples and tombs with strange letters and pictures which tell the history of Egypt. This is from the wall of a tomb where the paint is still fresh, though it is thousands of years old.

Cleopatra's Needle, once in Egypt, and now standing by the Thames in London, shows the strange writing on the Egyptian monuments.

The Rosetta Stone, which taught us to read the strange writing the Egyptians left behind. It said the same thing in three kinds of writing, and one kind was the Egyptian. Men knew one of the other kinds of writing, so that they were able to find out what the Egyptian writing meant.

There was no paper in old Egypt, and the people wrote on bricks and on the dried pith of the papyrus plant, here shown growing.

An early way of writing was to mark soft clay and bake it into a brick like this.

This is a piece of papyrus, showing how the Egyptians used it to write upon. Nearly all these things are in the British Museum.

Why Does Steam Put a Light Out?

Of course, it depends on the kind of light whether steam will or will not put it out, but it is certainly true that a fire or a lighted gas-jet or a lamp may be put out by steam.

For this there are at least two reasons. We use the word steam rather loosely, often meaning by it liquid water in the air—the steam that we can see. But sometimes we mean by it water-vapour. Wherever there is steam, there is water-vapour—that is to say, water in the air in the form of an invisible gas. Now, this water is already burnt; it can neither be burnt any more, nor can it sustain the burning of anything else.

In so far as the thing which produces the light is supplied with water-vapour in the air instead of oxygen, it is starved and must go out. But the presence of steam means also the presence of liquid water, and liquid water puts a light out because it so quickly swallows up into itself the heat which is near it, and makes the burning thing so cold that it cannot burn. Every man who smokes a pipe knows the great difference there is between smoking moist tobacco and dry tobacco.

What is Smoke Made of?

Smoke is the result of imperfect burning. Most of the things from which we get so much smoke—like coal—if they were properly burnt, would form nothing but gases, which we could not see, and which would very soon fly away and do no harm to anybody. But in order to burn coal properly some trouble and care are required. When we burn coal in an ordinary fire, we do not supply enough air to it. We put the fresh coal on at the top instead of at the bottom, as we should, and so we only partly burn the coal, and small specks of it, unburnt, are carried up in the draught, and make smoke. The chief stuff in smoke is simply coal in specks of various sizes. But the trouble is that a great deal of oily stuff comes out of the coal, and covers the specks of it in smoke, so that these stick to things. We all do wrong in this respect in our fires at home, and the time will come when we shall burn our coal in a better way.

At present the smoke makes black fogs in many cities, and cuts off a great quantity of the daylight by which we live, besides making everything dirty, destroying plants and trees, and filling our lungs with dirt which we never get rid of. There are few things about which we are more careless than smoke, and if we had sense enough we should stop making it, even if it were only for the reason that all the stuff in smoke might be burnt, and that in making smoke we waste a great deal of fuel.

What Makes Water Gurgle When it Comes Out of a Bottle?

We know that the air has pressure, and so, if there is an empty space anywhere, the air will press into it. Now, when we pour water out of a bottle which is full, there must be an empty space left behind in the bottle when the liquid comes out, and from moment to moment, as that empty space tends to be formed in the bottle, the air outside is bound to rush in to take its place. If the bottle has a wide mouth, like a tumbler, then, as we pour the liquid out, air can flow in evenly, and there is no gurgling.

But if we take a full ginger-beer bottle, and hold it upside down, then there is a series of fights going on between the liquid which is trying to get out and the air which is trying to get past the liquid to fill up the space in the bottle. Sometimes the air pushes back the ginger-beer, and sometimes the ginger-beer pushes back the air. This means that the air is thrown into little disturbances, which we hear as gurgles. We say that water gurgles, but really it is the air that is disturbed by this contest between it and the water, and we call these disturbances " gurgles."

Why Does a Glow-worm Glow?

A glow-worm is not a worm at all, but is really a kind of beetle seen during the summer months up to the end of August, on warm banks and hedgerows and in woods and pastures. As soon as the evening's dusk begins, this beautiful insect begins to show a most exquisite yellow-green light, caused by what are called luminous organs placed over the tail end.

The object of this light is not actually certain, but most of the wise men who study living creatures suppose that the female shows the light for the purpose of attracting males, which do not shine in this way. Whether this is the real reason or not we cannot be quite sure, but the glow-worm is only one of many animals which show light by means of what is called phosphorescence.

The Story of the Beautiful Things in the Treasure-House of the World

Three heads in the Sistine Chapel by Michael Angelo

LEONARDO AND MICHAEL ANGELO

HERE and there, in the progress of the world, Time and Fate turn author and tell a story, and the older the world grows the more fantastic the tale seems. Such a story comes in the growth of Southern Europe from the twelfth to the fifteenth centuries.

At the beginning of this period people were profoundly ignorant of the universe. Their only mathematics were simple addition, subtraction, and multiplication. Their idea of astronomy was a kind of chart of the heavens from which it was possible to understand certain simple phenomena, such as the habits of the Moon that controlled the Church festival of Eastertide. Greek and Roman culture, we must remember, had been stamped out of Italy by the repeated inroads of barbaric tribes from Central Europe, and now made its home in Byzantium.

Over the benighted continent a light of knowledge presently spread, directed from Spain, where the Moors were living as conquerors. Spain, in the twelfth century, was hundreds of years ahead of the rest of Europe; she had universities, astronomical observatories, and science laboratories, all the results of the Moorish occupation. The culture of the gifted Mohammedan peoples spread among the Christianised countries of Europe and aroused an intense curiosity.

It is difficult for us to realise how magical and wonderful was this awakening of an intellectually slothful continent. Men were like children at school, learning for the first time the secrets of the world; hunger for knowledge sent them, often barefoot, with the student's wallet, begging their way from one university to another. To be a scholar in those days was to be a member of a secret brotherhood, and to hold a sure claim on people's sympathy.

The same kind of curiosity was presently in the fifteenth century, to lead to the discovery of the New World and all the romantic and perilous voyages of our own Elizabethan seamen.

In the meantime a dormant sense of beauty had stirred, as we have seen, in the countries where the Gothic spirit was felt, and first the Sienese, then the Florentines, Umbrians, and Venetians were working and experimenting, generation by generation, toward a full realisation of what great art meant.

In the fifteenth century came another element into art. Sultan Mohammed II conquered Byzantium, and the Greeks, flying westward, took refuge in Italy,

PICTURES · STATUES · CARVINGS · BUILDINGS · IVORIES · CRAFTS

bringing with them their rich sense of beauty, their immortal traditions.

It seems strange that in Italy, at one time the stronghold of Greek and Roman culture, pagan beauty should ever have slumbered, and that the active presence of the Greeks should be necessary to remind the country of their old dominion; but that is one of the queer chapters in this medieval and awakened Italy.

The Christians of the early centuries were surrounded by the buildings and the arts of Rome and Greece, and seemed simply to be unaware of their merit. They pillaged the pagan halls for the pillars and capitals of their churches, taking from them all the marble they could; and this extraordinary indifference to the claims of the past persisted a thousand years, until the Greeks themselves, coming back, reminded them. Then the Italians looked about and tried to rescue from further destruction any monuments that remained, and they began to turn back to the ancients for study.

AN INTELLECTUAL AND ARTISTIC GENIUS TRIES TO FLY

Thus we see three marvellous forces at work to produce the paintings and sculpture of the fifteenth and sixteenth centuries in Italy—first the early renaissance in Tuscany, due to the Gothic spirit; then the growth of learning which infected artists and made them restless, unsatisfied with their own achievement; then again the inroad of Greek culture from the East.

All these forces centre in one Florentine painter, Leonardo da Vinci, who lived from 1452 to 1519. He was an intellectual as well as an artistic genius, a man of most brilliant gifts, any one of which would have put him apart and set him on a peak among his fellows. He, in his own person, should absolve artists for ever from the slur cast on them by men more practical and less imaginative.

There was scarcely a by-road, certainly there was not a highway of learning, that he did not explore. He foresaw several of the inventions which hundreds of years later was to revolutionise social life. He was philosopher, architect, engineer, physicist, chemist, geologist; he discovered the use of steam power and experimented in hydraulics. At one time he was military engineer to Caesar Borgia; when he was over 60, a guest

in the Vatican, he neglected painting pictures for the Pope in order to try once more to work out his idea of a machine that would fly in the air.

It would seem that to this man fortune had already come with both hands full; as if that were not enough, another gift was tossed to him—genius in art.

Unlike many painters and poets, there was no need for Leonardo to wait till he was dead to be called great; he was truly the living master, in himself his greatest picture—one of the most fascinating and compelling forces on a century already coloured with genius and gold-dusted with heavenly ideals.

LEONARDO'S FAMOUS PICTURE OF THE LAST SUPPER

Very little of Leonardo's art is left to us, and this is partly because of the accident of circumstance, partly the painter's own wilfulness—in one immortal instance—in working in a wrong medium, and partly his profound self distrust. His searchlight of criticism turned pitilessly on his own work, delaying its execution. There are four great paintings of his left to us, and one of these is but a ghost, a wreck of its own magnificence. It is the first of the two pictures which leap to the eye when the name of Leonardo da Vinci is mentioned—The Last Supper.

Many people, thinking of the story of the Last Supper as told in the Bible, think of Leonardo's picture of it—of that long table where Christ and the twelve disciples were seated, of the separate horror, fear, and curiosity chasing themselves across the faces of the apostles as the Master said: "One of you shall betray me"; and one after another they asked, "Lord, is it I?" The expression in this picture of those human feelings, and of Christ's own superb and sorrowful indifference, is sheer genuis.

THE PITIFUL DESTRUCTION OF A NOBLE MONUMENT

The Last Supper was painted in a method that peculiarly reveals the workings of the artist's wayward spirit. It was done for the Dominican Friars of St. Maria delle Grazie, at the command of Lodovico Sforza, the Duke of Milan, Leonardo's patron. The artist was engaged by this nobleman, at a handsome salary, to execute various works of art, the chief being an equestrian bronze statue of the duke's father.

PICTURES BY LEONARDO AND HIS PUPIL

The Man with the Red Cap   Beatrice d'Este or Bianca Sforza

PORTRAITS ONCE ATTRIBUTED TO LEONARDO BUT PROBABLY BY AMBROGIO DE PREDIS, HIS PUPIL

MARY, SAINT ANNE, AND THE INFANT JESUS
BY LEONARDO

THE MADONNA OF THE ROCKS
BY LEONARDO

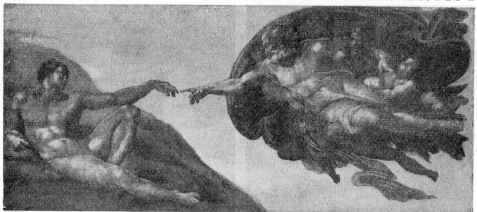

MICHAEL ANGELO'S CONCEPTION OF THE CREATION OF ADAM—FROM THE SISTINE CHAPEL

THE THREE FATES—BY MICHAEL ANGELO

MICHAEL ANGELO'S HOLY FAMILY

THREE OF THE NOBLE FIGURES ON THE CEILING OF THE SISTINE CHAPEL

THE HOLY FAMILY, BY MICHAEL ANGELO

Upon this work Leonardo spent the best of sixteen years, tortured by his inability to work out his own superb ideal, again and again making a new sketch and beginning the figures afresh. At the end of the sixteen years the model was ready to be cast in bronze and was temporarily set up in an archway outside the duke's home, Milan Castle. Its fate is one of the sad stories in Italian history. Sforza's enemies, the French, had long been threatening him; now they besieged Milan, and the equestrian statue was demolished by the archers of Louis the Twelfth.

LEONARDO MOST LABORIOUS WHEN HE WAS MOST IDLE

While Leonardo was busy on this group, however, he executed a great number of commissions, and among them the very important painting of the Last Supper on the walls of St. Maria delle Grazie. The artist received the order to execute this work with something approaching ecstasy; here was a subject he had yearned to paint. He made a great number of chalk studies, and the remnants of these are now widely scattered, the best being in the Accademia of Venice, and some rather fine heads in the library at Windsor. South Kensington Museum treasures some notes made by the artist describing the various attitudes and expressions of the Apostles.

Presently Leonardo began the actual painting, and soon was standing before it in his characteristic attitude of self-distrust and fastidious criticism, an ever-forward reaching to the ideal which was secret to his own soul.

Seized by an access of vigour, he would toil from dawn to dusk without food. Then there would come on him strange moods when he would stand motionless, staring at the composition for an hour or two; and after this spell of thought he would leave the painting untouched for several days. When questioned on these habits by the prior, who, good man, thought the artist was merely wasting time, Leonardo explained that when he was most idle he was really most laborious.

RAGS AND TATTERS OF GREATNESS CLING TO THE FRAGMENTS OF A PICTURE

For several years Leonardo divided his energy between The Last Supper and the equestrian statue. Sometimes the artist was seen to leave the group at Milan Castle and walk through the town in the hot midday to the convent beyond the gates. There he would add a few illuminating touches to the painting, and return to the castle.

In 1498 the picture was finished. It is our irreparable misfortune that the artist, refusing to work in fresco, which does not admit of the constant retouching that his ideals demanded, painted in oils on the stucco surface of the wall. In a very short time the fabric crumbled, and the picture stands now in ruin. Although many copies have been made, the rags and tatters of greatness clinging to the fragments of the original make the finest of them seem a sorry imitation.

The other most talked-of picture by Leonardo is of a very different kind—a simple portrait of a Neapolitan woman, called La Gioconda, and known as Mona Lisa. In this face the artist painted his mastery of knowledge of character.

As in the case of the Last Supper, he himself was standing apart, studying, as an intellectual exercise, the human emotions which stamp a face just as much as the definite features do. We can never feel, for instance, that Leonardo liked or disliked Peter or Judas, or liked or disliked Mona Lisa. He was fulfilling what he deemed was the artist's vocation in figure-painting—the delineation of the human soul.

PICTURE THAT MUST HAVE BEEN WORTH 4000 GOLD CROWNS

La Gioconda was just an ordinary woman, and she hid her thoughts under an elusive, inscrutable smile. Leonardo spent four years painting the smile, *and* her thoughts. In its early condition this masterpiece must have arrested all men's eyes, and have been well worth the 4000 gold crowns that Francis the First paid for it when Leonardo took it with him to France. The sky was very blue, and the Neapolitan's face was very fair, with sparkling eyes and pretty, red lips. Even now, with this brightness faded, it fulfils in itself Leonardo's own version of a very much older maxim—Mortal beauty perishes; Art remains.

Leonardo da Vinci is an eternal lesson to young students who want to paint before they can draw. Into the preliminary studies for his pictures he put an immense amount of care, and these charcoal drawings not only foreshadow the paintings but mirror the genius which inspired the artist in all his work.

LEONARDO'S SMILING LADY

MONA LISA, THE MOST FAMOUS PORTRAIT IN THE WORLD, BY LEONARDO DA VINCI

We have in our possession in England a treasure which many other nations envy, and by some curious fate it is tucked away in a corner of the Diploma Gallery at Burlington House—a collection of pictures very few people go to see. This treasure is a cartoon by Leonardo, one of the studies in charcoal for a Madonna group, now in the Louvre. The pure and lovely face of Mary is Leonardo's conception of the beauty of motherhood. It is the work of a supreme master.

There is a painting in the National Gallery which has long been attributed to Leonardo, but is now believed to be the

in Florence. It was part of the decoration of the Council Hall, and the work was entrusted to Leonardo and Michael Angelo. Thus two of the masters of the world, in whose two styles all styles met, were labouring under the same roof. They were already known to each other. Leonardo was over 50, Michael Angelo still young.

It would be difficult to find two men more differing from each other in the pursuit of a common ideal. There never was an artist who brought less feeling and emotion, and more intellectual force, to bear on his pictures than Leonardo da Vinci ; but in Michael Angelo thought

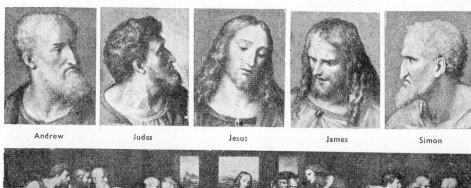

Andrew   Judas   Jesus   James   Simon

THE MASTERPIECE OF LEONARDO NOW CRUMBLING ON A WALL IN MILAN—THE LAST SUPPER

work of Ambrogio de Predis, one of his pupils. It is called the Madonna of the Rocks, and is a copy of the original picture of this name by Leonardo, now in the Louvre. The French thus own three of Leonardo's four great pictures—the Mona Lisa, the Madonna of the Rocks, the Madonna and Child and St. Anne. The ruins of the fourth, The Last Supper, are still to be seen in the Maria delle Grazie, Milan; and there also are two disputed portraits by Leonardo—Lodovico Sforza and either Beatrice d'Este or Bianca Sforza.

A great deal of the artist's work was destined to be lost. One of the paintings we should most like to have seen is a battle scene he worked at for some years

played little part; rather he flung his own joy, his own sorrow, into stone and into painted figures, a restless pent-up spirit throbbing its way to freedom. He was especially a sculptor, and his pictures show his vivid passion for line and form. To him, the body of man was indeed God's greatest work, and he paid little attention to landscape, light and shade, atmosphere, or any other aspect of natural objects.

Michael Angelo, sculptor, painter, architect, poet, was the last of the great Florentines. His work seemed like a mighty challenge to the rest of the world, and, heard across the centuries, those spiritual trumpets are still faintly booming. The old-new Greek culture had laid its hold on

MICHAEL ANGELO'S WONDERFUL CEILING

THE MAGNIFICENT CEILING OF THE SISTINE CHAPEL, PAINTED BY MICHAEL ANGELO, IS ONE OF THE CHIEF GLORIES OF ROME. THIS PICTURE GIVES SOME IDEA OF ITS GRANDEUR, BUT THE VASTNESS OF THE ARTIST'S CONCEPTION CANNOT BE REALLY SUGGESTED ON PAPER.

his imagination; he had already inherited close on three centuries of Tuscan art: two influences which were like live wires, twisted together, fire-making.

This impetuous and forcible genius was naturally a great leader, and he founded in Rome, where he chiefly worked, a school which influenced the energies of nearly all the artists of Italy.

In the realm of painting, Michael Angelo's greatest achievement was the decoration of the ceiling of the Sistine Chapel in the Vatican. This work he undertook not very willingly, at the command of Pope Julius II in 1508. He said to the Pope, rather querulously, that sculpture, not painting, was his trade, and that Raphael, the painter of Urbino, was much more likely to do the ceiling well. But the Pope insisted—for the great good fortune of us all—and Michael Angelo set to work, only reserving himself the final comment of henceforward signing all his letters, " Michael Angelo, *Scultore*."

A CHAPEL WHICH STANDS ALONE IN THE NOBLE HISTORY OF ART

It is difficult for people who have not seen the Sistine Chapel to realise this vast piece of painting, which stands alone in the history of art, stupendous, without the shadow of a rival. Michael Angelo accomplished it in four years, almost unaided, as the artists he summoned to Rome to help him did not fulfil his requirements, and he sent them away in disgust.

It would seem to us that the planning of this mighty work alone should have been one man's sole labour. In the central vault of the ceiling are nine large pictures telling the story of Creation, the Fall of Man, and the Deluge. Between the windows, spaces are filled with twelve figures of Prophets and Sybils who are foreshadowing the coming of Christ. In the spandrels are painted stories from the Old Testament, such as the Brazen Serpent and the Death of Goliath. The lunettes are filled with figures of David's descendants, and the ancestors of Mary. These large divisions complete, Michael Angelo used up all possible extra spaces to paint figures of youths and children. There are in all about two hundred figures, of immense size, painted in vigorous and sometimes unusual attitudes, the whole vast work charged with the extraordinary vividness, aliveness, and overweening strength which was the stamp of Michael

Angelo's creations. Looked at even now, after a lapse of 500 years, it would seem that those figures in the Sistine Chapel could quite easily step down, make some violent gestures, and speak in a high, heroic way.

THE COLOSSAL SHAPES EXPRESSIVE OF THE ARTIST'S SOUL

When Michael Angelo was about 70 he was ordered to paint The Last Judgment on the wall above the altar of the Sistine Chapel. This, his last fresco work, lacks the fire and force which mark the ceiling decorations, and shows what mannerisms without genius can do.

Very few other specimens of the mighty artist's paintings are left for us. He never carried out the fresco designed for the wall of the Council Hall in Florence, where Leonardo was working. The cartoon foreshadowed a magnificence even surpassing that of the Sistine ceiling, but this, like many other treasures, was destroyed. The Deposition in the National Gallery, attributed to Michael Angelo, gives some idea of his wild energy, his Titan-like strength. Another painting of his—the Holy Family—is in the Tribune of the Uffizi Gallery, Florence; and a very early picture of the same subject is in the National Gallery.

But when we think of Michael Angelo the painter, we think of the solitary and unrivalled magnificence of the Sistine Chapel, and we feel a little awed to think that one human being can be responsible for that immortal grandeur. We think of the artist toiling at the work, often through spells of great physical weariness and despondency, struggling to express his own soul in these colossal shapes.

THE LAST OF THE MIGHTY RACE OF FLORENTINE PAINTERS

His is a sad figure in a century of buoyant, happily-inspired artists. To him genius was indeed the sorrowful gift. By temperament a little unfriendly and irritable, he alienated many people who might have made his life happier. His patrons did not reward him too well; poverty and family trials burdened him. When he died, an old man of 89, all the rest of his brilliant generation had gone, Raphael and Leonardo over forty years before. With him died the mighty race of painters who for three hundred years had made the name of Florence famous.

The Wonderful House We Live In, and Our Place in the World

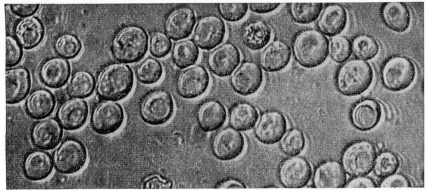

Magnified photographs of yeast cells, which breathe, digest, and multiply, and make alcohol out of sugar

OUR UNSEEN FRIENDS AND FOES

DIFFERENT kinds of microbes have different powers, and act sometimes in useful, sometimes in harmful ways. Some microbes, for instance, have special powers of making food material with the aid of the air which is found down in the soil. Air contains a very valuable element called nitrogen, which ordinary plants cannot use, and which we cannot use, though we breathe it into our blood along with the oxygen which we *do* use. But certain microbes can take this nitrogen and combine it with other elements so as to make compounds which are perfect food materials.

These particular microbes are specially fond of certain kinds of green plants which are not particularly useful in themselves; but the farmer knows that it is worth his while to grow these plants one year, so as to make the soil rich in food for his wheat in the next year. If he grows wheat every year the soil will become exhausted of its food materials, and so farmers have long practised what is called the *rotation of crops*. It is, of course, a very serious matter, for the farmer and for the country, that the farmer cannot grow wheat every year; but it is hoped that by using these special microbes in a particular way we may be able to grow wheat year after year in the same soil.

The dairyman should be no less interested in microbes than the farmer should be, for they are of the utmost importance in all his work. Among them are included his best friends and his most dangerous enemies. If we realise that microbes are everywhere, we shall understand that they invade milk from the moment it is drawn—microbes of all kinds, useful and dangerous, from the air, from dust, and from water.

Now, milk is one of the best things in the world in which to grow microbes, and so those which get into it grow very quickly, for good or for evil. It is the duty of the dairyman to keep out of his milk all dangerous microbes. It is the duty of everyone to know that milk, which is a perfect food for us, is also a perfect food for some of our most terrible enemies, such as the microbe (or tubercle bacillus) that causes the dreaded wasting disease called tuberculosis, usually referred to as t.b.

But here we are talking especially about the natural and proper work of microbes. There are quite a number of them which are, in a sense, natural in milk and are known as milk microbes.

They are certain to enter it, and are indeed very useful in it. These microbes exist in enormous numbers in cowsheds, and get into milk soon after it is drawn.

BODY, MIND, AND SOUL · CITIZENSHIP · ECONOMICS · GOVERNMENT

Now, the extraordinary thing about this is that as they grow and multiply in the milk they prevent other microbes which might be bad for us from growing there. In course of time they turn the milk sour, but sour milk is not bad for us, and, indeed, the microbes in sour milk, when they enter our bodies, help to protect us from other microbes which might do us harm. So they are really very good friends of ours, and nowadays, when people suffer from certain kinds of illness, they are sometimes given sour milk to make them better. The microbes in sour milk help us to digest our food, and they prevent other microbes which would hurt us from multiplying in our food after we have swallowed it.

But there is more to say than this. From milk we get cream, and from cream we get butter, but without the proper microbes of milk no butter could be made. It is the milk microbes which cause the cream to ripen so that butter can be made from it.

THE MICROBES THAT HELP US TO MAKE BUTTER AND CHEESE

The flavour of different kinds of butter depends on the particular kind of microbe that ripened the cream from which the butter was made, and nowadays we can cultivate just those kinds of microbes which help us to make butter with the kind of flavour people like. As the microbes start the process of butter-making, they are called " starters," and in some parts of the world men of science supply the best kind of " starters " to farmers to ripen their cream with.

Just as we could not have butter without microbes, so we could not have cheese. All cheese, of course, is really made from milk, and the milk produced by any particular kind of animal such as the cow is the same all the world over. Yet there are dozens of kinds of cheese, and their differences mostly depend on the particular kind of microbe which is used in their manufacture.

We owe our boots to microbes, too. Boots are made of leather, and all leather is made from the skins of animals by a process called tanning. But tanning would be impossible without microbes. Nor is this all. Every great city has to deal with the problem how to dispose of its waste matter, and one of the best ways

of dealing with sewage is by using microbes to do the work.

We see now that the tiniest of all living creatures play a great part in the world. Especially marvellous is the way, as we have already read, in which they destroy all dead creatures, animal, vegetable, and even human, so as to make room for those who are now living and those who yet shall be; and, more than that, turn the stuff of which these millions of dead bodies are made into fresh, wholesome, and pure food material to nourish the life of the Earth.

THE MICROBES OF THE PAST THAT LEARNED A LESSON

But we must be quite fair, of course, in talking about microbes. There are a certain number of microbes that live, not on dead matter, but in and upon the bodies of creatures that are still alive. Probably all microbes began by living on dead matter, but some of them learnt how to attack the bodies of very old or nearly dying plants, or animals, and so at last there were produced the present kinds of microbes which invade the living bodies of higher creatures and are a scourge and a menace to mankind.

Plants and animals and men may all suffer in this respect; but it is very interesting for us to learn that when creatures live wild, in their natural state in the open air of heaven, and in the light, they suffer little from microbes.

Wild animals and wild plants scarcely suffer at all. But when man takes various kinds of plants for his own purposes, and grows them in conditions which are not really natural, they are often attacked by microbes; and it is the same with domesticated animals.

MICROBES MORE DESTRUCTIVE THAN SNAKES AND TIGERS

This is a lesson for us. If wild creatures were meant to live in fresh air, with the sky as the roof over their heads, so also were men and women; and if we shut ourselves up, as we sometimes shut up cows and tigers, microbes will attack us, just as they attack them. The kinds of microbes which are useful to us, such as those that keep the earth sweet, those that help plants to grow, and so on, can thrive in the open air, and the light of day helps their work; but the dangerous microbes, and especially the microbe of tuberculosis—which kills far more human beings every day than all the snakes and tigers in the world kill in a year—are themselves killed if exposed to fresh air and sunlight.

At one time houses used to be built with windows made so that they could not be opened ; there were even houses with rooms which had no windows at all, and therefore no light. Human beings who were compelled to live in such conditions were exposed to constant danger of which they never knew. Fortunately, we know better than to build such houses today. More and more windows, more and more light, is the guiding principle of modern building, our schools being shining examples in this respect.

THE FRESH AIR THAT SAVES THE ZOO MONKEYS FROM TUBERCULOSIS

We cannot do without air and sunlight ; we must not be packed too closely together; and if we obey these laws microbes will scarcely injure us. If we can save the monkeys at the Zoo from the microbes of tuberculosis by giving them fresh air (as we do), we can also save each other in the same way.

One of the most important of these microbes is not usually called a microbe, but it might well be so called, for it is a close relative of microbes and lives in the same fashion.

This is the yeast plant, which turns sugar into alcohol and the gas called carbon dioxide. We use it every day in making bread. The alcohol is blown away as a gas, and the carbon dioxide forms in the flour and makes the bread rise.

But we also use the yeast plant to get the alcohol that it makes. This also is a very useful substance; it is used in hundreds of arts and industries; it is splendid for cleaning things and for preserving them; it burns beautifully and makes a splendid fuel; it is, perhaps, the cheapest and most easily made of all fuels for many purposes. If we had the sense to use alcohol only in useful ways, the tiny yeast plant which produces it would be among the best friends of man.

ALCOHOL A POISON FOR ALL LIVING CREATURES WITHOUT EXCEPTION

But men drink alcohol, *which is a poison to all living creatures without exception, men or animals or plants.* It is even a poison to the yeast plant that makes it, and when the amount of alcohol in the sugar which the yeast plant is feeding upon and changing rises to a fixed point, the yeast plant is killed, and if the process is to go on the alcohol has to be taken away as fast as it is made.

Alcohol is of no use to our bodies, but in time will cause disease in every part of them, especially the brain, which is the most important part of us. It is the great friend and ally of deadly microbes, for which it prepares the way by *making our bodies unable to resist them.*

In various ways, even when taken in moderation, alcohol reduces our power of fighting these deadly microbes. For it diminishes the vigour of activity of the white blood-cells which are the soldiers and scavengers of the body; it diminishes the power of the digestion and is apt to cause inflammation of the membrane of the stomach; and it damages the delicate nerve tissues.

All doctors, and insurance companies, know that people who abstain from alcohol have greater resistance to disease than people who take strong drink; and even when abstainers are stricken down with tuberculosis or any other disease, their chances of recovery are much greater than those of the drinkers.

TUBERCULOSIS THAT SLAYS THOUSANDS OF PEOPLE EVERY YEAR

The microbe of tuberculosis was found in the last half of the nineteenth century by a great German, Robert Koch, who took up the work of the Frenchman Louis Pasteur—the first man to understand and tell us about microbes.

Between eight and nine thousand people are killed by the microbe of tuberculosis every year in Britain. All over the world, wherever people are crowded together, this microbe destroys them; but medical science is making rapid strides in the treatment of tuberculosis, and the day will surely come when this disease will be numbered among the unhappy, far-off things of long ago.

Probably the microbe of tuberculosis is one of those microbes which can scarcely live at all except in the bodies of other living creatures, such as ourselves, and so, when we prevent it from attacking us, it will no doubt die out altogether.

But let us not forget that, though some microbes do us harm if we let them, and though some microbes kill us, yet without microbes we could not live at all.

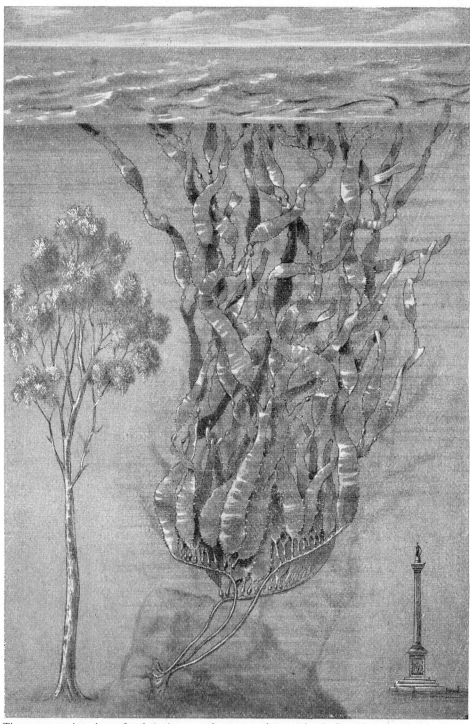

The most amazing plants, for their size, grow in water and not on land. Shackleton's ship, the Quest, found gigantic marine forests near Tierra del Fuego, and soundings showed that some of the monster seaweed plants peeping above the water were 600 feet high, over 100 feet taller than the tallest land tree—the Australian eucalyptus. This tree, and Nelson's Column, 172 feet high, are here compared.

The Story of the Marvellous Plants that Cover the Earth

PLANTS AND THEIR ANCESTORS

How living creatures began Science does not know, but some of the great events in their history are clear.

It is almost certain that plants had the start of animals, for plants are able to feed on air, water, and salts; while animals are seldom able to feed at such a low level.

It is almost certain that the first thoroughly successful creatures were microscopically small, that they swam about in the sea by means of a vibrating lash of living matter, that they possessed chlorophyll or some other colouring matter which enabled them to use the power of sunlight, and that they were nearer to plants than to animals.

Whenever and wherever well-lighted shallow waters were established, some of the pioneer free-swimming plants would anchor themselves, and thus began the history of fixed seaweeds. When we look at the beds of seaweed exposed at low tide, we are looking at a very old type of vegetation ; and it may be that some of the beautifully coloured and moulded kinds are extremely ancient forms of life.

When there was a buckling of the floor so that continents and ocean basins were established, and when the shores were slowly raised, as often happens, it is possible that some of the seaweeds were gradually transformed into land plants, getting true roots for absorbing water and salts from the soil, and true leaves for absorbing gases from the air. Or it may have been that some of the simple plants of the sea made their way up estuaries to rivers and lakes, and, after sojourning in swamps and marshes for ages, began at last to colonise the dry land.

Some of the liverworts of today may be representatives of the ancient pioneers. In any case the rock-story does not show any fossil land plants in the earlier strata, while there are plenty of traces of seaweeds, so that it is safe to conclude that plant life was at first aquatic. We may perhaps picture three great epochs:

1. The primeval Open Sea, teeming with small swimming green plants.

2. The floor of the illumined Shallow Sea, with anchored fronds, making endless experiments in body-building and in securing the continuance and spreading of their race.

3. The beginning of land vegetation, either from transformed seaweeds, or from active migrating plants which came on to dry land by a freshwater route.

In each age some kinds made themselves more and more at home where they were, while others pushed on to new adventures and conquests.

The simplest plants that live an independent life are among the seaweeds or the

BOTANY & ITS WONDERS · FLOWERS · TREES · HOW THINGS GROW

algae. Such are the diatoms, single-celled plants with beautifully sculptured shells of flint, which abound both in fresh and salt water. Such are the tiny plants that form a green coating on the windward side of trees and gate-posts.

But many of the seaweeds are very far from simple, and among the brown ones especially we find mimic roots and stems and leaves. The root, however, is only a holdfast, an anchor, and the leaves (or fronds) absorb water, not gas. In the brown seaweeds there is chlorophyll as in the green ones, but some yellow pigment is added. In the red seaweeds, though one can hardly believe it, there is chlorophyll again, but it is masked by an entirely different red pigment, which may perhaps help the plant to make more of the very blue light of moderately deep water.

On the shore the green seaweeds are most abundant in the shallow water, and red ones in the deeper water; the browns, like the bladder-wrack, are in between. Waving about like flags in the water are the great tangles, but we do not see much of them except at the very lowest tides. One of the giant tangles, much burned to yield potash and iodine, has a stem a hundred feet long and fronds of several hundred feet. In actual length these kelp-tangles exceed the height of the Big Trees of California, but they have no strength of tissue; they float in the water, buoyed by numerous gas-bladders.

THE PLANTS THAT FEED ON OTHER PLANTS OR ANIMALS

Parallel to the seaweeds or algae are what we call the Fungus family—moulds and mildews, mushrooms and toadstools. They are without chlorophyll and cannot live an independent life. Many of them feed on rotting matter; the others prey on living plants or animals. The simplest kind of fungus is the almost ever-present bacteria, single-celled plants of very small size, which are the causes of all rotting, of some kinds of fermentation, and of many diseases, such as plague, cholera, and tuberculosis. Many of them, however, are useful, as we read elsewhere.

A very interesting position is that of the encrusting lichens which we see on stones and trees, for they are " double plants," consisting of an alga and a fungus living together in a partnership which helps both. The fungus-partners serve to fix and to shelter; and they absorb the water and salts. The alga-partners have chlorophyll or some allied pigment and are able to build up carbon compounds. It sometimes happens that the fungus-partners get the upper hand and absorb the algae, but this means putting an end to their own existence, for they cannot continue long without their green allies.

THE PARASITE WHICH FORCES THE GREEN ALGAE TO BE ITS SLAVES

One of the discoverers of the secret of lichens writes of them very vividly:

The master is a fungus, a parasite which is accustomed to live upon others ; its slaves are green algae, which it has sought out, or indeed caught hold of and compelled into its service. It surrounds them, as a spider its prey, with a fibrous net of narrow meshes, which is gradually converted into an impenetrable covering; but while the spider sucks its prey and leaves it dead, the fungus incites the algae found in its net to more rapid activity—indeed, to more vigorous increase.

It should be mentioned here that in the lichens it is the fungus-partner that produces the spores, but the algae enter into the partnership almost from the very first. Lichens may be flat, or tufted, or hairy ; and their colours are often fine. Reindeer moss, on which reindeer largely depend, is a lichen; and so is Iceland moss, which is used in making a delicate food for invalids. Another interest of lichens is that they do a good deal in the way of weathering the rocks and beginning the formation of soil on the mountain-tops.

Lichens are a byway in evolution, they do not lead on to anything else; and, of course, the moulds and mildews and mushrooms and other funguses cannot be considered as leading to the higher plants, for they do not live independently. Therefore, it must not be supposed that the next step in evolution, after the seaweeds, was that which led to liverworts and mosses.

THE MYSTERY IN THE KNOB AT THE END OF THE STALK

Spreading on moist banks of clay, or on the rocks by the side of a waterfall, there are often flat, sprawling green liverworts. Many of them do not get beyond the level of prostrate fronds, but others are divided into lobes, which look like attempts to make leaves. These are often very well ventilated and provided with numerous internal spaces, in which the work of building up carbon compounds goes on effectively, though the light of the places where the liverworts flourish is often very dim. The liverworts make spores inside

THE LIFE-STORY OF A PIECE OF SEAWEED

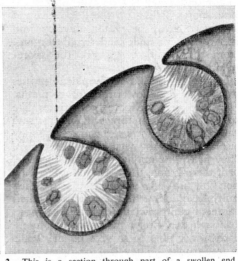

1. This is the common bladder wrack seaweed of our island coasts. Air bladders enable it to keep floating, and the ends of some of the branches are swollen and fitted with little dimples called conceptacles.

2. This is a section through part of a swollen end, showing two of the dimples. It will be seen that inside each is a mass of hairs which are the male organs of the seaweed, and globular bodies, which are the female organs.

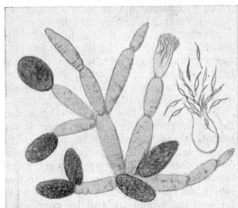

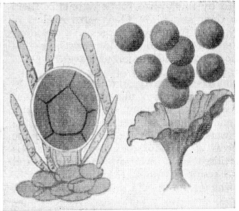

3. The male organs branch out as shown here, and the ends swell and become filled with yellow grains. When ripe the ends burst, and the grains, each with a pair of tiny hairs to help it to move in the water, are thrown out.

4. Here is the female organ of the bladder wrack surrounded by the male hairs. It contains eight little globules, which it discharges into the conceptacle, and then into the sea. On the right we see the globules escaping.

5. The female globule is now surrounded by the male grains, which are enabled to move about by hair-like attachments.

6. The male and female parts blend and form a fertile egg-cell ready to germinate.

7. The egg-cell develops into a young seaweed plant, with a tapering end, which grows sucker-like attachments.

8. The young plant now grows and branches, as shown here, and at last becomes a mature plant

a knob on the end of a delicate stalk; and these spores, falling on the damp ground or carried away by water, develop into liverworts with male and female organs. From the fertilised egg-cell, the spore-making generation arises.

Fond of moist and shady places, mosses are among the most beautiful of plants. They are very delicate—sometimes like tufts of hair, sometimes like prostrate feathers, sometimes forming spongy cushions, as in the well-known bog moss. They are what might be called sociable, for if there is one, there are many. They soon fill up any suitable place; they multiply quickly, and even a detached fragment can grow into a complete moss. Although they prefer moist places, many of them are able to survive on dry walls or tree-trunks. They can be dried until their leaves are crisp, but a heavy shower puts them right again. They absorb water by their whole green surface, and also by thread-like rootlets that fix them to their station. They form a class of pygmies, but they often show a considerable advance on the liverworts, having short stems and numerous leaves.

HOW THE EGG-CELLS OF THE MOSSES ARE FERTILISED BY SWIMMING CELLS

If we peer into the top of a vigorous moss-plant, we may see the male and female organs, sometimes called moss-flowers. The microscopic egg-cell, in the recess of a body shaped like a flask, is fertilised by a swimming male cell, and the result of the fertilisation is a spore borne on the tip of a delicate stalk. Thus, there are two generations: the ordinary leafy moss-plant, which has male and female organs, and then the spore-producing generation. The strange thing is that the second generation grows on the shoulders of the first. When a ripe spore-cell is carried from the burst capsule by wind or water or insect, and lights on a sudden moist place, it grows out into a delicate threadwork, and from this there arises the leafy moss-plant.

This complicated life-history is called *alternation of generations*. In one of the cave-mosses, where the light is very scanty, the threadwork gives out an emerald light, some of the cells acting like reflecting mirrors.

The liverworts and mosses are the simplest land plants of today, but there is no reason to believe that they led on to anything higher. To get on to the main line of ascent we must go back to the seaweeds from which the ferns made a fresh start in life.

It may be that this is the Golden Age of ferns, for there are as many living now as there have been in the past, and far more than in the ancient days of the Carboniferous Era. They are very varied, from delicate filmy ferns, which one might almost mistake for mosses, up to bracken six feet high; from the delicate maiden-hair ferns on the wall, to giants like the royal fern and the tree ferns. There are some 7000 different kinds, and they range from the Tropics to the Arctic. They show a great advance on mosses, for they have numerous vessels for transporting fluid materials within the plant.

THE LITTLE PLANT MANY PEOPLE HAVE NEVER SEEN

When we look at the underside of the fronds of a fern we see brown spore-making organs, and it is often easy to dust our hand with the minute spores.

When the spore of a fern lights on suitable moist soil it develops into a little plant which many people have never seen. This bears the male and female reproductive organs, and from its fertilised egg-cell there develops the spore-making fern plant.

In the time of the Old Red Sandstone the most prominent plants were ferns, horsetails, and club-mosses, along with some relatives of these, which are known only as fossils. There was a great vegetation of flowerless spore-plants, and it was from this stock that there arose the seed-plants, which by and by conquered the whole world.

FERNS AND MOSSES AS ANCESTORS OF FLOWERING PLANTS

It is a complicated story, and most of the chapters are still unread, but the main thing is that in very early times—probably in the age of the Old Red Sandstone—seed-plants arose from the great stock to which ferns, horsetails, and club-mosses belong. In the flowering plants that we are familiar with there are two kinds of spores, just as there are in water-ferns and some club-mosses—one kind of spore is represented by the pollen-grains produced by the spore-making organs we call stamens; and the other kind of spore is known as the embryo-sac, and is formed inside the spore-making organs we call *ovules*.

But the pollen grain (as we call the small spore of the flowering plant) contains, when ripe, three cells, and that is all that is left of the male generation. These three cells pass down the pollen tube which grows from the pollen grain when it is landed by wind or insect or otherwise on the tip of the pistil; and one of the three reaches the egg-cell inside the embryo-sac and fertilises it, so that a young plant begins to develop. It is interesting that in cycads, and in the maidenhair tree, the fertilising male cells should still be free-swimmers with many lashes, harking back to the free-swimming male cells of the great fern alliance. This shows the course of evolution.

THE EMBRYO AS THE GRANDCHILD OF THE PLANT IT GROWS ON

Turning to the other side of the flower, we find that the spores produced by the ovule are four embryo-sacs, one of which survives. This produces eight cells, and one of the eight is the egg-cell, which develops into a young plant in an ovule, and is called the seed. But, as Dr. Macgregor Skene has put it in his fine book on Common Plants, " the embryo is not the child of the plant on which it grows, by which, in the early stages of its life, it is nourished; it is the grandchild. Between the two there is an intermediate generation, reduced to a few cells, never having an independent existence, but still recognisable."

All this is difficult, but it is worth puzzling over, for it clears up the pedigree of plants in a wonderful way.

The passage from an ancient fern-stock to flowering plants was doubtless bound up with a more thorough conquest of the dry land, and with the more thoroughly aerial mode of life there came an elaborate protection of the offspring. The egg-cells and the embryos are carefully hidden away; the delicate offspring is bound in a close union with its parent; it is nursed, protected, and endowed with a legacy; and there are all sorts of arrangements securing that the seed is well scattered.

THE SEEDS THAT DRIFT ABOUT IN THE WIND

The young plant gets a good send-off in life. While the ancient spore-plants were spread about by spores, their successors, the seed-plants, are spread abroad by seeds; and this is the surer way.

In the geological Middle Ages (called the Mesozoic) there was a great wealth of cycad-like plants, along with their predecessors—the ferns, horsetails, clubmosses, and the extinct relatives of these. The cycads, the maidenhair trees, and the conifers are true seed-plants, but they do not quite rise to the level of flowering plants. In a pine tree the female cones bear on the upper surface of each scale two ovules which are quite naked. In early summer these scales open, and the pollen grains—each of which has two air-bladders or floats—are drifted by the wind and caught in a drop of sticky fluid on the tip of the exposed ovule. It is not till the next summer that the fertilisation of the egg-cell takes place, and it is not till the third year that the winged seeds are liberated and borne about by the wind.

The true flowering plants are divided into two great classes, the Dicotyledons—such as the buttercups, chickweeds, roses, and daisies; and the Monocotyledons—such as the lily and daffodil, the orchid and grass. Probably dicotyledons came first.

THE FLOWERING PLANTS THAT SURVIVED THROUGH CARING FOR THEIR YOUNG

Now, in the monocotyledons the leaves usually show a number of large strands joined by delicate cross connections; in dicotyledons the strands or bundles usually form a more noticeable network. The stem of a dicotyledon can go on growing in thickness indefinitely, but in most monocotyledons the stem does not increase in diameter after it is formed. Everyone is familiar with the tapering stem of an ordinary dicotyledonous tree, and the cylindrical stem of a monocotyledonous tree such as a palm. Finally the parts of the flower in monocotyledons are usually in threes, while the others are usually in fours or fives.

The different kinds of plants that belong to this vast Vegetable Kingdom are numbered in their tens of thousands, as is shown by the following list of the principal kinds which is compiled from estimates made by professors of Botany.

Group	Kinds
True Flowering Plants	200,000
Fungi	37,500
Seaweeds or Algae	14,000
Ferns	9300
Bacteria	2000

The large number of parasite plants is striking; but the Flowering Plants, with their great care for the young, have been the chief conquerors of the plant world.

THE CONQUEROR GOES HOME TO DIE

WILLIAM THE CONQUEROR IS BROUGHT TO THE ABBEY OF ST. GERVAIS TO DIE AMONG GREEN FIELDS

The Story of the Peoples of All Nations and Their Homelands

The Meeting of Harold and the Conqueror

THE CONQUEROR COMES

Now, when bands of Northmen were plundering and wasting England and Scotland, others went to the northern shores of what is now France, then the land of the Franks—formerly Caesar's Gaul—and settled there in the reign of Alfred. They gained the whole of the beautiful province called after them—Normandy, the land of the Northmen. They very soon left off speaking their own language, and learnt that of the Franks, which we call Norman-French.

These men were bold and very fierce, and they determined to take and keep all that came in their way. Their rulers were called Dukes. Emma, the wife of Ethelred the Unready, was the daughter of one called Richard the Fearless. Her son, Edward, was brought up in Normandy, after the family fled from England on account of the Danes, and as he grew up in a monastery he cared more for a quiet, learned life, and for attending services in church, than for fighting or looking after business.

So when the English had had enough of Danish kings—there were only three—and Edward was called back to be king, he was not at all fitted to take part in the stirring, anxious times in his fatherland,

and caused much discontent by favouring the Normans he brought with him.

A very strong English nobleman, Earl Godwin, kept him for a time in some measure to his duty. Edward's greatest pleasure was in building churches, and the most beautiful of all his churches was that of the Abbey at Westminster, built after the pattern of those he knew and loved so well in Normandy, with rounded windows and arches. This abbey church at Westminster was entirely rebuilt by later kings.

It is said that Edward promised his cousin, William of Normandy, that he should be King of England at his death; in any case William determined that King of England he would be. The gentle, white-haired, rosy-faced king—the Confessor, as he was afterwards called—died in January 1066. He was buried in his fine new church, finished only a few days before. Later, a beautiful tomb was raised over him, which we can see today in the heart of the Abbey.

The year 1066, which opened thus, was an important year for England, full of stirring history. The day after the weeping people had crowded the Abbey to see the funeral of Edward, they came back again to crown the successor whom they

THE FIVE CONTINENTS & 100 NATIONS & RACES THAT INHABIT THEM

had chosen—Harold, the son of Earl Godwin, whom they knew to be brave and wise, and a hater of the Normans.

And so, on that bright sunny day, in the keen north wind of January, the roof rang again with joyful shouts of " Yea! " when the old archbishop asked if they would have Harold for king.

When William heard that Harold had become king after Edward, he was furious and at once set to work to get an army and a fleet together to invade England and secure the crown he longed for. He said Harold had promised him the kingdom as well as Edward; but no one could really promise this, because it was the people's right to choose whom they would have as king.

THE BRIGHT SEPTEMBER DAY WHEN WILLIAM LANDED AT HASTINGS

When William landed at Pevensey, near Hastings, in bright September weather, Harold was at York. He marched his army down south by the great Roman road to London in nine days, and very quick that was, when so many had to go on foot. The battle of Hastings is one of the great battles of history. The Normans were led out by a singer on a fine prancing horse and the whole army caught up his song about the great hero of France and how he fought and won. The English did their best, but the Normans were too strong for them. Harold was killed, and the bravest of the best men of England fell fighting around him. This was on Saturday, October 14, 1066.

This battle, which greatly influenced our history for over 350 years, and had lasting effects on our language, has been pictured for us in tapestry scenes worked by Norman ladies who lived at the time.

The Bayeux Tapestry may still be seen in the ancient Norman town of Bayeux. It is worked with worsted on linen, like a sampler, in eight colours—by whom is not certain, though tradition says it was the Conqueror's wife who thus made history live with her busy fingers. Another tradition says it was William's half-brother Odo, Bishop of Bayeux, who, having fought in the battle, had the tapestry made to ornament his cathedral at Bayeux. Probably this is true, for Odo and his men are prominently represented on the tapestry. A third tradition says the great sampler was worked by Adela, William the Conqueror's daughter.

Whoever made it worked it while the scenes were fresh in the recollection of thousands, and it has continued in existence for at least 850 years, though a part at the end, showing the flight of the English, has perished. The tapestry is 231 feet long and 20 inches wide, and it tells the story of William's adventurous conquest in 72 scenes. It is by far the oldest picture of English history.

THE LONELY CROWNING OF WILLIAM THE CONQUEROR

By December William had forced the people of the south to own him as king, and he was crowned in Westminster Abbey on Christmas Day. No shouts of welcome, no bright faces, and when the question was asked, " Do you take William of Normandy to be your king? " there was but a sullen mutter; they *had* to say " Yes." William was almost alone on this great day.

Freedom for England was gone. The laws were changed, the poor were in utter misery. William gave much land and goods to his Norman followers, and, instead of paying rent in money, they had to promise to supply him with fighting men when he went to war. They made the men to whom they let land promise to do the same for them.

This feudal system, as it was called, lasted for many years in England. So that there should be no doubt how much land everyone had, and how many soldiers it was worth, William had a great book prepared, Domesday Book, in which is a description of all the great houses and estates in the kingdom.

THE WORK THAT THE CONQUEROR DID FOR ENGLAND

Another work of William's which lasts to this day was the making of the New Forest, in Hampshire. William made it to hunt in, and sorely distressed the poor folk who were turned out of their homes for his pleasure.

Some of the great castles William built to keep the English in order are still standing. Chief among them is the old part of the Tower of London, in which is a most perfect Norman chapel. It is said that from the gallery of this chapel William the Conqueror and his family looked down on the service below.

William spent a good deal of his time in Normandy, and in 1087 he died there. His sons behaved very badly to him, and he was alone in his death as he was at his

We give in these pages the famous Bayeux Tapestry, made for William the Conqueror not long after his conquest, and so eight centuries old. The original, about 19 inches high and over 200 feet long, is said to have been embroidered on linen by the Conqueror's wife, but that is uncertain. It has 623 men and women, 762 animals, 41 ships, and 37 buildings, the whole being here shown in the original colours.

28 z 1

Harold, sent to Normandy by King Edward the Confessor, rides to Bosham, on the Sussex coast.

Harold crosses the Channel in a fresh breeze, and makes for the lands of Count Guy of Ponthieu.

Adventure awaits Harold on French soil. As he lands from his vessel he is held a prisoner by Count Guy

Harold is taken as a prisoner to Beaurain in Normandy, but treated honourably by his captor.

Messengers from William reach Guy. The little figure holding the horses may represent perspective.

A messenger bearing the Count's answer delivers his dispatch to Duke William at his court.

Harold is brought to William. Guy rides ahead, and, nearing the Duke, points to his prisoner.

The party reaches the Duke's palace, where Harold explains to William his presence on French soil.

Harold marches with William to St. Michael's Mount, and rescues some of William's men at a ford.

The enemy is driven back to Rennes, but the final stand is made at Dinant, which is assaulted.

The town keys are surrendered. William rewards Harold by a gift of arms, and they march to Bayeux.

Here Harold takes a solemn oath to William on reliquaries. and returns home across the Channel.

Harold comes to the royal palace, where he is received by Edward, crowned and holding his staff with the feeble hand of a dying man.

King Edward dies, and his body is borne with signs of mourning and in solemn state to its resting-place in old Westminster Abbey.

This picture of the death of Edward follows that of his burying. Harold accepts the offered crown and other emblems of royalty.

On the left is Archbishop Stigand. On the right is a comet—probably Halley's comet—
at which the crowd is gazing in wonder.

The meaning of this incident is not clear, but it shows in detail an English ship making
ready to land on French soil.

Duke William takes the decisive step. Sitting in council he gives orders for a large
fleet to be built and equipped.

Here we see the building of the fleet, and men dragging the completed vessels to the water.

Loading of the fleet with supplies, including coats of mail, cross-bows, lances, and wine.

The invading fleet crossing the Channel to Pevensey. Note the large number of horses carried.

The Normans land on English soil. Note the horses coming ashore. Forage parties start out.

Bringing in captured supplies—sheep, cattle, and horses—by force of arms. The cooks at work.

A feast in progress; the meat is handed on spits. William in council with Bishop Odo and Robert of **Eu.**

The camp at Hastings is finished ; news of Harold arrives, and war begins with the burning of a house.

The Norman army marches out of camp eager to meet Harold and the sturdy defenders of English soil.

William (carrying a staff or mace) asks Vital for news of Harold's army. On the right are scouts at work.

A scout warns Harold of the approach of William's army. William addresses his men before the fight.

The Normans in battle array, inspired by their leader's words, advance against the foe.

The English are attacked on two sides and put up a stubborn fight against the charging horsemen.

The attack rages round Harold's bodyguard.   Here we see the slaying of his brothers Lewine and Gyrd.

Here the invaders are losing heavily.   Horses and men are falling, and the Saxons are hard beset.

Bishop Odo, holding a staff, heartens his men, and William lifts his visor to show that he has not fallen.

The last stand of the English takes place round Harold who is seen pulling an arrow from his face.

Harold and his standard-bearer having been slain resistance ends, and the victors pursue the fugitives.

This is an enlarged reproduction of part of one of the lower borders, representing farming operations.

coronation, when all but a few priests rushed out to join in the tumult going on outside the Abbey.

When Taillefer the minstrel led the Normans to victory at Hastings, tossing and catching his long sword as he rode forward on his gay, prancing horse, the words of his bold song were in French. What a roar of deep bass voices as the whole army behind him took up the air!

When the voice of the archbishop rang out in Westminster Abbey two months later, on Christmas Day, asking if it were the will of the people that William should be their king, he spoke first in French.

A HISTORY OF THE CONQUEST BY A MAN WHO KNEW THE MEN OF HASTINGS

There is in the British Museum a history of the Norman Conquest, in French, written by a man who knew many of those who had fought in the battle of Hastings. For many years authors wrote in French, because the king and his court, and nearly all the richest people in England, spoke French. There is an old poem written in French for the children of those times, with English meanings below, just as in the French lessons in this book. The writer of long ago says that he has so arranged it in order that the children may understand what they are reading, and when to use *son et sa, mon et ma, le et la*. Even the accounts of what was done in the law courts, and at the meetings of the Wise Men who helped the king to govern the country, were all in French.

But the use of the language spoken by Bede and Alfred did not die out, as some thought it would, any more than did the English nation, sorely oppressed as it was. By slow degrees the English and their language rose again; Normans married English wives, and naturally their children and grandchildren spoke both French and English. By slow degrees the use of French passed away, but the English which we speak now contains many words brought over by the Normans.

THE STORY OF THE NORMANS TOLD BY SIR WALTER SCOTT

If you read the fine story of Ivanhoe, by Sir Walter Scott—and everyone of us should read it, for it tells powerfully and with deep interest how the Normans and the English lived together more or less peacefully over a hundred years after the Conquest—you will find that English was enriched by being two languages welded together into one. There it is pointed out that the animals in the field, under the care of the English serving men, went by one name which was English, but when they were killed and placed on the table as food they took a French name. Thus the English cow in the pasture became changed into the French beef when it was cooked, and the English sheep appeared as French mutton; but now both these words have become equally good English.

Among other traces left by the Norman conquerors are the strong square towers, or *keeps*, to be seen not only by the banks of the Thames, but at Norwich and other places, especially at Rochester, where a magnificent tower still stands on the bank of the Medway as it stood in those Norman days. It is said that the Conqueror saw it. Most of these towers look strong enough now to stand a siege, and take us back to the days when the nobles shut themselves up in them, and sallied out to make prisoners and to steal and plunder. There was no redress for their unhappy neighbours.

THE CEASELESS COMING AND GOING ACROSS THE NARROW SEAWAY

All over England and the south of Scotland we find examples of the round arches and beautiful mouldings which go toward making what is called the Norman style. Some of the abbeys and cathedrals are still standing, having been repaired and added to through the centuries since the time of their founding; others are in ruins, without roofs, with grass and ivy showing up green against the grey stone. If we cross over to Normandy, we find many more of these buildings in the old home of the Normans; at Caen, where the Conqueror lies buried, and whence stone came in barges up the Thames to build old St. Paul's; at Bayeux, where the famous tapestry is kept; at Rouen, the old capital of Normandy, and scores of other places.

As we look out these places on the south side of the Channel let us think of the amount of coming and going there was across this arm of the sea, which lay in the midst of the dominions of the Dukes of Normandy who were also Kings of England. Barons and soldiers were constant travellers, for wars were unending then; traders, too, came and went; workmen and builders; fair ladies as brides, as well as the kings themselves, who had often to cross from side to side to look after their possessions. The pictures of the ships of those days, so beautifully painted by the monks in monasteries, suggest little comfort or room on board.

There was a man who fled over the Channel from Southampton and who must have felt in desperate anxiety for his ship to go quickly. He was a knight who on an August day in 1100 had been hunting in the New Forest with the king, who was the Conqueror's son William. Either by accident or not, the arrow he shot killed the king, and the knight was so frightened he rushed away to Normandy. You can see the stone set up in the beautiful forest to mark the spot. But there was no mourning for the Red King, William Rufus; people were glad and thankful when they saw the last of his red hair. His brother, Henry the First, was king after him. He was nicknamed Beauclerc, the French for "fine scholar." He began well by giving his people, three days after his brother's death, a letter in which he promised to set right the bad rule of his brother's time, and to keep the laws of Edward and Alfred.

INTERESTING THINGS TO BE SEEN IN THE BRITISH MUSEUM

There are many of these letters (or charters) that we can see in the Manuscript Room of the British Museum, promises of all kinds about lands and government, made through many years of history. The earliest belong to Saxon times, and we can find on them many names that we already know, such as Edgar, who rowed on the Dee; Canute the Dane, who rebuked the flattering courtiers when they asked him to command the waves of the sea to stop; and Edward the Confessor, who built old Westminster Abbey.

Henry had pleased the English very much by marrying a princess of Scotland, belonging to the old Royal Family of Alfred and Edgar. They felt now that they had some share in their country, and took heart once more. Queen Maud was a good woman, and she helped her husband in many ways. He put down the oppressive power of the nobles and destroyed many of their castles. He also helped the poor to get justice. Henry lost his only son when the boy was 18. He was drowned while crossing the Channel.

The fine new White Ship, in which Henry had been persuaded to let his son

travel, struck on a rock, and only one of all the passengers managed to hold on to the wreck till morning. The king never recovered from the great shock.

Though the nobles promised to take his daughter Matilda for their queen at his death, it was Henry's nephew Stephen who succeeded him in 1135.

THE WAILING OF THE PEOPLE WHEN THE LAND BORE NO CORN

In Henry's reign the Anglo-Saxon Chronicle begun by Alfred came to an end. Matilda and Stephen disputed long for the crown. One old Chronicle gives an account of Matilda escaping from Oxford with her companions over the Christmas snow all dressed in white, so as not to be seen. Fighting went on, and the barons began building castles again and taking people's property from them and doing as they liked till all the good Henry had tried to do in securing peace and quiet and justice was undone. "The land bare no corn," wails the historian. "You might as well try to till the sea as the land for the wickedness that is done in it."

When Stephen died, in 1154, Matilda's son became King Henry the Second. His wife Eleanor was a French princess, heiress of three provinces in France, while Henry was Duke of Normandy and overlord of Brittany, so that his dominions reached from the North of England to the Pyrenees, the great mountain range which separates France and Spain.

Much as he had, he was always going to war and planning to get more; especially he wanted to be king over the whole of the British Isles. After restoring order in England, by destroying castles and reestablishing the power of the courts of justice, he made the Scottish king give up Northumberland, Cumberland and Westmorland, all south of the Cheviot Hills.

THE WILD WAYS AND THE WILD CHIEFS OF THE IRISH

He tried to get Wales and Ireland, without success; but the only Englishman who was ever Pope of Rome lived at this time, and made Henry a present of Ireland, because it was said then that all islands belonged to the Pope, and that he could do what he liked with them.

Naturally, the Irish did not agree to this. They preferred their own wild ways, with wild chiefs always struggling and fighting together; and though Henry succeeded in getting some sort of order in the part of

THE WORK THE NORMANS LEFT BEHIND

The Manor House at Boothby Pagnell in Lincolnshire

The beautiful cloister court of Fountains Abbey in Yorkshire

Patrixbourne doorway in Kent

The north transept of Ely Cathedral

The gate at Kilpeck in Herefordshire

The Prior's doorway, Ely Cathedral

The Norman staircase at Canterbury

The old Norman Chapel at the Tower of London

The massive columns of Canterbury

The lofty nave of Rochester Cathedral

The magnificent interior of Old Shoreham Church in Sussex

Ireland that was nearest to England, things were as bad again, as soon as he was gone. A French king said of him with amazement: "The King of England is now in Ireland, now in England, now in Normandy. He may be rather said to fly than to go by horse or boat!"

If we go to Canterbury Cathedral we see the spot where the great archbishop of the time of Henry the Second met his death. His name was Thomas à Becket. He had quarrelled with the king about some Church affairs, chiefly about how the clergy were to be punished when they did wrong. It is said that the trouble began partly in the walls of the castle of Eynsford, which still stand in the valley of the River Darent, in Kent.

THE FOUR MEN WHO CAME FROM NORMANDY TO KILL A MAN

Henry, in a passion one day, said he wished someone would rid him of the troublesome archbishop. So four men hastened over from Normandy, where King Henry then was, and, taking the king at his word, killed Becket in his cathedral. The steps that lead to the spot where the archbishop was buried are worn by the knees of pilgrims who for long years went to pray at the tomb of the man who had suffered for boldly defending the clergy against the king.

Henry was not forgiven till he had walked barefooted and bareheaded to the chapel, and received a beating with rods from each of the monks in turn. Before he died he portioned out his great dominions to his sons; but they did not like his keeping the overlordship in his own hands, and there were miserable family quarrels in consequence. When the name of his favourite son John was found on the list of those fighting against him, the old man could bear no more. Turning his face to the wall, he said bitterly, " Let things now go as they will. I care no more for myself or for the world."

RICHARD THE CRUSADER, AND HOW HE GOT HIS MONEY FOR HIS WARS

His son Richard the First then became king. His statue, set up in front of the House of Lords at Westminster, shows him as a fine figure on a strong horse, clothed in armour made of little rings of metal, and holding aloft the long sword he used against enemies far away from England. During his reign (1189-1199) he was nearly always away fighting.

The great barons took advantage of Richard's absence to break out again, and the people suffered much from bad trade and bad cultivation of the fields, and from having nearly all the money they had squeezed out of them.

Of all things, Richard loved fighting and adventure best, and in his time the most exciting adventures were to be had in the Holy Land, at the eastern end of the Mediterranean Sea. The country and its capital, the scene of our Lord's life on Earth, had fallen into the hands of men who did not believe in Him, and who treated very badly the Christians who went to pray at the spots that were so sacred to them. So the Christians of Europe went on expeditions or Crusades, hoping to win back the Holy Land.

Anyone can see to this day in London a sight that carries the mind back to those chivalrous and stirring times. An Order of Knights was formed to patrol and guard the way by which pilgrims travelled from the sea coast of Palestine to the site of the Temple at Jerusalem, and the members of the Order were called Knights Templars. They belonged to all Christian lands, and one of their greatest and richest centres was in London.

RICHARD FORGIVES HIS ENEMY ON HIS DEATH-BED

If from the Strand you enter the Temple through an arched doorway you will find the Templars' ancient church. It has been greatly altered in recent years, but it is still a thrilling link with these Crusaders of old.

Richard joined the third of these expeditions, and he needed a great deal of money for the journey. He even sold a treaty which had been gained by his father from the Scottish king, in which he, Henry, was acknowledged as overlord for the whole of Scotland. Once the fever of the Crusades was on men, they seized what money and arms they could lay hands on, sewed strips of cloth like a cross on their arm, and hurried off by sea and by land to gain renown in fighting the enemies of Christ.

Round the base of Richard's statue in Westminster are shown the scenes of his death at the siege of a castle in France. On one side is the terrible fight going on; on the other the king lies on his bed, pardoning the man whose arrow caused the wound from which he is dying.

Illustrated Maps of All Countries with Many Thousand Pictures

THE MEN OF THE AGES—BRITON, ROMAN, SAXON, DANE, AND NORMAN, PASS DOWN THE ROAD OF TIME
THROUGH ENGLISH HISTORY

An Old Stone
Figure

Bronze Jug found
in Kent

A Gateway in the
Roman Wall

A Stone Figure of a
Lady

A Tessellated Pavement
from London

Sarcophagus found in London

Arches of a Roman House in Northumberland

The Heating Chamber in the Darenth Villa

Foundations of an Old Roman House

The Roman Wall at Rochester

Lion and its prey by a Roman Sculptor

A Roman Bowl from Darenth

A FEW VISIBLE FRAGMENTS OF ROMAN BRITAIN

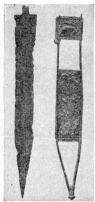

Small Statue found in Lincolnshire

A Sculpture found near Bishopsgate

An Altar, with Inscriptions

Iron Sword and its Bronze-plated Scabbard

Statue found in Suffolk

Hadrian's Wall across Britain

Roman Villa under a field at Darenth, in Kent

A Rare Bronze Tablet

A Stone Tablet with Figures

A Roman Spearman

A Beautiful Vase

Capital of a Roman Column

Figure of a Warrior

WHAT THE ROMANS LEFT BEHIND THEM

Stonehenge, one of the oldest monuments in Britain

A British house in the Bronze Age

Doorway of an ancient British house

An old British village and a stone there for grinding corn

A stone circle of the Bronze Age—probably the scene of great gatherings

HOUSES AND TEMPLES OF OLD ENGLAND

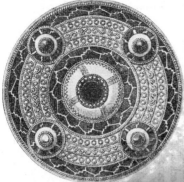

A Beautiful Brooch found at Sarre in Kent

A Saxon Cross at Hexham

The only authentic portrait of King Alfred

St. Martin's Cross and Ruins on Iona Island

The Fine Old Saxon Church at Bradford-on-Avon

A Buckle found in Kent Anglo-Saxon Pendants, a Ring, and a Necklace A Brooch Buckle

The Seat of Sanctuary in Hexham Abbey

St. Augustine's Chair in Canterbury Cathedral

The Old Saxon Tower of the church at Earls Barton

SOME OF THE THINGS THE SAXONS LEFT BEHIND

THE INTERESTING NATURAL FEATURES OF THE BRITISH ISLES

Scotland has 2500 miles of coast line, or one mile to every 12 square miles of area

The northern area of Scotland is largely moor and forest in which red deer are preserved

Fissure volcanoes, like those of Iceland, vents in the earth from which lava welled up, were once common in the Hebrides

Sea here is more than half a mile deep

Counting small islets the British Islands number about 5000

The sea here is nearly a mile deep

Fingals Cave   The Giants Causeway

Fingal's Cave, Staffa, and the Giant's Causeway, Antrim, were caused by lava shrinking as it cooled and splitting up into columns as drying starch splits

In some parts of Donegal the layers of rock have been bent up and folded over themselves

Lough Neagh, 150 square miles, the biggest lake in the British Isles

This coast is slowly rising out of the sea

Prevailing winds in this direction

STAFFA

FINGALS CAVE

GIANT'S CAUSEWAY

FOCHABERS

This coast is slowly rising out of the sea

ORKNEY ISLANDS

Here, at Fochabers, are earth pillars that have been washed by rain out of a mass of conglomerate that once filled the valley

Loch Lomond, 45 square miles, is the largest lake in Great Britain

GLASGOW

ARRAN

Arran was once a great glacier bed

At Partick Park, Glasgow, the remains of a coal measure forest can be seen with its tree trunks above ground

The isolated Bass Rock is the plug or neck of an ancient volcano

Active volcanoes once existed at Berwick

The lake district was once a great volcanic area

The sea here is 300 feet deep

In Yorkshire are many swallow holes, funnel shaped chasms in the limestone into which streams disappear

SHETLAND ISLANDS

The north of Shetland is as near to Norway as to the mainland of Scotland

The soil of the Orkneys is very shallow and only about a half of the area is cultivated

ORKNEY ISLANDS

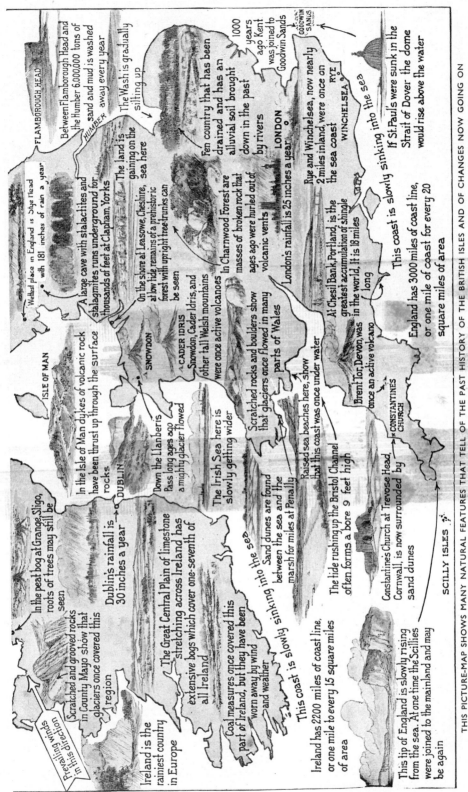

FLAMBOROUGH HEAD

Between Flamborough Head and the Humber 6,000,000 tons of sand and mud is washed away every year

HUMBER

The Wash is gradually silting up

Fen country that has been drained and has an alluvial soil brought down in the past by rivers

1000 years ago Kent was joined to Goodwin Sands

GOODWIN SANDS

LONDON

London's rainfall is 25 inches a year

Rye and Winchelsea, now nearly 2 miles inland, were once on the sea coast

RYE

WINCHELSEA

This coast is slowly sinking into the sea

If St Paul's were sunk in the Strait of Dover the dome would rise above the water

England has 3000 miles of coast line, or one mile of coast for every 20 square miles of area

At Chesil Bank, Portland, is the greatest accumulation of shingle in the world. It is 18 miles long

Brent Tor, Devon, was once an active volcano

CONSTANTINES CHURCH

Constantines Church at Trevose Head, Cornwall, is now surrounded by sand dunes

SCILLY ISLES

This tip of England is slowly rising from the sea. At one time the Scillies were joined to the mainland and may be again

The tide rushing up the Bristol Channel often forms a bore 9 feet high

Raised sea beaches here, show that this coast was once under water

Sand dunes are found between the sea and the marsh for miles at Penally

Scratched rocks and boulders show that glaciers once flowed in many parts of Wales

The Irish Sea here is slowly getting wider

This coast is slowly sinking into the sea

Ireland has 2200 miles of coast line, or one mile to every 15 square miles of area

Coal measures once covered this part of Ireland, but they have been worn away by wind and weather

The Great Central Plain of limestone stretching across Ireland has extensive bogs which cover one-seventh of all Ireland

Ireland is the rainiest country in Europe

Dublin's rainfall is 30 inches a year

DUBLIN

Down the Llanberis Pass long ages ago a mighty glacier flowed

CADER IDRIS

Snowdon, Cader Idris, and other tall Welsh mountains were once active volcanoes

SNOWDON

In Charnwood Forest are masses of broken rock that ages ago were hurled out of volcanic vents

On the shore at Leasowe, Cheshire, a low tide remains of a prehistoric forest with upright tree trunks can be seen

The land is gaining on the sea here

A large cave with stalactites and stalagmites runs underground for thousands of feet at Clapham, Yorks

In the Isle of Man dykes of volcanic rock have been thrust up through the surface rocks

ISLE OF MAN

Wettest place in England is Stye Head with 181 inches of rain a year

Scratched and grooved rocks in County Mayo show that glaciers once covered this region

In the peat bog at Grange, Sligo, roots of trees may still be seen

Prevailing winds in this direction

THIS PICTURE-MAP SHOWS MANY NATURAL FEATURES THAT TELL OF THE PAST HISTORY OF THE BRITISH ISLES AND OF CHANGES NOW GOING ON

THE LAST HEROISM OF SIR PHILIP SIDNEY

Sir Philip Sidney, lying on the battlefield at Zutphen in a raging fever, called for a cup of water, and was about to place it to his lips when his eye caught the gaze of a wounded comrade. Sir Philip stretched out his arm and gave the water to the dying man, saying : " Soldier, thy need is greater than mine."

One Thousand Poems of All Times and All Countries

ON SIR PHILIP SIDNEY

Sir Philip Sidney, who was born in 1554 and died in 1586 from the result of a wound received while fighting in the Netherlands, was one of the most beautiful characters of his time. Although we know him as one of the finest poets of the Elizabethan period, none of his poems was printed during his lifetime, and the fame which he enjoyed in his own day was largely due to his personal character. Whenever we wish to think of a true hero and a Christian gentleman, Sir Philip Sidney's name comes to mind. This poem was written by Sir Fulke Greville, who also wrote his life

SILENCE augmenteth grief, writing increaseth rage,
Staled are my thoughts, which loved and lost the wonder of our age;
Yet quickened now with fire, though dead with frost ere now,
Enraged I write I know not what; dead quick, I know not how.

HARD-HEARTED minds relent, and Rigour's tears abound,
And Envy strangely rues his end, in whom no fault she found;
Knowledge his light hath lost, Valour hath slain her knight:
Sidney is dead, dead is my friend, dead is the world's delight.

PLACE, pensive, wails his fall, whose presence was her pride;
Time crieth out, " My ebb is come, his life was my springtide ";
Fame mourns in that she lost the ground of her reports,
Each living wight laments his lack, and all in sundry sorts.

HE was—woe worth that word—to each well-thinking mind
A spotless friend, a matchless man, whose virtue ever shined,
Declaring in his thoughts, his life, and that he writ,
Highest conceits, longest foresights, and deepest works of wit.

HE only like himself was second unto none
Where death—though life—we rue, and wrong, and all in vain do moan,
Their loss, not him, wail they that fill the world with cries,
Death slew not him, but he made death his ladder to the skies.

NOW sink of sorrow I, who live, the more the wrong,
Who wishing death, whom death denies, whose thread is all too long,
Who tied to wretched life, who look for no relief,
Must spend my ever-dying days in neverending grief.

HEART's ease and only I like parallels run on,
Whose equal length keep equal breadth, and never meet in one,
Yet for not wronging him, my thoughts, my sorrow's cell,
Shall not run out, though leak they will, for liking him so well.

FAREWELL to you, my hopes, my wonted waking dreams !
Farewell sometime enjoyed joy, eclipsed are thy beams!
Farewell, self-pleasing thoughts which quietness brings forth,
And farewell friendship's sacred league uniting minds of worth.

POEMS · SONGS · BALLADS · VERSES AND RHYMES WITH MUSIC

And farewell, merry heart, the gift of
    guiltless minds,
And all sports which, for life's restore,
    variety assigns,
Let all that sweet is void! In me no
    mirth may dwell;
Philip, the cause of all this woe, my life's
    content, farewell!

Nor rime, the scourge of rage, which art
    no kin to skill,
And endless grief which deads my life, yet
    knows not how to kill,
Go seek that hapless tomb, which if ye
    hap to find,
Salute the stones that keep the lines that
    held so good a mind.

QUEEN MAB

Thomas Hood, who died in 1845, was a very gifted poet and
brave man. He wrote several poems that will never be forgotten, and when battling with ill-health and disease he
wrote many comic poems which have set everybody laughing who has read them. For he could be humorous as well
as pathetic, gay as well as sad. In Queen Mab he is
neither, but just fanciful, which suits young folk best of
all. Queen Mab, of course, reigns over the fairies.

A LITTLE fairy comes at night,
    Her eyes are blue, her hair is brown,
With silver spots upon her wings,
    And from the moon she flutters down.

She has a little silver wand,
    And when a good child goes to bed
She waves her wand from left to right,
    And makes a circle round its head.

And then it dreams of pleasant things,
    Of fountains filled with fairy fish,
And trees that bear delicious fruit,
    And bow their branches at a wish:

Of arbours filled with dainty scents
    From lovely flowers that never fade;
Bright flies that glitter in the sun,
    And glow-worms shining in the shade.

And singing birds with gifted tongues
    For singing songs and telling tales,
And pretty dwarfs to show the way
    Through fairy hills and fairy dales.

But when a bad child goes to bed,
    From left to right she weaves her rings,
And then it dreams all through the night
    Of only ugly, horrid things!

  .   .   .   .   .

Then wicked children wake and weep,
    And wish the long black gloom away;
But good ones love the dark, and find
    The night as pleasant as the day.

THE SANDS OF DEE

Charles Kingsley, who wrote this fine ballad, was a master
of this form of poetry. How much he can tell in so little
space! Notice how the weird picture of the cruel sea that
drowned poor Mary is brought before our mind's eye by the
repetition of certain words in the first three lines of the
second and fourth verses. It is a legend that the voice of
the drowned maiden can be heard still calling the cattle
home. This, of course, is one of those fancies that come to
our minds in listening to the strange noises of the sea.

O MARY, go and call the cattle home,
    And call the cattle home,
    And call the cattle home,
Across the sands of Dee.
The western wind was wild and dank with
    foam,
    And all alone went she.

The western tide crept up along the sand,
    And o'er and o'er the sand,
    And round and round the sand,
    As far as eye could see.
The rolling mist came down and hid the
    land;
    And never home came she.

" Oh! is it weed, or fish, or floating hair—
    A tress of golden hair,
    A drowned maiden's hair,
    Above the nets at sea? "
Was never salmon yet that shone so fair
    Among the stakes on Dee.

They rowed her in across the rolling foam,
    The cruel, crawling foam,
    The cruel, hungry foam,
    To her grave beside the sea.
But still the boatmen hear her call the
    cattle home
    Across the sands of Dee.

THE TEST

Emerson here suggests—as is indeed true—that Time will
at last winnow all the lines of the poets until only the sound
and the true remain indestructible—five lines from five
hundred it may be. By constant search wise readers and
critics seek to find from the poets of all the ages, and help
to treasure when found, those few deathless lines.

I HUNG my verses in the wind,
    Time and tide their faults may find.
All were winnowed through and through,
Five lines lasted sound and true;
Five were smelted in a pot
Than the South more fierce and hot;
These the siroc could not melt,
Fire their fiercer flaming felt,
And the meaning was more white
Than July's meridian light.
Sunshine cannot bleach the snow,
Nor time unmake what poets know.
Have you eyes to find the five
Which five hundred did survive?

TOM BOWLING

This song by Charles Dibdin is the most popular of all sea songs, and deservedly so for its pure and simple pathos.

HERE, a sheer hulk, lies poor Tom Bow-
    ling,
  The darling of our crew;
No more he'll hear the tempest howling,
  For death has broached him to.
His form was of the manliest beauty,
  His heart was kind and soft;
Faithful below he did his duty;
  But now he's gone aloft.

Tom never from his word departed,
  His virtues were so rare.
His friends were many and true-hearted,
  His Poll was kind and fair:
And then he'd sing, so blithe and jolly,
  Ah, many's the time and oft!
But mirth is turned to melancholy,
  For Tom is gone aloft.

Yet shall poor Tom find pleasant weather
  When He who all commands
Shall give, to call life's crew together,
  The word to pipe all hands.
Thus Death, who kings and tars dispatches,
  In vain Tom's life has doffed:
For, though his body's under hatches,
  His soul has gone aloft.

A CHILD'S THOUGHT OF GOD

Elizabeth Barrett Browning, the author of these beautiful verses, was a great poetess and the wife of Robert Browning, a great poet. Her pure and simple mind enabled her to see things with the clearness of a child's faith, and her power of words to express herself in noble poetry. Here she gives a wonderful idea of God's constant care and watchfulness over those of us who seek to do His will.

THEY say that God lives very high!
  But if you look above the pines
You cannot see our God. And why?

And if you dig down in the mines
  You never see Him in the gold,
Though from Him all that's glory shines.

God is so good, He wears a fold
  Of heaven and earth across His face—
Like secrets kept for love untold.

But still I feel that His embrace
  Slides down by thrills through all things
    made,
Through sight and sound of every place:

As if my tender mother laid
  On my shut lids her kisses' pressure,
Half waking me at night, and said:
  "Who kissed you through the dark,
    dear guesser?"

A RED, RED ROSE

The following is one of the most beautiful of the many love songs by Robert Burns. The style of the song is of an earlier day than his own, and different versions of it have been printed, but it is here given as it first appeared in a Scottish collection of songs to which the poet contributed.

O MY luve's like a red, red rose
    That's newly sprung in June;
O my luve's like the melodie
    That's sweetly played in tune.

As fair art thou, my bonnie lass,
    So deep in luve am I;
And I will luve thee still, my dear,
    Till a' the seas gang dry.

Till a' the seas gang dry, my dear,
    And the rocks melt wi' the sun;
I will luve thee still, my dear,
    While the sands o' life shall run.

And fare thee weel, my only luve!
    And fare thee weel a while!
And I will come again, my luve,
    Though it were ten thousand mile.

TRUE GREATNESS

The writer of this fine poem was Lady Elizabeth Carew, or Carey, who lived in the early years of the seventeenth century. She was a relative, on her mother's side, of the great poet Edmund Spenser, and died in the year 1635. The word seld in the last verse is, of course, the same as seldom, but even a poet would now hesitate to use the word, though our language has not changed greatly since the time of Elizabeth, when modern English was established.

THE fairest action of our human life
    Is scorning to revenge an injury:
For who forgives without a further strife
    His adversary's heart to him doth tie:
And 'tis a firmer conquest truly said
To win the heart than overthrow the head.

If we a worthy enemy do find,
    To yield to worth, it must be nobly
        done—
But if of baser metal be his mind,
    In base revenge there is no honour won.
Who would a worthy courage overthrow?
And who would wrestle with a worthless
        foe?

We say our hearts are great, and cannot
        yield;
    Because they cannot yield it proves
        them poor:
Great hearts are tasked beyond their power
        but seld:
    The weakest lion will the loudest roar.
Truth's school for certain does this same
        allow,
High-heartedness doth sometimes teach
    to bow.

SHAKESPEARE

Matthew Arnold in this fine sonnet conveys a splendid sense of Shakespeare's eminence over all the master-minds that have written in the English language. "Others abide our question" means that, while other great poets or thinkers may be open to question, Shakespeare speaks through his immortal verse with so divine a voice that we feel it is the very voice of truth itself and cannot be questioned.

OTHERS abide our question. Thou art free.
 We ask and ask—Thou smilest and art still,
Out-topping knowledge. For the loftiest hill
That to the stars uncrowns his majesty.

Planting his steadfast footsteps in the sea,
Making the heaven of heavens his dwelling-place,
Spares but the cloudy border of his base
To the foiled searching of mortality:

And thou, who didst the stars and sun-beams know,
Self-schooled, self-scanned, self-honoured, self-secure, [so!
Didst tread on earth unguessed at. Better

All pains the immortal spirit must endure,
All weakness that impairs, all griefs that bow,
Find their sole voice in that victorious brow.

THE FAIRIES

Written by William Allingham, who died in 1889, this is one of the most beautiful poems about fairies. Grown-up people used to believe in fairies, and in Ireland, not so very long ago, grown-ups would talk about fairies just as children do, so that Allingham, who was born in Ireland, no doubt got to know and love the "wee folk" he sings about.

UP the airy mountain,
 Down the rushy glen,
We daren't go a-hunting
 For fear of little men;
Wee folk, good folk,
 Trooping all together;
Green jacket, red cap,
 And white owl's feather!

Down along the rocky shore
 Some make their home,
They live on crispy pancakes
 Of yellow tide-foam;
Some in the reeds
 Of the black mountain-lake,
With frogs for their watch-dogs,
 All night awake.

High on the hill-top
 The old King sits;
He is now so old and grey
 He's nigh lost his wits.
With a bridge of white mist
 Columbkill he crosses,
On his stately journeys
 From Slieveleague to Rosses;

Or going up with music
 On cold, starry nights,
To sup with the Queen
 Of the gay Northern Lights.
They stole little Bridget
 For seven years long;
When she came down again
 Her friends were all gone.

They took her lightly back
 Between the night and morrow,
They thought that she was fast asleep,
 But she was dead with sorrow.
They have kept her ever since
 Deep within the lake,
On a bed of flag-leaves,
 Watching till she wake.

By the craggy hill-side,
 Through the mosses bare,
They have planted thorn-trees
 For pleasure here and there.
Is any man so daring
 As dig them up in spite,
He shall find their sharpest thorns
 In his bed at night.

Up the airy mountain,
 Down the rushy glen,
We daren't go a-hunting
 For fear of little men;
Wee folk, good folk,
 Trooping all together;
Green jacket, red cap,
 And white owl's feather!

GOOD-NIGHT, GOOD-NIGHT

Joanna Baillie was one of the most famous women writers in the first half of the last century. Her poetry was read throughout the English-speaking world, and several of her plays were performed with success. She wrote these lines.

THE sun is down, and time gone by,
 The stars are twinkling in the sky.
Nor torch nor taper longer may
Eke out a blithe but stinted day;
The hours have passed with stealthy flight,
We needs must part: good-night, good-night!

The lady in her curtained bed,
The herdsman in his wattled shed,
The clansmen in the heathered hall,
Sweet sleep be with you, one and all!
We part in hopes of days as bright
As this gone by: good-night, good-night!

Sweet sleep be with us one and all!
And if upon its stillness fall
The visions of a busy brain
We'll have our pleasures o'er again,
To warm the heart, to charm the sight.
Gay dreams to all! Good-night, good-night!

LITTLE VERSES FOR VERY LITTLE PEOPLE

JOY OF LIFE

THE sun is careering in glory and might
　　'Mid the deep blue sky and the
　　　clouds so bright;
The billow is tossing its foam on high,
And the summer breezes go lightly by;
The air and the water dance, glitter, and
　　play—
And why should not I be as merry as they?

The linnet is singing the wild wood
　　through,
The fawn's bounding footsteps skim over
　　the dew,
The butterfly flits round the blossoming
　　tree,
And the cowslip and bluebell are bent by
　　the bee:
All the creatures that dwell in the forest
　　are gay,
And why should not I be as merry as they?

Mary Russell Mitford

GENTLE, JESUS, MEEK AND MILD

GENTLE JESUS, meek and mild,
　　Look upon this little child;
Pity my simplicity,
Suffer me to come to Thee.

Fain I would to Thee be brought,
Gracious God, forbid it not;
In the kingdom of Thy grace
Grant Thy little child a place.

Charles Wesley

THE LITTLE STAR

TWINKLE, twinkle, little star;
　　How I wonder what you are!
Up above the world so high,
Like a diamond in the sky.

When the blazing sun is gone,
When he nothing shines upon,
Then you show your little light,
Twinkle, twinkle, all the night.

Then the traveller in the dark
Thanks you for your tiny spark;
He could not tell which way to go
If you did not twinkle so.

In the dark blue sky you keep,
And often through my curtains peep;
For you never shut your eye
Till the sun is in the sky.

As your bright and tiny spark
Lights the traveller in the dark,
Though I know not what you are,
Twinkle, twinkle, little star.

Jane Taylor

I MUST NOT TEASE MY MOTHER

I MUST not tease my mother,
　　For she is very kind;
And everything she says to me
　　I must directly mind;
For when I was a baby,
　　And could not speak or walk,
She let me in her bosom sleep,
　　And taught me how to talk.

I must not tease my mother;
　　And when she likes to read,
Or has the headache, I will step
　　Most silently indeed:
I will not choose a noisy play,
　　Nor trifling troubles tell,
But sit down quietly by her side,
　　And try to make her well.

I must not tease my mother;
　　I've heard dear father say.
When I was in my cradle sick
　　She nursed me night and day;
She lays me in my little bed,
　　She gives me clothes and food,
And I have nothing else to pay
　　But trying to be good.

I must not tease my mother;
　　She loves me all the day,
And she has patience with my faults,
　　And teaches me to pray.
How much I'll strive to please her
　　She every hour shall see;
For should she go away or die
　　What would become of me?

Mrs. Sigourney

WHAT MIGHT HAVE BEEN

THE little birds are singing
　　Above their speckled eggs,
The daddy-long-legs talks about
　　His children's lovely legs.

The red cow thinks her little calf
　　The best that there can be,
And my papa and my mamma
　　Are very proud of me!

And yet I might have been a bird,
　　And slept within a nest,
Or been a daddy-long-legs,
　　With scarcely any chest;

Or been a little calf or pig,
　　And grown to beef or ham;
I'm very, very, very glad
　　That I am what I am!

Frederic E. Weatherly

Upon yon nearest rock-top
  Can you see a dwelling stands?
Ah, 'tis the sweetest dwelling
  Found in these mountain lands!

It holds the sweetest lady!
  She is rich with golden hair,
Has clever, busy fingers,
  Though so small and lily fair.

They wash, they starch, they broider,
  They can spin, mix oaten cake,
And grind the white wheat finely
  The dainty loaves to bake.

And when that sweetest lady
  Shall be mine, my own to hold,
Ah, Earth to match her beauty
  Will wear a crown of gold!

&

Little Robin Redbreast sat upon a
    hurdle,
With a pair of speckled legs and a green
    girdle.

&

Baby and I
  Were baked in a pie,
The gravy was wonderful hot!
  We had nothing to pay
  To the baker that day,
And so we crept out of the pot.

&

Pretty flowers, tell me why
  All your leaves do open wide
Every morning when on high
  The noble sun begins to ride?

Rose dreamed she was a lily,
  Lily dreamed she was a rose;
Robin dreamed he was a sparrow;
  What the owl dreamed no one knows.

But they all woke up together
  As happy as could be.
Said each: "You're lovely, neighbour,
  But I'm very glad I'm me."

&

Pussy-cat ate the dumplings,
  Pussy-cat ate the dumplings!
Mamma stood by, and cried, Oh fie!
Why did you eat the dumplings?

&

The Robin and the Wren
  Fought about the porridge-pan;
And ere the Robin got a spoon
The Wren had ate the porridge down.

&

Bless you, bless you, bonnie bee!
  Say, when will my wedding be?
If it be tomorrow day
Take your wings and fly away.
Fly away east, or fly away west,
And show me where *he* lives who
  loves me the best!

&

Hey, my kitten, my kitten,
  And hey, my kitten, my deary!
Such a sweet pet as this
  Was neither fat nor weary.

A NURSERY RHYME OF THE CHILDREN OF FRANCE

Here is a French nursery rhyme. To the little French children it is as familiar as "Jack and Jill" and "Old Mother Hubbard" are to us. The English version does not pretend to be an exact translation of the French, because it would be impossible to find one to rhyme.

AU TEMPS JADIS

Le bon temps que c'était,
  Du temps que la reine Berthe filait!
Dans ce temps de miracles
Les docteurs guérissaient sans brevet,
Et comme des oracles
Les avocats parlaient sans bonnet,
Les rois que le temps prospère!
Alors n'avaient à faire
Que leurs quatre repas,
Et se croiser les bras;
Mais cela se passait
Du temps que la reine Berthe filait!

IN THE DAYS OF LONG AGO

Oh! what a happy time, 'tis said,
  When good Queen Bertha spun her
    thread!
For in that wonder-working day
The doctors cured, nor asked for pay;
The lawyers, men of great renown,
When pleading wore no wig and gown;
And kings who lived at that time, too,
Had very little else to do
Than eat four hearty meals a day,
Then simply fold their arms, they say;
But then this all took place, 'tis said,
When good Queen Bertha spun her
  thread!

734

The Story of Where Power Comes From, What It Does, & How It Works

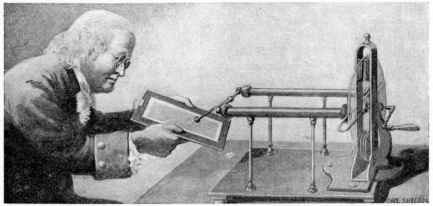

One of the first devices for storing electricity—Benjamin Franklin and his pane of glass

THE STORAGE BATTERY

As long as a dynamo is driven by a steam-engine, or some other kind of power, it continues to produce electricity. As soon as it stops, the electric current it has been generating stops too.

But electricity is provided by batteries as well as dynamos. The electrical energy comes from chemical energy which is freed when the electricity is taken from the battery cell.

The primary battery, the type which is used in pocket torches and portable radios, is exhausted when the chemical energy has been used up. The secondary battery, or accumulator, can be re-charged by connecting it to a suitable direct current electrical supply. Thus, this type can be used to store electricity, but only in comparatively small amounts. Large amounts, for example, for lighting a town, are nearly impossible to store, unless large quantities of water and suitable reservoirs are available.

There are many instances where a store of electricity is absolutely necessary. The case of the electric car is one. An electric delivery van can usually run for a distance of fifty or sixty miles, its supply of current being self-contained or stored up in a battery fixed in a box beneath the body. Every motor-car is provided with a storage battery. This is charged by a dynamo, driven by the petrol engine, and stores up energy as the car is running, which provides current for the lamps, the self-starter, radio, indicators, and often the wind-screen wiper.

One of the first instruments for storing electricity was invented by Benjamin Franklin and was known as Franklin's pane. It was a pane of glass with a large sheet of tinfoil pasted on each side, and by connecting it with a frictional machine it was possible to store a certain amount of static electricity. But static electricity, as we have seen, has entirely given place to the more powerful currents of the galvanic or voltaic battery, or the dynamo, and as such currents produce very pronounced chemical changes, it followed that the storage battery was devised.

A battery which could be charged with electricity and could be made to give the electricity back again was discovered in 1860 by Gaston Planté. It consisted of two sheets of lead rolled up together, with strips of some insulating material, such as flannel, between them, to prevent the two plates touching one another. This roll of the separated lead plates was placed in a mixture of sulphuric acid and water, and the current from a dynamo was connected

ELECTRICITY · WIRELESS · OIL · GAS · MOTORS · ENGINES · SHIPS

with the two plates until bubbles of gas were given off at their surface. On disconnecting the cell, and connecting its plates with some apparatus requiring a current, such as a lamp, it was found that the cell gave out the electric energy that had been produced and stored within it.

An electric storage cell may be looked upon as something capable of receiving, retaining, and giving up again the energy put into it from a dynamo or from an ordinary electric battery. Such a cell must not be thought to store electricity *as electricity*. The electric energy put into the cell is changed into chemical energy, and this chemical energy is again turned into electricity when the cell is discharged.

THE TRANSFORMATION OF MECHANICAL ENERGY INTO CHEMICAL ENERGY

Here, indeed, is a wonderful example of the different forms in which energy can exist.

A great rock high up on some mountain slope possesses potential energy, for if it were dislodged it could drop down upon something below and crush it. The stick of dynamite used by the miner to break up the rock is harmless enough to look at, yet on exploding it releases the energy of a hundred horses. In the accumulator, mechanical energy that has already been turned into electric energy is once again changed into chemical form energy. The joining up of the two ends of the accumulator with an electric motor will release the chemical energy and endow the motor with the power required to work a machine.

The modern accumulator, used on an immense scale in these days, is simple in construction. The positive and negative elements, or plates, are made in the form of flat grids, lead perforated or honeycombed, and filled with a paste of oxide of lead.

THE PRESSURE WHICH MAY EQUAL 200 TONS IN MAKING A CELL

In the type of plate invented by Faure red lead oxide is used in making the positive plates, and on the passage of an electric current gives a final hard paste of lead sulphate and lead peroxide. The negative plate, on the other hand, is filled with litharge, which becomes reduced to a spongy black form of lead when the cell is charged. These pastes are forced into the lead grids under tremendous pressure, sometimes being equal to as much as 200 tons.

The amount of electricity that can be stored in an accumulator depends very largely on the area of the plates, and in order to keep each cell of a convenient size the larger ones are made up of a number of positive and negative plates placed alternately in big vessels, all the negative and all the positive plates being connected together so that in each cell there are just the two terminals, positive and negative.

The average voltage of a cell is only two volts, so that where an accumulator battery is wanted for electric lighting, fifty or a hundred or more cells must be used, according to the voltage of the lamps. By connecting the positive of one cell to the negative of the next, and so on—which is called joining the cells *in series*—the voltage becomes multiplied by the number of cells.

The amount of electric energy that may be stored in a battery depends on the area of the surface of the positive plates in any one cell. If the battery could light a hundred lamps, each requiring an ampere of current for ten hours, the " capacity " of the battery would be 100 multiplied by 10, or 1000 *ampere-hours*.

THE STORAGE OF ELECTRIC POWER LIKE THE WINDING OF A SPRING

Six or twelve-volt accumulators used in motor-cars are usually of from 60 to 100 ampere-hours' capacity. Thus the *voltage* of an accumulator depends on the number of cells that are connected in series, and the *capacity* depends upon the number of square inches of surface of the positive plates in one of the cells.

What is the secret of these simple grids that lie inert-looking in a vessel of weak sulphuric acid? What happens when energy is stored up in the plates, or robbed from them?

The real elements that play their parts are very finely divided lead metal in the negative plate and peroxide of lead in the positive plate. When energy is being stored up in the cell, metallic lead is deposited on the negative plate, and sulphuric acid is generated, while oxygen is set free at the positive plate, forming oxide of lead.

These chemical changes represent the storage of electric energy. It is like winding the spring of a clock, which tries hard to unwind, and in so doing drives the clockwork mechanism until the spring is unwound. In a similar way the lead deposited on the negative plate tries to combine with the sulphuric acid to form sulphate of lead, and in so doing it releases hydrogen gas, which travels in the form of *ions* to the positive plate, combines with oxygen, and causes a compound of lead to be formed. This at once unites with the sulphuric acid to form sulphate of lead. The accumulator can be charged and discharged thousands of times.

WHY THE ACCUMULATOR MUST BE CHARGED FROM TIME TO TIME

So many small accumulators are used today for electric lighting and in motor-cars that some remarks may well be made about their general behaviour and upkeep.

There are two serious faults in the lead accumulator. One is the weight ; the other the fact that a charged battery when not in use will gradually lose its charge. Both these faults have been in some measure overcome within recent years.

Accumulators must be charged with current from time to time, and are quickly ruined if they are allowed to stand " empty " for any length of time.

When freshly charged, each cell will give rather less than two and a half volts, and if the accumulator be made to light a lamp the voltage will soon drop to two volts, and will then remain fairly constant until about three-fourths discharged, when it will drop in voltage by a quarter-volt.

THE ACID AND PURE WATER IN THE BATTERY CELLS

The lead grids must be always just covered with acid, and to make up for loss by evaporation a little distilled, or pure, water must be added from time to time.

In many batteries of the portable type, the acid is mixed with glass wool or a special kind of chemical jelly so that the acid cannot spill. A more recent invention is a *dry* storage battery, which is of course unspillable.

Edison invented a storage battery in which iron and nickel take the place of lead; these metals are only one-fourth of the weight of lead, though the complete battery is heavier than the lead type. Year after year the great American inventor toiled at his experiments, and ultimately he was rewarded with success.

In his battery the positive plates consist of tubes of nickel-plated steel held in a nickelled steel frame. The tubes are made from finely perforated strips and are filled with nickel hydroxide and thin layers of plate nickel. The negative plate has twenty-four flat pockets of nickel steel finely perforated and filled with oxide of iron. A solution of caustic potash is used in place of the sulphuric acid of the lead battery.

Edison was able to equip a comfortable little brougham type of car with a light battery containing sufficient electricity to drive it for fifty or sixty miles.

Many of these Edison batteries are used today, though they have by no means replaced the standard types of lead battery, because they are more expensive and have disadvantages for some uses. They are, however, very strong and will stand many knocks.

Thus the lead battery still possessed many advantages. It was left to a Canadian inventor to discover a form of accumulator that has put a new complexion on the problem of electric traffic. A lead accumulator was discovered which could not only be charged with electricity in a shorter time, but would retain the power imparted to it by a dynamo for a longer time. The new discovery showed a way of making a plate offer an immensely greater surface, and thus the weight of the battery could be reduced considerably.

SMALL BATTERIES WHICH RETAIN THEIR POWER FOR LONG PERIODS

Improvements in storage batteries have been made by many other people, and it is now possible to make lead plates of far less weight than before which will not only retain their charge for a long time but will occupy a much smaller space.

A later type of power battery was invented by an Irishman named Drumm. The Drumm battery could be charged, like the Edison, at a high speed and it would stand discharging at a great rate without injuring the plates. It is no longer made. Quick charging of traction batteries is very important, as it means that they can be charged with electricity in eight hours against the twelve hours or more which are required for the ordinary type of cell.

The motor-car dynamo automatically charges its battery. Other batteries are charged automatically by plugging in to a " charger " in a garage. When the mains voltage is alternating a metal rectifier is usually incorporated in the " charger," which rectifies the current to D.C.

The electric grid has largely modified the scope of the storage battery. The enormous voltages at which current can be transmitted for long distances with overhead cables makes it possible to supply a locomotive with direct power all the way along a line for hundreds of miles.

MODIFYING THE ALTERNATING CURRENT OF THE ELECTRIC GRID

The high tension electricity supplied by the grid is *alternating*. The poles of the dynamo become alternatively positive and negative in respect of each other many times every second. In order to charge an accumulator with current supplied by the grid it is necessary either to rectify it so that it can be applied to the battery afterwards in one direction, or it must be used to drive a motor which in turn will drive a direct current dynamo.

Suppose the electric car were of twenty horse-power and with a fully charged battery would run for ten hours. If the motorist wanted to refill his battery in half an hour he would have to " pour in " electric current on a scale of 400 horse-power! Special electric supply mains and switchboards would be required to deal out huge currents like this.

THE NUMEROUS WAYS IN WHICH THE STORAGE BATTERY IS USED

Nowadays the storage battery is used in a surprising number of ways. Anywhere electricity is required in a portable form provides a possible application. An interesting example is in ships, to supply emergency lighting. Small portable batteries are carried by miners to light the lamps in their caps when they go in their search for coal underground. The Telephone Exchanges are large users of batteries, and rely on them entirely for supplying the current to the telephone network. Every train carries a storage battery under each of its coaches. These are charged by dynamos coupled directly with one of the axles and provide the carriages with light. In some cases small trains themselves are being driven by power obtained from storage batteries. Battery-driven electric engines are used in mines for hauling coal and carrying men.

Many of us have seen the electric " pram " which the milkman or the baker brings round with him in place of his horse. The van in which he rides is often driven by batteries.

The battery-electric vehicle is clean, for there are no exhaust fumes. It is easy to drive because it has no gears and is supreme when short distances of about fifty miles have to be covered each day with many stops. For this reason battery-electric industrial trucks are much used for transporting goods in factories and docks.

There are many types of these trucks. Electric trucks are to be seen on the platforms of railway stations, pulling long lines of trailers loaded with luggage. The fork lift truck has a pair of prongs in front of it which can pick up bales and boxes. Not only can it carry them along but can also stack them up to about 15 feet high.

Some river launches and canoes are driven by electric motors which are supplied from batteries. But probably the best-known example of battery work is the submarine.

THE POTENTIAL ENERGY STORED-UP IN THE ACCUMULATOR GRID

An example of the use of small storage batteries is seen in obtaining power from the *wind*. Wind-wheels or miniature wind-mills are used in America for driving small electric generators which store up their current in an accumulator. The wind-wheel is automatically brought to face the wind, so that no wind power is wasted, and although at times there may be only light breezes, power is being continually stored up for use for lighting and other purposes. Experimental wind towers are being erected in Great Britain. In these the generators will be connected to the electric grid instead of to batteries.

A fascinating feature of the accumulator plate or grid is that when it is once charged with electricity in its liquid cells it can be actually removed, dried, and sent away to some distant place, when, as soon as it is set up again in a vessel filled with acid, it will give out its pent-up energy.

As surely as energy in the form of oil or petrol can be sent from the bowels of the earth to some other continent across the sea in a tank steamship, so electric energy can be sent from one spot to another in the form of " potential " energy stored up in the chemical composition of the accumulator grid.

Imperishable Thoughts of Men Enshrined in the Books of the World

Spenser reading one of his poems to Sir Walter Raleigh

THE POET WHO FOLLOWED CHAUCER

IF, five years before the death of Queen Elizabeth, anyone had asked in London who was the greatest poet of that time, when English literature was approaching its topmost height, the answer given would not have been William Shakespeare. The answer of the poets themselves, and they were many, would have been Edmund Spenser.

And we can understand, though no one would give the same answer now, that it was a natural reply to give then, and not absurd. For poetry had not at that time begun to include plays as the most splendid part of its wide domain.

Blank verse, the form in which our grandest poetry is written, had only recently come into use, and had not been enriched with the finest thought in the world of books outside religion. Poetry then was rhymed verse, and the greatest mass of English rhymed verse, sweet beyond all other verse in the English tongue, had been written by Edmund Spenser. If we were still thinking of poetry as rhymed verse only, or chiefly, we should give Spenser a place on the list of poets alongside the greatest.

So we must not pass him lightly by. He was the one great poet between Chaucer and Shakespeare—a period of 200 years —and he had as lasting an influence on English poetry as Chaucer had. Chaucer fixed the language and made it melodious; but his melody had not been sustained. Spenser revived the melody of our tongue, and so added to it that his tunefulness has been echoing through English poetry ever since. He is known especially as the poets' poet.

There are two reasons for this distinction. One is that nearly all his poems are purely fanciful. They do not deal with human life and character, as poetry did when it again enlarged its bounds by taking in great plays, as in the far-off days of the Greek drama. Spenser's poems are concerned with pleasing creations of the mind, dainty fancies, pretty parables with graceful and often useful meanings; but they are not concerned with the common stuff of plain life. It takes a poet to appreciate them fully. And, then again, they are deliciously sweet in their wording, and that feature can be appreciated best by fellow poets.

Yes, to the men of his own day he was their leading poet, though Shakespeare was alive, and no doubt knew Spenser. Shakespeare was twelve years younger than Spenser, and was a lad of fifteen when Spenser was acknowledged as the poet of his period. When Spenser died, thirteen years before Shakespeare died, the greater

ROMANCE · HISTORIES · DRAMAS · ESSAYS · WORLD CLASSICS

poet had not written his greatest works, and, indeed, Spenser, in his " Tears of the Muses," referred to " our pleasant Willy " :

That same gentle Spirit from whose pen
Large streams of honey and sweet nectar flow.

But Shakespeare was not then writing the works which made him famous; and it is now Spenser himself who somewhat more than satisfies us with his "honey and sweet nectar," while Shakespeare's bounty, left to all succeeding ages, is illimitable.

Chaucer, Spenser, and Milton are the only men in our list of the conspicuous English poets who lived an active public life apart from their work as poets. They were alike in being first and foremost poets born, yet they drudged at the kind of duties we now call Civil Service. Spenser frankly hated his work.

LONDON BOY WHO WROTE A CALENDAR FOR COUNTRYMEN

He was London born from a Lancashire stock, and on leaving Cambridge sought a career at the Court, where he was a friend of Sir Philip Sidney, and associated with the Earl of Leicester, an acquaintance that did him no good when that nobleman fell from royal favour.

Before he obtained official employment as Secretary to the Lord Lieutenant in Ireland he had published his Shepherd's Calendar, a pastoral poem that gave him the first place among contemporary poets, and showed his skill in using a wide variety of verse forms while commemorating the twelve months of the year.

The Shepherd's Calendar, an entirely artificial poem, as far from real life as the make-believe play of imaginative children, showed at least that Spenser had a quick sense of style in writing, and style was much admired in the days when the old literatures of Greece and Rome were being revived, and the newer literature of Italy was setting the fashion.

THE GROUP OF KINDRED SPIRITS WHO BRIGHTENED THEIR AGE

Spenser's greatest friend was Sir Philip Sidney, himself a poet and a most elaborate stylist in prose writing. Also Sidney was a man of singular purity of character and nobility of spirit, and Spenser showed himself a kindred spirit in all his writings. Walter Raleigh was another member of the same company. What a knightly group they must have made—Sidney, Spenser, Raleigh! Perhaps Sidney was fortunate in his early death, for he left a spotless name; while Spenser and Raleigh lived on into grave misfortune.

Sent to Ireland, then as now a land of strange violence, the poet felt himself to be in exile; but his value as a secretary was known—he proved it by writing a prose book on the state of Ireland—and he was kept there in spite of all his plans for release, and for employment under happier surroundings.

It was in Ireland that he planned the twelve books of his Faery Queen, the fanciful poem that preserves his fame; and there, too, he wrote six books of this work which still exist. Some of the poem was lost, and the rest not completed; but to us that does not matter, for we have as much of it as we want.

Spenser's weaknesses as a writer were, first that he had not the power of making a clear and manageable tale, but became involved as " in endless mazes lost; " and then that his writings were far off from real life. He lived in a twilight of romance, amid shadowy figures. And, as suited this fanciful world of the mind alone, his diction was continuously sweet and melodious, with words as well as tones that were, even then, purposely old-fashioned.

THE POEM OF THE FAERY QUEEN WITH A REAL QUEEN IN IT

And so he has sweetness without strength. But sweetness was what the literature of our country needed just then. It had more than sufficient ruggedness in the immediate past as it was splashed forth from the spluttering pens of poets like John Skelton.

The Faery Queen suited the age for which it was written, an age that has Sidney's Arcadia as its most popular prose romance. The poem was really a poetical dressing up of the old entertainment that was called a Morality Play. Certain virtues and their opposing vices were pictured as knights or ladies, or as monsters or tempting witcheries, and engaged in mildly adventurous contests.

Thus Holiness, Temperance, Chastity, Justice, Courtesy, and other benign figures came into contact with Falsehood, Pride, Unbelief, Lawlessness, and other harmful influences, amid surroundings that are wholly fanciful and strange. The poem is a collection of allegories; but it is complicated by the characters having a

POOR, TIRED, AND WORN OUT, SPENSER WAS LAID TO REST IN A GRAVE IN THE ABBEY, INTO WHICH HIS
POET FRIENDS THREW MOURNFUL POEMS AND THE PENS THAT HAD WRITTEN THEM

second meaning beyond their moral teaching. The more prominent of them were designed to represent living people, with Queen Elizabeth as the centre of the group. All this personal reference is useless lumber now, and only some of the moral suggestions remain; but what is left of real value is much pure poetry in singularly melodious words. Spenser, indeed, bequeathed to those who have followed him a style well worth knowing, but to be used with discretion.

THE POETS WHO FLUNG THEIR POEMS AND PENS INTO SPENSER'S GRAVE

How well his fellow poets appreciated him was seen when, driven from Ireland in great danger during one of the many insurrections that broke out, he arrived in London ill and impoverished, and there died before his sorry plight was fully understood. His funeral in Westminster Abbey was attended by a concourse of his fellow poets, who, acknowledging him as a master in the divine art, threw their pens and poems into his grave.

As examples of the mellowness of Spenser's fancies and of the tones in which they are expressed, we may take two scenes in which the good people he pictures are being lulled into a sense of peace and security in order that they may be the better tempted. The first is a gentle knight who finds himself resting in a magician's hut while passing through the wandering wood of Error.

And more to lull him in his slumber soft,
  A trickling stream from high rock tumbling down,
And ever drizzling rain upon the loft
  Mixed with a murmuring wind, much like the sound
Of swarming bees, did cast him in a swowne.
  No other wise, nor people's troublous cries
As still are wont t'annoy the wallèd town
  Might there be heard; but careless Quiet lies
Wrapt in eternal silence far from enemies.

THE MAJESTIC STANZA INVENTED BY EDMUND SPENSER

This is the nine-lined verse which Spenser invented, and which, known as the Spenserian stanza, has been used by many later poets, notably by Byron in Childe Harold. It consists of eight lines, each with ten syllables or five beats, followed by a ninth line of twelve syllables, or six beats, that ends the stanza with a lingering, restful sound that may, with the use of dignified words, become majestic. An even better example is to be heard in

the description of the Bower of Bliss of an enchantress, where all kinds of sweet sounds unite to charm those who are being tempted to their ruin.

Eftsoons they heard a most melodious sound
  Of all that might delight a dainty ear,
Such as at once might not on living ground,
  Save in this paradise, be heard elsewhere.
Right hard it was for wight who did it hear
  To rede what manner music that might be;
For all that pleasing is to living ear
  Was there consorted in one harmony—
Birds, voices, instruments, winds, waters, all agree !

The joyous birds, shrouded in cheerful shade,
  Their notes unto the voice attempered sweet
Th' angelical soft trembling voices made
  To th' instruments divine respondence mete ;
The silver-sounding instruments did meet
  With the bass murmur of the water's fall;
The water's fall, with difference discreet,
  Now soft, now loud, unto the wind did call;
The gentle warbling wind low answeréd to all.

THE MOST BEAUTIFUL WEDDING POEM IN THE ENGLISH LANGUAGE

Besides his Faery Queen and Shepherd's Calendar Spenser wrote with equal sweetness on love in its most refined forms.

His Epithalamion, written to commemorate his marriage when he had reached the substantial age of 42, is the most beautiful poem of its kind in the English language. It overflows with admiration of his bride's beauty, alike in form and character. His Prothalamion, hymning the marriage of two pairs of friends, is scarcely less successful. In it Spenser tells, in outline, the story of his own life, for he is one of the poets who, happily, has not hesitated to intermingle his personal affairs with his lyrical outpourings, and so provide posterity with facts that otherwise might not have been known. Even his courtship is traced in the sonnet form which he was foremost in introducing from the Italian tongue.

His personal poems, Mother Hubbard's Tale, and Colin Clout's Come Home Again expressing his longing to leave his Irish exile, and the Tears of the Muses, regretting the decline of poetry—a bad instance of misjudgment—are all interesting historically ; but it is his mixture of dainty fancy with the melody of words that gives him a secure place in our literature. As has been said by a fine critic, in words worthy of Spenser himself, in the pageant of the English poets Spenser should ride on a white horse and blow a silver trumpet.

The Great Words that Stir the Hearts and Minds of All Mankind

Immense Distance in space—Watching a star whose light left on its journey at the time of the defeat of the Spanish Armada by Sir Francis Drake, taking three hundred years to reach the Earth

DISTANCE

ONE night a lady said to a visitor : "We find it a great nuisance having our post-office half a mile away."

At that moment her husband entered the room. "I have been looking at Saturn," he said, "a glorious sight." "Ah," said the visitor, "that is farther off than your post-office !" "It is eight hundred and eighty-three million miles from the Sun," replied the astronomer.

Distance can be a great nuisance and a great blessing. Even a mile may be a nuisance when we are tired, or a quarter of a mile when a swimmer is seized with cramp at a distance from the shore; and yet what a blessing it is that the Sun is so far away from the Earth, and the Arctic regions from our British Isles!

The queer thing about distance is that it varies with circumstances. If you were staying at a house thirty miles away from a cathedral city, and the only means of getting there was a donkey-cart, the distance would seem for your purpose something like the distance of the Moon from the Earth. But if your host had a good pair of horses you would reckon your visit to the city as a day's work; if he kept a high-powered motor-car you would consider the visit as a morning's excursion;

if he had an aeroplane you would think of the city merely as a milestone on your way from one side of England to the other.

Like everything else in the world, distance is *relative*. You can think of it only in relation to something else. It is a good distance from London to York, but how trivial that distance seems when we think of the distance from Liverpool to Quebec. But the journey from London to York would seem infinitely farther than the journey from Liverpool to Quebec if we walked the one and made the other by an aeroplane.

There is another strange way of looking at distance. Many years ago an Indian student said to the writer, "The steamship has enormously increased the distance between England and India." What did he mean? In the old days of the sailing ships Englishmen returned home to the British Isles only at very long intervals of time; and so they lived for years together in India, and got to know the people intimately, and a real affection existed between them—the affection of knowledge. But the steamship made the journey so quickly that Englishmen went home almost every year, and no longer regarded India as their other home, with the result

LIBERTY · JUSTICE · SPACE · DISTANCE · MOVEMENT · TRUTH · FAITH

that *the distance between the Englishman and the Indian became greater than it was before the invention of the steamship.*

This moral distance is well worth thinking about. You may know one man for years, yet never know him at all. But you may meet another person for the first time and feel in half an hour that you know all about him; something in him destroys the distance between you. The French have a striking phrase of this "something:" they call it *le terrible don de la familiarité*, which means, "the terrible gift of intimacy." But it need not be terrible; the power which destroys the distance between one soul and another is affection, and this power must be unselfish to do its work.

One other aspect of moral distance is extremely interesting. There is no geographical distance so great as the distance between an illiterate person and the highest pleasures of human existence. A savage standing in the great reading-room of the British Museum would be as far away from the delight and beauty packed into those shelves as a butterfly in Devonshire from the chrysanthemums of Japan. A child who learns to read is building himself a plane which will annihilate the distance between him and El Dorado. He may be poor, yet richer than Solomon; he may be weak, yet stronger than Samson; he may be solitary, yet the friend of kings. What the steamship and the plane do to physical distance, education does to moral distance.

ONE OF THE GREATEST WORDS IN THE POLITICS OF THE WORLD

At the present moment distance is one of the greatest words in the politics of the world. Most people in the British Isles want to forget war, to banish hate, to settle down to work hard and live happily. But in some of the smaller countries people may exclaim: "Ah, you would change your tone if you had a powerful and ambitious country as your neighbour."

The answer we make to this objection shows how wonderfully the human mind is turning its attention more and more from mere physical distance to moral distance. We say to these people: "It is true that you are much nearer to a possible enemy than we are, and we sympathise with your anxieties, which are perfectly natural after recent wars; but we suggest to you that the moral distance between you is so tremendous that it makes your physical nearness a still greater inconvenience. We

think you would not be disturbed by that physical nearness if you destroyed the moral distance between you and your neighbours by sympathy and friendship."

This idea is the inspiration of those of us who believe in the United Nations. We say that wars are made by nations living at great moral distances from each other, and that if those distances can be destroyed we shall have peace on Earth, goodwill among men. We argue that if the railway, the steamship, the aeroplane, the cable, and wireless communication can destroy geographical distance, so the spiritual nature of man, if it is developed, can destroy the moral distances which imperil the world's peace and rob us all of a reasonable prosperity.

THE LIGHT OF STARS THAT PERISHED MILLIONS OF YEARS AGO

This same idea is to be found in all true religion. There are people who say: "How absurd it is to suppose that God takes any interest in our ridiculously little planet swimming like a grain of sand in the boundless ocean of ether! Consider the question of star distances. They overwhelm us, they crush us to the Earth, they annihilate the idea that we are of any importance to the universe.

"Why, so far away are the stars from this little Earth that their total light, as far as we are concerned, is represented by the effect of a one candle-power lamp at a distance of twelve yards. The distance of the nearest fixed star is three thousand times the diameter of the solar system. Think of this: 200,000 light years equals more than one million million million miles! Many of the stars we see in the sky may have perished millions of years ago, the light which still reaches us from them being vibrations in the ether, which began their journey before ever this Earth was made. And yet men speak of God, and a life after death!"

GOD THE CREATOR AND SPIRIT OF THE UNIVERSE

Religion replies to these people who say this by asking them: "How do you reach up into the heavens to take the diameter of the solar system, to measure the suns, to weigh the planets, to fix the position of invisible stars? You do that by means of instruments. You invent instruments which annihilate these immense distances. So we, by prayer and love, destroy the distance which separates the creature from the

Creator. Small our Earth may be, but it is a part of the universe; a thing of three-score-years-and-ten may be the creature man, but he is mind, and what else is real but mind? Nothing; not even distance."

Thus it comes about that men no longer think of God as a great potentate living at so crushing a distance from this planet that He neither sees us nor heeds us. We think of Him as the Spirit of the whole universe, and feel that He hears us even when we do not utter the thoughts and longings of our hearts, and that He cares for us even when we wander far from the path He has chosen for our advance.

Inspired men caught this idea of *God's immanence*, as we now call it, long before the era of modern science.

Whither shall I go from thy Spirit (cries the psalmist), or whither shall I flee from thy presence? If I take the wings of the morning and dwell in the uttermost parts of the sea, even there shall thy hand lead me, and thy right hand shall hold me.

The only distance which exists between the Creator and the creature is the moral distance made by sin. But even that distance vanishes away into unreality as soon as the hardened heart breaks with repentance. No utterance of human lips concerning distance is so moving as the words of Jesus in His story of the prodigal son: " *But while he was yet afar off* his father saw him, and was moved with compassion, and ran, and fell on his neck, and kissed him."

All distance exists only for those who are "afar off." There is no distance between Homer and our own day for the scholar of Greek literature; no distance between Earth and sky for astronomers and poets; no distance between God and man for those who love goodness. All distance is a relative thing, as Einstein and others have shown. Great is the distance between a

ALL DISTANCE IS CONQUERABLE BY KNOWLEDGE: ROMNEY'S PORTRAIT OF A READING GIRL

European navvy and a pygmy of Darkest Africa, but not greater than the distance between that navvy and men like Kelvin and Pasteur. To destroy distance we must destroy ignorance. Our sailors have destroyed the ignorance which kept the savage man in his hollowed tree trunk, our investigators of the ether have destroyed the ignorance which rested its faith in the telegraph wire and the deep-sea cable, our physicians have destroyed the ignorance which imprisoned the human mind in magic, and our idealists are destroying the ignorance which keeps the nations sundered by hate and fear.

All distance is conquerable by love and knowledge. The word means *standing apart*. It represents the *stance*—the position—of the human mind. Let that stance be one of love and longing, and the object, moved by compassion, comes toward us, compelled by that moral earnestness of our heart and mind to yield us its intimacy.

The thought of vast distances can never overwhelm a mind which has reflected deeply enough to see that all distances are its own creation. The philosopher learns from the astronomer that the Earth moves to points two hundred million miles apart, and from the physicist that it would take millions of atoms to cover an inch in a straight line, each of these atoms containing electrons which have as much space to move about in, relative to their size, as the Earth in the sky; and he hears these things with neither dismay nor despair, for he has learned to think of the whole universe as the creation of Mind.

Therefore, with quiet heart and steady gaze, he looks toward the infinitely Great and the infinitely Small, seeing them not separated by incalculable distances, but as a unity in which he too has his place.

AND JACOB WENT NEAR UNTO ISAAC HIS FATHER; AND HE FELT HIM, AND SAID, THE VOICE IS JACOB'S VOICE, BUT THE HANDS ARE THE HANDS OF ESAU

The Story of the Most Beautiful Book in the World

ISAAC AND HIS SONS

ISAAC, son of Abraham, was married to Rebekah, and he loved her tenderly.

He became a rich man. He not only increased his flocks and herds, but set himself to plough land and grow corn. His courage and his skill both helped to make his wealth. When famine came he did not sit down and mourn, but moved away to more fertile country, and made a fresh start.

When his wealth made other people envious, and they stopped up his well so that his flocks and herds might perish, he quietly set himself to dig other wells and prayed to God for His protection.

God, who had blessed Abraham, blessed his son Isaac, and appeared to him in the midst of his troubles, saying: I am the God of Abraham thy father; fear not, for I am with thee, and will bless thee, and multiply thy seed for my servant Abraham's sake.

Isaac rested in this promise. His character was so calm and noble, his life so honourable and beautiful, that even those who had sought to do him harm became his friends, and confessed that God had blessed him.

After nineteen years of marriage, Rebekah gave birth to two sons, Esau and Jacob. The joy of Isaac was now complete. His farming prospered, his heart was filled with peace, and his sons grew up in health and strength to rejoice the years of his old age.

These two boys were very different in character. Esau, the elder, was what we should call an outdoor lad; he loved riding and hunting, he was strong and powerful, he rejoiced in the splendid and dangerous risks of a wild life. Jacob, on the other hand, was a quiet and thoughtful lad; he was adored by his mother, who kept him at her side, and he preferred thinking to action.

We can imagine how his mother would tell him of his wonderful grandfather, the rich and powerful Abraham, who had seen visions of God, and to whom God had made the promise that his children should be a great nation. Jacob would think much of these things.

Esau probably thought little about Abraham and his dreams. All he cared about was the joy of hunting and the exercise of his bodily strength. In some ways he was a fine character, for he was free from avarice—he did not think how rich he would be when his father died, and he was not proud of being the eldest son and the heir.

He married women of a tribe which greatly displeased his father. He did not care. He probably laughed when his

GREAT FIGURES OF THE OLD TESTAMENT · THE LIFE OF JESUS

father reproved him. And yet we know that in spite of this disobedience Isaac loved his brave, gallant, and wilful son.

Reckless and wild was this bold hunter. He came home one day hot and weary from the chase, and found Jacob preparing a dish of food, the smell of which was very pleasant to him. He asked for it, and Jacob replied that the food should be Esau's if Esau would give him his birthright. Esau agreed; for a dish of food, because he was hungry and faint, he gave up his privilege as the eldest son of Abraham's son, Isaac.

HOW JACOB AND HIS MOTHER DECEIVED THE DYING ISAAC

Such were the characters of these two men. Esau, reckless and careless, but brave and generous; Jacob, gentle and thoughtful, but inclined to cunning.

When their father Isaac was an old man, and his eyes were dim, he called Esau to his side, and told him to take bow and arrow and go out to shoot venison and return to him with the meat, that he might lay his hands upon his eldest son and bless him.

Rebekah heard these words, and directly Esau had gone she whispered to Jacob that he should go and kill two kids, and she would make meat of them, and he should carry it to his father and receive the blessing. It was the advice of a mother tempted by love for her favourite child; and Jacob agreed to do as she desired, only saying that he feared to be discovered. "Behold, Esau my brother is a hairy man, and I am a smooth man: my father peradventure will feel me, and I shall seem to him as a deceiver."

THE STEALING OF THE BIRTHRIGHT AND THE GREAT BITTERNESS OF ESAU

Then Rebekah dressed him in Esau's clothes, and put the skins of animals on his arms and neck. They set themselves to deceive the blind, old, dying man.

Jacob carried the meat to his father, and his father was surprised. They spoke together in this manner, the father troubled by suspicion, the son trembling with shame and fear:

ISAAC : Who are thou, my son?

JACOB: I am Esau thy firstborn; I have done according as thou badest me. Arise, I pray thee, sit and eat of my venison, that thy soul may bless me !

ISAAC: How is it that thou hast found it so quickly, my son?

JACOB: Because the Lord thy God brought it to me.

ISAAC: Come near, I pray thee, that I may feel thee, my son, whether thou art my very son Esau or not. The voice is Jacob's voice, but the hands are the hands of Esau. Art thou my very son Esau ?

JACOB: I am.

Thus Jacob received the blessing.

When Jacob had gone out, and Isaac lay alone in the dim chamber, thinking of God's promises to his father Abraham, and praying that the son whom he had just blessed might receive the guidance of God, lo! there came in to the poor old man his son, his elder son, Esau, whom he loved with a deep passion.

Isaac, his father, said unto him, "Who art thou?" And he said, "I am thy son, thy firstborn Esau." And Isaac trembled, and said, "Who? Where is he that hath taken venison and brought it me, and I have eaten of all before thou camest, and have blessed him? Yea, and he shall be blessed."

When Esau heard the words of his father, he cried with a great and bitter cry, and said unto his father, "Bless me, even me also, O my father!"

ONE OF THE MOST PATHETIC SCENES IN THE BIBLE STORY

This scene is one of the most pathetic and beautiful in all the writings of the world. Who cannot see the horror in the dying, sightless eyes of the grand old farmer, and the bitter repentance of the reckless son as he knelt there, knowing, too late, that he had squandered his birthright? We can almost hear the sobbing of the hunter, and see the trembling of the dying patriarch.

Esau's fury against the brother who had supplanted him was deep and terrible. He vowed to kill him. But Rebekah heard of this, and, making a pretence that she wished Jacob to marry one of their own people, she persuaded Isaac to let Jacob go to her brother Laban, who lived far away, and there find a wife.

Her purpose was to send Jacob away only until Esau's wrath had vanished, but her purpose was frustrated by the will of God. She had sinned; she had taught Jacob to deceive, and her sin, though prompted by love, must meet its punishment.

(Next chapter in this group, page 865)

748

The Interests and Pleasures of Life for All Indoors and Out

A TOY TO MEASURE THE WIND

ANY boy can make an interesting toy that will enable him to appreciate the force of the wind, and even, to some extent, to tell its speed.

The first things required are two pieces of wood 3 inches square and half an inch thick. Through the middle of each square make a hole about three-eighths of an inch in diameter. Now take four pieces of wood 15 inches long, 2 inches wide and half an inch thick. Near one end of each of these pieces make a round hole 1 inch in diameter.

Now take the two square pieces and nail the four long pieces in position, as shown in picture 2, keeping the inside ends of the long pieces a little distance away from the hole in the middle of the square pieces. Care must be taken to place the four pieces exactly at right angles, and this can be tested by measuring the distances from tip to tip of any two adjoining ones. These distances should be all alike, and the result is something resembling the top of a signpost at two crossroads. Give it a coat of paint, any colour can be chosen, so that the wind measurer, as it could be called, may stand the weather.

Now get four tin funnels, or fillers, 4 or 6 inches diameter at the mouth, and into the spout of each put a cork that will close the end. Place these funnels in the round holes which were made near the tips of the wooden arms. They must be put in position, as seen in picture 1, so

1. The wind measurer ready for work

2. Fixing the arm

3. Complete for mounting

that the wind will blow into the mouth of each in turn as the arms spin round. Each funnel may be painted a different colour, and this will help in judging the speed at which the wind blows them round. Next, a post must be put up in the garden, so that the revolving toy may be mounted on top of it. If there are any wooden clothes-posts about, one of them would be ideal. Choose a post as far as possible from any walls that would prevent the wind from having a free course to reach the funnels.

The next thing to do is to get a washer—that is, a small flat ring of iron with a hole of, say, half-inch size ; also a round iron nail, not less than 5 inches long. Put the washer on top of the wooden post, right in the middle, put the measure with its arms and funnels on top of the washer, and drive the nail down through the hole in the centre, then through the washer and into the post, until the head of the nail is about half an inch above the top of the wind-measurer. Now let the wind do its work. It will send the toy merrily round when it blows briskly. Count how often the arms go round in a minute— the different colours of the funnels will make this easy. If one day the revolutions are more each minute than on another day, the wind is, of course, stronger, while the reverse is the case when the revolutions are fewer. A study of local weather announcements is useful, too.

CRAFTS · GAMES · NEEDLEWORK · PUZZLES · SCIENCE EXPERIMENTS

LITTLE PROBLEMS FOR ODD MOMENTS

THESE problems are continued from page 626, and their answers will be found, together with more questions, on page 872.

47. When Will They Meet Again ?

" My watch gains ten seconds an hour, and my clock loses ten seconds an hour," said Tomkinson. " I put them right at noon on June 1. When will they be together again? "

What is the answer?

48. How Much was the Picture ?

" You can have that picture framed," said the dealer, " for 42s., or in another frame only half the value of this for 36s."

How much was the picture unframed?

49. Could She Buy the Books ?

" That set of books is £5 5s.," said Joan, " and I am afraid I have not enough money." " But you have £2 2s. more than I have," said Janet, " and we have £9 between us."

Had Joan enough to buy the books?

50. Did He Lose Money ?

" I have just sold two houses," said Thomson, " for £990 each. On one I lost ten per cent and on the other I gained ten per cent." " Then you are exactly where you were," replied his friend.

Was he correct?

51. How were the Doctor's Visits Divided ?

" My doctor's bill for last quarter," said the squire, " came to £9 19s. 6d." " How often did the doctor come? " asked his friend. " Twelve times," replied the squire. " He charged me a guinea a visit for each night visit and half-a-guinea for each day visit."

How many night visits did the doctor put down on his bill?

52. Did He Catch the Train ?

" The station is twelve miles away," said a cyclist at a hotel, " and I have an hour and a half to catch the train. There are four miles uphill, which I must walk, and can do at four miles an hour; there are four miles downhill, where I can coast at twelve miles an hour; and there are four miles level, which I shall do at eight miles an hour. This is an average of eight miles an hour, and I shall be just in time."

Did he catch the train?

53. What were the Two Sums ?

" Here are two invoices," said the cashier, " which together amount to £34. In one the pounds, shillings, and pence are equal. In the other the pounds are twice the shillings and the shillings are twice the number of pence."

What were the two sums of money?

54. How Long to Mow the Field ?

Evans and Watson mowed a field in a certain time. If each had mown half the field, Evans would have worked one day less and Watson two days more.

How long were they mowing the field?

55. How Long did the Frog Take ?

A frog fell into a well that was 30 feet deep. He climbed up 3 feet every day and slipped back 2 feet every night.

How long did he take to reach the top?

56. How Many Trees in the Orchard ?

In an orchard there are only apple trees, pear trees, and cherry trees. One-third of the whole are apple, one-fourth are pear, and there are 30 cherry trees.

How many trees does the orchard contain?

THE ANSWERS TO THE PROBLEMS ON PAGE 626

39. Yes, the second farm was the bigger, and was more than twice as large as the other. Three miles square is 3 miles each way and contains 9 square miles, while the other farm contained only 4 square miles altogether.

40. He knew the name of the village from which he had come, and by supposing that the arm of the signpost with that name pointed in the direction from which he had cycled, he was able to tell what roads were indicated by the other arms.

41. She was right. Feathers are weighed by avoirdupois weight and gold by troy weight. An ounce troy has 480 grains, but 1 ounce avoirdupois has only 437½ grains.

42. If 225 men took 7 months to make 21 miles of railway, they would take 9⅔ months to make the remaining 29 miles. If 225 men would take 9⅔ months to do something, the same work could be done in 5 months by 435 men. He therefore engages an extra 210 men.

43. To walk at 4 miles an hour means 1 mile in 15 minutes, 5 miles an hour is 1 mile in 12 minutes.

So, at the quicker rate, William takes 3 minutes less for each mile, but for the whole distance he takes 15 minutes less. Therefore, the number of miles is the number of 3's in 15—that is, 5 miles.

44. There is an odd 2½d. in the total, and no shillings ; and the same is true of the cost of each rug. Therefore there must have been 1 rug more than a number which costs an exact number of pounds. Now, £1 is 96 times 2½d., so that 96 rugs is the smallest number which cost an exact number of pounds, the cost being £961. Therefore twice 96 cost £1922, which is within the right amount—that is, it consists of 4 figures, beginning with 1. Hence the number of rugs is 1 more than twice 96, which is 193 ; and the entry should have read : 193 rugs at £10 0s. 2½d. each = £1932 0s. 2½d.

45. 6000 tons. It is plain that 160 tons is the difference between three barge-loads and one barge-load, so that each barge held 80 tons. And there were 75 barge-loads in the cargo, so that the total was eighty times 75 tons—*i.e.*, 6000 tons.

46. Three ducks.

THE MAGIC OF A GLASS OF WATER

FOR every mystery there is an explanation, though sometimes this is a very long time forthcoming; but the more that is known about the true meaning and the properties of things the more mysteries it is possible to explain; and as soon as a mystery is understood it ceases to be one.

Look in a mirror. Why does the mirror show everything in front of it? Because it has the property of *reflection*. Throw this book into the air and see what happens. It falls downward. Why not upward? Why not sideways? It falls downward because of what we call *gravitation*.

Now try a curious experiment, which anyone who grasps what gravitation is will easily understand. It is necessary to have two tumblers, a little water, and a short piece of india-rubber tubing. Any sort of tubing would do, but it should be small and thin. Put a tumbler of water on some books on a table, or on anything that will cause it to stand a few inches higher than it would stand if put on the table.

Now put an empty tumbler on the table near the high tumbler. The tumbler holding water will then be higher than the empty tumbler. Put the end of the rubber tubing into the glass of water, letting it go down into the water. Now put the other end of the tubing into the mouth, and suck some of the water up. When the tubing is full of water, squeeze the end of the tube which is in the mouth. Take it between the finger and thumb, holding it tightly, and put this end into or over the empty tumbler, still keeping the other end of the tubing below the surface of the water in the high tumbler. The part of the tubing dangling over the side of the full tumbler should be longer than the part inside the full tumbler.

Now by taking away the fingers, thereby letting the lower end of the tubing open, the water will begin to flow, and will continue to flow until the high tumbler is empty, or until the water in the high tumbler is below the end of the tubing up which the water has been flowing. In this way has been made what is called a *syphon*—not the kind that holds soda water, for this is not a true syphon, but what men of science and engineers understand by the word.

What is the explanation? Imagine for example a string which has tied to one end a large stone or weight, and to the other end a small weight, and suppose that the middle of the string is put over a smooth rail.

What will happen? The heavy stone will immediately fall and pull up the little weight until this follows down the other side of the rail.

The water in the long end of the tube is like the heavy weight, and the water in the short one is like the small weight. But, someone says, the two weights would be tied together while water is not tied to water. That is true; but unless air gets into the tube of the syphon the effect is just as if the heavy column of the water were tied to the light column of water. Perhaps it would make it clearer to say that the heavy column of water falls down and *sucks* up the lighter column. The light column of water then becomes the heavy column, and sucks up more water, and so on until all the water possible has been sucked up and has flowed down the tube.

Try another experiment—how to make a penny rise up in water. It will not really rise up, but it will seem to do so, and the experiment is a very curious one. It shows that one does not see through water quite in the same way as through air.

Put a saucer on the table and put a penny in the middle of it. It will then look as shown in picture 2.

Now get someone to look at it. Ask him to sit a little lower until the penny is just hidden by the rim of the saucer. He will see the saucer, but not the penny. It will be like picture 3.

Now, while the friend sits still, pour water

1. A simple syphon showing how water will flow upward

2. Penny in saucer

3. Penny hidden from view

4. The difference in seeing through air and water

into the saucer. Do it very steadily so as not to spill the water. The penny will come into sight. It does not really rise. It is the water that makes it seem to do so. This is because, when looking through air, the vision is in a straight line. When looking through air and water, it is along two lines, as clearly illustrated in picture 4.

This curious property of water is called *refraction*, more about which will be learned by those beginning the study of the subject that is called *physics*.

5. Making the box

Another experiment shows yet another curious thing. To talk about a paper saucepan seems absurd, but it is not so ridiculous as it sounds. Water really can be made to boil in a paper saucepan without much difficulty. First make the saucepan. Take a piece of paper—ordinary writing paper will do. Fold it over something of square or oblong shape, as seen in picture 5. Put a pin through the folds at the sides, as seen in picture 6, to make the box keep its shape. Now put a thin piece of string round the parts of the two pins inside the box, and hang it up, or hold it in the hand. Pour some water into the paper box until it is almost full, doing this very gently, so as not to break it. Then hold the box over a fire or gas ring. The paper will not burn, as might be expected, but the water will get hotter and hotter until it boils. This result, which seems strange, comes about because the water will not allow the paper to retain the heat, but draws it to itself.

6. The box finished

The effect is due to what is called *radiation*, Instead of getting hotter and hotter until it burns, the paper gives its heat to the water, which gets hotter and hotter.

MAKING BREAD AND SCONES

Success in breadmaking is said to depend on the good temper of the cook while working, but, of course, it also comes through paying attention to important details, like putting the leavened dough—that is, the flour after yeast has been worked in—into a warmth-retaining wooden or earthenware bowl.

Often recipes for bread are given away with the bag of flour, but nothing is nicer than a home-made wholemeal loaf, and if you want to make one, this is how it is done.

Warm everything you intend to use—bowls, towels, bread tins. Thoroughly mix two pounds of *wholemeal* flour with two teaspoonfuls of salt in one of the bowls, and make a well in the centre. In a smaller basin cream an ounce of fresh yeast with one teaspoonful of soft brown or castor sugar, by working it with the back of a small wooden spoon till the mixture becomes liquid and begins stirring with tiny live bubbles. In 10 or 12 minutes it should be ready for mixing with one pint of water, or tepid *sour* milk and water, and this mixture should then be poured into the well in the flour.

Mix and knead all well together till the ball of sponge, as dough is sometimes called, comes away leaving the sides of the bowl quite clean. Return it to a clean, warm, floured basin, cover with a clean warm cloth, and leave it to rise in a temperature between 70° and 80° F. for one to one and a half hours.

Knead again, divide into pieces sufficient to one-third fill the well-warmed bread tins, previously rubbed with a little lard and dusted with a little flour. Cover them with a cloth and leave to rise for another 20 minutes or half an hour, then put the tins into an oven heated to between 350° and 375° F., and bake for 45 minutes to an hour.

Turn the bread out of the tins on to a wire tray when cooked, away from draught, to cool.

Perhaps, if you feel yeast bread is rather difficult for a beginner, you would like first to make a malt loaf which is delicious sliced and buttered for tea.

Sift into a basin half a pound of plain flour and a teaspoonful of baking-powder. Into a saucepan put two tablespoonfuls of syrup, and one tablespoonful of malt extract, which can be bought from the chemist. Warm slightly, so that the two blend together easily, add a pinch of salt, two ounces of seedless raisins and the sieved flour, and mix all well together in the saucepan with just under half a pint of milk in which half a teaspoonful of bi-carbonate of soda has been dissolved. Turn into a well-greased bread tin, and bake in a slow oven for about an hour and a half.

Scones are easy to make, too, and here is a simple standard recipe which can be varied by adding sultanas, currants, grated orange rind, or almost any flavouring you fancy.

Mix half a pound of sifted white flour in a bowl with half a teaspoonful of cream of tartar, half a teaspoonful of carbonate of soda, one ounce of sugar, and half a teaspoonful of salt. Rub in one to one and a half ounces of butter or margarine ; make into a soft dough with a quarter of a pint of *sour* milk ; roll out with a lightly-floured roller to half an inch thick; cut into portions and bake for 10 to 15 minutes in a hot oven. The next lesson is on cooking vegetables (see Index).

THE INEXHAUSTIBLE MATCHBOX

THE secret of this trick lies in the box which has been specially prepared, though in appearance it is just the ordinary full small safety matchbox it was originally.

To make it, with a sharp penknife split six or seven of the matches right down the middle. Take out the " drawer " portion of the box, turn it over, and smear the underside with glue or seccotine; then lay the half-matches, all pointing the same way, side by side upon it. If this is neatly done, the inverted drawer thus treated will give the appearance of a full one right side up. When the glue is dry, reverse the drawer again, replacing the matches that it contained. Push it half-way only into the outer case; and, into the opposite end of the other case, push the drawer portion also of another box. There will thus be two drawers in one case. The unprepared drawer is represented by *a;* the prepared one by *b.* In presenting the trick, bring this box forward as if it were one in ordinary use, taking care to keep the end *b* well covered by the right hand. Make some remark about the strange properties of matches of this brand, and with that, shake out the visible matches upon the table, and show the box empty. Remarking, " Now I will close the box again," bring the left hand up to it, as if merely to push in the drawer, but, as a matter of fact, press in *b* from the opposite

THE MAGIC MATCHBOX THAT ANY BOY CAN MAKE

end, thereby pushing out the empty drawer into the left hand, where it is hidden. Hold up the box fairly closed in the right hand.

This calls all eyes to the box, and gives an opportunity to drop the empty drawer into some convenient object placed beforehand on the table. Then, blowing upon the box, and pronouncing some magical formula, push open the box again, showing that it is still full of matches. This is done with the one hand only, the other falling carelessly on the matches, getting possession of a score or so of them, which are held against the palm by the pressure of the thumb. The second lot of matches is now shaken out upon the first, and again the box is closed. Once more the box is blown upon, and, under cover of this, turned upside down. When opened again, it is still apparently full, the matches glued to the bottom of the drawer being now brought into view. Transferring it to the opposite hand, give it a shake, allowing the matches concealed in that hand to fall from it as if out of the box, then again turn it to bring the empty side on top.

Now saying, " You can all testify that these matches came out of this box. To show there is no deception, we will try how many we can put back again," fill the box, which will, of course, only take about half the number on the table.

THE WIZARD'S HANDKERCHIEF

As its name implies, this handkerchief is a special one, being, in fact, two patterned handkerchiefs, exactly alike, sewn together all round the edges, except for an inch and a half each way at one corner, marked B in the picture. The space thus left between the two handkerchiefs makes the vanishing penny trick possible.

From the bottom of the opening at B to a point an inch short of the corner of C the two handkerchiefs must also be joined together by a diagonal line of stitching which should not be noticeable, so the darker and more closely-patterned the handkerchiefs are, the better.

Before beginning the show, hide a penny in some convenient place where no one else is likely to spot it. The handkerchief must be held spread out four-square, with the corner A between the thumb and fingers of the left hand, and the corner B between those of the right, but with the little mouth at B kept open by the tip of the forefinger. Then gather up the other corners to form a bag, and ask someone to drop a penny into this, in reality offering the opening at B, so that the coin falls between the two handkerchiefs. Prove that the coin is there by making it chink against the table, then let loose the corners C and D. Nothing falls, the penny running down the line of stitching to C. Pick up the corners again—the coin will then drop back to the centre of the bag—and order the penny to go to the place where the coin was put. Then shake out the handkerchief, and while the spectators are occupied in seeing whether the penny has obeyed, work the coin out and get rid of it.

CURIOUS WAYS OF PEELING AN ORANGE

THERE are various ways of peeling an orange which give very artistic effects, and which can be done quite easily with a little practice. With a sharp knife cut a number of slits from the top to about two-thirds the distance down the orange, and then gently and carefully pull away the peel all round from the white of the orange. Take the orange itself away, and open out the gores, or cuts, and there is a water-lily. If a night-light be put in the middle, and lighted, the effect is very pretty.

A more elaborate way of cutting the peel of an orange gives the beautiful result shown in the picture. First of all cut lines all round the orange as in picture 1; then on each side of these cuts, and about three-sixteenths of an inch away from them, cut other lines parallel to those already made, so that now the orange has a series of triple cuts as shown

A cleverly peeled orange

gently raise the peel everywhere from the body of the orange, taking care not to break any of the ribbons. Great patience is necessary, but at last the result is the figure shown in the picture. With care the orange can be removed from inside, piece by piece, or can be left to wither with the peel.

Another artistic method of peeling an orange is to cut it all round the centre up and down in small v's, or in squares like the key pattern, then to pull back the peel carefully and re-lease the orange so that two cups in the shape of a rose-bowl remain. In cutting and peeling oranges in these fancy ways one or two important points must be remembered and carefully followed.

First of all, choose a large orange, and it must not be over-ripe ; it should have a smooth skin and no blemishes. For the cutting have a sharp knife with a fine point,

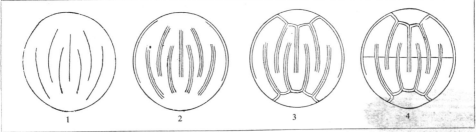

The different stages of cutting the peel of an orange to produce the artistic effect shown in the above picture

in picture 2. These cuts must now be joined up at the top and bottom of the orange as shown in picture 3, and then across the middle of the orange cut the peel between the lines, as shown in picture 4. All is now ready, and with a small, blunt penknife

and take care not to cut too deeply. But with a little care and patience any boy or girl can become quite expert in fancy orange peeling, and able to invent new and artistic designs.

When eating an orange, keep the peel, and use it to try out original ideas.

THE MYSTERIOUS BOTTLE OF WATER

A VERY amusing trick can be played upon a friend with the simple means of an ordinary glass bottle of any size or shape, but for preference it should be black or dark green in colour.

Get a few holes made in the bottom of the bottle with a glazier's diamond. Then place it in a large jug or pail of water, with the neck only above the surface. Now fill the bottle with water right up to the brim, and cork it very tightly with a sound cork, or if the bottle has a screw stopper screw it tightly. Then take the bottle out of the pail, dry the outside, and it is ready for use.

The trick is to give the bottle to a friend, and tell him that he will not be able to draw

the cork or unscrew the stopper without spilling all the water from the bottle. Of course he is quite sure he can do the task asked, and proceeds to uncork the bottle. But as soon as he does so the air gets in at the top, and the water flows freely through the holes at the bottom, greatly to his surprise.

When the bottle was quite full and tightly corked, the pressure of the air outside the holes, without any corresponding pressure inside the bottle, kept the water in, but the removal of the cork causes the air to press upon the top of the water, and it flows out.

Although anyone can do this, it is quite a good trick for the young magician to perform, for catches are always popular.

THE GAME OF ZOO-GUESS

EVERYONE at Mary's party was trying to think what a Zoo-guess could be, as a big board with two sheets of white paper pinned to it was placed on two chairs at one end of the room. At the other end Mary's mother sat at a table, and in front of her the children saw a bundle of little pink envelopes.

"First," the mother explained, "every boy must choose a partner."

"Now," she said, "I want two couples to come first. The boys will take these black chalks, and stand by the board. The girls will stand by me at the table. I shall give them each an envelope, and when I say Go! they must run to their partners and

and said: "Now run as quickly as you can, and remember that the one who gets back to me first with the right answer wins." Then she called out: "One, two, three—go!"

Both girls ran as hard as they could down the room till they reached the boys.

The boys read the names of the animals and then tried to draw them, but first they only made marks that did not seem to mean anything.

Then one of the girls saw a curly line that looked something like an elephant's trunk, and, without waiting for anything more, she rushed back and said: "It's an elephant."

"Wrong! Go back and look again."

Laughing Hyena

Leopard

Kangaroo

Alligator

Peacock

Parrot

Frog

Camel

Swan

SOME OF THE ANIMALS THE CHILDREN HAD TO GUESS

give them the envelopes. The boys will open the envelopes, and they will find pieces of paper inside with the names of animals written on them. Then, as quickly as possible, they must try to draw the animals named on the paper on the board, while their partners watch. The moment the girls can tell what the boys are trying to draw, they must run to me and say what the animals are meant for, and the girl who gets to me first will win a prize."

Two boys, with the black chalk ready, stood by the board, and their two girl partners stood at the table.

Mary's mother gave each girl an envelope,

The girl ran back to her partner and she saw now that the curly line she had mistaken for a trunk was meant for a swan's neck, but before she could run back the other girl had guessed what her partner was doing, and won.

Of course they made mistakes, because they were so anxious to tell Mary's mother what the animals were and win a prize, that they began to guess the moment they saw something they thought they knew.

Sometimes the two girls would guess what their partners were trying to draw at the same moment, and then there would be a tremendous race down the room, which was really the best part of the fun.

MAKING A KENNEL FOR A DOG

The size of the dog-kennel will, of course, depend upon the size of the dog that is to occupy it, so first consider the comfort of the animal for which it is to serve as a house and sleeping-place.

The length inside should be half as long again as the dog when he stretches himself out, and the width sufficient to allow him to turn round without any difficulty. The height of the sides should be a little more than the dog's height when standing up. If your pet is a puppy, the size of the kennel should be arranged to suit him when fully grown.

The kennel must stand a little way off the ground, to keep the floor dry when it is raining, for dogs take cold as well as human beings, and love warmth and comfort almost as much as we do.

The first part to make is the base. This should be of wood not less than one inch thick. Mark it the required length and cut as many pieces as are needed to make the necessary width. Fix these boards to two substantial cross-pieces long enough to reach across the full width of the base. Make certain that the floor-boards fit closely together without any cracks which will let in draughts. The ends of the boards must be straight and smooth and be flush with the cross-pieces, the best way to ensure this being to plane the edges after fixing.

The kennel and some of its parts—the front, a side, and the base.

The two sides are made by fixing boards which need not be quite as thick as the floor-boards, to cross-pieces made of timber one inch thick, and one inch shorter than the width of the sides, so that when the sides are fitted to the bottom they will overlap the floor-boards and can be screwed along the bottom edge.

The length of these side boards should be exactly the same as those for the floor, and their ends must be in line with the cross-pieces.

The method for the back is the same as for the sides, but the boards should be upright instead of running horizontally. At the top saw the ends off so that the boards slope at right-angles from the centre point as shown in the first illustration. Here the cross-pieces should be fitted together with a halved joint, which is described on page 379, and should be fitted at the top only; none is needed at the bottom as the end is fixed to the cross-piece of the kennel floor.

The front, which is the end shown here, is exactly the same as the back except that the middle board, or boards, are cut away to form the opening. An extra cross-piece must be fitted across the front, as shown, to which the base of the middle board can be fixed. The opening could be left square, or the rounded shape marked with a pencil and then cut out with a keyhole saw if you have one or, if not, with a chisel.

The kennel can now be put together. First fix the sides to the base by driving screws along the lower edge of each side and into the edges of the floor-boards; then screw the back and the front into the cross-pieces of the sides and the base.

Finally put on the roof. The boards for this should be four inches longer than the kennel. Fix the boards at the outside edges first, and let them project two inches over the sides, the front, and the back. Next arrange the boards up the slope of the ends, overlapping them as shown in the drawing. This method prevents rain getting inside, and also provides little triangular gaps between the roof and the ends which give ventilation. The last two boards should overlap, and two narrow pieces should be fitted to form a capping, as illustrated.

Galvanised nails should be used for making up the base, sides, and ends, and for fixing the roof. They would also do for putting the kennel together, but brass or galvanised screws are better. In fixing the boards to the cross-pieces, drive the nails in in alternate rows in order not to split the wood.

Last of all, give the inside of the kennel a coat of limewash, and paint the outside with two coats of paint, waiting until the first is thoroughly dry before applying the second. When this is quite dry, put some clean straw inside, and the dog's home is ready for him.

After this you may feel you want to make something for yourself ; so why not try the bookshelf and book-ends described on another page (See Index).

Simple Learning Made Easy for Very Little People

NUMBERS—THE SUMS GET HARDER

WHEN John and Jennifer had learned how to do addition sums, Mother showed them how to do subtraction, or "taking-away." First of all she showed them the little mark — which meant take-away.

"You have 10 fingers," she said, "5 on your right hand, and 5 on your left hand. What are 5 away from 10?"

The twins showed her their 10 fingers, and then put one hand behind them and found they had 5 fingers left.

$$5 + 5 = 10 \text{ then}$$
$$10 - 5 = 5.$$

"I see," said John. "I've got 2 eyes, and if I shut one you can only see one, so

$$1 + 1 = 2 \text{ and}$$
$$2 - 1 = 1."$$

"Yes," said Jennifer, "we've got 4 legs, and if I run away you can only see John's legs, so

$$2 + 2 = 4 \text{ and}$$
$$4 - 2 = 2."$$

Very soon John and Jennifer could do taking-away sums as well as adding up. They went round the house playing "take-aways." A chair has 4 legs, and 1 broke. How many are left?

$$4 - 1 = 3.$$

Mother made 10 little cakes, and we ate 4. How many were left for Daddy?

$$10 - 4 = 6.$$

Daddy brought home 4 pieces of chocolate, we had a piece each. How many were left? None. $4 - 4 = 0.$

"Seven sunflowers are growing in my garden," said Jennifer. "If I picked 4 for Mother how many should I have left?"

John said, "3." $7 - 4 = 3.$ "I have 9 soldiers," he went on, "some in scarlet coats, and some in khaki. Five are in scarlet. How many are in khaki?"

"That's easy," said Jennifer—"4." $9 - 5 = 4.$

When Daddy heard what they had been doing he said, "That's fine. Now you'll be able to do stock-taking in your café."

"Stock-taking," said Jennifer. "What a funny word! What ever does it mean?"

"Well," said Daddy, "when you have a shop, or a stores, or a café, you have to take stock of your goods to see how many new things you have to buy to restock your shop. For instance, if you have 12 bottles of lemonade, and you sold 6, you would have to order 6 new ones.

$$12 - 6 = 6.$$

"If you had 20 jam tarts and sold 17, you would find you had only 3 left, and would have to order 17 more.

$$20 - 17 = 3.$$

"Now, if you wanted 12 ice-cream cornets, and found you had only 4, how many would you have to order?"

"Oh dear!" said John and Jennifer together. "These sums are hard. Too hard to think about in our heads."

"Yes," said Mother, "they are hard,

READING · WRITING · ARITHMETIC · ART · MUSIC · FRENCH

so I have made you something to help."

She showed them 2 slats of wood, each with a string of 20 beads, fastened at each end like this:

"Now," she said, "think of that last sum. Daddy said 12 ice-cream cornets were wanted, and you had only 4. How many more would you have to order? First find your 12, and push the other beads down to the other end of the slat like this:

"Now move along the 4 you have, and see how many you have left to order."

"Why, 8," said John. "That makes it much easier!"

Then Mother showed them how to write it down.

12 − 4 = 8.

As soon as they could do this kind of sum Mother let them do upright sums, and made them a few sum cards like this:

$$8 \quad 6 \quad 7 \quad 5$$
$$-4 \quad -2 \quad -1 \quad -5$$

and with the help of their bead slats the twins loved "taking-away" and didn't find them at all hard. They learned what they called "taking-away rhymes," like:

Ten little nigger boys
As I was going to St. Ives

and

Two little dicky birds
Sat upon a wall.
Fly away Peter,
Fly away Paul.
Both had flown,
None left at all.

READING—SOME NEW WORDS

JOHN and Jennifer thought it was about time they wrote some more stories for their cinema. This time they wanted "hard" stories to read, and decided that as they were beginning to read well they could have much more story with their films. When they were showing them they could read the story out to the audience.

"There will be lots of words we can't read," said John.

"And lots we can't spell," said Jennifer, "and if I write them in my word book I shall never remember them all."

When Daddy came home they told him all about it, and he said, "Well, I brought home these lovely big sheets of cardboard. I wondered how we could use them—now I know! We'll have one card for things in the house; one for things in the street; one for shops; one for ships; in fact, one for everything you want."

"Yes," said John, "but how will that help us with our reading?"

Daddy said, "Tomorrow you can cut out all the pictures you find from old newspapers and magazines, and stick them on the cards. When I come home I will write the words underneath, and then when you want to write a story about a train, for instance, you can get the train card, and the pictures will tell you what the words say, and you won't have to ask Mother for every word you want."

Here is one of the cards:

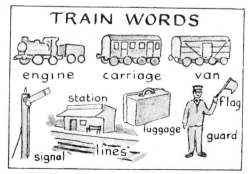

TRAIN WORDS

engine   carriage   van
station
luggage
signal   lines   guard   flag

When John and Jennifer had collected and stuck the pictures on the cards, and Daddy had written the words underneath, they each made up a story for their cinema.

This time, instead of painting pictures with a sentence written underneath, they wrote a whole page, and painted a picture about that part of the story. They then wrote another page, and so on.

John called his story:

A SAIL ON THE SEA

and Jennifer called hers:

MOTHERS AND FATHERS

Here is the beginning of John's story:

I went in a sailing boat. It sailed right out to sea.

And here is part of Jennifer's story:

My Daddy goes to town every day in the train.

The children took it in turns to show their films, and read their stories out loud. They practised a lot, reading to Mother first, and finding the words they did not know from their picture cards before inviting their friends to the cinema show. John turned the film for Jennifer and Jennifer turned it for John.

To help them to remember all the new words, Mother made them some more flash cards—not sentences this time, but words, much harder than sentences; but the twins were getting on with their reading, and were so interested that they liked doing hard things.

WRITING—COPYING THE NURSERY RHYMES

THE curtains the twins made for their cinema were made out of butter-muslin, painted with coloured inks.

To make them, Mother pinned the muslin out on to a thick padding of old newspapers, and with a big brush she made a wriggly line on the muslin. John and Jennifer made some more wriggly lines, and when these lines were dry, with another colour they filled up the spaces in between.

" It was quite easy, like making letters," said John, and the twins made both curtains. Here is one of them:

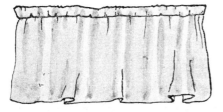

As we know, John and Jennifer were very fond of painting pictures, and one day they decided to paint a picture of every Nursery Rhyme they knew, and write the Nursery Rhyme underneath. They were getting on very well with their writing, and Mother said she would write out the rhymes for them to copy. If they really wrote them very neatly she would make a nursery rhyme sheet to hang on their bedroom wall. She would make it so that they could turn the rhymes over and have a new one every day, if they liked. John and Jennifer copied the rhymes that Mother wrote for them so neatly that they did not spoil one sheet. They each chose to write the rhymes they liked best. John wrote:

Little Boy Blue.
Humpty Dumpty.
Jack and Jill.
Hickory Dickory Dock
Baa, baa, black sheep.
Ride-a-cock horse.

Jennifer's list of Nursery Rhymes was :

Little Bo Peep.
Mary, Mary, quite contrary.
Little Miss Muffet.
Polly, put the kettle on.
Hush-a-bye baby.
The Queen of Hearts.

Here is one of their Nursery Rhyme sheets:

Humpty Dumpty sat on a wall,
Humpty Dumpty had a great fall.
Not all the king's horses, nor
all the king's men,
Could put Humpty Dumpty
together again.

When they were all finished Mother put the sheets one on top of the other, and sewed them together along the top. Then she got a piece of broom stick four inches longer than the width of the paper, which she nailed to the broom stick. She tied a picture cord to each end, so that she could hang up on their bedroom wall the whole Nursery Rhyme sheet.

Our Nursery Rhymes

The first thing the twins did every morning was to read the Nursery Rhyme that was showing, then turn it over and read the next one. Daddy said their writing was getting better with every rhyme they wrote.

In copying these Nursery Rhymes from Mother's copies, the twins learned a good deal about writing. They learned that every line and everyone's name must start with a capital letter. They learned that the small curly sign Mother put between some of the words was called a comma; and the dot at the end of a sentence was called a full stop.

Then they wrote the line:

Have you any wool ?

Mother told them that this curly mark was called a question mark. The last thing they learned was that we put a little comma when we are talking of other people's things. Like this:

All the king's horses
And all the king's men

MUSIC—MUSICAL DIALECTS

THE charm of our language lies in the different ways in which it is spoken in different parts of the world.

American English sounds different from Australian English. Lancashire people have one method of speech, Kentish people another. Not only does language change from place to place, but also from age to age. We should find Shakespeare's friends difficult to understand. They would find equal difficulty in understanding the friends of Chaucer.

Music, you may say, has nothing to do with words (except where they are joined together as in a song) ; surely a sonata is a sonata wherever or whenever it may have been composed. Yet when we look carefully at music we find that it, too, has its dialects. Listen to any piece by Dvorak (for example, the last movement from the New World symphony), and then listen to something by Mozart (such as the overture to The Magic Flute). They sound as though they come from different worlds. They speak with different accents.

Welsh people speak beautiful English, but it is different from that of English people. They go up where we go down! Up and down—that is the important phrase.

Let us look at our sol-fa syllables : And now sing them.
Doh—up one step *re*: up another step to *me*. *Me* to *fa*. This is only a little step. After that step, step, step, and one little step to the end. From

doh to *doh* we climb up a staircase. The musical staircase we call a *scale*. (This again comes from a Latin word, scalae, meaning a flight of stairs.)

The big steps, as from *doh* to *re*, we call tones ; the little steps semitones. When we arrive at a semitone we feel that we are on a landing. Flights of stairs differ from one another according to where their landings are placed. We can build quite a number of musical staircases:

You may either sing your way up these staircases, or you can play them on the piano—C to C (on the white notes), D to D, and so on.

Which among these sound familiar? No doubt you will answer the first— from *doh* to *doh*. The first step is *doh* and the last is *doh*. *Doh* is therefore the most important sound in this scale. In many of the tunes which you know *doh* is the most important note.

Which tune starts : **d d d r d d s₁?**

  ,,   ,,   ,,   **d d r t₁ d r?**

Which tune ends   **s f m d f r s f m r d?**

Look at the bottom of the page to see if you have found the answers.

The scale which makes *doh* so important has a name. It is called the Major Scale. Music written in the major scale is in

---

one of music's dialects. But it is not the only one.

Old music sounds " queer," some people say, because they are accustomed to one dialect. If you can hear a gramophone record of the last part of Dvorak's New World symphony you will hear ₁ t **d** t ₁ ₁ :

¹ s m s ¹: The first and last note is *lah* and the tune is, we say, in the *lah* scale. Its modern name is the Minor Scale.

Ask someone to play this melody; it is the beginning of the old Agincourt Song, composed to tell people about that famous battle. As you can see, it belongs

G line—

to a scale which runs from *re* to *re*. This was a scale much used in the olden days.

Here is part of another tune, one which you know quite well:

This tune has only five notes in it. The five-note scale is also an old one, and is often to be noticed in the music of Scotland. Some say that that scale was so much used in Scotland because it fitted the notes which the bagpipe could play.

There are two orchestral pieces which you might like to hear. Both show, at the beginning, melodies in this five-note (or, if you want a big word, *pentatonic*) scale. They are Laideronette (from the suite Mother Goose) by the French composer Ravel, and the overture to The Bartered Bride by the Czech, Smetana.

Then there are some weird scales sometimes to be heard. There is one with big steps (tones) only. This is called the Whole Tone Scale.

Ask someone to play this. Try to sing it.

---

(1) Good King Wenceslas.   (2) God Save the Queen. (3) Rule, Britannia.

You will find it very difficult to keep in tune. This is because it is much easier to sing a scale of tones **and** semitones than one consisting of only tones **or** semitones.

Here is the scale of semitones, called a Chromatic Scale:

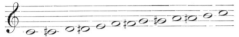

Now you have learned a lot about many scales. Perhaps you could now have them all played through to you. The Major Scale, the Minor Scale, the *re-re* Scale, and so on. Which of all these is the easiest to remember and the easiest to sing? You will say the Major Scale. Your second choice will be the Minor Scale. Because these have always been found the easiest to handle they have become the most popular.

But music is full of contrasts. So weird music has weird scales from which its melodies may be taken, sad music has sad scales, old music old scales. Perhaps you will never again find scales merely dull exercises, which annoy everyone else when we practise them! Scales are among the most interesting parts of music.

ART—WAYS OF MODELLING

MODELLING for most people means making things in clay. This clay may be the kind found in the banks of a river, or the spade lumps which the roadmen throw up when digging down to gas or water pipes, or the finely-made clay which you can get from a pottery. It is great fun to dig your own if there happens to be clay near your home or in the banks of a river.

The first thing to do is to get the clay in workable condition. For this you will need to wear an apron or overall, and to find a good firm table on which to bang the clay before using it. It is a bit like making dough for bread in that you have to mix it up and work it into the right state for use. If the clay is dry when found, it will have to be soaked in water beforehand.

While getting the clay ready for use, enjoy the feel of it and the way in which you can do things with it. It is quite a new experience from painting or cutting patterns. A big lump of clay in workable condition is a delight to handle and play with. You can quickly squeeze it in one place and pull it out in another, making all sorts of shapes which at the same time look like clay.

There is great satisfaction to be had from rolling out a long sausage of clay and getting it even in thickness all along its length. Try to do this. It is one way that is used for making pots. You will need many lengths about the thickness of your little finger. With one of these lengths make a coil like a " catharine wheel," and press the coil tightly together by working with your finger across it to the centre. When you have done one side turn the " wheel " over and do the same on the other side. It should then look something like a dinner mat. A small " wheel " will do to begin with, about the size of the bottom of a tea cup. Now begin to build up the sides in the same way, pressing down each length of clay on the top and running them together by working with your finger in a downward direction on the inside and outside of the pot.

Try to make a simple honeypot-shaped pot to begin with, and, when you get the feel of it, try larger sizes and more interesting shapes, like the beaker on page 132.

Another way to make a pot is to squeeze out the clay between your fingers, shaping it as you go along. Make a ball of clay in good condition first and then, pressing your thumb into the centre of it, gradually squeeze out the shape of the sides, keeping an even thickness all through.

Cut up your long sausages into even lengths about the thickness of the sausage itself. Having done this, pick up the pieces, one at a time, and roll them between your hands into balls like marbles. If you dry them very slowly for some days you can afterwards put them in a fire, where they will bake hard, and you can play with them.

If you make a hole through the balls of clay with a nail, wire, or metal meat-skewer, and fire them, you will have some beads which you can paint and wear.

Small, compact models of kings, queens, bishops, knights, and pawns for chessmen are very suitable subjects for modelling.

They must be simply made, and made to be looked at from all sides, and, at the same time, be pleasant things to feel and handle. If you make sure there are no air bubbles in the clay when you are modelling these little figures, and afterwards dry them very slowly so as to dry them right through and not just on the surface, you could have them fired in a potter's kiln.

It is also possible to do the firing in an ordinary fire at home. The important things to remember are that any air left in the clay or any dampness or sudden heating when firing will result in the models bursting to pieces.

WOMAN WITH BASKET

The pottery clay model of an old woman with her basket of fruit was modelled by a girl who had left school. It was her first attempt, however, and to make the figure suitable for firing in the pottery kiln it was hollowed out from underneath to leave a fairly even thickness of clay all through the model.

GRANDDAD AND GRANNY PUPPETS

If this were not done the firing would be uneven and result in the thin parts being fired before the thick, and the model cracking in the kiln.

While a good deal of modelling can best be done with the hands and fingers it is useful to have one or two modelling tools as well. You can buy them at the same shop which sells carving tools, but you can also make your own with wooden skewers, old toothbrush handles, or odd pieces of wood. Use them as little as possible, and keep to your fingers as long as you can.

MOTHER AND CHILD

The little figure of a mother and her baby was modelled in clay by a 10-year-old. It is a fine solid group, and there is something very attractive and motherly about it.

Modelling can be done in many other materials besides clay. One method is to make a wire skeleton first of the position of the body and limbs of the person or animal to be modelled. The wire should be made firm at the joints so as not to move. Thin copper wire is the kind to get for the purpose, and for some upright figures you can fix the wire in a thin piece of wood to hold the wire rigid. Over this wire frame you wrap bandages of scrap paper with paste until you get the required thickness of the limbs, which when dry you can paint with powder colours.

You can also model in Plasticine, as in the case of a puppet's head, and then paste over this several layers of little torn-up bits of paper until you have a thickness strong enough to be firm by itself, when dry.

Then cut the head vertically in two down each side and take apart. Remove the Plasticine. Afterwards put together round a finger a tube of coiled paper, and join with paper and paste. Let part of the tube serve for the neck and to attach the garment. For the hands make thimbles of card or paper to fit your thumb and middle finger ends, model the hands on them in Plasticine, and cover with layers of paper and paste. Do not remove the Plasticine from the hands unless you make very big ones.

The photograph of Granddad and Granny shows two glove puppets made by a girl of six. They are modelled in a paste made of torn-up bits of paper soaked in flour paste— called papier mâché. Up the inside of the heads is a tube of cardboard wide enough to take the index finger, and on this the paste of papier mâché is modelled. When dry, hair or beards made of darning wool can be stuck on.

FRENCH—HURRYING TO THE BOAT

OUR story tells us here how the party make their way to the boat. In reading remember that the first line under each picture is the French; the second line gives the English word for the French word above it; the third line shows how we make up the words in our own language.

Le bateau va bientôt partir.
The boat goes soon to start.
The boat will soon start.

Il y a beaucoup de voyageurs.
There are many of travellers.
There are many travellers.

Tout le monde se dépêche.
All the world itself hurries.
Everyone is hurrying.

On crie: " Monsieur Hawes! "
One cries : " Mr. Hawes! "
Someone calls: " Mr. Hawes! "

C'est un télégramme pour papa.
It is a telegram for Papa.
It is a telegram for Papa.

Papa l'ouvre; c'est de notre oncle.
Papa it opens ; it is from our uncle.
Papa opens it; it is from our uncle.

Il nous souhaite bon voyage.
He us wishes good journey.
He wishes us a good journey.

Nous sommes enfin sur le bateau.
We are at last on the boat.
At last we are on the boat.

Une vieille dame a perdu son perroquet.
An old lady has lost her parrot.
An old lady has lost her parrot.

La bonne aperçoit la cage.
The nurse sees the cage.
Nurse sees the cage.

La dame est enchantée.
The lady is delighted.
The lady is delighted.

La Cloche—The Bell

Il y a un bruit épouvantable!
There is a noise frightful!
There is a frightful noise!

La cloche sonne. Nous allons partir.
The bell rings. We go to start.
The bell rings. We are going to start.

Nous nous asseyons sur le pont.
We ourselves sit on the deck.
We sit on the deck.